SELECTED STATUTES ON TRUSTS AND ESTATES

1995 Edition

Compiled by

JOHN H. LANGBEIN
Chancellor Kent Professor of Law and Legal History
Yale University

LAWRENCE W. WAGGONER
Lewis M. Simes Professor of Law
University of Michigan

Westbury, New York
THE FOUNDATION PRESS, INC.
1995

3rd Reprint–1998

PREFACE

This collection of statutes is meant to provide law students with a single-volume source containing all the uniform acts needed in the trusts and estates course, together with some notable Commonwealth sources for comparative purposes.

In Part I we reproduce in full the Uniform Probate Code (UPC), Official 1990 Text, with 1991 and 1993 amendments and the full text of the official comments. The UPC's substantive law of intestacy, elective share, wills, and construction, contained in Article II, was extensively revised in 1990. The 1991 and 1993 revisions to Article II were technical in character, clarifying the 1990 reforms and improving the organization of the material. UPC Article VI, governing nonprobate transfers, was extensively revised in 1989. The present volume integrates the revised articles into the UPC. The pre-1990 text of Article II and the pre-1989 text of Article VI are preserved in two separate appendixes following the UPC.

In 1991 the Uniform Law Commission promulgated three free-standing acts based on the 1990 revisions of UPC Article II, for the convenience of jurisdictions that do not enact the UPC's procedural articles. They are (1) the Uniform Act on Intestacy, Wills, and Donative Transfers, which replicates all of UPC Article II together with some definitional material from other articles of the UPC; (2) the revised Uniform Testamentary Additions to Trusts Act, based on revised UPC § 2—513; and (3) the revised Uniform Simultaneous Death Act. The first two of these freestanding acts duplicate UPC Article II so closely in structure and text that it would be pointless to reproduce them in this volume. The new simultaneous death act, which consolidates several of the revised UPC provisions, is reproduced separately in Part II of this volume with the other uniform acts.

It should be remarked that the UPC incorporates in whole or in part several other freestanding acts: the Uniform Statutory Rule Against Perpetuities (UPC Art. 2, Part 9); the Uniform International Wills Act (UPC Art. 2, Part 10); the Uniform Durable Power of Attorney Act (UPC Art. 5, Part 5); the Uniform Guardianship and Protective Proceedings Act (amending UPC Art. 5, Parts 1–4); and the Uniform Nonprobate Transfers on Death Act, the Uniform Multiple-Person Accounts Act, and the Uniform TOD Security Registration Act (amending UPC Art. 6).

Part II of this book contains other uniform acts that may prove germane to a trusts and estates course, reproduced in the order that they were first promulgated by the National Conference of Commissioners on Uniform State Laws: the Revised Uniform Principal and Income Act, the Uniform Trustees' Powers Act, the Uniform Transfers to Minors Act, the Uniform Premarital Agreement Act, the Uniform Marital Property Act, the Uniform Statutory Rule Against Perpetuities, the Uniform Custodial Trust Act, the Uniform Status of Children of Assisted Conception Act, the Uniform Simultaneous Death Act, the Uniform Health-Care Decisions Act, and the Uniform Prudent Investor Act. All are reproduced with the full text of the official comments.

Part III reproduces non-uniform legislation: the Inheritance and Family Provision Act from England, somewhat abridged; brief statutes from two Australian and one Canadian jurisdiction excusing Wills Act execution errors; and North Dakota's ante-mortem probate measure.

JOHN H. LANGBEIN
LAWRENCE W. WAGGONER

September 1994

iv

TABLE OF CONTENTS

*

DETAILED TABLE OF CONTENTS FOR THE UNIFORM PROBATE CODE

Article I

GENERAL PROVISIONS, DEFINITIONS AND PROBATE JURISDICTION OF COURT

Part 1

SHORT TITLE, CONSTRUCTION, GENERAL PROVISIONS

Part 2

DEFINITIONS

Part 3

SCOPE, JURISDICTION AND COURTS

DETAILED TABLE OF CONTENTS

Part 4

NOTICE, PARTIES AND REPRESENTATION IN ESTATE LITIGATION AND OTHER MATTERS

Article II

INTESTACY, WILLS, AND DONATIVE TRANSFERS (1993)

Part 1

INTESTATE SUCCESSION

Part 2

ELECTIVE SHARE OF SURVIVING SPOUSE

DETAILED TABLE OF CONTENTS

Part 3

SPOUSE AND CHILDREN UNPROVIDED FOR IN WILLS

Part 4

EXEMPT PROPERTY AND ALLOWANCES

Part 5

WILLS, WILL CONTRACTS, AND CUSTODY AND DEPOSIT OF WILLS

DETAILED TABLE OF CONTENTS

Part 8

GENERAL PROVISIONS CONCERNING PROBATE AND NONPROBATE TRANSFERS

Part 9

STATUTORY RULE AGAINST PERPETUITIES; HONORARY TRUSTS

Subpart 1

STATUTORY RULE AGAINST PERPETUITIES

Subpart 2

[HONORARY TRUSTS]

Part 10

UNIFORM INTERNATIONAL WILLS ACT [INTERNATIONAL WILL; INFORMATION REGISTRATION]

DETAILED TABLE OF CONTENTS

Article III

PROBATE OF WILLS AND ADMINISTRATION

Part 1

GENERAL PROVISIONS

Part 2

VENUE FOR PROBATE AND ADMINISTRATION; PRIORITY TO ADMINISTER; DEMAND FOR NOTICE

Part 3

INFORMAL PROBATE AND APPOINTMENT PROCEEDINGS; SUCCESSION WITHOUT ADMINISTRATION

SUCCESSION WITHOUT ADMINISTRATION

DETAILED TABLE OF CONTENTS

Part 4

FORMAL TESTACY AND APPOINTMENT PROCEEDINGS

Part 5

SUPERVISED ADMINISTRATION

DETAILED TABLE OF CONTENTS

Part 8

CREDITORS' CLAIMS

DETAILED TABLE OF CONTENTS

DETAILED TABLE OF CONTENTS

DETAILED TABLE OF CONTENTS

DETAILED TABLE OF CONTENTS

DETAILED TABLE OF CONTENTS

Part 5

DURABLE POWER OF ATTORNEY

DETAILED TABLE OF CONTENTS

Article VI

NONPROBATE TRANSFERS ON DEATH (1989)

Part 1

PROVISIONS RELATING TO EFFECT OF DEATH

Part 2

MULTIPLE–PERSON ACCOUNTS

Subpart 1

DEFINITIONS AND GENERAL PROVISIONS

Subpart 2

OWNERSHIP AS BETWEEN PARTIES AND OTHERS

Subpart 3

PROTECTION OF FINANCIAL INSTITUTIONS

Part 3

UNIFORM TOD SECURITY REGISTRATION ACT

Article VII

TRUST ADMINISTRATION

Part 1

TRUST REGISTRATION

Part 2

JURISDICTION OF COURT CONCERNING TRUSTS

DETAILED TABLE OF CONTENTS

Part 3

DUTIES AND LIABILITIES OF TRUSTEES

Part 4

POWERS OF TRUSTEES

[GENERAL COMMENT ONLY]

Article VIII

EFFECTIVE DATE AND REPEALER

UPC APPENDICES

UNIFORM
PROBATE CODE

OFFICIAL 1990 TEXT
WITH 1991 AND 1993 AMENDMENTS AND COMMENTS

*

UNIFORM PROBATE CODE

OFFICIAL 1990 TEXT
WITH 1991 and 1993 AMENDMENTS
AND COMMENTS

**Official Text and Comments Approved by the
National Conference of Commissioners
on Uniform State Laws**

AN ACT

Relating to affairs of decedents, missing persons, protected persons, minors, incapacitated persons and certain others and constituting the Uniform Probate Code; consolidating and revising aspects of the law relating to wills and intestacy and the administration and distribution of estates of decedents, missing persons, protected persons, minors, incapacitated persons and certain others; ordering the powers and procedures of the Court concerned with the affairs of decedents and certain others; providing for the validity and effect of certain non-testamentary transfers, contracts and deposits which relate to death and appear to have testamentary effect; providing certain procedures to facilitate enforcement of testamentary and other trusts; making uniform the law with respect to decedents and certain others; and repealing inconsistent legislation.

COMMENT

The long title of the Code should be adapted to the constitutional, statutory requirements and practices of the enacting state. The concept of the Code is that the "affairs of decedents, missing persons, disabled persons, minors, and certain others" is a single subject of the law notwithstanding its many facets.

*

1

ARTICLE I

GENERAL PROVISIONS, DEFINITIONS AND PROBATE JURISDICTION OF COURT

Table of Sections

PART 1

SHORT TITLE, CONSTRUCTION, GENERAL PROVISIONS

PART 2

DEFINITIONS

PART 3

SCOPE, JURISDICTION AND COURTS

PART 4

NOTICE, PARTIES AND REPRESENTATION IN ESTATE LITIGATION AND OTHER MATTERS

3

PART 1

SHORT TITLE, CONSTRUCTION, GENERAL PROVISIONS

Section 1–101. [Short Title.]

This Act shall be known and may be cited as the Uniform Probate Code.

Section 1–102. [Purposes; Rule of Construction.]

(a) This Code shall be liberally construed and applied to promote its underlying purposes and policies.

(b) The underlying purposes and policies of this Code are:

(1) to simplify and clarify the law concerning the affairs of decedents, missing persons, protected persons, minors and incapacitated persons;

(2) to discover and make effective the intent of a decedent in distribution of his property;

(3) to promote a speedy and efficient system for liquidating the estate of the decedent and making distribution to his successors;

(4) to facilitate use and enforcement of certain trusts;

(5) to make uniform the law among the various jurisdictions.

Section 1–103. [Supplementary General Principles of Law Applicable.]

Unless displaced by the particular provisions of this Code, the principles of law and equity supplement its provisions.

Section 1–104. [Severability.]

If any provision of this Code or the application thereof to any person or circumstances is held invalid, the invalidity shall not affect other provisions or applications of the Code which can be given effect without the invalid provision or application, and to this end the provisions of this Code are declared to be severable.

Section 1–105. [Construction Against Implied Repeal.]

This Code is a general act intended as a unified coverage of its subject matter and no part of it shall be deemed impliedly repealed by subsequent legislation if it can reasonably be avoided.

4

Section 1–106. [Effect of Fraud and Evasion.]

Whenever fraud has been perpetrated in connection with any proceeding or in any statement filed under this Code or if fraud is used to avoid or circumvent the provisions or purposes of this Code, any person injured thereby may obtain appropriate relief against the perpetrator of the fraud or restitution from any person (other than a bona fide purchaser) benefitting from the fraud, whether innocent or not. Any proceeding must be commenced within 2 years after the discovery of the fraud, but no proceeding may be brought against one not a perpetrator of the fraud later than 5 years after the time of commission of the fraud. This section has no bearing on remedies relating to fraud practiced on a decedent during his lifetime which affects the succession of his estate.

COMMENT

This is an overriding provision that provides an exception to the procedures and limitations provided in the Code. The remedy of a party wronged by fraud is intended to be supplementary to other protections provided in the Code and can be maintained outside the process of settlement of the estate. Thus, if a will which is known to be a forgery is probated informally, and the forgery is not discovered until after the period for contest has run, the defrauded heirs still could bring a fraud action under this section. Or if a will is fraudulently concealed after the testator's death and its existence not discovered until after the basic three year period (section 3–108) has elapsed, there still may be an action under this section. Similarly, a closing statement normally provides binding protection for the personal representative after six months from filing (section 3–1005). However, if there is fraudulent misrepresentation or concealment in the preparation of the claim, a later suit may be brought under this section against the personal representative for damages; or restitution may be obtained from those distributees who benefit by the fraud. In any case innocent purchasers for value are protected.

Any action under this section is subject to usual rules of res judicata; thus, if a forged will has been informally probated, an heir discovers the forgery, and then there is a formal proceeding under section 3–1001 of which the heir is given notice, followed by an order of complete settlement of the estate, the heir could not bring a subsequent action under section 1–106 but would be bound by the litigation in which the issue could have been raised. The usual rules for securing relief for fraud on a court would govern, however.

The final limitation in this section is designed to protect innocent distributees after a reasonable period of time. There is no limit (other than the 2 years from discovery of the fraud) against the wrongdoer. But there ought to be some limit after which innocent persons who have built up expectations in good faith cannot be deprived of the property by a restitution action.

The time of "discovery" of a fraud is a fact question to be determined in the individual case. In some situations persons may not actually know that a fraud has been perpetrated but have such strong suspicion and evidence that a court may conclude there has been a discovery of the fraud at that stage. On the other hand there is no duty to exercise reasonable care to discover fraud; the burden should not be on the heirs and devisees to check on the honesty of the other interested persons or the fiduciary.

Section 1–107. [Evidence of Death or Status.]

In addition to the rules of evidence in courts of general jurisdiction, the following rules relating to determination of death and status apply:

(1) Death occurs when an individual [is determined to be dead under the Uniform Determination of Death Act] [has sustained either (i) irreversible cessation of circulatory and respiratory functions or (ii) irreversible cessation of all functions of the entire brain, including the brain stem. A determination of death must be made in accordance with accepted medical standards].

(2) A certified or authenticated copy of a death certificate purporting to be issued by an official or agency of the place where the death purportedly occurred is prima facie evidence of the fact, place, date and time of death and the identity of the decedent;

(3) A certified or authenticated copy of any record or report of a governmental agency, domestic or foreign, that an individual is missing, detained, dead, or alive is prima facie evidence of the status and of the dates, circumstances and places disclosed by the record or report;

(4) In the absence of prima facie evidence of death under paragraph (2) or (3), the fact of death may be established by clear and convincing evidence, including circumstantial evidence;

(5) An individual whose death is not established under the preceding paragraphs who is absent for a continuous period of 5 years, during which he [or she] has not been heard from, and whose absence is not satisfactorily explained after diligent search or inquiry is presumed to be dead. His [or her] death is presumed to have occurred at the end of the period unless there is sufficient evidence for determining that death occurred earlier.

(6) In the absence of evidence disputing the time of death stated on a document described in paragraph (2) or (3), a document described in paragraph (2) or (3) that states a time of death 120 hours or more after the time of death of another individual, however the time of death of the other individual is determined, establishes by clear and convincing evidence that the individual survived the other individual by 120 hours.

COMMENT

Paragraph (1) defines death by reference to the Uniform Determination of Death Act (UDDA). States that have adopted the UDDA should use the first set of bracketed language. States that have not adopted the UDDA should use the second set of bracketed language.

Note that paragraph (6) is made desirable by the fact that Sections 2–104 and 2–702 require that survival by 120 hours must be established by clear and convincing evidence.

Paragraph (4) is inconsistent with Section 1 of Uniform Absence as Evidence of Death and Absentees' Property Act (1938).

Proceedings to secure protection of property interests of an absent person may be commenced as provided in section 5–401.

Section 1–108. [Acts by Holder of General Power.]

For the purpose of granting consent or approval with regard to the acts or accounts of a personal representative or trustee, including relief from liability or penalty for failure to post bond, to register a trust, or to perform other duties, and for purposes of consenting to modification or termination of a trust or to deviation from its terms, the sole holder or all co-holders of a presently exercisable general power of appointment, including one in the form of a power of amendment or revocation, are deemed to act for beneficiaries to the extent their interests (as objects, takers in default, or otherwise) are subject to the power.

COMMENT

The status of a holder of a general power in estate litigation is dealt with by section 1–403.

This section permits the settlor of a revocable trust to excuse the trustee from registering the trust so long as the power of revocation continues.

"General power," as used in this section, is intended to refer to the common law concept, rather than to tax or other statutory meanings. A general power, as used herein, is one which enables the power holder to draw absolute ownership to himself.

PART 2

DEFINITIONS

Section 1–201. General Definitions.

Subject to additional definitions contained in the subsequent Articles that are applicable to specific Articles, parts, or sections, and unless the context otherwise requires, in this Code:

(1) "Agent" includes an attorney-in-fact under a durable or nondurable power of attorney, an individual authorized to make decisions concerning another's health care, and an individual authorized to make decisions for another under a natural death act.

(2) "Application" means a written request to the Registrar for an order of informal probate or appointment under Part 3 of Article III.

(3) "Beneficiary," as it relates to a trust beneficiary, includes a person who has any present or future interest, vested or contingent, and also includes the owner of an interest by assignment or other transfer; as it relates to a charitable trust, includes any person entitled to enforce the trust; as it relates to a "beneficiary of a beneficiary designation," refers to a beneficiary of an insurance or annuity policy, of an account with POD designation, of a security registered in beneficiary form (TOD), or of a pension, profit-sharing, retirement, or similar benefit plan, or other nonprobate transfer at death; and, as it relates to a "beneficiary designated in a governing instrument," includes a grantee of a deed, a devisee, a trust beneficiary, a beneficiary of a beneficiary designation, a donee, appointee, or taker in default of a power of appointment, and a person in whose favor a power of attorney or a power held in any individual, fiduciary, or representative capacity is exercised.

(4) "Beneficiary designation" refers to a governing instrument naming a beneficiary of an insurance or annuity policy, of an account with POD designation, of a security registered in beneficiary form (TOD), or of a pension, profit-sharing, retirement, or similar benefit plan, or other nonprobate transfer at death.

(5) "Child" includes an individual entitled to take as a child under this Code by intestate succession from the parent whose relationship is involved and excludes a person who is only a stepchild, a foster child, a grandchild, or any more remote descendant.

8

(6) "Claims," in respect to estates of decedents and protected persons, includes liabilities of the decedent or protected person, whether arising in contract, in tort, or otherwise, and liabilities of the estate which arise at or after the death of the decedent or after the appointment of a conservator, including funeral expenses and expenses of administration. The term does not include estate or inheritance taxes, or demands or disputes regarding title of a decedent or protected person to specific assets alleged to be included in the estate.

(7) "Court" means the [. . . . . . Court] or branch in this State having jurisdiction in matters relating to the affairs of decedents.

(8) "Conservator" means a person who is appointed by a Court to manage the estate of a protected person.

(9) "Descendant" of an individual means all of his [or her] descendants of all generations, with the relationship of parent and child at each generation being determined by the definition of child and parent contained in this Code.

(10) "Devise," when used as a noun, means a testamentary disposition of real or personal property and, when used as a verb, means to dispose of real or personal property by will.

(11) "Devisee" means a person designated in a will to receive a devise. For the purposes of Article III, in the case of a devise to an existing trust or trustee, or to a trustee on trust described by will, the trust or trustee is the devisee and the beneficiaries are not devisees.

(12) "Disability" means cause for a protective order as described in Section 5–401.

(13) "Distributee" means any person who has received property of a decedent from his [or her] personal representative other than as a creditor or purchaser. A testamentary trustee is a distributee only to the extent of distributed assets or increment thereto remaining in his [or her] hands. A beneficiary of a testamentary trust to whom the trustee has distributed property received from a personal representative is a distributee of the personal representative. For the purposes of this provision, "testamentary trustee" includes a trustee to whom assets are transferred by will, to the extent of the devised assets.

(14) "Estate" includes the property of the decedent, trust, or other person whose affairs are subject to this Code as originally constituted and as it exists from time to time during administration.

9

(15) "Exempt property" means that property of a decedent's estate which is described in Section 2–403.

(16) "Fiduciary" includes a personal representative, guardian, conservator, and trustee.

(17) "Foreign personal representative" means a personal representative appointed by another jurisdiction.

(18) "Formal proceedings" means proceedings conducted before a judge with notice to interested persons.

(19) "Governing instrument" means a deed, will, trust, insurance or annuity policy, account with POD designation, security registered in beneficiary form (TOD), pension, profit-sharing, retirement, or similar benefit plan, instrument creating or exercising a power of appointment or a power of attorney, or a dispositive appointive, or nominative instrument of any similar type.

(20) "Guardian" means a person who has qualified as a guardian of a minor or incapacitated person pursuant to testamentary or court appointment, but excludes one who is merely a guardian ad litem.

(21) "Heirs," except as controlled by Section 2–711, means persons, including the surviving spouse and the state, who are entitled under the statutes of intestate succession to the property of a decedent.

(22) "Incapacitated person" means an individual described in Section 5–103.

(23) "Informal proceedings" mean those conducted without notice to interested persons by an officer of the Court acting as a registrar for probate of a will or appointment of a personal representative.

(24) "Interested person" includes heirs, devisees, children, spouses, creditors, beneficiaries, and any others having a property right in or claim against a trust estate or the estate of a decedent, ward, or protected person. It also includes persons having priority for appointment as personal representative, and other fiduciaries representing interested persons. The meaning as it relates to particular persons may vary from time to time and must be determined according to the particular purposes of, and matter involved in, any proceeding.

(25) "Issue" of a person means descendant as defined in subsection (9).

(26) "Joint tenants with the right of survivorship" and "community property with the right of survivorship" includes co-owners

of property held under circumstances that entitle one or more to the whole of the property on the death of the other or others, but excludes forms of co-ownership registration in which the underlying ownership of each party is in proportion to that party's contribution.

(27) "Lease" includes an oil, gas, or other mineral lease.

(28) "Letters" includes letters testamentary, letters of guardianship, letters of administration, and letters of conservatorship.

(29) "Minor" means a person who is under [21] years of age.

(30) "Mortgage" means any conveyance, agreement, or arrangement in which property is encumbered or used as security.

(31) "Nonresident decedent" means a decedent who was domiciled in another jurisdiction at the time of his [or her] death.

(32) "Organization" means a corporation, business trust, estate, trust, partnership, joint venture, association, government or governmental subdivision or agency, or any other legal or commercial entity.

(33) "Parent" includes any person entitled to take, or who would be entitled to take if the child died without a will, as a parent under this Code by intestate succession from the child whose relationship is in question and excludes any person who is only a stepparent, foster parent, or grandparent.

(34) "Payor" means a trustee, insurer, business entity, employer, government, governmental agency or subdivision, or any other person authorized or obligated by law or a governing instrument to make payments.

(35) "Person" means an individual or an organization.

(36) "Personal representative" includes executor, administrator, successor personal representative, special administrator, and persons who perform substantially the same function under the law governing their status. "General personal representative" excludes special administrator.

(37) "Petition" means a written request to the Court for an order after notice.

(38) "Proceeding" includes action at law and suit in equity.

(39) "Property" includes both real and personal property or any interest therein and means anything that may be the subject of ownership.

(40) "Protected person" is as defined in Section 5–103.

11

(41) "Protective proceeding" means a proceeding described in Section 5–103.

(42) "Registrar" refers to the official of the Court designated to perform the functions of Registrar as provided in Section 1–307.

(43) "Security" includes any note, stock, treasury stock, bond, debenture, evidence of indebtedness, certificate of interest or participation in an oil, gas, or mining title or lease or in payments out of production under such a title or lease, collateral trust certificate, transferable share, voting trust certificate, and in general, any interest or instrument commonly known as a security, or any certificate of interest or participation, any temporary or interim certificate, receipt, or certificate of deposit for, or any warrant or right to subscribe to or purchase, any of the foregoing.

(44) "Settlement," in reference to a decedent's estate, includes the full process of administration, distribution, and closing.

(45) "Special administrator" means a personal representative as described by Sections 3–614 through 3–618.

(46) "State" means a state of the United States, the District of Columbia, the Commonwealth of Puerto Rico, or any territory or insular possession subject to the jurisdiction of the United States.

(47) "Successor personal representative" means a personal representative, other than a special administrator, who is appointed to succeed a previously appointed personal representative.

(48) "Successors" means persons, other than creditors, who are entitled to property of a decedent under his [or her] will or this Code.

(49) "Supervised administration" refers to the proceedings described in Article III, Part 5.

(50) "Survive" means that an individual has neither predeceased an event, including the death of another individual, nor is deemed to have predeceased an event under Section 2–104 or 2–702. The term includes its derivatives, such as "survives," "survived," "survivor," and "surviving."

(51) "Testacy proceeding" means a proceeding to establish a will or determine intestacy.

(52) "Testator" includes an individual of either sex.

(53) "Trust" includes an express trust, private or charitable, with additions thereto, wherever and however created. The term also includes a trust created or determined by judgment or decree under which the trust is to be administered in the manner of an express trust. The term excludes other constructive trusts and

excludes resulting trusts, conservatorships, personal representatives, trust accounts as defined in Article VI, custodial arrangements pursuant to [each state should list its legislation, including that relating to [gifts] [transfers] to minors, dealing with special custodial situations], business trusts providing for certificates to be issued to beneficiaries, common trust funds, voting trusts, security arrangements, liquidation trusts, and trusts for the primary purpose of paying debts, dividends, interest, salaries, wages, profits, pensions, or employee benefits of any kind, and any arrangement under which a person is nominee or escrowee for another.

(54) "Trustee" includes an original, additional, or successor trustee, whether or not appointed or confirmed by court.

(55) "Ward" means an individual described in Section 5–103.

(56) "Will" includes codicil and any testamentary instrument that merely appoints an executor, revokes or revises another will, nominates a guardian, or expressly excludes or limits the right of an individual or class to succeed to property of the decedent passing by intestate succession.

[FOR ADOPTION IN COMMUNITY PROPERTY STATES]

[(57) "Separate property" (if necessary, to be defined locally in accordance with existing concept in adopting state).

(58) "Community property" (if necessary, to be defined, locally in accordance with existing concept in adopting state).]

COMMENT

Special definitions for Articles V and VI are contained in Sections 5–103, 6–201, and 6–301. Except as controlled by special definitions applicable to these particular Articles, or applicable to particular sections, the definitions in Section 1–201 apply to the entire Code.

13

PART 3

SCOPE, JURISDICTION AND COURTS

Section 1–301. [Territorial Application.]

Except as otherwise provided in this Code, this Code applies to (1) the affairs and estates of decedents, missing persons, and persons to be protected, domiciled in this state, (2) the property of nonresidents located in this state or property coming into the control of a fiduciary who is subject to the laws of this state, (3) incapacitated persons and minors in this state, (4) survivorship and related accounts in this state, and (5) trusts subject to administration in this state.

Section 1–302. [Subject Matter Jurisdiction.]

(a) To the full extent permitted by the constitution, the Court has jurisdiction over all subject matter relating to (1) estates of decedents, including construction of wills and determination of heirs and successors of decedents, and estates of protected persons; (2) protection of minors and incapacitated persons; and (3) trusts.

(b) The Court has full power to make orders, judgments and decrees and take all other action necessary and proper to administer justice in the matters which come before it.

(c) The Court has jurisdiction over protective proceedings and guardianship proceedings.

(d) If both guardianship and protective proceedings as to the same person are commenced or pending in the same Court, the proceedings may be consolidated.

Section 1–303. [Venue; Multiple Proceedings; Transfer.]

(a) Where a proceeding under this Code could be maintained in more than one place in this state, the Court in which the proceeding is first commenced has the exclusive right to proceed.

(b) If proceedings concerning the same estate, protected person, ward, or trust are commenced in more than one Court of this state, the Court in which the proceeding was first commenced shall continue to hear the matter, and the other Courts shall hold the matter in abeyance until the question of venue is decided, and if the ruling Court determines that venue is properly in another Court, it shall transfer the proceeding to the other Court.

14

(c) If a Court finds that in the interest of justice a proceeding or a file should be located in another Court of this state, the Court making the finding may transfer the proceeding or file to the other Court.

Section 1–304. [Practice in Court.]

Unless specifically provided to the contrary in this Code or unless inconsistent with its provisions, the rules of civil procedure including the rules concerning vacation of orders and appellate review govern formal proceedings under this Code.

Section 1–305. [Records and Certified Copies.]

The [Clerk of Court] shall keep a record for each decedent, ward, protected person or trust involved in any document which may be filed with the Court under this Code, including petitions and applications, demands for notices or bonds, trust registrations, and of any orders or responses relating thereto by the Registrar or Court, and establish and maintain a system for indexing, filing or recording which is sufficient to enable users of the records to obtain adequate information. Upon payment of the fees required by law the clerk must issue certified copies of any probated wills, letters issued to personal representatives, or any other record or paper filed or recorded. Certificates relating to probated wills must indicate whether the decedent was domiciled in this state and whether the probate was formal or informal. Certificates relating to letters must show the date of appointment.

Section 1–306. [Jury Trial.]

(a) If duly demanded, a party is entitled to trial by jury in [a formal testacy proceeding and] any proceeding in which any controverted question of fact arises as to which any party has a constitutional right to trial by jury.

(b) If there is no right to trial by jury under subsection (a) or the right is waived, the Court in its discretion may call a jury to decide any issue of fact, in which case the verdict is advisory only.

Section 1–307. [Registrar; Powers.]

The acts and orders which this Code specifies as performable by the Registrar may be performed either by a judge of the Court or by a person, including the clerk, designated by the Court by a written order filed and recorded in the office of the Court.

Section 1–308. [Appeals.]

Appellate review, including the right to appellate review, interlocutory appeal, provisions as to time, manner, notice, appeal bond, stays, scope of review, record on appeal, briefs, arguments and power of the appellate court, is governed by the rules applicable to the appeals to the [Supreme Court] in equity cases from the [court of general jurisdiction], except that in proceedings where jury trial has been had as a matter of right, the rules applicable to the scope of review in jury cases apply.

Section 1–309. [Qualifications of Judge.]

A judge of the Court must have the same qualifications as a judge of the [court of general jurisdiction.]

COMMENT

In Article VIII, Section 8–101 on transition from old law to new law provision is made for the continuation in service of a sitting judge not qualified for initial selection.

Section 1–310. [Oath or Affirmation on Filed Documents.]

Except as otherwise specifically provided in this Code or by rule, every document filed with the Court under this Code including applications, petitions, and demands for notice, shall be deemed to include an oath, affirmation, or statement to the effect that its representations are true as far as the person executing or filing it knows or is informed, and penalties for perjury may follow deliberate falsification therein.

PART 4

NOTICE, PARTIES AND REPRESENTATION IN ESTATE LITIGATION AND OTHER MATTERS

Section 1–401. [Notice; Method and Time of Giving.]

(a) If notice of a hearing on any petition is required and except for specific notice requirements as otherwise provided, the petitioner shall cause notice of the time and place of hearing of any petition to be given to any interested person or his attorney if he has appeared by attorney or requested that notice be sent to his attorney. Notice shall be given:

(1) by mailing a copy thereof at least 14 days before the time set for the hearing by certified, registered or ordinary first class mail addressed to the person being notified at the post office address given in his demand for notice, if any, or at his office or place of residence, if known;

(2) by delivering a copy thereof to the person being notified personally at least 14 days before the time set for the hearing; or

(3) if the address, or identity of any person is not known and cannot be ascertained with reasonable diligence, by publishing at least once a week for 3 consecutive weeks, a copy thereof in a newspaper having general circulation in the county where the hearing is to be held, the last publication of which is to be at least 10 days before the time set for the hearing.

(b) The Court for good cause shown may provide for a different method or time of giving notice for any hearing.

(c) Proof of the giving of notice shall be made on or before the hearing and filed in the proceeding.

Section 1–402. [Notice; Waiver.]

A person, including a guardian ad litem, conservator, or other fiduciary, may waive notice by a writing signed by him or his attorney and filed in the proceeding. A person for whom a guardianship or other protective order is sought, a ward, or a protected person may not waive notice.

17

COMMENT

The subject of appearance is covered by Section 1–304.

Section 1–403. [Pleadings; When Parties Bound by Others; Notice.]

In formal proceedings involving trusts or estates of decedents, minors, protected persons, or incapacitated persons, and in judicially supervised settlements, the following apply:

(1) Interests to be affected shall be described in pleadings which give reasonable information to owners by name or class, by reference to the instrument creating the interests, or in other appropriate manner.

(2) Persons are bound by orders binding others in the following cases:

(i) Orders binding the sole holder or all co-holders of a power of revocation or a presently exercisable general power of appointment, including one in the form of a power of amendment, bind other persons to the extent their interests (as objects, takers in default, or otherwise) are subject to the power.

(ii) To the extent there is no conflict of interest between them or among persons represented, orders binding a conservator bind the person whose estate he controls; orders binding a guardian bind the ward if no conservator of his estate has been appointed; orders binding a trustee bind beneficiaries of the trust in proceedings to probate a will establishing or adding to a trust, to review the acts or accounts of a prior fiduciary and in proceedings involving creditors or other third parties; and orders binding a personal representative bind persons interested in the undistributed assets of a decedent's estate in actions or proceedings by or against the estate. If there is no conflict of interest and no conservator or guardian has been appointed, a parent may represent his minor child.

(iii) An unborn or unascertained person who is not otherwise represented is bound by an order to the extent his interest is adequately represented by another party having a substantially identical interest in the proceeding.

(3) Notice is required as follows:

(i) Notice as prescribed by Section 1–401 shall be given to every interested person or to one who can bind an interested

18

person as described in (2)(i) or (2)(ii) above. Notice may be given both to a person and to another who may bind him.

(ii) Notice is given to unborn or unascertained persons, who are not represented under (2)(i) or (2)(ii) above, by giving notice to all known persons whose interests in the proceedings are substantially identical to those of the unborn or unascertained persons.

(4) At any point in a proceeding, a court may appoint a guardian ad litem to represent the interest of a minor, an incapacitated, unborn, or unascertained person, or a person whose identity or address is unknown, if the Court determines that representation of the interest otherwise would be inadequate. If not precluded by conflict of interests, a guardian ad litem may be appointed to represent several persons or interests. The Court shall set out its reasons for appointing a guardian ad litem as a part of the record of the proceeding.

COMMENT

A general power, as used here and in Section 1–108, is one which enables the power holder to draw absolute ownership to himself. The section assumes a valid general power. If the validity of the power itself were in issue, the power holder could not represent others, as for example, the takers in default.

The general rules of civil procedure are applicable where not replaced by specific provision, see Section 1–304. Those rules would determine the mode of giving notice or serving process on a minor or the mode of notice in class suits involving large groups of persons made party to a suit.

*

ARTICLE II

INTESTACY, WILLS, AND DONATIVE TRANSFERS (1993)

Table of Sections

PART 1

INTESTATE SUCCESSION

PART 2

ELECTIVE SHARE OF SURVIVING SPOUSE

PART 3

SPOUSE AND CHILDREN UNPROVIDED FOR IN WILLS

PART 4

EXEMPT PROPERTY AND ALLOWANCES

PART 5

WILLS, WILL CONTRACTS, AND CUSTODY AND DEPOSIT OF WILLS

PART 6

RULES OF CONSTRUCTION APPLICABLE ONLY TO WILLS

Subpart 2. [Honorary Trusts]

PART 10

UNIFORM INTERNATIONAL WILLS ACT
[INTERNATIONAL WILL; INFORMATION REGISTRATION]

UNIFORM PROBATE CODE

PREFATORY NOTE

ARTICLE II REVISIONS

The Uniform Probate Code was promulgated in 1969. In 1990, Article II of the Code underwent significant revision. The 1990 revisions are the culmination of a systematic study of the Code conducted by the Joint Editorial Board for the Uniform Probate Code (JEB–UPC) and a special Drafting Committee to Revise Article II. The 1990 revisions concentrate on Article II, which is the article that covers the substantive law of intestate succession; spouse's elective share; omitted spouse and children; probate exemptions and allowances; execution and revocation of wills; will contracts; rules of construction; disclaimers; the effect of homicide and divorce on succession rights; and the rule against perpetuities and honorary trusts.

In the twenty or so years between the original promulgation of the Code and the 1990 revisions, several developments occurred that prompted the systematic round of review. Three themes were sounded: (1) the decline of formalism in favor of intent-serving policies; (2) the recognition that will substitutes and other inter-vivos transfers have so proliferated that they now constitute a major, if not the major, form of wealth transmission; (3) the advent of the multiple-marriage society, resulting in a significant fraction of the population being married more than once and having stepchildren and children by previous marriages and in the acceptance of a partnership or marital-sharing theory of marriage.

The 1990 revisions respond to these themes. The multiple-marriage society and the partnership/marital-sharing theory are reflected in the revised elective-share provisions of Part 2. As the General Comment to Part 2 explains, the revised elective share grants the surviving spouse a right of election that implements the partnership/marital-sharing theory by adjusting the elective share to the length of the marriage.

The children-of-previous-marriages and stepchildren phenomena are reflected most prominently in the revised rules on the spouse's share in intestacy.

The proliferation of will substitutes and other inter-vivos transfers is recognized, mainly, in measures tending to bring the law of probate and nonprobate transfers into greater unison. One aspect of this tendency is reflected in the restructuring of the rules of construction. Rules of construction are rules that supply presumptive meaning to dispositive and other provisions of governing instruments. Part 6 of the pre-1990 Code contained several rules of construction that applied only to wills. Some of those rules of construction appropriately applied only to wills; provisions relating to lapse, testamentary exercise of a power of appointment, and ademption of a devise by satisfaction exemplify such rules of construction. Other rules of construction, however, properly apply to all governing instruments, not just wills; the provision relating to inclusion of adopted persons in class gift language exemplifies this type of rule of construction. The 1990 revisions divide pre-1990 Part 6 into two parts—Part 6, containing rules of construction for wills only; and Part 7, containing rules of construction for wills and other governing instruments. A few new rules of construction are also added.

In addition to separating the rules of construction into two parts, and adding new rules of construction, the revocation-upon-divorce provision (section 2–804) is substantially revised so that divorce not only revokes devises, but also nonprobate beneficiary designations, in favor of the former spouse. Another feature of the 1990 revisions is a new section (section 2–503) that brings the execution formalities for wills more into line with those for nonprobate transfers.

The 1990 Article II revisions also respond to other modern trends. During the period from 1969 to 1990, many developments occurred in the case law and statutory law. Also, many specific topics in probate, estate, and future-interests law were examined in the scholarly literature. The influence of many of these developments is seen in the 1990 revisions of Article II.

PART 1

INTESTATE SUCCESSION

GENERAL COMMENT

The pre–1990 Code's basic pattern of intestate succession, contained in Part 1, was designed to provide suitable rules for the person of modest means who relies on the estate plan provided by law. The 1990 revisions are intended to further that purpose, by fine tuning the various sections and bringing them into line with developing public policy.

The principal features of the 1990 revisions are:

1. So-called negative wills are authorized, under which the decedent who dies intestate, in whole or in part, can by will disinherit a particular heir.

2. A surviving spouse receives the whole of the intestate estate, if the decedent left no surviving descendants and no parents or if the decedent's surviving descendants are also descendants of the surviving spouse and the surviving spouse has no descendants who are not descendants of the decedent. The surviving spouse receives the first $200,000 plus three-fourths of the balance if the decedent left no surviving descendants but a surviving parent. The surviving spouse receives the first $150,000 plus one-half of the balance of the intestate estate, if the decedent's surviving descendants are also descendants of the surviving spouse but the surviving spouse has one or more other descendants. The surviving spouse receives the first $100,000 plus one-half of the balance of the intestate estate, if the decedent has one or more surviving descendants who are not descendants of the surviving spouse.

3. A system of representation called per capita at each generation is adopted as a means of more faithfully carrying out the underlying premise of the pre–1990 UPC system of representation. Under the per-capita-at-each-generation system, all grandchildren (whose parent has predeceased the intestate) receive equal shares.

4. Although only a modest revision of the section dealing with the status of adopted children and children born of unmarried parents is made at this time, the question is under continuing review and further revisions may be presented in the future.

5. The section on advancements is revised so that it applies to partially intestate estates as well as to wholly intestate estates.

Section 2–101. Intestate Estate.

(a) Any part of a decedent's estate not effectively disposed of by will passes by intestate succession to the decedent's heirs as prescribed in this Code, except as modified by the decedent's will.

(b) A decedent by will may expressly exclude or limit the right of an individual or class to succeed to property of the decedent passing by intestate succession. If that individual or a member of that class survives the decedent, the share of the decedent's intestate estate to which that individual or class would have succeeded passes as if that individual or each member of that class had disclaimed his [or her] intestate share.

COMMENT

Purpose of Revision. The amendments to subsection (a) are stylistic, not substantive.

New subsection (b) authorizes the decedent, by will, to exclude or limit the right of an individual or class to share in the decedent's intestate estate, in effect disinheriting that individual or class. By specifically authorizing so-called negative wills, subsection (b) reverses the usually accepted common-law rule, which defeats a testator's intent for no sufficient reason. See Note, "The Intestate Claims of Heirs Excluded by Will: Should 'Negative Wills' Be Enforced?," 52 U. Chi. L. Rev. 177 (1985).

Whether or not in an individual case the decedent's will has excluded or limited the right of an individual or class to take a share of the decedent's intestate estate is a question of construction. A clear case would be one in which the decedent's will expressly states that an individual is to receive none of the decedent's estate. Examples would be testamentary language such as "my brother, Hector, is not to receive any of my property" or "Brother Hector is disinherited."

Another rather clear case would be one in which the will states that an individual is to receive only a nominal devise, such as "I devise $50.00 to my brother, Hector, and no more."

An individual need not be identified by name to be excluded. Thus, if brother Hector is the decedent's only brother, Hector could be identified by a term such as "my brother." A group or class of relatives (such as "my brothers and sisters") can also be excluded under this provision.

Subsection (b) establishes the consequence of a disinheritance— the share of the decedent's intestate estate to which the disinherited individual or class would have succeeded passes as if that individual or class had disclaimed the intestate share. Thus, if the decedent's will provides that brother Hector is to receive $50.00 and no more, Hector is entitled to the $50.00 devise (because Hector is *not* treated as having predeceased the decedent for purposes of *testate* succession), but the portion of the decedent's *intestate* estate to which Hector would have succeeded passes as if Hector had disclaimed his intestate share. The consequence of a disclaimer by Hector of his intestate share is governed by Section 2–801(d)(1), which provides that Hector's intestate share passes to Hector's descendants by representation.

Example: G died partially intestate. G is survived by brother Hector, Hector's 3 children (X, Y, and Z), and the child (V) of a

28

deceased sister. G's will excluded Hector from sharing in G's intestate estate.

Solution: V takes half of G's intestate estate. X, Y, and Z split the other half, i.e., they take 1/6 each. Sections 2–103(3); 2–106; 2–801(d)(1). Had Hector not been excluded by G's will, the share to which Hector would have succeeded would have been 1/2. Under section 2–801(d)(1), that half, not the whole of G's intestate estate, is what passes to Hector's descendants by representation as if Hector had disclaimed his intestate share.

Note that if brother Hector had *actually* predeceased G, or was treated as if he predeceased G by reason of not surviving G by 120 hours (see section 2–104), then no consequence flows from Hector's disinheritance: V, X, Y, and Z would each take 1/4 of G's intestate estate under sections 2–103(3) and 2–106.

Section 2–102. Share of Spouse.

The intestate share of a decedent's surviving spouse is:

(1) the entire intestate estate if:

(i) no descendant or parent of the decedent survives the decedent; or

(ii) all of the decedent's surviving descendants are also descendants of the surviving spouse and there is no other descendant of the surviving spouse who survives the decedent;

(2) the first [$200,000], plus three-fourths of any balance of the intestate estate, if no descendant of the decedent survives the decedent, but a parent of the decedent survives the decedent;

(3) the first [$150,000], plus one-half of any balance of the intestate estate, if all of the decedent's surviving descendants are also descendants of the surviving spouse and the surviving spouse has one or more surviving descendants who are not descendants of the decedent;

(4) the first [$100,000], plus one-half of any balance of the intestate estate, if one or more of the decedent's surviving descendants are not descendants of the surviving spouse.

COMMENT

Purpose and Scope of Revisions. This section is revised to give the surviving spouse a larger share than the pre–1990 UPC. If the decedent leaves no surviving descendants and no surviving parent or if the decedent does leave surviving descendants but neither the decedent nor the surviving spouse has other de-

29

scendants, the surviving spouse is entitled to all of the decedent's intestate estate.

If the decedent leaves no surviving descendants but does leave a surviving parent, the decedent's surviving spouse receives the first $200,000 plus three-fourths of the balance of the intestate estate.

If the decedent leaves surviving descendants and if the surviving spouse (but not the decedent) has other descendants, and thus the decedent's descendants are unlikely to be the *exclusive* beneficiaries of the surviving spouse's estate, the surviving spouse receives the first $150,000 plus one-half of the balance of the intestate estate. The purpose is to assure the decedent's own descendants of a share in the decedent's intestate estate when the estate exceeds $150,000.

If the decedent has other descendants, the surviving spouse receives $100,000 plus one half of the balance. In this type of case, the decedent's descendants who are not descendants of the surviving spouse are not natural objects of the bounty of the surviving spouse.

Note that in all the cases where the surviving spouse receives a lump sum plus a fraction of the balance, the lump sums must be understood to be in addition to the probate exemptions and allowances to which the surviving spouse is entitled under Part 4. These can add up to a minimum of $43,000.

Under the pre–1990 Code, the decedent's surviving spouse received the entire intestate estate only if there were neither surviving descendants nor parents. If there were surviving descendants, the descendants took one-half of the bal-

ance of the estate in excess of $50,-000 (for example, $25,000 in a $100,000 estate). If there were no surviving descendants, but there was a surviving parent or parents, the parent or parents took that one-half of the balance in excess of $50,-000.

References. The theory of this section is discussed in Waggoner, "The Multiple-Marriage Society and Spousal Rights Under the Revised Uniform Probate Code," 76 Iowa L.Rev. 223, 229–35 (1991).

Empirical studies support the increase in the surviving spouse's intestate share, reflected in the revisions of this section. The studies have shown that testators in smaller estates (which intestate estates overwhelmingly tend to be) tend to devise their *entire* estates to their surviving spouses, even when the couple has children. See C. Shammas, M. Salmon & M. Bahlin, Inheritance in America from Colonial Times to the Present 184–85 (1987); M. Sussman, J. Cates & D. Smith, The Family and Inheritance (1970); Browder, "Recent Patterns of Testate Succession in the United States and England," 67 Mich. L. Rev. 1303, 1307–08 (1969); Dunham, "The Method, Process and Frequency of Wealth Transmission at Death," 30 U. Chi. L. Rev. 241, 252 (1963); Gibson, "Inheritance of Community Property in Texas—A Need for Reform," 47 Texas L. Rev. 359, 364–66 (1969); Price, "The Transmission of Wealth at Death in a Community Property Jurisdiction," 50 Wash. L. Rev. 277, 283, 311–17 (1975). See also Fellows, Simon & Rau, "Public Attitudes About Property Distribution at Death and Intestate Succession Laws in the United States," 1978 Am. B. F. Research J. 319, 355–68;

Note, "A Comparison of Iowans' Dispositive Preferences with Selected Provisions of the Iowa and Uniform Probate Codes," 63 Iowa L. Rev. 1041, 1091–92 (1978).

Cross Reference. See Section 2–802 for the definition of spouse, which controls for purposes of intestate succession.

[ALTERNATIVE PROVISION FOR COMMUNITY PROPERTY STATES]

[Section 2–102A. Share of Spouse.

(a) The intestate share of a surviving spouse in separate property is:

(1) the entire intestate estate if:

(i) no descendant or parent of the decedent survives the decedent; or

(ii) all of the decedent's surviving descendants are also descendants of the surviving spouse and there is no other descendant of the surviving spouse who survives the decedent;

(2) the first [$200,000], plus three-fourths of any balance of the intestate estate, if no descendant of the decedent survives the decedent, but a parent of the decedent survives the decedent;

(3) the first [$150,000], plus one-half of any balance of the intestate estate, if all of the decedent's surviving descendants are also descendants of the surviving spouse and the surviving spouse has one or more surviving descendants who are not descendants of the decedent;

(4) the first [$100,000], plus one-half of any balance of the intestate estate, if one or more of the decedent's surviving descendants are not descendants of the surviving spouse.

(b) The one-half of community property belonging to the decedent passes to the [surviving spouse] as the intestate share.]

COMMENT

The brackets around the term "surviving spouse" in subsection (b) indicate that states are free to adopt a different scheme for the distribution of the decedent's half of the community property, as some community property states have done.

Section 2–103. Share of Heirs Other Than Surviving Spouse.

Any part of the intestate estate not passing to the decedent's surviving spouse under Section 2–102, or the entire intestate estate if there is no surviving spouse, passes in the following order to the individuals designated below who survive the decedent:

(1) to the decedent's descendants by representation;

(2) if there is no surviving descendant, to the decedent's parents equally if both survive, or to the surviving parent;

(3) if there is no surviving descendant or parent, to the descendants of the decedent's parents or either of them by representation;

(4) if there is no surviving descendant, parent, or descendant of a parent, but the decedent is survived by one or more grandparents or descendants of grandparents, half of the estate passes to the decedent's paternal grandparents equally if both survive, or to the surviving paternal grandparent, or to the descendants of the decedent's paternal grandparents or either of them if both are deceased, the descendants taking by representation; and the other half passes to the decedent's maternal relatives in the same manner; but if there is no surviving grandparent or descendant of a grandparent on either the paternal or the maternal side, the entire estate passes to the decedent's relatives on the other side in the same manner as the half.

COMMENT

This section provides for inheritance by descendants of the decedent, parents and their descendants, and grandparents and collateral relatives descended from grandparents; in line with modern policy, it eliminates more remote relatives tracing through great-grandparents.

Purpose and Scope of Revisions. The revisions are stylistic and clarifying, not substantive. The pre–1990 version of this section contained the phrase "if they are all of the same degree of kinship to the decedent they take equally (etc.)." That language has been removed.

It was unnecessary and confusing because the system of representation in Section 2–106 gives equal shares if the decedent's descendants are all of the same degree of kinship to the decedent.

The word "descendants" replaces the word "issue" in this section and throughout the revisions of Article II. The term issue is a term of art having a biological connotation. Now that inheritance rights, in certain cases, are extended to adopted children, the term descendants is a more appropriate term.

Section 2–104. Requirement That Heir Survive Decedent for 120 Hours.

An individual who fails to survive the decedent by 120 hours is deemed to have predeceased the decedent for purposes of homestead allowance, exempt property, and intestate succession, and the decedent's heirs are determined accordingly. If it is not established by clear and convincing evidence that an individual who would otherwise be an heir survived the decedent by 120 hours, it is deemed that the individual failed to survive for the required period. This section is not to be applied if its application would result in a taking of intestate estate by the state under Section 2–105.

COMMENT

This section is a limited version of the type of clause frequently found in wills to take care of the common accident situation, in which several members of the same family are injured and die within a few days of one another. The Uniform Simultaneous Death Act provides only a partial solution, since it applies only if there is no proof that the parties died otherwise than simultaneously. (Section 2–702 recommends revision of the Uniform Simultaneous Death Act.)

This section requires an heir to survive by five days in order to succeed to the decedent's intestate property; for a comparable provision as to wills and other governing instruments, see Section 2–702. This section avoids multiple administrations and in some instances prevents the property from passing to persons not desired by the decedent. The 120–hour period will not delay the administration of a decedent's estate because sections 3–302 and 3–307 prevent informal issuance of letters for a period of five days from death. The last sentence prevents the survivorship requirement from defeating inheritance by the last eligible relative of the intestate who survives him or her for any period.

In the case of a surviving spouse who survives the 120–hour period, the 120–hour requirement of survivorship does not disqualify the spouse's intestate share for the federal estate-tax marital deduction. See Int. Rev. Code § 2056(b)(3).

Section 2–105. No Taker.

If there is no taker under the provisions of this Article, the intestate estate passes to the [state].

Section 2–106. Representation.

(a) [Definitions.] In this section:

(1) "Deceased descendant," "deceased parent," or "deceased grandparent" means a descendant, parent, or grandparent who either predeceased the decedent or is deemed to have predeceased the decedent under Section 2–104.

(2) "Surviving descendant" means a descendant who neither predeceased the decedent nor is deemed to have predeceased the decedent under Section 2–104.

33

(b) [Decedent's Descendants.] If, under Section 2–103(1), a decedent's intestate estate or a part thereof passes "by representation" to the decedent's descendants, the estate or part thereof is divided into as many equal shares as there are (i) surviving descendants in the generation nearest to the decedent which contains one or more surviving descendants and (ii) deceased descendants in the same generation who left surviving descendants, if any. Each surviving descendant in the nearest generation is allocated one share. The remaining shares, if any, are combined and then divided in the same manner among the surviving descendants of the deceased descendants as if the surviving descendants who were allocated a share and their surviving descendants had predeceased the decedent.

(c) [Descendants of Parents or Grandparents.] If, under Section 2–103(3) or (4), a decedent's intestate estate or a part thereof passes "by representation" to the descendants of the decedent's deceased parents or either of them or to the descendants of the decedent's deceased paternal or maternal grandparents or either of them, the estate or part thereof is divided into as many equal shares as there are (i) surviving descendants in the generation nearest the deceased parents or either of them, or the deceased grandparents or either of them, that contains one or more surviving descendants and (ii) deceased descendants in the same generation who left surviving descendants, if any. Each surviving descendant in the nearest generation is allocated one share. The remaining shares, if any, are combined and then divided in the same manner among the surviving descendants of the deceased descendants as if the surviving descendants who were allocated a share and their surviving descendants had predeceased the decedent.

COMMENT

Purpose and Scope of Revisions. This section is revised to adopt the system of representation called per capita at each generation. The per-capita-at-each-generation system is more responsive to the underlying premise of the original UPC system, in that it always provides equal shares to those equally related; the pre–1990 UPC achieved this objective in most but not all cases. (See Variation 4, below, for an illustration of this point.) In addition, a recent survey of client preferences, conducted by Fellows of the American College of Trust and Estate Counsel, suggests that the per-capita-at-each-generation system of representation is preferred by most clients. See Young, "Meaning of 'Issue' and 'Descendants,'" 13 ACTEC Probate Notes 225 (1988). The survey results were striking: Of 761 responses, 541 (71.1%) chose the per-capita-at-each-generation system; 145 (19.1%) chose the per-stirpes system, and 70 (9.2%) chose the pre–1990 UPC system.

To illustrate the differences among the three systems, consider a family, in which G is the intestate. G has 3 children, A, B, and C. Child A has 3 children, U, V, and W. Child B has 1 child, X. Child C has 2 children, Y and Z. Consider four variations.

Variation 1: All three children survive G.

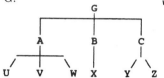

Solution: All three systems reach the same result: A, B, and C take 1/3 each.

Variation 2: One child, A, predeceases G; the other two survive G.

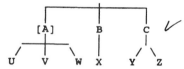

Solution: Again, all three systems reach the same result: B and C take 1/3 each; U, V, and W take 1/9 each.

Variation 3: All three children predecease G.

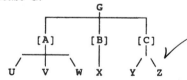

Solution: The pre–1990 UPC and the 1990 UPC systems reach the same result: U, V, W, X, Y, and Z take 1/6 each.

The per-stirpes system gives a different result: U, V, and W take 1/9 each; X takes 1/3; and Y and Z take 1/6 each.

Variation 4: Two of the three children, A and B, predecease G; C survives G.

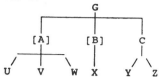

Solution: In this instance, the 1990 UPC system (per capita at each generation) departs from the pre–1990 UPC system. Under the 1990 UPC system, C takes 1/3 and the other two 1/3 shares are combined into a single share (amounting to 2/3 of the estate) and distributed as if C, Y and Z had predeceased G; the result is that U, V, W, and X take 1/6 each.

Although the pre–1990 UPC rejected the per-stirpes system, the result reached under the pre–1990 UPC was aligned with the per-stirpes system in this instance: C would have taken 1/3, X would have taken 1/3, and U, V, and W would have taken 1/9 each.

The 1990 UPC system furthers the *purpose* of the pre–1990 UPC. The pre–1990 UPC system was premised on a desire to provide equality among those equally related. The pre–1990 UPC system failed to achieve that objective in this instance. The 1990 system (per-capita-at-each-generation) remedies that defect in the pre–1990 system.

Reference. Waggoner, "A Proposed Alternative to the Uniform Probate Code's System for Intestate Distribution among Descendants," 66 Nw. U. L. Rev. 626 (1971).

Effect of Disclaimer. By virtue of Section 2–801(d)(1), an heir cannot use a disclaimer to effect a change in the division of an intestate's estate. To illustrate this point, consider the following example:

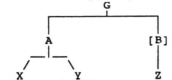

As it stands, G's intestate estate is divided into two equal parts: A takes half and B's child, Z, takes the other half. Suppose, however, that A files a disclaimer under Section 2–801. A cannot affect the basic division of G's intestate estate by this maneuver. Section 2–801(d)(1) provides that "the disclaimed interest devolves as if the disclaimant had predeceased the decedent, except that if by law or under the testamentary instrument the disclaimant's descendants would take the disclaimant's share by representation if the disclaimant actually predeceased the decedent, and if the disclaimant left descendants who survive the decedent, the disclaimed interest passes by representation to the disclaimant's descendants who survive the decedent." In this example, the "disclaimed interest" is A's share (1/2) of G's estate; thus the 1/2 interest renounced by A devolves to A's children, X and Y, who take 1/4 each.

If Section 2–801(d) had provided that G's "estate" is to be divided as if A predeceased G, A could have used his disclaimer to increase the share going to his children from 1/2 to 2/3 (1/3 for each child) and to decrease Z's share to 1/3. The careful wording of Section 2–801(d)(1), however, prevents A from manipulating the result by this method.

Section 2–107. Kindred of Half Blood.

Relatives of the half blood inherit the same share they would inherit if they were of the whole blood.

Section 2–108. Afterborn Heirs.

An individual in gestation at a particular time is treated as living at that time if the individual lives 120 hours or more after birth.

Section 2–109. Advancements.

(a) If an individual dies intestate as to all or a portion of his [or her] estate, property the decedent gave during the decedent's lifetime to an individual who, at the decedent's death, is an heir is treated as an advancement against the heir's intestate share only if (i) the decedent declared in a contemporaneous writing or the heir acknowledged in writing that the gift is an advancement or (ii) the decedent's contemporaneous writing or the heir's written acknowledgment otherwise indicates that the gift is to be taken into account in computing the division and distribution of the decedent's intestate estate.

36

(b) For purposes of subsection (a), property advanced is valued as of the time the heir came into possession or enjoyment of the property or as of the time of the decedent's death, whichever first occurs.

(c) If the recipient of the property fails to survive the decedent, the property is not taken into account in computing the division and distribution of the decedent's intestate estate, unless the decedent's contemporaneous writing provides otherwise.

COMMENT

Purpose of the Revisions. This section is revised so that an advancement can be taken into account with respect to the intestate portion of a partially intestate estate.

Other than these revisions, and a few stylistic and clarifying amendments, the original content of the section is maintained, under which the common law relating to advancements is altered by requiring written evidence of the intent that an inter-vivos gift be an advancement.

The statute is phrased in terms of the donee being an heir "at the decedent's death." The donee need not be a prospective heir at the time of the gift. For example, if the intestate, G, made an inter-vivos gift intended to be an advancement to a grandchild at a time when the intestate's child who is the grandchild's parent is alive, the grandchild would not then be a prospective heir. Nevertheless, if G's intent that the gift be an advancement is contained in a written declaration or acknowledgment as provided in subsection (a), the gift *is* regarded as an advancement if G's child (who is the grandchild's parent) predeceases G, making the grandchild an heir.

To be an advancement, the gift need not be an outright gift; it can be in the form of a will substitute, such as designating the donee as the beneficiary of the intestate's life-insurance policy or the beneficiary of the remainder interest in a revocable inter-vivos trust.

Most inter-vivos transfers today are intended to be absolute gifts or are carefully integrated into a total estate plan. If the donor intends that any transfer during the donor's lifetime be deducted from the donee's share of his estate, the donor may either execute a will so providing or, if he or she intends to die intestate, charge the gift as an advance by a writing within the present section.

This section applies to advances to the decedent's spouse and collaterals (such as nephews and nieces) as well as to descendants.

Computation of Shares—Hotchpot Method. This section does not specify the method of taking an advancement into account in distributing the decedent's intestate estate. That process, called the hotchpot method, is provided by the common law. The hotchpot method is illustrated by the following example.

Example: G died intestate, survived by his wife (W) and his three children (A, B, and C) by a prior marriage. G's probate estate is valued at $190,000. During his lifetime, G had advanced A $50,000 and B $10,000. G memorialized both gifts in a writing declaring his intent that they be advancements.

Solution. The first step in the hotchpot method is to add the value of the advancements to the value of G's probate estate. This combined figure is called the hotchpot estate.

In this case, G's hotchpot estate preliminarily comes to $250,000 ($190,000 + $50,000 + $10,000). W's intestate share of a $250,000 estate under section 2–102(4) is $175,000 ($100,-000 + 1/2 of $150,000). The remaining $75,000 is divided equally among A, B, and C, or $25,000 each. This calculation reveals that A has received an advancement greater than the share to which he is entitled; A can retain the $50,000 advancement, but is not entitled to any additional amount. A and A's $50,000 advancement are therefore disregarded and the process is begun over.

Once A and A's $50,000 advancement are disregarded, G's revised hotchpot estate is $200,-000 ($190,000 + $10,000). W's intestate share is $150,000 ($100,000 + 1/2 of $100,000). The remaining $50,000 is divided equally between B and C, or $25,000 each. From G's intestate estate, B receives $15,000 (B already having received $10,-000 of his ultimate $25,000 share as an advancement); and C receives $25,000. The final division of G's probate estate is

$150,000 to W, zero to A, $15,-000 to B, and $25,000 to C.

Effect if Advancee Predeceases the Decedent; Disclaimer. If a decedent had made an advancement to a person who predeceased the decedent, the last sentence of Section 2–109 provides that the advancement is not taken into account in computing the intestate share of the recipient's descendants (unless the decedent's declaration provides otherwise). The rationale is that there is no guarantee that the recipient's descendants received the advanced property or its value from the recipient's estate.

To illustrate the application of the last sentence of Section 2–109, consider this case: During her lifetime, G had advanced $10,000 to her son, A. G died intestate, leaving a probate estate of $50,000. G was survived by her daughter, B, and by A's child, X. A predeceased G.

G's advancement to A is *disregarded.* G's $50,000 intestate estate is divided into two equal shares, half ($25,000) going to B and the other half ($25,000) going to A's child, X.

Now, suppose that A survived G. In this situation, of course, the advancement to A *is* taken into account in the division of G's intestate estate. Under the hotchpot method, illustrated above, G's hotchpot estate is $60,000 (probate estate of $50,000 plus advancement to A of $10,000). A takes half of this $60,000 amount, or $30,000, but is charged with already having received $10,000 of it. Consequently, A takes only a 2/5 share ($20,-000) of G's intestate estate, and B takes the remaining 3/5 share ($30,-000).

Note that A cannot use a disclaimer under Section 2–801 in effect to give his child, X, a larger share than A was entitled to. Under Section 2–801(d)(1), the effect of a disclaimer by A is that the disclaimant's "interest" devolves to A's descendants as if the disclaimant had predeceased the decedent. The "interest" that A renounced was a right to a 2/5 share of G's estate, not a 1/2 share. Consequently, A's 2/5 share ($20,000) passes to A's child, X.

Section 2–110. Debts to Decedent.

A debt owed to a decedent is not charged against the intestate share of any individual except the debtor. If the debtor fails to survive the decedent, the debt is not taken into account in computing the intestate share of the debtor's descendants.

COMMENT

Section 2–110 supplements Section 3–903, Right of Retainer.

Effect of Disclaimer. Section 2–801(d)(1) prevents a living debtor from using the combined effects of the last sentence of Section 2–110 and a disclaimer to avoid a set-off. Although Section 2–110 provides that, if the debtor actually fails to survive the decedent, the debt is not taken into account in computing the intestate share of the debtor's descendants, the same result is not produced when a living debtor disclaims. Section 2–801(d) provides that the "interest" disclaimed, not the decedent's estate as a whole, devolves as though the disclaimant predeceased the decedent. The "interest" disclaimed by a living debtor is the share the *debtor* would have taken had he or she not disclaimed—his or her intestate share minus the debt.

Section 2–111. Alienage.

No individual is disqualified to take as an heir because the individual or an individual through whom he [or she] claims is or has been an alien.

COMMENT

This section eliminates the ancient rule that an alien cannot acquire or transmit land by descent, a rule based on the feudal notions of the obligations of the tenant to the King. Although there never was a corresponding rule as to personalty, the present section is phrased in light of the basic premise of the Code that distinctions between real and personal property should be abolished.

[Section 2–112. Dower and Curtesy Abolished.

The estates of dower and curtesy are abolished.]

COMMENT

The provisions of this Code replace the common-law concepts of dower and curtesy and their statutory counterparts. Those estates provided both a share in intestacy and a protection against disinheritance.

In states that have previously abolished dower and curtesy, or where those estates have never existed, the above section should be omitted.

Section 2–113. Individuals Related to Decedent Through Two Lines.

An individual who is related to the decedent through two lines of relationship is entitled to only a single share based on the relationship that would entitle the individual to the larger share.

COMMENT

This section prevents double inheritance. It has potential application in a case in which a deceased person's brother or sister marries the spouse of the decedent and adopts a child of the former marriage; if the adopting parent died thereafter leaving the child as a natural and adopted grandchild of its grandparents, this section prevents the child from taking as an heir from the grandparents in both capacities.

Section 2–114. Parent and Child Relationship.

(a) Except as provided in subsections (b) and (c), for purposes of intestate succession by, through, or from a person, an individual is the child of his [or her] natural parents, regardless of their marital status. The parent and child relationship may be established under [the Uniform Parentage Act] [applicable state law] [insert appropriate statutory reference].

(b) An adopted individual is the child of his [or her] adopting parent or parents and not of his [or her] natural parents, but adoption of a child by the spouse of either natural parent has no effect on (i) the relationship between the child and that natural parent or (ii) the right of the child or a descendant of the child to inherit from or through the other natural parent.

(c) Inheritance from or through a child by either natural parent or his [or her] kindred is precluded unless that natural parent has openly treated the child as his [or hers], and has not refused to support the child.

COMMENT

Subsection (a). Subsection (a) sets forth the general rule: For purposes of intestate succession, a child is the child of his or her natural parents, regardless of their marital status. In states that have enacted the Uniform Parentage Act (UPA), the parent and child relationship may be established under the UPA. Non–UPA states should insert a reference to its own statute or, if it has no statute on the question, should insert the phrase "applicable state law."

Subsection (b). Subsection (b) contains exceptions to the general rule of subsection (a). Subsection (b) states the rule that, for inheritance purposes, an adopted individual becomes part of the adopting family and is no longer part of the natural family.

The revision of subsection (b) affects only the exception from the rule pertaining to the adoption of an individual by that individual's stepparent. As revised, an individual who is adopted by his or her stepparent (the spouse of the custodial natural parent) becomes part of the adopting stepparent's family for inheritance purposes but also continues to be part of the family of the custodial natural parent. With respect to the noncustodial natural parent and that parent's family,

however, a different rule is promulgated. The adopted individual and the adopted individual's descendants continue to have a right of inheritance from and through that noncustodial natural parent, but that noncustodial natural parent and that noncustodial natural parent's family do not have a right to inherit from or through the adopted individual.

Subsection (c). Subsection (c) is revised to provide that neither natural parent (nor that natural parent's kindred) can inherit from or through a child unless that natural parent, mother or father, has openly treated the child as his or hers and has not refused to support the child. Prior to the revision, that rule was applied only to the father. The phrase "has not refused to support the child" refers to the time period during which the parent has a legal obligation to support the child.

Companion Statute. A state enacting this provision should also consider enacting the Uniform Status of Children of Assisted Conception Act (1988).

Historical Note. This Comment was revised in 1993. For the prior version, see 8 U.L.A. 118 (Supp. 1992).

PART 2

ELECTIVE SHARE OF SURVIVING SPOUSE

GENERAL COMMENT

The elective share of the surviving spouse was fundamentally revised in 1990 and was reorganized and clarified in 1993. The main purpose of the revisions is to bring elective-share law into line with the contemporary view of marriage as an economic partnership. The economic partnership theory of marriage is already implemented under the equitable-distribution system applied in both the common-law and community-property states when a marriage ends in divorce. When a marriage ends in death, that theory is also already implemented under the community-property system and under the system promulgated in the Uniform Marital Property Act. In the common-law states, however, elective-share law has not caught up to the partnership theory of marriage.

The general effect of implementing the partnership theory in elective-share law is to increase the entitlement of a surviving spouse in a long-term marriage in cases in which the marital assets were disproportionately titled in the decedent's name; and to decrease or even eliminate the entitlement of a surviving spouse in a long-term marriage in cases in which the marital assets were more or less equally titled or disproportionately titled in the surviving spouse's name. A further general effect is to decrease or even eliminate the entitlement of a surviving spouse in a short-term, later-in-life marriage in which neither spouse contributed much, if anything, to the acquisition of the other's wealth, except that a special supplemental elective-share amount is provided in cases in which the surviving spouse would otherwise be left without sufficient funds for support.

The Partnership Theory of Marriage

The partnership theory of marriage, sometimes also called the marital-sharing theory, is stated in various ways. Sometimes it is thought of "as an expression of the presumed intent of husbands and wives to pool their fortunes on an equal basis, share and share alike." M. Glendon, The Transformation of Family Law 131 (1989). Under this approach, the economic rights of each spouse are seen as deriving from an unspoken marital bargain under which the partners agree that each is to enjoy a half interest in the fruits of the marriage, i.e., in the property nominally acquired by and titled in the sole name of either partner during the marriage (other than in property acquired by gift or inheritance). A decedent who disinherits his or her surviving spouse is seen as having reneged on the bargain. Sometimes the theory is expressed in restitution-ary terms, a return-of-contribution notion. Under this approach, the law grants each spouse an entitlement to compensation for non-monetary contributions to the marital enterprise, as "a recognition of the activity of one spouse in the home and to compensate not only for this activity but for opportunities lost." Id.

No matter how the rationale is expressed, the community-property system, including that version of community law promulgated in the Uniform Marital Property Act, recognizes the partnership theory, but it is sometimes thought that the common-law system denies it. In the ongoing marriage, it is true that the basic principle in the common-law (title-based) states is that marital status does not affect the ownership of property. The regime is one of separate property. Each spouse owns all that he or she earns. By contrast, in the community-property states, each spouse acquires an ownership interest in half the property the other earns during the marriage. By granting each spouse *upon acquisition* an immediate half interest in the earnings of the other, the community-property regimes directly recognize that the couple's enterprise is in essence collaborative.

The common-law states, however, also give effect or purport to give effect to the partnership theory when a marriage is dissolved by divorce. If the marriage ends in divorce, a spouse who sacrificed his or her financial-earning opportunities to contribute so-called domestic services to the marital enterprise (such as child-rearing and homemaking) stands to be recompensed. All states now follow the equitable-distribution system upon divorce, under which "broad discretion [is given to] trial courts to assign to either spouse property acquired during the marriage, irrespective of title, taking into account the circumstances of the particular case and recognizing the value of the contributions of a nonworking spouse or homemaker to the acquisition of that property. Simply stated, the system of equitable distribution views marriage as essentially a shared enterprise or joint undertaking in the nature of a partnership to which both spouses contribute—directly and indirectly, financially and nonfinancially—the fruits of which are distributable at divorce." J. Gregory, The Law of Equitable Distribution ¶ 1.03, at p. 1–6 (1989).

The other situation in which spousal property rights figure prominently is disinheritance at death. The pre–1990 Uniform Probate Code, along with almost all other non-UPC common-law states, treats this as one of the few instances in American law where the decedent's testamentary freedom with respect to his or her title-based ownership interests must be curtailed. No matter what the decedent's intent, the pre–1990 Uniform Probate Code and almost all of the non-UPC common-law states recognize that the surviving spouse does have some claim to a portion of the decedent's estate. These statutes provide the spouse a so-called forced share. The forced share is expressed as an option that the survivor can elect or let lapse during the administration of the decedent's estate, hence in the UPC the forced share is termed the "elective" share.

Elective-share law in the common-law states, however, has not caught up to the partnership theory of marriage. Under typical American elective-share law, including the elective share provided by the pre–1990 Uniform Probate Code, a surviving spouse may claim a one-third share of the decedent's estate—not the 50 percent share of the couple's combined assets that the partnership theory would imply.

Long-term Marriages. To illustrate the discrepancy between the partnership theory and conventional elective-share law, consider first a long-term marriage, in which the couple's combined assets were accumulated mostly during the course of the marriage. The pre–1990 elective-share fraction of one-third of the decedent's estate plainly does not implement a partnership principle. The actual result depends on which spouse happens to die first and on how the property accumulated during the marriage was nominally titled.

Example 1—Long-term Marriage under Conventional Forced-share Law. Consider A and B, who were married in their twenties or early thirties; they never divorced, and A died at age, say, 70, survived by B. For whatever reason, A left a will entirely disinheriting B.

Throughout their long life together, the couple managed to accumulate assets worth $600,000, marking them as a somewhat affluent but hardly wealthy couple.

Under conventional elective-share law, B's ultimate entitlement depends on the manner in which these $600,000 in assets were nominally titled as between them. B could end up much poorer or much richer than a 50/50 partnership principle would suggest. The reason is that under conventional elective-share law, B has a claim to one-third of A's "estate."

Marital Assets Disproportionately Titled in Decedent's Name; Conventional Elective-share Law Frequently Entitles Survivor to Less Than Equal Share of Marital Assets. If all the marital assets were titled in A's name, B's claim against A's estate would only be for $200,000—well below B's $300,000 entitlement produced by the partnership/marital-sharing principle.

If $500,000 of the marital assets were titled in A's name, B's claim against A's estate would still only be for $166,500 ($1/3$ of $500,000), which when combined with B's "own" $100,000 yields a $266,500 cut for B— still below the $300,000 figure produced by the partnership/marital-sharing principle.

Marital Assets Equally Titled; Conventional Elective-share Law Entitles Survivor to Disproportionately Large Share. If $300,000 of the marital assets were titled in A's name, B would still have a claim against A's estate for $100,000, which when combined with B's "own" $300,000 yields a $400,000 cut for B—well above the $300,000 amount to which the partnership/marital-sharing principle would lead.

Marital Assets Disproportionately Titled in Survivor's Name; Conventional Elective-share Law Entitles Survivor to Magnify the Disproportion. If only $200,000 were titled in A's name, B would still have a claim against A's estate for $66,667 ($1/3$ of $200,000), even though B was *already* overcompensated as judged by the partnership/marital-sharing theory.

Short-term, Later-in-Life Marriages. Short-term marriages, particularly the short-term marriage later in life, present different considerations. Because each spouse in this type of marriage typically comes into the marriage owning assets derived from a former marriage, the one-third fraction of the decedent's estate far exceeds a 50/50 division of assets acquired during the marriage.

Example 2—Short-term, Later-in-Life Marriage under Conventional Elective-share Law. Consider B and C. A year or so after A's death, B married C. Both B and C are in their seventies, and after five years of marriage, B dies survived by C. Both B and C have adult children and a few grandchildren by their prior marriages, and each naturally would prefer to leave most or all of his or her property to those children.

The value of the couple's combined assets is $600,000, $300,000 of which is titled in B's name (the decedent) and $300,000 of which is titled in C's name (the survivor).

For reasons that are not immediately apparent, conventional elective-share law gives the survivor, C, a right to claim one-third of B's estate, thereby shrinking B's estate (and hence the share of B's children by B's prior marriage to A) by $100,000 (reducing it to $200,000) while supplementing C's assets (which will likely go to C's children by C's prior marriage) by $100,000 (increasing their value to $400,000).

Conventional elective-share law, in other words, basically rewards the children of the remarried spouse who manages to outlive the other, arranging for those children a windfall share of one third of the "loser's" estate. The "winning" spouse who chanced to survive gains a windfall, for this "winner" is unlikely to have made a contribution, monetary or otherwise, to the "loser's" wealth remotely worth one-third.

The Redesigned Elective Share

The redesigned elective share is intended to bring elective-share law into line with the partnership theory of marriage.

In the long-term marriage illustrated in Example 1, the effect of implementing a partnership theory is to increase the entitlement of the surviving spouse when the marital assets were disproportionately titled in the decedent's name; and to decrease or even eliminate the entitlement of the surviving spouse when the marital assets were more or less equally titled or disproportionately titled in the surviving spouse's name. Put differently, the effect is both to reward the surviving spouse who sacrificed his or her financial-earning opportunities in order to contribute so-called domestic services to the marital enterprise and to deny an additional windfall to the surviving spouse in whose name the fruits of a long-term marriage were mostly titled.

In the short-term, later-in-life marriage illustrated in Example 2, the effect of implementing a partnership theory is to decrease or even eliminate the entitlement of the surviving spouse because in such a marriage neither spouse is likely to have contributed much, if anything, to the acquisition of the other's wealth. Put differently, the effect is to deny a windfall to the survivor who contributed little to the decedent's wealth, and ultimately to deny a windfall to the survivor's children by a prior marriage at the expense of the decedent's children by a prior marriage. Bear in mind that in such a marriage, which produces no children, a decedent who disinherits or largely disinherits the surviving spouse may not be acting so much from malice or spite toward the surviving spouse, but from a natural instinct to want to leave most or all of his or her property to the children of his or her former, long-term marriage. In hardship cases, however, as explained later, a special supplemental elective-share amount is provided when the surviving spouse would otherwise be left without sufficient funds for support.

Specific Features of the Redesigned Elective Share

Because ease of administration and predictability of result are prized features of the probate system, the redesigned elective share implements the marital-partnership theory by means of a mechanically determined approximation system, which can be called an accrual-type elective share. Under the accrual-type elective share, there is no need to identify which of the couple's property was earned during the marriage and which was acquired prior to the marriage or acquired during the marriage by gift or inheritance. For further discussion of the reasons for choosing this method, see Waggoner, "Spousal Rights in Our Multiple–Marriage Society: The Revised Uniform Probate Code," 26 Real Prop.Prob. & Tr.J. 683 (1992).

Section 2–202(a)—The "Elective-share Percentage." Section 2–202(a) establishes the first step in the overall redesign of the elective share. Section 2–202(a) implements the accrual-type elective share by adjusting the surviving spouse's ultimate entitlement to the length of the marriage. The longer the marriage, the larger the "elective-share percentage." The sliding scale adjusts for the correspondingly greater contribution to the acquisition of the couple's marital property in a marriage of 15 years than in a marriage of 15 days. Specifically, the "elective-share percentage" starts low and increases annually according to a graduated schedule until it levels off at fifty percent. The schedule established in Section 2–202(a) starts by providing the surviving spouse, during the first year of marriage, a right to elect the "supplemental elective-share amount" only. (The supplemental-elective share amount is explained later.) After one year of marriage, the surviving spouse's "elective-share percentage" is three percent of the augmented estate and it increases with each additional year of marriage until it reaches the maximum 50 percent level after 15 years of marriage.

Section 2–203—the "Augmented Estate." The elective-share percentage determined under Section 2–202(a) is applied to the value of the "augmented estate." As defined in Section 2–203, the "augmented estate" equals the value of the couple's *combined* assets, not merely to the value of the assets nominally titled in the decedent's name, as described in Sections 2–204 through 2–207.

More specifically, the "augmented estate" is composed of the sum of four elements:

Section 2–204—the value of the decedent's net probate estate;

Section 2–205—the value of the decedent's nonprobate transfers to others, consisting of will-substitute-type inter-vivos transfers made by the decedent to others than the surviving spouse;

Section 2–206—the value of the decedent's nonprobate transfers to the surviving spouse, consisting of will-substitute-type inter-vivos transfers made by the decedent to the surviving spouse; and

Section 2–207—the value of the surviving spouse's net assets at the decedent's death, plus any property that would have been in the surviving spouse's nonprobate transfers to others under Section 2–205 had the surviving spouse been the decedent.

Section 2–202(a)—the "Elective-share Amount." Section 2–202(a) requires the elective-share percentage to be applied to the augmented estate. This calculation yields the "elective-share amount"—the amount to which the surviving spouse is entitled. If the elective-share percentage were to be applied only to the *decedent's* assets, a surviving spouse who has already been overcompensated in terms of the way the couple's marital assets have been nominally titled would receive a further windfall under the elective-share system. The couple's marital assets, in other words, would not be equalized. By applying the elective-share percentage to the augmented estate (the couple's combined assets), the redesigned system denies any significance to the possibly fortuitous factor of how the spouses happened to have taken title to particular assets.

Section 2–209—Satisfying the Elective-share Amount. Section 2–209 determines how the elective-share amount is to be satisfied. Under Section 2–209, the decedent's net probate estate and nonprobate transfers to others are liable to contribute to the satisfaction of the elective-share amount only to the extent the elective-share amount is not fully satisfied by the sum of the following amounts:

Subsection (a)(1)—amounts that pass or have passed from the decedent to the surviving spouse by testate or intestate succession and amounts included in the augmented estate under Section 2–206, i.e., the value of the decedent's nonprobate transfers to the surviving spouse; and

Subsection (a)(2)—twice the elective-share percentage, under Section 2–202(a), of the survivor's owned assets and nonprobate transfers to others, as determined under Section 2–207.

If the combined value of these amounts equals or exceeds the elective-share amount, the surviving spouse is not entitled to any further amount from the decedent's probate estate or recipients of the decedent's nonprobate transfers to others, unless the surviving spouse is entitled to a supplemental elective-share amount under Section 2–202(b).

Note that under Section 2–209(a)(2), the portion of the surviving spouse's assets that counts toward making up the elective-share amount is derived by applying a percentage to the survivor's assets equal to double the elective-share percentage. In a long-term marriage, the elective-share percentage will be 50%; thus, in such a marriage, *all* of the survivor's assets are counted toward making up the spouse's elective-share amount.

Example 3—15–Year or Longer Marriage under Redesigned Elective Share; Marital Assets Disproportionately Titled in Decedent's Name. A and B were married to each other more than 15 years. A died, survived by B. A's will left nothing to B, and A made no nonprobate transfers to B. A made no nonprobate transfers to others as defined in Section 2–205.

The augmented estate is the sum of the amounts described in Sections 2–204 through 2–207:

(1) A's net probate estate	$400,000
(2) A's nonprobate transfers to others....................	0
(3) A's nonprobate transfers to B	0
(4) B's assets and nonprobate transfers to others	$200,000
Augmented Estate	$600,000

The elective-share percentage for a 15–year or longer marriage is 50%. This means that B's elective-share amount is $300,000 (50% of $600,000).

Under Section 2–209(a)(2), the percentage of B's assets that counts first toward making up B's entitlement is 100% (twice the elective-share percentage of 50%), or $200,000. B, therefore, is treated as already having received $200,000 of B's ultimate entitlement of $300,000. Section 2–209(b) makes A's net probate estate liable for the unsatisfied balance of the elective-share amount, $100,000, which is the amount needed to bring B's own $200,000 up to the $300,000 level.

Example 4—15–Year or Longer Marriage under Redesigned Elective Share; Marital Assets Disproportionately Titled in Survivor's Name. As in Example 3, A and B were married to each other more than 15 years. A died, survived by B. A's will left nothing to B, and A made no nonprobate transfers to B. A made no nonprobate transfers to others as defined in Section 2–205.

The augmented estate is the sum of the amounts described in Sections 2–204 through 2–207:

(1) A's net probate estate	$200,000
(2) A's nonprobate transfers to others....................	0
(3) A's nonprobate transfers to B	0
(4) B's assets and nonprobate transfers to others	$400,000
Augmented Estate	$600,000

The elective-share percentage for a 15–year or longer marriage is 50%. This means that B's elective-share amount is $300,000 (50% of $600,000).

Under Section 2–209(a)(2), the percentage of B's assets that counts first toward making up B's entitlement is 100% (twice the elective-share percentage of 50%), or $400,000. B, therefore, is treated as already having received more than B's ultimate entitlement of $300,000. B has no claim on A's net probate estate.

In a marriage that has lasted less than 15 years, only a portion of the survivor's assets—not all—count toward making up the elective-share amount. This is because the elective-share percentage in these shorter-term marriages is less than 50% and, under Section 2–209(a)(2), the portion of the survivor's assets that count toward making up the elective-share amount is double the elective-share percentage.

To explain why this is appropriate requires further elaboration of the underlying theory of the redesigned system. The system avoids the tracing-to-source problem by applying an ever-increasing percentage to the couple's combined assets without regard to when or how those assets were acquired, rather than applying a constant percentage (50%) to an ever-growing accumulation of assets. By approximation, the redesigned system equates the elective-share percentage of the couple's combined assets with 50% of the couple's marital assets—assets subject to equalization under the partnership/marital-sharing theory. Thus, in a marriage that has endured long enough for the elective-share percentage to be 30%, Section 2–209(a)(2) in effect equates 30% of the couple's combined assets with 50% of the couple's marital assets. In the aggregate, Section 2–209(a)(2) equates 60% of the couple's combined assets with the assets subject to equalization.

Example 5—Under 15–Year Marriage under the Redesigned Elective Share; Marital Assets Disproportionately Titled in Decedent's Name. A and B were married to each other more than 5 but less than 6 years. A died, survived by B. A's will left nothing to B, and A made no nonprobate transfers to B. A made no nonprobate transfers to others as defined in Section 2–205.

The augmented estate is the sum of the amounts described in Sections 2–204 through 2–207:

(1) A's net probate estate $400,000
(2) A's nonprobate transfers to others.................... 0
(3) A's nonprobate transfers to B 0
(4) B's assets and nonprobate transfers to others $200,000
Augmented Estate $600,000

Under Section 2–202(a), the elective-share percentage for a 5–year marriage is 15%. This means that B's elective-share amount is $90,000 (15% of $600,000).

To say that B's entitlement is $90,000 presupposes (by approximation) that $180,000 of their $600,000 are marital assets—assets subject to equalization. Hence, B's entitlement is half of that amount, or $90,000. Exempted from equalization is the other $420,000 of their combined assets, some of which would have been A's individual or exempted property and the rest of which would have been B's individual or exempted property.

The redesigned system applies the same ratio to the asset mix of each spouse as it does to the couple's combined assets. To say that the elective-share percentage is 15% means that the combined assets are treated as being in a 30/70 ratio (30% marital, subject to equalization; 70% individual, exempted from equalization). This same ratio, in turn, governs the approximation of each spouse's mix of marital and individual property. Consequently, the redesigned system attributes 30% of A's $400,000 ($120,000) to marital property and the other 70% ($280,000) to individual property. And, the system does the same for B's $200,000, i.e., it treats 30% ($60,000) as marital property and 70% ($140,000) as individual property.

Accordingly, B is treated as already owning $60,000 of the $180,000 of marital property. Under Section 2–209(a)(2), $60,000 of B's $90,000 elective-share amount comes from B's own assets. Section 2–209(b) makes A's net probate estate liable for the unsatisfied balance—$30,000. (Remember that $120,000 of A's assets are attributed to marital property; thus, removing $30,000 of those $120,000 from A and adding that $30,000 to B's $60,000 in marital assets equalizes the aggregate $180,000 marital assets in a 50/50 split—$90,000 for A and $90,000 for B.)

The Support Theory

The partnership/marital-sharing theory is not the only driving force behind elective-share law. Another theoretical basis for elective-share law is that the spouses' mutual duties of support during their joint lifetimes should be continued in some form after death in favor of the survivor, as a claim on the decedent's estate. Current elective-share law implements this theory poorly. The fixed fraction, whether it is the typical one-third or some other fraction, disregards the survivor's actual need. A one-third share may be inadequate to the surviving spouse's needs, especially in a modest estate. On the other hand, in a very large estate, it may go far beyond the survivor's needs. In either a modest or a large estate, the survivor may or may not have ample independent means, and this factor, too, is disregarded in conventional elective-share law. The redesigned elective share system implements the support theory by granting the survivor a supplemental elective-share amount related to the survivor's actual needs. In implementing a support rationale, the length of the marriage is quite irrelevant. Because the duty of support is founded upon status, it arises at the time of the marriage.

Section 2–202(b)—the "Supplemental Elective-share Amount." Section 2–202(b) is the provision that implements the support theory by providing a supplemental elective-share amount of $50,000. The $50,000 figure is bracketed to indicate that individual states may wish to select a higher or lower amount.

In making up this $50,000 amount, the surviving spouse's own title-based ownership interests count first toward making up this supplemental amount; included in the survivor's assets for this purpose are amounts shifting to the survivor at the decedent's death and amounts owing to the survivor from the decedent's estate under the accrual-type elective-share apparatus discussed above, but excluded are (1) amounts going to the survivor under the Code's probate exemptions and allowances and (2) the survivor's Social Security benefits (and other governmental benefits, such as Medicare insurance coverage). If the survivor's assets are less than the $50,000 minimum, then the survivor is entitled to whatever additional portion of the decedent's estate is necessary, up to 100 percent of it, to bring the survivor's assets up to that minimum level. In the case of a late marriage, in which the survivor is perhaps aged in the mid-seventies, the minimum figure plus the probate exemptions and allowances (which under the Code amount to a minimum of another $43,000) is pretty much on target—in conjunction with Social Security payments and other governmental benefits—to provide the survivor with a fairly adequate means of support.

Example 6—Supplemental Elective-share Amount. After A's death in Example 1, B married C. Five years later, B died, survived by C. B's will left nothing to C, and B made no nonprobate transfers to C. B made no nonprobate transfers to others as defined in Section 2–205.

The augmented estate is the sum of the amounts described in Sections 2–204 through 2–207:

(1) B's net probate estate	$ 90,000
(2) B's nonprobate transfers to others	0
(3) B's nonprobate transfers to C	0
(4) C's assets and nonprobate transfers to others	$10,000
Augmented Estate	$100,000

The elective-share percentage for a 5–year marriage is 15%. This means that C's elective-share amount is $15,000 (15% of $100,000).

Solution under Redesigned Elective Share. Under Section 2–209(a)(2), $3,000 (30%) of C's assets count first toward making up C's elective-share amount; under Section 2–209(b), the remaining $12,000 elective-share amount would come from B's net probate estate.

Application of Section 2–202(b) shows that C is entitled to a supplemental elective-share amount. The sum of the amounts described in sections:

2–207	$10,000
2–209(a)(1)	0
Elective-share amount payable from decedent's probate estate under Section 2–209(b)	$12,000
Total	$22,000

The above calculation shows that C is entitled to a supplemental elective-share amount under Section 2–202(b) of $28,000 ($50,000 minus $22,000). The supplemental elective-share amount is payable entirely from B's net probate estate, as prescribed in Section 2–209(b).

The end result is that C is entitled to $40,000 ($12,000 + $28,000) by way of elective share from B's net probate estate (and nonprobate transfers to others, had there been any). Forty thousand dollars is the amount necessary to bring C's $10,000 in assets up to $50,000.

Decedent's Nonprobate Transfers to Others

The pre–1990 Code made great strides toward preventing "fraud on the spouse's share." The problem of "fraud on the spouse's share" arises when the decedent seeks to evade the spouse's elective share by engaging in various kinds of nominal inter-vivos transfers. To render that type of behavior ineffective, the pre–1990 Code adopted the augmented-estate concept, which extended the elective-share entitlement to property that was the subject of specified types of inter-vivos transfer, such as revocable inter-vivos trusts.

In the redesign of the elective share, the augmented-estate concept has been strengthened. The pre–1990 Code left several loopholes ajar in the augmented estate—a notable one being life insurance the decedent buys, naming someone other than his or her surviving spouse as the beneficiary. With appropriate protection for the insurance company that pays off before receiving notice of an elective-share claim, the redesigned elective-share system includes these types of insurance policies in the augmented estate as part of the decedent's nonprobate transfers to others under Section 2–205.

Historical Note. This General Comment was revised in 1993. For the prior version, see 8 U.L.A. 82 (Supp.1992).

Section 2–201. Definitions.

In this Part:

(1) As used in sections other than Section 2–205, "decedent's nonprobate transfers to others" means the amounts that are included in the augmented estate under Section 2–205.

(2) "Fractional interest in property held in joint tenancy with the right of survivorship," whether the fractional interest is unilaterally severable or not, means the fraction, the numerator of which is one and the denominator of which, if the decedent was a joint tenant, is one plus the number of joint tenants who survive the decedent and which, if the decedent was not a joint tenant, is the number of joint tenants.

(3) "Marriage," as it relates to a transfer by the decedent during marriage, means any marriage of the decedent to the decedent's surviving spouse.

(4) "Nonadverse party" means a person who does not have a substantial beneficial interest in the trust or other property arrangement that would be adversely affected by the exercise or nonexercise of the power that he [or she] possesses respecting the trust or other property arrangement. A person having a general power of appointment over property is deemed to have a beneficial interest in the property.

(5) "Power" or "power of appointment" includes a power to designate the beneficiary of a beneficiary designation.

(6) "Presently exercisable general power of appointment" means a power of appointment under which, at the time in question, the decedent, whether or not he [or she] then had the capacity to exercise the power, held a power to create a present or future interest in himself [or herself], his [or her] creditors, his [or her] estate, or creditors of his [or her] estate, and includes a power to revoke or invade the principal of a trust or other property arrangement.

(7) "Probate estate" means property that would pass by intestate succession if the decedent died without a valid will.

(8) "Property" includes values subject to a beneficiary designation.

(9) "Right to income" includes a right to payments under a commercial or private annuity, an annuity trust, a unitrust, or a similar arrangement.

(10) "Transfer," as it relates to a transfer by or of the decedent, includes (A) an exercise or release of a presently exercisable general power of appointment held by the decedent, (B) a lapse at death of a presently exercisable general power of appointment held by the decedent, and (C) an exercise, release, or lapse of a general power of appointment that the decedent created in himself [or herself] and of a power described in Section 2–205(2)(ii) that the decedent conferred on a nonadverse party.

Section 2–202.   Elective Share.

(a) [Elective–Share Amount.]   The surviving spouse of a decedent who dies domiciled in this State has a right of election, under the limitations and conditions stated in this Part, to take an elective-share amount equal to the value of the elective-share percentage of the augmented estate, determined by the length of time the spouse and the decedent were married to each other, in accordance with the following schedule:

If the decedent and the spouse were married to each other:	The elective-share percentage is:
Less than 1 year	Supplemental Amount Only.
1 year but less than 2 years	3% of the augmented estate.
2 years but less than 3 years	6% of the augmented estate.
3 years but less than 4 years	9% of the augmented estate.
4 years but less than 5 years	12% of the augmented estate.
5 years but less than 6 years	15% of the augmented estate.
6 years but less than 7 years	18% of the augmented estate.
7 years but less than 8 years	21% of the augmented estate.
8 years but less than 9 years	24% of the augmented estate.
9 years but less than 10 years	27% of the augmented estate.
10 years but less than 11 years	30% of the augmented estate.
11 years but less than 12 years	34% of the augmented estate.
12 years but less than 13 years	38% of the augmented estate.
13 years but less than 14 years	42% of the augmented estate.
14 years but less than 15 years	46% of the augmented estate.
15 years or more	50% of the augmented estate.

(b) [Supplemental Elective–Share Amount.] If the sum of the amounts described in Sections 2–207, 2–209(a)(1), and that part of the elective-share amount payable from the decedent's probate estate and nonprobate transfers to others under Section 2–209(b) and (c) is less than [$50,000], the surviving spouse is entitled to a supplemental elective-share amount equal to [$50,000], minus the sum of the amounts described in those sections. The supplemental elective-share amount is payable from the decedent's probate estate and from recipients of the decedent's nonprobate transfers to others in the order of priority set forth in Section 2–209(b) and (c).

(c) [Effect of Election on Statutory Benefits.] If the right of election is exercised by or on behalf of the surviving spouse, the surviving spouse's homestead allowance, exempt property, and family allowance, if any, are not charged against but are in addition to the elective-share and supplemental elective-share amounts.

(d) [Non–Domiciliary.] The right, if any, of the surviving spouse of a decedent who dies domiciled outside this State to take an elective share in property in this State is governed by the law of the decedent's domicile at death.

COMMENT

Pre–1990 Provision. The pre–1990 provisions granted the surviving spouse a one-third share of the augmented estate. The one-third fraction was largely a carry over from common-law dower, under which a surviving widow had a one-third interest for life in her deceased husband's land.

Purpose and Scope of Revisions. The revision of this section is the first step in the overall plan of implementing a partnership or marital-sharing theory of marriage, with a support theory back-up.

Subsection (a). Subsection (a) implements the partnership theory by increasing the maximum elective-share percentage of the augmented estate to fifty percent, but by phasing that ultimate entitlement in so that it does not reach the maximum fifty-percent level until the marriage has lasted at least 15 years. If the decedent and the surviving spouse were married to each other more than once, all periods of marriage to each other are added together for purposes of subsection (a); periods between marriages are not counted.

Subsection (b). Subsection (b) implements the support theory of the elective share by providing a [$50,000] supplemental elective-share amount, in case the surviving spouse's assets and other entitlements are below this figure.

Subsection (c). The homestead, exempt property, and family allowances provided by Article II, Part 4, are not charged to the electing spouse as a part of the elective share. Consequently, these allowances may be distributed from the probate estate without reference to whether an elective share right is asserted.

Cross Reference. To have the right to an elective share under subsection (a), the decedent's spouse must survive the decedent. Under Section 2–702(a), the requirement of survivorship is satisfied only if it can be established that the spouse survived the decedent by 120 hours.

Historical Note. This Comment was revised in 1993. For the prior version, see 8 U.L.A. 89 (Supp. 1992).

Section 2–203. Composition of the Augmented Estate.

Subject to Section 2–208, the value of the augmented estate, to the extent provided in Sections 2–204, 2–205, 2–206, and 2–207, consists of the sum of the values of all property, whether real or personal, movable or immovable, tangible or intangible, wherever situated, that constitute the decedent's net probate estate, the decedent's nonprobate transfers to others, the decedent's nonprobate transfers to the surviving spouse, and the surviving spouse's property and nonprobate transfers to others.

COMMENT

The elective-share percentage, determined by the length of the marriage under Section 2–202, is applied to the augmented estate. This section, added in 1993 as part of the reorganization and clarification of the elective-share provisions, operates as an umbrella section identifying the augmented estate as consisting of the sum of the values of four components. On the decedent's side are the values of (1) the decedent's net probate estate (Section 2–204) and (2) the decedent's nonprobate transfers to others (Section 2–205). Straddling between the decedent's side and the surviving spouse's side is the value of (3) the decedent's nonprobate transfers to the surviving spouse (Section 2–206). On the surviving spouse's side are the values of (4) the surviving spouse's net assets and the surviving spouse's nonprobate transfers to others (Section 2–207).

Historical Note. This Comment was added in 1993.

Section 2–204. Decedent's Net Probate Estate.

The value of the augmented estate includes the value of the decedent's probate estate, reduced by funeral and administration expenses, homestead allowance, family allowances, exempt property, and enforceable claims.

COMMENT

This section, which in the 1990 version appeared as a paragraph of a single, long section defining the augmented estate, establishes as the first component of the augmented estate the value of the decedent's probate estate, reduced by funeral and administration expenses, homestead allowance (Section 2–402), family allowances (Section 2–404), exempt property (Section 2–403), and enforceable claims. The term "claims" is defined in Section 1–201 as including "liabilities of the decedent or protected person whether arising in contract, in tort, or otherwise, and liabilities of the estate which arise at or after the death of the decedent or after the appointment of a conservator, including funeral expenses and expenses of administration. The term does not include estate or inheritance taxes, or demands or disputes regarding title of a decedent or protected person to specific assets alleged to be included in the estate."

Various aspects of Section 2–204 are illustrated by Examples 10, 11, and 12 in the Comment to Section 2–205, below.

Historical Note. This Comment was added in 1993.

Section 2–205. Decedent's Nonprobate Transfers to Others.

The value of the augmented estate includes the value of the decedent's nonprobate transfers to others, not included under Section 2–204, of any of the following types, in the amount provided respectively for each type of transfer:

(1) Property owned or owned in substance by the decedent immediately before death that passed outside probate at the decedent's death. Property included under this category consists of:

(i) Property over which the decedent alone, immediately before death, held a presently exercisable general power of appointment. The amount included is the value of the property subject to the power, to the extent the property passed at the decedent's death, by exercise, release, lapse, in default, or otherwise, to or for the benefit of any person other than the decedent's estate or surviving spouse.

(ii) The decedent's fractional interest in property held by the decedent in joint tenancy with the right of survivorship. The amount included is the value of the decedent's fractional interest, to the extent the fractional interest passed by right of survivorship at the decedent's death to a surviving joint tenant other than the decedent's surviving spouse.

(iii) The decedent's ownership interest in property or accounts held in POD, TOD, or co-ownership registration with the right of survivorship. The amount included is the value of the decedent's ownership interest, to the extent the decedent's ownership interest passed at the decedent's death to or for the benefit of any person other than the decedent's estate or surviving spouse.

(iv) Proceeds of insurance, including accidental death benefits, on the life of the decedent, if the decedent owned the insurance policy immediately before death or if and to the extent the decedent alone and immediately before death held a presently exercisable general power of appointment over the policy or its proceeds. The amount included is the value of the proceeds, to the extent they were payable at the decedent's death to or for the benefit of any person other than the decedent's estate or surviving spouse.

(2) Property transferred in any of the following forms by the decedent during marriage:

(i) Any irrevocable transfer in which the decedent retained the right to the possession or enjoyment of, or to the income from, the property if and to the extent the decedent's right terminated at or continued beyond the decedent's death. The amount included is the value of the fraction of the property to which the decedent's right related, to the extent the fraction of the property passed outside probate to or for the benefit of any person other than the decedent's estate or surviving spouse.

(ii) Any transfer in which the decedent created a power over income or property, exercisable by the decedent alone or in conjunction with any other person, or exercisable by a nonadverse party, to or for the benefit of the decedent, creditors of the decedent, the decedent's estate, or creditors of the decedent's estate. The amount included with respect to a power over property is the value of the property subject to the power, and the amount included with respect to a power over income is the value of the property that produces or produced the income, to the extent the power in either case was exercisable at the decedent's death to or for the benefit of any person other than the decedent's surviving spouse or to the extent the property passed at the decedent's death, by exercise, release, lapse, in default, or otherwise, to or for the benefit of any person other than the decedent's estate or surviving spouse. If the power is a power over both income and property and the preceding sentence produces different amounts, the amount included is the greater amount.

(3) Property that passed during marriage and during the two-year period next preceding the decedent's death as a result of a transfer by the decedent if the transfer was of any of the following types:

(i) Any property that passed as a result of the termination of a right or interest in, or power over, property that would have been included in the augmented estate under paragraph (1)(i), (ii), or (iii), or under paragraph (2), if the right, interest, or power had not terminated until the decedent's death. The amount included is the value of the property that would have been included under those paragraphs if the property were valued at the time the right, interest, or power terminated, and is included only to the extent the property passed upon termination to or for the benefit of any person other than the decedent or the decedent's estate, spouse, or surviving spouse. As used in this subparagraph, "termination," with respect to a right or interest in property, occurs when the right or interest terminated by the terms of the governing instrument or the decedent transferred or relinquished the right or interest, and, with respect to a power over property, occurs when the power terminated by exercise, release, lapse, default, or otherwise, but, with respect to a power described in paragraph (1)(i), "termination" occurs when the power terminated by exercise or release, but not otherwise.

(ii) Any transfer of or relating to an insurance policy on the life of the decedent if the proceeds would have been included in the augmented estate under paragraph (1)(iv) had the transfer not occurred. The amount included is the value of the insurance proceeds to the extent the proceeds were payable at the decedent's death to or for the benefit of any person other than the decedent's estate or surviving spouse.

(iii) Any transfer of property, to the extent not otherwise included in the augmented estate, made to or for the benefit of a person other than the decedent's surviving spouse. The amount included is the value of the transferred property to the extent the aggregate transfers to any one donee in either of the two years exceeded $10,000.

COMMENT

This section, which in the 1990 version appeared in substance as a paragraph of a single, long section defining the augmented estate, establishes as the second component of the augmented estate the value of the decedent's nonprobate transfers to others. In the 1990 version, the term "reclaimable estate" was used rather than the term "nonprobate transfers to others".

This component is divided into three basic categories: (1) property owned or owned in substance by the decedent immediately before death that passed outside probate to persons other than the surviving spouse; (2) property transferred by the decedent during marriage that passed outside probate to persons other than the surviving spouse; and (3) property transferred by the decedent during marriage and during the two-year period next preceding the decedent's death. Various aspects of each category and each subdivision within each category are discussed and illustrated below.

Paragraph (1)—Property Owned or Owned in Substance by the Decedent. This category covers property that the decedent owned or owned in substance immediately before death and that passed outside probate at the decedent's death to a person or persons other than the surviving spouse.

Paragraph (1) subdivides this category into four specific components:

(i) Property over which the decedent alone, immediately before death, held a presently exercisable general power of appointment. The amount included is the value of the property subject to the power, to the extent the property passed at the decedent's death, by exercise, release, lapse, in default, or otherwise, to or for the benefit of any person other than the decedent's estate or surviving spouse.

(ii) The decedent's fractional interest in property held by the decedent in joint tenancy with the right of survivorship. The amount included is the value of the decedent's fractional interest, to the extent the fractional interest passed by right of survivorship at the decedent's death to a surviving joint tenant other than the decedent's surviving spouse.

(iii) The decedent's ownership interest in property or accounts held in POD, TOD, or co-ownership registration with the right of survivorship. The amount included is the value of the decedent's ownership interest, to the extent the decedent's ownership interest passed at the decedent's death to or for the benefit of any person other than the decedent's estate or surviving spouse.

(iv) Proceeds of insurance, including accidental death benefits, on the life of the decedent, if the decedent owned the insurance policy immediately before death or if and to the extent the decedent alone and immediately before death held a presently exercisable general power of appointment over the policy or its proceeds. The amount included is the value of the proceeds, to the extent they were payable at the decedent's death to or for the benefit of any person other than the decedent's estate or surviving spouse.

With one exception for nonseverable joint tenancies (see Example 4 below), each of the above components covers a type of asset of which the decedent could have become the full, technical owner by merely exercising his or her power of appointment, incident of ownership, or right of severance or withdrawal. Had the decedent exercised these powers or rights to become the full, technical owner, the decedent could have controlled the devolution of these assets by his or her will; by not exercising these powers or rights, the decedent allowed the assets to pass outside probate to persons other than the surviving spouse. Thus, *in effect,* property covered by these components passes at the decedent's death by nonprobate transfer from the decedent to others. This is what justifies including these components in the augmented estate without regard to the person who *created* the decedent's substantive ownership interest, whether the decedent or someone else, and without regard to *when* it was created, whether before or after the decedent's marriage.

Although the augmented estate under the pre–1990 Code did not include life insurance, annuities, etc., payable to other persons, the revisions do include their value; this move recognizes that such arrangements were, under the pre–1990 Code, used to deplete the estate and reduce the spouse's elective-share entitlement.

Various aspects of paragraph (1) are illustrated by the following examples. Other examples illustrating various aspects of this paragraph are Example 19 in this Comment, below, and Examples 20 and 21 in the Comment to Section 2–206, below. In each of the following examples, G is the decedent and S is the decedent's surviving spouse.

Example 1—General Testamentary Power. G's mother, M, created a testamentary trust, providing for the income to go to G for life, remainder in corpus to such persons, including G, G's creditors, G's estate, or the creditors of G's estate, as G by will appoints; in default of appointment, to X. G died, survived by S and X. G's will did not exercise his power in favor of S.

The value of the corpus of the trust at G's death is not

60

included in the augmented estate under paragraph (1)(i), regardless of whether G exercised the power in favor of someone other than S or let the power lapse, so that the trust corpus passed in default of appointment to X. Section 2–205(1)(i) only applies to *presently exercisable* general powers; G's power was a general *testamentary* power. (Note that paragraph (2)(ii) does cover property subject to a general *testamentary* power, but only if the power was created by G during marriage. G's general testamentary power was created by M and hence not covered by paragraph (2)(ii).)

Example 2—Nongeneral Power and "5–and–5" Power. G's father, F, created a testamentary trust, providing for the income to go to G for life, remainder in corpus to such persons, except G, G's creditors, G's estate, or the creditors of G's estate, as G by will appoints; in default of appointment, to X. G was also given a noncumulative annual power to withdraw an amount equal to the greater of $5,000 or five percent of the trust corpus. G died, survived by S and X. G did not exercise her power in favor of S.

G's power over the remainder interest does not cause inclusion of the value of the full corpus in the augmented estate under paragraph (1)(i) because that power was a *nongeneral* power.

The value of the greater of $5,000 or five percent of the corpus of the trust *at G's death* is included in the augmented estate under paragraph (1)(i), to the extent that that property

passed at G's death, by exercise, release, lapse, in default, or otherwise, to or for the benefit of any person other than the decedent's estate or surviving spouse, because that portion of the trust corpus was subject to a *presently exercisable general* power of appointment held by G immediately before G's death. No additional amount is included, however, whether G exercised the withdrawal power or allowed it to lapse in the years prior to G's death. (Note that paragraph (3)(i) is inapplicable to this case. That paragraph only applies to property subject to powers *created by the decedent during marriage* that lapse within the two-year period next preceding the decedent's death.)

Example 3—Revocable Inter–Vivos Trust. G created a revocable inter-vivos trust, providing for the income to go to G for life, remainder in corpus to such persons, except G, G's creditors, G's estate, or the creditors of G's estate, as G by will appoints; in default of appointment, to X. G died, survived by S and X. G never exercised his power to revoke, and the corpus of the trust passed at G's death to X.

Regardless of whether G created the trust before or after marrying S, the value of the corpus of the trust at G's death is included in the augmented estate under paragraph (1)(i) because, immediately before G's death, the trust corpus was subject to a presently exercisable general power of appointment (the power to revoke: see Section 2–201(6)) held by G.

(Note that if G created the trust during marriage, paragraph (2)(ii) also requires inclusion of the value of the trust corpus. Because these two subparagraphs overlap, and because both subparagraphs include the same value, Section 2–208(c) provides that the value of the trust corpus is included under one but not both subparagraphs.)

Example 4—Joint Tenancy. G, X, and Y owned property in joint tenancy. G died, survived by S, X, and Y.

Because G's fractional interest in the property immediately before death was one-third, and because that one-third fractional interest passed by right of survivorship to X and Y at G's death, one-third of the value of the property at G's death is included in the augmented estate under paragraph (1)(ii). This is the result whether or not under local law G had the unilateral right to sever her fractional interest. See Section 2–201(2).

Example 5—TOD Registered Securities and POD Account. G registered securities that G owned in TOD form. G also contributed all the funds in a savings account that G registered in POD form. X was designated to take the securities and Y was designated to take the savings account on G's death. G died, survived by S, X, and Y.

Because G was the sole owner of the securities immediately before death (see Sections 6–302 and 6–306), and because ownership of the securities passed to X upon G's death (see Section 6–307), the full value of the securi-

ties at G's death is included in the augmented estate under paragraph (1)(iii). Because G contributed all the funds in the savings account, G's ownership interest in the savings account immediately before death was 100 percent. See Section 6–211. Because that 100 percentage ownership interest passed by right of survivorship to Y at G's death, the full value of the account at G's death is included in the augmented estate under paragraph (1)(iii).

Example 6—Joint Checking Account. G, X, and Y were registered as co-owners of a joint checking account. G contributed 75 percent of the funds in the account. G died, survived by S, X, and Y.

G's ownership interest in the account immediately before death, determined under Section 6–211, was 75 percent of the account. Because that percentage ownership interest passed by right of survivorship to X and Y at G's death, 75 percent of the value of the account at G's death is included in the augmented estate under paragraph (1)(iii).

Example 7—Joint Checking Account. G's mother, M, added G's name to her checking account so that G could pay her bills for her. M contributed all the funds in the account. The account was registered in co-ownership form with right of survivorship. G died, survived by S and M.

Because G had contributed none of his own funds to the account, G's ownership interest in the account immediately before death, determined under Section 6–211, was zero. Consequently, no part of the value of the account at G's death is included in the augmented estate under paragraph (1)(iii).

Example 8—Life Insurance. G, as owner of a life-insurance policy insuring her life, designated X and Y as the beneficiaries of that policy. G died owning the policy, survived by S, X, and Y.

The full value of the proceeds of that policy is included in the augmented estate under paragraph (1)(iv).

Paragraph (2)—Property Transferred by the Decedent During Marriage. This category covers property that the decedent transferred in specified forms during "marriage" (defined in Section 2–201(3) as "any marriage of the decedent to the decedent's surviving spouse"). If the decedent and the surviving spouse were married to each other more than once, transfers that took place during any of their marriages to each other count as transfers during marriage.

The word "transfer," as it relates to a transfer by or of the decedent, is defined in Section 2–201(10), as including "(A) an exercise or release of a presently exercisable general power of appointment held by the decedent, (B) a lapse at death of a presently exercisable general power of appointment held by the decedent, and (C) an exercise, release, or lapse of a general power of appointment that the decedent created in himself [or herself] and of a power described in Section 2–205(2)(ii) that the decedent conferred on a nonadverse party."

Paragraph (2) covers the following specific forms of transfer:

(i) Any irrevocable transfer in which the decedent retained the right to the possession or enjoyment of, or to the income from, the property if and to the extent the decedent's right terminated at or continued beyond the decedent's death. The amount included is the value of the fraction of the property to which the decedent's right related, to the extent the fraction of the property passed outside probate to or for the benefit of any person other than the decedent's estate or surviving spouse.

(ii) Any transfer in which the decedent created a power over income or property, exercisable by the decedent alone or in conjunction with any other person, or exercisable by a nonadverse party, to or for the benefit of the decedent, creditors of the decedent, the decedent's estate, or creditors of the decedent's estate. The amount included with respect to a power over property is the value of the property subject to the power, and the amount included with respect to a power over income is the value of the property that produces or produced the income, to the extent the power in either case was exercisable at the decedent's death to or for the benefit of any person other than the decedent's surviving spouse or to the extent the property passed at the decedent's death, by exercise, release, lapse, in default, or otherwise, to or for the benefit of any person other than the decedent's estate or surviving spouse. If the power is a power over both income and property and the preceding sentence produces different amounts, the amount included is the greater amount.

Various aspects of paragraph (2) are illustrated by the following examples. Other examples illustrating various aspects of this paragraph are Examples 1 and 3, above, and Example 22 in the Comment to Section 2–206, below. In the following examples, as in the examples above, G is the decedent and S is the decedent's surviving spouse.

Example 9—Retained Income Interest for Life. Before death, and during marriage, G created an irrevocable inter-vivos trust, providing for the income to be paid annually to G for life, then for the corpus of the trust to go to X. G died, survived by S and X.

The value of the corpus of the trust at G's death is included in the augmented estate under paragraph (2)(i). This paragraph applies to a retained income interest that terminates at the decedent's death, as here. The amount included is the value of the property that passes outside probate to any person other than the decedent's estate or surviving spouse, which in this case is the full value of the corpus that passes outside probate to X.

Had G retained the right to only one-half of the income, with the other half payable to Y for G's lifetime, only one half of the value of the corpus at G's death would have been included under paragraph (2)(i) because that paragraph specifies that "the amount included is the value of the fraction of the property to

which the decedent's right related." Note, however, that if G had created the trust within two years before death, paragraph (3)(iii) would require the inclusion of the value at the date the trust was established of the other half of the income interest for G's life and of the remainder interest in the other half of the corpus, each value to be reduced by as much as $10,000 as appropriate under the facts, taking into account other gifts made to Y and to X in the same year, if any.

Example 10—Retained Unitrust Interest for a Term. Before death, and during marriage, G created an irrevocable inter-vivos trust, providing for a fixed percentage of the value of the corpus of the trust (determined annually) to be paid annually to G for ten years, then for the corpus of the trust (and any accumulated income) to go to X. G died six years after the trust was created, survived by S and X.

The full value of the corpus at G's death is included in the augmented estate under a combination of Sections 2–204 and 2–205(2)(i).

Section 2–205(2)(i) requires the inclusion of the commuted value of X's remainder interest at G's death. This paragraph applies to a retained income interest, which under Section 2–201(9) includes a unitrust interest. Moreover, Section 2–205(2)(i) not only applies to a retained income interest that terminates at the decedent's death, but also applies to a retained income interest that continues beyond the decedent's death, as here. The amount included is the value of the interest that passes outside probate to a person other than the decedent's estate or surviving spouse, which in this case is the commuted value of X's remainder interest at G's death.

Section 2–204 requires the inclusion of the commuted value of the remaining four years of G's unitrust interest because that interest passes through G's probate estate to G's devisees or heirs.

Because both the four-year unitrust interest and the remainder interest that directly succeeds it are included in the augmented estate, there is no need to derive separate values for X's remainder interest and for G's remaining unitrust interest. The sum of the two values will equal the full value of the corpus, and that is the value that is included in the augmented estate. (Note, however, that *for purposes of Section 2–209 (Sources from Which Elective Share Payable)*, it might become necessary to derive separate values for these two interests.)

Had the trust been revocable, the end-result would have been the same. The only difference would be that the revocability of the trust would cause paragraph (2)(i) to be inapplicable, but would also cause overlapping application of paragraphs (1)(i) and (2)(ii) to X's remainder interest. Because each of these paragraphs yields the same value, Section 2–208(c) would require the commuted value of X's re-

mainder interest to be included in the augmented estate under any one, but only one, of them. Note that neither paragraphs (1)(i) nor (2)(ii) would apply to G's remaining four-year term because that four-year term would have passed to G's estate by lapse of G's power to revoke. As above, the commuted value of G's remaining four-year term would be included in the augmented estate under Section 2–204, obviating the need to derive separate valuations of G's four-year term and X's remainder interest.

Example 11—Personal Residence Trust. Before death, and during marriage, G created an irrevocable inter-vivos trust of G's personal residence, retaining the right to occupy the residence for ten years, then for the residence to go to X. G died six years after the trust was created, survived by S and X.

The full value of the residence at G's death is included in the augmented estate under a combination of Sections 2–204 and 2–205(2)(i).

Section 2–205(2)(i) requires the inclusion of the commuted value of X's remainder interest at G's death. This paragraph applies to a retained right to possession that continues beyond the decedent's death, as here. The amount included is the value of the interest that passes outside probate to a person other than the decedent's estate or surviving spouse, which in this case is the commuted value of X's remainder interest at G's death.

Section 2–204 requires the inclusion of the commuted value of G's remaining four-year term because that interest passes through G's probate estate to G's devisees or heirs.

As in Example 10, there is no need to derive separate valuations of the remaining four-year term and the remainder interest that directly succeeds it. The sum of the two values will equal the full value of the residence at G's death, and that is the amount included in the augmented estate. (Note, however, that *for purposes of Section 2–209 (Sources from Which Elective Share Payable)*, it might become necessary to derive separate values for these two interests.)

Example 12—Retained Annuity Interest for a Term. Before death, and during marriage, G created an irrevocable inter-vivos trust, providing for a fixed dollar amount to be paid annually to G for ten years, then for half of the corpus of the trust to go to X; the other half was to remain in trust for an additional five years, after which time the remaining corpus was to go to X. G died fourteen years after the trust was created, survived by S and X.

The value of the one-half of the corpus of the trust remaining at G's death is included in the augmented estate under a combination of Sections 2–204 and 2–205(2)(i). The other one-half of the corpus of the trust that was distributed to X four years before G's death is not included in the augmented estate.

Section 2–205(2)(i) requires the inclusion of the commuted value of X's remainder interest in half of the corpus of the trust. This section applies to a retained income interest, which under Section 2–201(9), includes an annuity interest that continues beyond the decedent's death, as here. The amount included is the value of the interest that passes outside probate to a person other than the decedent's estate or surviving spouse, which in this case is the commuted value of X's remainder interest at G's death.

Section 2–204 requires the inclusion of the commuted value of the remaining one year of G's annuity interest in half of the corpus of the trust, which passed through G's probate estate to G's devisees or heirs.

There is no need to derive separate valuations of G's remaining annuity interest and X's remainder interest that directly succeeds it. The sum of the two values will equal the full value of the remaining one-half of the corpus of the trust at G's death, and that is the amount included in the augmented estate. (Note, however, that *for purposes of Section 2–209 (Sources from Which Elective Share Payable)*, it might become necessary to derive separate values for these two interests.)

Had G died eleven years after the trust was created, so that the termination of half of the trust would have occurred within the two-year period next preceding G's death, the value of the half of the corpus of the trust that was distributed to X ten years after the trust was created would also have been included in the augmented estate under Section 2–205(3)(i).

Example   13—Commercial Annuity. Before G's death, and during marriage, G purchased three commercial annuities from an insurance company. Annuity One was a single-life annuity that paid a fixed sum to G annually and that contained a refund feature payable to X if G died within ten years. Annuity Two was a single-life annuity that paid a fixed sum to G annually, but contained no refund feature. Annuity Three was a self and survivor annuity that paid a fixed sum to G annually for life, and then paid a fixed sum annually to X for life. G died six years after purchasing the annuities, survived by S and X.

Annuity One: The value of the refund payable to X at G's death under Annuity One is included in the augmented estate under paragraph (2)(i). G retained an income interest, as defined in Section 2–201(9), that terminated at G's death. The amount included is the value of the interest that passes outside probate to a person other than the decedent's estate or surviving spouse, which in this case is the refund amount to which X is entitled.

Annuity Two: Annuity Two does not cause any value to be included in the augmented estate because it expired at G's death; although G retained an income interest, as defined in Section 2–201(9), that terminated at G's death, nothing passed outside probate to any person

other than G's estate or surviving spouse.

Annuity Three: The commuted value at G's death of the annuity payable to X under Annuity Three is included in the augmented estate under paragraph (2)(i). G retained an income interest, as defined in Section 2–201(9), that terminated at G's death. The amount included is the value of the interest that passes outside probate to a person other than the decedent's estate or surviving spouse, which in this case is the commuted value of X's right to the annuity payments for X's lifetime.

Example   14—Joint   Power. Before death, and during marriage, G created an inter-vivos trust, providing for the income to go to X for life, remainder in corpus at X's death to X's then-living descendants, by representation; if none, to a specified charity. G retained a power, exercisable only with the consent of X, allowing G to withdraw all or any portion of the corpus at any time during G's lifetime. G died without exercising the power, survived by S and X.

The value of the corpus of the trust at G's death is included in the augmented estate under paragraph (2)(ii). This paragraph applies to a power created by the decedent over the corpus of the trust that is exercisable by the decedent "in conjunction with any other person," who in this case is X. Note that the fact that X has an interest in the trust that would be adversely affected by the exercise of the power in favor of G is irrelevant.

The amount included is the full value of the corpus of the trust at G's death because the power related to the full corpus of the trust and the full corpus passed at the decedent's death, by lapse or default of the power, to a person other than the decedent's estate or surviving spouse—X, X's descendants, and the specified charity.

Example 15—Power in Nonadverse Party. Before death, and during marriage, G created an inter-vivos trust, providing for the income to go to X for life, remainder in corpus to X's then-living descendants, by representation; if none, to a specified charity. G conferred a power on the trustee, a bank, to distribute, in the trustee's complete and uncontrolled discretion, all or any portion of the trust corpus to G or to X. One year before G's death, the trustee distributed $50,000 of trust corpus to G and $40,000 of trust corpus to X. G died, survived by S and X.

The full value of the portion of the corpus of the trust remaining at G's death is included in the augmented estate under paragraph (2)(ii). This paragraph applies to a power created by the decedent over the corpus of the trust that is exercisable by a "nonadverse party." As defined in Section 2–201(4), the term "nonadverse party" is "a person who does not have a substantial beneficial interest in the trust or other property arrangement that would be adversely affected by the exercise or nonexercise of the power that he [or she] possesses respecting the trust or other property arrangement." The trustee in this case is a nonadverse party. The amount included is the full value of the corpus of the trust at G's death because the trustee's power related to the full corpus of the trust and the full corpus passed at the decedent's death, by lapse or default of the power, to a person other than the decedent's estate or surviving spouse—X, X's descendants, and the specified charity.

In addition to the full value of the remaining corpus at G's death, an additional amount is included in the augmented estate because of the $40,000 distribution of corpus to X within two years before G's death. As defined in Section 2–201(10), a transfer of the decedent includes the exercise "of a power described in Section 2–205(2)(ii) that the decedent conferred on a nonadverse party." Consequently, the $40,000 distribution to X is considered to be a transfer of the decedent within two years before death, and is included in the augmented estate under paragraph (3)(iii) to the extent it exceeded $10,000 of the aggregate gifts to X that year. If no other gifts were made to X in that year, the amount included would be $30,000 ($40,000 − $10,000).

Paragraph (3)—Property Transferred by the Decedent During Marriage and During the Two–Year Period Next Preceding the Decedent's Death. This paragraph—called the two-year rule—requires inclusion in the augmented estate of the value of property that the decedent transferred in specified forms during marriage and within two years of death. The word "transfer," as it relates to a transfer by or of the decedent, is defined in Section 2–201(10), as including "(A) an exercise or release of a presently exercisable general power of appointment held by the decedent, (B) a lapse at death of a presently exercisable general power of appointment held by the decedent, and (C) an exercise, release, or lapse of a general power of appointment that the decedent created in himself [or herself] and of a power described in Section 2–205(2)(ii) that the decedent conferred on a nonadverse party."

The two-year rule of paragraph (3) covers the following specific forms of transfer:

(i) Any property that passed as a result of the termination of a right or interest in, or power over, property that would have been included in the augmented estate under paragraph (1)(i), (ii), or (iii), or under paragraph (2), if the right, interest, or power had not terminated until the decedent's death. The amount included is the value of the property that would have been included under those paragraphs if the property were valued at the time the right, interest, or power terminated, and is included only to the extent the property passed upon termination to or for the benefit of any person other than the decedent or the decedent's estate, spouse, or surviving spouse. As used in this subparagraph, "termination," with respect to a right or interest in property, occurs when the right or interest terminated by the terms of the governing instru-

ment or the decedent transferred or relinquished the right or interest, and, with respect to a power over property, occurs when the power terminated by exercise, release, lapse, default, or otherwise, but, with respect to a power described in paragraph (1)(i), "termination" occurs when the power terminated by exercise or release, but not otherwise.

(ii) Any transfer of or relating to an insurance policy on the life of the decedent if the proceeds would have been included in the augmented estate under paragraph (1)(iv) had the transfer not occurred. The amount included is the value of the insurance proceeds to the extent the proceeds were payable at the decedent's death to or for the benefit of any person other than the decedent's estate or surviving spouse.

(iii) Any transfer of property, to the extent not otherwise included in the augmented estate, made to or for the benefit of a person other than the decedent's surviving spouse. The amount included is the value of the transferred property to the extent the aggregate transfers to any one donee in either of the two years exceeded $10,000.

Various aspects of paragraph (3) are illustrated by the following examples. Other examples illustrating various aspects of this paragraph are Examples 2, 9, 12, 14, and 15, above, and Examples 33 and 34 in the Comment to Section 2–207, below. In the following examples, as in the examples above, G is

69

the decedent and S is the decedent's surviving spouse.

Example 16—Retained Income Interest Terminating Within Two Years Before Death. Before death, and during marriage, G created an irrevocable inter-vivos trust, providing for the income to go to G for ten years, then for the corpus of the trust to go to X. G died 11 years after the trust was created, survived by S and X. G was married to S when the trust terminated.

The full value of the corpus of the trust at the date of its termination is included in the augmented estate under paragraph (3)(i). The full value of the corpus at death would have been included in the augmented estate under paragraph (2)(i) had G's income interest not terminated until death; G's income interest terminated within the two-year period next preceding G's death; G was married to S when the trust was created and when the income interest terminated; and the trust corpus upon termination passed to a person other than S, G, or G's estate.

Example 17—Personal Residence Trust Terminating Within Two Years Before Death. Before death, and during marriage, G created an irrevocable inter-vivos trust of G's personal residence, retaining the right to occupy the residence for ten years, then for the residence to go to X. G died eleven years after the trust was created, survived by S and X. G was married to S when the right to possession terminated.

The full value of the residence at the date the trust terminated is included in the augmented estate under paragraph (3)(i). The full value of the residence would have been included in the augmented estate under paragraph (2)(i) had G's right to possession not terminated until death; G's right to possession terminated within the two-year period next preceding G's death; G was married to S when the trust was created and when the right to possession terminated; and the residence passed upon termination to a person other than S, G, or G's estate.

Example 18—Irrevocable Assignment of Life–Insurance Policy Within Two Years Before Death. In Example 8, G irrevocably assigned the life-insurance policy to X and Y within two years preceding G's death. G was married to S when the policy was assigned. G died, survived by S, X, and Y.

The full value of the proceeds are included in the augmented estate under paragraph (3)(ii). The full value of the proceeds would have been included in the augmented estate under paragraph (1)(iv) had G owned the policy at death; G assigned the policy within the two-year period next preceding G's death; G was married to S when the policy was assigned; and the proceeds were payable to a person other than S or G's estate.

Example 19—Property Purchased in Joint Tenancy Within Two Years Before Death. Within two years before death, and during marriage, G and X purchased property in joint tenancy;

70

G contributed $75,000 of the $100,000 purchase price and X contributed $25,000. G died, survived by S and X.

Regardless of when or by whom the property was purchased, the value at G's death of G's fractional interest of one-half is included in the augmented estate under paragraph (1)(ii) because G's half passed to X as surviving joint tenant. Because the property was purchased within two years before death, and during marriage, and because G's contribution exceeded the value of G's fractional interest in the property, the excess contribution of $25,000 constitutes a gift to X within the two-year period next preceding G's death. Consequently, an additional $15,000 ($25,000 minus $10,000) is included in the augmented estate under paragraph (3)(iii) as a gift to X.

Had G provided all of the $100,000 purchase price, then paragraph (3)(iii) would require $40,000 ($50,000 minus $10,000) to be included in the augmented estate (in addition to the inclusion of one-half the value of the property at G's death under paragraph (1)(ii)).

Had G provided one-half or less of the $100,000 purchase price, then G would not have made a gift to X within the two-year period next preceding G's death. Half the value of the property at G's death would still be included in the augmented estate under paragraph (1)(ii), however.

Cross Reference. On obtaining written spousal consent to assure qualification for the charitable deduction for charitable remainder trusts or outright charitable donations, see the Comment to Section 2–208.

Historical Note. This Comment was added in 1993.

Section 2–206. Decedent's Nonprobate Transfers to the Surviving Spouse.

Excluding property passing to the surviving spouse under the federal Social Security system, the value of the augmented estate includes the value of the decedent's nonprobate transfers to the decedent's surviving spouse, which consist of all property that passed outside probate at the decedent's death from the decedent to the surviving spouse by reason of the decedent's death, including:

(1) the decedent's fractional interest in property held as a joint tenant with the right of survivorship, to the extent that the decedent's fractional interest passed to the surviving spouse as surviving joint tenant,

(2) the decedent's ownership interest in property or accounts held in co-ownership registration with the right of survivorship, to the extent the decedent's ownership interest passed to the surviving spouse as surviving co-owner, and

(3) all other property that would have been included in the augmented estate under Section 2–205(1) or (2) had it passed to or for the benefit of a person other than the decedent's spouse, surviving spouse, the decedent, or the decedent's creditors, estate, or estate creditors.

COMMENT

This section, which in the 1990 version appeared in substance as a paragraph of a single, long section defining the augmented estate, establishes as the third component of the augmented estate the value of the decedent's nonprobate transfers to the decedent's surviving spouse. Under this section, the decedent's nonprobate transfers to the decedent's surviving spouse:

consist of all property that passed outside probate at the decedent's death from the decedent to the surviving spouse by reason of the decedent's death, including:

(1) the decedent's fractional interest in property held as a joint tenant with the right of survivorship, to the extent that the decedent's fractional interest passed to the surviving spouse as surviving joint tenant,

(2) the decedent's ownership interest in property or accounts held in co-ownership registration with the right of survivorship, to the extent the decedent's ownership interest passed to the surviving spouse as surviving co-owner, and

(3) all other property that would have been included in the augmented estate under Section 2–205(1) or (2) had it passed to or for the benefit of a person other than the decedent's spouse, surviving spouse, the de-

cedent, or the decedent's creditors, estate, or estate creditors. Property passing to the surviving spouse under the federal Social Security system is excluded.

Various aspects of Section 2–206 are illustrated by the following examples. In these examples, as in the examples in the Comment to Section 2–205, above, G is the decedent and S is the decedent's surviving spouse.

Example 20—Tenancy by the Entirety. G and S own property in tenancy by the entirety. G died, survived by S.

Because the definition in Section 1–201 of "joint tenants with the right of survivorship" includes tenants by the entirety, the provisions of Section 2–206 relating to joint tenancies with right of survivorship apply to tenancies by the entirety.

In total, therefore, the full value of the property is included in the augmented estate—G's one-half under Section 2–206(1) and S's one-half under Section 2–207(a)(1)(i).

Section 2–206(1) requires the inclusion of the value of G's one-half fractional interest because it passed to S as surviving joint tenant.

Section 2–207(a)(1)(i) requires the inclusion of S's one-half fractional interest. Because G was a joint tenant immediately before G's death, S's fractional interest, for purposes of Section 2–207, is determined immediately before G's death, disregarding the fact that G predeceased S. Immediately before G's death, S's fractional interest was then a one-half fractional interest. Despite Section 2–205(1)(ii), none of S's fractional interest is included under Section 2–207(a)(2) because that provision does not apply to fractional interests that are included under Section 2–207(a)(1)(i). Consequently, the value of S's one-half interest is included under Section 2–207(a)(1)(i) but not under Section 2–207(a)(2).

Example 21—Joint Tenancy. G, S, and X own property in joint tenancy. G died more than two years after the property was titled in that form, survived by S and X.

In total, two-thirds of the value of the property at G's death is included in the augmented estate—one-sixth under Section 2–205, one-sixth under Section 2–206, and one-third under Section 2–207.

Section 2–205(1)(ii) requires the inclusion of half of the value of G's one-third fractional interest because that half passed by right of survivorship to X.

Section 2–206(1) requires the inclusion of the value of the other half of G's one-third fractional interest because that half passed to S as surviving joint tenant.

Section 2–207(a)(1)(i) requires the inclusion of the value of S's one-third interest. Because G was a joint tenant im-

mediately before G's death, S's fractional interest, for purposes of Section 2–207, is determined immediately before G's death, disregarding the fact that G predeceased S. Immediately before G's death, S's fractional interest was then a one-third fractional interest. Despite Section 2–205(1)(ii), none of S's fractional interest is included under Section 2–207(a)(2) because that provision does not apply to fractional interests that are included under Section 2–207(a)(1)(i). Consequently, the value of S's one-third fractional interest is included in the augmented estate under Section 2–207(a)(1)(i) but not under Section 2–207(a)(2).

Example 22—Income Interest Passing to Surviving Spouse. Before death, and during marriage, G created an irrevocable inter-vivos trust, providing for the income to go to G for life, then for the income to go to S for life, then for the corpus of the trust to go to X. G died, survived by S and X.

The full value of the corpus of the trust at G's death is included in the augmented estate under a combination of Sections 2–205 and 2–206.

Section 2–206(3) requires the inclusion of the commuted value of S's income interest. Note that, although S owns the income interest as of G's death, the value of S's income interest is not included under Section 2–207 because Section 2–207 only includes property interests that are not included under Section 2–206.

Section 2–205(2)(i) requires the inclusion of the commuted value of X's remainder interest.

Example 23—Corpus Passing to Surviving Spouse. Before death, and during marriage, G created an irrevocable inter-vivos trust, providing for the income to go to G for life, then for the corpus of the trust to go to S. G died, survived by S.

The value of the corpus of the trust at G's death is included in the augmented estate under Section 2–206(3). Note that, although S owns the corpus as of G's death, the value of S's ownership interest in the corpus is not included under Section 2–207 because Section 2–207 only includes property interests that are not included under Section 2–206.

Example 24—TOD Registered Securities, POD Account, and Life Insurance Payable to Surviving Spouse. In Examples 5 and 8 in the Comment to Section 2–205, G designated S to take the securities on death, registered S as the beneficiary of the POD savings account, and named S as the beneficiary of the life-insurance policy.

The same values that were included in the augmented estate under Section 2–205(1) in those examples are included in the augmented estate under Section 2–206.

Example 25—Joint Checking Account. G and S were registered as co-owners of a joint checking account. G contributed 75 percent of the funds in the account and S contributed 25 percent of the funds. G died, survived by S.

G's ownership interest in the account immediately before death, determined under Section 6–211, was 75 percent of the account. Because that percentage ownership interest passed by right of survivorship to S at G's death, 75 percent of the value of the account at G's death is included in the augmented estate under Section 2–206. The remaining 25 percent of the account is included in the augmented estate under Section 2–207.

Historical Note. This Comment was added in 1993.

Section 2–207. Surviving Spouse's Property and Non-probate Transfers to Others.

(a) [Included Property.] Except to the extent included in the augmented estate under Section 2–204 or 2–206, the value of the augmented estate includes the value of:

(1) property that was owned by the decedent's surviving spouse at the decedent's death, including:

(i) the surviving spouse's fractional interest in property held in joint tenancy with the right of survivorship,

(ii) the surviving spouse's ownership interest in property or accounts held in co-ownership registration with the right of survivorship, and

(iii) property that passed to the surviving spouse by reason of the decedent's death, but not including the spouse's right to homestead allowance, family allowance, exempt property, or payments under the federal Social Security system; and

(2) property that would have been included in the surviving spouse's nonprobate transfers to others, other than the spouse's fractional and ownership interests included under subsection (a)(1)(i) or (ii), had the spouse been the decedent.

(b) [Time of Valuation.] Property included under this section is valued at the decedent's death, taking the fact that the decedent predeceased the spouse into account, but, for purposes of subsection (a)(1)(i) and (ii), the values of the spouse's fractional and ownership interests are determined immediately before the decedent's death if the decedent was then a joint tenant or a co-owner of the property or accounts. For purposes of subsection (a)(2), proceeds of insurance that would have been included in the spouse's nonprobate transfers to others under Section 2–205(1)(iv) are not valued as if he [or she] were deceased.

(c) [Reduction for Enforceable Claims.] The value of property included under this section is reduced by enforceable claims against the surviving spouse.

COMMENT

This section, which in the 1990 version appeared in substance as a paragraph of a single, long section defining the augmented estate, establishes as the fourth component of the augmented estate the value of property owned by the surviving spouse at the decedent's death plus the value of amounts that would have been includible in the surviving spouse's nonprobate transfers to others had the spouse been the decedent, reduced by enforceable claims against that property or that spouse, as provided in Sections 2–207(c) and 2–208(b)(1).

Note that amounts that would have been includible in the surviving spouse's nonprobate transfers to others under Section 2–205(1)(iv) are not valued as if he or she were

deceased. Thus, if, at the decedent's death, the surviving spouse owns a $1 million life-insurance policy on his or her life, payable to his or her sister, that policy would not be valued at its face value of $1 million, but rather could be valued under the method used in the federal estate tax under Treas.Reg. § 20.2031–8.

The purpose of combining the estates and nonprobate transfers of both spouses is to implement a partnership or marital-sharing theory. Under that theory, there is a fifty/fifty split of the property acquired by *both* spouses. Hence the redesigned elective share includes the survivor's net assets in the augmented-estate entity. (Under a different rationale, no longer appropriate under the redesigned system, the pre–1990 version of Section 2–202 also added the value of property owned by the surviving spouse, but only to the extent the owned property had been derived from the decedent. An incidental benefit of the redesigned system is that this tracing-to-source feature of the pre–1990 version is eliminated.)

Various aspects of Section 2–207 are illustrated by the following examples. Other examples illustrating various aspects of this section are Examples 20, 21, 22, 23, and 25 in the Comment to Section 2–206. In the following examples, as in the examples in the Comments to Sections 2–205 and 2–206, above, G is the decedent and S is the decedent's surviving spouse.

Example 26—Inter–Vivos Trust Created by Surviving Spouse; Corpus Payable to Spouse at Decedent's Death. Before G's death, and during marriage, S created an irrevocable inter-vivos trust, providing for the income to go to G for life, then for the corpus of the trust to go to S. G died, survived by S.

The value of the corpus of the trust at G's death is included in the augmented estate under Section 2–207(a)(1) as either an interest owned by S at G's death or as an interest that passed to the spouse by reason of G's death.

Example 27—Inter–Vivos Trust Created by Another; Income Payable to Spouse for Life. Before G's death, X created an irrevocable inter-vivos trust, providing for the income to go to S for life, then for the income to go

to G for life, then for the corpus of the trust to go to Y. G died, survived by S and Y.

The commuted value of S's income interest as of G's death is included in the augmented estate under Section 2–207(a), as a property interest owned by the surviving spouse at the decedent's death.

Example 28—Inter–Vivos Trust Created by Another; Income Payable to Spouse for Life. Before G's death, X created an irrevocable inter-vivos trust, providing for the income to go to G for life, then for the income to go to S for life, then for the corpus of the trust to go to Y. G died, survived by S and Y.

The commuted value of S's income interest at the decedent's death is included in the augmented estate under Section 2–207(a)(1), as either a property interest owned by the surviving spouse at the decedent's death or a property interest that passed to the surviving spouse by reason of the decedent's death.

Example 29—Life Insurance on Decedent's Life Owned by Surviving Spouse; Proceeds Payable to Spouse. Before G's death, S bought a life-insurance policy on G's life, naming S as the beneficiary. G died, survived by S.

The value of the proceeds of the life-insurance policy is included in the augmented estate under Section 2–207(a)(1), as property owned by the surviving spouse at the decedent's death.

Example 30—Life Insurance on Decedent's Life Owned by Another; Proceeds Payable to Spouse. Before G's death, X bought a life-insurance policy on G's life, naming S as the beneficiary. G died, survived by S.

The value of the proceeds of the life-insurance policy is included in the augmented estate under Section 2–207(a)(1)(iii), as property that passed to the surviving spouse by reason of the decedent's death.

Example 31—Joint Tenancy Between Spouse and Another. S and Y own property in joint tenancy. G died, survived by S and Y.

The value of S's one-half fractional interest at G's death is included in the augmented estate under Section 2–207(a)(1)(i). Despite Section 2–205(1)(ii), none of S's fractional interest is included under Section 2–207(a)(2) because that provision does not apply to fractional interests required to be included under Section 2–207(a)(1)(i). Consequently, the value of S's one-half is included under Section 2–207(a)(1)(i) but not under Section 2–207(a)(2).

Example 32—Inter–Vivos Trust with Retained Income Interest Created by Surviving Spouse. Before G's death, and during marriage, S created an irrevocable inter-vivos trust, providing for the income to go to S for life, then for the income to go to G for life, then for the corpus of the trust to go to X. G died, survived by S and X.

The value of the trust corpus at G's death is included in the augmented estate under Section 2–207(a)(2) because, if S were the decedent, that value would be included in the spouse's non-probate transfers to others under Section 2–205(2)(i). Note that property included under Section 2–207 is valued at the decedent's death, taking the fact that the decedent predeceased the spouse into account. Thus, G's remainder in income for life is extinguished, and the full value of the corpus is included in the augmented estate under Section 2–207(a)(2). The commuted value of S's income interest would also be included under Section 2–207(a)(1) but for the fact that Section 2–208(c) provides that when two provisions apply to the same property interest, the interest is not included under both provisions, but is included under the provision yielding the highest value. Consequently, since Section 2–207(a)(2) yields a higher value (the full corpus) than Section 2–207(a)(1) (the income interest), and since the income interest is part of the value of the corpus, and hence both provisions apply to the same property interest, the full corpus is included under Section 2–207(a)(2) and nothing is included under Section 2–207(a)(1).

Example 33—Inter–Vivos Trust Created by Decedent; Income to Surviving Spouse. More than two years before G's death, and during marriage, G created an irrevocable inter-vivos trust, providing for the income to go to S for life, then for the corpus of the trust to go to X. G died, survived by S and X.

The commuted value of S's income interest as of G's death is included in the augmented estate under Section 2–207. If G had created the trust within the two-year period next preceding G's death, the commuted value of X's remainder interest as of the date of the creation of the trust (less $10,000, assuming G made no other gifts to X in that year) would also have been included in the augmented estate under Section 2–205(3)(iii).

Example 34—Inter–Vivos Trust Created by Surviving Spouse; No Retained Interest or Power. More than two years before G's death, and during marriage, S created an irrevocable inter-vivos trust, providing for the income to go to G for life, then for the corpus of the trust to go to Y. G died, survived by S and Y.

The value of the trust is not included in the augmented estate. If S had created the trust within the two-year period next preceding G's death, the commuted value of Y's remainder interest as of the date of the creation of the trust (less $10,000, assuming no other gifts to Y in that year) would have been included in the augmented estate under Section 2–207(a)(2) because if S were the decedent, the value of the remainder interest would have been included in S's nonprobate transfers to others under Section 2–205(3)(iii).

Historical Note. This Comment was added in 1993.

Section 2–208. Exclusions, Valuation, and Overlapping Application.

(a) [Exclusions]. The value of any property is excluded from the decedent's nonprobate transfers to others (i) to the extent the decedent received adequate and full consideration in money or money's worth for a transfer of the property or (ii) if the property was transferred with the written joinder of, or if the transfer was consented to in writing by, the surviving spouse.

(b) [Valuation.] The value of property:

(1) included in the augmented estate under Section 2–205, 2–206, or 2–207 is reduced in each category by enforceable claims against the included property; and

(2) includes the commuted value of any present or future interest and the commuted value of amounts payable under any trust, life insurance settlement option, annuity contract, public or private pension, disability compensation, death benefit or retirement plan, or any similar arrangement, exclusive of the federal Social Security system.

(c) [Overlapping Application; No Double Inclusion.] In case of overlapping application to the same property of the paragraphs or subparagraphs of Section 2–205, 2–206, or 2–207, the property is included in the augmented estate under the provision yielding the greatest value, and under only one overlapping provision if they all yield the same value.

COMMENT

Subsection (a). This subsection excludes from the decedent's nonprobate transfers to others the value of any property (i) to the extent that the decedent received adequate and full consideration in money or money's worth for a transfer of the property or (ii) if the property was transferred with the written joinder of, or if the transfer was consented to in writing by, the surviving spouse.

Consenting to Split–Gift Treatment Not Consent to the Transfer. Spousal consent to split-gift treatment under I.R.C. § 2513 does not constitute written joinder of or consent to the transfer by the spouse for purposes of subsection (a).

Obtaining the Charitable Deduction for Transfers Coming Within Section 2–205(2) or (3). Because, under Section 2–201(10), the term "right to income" includes a right to payments under an annuity trust or a unitrust, the value of a charitable remainder trust established by a married grantor without written spousal consent or joinder would be included in the decedent's nonprobate transfers to others under Section 2–205(2)(i). Consequently, a married grantor planning to establish a charitable remainder trust is advised to obtain the written consent of his or her spouse to the transfer, as provided in Section 2–208(a), in order to be assured of qualifying for the charitable deduction.

Similarly, outright gifts made by a married donor within two years

preceding death are included in the augmented estate under Section 2–205(3)(iii) to the extent that the aggregate gifts to any one donee exceed $10,000 in either of the two years. Consequently, a married donor planning to donate more than $10,000 to any charitable organization within a twelve-month period is advised to obtain the written consent of his or her spouse to the transfer, as provided in Section 2–208(a), in order to be assured of qualifying for the charitable deduction.

Spousal Waiver of ERISA Benefits. Under the Employee Retirement Income Security Act (ERISA), death benefits under an employee benefit plan subject to ERISA must be paid in the form of an annuity to the surviving spouse. A married employee wishing to designate someone other than the spouse must obtain a waiver from the spouse. As amended in 1984 by the Retirement Equity Act, ERISA requires each employee benefit plan subject to its provisions to provide that an election of a waiver shall not take effect unless

(i) the spouse of the participant consents in writing to such election, (ii) such election designates a beneficiary (or form of benefits) which may not be changed without spousal consent (or the consent of the spouse expressly permits designation by the participant without any requirement of further consent by the spouse), and (iii) the spouse's consent acknowledges the effect of such election and is witnessed by a plan representative or a notary public.

See 29 U.S.C. § 1055(c) (1988); Int. Rev.Code § 417(a). Any spousal waiver that complies with these requirements would satisfy Section 2–208(a) and would serve to exclude the value of the death benefits from the decedent's nonprobate transfers to others.

Cross Reference. See also Section 2–213 and Comment.

Subsection (c). The application of subsection (c) is illustrated in Example 32 in the Comment to Section 2–207.

Historical Note. This Comment was added in 1993.

Section 2–209. Sources From Which Elective Share Payable.

(a) [Elective–Share Amount Only.] In a proceeding for an elective share, the following are applied first to satisfy the elective-share amount and to reduce or eliminate any contributions due from the decedent's probate estate and recipients of the decedent's nonprobate transfers to others:

(1) amounts included in the augmented estate under Section 2–204 which pass or have passed to the surviving spouse by testate or intestate succession and amounts included in the augmented estate under Section 2–206; and

(2) amounts included in the augmented estate under Section 2–207 up to the applicable percentage thereof. For the purposes of this subsection, the "applicable percentage" is twice the elective-share percentage set forth in the schedule in Section 2–202(a) appropriate to the length of time the spouse and the decedent were married to each other.

(b) [Unsatisfied Balance of Elective–Share Amount; Supplemental Elective–Share Amount.] If, after the application of subsection (a), the elective-share amount is not fully satisfied or the surviving spouse is entitled to a supplemental elective-share amount, amounts included in the decedent's probate estate and in the decedent's nonprobate transfers to others, other than amounts included under Section 2–205(3)(i) or (iii), are applied first to satisfy the unsatisfied balance of the elective-share amount or the supplemental elective-share amount. The decedent's probate estate and that portion of the decedent's nonprobate transfers to others are so applied that liability for the unsatisfied balance of the elective-share amount or for the supplemental elective-share amount is equitably apportioned among the recipients of the decedent's probate estate and of that portion of the decedent's nonprobate transfers to others in proportion to the value of their interests therein.

(c) [Unsatisfied Balance of Elective–Share and Supplemental Elective–Share Amounts.] If, after the application of subsections (a) and (b), the elective-share or supplemental elective-share amount is not fully satisfied, the remaining portion of the decedent's nonprobate transfers to others is so applied that liability for the unsatisfied balance of the elective-share or supplemental elective-share amount is equitably apportioned among the recipients of the remaining portion of the decedent's nonprobate transfers to others in proportion to the value of their interests therein.

COMMENT

Purpose and Scope of Revisions. Section 2–209, as revised, is an integral part of the overall redesign of the elective share. It establishes the priority to be used in determining the sources from which the elective-share amount is payable.

Subsection (a). Subsection (a) applies only to the elective-share amount determined under Section 2–202(a), not to the supplemental elective-share amount determined under Section 2–202(b). Under subsection (a), the following are counted first toward satisfying the elective-share amount (to the extent they are included in the augmented estate):

(1) amounts included in the augmented estate under Section 2–204 which pass or have passed to the surviving spouse by testate or intestate succession and amounts included in the augmented estate under Section 2–206, i.e., the value of the decedent's nonprobate transfers to the surviving spouse, including the proceeds of insurance (including accidental death benefits) on the life of the decedent and benefits payable under a retirement plan in which the decedent was a participant, but excluding property passing under

the Federal Social Security system; and

(2) amounts included in the augmented estate under Section 2–207 up to the applicable percentage thereof, the applicable percentage being twice the elective-share percentage as determined under Section 2–202(a). (The phrase "amounts included in the augmented estate under Section 2–207" refers to the value of property owned by the surviving spouse at the decedent's death, plus the value of property that would have been includible in the spouse's nonprobate transfers to others had the surviving spouse been the decedent, reduced by enforceable claims against included property and against the surviving spouse.)

If the combined value of these amounts equals or exceeds the elective-share amount, the surviving spouse is not entitled to any further amount from the decedent's probate estate or recipients of the decedent's nonprobate transfers to others, unless the surviving spouse is entitled to a supplemental elective-share amount under Section 2–202(b).

Subsections (b) and (c). Subsections (b) and (c) apply to both the

81

elective-share amount and the supplemental elective-share amount, if any. As to the elective-share amount determined under Section 2–202(a), the decedent's probate estate and nonprobate transfers to others become liable only if and to the extent that the amounts described in subsection (a) are insufficient to satisfy the elective-share amount. The decedent's probate estate and nonprobate transfers to others are fully liable for the supplemental elective-share amount determined under Section 2–202(b), if any.

Subsections (b) and (c) establish a layer of priority within the decedent's probate estate and nonprobate transfers to others. The decedent's probate estate and that portion of the decedent's nonprobate transfers to others that was not included in the augmented estate under Section 2–205(3)(i) or (iii) are liable first. Only if and to the extent that those amounts are insufficient does the remaining portion of the decedent's nonprobate transfers to others become liable.

Note that the exempt property and allowances provided by Sections 2–401, 2–402, and 2–403 are not charged against, but are in addition to, the elective-share and supplemental elective-share amounts.

The provision that the spouse is charged with amounts that would have passed to the spouse but were disclaimed was deleted in 1993. That provision was introduced into the Code in 1975, prior to the addition of the QTIP provisions in the marital deduction of the federal estate tax. At that time, most devises to the surviving spouse were outright devises and did not require actuarial computation. Now, many if not most devises to the surviving spouse are in the form of an income interest that qualifies for the marital deduction under the QTIP provisions, and these devises require actuarial computations that should be avoided whenever possible.

Historical Note. This Comment was revised in 1993. For the prior version, see 8 U.L.A. 99 (Supp. 1992).

Section 2–210. Personal Liability of Recipients.

(a) Only original recipients of the decedent's nonprobate transfers to others, and the donees of the recipients of the decedent's nonprobate transfers to others, to the extent the donees have the property or its proceeds, are liable to make a proportional contribution toward satisfaction of the surviving spouse's elective-share or supplemental elective-share amount. A person liable to make contribution may choose to give up the proportional part of the decedent's nonprobate transfers to him [or her] or to pay the value of the amount for which he [or she] is liable.

(b) If any section or part of any section of this Part is preempted by federal law with respect to a payment, an item of property, or any other benefit included in the decedent's nonprobate transfers to others, a person who, not for value, receives the payment, item of property, or any other benefit is obligated to return the payment, item of property, or benefit, or is personally liable for the amount of the payment or the value of that item of property or benefit, as provided in Section 2–209, to the person who would have been entitled to it were that section or part of that section not preempted.

Section 2–211. Proceeding for Elective Share; Time Limit.

(a) Except as provided in subsection (b), the election must be made by filing in the court and mailing or delivering to the personal representative, if any, a petition for the elective share within nine months after the date of the decedent's death, or within six months after the probate of the decedent's will, whichever limitation later expires. The surviving spouse must give notice of the time and place set for hearing to persons interested in the estate and to the distributees and recipients of portions of the augmented estate whose interests will be adversely affected by the taking of the elective share. Except as provided in subsection (b), the decedent's nonprobate transfers to others are not included within the augmented estate for the purpose of computing the elective share, if the petition is filed more than nine months after the decedent's death.

(b) Within nine months after the decedent's death, the surviving spouse may petition the court for an extension of time for making an election. If, within nine months after the decedent's death, the spouse gives notice of the petition to all persons interested in the decedent's nonprobate transfers to others, the court for cause shown by the surviving spouse may extend the time for election. If the court grants the spouse's petition for an extension, the decedent's nonprobate transfers to others are not excluded from the augmented estate for the purpose of computing the elective-share and supplemental elective-share amounts, if the spouse makes an election by filing in the court and mailing or delivering to the personal representative, if any, a petition for the elective share within the time allowed by the extension.

(c) The surviving spouse may withdraw his [or her] demand for an elective share at any time before entry of a final determination by the court.

(d) After notice and hearing, the court shall determine the elective-share and supplemental elective-share amounts, and shall order its payment from the assets of the augmented estate or by contribution as appears appropriate under Sections 2–209 and 2–210. If it appears that a fund or property included in the augmented estate has not come into the possession of the personal representative, or has been distributed by the personal representative, the court nevertheless shall fix the liability of any person who has any interest in the fund or property or who has possession thereof, whether as trustee or otherwise. The proceeding may be maintained against fewer than all persons against whom relief could be sought, but no person is subject to contribution in any greater amount than he [or she] would have been under Sections 2–209 and 2–210 had relief been secured against all persons subject to contribution.

(e) An order or judgment of the court may be enforced as necessary in suit for contribution or payment in other courts of this State or other jurisdictions.

COMMENT

This section is revised to coordinate the terminology with that used in revised Section 2–205 and with the fact that an election can be made by a conservator, guardian, or agent on behalf of a surviving spouse, as provided in Section 2–212(a).

Historical Note. This Comment was revised in 1993. For the prior version, see 8 U.L.A. 98 (Supp. 1992).

Section 2–212. Right of Election Personal to Surviving Spouse; Incapacitated Surviving Spouse.

(a) [Surviving Spouse Must Be Living at Time of Election.] The right of election may be exercised only by a surviving spouse who is living when the petition for the elective share is filed in the court under Section 2–211(a). If the election is not exercised by the surviving spouse personally, it may be exercised on the surviving spouse's behalf by his [or her] conservator, guardian, or agent under the authority of a power of attorney.

(b) [Incapacitated Surviving Spouse.] If the election is exercised on behalf of a surviving spouse who is an incapacitated person, that portion of the elective-share and supplemental elective-share amounts due from the decedent's probate estate and recipients of the decedent's nonprobate transfers to others under Section 2–209(b) and (c) must be placed in a custodial trust for the benefit of the surviving spouse under the provisions of the [Enacting state] Uniform Custodial Trust Act, except as modified below. For the purposes of this subsection, an election on behalf of a surviving spouse by an agent under a durable power of attorney is presumed to be on behalf of a surviving spouse who is an incapacitated person. For purposes of the custodial trust established by this subsection, (i) the electing guardian, conservator, or agent is the custodial trustee, (ii) the surviving spouse is the beneficiary, and (iii) the custodial trust is deemed to have been created by the decedent spouse by written transfer that takes effect at the decedent spouse's death and that directs the custodial trustee to administer the custodial trust as for an incapacitated beneficiary.

(c) [Custodial Trust.] For the purposes of subsection (b), the [Enacting state] Uniform Custodial Trust Act must be applied as if Section 6(b) thereof were repealed and Sections 2(e), 9(b), and 17(a) were amended to read as follows:

(1) Neither an incapacitated beneficiary nor anyone acting on behalf of an incapacitated beneficiary has a power to terminate the custodial trust; but if the beneficiary regains capacity, the beneficiary then acquires the power to terminate the custodial trust by delivering to the custodial trustee a writing signed by the beneficiary declaring the termination. If not previously terminated, the custodial trust terminates on the death of the beneficiary.

(2) If the beneficiary is incapacitated, the custodial trustee shall expend so much or all of the custodial trust property as the custodial trustee considers advisable for the use and benefit of the beneficiary and individuals who were supported by the beneficiary when the beneficiary became incapacitated, or who are legally entitled to support by the beneficiary. Expenditures may be made in the manner, when, and to the extent that the custodial trustee determines suitable and proper, without court order but with regard to other support, income, and property of the beneficiary [exclusive of] [and] benefits of medical or other forms of assistance from any state or federal government or governmental agency for which the beneficiary must qualify on the basis of need.

(3) Upon the beneficiary's death, the custodial trustee shall transfer the unexpected custodial trust property in the following order: (i) under the residuary clause, if any, of the will of the beneficiary's predeceased spouse against whom the elective share was taken, as if that predeceased spouse died immediately after the beneficiary; or (ii) to that predeceased spouse's heirs under Section 2–711 of [this State's] Uniform Probate Code.

[STATES THAT HAVE NOT ADOPTED THE UNIFORM
CUSTODIAL TRUST ACT SHOULD ADOPT THE FOL-
LOWING ALTERNATIVE SUBSECTION (b) AND NOT
ADOPT SUBSECTION (b) OR (c) ABOVE]

[(b) [Incapacitated Surviving Spouse.] If the election is
exercised on behalf of a surviving spouse who is an incapacitated
person, the court must set aside that portion of the elective-share
and supplemental elective-share amounts due from the decedent's
probate estate and recipients of the decedent's nonprobate transfers to others under Section 2–209(b) and (c) and must appoint a
trustee to administer that property for the support of the surviving
spouse.   For the purposes of this subsection, an election on behalf
of a surviving spouse by an agent under a durable power of
attorney is presumed to be on behalf of a surviving spouse who is
an incapacitated person.   The trustee must administer the trust in
accordance with the following terms and such additional terms as
the court determines appropriate:

(1) Expenditures of income and principal may be made in
the manner, when, and to the extent that the trustee determines suitable and proper for the surviving spouse's support,
without court order but with regard to other support, income,
and property of the surviving spouse [exclusive of] [and] benefits
of medical or other forms of assistance from any state or federal
government or governmental agency for which the surviving
spouse must qualify on the basis of need.

(2) During the surviving spouse's incapacity, neither the
surviving spouse nor anyone acting on behalf of the surviving
spouse has a power to terminate the trust; but if the surviving
spouse regains capacity, the surviving spouse then acquires the
power to terminate the trust and acquire full ownership of the
trust property free of trust, by delivering to the trustee a
writing signed by the surviving spouse declaring the termination.

(3) Upon the surviving spouse's death, the trustee shall
transfer the unexpended trust property in the following order:
(i) under the residuary clause, if any, of the will of the predeceased spouse against whom the elective share was taken, as if
that predeceased spouse died immediately after the surviving
spouse; or (ii) to the predeceased spouse's heirs under Section
2–711.]

COMMENT

Subsection (a). Subsection (a) is revised to make it clear that the right of election may be exercised only by or on behalf of a living surviving spouse. If the election is not made by the surviving spouse personally, it can be made on behalf of the surviving spouse by the spouse's conservator, guardian, or agent. In any case, the surviving spouse must be alive when the election is made. The election cannot be made on behalf of a deceased surviving spouse.

Subsections (b) and (c). If the election is made on behalf of a surviving spouse who is an "incapacitated person," as defined in section 5–103(7), that portion of the elective-share and supplemental elective-share amounts which, under Section 2–209(b) and (c), are payable from the decedent's probate estate and nonprobate transfers to others must go into a custodial trust under the Uniform Custodial Trust Act, as adjusted in subsection (c).

If the election is made on behalf of the surviving spouse by his or her guardian or conservator, the surviving spouse is by definition an "incapacitated person." If the election is made by the surviving spouse's agent under a durable power of attorney, the surviving spouse is presumed to be an "incapacitated person"; the presumption is rebuttable.

The terms of the custodial trust are governed by the Uniform Custodial Trust Act, except as adjusted in subsection (c).

The custodial trustee is authorized to expend the custodial trust property for the use and benefit of the surviving spouse to the extent the custodial trustee considers it advisable. In determining the amounts, if any, to be expended for the spouse's benefit, the custodial trustee is directed to take into account the spouse's other support, income, and property; these items would include governmental benefits such as Social Security and Medicare.

Bracketed language in subsection (c)(2) (and in Alternative subsection (b)(1)) gives enacting states a choice as to whether governmental benefits for which the spouse must qualify on the basis of need, such as Medicaid, are also to be considered. If so, the enacting state should include the bracketed word "and" but not the bracketed phrase "exclusive of" in its enactment; if not, the enacting state should include the bracketed phrase "exclusive of" and not include the bracketed word "and" in its enactment.

At the surviving spouse's death, the remaining custodial trust property does not go to the surviving spouse's estate, but rather under the residuary clause of the will of the predeceased spouse whose probate estate and nonprobate transfers to others were the source of the property in the custodial trust, as if the predeceased spouse died immediately after the surviving spouse. In the absence of a residuary clause, the property goes to the predeceased spouse's heirs. See Section 2–711.

Alternative Subsection (b). For states that have not enacted the Uniform Custodial Trust Act, an Alternative subsection (b) is provided under which the court must set aside that portion of the elective-share and supplemental elective-share amounts which, under Section 2–209(b) and (c), are due from the decedent's probate estate and nonprobate transfers to others and must appoint a trustee to administer that property for the support of the surviving spouse, in accordance with the terms set forth in Alternative subsection (b).

Planning for an Incapacitated Surviving Spouse Not Disrupted. Note that the portion of the elective-share or supplemental elective-share amounts that go into the custodial or support trust is that portion due from the decedent's probate estate and nonprobate transfers to others under Section 2–209(b) and (c). These amounts constitute the involuntary transfers to the surviving spouse under the elective-share system. Amounts voluntarily transferred to the surviving spouse under the decedent's will, by intestacy, or by nonprobate transfer, if any, do not go into the custodial or support trust. Thus, estate planning measures deliberately established for a surviving spouse who is incapacitated are not disrupted. For example, the decedent's will might establish a trust that qualifies for or that can be elected as qualifying for the federal estate tax marital deduction. Although the value of the surviving spouse's interests in such a trust count toward satisfying the elective-share amount under Section 2–209(a)(1), the trust itself is not dismantled by virtue of Section 2–212(b) in order to force that proper-ty into the nonqualifying custodial or support trust.

Rationale. The approach of this section is based on a general expectation that most surviving spouses are, at the least, generally aware of and accept their decedents' overall estate plans and are not antagonistic to them. Consequently, to elect the elective share, and not have the disposition of that part of it that is payable from the decedent's probate estate and nonprobate transfers to others under Section 2–209(b) and (c) governed by subsections (b) and (c), the surviving spouse must not be an incapacitated person. When the election is made by or on behalf of a surviving spouse who is not an incapacitated person, the surviving spouse has personally signified his or her opposition to the decedent's overall estate plan.

If the election is made on behalf of a surviving spouse who is an incapacitated person, subsection (b) and (c) control the disposition of that part of the elective-share amount or supplemental elective-share amount payable under Section 2–209(b) and (c) from the decedent's probate estate and nonprobate transfers to others. The purpose of subsection (b) and (c), generally speaking, is to assure that that part of the elective share is devoted to the personal economic benefit and needs of the surviving spouse, but not to the economic benefit of the surviving spouse's heirs or devisees.

Historical Note. This Comment was revised in 1993. For the prior version, see 8 U.L.A. 95 (Supp. 1992).

Section 2–213. Waiver of Right to Elect and of Other Rights.

(a) The right of election of a surviving spouse and the rights of the surviving spouse to homestead allowance, exempt property, and family allowance, or any of them, may be waived, wholly or partially, before or after marriage, by a written contract, agreement, or waiver signed by the surviving spouse.

(b) A surviving spouse's waiver is not enforceable if the surviving spouse proves that:

(1) he [or she] did not execute the waiver voluntarily; or

(2) the waiver was unconscionable when it was executed and, before execution of the waiver, he [or she]:

(i) was not provided a fair and reasonable disclosure of the property or financial obligations of the decedent;

(ii) did not voluntarily and expressly waive, in writing, any right to disclosure of the property or financial obligations of the decedent beyond the disclosure provided; and

(iii) did not have, or reasonably could not have had, an adequate knowledge of the property or financial obligations of the decedent.

(c) An issue of unconscionability of a waiver is for decision by the court as a matter of law.

(d) Unless it provides to the contrary, a waiver of "all rights," or equivalent language, in the property or estate of a present or prospective spouse or a complete property settlement entered into after or in anticipation of separation or divorce is a waiver of all rights of elective share, homestead allowance, exempt property, and family allowance by each spouse in the property of the other and a renunciation by each of all benefits that would otherwise pass to him [or her] from the other by intestate succession or by virtue of any will executed before the waiver or property settlement.

COMMENT

This section incorporates the standards by which the validity of a premarital agreement is determined under the Uniform Premarital Agreement Act § 6.

The right to homestead allowance, exempt property and family allowance are conferred by the provisions of Part 4. The right to disclaim interests is recognized by Section 2–801. The provisions of this section, permitting a spouse or prospective spouse to waive all statutory rights in the other spouse's property, seem desirable in view of the common desire of parties to second and later marriages to insure that property derived from the prior spouse passes at death to the joint children (or descendants) of the prior marriage instead of to the later spouse. The operation of a property settlement in anticipation of separation or divorce as a waiver and renunciation takes care of most situations arising when a spouse dies while a divorce suit is pending.

Effect of Premarital Agreement or Waiver on ERISA Benefits. As amended in 1984 by the Retirement Equity Act, ERISA requires each employee benefit plan subject to its provisions to provide that an election of a waiver shall not take effect unless

> (i) the spouse of the participant consents in writing to such election, (ii) such election designates a beneficiary (or form of benefits) which may not be changed without spousal consent (or the consent of the spouse expressly permits designation by the participant without any requirement of further consent by the spouse), and (iii) the spouse's consent acknowledges the effect of such election and is witnessed by a plan representative or a notary public.

See 29 U.S.C. § 1055(c) (1988); Int. Rev.Code § 417(a).

In Hurwitz v. Sher, 982 F.2d 778 (2d Cir.1992), the court held that a premarital agreement was not an effective waiver of a wife's claims to spousal death benefits under a qualified profit sharing plan in which the deceased husband was the sole participant. The premarital agreement provided, in part, that "each party hereby waives and releases to the other party and to the other party's heirs, executor, administrators and assigns any and all rights and causes of action which may arise by reason of the marriage between the parties ... with respect to any property, real or personal, tangible or intangible ... now owned or hereafter acquired by the other party, as fully as though the parties had never married...." The court held that the premarital agreement was not an effective waiver because it "did not designate a beneficiary and did not acknowledge the effect of the waiver as required by ERISA." 982 F.2d at 781. Although the district court had held that the premarital agreement was also ineffective because the wife was not married to the participant when she signed the agreement, the Second Circuit "reserve[d] judgment on whether the [premarital] agreement might have operated as an effective waiver if its only deficiency were that it had been entered into before marriage." Id. at 781 n. 3. The court did, however, quote Treas.Reg. § 1.401(a)–20 (1991), which specifically states that "an agreement entered into prior to marriage does not satisfy the applicable consent requirements...." Id. at 782. Other cases involving the validity of premarital agreements on ERISA benefits include Callahan v. Hutsell, Callahan & Buchino, 813 F.Supp. 541 (W.D.Ky.1992); Zinn v. Donaldson Co., Inc., 799 F.Supp. 69 (D.Minn.1992); Estate of Hopkins, 574 N.E.2d 230 (Ill.App.Ct.1991); see also Howard v. Branham & Baker Coal Co., 1992 U.S.App. LEXIS 16247 (6th Cir.1992).

Cross Reference. See also Section 2–208 and Comment.

Historical Note. This Comment was revised in 1993. For the prior version, see 8 U.L.A. 97 (Supp. 1992).

Section 2–214. Protection of Payors and Other Third Parties.

(a) Although under Section 2–205 a payment, item of property, or other benefit is included in the decedent's nonprobate transfers to others, a payor or other third party is not liable for having made a payment or transferred an item of property or other benefit to a beneficiary designated in a governing instrument, or for having taken any other action in good faith reliance on the validity of a governing instrument, upon request and satisfactory proof of the decedent's death, before the payor or other third party received written notice from the surviving spouse or spouse's representative of an intention to file a petition for the elective share or that a petition for the elective share has been filed. A payor or other third party is liable for payments made or other actions taken after the payor or other third party received written notice of an intention to file a petition for the elective share or that a petition for the elective share has been filed.

(b) A written notice of intention to file a petition for the elective share or that a petition for the elective share has been filed must be mailed to the payor's or other third party's main office or home by registered or certified mail, return receipt requested, or served upon the payor or other third party in the same manner as a summons in a civil action. Upon receipt of written notice of intention to file a petition for the elective share or that a petition for the elective share has been filed, a payor or other third party may pay any amount owed or transfer or deposit any item of property held by it to or with the court having jurisdiction of the probate proceedings relating to the decedent's estate, or if no proceedings have been commenced, to or with the court having jurisdiction of probate proceedings relating to decedents' estates located in the county of the decedent's residence. The court shall hold the funds or item of property and, upon its determination under Section 2–211(d), shall order disbursement in accordance with the determination. If no petition is filed in the court within the specified time under Section 2–211(a) or, if filed, the demand for an elective share is withdrawn under Section 2–211(c), the court shall order disbursement to the designated beneficiary. Payments or transfers to the court or deposits made into court discharge the payor or other third party from all claims for amounts so paid or the value of property so transferred or deposited.

(c) Upon petition to the probate court by the beneficiary designated in a governing instrument, the court may order that all or part of the property be paid to the beneficiary in an amount and subject to conditions consistent with this Part.

COMMENT

This section provides protection to "payors" and other third parties who made payments or took any other action before receiving written notice of the spouse's intention to make an election under this Part or that an election has been made. The term "payor" is defined in Section 1–201 as meaning "a trustee, insurer, business entity, employer, government, governmental agency or subdivision, or any other person authorized or obligated by law or a governing instrument to make payments."

Historical Note. Although this Comment was added in 1993, the substance of the Comment previously appeared as the last paragraph of the Comment to Section 2–202, 8 U.L.A. 92, 93 (Supp.1992).

PART 3

SPOUSE AND CHILDREN UNPROVIDED FOR IN WILLS

Section 2–301. Entitlement of Spouse; Premarital Will.

(a) If a testator's surviving spouse married the testator after the testator executed his [or her] will, the surviving spouse is entitled to receive, as an intestate share, no less than the value of the share of the estate he [or she] would have received if the testator had died intestate as to that portion of the testator's estate, if any, that is neither devised to a child of the testator who was born before the testator married the surviving spouse and who is not a child of the surviving spouse nor devised to a descendant of such a child or passes under Sections 2–603 or 2–604 to such a child or to a descendant of such a child, unless:

(1) it appears from the will or other evidence that the will was made in contemplation of the testator's marriage to the surviving spouse;

(2) the will expresses the intention that it is to be effective notwithstanding any subsequent marriage; or

(3) the testator provided for the spouse by transfer outside the will and the intent that the transfer be in lieu of a testamentary provision is shown by the testator's statements or is reasonably inferred from the amount of the transfer or other evidence.

(b) In satisfying the share provided by this section, devises made by the will to the testator's surviving spouse, if any, are applied first, and other devises, other than a devise to a child of the testator who was born before the testator married the surviving spouse and who is not a child of the surviving spouse or a devise or substitute gift under Sections 2–603 or 2–604 to a descendant of such a child, abate as provided in Section 3–902.

COMMENT

Purpose and Scope of the Revisions. This section applies only to a premarital will, a will executed prior to the testator's marriage to his or her surviving spouse. If the decedent and the surviving spouse were married to each other more than once, a premarital will is a will executed by the decedent at any

93

time when they were not married to each other but not a will executed during a prior marriage. This section reflects the view that the intestate share of the spouse in that portion of the testator's estate not devised to certain of the testator's children, under trust or not, (or that is not devised to their descendants, under trust or not, or does not pass to their descendants under the antilapse statute) is what the testator would want the spouse to have if he or she had thought about the relationship of his or her old will to the new situation.

Under this section, a surviving spouse who married the testator after the testator executed his or her will may be entitled to a certain minimum amount of the testator's estate. The surviving spouse's entitlement under this section, if any, is granted automatically; it need not be elected. If the surviving spouse exercises his or her right to take an elective share, amounts provided under this section count toward making up the elective-share amount by virtue of the language in subsection (a) stating that the amount provided by this section is treated as "an intestate share." Under section 2–209(a)(1), amounts passing to the surviving spouse by intestate succession count first toward making up the spouse's elective-share amount.

Subsection (a). Subsection (a) is revised to make it clear that a surviving spouse who, by a premarital will, is devised, under trust or not, less than the share of the testator's estate he or she would have received had the testator died intestate as to that part of the estate, if any, not devised to certain of the testator's children, under trust or

not (or that is not devised to their descendants, under trust or not, or does not pass to their descendants under the antilapse statute) is entitled to be brought up to that share. Subsection (a) was amended in 1993 to make it clear that any lapsed devise that passes under section 2–604 to a child of the testator by a prior marriage, rather than only to a descendant of such a child, is covered.

> *Example.* G's will devised the residue of his estate "to my two children, A and B, in equal shares." A and B are children of G's prior marriage. G is survived by A and by G's new spouse, X. B predeceases G, without leaving any descendants who survived G by 120 hours. Under Section 2–604, B's half of the residue passes to G's child, A. A is a child of the testator's prior marriage but not a descendant of B. X's rights under Section 2–301 are to take an intestate share in that portion of G's estate not covered by the residuary clause.

The pre–1990 version of Section 2–301 was titled "*Omitted* Spouse," and the section used phrases such as "*fails* to provide" and "*omitted* spouse." The implication of the title and these phrases was that the section was inapplicable if the person the decedent later married was a devisee in his or her premarital will. It was clear, however, from the underlying purpose of the section that this was not intended. The courts recognized this and refused to interpret the section that way, but in doing so they have been forced to say that a premarital will containing a devise to the person to whom the testator was married at death could still be found to "fail to provide" for the survivor *in the survivor's capacity as spouse.* See Estate of Christensen, 665 P.2d 646 (Utah 1982); Estate of Ganier, 418 So.2d 256 (Fla. 1982); Note, "The Problem of the 'Un-omitted' Spouse Under Section 2–301 of the [Pre– 1990] Uniform Probate Code," 52 U. Chi. L. Rev. 481 (1985). By making the existence and amount of a premarital devise to the spouse irrelevant, the revisions of subsection (a) make the operation of the statute more purposive.

Subsection (a)(1), (2), and (3) Exceptions. The moving party has the burden of proof on the exceptions contained in subsections (a)(1), (2), and (3). For a case interpreting the language of subsection (a)(3), see Estate of Bartell, 776 P.2d 885 (Utah 1989). This section can be barred by a premarital agreement, marital agreement, or waiver as provided in Section 2–213.

Subsection (b). Subsection (b) is also revised to provide that the value of any premarital devise to the surviving spouse, equitable or legal, is used first to satisfy the spouse's entitlement under this section, before any other devises suffer abatement. This revision is made necessary by the revision of subsection (a): If the existence or amount of a premarital devise to the surviving spouse is irrelevant, the value of any such devise, equitable or legal, must be counted toward and not be in addition to the ultimate share to which the spouse is entitled. Normally, a devise in favor of the person whom the testator *later* marries will be a specific or general devise, not a residuary devise. The effect under the pre–1990 version of subsection (b) was that the surviving spouse could take the intestate share under Section 2–301, which in the pre–1990 version was satisfied out of the residue (under the rules of abatement in Section 3–902), *plus* the devise in his or her favor. The revision of subsection (b) prevents this "double dipping," so to speak.

Reference. The theory of this section is discussed in Waggoner, "Spousal Rights in Our Multiple-Marriage Society: The Revised Uniform Probate Code," 26 Real Prop. Prob. & Tr.J. 683, 748–51 (1992).

Historical Note. This Comment was revised in 1993. For the prior version, see 8 U.L.A. 101 (Supp. 1992).

Section 2–302. Omitted Children.

(a) Except as provided in subsection (b), if a testator fails to provide in his [or her] will for any of his [or her] children born or adopted after the execution of the will, the omitted after-born or after-adopted child receives a share in the estate as follows:

(1) If the testator had no child living when he [or she] executed the will, an omitted after-born or after-adopted child receives a share in the estate equal in value to that which the child would have received had the testator died intestate, unless the will devised all or substantially all the estate to the other parent of the omitted child and that other parent survives the testator and is entitled to take under the will.

(2) If the testator had one or more children living when he [or she] executed the will, and the will devised property or an interest in property to one or more of the then-living children, an omitted after-born or after-adopted child is entitled to share in the testator's estate as follows:

(i) The portion of the testator's estate in which the omitted after-born or after-adopted child is entitled to share is limited to devises made to the testator's then-living children under the will.

(ii) The omitted after-born or after-adopted child is entitled to receive the share of the testator's estate, as limited in subparagraph (i), that the child would have received had the testator included all omitted after-born and after-adopted children with the children to whom devises were made under the will and had given an equal share of the estate to each child.

(iii) To the extent feasible, the interest granted an omitted after-born or after-adopted child under this section must be of the same character, whether equitable or legal, present or future, as that devised to the testator's then-living children under the will.

(iv) In satisfying a share provided by this paragraph, devises to the testator's children who were living when the will was executed abate ratably. In abating the devises of the then-living children, the court shall preserve to the maximum extent possible the character of the testamentary plan adopted by the testator.

(b) Neither subsection (a)(1) nor subsection (a)(2) applies if:

(1) it appears from the will that the omission was intentional; or

(2) the testator provided for the omitted after-born or after-adopted child by transfer outside the will and the intent that the transfer be in lieu of a testamentary provision is shown by the testator's statements or is reasonably inferred from the amount of the transfer or other evidence.

(c) If at the time of execution of the will the testator fails to provide in his [or her] will for a living child solely because he [or she] believes the child to be dead, the child is entitled to share in the estate as if the child were an omitted after-born or after-adopted child.

(d) In satisfying a share provided by subsection (a)(1), devises made by the will abate under Section 3–902.

COMMENT

This section provides for both the case where a child was born or adopted after the execution of the will and not foreseen at the time and thus not provided for in the will, and the rare case where a testator omits one of his or her children because of the mistaken belief that the child is dead.

Basic Purposes and Scope of Revisions. This section is substantially revised. The revisions have two basic objectives. The first basic objective is to provide that a will that devised, under trust or not, all or substantially all of the testator's estate to the other parent of the omitted child prevents an after-born or after-adopted child from taking an intestate share if none of the testator's children was living when he or she executed the will. (Under this rule, the other parent must survive the testator and be entitled to take under the will.)

Under the pre–1990 Code, such a will prevented the omitted child's entitlement only if the testator had one or more children living when he or she executed the will. The rationale for the revised rule is found in the empirical evidence (cited in the Comment to section 2–102) that suggests that even testators with children tend to devise their entire estates to their surviving spouses, especially in smaller estates. The testator's purpose is not to disinherit the children; rather, such a will evidences a purpose to trust the surviving parent to use the property for the benefit of the children, as appropriate. This attitude of trust of the surviving parent carries over to the case where none of the children have been born when the will is executed.

The second basic objective of the revisions is to provide that if the testator had children when he or she executed the will, and if the will made provision for one or more of the then-living children, an omitted after-born or after-adopted child does not take a full intestate share (which might be substantially larger or substantially smaller than given to the living children). Rather, the omitted after-born or after-adopted child participates on a pro rata basis in the property devised, under trust or not, to the then-living children.

A more detailed description of the revised rules follows.

No Child Living When Will Executed. If the testator had no child living when he or she executed the will, subsection (a)(1) provides that an omitted after-born or after-adopted child receives the share he or she would have received had the testator died intestate, unless the will devised, under trust or not, all or substantially all of the estate to the other parent of the omitted child. If the will did devise, under trust or not, all or substantially all of the estate to the other parent of the omitted child, and if that other parent survives the testator and is entitled to take under the will, the omitted after-born or after-adopted child receives no share of the estate. In the case of an after-adopted child, the term "other parent" refers to the other adopting parent. (The other parent of the omitted child might survive the testator, but not be entitled to take under the will because, for example, that devise, under trust or not, to the other parent was revoked under Section 2–803 or 2–804.)

One or More Children Living When Will Executed. If the testator had one or more children living when the will was executed, subsection (a)(2), which implements the second basic objective stated above, provides that an omitted after-born or after-adopted child only receives a share of the testator's estate if the testator's will devised property or an equitable or legal interest in property to one or more of the children living at the time the will was executed; if not, the omitted after-born or after-adopted child receives nothing.

Subsection (a)(2) is modelled on N.Y. Est. Powers & Trusts Law § 5–3.2. Subsection (a)(2) is illustrated by the following example.

> *Example.* When G executed her will, she had two living children, A and B. Her will devised $7,500 to each child. After G executed her will, she had another child, C.
>
> C is entitled to $5,000. $2,500 (1/3 of $7,500) of C's entitlement comes from A's $7,500 devise (reducing it to $5,000); and $2,500 (1/3 of $7,500) comes from B's $7,500 devise (reducing it to $5,000).
>
> *Variation.* If G's will had devised $10,000 to A and $5,000 to B, C would be entitled to $5,000. $3,333 (1/3 of $10,000) of C's entitlement comes from A's $10,-000 devise (reducing it to $6,667); and $1,667 (1/3 of $5,000) comes from B's $5,000 devise (reducing it to $3,333).

Subsection (b) Exceptions. To preclude operation of subsection (a)(1) or (a)(2), the testator's will need not make any provision, even nominal in amount, for a testator's present or future children; under subsection (b)(1), a simple recital in the will that the testator intends to make no provision for then living children or any the testator thereafter may have would be sufficient.

For a case applying the language of subsection (b)(2), in the context of the omitted spouse provision, see Estate of Bartell, 776 P.2d 885 (Utah 1989).

The moving party has the burden of proof on the elements of subsections (b)(1) and (b)(2).

Subsection (c). Subsection (c) addresses the problem that arises if at the time of execution of the will the testator fails to provide in his or her will for a living child solely because he or she believes the child to be dead. Extrinsic evidence is admissible to determine whether the testator omitted the living child solely because he or she believed the child to be dead. Cf. Section 2–601, Comment. If the child was omitted solely because of that belief, the child is entitled to share in the estate as if the child were an omitted after-born or after-adopted child.

Abatement Under Subsection (d). Under subsection (d) and Section 3–902, any intestate estate would first be applied to satisfy the intestate share of an omitted after-born or after-adopted child under subsection (a)(1).

Historical Note. This Comment was revised in 1993. For the prior version, see 8 U.L.A. 103 (Supp. 1992).

98

PART 4

EXEMPT PROPERTY AND ALLOWANCES

GENERAL COMMENT

For decedents who die domiciled in this State, this part grants various allowances to the decedent's surviving spouse and certain children. The allowances have priority over unsecured creditors of the estate and persons to whom the estate may be devised by will. If there is a surviving spouse, all of the allowances described in this Part, which (as revised to adjust for inflation) total $25,000, plus whatever is allowed to the spouse for support during administration, normally pass to the spouse. If the surviving spouse and minor or dependent children live apart from one another, the minor or dependent children may receive some of the support allowance. If there is no surviving spouse, minor or dependent children become entitled to the homestead exemption of $15,000 and to support allowances. The exempt property section confers rights on the spouse, if any, or on all children, to $10,000 in certain chattels, or funds if the unencumbered value of chattels is below the $10,000 level. This provision is designed in part to relieve a personal representative of the duty to sell household chattels when there are children who will have them.

These family protection provisions supply the basis for the important small estate provisions of Article III, Part 12.

States adopting the Code may see fit to alter the dollar amounts suggested in these sections, or to vary the terms and conditions in other ways so as to accommodate existing traditions. Although creditors of estates would be aided somewhat if all family exemption provisions relating to probate estates were the same throughout the country, there is probably less need for uniformity of law regarding these provisions than for any of the other parts of this article. Still, it is quite important for all states to limit their homestead, support allowance and exempt property provisions, if any, so that they apply only to estates of decedents who were domiciliaries of the state.

Cross Reference. Notice that under Section 2–104 a spouse or child claiming under this Part must survive the decedent by 120 hours.

Section 2–401. Applicable Law.

This Part applies to the estate of a decedent who dies domiciled in this State. Rights to homestead allowance, exempt property, and family allowance for a decedent who dies not domiciled in this State are governed by the law of the decedent's domicile at death.

99

Section 2–402. Homestead Allowance.

A decedent's surviving spouse is entitled to a homestead allowance of [$15,000]. If there is no surviving spouse, each minor child and each dependent child of the decedent is entitled to a homestead allowance amounting to [$15,000] divided by the number of minor and dependent children of the decedent. The homestead allowance is exempt from and has priority over all claims against the estate. Homestead allowance is in addition to any share passing to the surviving spouse or minor or dependent child by the will of the decedent, unless otherwise provided, by intestate succession, or by way of elective share.

COMMENT

As originally adopted in 1969, the bracketed dollar amount was $5,000. To adjust for inflation, the bracketed amount was increased to $15,000 in 1990.

See Section 2–802 for the definition of "spouse," which controls in this Part. Also, see Section 2–104. Waiver of homestead is covered by Section 2–204. "Election" between a provision of a will and homestead is not required unless the will so provides.

A set dollar amount for homestead allowance was dictated by the desirability of having a certain level below which administration may be dispensed with or be handled summarily, without regard to the size of allowances under Section 2–404.

The "small estate" line is controlled largely, though not entirely, by the size of the homestead allowance. This is because Part 12 of Article III dealing with small estates rests on the assumption that the only justification for keeping a decedent's assets from his creditors is to benefit the decedent's spouse and children.

Another reason for a set amount is related to the fact that homestead allowance may prefer a decedent's minor or dependent children over his or her other children. It was felt desirable to minimize the consequence of application of an arbitrary age line among children of the decedent.

[Section 2–402A. Constitutional Homestead.

The value of any constitutional right of homestead in the family home received by a surviving spouse or child must be charged against the spouse or child's homestead allowance to the extent the family home is part of the decedent's estate or would have been but for the homestead provision of the constitution.]

COMMENT

This optional section is designed for adoption only in states with a constitutional homestead provision.

The value of the surviving spouse's constitutional right of homestead may be considerably less than the full value of the family home if the constitution gives him or her only a terminable life estate enjoyable in common with minor children.

Section 2–403. Exempt Property.

In addition to the homestead allowance, the decedent's surviving spouse is entitled from the estate to a value, not exceeding $10,000 in excess of any security interests therein, in household furniture, automobiles, furnishings, appliances, and personal effects. If there is no surviving spouse, the decedent's children are entitled jointly to the same value. If encumbered chattels are selected and the value in excess of security interests, plus that of other exempt property, is less than $10,000, or if there is not $10,000 worth of exempt property in the estate, the spouse or children are entitled to other assets of the estate, if any, to the extent necessary to make up the $10,000 value. Rights to exempt property and assets needed to make up a deficiency of exempt property have priority over all claims against the estate, but the right to any assets to make up a deficiency of exempt property abates as necessary to permit earlier payment of homestead allowance and family allowance. These rights are in addition to any benefit or share passing to the surviving spouse or children by the decedent's will, unless otherwise provided, by intestate succession, or by way of elective share.

COMMENT

As originally adopted in 1969, the dollar amount exempted was set at $3,500. To adjust for inflation, the amount was increased to $10,000 in 1990.

Unlike the exempt amount described in Sections 2–402 and 2–404, the exempt amount described in this section is available in a case in which the decedent left no spouse but left only adult children. The provision in this section that estab- lishes priorities is required because of possible difference between beneficiaries of the exemptions described in this section and those described in Sections 2–402 and 2–404.

Section 2–204 covers waiver of exempt property rights. This section indicates that a decedent's will may put a spouse to an election with reference to exemptions, but that no election is presumed to be required.

Section 2–404. Family Allowance.

(a) In addition to the right to homestead allowance and exempt property, the decedent's surviving spouse and minor children whom the decedent was obligated to support and children who were in fact being supported by the decedent are entitled to a reasonable allowance in money out of the estate for their maintenance during the period of administration, which allowance may not continue for longer than one year if the estate is inadequate to discharge allowed claims. The allowance may be paid as a lump sum or in periodic installments. It is payable to the surviving spouse, if living, for the use of the surviving spouse and minor and dependent children; otherwise to the children, or persons having their care and custody. If a minor child or dependent child is not living with the surviving spouse, the allowance may be made partially to the child or his [or her] guardian or other person having the child's care and custody, and partially to the spouse, as their needs may appear. The family allowance is exempt from and has priority over all claims except the homestead allowance.

(b) The family allowance is not chargeable against any benefit or share passing to the surviving spouse or children by the will of the decedent, unless otherwise provided, by intestate succession, or by way of elective share. The death of any person entitled to family allowance terminates the right to allowances not yet paid.

COMMENT

The allowance provided by this section does not qualify for the marital deduction under the federal estate tax because the interest is a non-deductible terminable interest. A broad code must be drafted to provide the best possible protection for the family in all cases, even though this may not provide desired tax advantages for certain larger estates. In the estates falling in the federal estate tax bracket where careful planning may be expected, it is important to the operation of formula clauses that the family allowance be clearly deductible or clearly non-deductible. With the section clearly creating a non-deductible interest, estate planners can create a plan that will operate with certainty. Finally, in order to facilitate administration of this allowance without court supervision it is necessary to provide a fairly simple and definite framework.

In determining the amount of the family allowance, account should be taken of both the previous standard of living and the nature of other resources available to the family to meet current living expenses until the estate can be administered and assets distributed. While the death of the principal income producer may necessitate some change in the standard of living, there must also be a period of adjustment. If the surviving spouse has a substantial income, this may be taken into account. Whether life insurance proceeds payable in a lump sum or periodic installments were intended by the decedent to be used for the period of adjustment or to be conserved as capital may be considered. A living trust may provide the needed income without resorting to the probate estate.

Obviously, need is relative to the circumstances, and what is reasonable must be decided on the basis of the facts of each individual case. Note, however, that under the next section the personal representative may not determine an allowance of more than $1500 per month for one year; a Court order would be necessary if a greater allowance is reasonably necessary.

Section 2–405. Source, Determination, and Documentation.

(a) If the estate is otherwise sufficient, property specifically devised may not be used to satisfy rights to homestead allowance or exempt property. Subject to this restriction, the surviving spouse, guardians of minor children, or children who are adults may select property of the estate as homestead allowance and exempt property. The personal representative may make those selections if the surviving spouse, the children, or the guardians of the minor children are unable or fail to do so within a reasonable time or there is no guardian of a minor child. The personal representative may execute an instrument or deed of distribution to establish the ownership of property taken as homestead allowance or exempt property. The personal representative may determine the family allowance in a lump sum not exceeding $18,000 or periodic installments not exceeding $1,500 per month for one year, and may disburse funds of the estate in payment of the family allowance and any part of the homestead allowance payable in cash. The personal representative or an interested person aggrieved by any selection, determination, payment, proposed payment, or failure to act under this section may petition the court for appropriate relief, which may include a family allowance other than that which the personal representative determined or could have determined.

(b) If the right to an elective share is exercised on behalf of a surviving spouse who is an incapacitated person, the personal representative may add any unexpended portions payable under the homestead allowance, exempt property, and family allowance to the trust established under Section 2–212(b).

COMMENT

Scope and Purpose of Revision. As originally adopted in 1969, the maximum family allowance the personal representative was authorized to determine without court order was a lump sum of $6,000 or periodic installments of $500 per month for one year. To adjust for inflation, the amounts are increased to $18,000 and $1,500 respectively.

A new subsection (b) is added to provide for the case where the right to an elective share is exercised on behalf of a surviving spouse who is an incapacitated person. In that case, the personal representative is authorized to add any unexpended portions under the homestead allowance, exempt property, and fam-

103

ily allowance to the custodial trust established by Section 2–212(b).

If Domiciliary Assets Insufficient. Note that a domiciliary personal representative can collect against out of state assets if domiciliary assets are insufficient.

Cross References. See Sections 3–902, 3–906, and 3–907.

Historical Note. This Comment was revised in 1993. For the prior version, see 8 U.L.A. 108 (Supp. 1992).

PART 5

WILLS, WILL CONTRACTS, AND CUSTODY AND DEPOSIT OF WILLS

GENERAL COMMENT

Part 5 of Article II is retitled to reflect the fact that it now includes the provisions on will contracts (pre–1990 section 2–701) and on custody and deposit of wills (pre–1990 sections 2–901 and 2–902).

Part 5 deals with capacity and formalities for execution and revocation of wills. The basic intent of the pre–1990 sections was to validate wills whenever possible. To that end, the minimum age for making wills was lowered to eighteen, formalities for a written and attested will were reduced, holographic wills written and signed by the testator were authorized, choice of law as to validity of execution was broadened, and revocation by operation of law was limited to divorce or annulment. In addition, the statute also provided for an optional method of execution with acknowledgment before a public officer (the self-proved will).

These measures have been retained, and the purpose of validating wills whenever possible has been strengthened by the addition of a new section, section 2–503, which allows a will to be upheld despite a harmless error in its execution.

Section 2–501. Who May Make Will.

An individual 18 or more years of age who is of sound mind may make a will.

COMMENT

This section states a uniform minimum age of eighteen for capacity to execute a will. "Minor" is defined in Section 1–201, and may involve an age different from that prescribed here.

Section 2–502. Execution; Witnessed Wills; Holographic Wills.

(a) Except as provided in subsection (b) and in Sections 2–503, 2–506, and 2–513, a will must be:

(1) in writing;

(2) signed by the testator or in the testator's name by some other individual in the testator's conscious presence and by the testator's direction; and

(3) signed by at least two individuals, each of whom signed within a reasonable time after he [or she] witnessed either the

105

signing of the will as described in paragraph (2) or the testator's acknowledgment of that signature or acknowledgment of the will.

(b) A will that does not comply with subsection (a) is valid as a holographic will, whether or not witnessed, if the signature and material portions of the document are in the testator's handwriting.

(c) Intent that the document constitute the testator's will can be established by extrinsic evidence, including, for holographic wills, portions of the document that are not in the testator's handwriting.

COMMENT

Scope and Purpose of Revision. Section 2–502 and pre–1990 Section 2–503 are combined to make room for new Section 2–503. Also, a cross reference to new section 2–503 is added, and fairly minor clarifying revisions are made.

Subsection (a). Three formalities for execution of a witnessed will are imposed. Subsection (a)(1) requires the will to be in writing. Any reasonably permanent record is sufficient. A tape-recorded will has been held not to be "in writing." Estate of Reed, 672 P.2d 829 (Wyo. 1983).

Under subsection (a)(2), the testator must sign the will or some other individual must sign the testator's name in the testator's presence and by the testator's direction. If the latter procedure is followed, and someone else signs the testator's name, the so-called "conscious presence" test is codified, under which a signing is sufficient if it was done in the testator's conscious presence, i.e., within the range of the testator's senses such as hearing; the signing need not have occurred within the testator's line of sight. For application of the "conscious-presence" test, see Cunning-

ham v. Cunningham, 80 Minn. 180, 83 N.W. 58 (1900) (conscious-presence requirement held satisfied where "the signing was within the sound of the testator's voice; he knew what was being done. . . ."); Healy v. Bartless, 73 N.H. 110, 59 A. 617 (1904) (individuals are in the decedent's conscious presence "whenever they are so near at hand that he is conscious of where they are and of what they are doing, through any of his senses, and where he can readily see them if he is so disposed."); Demaris' Estate, 166 Or. 36, 110 P.2d 571 (1941) ("[W]e do not believe that sight is the only test of presence. We are convinced that any of the senses that a testator possesses, which enable him to know whether another is near at hand and what he is doing, may be employed by him in determining whether [an individual is] in his [conscious] presence. . . .").

Under subsection (a)(3), at least two individuals must sign the will, each of whom witnessed at least one of the following: the signing of the will; the testator's acknowledgment

106

of the signature; or the testator's acknowledgment of the will.

Signing may be by mark, nickname, or initials, subject to the general rules relating to that which constitutes a "signature." There is no requirement that the testator "publish" the document as his or her will, or that he or she request the witnesses to sign, or that the witnesses sign in the presence of the testator or of each other. The testator may sign the will outside the presence of the witnesses, if he or she later acknowledges to the witnesses that the signature is his or hers (or that his or her name was signed by another) or that the document is his or her will. An acknowledgment need not be expressly stated, but can be inferred from the testator's conduct. Norton v. Georgia Railroad Bank & Tr. Co., 248 Ga. 847, 285 S.E.2d 910 (1982). The witnesses must sign as witnesses (see, e.g., Mossler v. Johnson, 565 S.W.2d 952 (Tex. Civ. App. 1978)), and must sign within a reasonable time after having witnessed the signing or acknowledgment. There is, however, no requirement that the witnesses sign before the testator's death; in a given case, the reasonable-time requirement could be satisfied even if the witnesses sign after the testator's death.

There is no requirement that the testator's signature be at the end of the will; thus, if he or she writes his or her name in the body of the will and intends it to be his or her signature, this would satisfy the statute. See Estate of Siegel, 214

N.J. Super. 586, 520 A.2d 798 (App. Div. 1987).

A will that does not meet these requirements may be valid under subsection (b) as a holograph or under Section 2–503.

Subsection (b). This subsection authorizes holographic wills. It enables a testator to write his or her own will in handwriting. There need be no witnesses. The only requirement is that the signature and the material portions of the document be in the testator's handwriting.

By requiring only the "material portions of the document" to be in the testator's handwriting (rather than requiring, as some existing statutes do, that the will be "entirely" in the decedent's handwriting), a holograph may be valid even though immaterial parts such as date or introductory wording are printed, typed, or stamped.

A valid holograph can also be executed on a printed will form if the material portions of the document are handwritten. The fact, for example, that the will form contains printed language such as "I give, devise, and bequeath to _____" does not disqualify the document as a holographic will, as long as the testator fills out the remaining portion of the dispositive provision in his or her own hand.

Under subsection (c), testamentary intent can be shown by extrinsic evidence, including for holographic wills the printed, typed, or stamped portions of the form or document.

Section 2–503. Writings Intended as Wills, etc.

Although a document or writing added upon a document was not executed in compliance with Section 2–502, the document or writing is treated as if it had been executed in compliance with that section if the proponent of the document or writing establishes by clear and convincing evidence that the decedent intended the document or writing to constitute (i) the decedent's will, (ii) a partial or complete revocation of the will, (iii) an addition to or an alteration of the will, or (iv) a partial or complete revival of his [or her] formerly revoked will or of a formerly revoked portion of the will.

COMMENT

Purpose of New Section. By way of dispensing power, this new section allows the probate court to excuse a harmless error in complying with the formal requirements for executing or revoking a will. The measure accords with legislation in force in the Canadian province of Manitoba and in several Australian jurisdictions. The Uniform Laws Conference of Canada approved a comparable measure for the Canadian Uniform Wills Act in 1987.

Legislation of this sort was enacted in the state of South Australia in 1975. The experience there has been closely studied by a variety of law reform commissions and in the scholarly literature. See, e.g., Law Reform Commission of British Columbia, Report on the Making and Revocation of Wills (1981); New South Wales Law Reform Commission, Wills: Execution and Revocation (1986); Langbein, Excusing Harmless Errors in the Execution of Wills: A Report on Australia's Tranquil Revolution in Probate Law, 87 Colum. L. Rev. 1 (1987). A similar measure has been in effect in Israel since 1965 (see British Columbia Report, supra, at 44–46; Langbein, supra, at 48–51).

Consistent with the general trend of the revisions of the UPC, section 2–503 unifies the law of probate and nonprobate transfers, extending to will formalities the harmless error principle that has long been applied to defective compliance with the formal requirements for nonprobate transfers. See, e.g., Annot., 19 A.L.R.2d 5 (1951) (life insurance beneficiary designations).

Evidence from South Australia suggests that the dispensing power will be applied mainly in two sorts of cases. See Langbein, supra, at 15–33. When the testator misunderstands the attestation requirements of Section 2–502(a) and neglects to obtain one or both witnesses, new Section 2–503 permits the proponents of the will to prove that the defective execution did not result from irresolution or from circumstances suggesting duress or trickery—in other words, that the defect was harmless to the purpose of the formality. The measure reduces the tension between holographic wills and the two-witness requirement for attested wills under Section 2–502(a). Ordinarily, the testator who attempts to make an attested will but blunders will still have achieved a level of formality that compares favorably with that permitted for holographic wills under the Code.

The other recurrent class of case in which the dispensing power has been invoked in South Australia entails alterations to a previously executed will. Sometimes the testator adds a clause, that is, the testator attempts to interpolate a defectively executed codicil. More frequently, the amendment has the character of a revision—the testator crosses out former text and inserts replacement terms. Lay persons do not always understand that the execution and revocation requirements of Section 2–502 call for fresh execution in order to modify a will; rather, lay persons often think that the original execution has continuing effect.

By placing the burden of proof upon the proponent of a defective instrument, and by requiring the proponent to discharge that burden by clear and convincing evidence (which courts at the trial and appellate levels are urged to police with rigor), Section 2–503 imposes procedural standards appropriate to the seriousness of the issue. Experience in Israel and South Australia strongly supports the view that a dispensing power like Section 2–503 will not breed litigation. Indeed, as an Israeli judge reported to the British Columbia Law Reform Commission, the dispensing power "actually prevents a great deal of unnecessary litigation," because it "eliminates disputes about technical lapses and limits the zone of dispute to the functional question of whether the instrument correctly expresses the testator's intent." British Columbia Report, supra, at 46.

The larger the departure from Section 2–502 formality, the harder it will be to satisfy the court that the instrument reflects the testator's intent. Whereas the South Australian and Israeli courts lightly excuse breaches of the attestation requirements, they have never excused noncompliance with the requirement that a will be in writing, and they have been extremely reluctant to excuse noncompliance with the signature requirement. See Langbein, supra, at 23–29, 49–50. The main circumstance in which the South Australian courts have excused signature errors has been in the recurrent class of cases in which two wills are prepared for simultaneous execution by two testators, typically husband and wife, and each mistakenly signs the will prepared for the other. E.g., Estate of Blakely, 32 S.A.S.R. 473 (1983). Recently, the New York Court of Appeals remedied such a case without aid of statute, simply on the ground "what has occurred is so obvious, and what was intended so clear." In re Snide, 52 N.Y.2d 193, 196, 418 N.E.2d 656, 657, 437 N.Y.S.2d 63, 64 (1981).

Section 2–503 means to retain the intent-serving benefits of Section 2–502 formality without inflicting intent-defeating outcomes in cases of harmless error.

Reference. The rule of this section is supported by the Restatement (Second) of Property (Donative Transfers) § 33.1 comment g (as approved by the American Law Institute at the 1990 annual meeting).

Section 2–504. Self–Proved Will.

(a) A will may be simultaneously executed, attested, and made self-proved, by acknowledgment thereof by the testator and affidavits of the witnesses, each made before an officer authorized to administer oaths under the laws of the state in which execution occurs and evidenced by the officer's certificate, under official seal, in substantially the following form:

I, _____, the testator, sign my name to this instrument this ___ day of _____, and being first duly sworn, do hereby declare to the undersigned authority that I sign and execute this instrument as my will and that I sign it willingly (or willingly direct another to sign for me), that I execute it as my free and voluntary act for the purposes therein expressed, and that I am eighteen years of age or older, of sound mind, and under no constraint or undue influence.

_____
Testator

We, _____, _____, the witnesses, sign our names to this instrument, being first duly sworn, and do hereby declare to the undersigned authority that the testator signs and executes this instrument as [his][her] will and that [he][she] signs it willingly (or willingly directs another to sign for [him][her]), and that each of us, in the presence and hearing of the testator, hereby signs this will as witness to the testator's signing, and that to the best of our knowledge the testator is eighteen years of age or older, of sound mind, and under no constraint or undue influence.

_____
Witness

_____
Witness

The State of _____
County of _____

Subscribed, sworn to and acknowledged before me by _____, the testator, and subscribed and sworn to before me by _____, and _____, witness, this ___ day of _____.

(Seal)

(Signed) _____

_____
(Official capacity of officer)

(b) An attested will may be made self-proved at any time after its execution by the acknowledgment thereof by the testator and the affidavits of the witnesses, each made before an officer authorized to administer oaths under the laws of the state in which the acknowledgment occurs and evidenced by the officer's certificate, under the official seal, attached or annexed to the will in substantially the following form:

The State of _____

County of _____

We, _____, _____, and _____, the testator and the witnesses, respectively, whose names are signed to the attached or foregoing instrument, being first duly sworn, do hereby declare to the undersigned authority that the testator signed and executed the instrument as the testator's will and that [he][she] had signed willingly (or willingly directed another to sign for [him][her]), and that [he][she] executed it as [his][her] free and voluntary act for the purposes therein expressed, and that each of the witnesses, in the presence and hearing of the testator, signed the will as witness and that to the best of [his][her] knowledge the testator was at that time eighteen years of age or older, of sound mind, and under no constraint or undue influence.

_____
Testator

_____
Witness

_____
Witness

Subscribed, sworn to and acknowledged before me by _____, the testator, and subscribed and sworn to before me by _____, and _____, witnesses, this ___ day of _____.

(Seal)

(Signed) _____

(Official capacity of officer)

(c) A signature affixed to a self-proving affidavit attached to a will is considered a signature affixed to the will, if necessary to prove the will's due execution.

111

COMMENT

A self-proved will may be admitted to probate as provided in Sections 3–303, 3–405, and 3–406 without the testimony of any subscribing witness, but otherwise it is treated no differently from a will not self proved. Thus, a self-proved will may be contested (except in regard to signature requirements), revoked, or amended by a codicil in exactly the same fashion as a will not self proved. The procedural advantage of a self-proved will is limited to formal testacy proceedings because Section 3–303, which deals with informal probate, dispenses with the necessity of testimony of witnesses even though the instrument is not self proved under this section.

A new subsection (c) is added to counteract an unfortunate judicial interpretation of similar self-proving will provisions in a few states, under which a signature on the self-proving affidavit has been held not to constitute a signature on the will, resulting in invalidity of the will in cases where the testator or witnesses got confused and only signed on the self-proving affidavit. See Mann, Self-proving Affidavits and Formalism in Wills Adjudication, 63 Wash. U. L.Q. 39 (1985); Estate of Ricketts, 773 P.2d 93 (Wash. Ct. App. 1989).

Section 2–505. Who May Witness.

(a) An individual generally competent to be a witness may act as a witness to a will.

(b) The signing of a will by an interested witness does not invalidate the will or any provision of it.

COMMENT

This section carries forward the position of the pre–1990 Code. The position adopted simplifies the law relating to interested witnesses. Interest no longer disqualifies a person as a witness, nor does it invalidate or forfeit a gift under the will. Of course, the purpose of this change is not to foster use of interested witnesses, and attorneys will continue to use disinterested witnesses in execution of wills. But the rare and innocent use of a member of the testator's family on a home-drawn will is not penalized.

This approach does not increase appreciably the opportunity for fraud or undue influence. A substantial devise by will to a person who is one of the witnesses to the execution of the will is itself a suspicious circumstance, and the devise might be challenged on grounds of undue influence. The requirement of disinterested witnesses has not succeeded in preventing fraud and undue influence; and in most cases of undue influence, the influencer is careful not to sign as a witness, but to procure disinterested witnesses.

Under Section 3–406, an interested witness is competent to testify to prove execution of the will.

112

Section 2–506. Choice of Law as to Execution.

A written will is valid if executed in compliance with Section 2–502 or 2–503 or if its execution complies with the law at the time of execution of the place where the will is executed, or of the law of the place where at the time of execution or at the time of death the testator is domiciled, has a place of abode, or is a national.

COMMENT

This section permits probate of wills in this state under certain conditions even if they are not executed in accordance with the formalities of Section 2–502 or 2–503. Such wills must be in writing but otherwise are valid if they meet the requirements for execution of the law of the place where the will is executed (when it is executed in another state or country) or the law of testator's domicile, abode or nationality at either the time of execution or at the time of death. Thus, if testator is domiciled in state 1 and executes a typed will merely by signing it without witnesses in state 2 while on vacation there, the Court of this state would recognize the will as valid if the law of either state 1 or state 2 permits execution by signature alone. Or if a national of Mexico executes a written will in this state which does not meet the requirements of Section 2–502 but meets the requirements of Mexican law, the will would be recognized as validly executed under this section. The purpose of this section is to provide a wide opportunity for validation of expectations of testators.

Section 2–507. Revocation by Writing or by Act.

↗ partial revoc'n

(a) A will or any part thereof is revoked:

(1) by executing a subsequent will that revokes the previous will or part expressly or by inconsistency; or

(2) by performing a revocatory act on the will, if the testator performed the act with the intent and for the purpose of revoking the will or part or if another individual performed the act in the testator's conscious presence and by the testator's direction. For purposes of this paragraph, "revocatory act on the will" includes burning, tearing, canceling, obliterating, or destroying the will or any part of it. A burning, tearing, or canceling is a "revocatory act on the will," whether or not the burn, tear, or cancellation touched any of the words on the will.

(b) If a subsequent will does not expressly revoke a previous will, the execution of the subsequent will wholly revokes the previous will by inconsistency if the testator intended the subsequent will to replace rather than supplement the previous will.

(c) The testator is presumed to have intended a subsequent will to replace rather than supplement a previous will if the subsequent will makes a complete disposition of the testator's estate. If this presumption arises and is not rebutted by clear and convincing evidence, the previous will is revoked; only the subsequent will is operative on the testator's death.

(d) The testator is presumed to have intended a subsequent will to supplement rather than replace a previous will if the subsequent will does not make a complete disposition of the testator's estate. If this presumption arises and is not rebutted by clear and convincing evidence, the subsequent will revokes the previous will only to the extent the subsequent will is inconsistent with the previous will; each will is fully operative on the testator's death to the extent they are not inconsistent.

COMMENT

Purpose and Scope of Revisions. Revocation of a will may be by either a subsequent will or an authorized act done to the document. Revocation by subsequent will cannot be effective unless the subsequent will is valid.

Revocation by Inconsistency. As originally promulgated, this section provided no standard by which the courts were to determine whether in a given case a subsequent will with no revocation clause revokes a prior will, wholly or partly, by inconsistency. Some courts seem to have been puzzled about the standard to be applied. New subsections (b), (c), and (d) codify the workable and common-sense standard set forth in the Restatement (Second) of Property (Donative Transfers) § 34.2 comment b (1991). Under these subsections, the question whether the subsequent will was intended to replace rather than supplement the previous will depends upon whether the second will makes a complete disposition of the testator's estate. If the second will does make a complete disposition of the testator's estate, a presumption arises that the

second will was intended to replace the previous will. If the second will does not make a complete disposition of the testator's estate, a presumption arises that the second will was intended to supplement rather than replace the previous will. The rationale is that, when the second will does not make a complete disposition of the testator's estate, the second will is more in the nature of a codicil to the first will. This standard has been applied in the cases without the benefit of a statutory provision to this effect. E.g., Gilbert v. Gilbert, 652 S.W.2d 663 (Ky. Ct. App. 1983).

> *Example.* Five years before her death, G executed a will (Will # 1), devising her antique desk to A; $20,000 to B; and the residue of her estate to C. Two years later, A died, and G executed another will (Will # 2), devising her antique desk to A's spouse, X; $10,000 to B; and the residue of her estate to C. Will # 2 neither expressly revoked Will # 1 nor made any other reference to it. G's net probate estate consisted of her antique desk (worth $10,000)

and other property (worth $90,-000). X, B, and C survived G by 120 hours.

Solution. Will # 2 was presumptively intended by G to replace Will # 1 because Will # 2 made a complete disposition of G's estate. Unless this presumption is rebutted by clear and convincing evidence, Will # 1 is wholly revoked; only Will # 2 is operative on G's death.

If, however, Will # 2 had not contained a residuary clause, and hence had not made a complete disposition of G's estate, "Will # 2" is more in the nature of a codicil to Will # 1, and the solution would be different. Now, Will # 2 would presumptively be treated as having been intended to supplement rather than replace Will # 1. In the absence of evidence clearly and convincingly rebutting this presumption, Will # 1 would be revoked only to the extent Will # 2 is inconsistent with it; both wills would be operative on G's death, to the extent they are not inconsistent. As to the devise of the antique desk, Will # 2 is inconsistent with Will # 1, and the antique desk would go to X. There being no residuary clause in Will # 2, there is nothing in Will # 2 that is inconsistent with the residuary clause in Will # 1, and so the residue would go to C. The more difficult question relates to the cash devises in the two wills. The question whether they are inconsistent with one another is a question of interpretation in the individual case. Section 2–507 does not establish a presumption one way or the other on that question. If the

court finds that the cash devises are inconsistent with one another, i.e., if the court finds that the cash devise in Will # 2 was intended to replace rather than supplement the cash devise in Will # 1, then B takes $10,000. But, if the court finds that the cash devises are not inconsistent with one another, B would take $30,000.

Revocatory Act. In the case of an act of revocation done to the document, subsection (a)(2) is revised to provide that a burning, tearing, or canceling is a sufficient revocatory act even though the act does not touch any of the words on the will. This is consistent with cases on burning or tearing (e.g., White v. Casten, 46 N.C. 197 (1853) (burning); Crampton v. Osburn, 356 Mo. 125, 201 S.W.2d 336 (1947) (tearing)), but inconsistent with most, but not all, cases on cancellation (e.g., Yont v. Eads, 317 Mass. 232, 57 N.E.2d 531 (1944); Kronauge v. Stoecklein, 33 Ohio App. 2d 229, 293 N.E.2d 320 (1972); Thompson v. Royall, 163 Va. 492, 175 S.E. 748 (1934); contra, Warner v. Warner's Estate, 37 Vt. 356 (1864)). By substantial authority, it is held that removal of the testator's signature—by, for example, lining it through, erasing or obliterating it, tearing or cutting it out of the document, or removing the entire signature page—constitutes a sufficient revocatory act to revoke the entire will. Board of Trustees of the University of Alabama v. Calhoun, 514 So.2d 895 (Ala. 1987) and cases cited therein.

Subsection (a)(2) is also revised to codify the "conscious-presence" test. As revised, subsection (a)(2) provides that, if the testator does not perform the revocatory act, but directs another to perform the act, the act is a sufficient revocatory act if the other individual performs it in the testator's conscious presence. The act need not be performed in the testator's line of sight. See the Comment to Section 2–502 for a discussion of the "conscious-presence" test.

Revocatory Intent. To effect a revocation, a revocatory act must be accompanied by revocatory intent. Determining whether a revocatory act was accompanied by revocatory intent may involve exploration of extrinsic evidence, including the testator's statements as to intent.

Partial Revocation. This section specifically permits partial revocation.

Dependent Relative Revocation. Each court is free to apply its own doctrine of dependent relative revocation. See generally Palmer, "Dependent Relative Revocation and Its Relation to Relief for Mistake," 69 Mich. L. Rev. 989 (1971). Note, however, that dependent relative revocation should less often be necessary under the revised provisions of the Code. Dependent relative revocation is the law of second best, i.e., its application does not produce the result the testator actually intended, but is designed to come as close as possible to that intent. A precondition to the application of dependent relative revocation is, or should be, good evidence of the testator's actual intention; without

that, the court has no basis for determining which of several outcomes comes the closest to that actual intention.

When there is good evidence of the testator's actual intention, however, the revised provisions of the Code would usually facilitate the effectuation of the result the testator actually intended. If, for example, the testator by revocatory act revokes a second will for the purpose of reviving a former will, the evidence necessary to establish the testator's intent to revive the former will should be sufficient under Section 2–509 to effect a revival of the former will, making the application of dependent relative revocation as to the second will unnecessary. If, by revocatory act, the testator revokes a will in conjunction with an effort to execute a new will, the evidence necessary to establish the testator's intention that the new will be valid should, in most cases, be sufficient under Section 2–503 to give effect to the new will, making the application of dependent relative revocation as to the old will unnecessary. If the testator lines out parts of a will or dispositive provision in conjunction with an effort to alter the will's terms, the evidence necessary to establish the testator's intention that the altered terms be valid should be sufficient under Section 2–503 to give effect to the will as altered, making dependent relative revocation as to the lined-out parts unnecessary.

Section 2–508. Revocation by Change of Circumstances.

Except as provided in Sections 2–803 and 2–804, a change of circumstances does not revoke a will or any part of it.

116

Section 2–509. Revival of Revoked Will.

(a) If a subsequent will that wholly revoked a previous will is thereafter revoked by a revocatory act under Section 2–507(a)(2), the previous will remains revoked unless it is revived. The previous will is revived if it is evident from the circumstances of the revocation of the subsequent will or from the testator's contemporary or subsequent declarations that the testator intended the previous will to take effect as executed.

(b) If a subsequent will that partly revoked a previous will is thereafter revoked by a revocatory act under Section 2–507(a)(2), a revoked part of the previous will is revived unless it is evident from the circumstances of the revocation of the subsequent will or from the testator's contemporary or subsequent declarations that the testator did not intend the revoked part to take effect as executed.

(c) If a subsequent will that revoked a previous will in whole or in part is thereafter revoked by another, later, will, the previous will remains revoked in whole or in part, unless it or its revoked part is revived. The previous will or its revoked part is revived to the extent it appears from the terms of the later will that the testator intended the previous will to take effect.

COMMENT

Purpose and Scope of Revisions. Although a will takes effect as a revoking instrument when it is executed, it takes effect as a dispositive instrument at death. Once revoked, therefore, a will is ineffective as a dispositive instrument unless it has been revived. This section covers the standards to be applied in determining whether a will (Will # 1) that was revoked by a subsequent will (Will # 2), either expressly or by inconsistency, has been revived by the revocation of the subsequent will, i.e., whether the revocation of Will # 2 (the revoking will) revives Will # 1 (the will that Will # 2 revoked).

As revised, this section is divided into three subsections. Subsections (a) and (b) cover the effect of revoking Will # 2 (the revoking will) by a revocatory act under Section 2–507(a)(2). Under subsection (a), if Will # 2 (the revoking will) wholly revoked Will # 1, the revocation of Will # 2 does not revive Will # 1 unless "it is evident from the circumstances of the revocation of [Will # 2] or from the testator's contemporary or subsequent declarations that the testator intended [Will # 1] to take effect as executed." This standard places the burden of persuasion on the proponent of Will # 1 to establish that the decedent's intention was that Will # 1 is to be his or her valid will. Testimony regarding the decedent's statements at the time he or she revokes Will # 2 or at a later date can be admitted. Indeed, all relevant evidence of intention is to be considered by the court on this question; the open-ended statutory language is not to be undermined by translating it into discrete subsidiary elements, all of which must be met, as the court did in Estate of Boysen, 309 N.W.2d 45 (Minn. 1981). See Langbein & Waggoner, "Reforming the Law of Gratuitous Transfers: The New Uniform Probate Code," 55 Alb.L.Rev. 871, 885–87 (1992).

The pre–1990 version of this section did not distinguish between complete and partial revocation. Regardless of whether Will # 2 wholly or partly revoked Will # 1, the pre–1990 version presumed against revival of Will # 1 when Will # 2 was revoked by act.

As revised, this section properly treats the two situations as distinguishable. The presumption against revival imposed by subsection (a) is justified because where Will # 2 *wholly* revoked Will No. 1, the testator understood or should have understood that Will # 1 had no continuing effect. Consequently, subsection (a) properly presumes that the testator's act of revoking Will # 2 was not accompanied by an intent to revive Will # 1.

Subsection (b) establishes the opposite presumption where Will # 2 (the revoking will) revoked Will # 1 only in part. In this case, the revo-cation of Will # 2 revives the re-voked part or parts of Will # 1 un-less "it is evident from the circum-stances of the revocation of [Will # 2] or from the testator's contem-porary or subsequent declarations that the testator did not intend the revoked part to take effect as exe-cuted." This standard places the burden of persuasion on the party arguing that the revoked part or parts of Will # 1 were not revived. The justification is that where Will # 2 only partly revoked Will # 1, Will # 2 is only a codicil to Will # 1, and the testator knows (or should know) that Will # 1 does have con-tinuing effect. Consequently, sub-section (b) properly presumes that the testator's act of revoking Will # 2 (the codicil) was accompanied by an intent to revive or reinstate the revoked parts of Will # 1.

Subsection (c) covers the effect on Will # 1 of revoking Will # 2 (the revoking will) by another, later, will (Will # 3). Will # 1 remains re-voked except to the extent that Will # 3 shows an intent to have Will # 1 effective.

Historical Note. This Comment was revised in 1993. For the prior version, see 8 U.L.A. 118 (Supp. 1992).

Section 2–510. Incorporation by Reference.

A writing in existence when a will is executed may be incorpo-rated by reference if the language of the will manifests this intent and describes the writing sufficiently to permit its identification.

COMMENT

This section codifies the common-law doctrine of incorporation by ref-erence, except that the sometimes troublesome requirement that the will refer to the document as being in existence when the will was exe-cuted has been eliminated.

Section 2–511. Testamentary Additions to Trusts.

(a) A will may validly devise property to the trustee of a trust established or to be established (i) during the testator's lifetime by the testator, by the testator and some other person, or by some other person, including a funded or unfunded life insurance trust, although the settlor has reserved any or all rights of ownership of the insurance contracts, or (ii) at the testator's death by the testator's devise to the trustee, if the trust is identified in the testator's will and its terms are set forth in a written instrument, other than a will, executed before, concurrently with, or after the execution of the testator's will or in another individual's will if that other individual has predeceased the testator, regardless of the existence, size, or character of the corpus of the trust. The devise is not invalid because the trust is amendable or revocable, or because the trust was amended after the execution of the will or the testator's death.

(b) Unless the testator's will provides otherwise, property devised to a trust described in subsection (a) is not held under a testamentary trust of the testator, but it becomes a part of the trust to which it is devised, and must be administered and disposed of in accordance with the provisions of the governing instrument setting forth the terms of the trust, including any amendments thereto made before or after the testator's death.

(c) Unless the testator's will provides otherwise, a revocation or termination of the trust before the testator's death causes the devise to lapse.

COMMENT

Purpose and Scope of Revisions. In addition to making a few stylistic changes, several substantive changes in this section are made.

As revised, it has been made clear that the "trust" need not have been established (funded with a trust res) during the decedent's lifetime, but can be established (funded with a res) by the devise itself. The pre–1990 version probably contemplated this result and reasonably could be so interpreted (because of the phrase "regardless of the *existence* ... of the corpus of the trust"). Indeed, a few cases have expressly stated that statutory language like the pre–1990 version of this section authorizes pour-over devises to unfunded trusts. E.g., Clymer v. Mayo, 473 N.E.2d 1084 (Mass. 1985); Trosch v. Maryland Nat'l Bank, 32 Md. App. 249, 359 A.2d 564 (1976). The authority of these pronouncements is problematic, however, because the trusts in these cases were so-called "unfunded" life-insurance trusts. An unfunded life-insurance trust is not a trust without a trust res; the trust res in an unfunded life-insurance trust is the contract right to the proceeds of the life-insurance policy conferred on the trustee by virtue of naming the trustee the beneficiary of the policy. See Gordon v. Portland Trust Bank, 201 Or. 648, 271 P.2d 653 (1954) ("[T]he [trustee as the] beneficiary [of the policy] is the owner of a promise to pay the proceeds at the death of the insured...."); Gurnett v. Mutual Life Ins. Co., 356 Ill. 612, 191 N.E. 250 (1934). Thus, the term "unfunded life-insurance trust" does not refer to an unfunded trust, but to a funded trust that has not received *additional* funding. For further indication of the problematic nature of the idea that the pre–1990 version of this section permits pour-over devises to unfunded trusts, see Estate of Daniels, 665 P.2d 594 (Colo. 1983) (pour-over devise failed; before signing the trust instrument, the decedent was advised by counsel that the "mere signing of the trust agreement would not activate it and that, before the trust could come into being, [the decedent] would have to fund it;" decedent then signed the trust agreement and returned it to counsel "to wait for further directions on it;" no further action was taken by the decedent prior to death; the decedent's will devised the residue of her estate to the trustee of the trust, but added that the residue should go elsewhere "if the trust created by said agreement is not in effect at my death.")

Additional revisions of this section are designed to remove obstacles to carrying out the decedent's intention that were contained in the pre–1990 version. These revisions allow the trust terms to be set forth in a written instrument executed after as well as before or concurrently with the execution of the will; require the devised property to be administered in accordance with the terms of the trust as amended after as well as before the decedent's death, even though the decedent's will does not so provide; and allow the decedent's will to provide that the devise is not to lapse even if the trust is revoked or terminated before the decedent's death.

Revision of Uniform Testamentary Additions to Trusts Act. The freestanding Uniform Testamentary Additions to Trusts Act (UTATA) was revised in 1991 in accordance with the revisions to UPC § 2–511. States that enact Section 2–511 need not enact the UTATA as revised in 1991 and should repeal the original version of the UTATA if previously enacted in the state.

Section 2–512. Events of Independent Significance.

A will may dispose of property by reference to acts and events that have significance apart from their effect upon the dispositions made by the will, whether they occur before or after the execution of the will or before or after the testator's death. The execution or revocation of another individual's will is such an event.

Section 2–513. Separate Writing Identifying Devise of Certain Types of Tangible Personal Property.

Whether or not the provisions relating to holographic wills apply, a will may refer to a written statement or list to dispose of items of tangible personal property not otherwise specifically disposed of by the will, other than money. To be admissible under this section as evidence of the intended disposition, the writing must be signed by the testator and must describe the items and the devisees with reasonable certainty. The writing may be referred to as one to be in existence at the time of the testator's death; it may be prepared before or after the execution of the will; it may be altered by the testator after its preparation; and it may be a writing that has no significance apart from its effect on the dispositions made by the will.

COMMENT

Purpose and Scope of Revision. As part of the broader policy of effectuating a testator's intent and of relaxing formalities of execution, this section permits a testator to refer in his or her will to a separate document disposing of tangible personalty other than money. The pre–1990 version precluded the disposition of "evidences of indebtedness, documents of title, and securities, and property used in a trade or business." These limitations are deleted in the revised version, partly to remove a source of confusion in the pre–1990 version, which arose because evidences of indebtedness, documents of title, and securities are not items of tangible personal property to begin with, and partly to permit the disposition of a broader range of items of tangible personal property.

The language "items of tangible personal property" does not require that the separate document specifically itemize each item of tangible personal property covered. The only requirement is that the document describe the items covered "with reasonable certainty." Consequently, a document referring to "all my tangible personal property other than money" or to "all my tangible personal property located in my office" or using similar catch-all type of language would normally be sufficient.

The separate document disposing of an item or items of tangible personal property may be prepared after execution of the will, so would not come within Section 2–510 on incorporation by reference. It may even be altered from time to time. The only requirement is that the document be signed by the testator. The pre–1990 version of this section gave effect to an unsigned document if it was in the testator's handwriting. The revisions remove the language giving effect to such an unsigned document. The purpose is to prevent a mere handwritten draft from becoming effective without sufficient indication that the testator intended it to be effective. The signature requirement is

121

designed to prevent mere drafts from becoming effective against the testator's wishes. An unsigned document could still be given effect under Section 2–503, however, if the proponent could carry the burden of proving by clear and convincing evidence that the testator intended the document to be effective.

The typical case covered by this section would be a list of personal effects and the persons whom the decedent desired to take specified items.

Sample Clause. Section 2–513 might be utilized by a clause in the decedent's will such as the following:

> I might leave a written statement or list disposing of items of tangible personal property. If I do and if my written statement or list is found and is identified as such by my Personal Representative no later than 30 days after the probate of this will, then my written statement or list is to be given effect to the extent authorized by law and is to take precedence over any con-

trary devise or devises of the same item or items of property in this will.

Section 2–513 only authorizes disposition of tangible personal property "not otherwise specifically disposed of by the will." The sample clause above is consistent with this restriction. By providing that the written statement or list takes precedence over any contrary devise in the will, a contrary devise is made conditional upon the written statement or list not contradicting it; if the written statement or list does contradict a devise in the will, the will does not otherwise specifically dispose of the property.

If, however, the clause in the testator's will does not provide that the written statement or list is to take precedence over any contrary devise in the will (or contain a provision having similar effect), then the written statement or list is ineffective to the extent it purports to dispose of items of property that were otherwise specifically disposed of by the will.

Section 2–514. Contracts Concerning Succession.

A contract to make a will or devise, or not to revoke a will or devise, or to die intestate, if executed after the effective date of this Article, may be established only by (i) provisions of a will stating material provisions of the contract, (ii) an express reference in a will to a contract and extrinsic evidence proving the terms of the contract, or (iii) a writing signed by the decedent evidencing the contract. The execution of a joint will or mutual wills does not create a presumption of a contract not to revoke the will or wills.

COMMENT

Section Relocated. No substantive revision of this section is made, but the section is relocated and re-

numbered to make room for new Part 7.

The purpose of this section is to tighten the methods by which contracts concerning succession may be proved. Oral contracts not to revoke wills have given rise to much litigation in a number of states; and in many states if two persons execute a single document as their joint will, this gives rise to a presumption that the parties had contracted not to revoke the will except by consent of both.

This section requires that either the will must set forth the material provisions of the contract, or the will must make express reference to the contract and extrinsic evidence

prove the terms of the contract, or there must be a separate writing signed by the decedent evidencing the contract. Oral testimony regarding the contract is permitted if the will makes reference to the contract, but this provision of the statute is not intended to affect normal rules regarding admissibility of evidence.

This section does not preclude recovery in quantum meruit for the value of services rendered the testator.

Section 2–515. Deposit of Will With Court in Testator's Lifetime.

A will may be deposited by the testator or the testator's agent with any court for safekeeping, under rules of the court. The will must be sealed and kept confidential. During the testator's lifetime, a deposited will must be delivered only to the testator or to a person authorized in writing signed by the testator to receive the will. A conservator may be allowed to examine a deposited will of a protected testator under procedures designed to maintain the confidential character of the document to the extent possible, and to ensure that it will be resealed and kept on deposit after the examination. Upon being informed of the testator's death, the court shall notify any person designated to receive the will and deliver it to that person on request; or the court may deliver the will to the appropriate court.

COMMENT

Many states already have statutes permitting deposit of wills during a testator's lifetime. Most of these statutes have elaborate provisions governing purely administrative matters: how the will is to be enclosed in a sealed wrapper, what is to be endorsed on the wrapper, the form of receipt or certificate given to the testator, the fee to be charged, how the will is to be opened after testator's death and who is to be notified. Under this

section, details have been left to Court rule, except as other relevant statutes such as one governing fees may apply.

It is, of course, vital to maintain the confidential nature of deposited wills. However, this obviously does not prevent the opening of the will after the death of the testator if necessary in order to determine the executor or other interested persons to be notified. Nor should it prevent opening the will to microfilm for confidential record storage, for example. These matters could again be regulated by Court rule.

The provision permitting examination of a will of a protected person by the conservator supplements Section 5–427.

Section 2–516. Duty of Custodian of Will; Liability.

After the death of a testator and on request of an interested person, a person having custody of a will of the testator shall deliver it with reasonable promptness to a person able to secure its probate and if none is known, to an appropriate court. A person who wilfully fails to deliver a will is liable to any person aggrieved for any damages that may be sustained by the failure. A person who wilfully refuses or fails to deliver a will after being ordered by the court in a proceeding brought for the purpose of compelling delivery is subject to penalty for contempt of court.

COMMENT

In addition to a registrar or clerk, a person authorized to accept delivery of a will from a custodian may be a universal successor or other person authorized under the law of another nation to carry out the terms of a will.

Section 2–517. Penalty Clause for Contest.

A provision in a will purporting to penalize an interested person for contesting the will or instituting other proceedings relating to the estate is unenforceable if probable cause exists for instituting proceedings.

COMMENT

This section replicates Section 3–905.

PART 6

RULES OF CONSTRUCTION
APPLICABLE ONLY
TO WILLS

GENERAL COMMENT

Parts 6 and 7 address a variety of construction problems that commonly occur in wills, trusts, and other types of governing instruments. All of the "rules" set forth in these parts yield to a finding of a contrary intention and are therefore rebuttable presumptions.

The rules of construction set forth in Part 6 apply only to wills. The rules of construction set forth in Part 7 apply to wills and other governing instruments.

The sections in Part 6 deal with such problems as death before the testator (lapse), the inclusiveness of the will as to property of the testator, effect of failure of a gift in the will, change in form of securities specifically devised, ademption by reason of fire, sale and the like, exoneration, and exercise of a power of appointment by general language in the will.

Section 2–601. Scope.

In the absence of a finding of a contrary intention, the rules of construction in this Part control the construction of a will.

COMMENT

Purpose and Scope of Revisions. Common-law rules of construction yield to a finding of a contrary intention. The pre–1990 version of this section provided that the rules of construction in Part 6 yielded only to a "contrary intention indicated by the will." To align the statutory rules of construction in Part 6 with those established at common law, this section is revised so that the rules of construction yield to a "finding of a contrary intention." As revised, evidence extrinsic to the will as well as the content of the will itself is admissible for the purpose of rebutting the rules of construction in Part 6.

As originally promulgated, this section began with the sentence: "The intention of a testator as expressed in his will controls the legal effect of his dispositions." This sentence is removed primarily because it is inappropriate and unnecessary in a part of the Code containing rules of construction. The deletion of this sentence does not signify a retreat from the widely accepted proposition that a testator's intention controls the legal effect of his or her dispositions.

A further reason for deleting this sentence is that a possible, though unintended, reading of this sentence might be that it prevents the

125

judicial adoption of a general reformation doctrine for wills, as approved by the American Law Institute in the Restatement (Second) of Property § 34.7 & comment d, illustration 11, and as advocated in Langbein & Waggoner, "Reformation of Wills on the Ground of Mistake: Change of Direction in American Law?," 130 U.Pa.L.Rev. 521 (1982). The striking of this sentence removes that possible impediment to the judicial adoption of a general reformation doctrine for wills as approved by the American Law Institute and as advocated in the Langbein–Waggoner article.

Cross Reference. See Section 8–101(b) for the application of the rules of construction in this Part to documents executed prior to the effective date of this Article.

Section 2–602. Will May Pass All Property and After–Acquired Property.

A will may provide for the passage of all property the testator owns at death and all property acquired by the estate after the testator's death.

COMMENT

Purpose and Scope of Revision. This section is revised to assure that, for example, a residuary clause in a will not only passes property owned at death that is not otherwise devised, even though the property was acquired by the testator after the will was executed, but also passes property acquired by a testator's estate after his or her death. This reverses a case like Braman Estate, 435 Pa. 573, 258 A.2d 492 (1969), where the court held that Mary's residuary devise to her sister Ruth "or her estate," which had passed to Ruth's estate where Ruth predeceased Mary by about a year, could not go to Ruth's residuary legatee. The court held that Ruth's will had no power to control the devolution of property acquired by Ruth's estate after her death; such property passed, instead, by intestate succession from Ruth. This section, applied to the Braman Estate case, would mean that the property acquired by Ruth's estate after her death would pass under her residuary clause.

The added language also makes it clear that items such as bonuses awarded to an employee after his or her death pass under his or her will.

Section 2–603. Antilapse; Deceased Devisee; Class Gifts.

(a) [Definitions.] In this section:

(1) "Alternative devise" means a devise that is expressly created by the will and, under the terms of the will, can take effect instead of another devise on the happening of one or more events, including survival of the testator or failure to survive the testator, whether an event is expressed in condition-prece-

126

dent, condition-subsequent, or any other form. A residuary clause constitutes an alternative devise with respect to a nonresiduary devise only if the will specifically provides that, upon lapse or failure, the nonresiduary devise, or nonresiduary devises in general, pass under the residuary clause.

(2) "Class member" includes an individual who fails to survive the testator but who would have taken under a devise in the form of a class gift had he [or she] survived the testator.

(3) "Devise" includes an alternative devise, a devise in the form of a class gift, and an exercise of a power of appointment.

(4) "Devisee" includes (i) a class member if the devise is in the form of a class gift, (ii) an individual or class member who was deceased at the time the testator executed his [or her] will as well as an individual or class member who was then living but who failed to survive the testator, and (iii) an appointee under a power of appointment exercised by the testator's will.

(5) "Stepchild" means a child of the surviving, deceased, or former spouse of the testator or of the donor of a power of appointment, and not of the testator or donor.

(6) "Surviving devisee" or "surviving descendant" means a devisee or a descendant who neither predeceased the testator nor is deemed to have predeceased the testator under Section 2–702.

(7) "Testator" includes the donee of a power of appointment if the power is exercised in the testator's will.

(b) [Substitute Gift.] If a devisee fails to survive the testator and is a grandparent, a descendant of a grandparent, or a stepchild of either the testator or the donor of a power of appointment exercised by the testator's will, the following apply:

(1) Except as provided in paragraph (4), if the devise is not in the form of a class gift and the deceased devisee leaves surviving descendants, a substitute gift is created in the devisee's surviving descendants. They take by representation the property to which the devisee would have been entitled had the devisee survived the testator.

(2) Except as provided in paragraph (4), if the devise is in the form of a class gift, other than a devise to "issue," "descendants," "heirs of the body," "heirs," "next of kin," "relatives," or "family," or a class described by language of similar import, a substitute gift is created in the surviving descendants of any deceased devisee. The property to which the devisees would have been entitled had all of them survived the testator passes

to the surviving devisees and the surviving descendants of the deceased devisees. Each surviving devisee takes the share to which he [or she] would have been entitled had the deceased devisees survived the testator. Each deceased devisee's surviving descendants who are substituted for the deceased devisee take by representation the share to which the deceased devisee would have been entitled had the deceased devisee survived the testator. For the purposes of this paragraph, "deceased devisee" means a class member who failed to survive the testator and left one or more surviving descendants.

(3) For the purposes of Section 2–601, words of survivorship, such as in a devise to an individual "if he survives me," or in a devise to "my surviving children," are not, in the absence of additional evidence, a sufficient indication of an intent contrary to the application of this section.

(4) If the will creates an alternative devise with respect to a devise for which a substitute gift is created by paragraph (1) or (2), the substitute gift is superseded by the alternative devise only if an expressly designated devisee of the alternative devise is entitled to take under the will.

(5) Unless the language creating a power of appointment expressly excludes the substitution of the descendants of an appointee for the appointee, a surviving descendant of a deceased appointee of a power of appointment can be substituted for the appointee under this section, whether or not the descendant is an object of the power.

(c) [More Than One Substitute Gift; Which One Takes.] If, under subsection (b), substitute gifts are created and not superseded with respect to more than one devise and the devises are alternative devises, one to the other, the determination of which of the substitute gifts takes effect is resolved as follows:

(1) Except as provided in paragraph (2), the devised property passes under the primary substitute gift.

(2) If there is a younger-generation devise, the devised property passes under the younger-generation substitute gift and not under the primary substitute gift.

(3) In this subsection:

(i) "Primary devise" means the devise that would have taken effect had all the deceased devisees of the alternative devises who left surviving descendants survived the testator.

(ii) "Primary substitute gift" means the substitute gift created with respect to the primary devise.

128

(iii) "Younger-generation devise" means a devise that (A) is to a descendant of a devisee of the primary devise, (B) is an alternative devise with respect to the primary devise, (C) is a devise for which a substitute gift is created, and (D) would have taken effect had all the deceased devisees who left surviving descendants survived the testator except the deceased devisee or devisees of the primary devise.

(iv) "Younger-generation substitute gift" means the substitute gift created with respect to the younger-generation devise.

COMMENT

Purpose and Scope of Revised Section. Revised Section 2–603 is a comprehensive antilapse statute that resolves a variety of interpretive questions that have arisen under standard antilapse statutes, including the antilapse statute of the pre–1990 Code.

Theory of Lapse. A will transfers property at the testator's death, not when the will was executed. The common-law rule of lapse is predicated on this principle and on the notion that property cannot be transferred to a deceased individual. Under the rule of lapse, all devises are automatically and by law conditioned on survivorship of the testator. A devise to a devisee who predeceases the testator fails (lapses); the devised property does not pass to the devisee's estate, to be distributed according to the devisee's will or pass by intestate succession from the devisee. (Section 2–702 modifies the rule of lapse by presumptively conditioning devises on a 120–hour period of survival.)

"Antilapse" Statutes—Rationale of Section 2–603. Statutes such as Section 2–603 are commonly called "antilapse" statutes. An antilapse statute is remedial in nature, tending to preserve equality of treatment among different lines of succession. Although Section 2–603 is a rule of construction, and hence under Section 2–601 yields to a finding of a contrary intention, the remedial character of the statute means that it should be given the widest possible latitude to operate in considering whether the testator had formed a contrary intent.

The 120–hour Survivorship Period. In effect, the requirement of survival of the testator's death means survival of the 120–hour period following the testator's death. This is because, under Section 2–702(a), "an individual who is not established to have survived an event ... by 120 hours is deemed to have predeceased the event." As made clear by subsection (a)(6), for the purposes of section 2–707, the "event" to which section 2–702(a) relates is the testator's death.

General Rule of Section 2–603— Subsection (b). Subsection (b) states the general rule of Section 2–603. Subsection (b)(1) applies to individual devises; subsection (b)(2) applies to devises in class gift form. Together, they show that the "antilapse" label is somewhat misleading. Strictly speaking, these subsections do not reverse the common-law rule of lapse. They do not abrogate the law-imposed condition of survivorship, so that devised property passes to the estates of predeceasing devisees. Subsections (b)(1) and (b)(2) leave the law-imposed condition of survivorship intact, but modify the devolution of lapsed devises by providing a statutory substitute gift in the case of specified relatives. The statutory substitute gift is to the devisee's descendants who survive the testator by 120 hours; they take the property to which the devisee would have been entitled had the devisee survived the testator by 120 hours.

Class Gifts. In line with modern policy, subsection (b)(2) continues the pre–1990 Code's approach of expressly extending the antilapse protection to class gifts. Subsection (b)(2) applies to class gifts in which one or more class members fail to survive the testator leaving descendants who survive the testator; in order for the subsection to apply, it is not necessary that any of the class members survive the testator. Class gifts to "issue," "descendants," "heirs of the body," "heirs," "next of kin," "relatives," "family," or a class described by language of similar import are excluded, however, because antilapse protection is unnecessary in class gifts of these types. They already contain within themselves the idea of representation, under which a deceased class member's descendants are substituted for him or her. See Sections 2–708, 2–709, 2–711.

"Void" Gifts. By virtue of subsection (a)(4), subsection (b) applies to the so-called "void" gift, where the devisee is dead at the time of execution of the will. Though contrary to some decisions, it seems

likely that the testator would want the descendants of a person included, for example, in a class term but dead when the will is made to be treated like the descendants of another member of the class who was alive at the time the will was executed but who dies before the testator.

Protected Relatives. The specified relatives whose devises are protected by this section are the testator's grandparents and their descendants and the testator's stepchildren or, in the case of a testamentary exercise of a power of appointment, the testator's (donee's) or donor's grandparents and their descendants and the testator's or donor's stepchildren.

Section 2–603 extends the "antilapse" protection to devises to the testator's own stepchildren. The term "stepchild" is defined in subsection (a)(5). Antilapse protection is not extended to devises to descendants of the testator's stepchildren or to stepchildren of any of the testator's relatives. As to the testator's own stepchildren, note that under Section 2–804 a devise to a stepchild might be revoked if the testator and the stepchild's adoptive or biological parent become divorced; the antilapse statute does not, of course, apply to a deceased stepchild's devise if it was revoked by Section 2–804. Subsections (b)(1) and (b)(2) give this result by providing that the substituted descendants take the property to which the deceased devisee or deceased class member would have been entitled if he or she had survived the testator. If a deceased stepchild whose devise was revoked by Section 2–804 had survived the testator, that stepchild would not have been entitled to his or her devise, and so his or her descendants take nothing, either.

Other than stepchildren, devisees related to the testator by affinity are not protected by this section.

Section 2–603 Applicable to Testamentary Exercise of a Power of Appointment Where Appointee Fails to Survive the Testator. Subsections (a)(3), (4), (5), (7), and (b)(5) extend the protection of this section to appointees under a power of appointment exercised by the testator's will. The extension of the antilapse statute to powers of appointment is a step long overdue. The extension brings the statute into line with the Restatement (Second) of Property (Donative Transfers) § 18.6 (1986).

Substituted Gift. The substitute gifts provided for by subsections (b)(1) and (b)(2) are to the deceased devisee's descendants. They include adopted persons and children of unmarried parents to the extent they would inherit from the devisee; see Sections 1–201 and 2–114.

The 120–hour survival requirement stated in Section 2–702 does not require descendants who would be substituted for their parent by this section to survive *their parent* by any set period.

The statutory substitute gift is divided among the devisee's descendants "by representation," a term defined in Section 2–709(b).

Section 2–603 Restricted to Wills. Section 2–603 is applicable only when a devisee of a *will* predeceases the testator. It does not apply to beneficiary designations in life-insurance policies, retirement plans, or transfer-on-death accounts, nor does it apply to inter-vivos trusts, whether revocable or irrevocable.

See, however, Sections 2–706 and 2–707 for rules of construction applicable when the beneficiary of a life-insurance policy, a retirement plan, or a transfer-on-death account predeceases the decedent or when the beneficiary of a future interest is not living when the interest is to take effect in possession or enjoyment.

Contrary Intention—the Rationale of Subsection (b)(3). An antilapse statute is a rule of construction, designed to carry out presumed intention. In effect, Section 2–603 declares that when a testator devises property "to A (a specified relative)," the testator (if he or she had thought further about it) is presumed to have wanted to add: "but if A is not alive (120 hours after my death), I devise the property in A's stead to A's descendants (who survive me by 120 hours)."

Under Section 2–601, the rule of Section 2–603 yields to a finding of a contrary intention. A foolproof means of expressing a contrary intention is to add to a devise the phrase "and not to [the devisee's] descendants." In the case of a power of appointment, the phrase "and not to an appointee's descendants" can be added by the donor of the power in the document creating the power of appointment, if the donor does not want the antilapse statute to apply to an appointment under a power. In addition, adding to the residuary clause a phrase such as "including all lapsed or failed devises," adding to a nonresiduary devise a phrase such as "if the devisee does not survive me, the devise is to pass under the residuary clause," or adding a separate clause providing generally that "if the devisee of any nonresiduary devise does not survive me, the devise is to pass under the residuary clause" makes the residuary clause an "alternative devise." Under subsection (b)(4), an alternative devise supersedes a substitute gift created by subsection (b)(1) or (b)(2) if an expressly designated devisee of the alternative devise is entitled to take under the will. See infra Example 3.

A much-litigated question is whether mere words of survivorship—such as in a devise "to my daughter, A, if A survives me" or "to my surviving children"—*automatically* defeat the antilapse statute. Lawyers who believe that the attachment of words of survivorship to a devise is a foolproof method of defeating an antilapse statute are mistaken. The very fact that the question is litigated so frequently is itself proof that the use of mere words of survivorship is far from foolproof. In addition, the results of the litigated cases are divided on the question. To be sure, many cases hold that mere words of survivorship do automatically defeat the antilapse statute. E.g., Estate of Stroble, 636 P.2d 236 (Kan.Ct. App.1981); Annot., 63 A.L.R.2d 1172, 1186 (1959); Annot., 92 A.L.R. 846, 857 (1934). Other cases, however, reach the opposite conclusion. E.g., Estate of Ulrikson, 290 N.W.2d 757 (Minn. 1980) (residuary devise to testator's brother Melvin and sister Rodine, and "in the event that either one of them shall predecease me, then to the other surviving brother or sister"; Melvin and Rodine predeceased testator, Melvin but not Rodine leaving descendants who survived testator; court held residue passed to Melvin's descendants under antilapse statute); Detzel v.

Nieberding, 219 N.E.2d 327 (Ohio P.Ct. 1966) (devise of $5,000 to sister "provided she be living at the time of my death"; sister predeceased testator; court held $5,000 devise passed under antilapse statute to sister's descendants); Henderson v. Parker, 728 S.W.2d 768 (Tex. 1987) (devise of all of testator's property "unto our surviving children of this marriage"; two of testator's children survived testator, but one child, William, predeceased testator leaving descendants who survived testator; court held that share William would have taken passed to William's descendants under antilapse statute; words of survivorship found ineffective to counteract antilapse statute because court interpreted those words as merely restricting the devisees to those living at the time the will was executed); see also Restatement (Second) of Property (Donative Transfers) § 27.2 comment f, illustration 5; cf. id. § 27.1 comment e, illustration 6. It may also be noted that the antilapse statutes in some other common-law countries expressly provide that words of survivorship do not defeat the statute. See, e.g., Queensland Succession Act 1981, § 33(2) ("A general requirement or condition that [protected relatives] survive the testator or attain a specified age is not a contrary intention for the purposes of this section.").

Subsection (b)(3) adopts the position that mere words of survivorship do not—by themselves, *in the absence of additional evidence*—lead to *automatic* defeat of the antilapse statute. As noted in French, "Antilapse Statutes Are Blunt Instruments: A Blueprint for Reform," 37 Hastings L. J. 335, 369 (1985), "courts have tended to accord too much significance to survival requirements when deciding whether to apply antilapse statutes."

A formalistic argument sometimes employed by courts adopting the view that words of survivorship automatically defeat the antilapse statute is that, when words of survivorship are used, there is nothing upon which the antilapse statute can operate; the devise itself, it is said, is eliminated by the devisee's having predeceased the testator. The language of subsections (b)(1) and (b)(2), however, nullify this formalistic argument by providing that the predeceased devisee's descendants take the property to which the devisee would have been entitled had the devisee survived the testator.

Another objection to applying the antilapse statute is that mere words of survivorship somehow establish a contrary intention. The argument is that attaching words of survivorship indicates that the testator thought about the matter and intentionally did not provide a substitute gift to the devisee's descendants. At best, this is an inference only, which may or may not accurately reflect the testator's actual intention. An equally plausible inference is that the words of survivorship are in the testator's will merely because the testator's lawyer used a will form with words of survivorship. The testator who went to lawyer X and ended up with a will containing devises with a survivorship requirement could by chance have gone to lawyer Y and ended up with a will containing devises with no survivorship requirement—with no different intent on

the testator's part from one case to the other.

Even a lawyer's deliberate use of mere words of survivorship to defeat the antilapse statute does not guarantee that the lawyer's intention represents the client's intention. Any linkage between the lawyer's intention and the client's intention is speculative unless the lawyer discussed the matter with the client. Especially in the case of younger-generation devisees, such as the client's children or nieces and nephews, it cannot be assumed that all clients, on their own, have anticipated the possibility that the devisee will predecease the client and will have thought through who should take the devised property in case the never-anticipated event happens.

If, however, evidence establishes that the lawyer did discuss the question with the client, and that the client decided that, for example, if the client's child predeceases the client, the deceased child's children (the client's grandchildren) should not take the devise in place of the deceased child, then the combination of the words of survivorship and the extrinsic evidence of the client's intention would support a finding of a contrary intention under Section 2–601. See Example 1, below. For this reason, Sections 2–601 and 2–603 will not expose lawyers to malpractice liability for the amount that, in the absence of the finding of the contrary intention, would have passed under the antilapse statute to a deceased devisee's descendants. The success of a malpractice claim depends upon sufficient evidence of a client's intention and the lawyer's failure to carry out that intention. In a case in which there is evidence that the client did not want the antilapse statute to apply, that evidence would support a finding of a contrary intention under Section 2–601, thus preventing the client's intention from being defeated by Section 2–603 and protecting the lawyer from liability for the amount that, in the absence of the finding of a contrary intention, would have passed under the antilapse statute to a deceased devisee's descendants.

Any inference about actual intention to be drawn from mere words of survivorship is especially problematic in the case of will substitutes such as life insurance, where it is less likely that the insured had the assistance of a lawyer in drafting the beneficiary designation. Although Section 2–603 only applies to wills, a companion provision is Section 2–706, which applies to will substitutes, including life insurance. Section 2–706 also contains language similar to that in subsection (b)(3), directing that words of survivorship do not, in the absence of additional evidence, indicate an intent contrary to the application of this section. It would be anomalous to provide one rule for wills and a different rule for will substitutes.

The basic operation of section 2–603 is illustrated in the following example:

> *Example 1.* G's will devised "$10,000 to my surviving children." G had two children, A and B. A predeceased G, leaving a child, X, who survived G by 120 hours. B also survived G by 120 hours.
>
> Solution: Under subsection (b)(2), X takes $5,000 and B takes $5,000. The substitute gift to A's descendant, X, is not defeated by the fact that the devise is a class gift nor, under subsection (b)(3), is it automatically defeated by the fact that the word "surviving" is used.

Note that subsection (b)(3) provides that words of survivorship are not by themselves to be taken as expressing a contrary intention for purposes of Section 2–601. Under Section 2–601, a finding of a contrary intention could appropriately be based on affirmative evidence that G deliberately used the words of survivorship to defeat the antilapse statute. In the case of such a finding, B would take the full $10,000 devise. Relevant evidence tending to support such a finding might be a pre-execution letter or memorandum to G from G's attorney stating that G's attorney used the word "surviving" for the purpose of assuring that if one of G's children were to predecease G, that child's descendants would not take the predeceased child's share under any statute or rule of law.

In the absence of persuasive evidence of a contrary intent, however, the antilapse statute, being remedial in nature, and tending to preserve equality among different lines of succession, should be given the widest possible chance to operate and should be defeated only by a finding of intention that *directly contradicts* the substitute gift created by the statute. Mere words of survivorship—by themselves—do not directly contradict the statutory substitute gift to the descendants of a deceased devisee. The common law of lapse already conditions all devises on survivorship (and Section 2–702 presumptively conditions all devises on survivorship by 120 hours). As noted above, the anti-lapse statute does not reverse the law-imposed requirement of survivorship in any strict sense; it merely alters the devolution of lapsed devises by substituting the deceased devisee's descendants in place of those who would otherwise take. Thus, mere words of survivorship merely *duplicate* the law-imposed survivorship requirement deriving from the rule of lapse, and do not contradict the statutory substitute gift created by subsection (b)(1) or (b)(2).

Subsection (b)(4). Under subsection (b)(4), a statutory substitute gift is superseded if the testator's will expressly provides for its own alternative devisee and if that alternative devisee is entitled to take under the will. For example, the statute's substitute gift would be superseded in the case of a devise "to A if A survives me; if not, to B," where B survived the testator but A predeceased the testator leaving descendants who survived the testator. Under subsection (b)(4), B, not A's descendants, would take. In the same example, however, it should be noted that A's descendants *would* take under the statute if B as well as A predeceased the testator, for in that case the "expressly designated devisee of the alternative devise" (B) would not be entitled to take under the will. This would be true even if B left descendants who survived the testator; B's descendants are not "expressly designated devisees of the alternative devise." (For an illustration of the meaning of "expressly

designated devisee" when the alternative devise is in the form of a class gift, see Example 6, below.)

It should also be noted that, for purposes of Section 2–601, an alternative devise might indicate a contrary intention even if subsection (b)(4) is inapplicable. To illustrate this point, consider a variation of Example 1. Suppose that in Example 1, G's will devised "$10,000 to my surviving children, *but if none of my children survives me, to the descendants of deceased children.*" The alternative devise to the descendants of deceased children would not cause the substitute gift to X to be superseded under subsection (b)(4) because the condition precedent to the alternative devise—"if none of my children survives me"—was not satisfied; one of G's children, B, survived G. Hence the alternative devisees would not be entitled to take under the will. Nevertheless, the italicized language would indicate that G did not intend to substitute descendants of deceased children unless all of G's children failed to survive G. Thus, although A predeceased G leaving a child, X, who survived G by 120 hours, X would not be substituted for A. B, G's surviving child, would take the whole $10,000 devise.

The above variation of Example 1 is to be distinguished from other variations, such as one in which G's will devised "$10,000 to my surviving children, *but if none of my children survives me, to my brothers and sisters.*" The italicized language in this variation would not indicate that G did not intend to substitute descendants of deceased children unless all of G's children failed to survive G. In addition, even if one or more of G's brothers and sisters survived G, the alternative devise would not cause the substitute gift to X to be superseded under subsection (b)(4); the alternative devisees would not be entitled to take under the will because the alternative devise is expressly conditioned on none of G's children surviving G. Thus, X would be substituted for A, allowing X and B to divide the $10,000 equally (as in the original version of Example 1.)

Subsection (b)(4) is further illustrated by the following examples:

Example 2. G's will devised "$10,000 to my sister, S" and devised "the rest, residue, and remainder of my estate to X–Charity." S predeceased G, leaving a child, N, who survived G by 120 hours.

Solution: S's $10,000 devise goes to N, not to X–Charity. The residuary clause does not create an "alternative devise," as defined in subsection (a)(1), because neither it nor any other language in the will specifically provides that S's $10,000 devise or lapsed or failed devises in general pass under the residuary clause.

Example 3. Same facts as Example 2, except that G's residuary clause devised "the rest, residue, and remainder of my estate, including all failed and lapsed devises, to X–Charity."

Solution: S's $10,000 devise goes to X–Charity, not to N. Under subsection (b)(4), the substitute gift to N created by subsection (b)(1) is superseded. The residuary clause expressly creates an "alternative devise," as defined in subsection (a)(1), in

favor of X–Charity and that alternative devisee, X–Charity, is entitled to take under the will.

Example 4. G's will devised "$10,000 to my two children, A and B, or to the survivor of them." A predeceased G, leaving a child, X, who survived G by 120 hours. B also survived G by 120 hours.

Solution: B takes the full $10,000. Because the takers of the $10,000 devise are both named and numbered ("my *two* children, A and B"), the devise is not in the form of a class gift. The substance of the devise is as if it read "half of $10,000 to A, but if A predeceases me, that half to B if B survives me and the other half of $10,000 to B, but if B predeceases me, that other half to A if A survives me." With respect to each half, A and B have alternative devises, one to the other. Subsection (b)(1) creates a substitute gift to A's descendant, X, with respect to A's alternative devise in each half. Under subsection (b)(4), however, that substitute gift to X with respect to each half is superseded by the alternative devise to B because the alternative devisee, B, survived G by 120 hours and is entitled to take under G's will.

Example 5. G's will devised "$10,000 to my two children, A and B, or to the survivor of them." A and B predeceased G. A left a child, X, who survived G by 120 hours; B died childless.

Solution: X takes the full $10,000. Because the devise itself is in the same form as the one in Example 4, the substance of the devise is as if it read "half of $10,000 to A, but if A predeceases me, that half to B if B survives me and the other half of $10,000 to B, but if B predeceases me, that other half to A if A survives me." With respect to each half, A and B have alternative devises, one to the other. As in Example 4, subsection (b)(1) creates a substitute gift to A's descendant, X, with respect to A's alternative devise in each half. Unlike the situation in Example 4, however, neither substitute gift to X is superseded under subsection (b)(4) by the alternative devise to B because, in this case, the alternative devisee, B, failed to survive G by 120 hours and is therefore not entitled to take either half under G's will.

Note that the order of deaths as between A and B is irrelevant. The phrase "or to the survivor" does not mean the survivor as between them if they both predecease G; it refers to the one who survives G if one but not the other survives G.

Example 6. G's will devised "$10,000 to my son, A, if he is living at my death; if not, to A's children." A predeceased G. A's child, X, also predeceased G. A's other child, Y, and X's children, M and N, survived G by 120 hours.

Solution: Half of the devise ($5,000) goes to Y. The other half ($5,000) goes to M and N.

Because A failed to survive G by 120 hours and left descendants who survived G by 120 hours, subsection (b)(1) substitutes A's descendants who survived G by 120 hours for A. But

that substitute gift is superseded under subsection (b)(4) by the alternative devise to A's children. Under subsection (b)(4), an alternative devise supersedes a substitute gift "if an expressly designated devisee of the alternative devise is entitled to take under the will." In this case, Y is an expressly designated devisee of the alternative devise who is entitled to take under the will. Note that a devisee of an alternative devise can be expressly designated by class designation, as here, as well as by name. Note also that only one member of the class needs to be entitled to take under the will in order for an alternative devise to supersede a substitute gift.

Because the alternative devise to A's children is a class gift, and because one of the class members, X, failed to survive G by 120 hours and left descendants who survived G by 120 hours, subsection (b)(2) applies and substitutes M and N for X.

Subsection (c). Subsection (c) is necessary because there can be cases in which subsections (b)(1) or (b)(2) create substitute gifts with respect to two or more alternative devises of the same property, and those substitute gifts are not superseded under the terms of subsection (b)(4). Subsection (c) provides the tie-breaking mechanism for such situations.

The initial step is to determine which of the alternative devises would take effect had all the devisees themselves survived the testator (by 120 hours). In subsection (c), this devise is called the "primary devise." Unless subsection (c)(2) applies, subsection (c)(1) provides that the devised property passes under substitute gift created with respect to the primary devise. This substitute gift is called the "primary substitute gift." Thus, the devised property goes to the descendants of the devisee or devisees of the primary devise.

Subsection (c)(2) provides an exception to this rule. Under subsection (c)(2), the devised property does not pass under the primary substitute gift if there is a "younger-generation devise"—defined as a devise that (A) is to a descendant of a devisee of the primary devise, (B) is an alternative devise with respect to the primary devise, (C) is a devise for which a substitute gift is created, and (D) would have taken effect had all the deceased devisees who left surviving descendants survived the testator except the deceased devisee or devisees of the primary devise. If there is a younger-generation devise, the devised property passes under the "younger-generation substitute gift"—defined as the substitute gift created with respect to the younger-generation devise.

Subsection (c) is illustrated by the following examples:

> *Example 7.* G's will devised "$5,000 to my son, A, if he is living at my death; if not, to my daughter, B" and devised "$7,500 to my daughter, B, if she is living at my death; if not, to my son, A." A and B predeceased G, both leaving descendants who survived G by 120 hours.
>
> Solution: A's descendants take the $5,000 devise as substitute takers for A, and B's descendants take the $7,500 devise as substitute takers for B. In the absence of a finding based on affirmative evidence such as described in the solution to Example 1, the mere words of survivorship do not by themselves indicate a contrary intent.

Both devises require application of subsection (c). In the case of both devises, the statute produces a substitute gift for the devise to A and for the devise to B, each devise being an alternative devise, one to the other. The question of which of the substitute gifts takes effect is resolved by determining which of the devisees themselves would take the devised property if both A and B had survived G by 120 hours.

With respect to the devise of $5,000, the primary devise is to A because A would have taken the devised property had both A and B survived G by 120 hours. Consequently, the primary substitute gift is to A's descendants and that substitute gift prevails over the substitute gift to B's descendants.

With respect to the devise of $7,500, the primary devise is to B because B would have taken the devised property had both A and B survived G by 120 hours, and so the substitute gift to B's descendants is the primary substitute gift and it prevails over the substitute gift to A's descendants.

Subsection (c)(2) is inapplicable because there is no younger-generation devise. Neither A nor B is a descendant of the other.

Example 8. G's will devised "$10,000 to my son, A, if he is living at my death; if not, to A's children, X and Y." A and X predeceased G. A's child, Y, and X's children, M and N, survived G by 120 hours.

Solution: Half of the devise ($5,000) goes to Y. The other half ($5,000) goes to M and N. The disposition of the latter half requires application of subsection (c).

Subsection (b)(1) produces substitute gifts as to that half for the devise of that half to A and for the devise of that half to X, each of these devises being alternative devises, one to the other. The primary devise is to A. But there is also a younger-generation devise, the alternative devise to X. X is a descendant of A, X would take if X but not A survived G by 120 hours, and the devise to X is one for which a substitute gift is created by subsection (b)(1). So, the younger-generation substitute gift, which is to X's descendants (M and N), prevails over the primary substitute gift, which is to A's descendants (Y, M, and N). Note that the outcome of this example is the same as in Example 6.

Example 9. Same facts as Example 5, except that both A and B predeceased the testator and both left descendants who survived the testator by 120 hours.

Solution: A's descendants take half ($5,000) and B's descendants take half ($5,000).

As to the half devised to A, subsection (b)(1) produces a substitute gift to A's descendants and a substitute gift to B's descendants (because the language "or to the survivor of them" created an alternative devise in B of A's half). As to the half devised to B, subsection (b)(1) produces a substitute gift to B's descendants and a substitute gift to A's descendants (because the language "or to the survivor of them" created an alternative devise in A of B's half). Thus, with respect to each half, resort must be had to subsection (c) to determine which substitute gift prevails.

Under subsection (c)(1), each half passes under the primary substitute gift. The primary devise as to A's half is to A and the primary devise as to B's half is to B because, if both A and B had survived G by 120 hours, A would have taken half ($5,000) and B would have taken half ($5,000). Neither A nor B is a descendant of the other, so subsection (c)(2) does not apply. Only if one were a descendant of the other would the other's descendants take it all, under the rule of subsection (c)(2).

Reference. This section is discussed in Halbach & Waggoner, "The UPC's New Survivorship and Antilapse Provisions," 55 Alb. L.Rev. 1091 (1992).

Historical Note. This Comment was revised in 1993. For the prior version, see 8 U.L.A. 127 (Supp. 1992).

Section 2–604. Failure of Testamentary Provision.

(a) Except as provided in Section 2–603, a devise, other than a residuary devise, that fails for any reason becomes a part of the residue.

(b) Except as provided in Section 2–603, if the residue is devised to two or more persons, the share of a residuary devisee that fails for any reason passes to the other residuary devisee, or to other residuary devisees in proportion to the interest of each in the remaining part of the residue.

COMMENT

This section applies only if Section 2–603 does not produce a substitute taker for a devisee who fails to survive the testator by 120 hours. There is also a special rule for disclaimers contained in Section 2–801; a disclaimed devise may be governed by either Section 2–603 or the present section, depending on the circumstances.

A devise of "all of my estate," or a devise using words of similar import, constitutes a residuary devise for purposes of this section.

Historical Note. This Comment was revised in 1993. For the prior version, see 8 U.L.A. 132 (Supp. 1992).

Section 2–605. Increase in Securities; Accessions.

(a) If a testator executes a will that devises securities and the testator then owned securities that meet the description in the will, the devise includes additional securities owned by the testator at death to the extent the additional securities were acquired by the testator after the will was executed as a result of the testator's ownership of the described securities and are securities of any of the following types:

(1) securities of the same organization acquired by reason of action initiated by the organization or any successor, related, or acquiring organization, excluding any acquired by exercise of purchase options;

(2) securities of another organization acquired as a result of a merger, consolidation, reorganization, or other distribution by the organization or any successor, related, or acquiring organization; or

(3) securities of the same organization acquired as a result of a plan of reinvestment.

(b) Distributions in cash before death with respect to a described security are not part of the devise.

COMMENT

Purpose and Scope of Revisions. The rule of subsection (a), as revised, relates to a devise of securities (such as a devise of 100 shares of XYZ Company), regardless of whether that devise is characterized as a general or specific devise. If the testator executes a will that makes a devise of securities and if the testator then owned securities that meet the description in the will, then the devisee is entitled not only to the described securities to the extent they are owned by the testator at death; the devisee is also entitled to any additional securities owned by the testator at death that were acquired by the testator during his or her lifetime after the will was executed and were acquired as a result of the testator's ownership of the described securities by reason of an action specified in subsections (a)(1), (a)(2), or (a)(3), such as the declaration of stock splits or stock dividends or spinoffs of a subsidiary.

The impetus for these revisions derives from the rule on stock splits enunciated by Bostwick v. Hurstel, 364 Mass. 282, 304 N.E.2d 186 (1973), and now codified in Massachusetts as to actions covered by subsections (a)(1) and (a)(2). Mass. Gen. Laws c. 191, § 1A(4).

Subsection (a) Not Exclusive. Subsection (a) is not exclusive, i.e., it is not to be understood as setting forth the only conditions under which additional securities of the types described in paragraphs (1), (2), and (3) are included in the devise. For example, the express terms of subsection (a) do not apply to a case in which the testator owned the described securities when he or she executed the will, but later sold (or otherwise disposed of) those securities, and then later purchased (or otherwise acquired) securities that meet the description in the will, following which additional securities of the type or types described in paragraphs (1), (2), or (3) are acquired as a result of the testator's ownership of the later-acquired securities. Nor do the express terms of subsection (a) apply to a similar (but less likely) case in which the testator did not own the described securities when he or she executed the will, but later purchased (or otherwise acquired) such securities. Subsection (a) does not preclude a court, in an appropriate case, from deciding that additional securities of the type described in paragraphs (1), (2), or (3) acquired as a result of the testator's ownership of the later-acquired securities pass under the devise in either of these two cases, or in other cases if appropriate.

Subsection (b) codifies existing law that distributions in cash, such as interest, accrued rent, or cash dividends declared and payable as of a record date before the testator's death, do not pass as a part of the devise. It makes no difference whether such cash distributions were paid before or after death. See Section 4 of the Revised Uniform Principal and Income Act.

Cross Reference. The term "organization" is defined in Section 1–201.

Section 2–606. Nonademption of Specific Devises; Unpaid Proceeds of Sale, Condemnation, or Insurance; Sale by Conservator or Agent.

(a) A specific devisee has a right to the specifically devised property in the testator's estate at death and:

(1) any balance of the purchase price, together with any security agreement, owing from a purchaser to the testator at death by reason of sale of the property;

(2) any amount of a condemnation award for the taking of the property unpaid at death;

(3) any proceeds unpaid at death on fire or casualty insurance on or other recovery for injury to the property;

(4) property owned by the testator at death and acquired as a result of foreclosure, or obtained in lieu of foreclosure, of the security interest for a specifically devised obligation;

(5) real or tangible personal property owned by the testator at death which the testator acquired as a replacement for specifically devised real or tangible personal property; and

(6) unless the facts and circumstances indicate that ademption of the devise was intended by the testator or ademption of the devise is consistent with the testator's manifested plan of distribution, the value of the specifically devised property to the extent the specifically devised property is not in the testator's estate at death and its value or its replacement is not covered by paragraphs (1) through (5).

(b) If specifically devised property is sold or mortgaged by a conservator or by an agent acting within the authority of a durable power of attorney for an incapacitated principal, or if a condemnation award, insurance proceeds, or recovery for injury to the property are paid to a conservator or to an agent acting within the authority of a durable power of attorney for an incapacitated principal, the specific devisee has the right to a general pecuniary devise equal to the net sale price, the amount of the unpaid loan, the condemnation award, the insurance proceeds, or the recovery.

(c) The right of a specific devisee under subsection (b) is reduced by any right the devisee has under subsection (a).

(d) For the purposes of the references in subsection (b) to a conservator, subsection (b) does not apply if after the sale, mortgage, condemnation, casualty, or recovery, it was adjudicated that the testator's incapacity ceased and the testator survived the adjudication by one year.

(e) For the purposes of the references in subsection (b) to an agent acting within the authority of a durable power of attorney for an incapacitated principal, (i) "incapacitated principal" means a principal who is an incapacitated person, (ii) no adjudication of incapacity before death is necessary, and (iii) the acts of an agent within the authority of a durable power of attorney are presumed to be for an incapacitated principal.

COMMENT

Purpose and Scope of Revisions. Under the "identity" theory followed by most courts, the common-law doctrine of ademption by extinction is that a specific devise is adeemed—rendered ineffective—if the specifically devised property is not owned by the testator at death. In applying the "identity" theory, courts do not inquire into the testator's intent to determine whether the testator's objective in disposing of the specifically devised property was to revoke the devise. The only thing that matters is that the property is no longer owned at death. The application of the "identity" theory of ademption has resulted in harsh results in a number of cases, where it was reasonably clear that the testator did not intend to revoke the devise. Notable examples include McGee v. McGee, 413 A.2d 72 (R.I.1980); Estate of Dungan, 73 A.2d 776 (Del.Ch.1950).

Recently, some courts have begun to break away from the "identity" theory and adopt instead the so-called "intent" theory. E.g., Estate of Austin, 113 Cal. App. 3d 167, 169 Cal. Rptr. 648 (1980). The major import of the revisions of this section is to adopt the "intent" theory in subsections (a)(5) and (a)(6).

Subsection (a)(5) does not import a tracing principle into the question of ademption, but rather should be seen as a sensible "mere change in form" principle.

Example 1. G's will devised to X "my 1984 Ford." After she executed her will, she sold her 1984 Ford and bought a 1988 Buick; later, she sold the 1988 Buick and bought a 1993 Chrysler. She still owned the 1993 Chrysler when she died. Under subsection (a)(5), X takes the 1993 Chrysler.

Variation. If G had sold her 1984 Ford (or any of the replacement cars) and used the proceeds to buy shares in a mutual fund, which she owned at death, subsection (a)(5) does not give X the shares in the mutual fund. If G owned an automobile at death as a replacement for her 1984 Ford, however, X would be entitled to that automobile, even though it was bought with funds other than the proceeds of the sale of the 1984 Ford.

Subsection (a)(6) applies only to the extent the specifically devised property is not in the testator's estate at death and its value or its replacement is not covered by the provisions of paragraphs (1) through (5). In that event, subsection (a)(6) creates a mild presumption against ademption by extinction, imposing on the party claiming that an ademption has occurred the burden of establishing that the facts and circumstances indicate that ademption of the devise was intended by the testator or that ademption of the devise is consistent with the testator's manifested plan of distribution.

Example 2. G's will devised to his son, A, "that diamond ring I inherited from grandfather" and devised to his daughter, B, "that diamond broach I inherited from grandmother." After G executed his will, a burglar entered his home and stole the diamond ring (but not the diamond broach, as it was in G's safety deposit box at his bank).

Under subsection (a)(6), the party claiming that A's devise was adeemed would be unlikely to be able to establish that G intended A's devise to be adeemed or that ademption is consistent with G's manifested plan of distribution. In fact, G's equalizing devise to B affirma-

tively indicates that ademption is inconsistent with G's manifested plan of distribution. The likely result is that, under subsection (a)(6), A would be entitled to the value of the diamond ring.

Example 3. G's will devised her painting titled *The Bar* by Edouard Manet to X. After executing her will, G donated the painting to a museum. G's deliberate act of giving away the specifically devised property is a fact and circumstance indicating that ademption of the devise was intended. In the absence of persuasive evidence to the contrary, therefore, X would not be entitled to the value of the painting.

Reference. Section 2–606 is discussed in Alexander, "Ademption and the Domain of Formality in Wills Law," 55 Alb.L.Rev. 1067 (1992).

Historical Note. This Comment was revised in 1993. For the prior version, see 8 U.L.A. 134 (Supp. 1992).

Section 2–607. Nonexoneration.

A specific devise passes subject to any mortgage interest existing at the date of death, without right of exoneration, regardless of a general directive in the will to pay debts.

COMMENT

See Section 3–814 empowering the personal representative to pay an encumbrance under some circumstances; the last sentence of that section makes it clear that such payment does not increase the right of the specific devisee. The present section governs the substantive rights of the devisee. The

common-law rule of exoneration of the specific devise is abolished by this section, and the contrary rule is adopted.

For the rule as to exempt property, see Section 2–403.

The rule of this section is not inconsistent with Section 2–606(b).

If a conservator or agent for an incapacitated principal mortgages specifically devised property, Section 2–606(b) provides that the specific devisee is entitled to a pecuniary devise equal to the amount of the unpaid loan. Section 2–606(b) does not contradict this section, which provides that the specific devise passes subject to any mortgage interest existing at the date of death, without right of exoneration.

Section 2–608. Exercise of Power of Appointment.

In the absence of a requirement that a power of appointment be exercised by a reference, or by an express or specific reference, to the power, a general residuary clause in a will, or a will making general disposition of all of the testator's property, expresses an intention to exercise a power of appointment held by the testator only if (i) the power is a general power and the creating instrument does not contain a gift if the power is not exercised or (ii) the testator's will manifests an intention to include the property subject to the power.

COMMENT

General Residuary Clause. As revised, this section, in conjunction with Section 2–601, provides that a general residuary clause (such as "All the rest, residue, and remainder of my estate, I devise to . . . .") in the testator's will or a will making general disposition of all of the testator's property (such as "All of my estate, I devise to . . . .") is presumed to express an intent to exercise a power of appointment held by the donee of the power only if one or the other of two circumstances or sets of circumstances are satisfied. One such circumstance (whether the power is general or nongeneral) is if the testator's will manifests an intention to include the property subject to the power. A simple example of a residuary clause that manifests such an intention is a so-called "blending" or "blanket-exercise" clause, such as "All the rest, residue, and remainder of my estate, including any property over which I have a power of appointment, I devise to . . . ."

The other circumstance under which a general residuary clause or a will making general disposition of all of the testator's property is presumed to express an intent to exercise a power is if the power is a *general* power *and* the instrument that created the power does not contain a gift over in the event the power is not exercised (a "gift in default"). In well planned estates, a general power of appointment will be accompanied by a gift in default. The gift-in-default clause is ordinarily expected to take effect; it is not merely an after-thought just in case the power is not exercised. The power is not expected to be exercised, and in fact is often conferred mainly to gain a tax benefit—the federal estate-tax marital deduction under section 2056(b)(5) of the Internal Revenue Code or, now, inclusion of the property in the gross estate of a younger-generation beneficiary under section 2041 of the Internal Revenue Code, in

145

order to avoid the possibly higher rates imposed by the new federal generation-skipping tax. See Blattmachr & Pennell, "Adventures in Generation Skipping, Or How We Learned to Love the 'Delaware Tax Trap,'" 24 Real Prop. Prob. & Tr. J. 75 (1989). A general power should not be exercised in such a case without clear evidence of an intent to appoint.

In poorly planned estates, on the other hand, there may be no gift-in-default clause. In the absence of a gift-in-default clause, it seems better to let the property pass under the donee's will than force it to return to the donor's estate, for the reason that the donor died before the donee died and it seems better to avoid forcing a reopening of the donor's estate.

Cross Reference. See also Section 2–704 for a provision governing the meaning of a requirement that a power of appointment be exercised by a reference (or by an express or specific reference) to the power.

Section 2–609. Ademption by Satisfaction.

(a) Property a testator gave in his [or her] lifetime to a person is treated as a satisfaction of a devise in whole or in part, only if (i) the will provides for deduction of the gift, (ii) the testator declared in a contemporaneous writing that the gift is in satisfaction of the devise or that its value is to be deducted from the value of the devise, or (iii) the devisee acknowledged in writing that the gift is in satisfaction of the devise or that its value is to be deducted from the value of the devise.

(b) For purposes of partial satisfaction, property given during lifetime is valued as of the time the devisee came into possession or enjoyment of the property or at the testator's death, whichever occurs first.

(c) If the devisee fails to survive the testator, the gift is treated as a full or partial satisfaction of the devise, as appropriate, in applying Sections 2–603 and 2–604, unless the testator's contemporaneous writing provides otherwise.

COMMENT

Scope and Purpose of Revisions. In addition to minor stylistic changes, this section is revised to delete the requirement that the gift in satisfaction of a devise be made to the devisee. The purpose is to allow the testator to satisfy a devise to A by making a gift to B. Consider why this might be desirable. G's will made a $20,000 devise to his child, A. G was a widower. Shortly before his death, G in consultation with his lawyer decided to take advantage of the $10,000 annual gift tax exclusion and sent a check for $10,000 to A and another check for $10,000 to A's spouse, B. The checks were accompanied by a letter from G explaining that the gifts were made for tax purposes and were in lieu of the $20,000 devise to

A. The removal of the phrase "to that person" from the statute allows the $20,000 devise to be fully satisfied by the gifts to A and B.

This section parallels Section 2–109 on advancements and follows the same policy of requiring written evidence that lifetime gifts are to be taken into account in the distribution of an estate, whether testate or intestate. Although courts traditionally call this "ademption by satisfaction" when a will is involved, and "advancement" when the estate is intestate, the difference in terminology is not significant.

Some wills expressly provide for lifetime advances by a hotchpot clause. Where the will contains no such clause, this section requires either the testator to declare in writing that the gift is in satisfaction of the devise or its value is to be deducted from the value of the devise or the devisee to acknowledge the same in writing.

To be a gift in satisfaction, the gift need not be an outright gift; it can be in the form of a will substitute, such as designating the devisee as the beneficiary of the testator's life-insurance policy or the beneficiary of the remainder interest in a revocable inter-vivos trust.

Subsection (b) on value accords with Section 2–109 and applies if, for example, property such as stock

is given. If the devise is specific, a gift of the specific property to the devisee during lifetime adeems the devise by extinction rather than by satisfaction, and this section would be inapplicable. Unlike the common law of satisfaction, however, specific devises are not excluded from the rule of this section. If, for example, the testator makes a devise of a specific item of property, and subsequently makes a gift of cash or other property to the devisee, accompanied by the requisite written intent that the gift satisfies the devise, the devise is satisfied under this section even if the subject of the specific devise is still in the testator's estate at death (and hence would not be adeemed under the doctrine of ademption by extinction).

Under subsection (c), if a devisee to whom a gift in satisfaction is made predeceases the testator and his or her descendants take under Section 2–603 or 2–604, they take the same devise as their ancestor would have taken had the ancestor survived the testator; if the devise is reduced by reason of this section as to the ancestor, it is automatically reduced as to the devisee's descendants. In this respect, the rule in testacy differs from that in intestacy; see Section 2–109(c).

PART 7

RULES OF CONSTRUCTION APPLICABLE TO WILLS AND OTHER GOVERNING INSTRUMENTS

GENERAL COMMENT

Part 7 contains rules of construction applicable to wills and other governing instruments, such as deeds, trusts, appointments, beneficiary designations, and so on. Like the rules of construction in Part 6 (which apply only to wills), the rules of construction in this Part yield to a finding of a contrary intention.

Some of the sections in Part 7 are revisions of sections contained in Part 6 of the pre–1990 Code. Although these sections originally applied only to wills, their restricted scope was inappropriate.

Some of the sections in Part 7 are new, having been added to the Code as desirable means of carrying out common intention.

Application to Pre–Existing Governing Instruments. Under Section 8–101(b), for decedents dying after the effective date of enactment, the provisions of this Code apply to governing instruments executed prior to as well as on or after the effective date of enactment. The Joint Editorial Board for the Uniform Probate Code has issued a statement concerning the constitutionality under the Contracts Clause of this feature of the Code. The statement, titled "Joint Editorial Board Statement Regarding the Constitutionality of Changes in Default Rules as Applied to Pre–Existing Documents," can be found at 17 Am.C.Tr. & Est.Couns.Notes 184 (1991) or can be obtained from the headquarters office of the National Conference of Commissioners on Uniform State Laws, 676 N. St. Clair St., Suite 1700, Chicago, IL 60611, Phone 312/915–0195, FAX 312/915–0187.

Historical Note. This General Comment was revised in 1993. For the prior version, see 8 U.L.A. 137 (Supp.1992).

Section 2–701. Scope.

In the absence of a finding of a contrary intention, the rules of construction in this Part control the construction of a governing instrument. The rules of construction in this Part apply to a governing instrument of any type, except as the application of a particular section is limited by its terms to a specific type or types of provision or governing instrument.

148

COMMENT

The rules of construction in this Part apply to governing instruments of any type, except as the application of a particular section is limited by its terms to a specific type or types of provision or governing instrument.

The term "governing instrument" is defined in Section 1–201 as "a deed, will, trust, insurance or annuity policy, account with POD designation, security registered in beneficiary form (TOD), pension, profit-sharing, retirement, or similar benefit plan, instrument creating or exercising a power of appointment or a power of attorney, or a dispositive, appointive, or nominative instrument of any similar type."

Certain of the sections in this Part are limited in their application to provisions or governing instruments of a certain type or types. Section 2–704, for example, applies only to a governing instrument creating a power of appointment. Section 2–706 applies only to governing instruments that are "beneficiary designations," a term defined in Section 1–201 as referring to "a governing instrument naming a beneficiary of an insurance or annuity policy, of an account with POD designation, of a security registered in beneficiary form (TOD), or of a pension, profit-sharing, retirement, or similar benefit plan, or other nonprobate transfer at death." Section 2–707 applies only to governing instruments creating a future interest under the terms of a trust.

Cross References. See the Comment to Section 2–601.

Historical Note. This comment was revised in 1993. For the prior version, see 8 U.L.A. 138 (Supp. 1992).

Section 2–702. Requirement of Survival by 120 Hours.

(a) [Requirement of Survival by 120 Hours Under Probate Code.] For the purposes of this Code, except as provided in subsection (d), an individual who is not established by clear and convincing evidence to have survived an event, including the death of another individual, by 120 hours is deemed to have predeceased the event.

(b) [Requirement of Survival by 120 Hours Under Governing Instrument.] Except as provided in subsection (d), for purposes of a provision of a governing instrument that relates to an individual surviving an event, including the death of another individual, an individual who is not established by clear and convincing evidence to have survived the event by 120 hours is deemed to have predeceased the event.

(c) [Co-owners With Right of Survivorship; Requirement of Survival by 120 Hours.] Except as provided in subsection (d), if (i) it is not established by clear and convincing evidence that one of two co-owners with right of survivorship survived the other co-owner by 120 hours, one-half of the property passes as if one had survived by 120 hours and one-half as if the other had survived by 120 hours and (ii) there are more than two co-owners and it is not established by clear and convincing evidence that at least one of them survived the others by 120 hours, the property passes in the proportion that one bears to the whole number of co-owners. For the purposes of this subsection, "co-owners with right of survivorship" includes joint tenants, tenants by the entireties, and other co-owners of property or accounts held under circumstances that entitles one or more to the whole of the property or account on the death of the other or others.

(d) [Exceptions.] Survival by 120 hours is not required if:

(1) the governing instrument contains language dealing explicitly with simultaneous deaths or deaths in a common disaster and that language is operable under the facts of the case;

(2) the governing instrument expressly indicates that an individual is not required to survive an event, including the death of another individual, by any specified period or expressly requires the individual to survive the event by a specified period; but survival of the event or the specified period must be established by clear and convincing evidence;

(3) the imposition of a 120–hour requirement of survival would cause a nonvested property interest or a power of appointment to fail to qualify for validity under Section 2–901(a)(1), (b)(1), or (c)(1) or to become invalid under Section 2–901(a)(2), (b)(2), or (c)(2); but survival must be established by clear and convincing evidence; or

(4) the application of a 120–hour requirement of survival to multiple governing instruments would result in an unintended failure or duplication of a disposition; but survival must be established by clear and convincing evidence.

(e) [Protection of Payors and Other Third Parties.]

(1) A payor or other third party is not liable for having made a payment or transferred an item of property or any other benefit to a beneficiary designated in a governing instrument who, under this section, is not entitled to the payment or item of property, or for having taken any other action in good faith reliance on the beneficiary's apparent entitlement under the terms of the governing instrument, before the payor or other third party received written notice of a claimed lack of entitlement under this section. A payor or other third party is liable

for a payment made or other action taken after the payor or other third party received written notice of a claimed lack of entitlement under this section.

(2) Written notice of a claimed lack of entitlement under paragraph (1) must be mailed to the payor's or other third party's main office or home by registered or certified mail, return receipt requested, or served upon the payor or other third party in the same manner as a summons in a civil action. Upon receipt of written notice of a claimed lack of entitlement under this section, a payor or other third party may pay any amount owed or transfer or deposit any item of property held by it to or with the court having jurisdiction of the probate proceedings relating to the decedent's estate, or if no proceedings have been commenced, to or with the court having jurisdiction of probate proceedings relating to decedents' estates located in the county of the decedent's residence. The court shall hold the funds or item of property and, upon its determination under this section, shall order disbursement in accordance with the determination. Payments, transfers, or deposits made to or with the court discharge the payor or other third party from all claims for the value of amounts paid to or items of property transferred to or deposited with the court.

(f) [Protection of Bona Fide Purchasers; Personal Liability of Recipient.]

(1) A person who purchases property for value and without notice, or who receives a payment or other item of property in partial or full satisfaction of a legally enforceable obligation, is neither obligated under this section to return the payment, item of property, or benefit nor is liable under this section for the amount of the payment or the value of the item of property or benefit. But a person who, not for value, receives a payment, item of property, or any other benefit to which the person is not entitled under this section is obligated to return the payment, item of property, or benefit, or is personally liable for the amount of the payment or the value of the item of property or benefit, to the person who is entitled to it under this section.

(2) If this section or any part of this section is preempted by federal law with respect to a payment, an item of property, or any other benefit covered by this section, a person who, not for value, receives the payment, item of property, or any other benefit to which the person is not entitled under this section is obligated to return the payment, item of property, or benefit, or is personally liable for the amount of the payment or the value

of the item of property or benefit, to the person who would have been entitled to it were this section or part of this section not preempted.

COMMENT

Scope and Purpose of Revision. This section parallels Section 2–104, which requires an heir to survive the intestate by 120 hours in order to inherit.

The scope of this section is expanded to cover all provisions of a governing instrument and this Code that relate to an individual surviving an event (including the death of another individual). As expanded, this section imposes the 120–hour requirement of survival in the areas covered by the Uniform Simultaneous Death Act. By 1993 technical amendment, an anomalous provision exempting securities registered under Part 3 of Article VI (Uniform TOD Security Registration Act) from the 120-hour survival requirement was eliminated. The exemption reflected a temporary concern attributable to UTODSRA's preparation prior to discussion of inserting a 120-hour survival requirement in the freestanding Uniform Simultaneous Death Act (USDA).

In the case of a multiple-party account, such as a joint checking account registered in the name of the decedent and his or her spouse with right of survivorship, the 120–hour requirement of survivorship will not, under the facility-of-payment provision of Section 6–222(1), interfere with the surviving spouse's ability to withdraw funds from the account during the 120–hour period following the decedent's death.

Note that subsection (d)(1) provides that the 120–hour requirement of survival is inapplicable if the governing instrument "contains language dealing explicitly with simultaneous deaths or deaths in a common disaster and that language is operable under the facts of the case." The application of this provision is illustrated by the following example.

Example. G died leaving a will devising her entire estate to her husband, H, adding that "in the event he dies before I do, at the same time that I do, or under circumstances as to make it doubtful who died first," my estate is to go to my brother Melvin. H died about 38 hours after G's death, both having died as a result of injuries sustained in an automobile accident.

Under subsection (b), G's estate passes under the alternative devise to Melvin because H's failure to survive G by 120 hours means that H is deemed to have predeceased G. The language in the governing instrument does not, under subsection (d)(1), nullify the provision that causes H, because of his failure to survive G by 120 hours, to be deemed to have predeceased G. Although the governing instrument does contain language dealing with simultaneous deaths, that language is not operable under the facts of the case because H did not die before G, at the same time as G, or under circumstances as to make it doubtful who died first.

Note that subsection (d)(4) provides that the 120–hour requirement of survival is inapplicable if "the application of this section to multiple governing instruments would result in an unintended failure or duplication of a disposition." The application of this provision is illustrated by the following example.

> *Example.* Pursuant to a common plan, H and W executed mutual wills with reciprocal provisions. Their intention was that a $50,-000 charitable devise would be made on the death of the survivor. To that end, H's will devised $50,000 to the charity if W predeceased him. W's will devised $50,000 to the charity if H predeceased her. Subsequently, H and W were involved in a common accident. W survived H by 48 hours.

> Were it not for subsection (d)(4), not only would the charitable devise in W's will be effective, because H in fact predeceased W, but the charitable devise in H's will would also be effective, because W's failure to survive H by 120 hours would result in her being deemed to have predeceased H. Because this would result in an unintended duplication of the $50,000 devise, subsection (d)(4) provides that the 120–hour requirement of survival is inapplicable. Thus, only the $50,000 charitable devise in W's will is effective.

> Subsection (d)(4) also renders the 120–hour requirement of survival inapplicable had H and W died in circumstances in which it could not be established by clear and convincing evidence that either survived the other. In such a case, an appropriate result might be to give effect to the common plan by paying half of the intended $50,000 devise from H's estate and half from W's estate.

ERISA Preemption of State Law. The Employee Retirement Income Security Act of 1974 (ERISA) federalizes pension and employee benefit law. Section 514(a) of ERISA, 29 U.S.C. § 1144(a), provides that the provisions of Titles I and IV of ERISA "shall supersede any and all State laws insofar as they may now or hereafter relate to any employee benefit plan" governed by ERISA. See the Comment to Section 2–804 for a discussion of the ERISA preemption question.

Revision of Uniform Simultaneous Death Act. The freestanding Uniform Simultaneous Death Act (USDA) was revised in 1991 in accordance with the revisions of this section. States that enact Sections 2–104 and 2–702 need not enact the USDA as revised in 1991 and should repeal the original version of the USDA if previously enacted in the state.

Reference. This section is discussed in Halbach & Waggoner, "The UPC's New Survivorship and Antilapse Provisions," 55 Alb. L.Rev. 1091 (1992).

Historical Note. This comment was revised in 1993. For the prior version, see 8 U.L.A. 140 (Supp. 1992).

Section 2-703. Choice of Law as to Meaning and Effect of Governing Instrument.

The meaning and legal effect of a governing instrument is determined by the local law of the state selected in the governing instrument, unless the application of that law is contrary to the provisions relating to the elective share described in Part 2, the provisions relating to exempt property and allowances described in Part 4, or any other public policy of this State otherwise applicable to the disposition.

COMMENT

Purpose and Scope of Revisions. The scope of this section is expanded to cover all governing instruments, not just wills. As revised, this section enables the law of a particular state to be selected in the governing instrument for purposes of interpreting the governing instrument without regard to the location of property covered thereby. So long as local public policy is accommodated, the section should be accepted as necessary and desirable.

Cross Reference. Choice of law rules regarding formal validity of a will are in Section 2-506. See also Sections 3-202 and 3-408.

Historical Note. This comment was revised in 1993. For the prior version, see 8 U.L.A. 141 (Supp. 1992).

Section 2-704. Power of Appointment; Meaning of Specific Reference Requirement.

If a governing instrument creating a power of appointment expressly requires that the power be exercised by a reference, an express reference, or a specific reference, to the power or its source, it is presumed that the donor's intention, in requiring that the donee exercise the power by making reference to the particular power or to the creating instrument, was to prevent an inadvertent exercise of the power.

COMMENT

Rationale of New Section. In the creation of powers of appointment, it has become common estate-planning practice to require that the donee of the power can exercise the power only by making reference (or express or specific reference) to it. The question of whether the donee has made a sufficiently specific reference is much litigated. The precise question often is whether a so-called blanket-exercise clause (also called a blending clause)—a clause referring to "any property over which I have a power of appointment"—constitutes a sufficient reference to a particular power to exercise that power. E.g., First National Bank v. Walker, 607 S.W.2d 469 (Tenn. 1980), and cases cited therein.

Section 2-704 sets forth the presumption that the donor's purpose in imposing a reference requirement was to prevent an inadvertent exercise of the power by the donee. Under this section, mere use by the donee of a blanket-exercise clause would be ineffective to exercise the power because such a clause would not make a sufficient reference to the particular power. If, however, it could be shown that the donee had knowledge of and intended to exercise the power, the blanket-exercise clause would be sufficient to exercise the power, unless the presumption of this section is overcome. Under Section 2–701, the presumption of this section would be overcome if it could be shown that the donor's intention was not merely to prevent an inadvertent exercise of the power but was to prevent any exercise of the power, intentional or inadvertent, that failed to identify in explicit terms the specific power or the creating instrument.

Reference. See Langbein & Waggoner, "Reformation of Wills on the Ground of Mistake: Change of Di-

rection in American Law?," 130 U. Pa. L. Rev. 521, 583 n.223 (1982), suggesting that a donee's will that omits a sufficiently specific reference to a particular power can be reformed to include the necessary reference *if* it can be shown by clear and convincing evidence that the omission was caused by a scrivener's mistake. This approach is not inconsistent with Section 2–704. See Sections 2–601 (and accompanying Comment); 2–701. See also Motes/Henes Trust v. Mote, 297 Ark. 380, 761 S.W.2d 938 (1988) (donee's intended exercise given effect despite use of blanket-exercise clause); In re Strobel, 149 Ariz. 213, 717 P.2d 892 (1986) (donee's intended exercise given effect despite defective reference to power).

Cross Reference. See Section 2–608 for a provision governing whether a general residuary clause in the donee's will exercises a power of appointment that does not require a reference (or an express or specific reference) by the donee of the power.

Section 2–705.   Class Gifts Construed to Accord With Intestate Succession.

(a) Adopted individuals and individuals born out of wedlock, and their respective descendants if appropriate to the class, are included in class gifts and other terms of relationship in accordance with the rules for intestate succession. Terms of relationship that do not differentiate relationships by blood from those by affinity, such as "uncles," "aunts," "nieces," or "nephews", are construed to exclude relatives by affinity. Terms of relationship that do not differentiate relationships by the half blood from those by the whole blood, such as "brothers," "sisters," "nieces," or "nephews", are construed to include both types of relationships.

(b) In addition to the requirements of subsection (a), in construing a dispositive provision of a transferor who is not the natural parent, an individual born to the natural parent is not considered the child of that parent unless the individual lived while a minor as a regular member of the household of that natural parent or of that parent's parent, brother, sister, spouse, or surviving spouse.

(c) In addition to the requirements of subsection (a), in construing a dispositive provision of a transferor who is not the adopting parent, an adopted individual is not considered the child of the adopting parent unless the adopted individual lived while a minor, either before or after the adoption, as a regular member of the household of the adopting parent.

COMMENT

Purpose and Scope of Revisions. This section facilitates a modern construction of gifts that identify the recipient by reference to a relationship to someone; usually these gifts will be class gifts. The rules set forth in this section are rules of construction, which under Section 2–701 are controlling in the absence of a finding of a contrary intention. With two exceptions, Section 2–705 invokes the rules pertaining to intestate succession as rules of construction for interpreting terms of relationship in private instruments.

The pre–1990 version of this section applied only to devises contained in wills. As revised and relocated in Part 7, this section is freed of that former restriction; it now applies to dispositive provisions of all governing instruments, as prescribed by Section 2–701.

Subsections (b) and (c) are based on Cal. Prob. Code § 6152. These subsections impose requirements for inclusion that are additional to the requirement of subsection (a). Put differently, a child must satisfy subsection (a) in all cases. In addition, if either subsection (b) or (c) applies, the child must also satisfy the requirements of that subsection to be included under the class gift or term of relationship.

The general theory of subsection (b) is that a transferor who is not the natural (biological) parent of a child would want the child to be included in a class gift as a child of the biological parent only if the child lived while a minor as a regular member of the household of that biological parent (or of specified relatives of that biological parent).

Example. G's will created a trust, income to G's son, A, for life, remainder in corpus to A's descendants who survive A, by representation. A fathered a child, X; A and X's mother, D, never married each other, and X never lived while a minor as a regular member of A's household or the household of A's parent, brother, sister, spouse, or surviving spouse. D later married E; D and E raised X as a member of their household.

Solution: Never having lived as a regular member of A's household or of the household of any of A's specified relatives, X would not be included as a member of the class of A's descendants who take the corpus of G's trust on A's death.

If, however, D's parent had created a similar trust, income to D for life, remainder in corpus to D's descendants who survive D, by representation, X would be included as a member of the class of D's descendants who take the corpus of this trust on D's death.

Also, if A executed a will containing a devise to his children or designated his children as beneficiary of his life insurance policy, X would be included in the class. Under Section 2–114, X would be A's child for purposes of intestate succession. Subsection (b) is inapplicable because the transferor, A, is the biological parent.

The general theory of subsection (c) is that a transferor who is not the adopting parent of an adopted child would want the child to be included in a class gift as a child of the adopting parent only if the child lived while a minor, either before or after the adoption, as a regular member of the household of that adopting parent.

Example. G's will created a trust, income to G's daughter, A, for life, remainder in corpus to A's descendants who survive A, by representation. A and A's husband adopted a 47–year old man, X, who never lived *while a*

minor as a regular member of A's household.

Solution: Never having lived while a minor as a regular member of A's household, X would not be included as a member of the class of A's descendants who take the corpus of G's trust on A's death.

If, however, A executed a will containing a devise to her children or designated her children as beneficiary of her life insurance policy, X would be included in the class. Under Section 2–114, X would be A's child for purposes of intestate succession. Subsection (c) is inapplicable because the transferor, A, is an adopting parent.

Companion Statute. A state enacting this provision should also consider enacting the Uniform Status of Children of Assisted Conception Act (1988).

Reference. Halbach, "Issues About Issue," 48 Mo. L. Rev. 333 (1983).

Historical Note. This comment was revised in 1993. For the prior version, see 8 U.L.A. 143 (Supp. 1992).

Section 2–706. Life Insurance; Retirement Plan; Account With POD Designation; Transfer-on-Death Registration; Deceased Beneficiary.

(a) [Definitions.] In this section:

(1) "Alternative beneficiary designation" means a beneficiary designation that is expressly created by the governing instrument and, under the terms of the governing instrument, can take effect instead of another beneficiary designation on the happening of one or more events, including survival of the decedent or failure to survive the decedent, whether an event is expressed in condition-precedent, condition-subsequent, or any other form.

(2) "Beneficiary" means the beneficiary of a beneficiary designation under which the beneficiary must survive the decedent and includes (i) a class member if the beneficiary designation is in the form of a class gift and (ii) an individual or class member who was deceased at the time the beneficiary designation was executed as well as an individual or class member who was then living but who failed to survive the decedent but excludes a joint tenant of a joint tenancy with the right of survivorship and a party to a joint and survivorship account.

(3) "Beneficiary designation" includes an alternative beneficiary designation and a beneficiary designation in the form of a class gift.

(4) "Class member" includes an individual who fails to survive the decedent but who would have taken under a beneficiary designation in the form of a class gift had he [or she] survived the decedent.

(5) "Stepchild" means a child of the decedent's surviving, deceased, or former spouse, and not of the decedent.

(6) "Surviving beneficiary" or "surviving descendant" means a beneficiary or a descendant who neither predeceased the decedent nor is deemed to have predeceased the decedent under Section 2–702.

(b) [Substitute Gift.] If a beneficiary fails to survive the decedent and is a grandparent, a descendant of a grandparent, or a stepchild of the decedent, the following apply:

(1) Except as provided in paragraph (4), if the beneficiary designation is not in the form of a class gift and the deceased beneficiary leaves surviving descendants, a substitute gift is created in the beneficiary's surviving descendants. They take by representation the property to which the beneficiary would have been entitled had the beneficiary survived the decedent.

(2) Except as provided in paragraph (4), if the beneficiary designation is in the form of a class gift, other than a beneficiary designation to "issue," "descendants," "heirs of the body," "heirs," "next of kin," "relatives," or "family," or a class described by language of similar import, a substitute gift is created in the surviving descendants of any deceased beneficiary. The property to which the beneficiaries would have been entitled had all of them survived the decedent passes to the surviving beneficiaries and the surviving descendants of the deceased beneficiaries. Each surviving beneficiary takes the share to which he [or she] would have been entitled had the

deceased beneficiaries survived the decedent.   Each deceased beneficiary's surviving descendants who are substituted for the deceased beneficiary take by representation the share to which the deceased beneficiary would have been entitled had the deceased beneficiary survived the decedent.   For the purposes of this paragraph, "deceased beneficiary" means a class member who failed to survive the decedent and left one or more surviving descendants.

(3) For the purposes of Section 2–701, words of survivorship, such as in a beneficiary designation to an individual "if he survives me," or in a beneficiary designation to "my surviving children," are not, in the absence of additional evidence, a sufficient indication of an intent contrary to the application of this section.

(4) If a governing instrument creates an alternative beneficiary designation with respect to a beneficiary designation for which a substitute gift is created by paragraph (1) or (2), the substitute gift is superseded by the alternative beneficiary designation only if an expressly designated beneficiary of the alternative beneficiary designation is entitled to take.

(c) [More Than One Substitute Gift; Which One Takes.] If, under subsection (b), substitute gifts are created and not superseded with respect to more than one beneficiary designation and the beneficiary designations are alternative beneficiary designations, one to the other, the determination of which of the substitute gifts takes effect is resolved as follows:

(1) Except as provided in paragraph (2), the property passes under the primary substitute gift.

(2) If there is a younger-generation beneficiary designation, the property passes under the younger-generation substitute gift and not under the primary substitute gift.

(3) In this subsection:

(i) "Primary beneficiary designation" means the beneficiary designation that would have taken effect had all the deceased beneficiaries of the alternative beneficiary designations who left surviving descendants survived the decedent.

(ii) "Primary substitute gift" means the substitute gift created with respect to the primary beneficiary designation.

(iii) "Younger-generation beneficiary designation" means a beneficiary designation that (A) is to a descendant of a beneficiary of the primary beneficiary designation, (B) is an alternative beneficiary designation with respect to the primary beneficiary designation, (C) is a beneficiary designation for which a substitute gift is created, and (D) would have taken effect had all the deceased beneficiaries who left surviving descendants survived the decedent except the deceased beneficiary or beneficiaries of the primary beneficiary designation.

(iv) "Younger-generation substitute gift" means the substitute gift created with respect to the younger-generation beneficiary designation.

(d) [Protection of Payors.]

(1) A payor is protected from liability in making payments under the terms of the beneficiary designation until the payor has received written notice of a claim to a substitute gift under this section. Payment made before the receipt of written notice of a claim to a substitute gift under this section discharges the payor, but not the recipient, from all claims for the amounts paid. A payor is liable for a payment made after the payor has received written notice of the claim. A recipient is liable for a payment received, whether or not written notice of the claim is given.

(2) The written notice of the claim must be mailed to the payor's main office or home by registered or certified mail, return receipt requested, or served upon the payor in the same manner as a summons in a civil action. Upon receipt of written notice of the claim, a payor may pay any amount owed by it to the court having jurisdiction of the probate proceedings relating to the decedent's estate or, if no proceedings have been commenced, to the court having jurisdiction of probate proceedings relating to decedents' estates located in the county of the decedent's residence. The court shall hold the funds and, upon its determination under this section, shall order disbursement in accordance with the determination. Payment made to the court discharges the payor from all claims for the amounts paid.

(e) [Protection of Bona Fide Purchasers; Personal Liability of Recipient.]

(1) A person who purchases property for value and without notice, or who receives a payment or other item of property in partial or full satisfaction of a legally enforceable obligation, is neither obligated under this section to return the payment, item of property, or benefit nor is liable under this section for the amount of the payment or the value of the item of property or benefit. But a person who, not for value, receives a payment, item of property, or any other benefit to which the person is not

entitled under this section is obligated to return the payment, item of property, or benefit, or is personally liable for the amount of the payment or the value of the item of property or benefit, to the person who is entitled to it under this section.

(2) If this section or any part of this section is preempted by federal law with respect to a payment, an item of property, or any other benefit covered by this section, a person who, not for value, receives the payment, item of property, or any other benefit to which the person is not entitled under this section is obligated to return the payment, item of property, or benefit, or is personally liable for the amount of the payment or the value of the item of property or benefit, to the person who would have been entitled to it were this section or part of this section not preempted.

COMMENT

Purpose of New Section. This new section provides an antilapse statute for "beneficiary designations" under which the beneficiary must survive the decedent. The term "beneficiary designation" is defined in Section 1–201 as "a governing instrument naming a beneficiary of an insurance or annuity policy, of an account with POD designation, of a security registered in beneficiary form (TOD), or of a pension, profit-sharing, retirement, or similar benefit plan, or other nonprobate transfer at death." Technical amendments in 1993 added language specifically excluding joint and survivorship accounts and joint tenancies with the right of survivorship; this amendment is consistent with the original purpose of the section.

The terms of this section parallel those of Section 2–603, except that the provisions relating to payor protection and personal liability of recipients have been added. The Comment to Section 2–603 contains an elaborate exposition of Section 2–603, together with the examples illustrating its application. That Comment, in addition to the examples given below, should aid understanding of Section 2–706. For a discussion of the reasons why Section 2–706 should not be preempted by federal law with respect to retirement plans covered by ERISA, see the Comment to Section 2–804.

Example 1. G is the owner of a life-insurance policy. When the policy was taken out, G was married to S; G and S had two young children, A and B. G died 45 years after the policy was taken out. S predeceased G. A survived G by 120 hours, and B predeceased G leaving three children (X, Y, and Z) who survived G by 120 hours. G's policy names S as the primary beneficiary of the policy, but because S predeceased G, the secondary (contingent) beneficiary designation became operative. The secondary (contingent) beneficiary designation of G's policy states: "equally to the then living children born of the marriage of G and S."

161

The printed terms of G's policy provide:

> If two or more persons are designated as beneficiary, the beneficiary will be the designated person or persons who survive the Insured, and if more than one survive, they will share equally.

Solution: The printed clause constitutes an "alternative beneficiary designation" for purposes of subsection (b)(4), which supersedes the substitute gift to B's descendants created by subsection (b)(2). A is entitled to all of the proceeds of the policy.

Example 2. The facts are the same as in Example 1, except that G's policy names "A and B" as secondary (contingent) beneficiaries. The printed terms of the policy provide:

> If any designated Beneficiary predeceases the Insured, the interest of such Beneficiary will terminate and shall be shared equally by such of the Beneficiaries as survive the Insured.

Solution: The printed clause constitutes an "alternative beneficiary designation" for purposes of subsection (b)(4), which supersedes the substitute gift to B's descendants created by subsection (b)(1). A is entitled to all of the proceeds of the policy.

Example 3. The facts are the same as Examples 1 or 2, except that the printed terms of the policy do not contain either quoted clause or a similar one.

Solution: Under Section 2-706, A would be entitled to half of the policy proceeds and X, Y,

and Z would divide the other half equally.

Example 4. The facts are the same as Example 3, except that the policy has a beneficiary designation that provides that, if the adjacent box is checked, the share of any deceased beneficiary shall be paid "in one sum and in equal shares to the children of that beneficiary who survive." G did *not* check the box adjacent to this option.

Solution: G's deliberate decision not to check the box providing for the share of any deceased beneficiary to go to that beneficiary's children constitutes a clear indication of a contrary intention for purposes of Section 2-701. A would be entitled to all of the proceeds of the policy.

Example 5. G's life-insurance policy names her niece, A, as primary beneficiary, and provides that if A does not survive her, the proceeds are to go to her niece B, as contingent beneficiary. A predeceased G, leaving children who survived G by 120 hours. B survived G by 120 hours.

Solution: The contingent beneficiary designation constitutes an "alternative beneficiary designation" for purposes of subsection (b)(4), which supersedes the substitute gift to A's descendants created by subsection (b)(1). The proceeds go to B, not to A's children.

Example 6. G's life-insurance policy names her niece, A, as primary beneficiary, and provides that if A does not survive her, the proceeds are to go to her niece B, as contingent beneficiary. The printed terms of the policy specifically state that if neither the primary nor secondary beneficiaries survive the policyholder, the proceeds are payable to the policyholder's estate. A predeceased G, leaving children who survived G by 120 hours. B also predeceased G, leaving children who survived G by 120 hours.

Solution: The second contingent beneficiary designation to G's estate constitutes an "alternative beneficiary designation" for purposes of subsection (b)(4),

which supersedes the substitute gifts to A's and B's descendants created by subsection (b)(1). The proceeds go to G's estate, not to A's children or to B's children.

Reference. This section is discussed in Halbach & Waggoner, "The UPC's New Survivorship and Antilapse Provisions," 55 Alb. L. Rev. 1091 (1992).

Historical Note. This Comment was revised in 1993. For the prior version, see 8 U.L.A. 146 (Supp. 1992).

Section 2–707. Survivorship With Respect to Future Interests Under Terms of a Trust; Substitute Takers.

(a) [Definitions.] In this section:

(1) "Alternative future interest" means an expressly created future interest that can take effect in possession or enjoyment instead of another future interest on the happening of one or more events, including survival of an event or failure to survive an event, whether an event is expressed in condition-precedent, condition-subsequent, or any other form. A residuary clause in a will does not create an alternative future interest with respect to a future interest created in a nonresiduary devise in the will, whether or not the will specifically provides that lapsed or failed devises are to pass under the residuary clause.

(2) "Beneficiary" means the beneficiary of a future interest and includes a class member if the future interest is in the form of a class gift.

(3) "Class member" includes an individual who fails to survive the distribution date but who would have taken under a future interest in the form of a class gift had he [or she] survived the distribution date.

(4) "Distribution date," with respect to a future interest, means the time when the future interest is to take effect in

163

possession or enjoyment. The distribution date need not occur at the beginning or end of a calendar day, but can occur at a time during the course of a day.

(5) "Future interest" includes an alternative future interest and a future interest in the form of a class gift.

(6) "Future interest under the terms of a trust" means a future interest that was created by a transfer creating a trust or to an existing trust or by an exercise of a power of appointment to an existing trust, directing the continuance of an existing trust, designating a beneficiary of an existing trust, or creating a trust.

(7) "Surviving beneficiary" or "surviving descendant" means a beneficiary or a descendant who neither predeceased the distribution date nor is deemed to have predeceased the distribution date under Section 2–702.

(b) [Survivorship Required; Substitute Gift.] A future interest under the terms of a trust is contingent on the beneficiary's surviving the distribution date. If a beneficiary of a future interest under the terms of a trust fails to survive the distribution date, the following apply:

(1) Except as provided in paragraph (4), if the future interest is not in the form of a class gift and the deceased beneficiary leaves surviving descendants, a substitute gift is created in the beneficiary's surviving descendants. They take by representation the property to which the beneficiary would have been entitled had the beneficiary survived the distribution date.

(2) Except as provided in paragraph (4), if the future interest is in the form of a class gift, other than a future interest to "issue," "descendants," "heirs of the body," "heirs," "next of kin," "relatives," or "family," or a class described by language of similar import, a substitute gift is created in the surviving descendants of any deceased beneficiary. The property to which the beneficiaries would have been entitled had all of them survived the distribution date passes to the surviving beneficiaries and the surviving descendants of the deceased beneficiaries. Each surviving beneficiary takes the share to which he [or she] would have been entitled had the deceased beneficiaries survived the distribution date. Each deceased beneficiary's surviving descendants who are substituted for the deceased beneficiary take by representation the share to which the deceased beneficiary would have been entitled had the deceased beneficiary survived the distribution date. For the purposes of this paragraph, "deceased beneficiary" means a class member who failed

to survive the distribution date and left one or more surviving descendants.

(3) For the purposes of Section 2–701, words of survivorship attached to a future interest are not, in the absence of additional evidence, a sufficient indication of an intent contrary to the application of this section. Words of survivorship include words of survivorship that relate to the distribution date or to an earlier or an unspecified time, whether those words of survivorship are expressed in condition-precedent, condition-subsequent, or any other form.

(4) If a governing instrument creates an alternative future interest with respect to a future interest for which a substitute gift is created by paragraph (1) or (2), the substitute gift is superseded by the alternative future interest only if an expressly designated beneficiary of the alternative future interest is entitled to take in possession or enjoyment.

(c) [More Than One Substitute Gift; Which One Takes.] If, under subsection (b), substitute gifts are created and not superseded with respect to more than one future interest and the future interests are alternative future interests, one to the other, the determination of which of the substitute gifts takes effect is resolved as follows:

(1) Except as provided in paragraph (2), the property passes under the primary substitute gift.

(2) If there is a younger-generation future interest, the property passes under the younger-generation substitute gift and not under the primary substitute gift.

(3) In this subsection:

(i) "Primary future interest" means the future interest that would have taken effect had all the deceased beneficiaries of the alternative future interests who left surviving descendants survived the distribution date.

(ii) "Primary substitute gift" means the substitute gift created with respect to the primary future interest.

(iii) "Younger-generation future interest" means a future interest that (A) is to a descendant of a beneficiary of the primary future interest, (B) is an alternative future interest with respect to the primary future interest, (C) is a future interest for which a substitute gift is created, and (D) would have taken effect had all the deceased beneficiaries who left surviving descendants survived the distribution date except

165

the deceased beneficiary or beneficiaries of the primary future interest.

    (iv) "Younger-generation substitute gift" means the substitute gift created with respect to the younger-generation future interest.

(d) [If No Other Takers, Property Passes Under Residuary Clause or to Transferor's Heirs.] Except as provided in subsection (e), if, after the application of subsections (b) and (c), there is no surviving taker, the property passes in the following order:

    (1) if the trust was created in a nonresiduary devise in the transferor's will or in a codicil to the transferor's will, the property passes under the residuary clause in the transferor's will; for purposes of this section, the residuary clause is treated as creating a future interest under the terms of a trust.

    (2) if no taker is produced by the application of paragraph (1), the property passes to the transferor's heirs under Section 2-711.

(e) [If No Other Takers and If Future Interest Created by Exercise of Power of Appointment.] If, after the application of subsections (b) and (c), there is no surviving taker and if the future interest was created by the exercise of a power of appointment:

    (1) the property passes under the donor's gift-in-default clause, if any, which clause is treated as creating a future interest under the terms of a trust; and

    (2) if no taker is produced by the application of paragraph (1), the property passes as provided in subsection (d). For purposes of subsection (d), "transferor" means the donor if the power was a nongeneral power and means the donee if the power was a general power.

COMMENT

Rationale of New Section. This new section applies only to future interests under the terms of a trust. For shorthand purposes, references in this Comment to the term "future interest" refer to a future interest under the terms of a trust.

The objective of this section is to project the antilapse idea into the area of future interests. The structure of this section substantially parallels the structure of the regular antilapse statute, Section 2-603, and the antilapse-type statute relating to beneficiary designations, Section 2-706. The rationale for restricting this section to future interests under the terms of a trust is that legal life estates in land, followed by indefeasibly vested remainder interests, are still created in some localities, often with respect to farmland. In such cases, the legal life tenant and the person holding the remainder interest can, together, give good title in the sale of the land. If the antilapse idea were injected into this type of situation, the ability of the parties to sell the land would be impaired if not destroyed because the antilapse idea would, in effect, create a contingent substitute remainder interest in the present and future descendants of the person holding the remainder interest.

Background. At common law, conditions of survivorship are not implied with respect to *future* interests (whether in trust or otherwise). For example, in the simple case of a trust, "income to husband, A, for life, remainder to daughter, B," B's interest is not defeated at common law if she predeceases A; B's interest would pass through her estate to her successors in interest (probably either her residuary legatees or heirs), who would become entitled to possession when A died. If any of B's successors in interest died before A, the interest held by that deceased successor in interest would likewise pass through his or her estate to his or her successors in interest; and so on.

The rationale for adopting a statutory provision reversing the common-law rule is to prevent cumbersome and costly distributions to and through the estates of deceased beneficiaries of future interests, who may have died long before the distribution date.

Subsection (b): Subsection (b) imposes a condition of survivorship on

future interests to the distribution date—defined as the time when the future interest is to take effect in possession or enjoyment.

The 120–hour Survivorship Period. In effect, the requirement of survival of the distribution date means survival of the 120–hour period following the distribution date. This is because, under Section 2–702(a), "an individual who is not established to have survived an event . . . by 120 hours is deemed to have predeceased the event." As made clear by subsection (a)(7), for the purposes of section 2–707, the "event" to which section 2–702(a) relates is the distribution date.

Note that the "distribution date" need not occur at the beginning or end of a calendar day, but can occur at a time during the course of a day, such as the time of death of an income beneficiary.

References in Section 2–707 and in this Comment to survival of the distribution date should be understood as referring to survival of the distribution date by 120 hours.

Ambiguous Survivorship Language. Subsection (b) serves another purpose. It resolves a frequently litigated question arising from ambiguous language of survivorship, such as in a trust, "income to A for life, remainder in corpus to my surviving children." Although some case law interprets the word "surviving" as merely requiring survival of the testator (e.g., Nass' Estate, 182 A. 401 (Pa.1936)), the predominant position at common law interprets "surviving" as requiring survival of the life tenant, A. Hawke v. Lodge, 77 A. 1090 (Del. Ch.1910); Restatement of Property § 251 (1940). The first sentence of subsection (b), in conjunction with paragraph (3), codifies the predominant common-law/Restatement position that survival relates to the distribution date.

The first sentence of subsection (b), in combination with paragraph (3), imposes a condition of survivorship to the distribution date (the time of possession or enjoyment) even when an express condition of survivorship to an earlier time has been imposed. Thus, in a trust like "income to A for life, remainder in corpus to B, but if B predeceases A, to B's children who survive B," the first sentence of subsection (b) combined with paragraph (3) requires B's children to survive (by 120 hours) the death of the income beneficiary, A.

Rule of Construction. Note that Section 2–707 is a rule of construction. It is qualified by the rule set forth in Section 2–701, and thus it yields to a finding of a contrary intention. Consequently, in trusts like "income to A for life, remainder in corpus to B whether or not B survives A," or "income to A for life, remainder in corpus to B or B's estate," this section would not apply and, should B predecease A, B's future interest would pass through B's estate to B's successors in interest, who would become entitled to possession or enjoyment at A's death.

Classification. Subsection (b) renders a future interest "contingent" on the beneficiary's survival of the distribution date. As a result, future interests are "nonvested" and subject to the Rule Against Perpetuities. To prevent an injustice from resulting because of this, the Uniform Statutory Rule Against Perpetuities, which has a wait-and-see el-

ement, is incorporated into the Code as Part 9.

Substitute Gifts. Section 2–707 not only imposes a condition of survivorship to the distribution date; like its antilapse counterparts, Sections 2–603 and 2–706, it provides substitute takers in cases of a beneficiary's failure to survive the distribution date.

The statutory substitute gift is divided among the devisee's descendants "by representation," a term defined in Section 2–709(b).

Subsection (b)(1)—Future Interests Not in the Form of a Class Gift: Subsection (b)(1) applies to non-class gifts, such as the "income to A for life, remainder in corpus to B" trust discussed above. If B predeceases A, subsection (b)(1) creates a substitute gift with respect to B's future interest; the substitute gift is to B's descendants who survive A.

Subsection (b)(2)—Class Gift Future Interests. Subsection (b)(2) applies to class gifts, such as in a trust "income to A for life, remainder in corpus to A's children." Suppose that A had two children, X and Y. X predeceases A; Y survives A. Subsection (b)(2) creates a substitute gift with respect to any of A's children who predecease A leaving descendants who survive A. Thus, if X left descendants who survived A, X's descendants would take X's share; if X left no descendants living at A's death, Y would take it all.

Subsection (b)(2) does not apply to future interests to classes such as "issue," "descendants," "heirs of the body," "heirs," "next of kin," "distributees," "relatives," "family," or the like. The reason is that these types of class gifts have their own internal systems of representation, and so the substitute gift provided by subsection (b)(1) would be out of place with respect to these types of future interests. The first sentence of subsection (a) and subsection (d) do apply, however. For example, suppose a nonresiduary devise "to A for life, remainder to A's issue, by representation." If A leaves issue surviving him, they take. But if A leaves no issue surviving him, the testator's residuary devisees are the takers.

Subsection (b)(4). Subsection (b)(4) provides that, if a governing instrument creates an alternative future interest with respect to a future interest for which a substitute gift is created by paragraph (1) or (2), the substitute gift is superseded by the alternative future interest only if an expressly designated beneficiary of the alternative future interest is entitled to take in possession or enjoyment. Consider, for example, a trust under the income is to be paid to A for life, remainder in corpus to B if B survives A, but if not to C if C survives A. If B predeceases A, leaving descendants who survive A, subsection (b)(1) creates a substitute gift to B's descendants. But, if C survives A, the alternative future interest in C supersedes the substitute gift to B's descendants. Upon A's death, the trust corpus passes to C.

Subsection (c). Subsection (c) is necessary because there can be cases in which subsections (b)(1) or (b)(2) create substitute gifts with respect to two or more alternative future interests, and those substitute gifts are not superseded under the terms of subsection (b)(4). Subsection (c) provides the tie-breaking mechanism for such situations.

The initial step is to determine which of the alternative future interests would take effect had all the beneficiaries themselves survived the distribution date (by 120 hours). In subsection (c), this future interest is called the "primary future interest." Unless subsection (c)(2) applies, subsection (c)(1) provides that the property passes under substitute gift created with respect to the primary future interest. This substitute gift is called the "primary substitute gift." Thus, the property goes to the descendants of the beneficiary or beneficiaries of the primary future interest.

Subsection (c)(2) provides an exception to this rule. Under subsection (c)(2), the property does not pass under the primary substitute gift if there is a "younger-generation future interest"—defined as a future interest that (A) is to a descendant of a beneficiary of the primary future interest, (B) is an alternative future interest with respect to the primary future interest, (C) is a future interest for which a substitute gift is created, and (D) would have taken effect had all the deceased beneficiaries who left surviving descendants survived the distribution date except the deceased beneficiary or beneficiaries of the primary future interest. If there is a younger-generation future interest, the property passes under the "younger-generation substitute gift"—defined as the substitute gift created with respect to the younger-generation future interest.

Subsection (d). Since it is possible that, after the application of subsections (b) and (c), there are no substitute gifts, a back-stop set of substitute takers is provided in subsection (d)—the transferor's residuary devisees or heirs. Note that the transferor's residuary clause is treated as creating a future interest and, as such, is subject to this section. Note also that the meaning of the back-stop gift to the transferor's heirs is governed by Section 2–711, under which the gift is to the transferor's heirs determined as if the transferor died when A died. Thus there will always be a set of substitute takers, even if it turns out to be the State. If the transferor's surviving spouse has remarried after the transferor's death but before A's death, he or she would not be a taker under this provision.

Examples. The application of Section 2–707 is illustrated by the following examples. Note that, in each example, the "distribution date" is the time of the income beneficiary's death. Assume, in each example, that an individual who is described as having "survived" the income beneficiary's death survived the income beneficiary's death by 120 hours or more.

Example 1. A nonresiduary devise in G's will created a trust, income to A for life, remainder in corpus to B if B survives A. G devised the residue of her estate to a charity. B predeceased A. At A's death, B's child, X, is living.

Solution: On A's death, the trust property goes to X, not to the charity. Because B's future interest is not in the form of a class gift, subsection (b)(1) applies, not (b)(2). Subsection (b)(1) creates a substitute gift with respect to B's future interest; the substitute gift is to B's child, X. Under subsection (b)(3), the words of survivorship attached to B's future interest

("to B if B survives A") do not indicate an intent contrary to the creation of that substitute gift. Nor, under subsection (b)(4), is that substitute gift superseded by an alternative future interest because, as defined in subsection (a)(1), G's residuary clause does not create an alternative future interest. In the normal lapse situation, a residuary clause does not supersede the substitute gift created by the antilapse statute, and the same analysis applies to this situation as well.

Example 2. Same as Example 1, except that B left no descendants who survived A.

Solution: Subsection (b)(1) does not create a substitute gift with respect to B's future interest because B left no descendants who survived A. This brings subsection (d) into operation, under which the trust property passes to the charity under G's residuary clause.

Example 3. G created an irrevocable inter-vivos trust, income to A for life, remainder in corpus to B if B survives A. B predeceased A. At A's death, G and X, B's child, are living.

Solution: X takes the trust property. Because B's future interest is not in the form of a class gift, subsection (b)(1) applies, not (b)(2). Subsection (b)(1) creates a substitute gift with respect to B's future interest; the substitute gift is to B's child, X. Under subsection (b)(3), the words of survivorship ("to B if B survives A") do not indicate an intent contrary to the creation of that substitute gift. Nor, under subsection (b)(4), is the substitute gift superseded by an alternative future interest; G's reversion is not an alternative future interest as defined in subsection (a)(1) because it was not *expressly* created.

Example 4. G created an irrevocable inter-vivos trust, income to A for life, remainder in corpus to B if B survives A; if not, to C. B predeceased A. At A's death, C and B's child are living.

Solution: C takes the trust property. Because B's future interest is not in the form of a class gift, subsection (b)(1) applies, not (b)(2). Subsection (b)(1) creates a substitute gift with respect to B's future interest; the substitute gift is to B's child, X. Under subsection (b)(3), the words of survivorship ("to B if B survives A") do not indicate an intent contrary to the creation of that substitute gift. But, under subsection (b)(4), the substitute gift to B's child is superseded by the alternative future interest held by C because C, having survived A (by 120 hours), is entitled to take in possession or enjoyment.

Example 5. G created an irrevocable inter-vivos trust, income to A for life, remainder in corpus to B, but if B predeceases A, to the person B appoints by will. B predeceased A. B's will exercised his power of appointment in favor of C. C survives A. B's child, X, also survives A.

Solution: B's appointee, C, takes the trust property, not B's child, X. Because B's future interest is not in the form of a class gift, subsection (b)(1) applies, not (b)(2). Subsection (b)(1) creates a substitute gift with respect to B's future interest; the substitute gift is to B's child, X. Under subsection (b)(3), the words of survivorship ("to B if B survives A") do not indicate an intent contrary to the creation of that substitute gift. But, under subsection (b)(4), the substitute gift to B's child is superseded by the alternative future interest held by C because C, having survived A (by 120 hours), is entitled to take in possession or enjoyment. Because C's future interest was created in "a" governing instrument (B's will), it counts as an "alternative future interest."

Example 6. G creates an irrevocable inter-vivos trust, income to A for life, remainder in corpus to A's children who survive A; if none, to B. A's children predecease A, leaving descendants, X and Y, who survive A. B also survives A.

Solution: On A's death, the trust property goes to B, not to X and Y. Because the future interest in A's children is in the form of a class gift, subsection (b)(2) applies, not (b)(1). Subsection (b)(2) creates a substitute gift with respect to the future interest in A's children; the substitute gift is to the descendants of A's children, X and Y. Under subsection (b)(3), the words of survivorship ("to A's children who survive A") do not indicate an intent contrary to the creation of that substitute gift. But, under subsection (b)(4), the alternative future interest to B supersedes the substitute gift to the descendants of A's children because B survived A.

Alternative Facts: One of A's children, J, survives A; A's other child, K, predeceases A, leaving descendants, X and Y, who survive A. B also survives A.

Solution: J takes half the trust property and X and Y split the other half. Although there is an alternative future interest (in B) and although B did survive A, the alternative future interest was conditioned on none of A's children surviving A. Because that condition was not satisfied, the expressly designated beneficiary of that alternative future interest, B, is not entitled to take in possession or enjoyment. Thus, the alternative future interest in B does not supersede the substitute gift to K's descendants, X and Y.

Example 7. G created an irrevocable inter-vivos trust, income to A for life, remainder in corpus to B if B survives A; if not, to C. B and C predecease A. At A's death, B's child and C's child are living.

Solution: Subsection (b)(1) produces substitute gifts with respect to B's future interest and with respect to C's future interest. B's future interest and C's future interest are alternative future interests, one to the other. B's future interest is expressly conditioned on B's surviving A. C's future interest is conditioned on B's predeceasing A and C's surviving A. The condition that C survive A does not arise from express language in G's trust but from the first sentence of subsection (b); that sentence makes C's future interest contingent on C's surviving A. Thus, because neither B nor C survived A, neither B nor C is entitled to take in possession or enjoyment. So, under subsection (b)(4), neither substitute gift, created with respect to the future interests in B and C, is superseded by an alternative future interest. Consequently, resort must be had to subsection (c) to break the tie to determine which substitute gift takes effect.

Under subsection (c), B is the beneficiary of the "primary future interest" because B would have been entitled to the trust property had both B and C survived A. Unless subsection (c)(2) applies, the trust property passes to B's child as the taker under the "primary substitute gift."

Subsection (c)(2) would only apply if C's future interest qualifies as a "younger-generation future interest." This depends upon whether C is a descendant of B, for C's future interest satisfies the other requirements necessary to make it a younger-generation future interest. If C was a descendant of B, the substitute gift to C's child would be a "younger-generation substitute gift" and would become effective instead of the "primary substitute gift" to B's descendants. But if C was not a descendant of B, the property would pass under the "primary substitute gift" to B's descendants.

Example 8. G created an irrevocable inter-vivos trust, income to A for life, remainder in corpus to A's children who survive A; if none, to B. All of A's children predecease A. X and Y, who are descendants of one or more of A's children, survive A. B predeceases A, leaving descendants, M and N, who survive A.

Solution: On A's death, the trust property passes to X and Y under the "primary substitute gift," unless B was a descendant of any of A's children.

Subsection (b)(2) produces substitute gifts with respect to A's children who predeceased A leaving descendants who survived A. Subsection (b)(1) creates a substitute gift with respect to B's future interest. A's children's future interest and B's future interest are alternative future interests, one to the other. A's children's future interest is expressly conditioned on surviving A. B's future interest is conditioned on none of A's children surviving A and on B's surviving A. The condition of survivorship as to B's future interest does not arise because of express language in G's trust but because of the first sentence of subsection (b); that sentence makes B's future interest contingent on B's surviving A. Thus, because none of A's children survived A, and because B did not survive A, none of A's children nor B is entitled to take in possession or enjoyment. So, under subsection (b)(4), neither substitute gift—i.e., neither the one created with respect to the future interest in A's children nor the one created with respect to the future interest in B—is superseded by an alternative future interest. Consequently, resort must be had to subsection

(c) to break the tie to determine which substitute gift takes effect.

Under subsection (c), A's children are the beneficiaries of the "primary future interest" because they would have been entitled to the trust property had all of them and B survived A. Unless subsection (c)(2) applies, the trust property passes to X and Y as the takers under the "primary substitute gift." Subsection (c)(2) would only apply if B's future interest qualifies as a "younger-generation future interest." This depends upon whether B is a descendant of any of A's children, for B's future interest satisfies the other requirements necessary to make it a "younger-generation future interest." If B was a descendant of one of A's children, the substitute gift to B's children, M and N, would be a "younger-generation substitute gift" and would become effective instead of the "primary substitute gift" to X and Y. But if B was not a descendant of any of A's children, the property would pass under the "primary substitute gift" to X and Y.

Example 9. G's will devised property in trust, income to niece Lilly for life, corpus on Lilly's death to her children; should Lilly die without leaving children, the corpus shall be equally divided among my nephews and nieces then living, the child or children of nieces who may be deceased to take the share their mother would have been entitled to if living.

Lilly never had any children. G had 3 nephews and 2 nieces in addition to Lilly. All 3 nephews and both nieces predeceased Lilly. A child of one of the nephews survived Lilly. One of the nieces had 8 children, 7 of whom survived Lilly. The other niece had one child, who did not survive Lilly. (This example is based on the facts of Bomberger's Estate, 32 A.2d 729 (Pa. 1943).)

Solution: The trust property goes to the 7 children of the nieces who survived Lilly. The substitute gifts created by subsection (b)(2) to the nephew's son or to the nieces' children are superseded under subsection (b)(4) because there is an alternative future interest (the "child or children of nieces who may be deceased") and expressly designated beneficiaries of that alternative future interest (the 7 children of the nieces) are living at Lilly's death and are entitled to take in possession or enjoyment.

Example 10. G devised the residue of his estate in trust, income to his wife, W, for life, remainder in corpus to their children, John and Florence; if either John or Florence should predecease W, leaving descendants, such descendants shall take the share their parent would have taken if living.

G's son, John, survived W. G's daughter, Florence, predeceased W. Florence never had any children. Florence's husband survived W. (This example is based on the facts of Matter of Kroos, 99 N.E.2d 222 (N.Y. 1951).)

Solution: John, of course, takes his half of the trust property. Because Florence left no descendants who survived W, subsection (b)(1) does not create a substitute gift with respect to Florence's future interest in her half. Subsection (d)(1) is inapplicable because G's trust was not created in a nonresiduary devise or in a codicil to G's will. Subsection (d)(2) therefore becomes applicable, under which Florence's half goes to G's heirs determined as if G died when W died, i.e., John. See Section 2-711.

Subsection (e). Subsection (e) was added in 1993 to clarify the passing of the property in cases in which the future interest is created by the exercise of a power of appointment.

Reference. This section is discussed in Halbach & Waggoner, "The UPC's New Survivorship and Antilapse Provisions," 55 Alb. L.Rev. 1091 (1992).

Historical Note. This Comment was revised in 1993. For the prior version, see 8 U.L.A. 148 (Supp. 1992).

Section 2-708. Class Gifts to "Descendants," "Issue," or "Heirs of the Body"; Form of Distribution if None Specified.

If a class gift in favor of "descendants," "issue," or "heirs of the body" does not specify the manner in which the property is to be distributed among the class members, the property is distributed among the class members who are living when the interest is to take effect in possession or enjoyment, in such shares as they would receive, under the applicable law of intestate succession, if the designated ancestor had then died intestate owning the subject matter of the class gift.

COMMENT

Purpose of New Section. This new section tracks Restatement (1st) of Property § 303(1), and does not accept the position taken in Restatement (Second) of Property, Donative Transfers § 28.2 (1988), under which a per stirpes form of distribution is presumed, regardless of the form of distribution used in the applicable law of intestate succession.

Section 2–709. Representation; Per Capita at Each Generation; Per Stirpes.

(a) **[Definitions.]** In this section:

(1) "Deceased child" or "deceased descendant" means a child or a descendant who either predeceased the distribution date or is deemed to have predeceased the distribution date under Section 2–702.

(2) "Distribution date," with respect to an interest, means the time when the interest is to take effect in possession or enjoyment. The distribution date need not occur at the beginning or end of a calendar day, but can occur at a time during the course of a day.

(3) "Surviving ancestor," "surviving child," or "surviving descendant" means an ancestor, a child, or a descendant who neither predeceased the distribution date nor is deemed to have predeceased the distribution date under Section 2–702.

(b) **[Representation; Per Capita at Each Generation.]** If an applicable statute or a governing instrument calls for property to be distributed "by representation" or "per capita at each generation," the property is divided into as many equal shares as there are (i) surviving descendants in the generation nearest to the designated ancestor which contains one or more surviving descendants (ii) and deceased descendants in the same generation who left surviving descendants, if any. Each surviving descendant in the nearest generation is allocated one share. The remaining shares, if any, are combined and then divided in the same manner among the surviving descendants of the deceased descendants as if the surviving descendants who were allocated a share and their surviving descendants had predeceased the distribution date.

175

(c) [Per Stirpes.] If a governing instrument calls for property to be distributed "per stirpes," the property is divided into as many equal shares as there are (i) surviving children of the designated ancestor and (ii) deceased children who left surviving descendants. Each surviving child, if any, is allocated one share. The share of each deceased child with surviving descendants is divided in the same manner, with subdivision repeating at each succeeding generation until the property is fully allocated among surviving descendants.

(d) [Deceased Descendant With No Surviving Descendant Disregarded.] For the purposes of subsections (b) and (c), an individual who is deceased and left no surviving descendant is disregarded, and an individual who leaves a surviving ancestor who is a descendant of the designated ancestor is not entitled to a share.

COMMENT

Purpose of New Section. This new section provides statutory definitions of "representation," "per capita at each generation," and "per stirpes." Subsection (b) applies to both private instruments and to provisions of applicable statutory law (such as Sections 2–603, 2–706, and 2–707) that call for property to be divided "by representation." The system of representation employed is the same as that which is adopted in Section 2–106 for intestate succession.

Subsection (c)'s definition of "per stirpes" accords with the predominant understanding of the term. In 1993, the phrase "if any" was added to subsection (c) to clarify the point that, under per stirpes, the initial division of the estate is made at the children generation even if no child survives the ancestor.

Historical Note. This Comment was revised in 1993. For the prior version, see 8 U.L.A. 154 (Supp. 1992).

Section 2–710. Worthier–Title Doctrine Abolished.

The doctrine of worthier title is abolished as a rule of law and as a rule of construction. Language in a governing instrument describing the beneficiaries of a disposition as the transferor's "heirs," "heirs at law," "next of kin," "distributees," "relatives," or "family," or language of similar import, does not create or presumptively create a reversionary interest in the transferor.

COMMENT

Purpose of New Section. This new section abolishes the doctrine of worthier title as a rule of law and as a rule of construction.

Cross Reference. See Section 2–711 for a rule of construction concerning the meaning of a disposition

to the heirs, etc., of a designated
person.

Section 2–711. Interests in "Heirs" and Like.

If an applicable statute or a governing instrument calls for a
present or future distribution to or creates a present or future
interest in a designated individual's "heirs," "heirs at law," "next
of kin," "relatives," or "family," or language of similar import, the
property passes to those persons, including the state under Section
2–105, and in such shares as would succeed to the designated
individual's intestate estate under the intestate succession law of
the designated individual's domicile if the designated individual
died when the disposition is to take effect in possession or enjoyment. If the designated individual's surviving spouse is living but
is remarried at the time the disposition is to take effect in possession or enjoyment, the surviving spouse is not an heir of the
designated individual.

COMMENT

Purpose of New Section. This new section provides a statutory definition of "heirs," etc., when contained in a dispositive provision or a statute (such as Section 2–707(h)). This section was amended in 1993 to make it applicable to present as well as future interests in favor of heirs and the like. Application of this section to present interests codifies the position of the Restatement (Second) of Property § 29.4 cmts. c & g (1987).

Cross Reference. See Section 2–710, abolishing the doctrine of worthier title.

Historical Note. This Comment was revised in 1993. For the prior version, see 8 U.L.A. 155 (Supp. 1992).

GENERAL PROVISIONS CONCERNING PROBATE AND NONPROBATE TRANSFERS

GENERAL COMMENT

Part 8 contains four general provisions that cut across probate and nonprobate transfers. Section 2–801 incorporates portions of the Uniform Disclaimer of Property Interests Act; these portions replace portions of the narrower Uniform Disclaimer of Transfers By Will, Intestacy or Appointment Act, which had been incorporated into the pre–1990 Code. The broader disclaimer provisions are now appropriate, given the broadened scope of Article II in covering nonprobate as well as probate transfers.

Section 2–802 deals with the effect of divorce and separation on the right to elect against a will, exempt property and allowances, and an intestate share.

Section 2–803 spells out the legal consequence of intentional and felonious killing on the right of the killer to take as heir and under wills and revocable inter-vivos transfers, such as revocable trusts and life-insurance beneficiary designations.

Section 2–804 deals with the consequences of a divorce on the right of the former spouse (and relatives of the former spouse) to take under wills and revocable inter-vivos transfers, such as revocable trusts and life-insurance beneficiary designations.

Application to Pre–Existing Governing Instruments. Under Section 8–101(b), for decedents dying after the effective date of enactment, the provisions of this Code apply to governing instruments executed prior to as well as on or after the effective date of enactment. The Joint Editorial Board for the Uniform Probate Code has issued a statement concerning the constitutionality under the Contracts Clause of this feature of the Code. The statement, titled "Joint Editorial Board Statement Regarding the Constitutionality of Changes in Default Rules as Applied to Pre–Existing Documents," can be found at 17 Am.C.Tr. & Est.Couns. Notes 184 (1991) or can be obtained from the headquarters office of the National Conference of Commissioners on Uniform State Laws, 676 N. St. Clair St., Suite 1700, Chicago, IL 60611, Phone 312/915–0195, FAX 312/915–0187.

Historical Note. This General Comment was revised in 1993. For the prior version, see 8 U.L.A. 156 (Supp.1992).

Section 2–801. Disclaimer of Property Interests.

(a) [**Right to Disclaim Interest in Property.**] A person, or the representative of a person, to whom an interest in or with respect to property or an interest therein devolves by whatever means may disclaim it in whole or in part by delivering or filing a written disclaimer under this section. The right to disclaim exists notwithstanding (i) any limitation on the interest of the disclaimant in the nature of a spendthrift provision or similar restriction or (ii) any restriction or limitation on the right to disclaim contained in the governing instrument. For purposes of this subsection, the "representative of a person" includes a personal representative of a decedent, a conservator of a disabled person, a guardian of a minor or incapacitated person, and an agent acting on behalf of the person within the authority of a power of attorney.

(b) [Time of Disclaimer.] The following rules govern the time when a disclaimer must be filed or delivered:

(1) If the property or interest has devolved to the disclaimant under a testamentary instrument or by the laws of intestacy, the disclaimer must be filed, if of a present interest, not later than [nine] months after the death of the deceased owner or deceased donee of a power of appointment and, if of a future interest, not later than [nine] months after the event determining that the taker of the property or interest is finally ascertained and his [or her] interest is indefeasibly vested. The disclaimer must be filed in the [probate] court of the county in which proceedings for the administration of the estate of the deceased owner or deceased donee of the power have been commenced. A copy of the disclaimer must be delivered in person or mailed by registered or certified mail, return receipt requested, to any personal representative or other fiduciary of the decedent or donee of the power.

(2) If a property or interest has devolved to the disclaimant under a nontestamentary instrument or contract, the disclaimer must be delivered or filed, if of a present interest, not later than [nine] months after the effective date of the nontestamentary instrument or contract and, if of a future interest, not later than [nine] months after the event determining that the taker of the property or interest is finally ascertained and his [or her] interest is indefeasibly vested. If the person entitled to disclaim does not know of the existence of the interest, the disclaimer must be delivered or filed not later than [nine] months after the person learns of the existence of the interest. The effective date of a revocable instrument or contract is the date on which the maker no longer has power to revoke it or to transfer to himself [or herself] or another the entire legal and equitable ownership of the interest. The disclaimer or a copy thereof must be delivered in person or mailed by registered or certified mail,

179

return receipt requested, to the person who has legal title to or possession of the interest disclaimed.

(3) A surviving joint tenant [or tenant by the entireties] may disclaim as a separate interest any property or interest therein devolving to him [or her] by right of survivorship. A surviving joint tenant [or tenant by the entireties] may disclaim the entire interest in any property or interest therein that is the subject of a joint tenancy [or tenancy by the entireties] devolving to him [or her], if the joint tenancy [or tenancy by the entireties] was created by act of a deceased joint tenant [or tenant by the entireties], the survivor did not join in creating the joint tenancy [or tenancy by the entireties], and has not accepted a benefit under it.

(4) If real property or an interest therein is disclaimed, a copy of the disclaimer may be recorded in the office of the [Recorder of Deeds] of the county in which the property or interest disclaimed is located.*

(c) [Form of Disclaimer.] The disclaimer must (i) describe the property or interest disclaimed, (ii) declare the disclaimer and extent thereof, and (iii) be signed by the disclaimant.

(d) [Effect of Disclaimer.] The effects of a disclaimer are:

(1) If property or an interest therein devolves to a disclaimant under a testamentary instrument, under a power of appointment exercised by a testamentary instrument, or under the laws of intestacy, and the decedent has not provided for another disposition of that interest, should it be disclaimed, or of disclaimed or failed interests in general, the disclaimed interest devolves as if the disclaimant had predeceased the decedent, but if by law or under the testamentary instrument the descendants of the disclaimant would share in the disclaimed interest by representation or otherwise were the disclaimant to predecease the decedent, then the disclaimed interest passes by representation, or passes as directed by the governing instrument, to the descendants of the disclaimant who survive the decedent. A future interest that takes effect in possession or enjoyment after the termination of the estate or interest disclaimed takes effect as if the disclaimant had predeceased the decedent. A disclaimer relates back for all purposes to the date of death of the decedent.

(2) If property or an interest therein devolves to a disclaimant under a nontestamentary instrument or contract and the

---

* If Torrens system is in effect, add provisions to comply with local law.

instrument or contract does not provide for another disposition of that interest, should it be disclaimed, or of disclaimed or failed interests in general, the disclaimed interest devolves as if the disclaimant had predeceased the effective date of the instrument or contract, but if by law or under the nontestamentary instrument or contract the descendants of the disclaimant would share in the disclaimed interest by representation or otherwise were the disclaimant to predecease the effective date of the instrument, then the disclaimed interest passes by representation, or passes as directed by the governing instrument, to the descendants of the disclaimant who survive the effective date of the instrument. A disclaimer relates back for all purposes to that date. A future interest that takes effect in possession or enjoyment at or after the termination of the disclaimed interest takes effect as if the disclaimant had died before the effective date of the instrument or contract that transferred the disclaimed interest.

(3) The disclaimer or the written waiver of the right to disclaim is binding upon the disclaimant or person waiving and all persons claiming through or under either of them.

(e) [Waiver and Bar.] The right to disclaim property or an interest therein is barred by (i) an assignment, conveyance, encumbrance, pledge, or transfer of the property or interest, or a contract therefor, (ii) a written waiver of the right to disclaim, (iii) an acceptance of the property or interest or a benefit under it, or (iv) a sale of the property or interest under judicial sale made before the disclaimer is made.

(f) [Remedy Not Exclusive.] This section does not abridge the right of a person to waive, release, disclaim, or renounce property or an interest therein under any other statute.

(g) [Application.] An interest in property that exists on the effective date of this section as to which, if a present interest, the time for filing a disclaimer under this section has not expired or, if a future interest, the interest has not become indefeasibly vested or the taker finally ascertained, may be disclaimed within [nine] months after the effective date of this section.

COMMENT

Purpose and Scope of Revisions. This section brings into the Code the Uniform Disclaimer of Property Interests Act, replacing the prior incorporation of the Uniform Disclaimer of Transfers by Will, Intestacy or Appointment Act. The reason for incorporating the broader Act is that the scope of Article II has now been expanded to cover dispositive provisions not contained in wills.

Explanation of Revisions. The Joint Editorial Board believes that this and the other Uniform Disclaimer Acts are in need of revision in several respects and intends to undertake further study of the question.

Subsection (a). Subsection (a) is revised in two respects. First, the right to disclaim is extended to a decedent through his or her personal representative. The Uniform Disclaimer of Property Interests Act does not authorize disclaimers on behalf of a deceased person. Second, the sentence authorizing a disclaimer despite a limitation or restriction in the governing instrument is clarified to leave no doubt that an explicit restriction or limitation on the right to disclaim in the governing instrument is ineffective.

Subsection (d). The third revision clarifies the effect of a disclaimer. The Uniform Disclaimer of Property Interests Act states that "it" shall devolve "as if the disclaimant had predeceased the decedent." Literally interpreted, the word "it" refers to "the disclaimed interest," not to the estate as a whole. (One of the changes above is to make this point unmistakable by replacing "it" with "the disclaimed interest.")

Unfortunately, even though the word "it" refers to the disclaimed interest, not to the estate as a whole, there is still a plausible interpretation of the phrase "the disclaimed interest devolves as if the disclaimant had predeceased the decedent" that does not produce the desired result. The desired result is to prevent an heir, for example, from using a disclaimer to effect a change in the division of an intestate's estate. To illustrate this point, consider the following example:

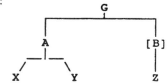

Under these facts, G's intestate estate is divided into two equal parts: A takes half and B's child, Z, takes the other half. Suppose, however, that A files a disclaimer. The desired effect of that disclaimer is to prevent A from affecting the basic division of G's intestate estate by this maneuver. If, however, the disclaimer statute merely provides that the "disclaimed interest" devolves as though the disclaimant (A) had predeceased the decedent, then A's one half interest would *not* pass *only* to X and Y, but to X, Y, *and* Z. To prevent this possible interpretation of that language, the "but if" phrase is added to (d)(1) and (d)(2). This added phrase explicitly provides that A's disclaimed interest passes to A's descendants, if A left any descendants.

Subsection (d)(1) and (2) were amended in 1993 to clarify the effect of a disclaimer in a case in which G, who died intestate, had two children, A and B. A had one child, X; B had two children, Y and Z. B actually predeceased G. A survived G, but disclaimed. The amendments make it clear that X takes A's disclaimed one-half by providing that if "the descendants of the disclaimant would share in the disclaimed interest by representation ... were the disclaimant to predecease the decedent ..., then the disclaimed interest passes by representation ... to the descendants of the disclaimant who survive the decedent...." In this case, were A actually to have predeceased G, A's descendants would share in the disclaimed interest under the representation system employed in the Code, but would not "take" all of the disclaimed interest. The amendments clarify the point that the fact that X would share in the disclaimed interest is enough to give that disclaimed interest to X as a result of A's disclaimer.

Time Allowed for Filing Disclaimer. It should be noted that there may be a discrepancy between the time allowed for filing a disclaimer under this section (and under the freestanding Uniform Acts) and the time allowed for filing a qualified disclaimer under the Internal Revenue Code § 2518. Lawyers are cautioned to check both the state and federal disclaimer statutes before advising clients, especially with respect to disclaimers of future interests.

Historical Note. This Comment was revised in 1993. For the prior version, see 8 U.L.A. 158 (Supp. 1992).

Section 2–802. Effect of Divorce, Annulment, and Decree of Separation.

(a) An individual who is divorced from the decedent or whose marriage to the decedent has been annulled is not a surviving spouse unless, by virtue of a subsequent marriage, he [or she] is married to the decedent at the time of death. A decree of separation that does not terminate the status of husband and wife is not a divorce for purposes of this section.

(b) For purposes of Parts 1, 2, 3, and 4 of this Article, and of Section 3–203, a surviving spouse does not include:

(1) an individual who obtains or consents to a final decree or judgment of divorce from the decedent or an annulment of their marriage, which decree or judgment is not recognized as valid in this State, unless subsequently they participate in a marriage ceremony purporting to marry each to the other or live together as husband and wife;

(2) an individual who, following an invalid decree or judgment of divorce or annulment obtained by the decedent, participates in a marriage ceremony with a third individual; or

(3) an individual who was a party to a valid proceeding concluded by an order purporting to terminate all marital property rights.

COMMENT

Clarifying Revision. The only substantive revision of this section is a clarifying revision of subsection (b)(2), making it clear that this subsection refers to an *invalid* decree of divorce or annulment.

Rationale. Although some existing statutes bar the surviving spouse for desertion or adultery, the present section requires some definitive legal act to bar the surviving spouse. Normally, this is divorce. Subsection (a) states an obvious proposition, but subsection (b) deals with the difficult problem of invalid divorce or annulment, which is particularly frequent as to foreign divorce decrees but may arise as to a local decree where there is some defect in jurisdiction; the basic principle underlying these provisions is estoppel against the surviving spouse. Where there is only a legal separation, rather than a divorce, succession patterns are not affected; but if the separation is accompanied by a complete property settlement, this may operate under Section 2–213 as a waiver or renunciation of benefits under a prior will and by intestate succession.

Cross Reference. See Section 2–804 for similar provisions relating to the effect of divorce to revoke devises and other revocable provisions to a former spouse.

Historical Note. This Comment was revised in 1993. For the prior version, see 8 U.L.A. 159 (Supp. 1992).

Section 2–803. Effect of Homicide on Intestate Succession, Wills, Trusts, Joint Assets, Life Insurance, and Beneficiary Designations.

(a) [Definitions.] In this section:

(1) "Disposition or appointment of property" includes a transfer of an item of property or any other benefit to a beneficiary designated in a governing instrument.

(2) "Governing instrument" means a governing instrument executed by the decedent.

(3) "Revocable," with respect to a disposition, appointment, provision, or nomination, means one under which the decedent, at the time of or immediately before death, was alone empowered, by law or under the governing instrument, to cancel the designation in favor of the killer, whether or not the decedent was then empowered to designate himself [or herself] in place of his [or her] killer and whether or not the decedent then had capacity to exercise the power.

(b) [Forfeiture of Statutory Benefits.] An individual who feloniously and intentionally kills the decedent forfeits all benefits under this Article with respect to the decedent's estate, including an intestate share, an elective share, an omitted spouse's or child's share, a homestead allowance, exempt property, and a family allowance. If the decedent died intestate, the decedent's intestate estate passes as if the killer disclaimed his [or her] intestate share.

(c) [Revocation of Benefits Under Governing Instruments.] The felonious and intentional killing of the decedent:

(1) revokes any revocable (i) disposition or appointment of property made by the decedent to the killer in a governing instrument, (ii) provision in a governing instrument conferring a general or nongeneral power of appointment on the killer, and (iii) nomination of the killer in a governing instrument, nominating or appointing the killer to serve in any fiduciary or representative capacity, including a personal representative, executor, trustee, or agent; and

(2) severs the interests of the decedent and killer in property held by them at the time of the killing as joint tenants with the right of survivorship [or as community property with the right of survivorship], transforming the interests of the decedent and killer into tenancies in common.

(d) [Effect of Severance.] A severance under subsection (c)(2) does not affect any third-party interest in property acquired for value and in good faith reliance on an apparent title by survivorship in the killer unless a writing declaring the severance has been noted, registered, filed, or recorded in records appropriate to the kind and location of the property which are relied upon, in the ordinary course of transactions involving such property, as evidence of ownership.

(e) [Effect of Revocation.] Provisions of a governing instrument are given effect as if the killer disclaimed all provisions revoked by this section or, in the case of a revoked nomination in a fiduciary or representative capacity, as if the killer predeceased the decedent.

(f) [Wrongful Acquisition of Property.] A wrongful acquisition of property or interest by a killer not covered by this section must be treated in accordance with the principle that a killer cannot profit from his [or her] wrong.

(g) [Felonious and Intentional Killing; How Determined.] After all right to appeal has been exhausted, a judgment of conviction establishing criminal accountability for the felonious and intentional killing of the decedent conclusively establishes the convicted individual as the decedent's killer for purposes of this section. In the absence of a conviction, the court, upon the petition of an interested person, must determine whether, under the preponderance of evidence standard, the individual would be found criminally accountable for the felonious and intentional killing of the decedent. If the court determines that, under that standard, the individual would be found criminally accountable for the felonious and intentional killing of the decedent, the determination conclusively establishes that individual as the decedent's killer for purposes of this section.

(h) [Protection of Payors and Other Third Parties.]

(1) A payor or other third party is not liable for having made a payment or transferred an item of property or any other benefit to a beneficiary designated in a governing instrument affected by an intentional and felonious killing, or for having taken any other action in good faith reliance on the validity of the governing instrument, upon request and satisfactory proof of the decedent's death, before the payor or other third party received written notice of a claimed forfeiture or revocation under this section. A payor or other third party is liable for a payment made or other action taken after the payor or other third party received written notice of a claimed forfeiture or revocation under this section.

(2) Written notice of a claimed forfeiture or revocation under paragraph (1) must be mailed to the payor's or other third party's main office or home by registered or certified mail, return receipt requested, or served upon the payor or other third party in the same manner as a summons in a civil action. Upon receipt of written notice of a claimed forfeiture or revocation under this section, a payor or other third party may pay any amount owed or transfer or deposit any item of property held by it to or with the court having jurisdiction of the probate proceedings relating to the decedent's estate, or if no proceedings have been commenced, to or with the court having jurisdiction of probate proceedings relating to decedents' estates located in the county of the decedent's residence. The court shall hold the funds or item of property and, upon its determination under this section, shall order disbursement in accordance with the determination. Payments, transfers, or deposits made to or with the court discharge the payor or other third party from all claims for the value of amounts paid to or items of property transferred to or deposited with the court.

(i) [Protection of Bona Fide Purchasers; Personal Liability of Recipient.]

(1) A person who purchases property for value and without notice, or who receives a payment or other item of property in partial or full satisfaction of a legally enforceable obligation, is neither obligated under this section to return the payment, item of property, or benefit nor is liable under this section for the amount of the payment or the value of the item of property or

benefit. But a person who, not for value, receives a payment, item of property, or any other benefit to which the person is not entitled under this section is obligated to return the payment, item of property, or benefit, or is personally liable for the amount of the payment or the value of the item of property or benefit, to the person who is entitled to it under this section.

(2) If this section or any part of this section is preempted by federal law with respect to a payment, an item of property, or any other benefit covered by this section, a person who, not for value, receives the payment, item of property, or any other benefit to which the person is not entitled under this section is obligated to return the payment, item of property, or benefit, or is personally liable for the amount of the payment or the value of the item of property or benefit, to the person who would have been entitled to it were this section or part of this section not preempted.

COMMENT

Purpose and Scope of Revisions. This section is substantially revised. Although the revised version does make a few substantive changes in certain subsidiary rules (such as the treatment of multiple party accounts, etc.), it does not alter the main thrust of the pre–1990 version. The major change is that the revised version is more comprehensive than the pre–1990 version. The structure of the section is also changed so that it substantially parallels the structure of Section 2–804, which deals with the effect of divorce on revocable benefits to the former spouse.

The pre–1990 version of this section was bracketed to indicate that it may be omitted by an enacting state without difficulty. The revised version omits the brackets because the Joint Editorial Board/Article II Drafting Committee believes that uniformity is desirable on the question.

As in the pre–1990 version, this section is confined to felonious and

intentional killing and excludes the accidental manslaughter killing. Subsection (g) leaves no doubt that, for purposes of this section, a killing can be "felonious and intentional," whether or not the killer has actually been convicted in a criminal prosecution. Under subsection (g), after all right to appeal has been exhausted, a judgment of conviction establishing criminal accountability for the felonious and intentional killing of the decedent conclusively establishes the convicted individual as the decedent's killer for purposes of this section. Acquittal, however, does not preclude the acquitted individual from being regarded as the decedent's killer for purposes of this section. This is because different considerations as well as a different burden of proof enter into the finding of criminal accountability in the criminal prosecution. Hence it is possible that the defendant on a murder charge may be found not guilty and acquitted, but if the same person claims as an heir, devisee, or beneficiary of a revocable beneficiary designation, etc. of the decedent, the probate court, upon the petition of an interested person, may find that, under a preponderance of the evidence standard, he or she would be found criminally accountable for the felonious and intentional killing of the decedent and thus be barred under this section from sharing in the affected property. In fact, in many of the cases arising under this section there may be no criminal prosecution because the killer has committed suicide.

It is now well accepted that the matter dealt with is not exclusively criminal in nature but is also a proper matter for probate courts. The concept that a wrongdoer may not profit by his or her own wrong is a civil concept, and the probate court is the proper forum to determine the effect of killing on succession to the decedent's property covered by this section. There are numerous situations where the same conduct gives rise to both criminal and civil consequences. A killing may result in criminal prosecution for murder and civil litigation by the decedent's family under wrongful death statutes. Another analogy exists in the tax field, where a taxpayer may be acquitted of tax fraud in a criminal prosecution but found to have committed the fraud in a civil proceeding.

The phrases "criminal accountability" and "criminally accountable" for the felonious and intentional killing of the decedent not only include criminal accountability as an actor or direct perpetrator, but also as an accomplice or co-conspirator.

Unlike the pre–1990 version, the revised version contains a subsection protecting payors who pay before receiving written notice of a claimed forfeiture or revocation under this section, and imposing personal liability on the recipient or killer.

The pre–1990 version's provision on the severance of joint tenancies and tenancies by the entirety also extended to "joint and multiple party accounts in banks, savings and loan associations, credit unions and other institutions, and any other form of co-ownership with survivorship incidents." Under subsection (c)(2) of the revised version, the severance applies only to "property held by [the decedent and killer] as joint tenants with the right of survivorship [or as community property with the right of survivorship]." The terms "joint tenants with the right of survivorship" and "community property with the right of survivorship" are defined in Section 1–201. That definition includes tenancies by the entirety, but excludes "forms of co-ownership registration in which the underlying ownership of each party is in proportion to that party's contribution." Under subsection (c)(1), any portion of the decedent's contribution to the co-ownership registration running in favor of the killer would be treated as a revocable and revoked disposition.

Subsection (e) was amended in 1993 to make it clear that the anti-lapse statute applies in appropriate cases in which the killer is treated as having disclaimed.

ERISA Preemption of State Law. The Employee Retirement Income Security Act of 1974 (ERISA) federalizes pension and employee benefit law. Section 514(a) of ERISA, 29

U.S.C. § 1144(a), provides that the provisions of Titles I and IV of ERISA "shall supersede any and all State laws insofar as they may now or hereafter relate to any employee benefit plan" governed by ERISA. See the Comment to Section 2–804 for a discussion of the ERISA preemption question.

Cross References. See Section 1–201 for definitions of "beneficiary designated in a governing instrument," "governing instrument," "joint tenants with the right of survivorship," "community property with the right of survivorship," and "payor."

Historical Note. This Comment was revised in 1993. For the prior version, see 8 U.L.A. 161 (Supp. 1992).

Section 2–804. Revocation of Probate and Nonprobate Transfers by Divorce; No Revocation by Other Changes of Circumstances.

(a) [Definitions.] In this section:

(1) "Disposition or appointment of property" includes a transfer of an item of property or any other benefit to a beneficiary designated in a governing instrument.

(2) "Divorce or annulment" means any divorce or annulment, or any dissolution or declaration of invalidity of a marriage, that would exclude the spouse as a surviving spouse within the meaning of Section 2–802. A decree of separation that does not terminate the status of husband and wife is not a divorce for purposes of this section.

(3) "Divorced individual" includes an individual whose marriage has been annulled.

(4) "Governing instrument" means a governing instrument executed by the divorced individual before the divorce or annulment of his [or her] marriage to his [or her] former spouse.

(5) "Relative of the divorced individual's former spouse" means an individual who is related to the divorced individual's former spouse by blood, adoption, or affinity and who, after the divorce or annulment, is not related to the divorced individual by blood, adoption, or affinity.

(6) "Revocable," with respect to a disposition, appointment, provision, or nomination, means one under which the divorced individual, at the time of the divorce or annulment, was alone empowered, by law or under the governing instrument, to cancel the designation in favor of his [or her] former spouse or former spouse's relative, whether or not the divorced individual was then empowered to designate himself [or herself] in place of his

189

[or her] former spouse or in place of his [or her] former spouse's relative and whether or not the divorced individual then had the capacity to exercise the power.

(b) [Revocation Upon Divorce.] Except as provided by the express terms of a governing instrument, a court order, or a contract relating to the division of the marital estate made between the divorced individuals before or after the marriage, divorce, or annulment, the divorce or annulment of a marriage:

(1) revokes any revocable (i) disposition or appointment of property made by a divorced individual to his [or her] former spouse in a governing instrument and any disposition or appointment created by law or in a governing instrument to a relative of the divorced individual's former spouse, (ii) provision in a governing instrument conferring a general or nongeneral power of appointment on the divorced individual's former spouse or on a relative of the divorced individual's former spouse, and (iii) nomination in a governing instrument, nominating a divorced individual's former spouse or a relative of the divorced individual's former spouse to serve in any fiduciary or representative capacity, including a personal representative, executor, trustee, conservator, agent, or guardian; and

(2) severs the interests of the former spouses in property held by them at the time of the divorce or annulment as joint tenants with the right of survivorship [or as community property with the right of survivorship], transforming the interests of the former spouses into tenancies in common.

(c) [Effect of Severance.] A severance under subsection (b)(2) does not affect any third-party interest in property acquired for value and in good faith reliance on an apparent title by survivorship in the survivor of the former spouses unless a writing declaring the severance has been noted, registered, filed, or recorded in records appropriate to the kind and location of the property which are relied upon, in the ordinary course of transactions involving such property, as evidence of ownership.

(d) [Effect of Revocation.] Provisions of a governing instrument are given effect as if the former spouse and relatives of the former spouse disclaimed all provisions revoked by this section or, in the case of a revoked nomination in a fiduciary or representative capacity, as if the former spouse and relatives of the former spouse died immediately before the divorce or annulment.

(e) [Revival if Divorce Nullified.] Provisions revoked solely by this section are revived by the divorced individual's remarriage to the former spouse or by a nullification of the divorce or annulment.

(f) [No Revocation for Other Change of Circumstances.] No change of circumstances other than as described in this section and in Section 2–803 effects a revocation.

(g) [Protection of Payors and Other Third Parties.]

(1) A payor or other third party is not liable for having made a payment or transferred an item of property or any other benefit to a beneficiary designated in a governing instrument affected by a divorce, annulment, or remarriage, or for having taken any other action in good faith reliance on the validity of the governing instrument, before the payor or other third party received written notice of the divorce, annulment, or remarriage. A payor or other third party is liable for a payment made or other action taken after the payor or other third party received written notice of a claimed forfeiture or revocation under this section.

(2) Written notice of the divorce, annulment, or remarriage under subsection (g)(2) must be mailed to the payor's or other third party's main office or home by registered or certified mail, return receipt requested, or served upon the payor or other third party in the same manner as a summons in a civil action. Upon receipt of written notice of the divorce, annulment, or remarriage, a payor or other third party may pay any amount owed or transfer or deposit any item of property held by it to or with the court having jurisdiction of the probate proceedings relating to the decedent's estate or, if no proceedings have been commenced, to or with the court having jurisdiction of probate proceedings relating to decedents' estates located in the county of the decedent's residence. The court shall hold the funds or item of property and, upon its determination under this section, shall order disbursement or transfer in accordance with the determination. Payments, transfers, or deposits made to or with the court discharge the payor or other third party from all claims for the value of amounts paid to or items of property transferred to or deposited with the court.

(h) [Protection of Bona Fide Purchasers; Personal Liability of Recipient.]

(1) A person who purchases property from a former spouse, relative of a former spouse, or any other person for value and without notice, or who receives from a former spouse, relative of a former spouse, or any other person a payment or other item of property in partial or full satisfaction of a legally enforceable

obligation, is neither obligated under this section to return the payment, item of property, or benefit nor is liable under this section for the amount of the payment or the value of the item of property or benefit. But a former spouse, relative of a former spouse, or other person who, not for value, received a payment, item of property, or any other benefit to which that person is not entitled under this section is obligated to return the payment, item of property, or benefit, or is personally liable for the amount of the payment or the value of the item of property or benefit, to the person who is entitled to it under this section.

(2) If this section or any part of this section is preempted by federal law with respect to a payment, an item of property, or any other benefit covered by this section, a former spouse, relative of the former spouse, or any other person who, not for value, received a payment, item of property, or any other benefit to which that person is not entitled under this section is obligated to return that payment, item of property, or benefit, or is personally liable for the amount of the payment or the value of the item of property or benefit, to the person who would have been entitled to it were this section or part of this section not preempted.

COMMENT

Purpose and Scope of Revision. The revisions of this section, pre–1990 Section 2–508, intend to unify the law of probate and nonprobate transfers. As originally promulgated, pre–1990 Section 2–508 revoked a predivorce devise to the testator's former spouse. The revisions expand the section to cover "will substitutes" such as revocable inter-vivos trusts, life-insurance and retirement-plan beneficiary designations, transfer-on-death accounts, and other revocable dispositions to the former spouse that the divorced individual established before the divorce (or annulment). As revised, this section also effects a severance of the interests of the former spouses in property that they held at the time of the divorce (or annulment) as joint tenants with the right of survivorship; their co-ownership in-terests become tenancies in common.

As revised, this section is the most comprehensive provision of its kind, but many states have enacted piecemeal legislation tending in the same direction. For example, Michigan and Ohio have statutes transforming spousal joint tenancies in land into tenancies in common upon the spouses' divorce. Mich. Comp. Laws Ann. § 552.102; Ohio Rev. Code Ann. § 5302.20(c)(5). Ohio, Oklahoma, and Tennessee have recently enacted legislation effecting a revocation of provisions for the settlor's former spouse in revocable inter-vivos trusts. Ohio Rev. Code Ann. § 1339.62; Okla. Stat. Ann. tit. 60, § 175; Tenn. Code Ann. § 35–50–115 (applies to revocable and irrevocable inter-vivos trusts). Statutes in Michigan, Ohio, Oklahoma, and Texas relate to the consequence of divorce on life-insurance and retirement-plan beneficiary designations. Mich. Comp. Laws Ann. § 552.101; Ohio Rev. Code Ann. § 1339.63; Okla. Stat. Ann. tit. 15, § 178; Tex. Fam. Code §§ 3.632–.633.

The courts have also come under increasing pressure to use statutory construction techniques to extend statutes like the pre–1990 version of section 2–508 to various will substitutes. In Clymer v. Mayo, 473 N.E.2d 1084 (Mass.1985), the Massachusetts court held the statute applicable to a revocable inter-vivos trust, but restricted its "holding to the particular facts of this case— specifically the existence of a revocable pour-over trust funded entirely at the time of the decedent's death." 473 N.E.2d at 1093. The trust in that case was an unfunded life-insurance trust; the life insurance was employer-paid life insurance. In Miller v. First Nat'l Bank & Tr. Co., 637 P.2d 75 (Okla. 1981), the court also held such a statute to be applicable to an unfunded life-insurance trust. The testator's will devised the residue of his estate to the trustee of the life-insurance trust. Despite the absence of meaningful evidence of intent to incorporate, the court held that the pour-over devise incorporated the life-insurance trust into the will by reference, and thus was able to apply the revocation-upon-divorce statute. In Equitable Life Assurance Society v. Stitzel, 1 Pa. Fiduc.2d 316 (C.P. 1981), however, the court held a statute similar to the pre–1990 version of section 2–508 to be inapplicable to effect a revocation of a life-insurance benefi-

ciary designation of the former spouse.

Revoking Benefits of the Former Spouse's Relatives. In several cases, including Clymer v. Mayo, 473 N.E.2d 1084 (Mass.1985), and Estate of Coffed, 387 N.E.2d 1209 (N.Y.1979), the result of treating the former spouse as if he or she predeceased the testator was that a gift in the governing instrument was triggered in favor of relatives of the former spouse who, after the divorce, were no longer relatives of the testator. In the Massachusetts case, the former spouse's nieces and nephews ended up with an interest in the property. In the New York case, the winners included the former spouse's child by a prior marriage. For other cases to the same effect, see Porter v. Porter, 286 N.W.2d 649 (Iowa 1979); Bloom v. Selfon, 555 A.2d 75 (Pa.1989); Estate of Graef, 368 N.W.2d 633 (Wis. 1985). Given that, during divorce process or in the aftermath of the divorce, the former spouse's relatives are likely to side with the former spouse, breaking down or weakening any former ties that may previously have developed between the transferor and the former spouse's relatives, seldom would the transferor have favored such a result. This section, therefore, also revokes these gifts.

Consequence of Revocation. The effect of revocation by this section is that the provisions of the governing instrument are given effect as if the divorced individual's former spouse (and relatives of the former spouse) disclaimed all provisions revoked by this section (see Section 2–801(d) for the effect of a disclaimer). Note that this means that the antilapse statute applies in appropriate cases in which the divorced individual or relative is treated as having disclaimed. In the case of a revoked nomination in a fiduciary or representative capacity, the provisions of the governing instrument are given effect as if the former spouse and relatives of the former spouse died immediately before the divorce or annulment. If the divorced individual (or relative of the divorced individual) is the donee of an unexercised power of appointment that is revoked by this section, the gift-in-default clause, if any, is to take effect, to the extent that the gift-in-default clause is not itself revoked by this section.

ERISA Preemption of State Law. The Employee Retirement Income Security Act of 1974 (ERISA) federalizes pension and employee benefit law. Section 514(a) of ERISA, 29 U.S.C. § 1144(a), provides that the provisions of Titles I and IV of ERISA "shall supersede any and all State laws insofar as they may now or hereafter relate to any employee benefit plan" governed by ERISA.

ERISA's preemption clause is extraordinarily broad. ERISA Section 514(a) does not merely preempt state laws that conflict with specific provisions in ERISA. Section 514(a) preempts "any and all State laws" insofar as they "relate to" any ERISA-governed employee benefit plan.

A complex case law has arisen concerning the question of whether to apply ERISA Section 514(a) to preempt state law in circumstances in which ERISA supplies no substantive regulation. For example, until 1984, ERISA contained no authorization for the enforcement of state domestic relations decrees against pension accounts, but the federal courts were virtually unanimous in refusing to apply ERISA preemption against such state decrees. See, e.g., American Telephone & Telegraph Co. v. Merry, 592 F.2d 118 (2d Cir. 1979). The Retirement Equity Act of 1984 amended ERISA to add Sections 206(d)(3) and 514(b)(7), confirming the judicially created exception for state domestic relations decrees.

The federal courts have been less certain about whether to defer to state probate law. In Board of Trustees of Western Conference of Teamsters Pension Trust Fund v. H.F. Johnson, Inc., 830 F.2d 1009 (9th Cir. 1987), the court held that ERISA preempted the Montana nonclaim statute (which is Section 3–803 of the Uniform Probate Code). On the other hand, in Mendez–Bellido v. Board of Trustees, 709 F. Supp. 329 (E.D. N.Y. 1989), the court applied the New York "slayer-rule" against an ERISA preemption claim, reasoning that "state laws prohibiting murderers from receiving death benefits are relatively uniform [and therefore] there is little threat of creating a 'patchwork scheme of regulations'" that ERISA sought to avoid.

It is to be hoped that the federal courts will continue to show sensitivity to the primary role of state law in the field of probate and nonprobate transfers. To the extent that the federal courts think themselves unable to craft exceptions to ERISA's preemption language, it is open to them to apply state law concepts as federal common law. Because the Uniform Probate Code contemplates multistate applicability, it is well suited to be the model for federal common law absorption.

Another avenue of reconciliation between ERISA preemption and the primacy of state law in this field is envisioned in subsection (h)(2) of this section. It imposes a personal liability for pension payments that pass to a former spouse or relative of a former spouse. This provision respects ERISA's concern that federal law govern the administration of the plan, while still preventing unjust enrichment that would result if an unintended beneficiary were to receive the pension benefits. Federal law has no interest in working a broader disruption of state probate and nonprobate transfer law than is required in the interest of smooth administration of pension and employee benefit plans.

Cross References. See Section 1–201 for definitions of "beneficiary designated in a governing instrument," "governing instrument," "joint tenants with the right of survivorship," "community property with the right of survivorship," and "payor."

References. The theory of this section is discussed in Waggoner, "Spousal Rights in Our Multiple-Marriage Society: The Revised Uniform Probate Code," 26 Real Prop. Prob. & Tr.J. 683, 689–701 (1992). See also Langbein, "The Nonprobate Revolution and the Future of the Law of Succession," 97 Harv. L. Rev. 1108 (1984).

Historical Note. This Comment was revised in 1993. For the prior version, see 8 U.L.A. 164 (Supp. 1992).

PART 9

STATUTORY RULE AGAINST PERPETUITIES; HONORARY TRUSTS

GENERAL COMMENT

Subpart 1 of this Part incorporates into the Code the Uniform Statutory Rule Against Perpetuities (USRAP or Uniform Statutory Rule) and Subpart 2 contains an optional section on honorary trusts and trusts for pets. Subpart 2 is under continuing review and, after appropriate study, might subsequently be revised to add provisions affecting certain types of commercial transactions respecting land, such as options in gross, that directly or indirectly restrain alienability.

In codifying Subparts 1 and 2, enacting states may deem it appropriate to locate them at some place other than in the probate code.

SUBPART 1. STATUTORY RULE AGAINST PERPETUITIES.

GENERAL COMMENT

Simplified Wait–and–See/Deferred–Reformation Approach Adopted. The Uniform Statutory Rule reforms the common-law Rule Against Perpetuities (common-law Rule) by adding a simplified wait-and-see element and a deferred-reformation element.

Wait-and-see is a two-step strategy. Step One (Section 2–901(a)(1)) preserves the validating side of the common-law Rule. By satisfying the common-law Rule, a nonvested future interest in property is valid at the moment of its creation. Step Two (Section 2–901(a)(2)) is a salvage strategy for future interests that would have been invalid at common law. Rather than invalidating such interests at creation, wait-and-see allows a period of time, called the permissible vesting period, during which the nonvested interests are permitted to vest according to the trust's terms.

The traditional method of measuring the permissible vesting period has been by reference to lives in being at the creation of the interest (the measuring lives) plus 21 years. There are, however, various difficulties and costs associated with identifying and tracing a set of actual measuring lives to see which one is the survivor and when he or she dies. In addition, it has been documented that the use of actual measuring lives plus 21 years does not produce a period of time that self-adjusts to each disposition, extending dead-hand control no further than necessary in each case; rather, the use of actual measuring lives (plus 21 years) generates a permissible vesting period whose length almost always exceeds by some arbitrary margin the point of actual vesting in cases traditionally validated by the wait-and-see strategy. The actual-measuring-lives approach, therefore, performs a margin-of-safety function. Given this fact, and given the costs and difficulties associated with the actual-measuring-lives approach, the Uniform Statutory Rule forgoes the use of actual measuring lives and uses instead a permissible vesting period of a flat 90 years.

The philosophy behind the 90–year period is to fix a period of time that approximates the average period of time that would traditionally be allowed by the wait-and-see doctrine. The flat-period-of-years method was not used as a means of increasing permissible dead-hand control by lengthening the permissible vesting period beyond its traditional boundaries. In fact, the 90–year period falls substantially short of the absolute maximum period of time that could theoretically be achieved under the common-law Rule itself, by the so-called "twelve-healthy-babies" ploy—a ploy that would average out to a period of about 115 years,[1] 25 years or 27.8% longer than the 90 years allowed by USRAP. The fact that the traditional period roughly averages out to a longish-sounding 90 years is a reflection of a quite different phenomenon: the dramatic increase in longevity that society as a whole has experienced in the course of the twentieth century.

The framers of the Uniform Statutory Rule derived the 90–year period as follows. The first point recognized was that if actual measuring lives were to have been used, the length of the permissible vesting period would, in the normal course of events, be governed by the life of the youngest measuring life. The second point recognized was that no matter what method is used to identify the measuring lives, the youngest measuring life, in standard trusts, is likely to be the transferor's youngest descendant living when the trust was created.[2] The 90–year period was premised on these propositions. Using four hypothetical families deemed to be representative of actual families, the framers of the Uniform Statutory Rule determined that, on average, the transferor's youngest descendant in being at the transferor's death—assuming the transferor's death to occur between ages 60 and 90, which is when 73 percent of the population die—is about 6 years old. See Waggoner, "Perpetuities: A Progress Report on the Draft Uniform Statutory Rule Against Perpetuities," 20 U. Miami Inst. on Est. Plan. Ch. 7 at 7–17 (1986). The remaining life expectancy of a 6–year–old is about 69 years. The 69 years, plus the 21–year tack-on period, gives a permissible vesting period of 90 years.

Acceptance of the 90–year–period Approach under the Federal Generation-skipping Transfer Tax. Federal regulations, to be promulgated by the U.S. Treasury Department under the generation-skipping transfer tax, will accept the Uniform Statutory Rule's 90–year period as a valid approximation of the period that, on average, would be produced by lives in being

---

1. Actuarially, the life expectancy of the longest living member of a group of twelve new-born babies is about 94 years; with the 21–year tack-on period, the "twelve-healthy-babies ploy" would produce, on average, a period of about 115 years (94 + 21).

2. Under section 2–707, the descendants of a beneficiary of a future interest are presumptively made substitute beneficiaries, almost certainly making those descendants in being at the creation of the interest measuring lives, were measuring lives to have been used.

plus 21 years. See Temp. Treas. Reg. § 26.2601–1(b)(1)(v)(B)(2) (as to be revised). When originally promulgated in 1988, this regulation was prepared without knowledge of the Uniform Statutory Rule Against Perpetuities, which had been promulgated in 1986; as first promulgated, the regulation only recognized a period measured by actual lives in being plus 21 years. After the 90–year approach of the Uniform Statutory Rule was brought to the attention of the U.S. Treasury Department, the Department issued a letter of intent to amend the regulation to treat the 90–year period as the equivalent of a lives–in–being–plus–21–years period. Letter from Michael J. Graetz, Deputy Assistant Secretary of the Treasury (Tax Policy), to Lawrence J. Bugge, President, National Conference of Commissioners on Uniform State Laws (Nov. 16, 1990). For further discussion of the coordination of the federal generation-skipping transfer tax with the Uniform Statutory Rule, see the Comment to Section 2–901(e), infra, and the Comment to Section 1(e) of the Uniform Statutory Rule Against Perpetuities.

The 90–year Period Will Seldom be Used Up. Nearly all trusts (or other property arrangements) will terminate by their own terms long before the 90–year permissible vesting period expires, leaving the permissible vesting period to extend unused (and ignored) into the future long after the contingencies have been resolved and the property distributed. In the unlikely event that the contingencies have not been resolved by the expiration of the permissible vesting period, Section 2–903 requires the disposition to be reformed by the court so that all contingencies are resolved within the permissible period.

In effect, wait-and-see with deferred reformation operates similarly to a traditional perpetuity saving clause, which grants a margin-of-safety period measured by the lives of the transferor's descendants in being at the creation of the trust or other property arrangement (plus 21 years).

No New Learning Required. The Uniform Statutory Rule does not require the practicing bar to learn a new and unfamiliar set of perpetuity principles. The effect of the Uniform Statutory Rule on the planning and drafting of documents for clients should be distinguished from the effect on the resolution of actual or potential perpetuity-violation cases. The former affects many more practicing lawyers than the latter.

With respect to the planning and drafting end of the practice, the Uniform Statutory Rule requires no modification of current practice and no new learning. *Lawyers can and should continue to use the same traditional perpetuity-saving/termination clause, using specified lives in being plus 21 years, they used before enactment.* Lawyers should not shift to a "later of" type clause that purports to operate upon the *later of* (A) 21 years after the death of the survivor of specified lives in being or (B) 90 years. As explained in more detail in the Comment to Section 2–901, such a clause is not effective. If such a "later of" clause is used in a trust that contains a violation of the common-law rule against perpetuities, Section 2–901(a), by itself, would render the clause ineffective, limit the maximum permissible vesting period to 90 years, and render the trust vulnerable to a reformation suit under Section 2–903.   Section 2–901(e), however, saves documents using this type of clause from this fate.   By limiting the effect of such clauses to the 21–year period following the death of the survivor of the specified lives, subsection (e) in effect transforms this type of clause into a traditional perpetuity-saving/termination clause, bringing the trust into compliance with the common-law rule against perpetuities and rendering it invulnerable to a reformation suit under Section 2–903.

Far fewer in number are those lawyers (and judges) who have an actual or potential perpetuity-violation case.   An actual or potential perpetuity-violation case will arise very infrequently under the Uniform Statutory Rule.   When such a case does arise, however, lawyers (or judges) involved in the case will find considerable guidance for its resolution in the detailed analysis contained in the commentary accompanying the Uniform Statutory Rule itself.   In short, the detailed analysis in the commentary accompanying the Uniform Statutory Rule need not be part of the general learning required of lawyers in the drafting and planning of dispositive documents for their clients.   The detailed analysis is supplied in the commentary for the assistance in the resolution of an actual violation.   Only then need that detailed analysis be consulted and, in such a case, it will prove extremely helpful.

General References.   Fellows, "Testing Perpetuity Reforms: A Study of Perpetuity Cases 1984–89," 25 Real Prop., Prob. & Tr. J. 597 (1991) (testing the various types of perpetuity reform measures and concluding, on the basis of empirical evidence, that the Uniform Statutory Rule is the best opportunity offered to date for a uniform perpetuity law that efficiently and effectively achieves a fair balance between present and future property owners); Waggoner, "The Uniform Statutory Rule Against Perpetuities: Oregon Joins Up," 26 Willamette L. Rev. 259 (1990) (explaining the operation of the Uniform Statutory Rule); Waggoner, "The Uniform Statutory Rule Against Perpetuities: The Rationale of the 90–Year Waiting Period," 73 Cornell L. Rev. 157 (1988) (explaining the derivation of the 90–year period); Waggoner, "The Uniform Statutory Rule Against Perpetuities," 21 Real Prop., Prob. & Tr. J. 569 (1986) (explaining the theory and operation of the Uniform Statutory Rule).

Section 2–901. Statutory Rule Against Perpetuities.

(a) [Validity of Nonvested Property Interest.]   A nonvested property interest is invalid unless:

> (1) when the interest is created, it is certain to vest or terminate no later than 21 years after the death of an individual then alive; or

> (2) the interest either vests or terminates within 90 years after its creation.

(b) [Validity of General Power of Appointment Subject to a Condition Precedent.]   A general power of appointment not presently exercisable because of a condition precedent is invalid unless:

(1) when the power is created, the condition precedent is certain to be satisfied or become impossible to satisfy no later than 21 years after the death of an individual then alive; or

(2) the condition precedent either is satisfied or becomes impossible to satisfy within 90 years after its creation.

(c) [Validity of Nongeneral or Testamentary Power of Appointment.] A nongeneral power of appointment or a general testamentary power of appointment is invalid unless:

(1) when the power is created, it is certain to be irrevocably exercised or otherwise to terminate no later than 21 years after the death of an individual then alive; or

(2) the power is irrevocably exercised or otherwise terminates within 90 years after its creation.

(d) [Possibility of Post-death Child Disregarded.] In determining whether a nonvested property interest or a power of appointment is valid under subsection (a)(1), (b)(1), or (c)(1), the possibility that a child will be born to an individual after the individual's death is disregarded.

(e) [Effect of Certain "Later-of" Type Language.] If, in measuring a period from the creation of a trust or other property arrangement, language in a governing instrument (i) seeks to disallow the vesting or termination of any interest or trust beyond, (ii) seeks to postpone the vesting or termination of any interest or trust until, or (iii) seeks to operate in effect in any similar fashion upon, the later of (A) the expiration of a period of time not exceeding 21 years after the death of the survivor of specified lives in being at the creation of the trust or other property arrangement or (B) the expiration of a period of time that exceeds or might exceed 21 years after the death of the survivor of lives in being at the creation of the trust or other property arrangement, that language is inoperative to the extent it produces a period of time that exceeds 21 years after the death of the survivor of the specified lives.

COMMENT

Section 2–901 codifies the validating side of the common-law Rule and implements the wait-and-see feature of the Uniform Statutory Rule Against Perpetuities. As provided in Section 2–906, this section and the other sections in Subpart 1 of Part 9 supersede the common-law Rule Against Perpetuities (common-law Rule) in jurisdictions previously adhering to it (or repeals any statutory version or variation thereof previously in effect in the jurisdiction). The common-law Rule (or the statutory version or variation thereof) is replaced by the Statutory Rule in Section 2–901 and by the other provisions of Subpart 1 of Part 9.

Section 2–901(a) covers nonvested property interests, and will be the subsection most often applicable. Subsections (b) and (c) cover powers of appointment.

Paragraph (1) of subsections (a), (b), and (c) is a codified version of the validating side of the common-law Rule. In effect, paragraph (1) of these subsections provides that nonvested property interests and powers of appointment that are valid under the common-law Rule Against Perpetuities, including those that are rendered valid because of a perpetuity saving clause, continue to be valid under the Statutory Rule and can be declared so at their inceptions. This means that no new learning is required of competent estate planners: The practice of lawyers who competently draft trusts and other property arrangements for their clients is undisturbed.

Paragraph (2) of subsections (a), (b), and (c) establishes the wait-and-see rule. Paragraph (2) provides that an interest or a power of appointment that is not validated by paragraph (1), and hence would have been invalid under the common-law Rule, is given a second chance: Such an interest is valid if it does not actually remain in existence and nonvested when the 90–year permissible vesting period expires; such a power of appointment is valid if it ceases to be subject to a

condition precedent or is no longer exercisable when the permissible 90–year period expires.

Subsection (d). The rule established in subsection (d) deserves a special comment. Subsection (d) declares that the possibility that a child will be born to an individual after the individual's death is to be disregarded. It is important to note that this rule applies only for the purpose of determining the validity of an interest (or a power of appointment) under paragraph (1) of subsection (a), (b), or (c). The rule of subsection (d) does not apply, for example, to questions such as whether a child who is born to an individual after the individual's death qualifies as a taker of a beneficial interest—as a member of a class or otherwise. Neither subsection (d), nor any other provision of Part 9, supersedes the widely accepted common-law principle, codified in Section 2–109, that a child in gestation (a child sometimes described as a child en ventre sa mere) who is later born alive (and, under Section 2–109, lives for 120 hours or more after birth) is regarded as alive during gestation.

The limited purpose of subsection (d) is to solve a perpetuity problem created by advances in medical science. The problem is illustrated by a case such as "to A for life, remainder to A's children who reach 21." When the common-law Rule was developing, the possibility was recognized, strictly speaking, that one or more of A's children might reach 21 more than 21 years after A's death. The possibility existed because A's wife (who might not be a life in being) might be pregnant when A died. If she was, and if the child was born viable a few months after A's death, the child could not reach his or her 21st birthday within 21 years after A's death. The device then invented to validate the interest of A's children was to "extend" the allowable perpetuity period by tacking on a period of gestation, if needed. As a result, the common-law perpetuity period was comprised of three components: (1) a life in being (2) plus 21 years (3) plus a period of gestation, when needed. Today, thanks to sperm banks, frozen embryos, and even the possibility of artificially maintaining the body functions of a deceased pregnant woman long enough to develop the fetus to viability—advances in medical science unanticipated when the common-law Rule was in its developmental stages—having a pregnant wife at death is no longer the only way of having children after death. These medical developments, and undoubtedly others to come, make the mere addition of a period of gestation inadequate as a device to confer initial validity under Section 2–901(a)(1) on the interest of A's children in the above example. The rule of subsection (d), however, does insure the initial validity of the children's interest. Disregarding the possibility that children of A will be born after his death allows A to be the validating life. None of his children, under this assumption, can reach 21 more than 21 years after his death.

Note that subsection (d) subsumes not only the case of children conceived after death, but also the more conventional case of children in gestation at death. With subsection (d) in place, the third component of the common-law perpetuity

period is unnecessary and has been jettisoned. The perpetuity period recognized in paragraph (1) of subsections (a), (b), and (c) has only two components: (1) a life in being (2) plus 21 years.

As to the legal status of conceived-after-death children, that question has not yet been resolved. For example, if in the above example A leaves sperm on deposit at a sperm bank and after A's death a woman (A's widow or another) becomes pregnant as a result of artificial insemination, the child or children produced thereby might not be included at all in the class gift. Cf. Restatement (Second) of Property (Donative Transfers) Introductory Note to Ch. 26 (1988). Without trying to predict how that question will be resolved in the future, the best way to handle the problem from the perpetuity perspective is the rule in subsection (d) requiring the possibility of post-death children to be disregarded.

Subsection (e)—Effect of Certain "Later-of" Type Language. Subsection (e) was added to the Uniform Statutory Rule in 1990. It primarily applies to a non-traditional type of "later of" clause (described below). Use of that type of clause might have produced unintended consequences, which are now rectified by the addition of subsection (e).

In general, perpetuity saving or termination clauses can be used in either of two ways. The predominant use of such clauses is as an override clause. That is, the clause is not an integral part of the dispositive terms of the trust, but operates independently of the dispositive terms; the clause provides that all interests must vest no later than at a specified time in the future, and sometimes also provides that the trust must then terminate, but only if any interest has not previously vested or if the trust has not previously terminated. The other use of such a clause is as an integral part of the dispositive terms of the trust; that is, the clause is the provision that directly regulates the duration of the trust. Traditional perpetuity saving or termination clauses do not use a "later of" approach; they mark off the maximum time of vesting or termination only by reference to a 21–year period following the death of the survivor of specified lives in being at the creation of the trust.

Subsection (e) applies to a nontraditional clause called a "later of" (or "longer of") clause. Such a clause might provide that the maximum time of vesting or termination of any interest or trust must occur no later than the later of (A) 21 years after the death of the survivor of specified lives in being at the creation of the trust or (B) 90 years after the creation of the trust.

Under the Uniform Statutory Rule as originally promulgated, this type of "later of" clause would not achieve a "later of" result. If used as an override clause in conjunction with a trust whose terms were, by themselves, valid under the common-law rule against perpetuities (common-law Rule), the "later of" clause did no harm. The trust would be valid under the common-

law Rule as codified in subsection (a)(1) because the clause itself would neither postpone the vesting of any interest nor extend the duration of the trust. But, if used either (1) as an override clause in conjunction with a trust whose terms were not valid under the common-law Rule or (2) as the provision that directly regulated the duration of the trust, the "later of" clause would not cure the perpetuity violation in case (1) and would create a perpetuity violation in case (2). In neither case would the clause qualify the trust for validity at common law under subsection (a)(1) because the clause would not guarantee that all interests will be certain to vest or terminate no later than 21 years after the death of an individual then alive.[3] In any given case, 90 years can turn out to be longer than the period produced by the specified–lives–in–being–plus–21–years language.

Because the clause would fail to qualify the trust for validity under the common-law Rule of subsection (a)(1), the nonvested interests in the trust would be subject to the wait-and-see element of subsection (a)(2) and vulnerable to a reformation suit under Section 2–903. Under subsection (a)(2), an interest that is not valid at common law is invalid unless it actually vests or terminates within 90 years after its creation. Subsection (a)(2) does not grant such nonvested interests a

---

3. By substantial analogous authority, the specified-lives-in-being-plus-21-years prong of the "later of" clause under discussion is not sustained by the separability doctrine (described in Part H of the Comment to § 1 of the Uniform Statutory Rule Against Perpetuities). See, e.g., Restatement of Property § 376

comments e & f & illustration 3 (1944); Easton v. Hall, 323 Ill. 397, 154 N.E. 216 (1926); Thorne v. Continental Nat. Bank & Trust Co., 305 Ill.App. 222, 27 N.E.2d 302 (1940). The inapplicability of the separability doctrine is also supported by perpetuity policy, as described in the text above.

permissible vesting period of either 90 years or a period of 21 years after the death of the survivor of specified lives in being. Subsection (a)(2) only grants such interests a period of 90 years in which to vest.

The operation of subsection (a), as outlined above, is also supported by perpetuity policy. If subsection (a) allowed a "later of" clause to achieve a "later of" result, it would authorize an improper use of the 90–year permissible vesting period of subsection (a)(2). The 90–year period of subsection (a)(2) is designed to approximate the period that, *on average,* would be produced by using actual lives in being plus 21 years. Because in any given case the period actually produced by lives in being plus 21 years can be shorter or longer than 90 years, an attempt to utilize a 90–year period in a "later of" clause improperly seeks to turn the 90–year *average* into a *minimum.*

Set against this background, the addition of subsection (e) is quite beneficial. Subsection (e) limits the effect of this type of "later of" language to 21 years after the death of the survivor of the specified lives, in effect transforming the clause into a traditional perpetuity saving/termination clause. By doing so, subsection (e) grants initial validity to the trust under the common-law Rule as codified in subsection (a)(1) and precludes a reformation suit under Section 2–903.

Note that subsection (e) covers variations of the "later of" clause described above, such as a clause that postpones vesting until the later of (A) *20* years after the death of the survivor of specified lives in being or (B) *89* years. Subsection (e) does not, however, apply to all dis-

positions that incorporate a "later of" approach. To come under subsection (e), the specified-lives prong must include a tack-on period of up to 21 years. Without a tack-on period, a "later of" disposition, unless valid at common law, comes under subsection (a)(2) and is given 90 years in which to vest. An example would be a disposition that creates an interest that is to vest upon "the later of the death of my widow or 30 years after my death."

Coordination of the Federal Generation-skipping Transfer Tax with the Uniform Statutory Rule. In 1990, the Treasury Department announced a decision to coordinate the tax regulations under the "grandfathering" provisions of the federal generation-skipping transfer tax with the Uniform Statutory Rule. Letter from Michael J. Graetz, Deputy Assistant Secretary of the Treasury (Tax Policy), to Lawrence J. Bugge, President, National Conference of Commissioners on Uniform State Laws (Nov. 16, 1990) (hereinafter *Treasury Letter*).

Section 1433(b)(2) of the Tax Reform Act of 1986 generally exempts ("grandfathers") trusts from the federal generation-skipping transfer tax that were irrevocable on September 25, 1985. This section adds, however, that the exemption shall apply "only to the extent that such transfer is not made out of corpus added to the trust after September 25, 1985." The provisions of Section 1433(b)(2) were first implemented by Temp. Treas. Reg. § 26.2601–1, promulgated by T.D. 8187 on March 14, 1988. Insofar as the Uniform Statutory Rule is concerned, a key feature of that temporary regulation is the concept that the statutory reference to "corpus added to the trust after September 25, 1985" not only covers actual post-9/25/85 transfers of new property or corpus to a grandfathered trust but "constructive" additions as well. Under the temporary regulation as first promulgated, a "constructive" addition occurs if, after 9/25/85, the donee of a nongeneral power of appointment exercises that power "in a manner that may postpone or suspend the vesting, absolute ownership or power of alienation of an interest in property for a period, measured from the date of creation of the trust, extending beyond any life in being at the date of creation of the trust plus a period of 21 years. If a power is exercised by creating another power it will be deemed to be exercised to whatever extent the second power may be exercised." Temp. Treas. Reg. § 26.2601–1(b)(1)(v)(B)(2) (1988).

Because the Uniform Statutory Rule was promulgated in 1986 and applies only prospectively, any "grandfathered" trust would have become irrevocable prior to the enactment of USRAP in any state. Nevertheless, the second sentence of Section 2–905(a) extends USRAP's wait-and-see approach to post-effective-date exercises of nongeneral powers even if the power itself was created prior to USRAP's effective date. Consequently, a post-USRAP-effective-date exercise of a nongeneral power of appointment created in a "grandfathered" trust could come under the provisions of the Uniform Statutory Rule.

The literal wording, then, of Temp. Treas. Reg. § 26.2601–1(b)(1)(v)(B)(2) (1988), as first promulgated, could have jeopardized the grandfathered status of an exempt trust if (1) the trust created a nongeneral power of appointment, (2) the donee exercised that nongeneral power, and (3) USRAP is the perpetuity law applicable to the donee's exercise. This possibility arose not only because the donee's exercise itself might come under the 90–year permissible vesting period of subsection (a)(2) if it otherwise violated the common-law Rule and hence was not validated under subsection (a)(1). The possibility also arose in a less obvious way if the donee's exercise created another nongeneral power. The last sentence of the temporary regulation states that "if a power is exercised by creating another power it will be deemed to be exercised to whatever extent the second power may be exercised."

In late March 1990, the National Conference of Commissioners on Uniform State Laws (NCCUSL) and the Joint Editorial Board for the Uniform Probate Code (JEB–UPC) filed a formal request with the Treasury Department asking that measures be taken to coordinate the regulation with USRAP. By the Treasury Letter referred to above, the Treasury Department responded by stating that it "will amend the temporary regulations to accommodate the 90–year period under USRAP as originally promulgated [in 1986] or as amended [in 1990 by the addition of subsection (e)]." This should effectively remove the possibility of loss of grandfathered status under the Uniform Statutory Rule merely because the donee of a nongeneral power created in a grandfathered trust inadvertently exercises that power in violation of the common-law Rule or merely because the donee exercises that power by creating a second nongeneral power that might, in the future, be inadvertently exercised in violation of the common-law Rule.

The Treasury Letter states, however, that any effort by the donee of a nongeneral power in a grandfathered trust to obtain a "later of" specified – lives – in – being – plus – 21–years or 90–years approach will be treated as a constructive addition, unless that effort is nullified by state law. As explained above, the Uniform Statutory Rule, as originally promulgated in 1986 or as amended in 1990 by the addition of subsection (e), nullifies any direct effort to obtain a "later of" approach by the use of a "later of" clause.

The Treasury Letter states that an indirect effort to obtain a "later of" approach would also be treated as a constructive addition that would bring grandfathered status to an end, unless the attempt to obtain the later-of approach is nullified by state law. The Treasury Letter indicates that an indirect effort to obtain a "later of" approach could arise if the donee of a nongeneral power successfully attempts to prolong the duration of a grandfathered trust by switching from a specified – lives – in – being – plus – 21–years perpetuity period to a 90–year perpetuity period, or vice versa. Donees of nongeneral powers in grandfathered trusts would therefore be well advised to resist any temptation to wait until it becomes clear or reasonably predictable which perpetuity period will be longer and then make a switch to the longer period if the governing instrument creating the power utilized the shorter period. No such attempted switch and no constructive addition will occur if in each instance a traditional specified–lives–in–being–plus–21–years perpetuity saving clause is used.

Any such attempted switch is likely in any event to be nullified by state law and, if so, the attempted switch will not be treated as a constructive addition. For example, suppose that the original grandfathered trust contained a standard perpetuity saving clause declaring that all interests in the trust must vest no later than 21 years after the death of the survivor of specified lives in being. In exercising a nongeneral power created in that trust, any indirect effort by the donee to obtain a "later of" approach by adopting a 90–year perpetuity saving clause will likely be nullified by subsection (e). If that exercise occurs at a time when it has become clear or reasonably predictable that the 90–year period will prove longer, the donee's exercise would constitute language in a governing instrument that seeks to operate in effect to postpone the vesting of any interest until the later of the specified – lives – in – being – plus – 21 – years period or 90 years. Under subsection (e), "that language is inoperative to the extent it produces a period of time that exceeds 21 years after the death of the survivor of the specified lives."

Quite apart from subsection (e), the relation-back doctrine generally recognized in the exercise of nongeneral powers stands as a doctrine that could potentially be invoked to nullify an attempted switch from one perpetuity period to the other perpetuity period. Under that doctrine, interests created by the exercise of a nongeneral power are considered created by the donor of that power. See, e.g., Restatement (Second) of Property, Donative Transfers § 11.1 comment b (1986). As such, the maximum vesting period applicable to interests created by the exercise of a nongeneral power would apparently be covered by the perpetuity saving clause in the document that created the power, not-

withstanding any different period the donee purports to adopt.

Reference. Section 2–901 is Section 1 of the Uniform Statutory Rule Against Perpetuities (Uniform Act). For further discussion of this section, with numerous examples illustrating its application, see the Official Comment to Section 1 of the Uniform Act.

Section 2–902. When Nonvested Property Interest or Power of Appointment Created.

(a) Except as provided in subsections (b) and (c) and in Section 2–905(a), the time of creation of a nonvested property interest or a power of appointment is determined under general principles of property law.

(b) For purposes of Subpart 1 of this Part, if there is a person who alone can exercise a power created by a governing instrument to become the unqualified beneficial owner of (i) a nonvested property interest or (ii) a property interest subject to a power of appointment described in Section 2–901(b) or (c), the nonvested property interest or power of appointment is created when the power to become the unqualified beneficial owner terminates. [For purposes of Subpart 1 of this Part, a joint power with respect to community property or to marital property under the Uniform Marital Property Act held by individuals married to each other is a power exercisable by one person alone.]

(c) For purposes of Subpart 1 of this Part, a nonvested property interest or a power of appointment arising from a transfer of property to a previously funded trust or other existing property arrangement is created when the nonvested property interest or power of appointment in the original contribution was created.

COMMENT

Section 2–902 defines the time when, for purposes of Subpart 1 of Part 9, a nonvested property interest or a power of appointment is created. The period of time allowed by Section 2–901 is measured from the time of creation of the nonvested property interest or power of appointment in question. Section 2–

905, with certain exceptions, provides that Subpart 1 of Part 9 applies only to nonvested property interests and powers of appointment created on or after the effective date of Subpart 1 of Part 9.

Subsection (a). Subsection (a) provides that, with certain exceptions, the time of creation of nonvested property interests and powers of appointment is determined under general principles of property law. Because a will becomes effective as a dispositive instrument upon the decedent's death, not upon the execution of the will, general principles of property law determine that a nonvested property interest or a power of appointment created by will is created at the decedent's death. With respect to an inter-vivos transfer, an interest or power is created on the date the transfer becomes effective for purposes of property law generally, normally the date of delivery of the deed or the funding of the trust.

Nonvested Property Interests and Powers of Appointment Created by the Exercise of a Power of Appointment. If a nonvested property interest or a power of appointment was created by the testamentary or inter-vivos exercise of a power of appointment, general principles of property law adopt the "relation-back" doctrine. Under that doctrine, the appointed interests or powers are created when the power was created, not when it was exercised, if the exercised power was a nongeneral power or a general testamentary power. If the nonvested property interest or power of appointment was created by the exercise of a nongeneral or a testamentary power of appointment that was itself created by the exercise of a nongeneral or a testamentary power of appointment, the relation-back doctrine is applied twice and the nonvested property interest or power of appointment was created when the first power of appointment was created, not when the second power was created or exercised.

Example 1. G's will created a trust that provided for the income to go to G's son, A, for life, remainder to such of A's descendants as A shall by will appoint.

A died leaving a will that exercised his nongeneral power of appointment, providing that the trust is to continue beyond A's death, paying the income to A's daughter, X, for her lifetime, remainder in corpus to such of X's descendants as X shall by will appoint; in default of appointment, to X's descendants who survive X, by representation.

A's exercise of his nongeneral power of appointment gave a nongeneral power of appointment to X and a nonvested property interest to X's descendants. For purposes of Section 2–901, X's power of appointment and the nonvested property interest in X's descendants is deemed to have been "created" at G's death when A's nongeneral power of appointment was created, not at A's death when he exercised his power of appointment.

Suppose that X subsequently dies leaving a will that exercises her nongeneral power of appointment. For purposes of Section 2–901, any nonvested property interest or power of appointment created by an exercise of X's nongeneral power of appointment is deemed to have been "created" at G's death, not at A's death or at X's death.

If the exercised power was a presently exercisable general power, the relation-back doctrine is not followed; the time of creation of the appointed property interests or appointed powers is regarded as the time when the power was irrevocably exercised, not when the power was created.

Example 2. The same facts as Example 1, except that A's will exercised his nongeneral power of appointment by providing that the trust is to continue beyond A's death, paying the income to A's daughter, X, for her lifetime, remainder in corpus to such person or persons, including X, her estate, her creditors, and the creditors of her estate, as X shall appoint; in default of appointment, to X's descendants who survive X, by representation.

A's exercise of his nongeneral power of appointment gave a presently exercisable general power of appointment to X. For purposes of Section 2–901, any nonvested property interest or power of appointment created by an exercise of X's presently exercisable general power of appointment is deemed to be "created" when X irrevocably exercises her power of appointment, not when her power of appointment or A's power of appointment was created.

A's exercise of his nongeneral power also granted a nonvested property interest to X's descendants (under the gift-in-default clause). Were it not for the presently exercisable general power granted to X, the nonvested property interest in X's surviving descendants would, under the relation-back doctrine, be deemed "created" for purposes of Section 2–901 at the time of G's death. However, under Section 2–902(b), the fact that X is granted the presently exercisable general power postpones the

time of creation of the nonvested property interest of X's descendants. Under Section 2–902(b), that nonvested property interest is deemed not to have been "created" for purposes of Section 2–901 at G's death but rather when X's presently exercisable general power "terminates." Consequently, the time of "creation" of the nonvested interest of X's descendants is postponed as of the time that X was granted the presently exercisable general power (upon A's death) and continues in abeyance until X's power terminates. X's power terminates by the first to happen of the following: X's irrevocable exercise of her power; X's release of her power; X's entering into a contract to exercise or not to exercise her power; X's dying without exercising her power; or any other action or nonaction that would have the effect of terminating her power.

Subsection (b). Subsection (b) provides that, if one person can exercise a power to become the unqualified beneficial owner of a nonvested property interest (or a property interest subject to a power of appointment described in Section 2–901(b) or 2–901(c)), the time of creation of the nonvested property interest (or the power of appointment) is postponed until the power to become the unqualified beneficial owner ceases to exist. This is in accord with existing common law. The standard example of the application of this subsection is a revocable inter-vivos trust. For perpetuity purposes, both at common law and under Subpart 1 of Part 9, the nonvested property interests and powers of appointment created in the trust are created when the power to revoke expires, usually at the settlor's death. For another example of the application of subsection (b), see the last paragraph of Example 2, above.

Subsection (c). Subsection (c) provides that nonvested property interests and powers of appointment arising out of transfers to a previously funded trust or other existing property arrangement are created when the nonvested property interest or power of appointment arising out of the original contribution was created. This avoids an administrative difficulty that can arise at common law when subsequent transfers are made to an existing irrevocable inter-vivos trust. Arguably, at common law, each transfer starts the period of the Rule running anew as to each transfer. The prospect of staggered periods is avoided by subsection (c). Subsection (c) is in accord with the saving-clause principle of wait-and-see embraced by Part 9. If the irrevocable inter-vivos trust had contained a saving clause, the perpetuity-period component of the clause would be measured by reference to lives in being when the original contribution to the trust was made, and the clause would cover subsequent contributions as well.

Reference. Section 2–902 is Section 2 of the Uniform Statutory Rule Against Perpetuities (Uniform Act). For further discussion of this section, with examples illustrating its application, see the Official Comment to Section 2 of the Uniform Act.

Section 2–903. Reformation.

Upon the petition of an interested person, a court shall reform a disposition in the manner that most closely approximates the transferor's manifested plan of distribution and is within the 90 years allowed by Section 2–901(a)(2), 2–901(b)(2), or 2–901(c)(2) if:

(1) a nonvested property interest or a power of appointment becomes invalid under Section 2–901 (statutory rule against perpetuities);

(2) a class gift is not but might become invalid under Section 2–901 (statutory rule against perpetuities) and the time has arrived when the share of any class member is to take effect in possession or enjoyment; or

(3) a nonvested property interest that is not validated by Section 2–901(a)(1) can vest but not within 90 years after its creation.

COMMENT

Section 2–903 implements the deferred-reformation feature of the Uniform Statutory Rule Against Perpetuities. Upon the petition of an interested person, the court is directed to reform a disposition within the limits of the allowable 90–year period, in the manner deemed by the court most closely to approximate the transferor's manifested plan of distribution, in any one of three circumstances. The "interested person" who would frequently bring the reformation suit would be the trustee.

Section 2–903 applies only to dispositions the validity of which is governed by the wait-and-see element of Section 2–901(a)(2), 2–901(b)(2), or 2–901(c)(2); it does not apply to dispositions that are initially valid under Section 2–901(a)(1), 2–901(b)(1), or 2–901(c)(1)—the codified version of the validating side of the common-law Rule.

Section 2–903 will seldom be applied. Of the fraction of trusts and other property arrangements that fail to meet the requirements for initial validity under the codified version of the validating side of the common-law Rule, almost all of them will have been settled under their own terms long before any of the circumstances requisite to reformation under Section 2–903 arise.

If, against the odds, one of the circumstances requisite to reformation does arise, it will be found easier than perhaps anticipated to determine how best to reform the disposition. The court is given two criteria to work with: (i) the transferor's manifested plan of distribution, and (ii) the allowable 90–year period. Because governing instruments are where transferors manifest their plans of distribution, the imaginary horrible of courts being forced to probe the minds of long-dead transferors will not materialize.

Subsection (1). The theory of Section 2–903 is to defer the right to reformation until reformation becomes truly necessary. Thus, the basic rule of Section 2–903(1) is that the right to reformation does not arise until a nonvested property interest or a power of appointment becomes invalid; under Section 2–901, this does not occur until the expiration of the 90–year permissible vesting period. This approach is more efficient than the "immediate cy pres" approach to perpetuity reform because it substantially reduces the number of reformation suits. It also is consistent with the saving-clause principle embraced by the Statutory Rule. Deferring the right to reformation until the permissible vesting period expires is the only way to grant every reasonable opportunity for the donor's disposition to work itself out without premature interference.

Subsection (2). Although, generally speaking, reformation is deferred until an invalidity has occurred, Section 2–903 grants an earlier right to reformation when it becomes necessary to do so or when there is no point in waiting the full 90–year period out. Thus subsection (2), which pertains to class gifts that are not yet but still might become invalid under the Statutory Rule, grants a right to reformation whenever the share of any class member whose share had vested within the permissible vesting period might otherwise have to wait out the remaining part of the 90 years before obtaining his or her share. Reformation under this subsection will seldom be needed, however, because of the common practice of structuring trusts to split into separate shares or separate trusts at the death of each income beneficiary, one such separate share or separate trust being created for each of the income beneficiary's then-living children; when this pattern is followed, the circumstances described in subsection (2) will not arise.

Subsection (3).   Subsection (3) also grants a right to reformation before the 90–year permissible vesting period expires.   The circumstances giving rise to the right to reformation under subsection (3) occurs if a nonvested property interest can vest but not before the 90–year period has expired.   Though unlikely, such a case can theoretically arise.   If it does, the interest— unless it terminates by its own terms earlier—is bound to become invalid under Section 2–901 eventually.   There is no point in deferring the right to reformation until the inevitable happens.   Section 2–903 provides for early reformation in such a case, just in case it arises.

Infectious Invalidity.   Given the fact that this section makes refor-

mation mandatory, not discretionary with the court, the common-law doctrine of infectious invalidity is superseded by this section.   In a state in which the courts have been particularly zealous about applying the infectious-invalidity doctrine, however, an express codification of the abrogation of this doctrine might be thought desirable.   If so, the above section could be made subsection (a), with the following new subsection (b) added:

> (b) The common-law rule known as the doctrine of infectious invalidity is abolished.

Reference.   Section 2–903 is Section 3 of the Uniform Statutory Rule Against Perpetuities (Uniform Act).   For further discussion of this section, with examples illustrating its application, see the Official Comment to Section 3 of the Uniform Act.

Section 2–904. Exclusions From Statutory Rule Against Perpetuities.

Section 2–901 (statutory rule against perpetuities) does not apply to:

(1) a nonvested property interest or a power of appointment arising out of a nondonative transfer, except a nonvested property interest or a power of appointment arising out of (i) a premarital or postmarital agreement, (ii) a separation or divorce settlement, (iii) a spouse's election, (iv) a similar arrangement arising out of a prospective, existing, or previous marital relationship between the parties, (v) a contract to make or not to revoke a will or trust, (vi) a contract to exercise or not to exercise a power of appointment, (vii) a transfer in satisfaction of a duty of support, or (viii) a reciprocal transfer;

(2) a fiduciary's power relating to the administration or management of assets, including the power of a fiduciary to sell, lease, or mortgage property, and the power of a fiduciary to determine principal and income;

(3) a power to appoint a fiduciary;

(4) a discretionary power of a trustee to distribute principal before termination of a trust to a beneficiary having an indefeasibly vested interest in the income and principal;

(5) a nonvested property interest held by a charity, government, or governmental agency or subdivision, if the nonvested property interest is preceded by an interest held by another charity, government, or governmental agency or subdivision;

(6) a nonvested property interest in or a power of appointment with respect to a trust or other property arrangement forming part of a pension, profit-sharing, stock bonus, health, disability, death benefit, income deferral, or other current or deferred benefit plan for one or more employees, independent contractors, or their beneficiaries or spouses, to which contributions are made for the purpose of distributing to or for the benefit of the participants or their beneficiaries or spouses the property, income, or principal in the trust or other property arrangement, except a nonvested property interest or a power of appointment that is created by an election of a participant or a beneficiary or spouse; or

(7) a property interest, power of appointment, or arrangement that was not subject to the common-law rule against perpetuities or is excluded by another statute of this State.

COMMENT

This section lists the interests and powers that are excluded from the Statutory Rule Against Perpetuities. This section is in part declaratory of existing common law but in part not. Under subsection (7), all the exclusions from the common-law Rule recognized at common law and by statute in the state are preserved.

The major departure from existing common law comes in subsection (1). In line with long-standing scholarly commentary, subsection (1) excludes nondonative transfers from the Statutory Rule. The Rule Against Perpetuities is an inappropriate instrument of social policy to use as a control of such arrangements. The period of the Rule—a life in being plus 21 years—is suit-

able for donative transfers only, and this point applies with equal force to the 90–year allowable waiting period under the wait-and-see element of Section 2–901. That period, as noted, represents an approximation of the period of time that would be produced, on average, by tracing a set of actual measuring lives and adding a 21–year period following the death of the survivor.

Certain types of transactions—although in some sense supported by consideration, and hence arguably nondonative—arise out of a domestic situation, and should not be excluded from the Statutory Rule. To avoid uncertainty with respect to such transactions, subsection (1) lists and restores such transactions, such as premarital or postmarital agreements, contracts to make or not to revoke a will or trust, and so on, to the donative-transfers category that does not qualify for an exclusion.

Reference. Section 2–904 is Section 4 of the Uniform Statutory Rule Against Perpetuities (Uniform Act). For further discussion of this section, with examples illustrating its application, see the Official Comment to Section 4 of the Uniform Act.

Section 2–905. Prospective Application.

(a) Except as extended by subsection (b), Subpart 1 of this Part applies to a nonvested property interest or a power of appointment that is created on or after the effective date of Subpart 1 of this Part. For purposes of this section, a nonvested property interest or a power of appointment created by the exercise of a power of appointment is created when the power is irrevocably exercised or when a revocable exercise becomes irrevocable.

(b) If a nonvested property interest or a power of appointment was created before the effective date of Subpart 1 of this Part and is determined in a judicial proceeding, commenced on or after the effective date of Subpart 1 of this Part, to violate this State's rule against perpetuities as that rule existed before the effective date of Subpart 1 of this Part, a court upon the petition of an interested person may reform the disposition in the manner that most closely approximates the transferor's manifested plan of distribution and is within the limits of the rule against perpetuities applicable when the nonvested property interest or power of appointment was created.

COMMENT

Section 2–905 provides that, except for Section 2–905(b), this Part applies only to nonvested property interests or powers of appointment created on or after the effective date of this Subpart. The second sentence of subsection (a) establishes a special rule for nonvested property interests (and powers of appointment) created by the exercise of a power of appointment. The import of this special rule, which applies to the exercise of all types of powers of appointment (general testamentary powers and nongeneral powers as well as presently exercisable general powers), is that all the provisions of this Subpart except Section 2–905(b) apply if the donee of a power of appointment exercises the power on or after the effective date of this Subpart, whether the donee's exercise is revocable or irrevocable. In addition, all the provisions of Subpart 1 except Section 2–905(b) apply if the donee exercised the power before the effective date of this Subpart if (i) that pre-effective-date exercise was revocable and (ii) that revocable exercise becomes irrevocable on or after the effective date of this Subpart. The special rule, in

214

other words, prevents the common-law doctrine of relation back from inappropriately shrinking the reach of this Subpart.

Although the Uniform Statutory Rule does not apply retroactively, Section 2–905(b) authorizes a court to exercise its equitable power of reform instruments that contain a violation of the state's former rule against perpetuities and to which the Uniform Statutory Rule does not apply because the offending property interest or power of appointment was created before the effective date of this Subpart. Courts are urged to consider reforming such dispositions by judicially inserting a perpetuity saving clause, because a perpetuity saving clause would probably have been used at the drafting stage of the disposition had it been drafted competently. To obviate any possibility of an inequitable exercise of the equitable power to reform, Section 2–905(b) limits the authority to reform to situations in which the violation of the former rule against perpetuities is determined in a judicial proceeding that is commenced on or after the effective date of this Subpart. The equitable power to reform would typically be exercised in the same judicial proceeding in which the invalidity is determined.

Reference. Section 2–905 is Section 5 of the Uniform Statutory Rule Against Perpetuities (Uniform Act). For further discussion of this section, with examples illustrating its application, see the Official Comment to Section 5 of the Uniform Act.

Section 2–906. [Supersession] [Repeal].

Subpart 1 of this Part [supersedes the rule of the common law known as the rule against perpetuities] [repeals (list statutes to be repealed)].

COMMENT

The first set of bracketed text is provided for states that follow the common-law Rule Against Perpetuities. The second set of bracketed text is provided for the repeal of statutory adoptions of the common-law Rule Against Perpetuities, statutory variations of the common-law Rule Against Perpetuities, or statutory prohibitions on the suspension of the power of alienation for more than a certain period. Some states may find it appropriate to enact both sets of bracketed text by joining them with the word "and." This would be appropriate in states having a statute that declares that the common-law Rule Against Perpetuities is in force in the state except as modified therein.

A cautionary note for states repealing listed statutes: If the statutes to be repealed contain exclusions from the rule against perpetuities, states should consider whether to repeal or retain those exclusions, in light of Section 2–904(7), which excludes from the Uniform Statutory Rule property interests, powers of appointment, and other arrangements "excluded by another statute of this State."

215

SUBPART 2. [HONORARY TRUSTS].

GENERAL COMMENT

Subpart 2 contains an optional provision on honorary trusts and trusts for pets. If this optional provision is enacted, a new subsection (8) should be added to Section 2–904 to avoid an overlap or conflict between Subpart 1 of Part 9 (USRAP) and Subpart 2 of Part 9. Subsection (8) makes it clear that Subpart 2 of Part 9 is the exclusive provision applicable to the property interests or arrangements subjected to a time limit by the provisions of Subpart 2. Subsection (8) states:

> (8) a property interest or arrangement subjected to a time limit under Subpart 2 of Part 9.

Additionally, the "or" at the end of Section 2–904(6) should be removed and placed after Section 2–904(7).

> *[Optional provision for validating and limiting the duration of so-called honorary trusts and trusts for pets.]*

[Section 2–907. Honorary Trusts; Trusts for Pets.

(a) [Honorary Trust.] Subject to subsection (c), if (i) a trust is for a specific lawful noncharitable purpose or for a lawful noncharitable purposes to be selected by the trustee and (ii) there is no definite or definitely ascertainable beneficiary designated, the trust may be performed by the trustee for [21] years but no longer, whether or not the terms of the trust contemplate a longer duration.

(b) [Trust for Pets.] Subject to this subsection and subsection (c), a trust for the care of a designated domestic or pet animal is valid. The trust terminates when no living animal is covered by the trust. A governing instrument must be liberally construed to bring the transfer within this subsection, to presume against the merely precatory or honorary nature of the disposition, and to carry out the general intent of the transferor. Extrinsic evidence is admissible in determining the transferor's intent.

(c) [Additional Provisions Applicable to Honorary Trusts and Trusts for Pets]. In addition to the provisions of subsection (a) or (b), a trust covered by either of those subsections is subject to the following provisions:

> (1) Except as expressly provided otherwise in the trust instrument, no portion of the principal or income may be converted to the use of the trustee or to any use other than for the trust's purposes or for the benefit of a covered animal.

(2) Upon termination, the trustee shall transfer the unexpended trust property in the following order:

(i) as directed in the trust instrument;

(ii) if the trust was created in a nonresiduary clause in the transferor's will or in a codicil to the transferor's will, under the residuary clause in the transferor's will; and

(iii) if no taker is produced by the application of subparagraph (i) or (ii), to the transferor's heirs under Section 2–711.

(3) For the purposes of Section 2–707, the residuary clause is treated as creating a future interest under the terms of a trust.

(4) The intended use of the principal or income can be enforced by an individual designated for that purpose in the trust instrument or, if none, by an individual appointed by a court upon application to it by an individual.

(5) Except as ordered by the court or required by the trust instrument, no filing, report, registration, periodic accounting, separate maintenance of funds, appointment, or fee is required by reason of the existence of the fiduciary relationship of the trustee.

(6) A court may reduce the amount of the property transferred, if it determines that that amount substantially exceeds the amount required for the intended use. The amount of the reduction, if any, passes as unexpended trust property under subsection (c)(2).

(7) If no trustee is designated or no designated trustee is willing or able to serve, a court shall name a trustee. A court may order the transfer of the property to another trustee, if required to assure that the intended use is carried out and if no successor trustee is designated in the trust instrument or if no designated successor trustee agrees to serve or is able to serve. A court may also make such other orders and determinations as shall be advisable to carry out the intent of the transferor and the purpose of this section.]

COMMENT

Subsection (a) of this section authorizes so-called honorary trusts and places a 21–year limit on their duration. The figure "21" is bracketed to indicate that an enacting state may select a different figure.

Subsection (b) provides more elaborate provisions for a particular type of honorary trust, the trust for the care of domestic or pet animals. Under subsection (b), a trust for the care of a designated domestic or pet animal is valid until the death of the animal.

Subsection (b) meets a concern of many pet owners by providing them a means for leaving funds to be used for the pet's care.

Historical Note. This Comment was revised in 1993. For the prior version, see 8 U.L.A. 180 (Supp. 1992).

PART 10

UNIFORM INTERNATIONAL WILLS ACT [INTERNATIONAL WILL; INFORMATION REGISTRATION]

PREFATORY NOTE

Introduction

The purpose of the Washington Convention of 1973 concerning international wills is to provide testators with a way of making wills that will be valid as to form in all countries joining the Convention. As proposed by the Convention, the objective would be achieved through uniform local rules of form, rather than through local or international law that makes recognition of foreign wills turn on choice of law rules involving possible application of foreign law. The international will provisions, prepared for the National Conference of Commissioners on Uniform State Laws by the Joint Editorial Board for the Uniform Probate Code which has functioned as a special committee of the Conference for the project, should be enacted by all states, including those that have not accepted the Uniform Probate Code. To that end, this statute is framed both as a free-standing act and as an added part of the Uniform Probate Code. The bracketed headings and numbers fit the proposal into UPC; the others present the proposal as a free-standing act.

Uniform state enactment of these provisions will permit the Washington Convention of 1973 to be implemented through state legislation familiar to will draftsmen. Thus, local proof of foreign law and reliance on federal legislation regarding wills can be avoided when foreign wills come into our states to be implemented. Also, the citizens of all states will have a will form available that should greatly reduce perils of proof and risks of invalidity that attend proof of American wills abroad.

History of the International Will

Discussions about possible international accord on an acceptable form of will led the Governing Council of UNIDROIT (International Institute for the Unification of Private Law) in 1960 to appoint a small committee of experts from several countries to develop proposals. Following week-long meetings at the Institute's quarters in Rome in 1963, and on two occasions in 1965, the Institute published and circulated a Draft Convention of December 1966 with an annexed uniform law that would be required to be enacted locally by those countries agreeing to the convention. The package and accompanying explanations were reviewed in this country by the Secretary of State's Advisory Committee on Private International Law. In turn, it referred the proposal to a special committee of American probate specialists drawn from members of NCCUSL's Special Committee on the Uniform Probate Code and its advisers and reporters. The resulting reports and recommendations were affirmative and urged the State Department to cooperate in continuing efforts to develop the 1966 Draft Convention, and to endeavor to interest other countries in the subject.

Encouraged by support for the project from this country and several others, UNIDROIT served as host for a 1971 meeting in Rome of an expanded group that included some of the original panel of experts and others from several countries that were not represented in the early drafting sessions. The result of this meeting was a revised draft of the proposed convention and annexed uniform law and this, in turn, was the subject of study and discussion by many more persons in this country. In mid–1973, the proposal from UNIDROIT was discussed in a joint program of the Real Property Probate and Trust Law Section, and the Section of International Law at the American Bar Association's annual meeting held that year in Washington, D.C. By late 1973, the list of published, scholarly discussions of the International Will proposals included Fratcher, "The Uniform Probate Code and the International Will", 66 Mich.L.Rev. 469 (1968); Wellman, "Recent Unidroit Drafts on the International Will", 6 The International Lawyer 205 (1973); and Wellman, "Proposed International Convention Concerning Wills", 8/4 Real Property, Probate and Trust Journal 622 (1973).

In October 1973, pursuant to a commitment made earlier to UNIDROIT representatives that it would provide leadership for the international will proposal if sufficient interest from other countries became evident, the United States served as host for the diplomatic Conference on Wills which met in Washington from October 10 to 26, 1973. 42 governments were represented by delegations, 6 by observers. The United States delegation of 8 persons plus 2 Congressional advisers and 2 staff advisers, was headed by Ambassador Richard D. Kearney, Chairman of the Secretary of State's Advisory Committee on Private International Law who also was selected president of the Conference. The result of the Conference was the Convention of October 26, 1973 Providing a Uniform Law on the Form of an International Will, an appended Annex, Uniform Law on the Form of an International Will, and a Resolution recommending establishment of state assisted systems for the safekeeping and discovery of wills. These three documents are reproduced at the end of these preliminary comments.

A more detailed account of the UNIDROIT project and the 1973 Convention, together with recommendations regarding United States implementation of the Convention, appears in Nadelmann, "The Formal Validity of Wills and the Washington Convention 1973 Providing the Form of an International Will", XXII The American Journal of Comparative Law, 365 (1974).

Description of the Proposal

The 1973 Convention obligates countries becoming parties to make the annexed uniform law a part of their local law. The proposed uniform law contemplates the involvement in will executions under this law of a state recognized expert who is referred to throughout the proposals as the "authorized person". Hence, the local law called for by the Convention must designate authorized persons, and prescribe the formalities for an international will and the role of authorized persons relating thereto. The Convention binds parties to respect the authority of another party's authorized persons and this obligation, coupled with local enactment of the common statute prescribing the role of such persons and according finality to their certificates regarding due execution of wills, assures recognition of international wills under local law in all countries joining the Convention.

The Convention and the annexed uniform law deal only with the formal validity of wills. Thus, the proposal is entirely neutral in relation to local laws dealing with revocation of wills, or those defining the scope of testamentary power, or regulating the probate, interpretation, and construction of wills, and the administration of decedents' estates. The proposal describes a highly formal mode of will execution; one that is sufficiently protective against imposition and mistake to command international approval as being safe enough. However, failure to meet the requirements of an international will does not necessarily result in invalidity, for the mode of execution described for an international will does not pre-empt or exclude other standards of testamentary validity.

The details of the prescribed mode of execution reflect a blend of common and civil law elements. Two attesting witnesses are required in the tradition of the English Statute of Wills of 1837 and its American counterparts. The authorized person whose participation in the ceremony of execution is required, and whose certificate makes the will self-proved, plays a role not unlike that of the civil law notary, though he is not required to retain custody of the will as is customary with European notaries.

The question of who should be given state recognition as authorized persons was resolved by designation of all licensed attorneys. The reasons for this can be seen in the observations about the role of Kurt H. Nadelmann, writing in The American Journal of Comparative Law:

The duties imposed by the Uniform Law upon the person doing the certifying go beyond legalization of signatures, the domain of the notary public. At least paralegal training is a necessity. Abroad, in countries with the law trained notary, the designation is likely to go to this class or at least to include it. Similarly, in countries with a closely supervised class of solicitors, their designation may be expected.

Attorneys are subject to training and licensing requirements everywhere in this country. The degree to which they are supervised after qualification varies considerably from state to state, but the trend is definitely in the direction of more rather than less supervision. Designation of attorneys in the uniform law permits a state to bring the statute into its local law books without undue delay.

Roles for Federal and State Law in Relation to International Will

Several alternatives are available for arranging federal and state laws on the subject of international wills. The 1973 Convention obligates nations becoming parties to introduce the annexed uniform law into their local law, and to recognize the authority, *vis a vis* will executions and certificates relating to wills, of persons designated as authorized by other parties to the Convention. But, the Convention includes a clause for federal states that may be used by the United States as it moves, through the process of Senate Advice and Consent, to accept the international compact. Through it, the federal government may limit the areas in this country to which the Convention will be applicable. Thus, Article XIV of the 1973 Convention provides:

1. If a state has two or more territorial units in which different systems of law apply in relation to matters respecting the form of wills, it may at the time of signature, ratification, or accession, declare that this Convention shall extend to all its territorial units or only to one or more of them, and may modify its declaration by submitting another declaration at any time.

2. These declarations shall be notified to the Depositary Government and shall state expressly the territorial units to which the Convention applies.

One alternative would be for the federal government to refrain from use of Article XIV and to accept the Convention as applicable to all areas of the country. The obligation to introduce the uniform law into local law then could be met by passage of a federal statute incorporating the uniform law and designating authorized persons who can assist testators desiring to use the international format, possibly leaving it open for state legislatures, if they wish, to designate other or additional groups of authorized persons. As to constitutionality, the federal statute on wills could be rested on the power of the federal government to bind the states by treaty and to implement a treaty obligation to bring agreed upon rules into local law by any appropriate method. Missouri v. Holland, 252 U.S. 416 (1920); Nadelmann, "The Formal Validity of Wills and the Washington Convention 1973 Providing the Form of An International Will", XXII The Am. Jn'l of Comp.L. 365, 375 (1974). Prof. Nadelmann favors this approach, arguing that new risks of invalidity of wills would arise if the treaty were limited so as to be applicable only in designated areas of the country, presumably those where state enactment of the uniform law already had occurred.

One disadvantage of this approach is that it would place a potentially important method for validating wills in federal statutes where probate practitioners, long accustomed to finding the statutes pertinent to their specialty in state compilations, simply would not discover it. Another, of course, relates to more generalized concerns that would attend any move by the federal government into an area of law traditionally reserved to the states.

Alternatively, the federal government might accept the Convention and uniform law as applicable throughout the land, so that international wills executed with the aid of authorized persons of other countries would be good anywhere in this country, but refrain from any designation of authorized persons, other than possibly of some minimum federal cadre, or of those who could function within the District of Columbia, leaving the selection of more useful groups of authorized persons entirely to the states. One result would be to greatly narrow the advantage of international wills to American testators who wanted to execute their instruments at home. In probable consequence, there would be pressure on state legislatures to enact the uniform law so as to make the advantages of the system available to local testators. Assuming some state legislatures respond to the pressure affirmatively and others negatively, a crazyquilt pattern of international will states would develop, leading possibly to some of the confusion and risk of illegality feared by Prof. Nadelmann. On the other hand, since execution of an international will involves use of an authorized person who derives authority from (on this assumption) state legislation, it seems somewhat unlikely that testators in states which have not designated authorized persons will be led to believe that they can make an international will unless they go to a state where authorized persons have been designated. Hence, the confusion may not be as great as if the Convention were inapplicable to portions of the country.

Finally, the federal government might use Article XIV as suggested earlier, and designate some but not all states as areas of the country in which the Convention applied. This seems the least desirable of all alternatives because it subjects international wills from abroad to the risk of non-recognition in some states, and offers the risk of confusion of American testators regarding the areas of the country where they can execute a will that will be received outside this country as an international will.

Under any of the approaches, the desirability of widespread enactment of state statutes embodying the uniform law and designating authorized persons, seems clear, as does the necessity for this project of the National Conference of Commissioners on Uniform State Laws.

Style

In preparing the International Will proposal, the special committee, after considerable discussion and consideration of alternatives, decided to stick as closely as possible to the wording of the Annex to the Convention of October 26, 1973. The Convention and its Annex were written in the English, French, Russian and Spanish languages, each version, as declared by Article XVI of the Convention, being equally authentic. Not surprisingly, the English version of the Annex has a style that is somewhat different than that to which the National Conference is accustomed. Nonetheless, from the view of those using languages other than English who may be reviewing our state statutes on the International Will to see if they adhere to the Annex, it is more important to stick with the agreed formulations than it is to re-style these expressions to suit our traditions. However, some changes from the Annex were made in the interests of clarity, and because some of the language of the Annex is plainly inappropriate in a local enactment. These changes are explained in the Comments.

Will Registration

A bracketed section 10[2–1010], is included in the International Will proposal to aid survivors in locating international and other wills that have been kept secret by testators during their lives. Differing from the section 2–901 of the Uniform Probate Code and the many existing statutes from which section 2–901 was derived which constitute the probate court as an agency for the safekeeping of wills deposited by living testators, the bracketed proposal is for a system of registering certain minimum information about wills, including where the instrument will be kept pending the death of the testator. It can be separated or omitted from the rest of the Act.

This provision for a state will registration system is derived from recommendations by the Council of Europe for common market countries. These recommendations were urged on the group that assembled in Rome in 1971, and were received with interest by representatives of United Kingdom, Canada and United States, where will-making laws and customs have not included any officially sanctioned system for safekeeping of wills or for locating information about wills, other than occasional statutes providing for ante-mortem deposit of wills with probate courts. Interest was expressed also by the notaries from civil law countries who have traditionally aided will-making both by formalizing execution and by being the source thereafter of official certificates about wills, the originals of which are retained with the official records of the notary and carefully protected and regulated by settled customs of the profession. All recognized that acceptance of the international will would tend to increase the frequency with which owners of property in several different countries relied on a single will to control all of their properties. This prospect, plus increasing mobility of persons between countries, indicates that new methods for safekeeping and locating wills after death should be developed. The Resolution adopted as the final act of the 1973 Conference on Wills shows that the problem also attracted the interest and attention of that assembly.

Apart from problems of wills that may have effect in more than one country, Americans are moving from state to state with increasing frequency. As the international will statute becomes enacted in most if not all states, our laws will tend to induce persons to rely on a single will as sufficient even though they may own land in two or more states, and to refrain from making new wills when they change domicile from one state to another. The spread of the Uniform Probate Code, tending as it does to give wills the same meaning and procedural status in all states, will have a similar effect.

General enactment of the will registration section should lead to development of new state and interstate systems to meet the predictable needs of testators and survivors that will follow as the law of wills is detached from provincial restraints. It is offered with the international will provisions because both meet obvious needs of the times.

Documents from 1973 Convention

Three documents representing the work of the 1973 Convention are reproduced here for the convenience of members of the Conference.

CONVENTION PROVIDING A UNIFORM LAW ON THE FORM OF AN INTERNATIONAL WILL

The States signatory to the present Convention,

DESIRING to provide to a greater extent for the respecting of last wills by establishing an additional form of will hereinafter to be called an "international will" which, if employed, would dispense to some extent with the search for the applicable law;

HAVE RESOLVED to conclude a Convention for this purpose and have agreed upon the following provisions:

Article I   1.   Each Contracting Party undertakes that not later than six months after the date of entry into force of this Convention in respect of that Party it shall introduce into its law the rules regarding an international will set out in the Annex to this Convention.

2.   Each Contracting Party may introduce the provisions of the Annex into its law either by reproducing the actual text, or by translating it into its official language or languages.

3.   Each Contracting Party may introduce into its law such further provisions as are necessary to give the provisions of the Annex full effect in its territory.

4.   Each Contracting Party shall submit to the Depositary Government the text of the rules introduced into its national law in order to implement the provisions of this Convention.

Article II   1.   Each Contracting Party shall implement the provisions of the Annex in its law, within the period provided for in the preceding article, by designating the persons who, in its territory, shall be authorized to act in connection with international wills.   It may also designate as a person authorized to act with regard to its nationals its diplomatic or consular agents abroad insofar as the local law does not prohibit it.

2.   The Party shall notify such designation, as well as any modifications thereof, to the Depositary Government.

Article III   The capacity of the authorized person to act in connection with an international will, if conferred in accordance with the law of a Contracting Party, shall be recognized in the territory of the other Contracting Parties.

Article IV   The effectiveness of the certificate provided for in Article 10 of the Annex shall be recognized in the territories of all Contracting Parties.

Article V   1.   The conditions requisite to acting as a witness of an international will shall be governed by the law under which the authorized person was designated.   The same rule shall apply as regards an interpreter who is called upon to act.

2.   Nonetheless no one shall be disqualified to act as a witness of an international will solely because he is an alien.

Article VI   1.   The signature of the testator, of the authorized person, and of the witnesses to an international will, whether on the will or on the certificate, shall be exempt from any legalization or like formality.

2.   Nonetheless, the competent authorities of any Contracting Party may, if necessary, satisfy themselves as to the authenticity of the signature of the authorized person.

Article VII   The safekeeping of an international will shall be governed by the law under which the authorized person was designated.

Article VIII   No reservation shall be admitted to this Convention or to its Annex.

Article IX   1.   The present Convention shall be open for signature at Washington from October 26, 1973, until December 31, 1974.

2.   The Convention shall be subject to ratification.

3.   Instruments of ratification shall be deposited with the Government of the United States of America, which shall be the Depositary Government.

Article X   1.   The Convention shall be open indefinitely for accession.

2.   Instruments of accession shall be deposited with the Depositary Government.

Article XI   1.   The present Convention shall enter into force six months after the date of deposit of the fifth instrument of ratification or accession with the Depositary Government.

2.   In the case of each State which ratifies this Convention or accedes to it after the fifth instrument of ratification or accession has been deposited, this Convention shall enter into force six months after the deposit of its own instrument of ratification or accession.

Article XII   1.   Any Contracting Party may denounce this Convention by written notification to the Depositary Government.

2.   Such denunciation shall take effect twelve months from the date on which the Depositary Government has received the notification, but such denunciation shall not affect the validity of any will made during the period that the Convention was in effect for the denouncing State.

Article XIII   1.   Any State may, when it deposits its instrument of ratification or accession or at any time thereafter, declare, by a notice addressed to the Depositary Government, that this Convention shall apply to all or part of the territories for the international relations of which it is responsible.

2.   Such declaration shall have effect six months after the date on which the Depositary Government shall have received notice thereof or, if at the end of such period the Convention has not yet come into force, from the date of its entry into force.

3. Each Contracting Party which has made a declaration in accordance with paragraph 1 of this Article may, in accordance with Article XII, denounce this Convention in relation to all or part of the territories concerned.

Article XIV 1. If a State has two or more territorial units in which different systems of law apply in relation to matters respecting the form of wills, it may at the time of signature, ratification, or accession, declare that this Convention shall extend to all its territorial units or only to one or more of them, and may modify its declaration by submitting another declaration at any time.

2. These declarations shall be notified to the Depositary Government and shall state expressly the territorial units to which the Convention applies.

Article XV If a Contracting Party has two or more territorial units in which different systems of law apply in relation to matters respecting the form of wills, any reference to the internal law of the place where the will is made or to the law under which the authorized person has been appointed to act in connection with international wills shall be construed in accordance with the constitutional system of the Party concerned.

Article XVI 1. The original of the present Convention, in the English, French, Russian and Spanish languages, each version being equally authentic, shall be deposited with the Government of the United States of America, which shall transmit certified copies thereof to each of the signatory and acceding States and to the International Institute for the Unification of Private Law.

2. The Depositary Government shall give notice to the signatory and acceding States, and to the International Institute for the Unification of Private Law, of:

(a) any signature;

(b) the deposit of any instrument of ratification or accession;

(c) any date on which this Convention enters into force in accordance with Article XI;

(d) any communication received in accordance with Article I, paragraph 4;

(e) any notice received in accordance with Article II, paragraph 2;

(f) any declaration received in accordance with Article XIII, paragraph 2, and the date on which such declaration takes effect;

(g) any denunciation received in accordance with Article XII, paragraph 1, or Article XIII, paragraph 3, and the date on which the denunciation takes effect;

(h) any declaration received in accordance with Article XIV, paragraph 2, and the date on which the declaration takes effect.

IN WITNESS WHEREOF, the undersigned Plenipotentiaries, being duly authorized to that effect, have signed the present Convention.

227

DONE at Washington this twenty-sixth day of October, one thousand nine hundred and seventy-three.

Annex

UNIFORM LAW ON THE FORM OF AN INTERNATIONAL WILL

Article 1 1. A will shall be valid as regards form, irrespective particularly of the place where it is made, of the location of the assets and of the nationality, domicile or residence of the testator, if it is made in the form of an international will complying with the provisions set out in Articles 2 to 5 hereinafter.

2. The invalidity of the will as an international will shall not affect its formal validity as a will of another kind.

Article 2 This law shall not apply to the form of testamentary dispositions made by two or more persons in one instrument.

Article 3 1. The will shall be made in writing.

2. It need not be written by the testator himself.

3. It may be written in any language, by hand or by any other means.

Article 4 1. The testator shall declare in the presence of two witnesses and of a person authorized to act in connection with international wills that the document is his will and that he knows the contents thereof.

2. The testator need not inform the witnesses, or the authorized person, of the contents of the will.

Article 5 1. In the presence of the witnesses and of the authorized person, the testator shall sign the will or, if he has previously signed it, shall acknowledge his signature.

2. When the testator is unable to sign, he shall indicate the reason therefor to the authorized person who shall make note of this on the will. Moreover, the testator may be authorized by the law under which the authorized person was designated to direct another person to sign on his behalf.

3. The witnesses and the authorized person shall there and then attest the will by signing in the presence of the testator.

Article 6 1. The signatures shall be placed at the end of the will.

2. If the will consists of several sheets, each sheet shall be signed by the testator or, if he is unable to sign, by the person signing on his behalf or, if there is no such person, by the authorized person. In addition, each sheet shall be numbered.

Article 7 1. The date of the will shall be the date of its signature by the authorized person.

2. This date shall be noted at the end of the will by the authorized person.

Article 8 In the absence of any mandatory rule pertaining to the safekeeping of the will, the authorized person shall ask the testator whether he wishes to make a declaration concerning the safekeeping of his will. If so and at the express request of the testator the place where he intends to have his will kept shall be mentioned in the certificate provided for in Article 9.

Article 9 The authorized person shall attach to the will a certificate in the form prescribed in Article 10 establishing that the obligations of this law have been complied with.

Article 10 The certificate drawn up by the authorized person shall be in the following form or in a substantially similar form:

CERTIFICATE

(Convention of October 26, 1973)

1. I, _____ (name, address and capacity), a person authorized to act in connection with international wills

2. Certify that on _____ (date) at _____ (place)

3. (testator) _____ (name, address, date and place of birth) in my presence and that of the witnesses

4.   (a) _____(name, address, date and place of birth)
     (b) _____ (name, address, date and place of birth) has declared that the attached document is his will and that he knows the contents thereof.
5. I furthermore certify that:
6.   (a) in my presence and in that of the witnesses
         (1) the testator has signed the will or has acknowledged his signature previously affixed.
       *(2) following a declaration of the testator stating that he was unable to sign his will for the following reason _____
          —I have mentioned this declaration on the will
        *—the signature has been affixed by _____ (name, address)
7.   (b) the witnesses and I have signed the will;
8. *(c) each page of the will has been signed by _____ and numbered;
9.   (d) I have satisfied myself as to the identity of the testator and of the witnesses as designated above;
10. (e) the witnesses met the conditions requisite to act as such according to the law under which I am acting;
11. *(f) the testator has requested me to include the following statement concerning the safekeeping of his will:

_____

_____

12. PLACE
13. DATE
14. SIGNATURE and, if necessary, SEAL
    *To be completed if appropriate

Article 11 The authorized person shall keep a copy of the certificate and deliver another to the testator.

Article 12 In the absence of evidence to the contrary, the certificate of the authorized person shall be conclusive of the formal validity of the instrument as a will under this Law.

229

Article 13 The absence or irregularity of a certificate shall not affect the formal validity of a will under this Law.

Article 14 The international will shall be subject to the ordinary rules of revocation of wills.

Article 15 In interpreting and applying the provisions of this law, regard shall be had to its international origin and to the need for uniformity in its interpretation.

RESOLUTION

The Conference

Considering the importance of measures to permit the safeguarding of wills and to find them after the death of the testator;

Emphasizing the special interest in such measures with respect to the international will, which is often made by the testator far from his home;

RECOMMENDS to the States that participated in the present Conference

—that they establish an internal system, centralized or not, to facilitate the safekeeping, search and discovery of an international will as well as the accompanying certificate, for example, along the lines of the Convention on the Establishment of a Scheme of Registration of Wills, concluded at Basel on May 16, 1972;

—that they facilitate the international exchange of information in these matters and, to this effect, that they designate in each state an authority or a service to handle such exchanges.

NUMBERING SECTIONS OF ACT

The Uniform International Wills Act may be adopted as a separate act or as part of the Uniform Probate Code. If adopted as a separate act, the unbracketed section numbers would govern. If adopted as part of the Probate Code, i.e., as Part 10 of Article 2, the section numbers in brackets would govern.

Section 1. [2–1001.] [Definitions.]

In this Act: [Part:]

(1) "International will" means a will executed in conformity with sections 2 [2–1002] through 5 [2–1005].

(2) "Authorized person" and "person authorized to act in connection with international wills" mean a person who by section 9 [2–1009], or by the laws of the United States including members of the diplomatic and consular service of the United States designated

by Foreign Service Regulations, is empowered to supervise the execution of international wills.

COMMENT

The term "international will" connotes only that a will has been executed in conformity with this act. It does not indicate that the will was planned for implementation in more than one country, or that it relates to an estate that has or may have international implications. Thus, it will be entirely appropriate to use an "international will" whenever a will is desired.

The reference in subsection (2) to persons who derive their authority to act from federal law, including Foreign Service Regulations, anticipates that the United States will become a party to the 1973 Convention, and that Congress, pursuant to the obligation of the Convention, will enact the annexed uniform law and include therein some designation, possibly of a cadre only, of authorized persons. See the discussion under "Roles for Federal and State Law in Relation to International Will", in the Prefatory Note, *supra*. If all states enact similar laws and designate all attorneys as authorized persons, the need for testators to resort to those designated by federal law may be minimal. It seems desirable, nonetheless, to associate whoever may be designated by federal law as suitable authorized persons for purposes of implementing state enactments of the uniform act. The resulting "borrowing" of those designated federally should minimize any difficulties that might arise from variances in the details of execution of international wills that may develop in the state and federal enactment process.

In the Explanatory Report of the 1973 Convention prepared by Mr. Jean–Pierre Plantard, Deputy Secretary–General of the International Institute for the Unification of Private Law (UNIDROIT) as published by the Institute in 1974, the following paragraphs that are relevant to this section appear:

"The Uniform Law gives no definition of the term will. The preamble of the Convention also uses the expression 'last wills'. The material contents of the document are of little importance as the Uniform Law governs only its form. There is, therefore, nothing to prevent this form being used to register last wishes that do not involve the naming of an heir and which in some legal systems are called by a special name, such as 'Kodizill' in Austrian Law (ABGB § 553).

"Although it is given the qualification 'international', the will dealt with by the Uniform Law can easily be used for a situation without any international element, for example, by a testator disposing in his own country of his assets, all of which are situated in that same country. The adjective 'international', therefore, only indicates what was had in mind at the time when this new will was conceived. Moreover, it would have been practically impossible to define a satisfactory sphere of application, had one intended to restrict its use to certain situations with an international element. Such an element could only be assessed by reference to several factors (nationality, residence, domicile of the testator, place where the will was drawn up, place where the assets are situated) and, moreover, these might vary considerably between when the will was drawn up and the beginning of the inheritance proceedings.

"Use of the international will should, therefore, be open to all testators who decide they want to use it. Nothing should prevent it from competing with the traditional forms if it offers advantages of convenience and simplicity over the other forms and guarantees the necessary certainty."

Section 2. [2–1002.] [International Will; Validity.]

(a) A will shall be valid as regards form, irrespective particularly of the place where it is made, of the location of the assets and of the nationality, domicile, or residence of the testator, if it is made in the form of an international will complying with the requirements of this Act. [Part.]

(b) The invalidity of the will as an international will shall not affect its formal validity as a will of another kind.

(c) This Act [Part] shall not apply to the form of testamentary dispositions made by two or more persons in one instrument.

COMMENT

This section combines what appears in Articles 1 and 2 of the Annex into a single section. Except for the reference to later sections, the first sentence is identical to Article 1, section 1 of the Annex, the second sentence is identical to Article 1, section 2, and the third is identical to Article 2.

Mr. Plantard's commentary that is pertinent to this section is as follows:

"The Uniform Law is intended to be introduced into the legal system of each Contracting State. Article 1, therefore, introduces into the internal law of each Contracting State the new, basic principle according to which the international will is valid irrespective of the country in which it was made, the nationality, domi-

cile or residence of the testator and the place where the assets forming the estate are located.

"The scope of the Uniform Law is thus defined in the first sentence. As was mentioned above, the idea behind it was to establish a new type of will, the form of which would be the same in all countries. The Law obviously does not affect the subsistence of all the other forms of will known under each national law....

"Some of the provisions relating to form laid down by the Uniform Law are considered essential. Violation of these provisions is sanctioned by the invalidity of the will as an international will. These are: that the will must be made in writing, the presence of two witnesses and of the authorised person, signature by the testator and by the persons involved (witnesses and authorised person) and the prohibition of joint wills. The other formalities, such as the position of the signature and date, the delivery and form of the certificate, are laid down for reasons of convenience and uniformity but do not affect the validity of the international will.

"Lastly, even when the international will is declared invalid because one of the essential provisions contained in Articles 2 to 5 has not been observed, it is not necessarily deprived of all effect. Paragraph 2 of Article 1 specifies that it may still be valid as a will of another kind, if it conforms with the requirements of the applicable national law. Thus, for example, a will written, dated and signed by the testator but handed over to an authorised person in the absence of witnesses or without the signature of the witnesses and the authorised person could quite easily be considered a valid holograph will. Similarly, an international will produced in the presence of a person who is not duly authorised might be valid as a will

witnessed in accordance with Common law rules.

"However, in these circumstances, one could no longer speak of an international will and the validity of the document would have to be assessed on the basis of the rules of internal law or of private international law.

"A joint will cannot be drawn up in the form of an international will. This is the meaning of Article 2 of the Uniform Law which does not give an opinion as to whether this prohibition on joint wills, which exists in many legal systems, is connected with its form or its substance.

"A will made in this international form by several people together in the same document would, therefore, be invalid as an international will but could possibly be valid as another kind of will, in accordance with Article 1, paragraph 2 of the Uniform Law.

"The terminology used in Article 2 is in harmony with that used in Article 4 of The Hague Convention on the Conflicts of Laws Relating to the Form of Testamentary Dispositions."

Section 3. [2–1003.]   [International Will; Requirements.]

(a) The will shall be made in writing. It need not be written by the testator himself. It may be written in any language, by hand or by any other means.

(b) The testator shall declare in the presence of two witnesses and of a person authorized to act in connection with international wills that the document is his will and that he knows the contents thereof. The testator need not inform the witnesses, or the authorized person, of the contents of the will.

(c) In the presence of the witnesses, and of the authorized person, the testator shall sign the will or, if he has previously signed it, shall acknowledge his signature.

(d) When the testator is unable to sign, the absence of his signature does not affect the validity of the international will if the testator indicates the reason for his inability to sign and the authorized person makes note thereof on the will. In these cases, it is permissible for any other person present, including the authorized person or one of the witnesses, at the direction of the testator to sign the testator's name for him, if the authorized person makes note of this also on the will, but it is not required that any person sign the testator's name for him.

(e) The witnesses and the authorized person shall there and then attest the will by signing in the presence of the testator.

COMMENT

The five subsections of this section correspond in content to Articles 3 through 5 of the Annex to the 1973 Convention. Article 1, section 1 makes it clear that compliance with all requirements listed in Articles 3 through 5 is necessary in order to achieve an international will. As re-organized for enactment in the United States, all mandatory requirements have been grouped in this section. Except for subsection (d), each of the sentences in the subsections corresponds exactly with a sentence in the Annex. Subsection (d), derived from Article 5, section 2 of the Annex, was reworded for the sake of clarity.

Mr. Plantard's comments on the requirements are as follows:

"Paragraph 1 of Article 3 lays down an essential condition for a will's validity as an international will: it must be made in writing.

"The Uniform Law does not explain what is meant by 'writing'. This is a word of everyday language which, in the opinion of the Law's authors, does not call for any definition but which covers any form of expression made by signs on a durable substance.

"Paragraphs 2 and 3 show the very liberal approach of the draft.

"Under paragraph 2, the will does not necessarily have to be written by the testator himself. This provision marks a moving away from the holograph will toward the other types of will: the public will or the mystic will and especially the Common law will. The latter, which is often very long, is only in exceptional cases written in the hand of the testator, who is virtually obliged to use a lawyer, in order to use the technical formulae necessary to give effect to his wishes. This is all the more so as wills frequently involve inter vivos family arrangements, and fiscal considerations play a very important part in this matter.

"This provision also allows for the will of illiterate persons, or persons who, for some other reason, cannot write themselves, for example paralysed or blind persons.

"According to paragraph 3 a will may be written in any language. This provision is in contrast with the rules accepted in various countries as regards public wills. It will be noted that the Uniform Law does not even require the will to be written in a language known by the testator.

The latter is, therefore, quite free to choose according to whichever suits him best: it is to be expected that he will usually choose his own language but, if he thinks it is better, he will sometimes also choose the language of the place where the will is drawn up or that of the place where the will is mainly to be carried out.   The important point is that he have full knowledge of the contents of his will, as is guaranteed by Articles 4 and 10.

"Lastly, a will may be written by hand or by any other method. This provision is the corollary of paragraph 2. What is mainly had in mind is a typewriter, especially in the case of a will drawn up by a lawyer advising the testator.

"The liberal nature of the principles set out in Article 3 calls for certain guarantees on the other hand.   These are provided by the presence of three persons, already referred to in the context of Articles III and V of the Convention, that is to say, the authorised person and the two witnesses.   It is evident that these three persons must all be simultaneously present with the testator during the carrying out of the formalities laid down in Articles 4 and 5.

"Paragraph 1 of Article 4 requires, first of all, that the testator declare, in the presence of these persons, that the document produced by him is his will and that he knows the contents thereof. The word 'declares' covers any unequivocal expression of intention, by way of words as well as by gestures or signs, as, for example, in the case of a testator who is dumb. This declaration must be made on pain of the

international will being invalid. This is justified by the fact that the will produced by the testator might have been materially drawn up by a person other than the testator and even, in theory, in a language which is not his own.

"Paragraph 2 of the article specifies that this declaration is sufficient: the testator does not need to 'inform' the witnesses or the authorised person 'of the contents of the will'. This rule makes the international will differ from the public will and brings it closer to the other types of will: the holograph will and especially the mystic will and the Common law will.

"The testator can, of course, always ask for the will to be read, a precaution which can be particularly useful if the testator is unable to read himself. The paragraph under consideration does not in any way prohibit this; it only aims at ensuring respect for secrecy, if the testator should so wish. The international will can therefore be a secret will without being a closed will.

"The declaration made by the testator under Article 4 is not sufficient: under Article 5, paragraph 1, he must also sign his will. However, the authors of the Uniform Law presumed that, in certain cases, the testator might already have signed the document forming his will before producing it. To require a second signature would be evidence of an exaggerated formalism and a will containing two signatures by the testator would be rather strange. That is why the same paragraph provides that, when he has already signed the will, the testator can merely acknowledge it. This acknowledgement is completely informal and is normally done by a simple declaration in the presence of the authorised person and witnesses.

"The Uniform Law does not explain what is meant by 'signature'. This is once more a word drawn from everyday language, the meaning of which is usually the same in the various legal systems. The presence of the authorised person, who will necessarily be a practising lawyer will certainly guarantee that there is a genuine signature correctly affixed.

"Paragraph 2 was designed to give persons incapable of signing the possibility of making an international will. All they have to do is indicate their incapacity and the reason therefor to the authorised person. The authorised person must then note this declaration on the will which will then be valid, even though it has not been signed by the testator. Indication of the reason for incapacity is an additional guarantee as it can be checked. The certificate drawn up by the authorised person in the form prescribed in Article 10 again reproduces this declaration.

"The authors of the Uniform Law were also conscious of the fact that in some legal systems—for example, English law—persons who are incapable of signing can name someone to sign in their place. Although this procedure is completely unknown to other systems in which a signature is exclusively personal, it was accepted that the testator can ask another person to sign in his name, if this is permitted under the law from which the authorised person derives his authority. This amounts to nothing more than giving satisfaction to the practice of

certain legal systems, as the authorised person must, in any case, indicate on the will that the testator declared that he could not sign, and give the reason therefor. This indication is sufficient to make the will valid. There will, therefore simply be a signature affixed by a third person instead of that of the testator. Although there is nothing stipulating this in the Uniform Law, one can expect the authorised person to explain the source of this signature on the document, all the more so as the signature of this substitute for the testator must also appear on the other pages of the will, by virtue of Article 6.

"This method over which there were some differences of opinion at the Diplomatic Conference, should not however interfere in any way with the legal systems which do not admit a signature in the name of someone else. Besides, its use is limited to the legal systems which admit it already and it is now implicitly accepted by the others when they recognise the validity of a foreign document drawn up according to this method. However, this situation can be expected to arise but rarely, as an international will made by a person who is incapable of signing it will certainly be a rare event.

"Lastly, Article 5 requires that the witnesses and authorised person also sign the will there and then in the presence of the testator. By using the words 'attest the will by signing', when only the word 'sign' had been used when referring to the testator, the authors of the Uniform Law intended to make a distinction between the person acknowledging the contents of a document and those who have only to affix their signature in order to certify their participation and presence.

"In conclusion, the international will will normally contain four signatures: that of the testator, that of the authorised person and those of the two witnesses. The signature of the testator might be missing: in this case, the will must contain a note made by the authorised person indicating that the testator was incapable of signing, adding his reason. All these signatures and notes must be made on pain of invalidity. Finally, if the signature of the testator is missing, the will could contain the signature of a person designated by the testator to sign in his name, in addition to the above-mentioned note made by the authorised person."

Section 4. [2–1004.] [International Will; Other Points of Form.]

(a) The signatures shall be placed at the end of the will. If the will consists of several sheets, each sheet will be signed by the testator or, if he is unable to sign, by the person signing on his behalf or, if there is no such person, by the authorized person. In addition, each sheet shall be numbered.

(b) The date of the will shall be the date of its signature by the authorized person. That date shall be noted at the end of the will by the authorized person.

(c) The authorized person shall ask the testator whether he wishes to make a declaration concerning the safekeeping of his will. If so and at the express request of the testator the place where he intends to have his will kept shall be mentioned in the certificate provided for in Section 5.

(d) A will executed in compliance with Section 3 shall not be invalid merely because it does not comply with this section.

COMMENT

Mr. Plantard's commentary about Articles 6, 7 and 8 of the Annex [*supra*] relate to subsections (a), (b) and (c) respectively of this section. Subsections (a) and (b) are identical to Articles 6 and 7; subsection (c) is the same as Article 8 of the Annex except that the prefatory language "In the absence of any mandatory rule pertaining to the safekeeping of the will ..." has been deleted because it is inappropriate for inclusion in a local statute designed for enactment by a state that has had no tradition or familiarity with mandatory rules regarding the safekeeping of the wills. Subsection (d) embodies the sense of Article 1, section 1 of the Annex which states that compliance with Articles 2 to 5 is necessary and so indicates that compliance with the remaining articles prescribing formal steps is not necessary.

Mr. Plantard's commentary is as follows:

"The provisions of Article 6 and those of the following articles are not imposed on pain of invalidity. They are nevertheless compulsory legal provisions which can involve sanctions, for example, the professional, civil and even criminal liability of the authorised person, according to the provisions of the law from which he derives his authority.

"The first paragraph, to guarantee a uniform presentation for international wills, simply indicates that signatures shall be placed at the end of international wills, that is, at the end of the text.

"Paragraph 2 provides for the frequent case in which the will consists of several sheets. Each sheet has to be signed by the testator, to guarantee its authenticity and to avoid substitutions. The use of the word 'signed' seems to imply that the signature must be in the same form as that at the end of the will. However, in the legal systems which merely require that the individual sheets be paraphed, usually by means of initials, this would certainly have the same value as signature, as a signature itself could simply consist of initials.

"The need for a signature on each sheet, for the purpose of authentifying each such sheet, led to the introduction of a special system for the case when the testator is incapable of signing. In this case it will generally be the authorised person who will sign each sheet in his place, unless, in accordance with Article 5, paragraph 2, the testator has designated another person to sign in his name. In this case, it will of course be this person who will sign each sheet.

"Lastly, it is prescribed that the sheets shall be numbered. Al-
though no further details are given on this subject, it will in practice be up to the authorised person to check if they have already been numbered and, if not, to number them or ask the testator to do so.

"The aim of this provision is obviously to guarantee the orderliness of the document and to avoid losses, subtractions or substitutions.

"The date is an essential element of the will and its importance is quite clear in the case of successive wills. Paragraph 1 of Article 7 indicates that the date of the will in the case of an international will is the date on which it was signed by the authorised person, this being the last of the formalities prescribed by the Uniform Law on pain of invalidity (Article 5, paragraph 3). It is, therefore, from the moment of this signature that the international will is valid.

"Paragraph 2 stipulates that the date shall be noted at the end of the will by the authorised person. Although this is compulsory for the authorised person, this formality is not sanctioned by the invalidity of the will which, as is the case in many legal systems such as English, German and Austrian law, remains fully valid even if it is not dated or is wrongly dated. The date will then have to be proved by some other means. It can happen that the will has two dates, that of its drawing up and the date on which it was signed by the authorised person as a result of which it became an international will. Evidently only this last date is to be taken into consideration.

"During the preparatory work it had been intended to organise the safekeeping of the international will

238

and to entrust its care to the authorised person. This plan caused serious difficulties both for the countries which do not have the notary as he is known in Civil law systems and for the countries in which wills must be deposited with a public authority, as is the case, for example, in the Federal Republic of Germany, where wills must be deposited with a court.

"The authors of the Uniform Law therefore abandoned the idea of introducing a unified system for the safekeeping of international wills. However, where a legal system already has rules on this subject, these rules of course also apply to the international will as well as to other types of will. Finally, the Washington Conference adopted, at the same time as the Convention, a resolution recommending States, in particular, to organise a system facilitating the safekeeping of international wills (see the commentary on this resolution, at the end of this Report). It should lastly be underlined that States desiring to give testators an additional guarantee as regards the international will will organise its safekeeping by providing, for example, that it shall be deposited with the authorised person or with a public officer. Complementary legislation of this kind could be admitted within the framework of paragraph 3 of Article 1 of the Convention, as was mentioned in our commentary on that article.

"These considerations explain why Article 8 starts by stipulating that it only applies 'in the absence of any mandatory rule pertaining to the safekeeping of the will'. If there happens to be such a rule in the national law from which the authorised person derives his authority this rule shall govern the safekeeping of the will. If there is no such rule, Article 8 requires the authorised person to ask the testator whether he wishes to make a declaration in this regard. In this way, the authors of the Uniform Law sought to reconcile the advantage of exact information so as to facilitate the discovery of the will after the death of the testator, on the one hand, and respect for the secrecy which the testator may want as regards the place where his will is kept, on the other hand. The testator is therefore quite free to make or not to make a declaration in this regard, but his attention is nevertheless drawn to the possibility left open to him, and particular to the opportunity he has, if he expressly asks for it, to have the details he thinks appropriate in this regard mentioned on the certificate provided for in Article 9. It will thus be easier to find the will again at the proper time, by means of the certificate made out in three copies, one of which remains in the hands of the authorised person."

Section 5. [2–1005.] [International Will; Certificate.]

The authorized person shall attach to the will a certificate to be signed by him establishing that the requirements of this Act [Part] for valid execution of an international will have been complied with. The authorized person shall keep a copy of the certificate and deliver another to the testator. The certificate shall be substantially in the following form:

CERTIFICATE

(Convention of October 26, 1973)

1. I, _____ (name, address and capacity), a person authorized to act in connection with international wills
2. Certify that on _____ (date) at _____ (place)
3. (testator) _____
    (name, address, date and place of birth) in my presence and that of the witnesses
4. (a) _____ (name, address, date and place of birth)
    (b) _____ (name, address, date and place of birth)
    has declared that the attached document is his will and that he knows the contents thereof.
5. I furthermore certify that:
6. (a) in my presence and in that of the witnesses
    (1) the testator has signed the will or has acknowledged his signature previously affixed.
    *(2) following a declaration of the testator stating that he was unable to sign his will for the following reasons _____, I have mentioned this declaration on the will
    * and the signature has been affixed by _____ (name and address)
7. (b) the witnesses and I have signed the will;
8. *   each page of the will has been signed by _____
    (c) and numbered;
9. (d) I have satisfied myself as to the identity of the testator and of the witnesses as designated above;
10. (e) the witnesses met the conditions requisite to act as such according to the law under which I am acting;
11. * (f) the testator has requested me to include the following statement concerning the safekeeping of his will:
    _____

12. PLACE OF EXECUTION
13. DATE
14. SIGNATURE and, if necessary, SEAL
    * to be completed if appropriate

COMMENT

This section embodies the content of Articles 9, 10 and 11 of the Annex with only minor, clarifying changes. Those familiar with the pre-proved will authorized by Uniform Probate Code § 2–504 should be comfortable with sections 5 and 6 of this act. Indeed, inclusion of these provisions in the Annex was the result of a concession by those familiar with civil law approaches to problems of execution and proof of

240

wills, to the English speaking countries where will ceremonies are divided between those occurring as testator acts, and those occurring later when the will is probated. Further, since English and Canadian practices reduce post-mortem probate procedures down to little more than the presentation of the will to an appropriate registry and so, approach civil law customs, the concession was largely to accommodate American states where post-mortem probate procedures are very involved. Thus, the primary purpose of the certificate, which provides conclusive proof of the formal validity of the will, is to put wills executed before a civil law notary and wills executed in the American tradition on a par; with the certificate, both are good without question insofar as formal requirements are concerned.

It should be noted that Article III of the Convention binds countries becoming parties to recognize the capacity of an authorized person to act in relation to an international will, as conferred by the law of another country that is a party. This means that an international will coming into one of our states that has enacted the uniform law will be entirely good under local law, and that the certificate from abroad will provide conclusive proof of its validity.

May an international will be contested? The answer is clearly affirmative as to contests based on lack of capacity, fraud, undue influence, revocation or ineffectiveness based on the contents of the will or substantive restraints on testamentary power. Contests based on failure to follow mandatory requirements of execution are not precluded because

the next section provides that the certificate is conclusive only "in the absence of evidence to the contrary". However, the Convention becomes relevant when one asks whether a probate court may require additional proof of the genuineness of signatures by testators and witnesses. It provides:

Article VI 1. The signature of the testator, of the authorized person, and of the witnesses to an international will, whether on the will or on the certificate, shall be exempt from any legalization or like formality.

2. Nonetheless, the competent authorities of any Contracting Party may, if necessary, satisfy themselves as to the authenticity of the signature of the authorized person. Presumably, the prohibition against legalization would not preclude additional proof of genuineness if evidence tending to show forgery is introduced, but without contrary proof, the certificate proves the will.

Mr. Plantard's commentary on the articles of the Annex that are pertinent to section 5, are as follows:

"This provision specifies that the authorised person must attach to the international will a certificate drawn up in accordance with the form set out in Article 10, establishing that the Uniform Law's provisions have been complied with. The term 'joint au testament' means that the certificate must be added to the will, that is, fixed thereto. The English text which uses the word 'attach' is perfectly clear on this point. Furthermore, it results from Article 11 that the certificate must be made out in three copies. This document, the contents of which are detailed in Article 10, is proof that the formalities required for the validity of the international will have been complied with. It also reveals the identity of the persons who participated in drawing up the document and may, in addition, contain a declaration by the testator as to the place where he intends his will to be kept. It should be stressed that the certificate is drawn up under the entire responsibility of the authorised person who is the only person to sign it.

"Article 10 sets out the form for the certificate. The authorised person must abide by it, in accordance with the provisions of Article 10 itself, laying down this or a substantially similar form. This last phrase could not be taken as authorising him to depart from this form: it only serves to allow for small changes of detail which might be useful in the interests of improving its comprehensibility or presentation, for example, the omission of the particulars marked with an asterisk indicating that they are to be completed where appropriate when in fact they do not need to be completed and thus become useless.

"Including the form of a certificate in one of the articles of a Uniform Law is unusual. Normally these appear in the annexes to Conventions. However, in this way, the authors of the Uniform Law underlined the importance of the certificate and its contents. Moreover, the Uniform Law already forms the Annex to the Convention itself.

"The 14 particulars indicated on the certificate are numbered. These numbers must be reproduced on each certificate, so as to facilitate its reading, especially when the

reader speaks a foreign language, as they will help him to find the relevant details more easily: the name of the authorised person and the testator, addresses, etc.

"The certificate contains all the elements necessary for the identification of the authorised person, testator and witnesses. It expressly mentions all the formalities which have to be carried out in accordance with the provisions of the Uniform Law. Furthermore, the certificate contains all the information required for the will's registration according to the system introduced by the Council of Europe Convention on the Establishment of a Scheme of Registration of Wills, signed at Basle on 16 May 1972.

"The authorised person must keep a copy of the certificate and deliver one to the testator. Seeing that another copy has to be attached to the will in accordance with Article 9, it may be deduced that the authorised person must make out altogether three copies of the certificate. These cannot be simple copies but have to be three signed originals. This provision is useful for a number of reasons. The fact that the testator keeps a copy of the certificate is a useful reminder for him, especially when his will is being kept by the authorised person or deposited with someone designated by national law. Moreover, discovery of the certificate among the testators' papers will inform his heirs of the existence of a will and will enable them to find it more easily. The fact that the authorised person keeps a copy of the certificate enables him to inform the heirs as well, if necessary. Lastly, the fact that there are sever-

al copies of the certificate is a guarantee against changes being made
to one of them and even, to a certain extent, against certain changes
to the will itself, for example as
regards its date."

Section 6. [2–1006.] [International Will; Effect of Certificate.]

In the absence of evidence to the contrary, the certificate of the
authorized person shall be conclusive of the formal validity of the
instrument as a will under this Act. [Part.] The absence or
irregularity of a certificate shall not affect the formal validity of a
will under this Act. [Part.]

COMMENT

This section, which corresponds
to Articles 11 and 12 of the Annex,
must be read with the definition of
"authorized person" in section 1,
and Articles III and IV of the 1973
Convention which will become binding on all states if and when the
United States joins that treaty. Articles III and IV of the Convention
provide:

Article III The capacity of the
authorized person to act in connection with an international will, if
conferred in accordance with the
law of a Contracting Party, shall be
recognized in the territory of the
other Contracting Parties.

Article IV The effectiveness of
the certificate provided for in Article 10 of the Annex shall be recognized in the territories of all Contracting Parties.

In effect, the state enacting this
law will be recognizing certificates
by authorized persons designated,
not only by this state, but by the
United States and other parties to
the 1973 Convention. Once the
identity of one making a certificate
on an international will is established, the will may be proved without more, assuming the presence of
the recommended form of certificate. Article IX(3) of the 1973 Convention constitutes the United
States as the Depositary under the
Convention, and Article II obligates
each country joining the Convention
to notify the Depositary Government of the persons designated by
its law as authorized to act in connection with international wills.
Hence, persons interested in local
probate of an international will
from another country will be enabled to determine from the Department of State whether the official
making the certificate in which they
are interested had the requisite authority.

In this connection, it should be
noted that under Article II of the
Convention, each contracting country may designate its diplomatic or
consular representatives abroad as
authorized persons insofar as the
local law does not prohibit it. Since
the Uniform Act will be the law
locally, and since it does not prohibit persons designated by foreign
states that are parties to the Convention from acting locally in respect to international wills, there
should be a considerable amount of
latitude in selecting authorized persons to assist with wills and a cor-

243

relative reduction in the chances of local non-recognition of an authorized person from abroad. Also, it should be noted that the Uniform Act does not restrict the persons which it constitutes as authorized persons in relation to the places where they can so function. This supports the view that local law as embodied in this statute should not be construed as restrictive in relation to local activities concerning international wills of foreign diplomatic and consular representatives who are resident here.

The certificate requires the authorized person to state that the witnesses had the requisite capacity. If the authorized person derives his authority from the law of a state other than that where he is acting, it would be advisable to have the certificate identify the applicable law.

The Uniform Act is silent in regard to methods of meeting local probate requirements contemplating deposit of the original will with the court. Section 3–409 of the Uniform Probate Code, or its counterpart in a state that has not adopted the uniform law on the point, becomes pertinent. The last sentence of UPC 3–409 provides:

> A will from a place which does not provide for probate of a will after death, may be proved for probate in this state by a duly authenticated certificate of its legal custodian that the copy introduced is a true copy and that the will has become effective under the law of the other place.

One final matter warrants mention. Implicit in local proof of an instrument by means of authentication provided by a foreign official, is the problem of proving the authority of the official. The traditional, exceedingly formalistic, method of accomplishing this has been through what has been known as "legalization", a process that involves a number of certificates. The capacity of the official who authenticates the signature of the party to the document, if derived from his status as a county official, is proved by the certificate of a high county official. In turn, the county official's status is proved by the certificate of the area's secretary of state, whose status is established by another and so on until, ultimately, the Department of State certifies to the identity of the highest state official in a format that will be persuasive to the receiving country's foreign relations representative.

Article VI of the 1973 Convention forbids legalization of the signature of testators and witnesses. It provides:

> 1. The signature of the testator, of the authorized person, and of the witnesses to an international will, whether on the will or on the certificate, shall be exempt from any legalization or like formality.

> 2. Nonetheless, the competent authorities of any Contracting Party may, if necessary, satisfy themselves as to the authenticity of the signature of the authorized person.

Thus, it would appear that if the United States, as contracting party, satisfies itself that the signature of a foreign authorized person is authentic, and so indicates to those interested in local probate of the document, the local court, though presumably able to receive and to act upon evidence to the contrary, cannot reject an international will for lack of proof. This is not to say, of course, that the authenticity of the signature of the foreign authorized person must be shown through the aid of the State Department; plainly, the point may be implied from the face of the document unless and until challenged.

Mr. Plantard's commentary on this portion of the uniform law is as follows:

"Article 12 states that the certificate is conclusive of the formal validity of the international will. It is therefore a kind of proof supplied in advance.

"This provision is only really understandable in those legal systems, like the United States, where a will can only take effect after it has been subjected to a preliminary procedure of verification ('Probate') designed to check on its validity. The mere presentation of the certificate should suffice to satisfy the requirements of this procedure.

"However, the certificate is not always irrefutable as proof, as is indicated by the words 'in the absence of evidence to the contrary'. If it is challenged, then the ensuing litigation will be solved in accordance with the legal procedure applicable in the Contracting State where the will and certificate are presented.

"The principle set out in Article 13 is already implied by Article 1, as only the provisions of Articles 2 to 5 are prescribed on pain of invalidity.

Besides, it is perfectly logical that the absence of or irregularities in a certificate should not affect the formal validity of the will, as the certificate is a document serving essentially for purposes of proof drawn up by the authorised person, without the testator taking any part either in drawing it up or in checking it. This provision is in perfect harmony with Article 12 which by the terms 'in the absence of evidence to the contrary' means that one can challenge what is stated in the certificate.

"In consideration of the fact that the authorised person will be a practising lawyer officially designated by each Contracting State, it is difficult to imagine him omitting or neglecting to draw up the certificate provided for by the national law to which he is subject. Besides, he would lay himself open to an action based on his professional and civil liability. He could even expose himself to sanctions laid down by his national law.

"However, the international will subsists, even if, by some quirk, the certificate which is a means of proof but not necessarily the only one, should be missing, be incomplete or contain particulars which are manifestly erroneous. In these undoubtedly very rare circumstances, proof that the formalities prescribed on pain of invalidity have been carried out will have to be produced in accordance with the legal procedures applicable in each State which has adopted the Uniform Law."

Section 7. [2–1007.] [International Will; Revocation.]

The international will shall be subject to the ordinary rules of revocation of wills.

COMMENT

Mr. Plantard's commentary on this portion of the uniform law is as follows:

"The authors of the Uniform Law did not intend to deal with the subject of the revocation of wills. There is indeed no reason why the international will should be submitted to a regime different from that of other kinds of will. Article 14 therefore merely gives expression to this idea. Whether or not there has been revocation—for example, by a subsequent will—is to be assessed in accordance with the law of each State which has adopted the Uniform Law, by virtue of Article 14. Besides, this is a question mainly concerning rules of substance which would thus overstep the scope of the Uniform Law."

Section 8. [2-1008.] [Source and Construction.]

Sections 1 [2-1001] through 7 [2-1007] derive from Annex to Convention of October 26, 1973, Providing a Uniform Law on the Form of an International Will. In interpreting and applying this Act [Part], regard shall be had to its international origin and to the need for uniformity in its interpretation.

COMMENT

Mr. Plantard's commentary on this portion of the uniform law is as follows:

"This Article contains a provision which is to be found in a similar form in several conventions or draft Uniform Laws. It seeks to avoid practising lawyers interpreting the Uniform Law solely in terms of the principles of their respective internal law, as this would prejudice the international unification being sought after. It requests judges to take the international character of the Uniform Law into consideration and to work towards elaborating a sort of common caselaw, taking account of the foreign legal systems which provided the foundation for the Uniform Law and the decisions handed down on the same text by the courts of other countries. The effort toward unification must not be limited to just bringing about the Law's adoption, but should be carried on into the process of putting it into operation."

Section 9. [2-1009.] [Persons Authorized to Act in Relation to International Will; Eligibility; Recognition by Authorizing Agency.]

Individuals who have been admitted to practice law before the courts of this state and who are in good standing as active law practitioners in this state, are hereby declared to be authorized persons in relation to international wills.

COMMENT

The subject of who should be designated to be authorized persons under the Uniform Law is discussed under the heading "Description of the Proposal" in the Prefatory Note.

The first draft of the Uniform Law presented to the National Conference at its 1975 meeting in Quebec City included provision for a special new licensing procedure through which others than attorneys might become qualified. The

ensuing discussion resulted in rejection of this approach in favor of the simpler approach of section 9. Among other difficulties with the special licensee approach, representatives of the State Department expressed concern about the attendant burden on the U.S. as Depositary Government, of receiving, keeping up to date, and interpreting to foreign governments the results of fifty different state licensing systems.

[Section 10. [2–1010.] [International Will Information Registration.]

The [Secretary of State] shall establish a registry system by which authorized persons may register in a central information center, information regarding the execution of international wills, keeping that information in strictest confidence until the death of the maker and then making it available to any person desiring information about any will who presents a death certificate or other satisfactory evidence of the testator's death to the center. Information that may be received, preserved in confidence until death, and reported as indicated is limited to the name, social-security or any other individual-identifying number established by law, address, and date and place of birth of the testator, and the intended place of deposit or safekeeping of the instrument pending the death of the maker. The [Secretary of State], at the request of the authorized person, may cause the information it receives about execution of any international will to be transmitted to the registry system of another jurisdiction as identified by the testator, if that other system adheres to rules protecting the confidentiality of the information similar to those established in this state.]

COMMENT

The relevance of this optional, bracketed section to the other sections constituting the uniform law concerning international wills is explained in the Prefatory Note. Also, Mr. Plantard's observations regarding the Resolution attached

to the 1973 Convention are pertinent. He writes:

"The Resolution adopted by the Washington Conference and annexed to its Final Act encourages States which adopt the Uniform Law to make additional provisions for the registering and safekeeping of the international will. The authors of the Uniform Law considered that it was not possible to lay down uniform rules on this subject on account of the differences in tradition and outlook, but several times, both during the preparatory work and during the final diplomatic phase, they underlined the importance of States making such provisions.

"The Resolution recommends organising a system enabling ... 'the safekeeping, search and discovery of an international will as well as the accompanying certificate' ...

"Indeed lawyers know that many wills are never carried out because the very existence of the will itself remains unknown or because the will is never found or is never produced. It would be quite possible to organise a register or index which would enable one to know after the death of a person whether he had drawn up a will. Some countries have already done something in this field, for example, Quebec, Spain, the Federal Republic of Germany, where this service is connected with the Registry of Births, Marriages and Deaths. Such a system could perfectly well be fashioned so as to ensure respect for the legitimate wish of testators to keep the very existence of their will secret.

"The Washington Conference also underlined that there is already an International Convention on this subject, namely the Council of Europe Convention on the Establishment of a Scheme of Registration of Wills, concluded at Basle on 16 May 1972, to which States which are not members of the Council of Europe may accede.

"In this Convention the Contracting States simply undertake to create an internal system for registering wills. The Convention stipulates the categories of will which should be registered, in terms which include the international will. Apart from national bodies in charge of registration, the Convention also provides for the designation by each Contracting State of a national body which must remain in contact with the national bodies of other States and communicate registrations and any information asked for. The Convention specifies that registration must remain secret during the life of the testator. This system, which will come into force between a number of European States in the near future, interested the authors of the Convention, even if they do not accede to it. The last paragraph of the Resolution follows the pattern of the Basle Convention by recommending, in the interests of facilitating an international exchange of information on this matter, the designation in each State of authorities or services to handle such exchanges.

"As for the organisation of the safekeeping of international wills, the resolution merely underlies the importance of this, without making any specific suggestions in this regard. This problem has already been discussed in connection with Article 8 of the Uniform Law.

"The Council of Europe Convention on the Establishment of a Scheme of Registration of Wills of May 16, 1972 and related documents were available to the reporter and provided the guidelines for section 10 of this Act."

ARTICLE III

PROBATE OF WILLS AND ADMINISTRATION

PART 1

GENERAL PROVISIONS

PART 2

VENUE FOR PROBATE AND ADMINISTRATION; PRIORITY TO ADMINISTER; DEMAND FOR NOTICE

PART 3

INFORMAL PROBATE AND APPOINTMENT PROCEEDINGS; SUCCESSION WITHOUT ADMINISTRATION

PART 4

FORMAL TESTACY AND APPOINTMENT PROCEEDINGS

PROBATE AND ADMINISTRATION

PART 5

SUPERVISED ADMINISTRATION

PART 6

PERSONAL REPRESENTATIVE; APPOINTMENT, CONTROL AND TERMINATION OF AUTHORITY

PART 7

DUTIES AND POWERS OF PERSONAL REPRESENTATIVES

PART 8

CREDITORS' CLAIMS

PART 9

SPECIAL PROVISIONS RELATING TO DISTRIBUTION

PROBATE AND ADMINISTRATION

253

GENERAL COMMENT

The provisions of this Article describe the Flexible System of Administration of Decedents' Estates. Designed to be applicable to both intestate and testate estates and to provide persons interested in decedents' estates with as little or as much by way of procedural and adjudicative safeguards as may be suitable under varying circumstances, this system is the heart of the Uniform Probate Code.

The organization and detail of the system here described may be expressed in varying ways and some states may see fit to reframe parts of this Article to better accommodate local institutions. Variations in language from state to state can be tolerated without loss of the essential purposes of procedural uniformity and flexibility, if the following essential characteristics are carefully protected in the redrafting process:

(1) Post-mortem probate of a will must occur to make a will effective and appointment of a personal representative by a public official after the decedent's death is required in order to create the duties and powers attending the office of personal representative. Neither are compelled, however, but are left to be obtained by persons having an interest in the consequence of probate or appointment. Estates descend at death to successors identified by any probated will, or to heirs if no will is probated, subject to rights which may be implemented through administration.

(2) Two methods of securing probate of wills which include a non-adjudicative determination (informal probate) on the one hand, and a judicial determination after notice to all interested persons (formal probate) on the other, are provided.

(3) Two methods of securing appointment of a personal representative which include appointment without notice and without final adjudication of matters relevant to priority for appointment (informal appointment), on the one hand, and appointment by judicial order after notice to interested persons (formal appointment) on the other, are provided.

(4) A five day waiting period from death preventing informal probate or informal appointment of any but a special administrator is required.

(5) Probate of a will by informal or formal proceedings or an adjudication of intestacy may occur without any attendant requirement of appointment of a personal representative.

(6) One judicial, in rem, proceeding encompassing formal probate of any wills (or a determination after notice that the decedent left no will), appointment of a personal representative and complete settlement of an estate under continuing supervision of the Court (supervised administration) is provided for testators and persons interested in a decedent's estate, whether testate or intestate, who desire to use it.

(7) Unless supervised administration is sought and ordered, persons interested in estates (including personal representatives, whether appointed informally or after notice) may use an "in and out" relationship to the Court so that any question or assumption relating to the estate, including the status of an estate as testate or intestate, matters relating to one or more claims, disputed titles, accounts of personal representatives, and distribution, may be resolved or established by adjudication after notice without necessarily subjecting the estate to the necessity of judicial orders in regard to other or further questions or assumptions.

(8) The status of a decedent in regard to whether he left a valid will or died intestate must be resolved by adjudication after notice in proceedings commenced within three years after his death. If not so resolved, any will probated informally becomes final, and if there is no such probate, the status of the decedent as intestate is finally determined, by a statute of limitations which bars probate and appointment unless requested within three years after death.

(9) Personal representatives appointed informally or after notice, and whether supervised or not, have statutory powers enabling them to collect, protect, sell, distribute and otherwise handle all steps in administration without further order of the Court, except that supervised personal representatives may be subjected to special restrictions on power as endorsed on their letters.

(10) Purchasers from personal representatives and from distributees of personal representatives are protected so that adjudications regarding the testacy status of a decedent or any other question going to the propriety of a sale are not required in order to protect purchasers.

(11) Provisions protecting a personal representative who distributes without adjudication are included to make nonadjudicated settlements feasible.

(12) Statutes of limitation bar creditors of the decedent who fail to present claims within four months after legal advertising of the administration and unsecured claims not previously barred by non-claim statutes are barred after three years from the decedent's death.

Overall, the system accepts the premise that the Court's role in regard to probate and administration, and its relationship to personal representatives who derive their power from public appointment, is wholly passive until some interested person invokes its power to secure resolution of a matter. The state, through the Court, should provide remedies which are suitable and efficient to protect any and all rights regarding succession, but should refrain from intruding into family affairs unless relief is requested, and limit its relief to that sought.

PART 1

GENERAL PROVISIONS

Section 3–101. [Devolution of Estate at Death; Restrictions.]

The power of a person to leave property by will, and the rights of creditors, devisees, and heirs to his property are subject to the restrictions and limitations contained in this Code to facilitate the prompt settlement of estates. Upon the death of a person, his real and personal property devolves to the persons to whom it is devised by his last will or to those indicated as substitutes for them in cases involving lapse, renunciation, or other circumstances affecting the devolution of testate estate, or in the absence of testamentary disposition, to his heirs, or to those indicated as substitutes for them in cases involving renunciation or other circumstances affecting devolution of intestate estates, subject to homestead allowance, exempt property and family allowance, to rights of creditors, elective share of the surviving spouse, and to administration.

ALTERNATIVE SECTION FOR COMMUNITY PROPERTY STATES

[Section 3–101A. [Devolution of Estate at Death; Restrictions.]

The power of a person to leave property by will, and the rights of creditors, devisees, and heirs to his property are subject to the restrictions and limitations contained in this Code to facilitate the prompt settlement of estates. Upon the death of a person, his separate property devolves to the persons to whom it is devised by his last will, or to those indicated as substitutes for them in cases involving lapse, renunciation or other circumstances affecting the devolution of testate estates, or in the absence of testamentary disposition to his heirs, or to those indicated as substitutes for them in cases involving renunciation or other circumstances affecting the devolution of intestate estates, and upon the death of a husband or wife, the decedent's share of their community property devolves to the persons to whom it is devised by his last will, or in the absence of testamentary disposition, to his heirs, but all of their community property which is under the management and control of the decedent is subject to his debts and administration, and that portion of their community property which is not under the management and control of the decedent but which is necessary to carry out the

256

provisions of his will is subject to administration; but the devolution of all the above described property is subject to rights to homestead allowance, exempt property and family allowances, to renunciation, to rights of creditors, [elective share of the surviving spouse] and to administration.]

COMMENT

In its present form, this section will not fit existing concepts concerning community property in all states recognizing community ownership. States differ in respect to how much testamentary power a decedent has over the community. Also, some changes of language may be necessary to reflect differing views concerning what estate is subject to "separate" and "communi-ty" debts. The reference to certain family rights is not intended to suggest that such rights relate to the survivor's interest in any community property. Rather, the assumption is that such rights relate only to property passing from the decedent at his death; e.g., his half of community property and his separate property.

Section 3–102. [Necessity of Order of Probate for Will.]

Except as provided in Section 3–1201, to be effective to prove the transfer of any property or to nominate an executor, a will must be declared to be valid by an order of informal probate by the Registrar, or an adjudication of probate by the Court.

COMMENT

The basic idea of this section follows Section 85 of the Model Probate Code. The exception referring to Section 3–1201 relates to affidavit procedures which are authorized for collection of estates worth less than $5,000.

Section 3–107 and various sections in Parts 3 and 4 of this Article make it clear that a will may be probated without appointment of a personal representative, including any nominated by the will.

The requirement of probate stated here and the limitations on probate provided in 3–108 mean that questions as to testacy may be eliminated simply by the running of time. Under these sections, an in-formally probated will cannot be questioned after the later of three years from the decedent's death or one year from the probate whether or not an executor was appointed, or, if an executor was appointed, without regard to whether the estate has been distributed. If the decedent is believed to have died without a will, the running of three years from death bars probate of a late-discovered will and so makes the assumption of intestacy conclusive.

The exceptions to the section (other than the exception relevant to small estates) are not intended to accommodate cases of late-discovered wills. Rather, they are designed to make the probate requirement inapplicable where circumstances led survivors of a decedent to believe that there was no point to probating a will of which they may have had knowledge. If any will was probated within three years of death, or if letters of administration were issued in this period, the exceptions to the section are inapplicable. If there has been no proceeding in probate, persons seeking to establish title by an unprobated will must show, with *reference to the estate they claim,* either that it has been possessed by those to whom it was devised or that it has been unknown to the decedent's heirs or devisees and not possessed by any.

It is to be noted, also, that devisees who are able to claim under one of the exceptions to this section may not obtain probate of the will or administration of the estate to assist them in their efforts to obtain the estate in question. The exceptions are to a rule which bars admission of a will into evidence, rather than to the section barring late probate and late appointment of personal representatives. Still, the exceptions should serve to prevent

two "hard" cases which can be imagined readily. In one, a surviving spouse fails to seek probate of a will, giving her the entire estate of the decedent because she is informed or believes that all of her husband's property was held by them jointly, with right of survivorship. Later, it is discovered that she was mistaken as to the nature of her husband's title. The other case involves a devisee who sees no point to securing probate of a will in his favor because he is unaware of any estate. Subsequently, valuable rights of the decedent are discovered.

In 1993, a technical amendment removed a two-pronged exception formerly occupying about 8 lines of text in the official text. The removed language permitted unprobated wills to be admitted in evidence in two limited categories of cases in which failure to probate a will within three years of the testator's death were deemed to be justified. The 1993 technical amendment to 3–108 so limits the three year time bar on probate and appointment proceedings as to make the 3–102 exception unnecessary.

Section 3–103. [Necessity of Appointment for Administration.]

Except as otherwise provided in Article IV, to acquire the powers and undertake the duties and liabilities of a personal representative of a decedent, a person must be appointed by order of the Court or Registrar, qualify and be issued letters. Administration of an estate is commenced by the issuance of letters.

COMMENT

This section makes it clear that appointment by a public official is required before one can acquire the status of personal representative.

"Qualification" is dealt with in Section 3–601. "Letters" are the subject of Section 1–305. Section 3–701 is also related, since it deals with the time of accrual of duties and powers of personal representatives.

See 3–108 for the time limit on requests for appointment of personal representatives.

In Article IV, Sections 4–204 and 4–205 permit a personal representative from another state to obtain the powers of one appointed locally by filing evidence of his authority with a local Court.

Section 3–104. [Claims Against Decedent; Necessity of Administration.]

No proceeding to enforce a claim against the estate of a decedent or his successors may be revived or commenced before the appointment of a personal representative. After the appointment and until distribution, all proceedings and actions to enforce a claim against the estate are governed by the procedure prescribed by this Article. After distribution a creditor whose claim has not been barred may recover from the distributees as provided in Section 3–1004 or from a former personal representative individually liable as provided in Section 3–1005. This section has no application to a proceeding by a secured creditor of the decedent to enforce his right to his security except as to any deficiency judgment which might be sought therein.

COMMENT

This and sections of Part 8, Article III, are designed to force creditors of decedents to assert their claims against duly appointed personal representatives. Creditors of a decedent are interested persons who may seek the appointment of a personal representative (Section 3–301). If no appointment is granted to another within 45 days after the decedent's death, a creditor may be eligible to be appointed if other persons with priority decline to serve or are ineligible (Section 3–203). But, if a personal representative has been appointed and has closed the estate under circumstances which leave a creditor's claim unbarred, the creditor is permitted to enforce his claims against distributees, as well as against the personal representative if any duty owed to creditors under 3–807 or 3–1003 has been breached. The methods for closing estates are outlined in Sections 3–1001 through 3–1003. Termination of appointment under Sections 3–608 et seq. may occur though the estate is *not* closed and so may be irrelevant to the question of whether creditors may pursue distributees.

Section 3–105. [Proceedings Affecting Devolution and Administration; Jurisdiction of Subject Matter.]

Persons interested in decedents' estates may apply to the Registrar for determination in the informal proceedings provided in this

Article, and may petition the Court for orders in formal proceedings within the Court's jurisdiction including but not limited to those described in this Article. The Court has exclusive jurisdiction of formal proceedings to determine how decedents' estates subject to the laws of this state are to be administered, expended and distributed. The Court has concurrent jurisdiction of any other action or proceeding concerning a succession or to which an estate, through a personal representative, may be a party, including actions to determine title to property alleged to belong to the estate, and of any action or proceeding in which property distributed by a personal representative or its value is sought to be subjected to rights of creditors or successors of the decedent.

COMMENT

This and other sections of Article III contemplate a non-judicial officer who will act on informal application and a judge who will hear and decide formal petitions. See Section 1–307 which permits the judge to perform or delegate the functions of the Registrar. *However, the primary purpose of Article III is to describe functions to be performed by various public officials, rather than to prescribe how these responsibilities should be assigned within a given state or county.* Hence, any of several alternatives to the organizational scheme assumed for purposes of this draft would be acceptable.

For example, a state might assign responsibility for maintenance of probate files and records, and for receiving and acting upon informal applications, to existing, limited power probate offices. Responsibility for hearing and deciding formal petitions would then be assigned to the court of general jurisdiction of each county or district.

If separate courts or offices are not feasible, it may be preferable to concentrate authority for allocating responsibility respecting formal and informal proceedings in the judge.

To do so helps fix responsibility for the total operation of the office. This is the assumption of this draft.

It will be up to each adopting state to select the organizational arrangement which best meets its needs.

If the office with jurisdiction to hear and decide formal petitions is the county or district court of general jurisdiction, there will be little basis for objection to the broad statement of concurrent jurisdiction of this section. However, if a more specialized "estates" court is used, there may be pressure to prevent it from hearing negligence and other actions involving jury trials, even though it may be given unlimited power to decide other cases to which a personal representative is a party. A system for certifying matters involving jury trials to the general trial court could be provided, although the alternative of permitting the estates court to empanel juries where necessary might not be unworkable. In any event, the jurisdiction of the "estates" or "probate" court in regard to negligence litigation would only be concurrent with that of the general trial court. The important point is that the estates court, whatever it is called, should have unlimited power to hear and finally dispose of all matters relevant to determination of the extent of the decedent's estate and of the claims against it. The jury trial question is peripheral.

See the comment to the next section regarding adjustments which might be made in the Code by a state with a single court of general jurisdiction for each county or district.

Section 3–106. [Proceedings Within the Exclusive Jurisdiction of Court; Service; Jurisdiction Over Persons.]

In proceedings within the exclusive jurisdiction of the Court where notice is required by this Code or by rule, and in proceedings to construe probated wills or determine heirs which concern estates that have not been and cannot now be open for administration, interested persons may be bound by the orders of the Court in respect to property in or subject to the laws of this state by notice in conformity with Section 1–401. An order is binding as to all who are given notice of the proceeding though less than all interested persons are notified.

COMMENT

The language in this and the preceding section which divides matters coming before the probate court between those within the court's "exclusive" jurisdiction and those within its "concurrent" jurisdiction would be inappropriate if probate matters were assigned to a branch of a single court of general jurisdiction. The Code could be adjusted to an assumption of a single court in various ways. Any adjusted version should contain a provision permitting the court to hear and settle certain kinds of matters after notice as provided in 1–401. It might be suitable to combine the second sentence of 3–105 and 3–106 into a single section as follows:

"The Court may hear and determine formal proceedings involving administration and distribution of decedents' estates after notice to interested persons

in conformity with Section 1–401. Persons notified are bound though less than all interested persons may have been given notice."

An adjusted version also might provide:

"Subject to general rules concerning the proper location of civil litigation and jurisdiction of persons, the Court (meaning the probate division) may hear and determine any other controversy concerning a succession or to which an estate through a personal representative, may be a party."

The propriety of this sort of statement would depend upon whether questions of docketing and assignment, including the division of matters between coordinate branches of

261

the Court, should be dealt with by legislation.

The Joint Editorial Board, in 1975, recommended the addition after "rule", of the language "and in proceedings to construe probated wills or determine heirs which concern estates that have not been and cannot now be opened for administration." This addition, coupled with the exceptions to the limita-

tions provisions in Section 3–108 that permit proceedings to construe wills and to determine heirs of intestates to be commenced more than three years after death, clarifies the purpose of the draftsmen to offer a probate proceeding to aid the determination of rights of inheritance of estates that were not opened for administration within the time permitted by Section 3–108.

Section 3–107. [Scope of Proceedings; Proceedings Independent; Exception.]

Unless supervised administration as described in Part 5 is involved, (1) each proceeding before the Court or Registrar is independent of any other proceeding involving the same estate; (2) petitions for formal orders of the Court may combine various requests for relief in a single proceeding if the orders sought may be finally granted without delay. Except as required for proceedings which are particularly described by other sections of this Article, no petition is defective because it fails to embrace all matters which might then be the subject of a final order; (3) proceedings for probate of wills or adjudications of no will may be combined with proceedings for appointment of personal representatives; and (4) a proceeding for appointment of a personal representative is concluded by an order making or declining the appointment.

COMMENT

This section and others in Article III describe a system of administration of decedents' estates which gives interested persons control of whether matters relating to estates will become occasions for judicial orders. Sections 3–501 through 3–505 describe supervised administration, a judicial proceeding which is continuous throughout administration. It corresponds with the theory of administration of decedents' estates which prevails in many states. See, section 62, Model Probate Code. If supervised adminis-

tration is not requested, persons interested in an estate may use combinations of the formal proceedings (order by judge after notice to persons concerned with the relief sought), informal proceedings (request for the limited response that nonjudicial personnel of the probate court are authorized to make in response to verified application) and filings provided in the remaining Parts of Article III to secure authority and protection needed to administer the estate. Nothing except self-interest will compel resort to the judge. When resort to the judge is necessary or desirable to resolve a dispute or to gain protection, the scope of the proceeding if not otherwise prescribed by the Code is framed by the petition. The securing of necessary jurisdiction over interested persons in a formal proceeding is facilitated by Sections 3–106 and 3–602. 3–201 locates venue for all proceedings at the place where the first proceeding occurred.

Section 3–108. [Probate, Testacy and Appointment Proceedings; Ultimate Time Limit.]

(a) No informal probate or appointment proceeding or formal testacy or appointment proceeding, other than a proceeding to probate a will previously probated at the testator's domicile and appointment proceedings relating to an estate in which there has been a prior appointment, may be commenced more than three years after the decedent's death, except:

(1) if a previous proceeding was dismissed because of doubt about the fact of the decedent's death, appropriate probate, appointment, or testacy proceedings may be maintained at any time thereafter upon a finding that the decedent's death occurred before the initiation of the previous proceeding and the applicant or petitioner has not delayed unduly in initiating the subsequent proceeding;

(2) appropriate probate, appointment or testacy proceedings may be maintained in relation to the estate of an absent, disappeared or missing person for whose estate a conservator has been appointed, at any time within three years after the conservator becomes able to establish the death of the protected person;

(3) a proceeding to contest an informally probated will and to secure appointment of the person with legal priority for appointment in the event the contest is successful, may be commenced within the later of twelve months from the informal probate or three years from the decedent's death;

(4) an informal appointment or a formal testacy or appointment proceeding may be commenced thereafter if no proceedings concerning the succession or estate administration has occurred within the three year period after decedent's death, but the personal representative has no right to possess estate assets as provided in Section 3–709 beyond that necessary to confirm title thereto in the successors to the estate and claims other than expenses of administration may not be presented against the estate; and

263

(5) a formal testacy proceeding may be commenced at any time after three years from the decedent's death for the purpose of establishing an instrument to direct or control the ownership of property passing or distributable after the decedent's death from one other than the decedent when the property is to be appointed by the terms of the decedent's will or is to pass or be distributed as a part of the decedent's estate or its transfer is otherwise to be controlled by the terms of the decedent's will.

(b) These limitations do not apply to proceedings to construe probated wills or determine heirs of an intestate.

(c) In cases under subsection (a) (1) or (2), the date on which a testacy or appointment proceeding is properly commenced shall be deemed to be the date of the decedent's death for purposes of other limitations provisions of this Code which relate to the date of death.

COMMENT

As originally approved and read with 3–102's requirement that wills be probated before being admissible in evidence, this section created a three-year-from death time period within which proceedings concerning a succession (other than a determination of heirs, or will interpretation or construction) must be commenced. Unless certain limited exceptions were met, an estate became conclusively intestate if no formal or informal estate proceeding was commenced within the three year period, and no administration could be opened in order to generate a deed of distribution for purposes of proving a succession.

Several of the original UPC states rejected the three year bar against late-offered wills and the related position that formal proceedings to determine heirs in previously unadministered estates were necessary to generate title muniments locating inherited land in lawful successors. Critics preferred continued availability of UPC's procedures for appointing p.r.'s whose distributive instruments gave protection to purchasers. The 1987 technical amendment to 3–108 reduced, but failed to eliminate, instances in which original probate and appointment proceedings were barred by the 3 year limitation period. The 1993 technical amendment eliminates the restriction altogether but limits the powers of a late appointed p.r. as appropriate for a proceeding initiated merely to confirm title in successors.

The 1993 technical amendment also added new (5) permitting initiation of a formal testacy proceeding to establish the terms of the will of a donee of a power of appointment for the sole purposes of determining title to property passing from one other than the decedent. The mere fact that an earlier estate proceeding occurred within the three year period following the decedent's death does not bar the proceeding sanctioned by the new subsection.

Section 3–109. [Statutes of Limitation on Decedent's Cause of Action.]

No statute of limitation running on a cause of action belonging to a decedent which had not been barred as of the date of his death, shall apply to bar a cause of action surviving the decedent's death sooner than four months after death. A cause of action which, but for this section, would have been barred less than four months after death, is barred after four months unless tolled.

PART 2

VENUE FOR PROBATE AND ADMINISTRATION; PRIORITY TO ADMINISTER; DEMAND FOR NOTICE

Section 3–201. [Venue for First and Subsequent Estate Proceedings; Location of Property.]

(a) Venue for the first informal or formal testacy or appointment proceedings after a decedent's death is:

(1) in the [county] where the decedent had his domicile at the time of his death; or

(2) if the decedent was not domiciled in this state, in any [county] where property of the decedent was located at the time of his death.

(b) Venue for all subsequent proceedings within the exclusive jurisdiction of the Court is in the place where the initial proceeding occurred, unless the initial proceeding has been transferred as provided in Section 1–303 or (c) of this section.

(c) If the first proceeding was informal, on application of an interested person and after notice to the proponent in the first proceeding, the Court, upon finding that venue is elsewhere, may transfer the proceeding and the file to the other court.

(d) For the purpose of aiding determinations concerning location of assets which may be relevant in cases involving non-domiciliaries, a debt, other than one evidenced by investment or commercial paper or other instrument in favor of a non-domiciliary is located where the debtor resides or, if the debtor is a person other than an individual, at the place where it has its principal office. Commercial paper, investment paper and other instruments are located where the instrument is. An interest in property held in trust is located where the trustee may be sued.

COMMENT

Sections 1–303 and 3–201 cover the subject of venue for estate proceedings. Sections 3–202, 3–301, 3–303 and 3–309 also may be relevant.

Provisions for transfer of venue appear in Section 1–303.

The interplay of these several sections may be illustrated best by examples.

266

(1) A formal probate or appointment proceeding is initiated in A County. Interested persons who believe that venue is in B County rather than A County must raise their question about venue in A County, because 1–303 gives the Court in which the proceeding is first commenced authority to resolve disputes over venue. If the Court in A County erroneously determines that it has venue, the remedy is by appeal.

(2) An informal probate or appointment application is filed and granted without notice in A County. If interested persons wish to challenge the registrar's determination of venue, they may not simply file a formal proceeding in the county of their choice and thus force the proponent in the prior proceeding to debate the question of venue in their county. 3–201(b) locates the venue of any subsequent proceeding where the first proceeding occurred. The function of (b) is obvious when one thinks of subsequent proceedings as those which relate to claims, or accounts, or to efforts to control a personal representative. It is less obvious when it seems to locate the forum for squabbles over venue at the place accepting the first informal application. Still, the applicant seeking an informal order must be careful about the statements he makes in his application because he may be charged with perjury under Section 1–310 if he is deliberately inaccurate. Moreover, the registrar must be satisfied that the allega-

tions in the application support a finding of venue. 3–201(c) provides a remedy for one who is upset about the venue-locating impact of a prior order in an informal proceeding and who does not wish to engage in full litigation about venue in the forum chosen by the other interested person unless he is forced to do so. Using it, he may succeed in getting the A County Court to transfer the proceedings to the county of his choice. He would be well advised to initiate formal proceedings if he gets the chance, for if he relies on informal proceedings, he, too, may be "bumped" if the judge in B County agrees with some movant that venue was not in B County.

(3) If the decedent's domicile was not in the state, venue is proper under 3–201 and 1–303 in any county where he had assets.

One contemplating starting administration because of the presence of local assets should have several other sections of the Code in mind. First, by use of the recognition provisions in Article IV, it may be possible to avoid administration in any state other than that in which the decedent was domiciled. Second, Section 3–203 may apply to give priority for local appointment to the representative appointed at domicile. Third, under Section 3–309, informal appointment proceedings in this state will be dismissed if it is known that a personal representative has been previously appointed at domicile.

Section 3–202.   [Appointment or Testacy Proceedings; Conflicting Claim of Domicile in Another State.]

If conflicting claims as to the domicile of a decedent are made in a formal testacy or appointment proceeding commenced in this state, and in a testacy or appointment proceeding after notice pending at the same time in another state, the Court of this state must stay, dismiss, or permit suitable amendment in, the proceeding here unless it is determined that the local proceeding was commenced before the proceeding elsewhere. The determination of domicile in the proceeding first commenced must be accepted as determinative in the proceeding in this state.

COMMENT

This section is designed to reduce the possibility that conflicting findings of domicile in two or more states may result in inconsistent administration and distribution of parts of the same estate. Section 3–408 dealing with the effect of adjudications in other states concerning testacy supports the same general purpose to use domiciliary law to unify succession of property located in different states.

Whether testate or intestate, succession should follow the presumed wishes of the decedent whenever possible. Unless a decedent leaves a separate will for the portion of his estate located in each different state, it is highly unlikely that he would want different portions of his estate subject to different rules simply because courts reach conflicting conclusions concerning his domicile. It is pointless to debate whether he would prefer one or the other of the conflicting rules, when the paramount inference is that the decedent would prefer that his estate be unified under either rule rather than wasted in litigation.

The section adds very little to existing law. If a previous estate proceeding in State A has determined that the decedent was a domiciliary of A, persons who were personally before the court in A would be precluded by the principles of res judicata or collateral estoppel (and full faith and credit) from relitigating the issue of domicile in a later proceeding in State B. Probably, it would not matter in this setting that domicile was a jurisdictional fact. Stoll v. Gottlieb, 59 S.Ct. 134, 305 U.S. 165, 83 L.Ed. 104 (1938). Even if the parties to a present proceeding were not personally before the court in an earlier proceeding in State A involving the same decedent, the prior judgment would be binding as to property subject to the power of the courts in A, on persons to whom due notice of the proceeding was given. Riley v. New York Trust Co., 62 S.Ct. 608, 315 U.S. 343, 86 L.Ed. 885 (1942); Mullane v. Central Hanover Bank and Trust Co., 70 S.Ct. 652, 339 U.S. 306, 94 L.Ed. 865 (1950).

Where a court learns that parties before it are also parties to previously initiated litigation involving a common question, traditional judicial reluctance to deciding unnecessary questions, as well as considerations of comity, are likely to lead it to delay the local proceedings to await the result in the other court. A somewhat more troublesome question is involved when one of the parties before the local court manifests a determination not to appear personally in the prior initiated proceedings so that he can preserve his ability to litigate contested points in a more friendly, or convenient, forum. But, the need to preserve all possible advantages available to particular litigants should be subordinated to the decedent's probable wish that his estate not be wasted in unnecessary litigation. Thus, the section requires that the local claimant either initiate litigation in the forum of his choice before litigation is started somewhere else, or accept the necessity of contesting unwanted views concerning the decedent's domicile offered in litigation pending elsewhere.

It is to be noted, in this connection, that the local suitor always will have a chance to contest the question of domicile in the other state. His locally initiated proceed-

ings may proceed to a valid judgment accepting his theory of the case unless parties who would oppose him appear and defend on the theory that the domicile question is currently being litigated elsewhere. If the litigation in the other state has proceeded to judgment, Section 3–408 rather than the instant section will govern. If this section applies, it will mean that the foreign proceedings are still pending, so that the local person's contention concerning domicile can be made therein even though until the defense of litigation elsewhere is offered in the local proceedings, he may not have been notified of the foreign proceeding.

Section 3–203. [Priority Among Persons Seeking Appointment as Personal Representative.]

(a) Whether the proceedings are formal or informal, persons who are not disqualified have priority for appointment in the following order:

(1) the person with priority as determined by a probated will including a person nominated by a power conferred in a will;

(2) the surviving spouse of the decedent who is a devisee of the decedent;

(3) other devisees of the decedent;

(4) the surviving spouse of the decedent;

(5) other heirs of the decedent;

(6) 45 days after the death of the decedent, any creditor.

(b) An objection to an appointment can be made only in formal proceedings. In case of objection the priorities stated in (a) apply except that

(1) if the estate appears to be more than adequate to meet exemptions and costs of administration but inadequate to discharge anticipated unsecured claims, the Court, on petition of creditors, may appoint any qualified person;

(2) in case of objection to appointment of a person other than one whose priority is determined by will by an heir or devisee appearing to have a substantial interest in the estate, the Court may appoint a person who is acceptable to heirs and devisees whose interests in the estate appear to be worth in total more than half of the probable distributable value, or, in default of this accord any suitable person.

(c) A person entitled to letters under (2) through (5) of (a) above, and a person aged [18] and over who would be entitled to letters but for his age, may nominate a qualified person to act as personal representative. Any person aged [18] and over may renounce his right to nominate or to an appointment by appropriate writing filed with the Court. When two or more persons share a priority, those of them who do not renounce must concur in nominating another to act for them, or in applying for appointment.

(d) Conservators of the estates of protected persons, or if there is no conservator, any guardian except a guardian ad litem of a minor or incapacitated person, may exercise the same right to nominate, to object to another's appointment, or to participate in determining the preference of a majority in interest of the heirs and devisees that the protected person or ward would have if qualified for appointment.

(e) Appointment of one who does not have priority, including priority resulting from renunciation or nomination determined pursuant to this section, may be made only in formal proceedings. Before appointing one without priority, the Court must determine that those having priority, although given notice of the proceedings, have failed to request appointment or to nominate another for appointment, and that administration is necessary.

(f) No person is qualified to serve as a personal representative who is:

(1) under the age of [21];

(2) a person whom the Court finds unsuitable in formal proceedings.

(g) A personal representative appointed by a court of the decedent's domicile has priority over all other persons except where the decedent's will nominates different persons to be personal representative in this state and in the state of domicile. The domiciliary personal representative may nominate another, who shall have the same priority as the domiciliary personal representative.

(h) This section governs priority for appointment of a successor personal representative but does not apply to the selection of a special administrator.

COMMENT

The priorities applicable to informal proceedings are applicable to formal proceedings. However, if the proceedings are formal, a person with a substantial interest may object to the selection of one having priority other than because of will provisions. The provision for majority approval which is triggered by such a protest can be handled in a formal proceeding since all interested persons will be before the court, and a judge capable of handling discretionary matters, will be involved.

In considering this section as it relates to a devise to a trustee for various beneficiaries, it is to be noted that "interested persons" is defined by 1–201(20) to include fiduciaries. Also, 1–403(2) and 3–912 show a purpose to make trustees serve as representatives of all beneficiaries. The provision in (d) is consistent.

If a state's statutes recognize a public administrator or public trustee as the appropriate agency to seek administration of estates in which the state may have an interest, it would be appropriate to indicate in this section the circumstances under which such an officer may seek administration. If no officer is recognized locally, the state could claim as heir by virtue of 2–105.

Subsection (g) was inserted in connection with the decision to abandon the effort to describe ancillary administration in Article IV. Other provisions in Article III which are relevant to administration of assets in a state other than that of the decedent's domicile are 1–301 (territorial effect), 3–201 (venue), 3–308 (informal appointment for non-resident decedent delayed 30 days), 3–309 (no informal appointment here if a representative has been appointed at domicile), 3–815 (duty of personal representative where administration is in more than one state) and 4–201 to 4–205 (local recognition of foreign personal representatives).

The meaning of "spouse" is determined by Section 2–802.

Section 3–204. [Demand for Notice of Order or Filing Concerning Decedent's Estate.]

Any person desiring notice of any order or filing pertaining to a decedent's estate in which he has a financial or property interest, may file a demand for notice with the Court at any time after the death of the decedent stating the name of the decedent, the nature of his interest in the estate, and the demandant's address or that of his attorney. The clerk shall mail a copy of the demand to the personal representative if one has been appointed. After filing of a demand, no order or filing to which the demand relates shall be made or accepted without notice as prescribed in Section 1–401 to the demandant or his attorney. The validity of an order which is issued or filing which is accepted without compliance with this requirement shall not be affected by the error, but the petitioner receiving the order or the person making the filing may be liable for any damage caused by the absence of notice. The requirement of notice arising from a demand under this provision may be waived in writing by the demandant and shall cease upon the termination of his interest in the estate.

COMMENT

The notice required as the result of demand under this section is regulated as far as time and manner requirements are concerned by Section 1–401.

This section would apply to any order which might be made in a supervised administration proceeding.

PART 3

INFORMAL PROBATE AND APPOINTMENT PROCEEDINGS; SUCCESSION WITHOUT ADMINISTRATION

Section 3–301. [**Informal Probate or Appointment Proceedings; Application; Contents.**]

(a) Applications for informal probate or informal appointment shall be directed to the Registrar, and verified by the applicant to be accurate and complete to the best of his knowledge and belief as to the following information:

(1) Every application for informal probate of a will or for informal appointment of a personal representative, other than a special or successor representative, shall contain the following:

(i) a statement of the interest of the applicant;

(ii) the name, and date of death of the decedent, his age, and the county and state of his domicile at the time of death, and the names and addresses of the spouse, children, heirs and devisees and the ages of any who are minors so far as known or ascertainable with reasonable diligence by the applicant;

(iii) if the decedent was not domiciled in the state at the time of his death, a statement showing venue;

(iv) a statement identifying and indicating the address of any personal representative of the decedent appointed in this state or elsewhere whose appointment has not been terminated;

(v) a statement indicating whether the applicant has received a demand for notice, or is aware of any demand for notice of any probate or appointment proceeding concerning the decedent that may have been filed in this state or elsewhere; and

(vi) that the time limit for informal probate or appointment as provided in this Article has not expired either because 3 years or less have passed since the decedent's death, or, if more than 3 years from death have passed, circumstances as described by Section 3–108 authorizing tardy probate or appointment have occurred.

273

(2) An application for informal probate of a will shall state the following in addition to the statements required by (1):

(i) that the original of the decedent's last will is in the possession of the court, or accompanies the application, or that an authenticated copy of a will probated in another jurisdiction accompanies the application;

(ii) that the applicant, to the best of his knowledge, believes the will to have been validly executed;

(iii) that after the exercise of reasonable diligence, the applicant is unaware of any instrument revoking the will, and that the applicant believes that the instrument which is the subject of the application is the decedent's last will.

(3) An application for informal appointment of a personal representative to administer an estate under a will shall describe the will by date of execution and state the time and place of probate or the pending application or petition for probate. The application for appointment shall adopt the statements in the application or petition for probate and state the name, address and priority for appointment of the person whose appointment is sought.

(4) An application for informal appointment of an administrator in intestacy shall state in addition to the statements required by (1):

(i) that after the exercise of reasonable diligence, the applicant is unaware of any unrevoked testamentary instrument relating to property having a situs in this state under Section 1–301, or, a statement why any such instrument of which he may be aware is not being probated;

(ii) the priority of the person whose appointment is sought and the names of any other persons having a prior or equal right to the appointment under Section 3–203.

(5) An application for appointment of a personal representative to succeed a personal representative appointed under a different testacy status shall refer to the order in the most recent testacy proceeding, state the name and address of the person whose appointment is sought and of the person whose appointment will be terminated if the application is granted, and describe the priority of the applicant.

(6) An application for appointment of a personal representative to succeed a personal representative who has tendered a resignation as provided in 3–610(c), or whose appointment has been terminated by death or removal, shall adopt the state-

ments in the application or petition which led to the appointment of the person being succeeded except as specifically changed or corrected, state the name and address of the person who seeks appointment as successor, and describe the priority of the applicant.

(b) By verifying an application for informal probate, or informal appointment, the applicant submits personally to the jurisdiction of the court in any proceeding for relief from fraud relating to the application, or for perjury, that may be instituted against him.

COMMENT

Forcing one who seeks informal probate or informal appointment to make oath before a public official concerning the details required of applications should deter persons who might otherwise misuse the no-notice feature of informal proceedings. The application is available as a part of the public record. If deliberately false representation is made, remedies for fraud will be available to injured persons without specified time limit (see Article I). The section is believed to provide important safeguards that may extend well beyond those presently available under supervised administration for persons damaged by deliberate wrongdoing.

Section 1–310 deals with verification.

In 1975, the Joint Editorial Board recommended the addition of subsection (b) to reflect an improvement accomplished in the first enactment in Idaho. The addition, which is a form of long-arm provision that affects everyone who acts as an applicant in informal proceedings, in conjunction with Section 1–106 provides a remedy in the court of probate against anyone who might make known misstatements in an application. The addition is not needed in the case of an applicant who becomes a personal representative as a result of his application for the implied consent provided in Section 3–602 would cover the matter. Also, the requirement that the applicant state that time limits on informal probate and appointment have not run, formerly appearing as (iv) under paragraph (2) was expanded to refer to informal appointment and moved into (1). Correcting an oversight in the original text, this change coordinates the statements required in an application with the limitations provisions of Section 3–108.

Section 3–302. [Informal Probate; Duty of Registrar; Effect of Informal Probate.]

Upon receipt of an application requesting informal probate of a will, the Registrar, upon making the findings required by Section 3–303 shall issue a written statement of informal probate if at least 120 hours have elapsed since the decedent's death. Informal probate is conclusive as to all persons until superseded by an order in a formal testacy proceeding. No defect in the application or procedure relating thereto which leads to informal probate of a will renders the probate void.

COMMENT

Model Probate Code Sections 68 and 70 contemplate probate by judicial order as the only method of validating a will. This "umbrella" section and the sections it refers to describe an alternative procedure called "informal probate". It is a statement of probate by the Registrar. A succeeding section describes cases in which informal probate is to be denied. "Informal probate" is subjected to safeguards which seem appropriate to a transaction which has the effect of making a will operative and which *may* be the only official reaction concerning its validity. "Informal probate", it is hoped, will serve to keep the simple will which generates no controversy from becoming involved in *truly* judicial proceedings. The procedure is very much like "probate in common form" as it is known in England and some states.

Section 3–303. [Informal Probate; Proof and Findings Required.]

(a) In an informal proceeding for original probate of a will, the Registrar shall determine whether:

(1) the application is complete;

(2) the applicant has made oath or affirmation that the statements contained in the application are true to the best of his knowledge and belief;

(3) the applicant appears from the application to be an interested person as defined in Section 1–201(20);

(4) on the basis of the statements in the application, venue is proper;

(5) an original, duly executed and apparently unrevoked will is in the Registrar's possession;

(6) any notice required by Section 3–204 has been given and that the application is not within Section 3–304; and

(7) it appears from the application that the time limit for original probate has not expired.

(b) The application shall be denied if it indicates that a personal representative has been appointed in another [county] of this state or except as provided in subsection (d) below, if it appears that this or another will of the decedent has been the subject of a previous probate order.

(c) A will which appears to have the required signatures and which contains an attestation clause showing that requirements of execution under Section 2–502, 2–503 or 2–506 have been met shall be probated without further proof. In other cases, the Registrar may assume execution if the will appears to have been properly executed, or he may accept a sworn statement or affidavit of any person having knowledge of the circumstances of execution, whether or not the person was a witness to the will.

(d) Informal probate of a will which has been previously probated elsewhere may be granted at any time upon written application by any interested person, together with deposit of an authenticated copy of the will and of the statement probating it from the office or court where it was first probated.

(e) A will from a place which does not provide for probate of a will after death and which is not eligible for probate under subsection (a) above, may be probated in this state upon receipt by the Registrar of a duly authenticated copy of the will and a duly authenticated certificate of its legal custodian that the copy filed is a true copy and that the will has become operative under the law of the other place.

COMMENT

The purpose of this section is to permit informal probate of a will which, from a simple attestation clause, appears to have been executed properly. It is not necessary that the will be notarized as is the case with "pre-proved" wills in some states. If a will is "pre-proved" as provided in Article II, it will, of course, "appear" to be well executed and include the recital necessary for easy probate here. If the instrument does not contain a proper recital by attesting witnesses, it may be probated informally on the strength of an affidavit by a person who can say what occurred at the time of execution.

Except where probate or its equivalent has occurred previously in another state, informal probate is available only where an original will exists and is available to be filed. Lost or destroyed wills must be established in formal proceedings. See Section 3–402. Under Section 3–401, pendency of formal testacy proceedings blocks informal probate or appointment proceedings.

Section 3–304. [Informal Probate; Unavailable in Certain Cases.]

Applications for informal probate which relate to one or more of a known series of testamentary instruments (other than a will and one or more codicils thereto), the latest of which does not expressly revoke the earlier, shall be declined.

COMMENT

The Registrar handles the informal proceeding, but is required to decline applications in certain cases where circumstances suggest that formal probate would provide desirable safeguards.

Section 3–305. [Informal Probate; Registrar Not Satisfied.]

If the Registrar is not satisfied that a will is entitled to be probated in informal proceedings because of failure to meet the requirements of Sections 3–303 and 3–304 or any other reason, he may decline the application. A declination of informal probate is not an adjudication and does not preclude formal probate proceedings.

COMMENT

The purpose of this section is to recognize that the Registrar should have some authority to deny probate to an instrument even though all stated statutory requirements may be said to have been met. Denial of an application for informal probate cannot be appealed. Rather, the proponent may initiate a formal proceeding so that the matter may be brought before the judge in the normal way for contested matters.

Section 3–306. [Informal Probate; Notice Requirements.]

[*] The moving party must give notice as described by Section 1–401 of his application for informal probate to any person demanding it pursuant to Section 3–204, and to any personal representative of the decedent whose appointment has not been terminated. No other notice of informal probate is required.

[(b) If an informal probate is granted, within 30 days thereafter the applicant shall give written information of the probate to the heirs and devisees. The information shall include the name and address of the applicant, the name and location of the court granting the informal probate, and the date of the probate. The information shall be delivered or sent by ordinary mail to each of the heirs and devisees whose address is reasonably available to the applicant. No duty to give information is incurred if a personal representative is appointed who is required to give the written information required by Section 3–705. An applicant's failure to give information as required by this section is a breach of his duty to the heirs and devisees but does not affect the validity of the probate.]

* This paragraph becomes (a) if optional subsection (b) is accepted.

COMMENT

This provision assumes that there will be a single office within each county or other area of jurisdiction of the probate court which can be checked for demands for notice relating to estates in that area. If there are or may be several registrars within a given area, provision would need to be made so that information concerning demands for notice might be obtained from the chief registrar's place of business.

In 1975, the Joint Editorial Board recommended the addition, as a bracketed, optional provision, of subsection (b). The recommendation was derived from a provision added to the Code in Idaho at the time of original enactment. The Board viewed the addition as interesting, possibly worthwhile, and worth being brought to the attention of enacting states as an optional addition. The Board views the

informational notice required by Section 3–705 to be of more importance in preventing injustices under the Code, because the opening of an estate via appointment of a personal representative instantly gives the estate representative powers over estate assets that can be used wrongfully and to the possible detriment of interested persons. Hence, the 3–705 duty is a part of the recommended Code, rather than a bracketed, optional provision. By contrast, the informal probate of a will that is not accompanied or followed by appointment of a personal representative only serves to shift the burden of making the next move to disinterested heirs who, inter alia, may initiate a Section 3–401 formal testacy proceeding to contest the will at any time within the limitations prescribed by Section 3–108.

Section 3–307. [Informal Appointment Proceedings; Delay in Order; Duty of Registrar; Effect of Appointment.]

(a) Upon receipt of an application for informal appointment of a personal representative other than a special administrator as provided in Section 3–614, if at least 120 hours have elapsed since the decedent's death, the Registrar, after making the findings required by Section 3–308, shall appoint the applicant subject to qualification and acceptance; provided, that if the decedent was a nonresident, the Registrar shall delay the order of appointment until 30 days have elapsed since death unless the personal representative appointed at the decedent's domicile is the applicant, or unless the decedent's will directs that his estate be subject to the laws of this state.

(b) The status of personal representative and the powers and duties pertaining to the office are fully established by informal appointment. An appointment, and the office of personal representative created thereby, is subject to termination as provided in Sections 3–608 through 3–612, but is not subject to retroactive vacation.

COMMENT

Section 3–703 describes the duty of a personal representative and the protection available to one who acts under letters issued in informal proceedings. The provision requiring a delay of 30 days from death before appointment of a personal representative for a non-resident decedent is new. It is designed to permit the first appointment to be at the decedent's domicile. See Section 3–203.

Section 3–308. [Informal Appointment Proceedings; Proof and Findings Required.]

(a) In informal appointment proceedings, the Registrar must determine whether:

(1) the application for informal appointment of a personal representative is complete;

(2) the applicant has made oath or affirmation that the statements contained in the application are true to the best of his knowledge and belief;

(3) the applicant appears from the application to be an interested person as defined in Section 1–201(20);

(4) on the basis of the statements in the application, venue is proper;

(5) any will to which the requested appointment relates has been formally or informally probated; but this requirement does not apply to the appointment of a special administrator;

(6) any notice required by Section 3–204 has been given;

(7) from the statements in the application, the person whose appointment is sought has priority entitling him to the appointment.

(b) Unless Section 3–612 controls, the application must be denied if it indicates that a personal representative who has not filed a written statement of resignation as provided in Section 3–610(c) has been appointed in this or another [county] of this state, that (unless the applicant is the domiciliary personal representative or his nominee) the decedent was not domiciled in this state and that a personal representative whose appointment has not been terminated has been appointed by a Court in the state of domicile, or that other requirements of this section have not been met.

COMMENT

Sections 3–614 and 3–615 make it clear that a special administrator may be appointed to conserve the estate during any period of delay in probate of a will. Even though the will has not been approved, Section 3–614 gives priority for appointment as special administrator to the person nominated by the will which has been offered for probate. Section 3–203 governs priorities for appointment. Under it, one or more of the same class may receive priority through agreement of the others.

The last sentence of the section is designed to prevent informal appointment of a personal representative in this state when a personal representative has been previously appointed at the decedent's domicile. Sections 4–204 and 4–205 may make local appointment unnecessary. Appointment in formal proceedings is possible, however.

Section 3–309. [Informal Appointment Proceedings; Registrar Not Satisfied.]

If the Registrar is not satisfied that a requested informal appointment of a personal representative should be made because of failure to meet the requirements of Sections 3–307 and 3–308, or for any other reason, he may decline the application. A declination of informal appointment is not an adjudication and does not preclude appointment in formal proceedings.

COMMENT

Authority to decline an application for appointment is conferred on the Registrar. Appointment of a personal representative confers broad powers over the assets of a decedent's estate. The process of declining a requested appointment for unclassified reasons should be one which a registrar can use quickly and informally.

Section 3–310. [Informal Appointment Proceedings; Notice Requirements.]

The moving party must give notice as described by Section 1–401 of his intention to seek an appointment informally: (1) to any person demanding it pursuant to Section 3–204; and (2) to any person having a prior or equal right to appointment not waived in writing and filed with the Court. No other notice of an informal appointment proceeding is required.

Section 3–311. [Informal Appointment Unavailable in Certain Cases.]

If an application for informal appointment indicates the existence of a possible unrevoked testamentary instrument which may relate to property subject to the laws of this state, and which is not filed for probate in this court, the Registrar shall decline the application.

SUCCESSION WITHOUT ADMINISTRATION

PREFATORY NOTE

This amendment to the Uniform Probate Code is an alternative to other methods of administering a decedent's estate. The Uniform Probate Code otherwise provides procedures for informal administration, formal administration and supervised administration. This amendment adds another alternative to the system of flexible administration provided by the Uniform Probate Code and permits the heirs of an intestate or residuary devisees of a testator to accept the estate assets without administration by assuming responsibility for discharging those obligations that normally would be discharged by the personal representative.

The concept of succession without administration is drawn from the civil law and is a variation of the method which is followed largely on the Continent in Europe, in Louisiana and in Quebec.

This proposed amendment contains cross-references to the procedures in the Uniform Probate Code and particularly implements the policies and concepts reflected in Sections 1–102, 3–101 and 3–901. These sections of the Uniform Probate Code provide in part:

SECTION 1–102. [Purposes; Rule of Construction.]

(a) This Code shall be liberally construed and applied to promote its underlying purposes and policies.

(b) The underlying purposes and policies of this Code are:

(1) to simplify and clarify the law concerning the affairs of decedents, missing persons, protected persons, minors and incapacitated persons;

(2) to discover and make effective the intent of a decedent in the distribution of his property;

(3) to promote a speedy and efficient system for liquidating the estate of the decedent and making distribution to his successors;

* * * * * * * * * *

SECTION 3–101. [Devolution of Estate at Death; Restrictions.]

The power of a person to leave property by will, and the rights of creditors, devisees, and heirs to his property are subject to the restrictions and limitations contained in this Code to facilitate the prompt settlement of estates. Upon the death of a person, his real and personal property devolves to the persons to whom it is devised by his last will or to those indicated as substitutes for them in cases involving lapse, renunciation, or other circumstances affecting the devolution of testate estate, or in the absence of testamentary disposition, to his heirs, or to those indicated as substitutes for them in cases involving renunciation or other circumstances affecting devolution of intestate estates, subject to homestead allowance, exempt property and family allowance, to rights of creditors, elective share of the surviving spouse, and to administration.

SECTION 3–901. [Successors' Rights if No Administration.]

In the absence of administration, the heirs and devisees are entitled to the estate in accordance with the terms of a probated will or the laws of intestate succession. Devisees may establish title by the probated will to devised property. Persons entitled to property by homestead allowance, exemption or intestacy may establish title thereto by proof of the decedent's ownership, his death, and their relationship to the decedent. Successors take subject to all charges incident to administration, including the claims of creditors and allowances of surviving spouse and dependent children, and subject to the rights of others resulting from abatement, retainer, advancement, and ademption.

Section 3–312. [Universal Succession; In General.]

The heirs of an intestate or the residuary devisees under a will, excluding minors and incapacitated, protected, or unascertained persons, may become universal successors to the decedent's estate by assuming personal liability for (1) taxes, (2) debts of the decedent, (3) claims against the decedent or the estate, and (4) distributions due other heirs, devisees, and persons entitled to property of the decedent as provided in Sections 3–313 through 3–322.

COMMENT

This section states the general policy of the Act to permit heirs or residuary legatees to take possession, control and title to a decedent's estate by assuming a personal obligation to pay taxes, debts, claims and distributions due to others entitled to share in the decedent's property by qualifying under the statute. Although the surviving spouse most often will be an heir or residuary devisee, he or she may also be a person otherwise entitled to property of the decedent as when a forced share is claimed.

This Act does not contemplate that assignees of heirs or residuary devisees will have standing to apply for universal succession since this involves undertaking responsibility for obligations of the decedent. Of course, after the statement of universal succession has been issued, persons may assign their beneficial interests as any other asset.

The Act excludes incapacitated and unascertained persons as universal successors because of the need for successors to deal with the property for various purposes. The procedure permits competent heirs and residuary devisees to proceed even where there are some others incompetent or unascertained. If any unascertained or incompetent heir or devisee wishes, they may require bonding or if unprotected they may force the estate into administration. Subsequent sections permit the conservator, guardian ad litem or other fiduciary of unascertained or incompetent heirs or devisees to object. The universal successors' obligations may be enforced by appropriate remedy. In Louisiana the procedure is available even though there are incompetent heirs for whom a tutor or guardian is appointed to act.

In restricting universal succession to competent heirs and residuary legatees, the act makes them responsible to incompetent heirs and legatees. This restriction is deemed appropriate to avoid the problems in dealing with the estate assets vested in an incompetent. This is a variation from the Louisiana practice. The procedure also contemplates that all competent heirs and

residuary devisees join and does not permit only part of the heirs to petition for succession without administration. This position means that succession without administration is essentially a consent procedure available when family members are in agreement.

This Act contemplates that known competent successors may proceed under it. Although all competent heirs are required to join in the informal process, the possibility of an unknown heir is not treated as jurisdictional. An unknown heir who appeared would be able to establish his or her rights as in administration unless barred by adjudication, estoppel or lapse of time.

Section 3–313. [Universal Succession; Application; Contents.]

(a) An application to become universal successors by the heirs of an intestate or the residuary devisees under a will must be directed to the [Registrar], signed by each applicant, and verified to be accurate and complete to the best of the applicant's knowledge and belief as follows:

(1) An application by heirs of an intestate must contain the statements required by Section 3–301(a)(1) and (4)(i) and state that the applicants constitute all the heirs other than minors and incapacitated, protected, or unascertained persons.

(2) An application by residuary devisees under a will must be combined with a petition for informal probate if the will has not been admitted to probate in this State and must contain the statements required by Section 3–301(a)(1) and (2). If the will has been probated in this State, an application by residuary devisees must contain the statements required by Section 3–301(a)(2)(iii). An application by residuary devisees must state that the applicants constitute the residuary devisees of the decedent other than any minors and incapacitated, protected, or unascertained persons. If the estate is partially intestate, all of the heirs other than minors and incapacitated, protected, or unascertained persons must join as applicants.

(b) The application must state whether letters of administration are outstanding, whether a petition for appointment of a personal representative of the decedent is pending in any court of this State, and that the applicants waive their right to seek appointment of a personal representative.

(c) The application may describe in general terms the assets of the estate and must state that the applicants accept responsibility for the estate and assume personal liability for (1) taxes, (2) debts of the decedent, (3) claims against the decedent or the estate and (4) distributions due other heirs, devisees, and persons entitled to property of the decedent as provided in Sections 3–316 through 3–322.

COMMENT

This section spells out in detail the form and requirements for application to the Registrar to become universal successors. The section requires the applicants to inform the Registrar whether the appointment of a personal representative has occurred or is pending in order to assure any administration is terminated before the application can be granted. The section requires applicants to waive their right to seek the appointment of a personal representative. The appointment of an executor would preclude or postpone universal succession by application for appointment unless the executor's appointment is avoided because of lack of interest in the estate. See Sections 3–611, 3–912.

The statements in the application are verified by signing and filing and deemed to be under oath as provided in Section 1–310. Like other informal proceedings under the U.P.C., false statements constitute fraud (U.P.C. 1–106).

Even though the presence of residuary devisees would seem to preclude partial intestacy (U.P.C. 2–605, 2–606), the last sentence of 3–313(a) regarding partial intestacy warns all parties that if there is a partial intestacy, the heirs must join. It avoids problems of determining whether the residuary takers are in all instances true residuary legatees, e.g., if a testator provides: "Lastly, I give ½ and only ½ of the rest of my estate to A." (cf. U.P.C. 2–603).

Section 3–313(c) provides that a general description of the assets may be included appropriate to the assets in the estate and adequate to inform the parties and the Registrar of the nature of the estate involved.

In the event an heir or residuary devisee were to disclaim prior to acceptance of the succession, those who would take in place of the disclaimant would be the successors who could apply to become universal successors. The disclaimant could not become a universal successor as to the disclaimed interest and would not be subject to liability as a universal successor.

Trustees of testamentary trusts have standing as devisees. If the trustee is a pecuniary devisee or a specific devisee other than a residuary devisee, he would administer the trust upon receipt of the assets from the universal successors and as a devisee could enforce distribution from the universal successors.

The trustee who is a residuary legatee has standing to qualify as a universal successor by acceptance of the decedent's assets, then to discharge the obligations of the universal successor, and finally to administer the residue under the trust without appointment of a personal representative. The will would be probated in any event. The residuary trustee could choose to insist on appointment of a personal representative and not seek universal succession. Neither alternative could alter the provisions of the residuary trust.

Section 3–314. [Universal Succession; Proof and Findings Required.]

(a) The [Registrar] shall grant the application if:

(1) the application is complete in accordance with Section 3–313;

(2) all necessary persons have joined and have verified that the statements contained therein are true, to the best knowledge and belief of each;

(3) venue is proper;

(4) any notice required by Section 3–204 has been given or waived;

(5) the time limit for original probate or appointment proceedings has not expired and the applicants claim under a will;

(6) the application requests informal probate of a will, the application and findings conform with Sections 3–301(a)(2) and 3–303(a)(c)(d) and (e) so the will is admitted to probate; and

(7) none of the applicants is a minor or an incapacitated or protected person.

(b) The [Registrar] shall deny the application if letters of administration are outstanding.

(c) Except as provided in Section 3–322, the [Registrar] shall deny the application if any creditor, heir, or devisee who is qualified by Section 3–605 to demand bond files an objection.

COMMENT

This section outlines the substantive requirements for universal succession and is the guideline to the Registrar for approval of the application. As in U.P.C. 3–303, review of the filed documents is all that is required, with the Registrar expected to determine whether to approve on the basis of information available to the Registrar. There is very little discretion in the Registrar except that if something appears lacking in the application, the Registrar would be able to request additional information. The analogy to U.P.C. 3–303 is rather direct and the authority of the Registrar is somewhat more limited because there is no parallel section to U.P.C. 3–305 as there is in probate. (See also U.P.C. 3–309.)

Section 3–314(a)(5) requires that the application for universal succession under a will be made before the time limit for original probate has expired. Against the background of U.P.C. 3–108 which limits administration proceedings after three years except for proof of heirship or will construction, the heirs could take possession of property and prove their title without the universal succession provisions.

The review of the application by the Registrar essentially is a clerical matter to determine if the application exhibits the appropriate circumstance for succession without administration. Hence, if there are letters of administration outstanding, the application must be denied under Section 3–314(b). Even though a disinterested executor under a will should not be able to preclude those interested in the estate from settling the estate without administration, coordination of the Registrar's action with the process of the probate court is imperative to protect the parties and the public. Consequently, any outstanding letters must be terminated before succession without administration is approved. Under the Uniform Probate Code, those with property interests in the estate are viewed as "interested persons" (U.P.C. 1–201(2)) and may initiate either informal (U.P.C. 3–105) or formal proceedings (U.P.C. 3–401); also the agreement of those interested in the estate is binding on the personal representative (U.P.C. 3–912, 3–

1101). These provisions appear adequate to preclude the personal representative who has no other interest in the estate from frustrating those interested from utilizing succession without administration.

There is need for coordination with other process within the probate court when a petition for letters is pending (i.e., not withdrawn) as when letters were outstanding. The appropriateness of the appointment of the personal representative, i.e., whether administration was necessary, could be determined on an objection to the appointment under U.P.C. Sections 3–414(b); cf., 3–608 to 3–612. If the appointment of a personal representative is denied, then the application for universal succession without administration could be approved in appropriate cases.

Section 3–314 does not require prior notice unless requested under U.P.C. 3–204. Information to other heirs and devisees is provided after approval of the application. See Section 3–319.

If, after universal succession is approved, a creditor or devisee were not paid or secured, in addition to suing the successor directly, the creditor or devisee could move for appointment of a personal representative to administer the estate properly. This pressure on the universal successors to perform seems desirable. In view of the availability of informal administration and other flexible alternatives under the U.P.C., if any person properly moves for appointment of a personal representative, succession without administration should be foreclosed or terminated.

Section 3–315. [Universal Succession; Duty of Registrar; Effect of Statement of Universal Succession.]

Upon receipt of an application under Section 3–313, if at least 120 hours have elapsed since the decedent's death, the [Registrar], upon granting the application, shall issue a written statement of universal succession describing the estate as set forth in the application and stating that the applicants (i) are the universal successors to the assets of the estate as provided in Section 3–312, (ii) have assumed liability for the obligations of the decedent, and (iii) have acquired the powers and liabilities of universal successors. The statement of universal succession is evidence of the universal successors' title to the assets of the estate. Upon its issuance, the powers and liabilities of universal successors provided in Sections 3–316 through 3–322 attach and are assumed by the applicants.

COMMENT

This section provides for a written statement issued by the Registrar evidencing the right and power of the universal successors to deal with the property of the decedent and serves as an instrument of distribution to them. Although the application for universal succession may be filed anytime after death, within the time limit for original probate, the Registrar may not act before 120 hours have elapsed since the testator's death. This period parallels provisions for other informal proceedings under the U.P.C., e.g., §§ 2–601, 3–302, 3–307.

Section 3–316. [Universal Succession; Universal Successors' Powers.]

Upon the [Registrar's] issuance of a statement of universal succession:

(1) Universal successors have full power of ownership to deal with the assets of the estate subject to the limitations and liabilities in this [Act]. The universal successors shall proceed expeditiously to settle and distribute the estate without adjudication but if necessary may invoke the jurisdiction of the court to resolve questions concerning the estate.

(2) Universal successors have the same powers as distributees from a personal representative under Sections 3–908 and 3–909 and third persons with whom they deal are protected as provided in Section 3–910.

(3) For purposes of collecting assets in another state whose law does not provide for universal succession, universal succes-

sors have the same standing and power as personal representatives or distributees in this State.

COMMENT

This section is the substantive provision (1) declaring the successors to be distributees and (2) to have the powers of owners so far as dealing with the estate assets subject to the obligations to others.

Details concerning the status of distributees under U.P.C. 3–908 and the power to deal with property are provided in U.P.C. 3–910.

Although one state cannot control the law of another, the universal successor should be recognized in other states as having the standing of either a foreign personal representative or a distributee of the claim to local assets. Paragraph (3) attempts to remove any limitation of this state in such a case.

Section 3–317. [Universal Succession; Universal Successors' Liability to Creditors, Other Heirs, Devisees and Persons Entitled to Decedent's Property; Liability of Other Persons Entitled to Property.]

(a) In the proportions and subject to the limits expressed in Section 3–321, universal successors assume all liabilities of the decedent that were not discharged by reason of death and liability for all taxes, claims against the decedent or the estate, and charges properly incurred after death for the preservation of the estate, to the extent those items, if duly presented, would be valid claims against the decedent's estate.

(b) In the proportions and subject to the limits expressed in Section 3–321, universal successors are personally liable to other heirs, devisees, and persons entitled to property of the decedent for the assets or amounts that would be due those heirs, were the estate administered, but no allowance having priority over devisees may be claimed for attorney's fees or charges for preservation of the estate in excess of reasonable amounts properly incurred.

(c) Universal successors are entitled to their interests in the estate as heirs or devisees subject to priority and abatement pursuant to Section 3–902 and to agreement pursuant to Section 3–912.

(d) Other heirs, devisees, and persons to whom assets have been distributed have the same powers and liabilities as distributees under Sections 3–908, 3–909, and 3–910.

(e) Absent breach of fiduciary obligations or express undertaking, a fiduciary's liability is limited to the assets received by the fiduciary.

COMMENT

The purpose of succession without administration is not to alter the relative property interests of the parties but only to facilitate the family's expeditious settlement of the estate. Consistent with this, the liability arising from the assumption of obligations is stated explicitly here to assist in understanding the coupling of power and liability. Subsection (b) includes an abatement reference that recognizes the possible adjustment that may be necessary by reason of excess claims under U.P.C. 3-902.

In succession without administration, there being no personal representative's notice to creditors, the short non-claim period under U.P.C. Section 3-803(a)(1) does not apply and creditors are subject to the statutes of limitations and the limitation of three years on decedent's creditors when no notice is published under U.P.C. Section 3-803(a)(2). The general statutes of limitation are suspended for four months following the decedent's death but resume thereafter under U.P.C. Section 3-802. The assumption of liability by the universal successors upon the issuance of the Statement of Universal Succession is deemed to be by operation of law and does not operate to extend or renew any statute of limitations that had begun to run against the decedent. The result is that creditors are barred by the general statutes of limitation or 3 years whichever is the shorter.

The obligation of the universal successors to other heirs, devisees and distributees is based on the promise to perform in return for the direct distribution of property and any limitation or laches begins to run on issuance of the statement of universal succession unless otherwise extended by action or assurance of the universal successor.

It should be noted that this statute does not deal with the consequences or obligations that arise under either federal or state tax laws. The universal successors will be subject to obligations for the return and payment of both income and estate taxes in many situations depending upon the tax law and the circumstances of the decedent and the estate. These tax consequences should be determined before electing to utilize succession without administration.

Section 3-318. [Universal Succession; Universal Successors' Submission to Jurisdiction; When Heirs or Devisees May Not Seek Administration.]

(a) Upon issuance of the statement of universal succession, the universal successors become subject to the personal jurisdiction of the courts of this state in any proceeding that may be instituted relating to the estate or to any liability assumed by them.

(b) Any heir or devisee who voluntarily joins in an application under Section 3-313 may not subsequently seek appointment of a personal representative.

COMMENT

This section imposes jurisdiction over the universal successors and bars them from seeking appointment as personal representative.

Section 3–319. [Universal Succession; Duty of Universal Successors; Information to Heirs and Devisees.]

Not later than thirty days after issuance of the statement of universal succession, each universal successor shall inform the heirs and devisees who did not join in the application of the succession without administration. The information must be delivered or be sent by ordinary mail to each of the heirs and devisees whose address is reasonably available to the universal successors. The information must include the names and addresses of the universal successors, indicate that it is being sent to persons who have or may have some interest in the estate, and describe the court where the application and statement of universal succession has been filed. The failure of a universal successor to give this information is a breach of duty to the persons concerned but does not affect the validity of the approval of succession without administration or the powers or liabilities of the universal successors. A universal successor may inform other persons of the succession without administration by delivery or by ordinary first class mail.

COMMENT

The problem of residuary legatees or some of the heirs moving for universal succession without the knowledge of others interested in the estate is similar to that of informal administration. By this provision those devisees and heirs who do not participate in the application are informed of the application and its approval and may move to protect any interest that they perceive. The provision parallels U.P.C. Section 3–705.

Section 3–320. [Universal Succession; Universal Successors' Liability for Restitution to Estate.]

If a personal representative is subsequently appointed, universal successors are personally liable for restitution of any property of the estate to which they are not entitled as heirs or devisees of the decedent and their liability is the same as a distributee under Section 3–909, subject to the provisions of Sections 3–317 and 3–321 and the limitations of Section 3–1006.

COMMENT

The liability of universal successors for restitution in the event a personal representative is appointed is spelled out in this section and keyed to the parallel sections in the U.P.C.

Section 3–321. [Universal Succession; Liability of Universal Successors for Claims, Expenses, Intestate Shares and Devises.]

The liability of universal successors is subject to any defenses that would have been available to the decedent. Other than liability arising from fraud, conversion, or other wrongful conduct of a universal successor, the personal liability of each universal successor to any creditor, claimant, other heir, devisee, or person entitled to decedent's property may not exceed the proportion of the claim that the universal successor's share bears to the share of all heirs and residuary devisees.

COMMENT

This is the primary provision for the successor's liability to creditors and others. The theory is that the universal successors as a group are liable in full to the creditors but that none have a greater liability than in proportion to the share of the estate received. Under the U.P.C., since informal administration is available with limited liability for the personal representative, the analogy to the Louisiana system would be to accept full responsibility for debts and claims if succession without administration is desired but to choose informal administration if protection of the inventory is desired.

This definition of liability assumes, first, that the devisees and heirs are subject to the usual priorities for creditors and devisees and abatement for them in §§ 3–316, 3–317. Second, it is assumed that if a creditor or a subsequently appointed personal representative were to proceed against the successors, having jurisdiction by submission, § 3–318, the liability would be on a theory of contribution by the successors with the burden on each universal successor to prove his or her own share of the estate and liability against that share.

Third, it is also assumed that, a creditor who is unprotected or unsecured under § 3–322, can object to universal succession under § 3–314(c) and if the creditor does not object, payments by the successors, like those by the decedent when alive, will be recognized as good without any theory of preferring creditors. Thus, until a creditor takes action to require administration, that creditor should be bound by the successors' non-fraudulent prior payment to other creditors. If a creditor suspects insolvency, he can put the estate into administration and after the appointment of a personal representative would have the usual priority as to remaining assets. This would be subject to the theory of fraud, i.e., a knowing and conscious design on the part of the successors to ignore the priority of the decedent's creditors to the harm of a creditor. This would constitute fraud that would defeat the limits on successor's liability otherwise available under the statute.

Section 3-322. [Universal Succession; Remedies of Creditors, Other Heirs, Devisees or Persons Entitled to Decedent's Property.]

In addition to remedies otherwise provided by law, any creditor, heir, devisee, or person entitled to decedent's property qualified under Section 3-605, may demand bond of universal successors. If the demand for bond precedes the granting of an application for universal succession, it must be treated as an objection under Section 3-314(c) unless it is withdrawn, the claim satisfied, or the applicants post bond in an amount sufficient to protect the demandant. If the demand for bond follows the granting of an application for universal succession, the universal successors, within 10 days after notice of the demand, upon satisfying the claim or posting bond sufficient to protect the demandant, may disqualify the demandant from seeking administration of the estate.

COMMENT

This section provides necessary protection to creditors and other heirs, devisees or persons entitled to distribution. Any person to whom a universal successor is obligated could pursue any available remedy, e.g., a proceeding to collect a debt or to secure specific performance. By this section, any creditor or other heir, devisee or person entitled to distribution may also demand protection and, if it is not forthcoming, put the estate into administration. This seems adequate to coerce performance from universal successors while assuring creditors their historical preference and other beneficiaries of the estate their rights.

PART 4

FORMAL TESTACY AND APPOINTMENT PROCEEDINGS

Section 3–401. [Formal Testacy Proceedings; Nature; When Commenced.]

A formal testacy proceeding is litigation to determine whether a decedent left a valid will. A formal testacy proceeding may be commenced by an interested person filing a petition as described in Section 3–402(a) in which he requests that the Court, after notice and hearing, enter an order probating a will, or a petition to set aside an informal probate of a will or to prevent informal probate of a will which is the subject of a pending application, or a petition in accordance with Section 3–402(b) for an order that the decedent died intestate.

A petition may seek formal probate of a will without regard to whether the same or a conflicting will has been informally probated. A formal testacy proceeding may, but need not, involve a request for appointment of a personal representative.

During the pendency of a formal testacy proceeding, the Registrar shall not act upon any application for informal probate of any will of the decedent or any application for informal appointment of a personal representative of the decedent.

Unless a petition in a formal testacy proceeding also requests confirmation of the previous informal appointment, a previously appointed personal representative, after receipt of notice of the commencement of a formal probate proceeding, must refrain from exercising his power to make any further distribution of the estate during the pendency of the formal proceeding. A petitioner who seeks the appointment of a different personal representative in a formal proceeding also may request an order restraining the acting personal representative from exercising any of the powers of his office and requesting the appointment of a special administrator. In the absence of a request, or if the request is denied, the commencement of a formal proceeding has no effect on the powers and duties of a previously appointed personal representative other than those relating to distribution.

294

COMMENT

The word "testacy" is used to refer to the general status of a decedent in regard to wills. Thus, it embraces the possibility that he left no will, any question of which of several instruments is his valid will, and the possibility that he died intestate as to a part of his estate, and testate as to the balance. See Section 1–201(44).

The formal proceedings described by this section may be: (i) an original proceeding to secure "solemn form" probate of a will; (ii) a proceeding to secure "solemn form" probate to corroborate a previous informal probate; (iii) a proceeding to block a pending application for informal probate, or to prevent an informal application from occurring thereafter; (iv) a proceeding to contradict a previous order of informal probate; (v) a proceeding to secure a declaratory judgment of intestacy and a determination of heirs in a case where no will has been offered. If a pending informal application for probate is blocked by a formal proceeding, the applicant may withdraw his application and avoid the obligation of going forward with pri-

ma facie proof of due execution. See Section 3–407. The petitioner in the formal proceedings may be content to let matters stop there, or he can frame his petition, or amend, so that he may secure an adjudication of intestacy which would prevent further activity concerning the will.

If a personal representative has been appointed prior to the commencement of a formal testacy proceeding, the petitioner must request confirmation of the appointment to indicate that he does not want the testacy proceeding to have any effect on the duties of the personal representative, or refrain from seeking confirmation, in which case, the proceeding suspends the distributive power of the previously appointed representative. If nothing else is requested or decided in respect to the personal representative, his distributive powers are restored at the completion of the proceeding, with Section 3–703 directing him to abide by the will. "Distribute" and "distribution" do not include payment of claims. See 1–201(10), 3–807 and 3–902.

Section 3–402. [Formal Testacy or Appointment Proceedings; Petition; Contents.]

(a) Petitions for formal probate of a will, or for adjudication of intestacy with or without request for appointment of a personal representative, must be directed to the Court, request a judicial order after notice and hearing and contain further statements as indicated in this section. A petition for formal probate of a will

(1) requests an order as to the testacy of the decedent in relation to a particular instrument which may or may not have been informally probated and determining the heirs,

(2) contains the statements required for informal applications as stated in the six subparagraphs under Section 3–

301(a)(1), the statements required by subparagraphs (ii) and (iii) of Section 3–301(a)(2), and

(3) states whether the original of the last will of the decedent is in the possession of the Court or accompanies the petition.

If the original will is neither in the possession of the Court nor accompanies the petition and no authenticated copy of a will probated in another jurisdiction accompanies the petition, the petition also must state the contents of the will, and indicate that it is lost, destroyed, or otherwise unavailable.

(b) A petition for adjudication of intestacy and appointment of an administrator in intestacy must request a judicial finding and order that the decedent left no will and determining the heirs, contain the statements required by (1) and (4) of Section 3–301(a) and indicate whether supervised administration is sought. A petition may request an order determining intestacy and heirs without requesting the appointment of an administrator, in which case, the statements required by subparagraph (ii) of Section 3–301(a)(4) above may be omitted.

COMMENT

If a petitioner seeks an adjudication that a decedent died intestate, he is required also to obtain a finding of heirship. A formal proceeding which is to be effective on all interested persons must follow reasonable notice to such persons. It seems desirable to force the proceedings through a formal determination of heirship because the finding will bolster the order, as well as preclude later questions that might arise at the time of distribution.

Unless an order of supervised administration is sought, there will be little occasion for a formal order concerning appointment of a personal representative which does not also adjudicate the testacy status of the decedent. If a formal order of appointment is sought because of disagreement over who should serve, Section 3–414 describes the appropriate procedure.

The words "otherwise unavailable" in the last paragraph of subsection (a) are not intended to be read restrictively.

Section 1–310 expresses the verification requirement which applies to all documents filed with the Courts.

Section 3–403. [Formal Testacy Proceedings; Notice of Hearing on Petition.]

(a) Upon commencement of a formal testacy proceeding, the Court shall fix a time and place of hearing. Notice shall be given in the manner prescribed by Section 1–401 by the petitioner to the persons herein enumerated and to any additional person who has filed a demand for notice under Section 3–204 of this Code.

Notice shall be given to the following persons: the surviving spouse, children, and other heirs of the decedent, the devisees and executors named in any will that is being, or has been, probated, or offered for informal or formal probate in the [county,] or that is known by the petitioner to have been probated, or offered for informal or formal probate elsewhere, and any personal representative of the decedent whose appointment has not been terminated. Notice may be given to other persons. In addition, the petitioner shall give notice by publication to all unknown persons and to all known persons whose addresses are unknown who have any interest in the matters being litigated.

(b) If it appears by the petition or otherwise that the fact of the death of the alleged decedent may be in doubt, or on the written demand of any interested person, a copy of the notice of the hearing on said petition shall be sent by registered mail to the alleged decedent at his last known address. The Court shall direct the petitioner to report the results of, or make and report back concerning, a reasonably diligent search for the alleged decedent in any manner that may seem advisable, including any or all of the following methods:

(1) by inserting in one or more suitable periodicals a notice requesting information from any person having knowledge of the whereabouts of the alleged decedent;

(2) by notifying law enforcement officials and public welfare agencies in appropriate locations of the disappearance of the alleged decedent;

(3) by engaging the services of an investigator.

The costs of any search so directed shall be paid by the petitioner if there is no administration or by the estate of the decedent in case there is administration.

COMMENT

Provisions governing the time and manner of notice required by this section and other sections in the Code are contained in 1–401.

The provisions concerning search for the alleged decedent are derived from Model Probate Code, Section 71.

Testacy proceedings involve adjudications that no will exists. Unknown wills as well as any which are brought to the attention of the Court are affected. Persons with potential interests under unknown wills have the notice afforded by death and by publication. Notice requirements extend also to persons named in a will that is known to the petitioners to exist, irrespective of whether it has been probated or offered for formal or informal probate, if their position may be affected adversely by granting of the petition. But, a rigid statutory requirement relating to such persons might cause undue difficulty. Hence, the statute merely provides that the petitioner may notify other persons.

It would not be inconsistent with this section for the Court to adopt rules designed to make petitioners exercise reasonable diligence in searching for as yet undiscovered wills.

Section 3–106 provides that an order is valid as to those given notice, though less than all interested persons were given notice. Section 3–1001(b) provides a means of extending a testacy order to previously unnotified persons in connection with a formal closing.

Section 3–404. [Formal Testacy Proceedings; Written Objections to Probate.]

Any party to a formal proceeding who opposes the probate of a will for any reason shall state in his pleadings his objections to probate of the will.

COMMENT

Model Probate Code section 72 requires a contestant to file written objections to any will he would oppose. The provision prevents potential confusion as to who must file what pleading that can arise from the notion that the probate of a will is in rem. The petition for probate of a revoking will is sufficient warning to proponents of the revoked will.

Section 3–405. [Formal Testacy Proceedings; Uncontested Cases; Hearings and Proof.]

If a petition in a testacy proceeding is unopposed, the Court may order probate or intestacy on the strength of the pleadings if satisfied that the conditions of Section 3–409 have been met, or conduct a hearing in open court and require proof of the matters necessary to support the order sought. If evidence concerning execution of the will is necessary, the affidavit or testimony of one of any attesting witnesses to the instrument is sufficient. If the affidavit or testimony of an attesting witness is not available, execution of the will may be proved by other evidence or affidavit.

COMMENT

For various reasons, attorneys handling estates may want interested persons to be gathered for a hearing before the Court on the formal allowance of the will. The Court is not required to conduct a hearing, however.

If no hearing is required, uncontested formal probates can be completed on the strength of the pleadings. There is no good reason for summoning attestors when no interested person wants to force the production of evidence on a formal probate. Moreover, there seems to be no valid distinction between litigation to establish a will, and other civil litigation, in respect to whether the court may enter judgment on the pleadings.

Section 3–406. [Formal Testacy Proceedings; Contested Cases; Testimony of Attesting Witnesses.]

(a) If evidence concerning execution of an attested will which is not self-proved is necessary in contested cases, the testimony of at least one of the attesting witnesses, if within the state, competent and able to testify, is required. Due execution of an attested or unattested will may be proved by other evidence.

(b) If the will is self-proved, compliance with signature requirements for execution is conclusively presumed and other requirements of execution are presumed subject to rebuttal without the testimony of any witness upon filing the will and the acknowledgment and affidavits annexed or attached thereto, unless there is proof of fraud or forgery affecting the acknowledgment or affidavit.

COMMENT

Model Probate Code section 76, combined with section 77, substantially unchanged. The self-proved will is described in Article II. See Section 2–504. The "conclusive presumption" described here would foreclose questions like whether the witnesses signed in the presence of the testator. It would not preclude proof of undue influence, lack of testamentary capacity, revocation or any relevant proof that the testator was unaware of the contents of the document. The balance of the section is derived from Model Probate Code sections 76 and 77.

Section 3–407. [Formal Testacy Proceedings; Burdens in Contested Cases.]

In contested cases, petitioners who seek to establish intestacy have the burden of establishing prima facie proof of death, venue, and heirship. Proponents of a will have the burden of establishing prima facie proof of due execution in all cases, and, if they are also petitioners, prima facie proof of death and venue. Contestants of a will have the burden of establishing lack of testamentary intent or capacity, undue influence, fraud, duress, mistake or revocation. Parties have the ultimate burden of persuasion as to matters with respect to which they have the initial burden of proof. If a will is opposed by the petition for probate of a later will revoking the former, it shall be determined first whether the later will is entitled to probate, and if a will is opposed by a petition for a declaration of intestacy, it shall be determined first whether the will is entitled to probate.

COMMENT

This section is designed to clarify the law by stating what is believed to be a fairly standard approach to questions concerning burdens of going forward with evidence in will contest cases.

Section 3–408. [Formal Testacy Proceedings; Will Construction; Effect of Final Order in Another Jurisdiction.]

A final order of a court of another state determining testacy, the validity or construction of a will, made in a proceeding involving notice to and an opportunity for contest by all interested persons must be accepted as determinative by the courts of this state if it includes, or is based upon, a finding that the decedent was domiciled at his death in the state where the order was made.

COMMENT

This section is designed to extend the effect of final orders of another jurisdiction of the United States. It should not be read to restrict the obligation of the local court to respect the judgment of another court when parties who were personally before the other court also are personally before the local court. An "authenticated copy" includes copies properly certified under the full faith and credit statute. If conflicting claims of domicile are made in proceedings which are commenced in different jurisdictions, Section 3–202 applies. This section is framed to apply where a formal proceeding elsewhere has been previously concluded. Hence, if a local proceeding is concluded before formal proceedings at domicile are concluded, local law will control.

Informal proceedings by which a will is probated or a personal representative is appointed are not proceedings which must be respected by a local court under either Section 3–202 or this section.

Nothing in this section bears on questions of what assets are included in a decedent's estate.

This section adds nothing to existing law as applied to cases where the parties before the local court were also personally before the foreign court, or where the property involved was subject to the power of the foreign court. It extends present law so that, for some purposes, the law of another state may become binding in regard to due execution or revocation of wills controlling local land, and to questions concerning the meaning of ambiguous words in wills involving local land. But, choice of law rules frequently produce a similar result. See § 240 Restatement of the Law, Second: Conflict of Laws, p. 73, Proposed Official Draft III, 1969.

This section may be easier to justify than familiar choice of law rules, for its application is limited to instances where the protesting party has had notice of, and an opportunity to participate in, previous litigation resolving the question he now seeks to raise.

Section 3–409. [Formal Testacy Proceedings; Order; Foreign Will.]

After the time required for any notice has expired, upon proof of notice, and after any hearing that may be necessary, if the Court finds that the testator is dead, venue is proper and that the proceeding was commenced within the limitation prescribed by Section 3–108, it shall determine the decedent's domicile at death, his heirs and his state of testacy. Any will found to be valid and unrevoked shall be formally probated. Termination of any previous informal appointment of a personal representative, which may be appropriate in view of the relief requested and findings, is governed by Section 3–612. The petition shall be dismissed or appropriate amendment allowed if the court is not satisfied that the alleged decedent is dead. A will from a place which does not provide for probate of a will after death, may be proved for probate in this state by a duly authenticated certificate of its legal custodian that the copy introduced is a true copy and that the will has become effective under the law of the other place.

COMMENT

Model Probate Code section 80(a), slightly changed. If the court is not satisfied that the alleged decedent is dead, it may permit amendment of the proceeding so that it would become a proceeding to protect the estate of a missing and therefore "disabled" person. See Article V of this Code.

Section 3–410. [Formal Testacy Proceedings; Probate of More Than One Instrument.]

If two or more instruments are offered for probate before a final order is entered in a formal testacy proceeding, more than one instrument may be probated if neither expressly revokes the other or contains provisions which work a total revocation by implication. If more than one instrument is probated, the order shall indicate what provisions control in respect to the nomination of an executor, if any. The order may, but need not, indicate how any provisions of a particular instrument are affected by the other instrument. After a final order in a testacy proceeding has been entered, no petition for probate of any other instrument of the decedent may be entertained, except incident to a petition to vacate or modify a previous probate order and subject to the time limits of Section 3–412.

COMMENT

Except as otherwise provided in Section 3–412, an order in a formal testacy proceeding serves to end the time within which it is possible to probate after-discovered wills, or to give effect to late-discovered facts concerning heirship. Determination of heirs is not barred by the three year limitation but a judicial determination of heirs is conclusive unless the order may be vacated.

This section authorizes a court to engage in some construction of wills incident to determining whether a will is entitled to probate. It seems desirable to leave the extent of this power to the sound discretion of the court. If wills are not construed in connection with a judicial probate, they may be subject to construction at any time. See Section 3–108.

Section 3–411. [Formal Testacy Proceedings; Partial Intestacy.]

If it becomes evident in the course of a formal testacy proceeding that, though one or more instruments are entitled to be probated, the decedent's estate is or may be partially intestate, the Court shall enter an order to that effect.

Section 3–412. [Formal Testacy Proceedings; Effect of Order; Vacation.]

Subject to appeal and subject to vacation as provided in this section and in Section 3–413, a formal testacy order under Sections 3–409 to 3–411, including an order that the decedent left no valid will and determining heirs, is final as to all persons with respect to all issues concerning the decedent's estate that the court considered or might have considered incident to its rendition relevant to the question of whether the decedent left a valid will, and to the determination of heirs, except that:

(1) the court shall entertain a petition for modification or vacation of its order and probate of another will of the decedent if it is shown that the proponents of the later-offered will: (i) were unaware of its existence at the time of the earlier proceeding; or (ii) were unaware of the earlier proceeding and were given no notice thereof, except by publication.

(2) If intestacy of all or part of the estate has been ordered, the determination of heirs of the decedent may be reconsidered if it is shown that one or more persons were omitted from the determination and it is also shown that the persons were unaware of their relationship to the decedent, were unaware of

his death, or were given no notice of any proceeding concerning his estate, except by publication.

(3) A petition for vacation under paragraph (1) or (2) must be filed prior to the earlier of the following time limits:

(i) if a personal representative has been appointed for the estate, the time of entry of any order approving final distribution of the estate, or, if the estate is closed by statement, six months after the filing of the closing statement;

(ii) whether or not a personal representative has been appointed for the estate of the decedent, the time prescribed by Section 3–108 when it is no longer possible to initiate an original proceeding to probate a will of the decedent; or

(iii) twelve months after the entry of the order sought to be vacated.

(4) The order originally rendered in the testacy proceeding may be modified or vacated, if appropriate under the circumstances, by the order of probate of the later-offered will or the order redetermining heirs.

(5) The finding of the fact of death is conclusive as to the alleged decedent only if notice of the hearing on the petition in the formal testacy proceeding was sent by registered or certified mail addressed to the alleged decedent at his last known address and the court finds that a search under Section 3–403(b) was made.

If the alleged decedent is not dead, even if notice was sent and search was made, he may recover estate assets in the hands of the personal representative. In addition to any remedies available to the alleged decedent by reason of any fraud or intentional wrongdoing, the alleged decedent may recover any estate or its proceeds from distributees that is in their hands, or the value of distributions received by them, to the extent that any recovery from distributees is equitable in view of all of the circumstances.

COMMENT

The provisions barring proof of late-discovered wills is derived in part from section 81 of Model Probate Code. The same section is the source of the provisions of (5) above. The provisions permitting vacation of an order determining heirs on certain conditions reflect the effort to offer parallel possibilities for adjudications in testate and intestate estates. See Section 3–401. An objective is to make it possible to handle an intestate estate exactly as a testate estate may be handled. If this is achieved, some of the pressure on persons to make wills may be relieved.

If an alleged decedent turns out to have been alive, heirs and distributees are liable to restore the "estate or its proceeds". If neither can be identified through the normal process of tracing assets, their liability depends upon the circumstances. The liability of distributees to claimants whose claims have

not been barred, or to persons shown to be entitled to distribution when a formal proceeding changes a previous assumption informally established which guided an earlier distribution, is different. See Sections 3-909 and 3-1004.

1993 technical amendments clarified the conditions intended in (1) and (2).

Section 3-413. [Formal Testacy Proceedings; Vacation of Order for Other Cause.]

For good cause shown, an order in a formal testacy proceeding may be modified or vacated within the time allowed for appeal.

COMMENT

See Sections 1-304 and 1-308.

Section 3-414. [Formal Proceedings Concerning Appointment of Personal Representative.]

(a) A formal proceeding for adjudication regarding the priority or qualification of one who is an applicant for appointment as personal representative, or of one who previously has been appointed personal representative in informal proceedings, if an issue concerning the testacy of the decedent is or may be involved, is governed by Section 3-402, as well as by this section. In other cases, the petition shall contain or adopt the statements required by Section 3-301(1) and describe the question relating to priority or qualification of the personal representative which is to be resolved. If the proceeding precedes any appointment of a personal representative, it shall stay any pending informal appointment proceedings as well as any commenced thereafter. If the proceeding is commenced after appointment, the previously appointed personal representative, after receipt of notice thereof, shall refrain from exercising any power of administration except as necessary to preserve the estate or unless the Court orders otherwise.

(b) After notice to interested persons, including all persons interested in the administration of the estate as successors under the applicable assumption concerning testacy, any previously appointed personal representative and any person having or claiming priority for appointment as personal representative, the Court shall determine who is entitled to appointment under Section 3–203, make a proper appointment and, if appropriate, terminate any prior appointment found to have been improper as provided in cases of removal under Section 3–611.

COMMENT

A petition raising a controversy concerning the priority or qualifications of a personal representative may be combined with a petition in a formal testacy proceeding. However, it is not necessary to petition formally for the appointment of a personal representative as a part of a formal testacy proceeding. A personal representative may be appointed on informal application either before or after formal proceedings which establish whether the decedent died testate or intestate or no appointment may be desired. See Sections 3–107, 3–301(a)(3), (4) and 3–307. Furthermore, procedures for securing the appointment of a new personal representative after a previous assumption as to testacy has been changed are provided by Section 3–612. These may be informal, or related to pending formal proceedings concerning testacy. A formal order relating to appointment may be desired when there is a dispute concerning priority or qualification to serve but no dispute concerning testacy. It is important to distinguish formal proceedings concerning appointment from "supervised administration". The former includes any proceeding after notice involving a request for an appointment. The latter originates in a "formal proceeding" and may be requested in addition to a ruling concerning testacy or priority or qualifications of a personal representative, but is descriptive of a special proceeding with a different scope and purpose than those concerned merely with establishing the bases for an administration. In other words, a personal representative appointed in a "formal" proceeding may or may not be "supervised".

Another point should be noted. The Court may not immediately issue letters even though a formal proceeding seeking appointment is involved and results in an order authorizing appointment. Rather, Section 3–601 et seq. control the subject of qualification. Section 1–305 deals with letters.

PART 5

SUPERVISED ADMINISTRATION

Section 3–501. [Supervised Administration; Nature of Proceeding.]

Supervised administration is a single in rem proceeding to secure complete administration and settlement of a decedent's estate under the continuing authority of the Court which extends until entry of an order approving distribution of the estate and discharging the personal representative or other order terminating the proceeding. A supervised personal representative is responsible to the Court, as well as to the interested parties, and is subject to directions concerning the estate made by the Court on its own motion or on the motion of any interested party. Except as otherwise provided in this Part, or as otherwise ordered by the Court, a supervised personal representative has the same duties and powers as a personal representative who is not supervised.

COMMENT

This and the following sections of this Part describe an optional procedure for settling an estate in one continuous proceeding in the Court. The proceeding is characterized as "in rem" to align it with the concepts described by the Model Probate Code. See Section 62, M.P.C. In cases where supervised administration is not requested or ordered, no compulsion other than self-interest exists to compel use of a formal testacy proceeding to secure an adjudication of a will or no will, because informal probate or appointment of an administrator in intestacy may be used. Similarly, unless administration is supervised, there is no compulsion other than self-interest to use a formal closing proceeding. Thus, even though an estate administration may be begun by use of a *formal* testacy proceeding which may involve an order concerning who is to be appointed personal representative, the proceeding is over when the order concerning testacy and appointment is entered. See Section 3–107. Supervised administration, therefore, is appropriate when an interested person desires assurance that the essential steps regarding opening and closing of an estate will be adjudicated. See the Comment following the next section.

Section 3–502. [Supervised Administration; Petition; Order.]

A petition for supervised administration may be filed by any interested person or by a personal representative at any time or the prayer for supervised administration may be joined with a petition in a testacy or appointment proceeding. If the testacy of the decedent and the priority and qualification of any personal representative have not been adjudicated previously, the petition for supervised administration shall include the matters required of a petition in a formal testacy proceeding and the notice requirements and procedures applicable to a formal testacy proceeding apply. If not previously adjudicated, the Court shall adjudicate the testacy of the decedent and questions relating to the priority and qualifications of the personal representative in any case involving a request for supervised administration, even though the request for supervised administration may be denied. After notice to interested persons, the Court shall order supervised administration of a decedent's estate: (1) if the decedent's will directs supervised administration, it shall be ordered unless the Court finds that circumstances bearing on the need for supervised administration have changed since the execution of the will and that there is no necessity for supervised administration; (2) if the decedent's will directs unsupervised administration, supervised administration shall be ordered only upon a finding that it is necessary for protection of persons interested in the estate; or (3) in other cases if the Court finds that supervised administration is necessary under the circumstances.

COMMENT

The expressed wishes of a testator regarding supervised administration should bear upon, but not control, the question of whether supervised administration will be ordered. This section is designed to achieve a fair balance between the wishes of the decedent, and the interests of successors in regard to supervised administration.

Since supervised administration normally will result in an adjudicated distribution of the estate, the issue of will or no will must be adjudicated. This section achieves this by forcing a petition for supervised administration to include matters necessary to put the issue of testacy before the Court. It is possible, however, that supervised administration will be requested be-

cause administrative complexities warranting it develop after the issue of will or no will has been resolved in a previously concluded formal testacy proceeding.

It should be noted that supervised administration, though it compels a judicial settlement of an estate, is not the only route to obtaining judicial review and settlement at the close of an administration. The procedures described in Sections 3–1101 and 3–1102 are available for use by or against personal representatives who are not supervised. Also efficient remedies for breach of duty by a personal representative who is not supervised are available under Part 6 of this Article. Finally, each personal representative consents to jurisdiction of the Court as invoked by mailed notice of any proceeding relating to the estate which may be initiated by an interested person. Also, persons interested in the estate may be subjected to orders of the Court following mailed notices made in proceedings initiated by the personal represen-tative. In combination, these possibilities mean that supervised administration will be valuable principally to persons who see some advantage in a single judicial proceeding which will produce adjudications on all major points involved in an estate settlement.

Section 3–503. [Supervised Administration; Effect on Other Proceedings.]

(a) The pendency of a proceeding for supervised administration of a decedent's estate stays action on any informal application then pending or thereafter filed.

(b) If a will has been previously probated in informal proceedings, the effect of the filing of a petition for supervised administration is as provided for formal testacy proceedings by Section 3–401.

(c) After he has received notice of the filing of a petition for supervised administration, a personal representative who has been appointed previously shall not exercise his power to distribute any estate. The filing of the petition does not affect his other powers and duties unless the Court restricts the exercise of any of them pending full hearing on the petition.

COMMENT

The duties and powers of personal representative are described in Part 7 of this Article. The ability of a personal representative to create a good title in a purchaser of estate assets is not hampered by the fact that the personal representative may breach a duty created by statute, court order or other circumstances in making the sale. See Section 3–715. However, formal proceedings against a personal representative may involve requests for qualification of the power normally possessed by personal representatives which, if granted, would subject the personal representative to the penalties for contempt of Court if he disregarded the restriction. See Section 3–607. If a proceeding also involved a demand that particular real estate be kept in the estate pending determination of a petitioner's claim thereto, notice of the pendency of the proceeding could be recorded as is usual under the jurisdiction's system for the lis pendens concept.

The word "restricts" in the last sentence is intended to negate the idea that a judicial order specially qualifying the powers and duties of a personal representative is a restraining order in the usual sense. The section means simply that some supervised personal representatives may receive the same powers and duties as ordinary personal representatives, except that they must obtain a Court order before paying claimants or distributing, while others may receive a more restricted set of powers. Section 3–607 governs petitions which seek to limit the power of a personal representative.

Section 3–504. [Supervised Administration; Powers of Personal Representative.]

Unless restricted by the Court, a supervised personal representative has, without interim orders approving exercise of a power, all powers of personal representatives under this Code, but he shall not exercise his power to make any distribution of the estate without prior order of the Court. Any other restriction on the power of a personal representative which may be ordered by the Court must be endorsed on his letters of appointment and, unless so endorsed, is ineffective as to persons dealing in good faith with the personal representative.

COMMENT

This section provides authority to issue letters showing restrictions of power of supervised administrators. In general, persons dealing with personal representatives are not bound to inquire concerning the authority of a personal representative, and are not affected by provisions in a will or judicial order unless they know of it. But, it is expected that persons dealing with personal representatives will want to see the personal representative's letters, and this section has the practical effect of requiring them to do so. No provision is made for noting restrictions in letters except in the case of supervised representatives. See Section 3–715.

Section 3–505. [Supervised Administration; Interim Orders; Distribution and Closing Orders.]

Unless otherwise ordered by the Court, supervised administration is terminated by order in accordance with time restrictions, notices and contents of orders prescribed for proceedings under Section 3–1001. Interim orders approving or directing partial distributions or granting other relief may be issued by the Court at any time during the pendency of a supervised administration on the application of the personal representative or any interested person.

COMMENT

Since supervised administration is a single proceeding, the notice requirement contained in 3–106 relates to the notice of institution of the proceedings which is described with particularity by Section 3–502. The above section makes it clear that an additional notice is required for a closing order. It was discussed whether provision for notice of interim orders should be included. It was decided to leave the point to be covered by court order or rule. There was a suggestion for a rule as follows: "Unless otherwise required by order, notice of interim orders in supervised administration need be given only to interested persons who request notice of all orders entered in the proceeding." 1–402 permits any person to waive notice by a writing filed in the proceeding.

A demand for notice under Section 3–204 would entitle any interested person to notice of any interim order which might be made in the course of supervised administration.

PART 6

PERSONAL REPRESENTATIVE; APPOINT-
MENT, CONTROL AND TERMINATION
OF AUTHORITY

Section 3–601. [Qualification.]

Prior to receiving letters, a personal representative shall qualify by filing with the appointing Court any required bond and a statement of acceptance of the duties of the office.

COMMENT

This and related sections of this Part describe details and conditions of appointment which apply to all personal representatives without regard to whether the appointment proceeding involved is formal or informal, or whether the personal representative is supervised. Sec- tion 1–305 authorizes issuance of copies of letters and prescribes their content. The section should be read with Section 3–504 which directs endorsement on letters of any restrictions of power of a supervised administrator.

Section 3–602. [Acceptance of Appointment; Consent to Jurisdiction.]

By accepting appointment, a personal representative submits personally to the jurisdiction of the Court in any proceeding relating to the estate that may be instituted by any interested person. Notice of any proceeding shall be delivered to the personal representative, or mailed to him by ordinary first class mail at his address as listed in the application or petition for appointment or as thereafter reported to the Court and to his address as then known to the petitioner.

COMMENT

Except for personal representatives appointed pursuant to Section 3–502, appointees are not deemed to be "officers" of the appointing court or to be parties in one continuous judicial proceeding that extends until final settlement. See Section 3–107. Yet, it is desirable to continue present patterns which prevent a personal representative who might make himself unavailable to service within the state from affecting the power of the appointing court to enter valid orders affecting him. See Michigan Trust Co. v. Ferry, 33 S.Ct. 550, 228 U.S. 346, 57 L.Ed. 867 (1912). The concept employed to accomplish this is that of requiring each appointee to consent in advance to the personal jurisdiction of the Court in any proceeding relating to the estate that may be instituted against him. The section requires that he be given notice of any such proceeding, which, when considered in the light of the responsibility he has undertaken, should make the procedure sufficient to meet the requirements of due process.

Section 3–603. [Bond Not Required Without Court Order, Exceptions.]

No bond is required of a personal representative appointed in informal proceedings, except (1) upon the appointment of a special administrator; (2) when an executor or other personal representative is appointed to administer an estate under a will containing an express requirement of bond or (3) when bond is required under Section 3–605. Bond may be required by court order at the time of appointment of a personal representative appointed in any formal proceeding except that bond is not required of a personal representative appointed in formal proceedings if the will relieves the personal representative of bond, unless bond has been requested by an interested party and the Court is satisfied that it is desirable. Bond required by any will may be dispensed with informal proceedings upon determination by the Court that it is not necessary. No bond is required of any personal representative who, pursuant to statute, has deposited cash or collateral with an agency of this state to secure performance of his duties.

COMMENT

This section must be read with the next three sections. The purpose of these provisions is to move away from the idea that bond always should be required of a probate fiduciary, or required unless a will excuses it. Also, it is designed to keep the registrar acting pursuant to applications in informal proceedings, from passing judgment in each case on the need for bond. The point is that the court and registrar are not responsible for seeing that personal representatives perform as they are supposed to perform. Rather, performance is coerced by the remedies available to interested persons. Interested persons are protected by their ability to demand prior notice of informal proceedings (Section 3–204), to contest a requested appointment by use of a formal testacy proceeding or by use of a formal proceeding seeking the appointment of another person. Section 3–105 gives general authority to the court in a formal proceeding to make appropriate orders as desirable incident to estate administration. This should be sufficient to make it clear that an informal application may be blocked by a formal petition which disputes the matters stated in the petition. Furthermore, an interested person has the remedies provided in Section 3–605 and 3–607. Finally, interested persons have assurance under this Code that their rights in respect to the values of a decedent's estate cannot be terminated without a judicial order after notice or before the passage of three years from the decedent's death.

It is believed that the total package of protection thus afforded may represent more real protection than a blanket requirement of bond. Surely, it permits a reduction in the procedures which must occur in uncomplicated estates where interested persons are perfectly willing to trust each other and the fiduciary.

Section 3–604. [Bond Amount; Security; Procedure; Reduction.]

If bond is required and the provisions of the will or order do not specify the amount, unless stated in his application or petition, the person qualifying shall file a statement under oath with the Registrar indicating his best estimate of the value of the personal estate of the decedent and of the income expected from the personal and real estate during the next year, and he shall execute and file a bond with the Registrar, or give other suitable security, in an amount not less than the estimate. The Registrar shall determine that the bond is duly executed by a corporate surety, or one or more individual sureties whose performance is secured by pledge of personal property, mortgage on real property or other adequate security. The Registrar may permit the amount of the bond to be reduced by the value of assets of the estate deposited with a domestic financial institution (as defined in Section 6–101) in a manner that prevents their unauthorized disposition. On petition of the personal representative or another interested person the Court may excuse a requirement of bond, increase or reduce the amount of the bond, release sureties, or permit the substitution of another bond with the same or different sureties.

COMMENT

This section permits estimates of value needed to fix the amount of required bond to be filed when it becomes necessary. A consequence of this procedure is that estimates of value of estates no longer need appear in the petitions and applications which will attend every ad-

ministered estate. Hence, a measure of privacy that is not possible under most existing procedures may be achieved. A co-signature arrangement might constitute adequate security within the meaning of this section.

Section 3–605. [Demand for Bond by Interested Person.]

Any person apparently having an interest in the estate worth in excess of [$1000], or any creditor having a claim in excess of

[$1000], may make a written demand that a personal representative give bond. The demand must be filed with the Registrar and a copy mailed to the personal representative, if appointment and qualification have occurred. Thereupon, bond is required, but the requirement ceases if the person demanding bond ceases to be interested in the estate, or if bond is excused as provided in Section 3–603 or 3–604. After he has received notice and until the filing of the bond or cessation of the requirement of bond, the personal representative shall refrain from exercising any powers of his office except as necessary to preserve the estate. Failure of the personal representative to meet a requirement of bond by giving suitable bond within 30 days after receipt of notice is cause for his removal and appointment of a successor personal representative.

COMMENT

The demand for bond described in this section may be made in a petition or application for appointment of a personal representative, or may be made after a personal representative has been appointed. The mechanism for compelling bond is designed to function without unnecessary judicial involvement. If demand for bond is made in a formal proceeding, the judge can determine the amount of bond to be required with due consideration for all circumstances. If demand is not made in formal proceedings, methods for computing the amount of bond are provided by statute so that the demand can be complied with without resort to judicial proceedings. The information which a personal representative is required by Section 3–705 to give each beneficiary includes a statement concerning whether bond has been required.

Section 3–606. [Terms and Conditions of Bonds.]

(a) The following requirements and provisions apply to any bond required by this Part:

(1) Bonds shall name the [state] as obligee for the benefit of the persons interested in the estate and shall be conditioned upon the faithful discharge by the fiduciary of all duties according to law.

(2) Unless otherwise provided by the terms of the approved bond, sureties are jointly and severally liable with the personal representative and with each other. The address of sureties shall be stated in the bond.

(3) By executing an approved bond of a personal representative, the surety consents to the jurisdiction of the probate court which issued letters to the primary obligor in any proceedings pertaining to the fiduciary duties of the personal representative and naming the surety as a party. Notice of any proceeding

shall be delivered to the surety or mailed to him by registered or certified mail at his address as listed with the court where the bond is filed and to his address as then known to the petitioner.

(4) On petition of a successor personal representative, any other personal representative of the same decedent, or any interested person, a proceeding in the Court may be initiated against a surety for breach of the obligation of the bond of the personal representative.

(5) The bond of the personal representative is not void after the first recovery but may be proceeded against from time to time until the whole penalty is exhausted.

(b) No action or proceeding may be commenced against the surety on any matter as to which an action or proceeding against the primary obligor is barred by adjudication or limitation.

COMMENT

Paragraph (2) is based, in part, on Section 109 of the Model Probate Code. Paragraph (3) is derived from Section 118 of the Model Probate Code.

Section 3–607. [Order Restraining Personal Representative.]

(a) On petition of any person who appears to have an interest in the estate, the Court by temporary order may restrain a personal representative from performing specified acts of administration, disbursement, or distribution, or exercise of any powers or discharge of any duties of his office, or make any other order to secure proper performance of his duty, if it appears to the Court that the personal representative otherwise may take some action which would jeopardize unreasonably the interest of the applicant or of some other interested person. Persons with whom the personal representative may transact business may be made parties.

(b) The matter shall be set for hearing within 10 days unless the parties otherwise agree. Notice as the Court directs shall be given to the personal representative and his attorney of record, if any, and to any other parties named defendant in the petition.

COMMENT

Cf. Section 3–401 which provides for a restraining order against a previously appointed personal representative incident to a formal testacy proceeding. The above section describes a remedy which is available for any cause against a previously appointed personal representative, whether appointed formally or informally.

This remedy, in combination with the safeguards relating to the process for appointment of a personal representative, permit "control" of a personal representative that is believed to be equal, if not superior to that presently available with respect to "supervised" personal representatives appointed by inferior courts. The request for a restraining order may mark the beginning of a new proceeding but the personal representative, by the consent provided in Section 3–602, is practically in the position of one who, on motion, may be cited to appear before a judge.

Section 3–608. [Termination of Appointment; General.]

Termination of appointment of a personal representative occurs as indicated in Sections 3–609 to 3–612, inclusive. Termination ends the right and power pertaining to the office of personal representative as conferred by this Code or any will, except that a personal representative, at any time prior to distribution or until restrained or enjoined by court order, may perform acts necessary to protect the estate and may deliver the assets to a successor representative. Termination does not discharge a personal representative from liability for transactions or omissions occurring before termination, or relieve him of the duty to preserve assets subject to his control, to account therefor and to deliver the assets. Termination does not affect the jurisdiction of the Court over the personal representative, but terminates his authority to represent the estate in any pending or future proceeding.

COMMENT

"Termination", as defined by this and succeeding provisions, provides definiteness respecting when the powers of a personal representative (who may or may not be discharged by court order) terminate.

It is to be noted that this section does not relate to jurisdiction over the estate in proceedings which may have been commenced against the personal representative prior to termination. In such cases, a substitution of successor or special representative should occur if the plaintiff desires to maintain his action against the estate.

It is important to note that "termination" is not "discharge". However, an order of the Court entered under 3–1001 or 3–1002 both terminates the appointment of, and discharges, a personal representative.

Section 3–609. [Termination of Appointment; Death or Disability.]

The death of a personal representative or the appointment of a conservator for the estate of a personal representative, terminates his appointment. Until appointment and qualification of a successor or special representative to replace the deceased or protected representative, the representative of the estate of the deceased or protected personal representative, if any, has the duty to protect the estate possessed and being administered by his decedent or ward at the time his appointment terminates, has the power to perform acts necessary for protection and shall account for and deliver the estate assets to a successor or special personal representative upon his appointment and qualification.

COMMENT

See Section 3–718, which establishes the rule that a surviving co-executor may exercise all powers incident to the office unless the will provides otherwise. Read together, this section and Section 3–718 mean that the representative of a deceased co-representative would not have any duty or authority in relation to the office held by his decedent.

Section 3–610. [Termination of Appointment; Voluntary.]

(a) An appointment of a personal representative terminates as provided in Section 3–1003, one year after the filing of a closing statement.

(b) An order closing an estate as provided in Section 3–1001 or 3–1002 terminates an appointment of a personal representative.

(c) A personal representative may resign his position by filing a written statement of resignation with the Registrar after he has given at least 15 days written notice to the persons known to be interested in the estate. If no one applies or petitions for appointment of a successor representative within the time indicated in the notice, the filed statement of resignation is ineffective as a termination of appointment and in any event is effective only upon the appointment and qualification of a successor representative and delivery of the assets to him.

COMMENT

Subparagraph (c) above provides a procedure for resignation by a personal representative which may occur without judicial assistance.

Section 3–611. [Termination of Appointment by Removal; Cause; Procedure.]

(a) A person interested in the estate may petition for removal of a personal representative for cause at any time. Upon filing of the petition, the Court shall fix a time and place for hearing. Notice shall be given by the petitioner to the personal representative, and to other persons as the Court may order. Except as otherwise ordered as provided in Section 3–607, after receipt of notice of removal proceedings, the personal representative shall not act except to account, to correct maladministration or preserve the estate. If removal is ordered, the Court also shall direct by order the disposition of the assets remaining in the name of, or under the control of, the personal representative being removed.

(b) Cause for removal exists when removal would be in the best interests of the estate, or if it is shown that a personal representative or the person seeking his appointment intentionally misrepresented material facts in the proceedings leading to his appointment, or that the personal representative has disregarded an order of the Court, has become incapable of discharging the duties of his office, or has mismanaged the estate or failed to perform any duty pertaining to the office. Unless the decedent's will directs otherwise, a personal representative appointed at the decedent's domicile, incident to securing appointment of himself or his nominee as ancillary personal representative, may obtain removal of another who was appointed personal representative in this state to administer local assets.

COMMENT

Thought was given to qualifying (a) above so that no formal removal proceedings could be commenced until after a set period from entry of any previous order reflecting judicial consideration of the qualifications of the personal representative. It was decided, however, that the matter should be left to the judgment of interested persons and the Court.

Section 3–612. [Termination of Appointment; Change of Testacy Status.]

Except as otherwise ordered in formal proceedings, the probate of a will subsequent to the appointment of a personal representative in intestacy or under a will which is superseded by formal probate of another will, or the vacation of an informal probate of a will subsequent to the appointment of the personal representative thereunder, does not terminate the appointment of the personal representative although his powers may be reduced as provided in Section 3–401. Termination occurs upon appointment in informal or formal appointment proceedings of a person entitled to appointment under the later assumption concerning testacy. If no request for new appointment is made within 30 days after expiration of time for appeal from the order in formal testacy proceedings, or from the informal probate, changing the assumption concerning testacy, the previously appointed personal representative upon request may be appointed personal representative under the subsequently probated will, or as in intestacy as the case may be.

COMMENT

This section and Section 3–401 describe the relationship between formal or informal proceedings which change a previous assumption concerning the testacy of the decedent, and a previously appointed personal representative. The basic assumption of both sections is that an appointment, with attendant powers of management, is separable from the basis of appointment; i.e., intestate or testate?; what will is the last will? Hence, a previously appointed personal representative continues to serve in spite of formal or informal proceedings that may give another a prior right to serve as personal representative. But, if the testacy status is changed in formal proceedings, the petitioner also may request appointment of the person who would be entitled to serve if his assumption concerning the decedent's will pre-

vails. Provision is made for a situation where all interested persons are content to allow a previously appointed personal representative to continue to serve even though another has a prior right because of a change relating to the decedent's will. It is not necessary for the continuing representative to seek reappointment under the new assumption for Section 3–703 is broad enough to require him to administer the estate as intestate, or under a later probated will, if either status is established after he was appointed. Under Section 3–403, notice of a formal testacy proceeding is required to be given to any previously appointed personal representative. Hence, the testacy status cannot be changed without notice to a previously appointed personal representative.

Section 3–613. [Successor Personal Representative.]

Parts 3 and 4 of this Article govern proceedings for appointment of a personal representative to succeed one whose appointment has been terminated. After appointment and qualification, a successor personal representative may be substituted in all actions and proceedings to which the former personal representative was a party, and no notice, process or claim which was given or served upon the former personal representative need be given to or served upon the successor in order to preserve any position or right the person giving the notice or filing the claim may thereby have obtained or preserved with reference to the former personal representative. Except as otherwise ordered by the Court, the successor personal representative has the powers and duties in respect to the continued administration which the former personal representative would have had if his appointment had not been terminated.

319

Section 3–614. [Special Administrator; Appointment.]

A special administrator may be appointed:

(1) informally by the Registrar on the application of any interested person when necessary to protect the estate of a decedent prior to the appointment of a general personal representative or if a prior appointment has been terminated as provided in Section 3–609;

(2) in a formal proceeding by order of the Court on the petition of any interested person and finding, after notice and hearing, that appointment is necessary to preserve the estate or to secure its proper administration including its administration in circumstances where a general personal representative cannot or should not act. If it appears to the Court that an emergency exists, appointment may be ordered without notice.

COMMENT

The appointment of a special administrator other than one appointed pending original appointment of a general personal representative must be handled by the Court. Appointment of a special administrator would enable the estate to participate in a transaction which the general personal representative could not, or should not, handle because of conflict of interest. If a need arises because of temporary absence or anticipated incapacity for delegation of the authority of a personal representative, the problem may be handled without judicial intervention by use of the delegation powers granted to personal representatives by Section 3–715(21).

Section 3–615. [Special Administrator; Who May Be Appointed.]

(a) If a special administrator is to be appointed pending the probate of a will which is the subject of a pending application or petition for probate, the person named executor in the will shall be appointed if available, and qualified.

(b) In other cases, any proper person may be appointed special administrator.

COMMENT

In some areas of the country, particularly where wills cannot be probated without full notice and hearing, appointment of special administrators pending probate is sought almost routinely. The provisions of this Code concerning informal probate should reduce the number of cases in which a fiduciary will need to be appointed pending probate of a will. Nonetheless, there will be instances where contests begin before probate and where it may be necessary to appoint a special administrator. The objective of this section is to reduce the likelihood that contestants will be encouraged to file contests as early as possible simply to gain some advantage via having a person who is sympathetic to their cause appointed special administrator. Most will contests are not successful. Hence, it seems reasonable to prefer the named executor as special administrator where he is otherwise qualified.

Section 3–616. [Special Administrator; Appointed Informally; Powers and Duties.]

A special administrator appointed by the Registrar in informal proceedings pursuant to Section 3–614(1) has the duty to collect and manage the assets of the estate, to preserve them, to account therefor and to deliver them to the general personal representative upon his qualification. The special administrator has the power of a personal representative under the Code necessary to perform his duties.

Section 3–617. [Special Administrator; Formal Proceedings; Power and Duties.]

A special administrator appointed by order of the Court in any formal proceeding has the power of a general personal representative except as limited in the appointment and duties as prescribed in the order. The appointment may be for a specified time, to perform particular acts or on other terms as the Court may direct.

Section 3–618. [Termination of Appointment; Special Administrator.]

The appointment of a special administrator terminates in accordance with the provisions of the order of appointment or on the appointment of a general personal representative. In other cases, the appointment of a special administrator is subject to termination as provided in Sections 3–608 through 3–611.

PART 7

DUTIES AND POWERS OF PERSONAL REPRESENTATIVES

Section 3–701. [Time of Accrual of Duties and Powers.]

The duties and powers of a personal representative commence upon his appointment. The powers of a personal representative relate back in time to give acts by the person appointed which are beneficial to the estate occurring prior to appointment the same effect as those occurring thereafter. Prior to appointment, a person named executor in a will may carry out written instructions of the decedent relating to his body, funeral and burial arrangements. A personal representative may ratify and accept acts on behalf of the estate done by others where the acts would have been proper for a personal representative.

COMMENT

This section codifies the doctrine that the authority of a personal representative relates back to death from the moment it arises. It also makes it clear that authority of a personal representative stems from his appointment. The sentence concerning ratification is designed to eliminate technical questions that might arise concerning the validity of acts done by others prior to appointment. Section 3–715(21) relates to delegation of authority after appointment. The third sentence accepts an idea found in the Illinois Probate Act, § 79 [S.H.A. ch. 3, § 79].

Section 3–702. [Priority Among Different Letters.]

A person to whom general letters are issued first has exclusive authority under the letters until his appointment is terminated or modified. If, through error, general letters are afterwards issued to another, the first appointed representative may recover any property of the estate in the hands of the representative subsequently appointed, but the acts of the latter done in good faith before notice of the first letters are not void for want of validity of appointment.

COMMENT

The qualification relating to "modification" of an appointment is intended to refer to the change that may occur in respect to the exclusive authority of one with letters upon later appointment of a co-rep-

322

resentative or of a special administrator.   The sentence concerning
erroneous dual appointment is derived from recent New York legislation.   See Section 704, Surrogate's
Court Procedure Act [McKinney's
SCPA 704].

Erroneous appointment of a second personal representative is possible if formal proceedings after notice are employed.   It might be desirable for a state to promulgate a

system whereby a notation of letters issued by each county probate
office would be relayed to a central
record keeping office which, in turn
could indicate to any other office
whether letters for a particular decedent, perhaps identified by social
security number, had been issued
previously.   The problem can arise
even though notice to known interested persons and by publication is
involved.

Section 3–703. [General Duties; Relation and Liability to Persons Interested in Estate; Standing to Sue.]

(a) A personal representative is a fiduciary who shall observe
the standards of care applicable to trustees as described by Section
7–302.   A personal representative is under a duty to settle and
distribute the estate of the decedent in accordance with the terms
of any probated and effective will and this Code, and as expeditiously and efficiently as is consistent with the best interests of the
estate.   He shall use the authority conferred upon him by this
Code, the terms of the will, if any, and any order in proceedings to
which he is party for the best interests of successors to the estate.

(b) A personal representative shall not be surcharged for acts of
administration or distribution if the conduct in question was authorized at the time.   Subject to other obligations of administration,
an informally probated will is authority to administer and distribute the estate according to its terms.   An order of appointment of a
personal representative, whether issued in informal or formal proceedings, is authority to distribute apparently intestate assets to
the heirs of the decedent if, at the time of distribution, the personal
representative is not aware of a pending testacy proceeding, a
proceeding to vacate an order entered in an earlier testacy proceeding, a formal proceeding questioning his appointment or fitness to
continue, or a supervised administration proceeding.   Nothing in
this section affects the duty of the personal representative to
administer and distribute the estate in accordance with the rights
of claimants, the surviving spouse, any minor and dependent children and any pretermitted child of the decedent as described
elsewhere in this Code.

(c) Except as to proceedings which do not survive the death of
the decedent, a personal representative of a decedent domiciled in
this state at his death has the same standing to sue and be sued in

the courts of this state and the courts of any other jurisdiction as his decedent had immediately prior to death.

COMMENT

This and the next section are especially important sections for they state the basic theory underlying the duties and powers of personal representatives. Whether or not a personal representative is supervised, this section applies to describe the relationship he bears to interested parties. If a supervised representative is appointed, or if supervision of a previously appointed personal representative is ordered, an additional obligation to the court is created. See Section 3–501.

The fundamental responsibility is that of a trustee. Unlike many trustees, a personal representative's authority is derived from appointment by the public agency known as the Court. But, the Code also makes it clear that the personal representative, in spite of the source of his authority, is to proceed with the administration, settlement and distribution of the estate by use of statutory powers and in accordance with statutory directions. See Sections 3–107 and 3–704. Subsection (b) is particularly important, for it ties the question of personal liability for administrative or distributive acts to the question of whether the act was "authorized at the time". Thus, a personal representative may rely upon and be protected by a will which has been probated without adjudication or an or-

der appointing him to administer which is issued in no-notice proceedings even though proceedings occurring later may change the assumption as to whether the decedent died testate or intestate. See Section 3–302 concerning the status of a will probated without notice and Section 3–102 concerning the ineffectiveness of an unprobated will. However, it does *not* follow from the fact that the personal representative distributed under authority that the distributees may not be liable to restore the property or values received if the assumption concerning testacy is later changed. See Sections 3–909 and 3–1004. Thus, a distribution may be "authorized at the time" within the meaning of this section, but be "improper" under the latter section.

Paragraph (c) is designed to reduce or eliminate differences in the amenability to suit of personal representatives appointed under this Code and under traditional assumptions. Also, the subsection states that so far as the law of the appointing forum is concerned, personal representatives are subject to suit in other jurisdictions. It, together with various provisions of Article IV, are designed to eliminate many of the present reasons for ancillary administrations.

Section 3–704. [Personal Representative to Proceed Without Court Order; Exception.]

A personal representative shall proceed expeditiously with the settlement and distribution of a decedent's estate and, except as otherwise specified or ordered in regard to a supervised personal representative, do so without adjudication, order, or direction of the Court, but he may invoke the jurisdiction of the Court, in proceedings authorized by this Code, to resolve questions concerning the estate or its administration.

COMMENT

This section is intended to confer authority on the personal representative to initiate a proceeding at any time when it is necessary to resolve a question relating to administration. Section 3–105 grants broad subject matter jurisdiction to the probate court which covers a proceeding initiated for any purpose other than those covered by more explicit provisions dealing with testacy proceedings, proceedings for supervised administration, proceedings concerning disputed claims and proceedings to close estates.

Section 3–705. [Duty of Personal Representative; Information to Heirs and Devisees.]

Not later than 30 days after his appointment every personal representative, except any special administrator, shall give information of his appointment to the heirs and devisees, including, if there has been no formal testacy proceeding and if the personal representative was appointed on the assumption that the decedent died intestate, the devisees in any will mentioned in the application for appointment of a personal representative. The information shall be delivered or sent by ordinary mail to each of the heirs and devisees whose address is reasonably available to the personal representative. The duty does not extend to require information to persons who have been adjudicated in a prior formal testacy proceeding to have no interest in the estate. The information shall include the name and address of the personal representative, indicate that it is being sent to persons who have or may have some interest in the estate being administered, indicate whether bond has been filed, and describe the court where papers relating to the estate are on file. The information shall state that the estate is being administered by the personal representative under the [State] Probate Code without supervision by the Court but that recipients are entitled to information regarding the administration from the personal representative and can petition the Court in any matter relating to the estate, including distribution of assets and expenses of administration. The personal representative's failure to give this information is a breach of his duty to the persons concerned but does not affect the validity of his appointment, his powers or other duties. A personal representative may inform other persons of his appointment by delivery or ordinary first class mail.

COMMENT

This section requires the personal representative to inform persons who appear to have an interest in the estate as it is being administered, of his appointment. Also, it requires the personal representative to give notice to persons who appear to be disinherited by the assumption concerning testacy under which the personal representative was appointed. The communication involved is not to be confused with the notice requirements relating to litigation. The duty applies even though there may have been a prior testacy proceeding after notice, except that persons who have been adjudicated to be without interest in the estate are excluded. The rights, if any, of persons in regard to estates cannot be cut off completely except by the running of the three year statute of limitations provided in Section 3–108, or by a formal judicial proceeding which will include full notice to all interested persons. The interests of some persons may be shifted from rights to specific property of the decedent to the proceeds from sale thereof, or to rights to values received by distributees. However, such a shift of protected interest from one thing to another, or to funds or obligations, is not new in relation to trust beneficiaries. A personal representative may initiate formal proceedings to determine whether persons, other than those appearing to have interests, may be interested in the estate, under Section 3–401 or, in connection with a formal closing, as provided by Section 3–1001.

No information or notice is required by this section if no personal representative is appointed.

Section 3–706. [Duty of Personal Representative; Inventory and Appraisement.]

Within 3 months after his appointment, a personal representative, who is not a special administrator or a successor to another representative who has previously discharged this duty, shall prepare and file or mail an inventory of property owned by the decedent at the time of his death, listing it with reasonable detail, and indicating as to each listed item, its fair market value as of the date of the decedent's death, and the type and amount of any encumbrance that may exist with reference to any item.

The personal representative shall send a copy of the inventory to interested persons who request it. He may also file the original of the inventory with the court.

COMMENT

This and the following sections eliminate the practice now required by many probate statutes under which the judge is involved in the selection of appraisers. If the personal representative breaches his duty concerning the inventory, he may be removed. Section 3–611.

Or, an interested person seeking to surcharge a personal representative for losses incurred as a result of his administration might be able to take advantage of any breach of duty concerning inventory. The section provides two ways in which a personal representative may handle an inventory. If the personal representative elects to send copies to all interested persons who request it, information concerning the assets of the estate need not become a part of the records of the probate court. The alternative procedure is to file the inventory with the court. This procedure would be indicated in estates with large numbers of interested persons, where the burden of sending copies to all would be substantial. The Court's role in respect to the second alternative is simply to receive and file the inventory with the file relating to the estate. See 3–204, which permits any interested person to demand notice of any document relating to an estate which may be filed with the Court.

In 1975, the Joint Editorial Board recommended elimination of the word "or" that separated the language dealing with the duty to send a copy of the inventory to interested persons requesting it, from the final part of the paragraph dealing with filing of the original. The purpose of the change was to prevent a literal interpretation of the original text that would have permitted a personal representative who filed the original inventory with the court to avoid compliance with requests for copies from interested persons.

Section 3–707. [Employment of Appraisers.]

The personal representative may employ a qualified and disinterested appraiser to assist him in ascertaining the fair market value as of the date of the decedent's death of any asset the value of which may be subject to reasonable doubt. Different persons may be employed to appraise different kinds of assets included in the estate. The names and addresses of any appraiser shall be indicated on the inventory with the item or items he appraised.

Section 3–708. [Duty of Personal Representative; Supplementary Inventory.]

If any property not included in the original inventory comes to the knowledge of a personal representative or if the personal representative learns that the value or description indicated in the original inventory for any item is erroneous or misleading, he shall make a supplementary inventory or appraisement showing the market value as of the date of the decedent's death of the new item or the revised market value or descriptions, and the appraisers or other data relied upon, if any, and file it with the Court if the original inventory was filed, or furnish copies thereof or information thereof to persons interested in the new information.

Section 3–709. [Duty of Personal Representative; Possession of Estate.]

Except as otherwise provided by a decedent's will, every personal representative has a right to, and shall take possession or control of, the decedent's property, except that any real property or tangible personal property may be left with or surrendered to the person presumptively entitled thereto unless or until, in the judgment of the personal representative, possession of the property by him will be necessary for purposes of administration. The request by a personal representative for delivery of any property possessed by an heir or devisee is conclusive evidence, in any action against the heir or devisee for possession thereof, that the possession of the property by the personal representative is necessary for purposes of administration. The personal representative shall pay taxes on, and take all steps reasonably necessary for the management, protection and preservation of, the estate in his possession. He may maintain an action to recover possession of property or to determine the title thereto.

COMMENT

Section 3–101 provides for the devolution of title on death. Section 3–711 defines the status of the personal representative with reference to "title" and "power" in a way that should make it unnecessary to discuss the "title" to decedent's assets which his personal representative acquires. This section deals with the personal representative's duty and right to possess assets. It proceeds from the assumption that it is desirable whenever possible to avoid disruption of possession of the decedent's assets by his devisees or heirs. But, if the personal representative decides that possession of an asset is necessary or desirable for purposes of administration, his judgment is made conclusive in any action for possession that he may need to institute against an heir or devisee. It may be possible for an heir or devisee to question the judgment of the personal representative in later action for surcharge for breach of fiduciary duty, but this possibility should not interfere with the personal representative's administrative authority as it relates to possession of the estate.

This Code follows the Model Probate Code in regard to partnership interests. In the introduction to the Model Probate Code, the following appears at p. 22:

"No provisions for the administration of partnership estates when a partner dies have been included. Several states have statutes providing that unless the surviving partner files a bond with the probate court, the personal representative of the deceased partner may administer the partnership estate upon giving an additional bond. Kan. Gen.Stat. (Supp.1943) §§ 59–1001 to 59–1005; Mo.Rev.Stat. Ann. (1942) §§ 81 to 93 [V.A.M.S. §§ 473.220 to 473.-

230]. In these states the administration of partnership estates upon the death of a partner is brought more or less completely under the jurisdiction of the probate court. While the provisions afford security to parties in interest, they have caused complications in the settlement of partnership estates and have produced much litigation. Woener, Administration (3rd ed., 1923) §§ 128 to 130; annotation, 121 A.L.R. 860. These statutes have been held to be inconsistent with section 37 of the Uniform Partnership Act providing for winding up by the surviving partner. Davis v. Hutchinson (C.C.A. 9th, 1929) 36 F.(2d) 309. Hence the Model Probate Code contains no provision regarding partnership property except for inclusion in the inventory of the decedent's proportionate share of any partnership. See § 120. However, it is suggested that the Uniform Partnership Act should be included in the statutes of the states which have not already enacted it."

Section 3–710. [Power to Avoid Transfers.]

The property liable for the payment of unsecured debts of a decedent includes all property transferred by him by any means which is in law void or voidable as against his creditors, and subject to prior liens, the right to recover this property, so far as necessary for the payment of unsecured debts of the decedent, is exclusively in the personal representative.

COMMENT

Model Probate Code section 125, with additions. See, also, Section 6–201, which saves creditors' rights in regard to non-testamentary transfers effective at death.

Section 3–711. [Powers of Personal Representatives; In General.]

Until termination of his appointment a personal representative has the same power over the title to property of the estate that an absolute owner would have, in trust however, for the benefit of the creditors and others interested in the estate. This power may be exercised without notice, hearing, or order of court.

COMMENT

The personal representative is given the broadest possible "power over title". He receives a *"power"*, rather than title, because the power concept eases the succession of assets which are not possessed by the personal representative. Thus, if the power is unexercised prior to its termination, its lapse clears the title of devisees and heirs. Purchasers from devisees or heirs who are "distributees" may be protected also by

329

Section 3–910. The power over title of an absolute owner is conceived to embrace all possible transactions which might result in a conveyance or encumbrance of assets, or in a change of rights of possession. The relationship of the personal representative to the estate is that of a trustee. Hence, personal creditors or successors of a personal representative cannot avail themselves of his title to any greater extent than is true generally of creditors and successors of trustees. Interested persons who are apprehensive of possible misuse of power by a personal representative may secure themselves by use of the devices implicit in the several sections of Parts 1 and 3 of this Article. See especially Sections 3–501, 3–605, 3–607 and 3–611.

Section 3–712. [Improper Exercise of Power; Breach of Fiduciary Duty.]

If the exercise of power concerning the estate is improper, the personal representative is liable to interested persons for damage or loss resulting from breach of his fiduciary duty to the same extent as a trustee of an express trust. The rights of purchasers and others dealing with a personal representative shall be determined as provided in Sections 3–713 and 3–714.

COMMENT

An interested person has two principal remedies to forestall a personal representative from committing a breach of fiduciary duty. (1) Under Section 3–607 he may apply to the Court for an order restraining the personal representative from performing any specified act or from exercising any power in the course of administration. (2) Under Section 3–611 he may petition the Court for an order removing the personal representative.

Evidence of a proceeding, or order, restraining a personal representative from selling, leasing, encumbering or otherwise affecting title to real property subject to administration, if properly recorded under the laws of this state, would be effective to prevent a purchaser from acquiring a marketable title under the usual rules relating to recordation of real property titles.

In addition Sections 1–302 and 3–105 authorize joinder of third persons who may be involved in contemplated transactions with a personal representative in proceedings to restrain a personal representative under Section 3–607.

Section 3–713. [Sale, Encumbrance or Transaction Involving Conflict of Interest; Voidable; Exceptions.]

Any sale or encumbrance to the personal representative, his spouse, agent or attorney, or any corporation or trust in which he has a substantial beneficial interest, or any transaction which is affected by a substantial conflict of interest on the part of the personal representative, is voidable by any person interested in the estate except one who has consented after fair disclosure, unless

(1) the will or a contract entered into by the decedent expressly authorized the transaction; or

(2) the transaction is approved by the Court after notice to interested persons.

COMMENT

If a personal representative violates the duty against self-dealing described by this section, a voidable title to assets sold results. Other breaches of duty relating to sales of assets will not cloud titles except as to purchasers with actual knowledge of the breach. See Section 3–714. The principles of bona fide purchase would protect a purchaser for value without notice of defect in the seller's title arising from conflict of interest.

Section 3–714. [Persons Dealing With Personal Representative; Protection.]

A person who in good faith either assists a personal representative or deals with him for value is protected as if the personal representative properly exercised his power. The fact that a person knowingly deals with a personal representative does not alone require the person to inquire into the existence of a power or the propriety of its exercise. Except for restrictions on powers of supervised personal representatives which are endorsed on letters as provided in Section 3–504, no provision in any will or order of court purporting to limit the power of a personal representative is effective except as to persons with actual knowledge thereof. A person is not bound to see to the proper application of estate assets paid or delivered to a personal representative. The protection here expressed extends to instances in which some procedural irregularity or jurisdictional defect occurred in proceedings leading to the issuance of letters, including a case in which the alleged decedent is found to be alive. The protection here expressed is not by substitution for that provided by comparable provisions of the laws relating to commercial transactions and laws simplifying transfers of securities by fiduciaries.

COMMENT

This section qualifies the effect of a provision in a will which purports to prohibit sale of property by a personal representative. The provisions of a will may prescribe the duties of a personal representative and subject him to surcharge or other remedies of interested persons if he disregards them. See

Section 3–703. But, the will's prohibition is not relevant to the rights of a purchaser unless he had actual knowledge of its terms. Interested persons who want to prevent a personal representative from having the power described here must use the procedures described in Sections 3–501 to 3–505. Each state will need to identify the relation between this section and other statutory provisions creating liens on estate assets for inheritance and other taxes. The section cannot control whether a purchaser takes free of the lien of unpaid federal estate taxes. Hence, purchasers from personal representatives appointed pursuant to this Code will have to satisfy themselves concerning whether estate taxes are paid, and if not paid, whether the tax lien follows the property they are acquiring. See Section 6234, Internal Revenue Code [26 U.S.C.A. § 6324].

The impact of formal recording systems beyond the usual probate procedure depends upon the particular statute. In states in which the recording system provides for recording wills as muniments of title, statutory adaptation should be made to provide that recording of wills should be postponed until the validity has been established by probate or limitation. Statutory limitation to this effect should be added to statutes which do not so provide to avoid conflict with power of the personal representative during administration. The purpose of the Code is to make the deed or instrument of distribution the usual muniment of title. See Sections 3–907, 3–908, 3–910. However, this is not available when no administration has occurred and in that event reliance upon general recording statutes must be had.

If a state continues to permit wills to be recorded as muniments of title, the above section would need to be qualified to give effect to the notice from recording.

Section 3–715. [Transactions Authorized for Personal Representatives; Exceptions.]

Except as restricted or otherwise provided by the will or by an order in a formal proceeding and subject to the priorities stated in Section 3–902, a personal representative, acting reasonably for the benefit of the interested persons, may properly:

(1) retain assets owned by the decedent pending distribution or liquidation including those in which the representative is personally interested or which are otherwise improper for trust investment;

(2) receive assets from fiduciaries, or other sources;

(3) perform, compromise or refuse performance of the decedent's contracts that continue as obligations of the estate, as he may determine under the circumstances. In performing enforceable contracts by the decedent to convey or lease land, the personal representative, among other possible courses of action, may:

(i) execute and deliver a deed of conveyance for cash payment of all sums remaining due or the purchaser's note for the sum remaining due secured by a mortgage or deed of trust on the land; or

(ii) deliver a deed in escrow with directions that the proceeds, when paid in accordance with the escrow agreement, be paid to the successors of the decedent, as designated in the escrow agreement;

(4) satisfy written charitable pledges of the decedent irrespective of whether the pledges constituted binding obligations of the decedent or were properly presented as claims, if in the judgment of the personal representative the decedent would have wanted the pledges completed under the circumstances;

(5) if funds are not needed to meet debts and expenses currently payable and are not immediately distributable, deposit or invest liquid assets of the estate, including moneys received from the sale of other assets, in federally insured interest-bearing accounts, readily marketable secured loan arrangements or other prudent investments which would be reasonable for use by trustees generally;

(6) acquire or dispose of an asset, including land in this or another state, for cash or on credit, at public or private sale; and manage, develop, improve, exchange, partition, change the character of, or abandon an estate asset;

(7) make ordinary or extraordinary repairs or alterations in buildings or other structures, demolish any improvements, raze existing or erect new party walls or buildings;

(8) subdivide, develop or dedicate land to public use; make or obtain the vacation of plats and adjust boundaries; or adjust differences in valuation on exchange or partition by giving or receiving considerations; or dedicate easements to public use without consideration;

(9) enter for any purpose into a lease as lessor or lessee, with or without option to purchase or renew, for a term within or extending beyond the period of administration;

(10) enter into a lease or arrangement for exploration and removal of minerals or other natural resources or enter into a pooling or unitization agreement;

(11) abandon property when, in the opinion of the personal representative, it is valueless, or is so encumbered, or is in condition that it is of no benefit to the state;

(12) vote stocks or other securities in person or by general or limited proxy;

(13) pay calls, assessments, and other sums chargeable or accruing against or on account of securities, unless barred by the provisions relating to claims;

(14) hold a security in the name of a nominee or in other form without disclosure of the interest of the estate but the personal representative is liable for any act of the nominee in connection with the security so held;

(15) insure the assets of the estate against damage, loss and liability and himself against liability as to third persons;

(16) borrow money with or without security to be repaid from the estate assets or otherwise; and advance money for the protection of the estate;

(17) effect a fair and reasonable compromise with any debtor or obligor, or extend, renew or in any manner modify the terms of any obligation owing to the estate. If the personal representative holds a mortgage, pledge or other lien upon property of another person, he may, in lieu of foreclosure, accept a conveyance or transfer of encumbered assets from the owner thereof in satisfaction of the indebtedness secured by lien;

(18) pay taxes, assessments, compensation of the personal representative, and other expenses incident to the administration of the estate;

(19) sell or exercise stock subscription or conversion rights; consent, directly or through a committee or other agent, to the reorganization, consolidation, merger, dissolution, or liquidation of a corporation or other business enterprise;

(20) allocate items of income or expense to either estate income or principal, as permitted or provided by law;

(21) employ persons, including attorneys, auditors, investment advisors, or agents, even if they are associated with the personal representative, to advise or assist the personal representative in the performance of his administrative duties; act without independent investigation upon their recommendations; and instead of acting personally, employ one or more agents to perform any act of administration, whether or not discretionary;

(22) prosecute or defend claims, or proceedings in any jurisdiction for the protection of the estate and of the personal representative in the performance of his duties;

(23) sell, mortgage, or lease any real or personal property of the estate or any interest therein for cash, credit, or for part cash and part credit, and with or without security for unpaid balances;

(24) continue any unincorporated business or venture in which the decedent was engaged at the time of his death (i) in the same business form for a period of not more than 4 months from the date of appointment of a general personal representative if continuation is a reasonable means of preserving the value of the business including good will, (ii) in the same business form for any additional period of time that may be approved by order of the Court in a formal proceeding to which the persons interested in the estate are parties; or (iii) throughout the period of administration if the business is incorporated by the personal representative and if none of the probable distributees of the business who are competent adults object to its incorporation and retention in the estate;

(25) incorporate any business or venture in which the decedent was engaged at the time of his death;

(26) provide for exoneration of the personal representative from personal liability in any contract entered into on behalf of the estate;

(27) satisfy and settle claims and distribute the estate as provided in this Code.

COMMENT

This section accepts the assumption of the Uniform Trustee's Powers Act that it is desirable to equip fiduciaries with the authority required for the prudent handling of assets and extends it to personal representatives. The section requires that a personal representative act reasonably and for the benefit of the interested person. Subject to this and to the other qualifications described by the preliminary statement, the enumerated transactions are made authorized transactions for personal representatives. Subparagraphs (27) and (18) support the other provisions of the Code, particularly Section 3–704, which contemplates that personal representatives will proceed with all of the business of administration without court orders.

In part, subparagraph (4) involves a substantive question of whether noncontractual charitable pledges of a decedent can be honored by his personal representative. It is believed, however, that it is not desirable from a practical standpoint to make much turn on whether a charitable pledge is, or is not, contractual. Pledges are rarely made the subject of claims. The effect of subparagraph (4) is to permit the personal representative to discharge pledges where he believes the decedent would have wanted him to do so without exposing himself to surcharge. The holder of a contractual pledge may, of course, pursue the remedies of a creditor. If a pledge provides that the obligation ceases on the death of the pledgor, no personal representative would be safe in assuming that the decedent would want the pledge completed under the circumstances.

Subsection (3) is not intended to affect the right to performance or to damages of any person who contracted with the decedent. To do so would constitute an unreasonable interference with private rights. The intention of the subsection is simply to give a personal representative who is obligated to carry out a decedent's contracts the same alternatives in regard to the contractual duties which the decedent had prior to his death.

Section 3-716. [Powers and Duties of Successor Personal Representative.]

A successor personal representative has the same power and duty as the original personal representative to complete the administration and distribution of the estate, as expeditiously as possible, but he shall not exercise any power expressly made personal to the executor named in the will.

Section 3-717. [Co-representatives; When Joint Action Required.]

If two or more persons are appointed co-representatives and unless the will provides otherwise, the concurrence of all is required on all acts connected with the administration and distribution of the estate. This restriction does not apply when any co-representative receives and receipts for property due the estate, when the concurrence of all cannot readily be obtained in the time reasonably available for emergency action necessary to preserve the estate, or when a co-representative has been delegated to act for the others. Persons dealing with a co-representative if actually unaware that another has been appointed to serve with him or if advised by the personal representative with whom they deal that he has authority to act alone for any of the reasons mentioned herein, are as fully protected as if the person with whom they dealt had been the sole personal representative.

COMMENT

With certain qualifications, this section is designed to compel co-representatives to agree on all matters relating to administration when circumstances permit. Delegation by one to another representative is a form of concurrence in acts that may result from the delegation. A co-representative who abdicates his responsibility to co-administer the estate by a blanket delegation breaches his duty to interested persons as described by Section 3-703. Section 3-715(21) authorizes some limited delegations, which are reasonable and for the benefit of interested persons.

Section 3–718. [Powers of Surviving Personal Representative.]

Unless the terms of the will otherwise provide, every power exercisable by personal co-representatives may be exercised by the one or more remaining after the appointment of one or more is terminated, and if one of 2 or more nominated as co-executors is not appointed, those appointed may exercise all the powers incident to the office.

COMMENT

Source, Model Probate Code section 102. This section applies where one of two or more co-representatives dies, becomes disabled or is removed. In regard to co-executors, it is based on the assumption that the decedent would not consider the powers of his fiduciaries to be personal, or to be suspended if one or more could not function. In regard to co-administrators in intestacy, it is based on the idea that the reason for appointing more than one ceases on the death or disability of either of them.

Section 3–719. [Compensation of Personal Representative.]

A personal representative is entitled to reasonable compensation for his services. If a will provides for compensation of the personal representative and there is no contract with the decedent regarding compensation, he may renounce the provision before qualifying and be entitled to reasonable compensation. A personal representative also may renounce his right to all or any part of the compensation. A written renunciation of fee may be filed with the Court.

COMMENT

This section has no bearing on the question of whether a personal representative who also serves as attorney for the estate may receive compensation in both capacities. If a will provision concerning a fee is framed as a condition on the nomination as personal representative, it could not be renounced.

Section 3–720. [Expenses in Estate Litigation.]

If any personal representative or person nominated as personal representative defends or prosecutes any proceeding in good faith, whether successful or not he is entitled to receive from the estate his necessary expenses and disbursements including reasonable attorneys' fees incurred.

COMMENT

Litigation prosecuted by a personal representative for the primary purpose of enhancing his prospects for compensation would not be in good faith.

A personal representative is a fiduciary for successors of the estate (Section 3–703). Though the will naming him may not yet be probated, the priority for appointment conferred by Section 3–203 on one named executor in a probated will means that the person named has an interest, as a fiduciary, in seeking the probate of the will. Hence, he is an interested person within the meaning of Sections 3–301 and 3–401. Section 3–912 gives the successors of an estate control over the executor, provided all are competent adults. So, if all persons possibly interested in the probate of a will, including trustees of any trusts created thereby, concur in directing the named executor to refrain from efforts to probate the instrument, he would lose standing to proceed. All of these observations apply with equal force to the case where the named executor of one instrument seeks to contest the probate of another instrument. Thus, the Code changes the idea followed in some jurisdictions that an executor lacks standing to contest other wills which, if valid, would supersede the will naming him, and standing to oppose other contests that may be mounted against the instrument nominating him.

Section 3–721. [Proceedings for Review of Employment of Agents and Compensation of Personal Representatives and Employees of Estate.]

After notice to all interested persons or on petition of an interested person or on appropriate motion if administration is supervised, the propriety of employment of any person by a personal representative including any attorney, auditor, investment advisor or other specialized agent or assistant, the reasonableness of the compensation of any person so employed, or the reasonableness of the compensation determined by the personal representative for his own services, may be reviewed by the Court. Any person who has received excessive compensation from an estate for services rendered may be ordered to make appropriate refunds.

COMMENT

In view of the broad jurisdiction conferred on the probate court by Section 3–105, description of the special proceeding authorized by this section might be unnecessary. But, the Code's theory that personal representatives may fix their own fees *and* those of estate attorneys marks an important departure from much existing practice under which fees are determined by the court in the first instance. Hence, it seemed wise to emphasize that any interested person can get judicial review of fees if he desires it. Also, if excessive fees have been paid, this section provides a quick and efficient remedy.

PART 8

CREDITORS' CLAIMS

GENERAL COMMENT

The need for uniformity of law regarding creditors' claims against estates is especially strong. Commercial and consumer credit depends upon efficient collection procedures. The cost of credit is pushed up by the cost of credit life insurance which becomes a practical necessity for lenders unwilling to bear the expense of understanding or using the cumbersome and provincial collection procedures found in 50 codes of probate.

The sections which follow facilitate collection of claims against decedents in several ways. First, a simple written statement mailed to the personal representative is a sufficient "claim." Allowance of claims is handled by the personal representative and is assumed if a claimant is not advised of disallowance. Also, a personal representative may pay any just claims without presentation and at any time, if he is willing to assume risks which will be minimal in many cases. The period of uncertainty regarding possible claims is only four months from first publication. This should expedite settlement and distribution of estates.

Section 3–801. [Notice to Creditors.]

(a) Unless notice has already been given under this section, a personal representative upon appointment [may] [shall] publish a notice to creditors once a week for three successive weeks in a newspaper of general circulation in the [county] announcing the appointment and the personal representative's address and notifying creditors of the estate to present their claims within four months after the date of the first publication of the notice or be forever barred.

(b) A personal representative may give written notice by mail or other delivery to a creditor, notifying the creditor to present his [or her] claim within four months after the published notice, if given as provided in subsection (a), or within 60 days after the mailing or other delivery of the notice, whichever is later, or be forever barred. Written notice must be the notice described in subsection (a) above or a similar notice.

(c) The personal representative is not liable to a creditor or to a successor of the decedent for giving or failing to give notice under this section.

340

COMMENT

Section 3–1203, relating to small estates, contains an important qualification on the duty created by this section.

In 1989, the Joint Editorial Board recommended replacement of the word "shall" with "[may] [shall]" in (a) to signal its approval of a choice between mandatory publication and optional publication of notice to creditors to be made by the legislature in an enacting state. Publication of notice to creditors is quite expensive in some populous areas of the country and, if *Tulsa Professional Collection Services v. Pope,* 108 S.Ct. 1340, 485 U.S. 478 (1988) applies to this code, is useless except to bar unknown creditors. Even if *Pope* does not apply, personal representatives for estates involving successors willing to assume the risk of unbarred claims should have (and have had under the code as a practical consequence of absence of court supervision and mandatory closings) the option of failing to publish.

Additional discussion of the impact of *Pope* on the Code appears in the Comment to Section 3–803, infra.

If a state elects to make publication of notice to creditors a duty for personal representatives, failure to advertise for claims would involve a breach of duty on the part of the personal representative. If, as a result of such breach, a claim is later asserted against a distributee under Section 3–1004, the personal representative may be liable to the distributee for costs related to discharge of the claim and the recovery of contribution from other distributees. The protection afforded personal representatives under Section 3–1003 would not be available, for that section applies only if the personal representative truthfully recites that the time limit for presentation of claims has expired.

Putting aside *Pope* case concerns regarding state action under this code, it might be appropriate, by legislation, to channel publications through the personnel of the probate court. See Section 1–401. If notices are controlled by a centralized authority, some assurance could be gained against publication in newspapers of small circulation. Also, the form of notices could be made uniform and certain efficiencies could be achieved. For example, it would be compatible with this section for the Court to publish a single notice each day or each week listing the names of personal representatives appointed since the last publication, with addresses and dates of non-claim.

Section 3–802. [Statutes of Limitations.]

(a) Unless an estate is insolvent, the personal representative, with the consent of all successors whose interests would be affected, may waive any defense of limitations available to the estate. If the defense is not waived, no claim barred by a statute of limitations at the time of the decedent's death may be allowed or paid.

(b) The running of a statute of limitations measured from an event other than death or the giving of notice to creditors is suspended for four months after the decedent's death, but resumes thereafter as to claims not barred by other sections.

(c) For purposes of a statute of limitations, the presentation of a claim pursuant to Section 3–804 is equivalent to commencement of a proceeding on the claim.

COMMENT

This section means that four months is added to the normal period of limitations by reason of a debtor's death before a debt is barred. It implies also that after the expiration of four months from death, the normal statute of limitations may run and bar a claim even though the non-claim provisions of Section 3–803 have not been triggered. Hence, the non-claim and limitation provisions of Section 3–803 are not mutually exclusive.

It should be noted that under Sections 3–803 and 3–804 it is possible for a claim to be barred by the process of claim, disallowance and failure by the creditor to commence a proceeding to enforce his claim prior to the end of the four month suspension period. Thus, the regular statute of limitations applicable during the debtor's lifetime, the non-claim provisions of Sections 3–803 and 3–804, and the three-year limitation of Section 3–803 all have potential application to a claim. The first of the three to accomplish a bar controls.

In 1975, the Joint Editorial Board recommended a change that makes it clear that only those successors who would be affected thereby, must agree to a waiver of a defense of limitations available to an estate. As the original text stood, the section appeared to require the consent of "all successors," even though this would include some who, under the rules of abatement, could not possibly be affected by allowance and payment of the claim in question.

In 1989, in connection with other amendments recommended in sequel to *Tulsa Professional Collection Services v. Pope,* 108 S.Ct. 1340, 485 U.S. 478 (1988), the Joint Editorial Board recommended the splitting out, into Subsections (b) and (c), of the last two sentences of what formerly was a four-sentence section. The first two sentences now appear as Subsection (a). The rearrangement aids understanding that the section deals with three separable ideas. No other change in language is involved, and the timing of the changes to coincide with *Pope* case amendments is purely coincidental.

Section 3–803. [Limitations on Presentation of Claims.]

(a) All claims against a decedent's estate which arose before the death of the decedent, including claims of the state and any subdivision thereof, whether due or to become due, absolute or contingent, liquidated or unliquidated, founded on contract, tort, or other legal basis, if not barred earlier by another statute of limitations or non-claim statute, are barred against the estate, the personal representative, and the heirs and devisees of the decedent, unless presented within the earlier of the following:

(1) one year after the decedent's death; or

(2) the time provided by Section 3–801(b) for creditors who are given actual notice, and within the time provided in 3–801(a) for all creditors barred by publication.

(b) A claim described in subsection (a) which is barred by the non-claim statute of the decedent's domicile before the giving of notice to creditors in this State is barred in this State.

(c) All claims against a decedent's estate which arise at or after the death of the decedent, including claims of the state and any subdivision thereof, whether due or to become due, absolute or contingent, liquidated or unliquidated, founded on contract, tort, or other legal basis, are barred against the estate, the personal representative, and the heirs and devisees of the decedent, unless presented as follows:

(1) a claim based on a contract with the personal representative, within four months after performance by the personal representative is due; or

(2) any other claim, within the later of four months after it arises, or the time specified in subsection (a)(1).

(d) Nothing in this section affects or prevents:

(1) any proceeding to enforce any mortgage, pledge, or other lien upon property of the estate;

(2) to the limits of the insurance protection only, any proceeding to establish liability of the decedent or the personal representative for which he is protected by liability insurance; or

(3) collection of compensation for services rendered and reimbursement for expenses advanced by the personal representative or by the attorney or accountant for the personal representative of the estate.

COMMENT

There was some disagreement among the Reporters over whether a short period of limitations, or of non-claim, should be provided for claims arising at or after death. Sub-paragraph (b) was finally inserted because most felt it was desirable to accelerate the time when unadjudicated distributions would be final. The time limits stated would not, of course, affect any personal liability in contract, tort, or by statute, of the personal representative. Under Section 3-808 a personal representative is not liable on transactions entered into on behalf of the estate unless he agrees to be personally liable or unless he breaches a duty by making the contract. Creditors of the estate and not of the personal representative thus face a special limitation that runs four months after performance is due from the personal representative. Tort claims normally will involve casualty insurance of the decedent or of the personal representative, and so will fall within the exception of subparagraph (d). If a personal representative is personally at fault in respect to a tort claim arising after the decedent's death, his personal liability would not be affected by the running of the special short period provided here.

In 1989, the Joint Editorial Board recommended amendments to Subsection (a). The change in (1) shortens the ultimate limitations period on claims against a decedent from 3 years after death to 1 year after death. Corresponding amendments were recommended for Sections 3-1003(a)(1) and 3-1006. The new one-year from death limitation (which applies without regard to whether or when an estate is opened for administration) is designed to prevent concerns stemming from the possible applicability to this Code of *Tulsa Professional Collection Services v. Pope,* 108 S.Ct. 1340, 485 U.S. 478 (1988) from unduly prolonging estate settlements and closings.

Subsection (a)(2), by reference to 3-801(a) and 3-801(b), adds an additional method of barring a prospective claimant of whom the personal representative is aware. The new bar is available when it is appropriate, under all of the circumstances, to send a mailed warning to one or more known claimants who have not presented claims that the recipient's claim will be barred if not presented within 60 days from the notice. This optional, mailed notice, described in accompanying new text in Section 3-801(b), is designed to enhance the ability of personal representatives to protect distributees against pass-through liability (under Section 3-1004) to possibly unbarred claimants. Personal representatives acting in the best interests of successors to the estate (see Section 3-703(a) and the definition of "successors" in Section 1-201(42)) may determine that successors are willing to assume risks (i) that *Pope,* supra, will be held to apply to this Code in spite of absence of any significant contact between an agency of the state and the acts of a personal representative operating independently of court supervision; and (ii) that a possibly unbarred claim is valid and will be pursued by its owner against estate distributees in time to avoid bar via the earliest to run of its own limitation period (which, under Section 3-802(b), resumes running four months after death), or the one-year from death limitation now provided by § 3-803(a)(1). If publication of notice as provided in Section 3-801 has occurred and if *Pope* either is inapplicable to this Code or is applicable but the late-arising claim in question is judged to have been unknown to the personal representative and unlikely to have been discovered by reasonable effort, an earlier, four months from first publication bar will apply.

The Joint Editorial Board recognized that the new bar running one year after death may be used by some sets of successors to avoid payment of claims against their decedents of which they are aware. Successors who are willing to delay receipt and enjoyment of inheritances may consider waiting out the non-claim period running from death simply to avoid any public record of an administration that might alert known and unknown creditors to pursue their claims. The scenario was deemed to be unlikely, however, for unpaid creditors of a decedent are interested persons (Section 1–201(20)) who are qualified to force the opening of an estate for purposes of presenting and enforcing claims. Further, successors who delay opening an administration will suffer from lack of proof of title to estate assets and attendant inability to enjoy their inheritances. Finally, the odds that holders of important claims against the decedent will need help in learning of the death and proper place of administration is rather small. Any benefit to such claimants of additional procedures designed to compel administrations and to locate and warn claimants of an impending non-claim bar, is quite likely to be heavily outweighed by the costs such procedures would impose on all estates, the vast majority of which are routinely applied to quick payment of the decedents' bills and distributed without any creditor controversy.

Note that the new bar described by Section 3–801(b) and Section 3–803(a)(2) is the earlier of one year from death or the period described by reference to § 3–801(b) and § 3–801(a) in § 3–803(a)(2). If publication of notice is made under § 3–801(a), and the personal representative thereafter gives actual notice to a known creditor, when is the creditor barred? If the actual notice is given less than 60 days prior to the expiration of the four months from first publication period, the claim will not be barred four months after first publication because the actual notice given by § 3–801(b) advises the creditor that it has no less than 60 days to present the claim. It is as if the personal representative gave the claimant a written waiver of any benefit the estate may have had by reason of the four month bar following published notice. (c.f., the ability of a personal representative, under § 3–802 to change claims from allowed to disallowed, and vice versa, and the 60 day period given by § 3–806(a) within which a claimant may contest a disallowance). The period ending with the running of 60 days from actual notice replaces the four month from publication period as the "time for original presentation" referred to in Section 3–806(a).

Note, too, that if there is no publication of notice as provided in Section 3–801(a), the giving of actual notice to known creditors establishes separate, 60 days from time of notice, non-claim periods for those so notified. The failure to publish also means that no general non-claim period, other than the one year period running from death, will be working for the estate. If an actual notice to a creditor is given before notice by publication is given, a question arises as to whether the 60 day period from actual notice, or the longer, four-month from publication applies. Subsections 3–801(a) and (b), which are pulled into Section 3–803(a)(2) by reference, make no distinction between actual notices given before publication and those given after publication. Hence, it would seem that the later time bar would control in either case. This reading also fits more satisfactorily with Section 3–806(a) and other code language referring in various contexts to "the time limit prescribed in § 3–803."

The proviso, formerly appended to 3–803(a)(1), regarding the effect in this state of the prior running of a non-claim statute of the decedent's domicile, has been restated as 3–803(b), and former subsections (b) and (c) have been redesignated as (c) and (d). The relocation of the proviso was made to improve the style of the section. No change of meaning is intended.

The second paragraph of the original comment has been deleted because of inconsistency with amended § 3–803(a).

The 1989 changes recommended by the Joint Editorial Board relat-

ing to former § 3–803(b) now designated as 3–803(c) are unrelated to the *Pope* case problem. The original text failed to describe a satisfactory non-claim period for claims arising at or after the decedent's death other than claims based on contract. The four months "after [any other claim] arises" period worked unjustly as to tort claims stemming from accidents causing the decedent's death by snuffing out claims too quickly, sometimes before an estate had been opened. The language added by the 1989 amendment assures such claimants against any bar working prior to the later of one year after death or four months from the time the claim arises.

The other change affecting what is now § 3–803(d) is the addition of a third class of items which are not barred by any time bar running from death, publication of notice to creditors, or any actual notice given to an estate creditor. The addition resembles a modification to the Code as enacted in Arizona.

Section 3–804. [Manner of Presentation of Claims.]

Claims against a decedent's estate may be presented as follows:

(1) The claimant may deliver or mail to the personal representative a written statement of the claim indicating its basis, the name and address of the claimant, and the amount claimed, or may file a written statement of the claim, in the form prescribed by rule, with the clerk of the Court. The claim is deemed presented on the first to occur of receipt of the written statement of claim by the personal representative, or the filing of the claim with the Court. If a claim is not yet due, the date when it will become due shall be stated. If the claim is contingent or unliquidated, the nature of the uncertainty shall be stated. If the claim is secured, the security shall be described. Failure to describe correctly the security, the nature of any uncertainty, and the due date of a claim not yet due does not invalidate the presentation made.

(2) The claimant may commence a proceeding against the personal representative in any Court where the personal representative may be subjected to jurisdiction, to obtain payment of his claim against the estate, but the commencement of the proceeding must occur within the time limited for presenting the claim. No presentation of claim is required in regard to matters claimed in proceedings against the decedent which were pending at the time of his death.

(3) If a claim is presented under subsection (1), no proceeding thereon may be commenced more than 60 days after the personal representative has mailed a notice of disallowance; but, in the case of a claim which is not presently due or which is contingent or unliquidated, the personal representative may consent to an extension of the 60–day period, or to avoid injustice the Court, on petition, may order an extension of the 60–day period, but in no event shall the extension run beyond the applicable statute of limitations.

COMMENT

The filing of a claim with the probate court under (2) of this section does not serve to initiate a proceeding concerning the claim. Rather, it serves merely to protect the claimant who may anticipate some need for evidence to show that his claim is not barred. The probate court acts simply as a depository of the statement of claim, as is true of its responsibility for an inventory filed with it under Section 3–706.

In reading this section it is important to remember that a regular statute of limitation may run to bar a claim before the non-claim provisions run. See Section 3–802.

Section 3–805. [Classification of Claims.]

(a) If the applicable assets of the estate are insufficient to pay all claims in full, the personal representative shall make payment in the following order:

(1) costs and expenses of administration;

(2) reasonable funeral expenses;

(3) debts and taxes with preference under federal law;

(4) reasonable and necessary medical and hospital expenses of the last illness of the decedent, including compensation of persons attending him;

(5) debts and taxes with preference under other laws of this state;

(6) all other claims.

(b) No preference shall be given in the payment of any claim over any other claim of the same class, and a claim due and payable shall not be entitled to a preference over claims not due.

COMMENT

In 1975, the Joint Editorial Board recommended the separation of funeral expenses from the items now accorded fourth priority. Under federal law, funeral expenses, but not debts incurred by the decedent can be given priority over claims of the United States.

Section 3–806. [Allowance of Claims.]

(a) As to claims presented in the manner described in Section 3–804 within the time limit prescribed in 3–803, the personal representative may mail a notice to any claimant stating that the claim has been disallowed. If, after allowing or disallowing a claim, the personal representative changes his decision concerning the claim, he shall notify the claimant. The personal representative may not change a disallowance of a claim after the time for the claimant to file a petition for allowance or to commence a proceeding on the claim has run and the claim has been barred. Every claim which is disallowed in whole or in part by the personal representative is barred so far as not allowed unless the claimant files a petition for allowance in the Court or commences a proceeding against the personal representative not later than 60 days after the mailing of the notice of disallowance or partial allowance if the notice warns the claimant of the impending bar. Failure of the personal representative to mail notice to a claimant of action on his claim for 60 days after the time for original presentation of the claim has expired has the effect of a notice of allowance.

(b) After allowing or disallowing a claim the personal representative may change the allowance or disallowance as hereafter provided. The personal representative may prior to payment change the allowance to a disallowance in whole or in part, but not after allowance by a court order or judgment or an order directing payment of the claim. He shall notify the claimant of the change to disallowance, and the disallowed claim is then subject to bar as provided in subsection (a). The personal representative may change a disallowance to an allowance, in whole or in part, until it is barred under subsection (a); after it is barred, it may be allowed and paid only if the estate is solvent and all successors whose interests would be affected consent.

(c) Upon the petition of the personal representative or of a claimant in a proceeding for the purpose, the Court may allow in whole or in part any claim or claims presented to the personal representative or filed with the clerk of the Court in due time and not barred by subsection (a) of this section. Notice in this proceeding shall be given to the claimant, the personal representative and those other persons interested in the estate as the Court may direct by order entered at the time the proceeding is commenced.

(d) A judgment in a proceeding in another court against a personal representative to enforce a claim against a decedent's estate is an allowance of the claim.

(e) Unless otherwise provided in any judgment in another court entered against the personal representative, allowed claims bear interest at the legal rate for the period commencing 60 days after the time for original presentation of the claim has expired unless based on a contract making a provision for interest, in which case they bear interest in accordance with that provision.

Section 3–807. [Payment of Claims.]

(a) Upon the expiration of the earlier of the time limitations provided in Section 3–803 for the presentation of claims, the personal representative shall proceed to pay the claims allowed against the estate in the order of priority prescribed, after making provision for homestead, family and support allowances, for claims already presented that have not yet been allowed or whose allowance has been appealed, and for unbarred claims that may yet be presented, including costs and expenses of administration. By petition to the Court in a proceeding for the purpose, or by appropriate motion if the administration is supervised, a claimant whose claim has been allowed but not paid may secure an order directing the personal representative to pay the claim to the extent funds of the estate are available to pay it.

(b) The personal representative at any time may pay any just claim that has not been barred, with or without formal presentation, but is personally liable to any other claimant whose claim is allowed and who is injured by its payment if:

(1) payment was made before the expiration of the time limit stated in subsection (a) and the personal representative failed to require the payee to give adequate security for the refund of any of the payment necessary to pay other claimants; or

(2) payment was made, due to negligence or willful fault of the personal representative, in such manner as to deprive the injured claimant of priority.

349

COMMENT

As recommended for amendment in 1989 by the Joint Editorial Board, the section directs the personal representative to pay allowed claims at the earlier of one year from the death or the expiration of 4 months from first publication. This interpretation reflects that distribution need not be delayed further on account of creditors' claims once a time bar running from death or publication has run, for known creditors who have failed to present claims by such time may have received an actual notice leading to a bar 60 days thereafter and in any event can and should be the occasion for withholding or the making of other provision by the personal representative to cover the possibility of later presentation and allowance of such claims. Distribution would also be appropriate whenever competent and solvent distributees expressly agree to indemnify the estate for any claims remaining unbarred and undischarged after the distribution.

Section 3–808. [Individual Liability of Personal Representative.]

(a) Unless otherwise provided in the contract, a personal representative is not individually liable on a contract properly entered into in his fiduciary capacity in the course of administration of the estate unless he fails to reveal his representative capacity and identify the estate in the contract.

(b) A personal representative is individually liable for obligations arising from ownership or control of the estate or for torts committed in the course of administration of the estate only if he is personally at fault.

(c) Claims based on contracts entered into by a personal representative in his fiduciary capacity, on obligations arising from ownership or control of the estate or on torts committed in the course of estate administration may be asserted against the estate by proceeding against the personal representative in his fiduciary capacity, whether or not the personal representative is individually liable therefor.

(d) Issues of liability as between the estate and the personal representative individually may be determined in a proceeding for accounting, surcharge or indemnification or other appropriate proceeding.

COMMENT

In the absence of statute an executor, administrator or a trustee is personally liable on contracts entered into in his fiduciary capacity unless he expressly excludes personal liability in the contract. He is commonly personally liable for obligations stemming from ownership or possession of the property (e.g., taxes) and for torts committed by servants employed in the management of the property. The claimant ordinarily can reach the estate only after exhausting his remedies against the fiduciary as an individual and then only to the extent that the fiduciary is entitled to indemnity from the property. This and the following sections are designed to make the estate a quasi-corporation for purposes of such liabilities. The personal representative would be personally liable only if an agent for a corporation would be under the same circumstances, and the claimant has a direct remedy against the quasi-corporate property.

Section 3–809. [Secured Claims.]

Payment of a secured claim is upon the basis of the amount allowed if the creditor surrenders his security; otherwise payment is upon the basis of one of the following:

(1) if the creditor exhausts his security before receiving payment, [unless precluded by other law] upon the amount of the claim allowed less the fair value of the security; or

(2) if the creditor does not have the right to exhaust his security or has not done so, upon the amount of the claim allowed less the value of the security determined by converting it into money according to the terms of the agreement pursuant to which the security was delivered to the creditor, or by the creditor and personal representative by agreement, arbitration, compromise or litigation.

Section 3–810. [Claims Not Due and Contingent or Unliquidated Claims.]

(a) If a claim which will become due at a future time or a contingent or unliquidated claim becomes due or certain before the distribution of the estate, and if the claim has been allowed or established by a proceeding, it is paid in the same manner as presently due and absolute claims of the same class.

(b) In other cases the personal representative or, on petition of the personal representative or the claimant in a special proceeding for the purpose, the Court may provide for payment as follows:

(1) if the claimant consents, he may be paid the present or agreed value of the claim, taking any uncertainty into account;

(2) arrangement for future payment, or possible payment, on the happening of the contingency or on liquidation may be made by creating a trust, giving a mortgage, obtaining a bond or security from a distributee, or otherwise.

Section 3–811. [Counterclaims.]

In allowing a claim the personal representative may deduct any counterclaim which the estate has against the claimant. In determining a claim against an estate a Court shall reduce the amount allowed by the amount of any counterclaims and, if the counterclaims exceed the claim, render a judgment against the claimant in the amount of the excess. A counterclaim, liquidated or unliquidated, may arise from a transaction other than that upon which the claim is based. A counterclaim may give rise to relief exceeding in amount or different in kind from that sought in the claim.

Section 3–812. [Execution and Levies Prohibited.]

No execution may issue upon nor may any levy be made against any property of the estate under any judgment against a decedent or a personal representative, but this section shall not be construed to prevent the enforcement of mortgages, pledges or liens upon real or personal property in an appropriate proceeding.

Section 3–813. [Compromise of Claims.]

When a claim against the estate has been presented in any manner, the personal representative may, if it appears for the best interest of the estate, compromise the claim, whether due or not due, absolute or contingent, liquidated or unliquidated.

Section 3–814. [Encumbered Assets.]

If any assets of the estate are encumbered by mortgage, pledge, lien, or other security interest, the personal representative may pay the encumbrance or any part thereof, renew or extend any obligation secured by the encumbrance or convey or transfer the assets to the creditor in satisfaction of his lien, in whole or in part, whether or not the holder of the encumbrance has presented a claim, if it appears to be for the best interest of the estate. Payment of an encumbrance does not increase the share of the distributee entitled to the encumbered assets unless the distributee is entitled to exoneration.

COMMENT

Section 2–609 establishes a rule of construction against exoneration. Thus, unless the will indicates to the contrary, a specific devisee of mortgaged property takes subject to the lien without right to have other assets applied to discharge the secured obligation.

In 1975, the Joint Editorial Board recommended substitution of the word "presented", in the first sentence, for the word "filed" in the original text. The change aligns this section with Section 3–804, which describes several methods, including mailing or delivery to the personal representative, as methods of protecting a claim against non-claim provisions of the Code.

Section 3–815. [Administration in More Than One State; Duty of Personal Representative.]

(a) All assets of estates being administered in this state are subject to all claims, allowances and charges existing or established against the personal representative wherever appointed.

(b) If the estate either in this state or as a whole is insufficient to cover all family exemptions and allowances determined by the law of the decedent's domicile, prior charges and claims, after satisfaction of the exemptions, allowances and charges, each claimant whose claim has been allowed either in this state or elsewhere in administrations of which the personal representative is aware, is entitled to receive payment of an equal proportion of his claim. If a preference or security in regard to a claim is allowed in another jurisdiction but not in this state, the creditor so benefited is to receive dividends from local assets only upon the balance of his claim after deducting the amount of the benefit.

(c) In case the family exemptions and allowances, prior charges and claims of the entire estate exceed the total value of the portions of the estate being administered separately and this state is not the state of the decedent's last domicile, the claims allowed in this state shall be paid their proportion if local assets are adequate for the purpose, and the balance of local assets shall be transferred to the domiciliary personal representative. If local assets are not sufficient to pay all claims allowed in this state the amount to which they are entitled, local assets shall be marshalled so that each claim allowed in this state is paid its proportion as far as possible, after taking into account all dividends on claims allowed in this state from assets in other jurisdictions.

COMMENT

Under Section 3–803(a)(1), if a local (property only) administration is commenced and proceeds to advertisement for claims before non-claim statutes have run at domicile, claimants may prove claims in the local administration at any time before the local non-claim period expires. Section 3–815 has the effect of subjecting all assets of the decedent, wherever they may be located and administered, to claims properly presented in any local administration. It is necessary, however, that the personal representative of any portion of the estate be aware of other administrations in order for him to become responsible for

claims and charges established against other administrations.

Section 3–816. [Final Distribution to Domiciliary Representative.]

The estate of a non-resident decedent being administered by a personal representative appointed in this state shall, if there is a personal representative of the decedent's domicile willing to receive it, be distributed to the domiciliary personal representative for the benefit of the successors of the decedent unless (1) by virtue of the decedent's will, if any, and applicable choice of law rules, the successors are identified pursuant to the local law of this state without reference to the local law of the decedent's domicile; (2) the personal representative of this state, after reasonable inquiry, is unaware of the existence or identity of a domiciliary personal representative; or (3) the Court orders otherwise in a proceeding for a closing order under Section 3–1001 or incident to the closing of a supervised administration. In other cases, distribution of the estate of a decedent shall be made in accordance with the other Parts of this Article.

PART 9

SPECIAL PROVISIONS RELATING TO DISTRIBUTION

Section 3–901. [Successors' Rights if No Administration.]

In the absence of administration, the heirs and devisees are entitled to the estate in accordance with the terms of a probated will or the laws of intestate succession. Devisees may establish title by the probated will to devised property. Persons entitled to property by homestead allowance, exemption or intestacy may establish title thereto by proof of the decedent's ownership, his death, and their relationship to the decedent. Successors take subject to all charges incident to administration, including the claims of creditors and allowances of surviving spouse and dependent children, and subject to the rights of others resulting from abatement, retainer, advancement, and ademption.

COMMENT

Title to a decedent's property passes to his heirs and devisees at the time of his death. See Section 3–101. This section adds little to Section 3–101 except to indicate how successors may establish record title in the absence of administration.

Section 3–902. [Distribution; Order in Which Assets Appropriated; Abatement.]

(a) Except as provided in subsection (b) and except as provided in connection with the share of the surviving spouse who elects to take an elective share, shares of distributees abate, without any preference or priority as between real and personal property, in the following order: (1) property not disposed of by the will; (2) residuary devises; (3) general devises; (4) specific devises. For purposes of abatement, a general devise charged on any specific property or fund is a specific devise to the extent of the value of the property on which it is charged, and upon the failure or insufficiency of the property on which it is charged, a general devise to the extent of the failure or insufficiency. Abatement within each classification is in proportion to the amounts of property each of the beneficiaries would have received if full distribution of the property had been made in accordance with the terms of the will.

355

(b) If the will expresses an order of abatement, or if the testamentary plan or the express or implied purpose of the devise would be defeated by the order of abatement stated in subsection (a), the shares of the distributees abate as may be found necessary to give effect to the intention of the testator.

(c) If the subject of a preferred devise is sold or used incident to administration, abatement shall be achieved by appropriate adjustments in, or contribution from, other interests in the remaining assets.

COMMENT

A testator may determine the order in which the assets of his estate are applied to the payment of his debts. If he does not, then the provisions of this section express rules which may be regarded as approximating what testators generally want. The statutory order of abatement is designed to aid in resolving doubts concerning the intention of a particular testator, rather than to defeat his purpose.

Hence, subsection (b) directs that consideration be given to the purpose of a testator. This may be revealed in many ways. Thus, it is commonly held that, even in the absence of statute, general legacies to a wife, or to persons with respect to which the testator is in loco parentis, are to be preferred to other legacies in the same class because this accords with the probable purpose of the legacies.

[Section 3–902A. [Distribution; Order in Which Assets Appropriated; Abatement.]

(addendum for adoption in community property states)

[(a) and (b) as above.]

(c) If an estate of a decedent consists partly of separate property and partly of community property, the debts and expenses of administration shall be apportioned and charged against the different kinds of property in proportion to the relative value thereof.

[(d) same as (c) in common law state.]]

COMMENT

(c) is suggested for inclusion in Section 3–902 in a community property state. Its inclusion causes (c) as drafted for common law states to be redesignated (d). As is the case

with other insertions suggested in the Code for community property states, the specific language of this draft is to be taken as illustrative of coverage that is desirable.

Section 3–903. [Right of Retainer.]

The amount of a non-contingent indebtedness of a successor to the estate if due, or its present value if not due, shall be offset against the successor's interest; but the successor has the benefit of any defense which would be available to him in a direct proceeding for recovery of the debt.

Section 3–904. [Interest on General Pecuniary Devise.]

General pecuniary devises bear interest at the legal rate beginning one year after the first appointment of a personal representative until payment, unless a contrary intent is indicated by the will.

COMMENT

Unlike the common law, this section provides that a general pecuniary devisee's right to interest begins one year from the time when administration was commenced, rather than one year from death. The rule provided here is similar to the common law rule in that the right to interest for delayed payment does not depend on whether the estate in fact realized income during the period of delay. The section is consistent with Section 5(b) of the Revised Uniform Principal and Income Act which allocates realized net income of an estate between various categories of successors.

Section 3–905. [Penalty Clause for Contest.]

A provision in a will purporting to penalize any interested person for contesting the will or instituting other proceedings relating to the estate is unenforceable if probable cause exists for instituting proceedings.

Section 3–906. [Distribution in Kind; Valuation; Method.]

(a) Unless a contrary intention is indicated by the will, the distributable assets of a decedent's estate shall be distributed in kind to the extent possible through application of the following provisions:

(1) A specific devisee is entitled to distribution of the thing devised to him, and a spouse or child who has selected particular assets of an estate as provided in Section 2–403 shall receive the items selected.

(2) Any homestead or family allowance or devise of a stated sum of money may be satisfied in kind provided

(i) the person entitled to the payment has not demanded payment in cash;

(ii) the property distributed in kind is valued at fair market value as of the date of its distribution, and

(iii) no residuary devisee has requested that the asset in question remain a part of the residue of the estate.

(3) For the purpose of valuation under paragraph (2) securities regularly traded on recognized exchanges, if distributed in kind, are valued at the price for the last sale of like securities traded on the business day prior to distribution, or if there was no sale on that day, at the median between amounts bid and offered at the close of that day. Assets consisting of sums owed the decedent or the estate by solvent debtors as to which there is no known dispute or defense are valued at the sum due with accrued interest or discounted to the date of distribution. For assets which do not have readily ascertainable values, a valuation as of a date not more than 30 days prior to the date of distribution, if otherwise reasonable, controls. For purposes of facilitating distribution, the personal representative may ascertain the value of the assets as of the time of the proposed distribution in any reasonable way, including the employment of qualified appraisers, even if the assets may have been previously appraised.

(4) The residuary estate shall be distributed in any equitable manner.

(b) After the probable charges against the estate are known, the personal representative may mail or deliver a proposal for distribution to all persons who have a right to object to the proposed distribution. The right of any distributee to object to the proposed distribution on the basis of the kind or value of asset he is to receive, if not waived earlier in writing, terminates if he fails to object in writing received by the personal representative within 30 days after mailing or delivery of the proposal.

COMMENT

This section establishes a preference for distribution in kind. It directs a personal representative to make distribution in kind whenever feasible and to convert assets to cash only where there is a special reason for doing so. It provides a reasonable means for determining value of assets distributed in kind. It is implicit in Sections 3–101, 3–901 and this section that each residuary beneficiary's basic right is to his proportionate share of each asset constituting the residue.

Section 3–907. [Distribution in Kind; Evidence.]

If distribution in kind is made, the personal representative shall execute an instrument or deed of distribution assigning, transferring or releasing the assets to the distributee as evidence of the distributee's title to the property.

COMMENT

This and sections following should be read with Section 3–709 which permits the personal representative to leave certain assets of a decedent's estate in the possession of the person presumptively entitled thereto. The "release" contemplated by this section would be used as evidence that the personal representative had determined that he would not need to disturb the possession of an heir or devisee for purposes of administration.

Under Section 3–711, a personal representative's relationship to as-

sets of the estate is described as the "same power over the title to property of the estate as an absolute owner would have." A personal representative may, however, acquire a full title to estate assets, as in the case where particular items are conveyed to the personal representative by sellers, transfer agents or others. The language of Section 3–907 is designed to cover instances where the instrument of distribution operates as a transfer, as well as those in which its operation is more like a release.

Section 3–908. [Distribution; Right or Title of Distributee.]

Proof that a distributee has received an instrument or deed of distribution of assets in kind, or payment in distribution, from a personal representative, is conclusive evidence that the distributee has succeeded to the interest of the estate in the distributed assets, as against all persons interested in the estate, except that the personal representative may recover the assets or their value if the distribution was improper.

COMMENT

The purpose of this section is to channel controversies which may arise among successors of a decedent because of improper distributions through the personal representative who made the distribution, or a successor personal repre-

sentative. Section 3–108 does not bar appointment proceedings initiated to secure appointment of a personal representative to correct an erroneous distribution made by a prior representative. But see Section 3–1006.

Section 3–909. [Improper Distribution; Liability of Distributee.]

Unless the distribution or payment no longer can be questioned because of adjudication, estoppel, or limitation, a distributee of property improperly distributed or paid, or a claimant who was improperly paid, is liable to return the property improperly received and its income since distribution if he has the property. If he does not have the property, then he is liable to return the value as of the date of disposition of the property improperly received and its income and gain received by him.

COMMENT

The term "improperly" as used in this section must be read in light of Section 3–703 and the manifest purpose of this and other sections of the Code to shift questions concerning the propriety of various distributions from the fiduciary to the distributees in order to prevent every administration from becoming an adjudicated matter. Thus, a distribution may be "authorized at the time" as contemplated by Section 3–703, and still be "improper" under this section. Section 3–703 is designed to permit a personal representative to distribute without risk in some cases, even though there has been no adjudication. When an unadjudicated distribution has occurred, the rights of persons to show that the basis for the distribution (e.g., an informally probated will, or informally issued letters of administration) is incorrect, or that the basis was improperly applied (erroneous interpretation, for example) is preserved against distributees by this section.

The definition of "distributee" to include the trustee and beneficiary of a testamentary trust in 1–201(10) is important in allocating liabilities that may arise under Sections 3–909 and 3–910 on improper distribution by the personal representative under an informally probated will. The provisions of 3–909 and 3–910 are based on the theory that liability follows the property and the fiduciary is absolved from liability by reliance upon the informally probated will.

Section 3–910. [Purchasers From Distributees Protected.]

If property distributed in kind or a security interest therein is acquired for value by a purchaser from or lender to a distributee who has received an instrument or deed of distribution from the personal representative, or is so acquired by a purchaser from or lender to a transferee from such distributee, the purchaser or lender takes title free of rights of any interested person in the estate and incurs no personal liability to the estate, or to any interested person, whether or not the distribution was proper or supported by court order or the authority of the personal representative was terminated before execution of the instrument or deed. This section protects a purchaser from or lender to a distributee who, as personal representative, has executed a deed of distribution to himself, as well as a purchaser from or lender to any other distributee or his transferee. To be protected under this provision, a purchaser or lender need not inquire whether a personal representative acted properly in making the distribution in kind, even if the authority of the personal representative had terminated before the distribution. Any recorded instrument described in this section on which a state documentary fee is noted pursuant to [insert appropriate reference] shall be prima facie evidence that such transfer was made for value.

COMMENT

The words "instrument or deed of distribution" are explained in Section 3–907. The effect of this section may be to make an instrument or deed of distribution a very desirable link in a chain of title involving succession of land. Cf. Section 3–901.

In 1975, the Joint Editorial Board recommended additions that

strengthen the protection extended by this section to bona fide purchasers from distributees. The additional language was derived from recommendations evolved with respect to the Colorado version of the Code by probate and title authorities who agreed on language to relieve title assurers of doubts they had identified in relation to some cases.

Section 3–911. [Partition for Purpose of Distribution.]

When two or more heirs or devisees are entitled to distribution of undivided interests in any real or personal property of the estate, the personal representative or one or more of the heirs or devisees may petition the Court prior to the formal or informal closing of the estate, to make partition. After notice to the interested heirs or devisees, the Court shall partition the property in the same manner as provided by the law for civil actions of partition. The Court may direct the personal representative to sell any property which cannot be partitioned without prejudice to the owners and which cannot conveniently be allotted to any one party.

COMMENT

Ordinarily heirs or devisees desiring partition of a decedent's property will resolve the issue by agreement without resort to the courts. (See Section 3–912.) If court deter-

mination is necessary, the court with jurisdiction to administer the estate has jurisdiction to partition the property.

Section 3–912. [Private Agreements Among Successors to Decedent Binding on Personal Representative.]

Subject to the rights of creditors and taxing authorities, competent successors may agree among themselves to alter the interests, shares, or amounts to which they are entitled under the will of the decedent, or under the laws of intestacy, in any way that they provide in a written contract executed by all who are affected by its provisions. The personal representative shall abide by the terms of the agreement subject to his obligation to administer the estate for the benefit of creditors, to pay all taxes and costs of administration, and to carry out the responsibilities of his office for the benefit of any successors of the decedent who are not parties. Personal representatives of decedents' estates are not required to see to the performance of trusts if the trustee thereof is another person who is willing to accept the trust. Accordingly, trustees of a testamentary trust are successors for the purposes of this section. Nothing herein relieves trustees of any duties owed to beneficiaries of trusts.

COMMENT

It may be asserted that this section is only a restatement of the obvious and should be omitted. Its purpose, however, is to make it clear that the successors to an estate have residual control over the way it is to be distributed. Hence, they may compel a personal representative to administer and distribute as they may agree and direct. Successors should compare the consequences and possible advantages of careful use of the power to renounce as described by Section 2–801 with the effect of agreement under this section. The most obvious difference is that an agreement among successors under this section would involve transfers by some participants to the extent it changed the pattern of distribution from that otherwise applicable.

Differing from a pattern that is familiar in many states, this Code does not subject testamentary trusts and trustees to special statutory provisions, or supervisory jurisdiction. A testamentary trustee is treated as a devisee with special duties which are of no particular concern to the personal representative. Article VII contains optional procedures extending the safeguards available to personal representatives to trustees of both inter vivos and testamentary trusts.

Section 3–913. [Distributions to Trustee.]

(a) Before distributing to a trustee, the personal representative may require that the trust be registered if the state in which it is to be administered provides for registration and that the trustee inform the beneficiaries as provided in Section 7–303.

(b) If the trust instrument does not excuse the trustee from giving bond, the personal representative may petition the appropriate Court to require that the trustee post bond if he apprehends that distribution might jeopardize the interests of persons who are not able to protect themselves, and he may withhold distribution until the Court has acted.

(c) No inference of negligence on the part of the personal representative shall be drawn from his failure to exercise the authority conferred by subsections (a) and (b).

COMMENT

This section is concerned with the fiduciary responsibility of the executor to beneficiaries of trusts to which he may deliver. Normally, the trustee represents beneficiaries in matters involving third persons, including prior fiduciaries. Yet, the executor may apprehend that delivery to the trustee may involve risks for the safety of the fund and for him. For example, he may be anxious to see that there is no equivocation about the devisee's willingness to accept the trust, and no problem of preserving evidence of the acceptance. He may have doubts about the integrity of the trustee, or about his ability to function satisfactorily. The testator's selection of the trustee may have been based on facts which are still current, or which are of doubtful relevance at the time of distribution. If the risks relate to the question of the trustee's intention to handle the fund without profit for himself, a conflict of interest problem is involved. If the risk relates to the ability of the trustee to manage prudently, a more troublesome question is posed for the executor. Is he, as executor, not bound to act in the best interests of the beneficiaries?

In many instances involving doubts of this sort, the executor probably will want the protection of a Court order. Sections 3–1001 and 3–1002 provide ample authority for an appropriate proceeding in the Court which issued the executor's letters.

In other cases, however, the executor may believe that he may be adequately protected if the acceptance of the trust by the devisee is unequivocal, or if the trustee is bonded. The purpose of this section is to make it clear that it is proper for the executor to require the trustee to register the trust and to notify beneficiaries before receiving distribution. Also, the section complements Section 7–304 by providing that the personal representative may petition an appropriate court to require that the trustee be bonded.

Status of testamentary trustees under the Uniform Probate Code. Under the Uniform Probate Code, the testamentary trustee by construction would be considered a devisee, distributee, and successor to whom title passes at time of the testator's death even though the will must be probated to prove the transfer. The informally probated will is conclusive until set aside and the personal representative may distribute to the trustee under the informally probated will or settlement agreement and the title of the trustee as distributee represented by the instrument or deed of distribution is conclusive until set aside on showing that it is improper. Should the informally probated will be set aside or the distribution to the trustee be shown to be improper, the trustee as distributee would be liable for value received but purchasers for value from the trustee as distributee under an instrument of distribution would be protected. Section 1–201's definition of "distributee" limits the distributee liability of the trustee and substitutes that of the trust beneficiaries to the extent of distributions by the trustee.

As a distributee as defined by 1–201, the testamentary trustee or beneficiary of a testamentary trust is liable to claimants like other distributees, would have the right of contribution from other distributees of the decedent's estate and would be protected by the same time limitations as other distributees (3–1006).

Incident to his standing as a distributee of the decedent's estate, the testamentary trustee would be an interested party who could petition for an order of complete settlement by the personal representative or for an order terminating testate administration. He also could appropriately receive the personal representative's account and distribution under a closing statement. As distributee he could represent his beneficiaries in compromise settlements in the decedent's estate which would be binding upon him and his beneficiaries. See Section 3–912.

The general fiduciary responsibilities of the testamentary trustee are not altered by the Uniform Probate Code and the trustee continues to have the duty to collect and reduce to possession within a reasonable time the assets of the trust estate including the enforcement of any claims on behalf of the trust against prior fiduciaries, including the personal representative, and third parties.

Section 3–914. [Disposition of Unclaimed Assets.]

(a) If an heir, devisee or claimant cannot be found, the personal representative shall distribute the share of the missing person to his conservator, if any, otherwise to the [state treasurer] to become a part of the [state escheat fund].

(b) The money received by [state treasurer] shall be paid to the person entitled on proof of his right thereto or, if the [state treasurer] refuses or fails to pay, the person may petition the Court which appointed the personal representative, whereupon the Court upon notice to the [state treasurer] may determine the person entitled to the money and order the [treasurer] to pay it to him. No interest is allowed thereon and the heir, devisee or claimant shall pay all costs and expenses incident to the proceeding. If no petition is made to the [court] within 8 years after payment to the [state treasurer], the right of recovery is barred.]

COMMENT

The foregoing section is bracketed to indicate that the National Conference does not urge the specific content as set forth above over recent comprehensive legislation on the subject which may have been enacted in an adopting state.

This section applies when it is believed that a claimant, heir or distributee exists but he cannot be located. See 2–105.

Section 3–915. [Distribution to Person Under Disability.]

(a) A personal representative may discharge his obligation to distribute to any person under legal disability by distributing in a manner expressly provided in the will.

(b) Unless contrary to an express provision in the will, the personal representative may discharge his obligation to distribute to a minor or person under other disability as authorized by Section 5–101 or any other statute. If the personal representative knows that a conservator has been appointed or that a proceeding for appointment of a conservator is pending, the personal representative is authorized to distribute only to the conservator.

(c) If the heir or devisee is under disability other than minority, the personal representative is authorized to distribute to:

(1) an attorney in fact who has authority under a power of attorney to receive property for that person; or

(2) the spouse, parent or other close relative with whom the person under disability resides if the distribution is of amounts not exceeding [$10,000] a year, or property not exceeding [$10,-000] in value, unless the court authorizes a larger amount or greater value.

Persons receiving money or property for the disabled person are obligated to apply the money or property to the support of that person, but may not pay themselves except by way of reimbursement for out-of-pocket expenses for goods and services necessary for the support of the disabled person. Excess sums must be preserved for future support of the disabled person. The personal representative is not responsible for the proper application of money or property distributed pursuant to this subsection.

COMMENT

Section 5–103 is especially important as a possible source of authority for a valid discharge for payment or distribution made on behalf of a minor.

Section 3–916. [Apportionment of Estate Taxes.]

(a) For purposes of this section:

(1) "estate" means the gross estate of a decedent as determined for the purpose of federal estate tax and the estate tax payable to this state;

(2) "person" means any individual, partnership, association, joint stock company, corporation, government, political subdivision, governmental agency, or local governmental agency;

(3) "person interested in the estate" means any person entitled to receive, or who has received, from a decedent or by reason of the death of a decedent any property or interest therein included in the decedent's estate. It includes a personal representative, conservator, and trustee;

(4) "state" means any state, territory, or possession of the United States, the District of Columbia, and the Commonwealth of Puerto Rico;

(5) "tax" means the federal estate tax and the additional inheritance tax imposed by _____ and interest and penalties imposed in addition to the tax;

(6) "fiduciary" means personal representative or trustee.

(b) Except as provided in subsection (i) and, unless the will otherwise provides, the tax shall be apportioned among all persons interested in the estate. The apportionment is to be made in the proportion that the value of the interest of each person interested in the estate bears to the total value of the interests of all persons interested in the estate. The values used in determining the tax are to be used for that purpose. If the decedent's will directs a method of apportionment of tax different from the method described in this Code, the method described in the will controls.

(c)(1) The Court in which venue lies for the administration of the estate of a decedent, on petition for the purpose may determine the apportionment of the tax.

(2) If the Court finds that it is inequitable to apportion interest and penalties in the manner provided in subsection (b), because of special circumstances, it may direct apportionment thereof in the manner it finds equitable.

(3) If the Court finds that the assessment of penalties and interest assessed in relation to the tax is due to delay caused by the negligence of the fiduciary, the Court may charge him with the amount of the assessed penalties and interest.

(4) In any action to recover from any person interested in the estate the amount of the tax apportioned to the person in accordance with this Code the determination of the Court in respect thereto shall be prima facie correct.

(d)(1) The personal representative or other person in possession of the property of the decedent required to pay the tax may withhold from any property distributable to any person interested in the estate, upon its distribution to him, the amount of tax attributable to his interest. If the property in possession of the personal representative or other person required to pay the tax and distributable to any person interested in the estate is insufficient to satisfy the proportionate amount of the tax determined to be due from the person, the personal representative or other person required to pay the tax may recover the deficiency from the person interested in the estate. If the property is not in the possession of the personal representative or the other person required to pay the tax, the personal representative or the other person required to pay the tax may recover from any person interested in the estate the amount of the tax apportioned to the person in accordance with this Act.

(2) If property held by the personal representative is distributed prior to final apportionment of the tax, the distributee shall provide a bond or other security for the apportionment liability in the form and amount prescribed by the personal representative.

(e)(1) In making an apportionment, allowances shall be made for any exemptions granted, any classification made of persons interested in the estate and for any deductions and credits allowed by the law imposing the tax.

(2) Any exemption or deduction allowed by reason of the relationship of any person to the decedent or by reason of the purposes of the gift inures to the benefit of the person bearing such relationship or receiving the gift; but if an interest is subject to a prior present interest which is not allowable as a deduction, the tax apportionable against the present interest shall be paid from principal.

(3) Any deduction for property previously taxed and any credit for gift taxes or death taxes of a foreign country paid by the decedent or his estate inures to the proportionate benefit of all persons liable to apportionment.

(4) Any credit for inheritance, succession or estate taxes or taxes in the nature thereof applicable to property or interests includable in the estate, inures to the benefit of the persons or interests chargeable with the payment thereof to the extent proportionately that the credit reduces the tax.

(5) To the extent that property passing to or in trust for a surviving spouse or any charitable, public or similar purpose is not an allowable deduction for purposes of the tax solely by reason of an inheritance tax or other death tax imposed upon and deductible from the property, the property is not included in the computation provided for in subsection (b) hereof, and to that extent no apportionment is made against the property. The sentence immediately preceding does not apply to any case

if the result would be to deprive the estate of a deduction otherwise allowable under Section 2053(d) of the Internal Revenue Code of 1954, as amended, of the United States, relating to deduction for state death taxes on transfers for public, charitable, or religious uses.

(f) No interest in income and no estate for years or for life or other temporary interest in any property or fund is subject to apportionment as between the temporary interest and the remainder. The tax on the temporary interest and the tax, if any, on the remainder is chargeable against the corpus of the property or funds subject to the temporary interest and remainder.

(g) Neither the personal representative nor other person required to pay the tax is under any duty to institute any action to recover from any person interested in the estate the amount of the tax apportioned to the person until the expiration of the 3 months next following final determination of the tax. A personal representative or other person required to pay the tax who institutes the action within a reasonable time after the 3 months' period is not subject to any liability or surcharge because any portion of the tax apportioned to any person interested in the estate was collectible at a time following the death of the decedent but thereafter became uncollectible. If the personal representative or other person required to pay the tax cannot collect from any person interested in the estate the amount of the tax apportioned to the person, the amount not recoverable shall be equitably apportioned among the other persons interested in the estate who are subject to apportionment.

(h) A personal representative acting in another state or a person required to pay the tax domiciled in another state may institute an action in the courts of this state and may recover a proportionate amount of the federal estate tax, of an estate tax payable to another state or of a death duty due by a decedent's estate to another state, from a person interested in the estate who is either domiciled in this state or who owns property in this state subject to attachment or execution. For the purposes of the action the determination of apportionment by the Court having jurisdiction of the administration of the decedent's estate in the other state is prima facie correct.

(i) If the liabilities of persons interested in the estate as prescribed by this act differ from those which result under the Federal Estate tax law, the liabilities imposed by the federal law will control and the balance of this Section shall apply as if the resulting liabilities had been prescribed herein.

COMMENT

Section 3–916 copies the Uniform Estate Tax Apportionment Act.

PART 10

CLOSING ESTATES

Section 3–1001. [Formal Proceedings Terminating Administration; Testate or Intestate; Order of General Protection.]

(a) A personal representative or any interested person may petition for an order of complete settlement of the estate. The personal representative may petition at any time, and any other interested person may petition after one year from the appointment of the original personal representative except that no petition under this section may be entertained until the time for presenting claims which arose prior to the death of the decedent has expired. The petition may request the Court to determine testacy, if not previously determined, to consider the final account or compel or approve an accounting and distribution, to construe any will or determine heirs and adjudicate the final settlement and distribution of the estate. After notice to all interested persons and hearing the Court may enter an order or orders, on appropriate conditions, determining the persons entitled to distribution of the estate, and, as circumstances require, approving settlement and directing or approving distribution of the estate and discharging the personal representative from further claim or demand of any interested person.

(b) If one or more heirs or devisees were omitted as parties in, or were not given notice of, a previous formal testacy proceeding, the Court, on proper petition for an order of complete settlement of the estate under this section, and after notice to the omitted or unnotified persons and other interested parties determined to be interested on the assumption that the previous order concerning testacy is conclusive as to those given notice of the earlier proceeding, may determine testacy as it affects the omitted persons and confirm or alter the previous order of testacy as it affects all interested persons as appropriate in the light of the new proofs. In the absence of objection by an omitted or unnotified person, evidence received in the original testacy proceeding shall constitute prima facie proof of due execution of any will previously admitted to probate, or of the fact that the decedent left no valid will if the prior proceedings determined this fact.

COMMENT

Subsection (b) is derived from § 64(b) of the Illinois Probate Act (1967) [S.H.A. ch. 3, § 64(b)]. Section 3–106 specifies that an order is binding as to all who are given notice even though less than all interested persons were notified. This section provides a method of curing an oversight in regard to notice which may come to light before the estate is finally settled. If the person who failed to receive notice of the earlier proceeding succeeds in obtaining entry of a different order from that previously made, others who received notice of the earlier proceeding may be benefitted. Still, they are not entitled to notice of the curative proceeding, nor should they be permitted to appear.

See, also, Comment following section 3–1002.

Section 3–1002. [Formal Proceedings Terminating Testate Administration; Order Construing Will Without Adjudicating Testacy.]

A personal representative administering an estate under an informally probated will or any devisee under an informally probated will may petition for an order of settlement of the estate which will not adjudicate the testacy status of the decedent. The personal representative may petition at any time, and a devisee may petition after one year, from the appointment of the original personal representative, except that no petition under this section may be entertained until the time for presenting claims which arose prior to the death of the decedent has expired. The petition may request the Court to consider the final account or compel or approve an accounting and distribution, to construe the will and adjudicate final settlement and distribution of the estate. After notice to all devisees and the personal representative and hearing, the Court may enter an order or orders, on appropriate conditions, determining the persons entitled to distribution of the estate under the will, and, as circumstances require, approving settlement and directing or approving distribution of the estate and discharging the personal representative from further claim or demand of any devisee who is a party to the proceeding and those he represents. If it appears that a part of the estate is intestate, the proceedings shall be dismissed or amendments made to meet the provisions of Section 3–1001.

COMMENT

Section 3–1002 permits a final determination of the rights between each other and against the personal representative of the devisees under a will when there has been no formal proceeding in regard to testacy.

Hence, the heirs in intestacy need not be made parties. Section 3-1001 permits a final determination of the rights between each other and against the personal representative of all persons interested in an estate. If supervised administra-tion is used, Section 3-505 directs that the estate be closed by use of procedures like those described in Section 3-1001. Of course, testacy will have been adjudicated before time for the closing proceeding if supervised administration is used.

Section 3-1003. [Closing Estates; By Sworn Statement of Personal Representative.]

(a) Unless prohibited by order of the Court and except for estates being administered in supervised administration proceedings, a personal representative may close an estate by filing with the court no earlier than six months after the date of original appointment of a general personal representative for the estate, a verified statement stating that the personal representatives or a previous personal representative, has:

(1) determined that the time limited for presentation of creditors' claims has expired.

(2) fully administered the estate of the decedent by making payment, settlement, or other disposition of all claims that were presented, expenses of administration and estate, inheritance and other death taxes, except as specified in the statement, and that the assets of the estate have been distributed to the persons entitled. If any claims remain undischarged, the statement must state whether the personal representative has distributed the estate subject to possible liability with the agreement of the distributees or state in detail other arrangements that have been made to accommodate outstanding liabilities; and

(3) sent a copy of the statement to all distributees of the estate and to all creditors or other claimants of whom the personal representative is aware whose claims are neither paid nor barred and has furnished a full account in writing of the personal representative's administration to the distributees whose interests are affected thereby.

(b) If no proceedings involving the personal representative are pending in the Court one year after the closing statement is filed, the appointment of the personal representative terminates.

COMMENT

The Code uses "termination" to refer to events which end a personal representative's authority. See

Sections 3–608, et seq. The word "closing" refers to circumstances which support the conclusions that the affairs of the estate either are, or have been alleged to have been, wound up. If the affairs of the personal representative are reviewed and adjudicated under either Sections 3–1001 or 3–1002, the judicial conclusion that the estate is wound up serves also to terminate the personal representative's authority. See Section 3–610(b). On the other hand, a "closing" statement under 3–1003 is only an affirmation by the personal representative that he believes the affairs of the estate to be completed. The statement is significant because it reflects that assets have been distributed. Any creditor whose claim has not been barred and who has not been paid is permitted by Section 3–1004 to assert his claim against distributees. The personal representative is also still fully subject to suit under Sections 3–602 and 3–608, for his authority is not "terminated" under Section 3–610(a) until one year after a closing statement is filed. Even if his authority is "terminated," he remains liable to suit unless protected by limitation or unless an adjudication settling his accounts is the reason for "termination". See Sections 3–1005 and 3–608.

From a slightly different viewpoint, a personal representative may obtain a complete discharge of his fiduciary obligations through a judicial proceeding after notice. Sections 3–1001 and 3–1002 describe two proceedings which enable a personal representative to gain protection from all persons or from devisees only. A personal representative who neither obtains a judicial order of protection nor files a closing statement, is protected by 3–703 in regard to acts or distributions which were authorized when done but which become doubtful thereafter because of a change in testacy status. On the other questions, the personal representative who does not take any of the steps described by the Code to gain more protection, has no protection against later claims of breach of his fiduciary obligation other than any arising from consent or waiver of individual distributees who may have bound themselves by receipts given to the personal representative.

This section increases the prospects of full discharge of a personal representative who uses the closing statement route over those of a personal representative who relies on receipts. Full protection follows from the running of the six months limitations period described in 3–1005. But, 3–1005's protection does not prevent distributees from claiming lack of full disclosure. Hence, it offers little more protection than a receipt. Still, it may be useful to decrease the likelihood of later claim of non-disclosure. Its more significant function, however, is to provide a means for terminating the office of personal representative in a way that will be obvious to third persons.

In 1989 the Joint Editorial Board recommended changing subparagraph (a)(1) to make the time reference correspond to changes recommended for Section 3–803.

Section 3–1004. [Liability of Distributees to Claimants.]

After assets of an estate have been distributed and subject to Section 3–1006, an undischarged claim not barred may be prosecuted in a proceeding against one or more distributees. No distributee shall be liable to claimants for amounts received as exempt property, homestead or family allowances, or for amounts in excess of the value of his distribution as of the time of distribution. As between distributees, each shall bear the cost of satisfaction of unbarred claims as if the claim had been satisfied in the course of administration. Any distributee who shall have failed to notify other distributees of the demand made upon him by the claimant in sufficient time to permit them to join in any proceeding in which the claim was asserted against him loses his right of contribution against other distributees.

COMMENT

This section creates a ceiling on the liability of a distributee of "the value of his distribution" as of the time of distribution. The section indicates that each distributee is liable for all that a claimant may prove to be due, provided the claim does not exceed the value of the defendant's distribution from the estate. But, each distributee may preserve a right of contribution against other distributees. The risk of insolvency of one or more, but less than all distributees is on the distributee rather than on the claimant.

In 1975, the Joint Editorial Board recommended the addition, after "claimants for amounts" in the second sentence, of "received as exempt property, homestead or family allowances, or for amounts . . ." The purpose of the addition was to prevent unpaid creditors of a decedent from attempting to enforce their claims against a spouse or child who had received a distribution of exempt values.

Section 3–1005. [Limitations on Proceedings Against Personal Representative.]

Unless previously barred by adjudication and except as provided in the closing statement, the rights of successors and of creditors whose claims have not otherwise been barred against the personal representative for breach of fiduciary duty are barred unless a proceeding to assert the same is commenced within 6 months after the filing of the closing statement. The rights thus barred do not include rights to recover from a personal representative for fraud, misrepresentation, or inadequate disclosure related to the settlement of the decedent's estate.

COMMENT

This and the preceding section make it clear that a claimant whose claim has not been barred may have alternative remedies when an estate has been distributed subject to his claim. Under this section, he has six months to prosecute an action against the personal representative if the latter breached any duty to the claimant. For example, the personal representative may be liable to a creditor if he violated the provisions of Section 3–807. The preceding section describes the fundamental liability of the distributees to unbarred claimants to the extent of the value received. The last sentence emphasizes that a personal representative who fails to disclose matters relevant to his liability in his closing statement and in the account of administration he furnished to distributees, gains no protection from the period described here. A personal representative may, however, use Section 3–1001, or, where appropriate, 3–1002 to secure greater protection.

Section 3–1006. [Limitations on Actions and Proceedings Against Distributees.]

Unless previously adjudicated in a formal testacy proceeding or in a proceeding settling the accounts of a personal representative or otherwise barred, the claim of a claimant to recover from a distributee who is liable to pay the claim, and the right of an heir or devisee, or of a successor personal representative acting in their behalf, to recover property improperly distributed or its value from any distributee is forever barred at the later of three years after the decedent's death or one year after the time of its distribution thereof, but all claims of creditors of the decedent, are barred one year after the decedent's death. This section does not bar an action to recover property or value received as a result of fraud.

COMMENT

This section describes an ultimate time limit for recovery by creditors, heirs and devisees of a decedent from distributees. It is to be noted: (1) Section 3–108 imposes a general limit of three years from death on one who must set aside an informal probate in order to establish his rights, or who must secure probate of a late-discovered will after an estate has been administered as intestate. Hence the time limit of 3–108 may bar one who would claim as an heir or devisee sooner than this section, although it would never cause a bar prior to three years from the decedent's death. (2) This section would not bar recovery by a supposed decedent whose estate has been probated. See Section 3–412. (3) The limitation of this section ends the possibility of appointment of a personal representative to correct an erroneous distribution as mentioned in Sections 3–1005 and 3–1008. If there have been no adjudications under Section 3–409, or possibly 3–1001 or 3–1002, estate of the decedent which is discovered after administration has been closed may be the subject of different distribution than that attending the estate originally administered.

The last sentence excepting actions or suits to recover property kept from one by the fraud of another may be unnecessary in view of the blanket provision concerning fraud in Article I. See Section 1–106.

In 1989, the Joint Editorial Board recommended changing the section so as to separate proceedings involving claims by claimants barred one year after decedent's death by Section 3–803(a)(1), and other proceedings by unbarred claimants or by omitted heirs or devisees.

Section 3–1007. [Certificate Discharging Liens Securing Fiduciary Performance.]

After his appointment has terminated, the personal representative, his sureties, or any successor of either, upon the filing of a verified application showing, so far as is known by the applicant, that no action concerning the estate is pending in any court, is entitled to receive a certificate from the Registrar that the personal representative appears to have fully administered the estate in question. The certificate evidences discharge of any lien on any property given to secure the obligation of the personal representative in lieu of bond or any surety, but does not preclude action against the personal representative or the surety.

COMMENT

This section does not affect the liability of the personal representative, or of any surety, but merely permits a release of security given by a personal representative, or his surety, when, from the passage of time and other conditions, it seems highly unlikely that there will be any liability remaining undischarged. See Section 3–607.

Section 3–1008. [Subsequent Administration.]

If other property of the estate is discovered after an estate has been settled and the personal representative discharged or after one year after a closing statement has been filed, the Court upon petition of any interested person and upon notice as it directs may appoint the same or a successor personal representative to administer the subsequently discovered estate. If a new appointment is made, unless the Court orders otherwise, the provisions of this Code apply as appropriate; but no claim previously barred may be asserted in the subsequent administration.

COMMENT

This section is consistent with Section 3–108 which provides a general period of limitations of three years from death for appointment proceedings, but makes appropriate exception for subsequent administrations.

PART 11

COMPROMISE OF CONTROVERSIES

Section 3–1101. [Effect of Approval of Agreements Involving Trusts, Inalienable Interests, or Interests of Third Persons.]

A compromise of any controversy as to admission to probate of any instrument offered for formal probate as the will of a decedent, the construction, validity, or effect of any governing instrument, the rights or interests in the estate of the decedent, of any successor, or the administration of the estate, if approved in a formal proceeding in the Court for that purpose, is binding on all the parties thereto including those unborn, unascertained or who could not be located. An approved compromise is binding even though it may affect a trust or an inalienable interest. A compromise does not impair the rights of creditors or of taxing authorities who are not parties to it.

COMMENT

1993 technical amendments to this and the following section clarified original intention that the described procedure would be available to resolve controversies other than those concerning a will.

Section 3–1102. [Procedure for Securing Court Approval of Compromise.]

The procedure for securing court approval of a compromise is as follows:

(1) The terms of the compromise shall be set forth in an agreement in writing which shall be executed by all competent persons and parents acting for any minor child having beneficial interests or having claims which will or may be affected by the compromise. Execution is not required by any person whose identity cannot be ascertained or whose whereabouts is unknown and cannot reasonably be ascertained.

(2) Any interested person, including the personal representative, if any, or a trustee, then may submit the agreement to the Court for its approval and for execution by the personal representative, the trustee of every affected testamentary trust, and other fiduciaries and representatives.

378

(3) After notice to all interested persons or their representatives, including the personal representative of any estate and all affected trustees of trusts, the Court, if it finds that the contest or controversy is in good faith and that the effect of the agreement upon the interests of persons represented by fiduciaries or other representatives is just and reasonable, shall make an order approving the agreement and directing all fiduciaries subject to its jurisdiction to execute the agreement. Minor children represented only by their parents may be bound only if their parents join with other competent persons in execution of the compromise. Upon the making of the order and the execution of the agreement, all further disposition of the estate is in accordance with the terms of the agreement.

COMMENT

This section and the one preceding it outline a procedure which may be initiated by competent parties having beneficial interests in a decedent's estate as a means of resolving controversy concerning the estate. If all competent persons with beneficial interests or claims which might be affected by the proposal and parents *properly* representing interests of their children concur, a settlement scheme differing from that otherwise governing the devolution may be substituted. The procedure for securing representation of minors and unknown or missing persons with interests must be followed. See Section 1–403. The ultimate control of the question of whether the substitute proposal shall be accepted is with the court which must find: "that the contest or controversy is in good faith and that the effect of the agreement upon the interests of parties represented by fiduciaries is just and reasonable."

The thrust of the procedure is to put the authority for initiating settlement proposals with the persons who have beneficial interests in the estate, and to prevent executors and testamentary trustees from vetoing any such proposal. The only reason for approving a scheme of devolution which differs from that framed by the testator or the statutes governing intestacy is to prevent dissipation of the estate in wasteful litigation. Because executors and trustees may have an interest in fees and commissions which they might earn through efforts to carry out testator's intention, the judgment of the court is substituted for that of such fiduciaries in appropriate cases. A controversy which the court may find to be in good faith, as well as concurrence of all beneficially interested and competent persons and parent-representatives provide prerequisites which should prevent the procedure from being abused. Thus, the procedure does not threaten the planning of a testator who plans and drafts with sufficient clarity and completeness to eliminate the possibility of good faith controversy concerning the meaning and legality of his plan.

See Section 1–403 for rules governing representatives and appointment of guardians ad litem.

These sections are modeled after Section 93 of the Model Probate Code. Comparable legislative provisions have proved quite useful in Michigan. See M.C.L.A. §§ 702.45–702.49.

PART 12

COLLECTION OF PERSONAL PROPERTY BY AFFIDAVIT AND SUMMARY ADMINISTRATION PROCEDURE FOR SMALL ESTATES

GENERAL COMMENT

The four sections which follow include two designed to facilitate transfer of small estates without use of a personal representative, and two designed to simplify the duties of a personal representative, who is appointed to handle a small estate.

The Flexible System of Administration described by earlier portions of Article III lends itself well to situations involving small estates. Letters may be obtained quickly without notice or judicial involvement. Immediately, the personal representative is in a position to distribute to successors whose deeds or transfers will protect purchasers. This route accommodates the need for quick and inexpensive transfers of land of small value as well as other assets. Consequently, it was unnecessary to frame complex provisions extending the affidavit procedures to land.

Indeed, transfers via letters of administration may prove to be less troublesome than use of the affidavit procedure. Still, it seemed desirable to provide a quick collection mechanism which avoids all necessity to visit the probate court. For one thing, unpredictable local variations in probate practice may produce situations where the alternative procedure will be very useful. For another, the provision of alternatives is in line with the overall philosophy of Article III to provide maximum flexibility.

Figures gleaned from a recent authoritative report of a major survey of probated estates in Cleveland, Ohio, demonstrate that more than one-half of all estates in probate had a gross value of less than $15,000. This means that the principal measure of the relevance of any legislation dealing with probate procedures is to be found in its impact on very small and moderate sized estates. Here is the area where probate affects most people.

Section 3–1201. [Collection of Personal Property by Affidavit.]

(a) Thirty days after the death of a decedent, any person indebted to the decedent or having possession of tangible personal property or an instrument evidencing a debt, obligation, stock or chose in action belonging to the decedent shall make payment of the indebtedness or deliver the tangible personal property or an instrument evidencing a debt, obligation, stock or chose in action to a person claiming to be the successor of the decedent upon being presented an affidavit made by or on behalf of the successor stating that:

(1) the value of the entire estate, wherever located, less liens and encumbrances, does not exceed $5,000;

(2) 30 days have elapsed since the death of the decedent;

(3) no application or petition for the appointment of a personal representative is pending or has been granted in any jurisdiction; and

(4) the claiming successor is entitled to payment or delivery of the property.

(b) A transfer agent of any security shall change the registered ownership on the books of a corporation from the decedent to the successor or successors upon the presentation of an affidavit as provided in subsection (a).

COMMENT

This section provides for an easy method for collecting the personal property of a decedent by affidavit prior to any formal disposition. Existing legislation generally permits the surviving widow or children to collect wages and other small amounts of liquid funds. Section 3–1201 goes further in that it allows the collection of personal property as well as money and permits any devisee or heir to make the collection. Since the appointment of a personal representative may be obtained easily under the Code, it is unnecessary to make the provisions regarding small estates applicable to realty.

Section 3–1202. [Effect of Affidavit.]

The person paying, delivering, transferring, or issuing personal property or the evidence thereof pursuant to affidavit is discharged and released to the same extent as if he dealt with a personal representative of the decedent. He is not required to see to the application of the personal property or evidence thereof or to inquire into the truth of any statement in the affidavit. If any person to whom an affidavit is delivered refuses to pay, deliver, transfer, or issue any personal property or evidence thereof, it may be recovered or its payment, delivery, transfer, or issuance compelled upon proof of their right in a proceeding brought for the purpose by or on behalf of the persons entitled thereto. Any person to whom payment, delivery, transfer or issuance is made is answerable and accountable therefor to any personal representative of the estate or to any other person having a superior right.

COMMENT

Sections 3–1201 and 3–1202 apply to any personal property located in this state whether or not the decedent died domiciled in this state, to any successor to personal property located in this state whether or not a resident of this state, and, to the extent that the laws of this state may control the succession to personal property, to personal property wherever located of a decedent who died domiciled in this state.

Section 3–1203. [Small Estates; Summary Administration Procedure.]

If it appears from the inventory and appraisal that the value of the entire estate, less liens and encumbrances, does not exceed homestead allowance, exempt property, family allowance, costs and expenses of administration, reasonable funeral expenses, and reasonable and necessary medical and hospital expenses of the last illness of the decedent, the personal representative, without giving notice to creditors, may immediately disburse and distribute the estate to the persons entitled thereto and file a closing statement as provided in Section 3–1204.

COMMENT

This section makes it possible for the personal representative to make a summary distribution of a small estate without the necessity of giving notice to creditors. Since the probate estate of many decedents will not exceed the amount specified in the statute, this section will prove useful in many estates.

Section 3–1204. [Small Estates; Closing by Sworn Statement of Personal Representative.]

(a) Unless prohibited by order of the Court and except for estates being administered by supervised personal representatives, a personal representative may close an estate administered under the summary procedures of Section 3–1203 by filing with the Court, at any time after disbursement and distribution of the estate, a verified statement stating that:

(1) to the best knowledge of the personal representative, the value of the entire estate, less liens and encumbrances, did not exceed homestead allowance, exempt property, family allowance, costs and expenses of administration, reasonable funeral expenses, and reasonable, necessary medical and hospital expenses of the last illness of the decedent;

383

(2) the personal representative has fully administered the estate by disbursing and distributing it to the persons entitled thereto; and

(3) the personal representative has sent a copy of the closing statement to all distributees of the estate and to all creditors or other claimants of whom he is aware whose claims are neither paid nor barred and has furnished a full account in writing of his administration to the distributees whose interests are affected.

(b) If no actions or proceedings involving the personal representative are pending in the Court one year after the closing statement is filed, the appointment of the personal representative terminates.

(c) A closing statement filed under this section has the same effect as one filed under Section 3–1003.

COMMENT

The personal representative may elect to close the estate under Section 3–1002 in order to secure the greater protection offered by that procedure.

The remedies for fraudulent statement provided in Section 1–106 of course would apply to any intentional misstatements by a personal representative.

ARTICLE IV

FOREIGN PERSONAL REPRESENTATIVES; ANCILLARY ADMINISTRATION

PART 1

DEFINITIONS

PART 2

POWERS OF FOREIGN PERSONAL REPRESENTATIVES

PART 3

JURISDICTION OVER FOREIGN REPRESENTATIVES

PART 4

JUDGMENTS AND PERSONAL REPRESENTATIVE

GENERAL COMMENT

This Article concerns the law applicable in estate problems which involve more than a single state. It covers the powers and responsibilities in the adopting state of personal representatives appointed in other states.

Some provisions of the Code covering local appointment of personal representatives for non-residents appear in Article III. These include the following: 3–201 (venue), 3–202 (resolution of conflicting claims regarding domicile), 3–203 (priority as personal representative of representative previously appointed at domicile), 3–307(a) (30 days delay required before appointment of a local representative for a non-resident), 3–803(a) (claims barred by non-claim at domicile before local administration commenced are barred locally) and 3–815 (duty of personal representative in regard to claims where estate is being administered in more than one state). See also 3–308, 3–611(a) and 3–816. Also, see Section 4–207.

The recognition provisions contained in Article IV and the various provisions of Article III which relate to administration of estates of non-residents are designed to coerce respect for domiciliary procedures and administrative acts to the extent possible.

The first part of Article IV contains some definitions of particular relevance to estates located in two or more states.

The second part of Article IV deals with the powers of foreign personal representatives in a jurisdiction adopting the Uniform Probate Code. There are different types of power which may be exercised. First, a foreign personal representative has the power under Section 4–201 to receive payments of debts owed to the decedent or to accept delivery of property belonging to the decedent. The foreign personal representative provides an affidavit indicating the date of death of the non-resident decedent, that no local administration has been commenced and that the foreign personal representative is entitled to payment or delivery. Payment under this provision can be made any time more than 60 days after the death of the decedent. When made in good faith the payment operates as a discharge of the debtor. A protection for local creditors of the decedent is provided in Section 4–203, under which local debtors of the non-resident decedent can be notified of the claims which local creditors have against the estate. This notification will prevent payment under this provision.

A second type of power is provided in Sections 4–204 to 4–206. Under these provisions a foreign personal representative can file with the appropriate court a copy of his appointment and official bond if he has one. Upon so filing, the foreign personal representative has all of the powers of a personal representative appointed by the local court. This would be all of the powers provided for in an unsupervised administration as provided in Article III of the Code.

The third type of power which may be obtained by a foreign personal representative is conferred by the priority the domiciliary personal representative enjoys in respect to local appointment. This is covered by Section 3–203. Also, see Section 3.611(b).

Part 3 provides for power in the local court over foreign personal representatives who act locally. If a local or ancillary administration has been started, provisions in Article III subject the appointee to the power of the court. See Section 3–602. In Part 3 of this Article, it is provided that a foreign personal representative submits himself to the jurisdiction of the local court by filing a copy of his appointment to get the powers provided in Section 4–205 or by doing any act which would give the state jurisdiction over him as an individual. In addition, the collection of funds as provided in Section 4–201 gives the court quasi-in-rem jurisdiction over the foreign personal representative to the extent of the funds collected.

Finally, Section 4–303 provides that the foreign personal representative is subject to the jurisdiction of the local court "to the same extent that his decedent was subject to jurisdiction immediately prior to death." This is similar to the typical non-resident motorist provision that provides for jurisdiction over the personal representative of a deceased non-resident motorist, see Note, 44 Iowa L.Rev. 384 (1959). It is, however, a much broader provision. Section 4–304 provides for the mechanical steps to be taken in serving the foreign personal representatives.

Part 4 of the Article deals with the res judicata effect to be given adjudications for or against a foreign personal representative. Any such adjudication is to be conclusive on a local personal representative "unless it resulted from fraud or collusion ... to the prejudice of the estate." This provision must be read with Section 3–408 which deals with certain out-of-state findings concerning a decedent's estate.

PART 1

DEFINITIONS

Section 4–101. [Definitions.]

In this Article

(1) "local administration" means administration by a personal representative appointed in this state pursuant to appointment proceedings described in Article III.

(2) "local personal representative" includes any personal representative appointed in this state pursuant to appointment proceedings described in Article III and excludes foreign personal representatives who acquire the power of a local personal representative pursuant to Section 4–205.

(3) "resident creditor" means a person domiciled in, or doing business in this state, who is, or could be, a claimant against an estate of a non-resident decedent.

COMMENT

Section 1–201 includes definitions of "foreign personal representative", "personal representative" and "non-resident decedent".

PART 2

POWERS OF FOREIGN PERSONAL
REPRESENTATIVES

Section 4–201. [Payment of Debt and Delivery of Property to Domiciliary Foreign Personal Representative Without Local Administration.]

At any time after the expiration of sixty days from the death of a nonresident decedent, any person indebted to the estate of the nonresident decedent or having possession or control of personal property, or of an instrument evidencing a debt, obligation, stock or chose in action belonging to the estate of the nonresident decedent may pay the debt, deliver the personal property, or the instrument evidencing the debt, obligation, stock or chose in action, to the domiciliary foreign personal representative of the nonresident decedent upon being presented with proof of his appointment and an affidavit made by or on behalf of the representative stating:

(1) the date of the death of the nonresident decedent,

(2) that no local administration, or application or petition therefor, is pending in this state,

(3) that the domiciliary foreign personal representative is entitled to payment or delivery.

COMMENT

Section 3–201(d) refers to the location of tangible personal estate and intangible personal estate which may be evidenced by an instrument. The instant section includes both categories. Transfer of securities is not covered by this section since that is adequately covered by Section 3 of the Uniform Act for Simplification of Fiduciary Security Transfers.

Section 4–202. [Payment or Delivery Discharges.]

Payment or delivery made in good faith on the basis of the proof of authority and affidavit releases the debtor or person having possession of the personal property to the same extent as if payment or delivery had been made to a local personal representative.

Section 4–203. [Resident Creditor Notice.]

Payment or delivery under Section 4–201 may not be made if a resident creditor of the nonresident decedent has notified the debtor of the nonresident decedent or the person having possession of the personal property belonging to the nonresident decedent that the debt should not be paid nor the property delivered to the domiciliary foreign personal representative.

COMMENT

Similar to provision in Colorado Revised Statute, 153–6–9.

Section 4–204. [Proof of Authority–Bond.]

If no local administration or application or petition therefor is pending in this state, a domiciliary foreign personal representative may file with a Court in this State in a [county] in which property belonging to the decedent is located, authenticated copies of his appointment and of any official bond he has given.

Section 4–205. [Powers.]

A domiciliary foreign personal representative who has complied with Section 4–204 may exercise as to assets in this state all powers of a local personal representative and may maintain actions and proceedings in this state subject to any conditions imposed upon nonresident parties generally.

Section 4–206. [Power of Representatives in Transition.]

The power of a domiciliary foreign personal representative under Section 4–201 or 4–205 shall be exercised only if there is no administration or application therefor pending in this state. An application or petition for local administration of the estate terminates the power of the foreign personal representative to act under Section 4–205, but the local Court may allow the foreign personal representative to exercise limited powers to preserve the estate. No person who, before receiving actual notice of a pending local administration, has changed his position in reliance upon the powers of a foreign personal representative shall be prejudiced by reason of the application or petition for, or grant of, local administration. The local personal representative is subject to all duties and obligations which have accrued by virtue of the exercise of the powers by the foreign personal representative and may be substituted for him in any action or proceedings in this state.

Section 4–207. [Ancillary and Other Local Administrations; Provisions Governing.]

In respect to a nonresident decedent, the provisions of Article III of this Code govern (1) proceedings, if any, in a Court of this state for probate of the will, appointment, removal, supervision, and discharge of the local personal representative, and any other order concerning the estate; and (2) the status, powers, duties and liabilities of any local personal representative and the rights of claimants, purchasers, distributees and others in regard to a local administration.

COMMENT

The purpose of this section is to direct attention to Article III for sections controlling local probates and administrations. See in particular, 1–301, 3–201, 3–202, 3–203, 3–307(a), 3–308, 3–611(b), 3–803(a), 3–815 and 3–816.

PART 3

JURISDICTION OVER FOREIGN REPRESENTATIVES

Section 4–301. [Jurisdiction by Act of Foreign Personal Representative.]

A foreign personal representative submits personally to the jurisdiction of the Courts of this state in any proceeding relating to the estate by (1) filing authenticated copies of his appointment as provided in Section 4–204, (2) receiving payment of money or taking delivery of personal property under Section 4–201, or (3) doing any act as a personal representative in this state which would have given the state jurisdiction over him as an individual. Jurisdiction under (2) is limited to the money or value of personal property collected.

COMMENT

The words "courts of this state" are sufficient under federal legislation to include a federal court having jurisdiction in the adopting state.

A foreign personal representative appointed at the decedent's domicile has priority for appointment in any local administration proceeding. See Section 3–203(g). Once appointed, a local personal representative remains subject to the jurisdiction of the appointing court under Section 3–602.

In 1975, the Joint Editorial Board recommended substitution of the word "personally" for "himself", in the preliminary language of the first sentence. Also, language restricting the submission to jurisdiction to cases involving the estate was added in 1975.

Section 4–302. [Jurisdiction by Act of Decedent.]

In addition to jurisdiction conferred by Section 4–301, a foreign personal representative is subject to the jurisdiction of the courts of this state to the same extent that his decedent was subject to jurisdiction immediately prior to death.

Section 4–303. [Service on Foreign Personal Representative.]

(a) Service of process may be made upon the foreign personal representative by registered or certified mail, addressed to his last reasonably ascertainable address, requesting a return receipt signed by addressee only. Notice by ordinary first class mail is sufficient

392

if registered or certified mail service to the addressee is unavailable. Service may be made upon a foreign personal representative in the manner in which service could have been made under other laws of this state on either the foreign personal representative or his decedent immediately prior to death.

(b) If service is made upon a foreign personal representative as provided in subsection (a), he shall be allowed at least [30] days within which to appear or respond.

COMMENT

The provision for ordinary mail as a substitute for registered or certified mail is provided because, under the present postal regulations, registered mail may not be available to reach certain addresses, 39 C.F.R. Sec. 51.3(c), and also certified mail may not be available as a process for service because of the method of delivery used, 39 C.F.R. Sec. 58.5(c) (rural delivery) and (d) (star route delivery.)

PART 4

JUDGMENTS AND PERSONAL REPRESENTATIVE

Section 4–401. [Effect of Adjudication for or Against Personal Representative.]

An adjudication rendered in any jurisdiction in favor of or against any personal representative of the estate is as binding on the local personal representative as if he were a party to the adjudication.

COMMENT

Adapted from Uniform Ancillary Administration of Estates Act, Section 8.

ARTICLE V

PROTECTION OF PERSONS UNDER DISABILITY AND THEIR PROPERTY

PART 1

GENERAL PROVISIONS AND DEFINITIONS

PART 2

GUARDIANS OF MINORS

PART 3

GUARDIANS OF INCAPACITATED PERSONS

Adoption of Uniform Guardianship and Protective Proceedings Act

In 1982, the National Conference of Commissioners on Uniform State Laws adopted the Uniform Guardianship and Protective Proceedings Act. The Act was designed to be either a separate, free-standing act or to be integrated into the Uniform Probate Code by amendments to Article V, Parts 1, 2, 3 and 4 thereof (see Prefatory Note, infra.).

PREFATORY NOTE

The Uniform Guardianship and Protective Proceedings Act is the product of a continuing review and study of laws in the area of probate matters by the National Conference of Commissioners on Uniform State Laws. In 1969, the National Conference adopted and promulgated the Uniform Probate Code. Since that time, various amendments and additions to the Uniform Probate Code have been adopted and promulgated.

Article V, Parts 1, 2, 3 and 4 of the original Uniform Probate Code cover guardianships for minors, guardianships for reasons other than minority, and protective proceedings seeking court-appointed conservators or other protective orders for the estate concerns of minors, adult incompetents, absentees and others. The following new provisions expand and extend Article V, Parts 1, 2, 3, and 4 of the original Uniform Probate Code to include the concept of "limited guardianships."

The impetus for adding a "limited guardianship" concept to the guardianship and conservator provisions of the Uniform Probate Code grew out of the recommendations of an American Bar Association project, the ABA Commission on the Mentally Disabled, which, in relation to guardianship other than for minors, recommended that state laws be changed to avoid an asserted "overkill" implicit in standard guardianship proceedings. In part, this occurs, it was asserted, because a finding of non compos mentis or incompetence has been the traditional threshold for the appointment of a guardian. As a result, in consequence of the appointment of a guardian, all personal and legal autonomy is stripped from the ward and vested in the appointing court and guardian. The call for "limited guardianship" was a call for more sensitive procedures and for appointments fashioned so that the authority of the protector would intrude only to the degree necessary on the liberties and prerogatives of the protected person. In short, rather than permitting an all-or-none status, there should be an intermediate status available to the courts through which the protected person will have

397

personal liberties and prerogatives restricted only to the extent necessary under the circumstances. The court should be admonished to look for a least-restrictive protection approach.

For a time, spokesmen for the Uniform Probate Code took the position that the formulations approved by the National Conference in 1969 should not be classified with "typical" guardianship legislation, and that Article V met the objectives of advocates of "limited guardianship." In particular, it was pointed out that appointment of a guardian of the person under the 1969 UPC (Art. V, Part 3) involves elaborate personal notices (1969 UPC § 5–303), and avoids a determination of "incompetence" because of a new standard describing an "incapacitated person" (1969 UPC § 5–101[1]). Further, it was noted that a UPC guardian, who has not gained the powers of a conservator (1969 UPC, Art. V, Part 4) has very limited authority over a ward's estate (see 1969 UPC § 5–312), meaning that a common, historic reason for guardianship proceedings has been removed. A "protective proceeding" pursuant to 1969 UPC, Art. V, Part 4, through which a court appointee having broad powers over the estate of another may be obtained, does not involve any restriction or finding regarding the legal capacity of a protected person (1969 UPC § 5–408[5]). Also, great flexibility regarding the precise dimension of a protective order or the legal authority of a conservator is provided by explicit statutory language (1969 UPC §§ 5–408, 5–409, & 5–426).

Nonetheless, Idaho, the first state to adopt the Uniform Probate Code, and other states acting in response to requests by followers of the ABA Commission's work, have been enacting new "limited guardianship" statutes. In Idaho, the new limited guardianship legislation was enacted without specific repeal of the provisions of the Uniform Probate Code that were already part of their statutory law. Other states were enacting rather short statutes that adopted the least-intrusive or least-restrictive concept of limited guardianship in skeleton form without further elaboration. These, and other similar instances of confusion, overlap and other problems born of hasty legislative acceptance of limited guardianship language demonstrated that the National Conference of Commissioners on Uniform State Laws should adjust its formulations on guardianship to include explicit language relative to the concept of "limited guardianships." The concept of "limited guardianships" certainly is consistent with the general policy considerations upon which the Uniform Probate Code, Article V, had been based in 1969. In addition, by making limited-guardianship concepts more explicit in the act, it was and is believed that some confusion could be eliminated and that this act could replace skeleton-type acts to make the concept workable.

The clearest and most explicit statements incorporating the "limited guardianship" philosophy of a least-intrusive approach to guardianships and protective proceedings are in §§ 5–306(a), 5–306(c) and 5–407(a) of the 1982 Uniform Probate Code. However, other language that appeared previously as Uniform Probate Code, Article V, Parts 1, 2, 3, and 4 has been reviewed, altered to achieve greater internal consistency and adjusted to accommodate the "limited guardianship" concept more clearly.

Indeed, the new work by the National Conference of Commissioners on Uniform State Laws of Article V of the Uniform Probate Code has resulted in two free-standing acts. These acts extend the Uniform Probate Code formulations, but each act has been designed to be enacted as a separate act should a state legislature wish to do so. The first of these, the Uniform Durable Power of Attorney Act, was completed and promulgated in 1979, and has been well received as an improved version of what was originally included as UPC Article V, Part 5. The second step has resulted in the Uniform Guardianship and Protective Proceedings Act.

In addition to the Commissioners on Uniform State Laws who worked on drafting this Uniform Guardianship and Protective Proceedings Act, the work and valuable contributions on the project of American Bar Association liaison persons, Messrs. Rodney N. Houghton, of Newark, New Jersey, and Russell E. Webb, III, of Idaho Falls, Idaho, is gratefully acknowledged.

PART 1

GENERAL PROVISIONS AND DEFINITIONS

Section 5–101. [Facility of Payment or Delivery.]

(a) Any person under a duty to pay or deliver money or personal property to a minor may perform the duty, in amounts not exceeding $5,000 a year, by paying or delivering the money or property to:

(1) the minor if 18 or more years of age or married;

(2) any person having the care and custody of the minor with whom the minor resides;

(3) a guardian of the minor; or

(4) a financial institution incident to a deposit in a state or federally insured savings account or certificate in the sole name of the minor with notice of the deposit to the minor.

(b) This section does not apply if the person making payment or delivery knows that a conservator has been appointed or proceedings for appointment of a conservator of the estate of the minor are pending.

(c) Persons, other than the minor or any financial institution, receiving money or property for a minor, are obligated to apply the money to the support and education of the minor, but may not pay themselves except by way of reimbursement for out-of-pocket expenses for goods and services necessary for the minor's support. Any excess sums must be preserved for future support and education of the minor and any balance not so used and any property received for the minor must be turned over to the minor when majority is attained. A person who pays or delivers money or property in accordance with provisions of this section is not responsible for the proper application thereof.

COMMENT

The source of this section is 1969 Uniform Probate Code (UPC) § 5–103.

Where a minor has only a small amount of property, it would be wasteful to require protective proceedings to deal with the property. This section makes it possible for other persons, possibly including a guardian, to handle the less complicated property affairs of the ward. Protective proceedings, including the possible establishment of a conservatorship, should be sought where substantial property is involved.

This section does not go as far as many facility of payment provisions found in trust instruments, which usually permit application of sums due a minor beneficiary to any expense or charge for the minor. It was felt that a grant of so large an area of discretion to any category of persons who might owe funds to a minor would be unwise. Nonetheless, the section as drafted should reduce the need for trust facility of payment provisions somewhat, while extending opportunities to insurance companies and other debtors to minors for relatively simple methods of gaining discharge.

The protection afforded by the section is unavailable if the person making payment or delivery knows that a conservator has been appointed for the minor's estate or knows that a proceeding seeking appointment of a conservator is pending. By way of contrast, the protection is available in spite of a payor's knowledge that a *guardian* for the minor has been appointed or may be appointed as a result of a pending proceeding. Guardianship proceedings affecting minors are described in Part 2 of this Article. A conservator for a minor comes into existence, if at all, incident to a protective proceeding as described in Part 4 of this Article. A guardian's powers, described in § 5–209, do not include the authority to *compel* payment of money due the ward, but include authority to receive payments made under the protection of this section. In contrast, a conservator has title to all assets of the minor's estate, except as otherwise provided in the case of a *limited* conservator. See § 5–419.

Section 5–102. [Delegation of Powers by Parent or Guardian.]

A parent or guardian of a minor or incapacitated person, by a properly executed power of attorney, may delegate to another person, for a period not exceeding 6 months, any power regarding care, custody or property of the minor child or ward, except the power to consent to marriage or adoption of a minor ward.

COMMENT

The source of this section is 1969 UPC § 5–104.

This section permits a temporary delegation of parental powers. For example, parents (or a guardian) of a minor plan to be out of the country for several months. They wish to empower a close relative (an uncle, e.g.) to take any necessary action regarding the child while they are away. Using this section, they could execute an appropriate power of attorney giving the uncle custody and power to consent. Then, if an emergency operation were required, the uncle could consent on behalf of the child; as a practical matter he would of course attempt to communicate with the parents before acting. The section is designed to reduce problems relating to consents for emergency treatment.

The problems touched by the section include some that would be eased but not eliminated if the jurisdiction has enacted the Model Health Care Consent Act. A guardian's authority over a ward, described in § 5–209 (guardians of mi- nors) and § 5–309 (guardians of in- capacitated persons), includes au- thority regarding the care, custody and control of the ward that goes well beyond consenting to health care.

In contrast to § 5–101, which re- lates only to certain business affairs of minors, this section is pertinent to the affairs of minors *and,* inca- pacitated persons for whom guard- ians have been appointed.

Section 5–103. [General Definitions.]

As used in Parts 1, 2, 3 and 4 of this Article:

(1) "Claims," in respect to a protected person, includes liabilities of the protected person, whether arising in contract, tort, or otherwise, and liabilities of the estate which arise at or after the appointment of a conservator, including expenses of administration.

(2) "Court" means the [_____] court.

(3) "Conservator" means a person who is appointed by a Court to manage the estate of a protected person and includes a limited conservator described in Section 5–419(a).

(4) "Disability" means cause for a protective order as de- scribed in Section 5–401.

(5) "Estate" includes the property of the person whose af- fairs are subject to this Article.

(6) "Guardian" means a person who has qualified as a guardian of a minor or incapacitated person pursuant to paren- tal or spousal nomination or court appointment and includes a limited guardian as described in Sections 5–209(e) and 5–306(c), but excludes one who is merely a guardian ad litem.

(7) "Incapacitated person" means any person who is im- paired by reason of mental illness, mental deficiency, physical illness or disability, chronic use of drugs, chronic intoxication, or other cause (except minority) to the extent of lacking sufficient understanding or capacity to make or communicate responsible decisions.

(8) "Lease" includes an oil, gas, or other mineral lease.

(9) "Letters" includes letters of guardianship and letters of conservatorship.

(10) "Minor" means a person who is under [21] years of age.

(11) "Mortgage" means any conveyance, agreement, or ar- rangement in which property is used as collateral.

(12) "Organization" includes a corporation, business trust, estate, trust, partnership, association, 2 or more persons having a joint or common interest, government, governmental subdivision or agency, or any other legal entity.

(13) "Parent" includes any person entitled to take, or who would be entitled to take if the child died without a will, as a parent by intestate succession from the child whose relationship is in question and excludes any person who is only a stepparent, foster parent, or grandparent.

(14) "Person" means an individual or an organization.

(15) "Petition" means a written request to the Court for an order after notice.

(16) "Proceeding" includes action at law and suit in equity.

(17) "Property" includes both real and personal property or any interest therein and means anything that may be the subject of ownership.

(18) "Protected person" means a minor or other person for whom a conservator has been appointed or other protective order has been made as provided in Sections 5–407 and 5–408.

(19) "Protective proceeding" means a proceeding under the provisions of Part 4 of this Article.

(20) "Security" includes any note, stock, treasury stock, bond, debenture, evidence of indebtedness, certificate of interest or participation in an oil, gas, or mining title or lease or in payments out of production under such a title or lease, collateral trust certificate, transferable share, voting trust certificate or, in general, any interest or instrument commonly known as a security, or any certificate of interest or participation, any temporary or interim certificate, receipt or certificate of deposit for, or any warrant or right to subscribe to or purchase any of the foregoing.

(21) "Visitor" means a person appointed in a guardianship or protective proceeding who is trained in law, nursing, or social work, is an officer, employee, or special appointee of the Court, and has no personal interest in the proceeding.

(22) "Ward" means a person for whom a guardian has been appointed. A "minor ward" is a minor for whom a guardian has been appointed solely because of minority.

COMMENT

The sources of this section are primarily 1969 UPC §§ 1–201 and 5–101.

In completing the definition of "court," an enacting jurisdiction should consider the power contemplated for the court described in § 1–302. Ideally, the tribunal designated should have the stature of a court of general jurisdiction. If constitutional allocations of subject matter jurisdiction of courts prevent use of a court of general jurisdiction as the court of guardianship, the court designated in § 5–103(2) should be staffed so as to generate community confidence in its ability to handle the formal and complicated proceedings contemplated by §§ 5–303 et seq. and 5–401 et seq. covering guardianship and protective proceedings. See § 1–309 option. Proceedings seeking appointment of a personal guardian for a minor without other disability as described in §§ 5–204 et seq. are somewhat less complicated, though formal in the sense that adjudications following notice and hearings are involved. The Act does not contemplate use in connection with guardianships and other protective proceedings of "summary" or "informal" proceedings of the sort utilized in decedent estate settlements for non-adjudicated probate of wills and appointment of personal representatives.

When read with § 5–407(d), the defined term "disability" plainly does not refer to lack of legal capacity, but only to the grounds described in warranting a protective proceeding as described in § 5–401.

The definition of "incapacitated person" supplies the substantive grounds for appointment of a guardian for reasons other than minority. See § 5–306(b).

The definition of "parent" is intended to include an adoptive parent, because an adoptive parent is eligible to inherit as a parent in intestate succession under the Uniform Probate Code and most statutes governing adoptions. The defined meaning of "parent" is especially significant when read with §§ 5–202 and 5–203 which prevent the appointment of a guardian of a minor, other than a temporary guardian under § 5–204(b), for whom a parent still has custodial rights.

The terms "ward" and "protected person" help distinguish persons over whom another holds personal, custodial authority from those whose property, or some part thereof, has been ordered into a statutory trusteeship or otherwise subjected to a protective court order. A person for whom a guardian has been named and whose property is the subject of a conservatorship or other protective order is both a ward and a protected person. In this connection, note that § 5–423(a) gives a conservator of a minor for whom no parent or guardian has parental rights of custody and control the duties and powers of a guardian. This section also specifies that the parental authority thus conferred on a conservator of a minor does not prevent appointment of another as guardian. In contrast, the existence of any other person having the custodial authority of a parent, a guardian by appointment of any court, or a guardian arising by parental appointment under § 5–202 or as a result of parental or spousal appointment under § 5–301, blocks any court appointment of a guardian.

Section 5–104. [Request for Notice; Interested Person.]

Upon payment of any required fee, an interested person who desires to be notified before any order is made in a guardianship proceeding, including any proceeding subsequent to the appointment of a guardian under Section 5–312, or in a protective proceeding under Section 5–401, may file a request for notice with the clerk of the court in which the proceeding is pending. The clerk shall mail a copy of the request to the guardian and to the conservator if one has been appointed. A request is not effective unless it contains a statement showing the interest of the person making it and the address of that person or an attorney to whom notice is to be given. The request is effective only as to proceedings occurring after the filing. Any governmental agency paying or planning to pay benefits to the person to be protected is an interested person in protective proceedings.

COMMENT

The source of this section is 1969 UPC § 5–406, which has been extended by this section to permit a request for notice in guardianship proceedings.

This Article does not define "interest" or "interested person" as used in this section. The definition of "interested person" in § 1–201(20) is too narrow as a test of would-be participants in guardianship and protective proceedings for it points only to persons having a property interest in the estate of the respondent or a claim against the estate. If extended to guardianship proceedings, this test would preclude non-owner children from participating in a proceeding concerning their parent.

This Article contains special provisions, differing somewhat as between the three types of court proceedings it describes, regarding persons entitled to initiate a proceeding, persons entitled to notice of a proceeding, and persons who may intervene. Sections 5–206(a), 5–303(a), and 5–404(a), respectively, control the identity of petitioners in a guardianship-for-a-minor proceeding, a guardianship proceeding for an incapacitated person, and a protective proceeding. The notice provisions applicable to the three proceedings are in §§ 5–206(b), 5–304(a), and 5–405(a). Provisions governing intervenors in guardianships for incapacitated persons and protective proceedings are in §§ 5–303(d) and 5–406(e).

PART 2

GUARDIANS OF MINORS

Section 5–201. [Appointment and Status of Guardian of Minor.]

A person may become a guardian of a minor by parental appointment or upon appointment by the Court. The guardianship status continues until terminated, without regard to the location from time to time of the guardian or minor ward.

COMMENT

The source of this section is 1969 UPC § 5–201.

One purpose of this section is to establish that a guardian created by parental appointment under §§ 5–202 and 5–203, infra, has the same legal status, as a guardian by court appointment under § 5–204 and following sections. Another purpose is to declare that the relationship of guardian and ward continues even though both persons involved may move to another jurisdiction. Thus, this Article makes the guardian and ward status more like the parent/child status it replaces. This is in contrast to the older concept that the court of guardianship, acting through the guardian as its appointee, carries the principal responsibility for wards under its jurisdiction. The older concept is not satisfactory as applied to instances where the persons involved leave the jurisdiction of the appointing court.

Section 5–202. [Parental Appointment of Guardian for Minor.]

(a) The parent of an unmarried minor may appoint a guardian for the minor by will, or other writing signed by the parent and attested by at least 2 witnesses.

(b) Subject to the right of the minor under Section 5–203, if both parents are dead or incapacitated or the surviving parent has no parental rights or has been adjudged to be incapacitated, a parental appointment becomes effective when the guardian's acceptance is filed in the Court in which a nominating instrument is probated, or, in the case of a non-testamentary nominating instrument, in the Court at the place where the minor resides or is present. If both parents are dead, an effective appointment by the parent who died later has priority.

(c) A parental appointment effected by filing the guardian's acceptance under a will probated in the state of the testator's domicile is effective in this State.

(d) Upon acceptance of appointment, the guardian shall give written notice of acceptance to the minor and to the person having the minor's care or the minor's nearest adult relative.

COMMENT

Derived from 1969 UPC § 5–502, the section confers authority on a parent to *appoint* a guardian; no action by any court is required. Unlike its UPC predecessor, the section enables a parent to exercise the appointing authority by deed as well as by will. Both forms of appointment become effective only when the appointee files an acceptance in the appropriate court *and* the other conditions of the statute are met. These conditions are: (1) the minor involved has not previously filed an unwithdrawn written objection to the appointment as provided in § 5–203; and (2) both parents are dead or incapacitated as defined in § 5–103(7), or the surviving parent has been adjudged incapacitated or has surrendered or been deprived of parental rights. The existence of a guardian who has gained authority from a parental appointment precludes any other appointment of another guardian for the same minor. This result follows from § 5–209(a) which confers the powers and responsibilities of a parent on a guardian, and from § 5–204(a) which prevents appointment of a guardian for a minor over whom another has parental rights of custody. However, the authority of a guardian arising by parental authority may be terminated by objection of the ward if 14 or more years old as provided by § 5–203 or § 5–210.

The ability of a single custodial parent to appoint a guardian by deed as well as by will is especially important where local procedures for the probate of a will require advance notice to all interested persons and representation of all interested persons who are minors. The document making the appointment is not required to be filed in a public office but it would be desirable practice for it, or a conformed copy, to be attached to the written acceptance by the nominee when the latter document is filed in order to complete the appointment. Also, in cases where there is a prospect that the authority of the parental nominee may be challenged, it might be desirable to attach other documentation to the filed acceptance, including copies of death certificates or other documents tending to show that all parental rights of custody have been terminated. In this connection, it should be noted that guardians for minors, whether created by parental or court appointment, lack authority to sell or mortgage real or personal assets of the ward. See § 5–209. Hence, the tendency of title examiners and insurers to insist on public record documentation regarding every possible question concerning title may be disregarded as one considers the extent and form of documentation to accompany a guardian's acceptance under this section. Notice, however, that a conservator arising by court appointment in a protective proceeding as provided in Part 4 of this Article has full authority as a statutory trustee of all assets transferred by the appointment. Also, under § 5–423(a) a conservator of the estate of an unmarried minor as to whom no one has parental rights, has the authority of a guardian. However, a parent is not empowered to appoint a conservator by deed or will. A parent with assets to use for the purpose may, of course, establish a trust for a minor or anyone else, but a trustee's authority would not include authority over the person of the beneficiary like that available to a guardian.

The final sentence of the section was added to 1969 UPC § 5–202 in 1975 following a recommendation of the Joint Editorial Board for the Uniform Probate Code. In making the recommendation, the JEB–UPC signalled that it approved a safeguard added to the section at the time of its first enactment in Idaho. Section 1–401 governs the method and time requirements of a notice as required in this section.

Section 5–203. [Objection by Minor of Fourteen or Older to Parental Appointment.]

A minor 14 or more years of age who is the subject of a parental appointment may prevent the appointment or cause it to terminate by filing in the Court in which the nominating instrument is filed a written objection to the appointment before it is accepted or within 30 days after receiving notice of its acceptance. An objection may be withdrawn. An objection does not preclude appointment by the Court in a proper proceeding of the parental nominee or any other suitable person.

COMMENT

The source of this section is 1969 UPC § 5–203.

A written objection of a minor to a parental appointment prevents a later accepted appointment from becoming effective. However, if the objection is withdrawn before the filing of the guardian's acceptance, the effect of the objection is cancelled. An objection filed within 30 days following the filing of an acceptance terminates the appointment but does not invalidate acts done previously in reliance on the guardian's authority. See § 5–210. It may be questioned, however, whether a post-acceptance objection that serves to terminate the authority of a parental guardian may be withdrawn so as to re-instate the guardian's authority. Safe practice in

such a case would dictate that those interested in establishing a legal guardianship petition the court for an appointment under § 5–204.

The final sentence in the section is not intended to imply that a court proceeding for appointment of a guardian is necessary or appropriate when there has been an effective parental appointment. It was inserted to indicate that a minor age 14 or more may not block a court appointment of one nominated as guardian by a parent even though the prospective ward is able to block or terminate a parental appointment that does not involve action by the court. In this connection, note that § 5–207, applicable to an appointment by the court, directs the court to respect the nomination of the prospective ward if 14 or more years of age. But, the court may conclude that appointment of the minor's nominee would be contrary to the best interest of the minor, clearing the way for appointment of a parental nominee or some other suitable person.

Section 5–204. [Court Appointment of Guardian of Minor; Conditions for Appointment.]

(a) The Court may appoint a guardian for an unmarried minor if all parental rights have been terminated or suspended by circumstances or prior Court order. A guardian appointed pursuant to Section 5–202 whose appointment has not been prevented or nullified under Section 5–203 has priority over any guardian who may be appointed by the Court, but the Court may proceed with another appointment upon a finding that the parental nominee has failed to accept the appointment within 30 days after notice of the guardianship proceeding.

(b) If necessary, and on appropriate petition or application, the Court may appoint a temporary guardian who shall have the full authority of a general guardian of a minor, but the authority of a temporary guardian may not last longer than 6 months. The appointment of a temporary guardian for a minor may occur even though the conditions described in subsection (a) have not been established.

COMMENT

The source of this section is 1969 UPC §§ 5–204 & 5–207(c).

This section and §§ 5–205 through 5–207 following cover proceedings to secure a court appointed guardian of a minor. Sections 5–208 through 5–212 are applicable to all guardians of minors who derive authority from parental appointment or court appointment as contemplated in this Part. Nothing in this Article is intended to deal with the status of a so-called natural guardian, with the authority of a parent over a child, or with authority over a child or children that may be conferred by other state laws.

The court is not authorized to appoint a guardian for one for whom a parent has custodial rights or for one who has a parental guardian. Two purposes are served by this restriction. First, it prevents use of guardianship proceedings as a weapon or tactic in a squabble between parents concerning child custody, thereby forcing these disputes to the court having jurisdiction over marital matters. Second, it establishes that a guardian by parental appointment is as completely endowed with authority as a guardian as one appointed by court order. A guardian by parental appointment may be replaced by one appointed by the court following removal in proceedings under § 5–212. If a court-appointed guardian comes into existence before a parental nomination is discovered or implemented by acceptance, it will be necessary to terminate the authority of the court-appointed guardian in order to clear the way for the parental nominee. See § 5–201. In this connection, the second sentence of § 5–204(a) may be invoked in appropriate cases by the proponent of the parental nomination. This would occur in proceedings incident to an application to the court for an order correcting the original appointment. Alternatively, the parental nominee may urge removal of the court-appointed guardian on the ground that the best interest of the minor as contemplated in § 5–212 would be served by termination of the prior appointment.

Subsection (b) gives the court having jurisdiction of guardianship matters important power regarding the welfare of a minor in the form of authority to appoint a temporary guardian in cases of necessity. The authority permits appointment of a temporary guardian even though one or both parents have parental authority. It is to be noted, however, that the appointment of a temporary guardian must be preceded by notice and hearing as required for appointment of any court appointed guardian. The authority might be particularly useful in a case where both parents have disappeared or simply departed without making adequate arrangements for their children. If the needs of minor children require the creation of guardianships before it is possible to prove the death of the parents, the subsection opens the way to appointment of one having parental authority for up to 6 months that does not require proof of the requirement of subsection (a) that "all parental rights of custody have been terminated or suspended by circumstances …"

In addition to guardians by parental appointment and court-appointed guardians, § 5–423(a) grants a conservator of the estate of a minor for whom no guardian or parent holds parental rights the powers of a guardian. The same section makes it clear that appointment of a conservator for the estate of a minor, even though it may create a form of guardianship authority over the minor, does not preclude court appointment of a guardian nor acceptance of a parental nomination. Thus, the statute enables persons interested in the affairs and welfare of a minor to secure a single authority competent to handle the personal and business needs of the minor. Alternatively, for cases where circumstances suggest that one person should be in charge of decisions regarding the minor's living conditions, health care, and education, and another in charge of management of the minor's property interests two appointments may be made.

Section 5–205. [Venue.]

The venue for guardianship proceedings for a minor is in the court at the place where the minor resides or is present at the time the proceedings are commenced.

COMMENT

The source of this section is 1969 UPC § 5–205. This section should be read with § 1–303 dealing with multiple venue proceedings and transfer of venue.

Section 5–206. [Procedure for Court–Appointment of Guardian of Minor.]

(a) A minor or any person interested in the welfare of the minor may petition for appointment of a guardian.

(b) After the filing of a petition, the Court shall set a date for hearing, and the petitioner shall give notice of the time and place of hearing the petition in the manner prescribed by Section 1–401 to:

(1) the minor, if 14 or more years of age and not the petitioner;

(2) any person alleged to have had the principal care and custody of the minor during the 60 days preceding the filing of the petition; and

(3) any living parent of the minor.

(c) Upon hearing, if the Court finds that a qualified person seeks appointment, venue is proper, the required notices have been given, the conditions of Section 5–204(a) have been met, and the welfare and best interest of the minor will be served by the requested appointment, it shall make the appointment and issue letters. In other cases, the Court may dismiss the proceedings or make any other disposition of the matter that will serve the best interest of the minor.

(d) If the Court determines at any time in the proceeding that the interests of the minor are or may be inadequately represented, it may appoint an attorney to represent the minor, giving consideration to the preference of the minor if the minor is 14 or more years of age.

COMMENT

The source of this section is 1969 UPC § 5–207.

Subsection (a) is new. It is intended to qualify as a potential petitioner any person with a serious interest or concern for a minor's welfare, including a relative or a non-relative having knowledge of the circumstances who completes a petition to the court, and any public official having official or personal concerns for the minor's welfare. If the court determines that the petitioner's concerns in the matter stem from interests that may not serve the welfare and best interest of the minor, it may dismiss the proceeding on the ground that the conditions for appointment as specified in subsection (b) have not been met.

The second sentence of subsection (b) may be interpreted to authorize an order directing that the petition be re-cast as a petition for a protective order under § 5–401. That authority is expressly conferred on the court by § 5–306 relating to a guardianship proceeding based on incapacity. The authority would be useful, for example, if the court determines that asset management is likely to be involved and that the person seeking appointment as guardian would be an appropriate person to serve as conservator with the power of a guardian. In these circumstances, two appointments could be avoided if the petitioner were willing to re-cast the petition as required by § 5–401.

Section 5–207. [Court Appointment of Guardian of Minor; Qualifications; Priority of Minor's Nominee.]

The Court may appoint as guardian any person whose appointment would be in the best interest of the minor. The Court shall appoint a person nominated by the minor, if the minor is 14 or more years of age, unless the Court finds the appointment contrary to the best interest of the minor.

COMMENT

The source of this section is 1969 UPC § 5–206.

Rather than provide for priorities among various classes of relatives, it was felt that the only priority should be for the person nominated by the minor. The important point is to locate someone whose appointment will be in the best interest of the minor. If there is contention among relatives over who should be named, it is not likely that a statutory priority keyed to degrees of kinship would help resolve the matter. For example, if the argument involved a squabble between relatives of the child's father and relatives of its mother, priority in terms of degrees of kinship would be useless.

Guardianships under this Article are not likely to be attractive positions for persons who are more interested in handling a minor's estate than in his or her personal well being. An order of a court having equity power is necessary if the guardian is to receive payment for services where there is no conservator for the minor's estate. Also, the powers of management of a ward's estate conferred on a guardian are restricted so that if a substantial estate is involved, a conservator will be needed to handle the financial matters.

Section 5–208. [Consent to Service by Acceptance of Appointment; Notice.]

By accepting a parental or court appointment as guardian, a guardian submits personally to the jurisdiction of the Court in any proceeding relating to the guardianship that may be instituted by any interested person. The petitioner shall cause notice of any proceeding to be delivered or mailed to the guardian at the guardian's address listed in the Court records and to the address then known to the petitioner. Letters of guardianship must indicate whether the guardian was appointed by court order or parental nomination.

COMMENT

The source of this section is 1969 UPC § 5–208.

The "long-arm" principle behind this section is well established. It seems desirable that the court in which acceptance is filed be able to serve its process on the guardian wherever he or she has moved. The continuing interest of that court in the welfare of the minor is ample to justify this provision. The consent to service is real rather than fictional in the guardianship situation, where the guardian acts voluntarily in filing acceptance. It is probable that the form of acceptance will expressly embody the provisions of this section, although the statute does not expressly require this.

Section 5–209. [Powers and Duties of Guardian of Minor.]

(a) A guardian of a minor ward has the powers and responsibilities of a parent regarding the ward's support, care, and education, but a guardian is not personally liable for the ward's expenses and is not liable to third persons by reason of the relationship for acts of the ward.

(b) In particular and without qualifying the foregoing, a guardian shall:

(1) become or remain personally acquainted with the ward and maintain sufficient contact with the ward to know of the ward's capacities, limitations, needs, opportunities, and physical and mental health;

(2) take reasonable care of the ward's personal effects and commence protective proceedings if necessary to protect other property of the ward;

(3) apply any available money of the ward to the ward's current needs for support, care, and education;

(4) conserve any excess money of the ward for the ward's future needs, but if a conservator has been appointed for the estate of the ward, the guardian, at least quarterly, shall pay to the conservator money of the ward to be conserved for the ward's future needs; and

413

(5) report the condition of the ward and of the ward's estate that has been subject to the guardian's possession or control, as ordered by the Court on petition of any person interested in the ward's welfare or as required by Court rule.

(c) A guardian may:

(1) receive money payable for the support of the ward to the ward's parent, guardian, or custodian under the terms of any statutory benefit or insurance system or any private contract, devise, trust, conservatorship, or custodianship, and money or property of the ward paid or delivered pursuant to Section 5–101;

(2) if consistent with the terms of any order by a court of competent jurisdiction relating to detention or commitment of the ward, take custody of the person of the ward and establish the ward's place of abode within or without this State;

(3) if no conservator for the estate of the ward has been appointed, institute proceedings, including administrative proceedings, or take other appropriate action to compel the performance by any person of a duty to support the ward or to pay sums for the welfare of the ward;

(4) consent to medical or other professional care, treatment, or advice for the ward without liability by reason of the consent for injury to the ward resulting from the negligence or acts of third persons unless a parent would have been liable in the circumstances;

(5) consent to the marriage or adoption of the ward; and

(6) if reasonable under all of the circumstances, delegate to the ward certain responsibilities for decisions affecting the ward's well-being.

(d) A guardian is entitled to reasonable compensation for services as guardian and to reimbursement for room, board and clothing personally provided to the ward, but only as approved by order of the Court. If a conservator, other than the guardian or one who is affiliated with the guardian, has been appointed for the estate of the ward, reasonable compensation and reimbursement to the guardian may be approved and paid by the conservator without order of the Court controlling the guardian.

(e) In the interest of developing self-reliance on the part of a ward or for other good cause, the Court, at the time of appointment or later, on its own motion or on appropriate petition or motion of the minor or other interested person, may limit the powers of a guardian otherwise conferred by this section and thereby create a limited guardianship. Any limitation on the statutory power of a guardian of a minor must be endorsed on the guardian's letters or, in the case of a guardian by parental appointment, must be reflected in letters that are issued at the time any limitation is imposed. Following the same procedure, a limitation may be removed and appropriate letters issued.

COMMENT

This section, derived in part from 1969 UPC § 5–209, represents an expansion and reorganization of the UPC section. Subsection (a) specifies that the parental powers and responsibilities entailed in a guardianship are those concerned with the ward's "support, care, and education." These terms, when read with subsection (b), obviously refer to all kinds of considerations that should be weighed and implemented on behalf of the ward by one invested with legal authority to control the ward's activities.

Subsection (b)(1) is new. It reflects a consensus of the drafting committee that a person who accepts a guardianship for a minor should be forewarned by explicit statutory language that the position entails responsibilities to make and maintain personal contact with the ward.

The basic duties of a guardian are described in the mandates of subsection (b). Subsection (c) outlines optional authority that is extended to every guardian by the statute. Subsection (d), dealing with the delicate question of compensation for a guardian, requires that a guardian obtain approval from an independent conservator of the minor's estate or from the court before taking sums as compensation from funds of the minor that have been received by the guardian. In contrast to 1969 UPC § 5–312(a)(4) which permitted a guardian for an incapacitated person to take funds of the ward by way of reimbursement for personal funds previously expended for certain purposes, this section requires court approval before any guardian's claim for reimbursement can be satisfied otherwise than through a conservator. Note, however, that no advance court approval is required in order to permit a guardian to use available funds of the ward for the ward's current needs as provided in subsection (b)(3).

The powers of a guardian regarding property of the ward are quite limited. Note, also, that the section does not encourage a guardian to apply to the appointing court for additional property power. Rather, the provisions are designed to encourage use of a protective proceeding under § 5–401 if property powers beyond those statutorily available to a guardian are needed. In this connection, it may be observed that subsection (c)(3), which contains one of the section's few references to use of the courts by a guardian, authorizes a guardian to institute proceedings to enforce a duty to support or pay money only if there is no conservator for the estate of the ward.

If the circumstances of a minor dictate that authority to control both person and property be obtained, protective proceedings under § 5–401 et seq. are indicated. Section 5–423(a) provides that a conservator for a minor as to whom no one has parental authority has the powers of a guardian as well as plenary power as a statutory trustee over the assets of the minor. In addition, as noted in the comment to § 5–204, the provisions of this Article enable interested persons to obtain appointment of the same or different persons as guardian and conservator for a minor even though § 5–423(a) makes it patently unnecessary to obtain two appointments in a case where a single person is to serve in both capacities.

Subsection (e) is new and extends the limited guardianship concept to guardians of minors by encouraging court orders limiting the already limited authority of a guardian. Using this provision, a court, at the time of appointment or on petition thereafter, might limit the authority of a guardian so that, for example, the guardian would not be able to direct the ward's religious training, or so that the guardian would be restricted in controlling the ward's place of abode by a condition that the ward's consent to any change of abode be given. The section provides that special restrictions of this sort may be removed or altered by further court order. Obviously, the drafters did not intend that the procedure for contracting and expanding special limitations on a guardian's power should be used to grant a guardian greater powers than are described in the section.

Section 5–210. [Termination of Appointment of Guardian; General.]

A guardian's authority and responsibility terminates upon the death, resignation, or removal of the guardian or upon the minor's death, adoption, marriage, or attainment of majority, but termination does not affect the guardian's liability for prior acts or the obligation to account for funds and assets of the ward. Resignation of a guardian does not terminate the guardianship until it has been approved by the Court. A parental appointment under an informally probated will terminates if the will is later denied probate in a formal proceeding.

COMMENT

The source of this section is 1969 UPC § 5–210.

The position taken in this section that termination of a guardian's authority and responsibility does not apply retroactively to nullify prior acts is intended to govern all forms of termination including termination by objection as described in § 5–203.

Any of various events, that may or may not appear from the records of the court that appointed a guardian may serve to terminate the guardian's authority and responsibility. The extremely limited authority of a guardian over the ward's money and property tends to reduce instances when third persons may be jeopardized by an unknown termination of a guardian's authority. Principles protecting third persons who rely to their detriment on an apparent authority that has been terminated without their knowledge should govern the occasional cases in which a prior, unknown termination clouds the legality of a guardian's act.

Section 5–211. [Proceedings Subsequent to Appointment; Venue.]

(a) The Court at the place where the ward resides has concurrent jurisdiction with the Court that appointed the guardian or in which acceptance of a parental appointment was filed over resignation, removal, accounting, and other proceedings relating to the guardianship.

(b) If the Court at the place where the ward resides is neither the appointing court nor the court in which acceptance of appointment is filed, the court in which proceedings subsequent to appointment are commenced in all appropriate cases shall notify the other court, in this or another state, and after consultation with that court determine whether to retain jurisdiction or transfer the proceedings to the other court, whichever is in the best interest of the ward. A copy of any order accepting a resignation or removing a guardian must be sent to the appointing court or the court in which acceptance of appointment is filed.

COMMENT

The source of this section is 1969 UPC § 5–211 with the substitution of "parental appointment" for "testamentary appointment."

Under §§ 5–103(2) and 1–302, the Court is designated as the proper court to handle matters relating to guardianship. The present section is intended to give jurisdiction to the forum where the ward resides as well as to the one where appointment initiated. This provision has primary importance where the ward's residence has been moved from the appointing state. Because the Court where acceptance of appointment is filed may as a practical matter be the only forum in which jurisdiction over the person of the guardian may be obtained (by reason of § 5–208), that Court is given concurrent jurisdiction.

Section 5–212. [Resignation, Removal, and Other Post–Appointment Proceedings.]

(a) Any person interested in the welfare of a ward or the ward, if 14 or more years of age, may petition for removal of a guardian on the ground that removal would be in the best interest of the ward or for any other order that is in the best interest of the ward. A guardian may petition for permission to resign. A petition for removal or for permission to resign may, but need not, include a request for appointment of a successor guardian.

(b) Notice of hearing on a petition for an order subsequent to appointment of a guardian must be given to the ward, the guardian, and any other person as ordered by the court.

(c) After notice and hearing on a petition for removal or for permission to resign, the Court may terminate the guardianship and make any further order that may be appropriate.

(d) If the Court determines at any time in the proceeding that the interest of the ward is or may be inadequately represented, it may appoint an attorney to represent the minor, giving consideration to the preference of the minor if the minor is 14 or more years of age.

COMMENT

The source of this section is 1969 UPC § 5–212. Subsection (a) of this section is identical to 1969 UPC § 5–212(a). Subsection (c) of this section also is identical to 1969 UPC § 5–212(b).

Subsection (b) of this section is new and identifies who must be given notice of any post-appointment proceedings affecting a guardianship. Section 1–401 describes methods and time requirements concerning notices required by this section. Section 1–402, which controls waiver of required notices, prevents waiver of notice by the ward. It would seem that a ward who is the petitioner in a post-appointment proceeding would not need to receive notice. However, a ward should be given notice of a petition initiated in the ward's name by a next friend.

PART 3

GUARDIANS OF INCAPACITATED PERSONS

Section 5–301. [Appointment of Guardian for Incapacitated Person by Will or Other Writing.]

(a) The parent of an unmarried incapacitated person may appoint by will, or other writing signed by the parent and attested by at least 2 witnesses, a guardian of the incapacitated person. If both parents are dead or the surviving parent is adjudged incapacitated, a parental appointment becomes effective when, after having given 7 days prior written notice of intention to do so to the incapacitated person and to the person having the care of the person or to the nearest adult relative, the guardian files acceptance of appointment in the court in which the will is [informally or formally] probated, or in the case of a non-testamentary nominating instrument, in the Court at the place where the incapacitated person resides or is present. The notice shall state that the appointment may be terminated by filing a written objection in the Court, as provided by subsection (d). If both parents are dead, an effective appointment by the parent who died later has priority.

(b) The spouse of a married incapacitated person may appoint by will, or other writing signed by the spouse and attested by at least 2 witnesses, a guardian of the incapacitated person. The appointment becomes effective when, after having given 7 days prior written notice of intention to do so to the incapacitated person and to the person having care of the incapacitated person or to the nearest adult relative, the guardian files acceptance of appointment in the Court in which the will is informally or formally probated or, in the case of non-testamentary nominating instrument, in the Court at the place where the incapacitated person resides or is present. The notice shall state that the appointment may be terminated by filing a written objection in the Court, as provided by subsection (d). An effective appointment by a spouse has priority over an appointment by a parent.

(c) An appointment effected by filing the guardian's acceptance under a will probated in the state of the decedent's domicile is effective in this State.

(d) Upon the filing in the Court in which the will was probated or, in the case of a non-testamentary nominating instrument, in the Court at the place where the incapacitated person resides or is present, of written objection to the appointment by the incapacitated person for whom a parental or spousal appointment of guardian has been made, the appointment is terminated. An objection does not prevent appointment by the Court in a proper proceeding of the parental or spousal nominee or any other suitable person upon an adjudication of incapacity in proceedings under the succeeding sections of this Part.

COMMENT

Derived from 1969 UPC § 5–301, this section confers authority on the spouse and a parent to appoint a guardian for an incapacitated person; no action by any court is required, but a condition of an effective parental or spousal appointment is that the appointee file an acceptance in an appropriate court. Such a filing does not initiate a court proceeding or require any response from the court. However, a parental or spousal guardian is entitled to a writing from the court showing that an acceptance has been filed and that a guardian's authority as provided by the statute (see § 1–305) appears to have been conferred.

The section differs from 1969 UPC § 5–301 only in that it authorizes a parental or spousal appointment to be made by a witnessed non-testamentary writing, as well as by will. This expansion is consistent with a parallel expansion of 1969 UPC § 5–202 by § 5–202 of this Article.

This section is modeled after § 5–202, but it differs from § 5–202 in several particulars. For one, it applies to guardians for persons who are incapacitated for reasons other than minority. See the definition of incapacity in § 5–103(7). Also, no advance written notice of intention to accept a parental appointment as a guardian for a minor

under § 5–202 is required while 7 days' advance notice is required for completion of a parental or spousal appointment under this section. Note, too, that termination by objection to an appointment under § 5–202 can be effected by virtue of § 5–203 only if the objection is filed within 30 days after the filing of the acceptance. In contrast, this section permits the ward to upset a parental or spousal appointment based on incapacity by written objection at any time.

Whether accomplished by deed or will, this section expressly provides that a parental appointment of a guardian based on the incapacity of a child cannot become effective until both parents are dead or the surviving parent has become incapacitated. Thus, a parent's appointing authority is limited to providing for a replacement of whatever authority might have been attached to the status of parent. A spousal appointment by will would be ambulatory and could not become effective until after the spouse's death. However, a spousal appointment by deed may become effective before the appointing spouse's death if the appointing instrument so provides and all other conditions of an effective appointment are met. Thus, a spouse of an incapacitated person is enabled to confer a guardian's authority over an incapacitated mate. The authority arising by spousal appointment may be helpful in cases where the appointing spouse plans to be absent, or in situations where some third person hesitates to respect the directions of an incompetent's spouse and insists on some form of guardianship paper.

The section provides several safeguards that attend the procedure. The case with which the authority available under this section may be ended by objection of the ward provides a safeguard against abuse of the procedure. For another safeguard, the absence of any adjudication of incapacity incident to a conferral of authority under the section means that a purported appointment is effective only if, upon challenge, it is determined by a court that the essential condition of incapacity existed when the appointment was accepted. Also, as noted earlier, the ward of a guardian who claims authority by virtue of the procedure described in this section may cause the authority to termi-

nate by filing a written objection at any time.

It may be questioned whether a legislature should bother to provide for an authority as fragile as that contemplated by the section. The drafters of the Uniform Probate Code believed that the procedure would be particularly helpful to parents of children suffering from congenital or other defects who require some lifetime care arrangements. These parents may desire some legal assurance that persons of their choice will be able to continue monitoring the care arrangements for their children when they become unable to do so. Since the role to be played calls principally for personal concern for the welfare of the incapacitated person, a prima facie showing of legal authority will suffice in many cases and it will be unimportant that the overseer's legal authority is not impregnable.

See the Comment following § 5–202 for additional observations regarding the utility of appointments of guardians by deed.

Section 5–302. [Venue.]

The venue for guardianship proceedings for an incapacitated person is in the place where the incapacitated person resides or is present at the time the proceedings are commenced. If the incapacitated person is admitted to an institution pursuant to order of a court of competent jurisdiction, venue is also in the [county] in which that court is located.

COMMENT

This section is identical to 1969 UPC § 5–302 and introduces the procedure for securing a court appointment of a guardian for an incapacitated person described in §§ 5–302 through 5–308.

Except for the case in which the authority of a parental or spousal guardian for an incapacitated person may be questioned or ended, the powers of a court-appointed guardian are the same as those of a spousal or parental guardian. Section 5–309 describes the powers. Perusal of § 5–309, of § 5–209 on which it is based, and of the Comments following § 5–209, is recommended. From these materials, it will be seen that most of the more traditional purposes of guardianships will not be served by the guardian's position described in this Article. Rather, a conservator, as described in Part 4 of this Article, will be much better equipped to handle financial affairs of an incapacitated person than a guardian. Consequently, the new guardianship as described in this Article is likely to be much less widely used than traditional guardianship procedures. Counsellors will be well advised to determine, in all cases where a guardianship may be suggested whether a guardianship, as distinguished from a conservatorship, will serve any useful purpose. Alternative methods of obtaining health and care services, including consent to medical treatment available under the Model Health Care Consent Act or comparable legislation and authority for voluntary or involuntary diagnostic or protective custodies under modern mental health legislation should be given careful consideration. Also, volunteer or paid companions, or placements with public or private nursing homes or other limited or total care providers, may be possible without the interposition of a court-appointed guardian.

Section 5–303. [Procedure for Court–Appointment of a Guardian of an Incapacitated Person.]

(a) An incapacitated person or any person interested in the welfare of the incapacitated person may petition for appointment of a guardian, limited or general.

(b) After the filing of a petition, the Court shall set a date for hearing on the issue of incapacity so that notices may be given as required by Section 5–304, and, unless the allegedly incapacitated person is represented by counsel, appoint an attorney to represent the person in the proceeding. The person so appointed may be granted the powers and duties of a guardian ad litem. The person alleged to be incapacitated must be examined by a physician or other qualified person appointed by the Court who shall submit a report in writing to the Court. The person alleged to be incapacitated also must be interviewed by a visitor sent by the Court. The visitor also shall interview the person who appears to have caused the petition to be filed and any person who is nominated to serve as guardian and visit the present place of abode of the person alleged to be incapacitated and the place it is proposed that the person will be detained or reside if the appointment is made and submit a report in writing to the Court. The Court may utilize the service of any public or charitable agency as an additional visitor to evaluate the condition of the allegedly incapacitated person and to make appropriate recommendations to the Court.

(c) A person alleged to be incapacitated is entitled to be present at the hearing in person. The person is entitled to be represented by counsel, to present evidence, to cross-examine witnesses, including the Court-appointed physician or other qualified person and any visitor[, and to trial by jury]. The issue may be determined at a closed hearing [or without a jury] if the person alleged to be incapacitated or counsel for the person so requests.

(d) Any person may apply for permission to participate in the proceeding, and the Court may grant the request, with or without hearing, upon determining that the best interest of the alleged incapacitated person will be served thereby. The Court may attach appropriate conditions to the permission.

COMMENT

The procedure described in this section involves three designations or appointments of persons as mandatory participants in a court-appointed guardianship proceeding based on incapacity. First, the respondent must be represented by counsel who also may be granted the powers and duties of a guardian ad litem and who may represent the respondent in all cases in which he or she lacks adequate counsel of choice. In context, the court probably should determine not only that private counsel is in the case, but that such counsel has been engaged by the respondent acting without undue pressure from others having some possible personal interest in the proceeding. Also, the court is required to designate a physician and a visitor to function as described. The roles of physician and visitor may be filled by a single person, provided the person has the requisite qualifications.

Mandatory participation by a visitor and physician (or other qualified person) is not mentioned in connection with guardianship proceedings based on minority. See § 5–206. These officials are mentioned in § 5–406 covering court proceedings seeking what has sometimes been called a "guardian of the estate" and is referred to in this Article as a conservator. However, in the protective proceedings described in § 5–406 the court has discretion concerning whether either or both of the functionaries should be involved.

Underlying the guardian ad litem, visitor and physician requirements in this section is the belief that an individual's liberty to select an abode, to receive or to refuse medical, psychiatric, vocational, or other therapy or attention should not be displaced by appointment of a guardian unless the appointment is clearly necessary. In order to properly evaluate the merits of a petition seeking appointment of a guardian, the court should have access to information regarding the respondent other than as provided by the petitioner and associated counsel. The precautionary procedures tend to reduce the risk that relatives of the respondent may use guardianship procedures to relieve themselves of burdensome but bearable responsibilities for care, or to prevent the respondent from dissipating assets they would like to inherit, or for other reasons that are not in the best interest of the respondent. Also, they are designed to increase the perceptions of the respondent available to the court and lessen the risk that honestly held but overly-narrow judgments regarding tolerable limits of eccentricity may cause the loss of an individual's liberty.

The mandatory features of a guardianship proceeding make the procedure somewhat more complex than a protective proceeding under § 5–401 et seq. seeking the appointment of a conservator. The differences may tend to discourage use of guardianships and so reduce the in-

stances in which persons may be declared to be without legal capacity. Loss of control over one's property is serious, to be sure, but there are reasons why it may be viewed as less serious than suffering a judgment that one is legally incapacitated and must be placed under the care of a guardian. First, one's property can and should be made available for support of legal dependents. Also, court-directed management of one's property does not impede the personal liberty of the protected person nor prevent the acquisition and enjoyment of assets that may be acquired thereafter. Finally, the interposition of another's control of one's personal freedom is rarely necessary or justified in non-criminal settings. Alternative methods of protecting persons with little ability to care for themselves should be encouraged.

Section 5–304. [Notice in Guardianship Proceeding.]

(a) In a proceeding for the appointment of a guardian of an incapacitated person, and, if notice is required in a proceeding for appointment of a temporary guardian, notice of hearing must be given to each of the following:

(1) the person alleged to be incapacitated and spouse, or, if none, adult children, or if none, parents;

(2) any person who is serving as guardian, conservator, or who has the care and custody of the person alleged to be incapacitated;

(3) in case no other person is notified under paragraph (1), at least one of the nearest adult relatives, if any can be found; and

(4) any other person as directed by the Court.

(b) Notice of hearing on a petition for an order subsequent to appointment of a guardian must be given to the ward, the guardian and any other person as ordered by the Court.

(c) Notice must be served personally on the alleged incapacitated person. Notices to other persons as required by subsection (a)(1) must be served personally if the person to be notified can be found within the state. In all other cases, required notices must be given as provided in Section 1–401.

(d) The person alleged to be incapacitated may not waive notice.

COMMENT

This section is based on 1969 UPC § 5–309. Like the source section, it requires that notice of the proceeding be served personally on the person alleged to be incapacitated. This appears in subsection (c), which qualifies both subsections (a) and (b). Subsection (b) applies to proceedings subsequent to the institution of a guardianship as covered in § 5–312.

It may be noted that personal service is not necessary for the required notice to a minor age 14 or over under § 5–206 governing proceedings seeking a court-appointed guardian for a minor. In this connection, it should be observed that the instant section, rather than § 5–206, governs if the petition seeks to establish that a minor is incapacitated for reasons other than minority and so is in need of a guardian who will continue to serve in spite of the respondent's attainment of majority. See § 5–210 and compare § 5–310.

Section 5–305. [Who May Be Guardian; Priorities.]

(a) Any qualified person may be appointed guardian of an incapacitated person.

(b) Unless lack of qualification or other good cause dictates the contrary, the Court shall appoint a guardian in accordance with the incapacitated person's most recent nomination in a durable power of attorney.

(c) Except as provided in subsection (b), the following are entitled to consideration for appointment in the order listed:

(1) the spouse of the incapacitated person or a person nominated by will of a deceased spouse or by other writing signed by the spouse and attested by at least 2 witnesses;

(2) an adult child of the incapacitated person;

(3) a parent of the incapacitated person, or a person nominated by will of a deceased parent or by other writing signed by a parent and attested by at least two witnesses;

(4) any relative of the incapacitated person with whom the person has resided for more than 6 months prior to the filing of the petition; and

(5) a person nominated by the person who is caring for or paying for the care of the incapacitated person.

(d) With respect to persons having equal priority, the Court shall select the one it deems best qualified to serve. The Court, acting in the best interest of the incapacitated person, may pass over a person having priority and appoint a person having a lower priority or no priority.

COMMENT

Subsection (a) limits those who may act as guardians for incapacitated persons to "qualified" persons. "Qualified" in its application to "persons" is not defined in this Article, meaning that an appointing court has considerable discretion regarding the suitability of an individual to serve as guardian for a particular ward. In exercising this discretion, the court should give careful consideration to the needs of the ward and to the experience or other qualifications of the applicant to react sensitively and positively to the ward's needs.

Subsections (b) and (c) govern priorities among persons who may seek appointment. Unless good cause or lack of qualification dictates otherwise, priority is with one nominated in an unrevoked power of attorney of the ward that remains effective though the ward has become incompetent since executing the power of attorney.

The source of this section is 1969 UPC § 5–311, which section also provided that a "suitable institution" might be appointed guardian. This suggestion was discussed thoroughly by the Uniform Law Commissioners for this Article and rejected. The reasoning for limiting appointments to "qualified persons" is that for a guardianship of the person, the needs, duties and responsibilities are so personal they should only be delegated to a person and not to an institution.

Section 5–306. [Findings; Order of Appointment.]

(a) The Court shall exercise the authority conferred in this Part so as to encourage the development of maximum self-reliance and independence of the incapacitated person and make appointive and other orders only to the extent necessitated by the incapacitated person's mental and adaptive limitations or other conditions warranting the procedure.

(b) The Court may appoint a guardian as requested if it is satisfied that the person for whom a guardian is sought is incapacitated and that the appointment is necessary or desirable as a means of providing continuing care and supervision of the person of the incapacitated person. The Court, on appropriate findings, may (i) treat the petition as one for a protective order under Section 5–401 and proceed accordingly, (ii) enter any other appropriate order, or (iii) dismiss the proceedings.

(c) The Court, at the time of appointment or later, on its own motion or on appropriate petition or motion of the incapacitated person or other interested person, may limit the powers of a guardian otherwise conferred by Parts 1, 2, 3 and 4 of this Article and thereby create a limited guardianship. Any limitation on the statutory power of a guardian of an incapacitated person must be endorsed on the guardian's letters or, in the case of a guardian by parental or spousal appointment, must be reflected in letters issued at the time any limitation is imposed. Following the same procedure, a limitation may be removed or modified and appropriate letters issued.

COMMENT

The purpose of subsections (a) and (c) is to remind an appointing court that a guardianship under this legislation should not confer more authority over the person of the ward than appears necessary to alleviate the problems caused by the ward's incapacity. This is a statement of the general principle underlying a "limited guardianship" concept. For example, if the principal reason for the guardianship is the ward's inability to comprehend a personal medical problem, the guardian's authority could be limited to making a judgment, after evaluation of all circumstances, concerning the advisability and form of treatment and to authorize actions necessary to carry out the decision. Or, if the ward's principal problem stems from memory lapses and associated wanderings, a guardian with authority limited to making arrangements for suitable security against this risk might be indicated. Subsection (c) facilitates use by the appointing court of a trial-and-error method to achieve a tailoring of the guardian's authority to changing needs and circumstances. Read with the last sentence of § 5–303(b) and with subsection (d) of § 5–303, the instant section authorizes use of any public or charitable agency that demonstrates interest and competence in evaluating the condition and needs of the ward in arriving at a decision regarding the appropriate powers of the guardian.

The section does not authorize enlargement of the powers of a guardian beyond those described in § 5–309 and related sections. Rather, *limitations* on a guardian's § 5–309 powers and duties may be imposed and removed. Thus, if the court determines that most of a respondent's demonstrated problems probably could be alleviated by the institution of an appropriate authority to manage the ward's property and make appropriate expenditures for the ward's well-being, the court should utilize subsection (b) to recast the proceedings so that a conservator, rather than a guardian, would be appointed. If the respondent's problems call for both a guardian and a conservator, subsection (b) authorizes the court to direct that the proceedings be recast to seek both forms of relief. In this connection, the case of an incapacitated person differs from that of a minor who needs both a personal guardian and a conservator. This difference is recognized in that the second sentence of § 5–423(a), which applies only to conservators of estates of unmarried minors, enables a minor's conservator, but not

a conservator for an incapacitated
person, to exercise the powers of a
personal guardian.

Section 5–307. [Acceptance of Appointment; Consent to Jurisdiction.]

By accepting appointment, a guardian submits personally to the jurisdiction of the Court in any proceeding relating to the guardianship that may be instituted by any interested person. Notice of any proceeding must be delivered or mailed to the guardian at the address listed in the Court records and at the address as then known to the petitioner.

COMMENT

This section is comparable to §§ 5–208 and 5–412. These three sections are derived from 1969 UPC §§ 5–208, 5–305 and 5–413.

The "long-arm" principle behind this section is well established. It seems desirable that the court in which acceptance is filed be able to serve its process on the guardian wherever he or she has moved. The continuing interest of that court in the welfare of the minor is ample to justify this provision. The consent to service is real rather than fictional in the guardianship situation, where the guardian acts voluntarily in filing acceptance. It is probable that the form of accep-

tance will expressly embody the provisions of this section, although the statute does not expressly require this.

The proceedings in this Article are flexible. The court should not appoint a guardian unless one is necessary or desirable for the care of the person. If it develops that the needs of the person who is alleged to be incapacitated are not those which would call for a guardian, the court may adjust the proceeding accordingly. By acceptance of the appointment, the guardian submits to the court's jurisdiction in much the same way as a personal representative.

Section 5–308. [Emergency Orders; Temporary Guardians.]

(a) If an incapacitated person has no guardian, an emergency exists, and no other person appears to have authority to act in the circumstances, on appropriate petition the Court may appoint a temporary guardian whose authority may not extend beyond [15 days] [the period of effectiveness of ex parte restraining orders], and who may exercise those powers granted in the order.

(b) If an appointed guardian is not effectively performing duties and the Court further finds that the welfare of the incapacitated person requires immediate action, it may appoint, with or without notice, a temporary guardian for the incapacitated person having the powers of a general guardian for a specified period not to exceed 6 months. The authority of any permanent guardian previously appointed by the Court is suspended as long as a temporary guardian has authority.

(c) The Court may remove a temporary guardian at any time. A temporary guardian shall make any report the Court requires. In other respects the provisions of Parts 1, 2, 3 and 4 of this Article concerning guardians apply to temporary guardians.

COMMENT

The source of this section generally is 1969 UPC § 5–310. However, subsection (a), while still requiring an "emergency" situation for its application, has been significantly revised as to the term of the appointment of this "temporary guardian." 1969 UPC § 5–310(a) permitted appointments of "temporary guardians" for "a specified period not to exceed 6 months." Subsection (a) offers alternative suggestions in bracketed language for permissible periods for appointment of "temporary guardians" in "emergencies." Of course, it is recognized in providing for a shorter period of appointment that a court can renew the appointment for an additional period or additional periods according to the exigencies of the emergency.

The language "and no other person appears to have authority to act in the circumstances" has been added to subsection (a). The added language should aid in preventing the mere institution of a guardianship proceeding from upsetting an arrangement for care under a durable power of attorney, or for nullifying an opportunity to use legislation like the Model Health Care Consent Act to resolve a problem involving the care of a person who is unable to care for himself or herself.

Under subsection (b), the appointing court retains authority to act on petition or on its own motion to suspend a guardian's authority by appointing a temporary guardian. The necessary finding, which need not follow notice to interested persons, is that the welfare of the incapacitated person requires action and the appointed guardian is not acting effectively.

Section 5–309. [General Powers and Duties of Guardian.]

Except as limited pursuant to Section 5–306(c), a guardian of an incapacitated person is responsible for care, custody, and control of the ward, but is not liable to third persons by reason of that responsibility for acts of the ward. In particular and without qualifying the foregoing, a guardian has the same duties, powers and responsibilities as a guardian for a minor as described in Section 5–209(b), (c) and (d).

429

COMMENT

The reference to § 5–306 coordinates this section with the limited guardian concept. All guardians, however appointed, have the powers and duties of a guardian of a minor as provided in § 5–209, subsections (b), (c), and (d). As discussed in the Comment to § 5–209, these powers do not enable a guardian to deal with property matters of the ward. A protective order under § 5–401 et seq. is indicated when property management is needed. Though the legislation does not contemplate that the statutory authority of a guardian may be increased by court order, the court, at the time of appointment or on motion or petition thereafter, may limit the power of a guardian in any respect. The provisions of § 5–304(b) requiring advance notice of a proceeding regarding a guardian's power instituted subsequent to appointment would apply to a post-appointment proceeding to impose or remove restrictions on a guardian's authority.

The language regarding a guardian's liability to third persons for acts of the ward is based on a somewhat differently worded statement in 1969 UPC § 5–310. Both formulations are intended merely to prevent any attribution of liability to a guardian on account of a ward's acts that might be thought to follow from the guardian's legal control of the ward. Neither version is intended to exonerate a guardian from the consequences of his or her own negligence.

Section 5–310. [Termination of Guardianship for Incapacitated Person.]

The authority and responsibility of a guardian of an incapacitated person terminates upon the death of the guardian or ward, the determination of incapacity of the guardian, or upon removal or resignation as provided in Section 5–311. Testamentary appointment under an informally probated will terminates if the will is later denied probate in a formal proceeding. Termination does not affect a guardian's liability for prior acts or the obligation to account for funds and assets of the ward.

COMMENT

The source of this section is 1969 UPC § 5–306 as amended in 1975. The comparable section of this Article, § 5–210, dealing with termination of the authority of a guardian whose authority derives solely from a ward's minority, differs from the instant section in that a guardian of a minor automatically loses authority when the minor attains the age of majority. Under the instant section, an adjudication is necessary to establish that a ward's incapacity has ended otherwise than upon the ward's death.

The concept that a guardian's authority may be terminated even though the guardian remains liable for prior acts or unaccounted funds is a corollary of the proposition that a guardian's authority to act for the ward should end automatically and without court order in certain circumstances. A more primitive concept to the effect that a guardian's authority derived from a court order continues until the court orders otherwise generates unnecessary and excessive use of the courts. Nonetheless, the question of whether a person's incapacity exists or continues and whether a guardian is necessary to provide continuing care and supervision of the ward is too complex to be resolved automatically save in the instances enumerated in this section. If a court determines that a ward's incapacity or

need for a guardian has ended, it may terminate the authority and make an appropriate, additional order regarding the guardian's liabilities for acts done or funds for which there has not been any accounting. The additional order might defer the determination regarding liabilities to a later time.

The penultimate sentence of this section should *not* be included in an enactment except in jurisdictions that have adopted the Uniform Probate Code or have similar legislation permitting the informal probate of wills.

Section 5-311. [Removal or Resignation of Guardian; Termination of Incapacity.]

(a) On petition of the ward or any person interested in the ward's welfare, the Court, after hearing, may remove a guardian if in the best interest of the ward. On petition of the guardian, the Court, after hearing, may accept a resignation.

(b) An order adjudicating incapacity may specify a minimum period, not exceeding six months, during which a petition for an adjudication that the ward is no longer incapacitated may not be filed without special leave. Subject to that restriction, the ward or any person interested in the welfare of the ward may petition for an order that the ward is no longer incapacitated and for termination of the guardianship. A request for an order may also be made informally to the Court and any person who knowingly interferes with transmission of the request may be adjudged guilty of contempt of court.

(c) Upon removal, resignation, or death of the guardian, or if the guardian is determined to be incapacitated, the Court may appoint a successor guardian and make any other appropriate order. Before appointing a successor guardian, or ordering that a ward's incapacity has terminated, the Court shall follow the same procedures to safeguard the rights of the ward that apply to a petition for appointment of a guardian.

COMMENT

The source of this section is 1969 UPC § 5-307.

The ward's incapacity is a question that usually may be reviewed at any time. However, provision is made for a discretionary restriction on review. In all review proceedings, the welfare of the ward is paramount.

The provisions of subsection (b) were designed to provide another protection against use of guardianship proceedings to secure a lock-up of a person who is not capable of looking out for his or her personal needs. If the safeguards imposed at the time of appointment fail to prevent an unnecessary guardianship, subsection (b) is intended to facilitate a ward's unaided or unassisted efforts to inform the court that an injustice has occurred as a result of the guardianship.

Section 5–312. [Proceedings Subsequent to Appointment; Venue.]

(a) The Court at the place where the ward resides has concurrent jurisdiction with the Court that appointed the guardian or in which acceptance of a parental or spousal appointment was filed over resignation, removal, accounting, and other proceedings relating to the guardianship, including proceedings to limit the authority previously conferred on a guardian or to remove limitations previously imposed.

(b) If the Court at the place where the ward resides is not the Court in which acceptance of appointment is filed, the Court in which proceedings subsequent to appointment are commenced, in all appropriate cases, shall notify the other Court, in this or another state, and after consultation with that Court determine whether to retain jurisdiction or transfer the proceedings to the other Court, whichever may be in the best interest of the ward. A copy of any order accepting a resignation, removing a guardian, or altering authority must be sent to the Court in which acceptance of appointment is filed.

COMMENT

The source of this section is 1969 UPC § 5–313. The source section has been expanded by the language in subsection (a) specifying that proceedings to alter the authority of the guardian, which may occur at any time subsequent to the original appointment of the guardian as provided in § 5–306(c), are included in the described concurrent jurisdiction.

The source section has been amended also to include recognition of appointments of guardians by non-testamentary written instruments executed by a parent or spouse.

PART 4

PROTECTION OF PROPERTY OF PERSONS UNDER DISABILITY AND MINORS

Section 5–401. [Protective Proceedings.]

(a) Upon petition and after notice and hearing in accordance with the provisions of this Part, the Court may appoint a conservator or make any other protective order for cause as provided in this section.

(b) Appointment of a conservator or other protective order may be made in relation to the estate and affairs of a minor if the Court determines that a minor owns money or property requiring management or protection that cannot otherwise be provided or has or may have business affairs that may be jeopardized or prevented by minority, or that funds are needed for support and education and that protection is necessary or desirable to obtain or provide funds.

(c) Appointment of a conservator or other protective order may be made in relation to the estate and affairs of a person if the Court determines that (i) the person is unable to manage property and business affairs effectively for such reasons as mental illness, mental deficiency, physical illness or disability, chronic use of drugs, chronic intoxication, confinement, detention by a foreign power, or disappearance; and (ii) the person has property that will be wasted or dissipated unless property management is provided or money is needed for the support, care, and welfare of the person or those entitled to the person's support and that protection is necessary or desirable to obtain or provide money.

COMMENT

This is the basic section of this Part providing for protective proceedings for minors and disabled persons. "Protective proceeding" is a generic term used to describe proceedings to establish conservatorships and obtain protective orders. Persons who may be subjected to the proceedings described here include a broad category of persons who, for a variety of different rea-sons, may be unable to manage their own property.

Since the problems of property management are generally the same for minors and disabled persons, it was thought undesirable to treat these problems in two separate parts. Where there are differences, these have been separately treated in specific sections.

The Comment to § 5–306, supra, points up the different meanings of

433

"incapacity" (warranting guardianship) and "disability."

The source of this section is 1969
UPC § 5–401.

Section 5–402. [Protective Proceedings; Jurisdiction of Business Affairs of Protected Persons.]

After the service of notice in a proceeding seeking the appointment of a conservator or other protective order and until termination of the proceeding, the Court in which the petition is filed has:

(1) exclusive jurisdiction to determine the need for a conservator or other protective order until the proceedings are terminated;

(2) exclusive jurisdiction to determine how the estate of the protected person which is subject to the laws of this State must be managed, expended, or distributed to or for the use of the protected person, the protected person's dependents, or other claimants; and

(3) concurrent jurisdiction to determine the validity of claims against the person or estate of the protected person and questions of title concerning any estate asset.

COMMENT

The source of this section is 1969 UPC § 5–402.

While the bulk of all judicial proceedings involving the conservator will be in the court supervising the conservatorship, third parties may bring suit against the conservator or the protected person on some matters in other courts. Claims against the conservator after appointment are dealt with by § 5–427.

Section 5–403. [Venue.]

Venue for proceedings under this Part is:

(1) in the Court at the place in this state where the person to be protected resides whether or not a guardian has been appointed in another place; or

(2) if the person to be protected does not reside in this State, in the Court at any place where property of the person is located.

COMMENT

The source of this section is 1969 UPC § 5–403.

Venue for protective proceedings lies in the county of residence (rather than domicile) or, in the case of a non-resident, where property of the protected person is located. Unitary management of the property is obtainable through easy transfer of proceedings (§ 1–303[b]) and easy collection of assets by foreign conservators (§ 5–430).

Section 5–404. [Original Petition for Appointment or Protective Order.]

(a) The person to be protected or any person who is interested in the estate, affairs, or welfare of the person, including a parent, guardian, custodian, or any person who would be adversely affected by lack of effective management of the person's property and business affairs may petition for the appointment of a conservator or for other appropriate protective order.

(b) The petition must set forth to the extent known the interest of the petitioner; the name, age, residence, and address of the person to be protected; the name and address of the guardian, if any; the name and address of the nearest relative known to the petitioner; a general statement of the person's property with an estimate of the value thereof, including any compensation, insurance, pension, or allowance to which the person is entitled; and the reason why appointment of a conservator or other protective order is necessary. If the appointment of a conservator is requested, the petition must also set forth the name and address of the person whose appointment is sought and the basis of the claim to priority for appointment.

COMMENT

The source of this section is 1969 UPC § 5–404 with some slight change of wording. For example, the word "business" has been inserted before "affairs" for clarification.

Section 5–405. [Notice.]

(a) On a petition for appointment of a conservator or other protective order, the requirements for notice described in Section 5–304 apply, but (i) if the person to be protected has disappeared or is otherwise situated so as to make personal service of notice impracticable, notice to the person must be given by publication as provided in Section 1–401, and (ii) if the person to be protected is a minor, the provisions of Section 5–206 also apply.

(b) Notice of hearing on a petition for an order subsequent to appointment of a conservator or other protective order must be given to the protected person, any conservator of the protected person's estate, and any other person as ordered by the Court.

COMMENT

The primary sections providing for notice in this Code are §§ 1–401 and 5–304. The source of this section is 1969 UPC § 5–405, but the provisions have been altered somewhat to make reference back to the primary notice provisions rather than repeating the requirements here again.

The provision relative to responding to requests for notice, which had been in 1969 UPC § 5–405, has been moved to and extended in § 5–104. This section intends to include responses to requests for notice through the provision for giving notice to other persons as ordered by the Court in subsection (b).

Section 5–406. [Procedure Concerning Hearing and Order on Original Petition.]

(a) Upon receipt of a petition for appointment of a conservator or other protective order because of minority, the Court shall set a date for hearing. If the Court determines at any time in the proceeding that the interests of the minor are or may be inadequately represented, it may appoint an attorney to represent the minor, giving consideration to the choice of the minor if 14 or more years of age. An attorney appointed by the Court to represent a minor may be granted the powers and duties of a guardian ad litem.

(b) Upon receipt of a petition for appointment of a conservator or other protective order for reasons other than minority, the Court shall set a date for hearing. Unless the person to be protected has chosen counsel, the Court shall appoint an attorney to represent the person who may be granted the powers and duties of a guardian ad litem. If the alleged disability is mental illness, mental deficiency, physical illness or disability, chronic use of drugs, or chronic intoxication, the Court may direct that the person to be protected be examined by a physician designated by the Court, preferably a physician who is not connected with any institution in which the person is a patient or is detained. The Court may send a visitor to interview the person to be protected. The visitor may be a guardian ad litem or an officer or employee of the Court.

(c) The Court may utilize, as an additional visitor, the service of any public or charitable agency to evaluate the condition of the person to be protected and make appropriate recommendations to the Court.

(d) The person to be protected is entitled to be present at the hearing in person. The person is entitled to be represented by counsel, to present evidence, to cross-examine witnesses, including any Court-appointed physician or other qualified person and any visitor[, and to trial by jury]. The issue may be determined at a closed hearing [or without a jury] if the person to be protected or counsel for the person so requests.

(e) Any person may apply for permission to participate in the proceeding and the Court may grant the request, with or without hearing, upon determining that the best interest of the person to be protected will be served thereby. The Court may attach appropriate conditions to the permission.

(f) After hearing, upon finding that a basis for the appointment of a conservator or other protective order has been established, the Court shall make an appointment or other appropriate protective order.

COMMENT

The section establishes a framework within which professionals, including the judge, attorney, and physician, if any, may be expected to exercise good judgment in regard to the minor or disabled person who is the subject of the proceeding. The National Conference accepts that it is desirable to rely on professionals rather than to attempt to draft detailed standards or conditions for appointment.

The source of subsections (a), (b), and (f) is 1969 UPC § 5–407. The phrase "if 14 or more years of age" has been changed for consistency within this Article.

Since there has not been any prior determination of incapacity, the person, for whom a protective order is sought, should be extended the same rights as any other person whose personal freedom may be restricted as a result of the proceedings. Subsection (d) expressly recognizes those rights. The hearing will be an open hearing, unless the protected person or counsel for the person requests a closed hearing.

Subsection (c) permits, but does not require, the court to utilize agencies, who may have a particular expertise, to aid in evaluating the person's condition when a protective order is sought. Subsection (e) permits a person, who might not otherwise be an "interested person," to request permission to participate in the proceeding. The court may or may not grant the permission and may attach conditions to the permission when granted. The court is given broad latitude in using public-interest agencies and in permitting persons, who do not otherwise qualify as "interested persons," in aiding the court to evaluate the case and in determining measures that will be in the best interest of the person for whom a protective order is sought. There are not any rights for these groups to participate in the proceedings—their involvement initially and the extent of their involvement is within the discretionary control of the court.

Section 5–407. [Permissible Court Orders.]

(a) The Court shall exercise the authority conferred in this Part to encourage the development of maximum self-reliance and independence of a protected person and make protective orders only to the extent necessitated by the protected person's mental and adaptive limitations and other conditions warranting the procedure.

(b) The Court has the following powers that may be exercised directly or through a conservator in respect to the estate and business affairs of a protected person:

(1) While a petition for appointment of a conservator or other protective order is pending and after preliminary hearing and without notice to others, the Court may preserve and apply the property of the person to be protected as may be required for the support of the person or dependents of the person.

(2) After hearing and upon determining that a basis for an appointment or other protective order exists with respect to a minor without other disability, the Court has all those powers over the estate and business affairs of the minor which are or may be necessary for the best interest of the minor and members of the minor's immediate family.

(3) After hearing and upon determining that a basis for an appointment or other protective order exists with respect to a person for reasons other than minority, the Court, for the benefit of the person and members of the person's immediate family, has all the powers over the estate and business affairs which the person could exercise if present and not under disability, except the power to make a will. Those powers include, but are not limited to, power to make gifts; to convey or release contingent and expectant interests in property, including marital property rights and any right of survivorship incident to joint tenancy or tenancy by the entirety; to exercise or release powers held by the protected person as trustee, personal representative, custodian for minors, conservator, or donee of a power of appointment; to enter into contracts; to create revocable or irrevocable trusts of property of the estate which may extend beyond the disability or life of the protected person; to exercise options of the protected person to purchase securities or other property; to exercise rights to elect options and change beneficiaries under insurance and annuity policies and to surrender the policies for their cash value; to exercise any right to an elective share in the estate of the person's deceased spouse and to renounce or disclaim any interest by testate or intestate succession or by inter vivos transfer.

(c) The Court may exercise or direct the exercise of the following powers only if satisfied, after notice and hearing, that it is in the best interest of the protected person, and that the person either is incapable of consenting or has consented to the proposed exercise of power:

(1) to exercise or release powers of appointment of which the protected person is donee;

(2) to renounce or disclaim interests;

(3) to make gifts in trust or otherwise exceeding 20 percent of any year's income of the estate; and

(4) to change beneficiaries under insurance and annuity policies.

(d) A determination that a basis for appointment of a conservator or other protective order exists has no effect on the capacity of the protected person.

COMMENT

The court which is supervising a conservatorship is given all the powers that the individual would have if the person were of full capacity. These powers are given to the court that is managing the protected person's property, because the exercise of these powers has important consequences with respect to the protected person's property.

The source of this section is 1969 UPC § 5–408. Subsection (a) has been added. It is the general admonition against an overly intrusive

exercise of its authority by the court adopting the concept of a limited guardianship. The court should not assume any greater authority over the protected person than the capacity and ability of that person necessitates.

There is some change of wording to provide consistency in terminology throughout this Article. Subparagraph (d) has been shortened, but it does not reflect a substantive change.

Section 5–408. [Protective Arrangements and Single Transactions Authorized.]

(a) If it is established in a proper proceeding that a basis exists as described in Section 5–401 for affecting the property and business affairs of a person, the Court, without appointing a conservator, may authorize, direct or ratify any transaction necessary or desirable to achieve any security, service, or care arrangement meeting the foreseeable needs of the protected person. Protective arrangements include payment, delivery, deposit, or retention of funds or property; sale, mortgage, lease, or other transfer of property; entry into an annuity contract, a contract for life care, a deposit contract, or a contract for training and education; or addition to or establishment of a suitable trust.

(b) If it is established in a proper proceeding that a basis exists as described in Section 5–401 for affecting the property and business affairs of a person, the Court, without appointing a conservator, may authorize, direct, or ratify any contract, trust, or other transaction relating to the protected person's property and business affairs if the Court determines that the transaction is in the best interest of the protected person.

(c) Before approving a protective arrangement or other transaction under this section, the Court shall consider the interests of creditors and dependents of the protected person and, in view of the disability, whether the protected person needs the continuing protection of a conservator. The Court may appoint a special conservator to assist in the accomplishment of any protective arrangement or other transaction authorized under this section who shall have the authority conferred by the order and serve until discharged by order after report to the Court of all matters done pursuant to the order of appointment.

COMMENT

It is important that the provision be made for the approval of single transactions or the establishment of protective arrangements as alternatives to full conservatorship. Under present law, a guardianship often must be established simply to make possible a valid transfer of land or securities. This section, consistent with the concept of a limited conservatorship, eliminates the necessity of the establishment of long-term arrangements in this situation.

The source of this section is 1969 UPC § 5–409. There have been some slight changes in terms, but there is not any substantive change from the 1969 UPC.

Section 5–409. [Who May Be Appointed Conservator; Priorities.]

(a) The Court may appoint an individual or a corporation with general power to serve as trustee or conservator of the estate of a protected person. The following are entitled to consideration for appointment in the order listed:

(1) a conservator, guardian of property, or other like fiduciary appointed or recognized by an appropriate court of any other jurisdiction in which the protected person resides;

(2) an individual or corporation nominated by the protected person 14 or more years of age and of sufficient mental capacity to make an intelligent choice;

(3) the spouse of the protected person;

(4) an adult child of the protected person;

(5) a parent of the protected person, or a person nominated by the will of a deceased parent;

(6) any relative of the protected person who has resided with the protected person for more than 6 months before the filing of the petition; and

(7) a person nominated by one who is caring for or paying benefits to the protected person.

(b) A person in priorities (1), (3), (4), (5), or (6) may designate in writing a substitute to serve instead and thereby transfer the priority to the substitute. With respect to persons having equal priority, the Court shall select the one it deems best qualified to serve. The Court, acting in the best interest of the protected person, may pass over a person having priority and appoint a person having a lower priority or no priority.

COMMENT

A flexible system of priorities for appointment as conservator has been provided. A parent may name a conservator for minor children in a will if the parent deems this to be desirable.

The source of this section is 1969 UPC § 5–410. There has been some slight changes in wording, particularly in subsection (b), for clarity without any intent to change substance.

Section 5–410. [Bond.]

The Court may require a conservator to furnish a bond conditioned upon faithful discharge of all duties of the trust according to law, with sureties as it shall specify. Unless otherwise directed, the bond must be in the amount of the aggregate capital value of the property of the estate in the conservator's control, plus one year's estimated income, and minus the value of securities deposited under arrangements requiring an order of the Court for their removal and the value of any land which the fiduciary, by express limitation of power, lacks power to sell or convey without Court authorization. The Court, in lieu of sureties on a bond, may accept other collateral for the performance of the bond, including a pledge of securities or a mortgage of land.

COMMENT

The bond requirements for conservators in this section are somewhat more strict than the requirements for personal representatives under Article III, Part 6 of this Code.

The source of this section is 1969 UPC § 5–411. Some slight changes

in words used, but there has not
been any change in substance.

Section 5–411. [Terms and Requirements of Bonds.]

(a) The following requirements and provisions apply to any
bond required under Section 5–410.

(1) Unless otherwise provided by the terms of the approved
bond, sureties are jointly and severally liable with the conservator and with each other.

(2) By executing an approved bond of a conservator, the
surety consents to the jurisdiction of the Court that issued
letters to the primary obligor in any proceeding pertaining to
the fiduciary duties of the conservator and naming the surety as
a party respondent. Notice of any proceeding must be delivered
to the surety or mailed by registered or certified mail to the
address listed with the Court at the place where the bond is filed
and to the address as then known to the petitioner.

(3) On petition of a successor conservator or any interested
person, a proceeding may be initiated against a surety for
breach of the obligation of the bond of the conservator.

(4) The bond of the conservator is not void after the first
recovery but may be proceeded against from time to time until
the whole penalty is exhausted.

(b) No proceeding may be commenced against the surety on any
matter as to which an action or proceeding against the primary
obligor is barred by adjudication or limitation.

COMMENT

The source of this section is 1969 UPC § 5–412. The word "respondent" has been substituted for "defendant" to be more accurate, perhaps. There is no substantive change in this section.

Section 5–412. [Effect of Acceptance of Appointment.]

By accepting appointment, a conservator submits personally to
the jurisdiction of the Court in any proceeding relating to the estate
which may be instituted by any interested person. Notice of any
proceeding must be delivered to the conservator or mailed by
registered or certified mail to the address as listed in the petition
for appointment or as thereafter reported to the Court and to the
address as then known to the petitioner.

COMMENT

The source of this section is 1969 UPC § 5–413 without substantive change.

Section 5–413. [Compensation and Expenses.]

If not otherwise compensated for services rendered, any visitor, attorney, physician, conservator, or special conservator appointed in a protective proceeding and any attorney whose services resulted in a protective order or in an order that was beneficial to a protected person's estate is entitled to reasonable compensation from the estate.

COMMENT

The source of this section is 1969 UPC § 5–414 without change.

Section 5–414. [Death, Resignation, or Removal of Conservator.]

The Court may remove a conservator for good cause, upon notice and hearing, or accept the resignation of a conservator. Upon the conservator's death, resignation, or removal, the Court may appoint another conservator. A conservator so appointed succeeds to the title and powers of the predecessor.

COMMENT

The source of this section is 1969 UPC § 5–415 without substantive change.

Section 5–415. [Petitions for Orders Subsequent to Appointment.]

(a) Any person interested in the welfare of a person for whom a conservator has been appointed may file a petition in the appointing court for an order:

(1) requiring bond or collateral or additional bond or collateral, or reducing bond;

(2) requiring an accounting for the administration of the trust;

(3) directing distribution;

(4) removing the conservator and appointing a temporary or successor conservator; or

(5) granting other appropriate relief.

(b) A conservator may petition the appointing court for instructions concerning fiduciary responsibility.

(c) Upon notice and hearing, the Court may give appropriate instructions or make any appropriate order.

COMMENT

Once a conservator has been appointed, the Court supervising the trust acts only upon the request of some moving party.

The source of this section is 1969 UPC § 5–416 without change.

Section 5–416. [General Duty of Conservator.]

A conservator, in relation to powers conferred by this Part, or implicit in the title acquired by virtue of the proceeding, shall act as a fiduciary and observe the standards of care applicable to trustees.

COMMENT

The source of this section is 1969 UPC § 5–417. The wording necessarily has been revised because 1969 UPC § 5–417 refers to the Standard of Care and Performance for trustees described in Article VII of the UPC. This section as revised adopts for conservators the standard of care and performance otherwise applicable to trustees in the enacting jurisdiction. If the enacting jurisdiction has enacted 1969 UPC § 7–302, or the standard of care and performance for trustees described in that section (i.e. the prudent-man rule) is otherwise the standard of the enacting jurisdiction, this section as revised will not effectuate any change in substance from 1969 UPC § 5–417.

Section 5–417. [Inventory and Records.]

(a) Within 90 days after appointment, each conservator shall prepare and file with the appointing Court a complete inventory of the estate subject to the conservatorship together with an oath or affirmation that the inventory is believed to be complete and accurate as far as information permits. The conservator shall provide a copy thereof to the protected person if practicable and the person has attained the age of 14 years and has sufficient mental capacity to understand the arrangement. A copy also shall be provided to any guardian or parent with whom the protected person resides.

(b) The conservator shall keep suitable records of the administration and exhibit the same on request of any interested person.

COMMENT

The source of this section is 1969 UPC § 5–418. There has not been any substantive change. In the second sentence, "if practicable" has been substituted for "if he can be located" and there has been some slight change in sentence structure for clarity.

Section 5–418. [Accounts.]

Each conservator shall account to the Court for administration of the trust not less than annually unless the Court directs otherwise, upon resignation or removal and at other times as the Court may direct. On termination of the protected person's minority or disability, a conservator shall account to the Court or to the formerly protected person or the successors of that person. Subject to appeal or vacation within the time permitted, an order after notice and hearing allowing an intermediate account of a conservator adjudicates as to liabilities concerning the matters considered in connection therewith; and an order, following notice and hearing, allowing a final account adjudicates as to all previously unsettled liabilities of the conservator to the protected person or the protected person's successors relating to the conservatorship. In connection with any account, the Court may require a conservator to submit to a physical check of the estate, to be made in any manner the Court specifies.

COMMENT

The persons who are to receive notice of intermediate and final accounts will be identified by court order as provided in § 5–405. Notice is given as described in § 1–401. In other respects, procedures applicable to accountings will be as provided by court rule.

The source of this section is 1969 UPC § 5–419 without substantive change.

Section 5–419. [Conservators; Title by Appointment.]

(a) The appointment of a conservator vests in the conservator title as trustee to all property, or to the part thereof specified in the order, of the protected person, presently held or thereafter acquired, including title to any property theretofore held for the protected person by custodians or attorneys-in-fact. An order specifying that only a part of the property of the protected person vests in the conservator creates a limited conservatorship.

(b) Except as otherwise provided herein, the interest of the protected person in property vested in a conservator by this section

445

is not transferrable or assignable by the protected person. An attempted transfer or assignment by the protected person, though ineffective to affect property rights, may generate a claim for restitution or damages which, subject to presentation and allowance, may be satisfied as provided in Section 5–427.

(c) Neither property vested in a conservator by this section nor the interest of the protected person in that property is subject to levy, garnishment, or similar process other than an order issued in the protective proceeding made as provided in Section 5–427.

COMMENT

This section permits independent administration of the property of the protected person once the appointment of a conservator has been obtained. Any interested person may require the conservator to account in accordance with § 5–418. As a trustee, a conservator holds title to the property of the protected person. The appointment of a conservator is a serious matter and the court must select the fiduciary with great care. Once appointed, the conservator is free to carry on all fiduciary responsibilities. If the conservator defaults in these in any way, the conservator may be made to account to the court.

Unlike a situation involving appointment of a guardian, the appointment of a conservator has no bearing on the capacity of the disabled person to contract or engage in other transactions except insofar as the spendthrift provisions of subsections (b) and (c) of this section apply to property transactions.

The source of this section is 1969 UPC § 5–420 generally. The phrase "or to the part thereof specified in the order," in the first sentence and the second sentence of subsection (a) have been added adopting the concept of a limited guardianship.

The provision in 1969 UPC § 5–420, that the appointment of a conservator is not a transfer or alienation within the meaning of those terms as used in statutes or other legal instrument restraining transfer or alienation, has not been included in this section, because it is believed that the statement is unnecessary.

Subsection (b) provides a spendthrift effect for property of the protected person vested in the conservator. An attempt by the protected person to transfer or alienate property may nevertheless generate a claim for restitution. This subsection was not a part of 1969 UPC § 5–420, but several suggestions have been made that the spendthrift provisions should be incorporated. The concept is analogous to spendthrift trust provisions often included when the beneficiary is incapable of managing his or her own property. The concept is also consistent with a conservatorship arrangement for protecting the estate of an incapacitated person.

Subsection (c) is the involuntary side of the spendthrift effect (subparagraph [b] is the voluntary restraint), which is also analogous to the spendthrift trust provisions and it was not a part of 1969 UPC § 5–420.

Section 5–420. [Recording of Conservator's Letters.]

(a) Letters of conservatorship are evidence of transfer of all assets, or the part thereof specified in the letters, of a protected person to the conservator. An order terminating a conservatorship is evidence of transfer of all assets subjected to the conservatorship from the conservator to the protected person, or to successors of the person.

(b) Subject to the requirements of general statutes governing the filing or recordation of documents of title to land or other property, letters of conservatorship and orders terminating conservatorships, may be filed or recorded to give record notice of title as between the conservator and the protected person.

COMMENT

The source of this section is 1969 UPC § 5–421. The phrases "or the part thereof specified in the letters," in the first sentence and "subjected to the conservatorship" in the second sentence have been added to recognize the concept of a limited conservatorship.

Section 5–421. [Sale, Encumbrance, or Transaction Involving Conflict of Interest; Voidable; Exceptions.]

Any sale or encumbrance to a conservator, the spouse, agent, attorney of a conservator, or any corporation, trust, or other organization in which the conservator has a substantial beneficial interest, or any other transaction involving the estate being administered by the conservator which is affected by a substantial conflict between fiduciary and personal interests is voidable unless the transaction is approved by the Court after notice as directed by the Court.

COMMENT

The source of this section is 1969 UPC § 5–422. The phrase, "or any other transaction involving the estate being administered by the conservator which is affected by a substantial conflict between fiduciary and personal interests ..." has been substituted for the phrase, "or any transaction which is affected by a substantial conflict of interest ..." for clarity. The phrase, "notice as directed by the Court" is a revision of wording and recognizes that notice may be to persons or agencies other than "interested parties" at the direction of the court, but the phrase is not a substantive

change from the provision in 1969
UPC § 5–422.

Section 5–422. [Persons Dealing With Conservators; Protection.]

(a) A person who in good faith either assists or deals with a conservator for value in any transaction other than those requiring a Court order as provided in Section 5–407 is protected as if the conservator properly exercised the power. The fact that a person knowingly deals with a conservator does not alone require the person to inquire into the existence of a power or the propriety of its exercise, but restrictions on powers of conservators which are endorsed on letters as provided in Section 5–425 are effective as to third persons. A person is not bound to see to the proper application of estate assets paid or delivered to a conservator.

(b) The protection expressed in this section extends to any procedural irregularity or jurisdictional defect occurred in proceedings leading to the issuance of letters and is not a substitution for protection provided by comparable provisions of the law relating to commercial transactions or to simplifying transfers of securities by fiduciaries.

COMMENT

The source of this section is 1969 UPC § 5–423 adopted without substantive change.

The section codifies the *b.f.p.* rule generally followed in transactions with fiduciaries. Nevertheless, any person dealing with a known conservator for another should examine the letters of appointment of the conservator for any limitations on the conservator's authority endorsed on the letters pursuant to § 5–425.

Section 5–423. [Powers of Conservator in Administration.]

(a) Subject to limitation provided in Section 5–425, a conservator has all of the powers conferred in this section and any additional powers conferred by law on trustees in this State. In addition, a conservator of the estate of an unmarried minor [under the age of 18 years], as to whom no one has parental rights, has the duties and powers of a guardian of a minor described in Section 5–209 until the minor attains [the age of 18 years] or marries, but the parental rights so conferred on a conservator do not preclude appointment of a guardian as provided in Part 2.

(b) A conservator without Court authorization or confirmation, may invest and reinvest funds of the estate as would a trustee.

(c) A conservator, acting reasonably in efforts to accomplish the purpose of the appointment, may act without Court authorization or confirmation, to

(1) collect, hold, and retain assets of the estate including land in another state, until judging that disposition of the assets should be made, and the assets may be retained even though they include an asset in which the conservator is personally interested;

(2) receive additions to the estate;

(3) continue or participate in the operation of any business or other enterprise;

(4) acquire an undivided interest in an estate asset in which the conservator, in any fiduciary capacity, holds an undivided interest;

(5) invest and reinvest estate assets in accordance with subsection (b);

(6) deposit estate funds in a state or federally insured financial institution, including one operated by the conservator;

(7) acquire or dispose of an estate asset, including land in another state, for cash or on credit, at public or private sale, and manage, develop, improve, exchange, partition, change the character of, or abandon an estate asset;

(8) make ordinary or extraordinary repairs or alterations in buildings or other structures; demolish any improvements; and raze existing or erect new party walls or buildings;

(9) subdivide, develop, or dedicate land to public use; make or obtain the vacation of plats and adjust boundaries; adjust differences in valuation or exchange or partition by giving or receiving considerations; and dedicate easements to public use without consideration;

(10) enter for any purpose into a lease as lessor or lessee with or without option to purchase or renew for a term within or extending beyond the term of the conservatorship;

(11) enter into a lease or arrangement for exploration and removal of minerals or other natural resources or enter into a pooling or unitization agreement;

(12) grant an option involving disposition of an estate asset and take an option for the acquisition of any asset;

(13) vote a security, in person or by general or limited proxy;

(14) pay calls, assessments, and any other sums chargeable or accruing against or on account of securities;

(15) sell or exercise stock-subscription or conversion rights;

(16) consent, directly or through a committee or other agent, to the reorganization, consolidation, merger, dissolution, or liquidation of a corporation or other business enterprise;

(17) hold a security in the name of a nominee or in other form without disclosure of the conservatorship so that title to the security may pass by delivery, but the conservator is liable for any act of the nominee in connection with the stock so held;

(18) insure the assets of the estate against damage or loss and the conservator against liability with respect to third persons;

(19) borrow money to be repaid from estate assets or otherwise; advance money for the protection of the estate or the protected person and for all expenses, losses, and liability sustained in the administration of the estate or because of the holding or ownership of any estate assets, for which the conservator has a lien on the estate as against the protected person for advances so made;

(20) pay or contest any claim; settle a claim by or against the estate or the protected person by compromise, arbitration, or otherwise; and release, in whole or in part, any claim belonging to the estate to the extent the claim is uncollectible;

(21) pay taxes, assessments, compensation of the conservator, and other expenses incurred in the collection, care, administration, and protection of the estate;

(22) allocate items of income or expense to either estate income or principal, as provided by law, including creation of reserves out of income for depreciation, obsolescence, or amortization, or for depletion in mineral or timber properties;

(23) pay any sum distributable to a protected person or dependent of the protected person by paying the sum to the distributee or by paying the sum for the use of the distributee to the guardian of the distributee, or, if none, to a relative or other person having custody of the distributee;

(24) employ persons, including attorneys, auditors, investment advisors, or agents, even though they are associated with the conservator, to advise or assist in the performance of administrative duties; act upon their recommendation without independent investigation; and instead of acting personally, employ

one or more agents to perform any act of administration, whether or not discretionary;

(25) prosecute or defend actions, claims, or proceedings in any jurisdiction for the protection of estate assets and of the conservator in the performance of fiduciary duties; and

(26) execute and deliver all instruments that will accomplish or facilitate the exercise of the powers vested in the conservator.

COMMENT

The source of this section is 1969 UPC § 5–424. There have been some minor stylistic changes, but there has not been any substantive change.

Any limitations or enlargements of the powers provided in this section for the conservator must be endorsed on the conservator's letters of appointment as provided in § 5–425.

Section 5–424. [Distributive Duties and Powers of Conservator.]

(a) A conservator may expend or distribute income or principal of the estate without Court authorization or confirmation for the support, education, care, or benefit of the protected person and dependents in accordance with the following principles:

(1) The conservator shall consider recommendations relating to the appropriate standard of support, education, and benefit for the protected person or dependent made by a parent or guardian, if any. The conservator may not be surcharged for sums paid to persons or organizations furnishing support, education, or care to the protected person or a dependent pursuant to the recommendations of a parent or guardian of the protected person unless the conservator knows that the parent or guardian derives personal financial benefit therefrom, including relief from any personal duty of support or the recommendations are clearly not in the best interest of the protected person.

(2) The conservator shall expend or distribute sums reasonably necessary for the support, education, care, or benefit of the protected person and dependents with due regard to (i) the size of the estate, the probable duration of the conservatorship, and the likelihood that the protected person, at some future time, may be fully able to be wholly self-sufficient and able to manage business affairs and the estate; (ii) the accustomed standard of living of the protected person and dependents; and (iii) other funds or sources used for the support of the protected person.

451

(3) The conservator may expend funds of the estate for the support of persons legally dependent on the protected person and others who are members of the protected person's household who are unable to support themselves, and who are in need of support.

(4) Funds expended under this subsection may be paid by the conservator to any person, including the protected person, to reimburse for expenditures that the conservator might have made, or in advance for services to be rendered to the protected person if it is reasonable to expect the services will be performed and advance payments are customary or reasonably necessary under the circumstances.

(5) A conservator, in discharging the responsibilities conferred by Court order and this Part, shall implement the principles described in Section 5–407(a), to the extent possible.

(b) If the estate is ample to provide for the purposes implicit in the distributions authorized by the preceding subsections, a conservator for a protected person other than a minor has power to make gifts to charity and other objects as the protected person might have been expected to make, in amounts that do not exceed in total for any year 20 percent of the income from the estate.

(c) When a minor who has not been adjudged disabled under Section 5–401(c) attains majority, the conservator, after meeting all claims and expenses of administration, shall pay over and distribute all funds and properties to the formerly protected person as soon as possible.

(d) If satisfied that a protected person's disability, other than minority, has ceased, the conservator, after meeting all claims and expenses of administration, shall pay over and distribute all funds and properties to the formerly protected person as soon as possible.

(e) If a protected person dies, the conservator shall deliver to the Court for safekeeping any will of the deceased protected person which may have come into the conservator's possession, inform the executor or beneficiary named therein of the delivery, and retain the estate for delivery to a duly appointed personal representative of the decedent or other persons entitled thereto. If, 40 days after the death of the protected person, no other person has been appointed personal representative and no application or petition for appointment is before the Court, the conservator may apply to exercise the powers and duties of a personal representative in order to be able to proceed to administer and distribute the decedent's estate. Upon application for an order granting the powers of a personal representative to a conservator, after notice to any person nominated personal representative by any will of which the applicant is aware, the Court may grant the application upon determining that there is no objection and endorse the letters of the conservator to note that the formerly protected person is deceased and that the conservator has acquired all of the powers and duties of a personal representative. The making and entry of an order under this section has the effect of an order of appointment of a personal representative [as provided in Section 3–308 and Parts 6 through 10 of Article III], but the estate in the name of the conservator, after administration, may be distributed to the decedent's successors without prior re-transfer to the conservator as personal representative.

COMMENT

This section sets out those situations wherein the conservator may distribute property or disburse funds during the continuance of or on termination of the trust. Section 5–415(b) makes it clear that a conservator may seek instructions from the court on questions arising under this section. Subsection (e) is derived in part from § 11.80.150 Revised Code of Washington (RCWA 11.80.150).

The source of this section is 1969 UPC § 5–425. There have been some stylistic changes in the wording.

Wording has been added to paragraphs (a)(1) and (a)(2) to make it clear that those provisions apply to dependents of the protected person as well as to the protected person. The additions are consistent with provisions in paragraphs (a)(3) and (a)(4).

Paragraph (a)(5) has been added in this section. It is a cross reference to the admonition in § 5–407(a) reiterating the principle that the conservator should continually be conscious of the policies of this Article against an overly intrusive exercise of control over property of the protected person.

The term "prior" has been deleted before the word "claims" in subsection (c). "Prior claims" is ambiguous in 1969 UPC § 5–425(c).

In the bracketed portion of subsection (e), the reference should be to the relevant statutes of the enacting jurisdiction pertaining to appointment proceedings for personal representatives in decedents' estates.

Section 5–425. [Enlargement or Limitation of Powers of Conservator.]

Subject to the restrictions in Section 5–407(c), the Court may confer on a conservator at the time of appointment or later, in addition to the powers conferred by Sections 5–423 and 5–424, any power that the Court itself could exercise under Sections 5–407(b)(2) and 5–407(b)(3). The Court, at the time of appointment or later, may limit the powers of a conservator otherwise conferred by Sections 5–423 and 5–424 or previously conferred by the Court and may at any time remove or modify any limitation. If the Court limits any power conferred on the conservator by Section 5–423 or Section 5–424, or specifies, as provided in Section 5–419(a), that title to some but not all assets of the protected person vest in the conservator, the limitation or specification of assets subject to the conservatorship must be endorsed upon the letters of appointment.

COMMENT

This section makes it possible to appoint a fiduciary whose powers are limited to part of the estate or who may conduct important transactions, such as sales and mortgages of land, only with special court authorization. In the latter case, a conservator would be in much the same position of a guardian of property under the law currently in force in most states, but he would have title to the property. The purpose of giving conservators title as trustees is to ensure that the provisions for protection of third parties have full effect. The Veterans Administration may insist, when it is paying benefits to a minor or disabled person, that the letters of conservatorship limit powers to those of a guardian under the Uniform Veteran's Guardianship Act and re-quire the conservator to file annual accounts.

The court may not only limit the powers of the conservator, but it may expand powers of the conservator so as to make it possible to act as the court itself might act.

The source of this section is 1969 UPC § 5–426. Although the UPC originally contemplated that limited conservatorships could be accommodated by application of the provisions of this section, the phrase "or specifies, as provided in Section 5–419(a), that title to some but not all assets of the protected person vest in the conservator,...." has been added to the last sentence to make it explicit and clearer that there can be a conservatorship limited both in terms of powers of the conservator and as to the property to which it applies.

Section 5–426. [Preservation of Estate Plan; Right to Examine.]

In (i) investing the estate, (ii) selecting assets of the estate for distribution under subsections (a) and (b) of Section 5–424, and (iii) utilizing powers of revocation or withdrawal available for the support of the protected person and exercisable by the conservator or the Court, the conservator and the Court shall take into account any estate plan of the protected person known to them, including a will, any revocable trust of which the person is settlor, and any contract, transfer, or joint ownership arrangement originated by the protected person with provisions for payment or transfer of benefits or interests at the person's death to another or others. The conservator may examine the will of the protected person.

COMMENT

The source of this section is 1969 UPC § 5–427 with some minor stylistic changes.

Section 5–427. [Claims Against Protected Person; Enforcement.]

(a) A conservator may pay or secure from the estate claims against the estate or against the protected person arising before or after the conservatorship upon their presentation and allowance in accordance with the priorities stated in subsection (c). A claim may be presented by either of the following methods:

(1) The claimant may deliver or mail to the conservator a written statement of the claim indicating its basis, the name and mailing address of the claimant, and the amount claimed; or

(2) The claimant may file a written statement of the claim, in the form prescribed by rule, with the clerk of Court and deliver or mail a copy of the statement to the conservator.

(b) A claim is deemed presented on the first to occur of receipt of the written statement of claim by the conservator or the filing of the claim with the Court. A presented claim is allowed if it is not disallowed by written statement mailed by the conservator to the claimant within 60 days after its presentation. The presentation of a claim tolls any statute of limitation relating to the claim until 30 days after its disallowance.

(c) A claimant whose claim has not been paid may petition the [appropriate] Court for determination of the claim at any time before it is barred by the applicable statute of limitation and, upon due proof, procure an order for its allowance, payment, or security from the estate. If a proceeding is pending against a protected person at the time of appointment of a conservator or is initiated against the protected person thereafter, the moving party shall give notice of the proceeding to the conservator if the proceeding could result in creating a claim against the estate.

(d) If it appears that the estate in conservatorship is likely to be exhausted before all existing claims are paid, the conservator shall distribute the estate in money or in kind in payment of claims in the following order:

(1) costs and expenses of administration;

(2) claims of the federal or state government having priority under other laws;

(3) claims incurred by the conservator for care, maintenance, and education, previously provided to the protected person or the protected person's dependents;

(4) claims arising prior to the conservatorship;

(5) all other claims.

(e) No preference may be given in the payment of any claim over any other claim of the same class, and a claim due and payable is not entitled to a preference over claims not due; but if it appears that the assets of the conservatorship are adequate to meet all existing claims, the Court, acting in the best interest of the protected person, may order the conservator to give a mortgage or other security on the conservatorship estate to secure payment at some future date of any or all claims in class 5.

COMMENT

The source of subsections (a) and (b) is 1969 UPC § 5–428(a) and (b) with the addition of a provision in subsection (a) recognizing that a priority for claims is established in subsection (c).

The sources of subsection (c) are 1969 UPC §§ 3–805 and 5–428(c)

generally. Since the priorities established in UPC § 3–805 apply to decedents' estates, the priorities established here for conservatorships are different. The establishment of preferences by categories of claims for conservatorships is new in this Article.

Section 5–428. [Personal Liability of Conservator.]

(a) Unless otherwise provided in the contract, a conservator is not personally liable on a contract properly entered into in fiduciary capacity in the course of administration of the estate unless the conservator fails to reveal the representative capacity and identify the estate in the contract.

(b) The conservator is personally liable for obligations arising from ownership or control of property of the estate or for torts committed in the course of administration of the estate only if personally at fault.

(c) Claims based on (i) contracts entered into by a conservator in fiduciary capacity, (ii) obligations arising from ownership or control of the estate, or (iii) torts committed in the course of administration of the estate, may be asserted against the estate by proceeding against the conservator in fiduciary capacity, whether or not the conservator is personally liable therefor.

(d) Any question of liability between the estate and the conservator personally may be determined in a proceeding for accounting, surcharge, or indemnification, or other appropriate proceeding or action.

COMMENT

The source of this section is 1969 UPC § 5–429 with some stylistic changes. There is not any change in substance.

Section 5–429. [Termination of Proceedings.]

The protected person, conservator, or any other interested person, may petition the Court to terminate the conservatorship. A protected person seeking termination is entitled to the same rights and procedures as in an original proceeding for a protective order. The Court, upon determining after notice and hearing that the minority or disability of the protected person has ceased, shall terminate the conservatorship. Upon termination, title to assets of the estate passes to the formerly protected person or to successors. The order of termination must provide for expenses of administration and direct the conservator to execute appropriate instruments to evidence the transfer.

COMMENT

Persons entitled to notice of a petition to terminate a conservatorship are identified by § 5–405.

Any interested person may seek the termination of a conservatorship if there is some question as to whether the trust is still needed. In some situations (e.g., the individual who returns after being missing) it may be perfectly clear that the person is no longer in need of a conservatorship.

An order terminating a conservatorship may be recorded as evidence of the transfer of title from the estate. See § 5–420.

The source of this section is 1969 UPC § 5–430 with some stylistic changes. The "personal representative" of the protected person has been deleted from specific enumeration in the first sentence because the "personal representative" also is covered by the term "other interested person".

Section 5–430. [Payment of Debt and Delivery of Property to Foreign Conservator Without Local Proceedings.]

(a) Any person indebted to a protected person or having possession of property or of an instrument evidencing a debt, stock, or chose in action belonging to a protected person may pay or deliver it to a conservator, guardian of the estate, or other like fiduciary appointed by a court of the state of residence of the protected person upon being presented with proof of appointment and an affidavit made by or on behalf of the fiduciary stating:

(1) that no protective proceeding relating to the protected person is pending in this State; and

(2) that the foreign fiduciary is entitled to payment or to receive delivery.

(b) If the person to whom the affidavit is presented is not aware of any protective proceeding pending in this State, payment or delivery in response to the demand and affidavit discharges the debtor or possessor.

COMMENT

Section 5–409(a)(1) gives a foreign conservator or guardian of property, appointed in the jurisdiction in which the disabled person resides, first priority for appointment as conservator in this State.

A foreign conservator may easily obtain any property in this State and take it to the residence of the protected person for management.

The source of this section is 1969 UPC § 5–431.

Section 5–431. [Foreign Conservator; Proof of Authority; Bond; Powers.]

If a conservator has not been appointed in this State and no petition in a protective proceeding is pending in this State, a conservator appointed in the state in which the protected person resides may file in a Court of this State in a [county] in which property belonging to the protected person is located, authenticated copies of letters of appointment and of any bond. Thereafter, the domiciliary foreign conservator may exercise as to assets in this State all powers of a conservator appointed in this State and may maintain actions and proceedings in this State subject to any conditions imposed upon non-resident parties generally.

COMMENT

The source of this section is 1969 UPC § 5–432 with some stylistic changes.

PART 5

DURABLE POWER OF ATTORNEY

Adoption of Uniform Durable Power of Attorney Act

Part 5 of Article V of the Uniform Probate Code was amended by the National Conference of Commissioners on Uniform State Laws in 1979. Sections 5–501 to 5–505, as enacted in 1979, are identical to sections 1 to 5 of the Uniform Durable Power of Attorney Act, also approved by the National Conference in 1979 as an alternative to Part 5 of Article V of the Uniform Probate Code. See Prefatory Note, infra.

PREFATORY NOTE

The National Conference included Sections 5–501 and 5–502 in Uniform Probate Code (1969) (1975) concerning powers of attorney to assist persons interested in establishing non-court regimes for the management of their affairs in the event of later incompetency or disability. The purpose was to recognize a form of senility insurance comparable to that available to relatively wealthy persons who use funded, revocable trusts for persons who are unwilling or unable to transfer assets as required to establish a trust.

The provisions included in the original UPC modify two principles that have controlled written powers of attorney. Section 5–501 (UPC (1969) (1975)), creating what has come to be known as a "durable power of attorney," permits a principal to create an agency in another that continues in spite of the principal's later loss of capacity to contract. The only requirement is that an instrument creating a durable power contain language showing that the principal intends the agency to remain effective in spite of his later incompetency.

Section 5–502 (UPC (1969) (1975)) alters the common law rule that a principal's death ends the authority of his agents and voids all acts occurring thereafter including any done in complete ignorance of the death. The new view, applicable to durable and nondurable, written powers of attorney, validates post-mortem exercise of authority by agents who act in good faith and without actual knowledge of the principal's death. The idea here was to encourage use of powers of attorney by removing a potential trap for agents in fact and third persons who decide to rely on a power at a time when they cannot be certain that the principal is then alive.

To the knowledge of the Joint Editorial Board for the Uniform Probate Code, the only statutes resembling the power of attorney sections of the UPC (1969) (1975) that had been enacted prior to the approval and promulgation of the Code were Sections 11–9.1 and 11–9.2 of Code of

Virginia [1950]. Since then, a variety of UPC inspired statutes adjusting agency rules have been enacted in more than thirty states.

This [Act] [Section] originated in 1977 with a suggestion from within the National Conference that a new free-standing uniform act, designed to make powers of attorney more useful, would be welcome in many states. For states that have yet to adopt durable power legislation, this new National Conference product represents a respected, collective judgment, identifying the best of the ideas reflected in the recent flurry of new state laws on the subject; additional enactments of a new and improved uniform act should result. For other states that have acted already, this new act offers a reason to consider amendments, including elimination of restrictions that no longer appear necessary.

In the course of preparing this [Act] [Section], the Joint Editorial Board for the Uniform Probate Code, acting as a Special Committee on the new project, evolved what it considers to be improvements in §§ 5–501 and 5–502 of the 1969 and 1975 versions of the Code. In the main, the changes reflect stylistic matters. However, the idea reflected in Section 3(a)—that draftsmen of powers of attorney may wish to anticipate the appointment of a conservator or guardian for the principal—is new, and a brief explanation is in order.

When the Code was originally drafted, the dominant idea was that durable powers would be used as alternatives to court-oriented, protective procedures. Hence, the draftsmen merely provided that appointment of a conservator for a principal who had granted a durable power to another did not automatically revoke the agency; rather, it would be up to the court's appointee to determine whether revocation was appropriate. The provision was designed to discourage the institution of court proceedings by persons interested solely in ending an agent's authority. It later appeared sensible to adjust the durable power concept so that it may be used either as an alternative to a protective procedure, or as a designed supplement enabling nomination of the principal's choice for guardian to an appointing court and continuing to authorize efficient estate management under the direction of a court appointee.

The sponsoring committee considered and rejected the suggestion that the word "durable" be omitted from the title. While it is true that the act describes "durable" and "non-durable" powers of attorney, this is merely the result of use of language to accomplish a purpose of making both categories of power more reliable for use than formerly. In the case of non-durable powers, the act extends validity by the provisions in Section [4] [5–504] protecting agents in fact and third persons who rely in good faith on a power of attorney when, unknown to them, the principal is incompetent or deceased. The general purpose of the act is to alter common law rules that created traps for the unwary by voiding powers on the principal's incompetency or death. The act does not purport to deal with other aspects of powers of attorney, and a label that would result from dropping "durable" would be misleading to the extent that it suggested otherwise.

Section 5–501. [Definition.]

A durable power of attorney is a power of attorney by which a principal designates another his attorney in fact in writing and the writing contains the words "This power of attorney shall not be affected by subsequent disability or incapacity of the principal, or lapse of time," or "This power of attorney shall become effective upon the disability or incapacity of the principal," or similar words showing the intent of the principal that the authority conferred shall be exercisable notwithstanding the principal's subsequent disability or incapacity, and unless it states a time of termination, notwithstanding the lapse of time since the execution of the instrument.

COMMENT

This section, derived from the first sentence of UPC 5–501 (1969) (1975), is a definitional section that supports use of the term "durable power of attorney" in the sections that follow. The second quoted expression was designed to emphasize that a durable power with postponed effectiveness is permitted. Some UPC critics have been bothered by the reference here to a later condition of "disability or incapacity," a circumstance that may be difficult to ascertain if it can be established without a court order. The answer, of course, is that draftsmen of durable powers are not limited in their choice of words to describe the later time when the principal wishes the authority of the agent in fact to become opera-

tive. For example, a durable power might be framed to confer authority commencing when two or more named persons, possibly including the principal's lawyer, physician or spouse, concur that the principal has become incapable of managing his affairs in a sensible and efficient manner and deliver a signed statement to that effect to the attorney in fact.

In this and following sections, it is assumed that the principal is competent when the power of attorney is signed. If this is not the case, nothing in this Act is intended to alter the result that would be reached under general principles of law.

Section 5–502. [Durable Power of Attorney Not Affected by Lapse of Time, Disability or Incapacity.]

All acts done by an attorney in fact pursuant to a durable power of attorney during any period of disability or incapacity of the principal have the same effect and inure to the benefit of and bind the principal and his successors in interest as if the principal were competent and not disabled. Unless the instrument states a time of termination, the power is exercisable notwithstanding the lapse of time since the execution of the instrument.

COMMENT

This section is derived from the second sentence of UPC 5–501 (1969) (1975) modified by deleting reference to the effect on a durable power of the principal's death, a matter that is now covered in Section [4] [5–504] which provides a single standard· for durable and non-durable powers.

The words "any period of disability or incapacity of the principal" are intended to include periods during which the principal is legally incompetent, but are not intended to be limited to such periods. In the Uniform Probate Code, the word "disability" is defined, and the term "incapacitated person" is defined. In the context of this section, however, the important point is that the terms embrace "legal incompetence," as well as less grievous disadvantages.

Section 5–503. [Relation of Attorney in Fact to Court–Appointed Fiduciary.]

(a) If, following execution of a durable power of attorney, a court of the principal's domicile appoints a conservator, guardian of the estate, or other fiduciary charged with the management of all of the principal's property or all of his property except specified exclusions, the attorney in fact is accountable to the fiduciary as well as to the principal. The fiduciary has the same power to revoke or amend the power of attorney that the principal would have had if he were not disabled or incapacitated.

(b) A principal may nominate, by a durable power of attorney, the conservator, guardian of his estate, or guardian of his person for consideration by the court if protective proceedings for the principal's person or estate are thereafter commenced. The court shall make its appointment in accordance with the principal's most recent nomination in a durable power of attorney except for good cause or disqualification.

COMMENT

Subsection (a) closely resembles the last two sentences of UPC § 5–501 (1969) (1975); most of the changes are stylistic. One change going beyond style states that an agent in fact is accountable *both* to the principal and a conservator or guardian if a court has appointed a fiduciary; the earlier version described accountability only to the fiduciary.

As explained in the introductory comment, the purpose of subsection (b) is to emphasize that agencies under durable powers and guardians or conservators may co-exist. It is not the purpose of the act to encourage resort to court for a fiduciary appointment that should be largely unnecessary when an alternative regime has been provided via a durable power. Indeed, the best reason for permitting a principal to use a durable power to express his preference regarding any future court appointee charged with the care and protection of his person or estate may be to secure the authority of the attorney in fact against upset by arranging matters so that the likely appointee in any future protective proceedings will be the attorney in fact or another equally congenial to the principal and his plans. However, the evolution of a free-standing durable power act increases the prospects that UPC–type statutes covering protective proceedings will not apply when a protective proceeding is commenced for one who has created a durable power. This means that a court receiving a petition for a guardian or conservator may not be governed by standards like those in UPC § 5–304 (personal guardians) and § 5–401(2) and related sections which are designed to deter unnecessary protective proceedings. Finally, attorneys and others may find various good uses for a regime in which a conservator directs exercise of an agent's authority under a durable power. For example, the combination would confer jurisdiction on the court handling the protective proceeding to approve or ratify a desirable transaction that might not be possible without the protection of a court order. The alternative of a declaratory judgment proceeding might be difficult or impossible in some states.

It is to be noted that the "fiduciary" described in subsection (a), to whom an attorney in fact under a durable power is accountable and who may revoke or amend the durable power, does not include a guardian of the person only. In subsection (b), however, the authority of a principal to nominate extends to a guardian of the person as well as to conservators and guardians of estates.

Discussion of this section in NCCUSL's Committee of the Whole involved the question of whether an agent's accountability, as described here, might be effectively countermanded by appropriate language in a power of attorney. The response was negative. The reference is to basic accountability like that owed by every fiduciary to his beneficiary and that distinguishes a fiduciary relationship from those involving gifts or general powers of appointment. The section is not intended to describe a particular form of accounting. Hence, the context differs from those involving statutory duties to account in court, or with specified frequency, where draftsmen of controlling instruments may be able to excuse statutory details relating to accountings without affecting the general principle of accountability.

Section 5–504. [Power of Attorney Not Revoked Until Notice.]

(a) The death of a principal who has executed a written power of attorney, durable or otherwise, does not revoke or terminate the agency as to the attorney in fact or other person, who, without actual knowledge of the death of the principal, acts in good faith under the power. Any action so taken, unless otherwise invalid or unenforceable, binds successors in interest of the principal.

(b) The disability or incapacity of a principal who has previously executed a written power of attorney that is not a durable power does not revoke or terminate the agency as to the attorney in fact or other person, who, without actual knowledge of the disability or incapacity of the principal, acts in good faith under the power. Any action so taken, unless otherwise invalid or unenforceable, binds the principal and his successors in interest.

COMMENT

UPC §§ 5–501 and 5–502 (1969) (1975) are flawed by different standards for durable and non-durable powers vis a vis the protection of an attorney in fact who purports to exercise a power after the principal has died. Section 5–501 (1969) (1975), applicable only to durable powers, expresses a most unsatisfactory standard; i.e. the attorney in fact is protected if the exercise occurs "during any period of uncertainty as to whether the principal is dead or alive...." Section 5–502 (1969) (1975), applicable only to non-durable powers, protects the agent who "without actual knowledge of the death ... of the principal, acts in good faith under the power of attorney...." Section [4] [5–504](a) expresses as a single test the standard now contained in § 5–502 (1969) (1975).

Subsection (b), applicable only to nondurable powers that are controlled by the traditional view that a principal's loss of capacity ends the authority of his agents, embodies the substance of UPC § 5–502 (1969) (1975).

The discussion in the Committee of the Whole established that the language "or other person" in subsections (a) and (b) is intended to refer to persons who transact business with the attorney in fact under the authority conferred by the power. Consequently, persons in this category who act in good faith and without the actual knowledge described in the subsections are protected by the statute.

Also, there was discussion of possible conflict between the actual knowledge test here prescribed for protection of persons relying on the continuance of a power and constructive notice concepts under statutes governing the recording of instruments affecting real estate. The view was expressed in the Committee of the Whole that the recording statutes would continue to control since those statutes are specifically designed to encourage public recording of documents affecting land titles. It was also suggested that "good faith," as required by this section, might be lacking in the unlikely case of one who, without actual knowledge of the principal's death or incompetency, accepted a conveyance executed by an attorney in fact without checking the public record where he would have found an instrument disclosing the principal's death or incompetency. If so, there would be no conflict between this act and recording statutes.

It is to be noted, also, that this section deals only with the effect of a principal's death or incompetency as a revocation of a power of attorney; it does not relate to an express revocation of a power or to the expiration of a power according to its terms. Further, since a durable power is not revoked by incapacity, the section's coverage of revocation of powers of attorney by the principal's incapacity is restricted to powers that are not durable. The only effect of the Act on rules governing express revocations of powers of attorney is as described in Section [5] [5-505].

Section 5–505. [Proof of Continuance of Durable and Other Powers of Attorney by Affidavit.]

As to acts undertaken in good faith reliance thereon, an affidavit executed by the attorney in fact under a power of attorney, durable or otherwise, stating that he did not have at the time of exercise of the power actual knowledge of the termination of the power by revocation or of the principal's death, disability, or incapacity is conclusive proof of the nonrevocation or nontermination of the power at that time. If the exercise of the power of attorney requires execution and delivery of any instrument that is recordable, the affidavit when authenticated for record is likewise recordable. This section does not affect any provision in a power of attorney for its termination by expiration of time or occurrence of an event other than express revocation or a change in the principal's capacity.

COMMENT

This section, embodying the substance and form of UPC 5–502(b) (1969) (1975), has been extended to apply to durable powers. It is unclear whether UPC 5–502(b) (1969) (1975) applies to durable powers. Affidavits protecting persons dealing with attorneys in fact extend the utility of powers of attorney and plainly should be available for use by all attorneys in fact.

The matters stated in an affidavit that are strengthened by this section are limited to the revocation of a power by the principal's voluntary act, his death, or, in the case of nondurable power, by his incompetence.

With one possible exception, other matters, including circumstances made relevant by the terms of the instrument to the commencement of the agency or to its termination by other circumstances, are not covered. The exception concerns the case of a power created to begin on "incapacity." The affidavit of the agent in fact that all conditions necessary to the valid exercise of the power might be aided by the statute in relation to the fact of incapacity. An affidavit as to the existence or non-existence of facts and circumstances not covered by this section nonetheless may be useful in establishing good faith reliance.

*

465

ARTICLE VI

NONPROBATE TRANSFERS ON DEATH (1989)

PART 1

PROVISIONS RELATING TO EFFECT OF DEATH

467

PART 3

UNIFORM TOD SECURITY REGISTRATION ACT

PREFATORY NOTE

This amendment of Uniform Probate Code Article VI (nonprobate transfers) replaces existing Article VI with a revised article. Part 1 (provisions relating to effect of death) of the revised article is amended and relocated from former Part 2. Part 2 (multiple-person accounts) of the revised article is amended and relocated from former Part 1. Part 3 (Uniform TOD Security Registration Act) of the revised article is new. This reorganization allows for general provisions at the beginning of the article, and permits parts to be divided into subparts that group related provisions together.

Multiple–Person Accounts

The amendment of Part 2 (multiple-person accounts) of the revised article simplifies drafting and terminology. It consolidates treatment of POD accounts and trust accounts so that the same rules apply to both, since both types of account operate identically and serve the same function of passing property to a beneficiary at the death of the account owner. The amendment likewise eliminates references to "joint" accounts, since the statute treats joint tenancy accounts and tenancy in common accounts the same for all purposes other than survivorship. Other terminological and drafting simplifications and standardizations are made throughout the statute. Treatment of existing accounts is included.

The amendment makes a few substantive changes in rules previously established in the multiple-person account statute. The changes include recognition of checks issued by an account owner before death and presented for payment after death, revision of the creditor rights procedure to enable a survivor or beneficiary to spread the burden among survivors and beneficiaries of other accounts of the decedent and to provide a uniform one-year limitation period for creditors, and a provision that a financial institution must have received notice at the appropriate office and have had a reasonable time to act before it is charged with knowledge that any

468

change in account circumstances has occurred. A provision is also added that on the death of a married person, beneficial ownership of the decedent's share in a survivorship account passes to the surviving spouse who is an account party in preference to other surviving account parties.

The amendment includes a number of important improvements designed to make multiple-person accounts more useful. An agency designation is authorized to enable an account owner to add another person to the account as a convenience in making withdrawals without creating any ownership or survivorship interest in the person identified as an agent. Optional statutory forms for multiple-person accounts are provided for the convenience and protection of financial institutions. Payment to a minor who is an account beneficiary is authorized pursuant to the Uniform Transfers to Minors Act. A provision is added to make clear that marital funds deposited in an account retain any community property incidents, and the law governing tenancy by the entireties is preserved where applicable.

The drafting committee believes that this amendment of the multiple-person account statute is a substantial improvement in an already successful law. This part of the Uniform Probate Code is one of the most broadly accepted, having been adopted either as part of the code or independently by over half the states. This amendment draws on useful improvements made by various states that have enacted the statute, and should make the statute even more attractive.

Uniform TOD Security Registration Act

The purpose of Part 3 (Uniform TOD Security Registration Act) of the revised article is to allow the owner of securities to register the title in transfer-on-death (TOD) form. Mutual fund shares and accounts maintained by brokers and others to reflect a customer's holdings of securities (so-called "street accounts") are also covered. The legislation enables an issuer, transfer agent, broker, or other such intermediary to transfer the securities directly to the designated transferee on the owner's death. Thus, TOD registration achieves for securities a certain parity with existing TOD and pay-on-death (POD) facilities for bank deposits and other assets passing at death outside the probate process.

The TOD registration under this part is designed to give the owner of securities who wishes to arrange for a nonprobate transfer at death an alternative to the frequently troublesome joint tenancy form of title. Because joint tenancy registration of securities normally entails a sharing of lifetime entitlement and control, it works satisfactorily only so long as the co-owners cooperate. Difficulties arise when co-owners fall into disagreement, or when one becomes afflicted or insolvent.

Use of the TOD registration form encouraged by this legislation has no effect on the registered owner's full control of the affected security during his or her lifetime. A TOD designation and any beneficiary interest arising under the designation ends whenever the registered asset is transferred, or whenever the owner otherwise complies with the issuer's conditions for

469

changing the title form of the investment. The part recognizes, in Section 6–302, that co-owners with right of survivorship may be registered as owners together with a TOD beneficiary designated to take if the registration remains unchanged until the beneficiary survives the joint owners. In such a case, the survivor of the joint owners has full control of the asset and may change the registration form as he or she sees fit after the other's death.

Implementation of the part is wholly optional with issuers. The drafting committee received the benefit of considerable advice and assistance from representatives of the mutual fund and stock transfer industries during the course of its three years of preparatory work. Accordingly, it is believed that this part takes full account of the practical requirements for efficient transfer within the securities industry.

Section 6–303 invites application of the legislation to locally owned securities though the statute may not have been locally enacted, so long as the part or similar legislation is in force in a jurisdiction of the issuer or transfer agent. Thus, if the principal jurisdictions in which securities issuers and transfer agents are sited enact the measure, its benefits will become generally available to persons domiciled in states that do not at once enact the statute.

The legislation has been drafted as a separate part, hence not interpolated as an expansion of the former UPC Article VI, Part 1, treating bank accounts ("multiple-party accounts"). Securities merit a distinct statutory regime, because a different principle has governed concurrent ownership of securities. By virtue either of statute or of account terms (contract), multiple-party bank accounts allow any one cotenant to consume or transfer account balances. See R. Brown, The Law of Personal Property § 65, at 217 (2d ed. 1955); Langbein, The Nonprobate Revolution and the Future of the Law of Succession, 97 Harv.L.Rev. 1108, 1112 (1984). The rule for securities, however, has been the rule that applies to real property: all cotenants must act together in transferring the securities. This difference in the legal regime reflects differences in function among the types of assets. Multiple-party bank accounts typically arise as convenience accounts, to facilitate frequent small transactions, often on an agency basis (as when spouses or relatives share an account). Securities resemble real estate in that the values are typically large and the transactions relatively infrequent, which is why the legal regime requires the concurrence of all concurrent owners for transfers affecting such assets.

Recently, of course, this distinction between bank accounts and securities has begun to crumble. Banks are offering certificates of deposit of large value under the same account forms that were devised for low-value convenience accounts. Meanwhile, brokerage houses with their so-called cash management accounts and mutual funds with their money market accounts have rendered securities subject to small recurrent transactions. In the latest developments, even the line between real estate and bank accounts is becoming indistinct, as the "home equity line of credit" creates a check-writing conduit to real estate values.

Nevertheless, even though new forms of contract have rendered the boundaries between securities and bank accounts less firm, the distinction seems intuitively correct for statutory default rules. True co-owners of securities, like owners of realty, should act together in transferring the asset.

The joint bank account and the Totten trust originated in ambiguous lifetime ownership forms, which required former UPC § 6–103 or comparable state legislation to clarify that an inter vivos transfer was not intended. In the securities field, by contrast, we start with unambiguous lifetime ownership rules. The sole purpose of the present statute is to facilitate a nonprobate TOD mechanism as an option for those owners.

For a comprehensive discussion of the issues entailed in this legislation, see Wellman, Transfer-on-Death Securities Registration: A New Title Form, 21 Ga.L.Rev. 789 (1987).

PART 1

PROVISIONS RELATING TO
EFFECT OF DEATH

Section 6–101. Nonprobate Transfers on Death.

(a) A provision for a nonprobate transfer on death in an insurance policy, contract of employment, bond, mortgage, promissory note, certificated or uncertificated security, account agreement, custodial agreement, deposit agreement, compensation plan, pension plan, individual retirement plan, employee benefit plan, trust, conveyance, deed of gift, marital property agreement, or other written instrument of a similar nature is nontestamentary. This subsection includes a written provision that:

(1) money or other benefits due to, controlled by, or owned by a decedent before death must be paid after the decedent's death to a person whom the decedent designates either in the instrument or in a separate writing, including a will, executed either before or at the same time as the instrument, or later;

(2) money due or to become due under the instrument ceases to be payable in the event of death of the promisee or the promisor before payment or demand; or

(3) any property controlled by or owned by the decedent before death which is the subject of the instrument passes to a person the decedent designates either in the instrument or in a separate writing, including a will, executed either before or at the same time as the instrument, or later.

(b) This section does not limit rights of creditors under other laws of this State.

COMMENT

This section is a revised version of former Section 6–201 of the original Uniform Probate Code, which authorized a variety of contractual arrangements that had sometimes been treated as testamentary in prior law. For example, most courts treated as testamentary a provision in a promissory note that if the payee died before making payment, the note should be paid to another named person; or a provision in a land contract that if the seller died before completing payment, the balance should be canceled and the property should belong to the vendee. These provisions often occurred in family arrangements. The result of holding such provisions testamentary was usually to invalidate them because not executed in accordance with the statute of wills. On the other hand, the same courts for years upheld beneficiary designations in life insurance contracts. The drafters of the original Uniform Probate Code declared in the Comment that they were unable to identify policy reasons for continuing to treat these varied arrangements as testamentary. The drafters said that the benign experience with such familiar will substitutes as the revocable inter vivos trust, the multiple-party bank account, and United States government bonds payable on death to named beneficiaries all demonstrated that the evils envisioned if the statute of wills were not rigidly enforced simply do not materialize. The Comment also observed that because these provisions often are part of a business transaction and are evidenced by a writing, the danger of fraud is largely eliminated.

Because the modes of transfer authorized by an instrument under this section are declared to be nontestamentary, the instrument does not have to be executed in compliance with the formalities for wills prescribed under Section 2–502; nor does the instrument have to be probated, nor does the personal representative have any power or duty with respect to the assets.

The sole purpose of this section is to prevent the transfers authorized

here from being treated as testamentary. This section does not invalidate other arrangements by negative implication. Thus, this section does not speak to the phenomenon of the oral trust to hold property at death for named persons, an arrangement already generally enforceable under trust law.

The reference to a "marital property agreement" in the introductory portion of subsection (a) of Section 6–101 includes an agreement made during marriage as well as a premarital contract.

The term "or other written instrument of a similar nature" in the introductory portion of subsection (a) replaces the former language "or any other written instrument effective as a contract, gift, conveyance or trust" in the original Section 6–201. The Supreme Court of Washington read that language to relieve against the delivery requirement of the law of deeds, a result that was not intended. Estate of O'Brien v. Woodhouse, 109 Wash.2d 913, 749 P.2d 154 (1988). The point was correctly decided in First National Bank in Minot v. Bloom, 264 N.W.2d 208, 212 (N.D.1978), in which the Supreme Court of North Dakota held that "nothing in [former Section 6–201] of the Uniform Probate Code ... eliminates the necessity of delivery of a deed to effectuate a conveyance from one living person to another."

PART 2

MULTIPLE–PERSON ACCOUNTS

SUBPART 1

DEFINITIONS AND GENERAL PROVISIONS

Section 6–201. Definitions.

In this part:

(1) "Account" means a contract of deposit between a depositor and a financial institution, and includes a checking account, savings account, certificate of deposit, and share account.

(2) "Agent" means a person authorized to make account transactions for a party.

(3) "Beneficiary" means a person named as one to whom sums on deposit in an account are payable on request after death of all parties or for whom a party is named as trustee.

(4) "Financial institution" means an organization authorized to do business under state or federal laws relating to financial institutions, and includes a bank, trust company, savings bank, building and loan association, savings and loan company or association, and credit union.

(5) "Multiple-party account" means an account payable on request to one or more of two or more parties, whether or not a right of survivorship is mentioned.

(6) "Party" means a person who, by the terms of an account, has a present right, subject to request, to payment from the account other than as a beneficiary or agent.

(7) "Payment" of sums on deposit includes withdrawal, payment to a party or third person pursuant to check or other request, and a pledge of sums on deposit by a party, or a set-off, reduction, or other disposition of all or part of an account pursuant to a pledge.

(8) "POD designation" means the designation of (i) a beneficiary in an account payable on request to one party during the party's lifetime and on the party's death to one or more beneficiaries, or to one or more parties during their lifetimes and on death of all of them to one or more beneficiaries, or (ii) a beneficiary in an account in the name of one or more parties as

trustee for one or more beneficiaries if the relationship is established by the terms of the account and there is no subject of the trust other than the sums on deposit in the account, whether or not payment to the beneficiary is mentioned.

(9) "Receive," as it relates to notice to a financial institution, means receipt in the office or branch office of the financial institution in which the account is established, but if the terms of the account require notice at a particular place, in the place required.

(10) "Request" means a request for payment complying with all terms of the account, including special requirements concerning necessary signatures and regulations of the financial institution; but, for purposes of this part, if terms of the account condition payment on advance notice, a request for payment is treated as immediately effective and a notice of intent to withdraw is treated as a request for payment.

(11) "Sums on deposit" means the balance payable on an account, including interest and dividends earned, whether or not included in the current balance, and any deposit life insurance proceeds added to the account by reason of death of a party.

(12) "Terms of the account" includes the deposit agreement and other terms and conditions, including the form, of the contract of deposit.

COMMENT

This and the sections that follow are designed to reduce certain questions concerning many forms of multiple-person accounts (including the so-called Totten trust account). A "payable on death" designation and an "agency" designation are also authorized for both single-party and multiple-party accounts. The POD designation is a more direct means of achieving the same purpose as a Totten trust account; this part therefore discourages creation of a Totten trust account and treats existing Totten trust accounts as POD designations.

An agent (paragraph (2)) may not be a party. The agency designation must be signed by all parties, and the agent is the agent of all parties. See Section 6–205 (designation of agent).

A "beneficiary" of a party (paragraph (3)) may be either a POD beneficiary or the beneficiary of a Totten trust; the two types of designations in an account serve the same function and are treated the same under this part. See paragraph (8) ("POD designation" defined). The definition of "beneficiary" refers to a "person," who may be an individual, corporation, organization, or other legal entity. Section 1–201(29). Thus a church, trust company, family corporation, or other entity, as well as any individual, may be designated as a beneficiary.

The term "multiple-party account" (paragraph (5)) is used in this part in a broad sense to include any account having more than one owner with a present interest in the account. Thus an account may be a "multiple-party account" within the meaning of this part regardless of whether the terms of the account refer to it as "joint tenancy" or as "tenancy in common," regardless of whether the parties named are coupled by "or" or "and," and regardless of whether any reference is made to survivorship rights, whether expressly or by abbreviation such as JTWROS or JT TEN. Survivorship rights in a multiple-party account are determined by the terms of the account and by statute, and survivorship is not a necessary incident of a multiple-party account. See Section 6–212 (rights at death).

Under paragraph (6), a "party" is a person with a present right to payment from an account. Therefore, present owners of a multiple-party account are parties, as is the present owner of an account with a POD designation. The beneficiary of an account with a POD designation is not a party, but is entitled to payment only on the death of all parties. The trustee of a Totten trust is a party but the beneficiary is not. An agent with the right of withdrawal on behalf of a party is not itself a party. A person claiming on behalf of a party such as a guardian or conservator, or claiming the interest of a party such as a creditor, is not itself a party, and the right of such a person to payment is governed by general law other than this part.

Various signature requirements may be involved in order to meet the payment requirements of the account. A "request" (paragraph (10)) involves compliance with these requirements. A party is one to whom an account is presently payable without regard to whose signature may be required for a "request."

Section 6–202. Limitation on Scope of Part.

This part does not apply to (i) an account established for a partnership, joint venture, or other organization for a business purpose, (ii) an account controlled by one or more persons as an agent or trustee for a corporation, unincorporated association, or charitable or civic organization, or (iii) a fiduciary or trust account in which the relationship is established other than by the terms of the account.

COMMENT

This part applies to accounts in this State. Section 1–301(4).

The reference to a fiduciary or trust account in item (iii) includes a regular trust account under a testamentary trust or a trust agreement that has significance apart from the account, and a fiduciary account arising from a fiduciary relation such as attorney-client.

Section 6–203. Types of Account; Existing Accounts.

(a) An account may be for a single party or multiple parties. A multiple-party account may be with or without a right of survivorship between the parties. Subject to Section 6–212(c), either a single-party account or a multiple-party account may have a POD designation, an agency designation, or both.

(b) An account established before, on, or after the effective date of this part, whether in the form prescribed in Section 6–204 or in any other form, is either a single-party account or a multiple-party account, with or without right of survivorship, and with or without a POD designation or an agency designation, within the meaning of this part, and is governed by this part.

COMMENT

In the case of an account established before (or after) the effective date of this part that is not in substantially the form provided in Section 6–204, the account is governed by the provisions of this part applicable to the type of account that most nearly conforms to the depositor's intent. See Section 6–204 (forms).

Thus, a tenancy in common account established before or after the effective date of this part would be classified as a "multiple-party account" for purposes of this part. See Section 6–201(5) ("multiple-party account" defined). On death of a party there would not be a right of survivorship since the tenancy in common title would be treated as a multiple-party account without right of survivorship. See Section 6–212(c). It should be noted that a POD designation may not be made in a multiple-party account without right of survivorship. See Sections 6–201(8) ("POD designation" defined), 6–204 (forms), and 6–212 (rights at death).

Under this section, a Totten trust account established before, on, or after the effective date of this part is governed by the provisions of this part applicable to an account with a POD designation. See Section 6–201(8) ("POD designation" defined) and the Comment to Section 6–201.

Section 6–204. Forms.

(a) A contract of deposit that contains provisions in substantially the following form establishes the type of account provided, and the account is governed by the provisions of this part applicable to an account of that type:

UNIFORM SINGLE– OR MULTIPLE–PARTY ACCOUNT FORM

PARTIES [Name One or More Parties]:
_____

OWNERSHIP [Select One And Initial]:
_____SINGLE–PARTY ACCOUNT

_____MULTIPLE–PARTY ACCOUNT
    Parties own account in proportion to net contributions unless there is clear and convincing evidence of a different intent.
RIGHTS AT DEATH [Select One And Initial]:
_____SINGLE–PARTY ACCOUNT
    At death of party, ownership passes as part of party's estate.
_____SINGLE–PARTY ACCOUNT WITH POD (PAY ON DEATH) DESIGNATION
    [Name One Or More Beneficiaries]:

_____   _____

    At death of party, ownership passes to POD beneficiaries and is not part of party's estate.
_____MULTIPLE–PARTY ACCOUNT WITH RIGHT OF SURVIV-ORSHIP
    At death of party, ownership passes to surviving parties.
_____MULTIPLE–PARTY ACCOUNT WITH RIGHT OF SURVIV-ORSHIP AND POD (PAY ON DEATH) DESIGNATION
    [Name One Or More Beneficiaries]:

_____   _____

    At death of last surviving party, ownership passes to POD beneficiaries and is not part of last surviving party's estate.
_____MULTIPLE–PARTY ACCOUNT WITHOUT RIGHT OF SURVIVORSHIP
    At death of party, deceased party's ownership passes as part of deceased party's estate.
AGENCY (POWER OF ATTORNEY) DESIGNATION [Optional]
    Agents may make account transactions for parties but have no ownership or rights at death unless named as POD beneficiaries.
    [To Add Agency Designation To Account, Name One Or More Agents]:

_____   _____

    [Select One And Initial]:
    _____AGENCY DESIGNATION SURVIVES DISABILITY OR INCAPACITY OF PARTIES
    _____AGENCY DESIGNATION TERMINATES ON DIS-ABILITY OR INCAPACITY OF PARTIES

  (b) A contract of deposit that does not contain provisions in substantially the form provided in subsection (a) is governed by the provisions of this part applicable to the type of account that most nearly conforms to the depositor's intent.

COMMENT

This section provides short forms for single- and multiple-party accounts which, if used, bring the accounts within the terms of this part. A financial institution that uses the statutory form language in its accounts is protected in acting in reliance on the form of the account. See also Section 6–226 (discharge).

The forms provided in this section enable a person establishing a multiple-party account to state expressly in the account whether

there are to be survivorship rights between the parties. The account forms permit greater flexibility than traditional account designations. It should be noted that no separate form is provided for a Totten trust account, since the POD designation serves the same function.

An account that is not substantially in the form provided in this section is nonetheless governed by this part. See Section 6–203 (types of account; existing accounts).

Section 6–205. Designation of Agent.

(a) By a writing signed by all parties, the parties may designate as agent of all parties on an account a person other than a party.

(b) Unless the terms of an agency designation provide that the authority of the agent terminates on disability or incapacity of a party, the agent's authority survives disability and incapacity. The agent may act for a disabled or incapacitated party until the authority of the agent is terminated.

(c) Death of the sole party or last surviving party terminates the authority of an agent.

COMMENT

An agent has no beneficial interest in the account. See Section 6–211 (ownership during lifetime). The agency relationship is governed by the general law of agency of the state, except to the extent this part provides express rules, including the rule that the agency survives the disability or incapacity of a party.

A financial institution may make payments at the direction of an

agent notwithstanding disability, incapacity, or death of the party, subject to receipt of a stop notice. Section 6–226 (discharge); see also Section 6–224 (payment to designated agent).

The rule of subsection (b) applies to agency designations on all types of accounts, including nonsurvivorship as well as survivorship forms of multiple-party accounts.

Section 6–206. Applicability of Part.

The provisions of Subpart 2 concerning beneficial ownership as between parties or as between parties and beneficiaries apply only to controversies between those persons and their creditors and other successors, and do not apply to the right of those persons to payment as determined by the terms of the account. Subpart 3 governs the liability and set-off rights of financial institutions that make payments pursuant to it.

SUBPART 2

OWNERSHIP AS BETWEEN PARTIES AND OTHERS

Section 6–211. Ownership During Lifetime.

(a) In this section, "net contribution" of a party means the sum of all deposits to an account made by or for the party, less all payments from the account made to or for the party which have not been paid to or applied to the use of another party and a proportionate share of any charges deducted from the account, plus a proportionate share of any interest or dividends earned, whether or not included in the current balance. The term includes deposit life insurance proceeds added to the account by reason of death of the party whose net contribution is in question.

(b) During the lifetime of all parties, an account belongs to the parties in proportion to the net contribution of each to the sums on deposit, unless there is clear and convincing evidence of a different intent. As between parties married to each other, in the absence of proof otherwise, the net contribution of each is presumed to be an equal amount.

(c) A beneficiary in an account having a POD designation has no right to sums on deposit during the lifetime of any party.

(d) An agent in an account with an agency designation has no beneficial right to sums on deposit.

COMMENT

This section reflects the assumption that a person who deposits funds in an account normally does not intend to make an irrevocable gift of all or any part of the funds represented by the deposit. Rather, the person usually intends no present change of beneficial ownership. The section permits parties to accounts to be as definite, or as indefinite, as they wish in respect to the matter of how beneficial ownership should be apportioned between them.

The assumption that no present change of beneficial ownership is intended may be disproved by showing that a gift was intended. For example, under subsection (c) it is presumed that the beneficiary of a POD designation has no present ownership interest during lifetime. However, it is possible that in the case of a POD designation in trust

480

form an irrevocable gift was intended.

It is important to note that the section is limited to ownership of an account while parties are alive. Section 6–212 prescribes what happens to beneficial ownership on the death of a party.

The section does not undertake to describe the situation between parties if one party withdraws more than that party is then entitled to as against the other party. Sections 6–221 and 6–226 protect a financial institution in that circumstance without reference to whether a withdrawing party may be entitled to less than that party withdraws as against another party. Rights between parties in this situation are governed by general law other than this part.

"Net contribution" as defined by subsection (a) has no application to the financial institution-depositor relationship. Rather, it is relevant only to controversies that may arise between parties to a multiple-party account.

The last sentence of subsection (b) provides a clear rule concerning the amount of "net contribution" in a case where the actual amount cannot be established as between spouses. This part otherwise contains no provision dealing with a failure of proof. The omission is deliberate. The theory of these sections is that the basic relationship of the parties is that of individual ownership of values attributable to their respective deposits and withdrawals, and not equal and undivided ownership that would be an incident of joint tenancy.

In a state that recognizes tenancy by the entireties for personal property, this section would not change the rule that parties who are married to each other own their combined net contributions to an account as tenants by the entireties. See Section 6–216 (community property and tenancy by the entireties).

Section 6–212. Rights at Death.

(a) Except as otherwise provided in this part, on death of a party sums on deposit in a multiple-party account belong to the surviving party or parties. If two or more parties survive and one is the surviving spouse of the decedent, the amount to which the decedent, immediately before death, was beneficially entitled under Section 6–211 belongs to the surviving spouse. If two or more parties survive and none is the surviving spouse of the decedent, the amount to which the decedent, immediately before death, was beneficially entitled under Section 6–211 belongs to the surviving parties in equal shares, and augments the proportion to which each survivor, immediately before the decedent's death, was beneficially entitled under Section 6–211, and the right of survivorship continues between the surviving parties.

(b) In an account with a POD designation:

(1) On death of one of two or more parties, the rights in sums on deposit are governed by subsection (a).

481

(2) On death of the sole party or the last survivor of two or more parties, sums on deposit belong to the surviving beneficiary or beneficiaries. If two or more beneficiaries survive, sums on deposit belong to them in equal and undivided shares, and there is no right of survivorship in the event of death of a beneficiary thereafter. If no beneficiary survives, sums on deposit belong to the estate of the last surviving party.

(c) Sums on deposit in a single-party account without a POD designation, or in a multiple-party account that, by the terms of the account, is without right of survivorship, are not affected by death of a party, but the amount to which the decedent, immediately before death, was beneficially entitled under Section 6–211 is transferred as part of the decedent's estate. A POD designation in a multiple-party account without right of survivorship is ineffective. For purposes of this section, designation of an account as a tenancy in common establishes that the account is without right of survivorship.

(d) The ownership right of a surviving party or beneficiary, or of the decedent's estate, in sums on deposit is subject to requests for payment made by a party before the party's death, whether paid by the financial institution before or after death, or unpaid. The surviving party or beneficiary, or the decedent's estate, is liable to the payee of an unpaid request for payment. The liability is limited to a proportionate share of the amount transferred under this section, to the extent necessary to discharge the request for payment.

COMMENT

The effect of subsection (a) is to make an account payable to one or more of two or more parties a survivorship arrangement unless a non-survivorship arrangement is specified in the terms of the account. This rule applies to community property as well as other forms of marital property. See Section 6–216 (community property and tenancy by the entireties). The section also applies to various forms of multiple-party accounts that may be in use at the effective date of the legislation. See Sections 6–203 (type of account; existing accounts) and 6–204 (forms).

Subsection (b) applies to both POD and Totten trust beneficiaries. See Section 6–201(8) ("POD designation" defined). It accepts the New York view that an account opened by "A" in A's name as "trustee for B" usually is intended by A to be an informal will of any balance remaining on deposit at A's death.

By technical amendment effective August 5, 1991, the word "part" was substituted for "section" in the first sentence of subsection (a). The amendment clarified the original purpose of the drafters and commissioners to permit a court to implement the intentions of parties to a joint account governed by Section 6–204(b) if it finds that the account was opened solely for the convenience of a party who supplied all funds reflected by the account and intended no present gift or death benefit for the other party.   In short, the account characteristics described in this section must be determined by reference to the form of the account *and* the impact of Sections 6–203 and 6–204 on the admissibility of extrinsic evidence tending to confirm or contradict intention as signalled by the form.

Section 6–213. Alteration of Rights.

(a) Rights at death under Section 6–212 are determined by the type of account at the death of a party. The type of account may be altered by written notice given by a party to the financial institution to change the type of account or to stop or vary payment under the terms of the account. The notice must be signed by a party and received by the financial institution during the party's lifetime.

(b) A right of survivorship arising from the express terms of the account, Section 6–212, or a POD designation, may not be altered by will.

COMMENT

Under this section, rights of parties and beneficiaries are determined by the type of account at the time of death. It is to be noted that only a "party" may give notice blocking the provisions of Section 6–212 (rights at death). "Party" is defined by Section 6–201(6). Thus if there is an account with a POD designation in the name of A and B with C as beneficiary, C cannot change the right of survivorship because C has no present right to payment and hence is not a party.

Section 6–214. Accounts and Transfers Nontestamentary.

Except as provided in Part 2 of Article II (elective share of surviving spouse) or as a consequence of, and to the extent directed by, Section 6–215, a transfer resulting from the application of Section 6–212 is effective by reason of the terms of the account involved and this part and is not testamentary or subject to Articles I through IV (estate administration).

COMMENT

The purpose of classifying the transactions contemplated by this part as nontestamentary is to bolster the explicit statement that their validity as effective modes of transfers on death is not to be determined by the requirements for wills. The section is consistent with Part 1 of Article VI (provisions relating to effect of death).

Section 6–215. Rights of Creditors and Others.

(a) If other assets of the estate are insufficient, a transfer resulting from a right of survivorship or POD designation under this part is not effective against the estate of a deceased party to the extent needed to pay claims against the estate and statutory allowances to the surviving spouse and children.

(b) A surviving party or beneficiary who receives payment from an account after death of a party is liable to account to the personal representative of the decedent for a proportionate share of the amount received to which the decedent, immediately before death, was beneficially entitled under Section 6–211, to the extent necessary to discharge the claims and allowances described in subsection (a) remaining unpaid after application of the decedent's estate. A proceeding to assert the liability may not be commenced unless the personal representative has received a written demand by the surviving spouse, a creditor, a child, or a person acting for a child of the decedent. The proceeding must be commenced within one year after death of the decedent.

(c) A surviving party or beneficiary against whom a proceeding to account is brought may join as a party to the proceeding a surviving party or beneficiary of any other account of the decedent.

(d) Sums recovered by the personal representative must be administered as part of the decedent's estate. This section does not affect the protection from claims of the personal representative or estate of a deceased party provided in Section 6–226 for a financial institution that makes payment in accordance with the terms of the account.

COMMENT

The sections of this article authorize transfers on death that reduce the estate to which the surviving spouse, creditors, and minor children normally must look for protection against a decedent's gifts by will. Accordingly, this section provides a remedy to these classes of persons that assures them that multiple-person accounts cannot be used to reduce the essential protection they would be entitled to if such accounts were deemed to per-

mit a special form of specific devise. This section provides a remedy for collection of amounts necessary to pay tax obligations incurred by the decedent during life, but not for death taxes. See Section 1–201(4) ("claims" defined). Apportionment and allocation of death taxes, and their collection, is governed by law other than this section.

Under this section a surviving spouse is automatically assured of some protection against a multiple-person account if the probate estate is insolvent; rights are limited, however, to sums needed for statutory allowances. The phrase "statutory allowances" includes the homestead allowance under Section 2–401, the family allowance under Section 2–403, and any allowance needed to make up the deficiency in exempt property under Section 2–402. In any case (including a solvent estate) the surviving spouse could proceed under Section 2–201 et seq. to claim an elective share in the account if the deposits by the decedent satisfy the requirements of Section 2–202 so that the account falls within the augmented net estate concept. In the latter situation the spouse is not proceeding as a creditor under this section.

Under subsection (b), a proceeding must be commenced within one year after the decedent's death.

This limitation period corresponds to the long term self-executing statute of limitations applicable under the code to creditors' claims generally.

By technical amendment effective August 5, 1991, the language referring to amounts the decedent owned beneficially immediately before death was added to make clear that the liability of a surviving party or beneficiary to account to the decedent's personal representative extends only to a proportionate share of funds transferred on death of the decedent, and not to funds already owned by the survivor or beneficiary. See subsection (a) (transfer not effective against estate). This is not a change in, but is a clarification of, the section. See also original UPC Section 6–107 (liability to account for amounts decedent owned beneficially immediately before death.)

Section 6–216. Community Property and Tenancy by the Entireties.

(a) A deposit of community property in an account does not alter the community character of the property or community rights in the property, but a right of survivorship between parties married to each other arising from the express terms of the account or Section 6–212 may not be altered by will.

(b) This part does not affect the law governing tenancy by the entireties.

COMMENT

Section 6–216 does not affect or limit the right of the financial institution to make payments pursuant to Subpart 3 (protection of financial institutions) and the deposit agreement. See Section 6–206 (applicability of part). For this reason, Section 6–216 does not affect the definiteness and certainty that the financial institution must have in order to be induced to make payments from the account and, at the same time, the section preserves the rights of the parties, creditors, and successors that arise out of the nature of the funds in the account—

community or separate, or tenancy
by the entireties.

SUBPART 3

PROTECTION OF FINANCIAL INSTITUTIONS

Section 6–221. Authority of Financial Institution.

A financial institution may enter into a contract of deposit for a multiple-party account to the same extent it may enter into a contract of deposit for a single-party account, and may provide for a POD designation and an agency designation in either a single-party account or a multiple-party account. A financial institution need not inquire as to the source of a deposit to an account or as to the proposed application of a payment from an account.

limits Banks liability (handwritten annotation)

COMMENT

The provisions of this subpart relate only to protection of a financial institution that makes payment as provided in the subpart. Nothing in this subpart affects the beneficial rights of persons to sums on deposit or paid out. Ownership as between parties, and others, is governed by Subpart 2. See Section 6–206 (applicability of part).

Section 6–222. Payment on Multiple–Party Account.

A financial institution, on request, may pay sums on deposit in a multiple-party account to:

(1) one or more of the parties, whether or not another party is disabled, incapacitated, or deceased when payment is requested and whether or not the party making the request survives another party; or

(2) the personal representative, if any, or, if there is none, the heirs or devisees of a deceased party if proof of death is presented to the financial institution showing that the deceased party was the survivor of all other persons named on the account either as a party or beneficiary, unless the account is without right of survivorship under Section 6–212.

COMMENT

A financial institution that makes payment on proper request under this section is protected unless the financial institution has received written notice not to. Section 6– 226 (discharge). Paragraph (1) applies to both a multiple-party account with right of survivorship and a multiple-party account without right of survivorship (including an

486

account in tenancy in common form). Paragraph (2) is limited to a multiple-party account with right of survivorship; payment to the personal representative or heirs or devisees of a deceased party to an account without right of survivorship is governed by the general law of the state relating to the authority of such persons to collect assets alleged to belong to a decedent.

Section 6–223. Payment on POD Designation.

A financial institution, on request, may pay sums on deposit in an account with a POD designation to:

(1) one or more of the parties, whether or not another party is disabled, incapacitated, or deceased when the payment is requested and whether or not a party survives another party;

(2) the beneficiary or beneficiaries, if proof of death is presented to the financial institution showing that the beneficiary or beneficiaries survived all persons named as parties; or

(3) the personal representative, if any, or, if there is none, the heirs or devisees of a deceased party, if proof of death is presented to the financial institution showing that the deceased party was the survivor of all other persons named on the account either as a party or beneficiary.

COMMENT

A financial institution that makes payment on proper request under this section is protected unless the financial institution has received written notice not to. Section 6–226 (discharge). Payment to the personal representative or heirs or devisees of a deceased beneficiary who would be entitled to payment under paragraph (2) is governed by the general law of the state relating to the authority of such persons to collect assets alleged to belong to a decedent.

Section 6–224. Payment to Designated Agent.

A financial institution, on request of an agent under an agency designation for an account, may pay to the agent sums on deposit in the account, whether or not a party is disabled, incapacitated, or deceased when the request is made or received, and whether or not the authority of the agent terminates on the disability or incapacity of a party.

COMMENT

This section is intended to protect a financial institution that makes a payment pursuant to an account with an agency designation even though the agency may have terminated at the time of the payment

487

due to disability, incapacity, or death of the principal. The protection does not apply if the financial institution has received notice under Section 6–226 not to make payment or that the agency has termi-nated. This section applies whether or not the agency survives the party's disability or incapacity under Section 6–205 (designation of agent).

Section 6–225. Payment to Minor.

If a financial institution is required or permitted to make payment pursuant to this part to a minor designated as a beneficiary, payment may be made pursuant to the Uniform Transfers to Minors Act.

COMMENT

Section 6–225 is intended to avoid the need for a guardianship or other protective proceeding in situations where the Uniform Transfers to Minors Act may be used.

Section 6–226. Discharge.

(a) Payment made pursuant to this part in accordance with the type of account discharges the financial institution from all claims for amounts so paid, whether or not the payment is consistent with the beneficial ownership of the account as between parties, beneficiaries, or their successors. Payment may be made whether or not a party, beneficiary, or agent is disabled, incapacitated, or deceased when payment is requested, received, or made.

(b) Protection under this section does not extend to payments made after a financial institution has received written notice from a party, or from the personal representative, surviving spouse, or heir or devisee of a deceased party, to the effect that payments in accordance with the terms of the account, including one having an agency designation, should not be permitted, and the financial institution has had a reasonable opportunity to act on it when the payment is made. Unless the notice is withdrawn by the person giving it, the successor of any deceased party must concur in a request for payment if the financial institution is to be protected under this section. Unless a financial institution has been served with process in an action or proceeding, no other notice or other information shown to have been available to the financial institution affects its right to protection under this section.

(c) A financial institution that receives written notice pursuant to this section or otherwise has reason to believe that a dispute exists as to the rights of the parties may refuse, without liability, to make payments in accordance with the terms of the account.

(d) Protection of a financial institution under this section does not affect the rights of parties in disputes between themselves or their successors concerning the beneficial ownership of sums on deposit in accounts or payments made from accounts.

COMMENT

The provision of subsection (a) protecting a financial institution for payments made after the death, disability, or incapacity of a party is a specific elaboration of the general protective provisions of this section and is drawn from Uniform Commercial Code Section 4–405.

Knowledge of disability, incapacity, or death of a party does not affect payment on request of an agent, whether or not the agent's authority survives disability or incapacity. See Section 6–224 (payment to designated agent). But under subsection (b), the financial institution may not make payments on request of an agent after it has received written notice not to, whether because the agency has terminated or otherwise.

Section 6–227. Set–Off.

Without qualifying any other statutory right to set-off or lien and subject to any contractual provision, if a party is indebted to a financial institution, the financial institution has a right to set-off against the account. The amount of the account subject to set-off is the proportion to which the party is, or immediately before death was, beneficially entitled under Section 6–211 or, in the absence of proof of that proportion, an equal share with all parties.

PART 3

UNIFORM TOD SECURITY REGISTRATION ACT

Section 6–301. Definitions.

In this part:

(1) "Beneficiary form" means a registration of a security which indicates the present owner of the security and the intention of the owner regarding the person who will become the owner of the security upon the death of the owner.

(2) "Register," including its derivatives, means to issue a certificate showing the ownership of a certificated security or, in the case of an uncertificated security, to initiate or transfer an account showing ownership of securities.

(3) "Registering entity" means a person who originates or transfers a security title by registration, and includes a broker maintaining security accounts for customers and a transfer agent or other person acting for or as an issuer of securities.

(4) "Security" means a share, participation, or other interest in property, in a business, or in an obligation of an enterprise or other issuer, and includes a certificated security, an uncertificated security, and a security account.

(5) "Security account" means (i) a reinvestment account associated with a security, a securities account with a broker, a cash balance in a brokerage account, cash, interest, earnings, or dividends earned or declared on a security in an account, a reinvestment account, or a brokerage account, whether or not credited to the account before the owner's death, or (ii) a cash balance or other property held for or due to the owner of a security as a replacement for or product of an account security, whether or not credited to the account before the owner's death.

COMMENT

"Security" is defined as provided in UCC § 8–102 and includes shares of mutual funds and other investment companies. The defined term "security account" is not intended to include securities held in the name of a bank or similar institution as nominee for the benefit of a trust.

"Survive" is not defined. No effort is made in this part to define survival as it is for purposes of intestate succession in UPC § 2–

490

104 which requires survival by an heir of the ancestor for 120 hours. For purposes of this part, survive is used in its common law sense of outliving another for any time interval no matter how brief. The drafting committee sought to avoid imposition of a new and unfamiliar meaning of the term on intermediaries familiar with the meaning of "survive" in joint tenancy registrations.

Section 6–302. Registration in Beneficiary Form; Sole or Joint Tenancy Ownership.

Only individuals whose registration of a security shows sole ownership by one individual or multiple ownership by two or more with right of survivorship, rather than as tenants in common, may obtain registration in beneficiary form. Multiple owners of a security registered in beneficiary form hold as joint tenants with right of survivorship, as tenants by the entireties, or as owners of community property held in survivorship form, and not as tenants in common.

COMMENT

This section is designed to prevent co-owners from designating any death beneficiary other than one who is to take only upon survival of *all* co-owners. It coerces co-owning registrants to signal whether they hold as joint tenants with right of survivorship (JT TEN), as tenants by the entireties (T ENT), or as owners of community property. Also, it imposes survivorship on co-owners holding in a beneficiary form that fails to specify a survivorship form of holding. Tenancy in common and community property otherwise than in a survivorship setting is negated for registration in beneficiary form because persons desiring to signal independent death beneficiaries for each individual's fractional interest in a co-owned security normally will split their holding into separate registrations of the number of units previously constituting their fractional share. Once divided, each can name his or her own choice of death beneficiary.

The term "individuals," as used in this section, limits those who may register as owner or co-owner of a security in beneficiary form to natural persons. However, the section does not restrict individuals using this ownership form as to their choice of death beneficiary. The definition of "beneficiary form" in Section 6–301 indicates that any "person" may be designated beneficiary in a registration in beneficiary form. "Person" is defined so that a church, trust company, family corporation, or other entity, as well as any individual, may be designated as a beneficiary. Section 1–201(29).

Section 6–303. Registration in Beneficiary Form; Applicable Law.

A security may be registered in beneficiary form if the form is authorized by this or a similar statute of the state of organization of the issuer or registering entity, the location of the registering entity's principal office, the office of its transfer agent or its office making the registration, or by this or a similar statute of the law of the state listed as the owner's address at the time of registration. A registration governed by the law of a jurisdiction in which this or similar legislation is not in force or was not in force when a registration in beneficiary form was made is nevertheless presumed to be valid and authorized as a matter of contract law.

COMMENT

This section encourages registrations in beneficiary form to be made whenever a state with which either of the parties to a registration has contact has enacted this or a similar statute. Thus, a registration in beneficiary form of X Company shares might rely on an enactment of this Act in X Company's state of incorporation, or in the state of incorporation of X Company's transfer agent. Or, an enactment by the state of the issuer's principal office, the transfer agent's principal office, or of the issuer's office making the registration also would validate the registration. An enactment of the state of the registering owner's address at time of registration also might be used for validation purposes.

The last sentence of this section is designed, as is UPC § 6–101, to establish a statutory presumption that a general principle of law is available to achieve a result like that made possible by this part.

Section 6–304. Origination of Registration in Beneficiary Form.

A security, whether evidenced by certificate or account, is registered in beneficiary form when the registration includes a designation of a beneficiary to take the ownership at the death of the owner or the deaths of all multiple owners.

COMMENT

As noted above in commentary to Section 6–302, this part places no restriction on who may be designated beneficiary in a registration in beneficiary form.

Section 6–305. Form of Registration in Beneficiary Form.

Registration in beneficiary form may be shown by the words "transfer on death" or the abbreviation "TOD," or by the words "pay on death" or the abbreviation "POD," after the name of the registered owner and before the name of a beneficiary.

COMMENT

The abbreviation POD is included for use without regard for whether the subject is a money claim against an issuer, such as its own note or bond for money loaned, or is a claim to securities evidenced by conventional title documentation. The use of POD in a registration in beneficiary form of shares in an investment company should not be taken as a signal that the investment is to be sold or redeemed on the owner's death so that the sums realized may be "paid" to the death beneficiary. Rather, only a transfer on death, not a liquidation on death, is indicated. The committee would have used only the abbreviation TOD except for the familiarity, rooted in experience with certificates of deposit and other deposit accounts in banks, with the abbreviation POD as signalling a valid nonprobate death benefit or transfer on death.

Section 6–306. Effect of Registration in Beneficiary Form.

The designation of a TOD beneficiary on a registration in beneficiary form has no effect on ownership until the owner's death. A registration of a security in beneficiary form may be canceled or changed at any time by the sole owner or all then surviving owners without the consent of the beneficiary.

COMMENT

This section simply affirms the right of a sole owner, or the right of all multiple owners, to end a TOD beneficiary registration without the assent of the beneficiary. The section says nothing about how a TOD beneficiary designation may be canceled, meaning that the registering entity's terms and conditions, if any, may be relevant. See Section 6–310. If the terms and conditions have nothing on the point, cancellation of a beneficiary designation presumably would be effected by a reregistration showing a different beneficiary or omitting reference to a TOD beneficiary.

Section 6–307. Ownership on Death of Owner.

On death of a sole owner or the last to die of all multiple owners, ownership of securities registered in beneficiary form passes to the beneficiary or beneficiaries who survive all owners. On proof of death of all owners and compliance with any applicable requirements of the registering entity, a security registered in beneficiary form may be reregistered in the name of the beneficiary or beneficiaries who survive the death of all owners. Until division of the security after the death of all owners, multiple beneficiaries surviving the death of all owners hold their interests as tenants in common. If no beneficiary survives the death of all owners, the security belongs to the estate of the deceased sole owner or the estate of the last to die of all multiple owners.

COMMENT

Even though multiple owners holding in the beneficiary form here authorized hold with right of survivorship, no survivorship rights attend the positions of multiple beneficiaries who become entitled to securities by reason of having survived the sole owner or the last to die of multiple owners. Issuers (and registering entities) who decide to accept registrations in beneficiary form involving more than one primary beneficiary also should provide by rule whether fractional shares will be registered in the names of surviving beneficiaries where the number of shares held by the deceased owner does not divide without remnant among the survivors. If fractional shares are not desired, the issuer may wish to provide for sale of odd shares and division of proceeds, for an uneven distribution with the first or last named to receive the odd share, or for other resolution. Section 6–308 deals with whether intermediaries have any obligation to offer beneficiary registrations of any sort; Section 6–310 enables issuers to adopt terms and conditions controlling the details of applications for registrations they decide to accept and procedures for implementing such registrations after an owner's death.

The reference to surviving, multiple TOD beneficiaries as tenants in common is not intended to suggest that a registration form specifying unequal shares, such as "TOD A (20%), B (30%), C (50%)," would be improper. Though not included in the beneficiary forms described for illustrative purposes in Section 6–310, the part enables a registering entity to accept and implement a TOD beneficiary designation like the one just suggested. If offered, such a registration form should be implemented by registering entity terms and conditions providing for disposition of the share of a beneficiary who predeceases the owner when two or more of a group of multiple beneficiaries survive the owner. For example, the terms might direct the share of the predeceased beneficiary to the survivors in the proportion that their original shares bore to each other. Unless unequal shares are specified in a registration in beneficiary form designating multiple beneficiaries, the shares of the beneficiaries would, of course, be equal.

The statement that a security registered in beneficiary form is in the deceased owner's estate when no beneficiary survives the owner is not intended to prevent application of any anti-lapse statute that might direct a nonprobate transfer on death to the surviving issue of a beneficiary who failed to survive the owner. Rather, the statement is intended only to indicate that the registering entity involved should transfer or reregister the security as directed by the decedent's personal representative.

See the Comment to Section 6–301 regarding the meaning of "survive" for purposes of this part.

Section 6–308. Protection of Registering Entity.

(a) A registering entity is not required to offer or to accept a request for security registration in beneficiary form. If a registration in beneficiary form is offered by a registering entity, the owner requesting registration in beneficiary form assents to the protections given to the registering entity by this part.

(b) By accepting a request for registration of a security in beneficiary form, the registering entity agrees that the registration will be implemented on death of the deceased owner as provided in this part.

(c) A registering entity is discharged from all claims to a security by the estate, creditors, heirs, or devisees of a deceased owner if it registers a transfer of the security in accordance with Section 6–307 and does so in good faith reliance (i) on the registration, (ii) on this part, and (iii) on information provided to it by affidavit of the personal representative of the deceased owner, or by the surviving beneficiary or by the surviving beneficiary's representatives, or other information available to the registering entity. The protections of this part do not extend to a reregistration or payment made after a registering entity has received written notice from any claimant to any interest in the security objecting to implementation of a registration in beneficiary form. No other notice or other information available to the registering entity affects its right to protection under this part.

(d) The protection provided by this part to the registering entity of a security does not affect the rights of beneficiaries in disputes between themselves and other claimants to ownership of the security transferred or its value or proceeds.

COMMENT

It is to be noted that the "request" for a registration in beneficiary form may be in any form chosen by a registering entity. This part does not prescribe a particular form and does not impose record-keeping requirements. Registering entities' business practices, including any industry standards or rules of transfer agent associations, will control.

The written notice referred to in subsection (c) would qualify as a notice under UCC § 8–403.

"Good faith" as used in this section is intended to mean "honesty in fact and the observance of reasonable commercial standards of fair dealing in the trade," as specified in UCC § 2–103(1)(b).

The protections described in this section are designed to meet any questions regarding registering entity protection that may not be foreclosed by issuer protections provided in the Uniform Commercial Code. Because persons interested in this part may wish to be reminded of relevant UCC provisions, a brief summary follows.

"U.C.C. § 8–403, 'Issuer's Duty as to Adverse Claims' contains detailed provisions regarding duties of inquiry by an issuer of a certificated or uncertificated security who is requested to effect a transfer, and the availability and use of 30 day notices to force adverse claimants to start litigation if further delay in transfer is desired. U.C.C. § 8–201's definition of 'issuer' for purposes of 'registration of transfer . . .' is simply 'a person on whose behalf transfer books are maintained'. U.C.C. § 8–403 is among the sections dealing with registration of transfers.

"U.C.C. sections 8–308 and 8–404(1) appear to exonerate an issuer who acts in response to transfer directions signalled by the 'necessary indorsement' on or with a certificated security or in response to 'an instruction originated by an appropriate person' in the case of an uncertificated security. Section 8–308 describes the meaning of 'appropriate person' in the case of a certificated security as 'the person specified by the certificated security . . . to be entitled to the security.' U.C.C. § 8–308(6) (1978). In the case of an uncertificated security, 'appropriate person' means the 'registered owner.' Id § 8–308(7). The survivor of owners listed as joint tenants with right of survivorship is specifically defined as an authorized person. Id. § 8–308(8)(d). The U.C.C. aspect of the problem could be met by an additional sub-paragraph to section 8–308(8) that would include a TOD beneficiary as an 'appropriate person' when the beneficiary has survived the owner.

"No U.C.C. addition would be necessary if a TOD beneficiary designation were viewed as a contingent order for transfer at the owner's death that may be safely implemented as a direction from the owner as an 'authorized person.' The owner's death before completion of the transfer would not pose U.C.C. problems because section 8–308(10) provides: 'Whether the person signing is appropriate is determined as of the date of signing and an indorsement made by or an instruction originated by him does not become unauthorized for the purposes of this Article by virtue of any subsequent change of circumstances.'

"It might be questioned whether a TOD direction, which may be revoked before it is carried into effect and is also contingent on the beneficiary's survival of the registrant, is within the transfer directions contemplated by the U.C.C. framers for purposes of issuer protection. However, since section 8–202 explicitly protects issuers against problems arising because of restrictions or conditions on transfers, only the novelty of revocable directions for transfer on death gives pause.

"In general, article 8 of the U.C.C. reflects a careful attempt to protect implementation of a wide range of transfer instructions so long as the signatures are genuine and are those of owners acting in conformity with duly imposed rules of the issuer organization. . . . Hence, existing U.C.C. protections should be adequate, . . ."

Wellman, Transfer–On–Death Securities Registration: A New Title Form, 21 Ga.L.Rev. 789, 823 n. 90 (1987).

Section 6–309. Nontestamentary Transfer on Death.

(a) A transfer on death resulting from a registration in beneficiary form is effective by reason of the contract regarding the registration between the owner and the registering entity and this part and is not testamentary.

(b) This part does not limit the rights of creditors of security owners against beneficiaries and other transferees under other laws of this State.

COMMENT

Subsection (a) is comparable to UPC § 6–214. Subsection (b) is similar to UPC § 6–101(b).

Section 6–310. Terms, Conditions, and Forms for Registration.

(a) A registering entity offering to accept registrations in beneficiary form may establish the terms and conditions under which it will receive requests (i) for registrations in beneficiary form, and (ii) for implementation of registrations in beneficiary form, including requests for cancellation of previously registered TOD beneficiary designations and requests for reregistration to effect a change of beneficiary. The terms and conditions so established may provide for proving death, avoiding or resolving any problems concerning fractional shares, designating primary and contingent beneficiaries, and substituting a named beneficiary's descendants to take in the place of the named beneficiary in the event of the beneficiary's death. Substitution may be indicated by appending to the name of the primary beneficiary the letters LDPS, standing for "lineal descendants per stirpes." This designation substitutes a deceased beneficiary's descendants who survive the owner for a beneficiary who fails to so survive, the descendants to be identified and to share in accordance with the law of the beneficiary's domicile at the owner's death governing inheritance by descendants of an intestate. Other forms of identifying beneficiaries who are to take on one or more contingencies, and rules for providing proofs and assurances needed to satisfy reasonable concerns by registering entities regarding conditions and identities relevant to accurate implementation of registrations in beneficiary form, may be contained in a registering entity's terms and conditions.

(b) The following are illustrations of registrations in beneficiary form which a registering entity may authorize:

497

(1) Sole owner-sole beneficiary: John S Brown TOD (or POD) John S Brown Jr.

(2) Multiple owners-sole beneficiary: John S Brown Mary B Brown JT TEN TOD John S Brown Jr.

(3) Multiple owners-primary and secondary (substituted) beneficiaries: John S Brown Mary B Brown JT TEN TOD John S Brown Jr SUB BENE Peter Q Brown *or* John S Brown Mary B Brown JT TEN TOD John S Brown Jr LDPS.

COMMENT

Use of "and" or "or" between the names of persons registered as co-owners is unnecessary under this part and should be discouraged. If used, the two words should have the same meaning insofar as concerns a title form; *i.e.,* that of "and" to indicate that both named persons own the asset.

Descendants of a named beneficiary who take by virtue of a "LDPS" designation appended to a beneficiary's name take as TOD beneficiaries rather than as intestate successors. If no descendant of a predeceased primary beneficiary survives the owner, the security passes as a part of the owner's estate as provided in Section 6–307.

[Section 6–311. Application of Part.

This part applies to registrations of securities in beneficiary form made before or after [effective date], by decedents dying on or after [effective date].]

COMMENT

Section 6–311 is an optional provision that may be particularly useful in a state that has previously enacted the Uniform Probate Code, since the general effective date and transitional provisions of UPC § 8–101 are not expressly adapted for

the addition of this part. A state newly enacting the Uniform Probate Code, including this part, may find that general Section 8–101 is adequate for this purpose and addition of optional Section 6–311 unnecessary.

ARTICLE VII

TRUST ADMINISTRATION

PART 1

TRUST REGISTRATION

PART 2

JURISDICTION OF COURT CONCERNING TRUSTS

PART 3

DUTIES AND LIABILITIES OF TRUSTEES

PART 4

POWERS OF TRUSTEES

[GENERAL COMMENT ONLY]

COMMENT

Several considerations explain the presence in the Uniform Probate Code of procedures applicable to inter vivos and testamentary trusts. The

499

most important is that the Court assumed by the Code is a full power court which appropriately may receive jurisdiction over trustees. Another is that personal representatives under Articles III and IV and conservators under Article V, have the status of trustees. It follows naturally that these fiduciaries and regular trustees should bear a similar relationship to the Court. Also, the general move of the Code away from the concept of supervisory jurisdiction over any fiduciary is compatible with the kinds of procedural provisions which are believed to be desirable for trustees.

The relevance of trust procedures to those relating to settlement of decedents' estates is apparent in many situations. Many trusts are created by will. In a substantial number of states, statutes now extend probate court control over decedents' estates to testamentary trustees, but the same procedures rarely apply to inter vivos trusts. For example, eleven states appear to require testamentary trustees to qualify and account in much the same manner as executors, though quite different requirements relate to trustees of inter vivos trusts in these same states. Twenty-four states impose some form of mandatory court accountings on testamentary trustees, while only three seem to have comparable requirements for inter vivos trustees.

From an estate planning viewpoint, probate court supervision of testamentary trustees causes many problems. In some states, testamentary trusts cannot be released to be administered in another state. This requires complicated planning if inconvenience to interested persons is to be avoided when the beneficiaries move elsewhere. Also, some states preclude foreign trust companies from serving as trustees of local testamentary trusts without complying with onerous or prohibitive qualification requirements. Regular accountings in court have proved to be more expensive than useful in relation to the vast majority of trusts and sometimes have led to the ill-advised use of legal life estates to avoid these burdens.

The various restrictions applicable to testamentary trusts have caused many planners to recommend use of revocable inter vivos trusts. The widely adopted Uniform Testamentary Addition to Trusts Act has accelerated this tendency by permitting testators to devise estates to trustees of previously established receptacle trusts which have and retain the characteristics of inter vivos trusts for purpose of procedural requirements.

The popularity of this legislation and the widespread use of pour-over wills indicates rather vividly the obsolescence and irrelevance of statutes contemplating supervisory jurisdiction.

One of the problems with inter vivos and receptacle trusts at the present time, however, is that persons interested in these arrangements as trustees or beneficiaries frequently discover that there are no simple and efficient statutory or judicial remedies available to them to meet the special needs of the trust relationship. Proceedings in equity before courts of general jurisdiction are possible, of course, but the difficulties of obtaining jurisdiction over all interested persons on each occasion when a judicial order may be necessary or desirable are commonly formidable. A few states offer simplified procedures on a voluntary basis for inter vivos as well as testamentary trusts. In some of these, however, the legislation forces inter vivos trusts into unpopular patterns involving supervisory control. Nevertheless, it remains true of the legislation in most states that there is too little for inter vivos trusts and too much for trusts created by will.

Other developments suggest that enactment of useful, uniform legislation on trust procedures is a matter of considerable social importance. For one thing, accelerating mobility of persons and estates is steadily increasing the pressure on locally oriented property institutions. The drafting and technical problems created by lack of uniformity of trust procedures in the several states are quite serious. If people cannot obtain efficient trust service to preserve and direct wealth because of state property rules, they will turn in time to national arrangements that eliminate property law problems. A general shift away from local management of trusteed wealth and increased reliance on various contractual claims against national funds seems the most likely consequence if the local law of trusts remains nonuniform and provincial.

Modestly endowed persons who are turning to inter vivos trusts to avoid probate are of more immediate concern. Lawyers in all parts of the country are aware of the trend toward reliance on revocable trusts as total substitutes for wills which recent controversies about probate procedures have stimulated. There would be little need for concern about this development if it could be assumed also that the people involved are seeking and getting competent advice and fiduciary assistance. But there are indications that many people are neither seeking nor receiving adequate information about trusts they are using. Moreover, professional fiduciaries are often not available as trustees for small estates. Consequently, neither settlors nor trustees of "do-it-yourself" trusts have much idea of what they are getting into. As a result, there are corresponding dangers to beneficiaries who are frequently uninformed or baffled by formidable difficulties in obtaining relief or information.

Enactment of clear statutory procedures creating simple remedies for persons involved in trust problems will not prevent disappointment for many of these persons but should help minimize their losses.

Several objectives of the Code are suggested by the preceding discussion. They may be summarized as follows:

1. To eliminate procedural distinctions between testamentary and inter vivos trusts.

2. To strengthen the ability of owners to select trustees by eliminating formal qualification of trustees and restrictions on the place of administration.

3. To locate nonmandatory judicial proceedings for trustees and beneficiaries in a convenient court fully competent to handle all problems that may arise.

4.   To facilitate judicial proceedings concerning trusts by comprehensive provisions for obtaining jurisdiction over interested persons by notice.

5.   To protect beneficiaries by having trustees file written statements of acceptance of trusts with suitable courts, thereby acknowledging jurisdiction and providing some evidence of the trust's existence for future beneficiaries.

6.   To eliminate routinely required court accountings, substituting clear remedies and statutory duties to inform beneficiaries.

PART 1

TRUST REGISTRATION

GENERAL COMMENT

Registration of trusts is a new concept and differs importantly from common arrangements for retained supervisory jurisdiction of courts of probate over testamentary trusts. It applies alike to inter vivos and testamentary trusts, and is available to foreign-created trusts as well as those locally created. The place of registration is related not to the place where the trust was created, which may lose its significance to the parties concerned, but is related to the place where the trust is primarily administered, which in turn is required (Section 7–305) to be at a location appropriate to the purposes of the trust and the interests of its beneficiaries. Sections 7–102 and 7–305 provide for transfer of registration. The procedure is more flexible than the typical retained jurisdiction in that it permits registration or submission to other appropriate procedures at another place, even in another state, in order to accommodate relocation of the trust at a place which becomes more convenient for its administration. (Cf. 20 [Purdon's] Pa.Stat. § 2080.309.) In addition, the registration acknowledges that a particular court will be accessible to the parties on a permissive basis without subjecting the trust to compulsory, continuing supervision by the court.

The process of registration requires no judicial action or determination but is accomplished routinely by simple acts on the part of the trustee which will place certain information on file with the court (Section 7–102). Although proceedings involving a registered trust will not be continuous but will be separate each time an interested party initiates a proceeding, it is contemplated that a court will maintain a single file for each registered trust as a record available to interested persons. Proceedings are facilitated by the broad jurisdiction of the court (Section 7–201) and the Code's representation and notice provisions (Section 1–403).

Section 7–201 provides complete jurisdiction over trust proceedings in the court of registration. Section 7–103 above provides for jurisdiction over parties. Section 7–104 should facilitate use of trusts involving assets in several states by providing for a single principal place of administration and reducing concern about qualification of foreign trust companies.

Section 7–101. [Duty to Register Trusts.]

The trustee of a trust having its principal place of administration in this state shall register the trust in the Court of this state at the principal place of administration. Unless otherwise designated in the trust instrument, the principal place of administration of a trust is the trustee's usual place of business where the records

503

pertaining to the trust are kept, or at the trustee's residence if he has no such place of business. In the case of co-trustees, the principal place of administration, if not otherwise designated in the trust instrument, is (1) the usual place of business of the corporate trustee if there is but one corporate co-trustee, or (2) the usual place of business or residence of the individual trustee who is a professional fiduciary if there is but one such person and no corporate co-trustee, and otherwise (3) the usual place of business or residence of any of the co-trustees as agreed upon by them. The duty to register under this Part does not apply to the trustee of a trust if registration would be inconsistent with the retained jurisdiction of a foreign court from which the trustee cannot obtain release.

COMMENT

This section rests on the assumption that a central "filing office" will be designated in each county where the Court may sit in more than one place.

The scope of this section and of Article VII is tied to the definition of "trustee" in Section 1–201. It was suggested that the definition should be expanded to include "land trusts." It was concluded, however that the inclusion of this term which has special meaning principally in Illinois, should be left for decision by enacting states. Under the definition of "trust" in this Code, custodial arrangements as contemplated by legislation dealing with gifts to minors, are excluded, as are "trust accounts" as defined in Article VI.

Section 7–102. [Registration Procedures.]

Registration shall be accomplished by filing a statement indicating the name and address of the trustee in which it acknowledges the trusteeship. The statement shall indicate whether the trust has been registered elsewhere. The statement shall identify the trust: (1) in the case of a testamentary trust, by the name of the testator and the date and place of domiciliary probate; (2) in the case of a written inter vivos trust, by the name of each settlor and the original trustee and the date of the trust instrument; or (3) in the case of an oral trust, by information identifying the settlor or other source of funds and describing the time and manner of the trust's creation and the terms of the trust, including the subject matter, beneficiaries and time of performance. If a trust has been registered elsewhere, registration in this state is ineffective until the earlier registration is released by order of the Court where prior registration occurred, or an instrument executed by the trustee and all beneficiaries, filed with the registration in this state.

COMMENT

Additional duties of the clerk of the Court are provided in Section 1–305. The duty to register trusts is stated in Section 7–101.

Section 7–103. [Effect of Registration.]

(a) By registering a trust, or accepting the trusteeship of a registered trust, the trustee submits personally to the jurisdiction of the Court in any proceeding under Section 7–201 of this Code relating to the trust that may be initiated by any interested person while the trust remains registered. Notice of any proceeding shall be delivered to the trustee, or mailed to him by ordinary first class mail at his address as listed in the registration or as thereafter reported to the Court and to his address as then known to the petitioner.

(b) To the extent of their interests in the trust, all beneficiaries of a trust properly registered in this state are subject to the jurisdiction of the court of registration for the purposes of proceedings under Section 7–201, provided notice is given pursuant to Section 1–401.

COMMENT

This section provides for jurisdiction over the parties. Subject matter jurisdiction for proceedings involving trusts is described in Sections 7–201 and 7–202. The basic jurisdictional concept in Section 7–103 is that reflected in widely adopted long-arm statutes, that a state may properly entertain proceedings when it is a reasonable forum under all the circumstances, provided adequate notice is given. Clearly the trustee can be deemed to consent to jurisdiction by virtue of registration. This basis for consent jurisdiction is in addition to and not in lieu of other bases of jurisdiction during or after registration. Also, incident to an order releasing registration under Section 7–305, the Court could condition the release on registration of the trust in another state or court. It also seems reasonable to require beneficiaries to go to the seat of the trust when litigation has been initiated there concerning a trust in which they claim beneficial interests, much as the rights of shareholders of a corporation can be determined at a corporate seat. The settlor has indicated a principal place of administration by his selection of a trustee or otherwise, and it is reasonable to subject rights under the trust to the jurisdiction of the Court where the trust is properly administered. Although most cases will fit within traditional concepts of jurisdiction, this section goes beyond established doctrines of in personam or quasi in rem jurisdiction as regards a nonresident beneficiary's interests in foreign land of chattels, but the National Conference believes the section affords due process and represents a worth-

505

while step forward in trust proceedings.

Section 7–104. [Effect of Failure to Register.]

A trustee who fails to register a trust in a proper place as required by this Part, for purposes of any proceedings initiated by a beneficiary of the trust prior to registration, is subject to the personal jurisdiction of any Court in which the trust could have been registered. In addition, any trustee who, within 30 days after receipt of a written demand by a settlor or beneficiary of the trust, fails to register a trust as required by this Part is subject to removal and denial of compensation or to surcharge as the Court may direct. A provision in the terms of the trust purporting to excuse the trustee from the duty to register, or directing that the trust or trustee shall not be subject to the jurisdiction of the Court, is ineffective.

COMMENT

Under Section 1–108, the holder of a presently exercisable general power of appointment can control all duties of a fiduciary to beneficiaries who may be changed by exercise of the power. Hence, if the settlor of a revocable inter vivos trust directs the trustee to refrain from registering a trust, no liability would follow even though another beneficiary demanded registration. The ability of the general power holder to control the trustee ends when the power is terminated.

Section 7–105. [Registration, Qualification of Foreign Trustee.]

A foreign corporate trustee is required to qualify as a foreign corporation doing business in this state if it maintains the principal place of administration of any trust within the state. A foreign co-trustee is not required to qualify in this state solely because its co-trustee maintains the principal place of administration in this state. Unless otherwise doing business in this state, local qualification by a foreign trustee, corporate or individual, is not required in order for the trustee to receive distribution from a local estate or to hold, invest in, manage or acquire property located in this state, or maintain litigation. Nothing in this section affects a determination of what other acts require qualification as doing business in this state.

COMMENT

Section 7–105 deals with non-resident trustees in a fashion which should correct a wide-spread deficiency in present regulation of trust activity. Provisions limiting business of foreign corporate trustees constitute an unnecessary limitation on the ability of a trustee to function away from its principal place of business. These restrictions properly relate more to continuous pursuit of general trust business by foreign corporations than to isolated instances of litigation and management of the assets of a particular trust. The ease of avoiding foreign corporation qualification statutes by the common use of local nominees or subtrustees, and the acceptance of these practices, are evidence of the futility and undesirability of more restrictive legislation of the sort commonly existing today. The position embodied in this section has been recommended by important segments of the banking and trust industry through a proposed model statute, and the failure to adopt this reform has been characterized as unfortunate by a leading trust authority. See 5 Scott on Trusts § 558 (3rd ed. 1967).

PART 2

JURISDICTION OF COURT CONCERNING TRUSTS

Section 7–201. [Court; Exclusive Jurisdiction of Trusts.]

(a) The Court has exclusive jurisdiction of proceedings initiated by interested parties concerning the internal affairs of trusts. Proceedings which may be maintained under this section are those concerning the administration and distribution of trusts, the declaration of rights and the determination of other matters involving trustees and beneficiaries of trusts. These include, but are not limited to, proceedings to:

(1) appoint or remove a trustee;

(2) review trustees' fees and to review and settle interim or final accounts;

(3) ascertain beneficiaries, determine any question arising in the administration or distribution of any trust including questions of construction of trust instruments, to instruct trustees, and determine the existence or nonexistence of any immunity, power, privilege, duty or right; and

(4) release registration of a trust.

(b) Neither registration of a trust nor a proceeding under this section result in continuing supervisory proceedings. The management and distribution of a trust estate, submission of accounts and reports to beneficiaries, payment of trustee's fees and other obligations of a trust, acceptance and change of trusteeship, and other aspects of the administration of a trust shall proceed expeditiously consistent with the terms of the trust, free of judicial intervention and without order, approval or other action of any court, subject to the jurisdiction of the Court as invoked by interested parties or as otherwise exercised as provided by law.

COMMENT

Derived in small part from Florida Statutes 1965, Chapters 737 and 87, and Title 20, Penna.Statutes, (Purdon) 32080.101 et seq.

Section 7–202. [Trust Proceedings; Venue.]

Venue for proceedings under Section 7–201 involving registered trusts is in the place of registration. Venue for proceedings under

508

Section 7–201 involving trusts not registered in this state is in any place where the trust properly could have been registered, and otherwise by the rules of civil procedure.

Section 7–203. [Trust Proceedings; Dismissal of Matters Relating to Foreign Trusts.]

The Court will not, over the objection of a party, entertain proceedings under Section 7–201 involving a trust registered or having its principal place of administration in another state, unless (1) when all appropriate parties could not be bound by litigation in the courts of the state where the trust is registered or has its principal place of administration or (2) when the interests of justice otherwise would seriously be impaired. The Court may condition a stay or dismissal of a proceeding under this section on the consent of any party to jurisdiction of the state in which the trust is registered or has its principal place of business, or the Court may grant a continuance or enter any other appropriate order.

COMMENT

While recognizing that trusts which are essentially foreign can be the subject of proceedings in this state, this section employs the concept of forum non conveniens to center litigation involving the trustee and beneficiaries at the principal place of administration of the trust but leaves open the possibility of suit elsewhere when necessary in the interests of justice. It is assumed that under this section a court would refuse to entertain litigation involving the foreign registered trust unless for jurisdictional or other reasons, such as the nature and location of the property or unusual interests of the parties, it is manifest that substantial injustice would result if the parties were referred to the court of registration. As regards litigation involving third parties, the trustee may sue and be sued as any owner and manager of property under the usually applicable rules of civil procedure and also as provided in Section 7–203.

The concepts of res judicata and full faith and credit applicable to any managing owner of property have generally been applicable to trustees. Consequently, litigation by trustees has not involved the artificial problems historically found when personal representatives maintain litigation away from the state of their appointment, and a prior adjudication for or against a trustee rendered in a foreign court having jurisdiction is viewed as conclusive and entitled to full faith and credit. Because of this, provisions changing the law, analogous to those relating to personal representatives in Section 4–401 do not appear necessary. See also Section 3–408. In light of the foregoing, the issue is essentially only one of forum non conveniens in having litigation proceed in the most appropriate forum. This is the function of this section.

Section 7–204. [Court; Concurrent Jurisdiction of Litigation Involving Trusts and Third Parties.]

The Court of the place in which the trust is registered has concurrent jurisdiction with other courts of this state of actions and proceedings to determine the existence or nonexistence of trusts created other than by will, of actions by or against creditors or debtors of trusts, and of other actions and proceedings involving trustees and third parties. Venue is determined by the rules generally applicable to civil actions.

Section 7–205. [Proceedings for Review of Employment of Agents and Review of Compensation of Trustee and Employees of Trust.]

On petition of an interested person, after notice to all interested persons, the Court may review the propriety of employment of any person by a trustee including any attorney, auditor, investment advisor or other specialized agent or assistant, and the reasonableness of the compensation of any person so employed, and the reasonableness of the compensation determined by the trustee for his own services. Any person who has received excessive compensation from a trust may be ordered to make appropriate refunds.

COMMENT

In view of the broad jurisdiction conferred on the probate court, description of the special proceeding authorized by this section might be unnecessary. But the Code's theory that trustees may fix their own fees and those of their attorneys marks an important departure from much existing practice under which fees are determined by the Court in the first instance. Hence, it seems wise to emphasize that any interested person can get judicial review of fees if he desires it. Also, if excessive fees have been paid, this section provides a quick and efficient remedy. This review would meet in part the criticism of the broad powers given in the Uniform Trustees' Powers Act.

Section 7–206. [Trust Proceedings; Initiation by Notice; Necessary Parties.]

Proceedings under Section 7–201 are initiated by filing a petition in the Court and giving notice pursuant to Section 1–401 to interested parties. The Court may order notification of additional persons. A decree is valid as to all who are given notice of the proceeding though fewer than all interested parties are notified.

PART 3

DUTIES AND LIABILITIES OF TRUSTEES

Section 7–301. [General Duties Not Limited.]

Except as specifically provided, the general duty of the trustee to administer a trust expeditiously for the benefit of the beneficiaries is not altered by this Code.

Section 7–302. [Trustee's Standard of Care and Performance.]

Except as otherwise provided by the terms of the trust, the trustee shall observe the standards in dealing with the trust assets that would be observed by a prudent man dealing with the property of another, and if the trustee has special skills or is named trustee on the basis of representations of special skills or expertise, he is under a duty to use those skills.

COMMENT

This is a new general provision designed to make clear the standard of skill expected from trustees, both individual and corporate, nonprofessional and professional. It differs somewhat from the standard stated in § 174 of the Restatement of Trusts, Second, which is as follows:

"The trustee is under a duty to the beneficiary in administering the trust to exercise such care and skill as a man of ordinary prudence would exercise in dealing with his own property; and if the trustee has or procures his appointment as trustee by representing that he has greater skill than that of a reasonable man of ordinary prudence, he is under a duty to exercise such skill."

By making the basic standard align to that observed by a prudent man in dealing with the property of another, the section accepts a standard as it has been articulated in some decisions regarding the duty of a trustee concerning investments. See Estate of Cook, (Del. Chanc.1934) 20 Del.Ch. 123, 171 A. 730. Also, the duty as described by the above section more clearly conveys the idea that a trustee must comply with an external, rather than with a personal, standard of care.

Section 7–303. [Duty to Inform and Account to Beneficiaries.]

The trustee shall keep the beneficiaries of the trust reasonably informed of the trust and its administration. In addition:

(a) Within 30 days after his acceptance of the trust, the trustee shall inform in writing the current beneficiaries and if possible, one

511

or more persons who under Section 1–403 may represent beneficiaries with future interests, of the Court in which the trust is registered and of his name and address.

(b) Upon reasonable request, the trustee shall provide the beneficiary with a copy of the terms of the trust which describe or affect his interest and with relevant information about the assets of the trust and the particulars relating to the administration.

(c) Upon reasonable request, a beneficiary is entitled to a statement of the accounts of the trust annually and on termination of the trust or change of the trustee.

COMMENT

Analogous provisions are found in Section 3–705.

This provision does not require regular accounting to the Court nor are copies of statements furnished beneficiaries required to be filed with the Court. The parties are expected to assume the usual ownership responsibility for their interests including their own record keeping. Under Section 1–108, the holder of a general power of appointment or of revocation can negate the trustee's duties to any other person.

This section requires that a reasonable selection of beneficiaries is entitled to information so that the interests of the future beneficiaries may adequately be protected. After mandatory notification of registration by the trustee to the beneficiaries, further information may be obtained by the beneficiary upon request. This is to avoid extensive mandatory formal accounts and yet provide the beneficiary with adequate protection and sources of information. In most instances, the trustee will provide beneficiaries with copies of annual tax returns or tax statements that must be filed. Usually this will be accompanied by a narrative explanation by the trustee. In the case of the charitable trust, notice need be given only to the attorney general or other state officer supervising charitable trusts and in the event that the charitable trust has, as its primary beneficiary, a charitable corporation or institution, notice should be given to that charitable corporation or institution. It is not contemplated that all of the individuals who may receive some benefit as a result of a charitable trust be informed.

Section 7–304. [Duty to Provide Bond.]

A trustee need not provide bond to secure performance of his duties unless required by the terms of the trust, reasonably requested by a beneficiary or found by the Court to be necessary to protect the interests of the beneficiaries who are not able to protect themselves and whose interests otherwise are not adequately represented. On petition of the trustee or other interested person the Court may excuse a requirement of bond, reduce the amount of the bond, release the surety, or permit the substitution of another bond with the same or different sureties. If bond is required, it shall be filed in the Court of registration or other appropriate Court in amounts and with sureties and liabilities as provided in Sections 3–604 and 3–606 relating to bonds of personal representatives.

COMMENT

See Sections 3–603 and 3–604; 60 Okla.Stats.1961, § 175.24 [60 Okl. St.Ann. § 175.24]; Pa.Fid.Act, 1949, § 390.911(b) [20 Purdon's Pa. Stat. § 390.911(b)]; cf. Tenn.Code Ann. § 35–113.

Section 7–305. [Trustee's Duties; Appropriate Place of Administration; Deviation.]

A trustee is under a continuing duty to administer the trust at a place appropriate to the purposes of the trust and to its sound, efficient management. If the principal place of administration becomes inappropriate for any reason, the Court may enter any order furthering efficient administration and the interests of beneficiaries, including, if appropriate, release of registration, removal of the trustee and appointment of a trustee in another state. Trust provisions relating to the place of administration and to changes in the place of administration or of trustee control unless compliance would be contrary to efficient administration or the purposes of the trust. Views of adult beneficiaries shall be given weight in determining the suitability of the trustee and the place of administration.

COMMENT

This section and 7–102 are related. The latter section makes it clear that registration may be released without Court order if the trustee and beneficiaries can agree on the matter. Section 1–108 may be relevant, also.

The primary thrust of Article VII is to relate trust administration to the jurisdiction of courts, rather than to deal with substantive matters of trust law. An aspect of deviation, however, is touched here.

Section 7–306. [Personal Liability of Trustee to Third Parties.]

(a) Unless otherwise provided in the contract, a trustee is not personally liable on contracts properly entered into in his fiduciary capacity in the course of administration of the trust estate unless he fails to reveal his representative capacity and identify the trust estate in the contract.

(b) A trustee is personally liable for obligations arising from ownership or control of property of the trust estate or for torts committed in the course of administration of the trust estate only if he is personally at fault.

(c) Claims based on contracts entered into by a trustee in his fiduciary capacity, on obligations arising from ownership or control of the trust estate, or on torts committed in the course of trust administration may be asserted against the trust estate by proceeding against the trustee in his fiduciary capacity, whether or not the trustee is personally liable therefor.

(d) The question of liability as between the trust estate and the trustee individually may be determined in a proceeding for accounting, surcharge or indemnification or other appropriate proceeding.

COMMENT

The purpose of this section is to make the liability of the trust and trustee the same as that of the decedent's estate and personal representative.

Ultimate liability as between the estate and the fiduciary need not necessarily be determined whenever there is doubt about this question. It should be permissible, and often it will be preferable, for judgment to be entered, for example, against the trustee individually for purposes of determining the claimant's rights without the trustee placing that matter into controversy. The question of his right of reimbursement may be settled informally with beneficiaries or in a separate proceeding in the probate court involving reimbursement. The section does not preclude the possibility, however, that beneficiaries might be permitted to intervene in litigation between the trustee and a claimant and that all questions might be resolved in that action.

Section 7–307. [Limitations on Proceedings Against Trustees After Final Account.]

Unless previously barred by adjudication, consent or limitation, any claim against a trustee for breach of trust is barred as to any beneficiary who has received a final account or other statement fully disclosing the matter and showing termination of the trust relationship between the trustee and the beneficiary unless a proceeding to assert the claim is commenced within [6 months] after receipt of the final account or statement. In any event and notwithstanding lack of full disclosure a trustee who has issued a final account or statement received by the beneficiary and has informed the beneficiary of the location and availability of records for his examination is protected after 3 years. A beneficiary is deemed to have received a final account or statement if, being an adult, it is received by him personally or if, being a minor or disabled person, it is received by his representative as described in Section 1–403(1) and (2).

514

COMMENT

Final accounts terminating the trustee's obligations to the trust beneficiaries may be formal or informal. Formal judicial accountings may be initiated by the petition of any trustee or beneficiary. Informal accounts may be conclusive by consent or by limitation. This section provides a special limitation supporting informal accounts. With regard to facilitating distribution see Section 5–103.

Section 1–108 makes approval of an informal account or settlement with a trustee by the holder of a presently exercisable general power of appointment binding on all beneficiaries. In addition, the equitable principles of estoppel and laches, as well as general statutes of limitation, will apply in many cases to terminate trust liabilities.

PART 4

POWERS OF TRUSTEES

GENERAL COMMENT

There has been considerable interest in recent years in legislation giving trustees extensive powers. The Uniform Trustees' Powers Act, approved by the National Conference in 1964 has been adopted in Idaho, Kansas, Mississippi and Wyoming. New York and New Jersey have adopted similar statutes which differ somewhat from the Uniform Trustees' Powers Act, and Arkansas, California, Colorado, Florida, Iowa, Louisiana, Oklahoma, Pennsylvania, Virginia and Washington have comprehensive legislation which differ in various respects from other models. The legislation in Connecticut, North Carolina and Tennessee provides lists of powers to be incorporated by reference as draftsmen wish.

Comprehensive legislation dealing with trustees' powers appropriately may be included in the Code package at this point.

ARTICLE VIII

EFFECTIVE DATE AND REPEALER

Section 8–101. [Time of Taking Effect; Provisions for Transition.]

(a) This Code takes effect on January 1, 19___.

(b) Except as provided elsewhere in this Code, on the effective date of this Code:

(1) the Code applies to governing instruments executed by decedents dying thereafter;

(2) the Code applies to any proceedings in Court then pending or thereafter commenced regardless of the time of the death of decedent except to the extent that in the opinion of the Court the former procedure should be made applicable in a particular case in the interest of justice or because of infeasibility of application of the procedure of this Code;

(3) every personal representative including a person administering an estate of a minor or incompetent holding an appointment on that date, continues to hold the appointment but has only the powers conferred by this Code and is subject to the duties imposed with respect to any act occurring or done thereafter;

(4) an act done before the effective date in any proceeding and any accrued right is not impaired by this Code. If a right is acquired, extinguished or barred upon the expiration of a prescribed period of time which has commenced to run by the provisions of any statute before the effective date, the provisions shall remain in force with respect to that right;

(5) any rule of construction or presumption provided in this Code applies to governing instruments executed before the effective date unless there is a clear indication of a contrary intent;

(6) a person holding office as judge of the Court on the effective date of this Act may continue the office of judge of this Court and may be selected for additional terms after the effec-

tive date of this Act even though he does not meet the qualifications of a judge as provided in Article I.

Section 8–102. [Specific Repealer and Amendments.]

(a) The following Acts and parts of Acts are repealed:

   (1)

   (2)

   (3)

(b) The following Acts and parts of Acts are amended:

   (1)

   (2)

   (3)

UPC APPENDICES

APPENDIX A: PRE-1990 UPC ARTICLE II

INTESTATE SUCCESSION AND WILLS

PART 1

INTESTATE SUCCESSION

PART 2

ELECTIVE SHARE OF SURVIVING SPOUSE

PART 3

SPOUSE AND CHILDREN UNPROVIDED FOR IN WILLS

PART 4

EXEMPT PROPERTY AND ALLOWANCES

APPENDIX A

PART 8

GENERAL PROVISIONS

PART 9

CUSTODY AND DEPOSIT OF WILLS

PART 10

UNIFORM INTERNATIONAL WILLS ACT
[INTERNATIONAL WILL; INFORMATION REGISTRATION]

PART 1

INTESTATE SUCCESSION

COMMENT

Part 1 of Article II contains the basic pattern of intestate succession historically called descent and distribution. It is no longer meaningful to have different patterns for real and personal property, and under the proposed statute all property not disposed of by a decedent's will passes to his heirs in the same manner. The existing statutes on descent and distribution in the United States vary from state to state. The most common pattern for the immediate family retains the imprint of history, giving the widow a third of realty (sometimes only for life by her dower right) and a third of the personalty, with the balance passing to issue. Where the decedent is survived by no issue, but leaves a spouse and collateral blood relatives, there is wide variation in disposition of the intestate estate, some states giving all to the surviving spouse, some giving substantial shares to the blood relatives. The Code attempts to reflect the normal desire of the owner of wealth as to disposition of his property at death, and for this purpose the prevailing patterns in wills are useful in determining what the owner who fails to execute a will would probably want.

A principal purpose of this Article and Article III of the Code is to provide suitable rules and procedures for the person of modest means who relies on the estate plan provided by law. For a discussion of this important aspect of the Code, see 3 Real Property, Probate and Trust Journal (Fall 1968) p. 199.

The principal features of Part 1 are:

(1) A larger share is given to the surviving spouse, if there are issue, and the whole estate if there are no issue or parent.

(2) Inheritance by collateral relatives is limited to grandparents and those descended from grandparents. This simplifies proof of heirship and eliminates will contests by remote relatives.

(3) An heir must survive the decedent for five days in order to take under the statute. This is an extension of the reasoning behind the Uniform Simultaneous Death Act and is similar to provisions found in many wills.

(4) Adopted children are treated as children of the adopting parents for all inheritance purposes and cease to be children of natural parents; this reflects modern policy of recent statutes and court decisions.

(5) In an era when inter vivos gifts are frequently made within the family, it is unrealistic to preserve concepts of advancement developed when such gifts were rare. The statute provides that gifts during

523

lifetime are not advancements unless declared or acknowledged in writing.

While the prescribed patterns may strike some as rules of law which may in some cases defeat intent of a decedent, this is true of every statute of this type. In assessing the changes it must therefore be borne in mind that the decedent may always choose a different rule by executing a will.

Section 2–101. [Intestate Estate.]

Any part of the estate of a decedent not effectively disposed of by his will passes to his heirs as prescribed in the following sections of this Code.

Section 2–102. [Share of the Spouse.]

The intestate share of the surviving spouse is:

(1) if there is no surviving issue or parent of the decedent, the entire intestate estate;

(2) if there is no surviving issue but the decedent is survived by a parent or parents, the first [$50,000], plus one-half of the balance of the intestate estate;

(3) if there are surviving issue all of whom are issue of the surviving spouse also, the first [$50,000], plus one-half of the balance of the intestate estate;

(4) if there are surviving issue one or more of whom are not issue of the surviving spouse, one-half of the intestate estate.

COMMENT

This section gives the surviving spouse a larger share than most existing statutes on descent and distribution. In doing so, it reflects the desires of most married persons, who almost always leave all of a moderate estate or at least one-half of a larger estate to the surviving spouse when a will is executed. A husband or wife who desires to leave the surviving spouse less than the share provided by this section may do so by executing a will, subject of course to possible election by the surviving spouse to take an elective share of one-third under

Part 2 of this Article. Moreover, in the small estate (less than $50,000 after homestead allowance, exempt property, and allowances) the surviving spouse is given the entire estate if there are only children who are issue of both the decedent and the surviving spouse; the result is to avoid protective proceedings as to property otherwise passing to their minor children.

See Section 2–802 for the definition of spouse which controls for purposes of intestate succession.

ALTERNATIVE PROVISION FOR COMMUNITY PROPERTY STATES

[Section 2–102A. [Share of the Spouse.]

The intestate share of the surviving spouse is as follows:

(1) as to separate property

(i) if there is no surviving issue or parent of the decedent, the entire intestate estate;

(ii) if there is no surviving issue but the decedent is survived by a parent or parents, the first [$50,000], plus one-half of the balance of the intestate estate;

(iii) if there are surviving issue all of whom are issue of the surviving spouse also, the first [$50,000], plus one-half of the balance of the intestate estate;

(iv) if there are surviving issue one or more of whom are not issue of the surviving spouse, one-half of the intestate estate.

(2) as to community property

(i) the one-half of community property which belongs to the decedent passes to the [surviving spouse].]

Section 2–103. [Shares of Heirs Other Than Surviving Spouse.]

The part of the intestate estate not passing to the surviving spouse under Section 2–102, or the entire intestate estate if there is no surviving spouse, passes as follows:

(1) to the issue of the decedent; if they are all of the same degree of kinship to the decedent they take equally, but if of unequal degree, then those of more remote degree take by representation;

(2) if there is no surviving issue, to his parent or parents equally;

(3) if there is no surviving issue or parent, to the issue of the parents or either of them by representation;

(4) if there is no surviving issue, parent or issue of a parent, but the decedent is survived by one or more grandparents or issue of grandparents, half of the estate passes to the paternal grandparents if both survive, or to the surviving paternal grandparent, or to the issue of the paternal grandparents if both are deceased, the issue taking equally if they are all of the same degree of kinship to the decedent, but if of unequal degree those of more remote degree take by representation; and the other half passes to the maternal relatives in the same manner; but if there be no surviving grandparent or issue of grandparent on either the paternal or the maternal side, the entire estate passes to the relatives on the other side in the same manner as the half.

COMMENT

This section provides for inheritance by lineal descendants of the decedent, parents and their descendants, and grandparents and collateral relatives descended from grandparents; in line with modern policy, it eliminates more remote relatives tracing through great-grandparents.

In general the principle of representation (which is defined in Section 2–106) is adopted as the pattern which most decedents would prefer.

If the pattern of this section is not desired, it may be avoided by a properly executed will or, after the decedent's death, by renunciation by particular heirs under Section 2–801.

In 1975, the Joint Editorial Board recommended replacement of the original text of subsection (3) which referred to "brothers and sisters" of the decedent, and to their issue. The new language is much simpler, and it avoids the problem that "brother" and "sister" are not defined terms. "Issue" by contrast is defined in Section 1–201(21). The definition refers to other defined terms, "parent" and "child", both of which refer to Section 2–109 where the effect of illegitimacy and adoption on relationships for inheritance purposes is spelled out.

The Joint Editorial Board gave careful consideration to a change in the Code's system for distribution among issue as recommended in Waggoner, "A Proposed Alternative to the Uniform Probate Code's System for Intestate Distribution Among Descendants," 66 Nw. U.L.Rev. 626 (1971). Though favored as a recommended change in the Code by a majority of the Board, others opposed on the ground that the original text had been enacted already in several states, and that a change in this basic section of the Code would weaken the case for uniformity of probate law in all states. Nonetheless, since some states as of 1975 had adopted versions of the Code containing deviations from the original text of this and related sections, it was the consensus that Prof. Waggoner's recommendation and the statutory changes that would be necessary to implement it, should be described in Code commentary.

The changes involved would appear in this section and in Section 2–106. The old and the revised text of these sections would be as follows if the Waggoner recommendation is accepted by an enacting state which decides that unifor-mity of the substantive rules of intestate succession is not vital:

Change Section 2–103(1), (3) and (4) by altering, in each instance, the language referring to taking per capita or by representation, as follows:

2–103   . . .

(1) to the issue of the decedent; *to be distributed per capita at each generation as defined in Section 2–106;* if they are all of the same degree of kinship to the decedent they take equally, but if of unequal degree then those of more remote degree take by representation;

(3) if there is no surviving issue or parent, to the issue of the parents or either of them *to be distributed per capita at each generation as defined in Section 2–106;* by representation;

(4) . . . or to the issue of the paternal grandparents if both are deceased *to be distributed per capita at each generation as defined in Section 2–106;* the issue taking equally if they are all of the same degree of kinship to the decedent, but if of unequal degree those of more remote degree take by representation.

Also, alter 2–106 as follows:

SECTION 2–106. [*Per Capita at Each Generation.*]

If per capita at each generation representation is called for by this Code, the estate is divided into as many shares as there are surviving heirs in the nearest degree of kinship *which contains any surviving heirs* and deceased persons in the same degree who left issue who survive the decedent, ;e Each surviving heir in the nearest degree *which contains any surviving heir is allocated one share and the remainder of the estate is divided in the same manner as if the heirs already allocated a share and their issue had predeceased the decedent.* receiving one share and the share of each deceased person in the same degree being divided among his issue in the same manner.

Section 2–104. [Requirement That Heir Survive Decedent For 120 Hours.]

Any person who fails to survive the decedent by 120 hours is deemed to have predeceased the decedent for purposes of homestead allowance, exempt property and intestate succession, and the decedent's heirs are determined accordingly. If the time of death of the decedent or of the person who would otherwise be an heir, or the times of death of both, cannot be determined, and it cannot be established that the person who would otherwise be an heir has survived the decedent by 120 hours, it is deemed that the person failed to survive for the required period. This section is not to be applied where its application would result in a taking of intestate estate by the state under Section 2–105.

COMMENT

This section is a limited version of the type of clause frequently found in wills to take care of the common accident situation, in which several members of the same family are injured and die within a few days of each other. The Uniform Simultaneous Death Act provides only a partial solution, since it applies only if there is no proof that the parties died otherwise than simultaneously. This section requires an heir to survive by five days in order to succeed to decedent's intestate property; for a comparable provision as to wills, see Section 2–601. This section avoids multiple administrations and in some instances prevents the property from passing to persons not desired by the decedent. The five-day period will not hold up administration of a decedent's estate because sections 3–302 and 3–307 prevent informal probate of a will or informal issuance of letters for a period of five days from death. The last sentence prevents the survivorship requirement from affecting inheritances by the last eligible relative of the intestate who survives him for any period.

I.R.C. § 2056(b)(3) makes it clear that an interest passing to a surviving spouse is *not* made a "terminable interest" and thereby disqualified for inclusion in the marital deduction by its being conditioned on failure of the spouse to survive a period not exceeding six months after the decedent's death, if the spouse in fact lives for the required period. Thus, the intestate share of a spouse who survives the decedent by five days is available for the marital deduction. To assure a marital deduction in cases where one spouse fails to survive the other by the required period, the decedent must leave a will. The marital deduction is not a problem in the typical intestate estate. The draftsmen and Special Committee concluded that the statute should accommodate the typical estate to which it applies, rather than the unusual case of an unplanned estate involving large sums of money.

Section 2–105. [No Taker.]

If there is no taker under the provisions of this Article, the intestate estate passes to the [state].

Section 2–106. [Representation.]

If representation is called for by this Code, the estate is divided into as many shares as there are surviving heirs in the nearest degree of kinship and deceased persons in the same degree who left issue who survive the decedent, each surviving heir in the nearest degree receiving one share and the share of each deceased person in the same degree being divided among his issue in the same manner.

COMMENT

Under the system of intestate succession in effect in some states, property is directed to be divided "per stirpes" among issue or descendants of identified ancestors. Applying a meaning commonly associated with the quoted words, the estate is first divided into the number indicated by the number of children of the ancestor who survive, *or* who leave issue who survive. If, for example, the property is directed to issue "per stirpes" of the intestate's parents, the first division would be by the number of children of parents (other than the intestate) who left issue surviving even though no person of this generation survives. Thus, if the survivors are a child and a grandchild of a deceased brother

of the intestate and five children of his deceased sister, the brother's descendants would divide one-half and the five children of the sister would divide the other half. Yet, if the parent of the brother's grandchild also had survived, most statutes would give the seven nephews and nieces equal shares because it is commonly provided that if all surviving kin are in equal degree, they take per capita.

The draft rejects this pattern and keys to a system which assures that the first and principal division of the estate will be with reference to a generation which includes one or more living members.

Section 2–107. [Kindred of Half Blood.]

Relatives of the half blood inherit the same share they would inherit if they were of the whole blood.

Section 2–108. [Afterborn Heirs.]

Relatives of the decedent conceived before his death but born thereafter inherit as if they had been born in the lifetime of the decedent.

Section 2–109. [Meaning of Child and Related Terms.]

If, for purposes of intestate succession, a relationship of parent and child must be established to determine succession by, through, or from a person,

(1) an adopted person is the child of an adopting parent and not of the natural parents except that adoption of a child by the spouse of a natural parent has no effect on the relationship between the child and either natural parent.

(2) In cases not covered by Paragraph (1), a person is the child of its parents regardless of the marital status of its parents and the parent and child relationship may be established under the [Uniform Parentage Act].

*Alternative subsection (2) for states that have not
adopted the Uniform Parentage Act.*

[(2) In cases not covered by Paragraph (1), a person born out of wedlock is a child of the mother. That person is also a child of the father, if:

(i) the natural parents participated in a marriage ceremony before or after the birth of the child, even though the attempted marriage is void; or

(ii) the paternity is established by an adjudication before the death of the father or is established thereafter by clear and convincing proof, but the paternity established under this subparagraph is ineffective to qualify the father or his kindred to inherit from or through the child unless the father has openly treated the child as his, and has not refused to support the child.]

COMMENT

The definition of "child" and "parent" in Section 1–201 incorporates the meanings established by this section, thus extending them for all purposes of the Code. See Section 2–802 for the definition of "spouse" for purposes of intestate succession.

The change in 1975 from "that" to "either" as the third from the last word in subsection (1) was recommended by the Joint Editorial Board so that children would not be detached from any natural relatives for inheritance purposes because of adoption by the spouse of one of its natural parents. The change in this section, which is referred to by the definitions in Section 1–201 of "child", "issue" and "parent", affects, inter alia, the meaning of Sections 2–102, 2–103, 2–106, 2–302, 2–401, 2–402, 2–403, 2–404 and 2–605. As one consequence, the child of a deceased father who has been adopted by the mother's new spouse does not cease to be "issue" of his father and his parents, and so, under Section 2–605, would take a devise from one of his natural, paternal grandparents in favor of the child's deceased father who predeceased the testa-

tor. This situation is suggested by In re Estate of Bissell, 342 N.Y.S.(2d) 718.

The recommended addition of a new section, Section 2–114, dealing with the possibility of double inheritance where a person establishes relationships to a decedent through two lines of relatives is attributable, in part, to the change recommended in Section 2–109(1).

The approval in 1973 by the National Conference of Commissioners on Uniform State Laws of the Uniform Parentage Act reflects a change of policy by the Conference regarding the status of children born out of wedlock to one which is inconsistent with Section 2–109(2) of the Code as approved in 1969. The new language of 2–109(2) conforms the Uniform Probate Code to the Uniform Parentage Act. In view of the fact that eight states [as of 1975] have enacted the 1969 version of 2–109(2), the former language is retained, in brackets, to indicate that states, consistently with enactment of the Uniform Probate Code, may accept either form of approved language.

Section 2–110. [Advancements.]

If a person dies intestate as to all his estate, property which he gave in his lifetime to an heir is treated as an advancement against the latter's share of the estate only if declared in a contemporaneous writing by the decedent or acknowledged in writing by the heir to be an advancement. For this purpose the property advanced is valued as of the time the heir came into possession or enjoyment of the property or as of the time of death of the decedent, whichever first occurs. If the recipient of the property fails to survive the decedent, the property is not taken into account in computing the intestate share to be received by the recipient's issue, unless the declaration or acknowledgment provides otherwise.

COMMENT

This section alters the common law relating to advancements by requiring written evidence of the intent that an inter vivos gift be an advancement. The statute is phrased in terms of the donee being an "heir" because the transaction is regarded as of decedent's death; of course, the donee is only a prospective heir at the time of the transfer during lifetime. Most inter vivos transfers to-day are intended to be absolute gifts or are carefully integrated into a total estate plan. If the donor intends that any transfer during lifetime be deducted from the donee's share of his estate, the donor may either execute a will so providing or, if he intends to die intestate, charge the gift as an advance by a writing within the present section. The present section applies only when the decedent died intestate and not when he leaves a will.

This section applies to advances to collaterals (such as nephews and nieces) as well as to lineal descendants. The statute does not spell out the method of taking account in the advance, since this process is well settled by the common law and is not a source of litigation.

Section 2–111. [Debts to Decedent.]

A debt owed to the decedent is not charged against the intestate share of any person except the debtor. If the debtor fails to survive the decedent, the debt is not taken into account in computing the intestate share of the debtor's issue.

COMMENT

This supplements the content of Section 3–903, *infra*.

Section 2–112. [Alienage.]

No person is disqualified to take as an heir because he or a person through whom he claims is or has been an alien.

COMMENT

The purpose of this section is to eliminate the ancient rule that an alien cannot acquire or transmit land by descent, a rule based on the feudal notions of the obligations of the tenant to the King. Although there never was a corresponding rule as to personalty, the present section is phrased in light of the basic premise of the Code that distinctions between real and personal property should be abolished.

This section has broader vitality in light of the recent decision of the United

States Supreme Court in Zschernig v. Miller, 88 S.Ct. 664, 389 U.S. 429, 19 L.Ed.2d 683 (1968) holding unconstitutional a state statute providing for escheat if a nonresident alien cannot meet three requirements: the existence of a reciprocal right of a United States citizen to take property on the same terms as a citizen or inhabitant of the foreign country, the right of United States citizens to receive payment here of funds from estates in the foreign country, and the right of the foreign heirs to receive the proceeds of the local estate without confiscation by the foreign government. The rationale was that such a statute involved the local probate court in matters which essentially involve United States foreign policy, whether or not there is a governing treaty with the foreign country. Hence, the statute is "an intrusion by the State into the field of foreign affairs which the Constitution entrusts to the President and the Congress".

[Section 2–113. [Dower and Curtesy Abolished.]

The estates of dower and curtesy are abolished.]

COMMENT

The provisions of this Code replace the common law concepts of dower and curtesy and their statutory counterparts. Those estates provided both a share in intestacy and a protection against disinheritance.

In states which have previously abolished dower and curtesy, or where those estates have never existed, the above section should be omitted.

Section 2–114. [Persons Related to Decedent Through Two Lines.]

A person who is related to the decedent through 2 lines of relationship is entitled to only a single share based on the relationship which would entitle him to the larger share.

COMMENT

This section was added in 1975. The language is identical to that appearing as Section 2–112 in U.P.C. Working Drafts 3 and 4, and as Section 2–110 in Working Draft 5. The section was dropped because, with adoptions serving to transplant adopted children from all natural relationships to full relationship with adoptive relatives, and inheritance eliminated as between persons more distantly related than descendants of a common grandparent, the prospects of double inheritance seemed too remote to warrant the burden of an extra section. The changes recommended in Section 2–109(1) increase the prospects of double inheritance to the point where the addition of Section 2–114 seemed desirable. The section would have potential application in the not uncommon case where a deceased person's brother or sister marries the spouse of the decedent and adopts a child of the former marriage; it would block inheritance through two lines if the adopting parent died thereafter leaving the child as a natural and adopted grandchild of its grandparents.

PART 2

ELECTIVE SHARE OF SURVIVING SPOUSE

GENERAL COMMENT

The sections of this Part describe a system for common law states designed to protect a spouse of a decedent who was a domiciliary against donative transfers by will and will substitutes which would deprive the survivor of a "fair share" of the decedent's estate. Optional sections adapting the elective share system to community property jurisdictions were contained in preliminary drafts, but were dropped from the final Code. Problems of disherison of spouses in community states are limited to situations involving assets acquired by domiciliaries of common law states who later become domiciliaries of a community property state, and to instances where substantially all of a deceased spouse's property is separate property. Representatives of community property states differ in regard to whether either of these problem areas warrant statutory solution.

Almost every feature of the system described herein is or may be controversial. Some have questioned the need for any legislation checking the power of married persons to transfer their property as they please. See Plager, "The Spouse's Nonbarrable Share: A Solution in Search of a Problem", 33 Chi.L.Rev. 681 (1966). Still, virtually all common law states impose some restriction on the power of a spouse to disinherit the other. In some, the ancient concept of dower continues to prevent free transfer of land by a married person. In most states, including many which have abolished dower, a spouse's protection is found in statutes which give a surviving spouse the power to take a share of the decedent's probate estate upon election rejecting the provisions of the decedent's will. These statutes expand the spouse's protection to all real and personal assets owned by the decedent at death, but usually take no account of various will substitutes which permit an owner to transfer ownership at his death without use of a will. Judicial doctrines identifying certain transfers to be "illusory" or to be in "fraud" of the spouse's share have been evolved in some jurisdictions to offset the problems caused by will substitutes, and in New York and Pennsylvania, statutes have extended the elective share of a surviving spouse to certain non-testamentary transfers.

Questions relating to the proper size of a spouse's protected interest may be raised in addition to those concerning the need for, and method of assuring, any protection. The traditions in both common law and community property states point toward some capital sum related to the size of the deceased spouse's holdings rather than to the needs of the surviving spouse. The community property pattern produces one-half for the surviving spouse, but is somewhat misleading as an analogy, for it takes no account of the decedent's separate property. The fraction of one-third, which is stated in Section 2–201, has the advantage of familiarity, for it is used in many forced share statutes.

Although the system described herein may seem complex, it should not complicate administration of a married person's estate in any but very unusual cases. The surviving spouse rather than the executor or the probate court has the burden of asserting an election, as well as the burden of proving the matters which must be shown in order to make a successful claim to more than he or she has received. Some of the apparent complexity arises from Section 2–202, which has the effect of compelling an electing spouse to allow credit for all funds attributable to the decedent when the spouse, by electing, is claiming that more is due. This feature should serve to reduce the number of instances in which an elective share will be asserted. Finally, Section 2–204 expands the effectiveness of attempted waivers and releases of rights to claim an elective share. Thus, means by which estate planners can assure clients that their estates will not become embroiled in election litigation are provided.

Uniformity of law on the problems covered by this Part is much to be desired. It is especially important that states limit the applicability of rules protecting spouses so that only estates of domiciliary decedents are involved.

Section 2–201. [Right to Elective Share.]

(a) If a married person domiciled in this state dies, the surviving spouse has a right of election to take an elective share of one-third of the augmented estate under the limitations and conditions hereinafter stated.

(b) If a married person not domiciled in this state dies, the right, if any, of the surviving spouse to take an elective share in property in this state is governed by the law of the decedent's domicile at death.

COMMENT

See Section 2–802 for the definition of "spouse" which controls in this Part.

Under the common law a widow was entitled to dower, which was a life estate in a fraction of lands of which her husband was seized of an estate of inheritance at any time during the marriage. Dower encumbers titles and provides inadequate protection for widows in a society which classifies most wealth as personal property. Hence the states have tended to substitute a forced share in the whole estate for dower and the widower's comparable common law right of curtesy. Few existing forced share stat-

utes make adequate provisions for transfers by means other than succession to the surviving spouse and others. This and the following sections are designed to do so. The theory of these sections is discussed in Fratcher, "Toward Uniform Succession Legislation," 41 N.Y.U.L.Rev. 1037, 1050–1064 (1966). The existing law is discussed in Mac-Donald, Fraud on the Widow's Share (1960). Legislation comparable to that suggested here became effective in New York on Sept. 1, 1966. See Decedent Estate Law, § 18.

Section 2–202. [Augmented Estate.]

The augmented estate means the estate reduced by funeral and administration expenses, homestead allowance, family allowances and exemptions, and enforceable claims, to which is added the sum of the following amounts:

(1) The value of property transferred to anyone other than a bona fide purchaser by the decedent at any time during marriage, to or for the benefit of any person other than the surviving spouse, to the extent that the decedent did not receive adequate and full consideration in money or money's worth for the transfer, if the transfer is of any of the following types:

(i) any transfer under which the decedent retained at the time of his death the possession or enjoyment of, or right to income from, the property;

(ii) any transfer to the extent that the decedent retained at the time of his death a power, either alone or in conjunction with any other person, to revoke or to consume, invade or dispose of the principal for his own benefit;

(iii) any transfer whereby property is held at the time of decedent's death by decedent and another with right of survivorship;

(iv) any transfer made to a donee within two years of death of the decedent to the extent that the aggregate transfers to any one donee in either of the years exceed $3,000.00.

Any transfer is excluded if made with the written consent or joinder of the surviving spouse. Property is valued as of the decedent's death except that property given irrevocably to a donee during lifetime of the decedent is valued as of the date the donee came into possession or enjoyment if that occurs first. Nothing herein shall cause to be included in the augmented estate any life insurance, accident insurance, joint annuity, or pension payable to a person other than the surviving spouse.

(2) The value of property owned by the surviving spouse at the decedent's death, plus the value of property transferred by the spouse at any time during marriage to any person other than the decedent which would have been includible in the spouse's augmented estate if the surviving spouse had predeceased the decedent to the extent the owned or transferred property is derived from the decedent by any means other than testate or intestate succession without a full consideration in money or money's worth. For purposes of this paragraph:

(i) Property derived from the decedent includes, but is not limited to, any beneficial interest of the surviving spouse in a trust created by the decedent during his lifetime, any property appointed to the spouse by the decedent's exercise of a general or special power of appointment also exercisable in favor of others than the spouse, any proceeds of insurance (including accidental death benefits) on the life of the decedent attributable to premiums paid by him, any lump sum immediately payable and the commuted value of the proceeds of annuity contracts under which the decedent was the primary annuitant attributable to premiums paid by him, the commuted value of amounts payable after the decedent's death under any public or private pension, disability compensation, death benefit or retirement plan, exclusive of the Federal Social Security system, by reason of service performed or disabilities incurred by the decedent, any property held at the time of decedent's death by decedent and the surviving spouse with right of survivorship, any property held by decedent and transferred by contract to the surviving spouse by reason of the decedent's death and the value of the share of the surviving spouse resulting from rights in community property in this or any other state formerly owned with the decedent. Premiums paid by the decedent's employer, his partner, a partnership of which he was a member, or his creditors, are deemed to have been paid by the decedent.

(ii) Property owned by the spouse at the decedent's death is valued as of the date of death. Property transferred by the spouse is valued at the time the transfer became irrevocable, or at the decedent's death, whichever occurred first. Income earned by included property prior to the decedent's death is not treated as property derived from the decedent.

(iii) Property owned by the surviving spouse as of the decedent's death, or previously transferred by the surviving spouse, is presumed to have been derived from the decedent except to the extent that the surviving spouse establishes that it was derived from another source.

(3) For purposes of this section a bona fide purchaser is a purchaser for value in good faith and without notice of any adverse claim. Any recorded instrument on which a state documentary fee is noted pursuant to [insert appropriate reference] is prima facie evidence that the transfer described therein was made to a bona fide purchaser.

COMMENT

The purpose of the concept of augmenting the probate estate in computing the elective share is twofold: (1) to prevent the owner of wealth from making arrangements which transmit his property to others by means other than probate deliberately to defeat the right of the surviving spouse to a share, and (2) to prevent the surviving spouse from electing a share of the probate estate when the spouse has received a fair share of the total wealth of the decedent either during the lifetime of the decedent or at death by life insurance, joint tenancy assets and other nonprobate arrangements. Thus essentially two separate groups of property are added to the net probate estate to arrive at the augmented net estate which is the basis for computing the one-third share of the surviving spouse. In the first category

are transfers by the decedent during his lifetime which are essentially will substitutes, arrangements which give him continued benefits or controls over the property. However, only transfers during the marriage are included in this category. This makes it possible for a person to provide for children by a prior marriage, as by a revocable living trust, without concern that such provisions will be upset by later marriage. The limitation to transfers during marriage reflects some of the policy underlying community property. What kinds of transfers should be included here is a matter of reasonable difference of opinion. The finespun tests of the Federal Estate Tax Law might be utilized, of course. However, the objectives of a tax law are different from those involved here in the Probate Code, and the present section is therefore more limited. It is intended to reach the kinds of transfers readily usable to defeat an elective share in only the probate estate.

In the second category of assets, property of the surviving spouse derived from the decedent and property derived from the decedent which the spouse has, in turn, given away in a transaction that is will-like in effect or purpose, the scope is much broader. Thus a person can during his lifetime make outright gifts to relatives and they are not included in this first category unless they are made within two years of death (the exception being designed to prevent a person from depleting his estate in contemplation of death). But the time when the surviving spouse derives her wealth from the decedent is immaterial; thus if a husband has purchased a home in the wife's name and made systematic gifts to the wife over many years, the home and accumulated wealth she owns at his death as a result of such gifts ought to, and under this section do, reduce her share of the augmented estate. Likewise, for policy reasons life insurance is not included in the first category of transfers to other persons, because it is not ordinarily purchased as a way of depleting the probate estate and avoiding the elective share of the spouse; but life insurance proceeds payable to the surviving spouse are included in the second category, because it seems unfair to allow a surviving spouse to disturb the decedent's estate plan if the spouse has received ample provision from life insurance. In this category no distinction is drawn as to whether the transfers are made before or after marriage.

Depending on the circumstances it is obvious that this section will operate in the long run to decrease substantially the number of elections. This is because the statute will encourage and provide a legal base for counseling of testators against schemes to disinherit the spouse, and because the spouse can no longer elect in cases where substantial provision is made by joint tenancy,

life insurance, lifetime gifts, living trusts set up by the decedent, and the other numerous nonprobate arrangements by which wealth is today transferred. On the other hand the section should provide realistic protection against disinheritance of the spouse in the rare case where decedent tries to achieve that purpose by depleting his probate estate.

The augmented net estate approach embodied in this section is relatively complex and assumes that litigation may be required in cases in which the right to an elective share is asserted. The proposed scheme should not complicate administration in well-planned or routine cases, however, because the spouse's rights are freely releasable under Section 2–204 and because of the time limits in Section 2–205. Some legislatures may wish to consider a simpler approach along the lines of the Pennsylvania Estates Act provision reading:

"A conveyance of assets by a person who retains a power of appointment by will, or a power of revocation or consumption over the principal thereof, shall at the election of his surviving spouse, be treated as a testamentary disposition so far as the surviving spouse is concerned to the extent to which the power has been reserved, but the right of the surviving spouse shall be subject to the rights of any income beneficiary whose interest in income becomes vested in enjoyment prior to the death of the conveyor. The provisions of this subsection shall not apply to any contract of life insurance purchased by a decedent, whether payable in trust or otherwise."

In passing, it is to be noted that a Pennsylvania widow apparently may claim against a revocable trust or will even though she has been amply provided for by life insurance or other means arranged by the decedent. Penn.Stats.Annot. title 20, § 301.11(a).

The New York Estates, Powers and Trusts Law § 5–1.1(b) also may be suggested as a model. It treats as testamentary dispositions all gifts causa mortis, money on deposit by the decedent in trust for another, money deposited in the decedent's name payable on death to another, joint tenancy property, and transfers by decedent over which he has a power to revoke or invade. The New York law also expressly excludes life insurance, pension plans, and United States savings bonds payable to a designated person. One of the drawbacks of the New York legislation is its complexity, much of which is attributable to the effort to prevent a spouse from taking an elective share when the deceased spouse has followed certain prescribed procedures. The scheme described by Sections 2–201 et seq. of this draft, like that of all states except New York, leaves the question of whether a spouse may or may not elect to be controlled by the economics of the situation, rather than by conditions on the statutory right. Further, the New York system gives the spouse election rights in spite of the possibility that the spouse has been well provided for by insurance or other gifts from the decedent.

In 1975, the Joint Editorial Board recommended the addition of reference to bona fide purchaser in paragraph (1),

"to a donee" in paragraph (1)(iv) and the addition of paragraph (3) to the above section to reflect recommendations evolved in discussions by committees of the Colorado Bar Association to meet title problems that had been identified under the Code as originally enacted. One problem that should be cured by the amendments arose when real property experts in Colorado took the position that, since any transfer might be found to be for less than "adequate and full consideration in money or money's worth," the language of the original text, all deeds from married persons had to be joined in by the spouse, lest the grantor die within two years and the grantee be subjected to the claim that the value involved was a part of the augmented estate.

Also, the Joint Editorial Board in 1975 recommended the addition in Section 2–202(2)(i) of language referring to property moving to the surviving spouse via joint and survivorship holdings with the decedent. The addition would not, in all probability, change the meaning of the subsection, but it would clarify it in relation to jointly held property which will be present in a great number of cases.

Section 2–203. [Right of Election Personal to Surviving Spouse.]

The right of election of the surviving spouse may be exercised only during his lifetime by him. In the case of a protected person, the right of election may be exercised only by order of the court in which protective proceedings as to his property are pending, after finding that exercise is necessary to provide adequate support for the protected person during his probable life expectancy.

COMMENT

See Section 5–101 for definitions of protected person and protective proceedings.

Section 2–204. [Waiver of Right to Elect and of Other Rights.]

The right of election of a surviving spouse and the rights of the surviving spouse to homestead allowance, exempt property and family allowance, or any of them, may be waived, wholly or partially, before or after marriage, by a written contract, agreement or waiver signed by the party waiving after fair disclosure. Unless it provides to the contrary, a waiver of "all rights" (or equivalent language) in the property or estate of a present or prospective spouse or a complete property settlement entered into after or in anticipation of separation or divorce is a waiver of all rights to elective share, homestead allowance, exempt property and family allowance by each spouse in the property of the other and a renunciation by each of all benefits which would otherwise pass to him from the other by intestate succession or by virtue of the provisions of any will executed before the waiver or property settlement.

COMMENT

The right to homestead allowance is conferred by Section 2–401, that to exempt property by Section 2–402, and that to family allowance by Section 2–403. The right to renounce interests passing by testate or intestate succession is recognized by Section 2–801. The provisions of this section, permitting a spouse or prospective spouse to waive all statutory rights in the other spouse's property seem desirable in view of the common and commendable desire of parties to second and later marriages to insure that property derived from prior spouses passes at death to the issue of the prior spouses instead of to the newly acquired spouse. The operation of a property settlement as a waiver and renunciation takes care of the situation which arises when a spouse dies while a divorce suit is pending.

Section 2–205. [Proceeding for Elective Share; Time Limit.]

(a) The surviving spouse may elect to take his elective share in the augmented estate by filing in the Court and mailing or delivering to the personal representative, if any, a petition for the elective share within 9 months after the date of death, or within 6 months after the probate of the decedent's will, whichever limitation last expires. However, non-probate transfers, described in Section 2–202(1), shall not be included within the augmented estate for the purpose of computing the elective share, if the petition is filed later than 9 months after death.

The Court may extend the time for election as it sees fit for cause shown by the surviving spouse before the time for election has expired.

(b) The surviving spouse shall give notice of the time and place set for hearing to persons interested in the estate and to the distributees and recipients of portions of the augmented net estate whose interests will be adversely affected by the taking of the elective share.

(c) The surviving spouse may withdraw his demand for an elective share at any time before entry of a final determination by the Court.

(d) After notice and hearing, the Court shall determine the amount of the elective share and shall order its payment from the assets of the augmented net estate or by contribution as appears appropriate under Section 2–207. If it appears that a fund or property included in the augmented net estate has not come into the possession of the personal representative, or has been distributed by the personal representative, the Court nevertheless shall fix the liability of any person who has any interest in the fund or property or who has possession thereof, whether as trustee or otherwise. The proceeding may be maintained against fewer than all persons against whom relief could be sought, but no person is subject to contribution in any greater amount than he would have been if relief had been secured against all persons subject to contribution.

(e) The order or judgment of the Court may be enforced as necessary in suit for contribution or payment in other courts of this state or other jurisdictions.

COMMENT

In 1975, the Joint Editorial Board recommended changes in subsection (a) that were designed to meet a question, arising under the original text, of whether the right to an elective share was ever barred in cases of unadministered estates. The new language also has the effect of clearing included, non-probate transfers to persons other than the surviving spouse of the lien of any possible elective share proceeding unless the spouse's action is commenced within nine months after death. This bar on efforts to recapture non-probate assets for an elective share does not apply to probate assets. Probate assets may be controlled by a will that may not be offered for probate until as late as three years from death. As to these, the limitation on the surviving spouse's proceeding is six months after the probate.

Section 2–206. [Effect of Election on Benefits by Will or Statute.]

A surviving spouse is entitled to homestead allowance, exempt property, and family allowance, whether or not he elects to take an elective share.

COMMENT

The election does not result in a loss of benefits under the will (in the absence of renunciation) because those benefits are charged against the elective share under Sections 2–201, 2–202 and 2–207(a).

In 1975, the Joint Editorial Board recommended changes in this and the following section that reverse the position of the original text which permitted an electing spouse to accept or reject particular benefits as provided him by the decedent without reducing the dollar value of his elective share. The new language in this section, replacing former Section 2–206(a) and (b), does not mention renunciation of transfers which is now dealt with in Section 2–207. The remaining content of this section is restricted to a simple statement indicating that the family exemptions described by Article II, Part 4 may be distributed from the probate estate without reference to whether an elective share right is asserted, and without being charged to the electing spouse as a part of the elective share. In the view of the Board, deletion of language in the original form of Section 2–206(b), dealing with devises that are intended to be in lieu of family exemptions, does not alter the ability of a testator, by express provision in the will, from putting a surviving spouse to an election between accepting the devises provided or accepting the family exemptions provided by law. This matter

is dealt with in Sections 2–401, 2–402,
2–403 and 2–404.

Section 2–207. [Charging Spouse With Gifts Received; Liability of Others for Balance of Elective Share.]

(a) In the proceeding for an elective share, values included in the augmented estate which pass or have passed to the surviving spouse, or which would have passed to the spouse but were renounced, are applied first to satisfy the elective share and to reduce any contributions due from other recipients of transfers included in the augmented estate. For purposes of this subsection, the electing spouse's beneficial interest in any life estate or in any trust shall be computed as if worth one half of the total value of the property subject to the life estate, or of the trust estate, unless higher or lower values for these interests are established by proof.

(b) Remaining property of the augmented estate is so applied that liability for the balance of the elective share of the surviving spouse is equitably apportioned among the recipients of the augmented estate in proportion to the value of their interests therein.

(c) Only original transferees from, or appointees of, the decedent and their donees, to the extent the donees have the property or its proceeds, are subject to the contribution to make up the elective share of the surviving spouse. A person liable to contribution may choose to give up the property transferred to him or to pay its value as of the time it is considered in computing the augmented estate.

COMMENT

Sections 2–401, 2–402 and 2–403 have the effect of giving a spouse certain exempt property and allowances in addition to the amount of the elective share.

In 1975, the Joint Editorial Board recommended changes in Section 2–206 and subsection (a) of this section which have the effect of protecting a decedent's plan as far as it provides values for the surviving spouse. The spouse is not compelled to accept the benefits devised by the decedent, but if these benefits are rejected, the values involved are charged to the electing spouse as if the devises were accepted. The second sentence of new subsection (a) provides a rebuttable presumption of the value of a life estate or an interest in a trust, when this form of benefit is provided for an electing spouse by the decedent's plan.

PART 3

SPOUSE AND CHILDREN UNPROVIDED FOR IN WILLS

Section 2–301. [Omitted Spouse.]

(a) If a testator fails to provide by will for his surviving spouse who married the testator after the execution of the will, the omitted spouse shall receive the same share of the estate he would have received if the decedent left no will unless it appears from the will that the omission was intentional or the testator provided for the spouse by transfer outside the will and the intent that the transfer be in lieu of a testamentary provision is shown by statements of the testator or from the amount of the transfer or other evidence.

(b) In satisfying a share provided by this section, the devises made by the will abate as provided in Section 3–902.

COMMENT

Section 2–508 provides that a will is not revoked by a change of circumstances occurring subsequent to its execution other than as described by that section. This section reflects the view that the intestate share of the spouse is what the decedent would want the spouse to have if he had thought about the relationship of his old will to the new situation. One effect of this section should be to reduce the number of instances where a spouse will claim an elective share.

Section 2–302. [Pretermitted Children.]

(a) If a testator fails to provide in his will for any of his children born or adopted after the execution of his will, the omitted child receives a share in the estate equal in value to that which he would have received if the testator had died intestate unless:

(1) it appears from the will that the omission was intentional;

(2) when the will was executed the testator had one or more children and devised substantially all his estate to the other parent of the omitted child; or

(3) the testator provided for the child by transfer outside the will and the intent that the transfer be in lieu of a testamentary provision is shown by statements of the testator or from the amount of the transfer or other evidence.

(b) If at the time of execution of the will the testator fails to provide in his will for a living child solely because he believes the child to be dead, the child receives a share in the estate equal in value to that which he would have received if the testator had died intestate.

541

(c) In satisfying a share provided by this section, the devises made by the will abate as provided in Section 3–902.

COMMENT

This section provides for both the case where a child was born or adopted after the execution of the will and not foreseen at the time and thus not provided for in the will, and the rare case where a testator omits one of his existing children because of mistaken belief that the child is dead.

Although the sections dealing with advancement and ademption by satisfaction (2–110 and 2–612) provide that a gift during lifetime is not an advancement or satisfaction unless the testator's intent is evidenced in writing, this section permits oral evidence to establish a testator's intent that lifetime gifts or nonprobate transfers such as life insurance or joint accounts are in lieu of a testamentary provision for a child born or adopted after the will. Here there is no real contradiction of testamentary intent, since there is no provision in the will itself for the omitted child.

To preclude operation of this section it is not necessary to make any provision, even nominal in amount, for a testator's present or future children; a simple recital in the will that the testator intends to make no provision for then living children or any the testator thereafter may have would meet the requirement of (a)(1).

Under subsection (c) and Section 3–902, any intestate estate would first be applied to satisfy the share of a pretermitted child.

This section is not intended to alter the rules of evidence applicable to statements of a decedent.

PART 4

EXEMPT PROPERTY AND ALLOWANCES

GENERAL COMMENT

This part describes certain rights and values to which a surviving spouse and certain children of a deceased *domiciliary* are entitled in preference over unsecured creditors of the estate and persons to whom the estate may be devised by will. If there is a surviving spouse, all of the values described in this Part, which total $8,500 plus whatever is allowed to the spouse for support during administration, pass to the spouse. Minor or dependent children become entitled to the homestead exemption of $5,000 and to support allowances if there is no spouse, and may receive some of the support allowance if they live apart from the surviving spouse. The exempt property section confers rights on the spouse, if any, or on all children, to $3,500 in certain chattels, or funds if the unencumbered value of chattels is below the $3,500 level. This provision is designed in part to relieve a personal representative of the duty to sell household chattels when there are children who will have them.

These family protection provisions supply the basis for the important small estate provisions of Article III, Part 12.

States adopting the Code may see fit to alter the dollar amounts suggested in these sections, or to vary the terms and conditions in other ways so as to accommodate existing traditions. Although creditors of estates would be aided somewhat if all family exemption provisions relating to probate estates were the same throughout the country, there is probably less need for uniformity of law regarding these provisions than for any of the other parts of this article. Still, it is quite important for all states to limit their homestead, support allowance and exempt property provisions, if any, so that they apply only to estates of decedents who were domiciliaries of the state.

Notice that Section 2–104 imposes a requirement of survival of the decedent for 120 hours on any spouse or child claiming under this Part.

Section 2–401. [Homestead Allowance.]

A surviving spouse of a decedent who was domiciled in this state is entitled to a homestead allowance of [$5,000]. If there is no surviving spouse, each minor child and each dependent child of the decedent is entitled to a homestead allowance amounting to [$5,000] divided by the number of minor and dependent children of the decedent. The homestead allowance is exempt from and has priority over all claims against the estate. Homestead allowance is in addition to any share passing to the surviving spouse or minor or dependent child by the will of the decedent

543

unless otherwise provided, by intestate succession or by way of elective share.

COMMENT

See Section 2–802 for the definition of "spouse" which controls in this Part. Also, see Section 2–104. Waiver of homestead is covered by Section 2–204. "Election" between a provision of a will and homestead is not required unless the will so provides.

A set dollar amount for homestead allowance was dictated by the desirability of having a certain level below which administration may be dispensed with or be handled summarily, without regard to the size of allowances under Section 2–402. The "small estate" line is controlled largely, though not entirely by

the size of the homestead allowance. This is because Part 12 of Article III dealing with small estates rests on the assumption that the only justification for keeping a decedent's assets from his creditors is to benefit the decedent's spouse and children.

Another reason for a set amount is related to the fact that homestead allowance may prefer a decedent's minor or dependent children over his other children. It was felt desirable to minimize the consequence of application of an arbitrary age line among children of the testator.

[Section 2–401A. [Constitutional Homestead.]

The value of any constitutional right of homestead in the family home received by a surviving spouse or child shall be charged against that spouse or child's homestead allowance to the extent that the family home is part of the decedent's estate or would have been but for the homestead provision of the constitution.]

COMMENT

This optional section is designed for adoption only in states with a constitutional homestead provision. The value of the surviving spouse's constitutional right of homestead may be considerably

less than the full value of the family home if the constitution gives her only a terminable life estate enjoyable in common with minor children.

Section 2–402. [Exempt Property.]

In addition to the homestead allowance, the surviving spouse of a decedent who was domiciled in this state is entitled from the estate to value not exceeding $3,500 in excess of any security interests therein in household furniture, automobiles, furnishings, appliances and personal effects. If there is no surviving spouse, children of the decedent are entitled jointly to the same value. If encumbered chattels are selected and if the value in excess of security interests, plus that of other exempt property, is less than $3,500, or if there is not $3,500 worth of exempt property in the estate, the spouse or children are entitled to other assets of the estate, if any, to the extent necessary to make up the $3,500 value. Rights to exempt property and assets needed to make up a deficiency of exempt property have priority over all claims against the estate, except that the right to any assets to make up a deficiency of exempt property shall abate as necessary to permit prior payment of homestead allowance and family allowance. These rights are in addition to any benefit or share passing to the surviving spouse or children by the will of the decedent unless otherwise provided, by intestate succession, or by way of elective share.

COMMENT

Unlike the exempt values described in Sections 2–401 and 2–403, the exempt values described in this section are available in a case where the decedent left no spouse but left only adult children. The possible difference between beneficiaries of the exemptions described by Sections 2–401 and 2–403, and this section, ex-plain the provision in this section which establishes priorities.

Section 2–204 covers waiver of exempt property rights. This section indicates that a decedent's will may put a spouse to an election with reference to exemptions, but that no election is presumed to be required.

Section 2–403. [Family Allowance.]

In addition to the right to homestead allowance and exempt property, if the decedent was domiciled in this state, the surviving spouse and minor children whom the decedent was obligated to support and children who were in fact being supported by him are entitled to a reasonable allowance in money out of the estate for their maintenance during the period of administration, which allowance may not continue for longer than one year if the estate is inadequate to discharge allowed claims. The allowance may be paid as a lump sum or in periodic installments. It is payable to the surviving spouse, if living, for the use of the surviving spouse and minor and dependent children; otherwise to the children, or persons having their care and custody; but in case any minor child or dependent child is not living with the surviving spouse, the allowance may be made partially to the child or his guardian or other person having his care and custody, and partially to the spouse, as their needs may appear. The family allowance is exempt from and has priority over all claims but not over the homestead allowance.

The family allowance is not chargeable against any benefit or share passing to the surviving spouse or children by the will of the decedent unless otherwise provided, by intestate succession, or by way of elective share. The death of any person entitled to family allowance terminates his right to allowances not yet paid.

COMMENT

The allowance provided by this section does not qualify for the marital deduction under the Federal Estate Tax Act because the interest is terminable. A broad code must be drafted to provide the best possible protection for the family in all cases, even though this may not provide desired tax advantages for certain larger estates. In the estates falling in the federal estate tax bracket where careful planning may be expected, it is important to the operation of formula clauses that the family allowance be clearly terminable or clearly nonterminable. With the proposed section clearly creating a terminable interest, estate planners can create a plan which will operate with certainty. Finally, in order to facilitate administration of this allowance without court supervision it is necessary to provide a fairly simple and definite framework.

In determining the amount of the family allowance, account should be taken of both the previous standard of living and the nature of other resources available to the family to meet current living expenses until the estate can be administered and assets distributed. While the death of the principal income producer may necessitate some change in the standard of living, there must also be a period of adjustment. If the surviving spouse has a substantial income, this may be taken into account. Whether life insurance proceeds payable in a lump sum or periodic installments were intended by the decedent to be used for the period of adjustment or to be conserved as capital may be considered. A living trust may provide the needed income without resorting to the probate estate. If a husband has been the principal source of family support, a wife should not be expected to use her capital to support the family.

Obviously, need is relative to the circumstances, and what is reasonable must be decided on the basis of the facts of each individual case. Note, however, that under the next section the personal representative may not determine an allowance of more than $500 per month for one year; a Court order would be necessary if a greater allowance is reasonably necessary.

Section 2–404. [Source, Determination and Documentation.]

If the estate is otherwise sufficient, property specifically devised is not used to satisfy rights to homestead and exempt property. Subject to this restriction, the surviving spouse, the guardians of the minor children, or children who are adults may select property of the estate as homestead allowance and exempt property. The personal representative may make these selections if the surviving spouse, the children or the guardians of the minor children are unable or fail to do so within a reasonable time or if there are no guardians of the minor children. The personal representative may execute an instrument or deed of distribution to establish the ownership of property taken as homestead allowance or exempt property. He may determine the family allowance in a lump sum not exceeding $6,000 or periodic installments not exceeding $500 per month for one year, and may disburse funds of the estate in payment of the family allowance and any part of the homestead allowance payable in cash. The personal representative or any interested person aggrieved by any selection, determination, payment, proposed payment, or failure to act under this section may petition the Court for appropriate relief, which relief may provide a family allowance larger or smaller than that which the personal representative determined or could have determined.

COMMENT

See Sections 3–902, 3–906 and 3–907.

PART 5

WILLS

GENERAL COMMENT

Part 5 of Article II deals with capacity and formalities for execution and revocation of wills. If the will is to be restored to its role as the major instrument for disposition of wealth at death, its execution must be kept simple. The basic intent of these sections is to validate the will whenever possible. To this end, the age for making wills is lowered to eighteen, formalities for a written and attested will are kept to a minimum, holographic wills written and signed by the testator are authorized, choice of law as to validity of execution is broadened, and revocation by operation of law is limited to divorce or annulment. However, the statute also provides for a more formal method of execution with acknowledgment before a public officer (the self-proved will).

Section 2–501. [Who May Make a Will.]

Any person 18 or more years of age who is of sound mind may make a will.

COMMENT

This section states a uniform minimum age of eighteen for capacity to execute a will. "Minor" is defined in Section 1–201, and may involve a different age than that prescribed here.

Section 2–502. [Execution.]

Except as provided for holographic wills, writings within Section 2–513, and wills within Section 2–506, every will shall be in writing signed by the testator or in the testator's name by some other person in the testator's presence and by his direction, and shall be signed by at least 2 persons each of whom witnessed either the signing or the testator's acknowledgment of the signature or of the will.

COMMENT

The formalities for execution of a witnessed will have been reduced to a minimum. Execution under this section normally would be accomplished by signature of the testator and of two witnesses; each of the persons signing as witnesses must "witness" any of the following: the signing of the will by the testator, an acknowledgment by the testator that the signature is his, or an acknowledgment by the testator that the document is his will. Signing by the testator may be by mark under general rules relating to what constitutes a signature; or the will may be signed on behalf of the testator by another person signing the testator's name at his direction and in his presence. There is no requirement that the testator publish

547

the document as his will, or that he request the witnesses to sign, or that the witnesses sign in the presence of the testator or of each other. The testator may sign the will outside the presence of the witnesses if he later acknowledges to the witnesses that the signature is his or that the document is his will, and they sign as witnesses. There is no requirement that the testator's signature be at the end of the will; thus, if he writes his name in the body of the will and intends it to be his signature, this would satisfy the statute. The intent is to validate wills which meet the minimal formalities of the statute.

A will which does not meet these requirements may be valid under Section 2–503 as a holograph.

Section 2–503. [Holographic Will.]

A will which does not comply with Section 2–502 is valid as a holographic will, whether or not witnessed, if the signature and the material provisions are in the handwriting of the testator.

COMMENT

This section enables a testator to write his own will in his handwriting. There need be no witnesses. The only requirement is that the signature and the material provisions of the will be in the testator's handwriting. By requiring only the "material provisions" to be in the testator's handwriting (rather than requiring, as some existing statutes do, that the will be "entirely" in the testator's handwriting) a holograph may be valid even though immaterial parts such as date or introductory wording be printed or stamped. A valid holograph might even be executed on some printed will forms if the printed portion could be eliminated and the handwritten portion could evidence the testator's will. For persons unable to obtain legal assistance, the holographic will may be adequate.

Section 2–504. [Self-Proved Will.]

(a) Any will may be simultaneously executed, attested, and made self-proved, by acknowledgment thereof by the testator and affidavits of the witnesses, each made before an officer authorized to administer oaths under the laws of the state where execution occurs and evidenced by the officer's certificate, under official seal, in substantially the following form:

I, _____, the testator, sign my name to this instrument this _____ day of _____, 19__, and being first duly sworn, do hereby declare to the undersigned authority that I sign and execute this instrument as my last will and that I sign it willingly (or willingly direct another to sign for me), that I execute it as my free and voluntary act for the purposes therein expressed, and that I am eighteen years of age or older, of sound mind, and under no constraint or undue influence.

_____

Testator

We, _____, _____, the witnesses, sign our names to this instrument, being first duly sworn, and do hereby declare to the undersigned authority that the testator signs and executes this instrument as his last will and that he signs it willingly (or willingly directs another to sign for him), and that each of us, in the presence and hearing of the testator, hereby signs this will as witness to the testator's signing, and that to the best of our knowledge the testator is eighteen years of age or older, of sound mind, and under no constraint or undue influence.

_____
Witness

_____
Witness

The State of _____
County of _____

   Subscribed, sworn to and acknowledged before me by _____, the testator, and subscribed and sworn to before me by _____, and _____, witnesses, this _____ day of _____.

(Seal)

                     (Signed) _____

                     _____
                     (Official capacity of officer)

   (b) An attested will may at any time subsequent to its execution be made self-proved by the acknowledgment thereof by the testator and the affidavits of the witnesses, each made before an officer authorized to administer oaths under the laws of the state where the acknowledgment occurs and evidenced by the officer's certificate, under the official seal, attached or annexed to the will in substantially the following form:

The State of _____
County of _____

   We, _____, _____, and _____, the testator and the witnesses, respectively, whose names are signed to the attached or foregoing instrument, being first duly sworn, do hereby declare to the undersigned authority that the testator signed and executed the instrument as his last will and that he had signed willingly (or willingly directed another to sign for him), and that he executed it as his free and voluntary act for the purposes therein expressed, and that each of the witnesses, in the presence and hearing of the testator, signed the will as witness and that to the best of his knowledge the testator was at that time eighteen years of age or older, of sound mind and under no constraint or undue influence.

_____
Testator

Witness

Witness

Subscribed, sworn to and acknowledged before me by _____, the testator, and subscribed and sworn to before me by _____, and _____, witnesses, this _____ day of _____.

(Seal)

(Signed) _____

(Official capacity of officer)

COMMENT

A self-proved will may be admitted to probate as provided in Sections 3–303, 3–405 and 3–406 without the testimony of any subscribing witness, but otherwise it is treated no differently than a will not self-proved. Thus, a self-proved will may be contested (except in regard to signature requirements), revoked, or amended by a codicil in exactly the same fashion as a will not self-proved. The significance of the procedural advantage for a self-proved will is limited to formal testacy proceedings because Section 3–303 dealing with informal probate dispenses with the necessity of testimony of witnesses even though the instrument is not self-proved under this section.

The original text of this section directed that the officer who assisted the execution of a self-proved will be authorized to act by virtue of the laws of "this State", thereby restricting this mode of execution to wills offered for probate in the state where they were executed. Also, the original text authorized only the addition to an already signed and witnessed will, of an acknowledgment of the testator and affidavits of the witnesses, thereby requiring testator and witnesses, to sign twice even though the entire execution ceremony occurred in the presence of a notary or other official. In 1975, the Joint Editorial Board recommended the substitution of new text that eliminates these problems.

Section 2–505. [Who May Witness.]

(a) Any person generally competent to be a witness may act as a witness to a will.

(b) A will or any provision thereof is not invalid because the will is signed by an interested witness.

COMMENT

This section simplifies the law relating to interested witnesses. Interest no longer disqualifies a person as a witness, nor does it invalidate or forfeit a gift under the will. Of course, the purpose of this change is not to foster use of interested witnesses, and attorneys will continue to use disinterested witnesses in execution of wills. But the rare and innocent use of a member of the testator's family on a home-drawn will would no longer be penalized. This change

550

does not increase appreciably the opportunity for fraud or undue influence. A substantial gift by will to a person who is one of the witnesses to the execution of the will would itself be a suspicious circumstance, and the gift could be challenged on grounds of undue influence. The requirement of disinterested witnesses has not succeeded in preventing fraud and undue influence; and in most cases of undue influence, the influencer is careful not to sign as witness but to use disinterested witnesses.

An interested witness is competent to testify to prove execution of the will, under Section 3–406.

Section 2–506. [Choice of Law as to Execution.]

A written will is valid if executed in compliance with Section 2–502 or 2–503 or if its execution complies with the law at the time of execution of the place where the will is executed, or of the law of the place where at the time of execution or at the time of death the testator is domiciled, has a place of abode or is a national.

COMMENT

This section permits probate of wills in this state under certain conditions even if they are not executed in accordance with the formalities of Section 2–502. Such wills must be in writing but otherwise are valid if they meet the requirements for execution of the law of the place where the will is executed (when it is executed in another state or country) or the law of testator's domicile, abode or nationality at either the time of execution or at the time of death. Thus, if testator is domiciled in state 1 and executes a typed will merely by signing it without witnesses in state 2 while on vacation there, the Court of this state would recognize the will as valid if the law of either state 1 or state 2 permits execution by signature alone.

Or if a national of Mexico executes a written will in this state which does not meet the requirements of Section 2–502 but meets the requirements of Mexican law, the will would be recognized as validly executed under this section. The purpose of this section is to provide a wide opportunity for validation of expectations of testators. When the Uniform Probate Code is widely adopted, the impact of this section will become minimal.

A similar provision relating to choice of law as to revocation was considered but was not included. Revocation by subsequent instruments are covered. Revocations by act, other than partial revocations, do not cause much difficulty in regard to choice of laws.

Section 2–507. [Revocation by Writing or by Act.]

A will or any part thereof is revoked

(1) by a subsequent will which revokes the prior will or part expressly or by inconsistency; or

(2) by being burned, torn, canceled, obliterated, or destroyed, with the intent and for the purpose of revoking it by the testator or by another person in his presence and by his direction.

COMMENT

Revocation of a will may be by either a subsequent will or an act done to the document. If revocation is by a subsequent will, it must be properly executed. This section employs the traditional language which has been interpreted by the courts in many cases. It leaves to the Court the determination of whether a subsequent will which has no express revocation clause is inconsistent with the prior will so as to revoke it wholly or partially, and in the case of an act done to the document the determination of whether the act is a sufficient burning, tearing, canceling, obliteration or destruction and was done with the intent and for the purpose of revoking. The latter necessarily involves exploration of extrinsic evidence, including statements of testator as to intent.

The section specifically permits partial revocation. Each Court is free to apply its own doctrine of dependent relative revocation.

The section does not affect present law in regard to the case of accidental destruction which is later confirmed by revocatory intention.

Section 2–508. [Revocation by Divorce; No Revocation by Other Changes of Circumstances.]

If after executing a will the testator is divorced or his marriage annulled, the divorce or annulment revokes any disposition or appointment of property made by the will to the former spouse, any provision conferring a general or special power of appointment on the former spouse, and any nomination of the former spouse as executor, trustee, conservator, or guardian, unless the will expressly provides otherwise. Property prevented from passing to a former spouse because of revocation by divorce or annulment passes as if the former spouse failed to survive the decedent, and other provisions conferring some power or office on the former spouse are interpreted as if the spouse failed to survive the decedent. If provisions are revoked solely by this section, they are revived by testator's remarriage to the former spouse. For purposes of this section, divorce or annulment means any divorce or annulment which would exclude the spouse as a surviving spouse within the meaning of Section 2–802(b). A decree of separation which does not terminate the status of husband and wife is not a divorce for purposes of this section. No change of circumstances other than as described in this section revokes a will.

COMMENT

The section deals with what is sometimes called revocation by operation of law. It provides for revocation by a divorce or annulment only. No other change in circumstances operate to revoke the will; this is intended to change the rule in some states that subsequent marriage or marriage plus birth of issue operate to revoke a will. Of course, a specific devise may be adeemed by transfer of the property during the testator's lifetime except as otherwise provided in this Code; although this is occasionally called revocation, it is not within the present section. The provisions with regard to invalid divorce decrees parallel those in Section 2–802. Neither this section nor 2–802 includes "divorce from bed and board" as an event which affects devises or marital rights on death.

But see Section 2–204 providing that a complete property settlement entered into after or in anticipation of separation or divorce constitutes a renunciation of all benefits under a prior will, unless the settlement provides otherwise.

Although this Section does not provide for revocation of a will by subsequent marriage of the testator, the spouse may be protected by Section 2–301 or an elective share under Section 2–201.

Section 2–509. [Revival of Revoked Will.]

(a) If a second will which, had it remained effective at death, would have revoked the first will in whole or in part, is thereafter revoked by acts under Section 2–507, the first will is revoked in whole or in part unless it is evident from the circumstances of the revocation of the second will or from testator's contemporary or subsequent declarations that he intended the first will to take effect as executed.

(b) If a second will which, had it remained effective at death, would have revoked the first will in whole or in part, is thereafter revoked by a third will, the first will is revoked in whole or in part, except to the extent it appears from the terms of the third will that the testator intended the first will to take effect.

COMMENT

This section adopts a limited revival doctrine. If testator executes will no. 1 and later executes will no. 2, revoking will no. 1 and still later revokes will no. 2 by act such as destruction, there is a question as to whether testator intended to die intestate or have will no. 1 revived as his last will. Under this section will no. 1 can be probated as testator's last will if his intent to that effect can be established. For this purpose testimony as to his statements at the time he revokes will no. 2 or at a later date can be admitted. If will no. 2 is revoked by a third will, will no. 1 would remain revoked except to the extent that will no. 3 showed an intent to have will no. 1 effective.

Section 2–510. [Incorporation by Reference.]

Any writing in existence when a will is executed may be incorporated by reference if the language of the will manifests this intent and describes the writing sufficiently to permit its identification.

Section 2–511. [Testamentary Additions to Trusts.]

A devise or bequest, the validity of which is determinable by the law of this state, may be made by a will to the trustee of a trust established or to be established by the testator or by the testator and some other person or by some other person (including a funded or unfunded life insurance trust, although the trustor has reserved any or all rights of ownership of the insurance contracts) if the trust is identified in the testator's will and its terms are set forth in a written instrument (other than a will) executed before or concurrently with the execution of the testator's will or in the valid last will of a person who has predeceased the testator (regardless of the existence, size, or character of the corpus of the trust). The devise is not invalid because the trust is amendable or revocable, or because the trust was amended after the execution of the will or after the death of the testator. Unless the testator's will provides otherwise, the property so

553

devised (1) is not deemed to be held under a testamentary trust of the testator but becomes a part of the trust to which it is given and (2) shall be administered and disposed of in accordance with the provisions of the instrument or will setting forth the terms of the trust, including any amendments thereto made before the death of the testator (regardless of whether made before or after the execution of the testator's will), and, if the testator's will so provides, including any amendments to the trust made after the death of the testator. A revocation or termination of the trust before the death of the testator causes the devise to lapse.

COMMENT

This is Section 1 of the Uniform Testamentary Additions to Trusts Act.

Section 2–512. [Events of Independent Significance.]

A will may dispose of property by reference to acts and events which have significance apart from their effect upon the dispositions made by the will, whether they occur before or after the execution of the will or before or after the testator's death. The execution or revocation of a will of another person is such an event.

Section 2–513. [Separate Writing Identifying Bequest of Tangible Property.]

Whether or not the provisions relating to holographic wills apply, a will may refer to a written statement or list to dispose of items of tangible personal property not otherwise specifically disposed of by the will, other than money, evidences of indebtedness, documents of title, and securities, and property used in trade or business. To be admissible under this section as evidence of the intended disposition, the writing must either be in the handwriting of the testator or be signed by him and must describe the items and the devisees with reasonable certainty. The writing may be referred to as one to be in existence at the time of the testator's death; it may be prepared before or after the execution of the will; it may be altered by the testator after its preparation; and it may be a writing which has no significance apart from its effect upon the dispositions made by the will.

COMMENT

As part of the broader policy of effectuating a testator's intent and of relaxing formalities of execution, this section permits a testator to refer in his will to a separate document disposing of certain tangible personalty. The separate document may be prepared after execution of the will, so would not come within Section 2–510 on incorporation by reference. It may even be altered from time to time. It need only be either in the testator's handwriting or signed by him. The typical case would be a list of personal effects and the persons whom the testator desired to take specified items.

PART 6

RULES OF CONSTRUCTION

GENERAL COMMENT

Part 6 deals with a variety of construction problems which commonly occur in wills. All of the "rules" set forth in this part yield to a contrary intent expressed in the will and are therefore merely presumptions. Some of the sections are found in all states, with some variation in wording; others are relatively new. The sections deal with such problems as death before the testator (lapse), the inclusiveness of the will as to property of the testator, effect of failure of a gift in the will, change in form of securities specifically devised, ademption by reason of fire, sale and the like, exoneration, exercise of power of appointment by general language in the will, and the kinds of persons deemed to be included within various class gifts which are expressed in terms of family relationships.

Section 2–601. [Requirement That Devisee Survive Testator by 120 Hours.]

A devisee who does not survive the testator by 120 hours is treated as if he predeceased the testator, unless the will of decedent contains some language dealing explicitly with simultaneous deaths or deaths in a common disaster, or requiring that the devisee survive the testator or survive the testator for a stated period in order to take under the will.

COMMENT

This parallels Section 2–104 requiring an heir to survive by 120 hours in order to inherit.

Section 2–602. [Choice of Law as to Meaning and Effect of Wills.]

The meaning and legal effect of a disposition in a will shall be determined by the local law of a particular state selected by the testator in his instrument unless the application of that law is contrary to the provisions relating to the elective share described in Part 2 of this Article, the provisions relating to exempt property and allowances described in Part 4 of this Article, or any other public policy of this State otherwise applicable to the disposition.

COMMENT

New York Estates, Powers & Trusts Law Sec. 3–5.1(h) and Illinois Probate Act Sec. 896(b) direct respect for a testa-tor's choice of local law with reference to personal and intangible property situat-

555

ed in the enacting state. This provision goes further and enables a testator to select the law of a particular state for purposes of interpreting his will without regard to the location of property covered thereby. So long as local public policy is accommodated, the section should be accepted as necessary and desirable to add to the utility of wills. Choice of law regarding formal validity of a will is in Sec. 2–506. See also Sections 3–202 and 3–408.

In 1975, the Joint Editorial Board recommended the addition of explicit reference to the elective share described in Article II, Part 2, and the exemptions and allowances described in Article II, Part 4, as embodying policies of this state which may not be circumvented by a testator's choice of applicable law.

Section 2–603. [Rules of Construction and Intention.]

The intention of a testator as expressed in his will controls the legal effect of his dispositions. The rules of construction expressed in the succeeding sections of this Part apply unless a contrary intention is indicated by the will.

Section 2–604. [Construction That Will Passes All Property; After–Acquired Property.]

A will is construed to pass all property which the testator owns at his death including property acquired after the execution of the will.

Section 2–605. [Anti-lapse; Deceased Devisee; Class Gifts.]

If a devisee who is a grandparent or a lineal descendant of a grandparent of the testator is dead at the time of execution of the will, fails to survive the testator, or is treated as if he predeceased the testator, the issue of the deceased devisee who survive the testator by 120 hours take in place of the deceased devisee and if they are all of the same degree of kinship to the devisee they take equally, but if of unequal degree than those of more remote degree take by representation. One who would have been a devisee under a class gift if he had survived the testator is treated as a devisee for purposes of this section whether his death occurred before or after the execution of the will.

COMMENT

This section prevents lapse by death of a devisee before the testator if the devisee is a relative and leaves issue who survives the testator. A relative is one related to the testator by kinship and is limited to those who can inherit under Section 2–103 (through grandparents); it does not include persons related by marriage. Issue include adopted persons and illegitimates to the extent they would inherit from the devisee; see Sections 1–201 and 2–109. Note that the section is broader than some existing anti-lapse statutes which apply only to devises to children and other descendants, but is narrower than those which apply to devises to any person. The section is expressly applicable to class gifts, thereby eliminating a frequent source of litigation. It also applies to the so-called "void" gift, where the devisee is dead at the time of execution of the will. This, though contrary to some decisions, seems justified. It still seems likely that the testator would want the issue of a person included in a class term but dead when the will is made to be treated like the issue of another member of the class who was alive at the time the will was executed but who died before the testator.

The five day survival requirement stated in Section 2-601 does not require issue who would be substituted for their parent by this section to survive *their parent* by any set period.

Section 2-106 describes the method of division when a taking by representation is directed by the Code.

Section 2-606. [Failure of Testamentary Provision.]

(a) Except as provided in Section 2-605 if a devise other than a residuary devise fails for any reason, it becomes a part of the residue.

(b) Except as provided in Section 2-605 if the residue is devised to two or more persons and the share of one of the residuary devisees fails for any reason, his share passes to the other residuary devisee, or to other residuary devisees in proportion to their interests in the residue.

COMMENT

If a devise fails by reason of lapse and the conditions of Section 2-605 are met, the latter section governs rather than this section. There is also a special rule for renunciation contained in Section 2-801; a renounced devise may be governed by either Section 8-605 or the present section, depending on the circumstances.

Section 2-607. [Change in Securities; Accessions; Nonademption.]

(a) If the testator intended a specific devise of certain securities rather than the equivalent value thereof, the specific devisee is entitled only to:

(1) as much of the devised securities as is a part of the estate at time of the testator's death;

(2) any additional or other securities of the same entity owned by the testator by reason of action initiated by the entity excluding any acquired by exercise of purchase options;

(3) securities of another entity owned by the testator as a result of a merger, consolidation, reorganization or other similar action initiated by the entity; and

(4) any additional securities of the entity owned by the testator as a result of a plan of reinvestment.

(b) Distributions prior to death with respect to a specifically devised security not provided for in subsection (a) are not part of the specific devise.

557

COMMENT

The Joint Editorial Board considered amending Subsection (a)(2) so as to exclude additional securities of the same entity that were not acquired by testator as a result of his ownership of the devised securities. It concluded that, in context, the present language is clear enough to make the proposed amendment unnecessary.

Subsection (b) is intended to codify existing law to the effect that cash dividends declared and payable as of a record date occurring before the testator's death do not pass as a part of the specific devise even though paid after death. See Section 4, Revised Uniform Principal and Income Act.

Section 2–608. [Nonademption of Specific Devises in Certain Cases; Unpaid Proceeds of Sale, Condemnation or Insurance; Sale by Conservator.]

(a) A specific devisee has the right to the remaining specifically devised property and:

(1) any balance of the purchase price (together with any security interest) owing from a purchaser to the testator at death by reason of sale of the property;

(2) any amount of a condemnation award for the taking of the property unpaid at death;

(3) any proceeds unpaid at death on fire or casualty insurance on the property; and

(4) property owned by testator at his death as a result of foreclosure, or obtained in lieu of foreclosure, of the security for a specifically devised obligation.

(b) If specifically devised property is sold by a conservator or an agent acting within the authority of a durable power of attorney for a principal who is under a disability, or if a condemnation award or insurance proceeds are paid to a conservator or an agent acting within the authority of a durable power of attorney for a principal who is under a disability as a result of condemnation, fire, or casualty, the specific devisee has the right to a general pecuniary devise equal to the net sale price, the condemnation award, or the insurance proceeds. This subsection does not apply if after the sale, condemnation or casualty, it is adjudicated that the disability of the testator has ceased and the testator survives the adjudication by one year. The right of the specific devisee under this subsection is reduced by any right he has under subsection (a).

COMMENT

In 1975, the Joint Editorial Board recommended a re-ordering of the title of this section and a reversal of the original order of the subsections. This recommendation was designed to correct

an unintended interpretation of the section to the effect that all of the events described in subsections (a) and (b) had relevance only when the testator was under a conservatorship. The original intent of the section, made more apparent by this re-ordering, was to prevent ademption in all cases involving sale, condemnation or destruction of specifically devised assets where testator's death occurred before the proceeds of the sale, condemnation or any insurance, had been paid to the testator.

Section 2–609. [Non–exoneration.]

A specific devise passes subject to any mortgage interest existing at the date of death, without right of exoneration, regardless of a general directive in the will to pay debts.

COMMENT

See Section 3–814 empowering the personal representative to pay an encumbrance under some circumstances; the last sentence of that section makes it clear that such payment does not increase the right of the specific devisee. The present section governs the substantive rights of the devisee. The common law rule of exoneration of the specific devise is abolished by this section, and the contrary rule is adopted.

For the rule as to exempt property, see Section 2–402.

Section 2–610. [Exercise of Power of Appointment.]

A general residuary clause in a will, or a will making general disposition of all of the testator's property, does not exercise a power of appointment held by the testator unless specific reference is made to the power or there is some other indication of intention to include the property subject to the power.

COMMENT

Although there is some indication that more states will adopt special legislation on powers of appointment, and this Code has therefore generally avoided any provisions relating to powers of appointment, there is great need for uniformity on the subject of exercise by a will purporting to dispose of all of the donee's property, whether by a standard residuary clause or a general recital of property passing under the will. Although a substantial number of states have legislation to the effect that a will with a general residuary clause does manifest an intent to exercise a power, the contrary rule is stated in the present section for two reasons: (1) this is still the majority rule in the United States, and (2) most powers of appointment are created in marital deduction trusts and the donor would prefer to have the property pass under his trust instrument unless the donee affirmatively manifests an intent to exercise the power.

Under this section and Section 2–603 the intent to exercise the power is effective if it is "indicated by the will." This wording permits a Court to find the manifest intent if the language of the will interpreted in light of all the surrounding circumstances shows that the donee intended an exercise, except, of course, if the donor has conditioned exercise on an express reference to the original creating instrument. In other words, the modern liberal rule on interpretation of the donee's will would be available.

Section 2–611. [Construction of Generic Terms to Accord with Relationships as Defined for Intestate Succession.]

Halfbloods, adopted persons, and persons born out of wedlock are included in class gift terminology and terms of relationship in accordance with rules for determining relationships for purposes of intestate succession. [However, a person born out of wedlock is not treated as the child of the father unless the person is openly and notoriously so treated by the father.]

COMMENT

The purpose of this section is to facilitate a modern construction of gifts, usually class gifts, in wills.

In 1975, the Joint Editorial Board recommended that the section end with the words, "of intestate succession", in order to align the section with the Uniform Parentage Act of 1973. The Board also recommended retention, as a bracketed alternative form for states that do not enact the Uniform Parentage Act, of the language of the 1969 text beginning with "but a person born out of wedlock", and continuing through to the end of the original section.

Section 2–612. [Ademption by Satisfaction.]

Property which a testator gave in his lifetime to a person is treated as a satisfaction of a devise to that person in whole or in part, only if the will provides for deduction of the lifetime gift, or the testator declares in a contemporaneous writing that the gift is to be deducted from the devise or is in satisfaction of the devise, or the devisee acknowledges in writing that the gift is in satisfaction. For purpose of partial satisfaction, property given during lifetime is valued as of the time the devisee came into possession or enjoyment of the property or as of the time of death of the testator, whichever occurs first.

COMMENT

This section parallels Section 2–110 on advancements and follows the same policy of requiring written evidence that lifetime gifts are to be taken into account in distribution of an estate, whether testate or intestate. Although Courts traditionally call this "ademption by satisfaction" when a will is involved, and "advancement" when the estate is intestate, the difference in terminology is not significant. Some wills expressly provide for lifetime advances by a hotchpot clause. Where the will is silent, the above section would require either the testator to declare in writing that the gift is an advance or satisfaction or the devisee to acknowledge the same in writing. The second sentence on value accords with Section 2–110 and would apply if property such as stock is given. If the devise is specific, a gift of the specific property during lifetime would adeem the devise by extinction rather than by satisfaction, and this section would be inapplicable. If a devisee to whom an advancement is made predeceases the testator and his issue take under 2–605, they take the same devise as their ancestor; if the devise is reduced by reason of this section as to the ancestor, it is automatically reduced as to his issue. In this respect the rule in testacy differs from that in intestacy; see Section 2–110.

PART 7

CONTRACTUAL ARRANGEMENTS RELATING TO DEATH

(See, also, Article VI, Non–Probate Transfers)

Section 2–701. [Contracts Concerning Succession.]

A contract to make a will or devise, or not to revoke a will or devise, or to die intestate, if executed after the effective date of this Act, can be established only by (1) provisions of a will stating material provisions of the contract; (2) an express reference in a will to a contract and extrinsic evidence proving the terms of the contract; or (3) a writing signed by the decedent evidencing the contract. The execution of a joint will or mutual wills does not create a presumption of a contract not to revoke the will or wills.

COMMENT

It is the purpose of this section to tighten the methods by which contracts concerning succession may be proved. Oral contracts not to revoke wills have given rise to much litigation in a number of states; and in many states if two persons execute a single document as their joint will, this gives rise to a presumption that the parties had contracted not to revoke the will except by consent of both.

This section requires that either the will must set forth the material provi-sions of the contract, or the will must make express reference to the contract and extrinsic evidence prove the terms of the contract, or there must be a separate writing signed by the decedent evidencing the contract. Oral testimony regarding the contract is permitted if the will makes reference to the contract, but this provision of the statute is not intended to affect normal rules regarding admissibility of evidence.

PART 8

GENERAL PROVISIONS

GENERAL COMMENT

Part 8 contains three general provisions which cut across both testate and intestate succession. The first section permits renunciation; the existing law in most states permits renunciation of gifts by will but not by intestate succession, a distinction which cannot be defended on policy grounds. The second section deals with the effect of divorce and separation on the right to elect against a will, exempt property and allowances, and an intestate share. The last section, an optional provision, spells out the legal consequence of murder on the right of the murderer to take as heir, devisee, joint tenant or life insurance beneficiary.

Section 2–801. [Renunciation of Succession.]

(a) A person or the representative of an incapacitated or protected person, who is an heir, devisee, person succeeding to a renounced interest, beneficiary under a testamentary instrument, or appointee under a power of appointment exercised by a testamentary instrument, may renounce in whole or in part the right of succession to any property or interest therein, including a future interest, by filing a written renunciation under this Section. The right to renounce does not survive the death of the person having it. The instrument shall (1) describe the property or interest renounced, (2) declare the renunciation and extent thereof, and (3) be signed by the person renouncing.

Comment to Subsection (a)

Who May Disclaim: At common law it was settled that the taker of property under a will had the right to accept or reject a legacy or devise (per Abbott, C.J., in *Townson v. Tickell,* 3 B & Ald 3, 136, 106 Eng.Rep. 575, 576). The same rule prevails in the United States (*Peter v. Peter,* 343 Ill. 493, 175 N.E. 846 (1931) 75 ALR 890). It is said that no one can make another an owner of an estate against his consent by devising it to him. See, for example, *People v. Flanagin,* 331 Ill. 203, 162 N.E. 848, (1928) 60 ALR 305:

> "The law is clear that a legatee or devisee is under no obligation to accept a testamentary gift ... and he may renounce the gift, by which act

the estate will descend to the heir or pass in some other direction under the will ..."

Under the rule permitting the disclaimer of testate successions, the disclaimed interest related back to the date of the testator's death so that the interest did not vest in the grantee but remained in the original owner as if the will had never been executed (*People v. Flanagin,* supra).

Unlike the devisee or legatee, an heir had no common law power to prevent passage of title to himself by disclaimer. "An heir at law is the only person in whom the law of England vests property, whether he will or not," declares

Williams on Real Property, and adds, "No disclaimer that he may make will have any effect, though, of course, he may as soon as he pleases dispose of the property by ordinary conveyance." (Williams on Law of Real Property 75 [2d Am.Ed.1857]. See also 6 Page on Wills [Bowe–Parker Revision] Section 49.1.)

The difference between testate and intestate successions in respect to the right to disclaim, has produced a number of illogical and undesirable consequences. An heir who sought to reject his inheritance was subjected to the Federal gift tax on the theory that since he could not prevent the passage of title to himself, any act done to rid himself of the interest necessarily involved a transfer subject to gift tax liability [*Hardenberg v. Com'r,* 198 F.2d 63 (8th Cir.) cert. denied, 344 U.S. 863, (1952) aff'g 17 T.C. 166 (1951); *Maxwell v. Com'r,* 17 T.C. 1589 (1952). See Lauritzen, Only God Can Make An Heir, 48 NWL Rev. 568; Annotation 170 ALR 435.] On the other hand, a legatee or devisee who rejected a legacy or devise under the will incurred no such tax consequences [*Brown v. Routzahn,* 63 F.2d 914 (6th Cir.) cert. denied, 290 U.S. 641 (1933)].

Subsection (a) places an heir on the same basis as a devisee or legatee and provides that he and others upon whom successions may devolve, have the full right to disclaim in whole or in part the passage of property to them, with the same legal consequences applying in all such cases.

Successive disclaimers are permitted by the express inclusion of "person succeeding to a disclaimed interest" among those who may disclaim.

Beneficiary: The term beneficiary is used in a broad sense to include any person entitled, but for his disclaimer, to possess or enjoy an equitable or legal interest, present or future, in the property or interest, including a power to consume, appoint, or apply it for any purpose or to enforce the transfer in any respect.

Subsection (a) extends the right to disclaim to the representative of an incapacitated or protected person. This accords with the general rule that the probate or surrogate court in the exercise of its traditional jurisdiction over the person and estate of a minor or incompetent may authorize or direct the guardian, conservator or committee to exercise the right on behalf of his ward when it is in the ward's interest to do so. *Davis v. Mather,* 309 Ill. 284, 141 N.E. 209 (1923).

On the other hand, absent a statute, the general rule is that the right to disclaim is personal to the person entitled to exercise it, and dies with him in the absence of fraud or concealment or conflict of interest of his representative, even though the time within which the right might have been utilized has not expired and even though he may be incompetent. *Rock Island Bank & Trust Co. v. First Nat. Bank of Rock Island,* 26 Ill.2d 47, 185 N.E.2d 890, (1962), 3 ALR3d 114. Subsection (a) adopts this position by stating that the right to disclaim does not survive the death of the person having it.

The Act makes no provision here or elsewhere, for an extension of time to disclaim or other relief from a strict observance of the statutory requirements for disclaimer and the time limitations for expressing the right of disclaimer apply to persons under disability as well as to others.

What May be Disclaimed: Subsection (a) specifies that the "succession" to any property, real or personal or interest therein, may be disclaimed, and it is immaterial whether it derives by way of will, intestacy, exercise of a power of appointment or disclaimer. It would include the right to renounce any survivorship interest in the community in a community property state. Cf. *U.S. v. Mitchell,* 403 U.S. 190 (1971), rev'g 430 F.2d (5th Cir.1970), aff'g 51 T.C. 641 (1969).

Future Interests: Subsection (a) contemplates the disclaimer of future interests by reference to "beneficiary under a testamentary instrument" and "appointee under a power of appointment." The time for making such a disclaimer is dealt with in Subsection (b).

Partial Disclaimer: The status of partial disclaimers has been uncertain in many states. The result has often turned on whether the gift is "severable" or constitutes a "single, aggregate" gift [*Olgesby v. Springfield Marine Bank,* 395 Ill. 37, 69 N.E.2d 269 (1946); *Brown v. Routzahn,* supra]. Subsection (a) makes it clear that a partial, as well as a total, disclaimer is permitted.

Discretionary administrative and investment powers under a trust have been held to constitute a "severable" interest and subject to partial disclaimer. *Estate of Harry C. Jaecker,* 58 T.C. 166, CCH Dec. 31,356 (1972).

Method of Disclaiming: In many states no satisfactory case law has existed as to the form and manner of making disclaimers of devises or legacies under wills. See Annotation 93 ALR2d 8— What Constitutes or Establishes Beneficiary's Acceptance of Renunciation of Bequest or Devise. Because certainty of titles and the expeditious administration of estates makes definiteness desirable in this area. Subsection (a) requires a disclaimer to (i) describe the property or interest disclaimed; (ii) declare the disclaimer and the extent thereof; and (iii) be signed by the disclaimant.

(b)(1) An instrument renouncing a present interest shall be filed not later than [9] months after the death of the decedent or the donee of the power.

(2) An instrument renouncing a future interest may be filed not later than [9] months after the event determining that the taker of the property or interest is finally ascertained and his interest is indefeasibly vested.

(3) The renunciation shall be filed in the [probate] court of the county in which proceedings have been commenced for the administration of the estate of the deceased owner or deceased donee of the power or, if they have not been commenced, in which they could be commenced. A copy of the renunciation shall be delivered in person or mailed by registered or certified mail to any personal representative, or other fiduciary of the decedent or donee of the power. If real property or an interest therein is renounced, a copy of the renunciation may be recorded in the office of the [Recorder of Deeds] of the county in which the real estate is situated.*

* If Torrens system is in effect, add provisions to comply with local law.

Comment to Subsection (b)

Time for Making Disclaimer: At common law, no specific time evolved within which disclaimer had to be made. The only requirement was that it be within a "reasonable" time (*In re Wilson's Estate,* 298 N.Y. 398, 83 N.E.2d 852 (1949); *Ewing v. Rountree,* 228 F.Supp. 137 (D.C.Tenn.1964)). As a result, divergent holdings were reached by the courts (*Brown v. Routzahn,* 63 F.2d 914, (6th Cir.), cert. denied, 290 U.S. 641 (1933)). Subsection (b) fixes a definite time for filing of disclaimers. This approach follows the pattern of the Federal estate tax law which prescribed the time for filing estate tax returns in terms of the decedent's death. The time allowed should overlast the time for filing claims and contesting the will and enable the executor or administrator to know with certainty who the takers of the estate will be. On the other hand, it should not be so long as to work against an early determination of the acceptance or rejection of succession to an estate, or increase the risk of inadvertent acceptance of the benefits of the property, creating an estoppel. In the case of future interests the disclaimer period should run from the time the takers of the interest are finally ascertained and their interest indefeasibly fixed. *Seifner v. Weller,* 171 S.W.2d 617 (Mo., 1943). For the consequence of selecting too short a period, see *Brodhag v. U.S.,* 319 F.Supp. 747 (S.D.W.Va., 1970) involving a 2–month period fixed by West Virginia law.

In the case of future interests it should be noted that the person need not wait until the occurrence of the determinative event before filing a disclaimer, but may do so at any time after the death of the decedent or donee, so long as it is made "not later than" the prescribed period.

Federal Gift Tax Implications: Disclaimers have significance under the Federal gift tax law. Section 2511(a) of the Internal Revenue Code imposes a gift tax upon the transfer of property by gift whether the transfer is in trust or otherwise, and whether the gift is direct or indirect. The Treasury regulations under this section state that where local law gives the beneficiary, heir or next of kin an unqualified right to refuse to accept ownership of property transferred from a decedent, whether by will or by intestacy, a refusal to accept ownership does not constitute the making of a gift if the refusal is made within a "reason-able time" after knowledge of the existence of the transfer.

A "reasonable time" for gift tax purposes is not defined in the Code or regulations. It has been held that the courts will look to the law of the states in determining the question. (*Brown v. Routzahn,* 63 F.2d 914 (6th Cir.) cert. denied 290 U.S. 641 (1933)), not conclusively, but as relevant and having probative value (*Keinath v. C.I.R.,* 480 F.2d 57 (8th Cir.,1973), rev'g 58 T.C. 352, (1972)), and that an unequivocal disclaimer filed within 6 months of the determinative event is made within a "reasonable time." It has been held, further, that as regards future interests, the "reasonable time" period runs from the termination of the preceding estate or interest, and not from the time the transfer was made, *Keinath v. C.I.R.,* supra.

Place of Filing Disclaimer: Subsection (b) requires a disclaimer to be filed in the probate court. If real property or an interest therein is involved, a copy of the disclaimer may also be recorded in the office of the recorder of deeds or other appropriate office in the county in which the real estate is situated. If the Torrens system is in effect, appropriate provisions should be added to comply with local law.

Notice: A copy of the disclaimer is required to be delivered in person or mailed by registered or certified mail to the personal representative or other fiduciary of the decedent or of the donee of the power as the case may be.

(c) Unless the decedent or donee of the power has otherwise provided, the property or interest renounced devolves as though the person renouncing had predeceased the decedent or, if the person renouncing is designated to take under a power of appointment exercised by a testamentary instrument, as though the person renouncing had predeceased the donee of the power. A future interest that takes effect in possession or enjoyment after the termination of the estate or interest renounced takes effect as though the person renouncing had predeceased the decedent or the donee of the power. A renunciation relates back for all purposes to the date of the death of the decedent or the donee of the power.

Comment to Subsection (c)

Devolution of Disclaimed Property: When a beneficiary disclaims his interest under a will, the question arises as to what happens to the rejected interest. In *People v. Flanagin,* 331 Ill. 203, 162 N.E. 848 (1928), 60 ALR 305, the court, quoting the New York case of *Burritt v. Sillman,* 13 N.Y. 93 (1855) said that the disclaimed property will "descend to the heir or pass in some other direction under the will." From this, it may be assumed that the court meant that if the decedent left no will, the renounced interest passed according to the rules of descent, but if he left a will, it passed according to its terms.

It has been generally thought that devolution in the case of disclaimer should be the same as in the case of lapse, which is controlled by sections of the probate law. Subsection (c) takes this approach. It provides that unless the will of the decedent or the donee of the power has otherwise provided, the disclaimed interest devolves as if the disclaimant had predeceased the decedent or the donee of the power. In every case the disclaimer relates back to the date of the death of the decedent or of the donee. The provision that the disclaimer "relates back", codifies the rule that a renunciation of a devise or legacy relates to the date of death of the decedent or donee and prevents the succession from becoming operative in favor of the disclaimant. See *In re Wilson's Estate,* 298 N.Y. 398, 83 N.E.2d 852 (1949). Also, *Bouse, for use of State v. Hull,* 168 Md. 1, 176 A. 645 (1935).

Acceleration of Future Interests: If a life estate or other future interest is disclaimed, the problem is raised of whether succeeding interests or estates accelerate in possession or enjoyment or whether the disclaimed interest must be marshalled to await the actual happening of the contingency. Subsection (c) provides that remainder interests are accelerated, the second sentence specifically stating that any future interest which is to take effect in possession or enjoy-

ment after the termination of the estate or interest disclaimed, takes effect as if the disclaimant had predeceased the deceased owner or deceased donee of the power. Thus, if T leaves his estate in trust to pay the income to his son for life, remainder to his son's children who survive him, and S disclaims with two children then living, the remainder in the children accelerates; the trust terminates and the children receive possession and enjoyment, even though the son may subsequently have other children or that one or more of the living children may die during their father's lifetime.

Effect of Death or Disability of Person Entitled to Disclaim: The effect of death of a person entitled to disclaim, including one under disability, is discussed under Subsection (a). A guardian or conservator of the estate of an incapacitated or protected person may disclaim for the ward. Subsection (b) makes no provision for an extension of time or for other relief in case of disability for the observance of the statutory requirements for effective disclaimer. The intent is that the period for disclaimer applies to a person under disability as well as to others, and includes a court which purports to act on behalf of one under disability in the absence of fraud, misconduct or other unusual circumstances. *Pratt v. Baker,* 48 Ill.App.2d 442, 199 N.E.2d 307 (1964).

Rights of Creditors and Others: As regards creditors, taxing authorities and others, the provision for "relation back" has the legal effect of preventing a succession from becoming operative in favor of the disclaimant. The relation back is "for all purposes" which would include, among others for the purpose of rights of creditors, taxing authorities and assertion of dower. It is immaterial that the effect is to avoid the imposition of a higher death tax than would be the case if the interest had been accepted: *Estate of Aylsworth,* 74 Ill.App.2d 375, 219

N.E.2d 779 (1966) [motive for the disclaimer is immaterial]; *People v. Flanagin,* 331 Ill. 203, 162 N.E. 848 (1928), 60 ALR 305; *Cook v. Dove,* 32 Ill.2d 109, 203 N.E.2d 892 (1965) [upholding for inheritance tax the right of appointees to take by default rather than under the power-holder's exercise of power]; *Matter of Wolfe's Estate,* 179 N.Y. 599, 72 N.E. 1152 (1904); aff'g 89 App.Div. 349, 83 N.Y.Supp. 949 (1903); *Brown v. Routzahn,* 63 F.2d 914 (6th Cir.), cert. denied 290 U.S. 641 (1933); *In re Stone's Estate,* 132 Ia. 136, 109 N.W. 455 (1906); *Tax Commission v. Glass,* 119 Ohio St. 389, 164 N.E. 425 (1929); *U.S. v. McCrackin,* 189 F.Supp. 632 (S.D.Ohio 1960).

Similarly, numerous cases have held that a devisee or legatee can disclaim a devise or legacy despite the claims of creditors: *Hoecker v. United Bank of Boulder,* 476 F.2d 838 (CA 10, 1973) aff'g 334 F.Supp. 1080 (D.Colo.1971) (bankruptcy); *U.S. v. McCrackin,* supra (Federal income tax liens); *Shoonover v. Osborne,* 193 Ia. 474, 187 N.W. 20 (1922), *Bradford v. Calhoun,* 120 Tenn. 53, 109 S.W. 502 (1908), *Carter v. Carter,* 63 N.J.Eq. 726, 53 A. 160 (1902), *Estate of Hansen,* 109 Ill.App.2d 283, 248 N.E.2d 709 (1969) (judgment creditor); 37 Mich.L.Rev. 1168; 43 Yale L.J. 1030; 27 ALR 477; 133 ALR 1428. A creditor is not entitled to notice of the disclaimer (*In re Estate of Hansen,* 109 Ill.App.2d 283, 248 N.E.2d 709 (1969)).

(d)(1) The right to renounce property or an interest therein is barred by (i) an assignment, conveyance, encumbrance, pledge, or transfer of the property or interest, or a contract therefor, (ii) a written waiver of the right to renounce, (iii) an acceptance of the property or interest or benefit thereunder, or (iv) a sale of the property or interest under judicial sale made before the renunciation is effected.

(2) The right to renounce exists notwithstanding any limitation on the interest of the person renouncing in the nature of a spendthrift provision or similar restriction.

(3) A renunciation or a written waiver of the right to renounce is binding upon the person renouncing or person waiving and all persons claiming through or under him.

Comment to Subsection (d)

Bars to Disclaimer—Waiver—Estoppel: It may be necessary or advisable to sell real estate in a decedent's estate before the expiration of the period permitted for disclaimer. In such case, the possibility of a disclaimer being filed within the period, could be a deterrent to sale and delivery of good title. Subsection (d) expressly authorizes an heir, devisee, legatee or other person entitled to disclaim, to indicate in writing his intention to "waive" his right of disclaimer, and thus avoid any delay in the completion of a sale or other disposition of estate assets. The written waiver bars the right of the person subsequently to disclaim the property or interest

therein and is binding on persons claiming through or under him.

Similarly, Subsection (d) provides that various acts of a person entitled to disclaim in regard to property or an interest therein, such as making an assignment, conveyance, encumbrance, pledge or transfer of the property or interest, or a contract therefor, bars the right of the person to disclaim and is binding on all persons claiming through or under him.

Spendthrift Provisions: The existence of a limitation on the interest of an heir, legatee, devisee or other disclaimant in the nature of a spendthrift provision or similar restriction is expressly declared not to affect the right to disclaim. Without this provision, there might be a question as to whether the beneficiary of a spendthrift trust can disclaim under the statute (Griswold, Spendthrift Trust [2d Ed.] Section 524, p. 603). If a person who is under no legal disability wishes to refuse a beneficial interest under a trust, he should not be powerless to make an effective disclaimer even though the intended interest once accepted by him would be inalienable. (Scott on Trusts, Section 337.7, p. 2683, 3d Ed.)

When a beneficial interest is accepted by a beneficiary, he cannot thereafter disclaim or release it (Griswold, supra, Section 534, p. 603 note 48). As to what conduct amounts to an acceptance, see *In Re Wilson's Estate,* 298 N.Y. 398, 83 N.E.2d 852 (1949).

Judicial Sale: The section provides that the right to disclaim is barred by a sale of the property or interest under a judicial sale. Judicial sales are ordered in many different types of proceeding such as foreclosure of mortgage or trust deed, enforcement of lien, partition proceedings and proceedings for the sale of real property of a decedent or ward for certain purposes. Probate laws frequently permit a representative to mortgage or pledge property of the decedent or ward in certain circumstances. Execution sales are made pursuant to a writ to satisfy a money judgment. Subsection (d) has the effect of providing that the making of a judicial sale for the account of the heir, devisee, or beneficiary, bars him from renouncing the property or interest. To be distinguished from a judicial sale, is a taking pursuant to eminent domain, which is considered to be a taking of property without the owner's consent and unrelated to his obligations or commitments. The right to disclaim the proceeds of a condemnation action if otherwise timely and in accordance with this Section, should not, therefore, be barred under Subsection (d).

(e) This Section does not abridge the right of a person to waive, release, disclaim, or renounce property or an interest therein under any other statute.

Comment to Subsection (e)

Subsection (e) provides that the right to disclaim under the law does not abridge the right of any person to waive, release, disclaim or renounce any property or interest therein under any other statute. The principal statutes to which this provision is pointed are those dealing with spousal renunciations and release of powers.

Being a codification of the common law in regard to the renunciation of the property, this Section is intended to constitute an *exclusive remedy* for the disclaimer of testamentary successions apart from those provided by other statutes, and supplants the common law right to disclaim.

(f) An interest in property existing on the effective date of this Section as to which the time for filing a renunciation under this Section would have begun to run were this Section in effect when the interest was created, may be renounced within [9] months after the effective date of this Section.

Comment to Subsection (f)

Subsection (f) deals with the application of this Section to property interests under instruments or in estates in existence on the effective date. If the interest is a present one and the filing time has not expired, the holder is given a full period after enactment within which to disclaim the interest. If the interest is a future one, the holder is given a full period after the interest becomes indefeasibly vested or the takers finally ascertained, after enactment in which to disclaim it. If T dies in 1960 trusteeing his estate to W for life, remainder to such of T's sons as are living at W's death and W dies in 1975, this Section permits a son to disclaim his remainder interest after it ripens even though it arises under an instrument predating the effective date of this Section. The application of statute to pre-existing instruments in like situations finds support in cases such as Will of Allis, 6 Wis.2d 1, 94 N.W.2d 226, (1959) 69 ALR2d 1128.

Comment to Section 2–801

The above text, consists of Sections 1 through 6 of Uniform Disclaimer of Transfers By Will, Intestacy or Appointment Act of 1973, redesignated as subsections (a) through (f).

The Comments following each subsection are the Official Comments to the 1973 statute. The word "renunciation" has been substituted for "disclaimer" because the original Section 2–801 used the term "renunciation" and several cross-references to this term appear in other sections of this Code. It is the view of the Joint Editorial Board that the terms "renunciation" and "disclaimer" have the same meaning.

The principal substantive difference between original Section 2–801 and the 1973 replacement therefor is that the former permitted renunciation by the personal representative of a person who might have renounced during his lifetime. Under the new uniform act, which is now the official text of Section 2–801, the right to renounce terminates upon the death of the person who might have renounced during his lifetime. Also, the original version was less precise than the present version in the important provisions of subsection (b) which govern the time for renunciation.

This Section is designed to facilitate renunciation in order to aid postmortem planning. Although present law in all states permits renunciation of a devise under a will, the common law did not permit renunciation of an intestate share. There is no reason for such a distinction, and some states have already adopted legislation permitting renunciation of an intestate share. Renunciation may be made for a variety of reasons, including carrying out the decedent's wishes not expressed in a properly executed will.

Under the rule of this Section, renounced property passes as if the renouncing person had failed to survive the decedent. In the case of intestate property, the heir who would be next in line in succession would take; often this will be the issue of the renouncing person, taking by representation. For consistency the same rule is adopted for renunciation by a devisee; if the devisee is a relative who leaves issue surviving the testator, the issue will take under Section 2–605; otherwise disposition will be governed by Section 2–606 and general rules of law.

The Section limits renunciation to nine months after the death of the decedent or if the taker of the property is not ascertained at that time, then nine months after he is ascertained. If the personal representative is concerned about closing the estate within that nine months period in order to make distribution, he can obtain a waiver of the right to renounce. Normally this should be no problem, since the heir or devisee cannot renounce once he has taken possession of the property.

The presence of a spendthrift clause does not prevent renunciation under this Section.

Section 2–802. [Effect of Divorce, Annulment, and Decree of Separation.]

(a) A person who is divorced from the decedent or whose marriage to the decedent has been annulled is not a surviving spouse unless, by virtue of a subsequent marriage, he is married to the decedent at the time of death. A decree of separation which does not terminate the status of husband and wife is not a divorce for purposes of this section.

(b) For purposes of Parts 1, 2, 3 & 4 of this Article, and of Section 3–203, a surviving spouse does not include:

(1) a person who obtains or consents to a final decree or judgment of divorce from the decedent or an annulment of their marriage, which decree or judgment is not recognized as valid in this state, unless they subsequently participate in a marriage ceremony purporting to marry each to the other, or subsequently live together as man and wife;

(2) a person who, following a decree or judgment of divorce or annulment obtained by the decedent, participates in a marriage ceremony with a third person; or

(3) a person who was a party to a valid proceeding concluded by an order purporting to terminate all marital property rights.

COMMENT

See Section 2–508 for similar provisions relating to the effect of divorce to revoke devises to a spouse.

Although some existing statutes bar the surviving spouse for desertion or adultery, the present section requires some definitive legal act to bar the surviving spouse. Normally, this is divorce. Subsection (a) states an obvious proposition, but subsection (b) deals with the difficult problem of invalid divorce or annulment, which is particularly frequent as to foreign divorce decrees but may arise as to a local decree where there is some defect in jurisdiction; the basic principle underlying these provisions is estoppel against the surviving spouse. Where there is only a legal separation, rather than a divorce, succession patterns are not affected; but if the separation is accompanied by a complete property settlement, this may operate under Section 2–204 as a renunciation of benefits under a prior will and by intestate succession.

In 1975, the Joint Editorial Board recommended the addition, in the preliminary statement of subsection (b), of explicit reference to Section 3–203 which controls priorities for appointment as personal representative.

[Section 2–803. [Effect of Homicide on Intestate Succession, Wills, Joint Assets, Life Insurance and Beneficiary Designations.]

(a) A surviving spouse, heir or devisee who feloniously and intentionally kills the decedent is not entitled to any benefits under the will or under this Article, and the estate of decedent passes as if the killer had predeceased the decedent. Property appointed by the will of the decedent to or for the benefit of the killer passes as if the killer had predeceased the decedent.

(b) Any joint tenant who feloniously and intentionally kills another joint tenant thereby effects a severance of the interest of the decedent so that the share of the decedent passes as his property and the killer has no rights by survivorship. This provision applies to joint tenancies [and tenancies by the entirety] in real and personal property, joint and multiple-party accounts in banks, savings and loan associations, credit unions and other institutions, and any other form of co-ownership with survivorship incidents.

(c) A named beneficiary of a bond, life insurance policy, or other contractual arrangement who feloniously and intentionally kills the principal obligee or the person upon whose life the policy is issued is not entitled to any benefit under the bond, policy or other contractual arrangement, and it becomes payable as though the killer had predeceased the decedent.

(d) Any other acquisition of property or interest by the killer shall be treated in accordance with the principles of this section.

(e) A final judgment of conviction of felonious and intentional killing is conclusive for purposes of this section. In the absence of a conviction of felonious and intentional killing the Court may determine by a preponderance of evidence whether the killing was felonious and intentional for purposes of this section.

(f) This section does not affect the rights of any person who, before rights under this section have been adjudicated, purchases from the killer for value and without notice property which the killer would have acquired except for this section, but the killer is liable for the amount of the proceeds or the value of the property. Any insurance company, bank, or other obligor making payment according to the terms of its policy or obligation is not liable by reason of this section unless prior to payment it has received at its home office or principal address written notice of a claim under this section.]

COMMENT

This section is bracketed to indicate that it may be omitted by an enacting state without difficulty.

A growing group of states have enacted statutes dealing with the problems covered by this section, and uniformity appears desirable. The section is confined to intentional and felonious homicide and excludes the accidental manslaughter killing.

At first it may appear that the matter dealt with is criminal in nature and not a proper matter for probate courts. However, the concept that a wrongdoer may not profit by his own wrong is a civil concept, and the probate court is the proper forum to determine the effect of killing on succession to property of the decedent. There are numerous situations where the same conduct gives rise to both criminal and civil consequences. A killing may result in criminal prosecution for murder and civil litigation by the murdered person's family under wrongful death statutes. While conviction in the criminal prosecution under this section is treated as conclusive on the matter of succession to the murdered person's property, acquittal does not have the same consequences. This is because different considerations as well as a different burden of proof enter into the finding of guilty in the criminal prosecution. Hence it is possible that the defendant on a murder charge may be found not guilty and acquitted, but if the same person claims as an heir or devisee of the decedent, he may in the probate court be found to have feloniously and intentionally killed the decedent and thus be barred under this section from sharing in the estate. An analogy exists in the tax field, where a taxpayer may be acquitted of tax fraud in a criminal prosecution but found to have committed the fraud in a civil proceeding. In many of the cases arising under this section there may be no criminal prosecution because the murderer has committed suicide.

PART 9

CUSTODY AND DEPOSIT OF WILLS

Section 2–901. [Deposit of Will With Court in Testator's Lifetime.]

A will may be deposited by the testator or his agent with any Court for safekeeping, under rules of the Court. The will shall be kept confidential. During the testator's lifetime a deposited will shall be delivered only to him or to a person authorized in writing signed by him to receive the will. A conservator may be allowed to examine a deposited will of a protected testator under procedures designed to maintain the confidential character of the document to the extent possible, and to assure that it will be resealed and left on deposit after the examination. Upon being informed of the testator's death, the Court shall notify any person designated to receive the will and deliver it to him on request; or the Court may deliver the will to the appropriate Court.

COMMENT

Many states already have statutes permitting deposit of wills during a testator's lifetime. Most of these statutes have elaborate provisions governing purely administrative matters: how the will is to be enclosed in a sealed wrapper, what is to be endorsed on the wrapper, the form of receipt or certificate given to the testator, the fee to be charged, how the will is to be opened after testator's death and who is to be notified. Under this section, details have been left to Court rule, except as other relevant statutes such as one governing fees may apply.

It is, of course, vital to maintain the confidential nature of deposited wills. However, this obviously does not prevent the opening of the will after the death of the testator if necessary in order to determine the executor or other interested persons to be notified. Nor should it prevent opening the will to

microfilm for confidential record storage, for example. These matters could again be regulated by Court rule.

It is suggested that in the near future it may be desirable to develop a central filing system regarding the presence of deposited wills, because the mobility of our modern population makes it probable that the testator will not die in the county where his will is deposited. Thus a statute might require that the local registrar notify an appropriate official, that the will is on file; the state official would in effect provide a clearing-house for information on location of deposited wills without disrupting the local administration.

The provision permitting examination of a will of a protected person by the conservator supplements Section 5–427.

Section 2–902. [Duty of Custodian of Will; Liability.]

After the death of a testator and on request of an interested person, any person having custody of a will of the testator shall deliver it with reasonable promptness to a person able to secure its probate and if none is

574

known, to an appropriate Court. Any person who wilfully fails to deliver a will is liable to any person aggrieved for the damages which may be sustained by the failure. Any person who wilfully refuses or fails to deliver a will after being ordered by the Court in a proceeding brought for the purpose of compelling delivery is subject to penalty for contempt of Court.

COMMENT

Model Probate Code Section 63, slightly changed. A person authorized by a Court to accept delivery of a will from a custodian may, in addition to a registrar or clerk, be a universal successor or other person authorized under the law of another nation to carry out the terms of a will.

APPENDIX B: PRE–1989 UPC ARTICLE VI

NON–PROBATE TRANSFERS

PART 1

MULTIPLE–PARTY ACCOUNTS

PART 2

PROVISIONS RELATING TO EFFECT OF DEATH

PART 1

MULTIPLE–PARTY ACCOUNTS

Section 6–101. [Definitions.]

In this part, unless the context otherwise requires:

(1) "account" means a contract of deposit of funds between a depositor and a financial institution, and includes a checking account, savings account, certificate of deposit, share account and other like arrangement;

(2) "beneficiary" means a person named in a trust account as one for whom a party to the account is named as trustee;

(3) "financial institution" means any organization authorized to do business under state or federal laws relating to financial institutions, including, without limitation, banks and trust companies, savings banks, building and loan associations, savings and loan companies or associations, and credit unions;

(4) "joint account" means an account payable on request to one or more of two or more parties whether or not mention is made of any right of survivorship;

(5) a "multiple-party account" is any of the following types of account: (i) a joint account, (ii) a P.O.D. account, or (iii) a trust account. It does not include accounts established for deposit of funds of a partnership, joint venture, or other association for business purposes, or accounts controlled by one or more persons as the duly authorized agent or trustee for a corporation, unincorporated association, charitable or civic organization or a regular fiduciary or trust account where the relationship is established other than by deposit agreement;

(6) "net contribution" of a party to a joint account as of any given time is the sum of all deposits thereto made by or for him, less all withdrawals made by or for him which have not been paid to or applied to the use of any other party, plus a pro rata share of any interest or dividends included in the current balance. The term includes, in addition, any proceeds of deposit life insurance added to the account by reason of the death of the party whose net contribution is in question;

(7) "party" means a person who, by the terms of the account, has a present right, subject to request, to payment from a multiple-party account. A P.O.D. payee or beneficiary of a trust account is a party only after the account becomes payable to him by reason of his surviving the original payee or trustee. Unless the context otherwise requires, it includes a guardian, conservator, personal representative, or assignee, including an attaching creditor, of a party. It also includes a person identified as a trustee of an account for another whether or not a beneficiary is named,

577

but it does not include any named beneficiary unless he has a present right of withdrawal;

(8) "payment" of sums on deposit includes withdrawal, payment on check or other directive of a party, and any pledge of sums on deposit by a party and any set-off, or reduction or other disposition of all or part of an account pursuant to a pledge;

(9) "proof of death" includes a death certificate or record or report which is prima facie proof of death under Section 1–107;

(10) "P.O.D. account" means an account payable on request to one person during his lifetime and on his death to one or more P.O.D. payees, or to one or more persons during their lifetimes and on the death of all of them to one or more P.O.D. payees;

(11) "P.O.D. payee" means a person designated on a P.O.D. account as one to whom the account is payable on request after the death of one or more persons;

(12) "request" means a proper request for withdrawal, or a check or order for payment, which complies with all conditions of the account, including special requirements concerning necessary signatures and regulations of the financial institution; but if the financial institution conditions withdrawal or payment on advance notice, for purposes of this part the request for withdrawal or payment is treated as immediately effective and a notice of intent to withdraw is treated as a request for withdrawal;

(13) "sums on deposit" means the balance payable on a multiple-party account including interest, dividends, and in addition any deposit life insurance proceeds added to the account by reason of the death of a party;

(14) "trust account" means an account in the name of one or more parties as trustee for one or more beneficiaries where the relationship is established by the form of the account and the deposit agreement with the financial institution and there is no subject of the trust other than the sums on deposit in the account; it is not essential that payment to the beneficiary be mentioned in the deposit agreement. A trust account does not include a regular trust account under a testamentary trust or a trust agreement which has significance apart from the account, or a fiduciary account arising from a fiduciary relation such as attorney-client;

(15) "withdrawal" includes payment to a third person pursuant to check or other directive of a party.

COMMENT

This and the sections which follow are designed to reduce certain questions concerning many forms of joint accounts and the so-called Totten trust account. An account "payable on death" is also authorized.

As may be seen from examination of the sections that follow, "net contribution" as defined by subsection (f) has no application to the financial institution-depositor relationship. Rather, it is relevant only to controversies that may arise between parties to a multiple-party account.

Various signature requirements may be involved in order to meet the withdrawal requirements of the account. A "request" involves compliance with these requirements. A "party" is one to whom an account is presently payable without regard for whose signature may be required for a "request."

Section 6–102. [Ownership as Between Parties, and Others; Protection of Financial Institutions.]

The provisions of Sections 6–103 to 6–105 concerning beneficial ownership as between parties, or as between parties and P.O.D. payees or beneficiaries of multiple-party accounts, are relevant only to controversies between these persons and their creditors and other successors, and have no bearing on the power of withdrawal of these persons as determined by the terms of account contracts. The provisions of Sections 6–108 to 6–113 govern the liability of financial institutions who make payments pursuant thereto, and their set-off rights.

COMMENT

This section organizes the sections which follow into those dealing with the relationship between parties to multiple-party accounts, on the one hand, and those relating to the financial institution-depositor (or party) relationship, on the other. By keeping these relationships separate, it is possible to achieve the degree of definiteness that financial institutions must have in order to be induced to offer multiple-party accounts for use by their customers, while preserving the opportunity for individuals involved in multiple-party accounts to show various intentions that may have attended the original deposit, or any unusual transactions affecting the account thereafter. The separation thus permits individuals using accounts of the type dealt with by these sections to avoid unconsidered and unwanted definiteness in regard to their relationship with each other. In a sense, the approach is to implement a layman's wish to "trust" a co-depositor by leaving questions that may arise between them essentially unaffected by the form of the account.

Section 6–103. [Ownership During Lifetime.]

(a) A joint account belongs, during the lifetime of all parties, to the parties in proportion to the net contributions by each to the sums on deposit, unless there is clear and convincing evidence of a different intent.

(b) A P.O.D. account belongs to the original payee during his lifetime and not to the P.O.D. payee or payees; if two or more parties are named as original payees, during their lifetimes rights as between them are governed by subsection (a) of this section.

(c) Unless a contrary intent is manifested by the terms of the account or the deposit agreement or there is other clear and convincing evidence of an irrevocable trust, a trust account belongs beneficially to the trustee during his lifetime, and if two or more parties are named as trustee on the account, during their lifetimes beneficial rights as between them are governed by subsection (a) of this section. If there is an irrevocable trust, the account belongs beneficially to the beneficiary.

COMMENT

This section reflects the assumption that a person who deposits funds in a multiple-party account normally does not intend to make an irrevocable gift of all or any part of the funds represented by the deposit. Rather, he usually intends no present change of beneficial ownership. The assumption may be disproved by proof that a gift was intended. Read with Section 6–101(6) which defines "net contributions," the section permits parties to certain kinds of multiple-party accounts to be as definite, or as indefinite, as they wish in respect to the matter of how beneficial ownership should be apportioned between them. It is important to note that the section is limited to describe ownership of an account while original parties are alive. Section 6–104 prescribes what happens to beneficial ownership on the death of a party. The section does not undertake to describe the situation between parties if one withdraws more than he is then entitled to as against the other party. Sections 6–108 and 6–112 protect a financial institution in such circumstances without reference to whether a withdrawing party may be entitled to less than he withdraws as against another party. Presumably, overwithdrawal leaves the party making the excessive withdrawal liable to the beneficial owner

as a debtor or trustee. Of course, evidence of intention by one to make a gift to the other of any sums withdrawn by the other in excess of his ownership should be effective.

The final Code contains no provision dealing with division of the account when the parties fail to prove net contributions. The omission is deliberate. Undoubtedly a court would divide the account equally among the parties to the extent that net contributions cannot be proven; but a statutory section explicitly embodying the rule might undesirably narrow the possibility of proof of partial contributions and might suggest that gift tax consequences applicable to creation of a joint tenancy should attach to a joint account. The theory of these sections is that the basic relationship of the parties is that of individual ownership of values attributable to their respective deposits and withdrawals; the right of survivorship which attaches unless negated by the form of the account really is a right to the values theretofore owned by another which the survivor receives for the first time at the death of the owner. That is to say, the account operates as a valid disposition at death rather than as a present joint tenancy.

Section 6–104. [Right of Survivorship.]

(a) Sums remaining on deposit at the death of a party to a joint account belong to the surviving party or parties as against the estate of the decedent unless there is clear and convincing evidence of a different intention at the time the account is created. If there are 2 or more surviving parties, their respective ownerships during lifetime shall be in proportion to their previous ownership interests under Section 6–103 augmented by an equal share for each survivor of any interest the decedent may have owned in the account immediately before his death; and the right of survivorship continues between the surviving parties.

(b) if the account is a P.O.D. account;

(1) on death of one of 2 or more original payees the rights to any sums remaining on deposit are governed by subsection (a);

(2) on death of the sole original payee or of the survivor of two or more original payees, any sums remaining on deposit belong to the P.O.D. payee or payees if surviving, or to the survivor of them if one or more die before the original payee; if 2 or more P.O.D. payees survive, there is no right of survivorship in the event of death of a P.O.D. payee thereafter unless the terms of the account or deposit agreement expressly provide for survivorship between them.

(c) if the account is a trust account;

(1) on death of one of 2 or more trustees, the rights to any sums remaining on deposit are governed by subsection (a);

(2) on death of the sole trustee or the survivor of 2 or more trustees, any sums remaining on deposit belong to the person or persons named as beneficiaries, if surviving, or to the survivor of them if one or more die before the trustee, unless there is clear evidence of a contrary intent; if 2 or more beneficiaries survive, there is no right of survivorship in event of death of any beneficiary thereafter unless the terms of the account or deposit agreement expressly provide for survivorship between them.

(d) In other cases, the death of any party to a multiple-party account has no effect on beneficial ownership of the account other than to transfer the rights of the decedent as part of his estate.

(e) A right of survivorship arising from the express terms of the account or under this section, a beneficiary designation in a trust account, or a P.O.D. payee designation, cannot be changed by will.

COMMENT

The effect of (a) of this section, when read with the definition of "joint account" in 6–101(4), is to make an account payable to one or more of two or more parties a survivorship arrangement unless "clear and convincing evidence of a different contention" is offered.

The underlying assumption is that most persons who use joint accounts want the survivor or survivors to have all balances remaining at death. This assumption may be questioned in states like Michigan where existing statutes and decisions do not provide any safe and wholly practical method of establishing a joint account which is not survivorship. See Leib v. Genesee Merchants Bank, 371 Mich. 89, 123 N.W.(2d) 140 (1962). But, use of a form negating survivorship would make (d) of this section applicable. Still, the finan-

cial institution which paid after the death of a party would be protected by 6–108 and 6–109. Thus, a safe nonsurvivorship account form is provided. Consequently, the presumption stated by this section should become increasingly defensible.

The section also is designed to apply to various forms of multiple-party accounts which may be in use at the effective date of the legislation. The risk that it may turn nonsurvivorship accounts into unwanted survivorship arrangements is meliorated by various considerations. First of all, there is doubt that many persons using any form of multiple name account would not want survivorship rights to attach. Secondly, the survivorship incidents described by this section may be shown to have been against the intention of the parties. Finally, it would be wholly consistent with the purpose of the legislation to provide for a delayed effective date so that financial institutions could get notices to customers warning them of possible review of accounts which may be desirable because of the legislation.

Subsection (c) accepts the New York view that an account opened by "A" in his name as "trustee for B" usually is intended by A to be an informal will of any balance remaining on deposit at his death. The section is framed so that accounts with more than one "trustee," or more than one "beneficiary" can be accommodated. Section 6–103(c) would apply to such an account during the lifetimes of "all parties." "Party" is defined by 6–101(7) so as to exclude a beneficiary who is not described by the account as having a present right of withdrawal.

In the case of a trust account for two or more beneficiaries, the section prescribes a presumption that all beneficiaries who survive the last "trustee" to die own equal and undivided interests in the account. This dovetails with Sections 6–111 and 6–112 which give the financial institution protection only if it pays to all beneficiaries who show a right to withdraw by presenting appropriate proof of death. No further survivorship between surviving beneficiaries of a trust account is presumed because these persons probably have had no control over the form of the account prior to the death of the trustee. The situation concerning further survivorship between two or more surviving parties to a joint account is different.

In 1975, the Joint Editorial Board recommended expansion of subsections (b) and (c) so that the subsections now deal explicitly with cases involving multiple original payees in P.O.D. accounts, and multiple trustees in trust accounts. These changes were conceived to clarify, rather than to change, the text.

Section 6–105. [Effect of Written Notice to Financial Institution.]

The provisions of Section 6–104 as to rights of survivorship are determined by the form of the account at the death of a party. This form may be altered by written order given by a party to the financial institution to change the form of the account or to stop or vary payment under the terms of the account. The order or request must be signed by a party, received by the financial institution during the party's lifetime, and not countermanded by other written order of the same party during his lifetime.

COMMENT

It is to be noted that only a "party" may issue an order blocking the provisions of Section 6–104. "Party" is defined by Section 6–101(7). Thus if there is a trust account in the name of A or B in trust for C, C cannot change the right of survivorship because he has no present right of withdrawal and hence is not a party.

Section 6–106. [Accounts and Transfers Nontestamentary.]

Any transfers resulting from the application of Section 6–104 are effective by reason of the account contracts involved and this statute and are not to be considered as testamentary or subject to Articles I through IV, except as provided in Sections 2–201 through 2–207, and except as a consequence of, and to the extent directed by, Section 6–107.

COMMENT

The purpose of classifying the transactions contemplated by Article VI as nontestamentary is to bolster the explicit statement that their validity as effective modes of transfers at death is not to be determined by the requirements for wills. The section is consistent with Part 2 of Article VI.

The closing reference to Article II, Part 2, and to 6–107 was added in 1975 at the recommendation of the Joint Editorial Board to clarify the intention of the original text.

Section 6–107. [Rights of Creditors.]

No multiple-party account will be effective against an estate of a deceased party to transfer to a survivor sums needed to pay debts, taxes, and expenses of administration, including statutory allowances to the surviving spouse, minor children and dependent children, if other assets of the estate are insufficient. A surviving party, P.O.D. payee, or beneficiary who receives payment from a multiple-party account after the death of a deceased party shall be liable to account to his personal representative for amounts the decedent owned beneficially immediately before his death to the extent necessary to discharge the claims and charges mentioned above remaining unpaid after application of the decedent's estate. No proceeding to assert this liability shall be commenced unless the personal representative has received a written demand by a surviving spouse, a creditor or one acting for a minor or dependent child of the decedent, and no proceeding shall be commenced later than two years following the death of the decedent. Sums recovered by the personal representative shall be administered as part of the decedent's estate. This section shall not affect the right of a financial institution to make payment on multiple-party accounts according to the terms thereof, or make it liable to the estate of a deceased party unless before payment the institution has been served with process in a proceeding by the personal representative.

COMMENT

The sections of this Article authorize transfers at death which reduce the estate to which the surviving spouse, creditors and minor children normally must look for protection against a decedent's gifts by will. Accordingly, it seemed desirable to provide a remedy to these classes of persons which should assure them that multiple-party accounts cannot be used to reduce the essential protection they would be entitled to if such accounts were deemed to permit a special form of specific devise. Under this Section a surviving spouse is automatically assured of some protection against a multiple-party account if the probate

estate is insolvent; rights are limited, however, to sums needed for statutory allowances. The phrase "statutory allowances" includes the homestead allowance under Section 2–401, the family allowance under Section 2–403, and any allowance needed to make up the deficiency in exempt property under Section 2–402. In any case (including a solvent estate) the surviving spouse could proceed under Section 2–201 et seq. to claim an elective share in the account if the deposits by the decedent satisfy the requirements of Section 2–202 so that the account falls within the augmented net estate concept. In the latter situa-

tion the spouse is not proceeding as a
creditor under this section.

Section 6–108. [Financial Institution Protection; Payment on Signature of One Party.]

Financial institutions may enter into multiple-party accounts to the same extent that they may enter into single-party accounts. Any multiple-party account may be paid, on request, to any one or more of the parties. A financial institution shall not be required to inquire as to the source of funds received for deposit to a multiple-party account, or to inquire as to the proposed application of any sum withdrawn from an account, for purposes of establishing net contributions.

Section 6–109. [Financial Institution Protection; Payment After Death or Disability; Joint Account.]

Any sums in a joint account may be paid, on request, to any party without regard to whether any other party is incapacitated or deceased at the time the payment is demanded; but payment may not be made to the personal representative or heirs of a deceased party unless proofs of death are presented to the financial institution showing that the decedent was the last surviving party or unless there is no right of survivorship under Section 6–104.

Section 6–110. [Financial Institution Protection; Payment of P.O.D. Account.]

Any P.O.D. account may be paid, on request, to any original party to the account. Payment may be made, on request, to the P.O.D. payee or to the personal representative or heirs of a deceased P.O.D. payee upon presentation to the financial institution of proof of death showing that the P.O.D. payee survived all persons named as original payees. Payment may be made to the personal representative or heirs of a deceased original payee if proof of death is presented to the financial institution showing that his decedent was the survivor of all other persons named on the account either as an original payee or as P.O.D. payee.

Section 6–111. [Financial Institution Protection; Payment of Trust Account.]

Any trust account may be paid, on request, to any trustee. Unless the financial institution has received written notice that the beneficiary has a vested interest not dependent upon his surviving the trustee, payment may be made to the personal representative or heirs of a deceased trustee if proof of death is presented to the financial institution showing that his decedent was the survivor of all other persons named on the account either as trustee or beneficiary. Payment may be made, on request, to the beneficiary upon presentation to the financial institution of proof of death showing that the beneficiary or beneficiaries survived all persons named as trustees.

Section 6–112. [Financial Institution Protection; Discharge.]

Payment made pursuant to Sections 6–108, 6–109, 6–110 or 6–111 discharges the financial institution from all claims for amounts so paid whether or not the payment is consistent with the beneficial ownership of the account as between parties, P.O.D. payees, or beneficiaries, or their successors. The protection here given does not extend to payments made after a financial institution has received written notice from any party able to request present payment to the effect that withdrawals in accordance with the terms of the account should not be permitted. Unless the notice is withdrawn by the person giving it, the successor of any deceased party must concur in any demand for withdrawal if the financial institution is to be protected under this section. No other notice or any other information shown to have been available to a financial institution shall affect its right to the protection provided here. The protection here provided shall have no bearing on the rights of parties in disputes between themselves or their successors concerning the beneficial ownership of funds in, or withdrawn from, multiple-party accounts.

Section 6–113. [Financial Institution Protection; Set-Off.]

Without qualifying any other statutory right to set-off or lien and subject to any contractual provision, if a party to a multiple-party account is indebted to a financial institution, the financial institution has a right to set-off against the account in which the party has or had immediately before his death a present right of withdrawal. The amount of the account subject to set-off is that proportion to which the debtor is, or was immediately before his death, beneficially entitled, and in the absence of proof of net contributions, to an equal share with all parties having present rights of withdrawal.

PART 2

PROVISIONS RELATING TO EFFECT OF DEATH

Section 6–201. [Provisions for Payment or Transfer at Death.]

(a) Any of the following provisions in an insurance policy, contract of employment, bond, mortgage, promissory note, deposit agreement, pension plan, trust agreement, conveyance or any other written instrument effective as a contract, gift, conveyance, or trust is deemed to be nontestamentary, and this Code does not invalidate the instrument or any provision:

(1) that money or other benefits theretofore due to, controlled or owned by a decedent shall be paid after his death to a person designated by the decedent in either the instrument or a separate writing, including a will, executed at the same time as the instrument or subsequently;

(2) that any money due or to become due under the instrument shall cease to be payable in event of the death of the promisee or the promissor before payment or demand; or

(3) that any property which is the subject of the instrument shall pass to a person designated by the decedent in either the instrument or a separate writing, including a will, executed at the same time as the instrument or subsequently.

(b) Nothing in this section limits the rights of creditors under other laws of this state.

COMMENT

This section authorizes a variety of contractual arrangements which have in the past been treated as testamentary. For example most courts treat as testamentary a provision in a promissory note that if the payee dies before payment is made the note shall be paid to another named person, or a provision in a land contract that if the seller dies before payment is completed the balance shall be cancelled and the property shall belong to the vendee. These provisions often occur in family arrangements. The result of holding the provisions testamentary is usually to invalidate them because not executed in accordance with the statute of wills. On the other hand the same courts have for years upheld beneficiary designations in life insurance contracts. Similar kinds of problems are arising in regard to beneficiary designations in pension funds and under annuity contracts. The analogy of the power of appointment provides some historical base for solving some of these problems aside from a validating statute. However, there appear to be no policy reasons for continuing to treat these varied arrangements as testamentary. The revocable living trust and the multiple-party bank accounts, as well as the experience with United States government bonds payable on death to named beneficiaries, have demonstrated that the evils envisioned if the statute of wills is not rigidly enforced simply do not materialize. The fact that these provisions often are part of a business transaction and in any event are evidenced by a writing eliminate the danger of "fraud."

Because the types of provisions described in the statute are characterized as nontestamentary, the instrument does not have to be executed in compliance with Section 2–502; nor does it have to be probated, nor does the personal representative have any power or duty with respect to the assets involved.

The sole purpose of this section is to eliminate the testamentary characterization from the arrangements falling within the terms of the section. It does not invalidate other arrangements by negative implication. Thus it is not intended by this section to embrace oral trusts to hold property at death for named persons; such arrangements are already generally enforceable under trust law.

*

SELECTED
UNIFORM ACTS

REVISED UNIFORM PRINCIPAL
AND INCOME ACT

PREFATORY NOTE

In 1959 the National Conference of Commissioners on Uniform State Laws created a committee of its members to prepare a revision of the Uniform Principal and Income Act which had been approved by the Commissioners in 1931. Early in its deliberations the committee proposed to submit a revised Act rather than a series of correcting amendments to the existing Act. The committee submitted three different drafts of an Act to three separate annual conferences from 1960 to 1962. In the latter year the final draft of the Uniform Revised Principal and Income Act was approved by the Commissioners and later was approved by the American Bar Association.

Request for revision of the old Act came from several sources, particularly from trustees who found it difficult to administer trusts under the older Act due to the development of new forms of investment property for trustees. This new development was especially true in the field of corporate distributions and also in the holding of mineral resources as a trust investment. The revised Act provides as did the original Act that the settlor's intent is the guiding principle which should control the disposition of all receipts. But settlors have not always foreseen the multitude of problems which may have to be faced and even draftsmen have found it difficult to foresee all the possible kinds of receipts and disbursements. It is important, therefore, to set forth some clear and uniform standards to assist those to whom the power of decision has been committed, that is, the trustees, and this Act attempts to provide these standards.

The aim of the revised Act is simplicity and convenience of administration of the estate. Of course, fairness to all beneficiaries both present and future has also been considered. Because simplicity and convenience were a primary aim of the revised Act, the revised Act unlike the original Act is made applicable to all trusts and estates whether in existence at the time the revised Act becomes law or not. A trustee who administers several trusts, it was thought, would have difficulty attempting to administer the various trusts under different rules for distribution of receipts and allocation of disbursements and it was thought better, therefore, to make the Act applicable to all trusts. The original Act had no section treating with income earned during administration of a decedent's estate. Several years before it was decided to revise the Uniform Act the Commissioners had promulgated an amendment to the original Act dealing with this problem and this amendment is in substance carried forward into the revised Act.

The original Act followed the so-called "Massachusetts Rule" of awarding cash dividends on corporate stock to income and stock dividends to principal, thereby rejecting the Pennsylvania Rule or some variation of it requiring apportionment between the two funds. The revised Act continues to follow the Massachusetts Rule but provides for some newer problems which have arisen since the original Act was promulgated. Thus provision is now made for corporate distributions pursuant to a court decree such as a divestiture order in an antitrust suit. Provision is also made for treatment of the distributions of a regulated investment company or real estate investment trust. Since the original Act was promulgated development has occurred in methods of issuing bonds, notably the discount type of bond such as the Series E bond of the United States government and provision has been made for allocating the increment in value between principal and income. When the various states considered and adopted the original Act there were a lot of changes made in the section concerning disposition of natural resources. The revised Act attempts to collect the most common of these variations and provides for an allocation of natural resources substantially different from that provided in the original Act but not substantially different form the rules adopted in many of the states producing natural resources. Because of the difficulty of apportioning receipts from extraction of natural resources among the income and principal beneficiaries it is provided in the revised Act that an arbitrary allocation should occur, that is, 27½% of the gross receipts shall be added to principal as a "depletion reserve," and the balance should be payable to the income beneficiary. Attempts to apportion the receipts on the relation of the amount of minerals extracted to the amount of minerals remaining in the ground have proved difficult of calculation and this method of allocation was accordingly rejected in favor of simplicity.

While the revised Act continues to deal specifically with a number of subjects as did the original Act, the revised Act also contains a "catch-all" providing for disposition of receipts where there is no specific section in the Act dealing with the allocation. A form of "prudent man" rule has been adopted to handle this situation.

The Act, therefore, sets forth simple and workable rules of administration which are believed to be consistent with the wishes of settlors upon the subject treated unless the settlor specifically provides for a different treatment in his own trust instrument.

Table of Sections

Section 1. [*Definitions.*]

As used in this Act:

(1) "income beneficiary" means the person to whom income is presently payable or for whom it is accumulated for distribution as income;

(2) "inventory value" means the cost of property purchased by the trustee and the market value of other property at the time it became subject to the trust, but in the case of a testamentary trust the trustee may use any value finally determined for the purposes of an estate or inheritance tax;

(3) "remainderman" means the person entitled to principal, including income which has been accumulated and added to principal;

(4) "trustee" means an original trustee and any successor or added trustee.

Section 2. [*Duty of Trustee as to Receipts and Expenditures.*]

(a) A trust shall be administered with due regard to the respective interests of income beneficiaries and remaindermen. A trust is so administered with respect to the allocation of receipts and expenditures if a receipt is credited or an expenditure is charged to income or principal or partly to each—

(1) in accordance with the terms of the trust instrument, notwithstanding contrary provisions of this Act;

(2) in the absence of any contrary terms of the trust instrument, in accordance with the provisions of this Act; or

(3) if neither of the preceding rules of administration is applicable, in accordance with what is reasonable and equitable in view of the interests of those entitled to income as well as of those entitled to principal, and in view of the manner in which men of ordinary prudence, discretion and judgment would act in the management of their own affairs.

(b) If the trust instrument gives the trustee discretion in crediting a receipt or charging an expenditure to income or principal or partly to each, no inference of imprudence or partiality arises from the fact that the trustee has made an allocation contrary to a provision of this Act.

Section 3. [*Income; Principal; Charges.*]

(a) Income is the return in money or property derived from the use of principal, including return received as

(1) rent of real or personal property, including sums received for cancellation or renewal of a lease;

(2) interest on money lent, including sums received as consideration for the privilege of prepayment of principal except as provided in section 7 on bond premium and bond discount;

(3) income earned during administration of a decedent's estate as provided in section 5;

(4) corporate distributions as provided in section 6;

(5) accrued increment on bonds or other obligations issued at discount as provided in section 7;

(6) receipts from business and farming operations as provided in section 8;

(7) receipts from disposition of natural resources as provided in sections 9 and 10;

(8) receipts from other principal subject to depletion as provided in section 11;

(9) receipts from disposition of underproductive property as provided in section 12.

(b) Principal is the property which has been set aside by the owner or the person legally empowered so that it is held in trust eventually to be delivered to a remainderman while the return or use of the principal is in the meantime taken or received by or held for accumulation for an income beneficiary. Principal includes

(1) consideration received by the trustee on the sale or other transfer of principal or on repayment of a loan or as a refund or replacement or change in the form of principal;

(2) proceeds of property taken on eminent domain proceedings;

(3) proceeds of insurance upon property forming part of the principal except proceeds of insurance upon a separate interest of an income beneficiary;

(4) stock dividends, receipts on liquidation of a corporation, and other corporate distributions as provided in section 6;

(5) receipts from the disposition of corporate securities as provided in section 7;

(6) royalties and other receipts from disposition of natural resources as provided in sections 9 and 10;

(7) receipts from other principal subject to depletion as provided in section 11;

(8) any profit resulting from any change in the form of principal except as provided in section 12 on underproductive property;

(9) receipts from disposition of underproductive property as provided in section 12;

(10) any allowances for depreciation established under sections 8 and 13(a)(2).

(c) After determining income and principal in accordance with the terms of the trust instrument or of this Act, the trustee shall charge to income or principal expenses and other charges as provided in section 13.

Section 4. [When Right to Income Arises; Apportionment of Income.]

(a) An income beneficiary is entitled to income from the date specified in the trust instrument, or, if none is specified, from the date an asset becomes subject to the trust. In the case of an asset becoming subject to a trust by reason of a will, it becomes subject to the trust as of the date of the death of the testator even though there is an intervening period of administration of the testator's estate.

(b) In the administration of a decedent's estate or an asset becoming subject to a trust by reason of a will

(1) receipts due but not paid at the date of death of the testator are principal;

(2) receipts in the form of periodic payments (other than corporate distributions to stockholders), including rent, interest, or annuities, not due at the date of the death of the testator shall be treated as accruing from day to day. That portion of the receipt accruing before the date of death is principal, and the balance is income.

(c) In all other cases, any receipt from an income producing asset is income even though the receipt was earned or accrued in whole or in part before the date when the asset became subject to the trust.

(d) On termination of an income interest, the income beneficiary whose interest is terminated, or his estate, is entitled to

(1) income undistributed on the date of termination;

(2) income due but not paid to the trustee on the date of termination;

(3) income in the form of periodic payments (other than corporate distributions to stockholders), including rent, interest or annuities, not due on the date of termination, accrued from day to day.

(e) Corporate distributions to stockholders shall be treated as due on the day fixed by the corporation for determination of stockholders of record entitled to distribution or, if no date is fixed, on the date of declaration of the distribution by the corporation.

Section 5. [*Income Earned During Administration of a Decedent's Estate.*]

(a) Unless the will otherwise provides and subject to subsection (b), all expenses incurred in connection with the settlement of a decedent's estate, including debts, funeral expenses, estate taxes, interest and penalties concerning taxes, family allowances, fees of attorneys and personal representatives, and court costs shall be charged against the principal of the estate.

(b) Unless the will otherwise provides, income from the assets of a decedent's estate after the death of the testator and before distribution, including income from property used to discharge liabilities, shall be determined in accordance with the rules applicable to a trustee under this Act and distributed as follows:

(1) to specific legatees and devisees, the income from the property bequeathed or devised to them respectively, less taxes, ordinary repairs, and other expenses of management and operation of the property, and an appropriate portion of interest accrued since the death of the testator and of taxes imposed on income (excluding taxes on capital gains) which accrue during the period of administration;

(2) to all other legatees and devisees, except legatees of pecuniary bequests not in trust, the balance of the income, less the balance of taxes, ordinary repairs, and other expenses of management and operation of all property from which the estate is entitled to income, interest accrued since the death of the testator, and taxes imposed on income (excluding taxes on capital gains) which accrue during the period of administration, in proportion to their respective interests in the undistributed assets of the estate computed at times of distribution on the basis of inventory value.

(c) Income received by a trustee under subsection (b) shall be treated as income of the trust.

Section 6. [*Corporate Distributions.*]

(a) Corporate distributions of shares of the distributing corporation, including distributions in the form of a stock split or stock dividend, are principal. A right to subscribe to shares or other securities issued by the distributing corporation accruing to stockholders on account of their stock ownership and the proceeds of any sale of the right are principal.

(b) Except to the extent that the corporation indicates that some part of a corporate distribution is a settlement of preferred or guaranteed dividends accrued since the trustee became a stockholder or is in lieu of an ordinary cash dividend, a corporate distribution is principal if the distribution is pursuant to

(1) a call of shares;

(2) a merger, consolidation, reorganization, or other plan by which assets of the corporation are acquired by another corporation; or

(3) a total or partial liquidation of the corporation, including any distribution which the corporation indicates is a distribution in total or partial liquidation or any distribution of assets, other than cash, pursuant to a court decree or final administrative order by a government agency ordering distribution of the particular assets.

(c) Distributions made from ordinary income by a regulated investment company or by a trust qualifying and electing to be taxed under federal law as a real estate investment trust are income. All other distributions made by the company or trust, including distributions from capital gains, depreciation, or depletion, whether in the form of cash or an option to take new stock or cash or an option to purchase additional shares, are principal.

(d) Except as provided in subsections (a), (b), and (c), all corporate distributions are income, including cash dividends, distributions of or rights to subscribe to shares or securities or obligations of corporations other than the distributing corporation, and the proceeds of the rights or property distributions. Except as provided in subsections (b) and (c), if the distributing corporation gives a stockholder an option to receive a distribution either in cash or in its own shares, the distribution chosen is income.

(e) The trustee may rely upon any statement of the distributing corporation as to any fact relevant under any provision of this Act concerning the source or character of dividends or distributions of corporate assets.

Section 7. [*Bond Premium and Discount.*]

(a) Bonds or other obligations for the payment of money are principal at their inventory value, except as provided in subsection (b) for discount bonds. No provision shall be made for amortization of bond premiums or for accumulation for discount. The proceeds of sale, redemption, or other disposition of the bonds or obligations are principal.

(b) The increment in value of a bond or other obligation for the payment of money payable at a future time in accordance with a fixed schedule of appreciation in excess of the price at which it was issued is distributable as income. The increment in value is distributable to the beneficiary who was the income beneficiary at the time of increment from the first principal cash available or, if none is available, when realized by sale, redemption, or other disposition. Whenever unrealized increment is distributed as income but out of principal, the principal shall be reimbursed for the increment when realized.

Section 8. [*Business and Farming Operations.*]

(a) If a trustee uses any part of the principal in the continuance of a business of which the settlor was a sole proprietor or a partner, the net profits of the business, computed in accordance with generally accepted accounting principles for a comparable business, are income. If a loss results in any fiscal or calendar year, the loss falls on principal and shall not be carried into any other fiscal or calendar year for purposes of calculating net income.

(b) Generally accepted accounting principles shall be used to determine income from an agricultural or farming operation, including the raising of animals or the operation of a nursery.

Section 9. [*Disposition of Natural Resources.*]

(a) If any part of the principal consists of a right to receive royalties, overriding or limited royalties, working interests, production payments, net profit interests, or other interests in minerals or other natural resources in, on or under land, the receipts from taking the natural resources from the land shall be allocated as follows:

(1) If received as rent on a lease or extension payments on a lease, the receipts are income.

(2) If received from a production payment, the receipts are income to the extent of any factor for interest or its equivalent provided in the governing instrument. There shall be allocated to principal the fraction of the balance of the receipts which the unrecovered cost of the production payments bears to the balance owed on the production payment, exclusive of any factor for interest or its equivalent. The receipts not allocated to principal are income.

(3) If received as a royalty, overriding or limited royalty, or bonus, or from a working, net profit, or any other interest in minerals or other natural resources, receipts not provided for in the preceding paragraphs of this section shall be apportioned on a yearly basis in accordance with this paragraph whether or not any natural resource was being taken from the land at the time the trust was established. Twenty-seven and one-half per cent of the gross receipts (but not to exceed 50% of the net receipts remaining after payment of all expenses, direct and indirect, computed without allowance for depletion) shall be added to principal as an allowance for depletion. The balance of the gross receipts, after payment therefrom of all expenses, direct and indirect, is income.

(b) If a trustee, on the effective date of this Act, held an item of depletable property of a type specified in this section he shall allocate receipts from the property in the manner used before the effective date of this Act, but as to all depletable property acquired after the effective date of this Act by an existing or new trust, the method of allocation provided herein shall be used.

(c) This section does not apply to timber, water, soil, sod, dirt, turf, or mosses.

Section 10. *[Timber.]*

If any part of the principal consists of land from which merchantable timber may be removed, the receipts from taking the timber from the land shall be allocated in accordance with section 2(a)(3).

Section 11. *[Other Property Subject to Depletion.]*

Except as provided in sections 9 and 10, if the principal consists of property subject to depletion, including leaseholds, patents, copyrights, royalty rights, and rights to receive payments on a contract for deferred compensation, receipts from the property, not in excess of 5% per year of its inventory value, are income, and the balance is principal.

Section 12. *[Underproductive Property.]*

(a) Except as otherwise provided in this section, a portion of the net proceeds of sale of any part of principal which has not produced an average net income of at least 1% per year of its inventory value for more than a year (including as income the value of any beneficial use of the property by the income beneficiary) shall be treated as delayed income to which the income beneficiary is entitled as provided in this section. The net proceeds of sale are the gross proceeds received, including the value of any property received in substitution for the property disposed of, less the expenses, including capital gains tax, if any, incurred in disposition and less any carrying charge paid while the property was underproductive.

(b) The sum allocated as delayed income is the difference between the net proceeds and the amount which, had it been invested at simple interest at [4%] per year while the property was underproductive, would have produced the net proceeds. This sum, plus any carrying charges and expenses previously charged against income while the property was underproductive, less any income received by the income beneficiary from the property and less the value of any beneficial use of the property by the income beneficiary, is income, and the balance is principal.

(c) An income beneficiary or his estate is entitled to delayed income under this section as if it accrued from day to day during the time he was a beneficiary.

(d) If principal subject to this section is disposed of by conversion into property which cannot be apportioned easily, including land or mortgages (for example, realty acquired by or in lieu of foreclosure), the income beneficiary is entitled to the net income from any property or obligation into which the original principal is converted while the substituted property or obligation is held. If within 5 years after the conversion the substituted property has not been further converted into easily apportionable property, no allocation as provided in this section shall be made.

Section 13. [Charges Against Income and Principal.]

(a) The following charges shall be made against income:

(1) ordinary expenses incurred in connection with the administration, management, or preservation of the trust property, including regularly recurring taxes assessed against any portion of the principal, water rates, premiums on insurance taken upon the interests of the income beneficiary, remainderman, or trustee, interest paid by the trustee, and ordinary repairs;

(2) a reasonable allowance for depreciation on property subject to depreciation under generally accepted accounting principles, but no allowance shall be made for depreciation of that portion of any real property used by a beneficiary as a residence or for depreciation of any property held by the trustee on the effective date of this Act for which the trustee is not then making an allowance for depreciation;

(3) one-half of court costs, attorney's fees, and other fees on periodic judicial accounting, unless the court directs otherwise;

(4) court costs, attorney's fees, and other fees on other accountings or judicial proceedings if the matter primarily concerns the income interest, unless the court directs otherwise;

(5) one-half of the trustee's regular compensation, whether based on a percentage of principal or income, and all expenses reasonably incurred for current management of principal and application of income;

(6) any tax levied upon receipts defined as income under this Act or the trust instrument and payable by the trustee.

(b) If charges against income are of unusual amount, the trustee may by means of reserves or other reasonable means charge them over a reasonable period of time and withhold from distribution sufficient sums to regularize distributions.

(c) The following charges shall be made against principal:

(1) trustee's compensation not chargeable to income under subsections (a)(4) and (a)(5), special compensation of trustees, expenses reasonably incurred in connection with principal, court costs and attorney's fees primarily concerning matters of principal, and trustee's compensation computed on principal as an acceptance, distribution, or termination fee;

(2) charges not provided for in subsection (a), including the cost of investing and reinvesting principal, the payments on principal of an indebtedness (including a mortgage amortized by periodic payments of principal), expenses for preparation of property for rental or sale, and, unless the court directs otherwise, expenses incurred in maintaining or defending any action to construe the trust or protect it or the property or assure the title of any trust property;

(3) extraordinary repairs or expenses incurred in making a capital improvement to principal, including special assessments, but, a trustee may establish an allowance for depreciation out of income to the extent permitted by subsection (a)(2) and by section 8;

(4) any tax levied upon profit, gain, or other receipts allocated to principal notwithstanding denomination of the tax as an income tax by the taxing authority;

(5) if an estate or inheritance tax is levied in respect of a trust in which both an income beneficiary and a remainderman have an interest, any amount apportioned to the trust, including interest and penalties, even though the income beneficiary also has rights in the principal.

(d) Regularly recurring charges payable from income shall be apportioned to the same extent and in the same manner that income is apportioned under section 4.

Section 14. [*Application of Act.*]

Except as specifically provided in the trust instrument or the will or in this Act, this Act shall apply to any receipt or expense received or incurred after the effective date of this Act by any trust or decedent's estate whether established before or after the effective date of this Act and whether the asset involved was acquired by the trustee before or after the effective date of this Act.

Section 15. [*Uniformity of Interpretation.*]

This Act shall be so construed as to effectuate its general purpose to make uniform the law of those states which enact it.

Section 16. [*Short Title.*]

This Act may be cited as the Revised Uniform Principal and Income Act.

Section 17. [*Severability.*]

If any provision of this Act or the application thereof to any person or circumstance is held invalid, the invalidity does not affect other provisions or applications of the Act which can be given effect without the invalid provision or application and to this end the provisions of this Act are severable.

Section 18. [*Repeal.*]

[The following acts and parts of acts are repealed:

(1)

(2)

(3)   .]

Section 19. [*Time of Taking Effect.*]

This Act shall take effect on _____.

UNIFORM TRUSTEES' POWERS ACT

PREFATORY NOTE

Increased flexibility in the exercise of investment powers attendant upon the enactment of prudent man rule investment statutes has suggested the advisability of extending the same principle to the field of trustees' powers generally. Greater reliance is thereby placed upon trustee self-regulation rather than upon trustor restriction to protect the fulfillment of trust purposes without depriving a trustor of power to impose trust power restrictions if he wishes so to do.

The Uniform Trustees' Powers Act proceeds upon the premise that in the trusts to which the Act applies (Section 1) the trustees' powers, subject to trust restrictions thereon imposed by the trust or by other statutes (Section 2), should be commensurate with the duties of the trustee acting as a prudent man to perform the purposes of the trust. Accordingly, the trustee is empowered "to perform, without Court authorization, every act which a prudent man would perform for the purposes of the trust" whether or not but for the Act, decisional restrictions on the scope of the powers conferred would exist (Section 3(a)(c)). The list of specific powers in Section 3(c) is illustrative of the broad power conferred in Section 3(a) and certain of such illustrative powers change the common law rule; e.g., the power to delegate discretion (Section 3(c)(24)). Self-dealing powers are permitted only in certain instances (Section 3(c)(1), (4), (6), (18) and (24)) (Section 5(b)). The Act does not affect the power of a Court for cause shown to relieve a trustee from any restriction on his power (Section 5) and provision is made concerning powers exercisable by joint trustees (Section 6).

Notwithstanding the broad powers conferred, it is expressly provided that the trustee has a duty to act, with due regard to his obligation as a fiduciary, including a duty not to exercise any power in such a way as to deprive the trust or a donor of a trust asset of an otherwise available tax exemption, deduction or credit, or operate to impose a tax upon a donor or other person as owner of any portion of the trust (Section 3(b)). The trustee may not transfer his office or delegate the entire administration of the trust to a co-trustee or another (Section 4).

A third person, without actual knowledge of breach of trust, dealing with the trustee is protected. Accordingly, a third person has no duty of inquiry concerning the existence or proper exercise of trust power. A third person without actual knowledge to the contrary, may assume that the requisite power exists and is properly exercised. He is not bound to assure the proper application of trust assets paid or delivered to the trustee (Section 7).

The Act applies to future trusts, but the Legislature may make the Act applicable to existing trusts (Section 8).

For a basic review of the underlying theory of the Uniform Trustees' Powers Act, see Professor William F. Fratcher's article entitled "Trustees' Powers Legislation" published in *New York University Law Review, June, 1962, Vol. 37, No. 4, pp. 627–664.*

Table of Sections

Section 1. [*Definitions.*]

As used in this Act:

(1) "trust" means an express trust created by a trust instrument, including a will, whereby a trustee has the duty to administer a trust asset for the benefit of a named or otherwise described income or principal beneficiary, or both; "trust" does not include a resulting or constructive trust, a business trust which provides for certificates to be issued to the beneficiary, an investment trust, a voting trust, a security instrument, a trust created by the judgment or decree of a court, a liquidation trust, or a trust for the primary purpose of paying dividends, interests, interest coupons, salaries, wages, pensions or profits, or employee benefits of any kind, an instrument wherein a person is nominee or escrowee for another, a

trust created in deposits in any financial institution, or other trust the nature of which does not admit of general trust administration;

(2) "trustee" means an original, added, or successor trustee;

(3) "prudent man" means a trustee whose exercise of trust powers is reasonable and equitable in view of the interests of income or principal beneficiaries, or both, and in view of the manner in which men of ordinary prudence, diligence, discretion, and judgment would act in the management of their own affairs.

COMMENT

What is "reasonable and equitable" in the exercise of trust powers will be determined as of the time of exercise.

Section 2. [*Powers of Trustee Conferred by Trust or by Law.*]

(a) The trustee has all powers conferred upon him by the provisions of this Act unless limited in the trust instrument [and except as is otherwise provided in _____].

(b) An instrument which is not a trust under section 1(1) may incorporate any part of this Act by reference.

Section 3. [*Powers of Trustees Conferred by This Act.*]

(a) From time of creation of the trust until final distribution of the assets of the trust, a trustee has the power to perform, without court authorization, every act which a prudent man would perform for the purposes of the trust including but not limited to the powers specified in subsection (c).

(b) In the exercise of his powers including the powers granted by this Act, a trustee has a duty to act with due regard to his obligation as a fiduciary, including a duty not to exercise any power under this Act in such a way as to deprive the trust of an otherwise available tax exemption, deduction, or credit for tax purposes or deprive a donor of a trust asset of a tax exemption, deduction, or credit or operate to impose a tax upon a donor or other person as owner of any portion of the trust. "Tax" includes, but is not limited to, any federal, state, or local income, gift, estate, or inheritance tax.

(c) A trustee has the power, subject to subsections (a) and (b):

(1) to collect, hold, and retain trust assets received from a trustor until, in the judgment of the trustee, disposition of the assets should be made; and the assets may be retained even

though they include an asset in which the trustee is personally interested;

(2) to receive additions to the assets of the trust;

(3) to continue or participate in the operation of any business or other enterprise, and to effect incorporation, dissolution, or other change in the form of the organization of the business or enterprise;

(4) to acquire an undivided interest in a trust asset in which the trustee, in any trust capacity, holds an undivided interest;

(5) to invest and reinvest trust assets in accordance with the provisions of the trust or as provided by law;

(6) to deposit trust funds in a bank, including a bank operated by the trustee;

(7) to acquire or dispose of an asset, for cash or on credit, at public or private sale; and to manage, develop, improve, exchange, partition, change the character of, or abandon a trust asset or any interest therein; and to encumber, mortgage, or pledge a trust asset for a term within or extending beyond the term of the trust, in connection with the exercise of any power vested in the trustee;

(8) to make ordinary or extraordinary repairs or alterations in buildings or other structures, to demolish any improvements, to raze existing or erect new party walls or buildings;

(9) to subdivide, develop, or dedicate land to public use; or to make or obtain the vacation of plats and adjust boundaries; or to adjust differences in valuation on exchange or partition by giving or receiving consideration; or to dedicate easements to public use without consideration;

(10) to enter for any purpose into a lease as lessor or lessee with or without option to purchase or renew for a term within or extending beyond the term of the trust;

(11) to enter into a lease or arrangement for exploration and removal of minerals or other natural resources or enter into a pooling or unitization agreement;

(12) to grant an option involving disposition of a trust asset, or to take an option for the acquisition of any asset;

(13) to vote a security, in person or by general or limited proxy;

(14) to pay calls, assessments, and any other sums chargeable or accruing against or on account of securities;

(15) to sell or exercise stock subscription or conversion rights; to consent, directly or through a committee or other agent, to the reorganization, consolidation, merger, dissolution, or liquidation of a corporation or other business enterprise;

(16) to hold a security in the name of a nominee or in other form without disclosure of the trust, so that title to the security may pass by delivery, but the trustee is liable for any act of the nominee in connection with the stock so held;

(17) to insure the assets of the trust against damage or loss, and the trustee against liability with respect to third persons;

(18) to borrow money to be repaid from trust assets or otherwise; to advance money for the protection of the trust, and for all expenses, losses, and liability sustained in the administration of the trust or because of the holding or ownership of any trust assets, for which advances with any interest the trustee has a lien on the trust assets as against the beneficiary;

(19) to pay or contest any claim; to settle a claim by or against the trust by compromise, arbitration, or otherwise; and to release, in whole or in part, any claim belonging to the trust to the extent that the claim is uncollectible;

(20) to pay taxes, assessments, compensation of the trustee, and other expenses incurred in the collection, care, administration, and protection of the trust;

(21) to allocate items of income or expense to either trust income or principal, as provided by law, including creation of reserves out of income for depreciation, obsolescence, or amortization, or for depletion in mineral or timber properties;

(22) to pay any sum distributable to a beneficiary under legal disability, without liability to the trustee, by paying the sum to the beneficiary or by paying the sum for the use of the beneficiary either to a legal representative appointed by the court, or if none, to a relative;

(23) to effect distribution of property and money in divided or undivided interests and to adjust resulting differences in valuation;

(24) to employ persons, including attorneys, auditors, investment advisors, or agents, even if they are associated with the trustee, to advise or assist the trustee in the performance of his administrative duties; to act without independent investigation upon their recommendations; and instead of acting personally, to employ one or more agents to perform any act of administration, whether or not discretionary;

(25) to prosecute or defend actions, claims, or proceedings for the protection of trust assets and of the trustee in the performance of his duties;

(26) to execute and deliver all instruments which will accomplish or facilitate the exercise of the powers vested in the trustee.

Section 4. *[Trustee's Office Not Transferable.]*

The trustee shall not transfer his office to another or delegate the entire administration of the trust to a cotrustee or another.

Section 5. *[Power of Court to Permit Deviation or to Approve Transactions Involving Conflict of Interest.]*

(a) This Act does not affect the power of a court of competent jurisdiction for cause shown and upon petition of the trustee or affected beneficiary and upon appropriate notice to the affected parties to relieve a trustee from any restrictions on his power that would otherwise be placed upon him by the trust or by this Act.

(b) If the duty of the trustee and his individual interest or his interest as trustee of another trust, conflict in the exercise of a trust power, the power may be exercised only by court authorization (except as provided in sections 3(c)(1), (4), (6), (18), and (24)) upon petition of the trustee. Under this section, personal profit or advantage to an affiliated or subsidiary company or association is personal profit to any corporate trustee.

Section 6. *[Powers Exercisable by Joint Trustees–Liability.]*

(a) Any power vested in 3 or more trustees may be exercised by a majority, but a trustee who has not joined in exercising a power is not liable to the beneficiaries or to others for the consequences of the exercise; and a dissenting trustee is not liable for the consequences of an act in which he joins at the direction of the majority of the trustees, if he expressed his dissent in writing to any of his cotrustees at or before the time of the joinder.

(b) If 2 or more trustees are appointed to perform a trust, and if any of them is unable or refuses to accept the appointment, or, having accepted, ceases to be a trustee, the surviving or remaining trustees shall perform the trust and succeed to all the powers, duties, and discretionary authority given to the trustees jointly.

(c) This section does not excuse a cotrustee from liability for failure either to participate in the administration of the trust or to attempt to prevent a breach of trust.

Section 7. [*Third Persons Protected in Dealing With Trustee.*]

With respect to a third person dealing with a trustee or assisting a trustee in the conduct of a transaction, the existence of trust powers and their proper exercise by the trustee may be assumed without inquiry. The third person is not bound to inquire whether the trustee has power to act or is properly exercising the power; and a third person, without actual knowledge that the trustee is exceeding his powers or improperly exercising them, is fully protected in dealing with the trustee as if the trustee possessed and properly exercised the powers he purports to exercise. A third person is not bound to assure the proper application of trust assets paid or delivered to the trustee.

Section 8. [*Application of Act.*]

Except as specifically provided in the trust, the provisions of this Act apply to any trust established [before or] after the effective date of this Act and to any trust asset acquired by the trustee [before or] after the effective date of this Act.

COMMENT

If the bracketed provisions are included in the Act as adopted, the provisions of this section will not affect the validity of any act of the trustee performed prior to its enactment.

Section 9. [*Uniformity of Interpretation.*]

This Act shall be construed to effectuate its general purpose to make uniform the law of those states which enact it.

Section 10. [*Short Title.*]

This Act may be cited as the "Uniform Trustees' Powers Act."

Section 11. [*Severability.*]

If any provision of this Act or the application thereof to any person or circumstance is held invalid, the invalidity does not affect other provisions or applications of the Act which can be given effect without the invalid provision or application, and to this end the provisions of this Act are severable.

Section 12. [*Repeal.*]

The following acts are repealed:

(1)

(2)

(3)

Section 13. [*Time of Taking Effect.*]

This Act takes effect _____.

UNIFORM TRANSFERS TO MINORS ACT

PREFATORY NOTE

This Act revises and restates the Uniform Gifts to Minors Act (UGMA), one of the Conference's most successful products, some version of which has been enacted in every American jurisdiction.

The original version of UGMA was adopted by the Conference in 1956 and closely followed a model "Act concerning Gifts of Securities to Minors" which was sponsored by the New York Stock Exchange and the Association of Stock Exchange Firms and which had been adopted in 14 states. The 1956 version of UGMA broadened the model act to cover gifts of money as well as securities but made few other changes.

In 1965 and 1966 the Conference revised UGMA to expand the types of financial institutions which could serve as depositories of custodial funds, to facilitate the designation of successor custodians, and to add life insurance policies and annuity contracts to the types of property (cash and securities) that could be made the subject of a gift under the Act.

Not all states adopted the 1966 revisions; some 11 jurisdictions retained their versions of the 1956 Act. More importantly, however, many states since 1966 have substantially revised their versions of UGMA to expand the kinds of property that may he made the subject of a gift under the Act, and a few states permit transfers to custodians from other sources, such as trusts and estates, as well as lifetime gifts. As a result, a great deal of non-uniformity has arisen among the states. Uniformity in this area is important, for the Conference has cited UGMA as an example of an act designed to avoid conflicts of law when the laws of more than one state may apply to a transaction or a series of transactions.

This Act follows the expansive approach taken by several states and allows any kind of property, real or personal, tangible or intangible, to be made the subject of a transfer to a custodian for the benefit of a minor (SECTION 1(6)). In addition, it permits such transfers not only by lifetime outright gifts (SECTION 4), but also from trusts, estates and guardianships, whether or not specifically authorized in the governing instrument (SECTIONS 5 and 6), and from other third parties indebted to a minor who does not have a conservator, such as parties against whom a minor has a tort claim or judgment, and depository institutions holding deposits or insurance companies issuing policies payable on death to a minor

(SECTION 7). For this reason, and to distinguish the enactment of this statute from the 1956 and 1966 versions of UGMA, the title of the Act has been changed to refer to "Transfers" rather than to "Gifts," a much narrower term.

As so expanded, the Act might be considered a statutory form of trust or guardianship that continues until the minor reaches 21. Note, however, that unlike a trust, a custodianship is not a separate legal entity or taxpayer. Under SECTION 11(b) of this Act, the custodial property is indefeasibly vested in the minor, not the custodian, and thus any income received is attributable to and reportable by the minor, whether or not actually distributed to the minor.

The expansion of the Act to permit transfers of any kind of property to a custodian creates a significant problem of potential personal liability for the minor or the custodian arising from the ownership of property such as real estate, automobiles, general partnership interests, and business proprietorships. This problem did not exist under UGMA under which custodial property was limited to bank deposits, securities and insurance. In response, SECTION 17 of this Act generally limits the claims of third parties to recourse against the custodial property, with the minor insulated against personal liability unless he is personally at fault. The custodian is similarly insulated unless he is personally at fault or fails to disclose his custodial capacity in entering into a contract.

Nevertheless, the Act should be used with caution with respect to property such as real estate or general partnership interests from which liabilities as well as benefits may arise. Many of the possible risks can and should be insured against, and the custodian has the power under SECTION 13(a) to purchase such insurance, at least when other custodial assets are sufficient to do so. If the assets are not sufficient, there is doubt that a custodian will act, or there are significant uninsurable risks, a transferor should consider a trust with spendthrift provisions, such as a minority trust under Section 2503(c), IRC, rather than a custodianship, to make a gift of such property to a minor.

The Act retains (or reverts to) 21 as the age of majority or, more accurately, the age at which the custodianship terminates and the property is distributed. Since tax law permits duration of Section 2503(c) trusts to 21, even though the statutory age of majority is 18 in most states, this age should be retained since most donors and other transferors wish to preserve a custodianship as long as possible.

Finally, the Act restates and rearranges, rather than amends, the 1966 Act. The addition of other forms of property and other forms of dispositions made adherence to the format and language of the prior act very unwieldy. In addition, the 1966 and 1956 Acts closely followed the language of the earlier model act, which had already been adopted in several states, even though it did not conform to Conference style. It is hoped that this rewriting and revision of UGMA will improve its clarity while also expanding its coverage.

Table of Sections

§ 1. Definitions

In this [Act]:

(1) "Adult" means an individual who has attained the age of 21 years.

(2) "Benefit plan" means an employer's plan for the benefit of an employee or partner.

(3) "Broker" means a person lawfully engaged in the business of effecting transactions in securities or commodities for the person's own account or for the account of others.

(4) "Conservator" means a person appointed or qualified by a court to act as general, limited, or temporary guardian of a minor's property or a person legally authorized to perform substantially the same functions.

(5) "Court" means [_____ court].

(6) "Custodial property" means (i) any interest in property transferred to a custodian under this [Act] and (ii) the income from and proceeds of that interest in property.

(7) "Custodian" means a person so designated under Section 9 or a successor or substitute custodian designated under Section 18.

(8) "Financial institution" means a bank, trust company, savings institution, or credit union, chartered and supervised under state or federal law.

(9) "Legal representative" means an individual's personal representative or conservator.

(10) "Member of the minor's family" means the minor's parent, stepparent, spouse, grandparent, brother, sister, uncle, or aunt, whether of the whole or half blood or by adoption.

(11) "Minor" means an individual who has not attained the age of 21 years.

(12) "Person" means an individual, corporation, organization, or other legal entity.

(13) "Personal representative" means an executor, administrator, successor personal representative, or special administrator of a decedent's estate or a person legally authorized to perform substantially the same functions.

(14) "State" includes any state of the United States, the District of Columbia, the Commonwealth of Puerto Rico, and any territory or possession subject to the legislative authority of the United States.

(15) "Transfer" means a transaction that creates custodial property under Section 9.

(16) "Transferor" means a person who makes a transfer under this [Act].

(17) "Trust company" means a financial institution, corporation, or other legal entity, authorized to exercise general trust powers.

COMMENT

To reflect the broader scope and the unlimited types of property to which the new Act will apply, a number of definitional changes have been made from the 1966 Act. In addition, several definitions specifically applicable to the limited types of property (cash, securities and insurance policies) subject to the 1966 Act have been eliminated as unnecessary. These include the definitions of "bank," "issuer," "life insurance policy or annuity contract," "security," and "transfer agent." No change in the meaning or construction of these terms as used in this Act is intended by such deletions.

The definitions of "domestic financial institution" and "insured financial institution" have been eliminated because few if any states limit deposits by custodians to local institutions, and the prudent person rule of SECTION 12(b) of this Act may dictate the use of insured institutions as depositories, without having the Act so specify.

The principal changes or additions to the remaining definitions are discussed below.

Paragraph (2). The definition of "benefit plan" is intentionally very broad and is meant to cover any contract, plan, system, account or trust such as a pension plan, retirement plan, death benefit plan, deferred compensation plan, employment agency arrangement or, stock bonus, option or profit sharing plan.

Paragraph (4). The term "conservator" rather than "guardian of the estate" has been employed in the Act to conform to Uniform Probate Code terminology. The term includes a guardian of the minor's property, whether general, limited or temporary, and includes a committee, tutor, or curator of the minor's property.

Paragraph (6). The definition of "custodial property" has been generalized and expanded to encompass every conceivable legal or equitable interest in property of any kind, including real estate and tangible or intangible personal property. The term is intended, for example, to include joint interests with right of survivorship, beneficial interests in land trusts, as well as all other intangible interests in property. Contingent or expectancy interests such as the designation as a beneficiary under insurance policies or benefit plans become "custodial property" only if the designation is irrevocable, or when it becomes so, but the Act specifically authorizes the "nomination" of a future custodian as beneficiary of such interests (see SECTION 3). Proceeds of custodial property, both immediate and remote, are themselves custodial property, as is the case under UGMA.

Custodial property is defined without reference to the physical location of the property, even if it has one. No, useful purpose would be served by restricting the application of the Act to, for example, real estate "located in this state," since a conveyance recorded in the state of the property's location, if done with proper formalities, should be effective even if that state has not enacted this Act. The rights, duties and powers of the custodian should be determined by reference to the law of the state under which the custodianship is created, assuming there is sufficient nexus under SECTION 2 between that state and the transferor, the minor or the custodian.

Paragraph (11). This definition of "minor" retains the historical age of 21 as the age of majority, even though most states have lowered the age for most other purposes, as well as in their versions of the 1966 Act. Nevertheless, because the Internal Revenue Code continues to permit "minority trusts" under Section 2503(c), IRC, to continue in effect until age 21, and because it is believed that most donors creating minority trusts or custodianships prefer to retain the property under management for the benefit of the young person as long as possible, it is strongly suggested that the age of 21 be retained as the age of majority under this Act. For states that have reduced the age of majority in their versions of the 1966 Act, SECTION 22(c) of

this Act provides that a change back to 21 will not affect custodianships that have already terminated at an earlier age.

Paragraph (13). The definition of the term "personal representative" is based upon that definition in Sec. 1–201(30) of the Uniform Probate Code.

Paragraph (15). The new definition of "transfer" is necessary to reflect the application of the Act not only to gifts, but also to distributions from trusts and estates, obligors of the minor, and transfers of the minor's own assets to a custodianship by the legal representative of a minor, all of which are now permitted by this Act.

Paragraph (16). The new definition of "transferor" is required because the term includes not only the maker of a gift, i.e., a donor in the usual sense, but also fiduciaries and obligors who control or own property that is the subject of the transfer. Nothing in this Act requires that a transferor be an "adult." If permitted under other law of the enacting state relating to emancipation or competence to make a will, gift, or other transfer, a minor may make an effective transfer of property to a custodian for his benefit or for the benefit of another minor.

Paragraph (17). Only entities authorized to exercise "general" trust powers qualify as "trust companies"; that is, the authority to exercise only limited fiduciary responsibilities, such as the authority to accept Individual Retirement Account deposits, is not sufficient.

§ 2. Scope and Jurisdiction

(a) This [Act] applies to a transfer that refers to this [Act] in the designation under Section 9(a) by which the transfer is made if at the time of the transfer, the transferor, the minor, or the custodian is a resident of this State or the custodial property is located in this State. The custodianship so created remains subject to this [Act] despite a subsequent change in residence of a transferor, the minor, or the custodian, or the removal of custodial property from this State.

(b) A person designated as custodian under this [Act] is subject to personal jurisdiction in this State with respect to any matter relating to the custodianship.

(c) A transfer that purports to be made and which is valid under the Uniform Transfers to Minors Act, the Uniform Gifts to Minors Act, or a substantially similar act, of another state is governed by the law of the designated state and may be executed and is enforceable in this State if at the time of the transfer, the transferor, the minor, or the custodian is a resident of the designated state or the custodial property is located in the designated state.

COMMENT

This section has no counterpart in the 1966 Act. It attempts to resolve uncertainties and conflicts-of-laws questions that have frequently arisen because of the present nonuniformity of UGMA in the various states and which may continue to arise during the transition from UGMA to this Act.

The creation of a custodianship must invoke the law of a particular state because of the form of the transfer required under SECTION 9(a). This section provides that a choice of the UTMA of the enacting state is appropriate and effective if any of the nexus factors specified in subsection (a) exists at the time of the transfer. This Act continues to govern, and subsection (b) makes the custodian accountable and subject to personal jurisdiction in the courts of the enacting state for the duration of the custodianship, despite subsequent relocation of the parties or the property.

Subsection (c) recognizes that residents of the enacting state may elect to have the law of another state apply to a transfer. That choice is valid if a nexus with the chosen state exists at the time of the transfer. If personal jurisdiction can be obtained in the enacting state under other law apart from this Act, the custodianship may be enforced in its courts, which are directed to apply the law of the state elected by the transferor.

If the choice of law under subsection (a) or (c) is ineffective because of the absence of the required nexus, the transfer may still be effective under the Act of another state with which a nexus does exist. See SECTION 21.

§ 3. Nomination of Custodian

(a) A person having the right to designate the recipient of property transferable upon the occurrence of a future event may revocably nominate a custodian to receive the property for a minor beneficiary upon the occurrence of the event by naming the custodian followed in substance by the words: "as custodian for _____ (name of minor) under the [name of Enacting State] Uniform Transfers to Minors Act." The nomination may name one or more persons as substitute custodians to whom the property must be transferred, in the order named, if the first nominated custodian dies before the transfer or is unable, declines, or is ineligible to serve. The nomination may be made in a will, a trust, a deed, an instrument exercising a power of appointment, or in a writing designating a beneficiary of contractual rights which is registered with or delivered to the payor, issuer, or other obligor of the contractual rights.

(b) A custodian nominated under this section must be a person to whom a transfer of property of that kind may be made under Section 9(a).

(c) The nomination of a custodian under this section does not create custodial property until the nominating instrument becomes irrevocable or a transfer to the nominated custodian is completed under Section 9. Unless the nomination of a custodian has been revoked, upon the occurrence of the future event the custodianship becomes effective and the custodian shall enforce a transfer of the custodial property pursuant to Section 9.

COMMENT

This section is new and permits a future custodian for a minor to be nominated to receive a distribution under a will or trust, or as a beneficiary of a power of appointment, or of contractual rights such as a life or endowment insurance policy, annuity contract, P.O.D. Account, benefit plan, or similar future payment right. Nomination of a future custodian does not constitute a "transfer" under this Act and does not create custodial property. If it did, the nomination and beneficiary designation would have to be permanent, since a "transfer" is irre-

vocable and indefeasibly vests ownership of the interest in the minor under SECTION 11(b).

Instead, this section permits a revocable beneficiary designation that takes effect only when the donor dies, or when a lifetime transfer to the custodian for the minor beneficiary occurs, such as a distribution under an inter vivos trust. However, an unrevoked nomination under this section is binding on a personal representative or trustee (see SECTION 5(b)) and on insurance companies and other obligors who contract to pay in the future (see SECTION 7(b)).

The person making the nomination may name contingent or successive future custodians to serve, in the order named, in the event that the person first nominated dies, or is unable, declines, or is ineligible to serve. Such a substi- tute future custodian is a custodian "nominated . . . under Section 3" to whom the transfer must be made under SECTIONS 5(b) and 7(b).

Any person nominated as future custodian may decline to serve before the transfer occurs and may resign at any time after the transfer. See SECTION 18.

§ 4. Transfer by Gift or Exercise of Power of Appointment

A person may make a transfer by irrevocable gift to, or the irrevocable exercise of a power of appointment in favor of, a custodian for the benefit of a minor pursuant to Section 9.

COMMENT

To emphasize the different kinds of transfers that create presently effective custodianships under this Act, they are separately described in SECTIONS 4, 5, 6 and 7. This section in part corresponds to Section 2(a) of the 1966 Act and covers the traditional lifetime gift that was the only kind of transfer authorized by the 1966 Act. It also covers an irrevocable exercise of a power of appointment in favor of a custodian, as distinguished from the exercise of a power in a revocable instrument that results only in the nomination of a future custodian under SECTION 3.

§ 5. Transfer Authorized by Will or Trust

(a) A personal representative or trustee may make an irrevocable transfer pursuant to Section 9 to a custodian for the benefit of a minor as authorized in the governing will or trust.

(b) If the testator or settlor has nominated a custodian under Section 3 to receive the custodial property, the transfer must be made to that person.

(c) If the testator or settlor has not nominated a custodian under Section 3, or all persons so nominated as custodian die before the transfer or are unable, decline, or are ineligible to serve, the personal representative or the trustee, as the case may be, shall designate the custodian from among those eligible to serve as custodian for property of that kind under Section 9(a).

COMMENT

This section is new and has no counterpart in the 1966 Act. It is based on nonuniform provisions adopted by Connecticut, Illinois,

Wisconsin and other states to validate distributions from trusts and estates to a custodian for a minor beneficiary, when the use of a custodian is expressly authorized by the governing instrument. It also covers the designation of the custodian whenever the settlor or testator fails to make a nomination, or the future custodian nominated under SECTION 3 (and any alternate named) fails to qualify.

§ 6. Other Transfer by Fiduciary

(a) Subject to subsection (c), a personal representative or trustee may make an irrevocable transfer to another adult or trust company as custodian for the benefit of a minor pursuant to Section 9, in the absence of a will or under a will or trust that does not contain an authorization to do so.

(b) Subject to subsection (c), a conservator may make an irrevocable transfer to another adult or trust company as custodian for the benefit of the minor pursuant to Section 9.

(c) A transfer under subsection (a) or (b) may be made only if (i) the personal representative, trustee, or conservator considers the transfer to be in the best interest of the minor, (ii) the transfer is not prohibited by or inconsistent with provisions of the applicable will, trust agreement, or other governing instrument, and (iii) the transfer is authorized by the court if it exceeds [$10,000] in value.

COMMENT

This section is new and has no counterpart in the 1966 Act. It covers a new concept, already authorized by the law of some states through nonuniform amendments to the 1966 Act, to permit custodianships to be used as guardianship or conservator substitutes, even though not specifically authorized by the person whose property is the subject of the transfer. It also permits the legal representative of the minor, such as a conservator or guardian, to transfer the minor's own property to a new or existing custodianship for the purposes of convenience or economies of administration.

A custodianship may be created under this section even though not specifically authorized by the transferor, the testator, or the settlor of the trust if three tests are satisfied. First, the fiduciary making the transfer must determine in good faith and in his fiduciary capacity that a custodianship will be in the best interests of the minor. Second, a custodianship may not be prohibited by, or inconsistent with, the terms of any governing instrument. Inconsistent terms would include, for example, a spendthrift clause in a governing trust, provisions terminating a governing trust for the minor's benefit at a time other than the time of the minor's age of majority, and provisions for mandatory distributions of income or principal at specific times or periodic intervals. Provisions for other outright distributions or bequests would not be inconsistent with the creation of a custodianship under this section. Third, the amount of property transferred, (as measured by its value) must be of such relatively small amount that the lack of court supervision and the typically stricter investment standards that would apply to the conservator otherwise required will not be important. However, if the property is of significant size, transfer to a custo-

dian may still be made if the court approves and if the other two tests are met.

The custodianship created under this section without express authority in the governing instrument will terminate upon the minor's attainment of the statutory age of majority of the enacting state apart from this Act, i.e., at the same age a conservatorship of the minor would end. See SECTION 20(b) and the Comment thereto.

§ 7. Transfer by Obligor

(a) Subject to subsections (b) and (c), a person not subject to Section 5 or 6 who holds property of or owes a liquidated debt to a minor not having a conservator may make an irrevocable transfer to a custodian for the benefit of the minor pursuant to Section 9.

(b) If a person having the right to do so under Section 3 has nominated a custodian under that section to receive the custodial property, the transfer must be made to that person.

(c) If no custodian has been nominated under Section 3, or all persons so nominated as custodian die before the transfer or are unable, decline, or are ineligible to serve, a transfer under this section may be made to an adult member of the minor's family or to a trust company unless the property exceeds [$10,000] in value.

COMMENT

This section is new and, like SECTION 6, permits a custodianship to be established as a substitute for a conservator to receive payments due a minor from sources other than estates, trusts, and existing guardianships covered by SECTIONS 5 and 6. For example, a tort judgment debtor of a minor, a bank holding a joint or P.O.D. account of which a minor is the surviving payee, or an insurance company holding life insurance policy or benefit plan proceeds payable to a minor may create a custodianship under this section.

Use of this section is mandatory when a future custodian has been nominated under SECTION 3 as a named beneficiary of an insurance policy, benefit plan, deposit account, or the like, because the original owner of the property specified a custodianship (and a future custodian) to receive the property. If that custodian (or any alternate named) is not available, if none was nominated, or none could have been nominated (as in the case of a tort judgment payable to the minor), this section is permissive and does not preclude the obligor from re-

quiring the appointment of a conservator to receive payment. It allows the obligor to transfer to a
custodian unless the property ex-

ceeds the stated value, in which
case a conservator must be appointed to receive it.

§ 8. Receipt for Custodial Property

A written acknowledgment of delivery by a custodian constitutes
a sufficient receipt and discharge for custodial property transferred
to the custodian pursuant to this [Act].

COMMENT

This section discharges transferors from further responsibility for
custodial property delivered to and
receipted for by the custodian. See
also SECTION 16 which protects
transferors and other third parties
dealing with custodians. Because a
discharge or release for a donative
transfer is not necessary, this section had no counterpart in the 1966
Act.

This section does not authorize
an existing custodian, or a custodian to whom an obligor makes a
transfer under SECTION 7, to settle or release a claim of the minor
against a third party. Only a conservator, guardian ad litem or other
person authorized under other law
to act for the minor may release
such a claim.

§ 9. Manner of Creating Custodial Property and Effect-ing Transfer; Designation of Initial Custodian; Control

(a) Custodial property is created and a transfer is made whenever:

(1) an uncertificated security or a certificated security in
registered form is either:

(i) registered in the name of the transferor, an adult
other than the transferor, or a trust company, followed in
substance by the words: "as custodian for _____
_____(name of minor) under the [Name of Enacting
State] Uniform Transfers to Minors Act"; or

(ii) delivered if in certificated form, or any document
necessary for the transfer of an uncertificated security is
delivered, together with any necessary endorsement to an
adult other than the transferor or to a trust company as
custodian, accompanied by an instrument in substantially
the form set forth in subsection (b);

(2) money is paid or delivered, or a security held in the name
of a broker, financial institution, or its nominee is transferred,
to a broker or financial institution for credit to an account in

the name of the transferor, an adult other than the transferor, or a trust company, followed in substance by the words: "as custodian for _____ (name of minor) under the [Name of Enacting State] Uniform Transfers to Minors Act";

(3) the ownership of a life or endowment insurance policy or annuity contract is either:

(i) registered with the issuer in the name of the transferor, an adult other than the transferor, or a trust company, followed in substance by the words: "as custodian for _____ (name of minor) under the [Name of Enacting State] Uniform Transfers to Minors Act"; or

(ii) assigned in a writing delivered to an adult other than the transferor or to a trust company whose name in the assignment is followed in substance by the words: "as custodian for _____ (name of minor) under the [Name of Enacting State] Uniform Transfers to Minors Act";

(4) an irrevocable exercise of a power of appointment or an irrevocable present right to future payment under a contract is the subject of a written notification delivered to the payor, issuer, or other obligor that the right is transferred to the transferor, an adult other than the transferor, or a trust company, whose name in the notification is followed in substance by the words: "as custodian for _____ (name of minor) under the [Name of Enacting State] Uniform Transfers to Minors Act";

(5) an interest in real property is recorded in the name of the transferor, an adult other than the transferor, or a trust company, followed in substance by the words: "as custodian for _____ (name of minor) under the [Name of Enacting State] Uniform Transfers to Minors Act";

(6) a certificate of title issued by a department or agency of a state or of the United States which evidences title to tangible personal property is either:

(i) issued in the name of the transferor, an adult other than the transferor, or a trust company, followed in substance by the words: "as custodian for _____ (name of minor) under the [Name of Enacting State] Uniform Transfers to Minors Act"; or

(ii) delivered to an adult other than the transferor or to a trust company, endorsed to that person followed in substance by the words: "as custodian for _____ (name of minor) under the [Name of Enacting State] Uniform Transfers to Minors Act"; or

(7) an interest in any property not described in paragraphs (1) through (6) is transferred to an adult other than the transferor or to a trust company by a written instrument in substantially the form set forth in subsection (b).

(b) An instrument in the following form satisfies the requirements of paragraphs (1)(ii) and (7) of subsection (a):

"TRANSFER UNDER THE [NAME OF ENACTING STATE] UNIFORM TRANSFER TO MINORS ACT

I, _____ (name of transferor or name and representative capacity if a fiduciary) hereby transfer to _____ (name of custodian), as custodian for _____ (name of minor) under the [Name of Enacting State] Uniform Transfers to Minors Act, the following: (insert a description of the custodial property sufficient to identify it).

Dated: _____

_____

(Signature)

_____ (name of custodian) acknowledges receipt of the property described above as custodian for the minor named above under the [Name of Enacting State] Uniform Transfers to Minors Act.

Dated: _____

_____"

(Signature of Custodian)

(c) A transferor shall place the custodian in control of the custodial property as soon as practicable.

COMMENT

The 1966 Act contained optional bracketed language permitting an adopting state to limit the class of eligible initial custodians to an adult member of the minor's family or a guardian of the minor. This optional limitation has been deleted because it would preclude the use of an individual and uncompensated custodian if no qualified or willing family member is available.

Otherwise, with respect to transfers of securities, cash, and insurance or annuity contracts, this section tracks the cognate provisions of subsection 2(a) of the 1966 Act, with one exception. Under subsection (a)(1)(ii) of this section, a transfer of securities in registered form may be accomplished without registering the transfer in the name of the custodian so that transfers may be accomplished more expeditiously, and so that securities may be held by custodians in street name. In other words, subsection (a)(1)(i) is not the exclusive manner for making effective transfers of securities in registered form.

In addition, subsection (a) creates new procedures for handling the additional types of property now subject to the Act; specifically:

Paragraph (3) covers the irrevocable transfer of ownership of like and endowment insurance policies and annuity contracts.

Paragraph (4) covers the *irrevocable* exercise of a power of appointment and the *irrevocable* present assignment of future payment rights, such as royalties, interest and principal payments under a promissory note, or beneficial interests under life or endowment or annuity insurance contracts or benefit plans. The payor, issuer, or obligor may require additional formalities such as completion of a specific assignment form and an endorsement, but the transfer is effective upon delivery of the notification. See SECTION 3 and the Comment thereto for the procedure for revocably "nominating" a future custodian as a beneficiary of a power of appointment or such payment rights.

Paragraph (5) is the exclusive method for the transfer of real estate and includes a disposition effected by will. Under the law of those states in which a devise of real estate vests in the devisee without the need for a deed from the personal representative of the decedent, a document such as the will must still be "recorded" under this provision to make the transfer effective. For inter vivos transfers, of course, a conveyance in recordable form would be employed for dispositions of real estate to a custodian.

Paragraph (6) covers the transfer of personal property such as automobiles, aircraft, and other property subject to registration of ownership with a state or federal agency. Either registration of the transfer in the name of the custodian or delivery of the endorsed certificate in registerable form makes the transfer effective.

Paragraph (7) is a residual classification, covering all property not otherwise covered in the preceding paragraphs. Examples would include nonregistered securities, partnership interests, and tangible personal property not subject to title certificates.

The form of transfer document recommended and set forth in subsection (b) contains an acceptance that must be executed by the custodian to make the disposition effective. While such a form of written acceptance is not specifically required in the case of registered securities under subsection (a)(1), money under (a)(2), insurance contracts or interests under (a)(3) or (4), real estate under (a)(5), or titled personal property under (a)(6), it is certainly the better and recommended practice to obtain the acknowledgment, consent, and acceptance of the designated custodian on the instrument of transfer, or otherwise.

A transferor may create a custodianship by naming himself as custodian, except for transfers of securities under subsection (a)(1)(ii), insurance and annuity contracts under (a)(3)(ii), and titled personalty under (a)(6)(ii), which are made without registering them in the name of the custodian, and transfers of the residual class of property covered by (a)(7). In all of these cases a transfer of possession and control to a third party is necessary to establish donative intent and consummation of the transfer, and designation of the transferor as custodian renders the transfer invalid under SECTION 11(a)(2).

Note, also, that the Internal Revenue Service takes the position that custodial property is includable in the gross estate of the donor if he appoints himself custodian and dies while serving in that capacity before the minor attains the age of 21. Rev.Rul. 57–366, C.B. 1957–2, 618; Rev.Rul. 59–357, C.B. 1959–2, 212; Rev.Rul. 70–348, C.B. 1970–2, 193; Estate of Prudowsky v. Comm'r, 55 T.C. 890 (1971), affd. per curiam, 465 F.2d 62 (7th Cir. 1972).

This Act has been drafted in an attempt to avoid income attribution to the parent or inclusion of custodial insurance policies on a custodian's life in the estate of the custodian through the changes made in the standards for expenditure of custodial property and the custodian's incidents of ownership in custodial property. See SECTIONS 13 and 14 and the Comments thereto. However, the much greater problem of inclusion of custodial property in the estate of the donor who serves as custodian remains. Therefore, despite the fact that this section of the Act permits it in the case of registered securities, money, life insurance, real estate, and personal property subject to titling laws, it is generally still inadvisable for a donor to appoint himself custodian or for a parent of the minor to serve as custodian. See, generally Sections 2036 and 2038 I.R.C. and Rulings and cases cited above; with respect to gifts of closely held stock when a donor retains voting rights by serving as custodian, see Section 2036(b), I.R.C., overruling U.S. v. Byrum, 408 U.S. 125 (1972), rehearing denied 409 U.S. 898.

Subsection (c) tracks in substance Section 2(c) of the 1966 Act. However, it replaces the requirement that the transferor "promptly do all things within his power" to complete the transfer, with the requirement that such action must be taken "as soon as practicable." This change is intended only to reflect the fact that possession and control of property transferred from an estate can rarely be accomplished with the immediacy that the term "promptly" may have implied. In the case of inter vivos transfers, no relaxation of the former requirement is intended, since "prompt" transfer of dominion is usually practicable.

§ 10. Single Custodianship

A transfer may be made only for one minor, and only one person may be the custodian. All custodial property held under this [Act] by the same custodian for the benefit of the same minor constitutes a single custodianship.

COMMENT

The first sentence follows Section 2(b) of the 1966 Act. The second sentence states what was implicit in the 1966 Act, that additional transfers at different times and from different sources may be made to an existing custodian for the minor and do not create multiple custodianships. This provision also permits an existing custodian to be named as successor custodian by another custodian for the same minor who resigns under SECTION 18 for the purpose of consolidating the assets in a single custodianship.

Note, however, that these results are limited to transfers made "under this Act." Gifts previously made under the enacting state's UGMA or under the UGMA or UTMA of another state must be treated as separate custodianships, even though the same custodian and minor are involved, because of possible differences in the age of distribution and custodian's powers under those other Acts.

Even when all transfers to a single custodian are made "under this Act" and a single custodianship results, custodial property transferred under SECTIONS 6 and 7 must be accounted for separately from property transferred under SECTIONS 4 and 5 because the custodianship will terminate sooner with respect to the former property if the enacting state has a statutory age of majority lower than 21. See SECTION 20 and the Comment thereto.

§ 11. Validity and Effect of Transfer

(a) The validity of a transfer made in a manner prescribed in this [Act] is not affected by:

(1) failure of the transferor to comply with Section 9(c) concerning possession and control;

(2) designation of an ineligible custodian, except designation of the transferor in the case of property for which the transferor is ineligible to serve as custodian under Section 9(a); or

(3) death or incapacity of a person nominated under Section 3 or designated under Section 9 as custodian or the disclaimer of the office by that person.

(b) A transfer made pursuant to Section 9 is irrevocable, and the custodial property is indefeasibly vested in the minor, but the custodian has all the rights, powers, duties, and authority provided in this [Act], and neither the minor nor the minor's legal representative has any right, power, duty, or authority with respect to the custodial property except as provided in this [Act].

(c) By making a transfer, the transferor incorporates in the disposition all the provisions of this [Act] and grants to the custodian, and to any third person dealing with a person designated as custodian, the respective powers, rights, and immunities provided in this [Act].

COMMENT

Subsection (a) generally tracks Section 2(c) of the 1966 Act, except that the transferor's designation of himself as custodian of property for which he is not eligible to serve under SECTION 9(a) makes the transfer ineffective. See Comment to SECTION 9.

The balance of this section generally tracks Section 3 of the 1966 Act with a number of necessary, and perhaps significant, changes required by the new kinds of property subject to custodianships. The 1966 Act provides that a transfer made in accordance with its terms "conveys to the minor indefeasibly vested legal title to the [custodial property]." Because equitable interests in property may be the subject of a transfer under this Act, the reference to "legal title" has been deleted, but no change concerning the effect or finality of the transfer is intended.

However, subsection (b) qualifies the rights of the minor in the property, by making them subject to "the rights, powers, duties and authority" of the custodian under this Act, a concept that may have been implicit and intended in the 1966 Act, but not expressed. The concept is important because of the kinds of property, particularly real estate, now subject to custodianship. If the minor is married, it would be possible for homestead, dower, or community property rights to attach to real estate (or other property) acquired after marriage by the minor through a transfer to a custodianship for his benefit. The quoted language qualifying the minor's interest in the property is intended to override these rights insofar as they may conflict with the custodian's ability and authority to manage, sell, or transfer such property while it is custodial property. Upon termination of the custodianship and transfer of the custodial property to the former minor, the custodial property would then become subject to such spousal rights for the first time.

For a list of the immunities enjoyed by third persons under subsection (c), see SECTION 16 and the Comment thereto.

Because a custodianship under this Act can extend beyond the age of majority in many states, or beyond emancipation of a minor through marriage or otherwise, the Drafting Committee considered the addition of a spendthrift clause to this section. The idea was rejected because neither the 1966 Act nor its predecessors had such a provision, because spendthrift protection would extend only until 21 in any event and judgments against the minor would then be enforceable, and because the spendthrift qualification on the interest of the minor in the property may be inconsistent with the theory of the Act to convey the property indefeasibly to the minor.

§ 12. Care of Custodial Property

(a) A custodian shall:

(1) take control of custodial property;

(2) register or record title to custodial property if appropriate; and

(3) collect, hold, manage, invest, and reinvest custodial property.

(b) In dealing with custodial property, a custodian shall observe the standard of care that would be observed by a prudent person dealing with property of another and is not limited by any other statute restricting investments by fiduciaries. If a custodian has a special skill or expertise or is named custodian on the basis of representations of a special skill or expertise, the custodian shall use that skill or expertise. However, a custodian, in the custodian's discretion and without liability to the minor or the minor's estate, may retain any custodial property received from a transferor.

(c) A custodian may invest in or pay premiums on life insurance or endowment policies on (i) the life of the minor only if the minor or the minor's estate is the sole beneficiary, or (ii) the life of another person in whom the minor has an insurable interest only to the extent that the minor, the minor's estate, or the custodian in the capacity of custodian, is the irrevocable beneficiary.

(d) A custodian at all times shall keep custodial property separate and distinct from all other property in a manner sufficient to identify it clearly as custodial property of the minor. Custodial property consisting of an undivided interest is so identified if the minor's interest is held as a tenant in common and is fixed. Custodial property subject to recordation is so identified if it is recorded, and custodial property subject to registration is so identified if it is either registered, or held in an account designated, in the name of the custodian, followed in substance by the words: "as a custodian for _____ (name of minor) under the [Name of Enacting State] Uniform Transfers to Minors Act."

(e) A custodian shall keep records of all transactions with respect to custodial property, including information necessary for the preparation of the minor's tax returns, and shall make them available for inspection at reasonable intervals by a parent or legal representative of the minor or by the minor if the minor has attained the age of 14 years.

COMMENT

Subsection (a) expands Section 4(a) of the 1966 Act to include the duties to take control and appropriately register or record custodial property in the name of the custodian.

Subsection (b) restates and makes somewhat stricter the prudent man fiduciary standard for the custodian, since it is now cast in terms of a prudent person "dealing with property *of another*" rather than one "who is seeking a reasonable income and the preservation of *his* capital," as under the 1966 Act. The rule also adds a slightly higher standard for professional fiduciaries. The rule parallels section 7–302 of the Uniform Probate Code in order to refer to the existing and growing body of law interpreting that standard. The 1966 Act permitted a custodian to retain any security or bank account received, without the obligation to diversify investment. This subsection extends that rule to any property received.

In order to eliminate any uncertainty that existed under the 1966 Act, subsection (c) grants specific authority to invest custodial property in life insurance on the minor's life, provided the minor's estate is the sole beneficiary, or on the life of another person in whom the minor has an insurable interest, provided the minor, the minor's estate, or the custodian in his custodial capacity is made the beneficiary of such policies.

Subsection (d) generally tracks Section 4(g) of the 1966 Act but adds the provision requiring that custodial property consisting of an undivided interest be held as a tenant in common. This provision permits the custodian to invest custodial property in common trust funds, mutual funds, or in a proportional interest in a "jumbo" certificate of deposit. Investment in property held in joint tenancy with right of survivorship is not permitted, but the Act does not preclude a transfer of such an interest to a custodian, and the custodian is authorized under subsection (b) to retain a joint tenancy interest so received.

Subsection (e) follows Section 4(h) of the 1966 Act, but adds the requirement that income tax information be maintained and made available for preparation of the minor's tax returns. Because the custodianship is not a separate legal entity or taxpayer, the minor's tax identification number should be used to identify all custodial property accounts.

§ 13. Powers of Custodian

(a) A custodian, acting in a custodial capacity, has all the rights, powers, and authority over custodial property that unmarried adult owners have over their own property, but a custodian may exercise those rights, powers, and authority in that capacity only.

(b) This section does not relieve a custodian from liability for breach of Section 12.

COMMENT

Subsection (a) replaces the specific list of custodian's powers in Section 4(f) of the 1966 Act which related only to securities, money, and insurance, then the only permitted kinds of custodial property. It was determined not to expand the list to try to deal with all forms of property now covered by the Act and to specify all powers that might be appropriate for each kind of property, or to refer to an existing body of state law, such as the Trustee's Powers Act, since such powers would not be uniform. Instead, this provision grants the custodian the very broad and general powers of an unmarried adult owner of the property, subject to the prudent person rule and to the duties of segregation and record keeping specified in SECTION 12. This approach permits the Act to be self-contained and more readily understandable by volunteer, non-professional fiduciaries, who most often serve as custodians. It is intended that the authority granted includes the powers most often suggested for custodians, such as the power to borrow, whether at interest or interest free, the power to invest in common trust funds, and the power to enter contracts that extend beyond the termination of the custodianship.

Subsection (a) further specifies that the custodian's powers or incidents of ownership in custodial property such as insurance policies may be exercised only in his capacity as custodian. This provision is intended to prevent the exercise of those powers for the direct or indirect benefit of the custodian, so as to avoid as nearly as possible the result that a custodian who dies while holding an insurance policy on his own life for the benefit of a minor will have the policy taxed in his estate. See, Section 2042, I.R.C.; but compare Terriberry v. U.S., 517 F.2d 286 (5th Cir. 1975), and Rose v. U.S., 511 F.2d 259 (5th Cir. 1975).

§ 14. Use of Custodial Property

(a) A custodian may deliver or pay to the minor or expend for the minor's benefit so much of the custodial property as the custodian considers advisable for the use and benefit of the minor, without court order and without regard to (i) the duty or ability of the custodian personally or of any other person to support the minor, or (ii) any other income or property of the minor which may be applicable or available for that purpose.

(b) On petition of an interested person or the minor if the minor has attained the age of 14 years, the court may order the custodian to deliver or pay to the minor or expend for the minor's benefit so much of the custodial property as the court considers advisable for the use and benefit of the minor.

(c) A delivery, payment, or expenditure under this section is in addition to, not in substitution for, and does not affect any obligation of a person to support the minor.

COMMENT

Subsections (a) and (b) track subsections (b) and (c) of Section 4 of the 1966 Act, but with two significant changes. The standard for expenditure of custodial property has been amended to read "for the use and benefit of the minor," rather than "for the support, maintenance, education and benefit of the minor" as specified under the 1966 Act. This change is intended to avoid the implication that the custodial property can be used only for the required support of the minor.

The IRS has taken the position that the income from custodial property, to the extent it is used for the support of the minor-donee, is includable in the gross income of any person who is legally obligated to support the minor-donee, whether or not that person or parent is serving as the custodian. Rev.Rul. 56–484, C.B. 1956–2, 23; Rev.Rul. 59–357, C.B. 1959–2, 212. However, Reg. 1.662(a)–4 provides that the term "legal obligation" includes a legal obligation to support another person if, and only if, the obligation is not affected by the adequacy of the dependent's own resources. Thus, if under local law a parent may use the resources of a child for the child's support in lieu of supporting the child himself or herself, no obligation of support exists, whether or not income is actually used for support, at least if the child's resources are adequate. See, Bittker, *Federal Taxation of Income Estates and Gifts* ¶80.44 (1981).

For this reason, new subsection (c) has been added to specify that distributions or expenditures may be made for the minor without regard to the duty or ability of any other person to support the minor and that distributions or expenditures are not in substitution for, and shall not affect, the obligation of any person to support the minor. Other possible methods of avoiding the attribution of custodial property income to the person obligated to support the minor would be to prohibit the use of custodial property or its income for that purpose, or to provide that any such use gives rise to a cause of action by the minor against his parent to the extent that custodial property or income is so used. The first alternative was rejected as too restrictive, and the second as too cumbersome.

The "use and benefit" standard in subsections (a) and (b) is intended to include payment of the minor's legally enforceable obligations such as tax or child support obligations or tort claims. Custodial property could be reached by levy of a judgment creditor in any event, so there is no reason not to permit custodian or court-ordered expenditures for enforceable claims.

An "interested person" entitled to seek court ordered distributions under subsection (b) would include not only the parent or conservator or guardian of the minor and a transferor or a transferor's legal representative, but also a public agency or official with custody of the minor and a third party to whom the minor owes legally enforceable debts.

§ 15. Custodian's Expenses, Compensation, and Bond

(a) A custodian is entitled to reimbursement from custodial property for reasonable expenses incurred in the performance of the custodian's duties.

(b) Except for one who is a transferor under Section 4, a custodian has a non-cumulative election during each calendar year to charge reasonable compensation for services performed during that year.

(c) Except as provided in Section 18(f), a custodian need not give a bond.

COMMENT

This section parallels and restates Section 5 of the 1966 Act. It deletes the statement that a custodian may act without compensation for services, since that concept is implied in the retained provision that a custodian has an "election" to be compensated. However, to prevent abuse, the latter provision for permissive compensation is denied to a custodian who is also the donor of the custodial property.

The custodian's election to charge compensation must be exercised (although the compensation need not be actually paid) at least annually or it lapses and may not be exercised later. This provision is intended to avoid imputed income to the custodian who waives compensation, and also to avoid the accumulation of a large unanticipated claim for compensation exercisable at termination of the custodianship.

This section deletes as surplusage the bracketed optional standards contained in the 1966 Act for determining "reasonable compensation" which included, "in the order stated," a direction by the donor, statutes governing compensation of custodians or guardians, or court order. While compensation of custodians becomes a more likely occurrence and a more important issue under this Act because property requiring increased management may now be subject to custodianship, compensation can still be determined by agreement, by reference to a statute or by court order, without the need to so state in this Act.

§ 16. Exemption of Third Person From Liability

A third person in good faith and without court order may act on the instructions of or otherwise deal with any person purporting to make a transfer or purporting to act in the capacity of a custodian and, in the absence of knowledge, is not responsible for determining:

(1) the validity of the purported custodian's designation;

(2) the propriety of, or the authority under this [Act] for, any act of the purported custodian;

(3) the validity or propriety under this [Act] of any instrument or instructions executed or given either by the person purporting to make a transfer or by the purported custodian; or

(4) the propriety of the application of any property of the minor delivered to the purported custodian.

COMMENT

This section carries forward, but shortens and simplifies, Section 6 of the 1966 Act, with no substantive change intended. The 1966 revision permitted a 14-year old minor to appoint a successor custodian and specifically provided that third parties were entitled to rely on the appointment. Because this section refers to any custodian, and "custodian" is defined to include successor custodians (SECTION 1(7)), a successor custodian appointed by the minor is included among those upon whom third parties may rely.

Similarly, because this section protects any third "persons," it is not necessary to specify here or in SECTION 11(c) that it extends to any "issuer, transfer agent, bank, life insurance company, broker, or other person or financial institu-

tion," as did the 1966 Act. See the definition of "person" in SECTION 1(12).

This section excludes from its protection persons with "knowledge" of the irregularity of a transaction, a concept not expressed but probably implied in Section 6 of the 1966 Act. See, e.g., State ex rel. Paden v. Currel, 597 S.W.2d 167 (Mo.App.1980) disapproving the pledge of custodial property to secure a personal loan to the custodian.

Similarly, this section does not alter the requirements for bona fide purchaser or holder in due course status under other law for persons who acquire from a custodian custodial property subject to recordation or registration.

§ 17. Liability to Third Persons

(a) A claim based on (i) a contract entered into by a custodian acting in a custodial capacity, (ii) an obligation arising from the ownership or control of custodial property, or (iii) a tort committed during the custodianship, may be asserted against the custodial property by proceeding against the custodian in the custodial capacity, whether or not the custodian or the minor is personally liable therefor.

(b) A custodian is not personally liable:

(1) on a contract properly entered into in the custodial capacity unless the custodian fails to reveal that capacity and to identify the custodianship in the contract; or

(2) for an obligation arising from control of custodial property or for a tort committed during the custodianship unless the custodian is personally at fault.

(c) A minor is not personally liable for an obligation arising from ownership of custodial property or for a tort committed during the custodianship unless the minor is personally at fault.

COMMENT

This section has no counterpart in the 1966 Act and is based upon Section 5–429 of the Uniform Probate Code, relating to limitations on the liability of conservators. Because some forms of custodial property now permitted under this Act can give rise to liabilities as well as benefits (e.g., general partnership interests, interests in real estate or business proprietorships, automobiles, etc.) the Committee believes it is necessary to protect the minor and other assets he might have or acquire from such liabilities, since the minor is unable to disclaim a transfer to a custodian for his benefit. Similar protection for the custodian is necessary so as not to discourage nonprofessional or uncompensated persons from accepting the office. Therefore this section generally limits the claims of third parties to recourse against the custodial property, as third parties dealing with a trust are generally limited to recourse against the trust corpus.

The custodian incurs personal liability only as provided in subsection (b) for actual fault or for failure to disclose his custodial capacity "in the contract" when contracting with third parties. In oral contracts, oral disclosure of the custodial capacity is sufficient. The minor, on the other hand, incurs personal liability under subsection (c) only for actual fault.

When custodial property is subjected to claims of third parties under this section, the minor or his legal representative, if not a party to the action by which the claim is successfully established, may seek to recover the loss from the custodian in a separate action. See SECTION 19 and the Comment thereto.

§ 18. Renunciation, Resignation, Death, or Removal of Custodian; Designation of Successor Custodian

(a) A person nominated under Section 3 or designated under Section 9 as custodian may decline to serve by delivering a valid disclaimer [under the Uniform Disclaimer of Property Interests Act of the Enacting State] to the person who made the nomination or to the transferor or the transferor's legal representative. If the event giving rise to a transfer has not occurred and no substitute custodian able, willing, and eligible to serve was nominated under Section 3, the person who made the nomination may nominate a substitute custodian under Section 3; otherwise the transferor or the transferor's legal representative shall designate a substitute custodian at the time of the transfer, in either case from among the persons eligible to serve as custodian for that kind of property under Section 9(a). The custodian so designated has the rights of a successor custodian.

(b) A custodian at any time may designate a trust company or an adult other than a transferor under Section 4 as successor custodian by executing and dating an instrument of designation before a subscribing witness other than the successor. If the instrument of designation does not contain or is not accompanied by the resignation of the custodian, the designation of the successor does not take effect until the custodian resigns, dies, becomes incapacitated, or is removed.

(c) A custodian may resign at any time by delivering written notice to the minor if the minor has attained the age of 14 years and to the successor custodian and by delivering the custodial property to the successor custodian.

(d) If a custodian is ineligible, dies, or becomes incapacitated without having effectively designated a successor and the minor has attained the age of 14 years, the minor may designate as successor custodian, in the manner prescribed in subsection (b), an adult member of the minor's family, a conservator of the minor, or a trust company. If the minor has not attained the age of 14 years or fails to act within 60 days after the ineligibility, death, or incapacity, the conservator of the minor becomes successor custodian. If the minor has no conservator or the conservator declines to act, the transferor, the legal representative of the transferor or of the custodian, an adult member of the minor's family, or any other interested person may petition the court to designate a successor custodian.

(e) A custodian who declines to serve under subsection (a) or resigns under subsection (c), or the legal representative of a deceased or incapacitated custodian, as soon as practicable, shall put the custodial property and records in the possession and control of the successor custodian. The successor custodian by action may enforce the obligation to deliver custodial property and records and becomes responsible for each item as received.

(f) A transferor, the legal representative of a transferor, an adult member of the minor's family, a guardian of the person of the minor, the conservator of the minor, or the minor if the minor has attained the age of 14 years may petition the court to remove the custodian for cause and to designate a successor custodian other than a transferor under Section 4 or to require the custodian to give appropriate bond.

COMMENT

This section tracks but condenses Section 7 of the 1966 Act to provide that the custodian, or if the custodian does not do so, the minor if he is 14, may appoint the successor custodian, or failing that, that the conservator of the minor or a court appointee shall serve. It also covers disclaimer of the office by designated or successor custodians or by nominated future custodians who decline to serve.

This Act broadens the category of persons who may be designated by the initial custodian as successor custodian from an adult member of the minor's family, his conservator, or a trust company to any adult or trust company. However, the minor's designation remains limited to an adult member of his family (expanded to include a spouse and a stepparent, see SECTION 1(10)), his conservator, or a trust company.

§ 19. Accounting by and Determination of Liability of Custodian

(a) A minor who has attained the age of 14 years, the minor's guardian of the person or legal representative, an adult member of the minor's family, a transferor, or a transferor's legal representative may petition the court (i) for an accounting by the custodian or the custodian's legal representative; or (ii) for a determination of responsibility, as between the custodial property and the custodian personally, for claims against the custodial property unless the responsibility has been adjudicated in an action under Section 17 to which the minor or the minor's legal representative was a party.

(b) A successor custodian may petition the court for an accounting by the predecessor custodian.

(c) The court, in a proceeding under this [Act] or in any other proceeding, may require or permit the custodian or the custodian's legal representative to account.

(d) If a custodian is removed under Section 18(f), the court shall require an accounting and order delivery of the custodial property and records to the successor custodian and the execution of all instruments required for transfer of the custodial property.

COMMENT

This section carries forward Section 8 of the 1966 Act, but expands the class of parties who may require an accounting by the custodian to include any person who made a transfer to him (or any such person's legal representative), the mi-

nor's guardian of the person, and the successor custodian.

Subsection (b) authorizes but does not obligate a successor custodian to seek an accounting by the predecessor custodian. Since the minor and other persons mentioned in subsection (a) may also seek an accounting from the predecessor at any time, it is anticipated that the exercise of this right by the successor should be rare.

Subsection (a) also gives the same parties (other than a successor custodian) the right to seek recovery from the custodian for loss or diminution of custodial property resulting from successful claims by third persons under SECTION 17, unless that issue has already been adjudicated in an action under that section to which the minor was a party.

This section does not contain a separate statute of limitations pre-cluding petitions for accounting after termination of the custodianship. Because custodianships can be created without the knowledge of the minor, a person might learn of a custodian's failure to turn over custodial property long after reaching majority, and should not be precluded from asserting his rights in the case of such fraud. In addition, the 1966 Act has no such preclusion and seems to have worked well. Other law, such as general statutes of limitation and the doctrine of laches, should serve adequately to protect former custodians from harassment.

§ 20. Termination of Custodianship

The custodian shall transfer in an appropriate manner the custodial property to the minor or to the minor's estate upon the earlier of:

(1) the minor's attainment of 21 years of age with respect to custodial property transferred under Section 4 or 5;

(2) the minor's attainment of [majority under the laws of this State other than this [Act]] [age 18 or other statutory age of majority of Enacting State] with respect to custodial property transferred under Section 6 or 7; or

(3) the minor's death.

COMMENT

This section tracks Section 4(d) of the 1966 Act, but provides that custodianships created by fiduciaries without express authority from the donor of the property under SECTION 6 and by obligors of the minor under SECTION 7 terminate upon the minor's attaining the age of majority under the general laws of the state, since these custodianships are substitutes for conservatorships that would otherwise terminate at that time. Because property in a single custodianship may be distributable at different times, separate accounting for custodial property by source may be required. See Comment to SECTION 10.

§ 21. Applicability

This [Act] applies to a transfer within the scope of Section 2 made after its effective date if:

(1) the transfer purports to have been made under [the Uniform Gifts to Minors Act of the Enacting State]; or

(2) the instrument by which the transfer purports to have been made uses in substance the designation "as custodian under the Uniform Gifts to Minors Act" or "as custodian under the Uniform Transfers to Minors Act" of any other state, and the application of this [Act] is necessary to validate the transfer.

COMMENT

This section is new and has two purposes. First, it operates as a "savings clause" to validate transfers made after its effective date which mistakenly refer to the enacting state's UGMA rather than to this Act. Second, it validates transfers attempted under the UGMA of another state which would not permit transfers from that source or of property of that kind or under the UTMA of another state with no nexus to the transaction, provided in each case that the enacting state has a sufficient nexus to the transaction under SECTION 2.

§ 22. Effect on Existing Custodianships

(a) Any transfer of custodial property as now defined in this [Act] made before [the effective date of this Act] is validated notwithstanding that there was no specific authority in [the Uniform Gifts to Minors Act of the Enacting State] for the coverage of custodial property of that kind or for a transfer from that source at the time the transfer was made.

(b) This [Act] applies to all transfers made before the effective date of this [Act] in a manner and form prescribed in [the Uniform Gifts to Minors Act of the Enacting State], except insofar as the application impairs constitutionally vested rights or extends the duration of custodianships in existence on the effective date of this [Act].

[(c) Sections 1 and 20 with respect to the age of a minor for whom custodial property is held under this [Act] do not apply to custodial property held in a custodianship that terminated because of the minor's attainment of the age of [18] after [date prior Act was amended to specify [18] as age of majority] and before [the effective date of this Act].]

COMMENT

Subsection (a) is new and is based on Section 45–109a of the Connecticut Act which validates gifts of real estate and partnership interests made prior to their inclusion as "custodial property" under that Act. However, this provision goes further and purports also to val-

639

idate prior transfers of the kind now covered by the Act, i.e., transfers from estates, trusts, guardianships, and obligors.

All states have previously enacted some version of UGMA, and it will be more orderly to subject gifts or other transfers under the prior Act to the procedures of this Act, rather than to keep both Acts in force, presumably for 18 or 21 years until all custodianships created under prior law have terminated. Subsection (b) is intended to apply this Act to prior gifts and existing custodianships insofar as it is constitutionally permissible to do so. However, pri-

or custodianships will continue to terminate at the age prescribed under the prior Act.

Optional subsection (c) is also new and is based upon Section 45–109b of the Connecticut Act. It is intended for adoption in those states that amended their Acts to reduce the age of majority to 18, but which adopt the recommended return to 21 as the age at which custodianships terminate. Its purpose is to avoid resurrecting custodianships for persons not yet 21 which terminated during the period that the age of 18 governed termination.

§ 23. Uniformity of Application and Construction

This [Act] shall be applied and construed to effectuate its general purpose to make uniform the law with respect to the subject of this [Act] among states enacting it.

§ 24. Short Title

This [Act] may be cited as the "[Name of Enacting State] Uniform Transfers to Minors Act."

§ 25. Severability

If any provisions of this [Act] or its application to any person or circumstance is held invalid, the invalidity does not affect other provisions or applications of this [Act] which can be given effect without the invalid provision or application, and to this end provisions of this [Act] are severable.

§ 26. Effective Date

This [Act] takes effect _____.

§ 27. Repeals

[Insert appropriate reference to the existing Gifts to Minors Act of the Enacting State or other jurisdiction] is hereby repealed. To the extent that this [Act], by virtue of Section 22(b), does not apply to transfers made in a manner prescribed in [the Gifts to Minors Act of the Enacting State] or to the powers, duties, and immunities conferred by transfers in that manner upon custodians and persons dealing with custodians, the repeal of [the Gifts to Minors Act of the Enacting State] does not affect those transfers or those powers, duties, and immunities.

UNIFORM PREMARITAL AGREEMENT ACT

PREFATORY NOTE

The number of marriages between persons previously married and the number of marriages between persons each of whom is intending to continue to pursue a career is steadily increasing. For these and other reasons, it is becoming more and more common for persons contemplating marriage to seek to resolve by agreement certain issues presented by the forthcoming marriage. However, despite a lengthy legal history for these premarital agreements, there is a substantial uncertainty as to the enforceability of all, or a portion, of the provisions of these agreements and a significant lack of uniformity of treatment of these agreements among the states. The problems caused by this uncertainty and nonuniformity are greatly exacerbated by the mobility of our population. Nevertheless, this uncertainty and nonuniformity seem reflective not so much of basic policy differences between the states but rather a result of spasmodic, reflexive response to varying factual circumstances at different times. Accordingly, uniform legislation conforming to modern social policy which provides both certainty and sufficient flexibility to accommodate different circumstances would appear to be both a significant improvement and a goal realistically capable of achievement.

This Act is intended to be relatively limited in scope. Section 1 defines a "premarital agreement" as "an agreement between prospective spouses made in contemplation of marriage and to be effective upon marriage." Section 2 requires that a premarital agreement be in writing and signed by both parties. Section 4 provides that a premarital agreement becomes effective upon the marriage of the parties. These sections establish significant parameters. That is, the Act does not deal with agreements between persons who live together but who do not contemplate marriage or who do not marry. Nor does the Act provide for postnuptial or separation agreements or with oral agreements.

On the other hand, agreements which are embraced by the act are permitted to deal with a wide variety of matters and Section 3 provides an *illustrative* list of those matters, including spousal support, which may properly be dealt with in a premarital agreement.

Section 6 is the key operative section of the Act and sets forth the conditions under which a premarital agreement is not enforceable. An agreement is not enforceable if the party against whom enforcement is sought proves that (a) he or she did not execute the agreement voluntarily or that (b) the agreement was unconscionable when it was executed and, before execution of the agreement, he or she (1) was not provided a fair and reasonable disclosure of the property or financial obligations of the other party, (2) did not voluntarily and expressly waive, in writing, any right to disclosure of the property or financial obligations of the other party beyond the disclosure provided, *and* (3) did not have, or reasonably could not have had, an adequate knowledge of the property and financial obligations of the other party.

Even if these conditions are not proven, if a provision of a premarital agreement modifies or eliminates spousal support, and that modification or elimination would cause a party to be eligible for support under a program of public assistance at the time of separation, marital dissolution, or death, a court is authorized to order the other party to provide support to the extent necessary to avoid that eligibility.

These sections form the heart of the Act; the remaining sections deal with more tangential issues. Section 5 prescribes the manner in which a premarital agreement may be amended or revoked; Section 7 provides for very limited enforcement where a marriage is subsequently determined to be void; and Section 8 tolls any statute of limitations applicable to an action asserting a claim for relief under a premarital agreement during the parties' marriage.

Table of Sections

§ 1. Definitions

As used in this Act:

(1) "Premarital agreement" means an agreement between prospective spouses made in contemplation of marriage and to be effective upon marriage.

(2) "Property" means an interest, present or future, legal or equitable, vested or contingent, in real or personal property, including income and earnings.

COMMENT

The definition of "premarital agreement" set forth in subsection (1) is limited to an agreement between prospective spouses made in contemplation of and to be effective upon marriage. Agreements between persons living together but not contemplating marriage (see Marvin v. Marvin, 18 Cal.3d 660 (1976), judgment after trial modified, 122 Cal.App.3d 871 (1981)) and post-nuptial or separation agreements are outside the scope of this Act. Formal requirements are pre-scribed by Section 2. An illustrative list of matters which may be included in an agreement is set forth in Section 3.

Subsection (2) is designed to embrace all forms of property and interests therein. These may include rights in a professional license or practice, employee benefit plans, pension and retirement accounts, and so on. The reference to income or earnings includes both income from property and earnings from personal services.

§ 2. Formalities

A premarital agreement must be in writing and signed by both parties. It is enforceable without consideration.

COMMENT

This section restates the common requirement that a premarital agreement be reduced to writing and signed by both parties (see Ariz.Rev.Stats. § 25–201; Ark. Stats. § 55–310; Cal.Civ.C. § 5134; 13 Dela.Code 1974 § 301; Idaho Code § 32–917; Ann.Laws Mass. ch. 209, § 25; Minn.Stats.Ann. § 519.11; Montana Rev.C. § 36–123; New Mex. Stats.Ann.1978 40–2–4; Ore.Rev.Stats. § 108.140; Vernon's Texas Codes Ann. § 5.44; Vermont Stats.Ann. Title 12, § 181). Many states also require other formalities, including notarization or an acknowledgement (see, e.g., Arizona, Arkansas, California, Idaho, Montana, New Mexico) but may then permit the formal statutory requirement to be avoided or satisfied subsequent to execution (see In re Marriage of Cleveland, 76 Cal.App.3d 357 (1977) (premarital agreement never acknowledged but "proved" by sworn testimony of parties in dissolution proceeding)). This act dispenses with all formal requirements except a writing signed by both parties. Although the section is framed in the singular, the agreement may consist of one or more documents intended to be part of the agreement and executed as required by this section.

Section 2 also restates what appears to be the almost universal rule regarding the marriage as consideration for a premarital agreement (see, e.g., Ga.Code § 20–303; Barnhill v. Barnhill, 386 So.2d 749 (Ala.Civ.App.1980); Estate of Gillilan v. Estate of Gillilan, 406 N.E.2d 981 (Ind.App.1980); Friedlander v. Friedlander, 494 P.2d 208 (Wash. 1972); but cf. Wilson v. Wilson, 170 A.2d 679, 685 (Me.1961)). The primary importance of this rule has been to provide a degree of mutuality of benefits to support the enforceability of a premarital agreement. A marriage is a prerequisite for the effectiveness of a premarital agreement under this act (see Section 4). This requires that there be a ceremonial marriage. Even if this marriage is subsequently determined to have been void, Section 7 may provide limits of enforceability of an agreement entered into in contemplation of that marriage. Consideration as such is not required and the standards for en-

forceability are established by Sections 6 and 7. Nevertheless, this provision is retained here as a desirable, if not essential, restatement of the law. On the other hand, the fact that marriage is deemed to be consideration for the purpose of this act does not change the rules applicable in other areas of law (see, e.g., 26 U.S.C.A. §§ 2043) release of certain marital rights not treated as consideration for federal estate tax, 2512; Merrill v. Fahs, 324 U.S. 308, rehearing denied 324 U.S. 888 (release of marital rights in premarital agreement not adequate and full consideration for purposes of federal gift tax).

Finally, a premarital agreement is a contract. As required for any other contract, the parties must have the capacity to contract in order to enter into a binding agreement. Those persons who lack the capacity to contract but who under other provisions of law are permitted to enter into a binding agreement may enter into a premarital agreement under those other provisions of law.

§ 3. Content

(a) Parties to a premarital agreement may contract with respect to:

(1) the rights and obligations of each of the parties in any of the property of either or both of them whenever and wherever acquired or located;

(2) the right to buy, sell, use, transfer, exchange, abandon, lease, consume, expend, assign, create a security interest in, mortgage, encumber, dispose of, or otherwise manage and control property;

(3) the disposition of property upon separation, marital dissolution, death, or the occurrence or nonoccurrence of any other event;

(4) the modification or elimination of spousal support;

(5) the making of a will, trust, or other arrangement to carry out the provisions of the agreement;

(6) the ownership rights in and disposition of the death benefit from a life insurance policy;

(7) the choice of law governing the construction of the agreement; and

(8) any other matter, including their personal rights and obligations, not in violation of public policy or a statute imposing a criminal penalty.

(b) The right of a child to support may not be adversely affected by a premarital agreement.

COMMENT

Section 3 permits the parties to contract in a premarital agreement with respect to any matter listed and any other matter not in violation of public policy or any statute imposing a criminal penalty. The matters are intended to be illustrative, not exclusive. Paragraph (4) of subsection (a) specifically authorizes the parties to deal with spousal support obligations. There is a split in authority among the states as to whether a premarital agreement may control the issue of spousal support. Some few states do not permit a premarital agreement to control this issue (see, e.g., In re Marriage of Winegard, 278 N.W.2d 505 (Iowa 1979); Fricke v. Fricke, 42 N.W.2d 500 (Wis.1950)). However, the better view and growing trend is to permit a premarital agreement to govern this matter if the agreement and the circumstances of its execution satisfy certain standards (see, e.g., Newman v. Newman, 653 P.2d 728 (Colo.Sup. Ct.1982); Parniawski v. Parniawski, 359 A.2d 719 (Conn.1976); Volid v. Volid, 286 N.E.2d 42 (Ill.1972); Osborne v. Osborne, 428 N.E.2d 810 (Mass.1981); Hudson v. Hudson, 350 P.2d 596 (Okla.1960); Unander v. Unander, 506 P.2d 719 (Ore.1973)) (see Sections 7 and 8).

Paragraph (8) of subsection (a) makes clear that the parties may also contract with respect to other matters, including personal rights and obligations, not in violation of public policy or a criminal statute. Hence, subject to this limitation, an agreement may provide for such matters as the choice of abode, the freedom to pursue career opportunities, the upbringing of children, and so on. However, subsection (b) of this section makes clear that an agreement may not adversely affect what would otherwise be the obligation of a party to a child.

§ 4. Effect of Marriage

A premarital agreement becomes effective upon marriage.

COMMENT

This section establishes a marriage as a prerequisite for the effectiveness of a premarital agreement. As a consequence, the act does not provide for a situation where persons live together without marrying. In that situation, the parties must look to the other law of the jurisdiction (see Marvin v. Marvin, 18 Cal.3d 660 (1976); judgment after trial modified, 122 Cal.App.3d 871 (1981)).

§ 5. Amendment, Revocation

After marriage, a premarital agreement may be amended or revoked only by a written agreement signed by the parties. The amended agreement or the revocation is enforceable without consideration.

COMMENT

This section requires the same formalities of execution for an amendment or revocation of a premarital agreement as are required for its original execution (cf. Estate of Gillilan v. Estate of Gillilan, 406 N.E.2d 981 (Ind.App.1980) (agreement may be altered by subsequent agreement but not simply by inconsistent acts)).

§ 6. Enforcement

(a) A premarital agreement is not enforceable if the party against whom enforcement is sought proves that:

(1) that party did not execute the agreement voluntarily; or

(2) the agreement was unconscionable when it was executed and, before execution of the agreement, that party:

(i) was not provided a fair and reasonable disclosure of the property or financial obligations of the other party;

(ii) did not voluntarily and expressly waive, in writing, any right to disclosure of the property or financial obligations of the other party beyond the disclosure provided; and

(iii) did not have, or reasonably could not have had, an adequate knowledge of the property or financial obligations of the other party.

(b) If a provision of a premarital agreement modifies or eliminates spousal support and that modification or elimination causes one party to the agreement to be eligible for support under a program of public assistance at the time of separation or marital dissolution, a court, notwithstanding the terms of the agreement, may require the other party to provide support to the extent necessary to avoid that eligibility.

(c) An issue of unconscionability of a premarital agreement shall be decided by the court as a matter of law.

COMMENT

This section sets forth the conditions which must be proven to avoid the enforcement of a premarital agreement. If prospective spouses enter into a premarital agreement and their subsequent marriage is determined to be void, the enforceability of the agreement is governed by Section 7.

The conditions stated under subsection (a) are comparable to concepts which are expressed in the statutory and decisional law of many jurisdictions. Enforcement based on disclosure and voluntary execution is perhaps most common (see, e.g., Ark.Stats. § 55–309; Minn.Stats.Ann. § 519.11; In re Kaufmann's Estate, 171 A.2d 48 (Pa.1961) (alternate holding)). However, knowledge or reason to know, together with voluntary execution, may also be sufficient (see, e.g., Tenn.Code Ann. § 36–606; Barnhill v. Barnhill, 386 So.2d 479 (Ala.Civ.App.1980); Del Vecchio v. Del Vecchio, 143 So.2d 17 (Fla. 1962); Coward and Coward, 582 P.2d 834 (Or.App.1978); but see Matter of Estate of Lebsock, 618 P.2d 683 (Colo.App.1980)) and so may a voluntary, knowing waiver (see Hafner v. Hafner, 295 N.W.2d 567 (Minn.1980)). In each of these situations, it should be underscored that execution must have been voluntary (see Lutgert v. Lutgert, 338 So.2d 1111 (Fla.1976); see also 13 Dela.Code 1974, § 301 (10 day waiting period)). Finally, a premarital agreement is enforceable if enforcement would not have been unconscionable at the time the agreement was executed (cf. Hartz v. Hartz,

234 A.2d 865 (Md.1967) (premarital agreement upheld if no disclosure but agreement was fair and equitable under the circumstances)).

The test of "unconscionability" is drawn from Section 306 of the Uniform Marriage and Divorce Act (UMDA) (see Ferry v. Ferry, 586 S.W.2d 782 (Mo.1979); see also Newman v. Newman, 653 P.2d 728 (Colo.Sup.Ct.1982) (maintenance provisions of premarital agreement tested for unconscionability at time of marriage termination)). The following discussion set forth in the Commissioner's Note to Section 306 of the UMDA is equally appropriate here:

"Subsection (b) undergirds the freedom allowed the parties by making clear that the terms of the agreement respecting maintenance and property disposition are binding upon the court unless those terms are found to be unconscionable. The standard of unconscionability is used in commercial law, where its meaning includes protection against one-sidedness, oppression, or unfair surprise (see section 2–302. Uniform Commercial Code), and in contract law, Scott v. U. S., 12 Wall (U.S.) 443 (1870) ('contract ... unreasonable and unconscionable but not void for fraud'); Stiefler v. McCullough, 174 N.E. 823, 97 Ind. App. 123 (1931); Terre Haute Cooperage v. Branscome, 35 So.2d 537, 203 Miss. 493 (1948); Carter v. Boone County Trust Co., 92 S.W.2d 647, 338 Mo. 629 (1936). It has been used in cases respecting divorce settlements or awards. Bell v. Bell, 371 P.2d 773, 150 Colo. 174 (1962) ('this division of property is manifestly unfair, inequitable and unconscionable'). Hence the act does not introduce a novel standard unknown to the law. In the context of negotiations between spouses as to the financial incidents of their marriage, the standard includes protection against overreaching, concealment of assets, and sharp dealing not consistent with the obligations of marital partners to deal fairly with each other.

"In order to determine whether the agreement is unconscionable, the court may look to the economic circumstances of the parties resulting from the agreement, and any other relevant evidence such as the conditions under which the agreement was made, including the knowledge of the other party. If the court finds the agreement not unconscionable, its terms respecting property division and maintenance may not be altered by the court at the hearing."

(Commissioner's Note, Sec. 306, Uniform Marriage and Divorce Act.)

Nothing in Section 6 makes the absence of assistance of independent legal counsel a condition for the unenforceability of a premarital agreement. However, lack of that assistance may well be a factor in determining whether the conditions stated in Section 6 may have existed (see, e. g., Del Vecchio v. Del Vecchio, 143 So.2d 17 (Fla.1962)).

Even if the conditions stated in subsection (a) are not proven, if a provision of a premarital agreement modifies or eliminates spousal support, subsection (b) authorizes a court to provide very limited relief to a party who would otherwise be

eligible for public welfare (see, e. g., Osborne v. Osborne, 428 N.E.2d 810 (Mass.1981) (dictum); Unander v. Unander, 506 P.2d 719, (Ore. 1973) (dictum)).

No special provision is made for enforcement of provisions of a premarital agreement relating to personal rights and obligations. However, a premarital agreement is a contract and these provisions may be enforced to the extent that they are enforceable are under otherwise applicable law (see Avitzur v. Avitzur, 459 N.Y.S.2d 572 (Ct.App.)).

Section 6 is framed in a manner to require the party who alleges that a premarital agreement is not enforceable to bear the burden of proof as to that allegation. The statutory law conflicts on the issue of where the burden of proof lies (contrast Ark.Stats. § 55–313; 31 Minn.Stats.Ann. § 519.11 with Vernon's Texas Codes Ann. § 5.45). Similarly, some courts have placed the burden on the attacking spouse to prove the invalidity of the agreement. Linker v. Linker, 470 P.2d 921 (Colo.1970); Matter of Estate of Benker, 296 N.W.2d 167 (Mich. App.1980); In re Kaufmann's Estate, 171 A.2d 48 (Pa.1961). Some have placed the burden upon those relying upon the agreement to prove its validity. Hartz v. Hartz, 234 A.2d 865 (Md.1967). Finally, several have adopted a middle ground by stating that a premarital agreement is presumptively valid but if a disproportionate disposition is make for the wife, the husband bears the burden of proof of showing adequate disclosure. (Del Vecchio v. Del Vecchio, 143 So.2d 17 (Fla.1962); Christians v. Christians, 44 N.W.2d 431 (Iowa 1950); In re

Neis' Estate, 225 P.2d 110 (Kans.1950); Truitt v. Truitt's Adm'r, 162 S.W.2d 31 (Ky.1942); In re Estate of Strickland, 149 N.W.2d 344 (Neb.1967); Kosik v. George, 452 P.2d 560 (Or.1969); Friedlander v. Friedlander, 494 P.2d 208 (Wash.1972)).

§ 7. Enforcement: Void Marriage

If a marriage is determined to be void, an agreement that would otherwise have been a premarital agreement is enforceable only to the extent necessary to avoid an inequitable result.

COMMENT

Under this section a void marriage does not completely invalidate a premarital agreement but does substantially limit its enforceability. Where parties have married and lived together for a substantial period of time and one or both have relied on the existence of a premarital agreement, the failure to enforce the agreement may well be inequitable. This section, accordingly, provides the court discretion to enforce the agreement to the extent necessary to avoid the inequitable result (see Annot., 46 A.L.R.3d 1403).

§ 8. Limitation of Actions

Any statute of limitations applicable to an action asserting a claim for relief under a premarital agreement is tolled during the marriage of the parties to the agreement. However, equitable defenses limiting the time for enforcement, including laches and estoppel, are available to either party.

COMMENT

In order to avoid the potentially disruptive effect of compelling litigation between the spouses in order to escape the running of an applicable statute of limitations, Section 8 tolls any applicable statute during the marriage of the parties (contrast Dykema v. Dykema, 412 N.E.2d 13 (Ill.App.1980) (statute of limitations not tolled where fraud not adequately pleaded, hence premarital agreement enforced at death)). However, a party is not completely free to set on his or her rights because the section does preserve certain equitable defenses.

§ 9. Application and Construction

This [Act] shall be applied and construed to effectuate its general purpose to make uniform the law with respect to the subject of this [Act] among states enacting it.

COMMENT

Section 9 is a standard provision in all Uniform Acts.

§ 10. Short Title

This [Act] may be cited as the Uniform Premarital Agreement Act.

COMMENT

This is the customary "short title" clause, which may be placed in that order in the bill for enactment as the legislative practice of the state prescribes.

§ 11. Severability

If any provision of this [Act] or its application to any person or circumstance is held invalid, the invalidity does not affect other provisions or applications of this [Act] which can be given effect without the invalid provision or application, and to this end the provisions of this [Act] are severable.

COMMENT

Section 11 is a standard provision included in certain Uniform Acts.

§ 12. Time of Taking Effect

This [Act] takes effect _____ and applies to any premarital agreement executed on or after that date.

§ 13. Repeal

The following acts and parts of acts are repealed:

(a)

(b)

(c)

UNIFORM MARITAL PROPERTY ACT

PREFATORY NOTE

"The institution of property is the embodiment of accidents, events, and the wisdom of the past. It is before us as clay into which we can introduce the coloration and configuration representing our wisdom. How great, how useful this new ingredient may be will largely determine the future happiness, and perhaps the continued existence of our society." Powell, *The Law of Real Property* (Rohan 4th ed. 1977).

Marriages have beginnings and endings. For their participants, the period between these points *is* the marriage. This Act is a property law. It functions to recognize the respective contributions made by men and women during a marriage. It discharges that function by raising those contributions to the level of defined, shared and enforceable property rights at the time the contributions are made.

The challenge to create such a framework is not new. Basic differences in approaches to marital economics go back for many centuries. *See* Donahue, *What Causes Fundamental Legal Ideas? Marital Property in England and France in the Thirteenth Century,* 78 Mich.L.Rev. 59 (1979); Younger, *Marital Regimes: A Story of Compromise and Demoralization, Together with Criticism and Suggestions for Reform,* 67 Cornell L.Rev. 45 (1981). In modern times the challenge was well articulated twenty years ago by the Report of the Committee on Civil and Political Rights to the President's Commission on the Status of Women. In 1963 that Report said:

Marriage is a partnership to which each spouse makes a different but equally important contribution. This fact has become increasingly recognized in the realities of American family living. While the laws of other countries have reflected this trend, family laws in the United States have lagged behind. Accordingly, the Committee concludes that during marriage each spouse should have a legally defined and substantial right in the earnings of the other spouse and in the real and personal property acquired as a result of such earnings, as well as in the management of such earnings and property. Such right should survive the marriage and be legally recognized in the event of its termination by annulment, divorce, or death. This policy should be appropriately implemented by legislation which would

652

safeguard either spouse against improper alienation of property by the other.

In the twenty years after those words much has changed regarding the institution of marriage, even though the challenge has not been fully met.

A prime example is the very demography of marriage and its terminal events. In 1963, 66.31% of all terminated marriages ended by death and 33.69% by divorce. By 1979 only 42.77% terminated by death, while 57.23% ended by dissolution. For half a decade the ratio of marriages to dissolution has been about two to one. The latest figures were 2,438,000 marriages and 1,219,000 divorces in 1981. The two to one ratio contrasts with 1930, when there were six marriages to every dissolution.

Statistics are not the only evidence of dramatic change. Statehouses have reflected it. Beginning with California at the end of the 60's and promulgation of the Uniform Marriage and Divorce Act in the early 70's, no-fault divorce has swept the statute books. In 1983 Illinois and South Dakota stand alone in adhering to fault-based divorce, and efforts to change to no-fault continue in Illinois. "Equitable distribution" of property became the handmaiden of no-fault divorce in the Uniform Marriage and Divorce Act and in most other reforms. Forty-one traditional common law jurisdictions now use some form of *property division* as a principal means of resolving economic dilemmas on dissolution. Adding the eight community property jurisdictions in which such a division is an inherent aspect of spousal property rights yields a total of 49. The one state missing on the property division roster is Mississippi. These property division developments address and typically adopt sharing concepts and bring many common law jurisdictions close to a deferred community property approach to divorce. Cheadle, *The Development of Sharing Principles in Common Law Marital Property States,* 28 UCLA L.Rev. 1269 (1981); *see also* Younger, *op. cit., supra.*

The ferment of change has not been limited to dissolution. The Uniform Probate Code was promulgated in 1969. Fourteen states are now listed as Code states or as substantially conforming states. Article II of the Code contains the concept of an augmented estate. It borrows heavily from New York's 1966 version of the idea. It is an advance on traditional forced-share procedures, operating by the creation of a larger universe of property against which a spousal right of election is exercisable. It accomplishes this by penetrating the veil of title and other techniques which have developed to insulate assets from the reach of forced-share statutes. In the official comment to the Code the augmented estate provisions are described as preventing arrangements by the owner of wealth which would transmit property to others than a surviving spouse by means other than probate for the deliberate purpose of defeating the rights of a surviving spouse.

It is worth noting that the Code's provisions, as well as conventional forced-share provisions in common law states, leave a gap. They transform assets into a sharing mode in a meaningful way only when the "have-not" spouse survives. If the sequence of death is the opposite, the have-not spouse has no power to dispose of assets over which he or she has no title in any common law jurisdiction.

The long-arm augmented estate provisions of the Uniform Probate Code may not go far enough to accommodate the perception of most laymen. A significant empirical study published in 1978 indicates a widespread public preference for a distribution of an *entire* intestate estate to a surviving spouse, whether or not there are surviving children. Fellows, Simon & Rau, *Public Attitudes About Distribution At Death And Intestate Succession Laws In The United States,* 1978 Am. B. Found. Research J. 319.

Obviously the "everything to each other" mode is confined to dispositions at death. An imposing body of case law testifies to a paradigm shift in this view when the question of "Who should get what and when?" is asked at a dissolution! And it is the equitable distribution court's demanding role in the judicial process to monitor and referee the ensuing contests in the divorce courts. Burgeoning advance sheets clearly indicate just how difficult the referee's job is when it must be done well over a million times a year!

In 1981 yet another shift was added to the catalog of change. After years of debate, tax-free interspousal transfers entered the stage under the auspices of the Economic Recovery Tax Act of 1981. *Wall Street Journal* columnist Vermont Royster furnished a characteristically succinct summary of it all:

"The marriage ceremony may say you two are now one and even include that phrase about with all my worldly goods I thee endow. The Internal Revenue Service has always taken a different view. It's wanted its share.

. . . wait until January 1, 1982, and . . . after that magic date you can share with your spouse as much as you please of those worldly goods . . . without so much as a by-your-leave from the federal tax man. In 1982 no more gift and estate taxes between spouses." Wall St. J., Sept. 2, 1981.

Heavy economic responsibilities of married couples and methods of coping with them point to yet another trendline of the last few decades. It is that of the two-worker households in which sharing the burden of producing family income is becoming routine. In more than half of American marriages with two spouses present there is a working wife and the number is growing. When there are children, the ratio is even higher. In more than two-thirds of current upper income marriages ($24,000 or more) there are two wage earners. Sharing of responsibility for wages from *outside* the home is altering traditional spousal roles and particularly economic roles rights, and responsibilities.

Thus the stage is set by substantial social and legislative change in the duration of marriages and in the economics of the termination of marriages by dissolution and death.

The Uniform Marital Property Act makes its appearance on that stage to offer a means of establishing present shared property rights of spouses *during* the marriage. This approach is bottomed on two propositions. The first is creation of an immediate sharing mode of ownership. The second proposition is that the sharing mode during marriage is an ownership right already in existence at the end of a marriage. Thus recognition and perfection of shared and vested ownership rights in marital property are in place at divorce or death. They do not have to come to fruition as a result of a court-ordained and possibly adversary "division" or by a statutorily-sanctioned "transfer."

Is the Uniform Marital Property Act a panacea for the malaise of marriage? Will it lower the divorce rate? Save the family? Eliminate marital violence? Be fully comprehensible? Be welcomed by all? Lower the cost of the family house? Create better parents? Solve child abuse? Avoid probate? Lower the cost of death or divorce?

Perhaps some but certainly not all of the above. If it does affect any of those considerations, it will take time and the process will be subtle. The disintegrating forces operating on marriages and families are many and complex. It would be a bold claim to suggest that any legislation could fully identify and rectify the problems in such an area. But the obvious and apparent existence of problems in the economic area of marriage certainly justifies an effort to identify and rectify them. The Uniform Marital Property Act is precisely such an effort.

What are the root concepts?

FIRST: Property acquired during marriage by the effort of spouses is shared and is something the couple can truly style as "ours." Rather than an evanescent hope, the idea of sharing implicit in viewing property as "ours" becomes reality as a result of a present, vested ownership right which each spouse has in all property acquired by the personal efforts of either during the marriage. That property is "marital property." (Section 4).

Except for its income, property brought into the marriage or acquired afterward by gift or devise is not marital but "individual property." Its *appreciation* remains individual property. However, the *income* of that property becomes marital property, so that *all* income of a couple is marital property. (Section 4).

Property already owned when the Act becomes effective or owned by couples moving into an adopting state will take on the characteristics of marital property only at death or marital dissolution and then only if it would have been marital property under the Act had the Act been in effect when and where the property was acquired. Prior to death or dissolution the Act ordains no change in the classification of property of a couple acquired at a time when the Act did not apply. (Sections 4(h), 17 and 18).

SECOND: The system which the Act creates to manage and control marital property accords a considerable measure of individual option. "Management and control" is a phrase of art in the Act. Basically management and control rights flow from the form in which title to property is held. If only one spouse holds property there is no requirement for the other spouse to participate in management and control functions. If both spouses hold property they must both participate in management and control unless the holding is in an alternative ("A *or* B") form. Couples can select their own options as they deem appropriate. (Sections 3, 5, 10 and 11). Management and control is different from ownership. Ownership rights are not lost by relinquishing or even neglecting management and control rights. In essence, the Act's management and control system is substantially similar to the existing procedures of title based management in common law states. (Section 5).

To guard against possible abuses by a spouse with sole title, a court can implement the addition of the name of the other spouse to marital property so that it is held, managed and controlled by both spouses. (Section 15).

The rule on gifts of marital property to third parties provides a safe harbor for smaller gifts. Unless aggregate gifts of marital property by one spouse to a third party in a calendar year are less than a specified dollar amount or are reasonable in amount with respect to the economic position of the spouses when made, both spouses must join in making the gift. A failure to procure that joinder renders the gift voidable at the option of the non-participating spouse. (Section 6).

THIRD: The varying patterns of today's marriages are accommodated by an opportunity to create custom systems by "marital property agreements." Full freedom to contract with respect to virtually all property matters is possible under the Act. By a marital property agreement a couple could opt out of the provisions of the Act in whole or in part. Conversely, they could opt in by agreeing that the Act's provisions will apply to all or a part of the property they own before they became subject to its terms.

As a protection and to ease matters of proof, the Act requires that marital property agreements be made in writing and signed by both spouses. (Section 10). Marital property agreements are enforceable without consideration.

FOURTH: On dissolution the structure of the Act as a *property statute* comes into full play. The Act takes the parties "to the door of the divorce court" only. It leaves to existing dissolution procedures in the several states the selection of the appropriate procedures for dividing property. On the other hand the Act has the function of confirming the *ownership* of property as the couple enters the process. Thus reallocation of property derived from the effort of both spouses during the marriage starts from a basis of the equal undivided ownership that the spouses share in their marital property. A given state's equitable distribution or other property division procedures could mean that the ownership will end that way, or that it could be substantially altered, but that will depend on other applicable state law and judicial determinations. An analogous situation obtains at death, with the Act operating primarily as a property statute rather than a probate statute.

At divorce and death special provisions will apply to property of a couple acquired before the Act applied to that couple. If any of that property would have been marital property under the Act, had the Act been in effect when and where it was acquired, then such property will be treated as if it were marital property at divorce. Property of the deceased spouse having that characteristic will be treated in that manner at death. This represents a deferred approach to reclassification of the property of spouses which does not otherwise have the characteristics of marital property due to the time or place of its acquisition. The deferral is to the time of marital termination at divorce or death. Those are events at which states have long altered the classification of their citizens' property by equitable distribution provisions or by forced share and augmented estate provisions. The Act builds on those established patterns already followed by the states by creating the deferred classification with respect to property owned by couples before the Act applied to them. A provision effecting automatic reclassification of such property with the passage of the Act would amount to retroactive legislation and would risk constitutional attack. *See* Irish, *A Common Law State Considers A Shift to Community Property,* 5 Community Prop. J. 227 (1978). On the other hand, the deferred approach of the Act operates only prospectively, tracking the procedure of the bulk of existing state legislation that prescribes forms of marital sharing effective only at divorce or death. (Sections 17 and 18).

FIFTH: Creditors may have claims that arise before marriage and after marriage. The premarital creditor is denied a bonanza by a marriage. (Section 8(b)(iii)). That creditor can only reach what would have been reached had there been no marriage. Postmarital obligations may subject both marital and individual property to claims. Obligations incurred by a spouse during marriage are presumed to be incurred in the interest of the marriage and the family and those obligations may be satisfied from all marital property and the other property of the incurring spouse. (Section 8(a) and (b)(ii)).

SIXTH: Bona fide purchasers of property for value are protected in their transactions with spouses by reliance on the manner in which property is held. They are under no duty to look "underneath" the manner of holding and are fully protected for not doing so. (Section 9).

In addition to those root concepts, a series of enabling provisions offer convenient support for the system. These include special methods of holding property, including a survivorship form of ownership (Section 11); dispositions by a probate avoidance feature in marital property agreements (Section 10(c)(6)); and remedies for disputes between the spouses affecting their property, including interspousal property accountings (Section 15). There are procedures to deal with marital and individual property which becomes intermixed. (Section 14). Special rules deal with complex property rights in life insurance and deferred employee benefits. (Sections 12 and 13). Conventional concurrent and survivorship forms may be used for marital property. (Section 11(d)). As an option for use in states that recognize tenancy by the entireties, existing tenancy by the entireties property continues to be available to perpetuate the creditor protection it affords. (Section 19).

Some of the root concepts can be traced to the sharing ideal which is at the center of the historical community property approach. The fundamental principle that ownership of all of the economic rewards from the personal effort of each spouse during marriage is shared by the spouses in vested, present, and equal interests is the heart of the community property system. It is also the heart of the Uniform Marital Property Act. Common law states have been moving closer and closer to the sharing concept in both divorce and probate legislation, and the Uniform Marital Property Act builds on the direction of that movement. Sharing is seen as a system of elemental fairness and justice so that those who share in the many and diverse forms of work involved in establishing and maintaining a marriage will have a protected share in the material acquisitions of that marriage. The Act creates and protects that share without forcing a spouse to await the completion of a gift from the other spouse or the garnering of proof of dollar-for-dollar contributions to the purchase price of assets acquired over the years of marriage. Under the Act, the sharing of property is recognized by creation of a present interest simultaneously with acquisition of property by effort during marriage. The interest is legally defined and enforceable. It permeates assets as they are acquired and continues to permeate them as they are invested and reinvested, as they are exchanged and transferred, and as they grow or diminish.

Such a law translates the emotional and perceived concept of "ours" into a verified legal reality. And while that parallels sharing under community property systems, the Act is more accurately characterized as a *sui generis* approach, and as one which utilizes equally useful ideas developed in common law jurisdictions, such as title based management and control. In addition, it is a response to the twenty-year-long challenge of the President's Commission on the Status of Women issued in 1963 to face the reality that each spouse makes a different but equally important contribution in a marriage. Though drafted with an awareness of various community property statutes and cases, the Uniform Marital Property Act is not an image of any of them. It is a statute speaking to the realities and equities of marriages in America in the Eighties.

Table of Sections

---

§ 1. General Definitions

In this [Act]:

(1) "Acquire" in relation to property includes reduction of indebtedness on encumbered property and obtaining a lien on or security interest in property.

(2) "Appreciation" means a realized or unrealized increase in the value of property.

(3) "Decree" means a judgment or other order of a court.

(4) "Deferred employment benefit" means a benefit under a plan, fund, program, or other arrangement under which compensation or benefits from employment are expressly, or as a result of surrounding circumstances, deferred to a later date or the happening of a future event. Such an arrangement includes a pension, profit sharing, or stock-bonus plan; an employee stock-ownership or stock-purchase plan; a savings or thrift plan; an annuity plan; a qualified bond-purchase plan; a self-employed retirement plan; a simplified employee pension; and a deferred compensation agreement or plan. It does not include life, health, accident, or other insurance, or a plan, fund, pro-

gram, or other arrangement providing benefits comparable to insurance benefits, except to the extent that benefits under the arrangement: (i) have a present value that is immediately realizable in cash at the option of the employee; (ii) constitute an unearned premium for the coverage; (iii) represent a right to compensation for loss of income during disability; or (iv) represent a right to payment of expenses incurred before time of valuation.

(5) "Determination date" means the last to occur of the following: (i) marriage; (ii) 12:01 a.m. on the date of establishment of a marital domicile in this State; or (iii) 12:01 a.m. on the effective date of this [Act].

(6) "Disposition at death" means transfer of property by will, intestate succession, nontestamentary transfer, or other means that take effect at the transferor's death.

(7) "Dissolution" means: (i) termination of a marriage by a decree of dissolution, divorce, annulment, or declaration of invalidity; or (ii) entry of a decree of legal separation or separate maintenance.

(8) "During marriage" means a period that begins at marriage and ends at dissolution or at the death of a spouse.

(9) Property is "held" by a person only if a document of title to the property is registered, recorded, or filed in a public office in the name of the person or a writing that customarily operates as a document of title to the type of property is issued for the property in the person's name.

(10) "Income" means wages, salaries, commissions, bonuses, gratuities, payments in kind, deferred employment benefits, proceeds, other than death benefits, of a health, accident, or disability insurance policy, or of a plan, fund, program, or other arrangement providing benefits comparable to those forms of insurance, other economic benefits having value which are attributable to the effort of a spouse, dividends, interest, income from trusts, and net rents and other net returns attributable to investment, rental, licensing, or other use of property, unless attributable to a return of capital or to appreciation.

(11) "Management and control" means the right to buy, sell, use, transfer, exchange, abandon, lease, consume, expend, assign, create a security interest in, mortgage, encumber, dispose of, institute or defend a civil action regarding, or otherwise deal with, property as if it were property of an unmarried person.

661

(12) "Marital property agreement" means an agreement that complies with Section 10.

(13) A person has "notice" of a fact if the person has knowledge of it, receives a notification of it, or has reason to know that it exists from the facts and circumstances known to the person.

(14) "Presumption" or a "presumed" fact means the imposition on the person against whom the presumption or presumed fact is directed of the burden of proving that the nonexistence of the presumed condition or fact is more probable than its existence.

(15) "Property" means an interest, present or future, legal or equitable, vested or contingent, in real or personal property.

(16) "Written consent" means a document signed by a person against whose interests it is sought to be enforced.

COMMENT

(1) The definition of "acquiring" assures the inclusion in the word of all transactions which increase dominion and control over assets. In a typical marital situation, payment on a mortgage will be an important means of building assets. The definition makes it clear that this is a means of acquisition.

(2) "Appreciation" has certain differential consequences, depending on whether it is from individual property or is created or enhanced by the effort of one spouse expended on individual property of the other spouse. The definition makes it clear that a specific realization, such as a sale, is *not* necessary for it to be a factor in marital property economics.

(4) The major provisions of the definition are derived from The Employee Retirement Income Security Act of 1974 ("ERISA"), Pub.L. No. 93–406. In the Act the definition is intended to cover and include plans of both private and public employers.

(5) The Act will apply to those couples now domiciled in an adopting state as well as those who move to one in the future. It will also apply to couples who marry in an adopting state after the Act is in effect. The definition of "determination date" creates a flexible formula to establish for individual couples in these three separate configurations the specific date as of which the Act is in effect with respect to their property. Use of 12:01 a. m. as the triggering incident of the determination date eliminates the necessity of referring throughout the Act to events occurring "*on or after*" the determination date.

(7) A legal separation or decree of separate maintenance is a dissolution. Specific authority to deal with the consequences of a legal separation is included as bracketed Subsection (4) of Section 17 for states in which this procedure is still in use. It is suggested that the term should remain in the defini-

tion even if this subsection is not enacted in order to deal with possible multi-state problems that could involve a state still using the procedure.

(8) The Act concerns the property of married persons. If a man and a women are not married, the property they own is *not* marital property. It may have been marital property if their marriage has been dissolved, or if one of them is deceased, but on the occurrence of such an event it loses its classification as marital property. Consequently the term "during marriage" applies throughout the Act and describes a particular status. The period when certain property will be marital is during marriage and the Act's provisions addressed to "spouses" will apply then as well. Without marriage, a man and a woman are not spouses. When they are referred to as spouses, the connotation is that the event or relationship referred to takes place during marriage.

(9) The word "title" is often viewed as the equivalent of "ownership." In the Act the method of referring to property to which there is a typical and usual form of documentation of title is that of identifying it as being "held" by a person named in the documentation, since title is *not* synonymous with ownership in the Act. The concept of holding is used to avoid a continued reference to title and a construction that might encourage overlooking the separate legal status of title and ownership, which is a fundamental aspect of the Act. The result of the definition is that there will be some types of property that will not be held by either spouse. This is obviously true with respect to classic

forms of bearer property without the Act, and the Act does not disturb that circumstance.

(10) Section 4 classifies all income earned or accrued during marriage and after the determination date from any source as marital property. The "income" definition is a broad one and is intended to cover all forms of income and earnings, but to exclude returns of capital and appreciation.

(11) Management and control issues are faced daily by partners and owners of various concurrent interests. They are solved daily as well. The management and control function is central to the Act, and the way in which the definition is applied is covered in Section 5.

(14) The presumption provisions are derived from Rule 301(a) of the Uniform Rules of Evidence.

(16) There are two types of writings that have special significance under the Act. One is a marital property agreement, fully described in Section 10. The other is the "written consent." This is a writing that states facts or consequences chargeable to and enforceable against a signatory. A written consent may have one or more signatories. It could be a conventional contract signed by two or more persons or it could be a simple memorandum of a type that would satisfy a statute of frauds requirement, signed by only one person. As an example, a creditor can relinquish a right to proceed against marital property by the terms of Section 8(d). This is accomplished by a written consent, and that would be a one-signatory document affirming the relinquishment. As additional examples, Section 12(c)(5) specifies

that a written consent of one spouse permits relinquishment of rights in a life insurance policy, while in Section 12(c)(6) the written consents of both spouses are prerequisites to another method of dealing with life insurance.

§ 2. Responsibility Between Spouses

(a) Each spouse shall act in good faith with respect to the other spouse in matters involving marital property or other property of the other spouse. This obligation may not be varied by a marital property agreement.

(b) Management and control by a spouse of that spouse's property that is not marital property in a manner that limits, diminishes, or fails to produce income from that property does not violate subsection (a).

COMMENT

Spouses are not trustees or guarantors toward each other. Neither are they simple parties to a contract endeavoring to further their individual interests. The duty is between, and is one of good faith. A spouse is not bound always to succeed in matters involving marital property ventures, but while endeavoring to succeed in a venture, must proceed with an appropriate regard for the property interests of the other spouse and without taking unfair advantage of the other spouse. *See* Cal.Civ. Code § 5125(e) (Supp.1980) for a similar provision in use in that state. *See also* Reppy, *Community Property in*

California, pp. 174–75, 177 (1980). This is one of four provisions in the Act that cannot be varied by a marital property agreement. (Section 10(c)).

Subsection (b) clarifies the right of a spouse to regulate the income stream of property of that spouse that is not marital property without violating the Section. Since all income of that property during marriage and after the determination date is marital property, a question might arise regarding the application of Subsection (a) to the income stream. Subsection (b) resolves that question.

§ 3. Variation by Marital Property Agreement

Except as provided in Sections 2, 8(e), 9(c) and 10(b), a marital property agreement may vary the effect of this [Act].

COMMENT

This section is modeled on UCC Section 1–102(3). It is placed at this point in the chronology in the Act in order that its message be conveyed early and emphatically.

The Act's property system applies if it is not changed. However, with four very limited exceptions (those of the good faith duty of Section 2, the protection of third parties under

Sections 8(e) and 9(c), and the support of dependent children under Section 10(b)), there is freedom to change the Act by a marital property agreement. Thus a couple may opt-out, opt-in, or do both in part. Custom-tailored marital property regimes are possible. The Act permits a couple to move its marital economics from status to contract and encourages a type of interspousal contractual freedom little known in common law states. It is important to the operation of the Act that the significance of this section be carried through to the use and application of its various provisions. For example, it is clearly intended that contractual variance is possible with respect to Section 4 (classification generally), Section 5 (management and control), Section 12 (life insurance classification), Section 13 (classification of employee benefits), Section 17 (marital dissolution), and Section 18 (disposition at death), although these are only examples. The provisions of this Section and Section 10 should always be read as a part of every other provision of the Act.

§ 4. Classification of Property of Spouses

(a) All property of spouses is marital property except that which is classified otherwise by this [Act].

(b) All property of spouses is presumed to be marital property.

(c) Each spouse has a present undivided one-half interest in marital property.

(d) Income earned or accrued by a spouse or attributable to property of a spouse during marriage and after the determination date is marital property.

(e) Marital property transferred to a trust remains marital property.

(f) Property owned by a spouse at a marriage after the determination date is individual property.

(g) Property acquired by a spouse during marriage and after the determination date is individual property if acquired:

(1) by gift or a disposition at death made by a third person to the spouse and not to both spouses;

(2) in exchange for or with the proceeds of other individual property of the spouse;

(3) from appreciation of the spouse's individual property except to the extent that the appreciation is classified as marital property under Section 14;

(4) by a decree, marital property agreement, written consent, or reclassification under Section 7(b) designating it as the individual property of the spouse;

(5) as a recovery for damage to property under Section 15, except as specifically provided otherwise in a decree, marital property agreement, or written consent; or

(6) as a recovery for personal injury except for the amount of that recovery attributable to expenses paid or otherwise satisfied from marital property.

(h) Except as provided otherwise in this [Act] the enactment of this [Act] does not alter the classification and ownership rights of property acquired before the determination date.

(i) Except as provided otherwise in this [Act] and to the extent it would affect the ownership rights of the spouse that existed in the property before the determination date, during marriage the interest of a spouse in property owned immediately before the determination date is treated as if it were individual property.

COMMENT

The Section creates the heart of the Act. It contains a general presumption, a series of property rules, an income rule, classification rules, and transition rules.

Classification: "Classification" is an essential process in applying the Act. In classification the essential sorting process is taking place: What is a given item or aggregation of property? Marital property? Individual property? Property owned before the determination date which had a wholly different set of ownership incidents not established by the Act at all? All property has a classification—a generic and basic set of characteristics—and the process is devoted to establishing those precise characteristics and answering those questions. The most important parts of the answer depend on *source* and *time of acquisition.* Title is *not* an answer since title functions under the Act principally to establish management and control rights and the facilitation of third party transactions flowing from the exercise of management and control rights. Under the Act title does *not* function as a classification index. Reclassification is just what the word implies—it is a change in classification, generally from marital to individual or vice versa.

The General Presumption: The first building block in the Act's operation is the general presumption in Subsection (b). The bias of the presumption favors classifying spousal assets as marital property. Thus at the beginning of any process of classifying spousal assets, everything is presumed to be marital property. When there is adequate proof to overcome the general presumption, then the proof will prevail and classification will be otherwise. But the "easy way," when there are no records or proof, will result in the operation of the presumption and in the classification of all spousal property as marital.

The Present Interest: A second building block is the creation of a *present* equal undivided interest for each spouse. This is a distinct de-

666

parture from existing versions of "marital property" arising out of equitable distribution developments in family law. Those family-law interests set forth in marital property definitions in equitable distribution statutes are delayed-action in nature and come to maturity only during the dissolution process. Marital property under the Act is created *as assets are acquired* by the spouses, whether from income from the effort of either spouse during marriage, as income attributable to passive or investment sources, or as appreciation of or in an exchange for or rollover of existing marital property. When the assets are acquired from such sources, the incidents and attributes of marital property, including the creation of a present legal interest, attach simultaneously with the acquisition. The assets so acquired are instantly classified or characterized as marital property. The classification persists until the marriage terminates by dissolution or death, or until occurrence of a "reclassification" by one or another of the methods provided in the Act.

The Income Rule: The third feature is an income rule, creating an easily comprehended system. By treating all income from any source as marital property, the Act affords a simple and understandable arrangement. In the majority of marriages, most income will be spent sooner or later. In those so affluent that this does not happen, the rule can either be followed or changed by marital property agreement. In the latter group of marriages, some extra record-keeping following an agreed bifurcation of income from marital and individual property should not pose an undue burden.

The income rule poses some "front-end" and "tail-end" problems. The "front-end" problem pertains to income received shortly after the determination date from effort or accrual of rights before the determination date. Actual ownership of such income became fixed before the determination date and it should not be and is not classified as marital property. This is handled by providing that income is marital only if "earned or accrued" after the determination date *and* during marriage.

With a disintegrating marriage in a state which has had the Act for a reasonable period of time, a cash basis or actual receipt rule at dissolution could give rise to significant abuses. This is the potential "tail-end" problem. Receipt of income under the management and the control of one spouse could be delayed voluntarily until the dissolution was complete, to the prejudice of the former spouse who was not in such a position of control. Hence the earned or accrued rule of the Act also addresses this problem. The accounting and classification problems of the accrual or constructive receipt system used in the Act to deal with the tail-end problem obviously could necessitate tracing activities, but the potential for manipulation and diversion with a cash basis rule is such that the difficulty is justified.

Transition to the Income Rule: There is an additional important element in the treatment of income. All property of couples already married when the Act becomes law in an adopting state has a set of characteristics not created by the Act.

667

The Act has been drafted to avoid altering those characteristics during the on-going marriage as far as the *principal* of the pre-adoption property is concerned. However the income rule obviously affects post-adoption income, classifying it as marital property. Post-adoption income is just that. It is not principal, and it is received and regulated by the Act's provisions only when the claim of right to it occurs by virtue of its having been earned or accrued *after* adoption. Hence the Act's income rule is not retroactive.

Trusts: Marital property transferred to a trust remains marital property and does not become "something else" under Subsection (e). A marital property agreement could provide otherwise. The subsection's principal enabling function is to permit the creation of revocable living trusts by one or both spouses without any automatic reclassification of property committed to the trust. If the trust is created by both spouses, or if created by one and consented to by the other, it would itself be a sufficient written form of marital property agreement to effect any reclassification directed by its terms if the other requirements of Section 10 are met. A trust created by one spouse would necessarily be measured by the good faith provisions of Section 2. The subsection would have no application to testamentary trusts, since marital property is the property of spouses. When a former spouse dies leaving a will that creates a trust, the property funding the trust can no longer be marital property. It could, and ordinarily would, be the decedent's share of *former* marital property.

Appreciation of Individual Property: Individual property definitions for post-determination date acquisitions are furnished in a listed format. In addition to such acquisitions by gift or inheritance, there are other obvious inclusions. One of special importance concerns *appreciation* of individual property. Assume that one spouse comes to a marriage subject to the Act as the owner of a valuable piece of real estate. It is individual property. If it quadruples in value, it is *still* individual property. While its income is marital property, the property itself *and* its appreciation in value is almost always individual property. One exception is the special rule announced in Section 14(b). That rule is concerned with the application to the individual property of one spouse of personal effort by the other spouse. It could apply in limited situations, but establishing it requires a very strong showing. Another possible exception could arise from mixing marital property with the individual property, also dealt with in Section 14. If the components of the mixed property can be traced, then no reclassification will occur. Monetary contributions to real estate acquisition or improvement are typically traceable, so that this form of reclassification regarding real estate should not be a frequent issue.

Donated Property: The rule treating property received by gift as individual property applies to gifts made to only one spouse. If a gift is made to both spouses, the donated property is marital property. This would apply to gifts to both in any form, including transfers to them as joint tenants, tenants in common, or in one of the title forms included in Section 11.

Effect on Existing Property: Subsection (h) states an important transitional rule. It can be assumed that in an adopting state one spouse might own property absolutely, and that a couple might also own property concurrently or as community property. The latter would be true of a couple which moved into an adopting state from one of the existing community property states as well as a couple in an adopting community property state. All of the property of a married couple in an adopting state on hand at the determination date would have a particular classification. Certain incidents would already have attached to the manner of ownership. Survivorship would be an incident of jointly held or entireties property. A tenancy in common would consist of undivided interests, with each interest subject to individual rights of disposition. Community property would have the incidents described in the *Uniform Disposition of Community Property Rights at Death Act,* and possibly others developed between the spouses by agreement. Trust interests would be regulated by governing instruments. The Act is *not* designed to alter these various incidents of ownership or to reclassify such property.

With minor exceptions, the arrival of the determination date for such a couple would neither reclassify any of their property as marital property nor as *any* type of property other than what it was prior to the determination date. The exceptions all operate on that property only *after* the determination date. They are limited and include only

the "deferred marital property" approach at dissolution and death set forth in Sections 17 and 18, the income treatment set forth in Subsection (d), and the specific provisions of Subsection (i).

Note that Subsection (h) applies to property of *spouses* owned before the determination date. On the other hand Subsection (f) deals specifically with property owned *before marriage* by persons marrying in an adopting state after the Act is effective. It follows the traditional pattern of community property and dissolution-based marital property statutes in clearly classifying solely owned property owned before marriage as individual property effective with the marriage. Except for its income, individual property under the Act is analogous to solely owned property in a common law state or to separate property in an American community property state. Texas, Louisiana and Idaho separate property is even more kindred, since the income of separate property in those states is community property.

The "As If" Treatment: Subsection (i) is a statutory statement to identify pre-determination date property that is solely owned as functioning with a "fraternal twin" relationship to individual property under the Act. It is a transitional rule, stated as it is to avoid a direct substantive reclassification of pre-determination date property, but to clarify the functional treatment of it in applying the Act. It is important that it be read as the "as if" rule that it is, and not as a reclassification statute.

The exceptions in Subsection (i) are intended to avoid any interference with actual ownership incidents in property owned prior to the determination date. For example, community property owned prior to the determination date should not be treated functionally as individual property in applying the Act. On the other hand, tenancy in common property could function as if it were individual property under the Act's provisions with each owner's undivided interest being treated as though it were individual property. A tenancy in common of individual property of the respective spouses is possible under the Act.

Property "that is not marital property": There are references in the Act to property of a spouse " . . . that is not marital property . . ." (Sections 8(b) and 14(a)); property " . . . having any other classification . . ." (Section 14(a)); " . . . property of the designated owner of the policy . . ." (Section 12(c)(4)); " . . . all property then owed by the spouses . . . which would have been marital property . . ." (Section 17(1)); or " . . . all property then owned by the spouse . . . which would have been marital property . . ." (Section 18(a)). It is reason-able to ask why such references are not to *individual* property and to ask further whether the Act fractionalizes all property of spouses into marital *or* individual property. The explanation is part of the transition problem and is consonant with Subsections (b) and (i). Property in existence prior to adoption is *not* individual property, by definition, since the classification of individual property is a creation of the Act. Property in existence prior to adoption of the Act is whatever it is without the Act. Subsection (h) makes it clear that the Act does not go about reclassifying that property. Hence there will be a multitude of couples that will have property that is "something else" than marital property or the individual property established by the Act. That "something else" type of property is property of a spouse that " . . . is not marital property . . ." property, " . . . having any other classification . . ." and the like. Hence such descriptions are intentional in the reference they make to the "something else" or predetermination date property to which they point.

§ 5. Management and Control of Property of Spouses

(a) A spouse acting alone may manage and control:

(1) that spouse's property that is not marital property;

(2) except as provided in subsections (b) and (c), marital property held in that spouse's name alone or not held in the name of either spouse;

(3) a policy of insurance if that spouse is designated as the owner on the records of the issuer of it;

(4) the rights of an employee under an arrangement for deferred employment benefits that accrue as a result of that spouse's employment;

(5) a claim for relief vested in that spouse by other law; and

(6) marital property held in the names of both spouses in the alternative, including a manner of holding using the names of both spouses and the word "or".

(b) Spouses may manage and control marital property held in the names of both spouses other than in the alternative only if they act together.

(c) The right to manage and control marital property transferred to a trust is determined by the terms of the trust.

(d) The right to manage and control marital property does not determine the classification of property of the spouses and does not rebut the presumption of Section 4(b).

(e) The right to manage and control marital property permits gifts of that property only to the extent provided in Section 6.

(f) The right to manage and control any property of spouses acquired before the determination date is not affected by this [Act].

(g) A court may appoint a [conservator, guardian] to exercise a disabled spouse's right to manage and control marital property.

COMMENT

Title Based System: If Section 4 is the heart of the Act, then Section 5 and its management and control system is its aorta. Management and control is a title based system and to that extent will parallel the management and control rights which typically follow title in common law states. However, there is a very basic difference. While title is virtually synonymous with ownership in the common law system, it is perhaps best understood as a *nominee* relationship under the Act. Title can be viewed as something of a permeable membrane that presents one state of affairs to third parties while encompassing an ownership relationship between the spouses within that relationship which may well be different from the title-side of the membrane. To lawyers long attuned to common law concepts of the impermeable membrane view of title, the thrust is a new one. A fairly useful illustrative analogy is the fractionalization of title which occurs when a trust is created. A trustee has "legal title" (and management rights) while a beneficiary (usually undisclosed on legal title) has equitable and beneficial rights. Two sets of rights coexist, yet the outside world need deal only with the trustee as apparent owner, notwithstanding the beneficiary's completely valid, enforceable, coexisting, but usually undisclosed rights. In the marital property situation, the spouses as co-owners are analogous to the beneficiaries and a spouse as sole holder of marital property is analogous to the trustee as title holder. This comment is *not* intended to imply that marital property creates a trust, but simply to use an analogy to illustrate the coexisting relationships that are present in both situations.

Sole Management: Under Section 5 either spouse has sole management and control rights of a marital property asset which that spouse "holds" alone. No joinder for management and control functions would be required for that property. Holding is defined in Section 1(9) and that definition and this Section function together to treat conventional title as the method of determining holding.

Concurrent Holding: Management and control of concurrently held assets is dealt with specifically. The rights are related to the use of "and" or "or" in the title. If "and" is used in the concurrent title, *both* spouses manage and control, and joinder of both is required to discharge management and control functions. If "or" is used, it means what it says, and either spouse may manage and control the asset. Section 11(c) effectively applies the provisions on management and control of concurrent property not only to the special optional forms authorized by Section 11, but

to conventional forms already in use in adopting states.

Bearer property and other property not "held" can be managed and controlled by either spouse, and no joinder is required. (Section 5(a)(2)). Section 5(a)(2) permits a spouse to manage and control property not held in the name of either spouse; this covers bearer property. The term "held" in Section 1(9) does not extend to bearer property, and the provisions of Section 5(a)(2) integrate with that by permitting one spouse to manage and control any marital property that does not come within the purview of the holding definition in Section 1(9).

Special rules apply to insurance and employee benefits, and claims for relief. Insurance is managed and controlled by its owner. Employee benefits are managed and controlled by the employee on whose behalf they accrue. A claim for relief is managed and controlled by the spouse in whom the claim is vested by other law. (Section 5(a)(3), (4) and (5)).

§ 6. Gifts of Marital Property to Third Persons

(a) A spouse acting alone may give to a third person marital property that the spouse has the right to manage and control only if the value of the marital property given to the third person does not aggregate more than [$500] in a calendar year, or a larger amount if, when made, the gift is reasonable in amount considering the economic position of the spouses. Any other gift of marital property to a third person is subject to subsection (b) unless both spouses act together in making the gift.

(b) If a gift of marital property by a spouse does not comply with subsection (a), the other spouse may bring an action to recover the property or a compensatory judgment in place of the property, to the extent of the noncompliance. The other spouse may bring the action against the donating spouse, the recipient of the gift, or both. The action must be commenced within the earlier of one year after the other spouse has notice of the gift or 3 years after the gift. If the recovery occurs during marriage, it is marital property. If the recovery occurs after a dissolution or the death of either spouse, it is limited to one-half of the value of the gift and is individual property.

COMMENT

Since each spouse has a present undivided ownership in marital property, unrestricted gifts of marital property to a third person by one spouse of property managed and controlled by that spouse could defeat the interest of the other spouse in the donated property. Section 6 deals with gifts to third persons by spouses who have sole management and control rights. It has an absolute safe-harbor provision permitting gifts of a specified dollar amount per year to one individual. The amount is bracketed and should be set at any level deter-mined to be appropriate in an adopting state. It also has a less objective test of reasonableness with reference to the economic position of the spouses when made. The section has teeth in the form of a right of recovery. The section is specific in authorizing a recovery of only the portion of the gift that exceeds the permissible limit, rather than the entire gift. If the gift was of a specific item, the alternative recovery of a compensatory judgment is available to avoid awkward fractionalized ownership of such an item after the recovery action.

§ 7. Property Transactions Between Spouses

(a) Restrictions on the power of spouses to enter into property transactions with each other are abolished.

(b) Spouses may reclassify their property by gift or marital property agreement.

§ 8. Obligations of Spouses

(a) An obligation incurred by a spouse during marriage, including one attributable to an act or omission during marriage, is presumed to be incurred in the interest of the marriage or the family.

(b) After the determination date:

(i) a spouse's obligation to satisfy a duty of support owed to the other spouse or to a child of the marriage may be satisfied only from all marital property and all other property of the obligated spouse that is not marital property;

(ii) an obligation incurred by a spouse in the interest of the marriage or the family may be satisfied only from all marital property and all other property of that spouse that is not marital property;

(iii) an obligation incurred by a spouse before or during marriage that is attributable to an obligation arising before marriage or to an act or omission occurring before marriage may be satisfied only from property of that spouse that is not marital property and that part of marital property which would have been the property of that spouse, but for the marriage; and

(iv) any other obligation incurred by a spouse during marriage, including one attributable to an act or omission during marriage, may be satisfied only from property of that spouse that is not marital property and that spouse's interest in marital property and in that order.

(c) This [Act] does not alter the relationship between spouses and their creditors with respect to any property or obligation in existence on the determination date.

(d) Provisions of a written consent signed by a creditor which diminish the rights of the creditor provided in this section are binding on the creditor.

(e) No provision of a marital property agreement adversely affects the interest of a creditor unless the creditor had actual knowledge of that provision when the obligation to that creditor was incurred. The effect of this subsection may not be varied by a marital property agreement.

(f) This [Act] does not affect the exemption of any property of spouses under other law.

COMMENT

Basic Doctrine: The section builds on a doctrine that has been developed and followed in Arizona, Louisiana and Washington. Ariz. Rev.Stat.Ann. § 25–215 (1956); La. Rev.Civ.Code Ann. art. 2360; Wash. Rev.Code Ann. § 26.16.205 (1974). *See also* McClanahan, *Community Property Law in the United States,* § 10.4 (1982). The doctrine may be described as a "family purpose" doctrine, and it concerns the obligations incurred during the marriage and establishes a bifurcation separating those obligations that have a relation to the marriage, or the family, or the community, from those obligations incurred for the

purely personal purposes of an incurring spouse. The Louisiana statute uses the terms "... for the common interests of the spouses ..." in its definition of obligations having a relation to the marriage. The obligation having a relation to the marriage is treated in the three states as a community obligation. Obligations for personal purposes are treated as those of the incurring spouse, and that spouse's separate property is available to satisfy them, along with the spouse's interest in community property. *See Cosper v. Valley Bank,* 28 Ariz. 373, 237 P. 175 (1925); *Garrett v. Shannon,* 13 Ariz.App. 332, 476 P.2d 538

(1970); *Beyers v. Moore,* 45 Wash.2d 68, 272 P.2d 626 (1954).

The method used in the Act is to begin with a presumption. The same technique is used in Louisiana. La.Rev.Civ.Code Ann. art. 2361. An obligation incurred by a spouse during marriage is presumed to be incurred in the interest of the marriage or the family. The presumption specifically includes obligations arising out of an act or omission and thus covers the tort field. This is consistent with the development of the underlying family purpose doctrine. *See De Pinto v. Provident Security Life Ins. Co.,* 375 F.2d 50 (9th Cir. 1967); *McHenry v. Short,* 29 Wash.2d 263, 186 P.2d 900 (1947); *McFadden v. Watson,* 51 Ariz. 110, 74 P.2d 118 (1938); *Benson v. Bush,* 3 Wash. App. 815, 502 P.2d 1245 (1972).

With the presumption as a background, the section proceeds to establish four categories of obligations with which a couple may be involved, and to clarify what property is available to satisfy those different categories of obligations.

Support: All marital property and all other property of the obligated spouse is available to satisfy an obligation of support owed to the other spouse or a child of the marriage.

Family Purposes: Obligations falling within the presumption, being for the interest of the marriage, may be satisfied from all marital property and from the property of the incurring spouse that is not marital property. *See* Comment to Section 4 for discussion of "property that is not marital property."

Premarital Obligations: A premarital obligation or an obligation incurred during marriage but attributable to an act or omission before marriage is to be satisfied from the property of the incurring spouse that is not marital property and from the marital property that would have been the property of the incurring spouse but for the marriage. This latter quantum of property is different from a spouse's undivided half-interest in marital property. Assume a marriage with only one spouse earning wages and assume that that spouse had a premarital obligation for child support of a child of a prior marriage. The obligation could be satisfied from any property of the obligated spouse that was not marital property. It could also be satisfied from the wages or the savings from the wages earned during the marriage. If marriage had not occurred, the wages would have been the solely owned property of the obligated spouse. Thus Subsection (b)(iii) renders all of those wages available, even though the wages would typically have created marital property. In the converse situation, if the obligation had been that of the spouse creating no wages, none of the employed spouse's wages, *nor any marital property created with them,* would be available for such an obligation. This prevents a windfall to the premarital creditor by a marriage, for no interest in marital property attributable to the effort of the new spouse of the obligated party becomes available to enhance the assets available to that creditor to satisfy a debt of the obligated spouse. The objective is that the marriage should be neutral as far as the premarital creditor is concerned, neither adding to nor detracting from the assets available for satisfaction of the claim.

All Other Obligations: Obligations not covered by the first three categories may be satisfied out of the property of the incurring spouse that is not marital property and from the interest of the incurring spouse in marital property. Subsection (b)(iv) specifically establishes the order of satisfaction by requiring that marital property should be reached after other property is exhausted. In this instance the marital property to be reached is the undivided one-half interest of the incurring spouse and is not the same as the property which the premarital creditor can reach. Under this fourth category would fall obligations incurred during marriage that were not incurred in the interest of the marriage or the family. *See de Elche v. Jacobsen,* 95 Wash.2d 237, 622 P.2d 835 (1980).

The provisions of the section can be altered if a creditor is willing to diminish the rights established by the section. For example, one spouse with substantial amounts of individual property might wish to limit the possible obligation of the other spouse, even though the purpose of the obligation was clearly in the interest of the marriage. That spouse could obtain a writing from a creditor under Subsection (d) which would accomplish this. In the absence of it, Subsection (b)(ii) would subject the interest of the nonincurring spouse in marital property to the obligation. *See* N.M.Stat.Ann. § 40–3–9A(4).

Marital Property Agreements: For purposes of a creditor's rights under the section, a marital property agreement may not redefine or reclassify marital property in a manner that has any adverse effect on the creditor unless the creditor had actual knowledge of the adverse provision when the credit was extended.

§ 9. Protection of Bona Fide Purchasers Dealing With Spouses

(a) In this section:

(1) "Bona fide purchaser" means a purchaser of property for value who: (i) has not knowingly been a party to fraud or illegality affecting the interest of the spouses or other parties to the transaction; (ii) does not have notice of an adverse claim by a spouse; and (iii) has acted in the transaction in good faith.

(2) "Purchase" means to acquire property by sale, lease, discount, negotiation, mortgage, pledge, or lien or otherwise to deal with property in a voluntary transaction other than a gift.

(3) A purchaser gives "value" for property acquired: (i) in return for a binding commitment to extend credit; (ii) as security for or in total or partial satisfaction of a pre-existing claim; (iii) by accepting delivery pursuant to a pre-existing contract for purchase; or (iv) generally, in return for any other consideration sufficient to support a simple contract.

676

(b) Notice of the existence of a marital property agreement, a marriage, or the termination of a marriage does not affect the status of a purchaser as a bona fide purchaser.

(c) Marital property purchased by a bona fide purchaser from a spouse having the right to manage and control the property under Section 5 is acquired free of any claim of the other spouse. The effect of this subsection may not be varied by a marital property agreement.

COMMENT

Third parties will deal with the spouse or spouses who manage and control, and that in turn depends on which spouse "holds" marital property. When one who satisfies the bona fide purchaser requirements deals with a spouse who has management and control rights under Section 5, the transaction is free from the claim of the other spouse. This section is one of three parts of the Act that cannot be altered by a marital property agreement. (Section 10(c)). Between the spouses, the section does not function to eliminate any claim, since it is addressed solely to the protection of bona fide purchasers. The definition of "purchase" follows UCC § 1–201(32). The effect of a marital property agreement on a creditor is discussed in the Comment to Section 8.

§ 10. Marital Property Agreement

(a) A marital property agreement must be a document signed by both spouses. It is enforceable without consideration.

(b) A marital property agreement may not adversely affect the right of a child to support.

(c) Except as provided in Sections 2, 8(e), and 9(c) and in subsection (b), in a marital property agreement spouses may agree with respect to:

(1) rights and obligations in any of their property whenever and wherever acquired or located;

(2) management and control of any of their property;

(3) disposition of any of their property on dissolution, death, or the occurrence or nonoccurrence of any other event;

(4) modification or elimination of spousal support;

(5) making a will, trust, or other arrangement to carry out the agreement;

(6) a provision that upon the death of either of them, any of their property, including after-acquired property, will pass with-

out probate to a designated person, trust, or other entity by nontestamentary disposition;

(7) choice of law governing construction of the agreement; and

(8) any other matter affecting their property not in violation of public policy or a statute imposing a criminal penalty.

(d) A marital property agreement may be amended or revoked only by a later marital property agreement. The amended agreement or the revocation is enforceable without consideration.

(e) Persons intending to marry each other may enter into a marital property agreement as if married, but the agreement becomes effective only upon their marriage.

(f) A marital property agreement executed during marriage is not enforceable if the spouse against whom enforcement is sought proves that:

(1) the agreement was unconscionable when made; or

(2) that spouse did not execute the agreement voluntarily; or

(3) before execution of the agreement, that spouse:

(i) was not provided a fair and reasonable disclosure of the property or financial obligations of the other spouse;

(ii) did not voluntarily sign a written consent expressly waiving any right to disclosure of the property or financial obligations of the other spouse beyond the disclosure provided; and

(iii) did not have notice of the property or financial obligations of the other spouse.

(g) A marital property agreement executed before marriage is not enforceable if the spouse against whom enforcement is sought proves that:

(1) that spouse did not execute the agreement voluntarily; or

(2) the agreement was unconscionable when made and before execution of the agreement that spouse:

(i) was not provided a fair and reasonable disclosure of the property or financial obligations of the other spouse;

(ii) did not voluntarily sign a written consent expressly waiving any right to disclosure of the property or financial obligations of the other spouse beyond the disclosure provided; and

    (iii) did not have notice of the property or financial obligations of the other spouse.

(h) An issue of unconscionability of a marital property agreement is for decision by the court as a matter of law.

(i) If a provision of a marital property agreement modifies or eliminates spousal support and that modification or elimination causes one spouse to be eligible for support under a program of public assistance at the time of dissolution, the court may require the other spouse to provide support to the extent necessary to avoid that eligibility, notwithstanding the terms of the agreement.

(j) A document signed before the effective date of this [Act] by spouses or unmarried persons who subsequently married each other which affects the property of either of them and is enforceable by either of them without reference to this [Act] is not affected by this [Act] except as provided otherwise in a marital property agreement made after the determination date.

COMMENT

The Act provides almost unlimited contractual freedom for persons who want to amend, avoid or adopt its provisions. This is codified in this section. An important characteristic of a marital property agreement is that it will usually be a postmarital agreement. On the other hand, a premarital agreement precedes the marriage by definition. Conceptually, the typical attitude toward a premarital agreement is that it will be changed infrequently after the marriage, if at all. On the other hand, the approach in this Act toward marital property agreements is that there may, and usually will, be many of them made at numerous times during a marriage. Section 10(e) specifically sanctions entry into a marital property agreement before marriage, but provides that it becomes effective only upon marriage of the parties to it. If they do not marry, the agreement would be a nullity.

Multiple Agreements: A number of separate and distinct marital property agreements might be in existence in a given marriage. In adopting states, spouses would be able to execute as many of these agreements as needed during their marriage. The policy announced by the section is that any arrangement that changes the application of the Act should be a marital property agreement. In turn it should conform with Section 10.

Scope: The specific group of matters which a marital property agreement can cover, set out in Subsection (c), is not exclusive. Paragraph 8 of the subsection extends the opportunity for contracting between spouses to any other matters not in violation of public policy or any statute imposing a criminal penalty.

Enforceability: There are two sets of provisions regarding enforceability. One is parallel to the *Uniform Premarital Agreements Act.* (Subsection (g)). These provisions apply to marital property agreements made before marriage. The second set of provisions applies to marital property agreements made after marriage. (Subsection (f)). The postmarital requirements elevate the test of "unconscionable when made" as a disqualifying factor. In the postmarital agreement an agreement may not be enforced against a spouse who proves that the agreement was unconscionable when made.

Although the Act sets forth a specific group of requirements for enforceability, they are not exclusive. Ordinary contract defenses not specifically ruled out by the Act (as lack of consideration is) remain available.

Dispositions At Death: Paragraph 6 of Subsection (c) contains provisions substantially similar to those in Washington law. Wash.Rev.Code Ann. § 26.16.120 (1974). These have been in effect in Washington since 1881, and they constitute a valuable and useful method of non-probate disposition. The language in the Act contains after-acquired property provisions. It is intended to be used on an omnibus basis with respect to all property, or on a more limited basis with respect to a specified asset or group of assets. It constitutes a statutory authorization for a disposition other than one under the Statute of Wills. In that respect, it also follows certain of the policies announced in Section 6.201 of the *Uniform Probate Code,* although the latter is seen by many as being drafted to apply on an as-set-by-asset basis rather than on the omnibus basis available in Subsection (c)(6). It should be noted that since the provisions of this type of agreement are incorporated in a marital property agreement, they may not be altered unilaterally. A discussion of the use of the agreements in Washington appears in Cross, *The Community Property Law of Washington,* 49 Wash.L.Rev. 729, 798, 805 (1974). A version of the arrangement in use in another state can be found in Idaho Code § 15–6–201 which incorporates the idea into Idaho's version of § 6.201 of the *Uniform Probate Code. See also* Bell, *Statutory Survivorship Contracts in the State of Washington,* 1 Community Prop.J. 239 (1974); Note, *The Community Property Agreement: A Probate Cure With Side Effects,* 18 Gonz.L.Rev. 121 (1983); Note, *A First Look at the Community Property Agreement in Idaho,* 12 Idaho L.Rev. 41 (1975).

No Consideration Required; Formalities: No consideration is required for a marital property agreement, and the agreement, amendments, and revocations of the agreement require the signature of *both* spouses. Subsection (d) relates to amendments and revocations and requires that these be by later marital property agreements. These would necessarily be documents signed by both spouses, since Subsection (a) requires that all marital property agreements be signed by both spouses.

Existing Agreements: Subsection (j) deals with a transitional problem. From the point of view of comprehensibility and ease of administration, it would be desirable to convert agreements relating to the subject matter of the Act to marital property agreements under the Act with the adoption of the Act. However, such legislation could be seen as impairing the obligation of those agreements and as retroactive, and it is therefore avoided. Thus a predetermination date agreement dealing with subject matter such as that in the Act will simply continue to stand on such authority as it had without the Act, and the Act neither helps nor hinders that agreement.

§ 11. Optional Forms of Holding Property, Including Use of "And" or "Or"; Survivorship Ownership

(a) Spouses may hold marital property in a form that designates the holders of it by the words "(name of one spouse) or (name of other spouse) as marital property." Marital property held in that form is subject to Section 5(a)(6).

(b) Spouses may hold marital property in a form that designates the holder of it by the words "(name of one spouse) and (name of other spouse) as marital property." Marital property held in that form is subject to Section 5(b).

(c) A spouse may hold individual property in a form that designates the holder of it by the words "(name of spouse) as individual property." Individual property held in that form is subject to Section 5(a)(1).

(d) Spouses may hold property in any other form permitted by law, including a concurrent form or a form that provides for survivorship ownership.

(e) If the words "survivorship marital property" are used instead of the words "marital property" in the form described in subsection (a) or (b), marital property so held is survivorship marital property. On the death of a spouse, the ownership rights of that spouse in survivorship marital property vest solely in the surviving spouse by nontestamentary disposition at death. The first deceased spouse does not have a right of disposition at death of any interest in survivorship marital property. Holding marital property in a form described in subsection (a) or (b) does not alone establish survivorship ownership between the spouses with respect to the property held in that form.

COMMENT

Although the provisions of the Act do not require any particular form of labeling of title-documented property, that kind of labeling will be desirable in an adopting state. For a couple wishing to be specific and definite with respect to the classification of property, the labeling device provided by the section is a desirable provision for holding property.

Relationship to Management and Control: The section goes beyond mere labeling and provides specific confirmation of management and control rights with respect to types of labeling which are congruent with Section 5. Use of the Act's designation of property as marital property in a conjunctive or a disjunctive form will have different effects on management and control rights. The conjunctive ("and") form will require management and control by both spouses and joinder of both in transactions affecting the property. The disjunctive ("or") form permits management and control by either spouse without the necessity of joinder by the other.

Other Forms: Affirmative recognition of the ability to hold marital property in any form permitted by other law is provided by Subsection (d). This is consistent with the underlying difference under the Act between ownership and the integrated matters of title or holding and management and control.

Survivorship Ownership: An important substantive addition made by the section is a survivorship ownership feature. If the appropriate words described in the section are added to the designation by which the property is held, then survivorship ownership will follow that. If those words are not used, there is a specific statement that survivorship is not achieved by using the marital property form in either the conjunctive or the disjunctive form. It is important to note that survivorship marital property can be created with respect to marital property held in *either* the disjunctive form or the conjunctive form. This feature creates a wider option than would be afforded by limiting survivorship to the disjunctive form only. Management and control rights are unaffected by the addition of the survivorship language and relate back to the provisions in the last sentences of Subsections (a) and (b). The survivorship estate is not a form of joint tenancy but is a new statutory estate created by the section. It is not intended to carry on the arcane doctrines of joint tenancy but simply to establish a nonprobate survivorship incident by the utilization of the appropriate words on a document of title or other medium by which property is held. It is consistent with the policy of Section 10(c)(6) and Section 6.201 of the *Uniform Probate Code.*

An adopting state will wish to review banking statutes dealing with concurrent ownership rights to assure appropriate recognition of the provisions of the section and coordination with existing provisions of banking statutes.

§ 12. Classification of Life Insurance Policies and Proceeds

(a) In this section:

(1) "Owner" means a person appearing on the records of the policy issuer as the person having the ownership interest or, if no person other than the insured appears on those records as a person having that interest, it means the insured.

(2) "Ownership interest" means the rights of an owner under a policy.

(3) "Policy" means an insurance policy insuring the life of a spouse and providing for payment of death benefits at the spouse's death.

(4) "Proceeds" means the death benefit from a policy and all other economic benefits from it, whether they accrue or become payable as a result of the death of an insured person or upon the occurrence or nonoccurrence of another event.

(b) If a policy issuer makes payments or takes actions in accordance with the policy and the issuer's records, the issuer is not liable because of those payments or actions unless, at the time of the payments or actions, it had actual knowledge of inconsistent provisions of a decree or marital property agreement or of an adverse claim by a spouse, former spouse, surviving spouse, or persons claiming under a deceased spouse's disposition at death.

(c) Except as provided in subsections (d), (e), and (f):

(1) The ownership interest and proceeds of a policy issued after the determination date which designates the insured as the owner are marital property without regard to the classification of property used to pay premiums on the policy.

(2) The ownership interest and proceeds of a policy issued before the determination date which designates the insured as the owner are mixed property if a premium on the policy is paid from marital property after the determination date without regard to the classification of property used to pay premiums on that policy after the initial payment of a premium on it from marital property. The marital property component of the ownership interest and proceeds is the part resulting from multiplying the entire ownership interest and proceeds by a fraction of which the numerator is the period during marriage that the policy was in effect after the date on which a premium was paid from marital property and the denominator is the entire period the policy was in effect.

(3) The ownership interest and proceeds of a policy issued during marriage which designates the spouse of the insured as the owner are individual property of its owner without regard to the classification of property used to pay premiums on the policy.

(4) The ownership interest and proceeds of a policy that designates a person other than either of the spouses as the owner are not affected by this [Act] if no premium on the policy

683

is paid from marital property after the determination date. If a premium on the policy is paid from marital property after the determination date, the ownership interest and proceeds of the policy are in part property of the designated owner of the policy and in part marital property of the spouses without regard to the classification of property used to pay premiums on that policy after the initial payment of a premium on it from marital property. The marital property component of the ownership interest and proceeds is the part resulting from multiplying the entire ownership interest and proceeds by a fraction of which the numerator is the period during marriage that the policy was in effect after the date on which a premium was paid from marital property and the denominator is the entire period the policy was in effect.

(5) Written consent by a spouse to the designation of another person as the beneficiary of the proceeds of a policy is effective to relinquish that spouse's interest in the ownership interest and proceeds of the policy without regard to the classification of property used by a spouse or another to pay premiums on that policy. A designation by either spouse of a parent or child of either of the spouses as the beneficiary of the proceeds of a policy is presumed to have been made with the consent of the other spouse.

(6) Unless the spouses provide otherwise in a marital property agreement, designation of a trust as the beneficiary of the proceeds of a policy with a marital property component does not reclassify that component.

(d) This section does not affect a creditor's interest in the ownership interest or proceeds of a policy assigned or made payable to the creditor as security.

(e) The interest of a person as owner or beneficiary of a policy acquired under a decree or property settlement agreement incident to a prior marriage or parenthood is not marital property without regard to the classification of property used to pay premiums on that policy.

(f) This section does not affect the ownership interest or proceeds of a policy if neither spouse is designated as an owner in the policy or the records of the policy issuer and no marital property is used to pay a premium on the policy.

COMMENT

The section sets forth a series of rules regarding the classification of life insurance policies and the proceeds of them.

As with other provisions of the Act, it is important to review the section with an awareness that a marital property agreement can change its provisions.

Protected Parties: A series of definite rules operating on described objective facts protects certain parties to insurance policy transactions. The first protected party is the issuing insurance company. Subsection (b) relieves it from liability if it proceeds on the basis of the policy and its own records unless it has *actual knowledge* of other facts which would affect claims under the policy or those records.

The second protected party is a creditor to whom a policy is assigned or made payable. Subsection (d) provides that the section does not affect that creditor's interest in the policy, so that its provisions do not concern or impair the rights of the creditor.

The third protected party is a person who is an owner or beneficiary by virtue of provisions made in the dissolution of a prior marriage or as an incident to parenthood. In many dissolutions the maintenance of a life insurance policy for children of the marriage or for a former spouse is required. Subsection (e) accords to persons intended to be benefited from that type of provision protection from the other provisions of the section.

Finally, Subsection (f) provides that if neither spouse is an owner of a policy and no marital property is used to pay a premium on the policy, the section will have no effect on the policy or its proceeds. Thus a typical business-based life insurance policy would ordinarily be unaffected by any provision of the section. Similarly, insurance owned and paid for by a child on the life of a parent would be unaffected by the section.

Carving out those four groups of protected persons leaves six separate situations with which the section deals.

The Basic Rule: The basic rule is found in Subsection (c)(1). If a policy is issued *after the determination date* and an insured spouse is the owner, it is a marital property policy, *without regard to the source of premium payments*. This situation is the typical garden-variety transaction in which one spouse is the owner of a policy on his or her life. The section offers a rule of comparative simplicity for that policy—it is marital property.

Straddles: The next situation dealt with is a "straddle." Subsection (c)(2) speaks of a policy that existed before the determination date which is owned by the insured and continues in force after the determination date. Payment of *any* premium on such a policy at any time *after* the determination date will operate as a reclassification of the policy ownership and proceeds. A formula is set forth in the section to establish the marital property component.

Spouse-Owned Insurance: Under Subsection (c)(3), the frequently used transaction of spouse-owned insurance is treated. The Act assumes that a designation of a spouse of an insured as an owner will typically be used if the parties desire that the non-insured spouse be the owner for all purposes. The effect of the Act is to perfect that treatment. While the spouses could always agree to an alternative treatment, unless they do, a policy owned by one on the life of the other will be individual property of the owner without regard to the source of premium payments.

Third Person Ownership: A fourth situation, dealt with in Subsection (c)(4), concerns a policy owned by third persons with premiums paid from marital property. The "straddle" system and accompanying formula is used to deal with the ownership interest and

proceeds. The straddle is again initiated by the first payment of a premium from marital property.

Parent or Child As Beneficiary: Subsection (c)(5) presents a means of relinquishing marital property interests in life insurance and contains a presumption that the designation by a spouse of a parent or a child of either spouse as a beneficiary is made with the consent of the other spouse.

Trust As Beneficiary: The marital property component of a policy retains that classification even if a trust is designated as a beneficiary under Subsection (c)(6). Consent of both spouses to another classification is possible to alter this result.

§ 13. Classification of Deferred Employment Benefits

(a) A deferred employment benefit attributable to employment of a spouse occurring after the determination date is marital property.

(b) A deferred employment benefit attributable to employment of a spouse occurring during marriage and partly before and partly after the determination date is mixed property. The marital property component of that mixed property is the part resulting from multiplying the entire benefit by a fraction of which the numerator is the period of employment giving rise to the benefit that occurred after the determination date and during marriage and the denominator is the total period of the employment. Unless provided otherwise in a decree, marital property agreement, or written consent, valuation of a deferred employment benefit that is mixed property shall be made as of the death of a spouse or a dissolution.

(c) Ownership or disposition provisions of a deferred employment benefit which conflict with subsections (a) and (b) are ineffective between spouses, former spouses, or between a surviving spouse and a person claiming under a deceased spouse's disposition at death.

(d) If an administrator of an arrangement for deferred employment benefits makes payments or takes actions in accordance with the arrangement and the administrator's records, the administrator is not liable because of those payments or actions unless, at the time of the payments or actions, it had actual knowledge of inconsistent provisions of a decree or marital property agreement or of an adverse claim by a spouse, former spouse, surviving spouse, or a person claiming under a deceased spouse's disposition at death.

COMMENT

This section deals with marital property rights in employment benefits. Its provisions may be varied by a marital property agreement.

Protection: As with the payment of life insurance proceeds under Section 12, Subsection (d) protects an entity which makes payments in accordance with the employee benefit plan and its own records. Unless it has actual knowledge that a decree or marital property agreement requires some other payment, or actual knowledge of an adverse claim by a spouse or surviving spouse, that entity has no liability even though its payments may be inconsistent with such rights or claims.

The Two Formats: The section deals with two situations. A deferred employment benefit attributable to employment *after* the determination date is marital property under Subsection (a). Such a benefit attributable to employment during marriage and *before and after* the determination date is subject to a formula which uses time periods.

The Array of Problems: There are many significant and important problems regarding employee benefits which the Act does not address specifically. As a property statute, the thrust of the Act is to treat an appropriate quantum of an employee benefit as marital property. From that point on, a court dealing with the matter will have before it the many other problems in the field. These include valuation problems, questions regarding the time at which an interest is to be quantified and delivered, questions relating to whether the plan is or is not in pay status, problems with respect to events affecting the plan which can occur with the passage of time, federal preemption problems, problems with respect to the claims of prior spouses, and many other problems that are now being heard on a daily basis in courts throughout the nation. *See 3 Equitable Distribution Rep.* 109 (Special Pension Issue, April 1983); McClanahan, *Community Property Law in the United States*, § 12.15 (1982); O'Neill, *Pensions As Marital Property: Valuation, Allocation and Related Mysteries.* 16 Creighton L.Rev. 743 (1983); Campbell, *Pension Plan Benefits as an Asset in Dissolution-of-Marriage Cases,* 61 Taxes 583 (1983); *Kalinoski v. Kalinoski,* 9 Fam.L.Rep. 3033 (Pa.Ct. of Comm.Pl.1983). There is no consensus in the existing state of the law that justifies the formulation of more than the general policy in the section. Adopting states will already have dealt with many of these problems and the Act does not alter that case law, but simply operates to establish an appropriate marital property interest. The existing body of state case law may be applied to that property interest.

Some federal benefit programs, such as the Railroad Retirement Act (45 U.S.C. § 231 *et seq.*), preempt state definitions of property which include pension benefits in dissolution property settlements. *Hisquierdo v. Hisquierdo,* 439 U.S. 572 (1979). *See also Fritz v. Railroad Retirement Board,* 449 U.S. 166 (1980). Where there is federal preemption former spouses may themselves qualify as independent beneficiaries. In the case of the Railroad Retirement Act, *see* 45 U.S.C. § 231a(c)(4) (divorced spouse annuity), and 45 U.S.C. § 231a(d)(1)(v) (surviving divorced wife). *See also* the Uniformed Services Former

Spouses' Protection Act, 10 U.S.C. § 1408, reversing the United States Supreme Court decision in *McCarty v. McCarty,* 453 U.S. 210 (1981), and enacting into law a time period formula bearing some analogy to that used in the section. The preemption problem exists independently of the Act, and obviously cannot be solved by actual or proposed state legislation in any event. *See* Reppy and Samuels, *Community Property in the United States,* p. 396 et seq. (1982).

§ 14. Mixed Property

(a) Except as provided otherwise in Sections 12 and 13, mixing marital property with property having any other classification reclassifies the other property to marital property unless the component of the mixed property which is not marital property can be traced.

(b) Application by one spouse of substantial labor, effort, inventiveness, physical or intellectual skill, creativity, or managerial activity on individual property of the other spouse creates marital property attributable to that application if:

(i) reasonable compensation is not received for the application; and

(ii) substantial appreciation of the individual property of the other spouse results from the application.

COMMENT

Commingling of the assets of spouses is an everyday occurrence without the Act, and will continue with or without it. The Act supplies a rule to deal with it. Under that rule, mixing properties that cannot be identified or traced after the mixing will result in a reclassification. Since the general presumption of Section 4(b) operates to classify all spousal property as marital property, that will be the result in the absence of the ability to trace.

Tracing: The basic rule of Section 14 requires a tracing in order to "unmix" property. In turn the tracing would necessarily be done under the appropriate tracing rules of an adopting state. *See* McClanahan, *Community Property Law in the United States,* §§ 6.7 and 6.8 (1982) and Reppy and Samuels, *Community Property in the United States,* Chapter 10 (1982), for discussion of tracing principles. U.C.C. § 9–306 also supplies a version of tracing rules. The policy of the Act is to enhance the procedures and practices which create marital property. Consequently this section would have the effect of treating mixed property as marital property unless tracing was a possibility.

What of De Minimis Mixing? An obvious matter of concern is the possibility of serious injustice that could result from mixing a minimal amount of marital property with a substantial amount of other property. *See* Reppy and Samuels, *Community Property in the United States,* p. 128ff (1982). For example, one principal payment might be made from marital property on a large mortgage on a valuable piece of individual real property. This would mix marital and individual property. Another example might be one deposit of marital property to a very large individual bank account. However these types of transactions lend themselves to solution by an application of tracing, since the underlying types of property are very much record-oriented. Meeting the burden of proof in a tracing process from the records should usually be possible.

A more difficult case is that of fungible properties—a large stamp, coin or precious gem collection, for example. These will create the same types of problems that they already create when they are not in unified ownership. Commingling of fungible goods without being willing to sacrifice ownership is a highly dangerous practice and would remain so under the Act. In reality the spouse who stands to gain from a reclassification arising from a "tainting" of a large collection of fungibles with a small amount of marital property will have to carry the burden of proving that a mixing even occurred. In a sense that imposes the burden on that spouse to trace the marital property *into* the mixed property, which will be an effective though backward threshold method of tracing.

Commingled Accounts: Commingled accounts (such as bank accounts and mutual fund accounts to which continuing payments for new purchases are made) and increased value resulting from payments on liens on property are examples of types of mixed property which will undoubtedly occur and which will typically require solutions. Those problems and solutions for them already exist in dissolution and probate matters. The Act would necessarily build on the procedures for tracing that exist in an adopting state. In addition, accounts of that type are frequently accompanied by normal and routine documentation and records which would ease the tracing process.

One rather common mixing process will undoubtedly occur. Many bank accounts, mutual fund accounts and common-stock dividend reinvestment programs provide automatic reinvestment of dividends and interest. Under the Act, income is marital property. Hence the automatic reinvestment of income will be a mixing of marital property with other property if the accounts or common stock are not already marital property. Under the section this will reclassify the accounts or common stock to marital property absent tracing. Spouses wishing to avoid this result could avoid automatic reinvestment of dividends or interest in such programs or could create an individual property classification for the reinvested income by a marital property agreement.

Physical Labor: The section deals with another extremely important issue. It is the situation arising from the application to the individual property of one spouse of personal effort by the other spouse and carrying the burden of proving its elements will be difficult. The rule of the section is strict. It articulates a bias against creation of marital property from such an act unless the effort has been substantial and has been responsible for substantial appreciation. Routine, normal, and usual effort is not substantial. Though drawing a precise line as to what is substantial and what is not is not possible, the section does not create opportunity to translate for recognizing minimal effort to a property interest. The section is only satisfied by proof of (1) a truly substantial effort followed by (2) a truly substantial appreciation *attributable to the effort* for which (3) no reasonable compensation was received. Many situations can be visualized. Real property transactions are those in which the problem will typically occur. One spouse will bring real property into the marriage. After the marriage, that real property will be an important element in the economic life of the couple. The other spouse will improve it by physical labor. This might be work on a farm, or improvements or additions to a home or to a piece of commercial real estate. The statute operates to avoid the creation of marital proper-

ty if reasonable compensation for the effort was paid at the time that it occurred. If the compensation was nominal or nonexistent, then the provisions of the section still require a showing that the effort was substantial and that substantial appreciation resulted from it. Otherwise there can be no quantification of the marital property created by the effort and the spouse expending the effort will simply have done so without anything demonstrable to show for it.

What is the Laborer's Right? Section 14(b) provides that the physical labor creates *marital property* when it is applicable. That would mean that the right of the spouse who created the marital property is to an interest in the asset, and not to a right of reimbursement or a lien for a specific amount. As the marital property component rises and falls in value, the interest rises and falls.

Burden of Proof: Many mixing problems that might otherwise exist will be resolved by burden of proof requirements. A spouse claiming a particular classification for an asset contrary to the general presumption of Section 4(b) will have the burden of proof on that claim, and failure to meet it would render any mixing issue moot. In particular meeting the burden of proof should be helpful in the *de minimis* mixing situations, since proving mixing, even of small amounts, is itself a form of tracing.

§ 15. Interspousal Remedies

(a) A spouse has a claim against the other spouse for breach of the duty of good faith imposed by Section 2 resulting in damage to the claimant spouse's present undivided one-half interest in marital property.

(b) A court may order an accounting of the property and obligations of the spouses and may determine rights of ownership in, beneficial enjoyment of, or access to, marital property and the classification of all property of the spouses.

(c) A court may order that the name of a spouse be added to marital property held in the name of the other spouse alone, except with respect to:

(1) a partnership interest held by the other spouse as a general partner;

(2) an interest in a professional corporation, professional association, or similar entity held by the other spouse as a stockholder or member;

(3) an asset of an unincorporated business if the other spouse is the only spouse involved in operating or managing the business; or

(4) any other property if the addition would adversely affect the rights of a third person.

(d) Except as provided otherwise in Section 6(b), a spouse must commence an action against the other spouse under subsection (a) not later than 3 years after acquiring actual knowledge of the facts giving rise to the claim.

COMMENT

The section will create a change in the law of those states which prohibit litigation between spouses regarding property rights during an ongoing marriage. Since the Act creates respective vested interests in marital property while still permitting individual management and control of that property, there is an obvious possibility that management and control rights could be exercised in a way that damages or eliminates the interest of the spouse who does not hold the property. This section creates a remedy for this type of conduct. An important purpose of the section is creation of a remedy for a violation of the good faith responsibility between spouses required by Section 2. *See* McClanahan, *Community Property Law in* *the United States,* § 9.12 (1982); Reppy and Samuels, *Community Property in the United States,* p. 243 ff. (1982); Comment, *California's New Community Property Law—Its Effect on Interspousal Mismanagement Litigation,* 5 Pac.L.J. 723 (1974). It also affords a remedy for violations of specific provisions contained throughout the Act. However, it is not intended to reverse interspousal immunity beyond its terms unless an adopting state should choose to do so. Note that Section 6, dealing with gifts, also creates rights for one spouse to proceed against the other spouse. Those rights are in addition to the provisions of this section.

The Basis: The rationale of the section is well explained in De Funiak and Vaughn, *Principles of Community Property,* § 151 (1971). There it is pointed out that in community property jurisdictions

". . . it must follow as a logical result that each is entitled to protect or enforce against the other his or her rights in the common property or to enforce or protect as against the other his or her rights in separate property, even by civil action. . . . the common law fiction that husband and wife are one person, so that one cannot sue the other during coverture, is alien to the community property system's view of the spouses as individuals in their own right. . . if this right to sue did not exist, one spouse, especially if the title to the property were in his or her name, might be enabled to appropriate community property to his or her own use or otherwise deny or injure the rights therein of the other spouse without the other spouse having any remedy whereby to defeat such conduct."

Accounting: The accounting remedy contemplated is a form of balancing of the property rights between the spouses. It is not intended that such an accounting would be the classic fiduciary accounting in either style or substance. In particular, it is not intended that such an accounting should prevent the balancing of losses and gains or that it should charge one spouse with losses while not crediting gains. Rather, the accounting would simply establish what is marital property and what is not. If an "unmixing" under Section 14 was appropriate, that would be accomplished in the accounting. In addition to the accounting, the rights of the spouses by way of ownership or beneficial enjoyment of or access to marital property or other property is a contemplated form of relief under the Act. The remedy could well include some form of separation of property if needed to protect the ownership or beneficial enjoyment of the spouses in any of their property. *See* Reppy and Samuels, *Community Property in the United States,* p. 247ff (1982).

"Add-A-Name": One of the ways in which a spouse's interest could be injured would follow utilization of a one-spouse method of holding property and management or disposition of that property to the prejudice of the other spouse. In order to prevent this, the section has a specific provision for adding the name of a spouse to the form in which marital property is held. However, this procedure has certain safeguards and prohibitions. The "add-a-name" function cannot occur with respect to general partnership interests, professional entities, unincorporated businesses operated by the other spouse, or other property if a third party's interests would be adversely affected.

Statute of Limitations: The section contains a statute of limitations. This is intended to function as a means of clearing the records. It operates in a manner similar to that used in fraud-type statutes of limitations. The time period runs only after actual knowledge of facts which would give rise to a claim. If there is a dissolution or death, the statute of limitation provisions would be subject to an adopting state's limiting provisions for actions between parties to a dissolution and for claims against an estate set out in its dissolution and probate statutes.

If the statute of limitations operates during the course of a marriage to bar any actions, that bar will be in effect at death or dissolution. That could mean frustration in some circumstances, so that consideration of enforcement of rights under the section during the course of a marriage will be appropriate.

While it is not the purpose of the section to open the door to a torrent of interspousal "economic fault" litigation, it is nonetheless necessary to provide remedies for conduct that injures the interest of one of the spouses. The dominant theme of the relationship between the spouses toward their property is established by the good faith requirement of Section 2. As stated in the

comment to that section, a spouse is not bound to succeed in an economic sense. An appropriate regard for the property interests of the other spouse and an avoidance of an unfair advantage are the norm under the good faith requirement. This section provides a remedy for interference or damage. If that can be proven, particularly against an allegation of good faith conduct by the other spouse, a remedy is appropriate. However, such matters should not be dredged up after the apparent ratification that would be implied by the passage of time. The specific statute of limitations has been added for that reason and in order to operate as something of a "cleansing" process in matters of marital economics.

§ 16. Invalid Marriages

If a marriage is invalidated by a decree, a court may apply so much of this [Act] to the property of the persons who were parties to the invalid marriage as is necessary to avoid an inequitable result.

COMMENT

The section should be read with Sections 208 and 209 of the *Uniform Marriage and Divorce Act* dealing with declarations of invalidity and putative spouses. Adopting states should also review their an-

nulment provisions if they do not follow Section 208. The section is intended to deal only with spousal relations and not with unmarried cohabitation.

§ 17. Treatment of Certain Property at Dissolution

Except as provided in Section 16:

(1) In a dissolution, all property then owned by the spouses that was acquired during marriage and before the determination date which would have been marital property under this [Act] if acquired after the determination date must be treated as if it were marital property.

(2) In a dissolution, any property of either spouse which can be traced to property received by a spouse after the determina-

tion date as a recovery for a loss of earning capacity during marriage must be treated as if it were marital property.

(3) After a dissolution, each former spouse owns an undivided one-half interest in the former marital property as a tenant in common except as provided otherwise in a decree or written consent.

[(4) In an action for legal separation, the court may decree the extent to which property acquired by the spouses after the legal separation is marital property and the responsibility of each spouse for obligations incurred after the decree of legal separation.]

COMMENT

The Act contains no provision which would make an immediate alteration in the classification of the property of couples to which it becomes applicable who had married before its effective date. *See* Comment to Section 4. That property will continue to have whatever characteristics it had before the Act became applicable to its owners. The policy reason for this approach is avoidance of constitutional problems which would attend any effort to alter existing rights in property acquired before the Act was effective.

The Concept of Deferral: To that extent, the Act parallels procedures followed when states adopt changes in intestate share and forced heirship provisions or changes which create equitable distribution structures to apply at dissolution. Such changes make no *immediate* change in the rights in property which existed at the time the changes become effective. However, with respect to all of that existing property, as well as property acquired after the statutory change, when a time of dissolution is subsequently reached, such statutes typically create a state-authorized system of di-

vision and disposition which is applied to that property. It is accepted that a state has an appropriate role in determining the disposition of property at dissolution. It has also been settled that provisions in state dissolution property settlement statutes can affect not only property which came into being after those statutes were enacted, but property which came into being before that. *Kujawinski v. Kujawinski,* 71 Ill.2d 563, 376 N.E.2d 1382 (1978); *Fournier v. Fournier,* 376 A.2d 100 (Me. 1977); *Rothman v. Rothman,* 65 N.J. 219, 320 A.2d 496 (1974).

In addition, it appears to be settled that the domiciliary state's property division provisions will generally affect all property of the spouses, even though originally created or acquired in another state. Clark, *Law of Domestic Relations,* § 11.4 (1968): Leflar *Conflict of Laws: Dividing Property When Marriage Ends,* 1 Fairshare #8 at p. 9 (Aug. 1981). Certain residual problems continue to arise regarding real property outside the domiciliary state, but as a practical matter, those are usually settled by *in personam* jurisdiction of the dissolution court over the parties and its authority to decree certain actions by those persons before it in a litigated case. Leflar, *op. cit.* at p. 10.

The Act as a Property Statute: Under the Act, property which a couple acquires from their respective efforts, as well as all income earned or accrued after the Act becomes applicable to that couple will be marital property. Each spouse will own an undivided one-half interest in that marital property. Consequently, in analyzing the property marshalled in a dissolution proceeding, each spouse is the *owner* of half of the marital property. If a state has provisions authorizing the alteration of property ownership by equitable distribution at divorce after the application of appropriate factors, then those factors and that authorized division would apply to marital property as it applies to the property each spouse owns prior to the adoption of the Act. Assume, as an example, that in a common law state without the Act spouses own all of their property as tenants in common, and that the state has an equitable distribution statute authorizing reallocation of property ownership in dissolution after the application of a set of factors. Also assume that after the application of the factors, a determination is reached that Spouse A should receive sixty percent of the total divisible property and Spouse B should receive forty percent. The dissolution court would have jurisdiction to reallocate ten percent of the property of one of the two tenants in common in favor of the other one in order to create the sixty-forty ratio of ownership.

If instead, all property of the couple was marital property under the Act, with everything else being identical, the same court could and should attain the same result. In both instances, property "owned" by one spouse is being reallocated in an equitable distribution proceeding to the other spouse. That is the precise way in which the ownership element in marital property should be applied and administered by a dissolution court under its equitable distribution statutes or procedures.

Possible Adopting State Revisions: Obviously an adopting state may wish to review its equitable distribution procedures and consider revising them after giving recognition to the effect of the adoption of the Act. However, the Act can and should function in a cognate fashion with respect to existing dissolution legislation. Coordination would certainly be necessary if an existing body of statutory law establishes a defined class of "marital property" to be marshalled and divided in the dissolution process only. That definition would have to be altered or omitted so that the definition of marital property in the Act would not conflict. However, not all states applying equitable distribution procedures follow a *statutory* definition of marital property. Some states apply their equitable distribution procedures to *all* property whenever and from wherever derived (Connecticut, Massachusetts). Some have *judicial* definitions of the universe of property to which their statutes apply (Florida, Ohio). Others have presumptions as to an appropriate division (Arkansas, North Carolina, Wisconsin). Still others have developed patterns of division which may have the same effect as a presumption (Pennsylvania). There are some fifty different systems in use, and virtually none of them is identical with any of the rest. *See* Freed, *Equitable Distribution as of December 1982*, 9 Fam.L.Rep. 4001 (1983) and Freed, *Family Law in the Fifty States: An Overview*, 4 Fam.L.Q. 289 (1983). Even if substantial statutory identity exists, case law has developed different answers to identical questions in different jurisdictions.

Division in an Adopting State May Be Unequal or Equal: It is not the mission of the Act to enter into the territory of equitable distribution or other systems of property division at dissolution. It is intended to operate as a property statute and to establish that a definite vested property interest exists in marital property from the instant of the creation of that property which traces through investment and reinvestment of the original property to property acquired with its proceeds. Consequently, a distribution different from an equal one in a dissolution of spouses owning marital property would simply be a property division dealing with the existing property rights of the spouses in marital property and reaching a particular result to achieve an equitable distribution of the marital property. Dealing with vested property rights in such a division is already a typical part of equitable distribution procedures. The Act is not designed to interfere with such a division under the statutes and cases in an adopting state or to ordain an equal division when that is not otherwise indicated. What the Act will do is to create a different balance of ownership *going in* to the equitable division procedure from one which typically exists in

common law jurisdictions in which title and ownership are synonymous.

"Other Than Marital" Property At Dissolution: What has been said relates to actual marital property, which is property acquired by efforts of a couple and from their income from all sources after the Act applies to them. Such a couple could be a couple married after the Act is adopted. It could be a couple living in an adopting state, both before and after the Act was adopted. It could also be a couple domiciled elsewhere and moving into an adopting state after the adoption. The "determination date" will be that event which renders the Act applicable to the property of each couple coming under its provisions. In the three situations, there will only be one in which the provisions of the Act would cover all post-marital income and all property acquired by productive efforts of the couple from and after their marriage so long as they live in the adopting state. That will be the couple marrying in an adopting state after the Act becomes effective and remaining in it until dissolution. As to couples in the other two situations, presumably they would have some accumulation of "other than marital" property which existed before the determination date and which could well have been marital property if the Act had been in effect when and where that property was acquired. That is obvious in the case of a couple marrying in and living in an adopting state both before and after the Act becomes effective. All of the income earned or accrued and the property acquired by productive efforts of that couple during their marriage would have

been marital property if the Act had been in effect when it was acquired. Similarly, with a couple moving into an adopting state following adoption but bringing with them property which they had acquired in other jurisdictions, their income earned or accrued and ·property acquired by their productive efforts which was owned prior to moving into the state would have been marital property if in fact the Act had applied when and where it was acquired.

The Deferred Approach: The situation calls for an approach to deal with the property of couples who are seeking a divorce but who own something "other than marital" property. Section 17 applies a *deferred* marital property concept to that other property. An example will help to illustrate how it operates. Assume a couple always lived in an adopting state but lived there before the adoption. Before the adoption but during marriage, they acquired Blackacre with the proceeds of the employment of one or both of them. After adoption of the Act, they acquired Whiteacre with proceeds of employment occurring after the adoption. Their marriage is now dissolving. Whiteacre is clearly marital property and is owned in the equal undivided interests specified by the Act because it was acquired after the Act as the result of personal effort of one or both spouses and was marital property from its inception. On the other hand, Blackacre is some form of property other than marital property. That is because the Act does not operate retroactively, and Blackacre was owned before the Act applied to the couple. However, with the filing of the divorce suit, Blackacre is treated *as if* the Act

had been in force when it was acquired, and will therefore be treated in the dissolution proceeding in a manner similar to Whiteacre.

Comparison With Existing Approaches: The way in which the section and the deferral concept operates is not substantially different from much existing equitable distribution legislation which provides that as of dissolution all of the property of the couple takes on the characteristics either of marital property or separate property (e.g., Colorado, Illinois, Missouri). That constitutes a deferred approach to such property, creating a class of dissolution-only marital property as of a deferred time namely the institution of the dissolution proceeding. A number of such statutes and procedures are in place in the several states, and the way this section operates is to follow the technique used in those statutes with respect to property which *would have been* marital property if the Act had been in effect as to the couple when and where the property was acquired. *See* Freed, *op. cit.*

Certain Personal Injury Recoveries: Subsection (b) deals with a matter related to Section 4(g)(6). The latter provision classifies as individual property a recovery for personal injury except for the component of the amount of the recovery attributable to expenses paid from marital property. Under Subsection (b) there is a deferred reclassification of any of that recovery that can be traced to the personal injury recovery as allocable to a loss of earning capacity. In the first instance, Section 4(g)(6) avoids the necessity of an allocation. That should make the personal injury action simpler. Ultimately, an allocation would be possible under Subsection (b) but only if there was still on hand at dissolution a traceable portion of the personal injury recovery allocable to a loss of earning capacity during marriage.

An example is illustrative. Assume a massive personal injury and a recovery of $1,000,000. Assume no expenses were paid from marital property, so that the provisions of Section 4(g)(6) classified the entire amount as individual property. In a dissolution, some years later, the uninjured spouse is able to show that $200,000 of the amount still on hand is fairly allocable to a loss of earning capacity. Then $200,000 would be treated *as if* it were marital property, giving the uninjured spouse an opportunity to show that *before* the application of the appropriate equitable distribution factors, $100,000 could be treated as his or her marital property in the dissolution proceeding.

The rationale for the Subsection (b) treatment is that earnings are ordinarily marital property. By creating the possibility that residual amounts allocable to lost earnings could be marital property, an opportunity to achieve an equitable result in an appropriate case is presented. Loss of earning power is singled out because earnings would themselves have created marital property if they had not been lost. At dissolution it is appropriate to create some protection and replacement for the other spouse for the marital property that would have been there but for the injury. On the other hand, to have forced this determination at the time of the injury would impair the litigating posture, hence it is delayed to a point at which the issue significantly affects the interests of the uninjured spouse.

Oversight Problems: Subsection (c) is an "oversight" section. As pointed out in the Comments to Section 1(8), persons must be married to hold marital property. Ordinarily in a dissolution a disposition of all the property of the spouses will be made by decree or an agreement. Subsection (c) anticipates that this will occur, but makes a provision for a tenancy-in-common if satisfactory action has been omitted as to any former marital property. It is *not* a presumption or other indication that an equal division is either appropriate or required. Rather it deals only with oversight situations to clarify rights of former spouses when those rights have not been clarified by other documentation incident to the dissolution.

Subsection (d) is a bracketed section which would be appropriate in states in which a legal separation is recognized.

Contractual Variance: As with all provisions of the Act that contain no specific prohibition against contractual variance, the provisions of the section may be varied by a marital property agreement.

§ 18. Treatment of Certain Property at Death of Spouse

(a) At the death of a spouse domiciled in this State, all property then owned by the spouse that was acquired during marriage and before the determination date which would have been marital property under this [Act] if acquired after the determination date must be treated as if it were marital property.

(b) At the death of a spouse domiciled in this State, any property of the spouse which can be traced to property received by the spouse after the determination date as a recovery for a loss of earning capacity during marriage must be treated as if it were marital property.

COMMENT

The Deferred Approach At Death: The deferred approach used in Section 17 at dissolution is also appropriate at death, and the reasons are substantially the same. A leading text explains the rationale:

"[T]here was almost universal acceptance of the rule that, when spouses changed their domicile, taking their property with them, the move did not change the classification of the property in the new domicile. . . . [I]f this move were from one state to another state having the same system of marital-property law, no serious problems arose. But when the move was from a common law state to a community property state, serious problems arose and inequitable results were the rule, not the exception. To hold that separate property from a common law state was also the husband's separate property in the community property state, and then to subject it to the laws of wills and succession of the community property state relating to separate property, changed its attributes and legal characteristics, and the rights and interests of the spouses in this property in a major way. What had happened in all these cases was that the wife had lost the protection furnished to her in the common law state by dower, or a statutory interest in lieu

thereof, and had acquired no protection of any kind under the laws of the community property state. . . . It was noticed that, in most of the cases which reached the reviewing courts, nearly all of the property brought from the common law states was in the name of the husband and, under their law, was his separate property. When this was treated as the husband's separate property in the community property state, he could devise it by will to others than the spouse, and often did, the wife receiving no part of the estate." McClanahan, *Community Property Law in the United States,* § 13.9 (1982).

California developed the initial response to the problem described by McClanahan and its solution appears in Cal.Prob.Code § 201.5. Idaho has followed the California approach in Idaho Code §§ 15–2–202 and 15–2–203. *See also* Reppy, *Community Property in California,* p. 292 ff (1980). Section 18 is similar to this legislation, although it does not use the same terminology. The approach is to create a *deferred* property right which applies at death. When it applies, property of the *deceased* spouse which would have been marital after acquisition if it had been originally acquired under the Act is treated *as if* it had been so acquired for purposes of disposition at death. A provision regarding personal injury recoveries analogous to that in Section 17 is also included as Subsection (b).

The Property Right: There is an important parallel between the treatment of marital property at death and dissolution. It is that of the property right of the deceased spouse in the marital property as just that: a property right. The deceased spouse is the *owner* of a one-half undivided interest in marital property and it is subject to disposition at death as any other owned property. The ownership right is an integral part of the Act, expressly stated in Section 4(c). As with the same ownership right at divorce, it must be dealt with as an ownership right, and integrated into the probate system as property subject to disposition at death. If the spouse dies testate and the half interest in marital property is not disposed of by a nontestamentary method, it is subject to disposition as part of the testate estate. An attempt to dispose of *more* than the decedent's interest in marital property would be no different from an attempt to dispose of any other property a person did not own—it would be a nullity. It would amount to interference with the ownership right of the other spouses, subject to being dealt with as any such interference is already dealt with by applicable law.

Appropriate Intestacy Provisions: If a deceased spouse dies intestate, and an adopting state makes no change in its intestacy laws, the marital property interest of the decedent will be subject to intestate disposition. This raises interesting questions as to appropriate action in an adopting state. In the American community property states

intestate disposition of separate property follows a pattern that varies from state to state as it does in common law states. All of the American community property states follow one pattern for disposing of community property and another for separate property. Obviously common law states have had no occasion for such a dual system and none is in place.

The typical intestate disposition of the first deceased spouse's interest in *community* property is in favor of the surviving spouse. However, that is not the universal rule. In California, Idaho, Nevada, New Mexico and Washington, upon the death of either spouse intestate, the decedent's half of the community property does pass to the surviving spouse. However, in Arizona, Louisiana and Texas, the decedent's half of the community property passes to the surviving spouse if there are no descendants. If there are descendants, the proportions vary from 100%, if all the surviving descendants are also descendants of the surviving spouse (Arizona), to one-half (Texas), to legal usufruct (life estate) only (Louisiana), to none, if one or more of the surviving descendants are not also descendants of the surviving spouse (Arizona).

Uniform Probate Code Provisions: There were significant historical reasons in the American community property states for bifurcating their intestate treatment of community and separate property which have never been present in American common law states. There would appear to be at least one element of community property intestacy law that ought to be followed by an appropriate alteration of intestacy laws by an American common law state adopting the Act. That would constitute following the recommendation set forth in Section 2.102A of the Uniform Probate Code. With respect to community property disposed of in intestacy, the recommendation was that "the one-half of community property which belongs to the decedent spouse passes to the [surviving spouse]." Apart from such an alteration, adopted to refer to marital property rather than community property, adopting states should *require* no substantial change in intestacy laws. Property other than marital property could remain subject to present patterns with the local preferences for particular schemes perpetuated. The logic of the alteration with respect to marital property is the logic at the heart of the Act, which is that of a sharing mode for marital acquisitions. A spouse who disapproves would have testamentary disposition as an option, and as noted below the testamentary disposition should not be subject to forced-share election.

Forced or Elective Shares: A corollary problem to intestate distribution is the elective share of a surviving spouse in testate dispositions. Among American community property states, only Louisiana's forced heirship provisions (in favor of others than the surviving spouse) interfere with the *first* deceased spouse's right of disposition of his or her share of the community. An adopting state should follow the majority rule and bar the enforcement of elective share rights of a surviving spouse against the interest in marital property of the first deceased spouse. The same reasoning would apply to the deferred marital

property created by Section 18. The section itself establishes in the surviving spouse a half interest in the deferred marital property of the *deceased* spouse. Hence there is an effective statutory sharing in favor of the survivor in that property already established by the Act, and no further elective right in that property is needed or appropriate for that survivor. The result is that elective rights should be limited, if they are in fact perpetuated by an adopting state. They should apply only to individual property and other property in which the surviving spouse acquires no interest by the terms of the Act.

The Novel Question For Adopting States: With respect to elective share rights in an adopting state against property other than marital property or Section 18 deferred marital property, a substantial and novel question is presented. In community property states, separate property is not subject to elective rights by the other spouse. McClanahan, *op. cit.,* § 11.4. The policy rationale is that community property rights are adequate protection and separate property is separate and should be under the unfettered control of its owner. However, if an adopting state followed that pattern it would represent a considerable retreat from existing spousal protection in most common law states. It would appear appropriate for an adopting state to retain elective rights against all property other than marital property and Section 18 deferred marital property, rather than to switch to the community property structure. However a major policy issue is presented by this question which each adopting state will necessarily consider for itself. A compromise might be the use of a lesser forced-share percentage against individual property than is presently in place. Here the issue of sharing will necessarily be considered in its fullest form, and the issues confronted will be *de novo,* since they have not previously been considered in this form in either common law or community property states. The closest approach was California's debate over quasi-community property which resulted in Cal.Prob.Code § 201.5, previously discussed, but this did not present identical issues. In considering any possible revisions, an adopting state may wish to consider the data revealed and discussed in Fellows, Simon & Rau, *Public Attitudes About Distribution At Death and Intestate Succession Laws in the United States,* 1978 Am.B.Found. Research J. 319; *See also* Price, *The Transmission of Wealth at Death in a Community Property Jurisdiction,* 50 Wash. L.Rev. 277 (1975).

Section 18 Protects the Survivor: Section 18 is itself a statute that emphasizes protection to the survivor rather than the decedent. It does not treat all property of *either* spouse in the deferred mode, but only property acquired by the *decedent.* Thus the survivor will acquire a one-half interest in that property without the necessity of any election and without regard to will provisions. As with marital property, the surviving spouse will own a share of the deferred marital property as a property right and not as a result of exercising any elective right. Review of elective share provisions regarding this property is necessary. If appropriate in a state's statutory scheme, an at-

tempt by a first decedent to defeat the operation of Section 18 should be barred by appropriate elective share provisions which would confirm Section 18 rights in favor of the surviving spouse. In Idaho the interest of a survivor in Idaho quasi-community property is protected by forced-share provisions. Idaho Code §§ 15–2–202, 203. In California the quasi-community interest is simply stated as a property interest of the survivor. Cal.Prob.Code. § 201.5.

The Administration Issue: Historically the entire community was administered when a spouse died. *See* De Funiak and Vaughn, *Principles of Community Property,* §§ 205–07 (1971). This pattern has been eroding. At this time, California and Nevada require administration only of the decedent's interest in the community. Arizona, Idaho, New Mexico and Washington follow the traditional pattern, though all four have simplified administration procedures under their versions of the *Uniform Probate Code* or Washington's non-intervention provision. Texas and Louisiana have simplified procedures when there is a surviving spouse but no issue, in Texas, or when succession without administration occurs, in Louisiana. In addition, Texas has independent administration as a possibility. *See* Mennell, *Community Property,* p. 355 ff (1982). An adopting state will necessarily face the administration issue and will be forced to consider whether the California and Nevada solution represents the appropriate trend.

The following sums up state intestacy, elective share and probate law provisions that would be appropriate for consideration by an adopting state for application on the death of a spouse subject to the Act:

(1) Type of Property Subject to Testamentary Disposition	(2) Amount Subject to Disposition By Decedent	(3) What Are Survivor's Rights of Election as To Amount In Column 2?	(4) Intestate Disposition As to Amount In Column 2
Marital Property	One-half	None (already owns other half of marital property)	To surviving spouse. If no surviving spouse (because of simultaneous death) by existing law in adopting state
"Deferred Marital" or Section 18 Property	One-half	None, but should be given elective right to secure survivor's half if necessary as in Idaho	Same
All other property subject to disposition at death by decedent	All	As provided by existing law in adopting state	As provided by existing law in adopting state, including appropriate augmented estate provisions

As with all provisions of the Act that contain no specific prohibition against contractual variance, the provisions of the section may be varied by a marital property agreement.

[§ 19. Estate by Entireties

This [Act] does not affect the relationship between spouses and their creditors with respect to property held by spouses in an estate by entireties after the determination date.]

COMMENT

This is a bracketed section which would apply only in jurisdictions in which estates by entireties are used. The effect of the section would be to permit the continuation of the creditor protection afforded by the tenancy by entirety provisions. See 41 Am.Jur.2d *Husband & Wife* § 55.

§ 20. Rules of Construction

Unless displaced by this [Act], the principles of law and equity supplement its provisions.

§ 21. Uniformity of Application and Construction

This [Act] shall be applied and construed to effectuate its general purpose to make uniform the law with respect to the subject of this [Act] among states enacting it.

§ 22. Short Title

This [Act] may be cited as the "Uniform Marital Property Act."

§ 23. Severability

If any provision of this [Act] or its application to any person or circumstance is held invalid, the invalidity does not affect other provisions or applications of this [Act] which can be given effect without the invalid provision or application, and to this end the provisions of this [Act] are severable.

§ 24. Time of Taking Effect

This [Act] takes effect on January 1, 19[—].

§ 25. Repeal

The following Acts and parts of Acts are repealed:

COMMENT

In an adopting state, it would be necessary to consider the interrelationship between provisions of the *Uniform Marital Property Act* and all other statutes of the state that affect the property rights of spouses. In particular, Section 15 would require attention to provisions concerning interspousal immunity from suits. Section 18 would require attention to intestacy and forced share provisions of probate laws.

§ 26. Laws Not Repealed

This [Act] does not repeal:

(1)

(2)

(3)

UNIFORM STATUTORY RULE AGAINST PERPETUITIES

PREFATORY NOTE

The Uniform Statutory Rule Against Perpetuities (Statutory Rule) alters the Common-law Rule Against Perpetuities by installing a workable wait-and-see element. See Fellows, *Testing Perpetuity Reforms: A Study of Perpetuity Cases 1984–89*, 25 Real Prop., Prob., and Tr. J. 597 (1991); Waggoner, *The Uniform Statutory Rule Against Perpetuities*, 21 Real Prop., Prob., and Tr. J. 569 (1986).

Under the Common-law Rule Against Perpetuities (Common-law Rule), the validity or invalidity of a nonvested property interest is determined, once and for always, on the basis of the facts existing *when the interest was created*. Like most rules of property law, the Common-law Rule has two sides—a validating side and an invalidating side. Both sides are evident from, but not explicit in, John Chipman Gray's formulation of the Common-law Rule:

> No [nonvested property] interest is good unless it must vest, if at all, not later than 21 years after some life in being at the creation of the interest.

J. GRAY, THE RULE AGAINST PERPETUITIES § 201 (4th ed. 1942).

With its validating and invalidating sides explicitly separated, the Common-law Rule is as follows:

> *Validating Side of the Common-law Rule:* A nonvested property interest is valid when it is created (initially valid) if it is then *certain* to vest or terminate (fail to vest)—one or the other—no later than 21 years after the death of an individual then alive.

> *Invalidating Side of the Common-law Rule:* A nonvested property interest is invalid when it is created (initially invalid) if there is no such certainty.

Notice that the invalidating side focuses on a lack of *certainty*, which means that invalidity under the Common-law Rule is *not* dependent on *actual* post-creation events but only on *possible* post-creation events. Since *actual* post-creation events are irrelevant at common law, even those that are known at the time of the lawsuit, interests that are likely to and in fact would (if given the chance), vest well within the period of a life in being plus 21 years are nevertheless invalid if at the time of the interest's creation there was a possibility, no matter how remote, that they might not have done so. This is what makes the *invalidating* side of the Common-law Rule so harsh: It can invalidate interests on the ground of post-creation events that, though possible, are extremely unlikely to happen and in actuality almost never do happen, if ever. Reasonable dispositions can be rendered invalid because of such remote possibilities as a woman, after menopause, giving birth to (or adopting) additional children (see Example (7) in the Comment to Section 1), the probate of an estate taking more than 21 years to complete (see Example (8) in the Comment to Section 1), or a married man or woman in his or her middle or late years later becoming remarried to a person born after the testator's death (see Example (9) in the Comment to Section 1). None of these dispositions offends the public policy of preventing people from tying up property in long term or even perpetual family trusts. In fact, each disposition seems quite reasonable, and violates the Common-law Rule on technical grounds only.

The Wait-and-See Reform Movement. The prospect of invalidating such interests led some decades ago to thoughts about reforming the Common-law Rule. Since the chains of events that make such interests invalid are so unlikely to happen, it was rather natural to propose that the criterion be shifted from *possible* post-creation events to *actual* post-creation events. Instead of invalidating an interest because of what *might* happen, waiting to see what *does* happen seemed then and still seems now to be more sensible.

The Uniform Statutory Rule Against Perpetuities follows the lead of the American Law Institute's Restatement (Second) of Property (Donative Transfers) § 1.3 (1983) in adopting the approach of waiting to see what does happen. This approach is known as the wait-and-see method of perpetuity reform.

In line with the Restatement (Second), the Uniform Act does not alter the *validating* side of the Common-law Rule. Consequently, dispositions that would have been valid under the Common-law Rule, *including those that are rendered valid because of a perpetuity saving clause,* remain valid as of their creation. *The practice of lawyers who competently draft trusts and other property arrangements for their clients is undisturbed.*

Under the Uniform Act, as well as under the Restatement (Second), the wait-and-see element is applied only to interests that fall under the *invalidating* side of the Common-law Rule. Interests that would be invalid at common law are saved from being rendered *initially invalid.* They are, as it were, given a second chance: Such interests are valid if they actually vest within the permissible vesting period, and become invalid only if they remain in existence but still nonvested at the expiration of the permissible vesting period.

In consequence, the Uniform Act recasts the validating and invalidating sides of the Rule Against Perpetuities as follows:

Validating Side of the Statutory Rule: A nonvested property interest is initially valid if, when it is created, it is then *certain* to vest or terminate (fail to vest) no later than 21 years after the death of an individual then alive. A nonvested property interest that is not *initially* valid is not necessarily invalid. Such an interest is valid if it vests within the permissible vesting period after its creation.

Invalidating Side of the Statutory Rule: A nonvested property interest that is not *initially* valid becomes invalid (and, as explained later, subject to reformation to make it valid) if it neither vests nor terminates within the permissible vesting period after its creation.

Shifting the focus from possible to actual post-creation events has great attraction. It eliminates the harsh consequences of the Common-law Rule's approach of invalidating interests because of what *might* happen, without sacrificing the basic policy goal of preventing property from being tied up for too long a time in very long term or even perpetual family trusts or other arrangements.

One of the early objections to wait-and-see should be mentioned at this point, because it has long since been put to rest. It was once argued that wait-and-see could cause harm because it puts the validity of property interests in abeyance—no one could determine whether an interest was valid or not. This argument has been shown to be false. Keep in mind that the wait-and-see element is applied only to interests that would be invalid were it not for wait-and-see. Such interests, otherwise invalid, are always nonvested future interests. It is now understood that wait-and-see does nothing more than affect that type of future interest with an *additional* contingency. To vest, the other contingencies must not only be satisfied—they must be satisfied within a certain period of time. *If* that period of time—the permissible vesting period—is easily determined, as it is under the Uniform Act, then the additional contingency causes no more uncertainty in the state of the title than would have been the case had the additional contingency been originally expressed in the governing instrument. It should also be noted that only the status of the affected future interest in the trust or other property arrangement is deferred. In the interim, the other interests, such as the interests of current income beneficiaries, are carried out in the normal course without obstruction.

The Permissible Vesting Period. Despite its attraction, wait-and-see has not been widely adopted. The greatest controversy over wait-and-see concerns how to determine the permissible vesting period, the time allotted for the contingencies attached to a nonvested property interest to be validly worked out to a final resolution.

The wait-and-see reform movement has always proceeded on the unexamined assumption that the permissible vesting period should be determined by reference to so-called measuring lives who are in being at the creation of the interest; the permissible vesting period under this assumption expires 21 years after the death of the last surviving measuring life. The controversy has raged over who the measuring lives should be and how the law should identify them. Competing methods have been advanced, rather stridently on occasion.

The Drafting Committee of the Uniform Act began its work in 1984 operating on the same basic assumption—that the permissible vesting period was to be determined by reference to measuring lives. The draft presented to the Conference for first reading in the summer of 1985 utilized that method.

The Saving-Clause Principle of Wait-and-See. The measuring lives selected in that earlier draft were patterned after the measuring lives listed in the Restatement (Second), which adopts the saving-clause principle of wait-and-see. Under the saving-clause principle, the measuring lives are those individuals who might appropriately have been selected in a well-drafted perpetuity saving clause.

A perpetuity saving clause typically contains two components, the *perpetuity-period component* and the *gift-over component.* The perpetuity-period component expressly requires interests in the trust or other arrangement to vest (or terminate) no later than 21 years after the death of the last survivor of a group of individuals designated in the governing instrument by name or class. The gift-over component expressly creates a gift over that is guaranteed to vest at the expiration of the period set forth in the perpetuity-period component, but only if the interests in the trust or other arrangement have neither vested nor terminated earlier in accordance with their other terms.

In most cases, the saving clause not only avoids a violation of the Common-law Rule; it also, in a sense, over-insures the client's disposition against the gift over from ever taking effect, because the period of time determined by the perpetuity-period component provides a margin of safety. Its length is sufficient to exceed—usually by a substantial margin—the time when the interests in the trust or other arrangement actually vest (or terminate) by their own terms. The clause, therefore, is usually a formality that validates the disposition without affecting the substance of the disposition at all.

In effect, the perpetuity-period component of the saving clause constitutes a privately established wait-and-see rule. Conversely, the principle supporting the adoption and operation of wait-and-see is that it provides, in effect, a saving clause for dispositions that violate the Common-law Rule, dispositions that had they been competently drafted would have included a saving clause to begin with. This is the principle embraced by the Uniform Act and the principle reflected in the Restatement (Second). The permissible vesting period under wait-and-see is the equivalent of the perpetuity-period component of a well-conceived saving clause.

The Uniform Act and the Restatement (Second) round out the saving clause by providing the near-equivalent of a gift-over component via a provision for judicial reformation of a disposition in case the interest is still in existence and nonvested when the permissible vesting period expires.

The Permissible Vesting Period: Why the Uniform Act Foregoes the Use of Actual Measuring Lives and Uses a Proxy Instead. The Uniform Act departs from and improves on the Restatement (Second) in a very important particular. The Uniform Act foregoes the use of *actual* measuring lives and instead marks off the permissible vesting period by reference to a reasonable approximation of—a proxy for—the period of time that would, *on average,* be produced through the use of a set of actual measuring lives identified by statute and then adding the traditional 21-year tack-on period after the death of the survivor. The proxy utilized in the Uniform Act is a flat period of 90 years. The rationale for this period is discussed below.

The use of a proxy, such as the flat 90-year period utilized in the Uniform Act, is greatly to be preferred over the conventional approach of using actual measuring lives plus 21 years. The conventional approach has serious disadvantages: Wait-and-see measuring lives are difficult to describe in statutory language and they are difficult to identify and trace so as to determine which one is the survivor and when he or she died.

709

Drafting statutory language that unambiguously identifies actual measuring lives under wait-and-see is immensely more difficult than drafting an actual perpetuity saving clause. An actual perpetuity saving clause can be tailored on a case by case basis to the terms and beneficiaries of each trust or other property arrangement. A statutory saving clause, however, cannot be redrafted for each new disposition. It must be drafted so that one size fits all. As a result of the difficulty of drafting such a one-size-fits-all clause, any list of measuring lives is likely to contain ambiguities, at least at the margin.

Quite apart from the difficulty of drafting unambiguous and uncomplicated statutory language, another serious problem connected to the actual-measuring-lives approach is that it imposes a costly administrative burden. The Common-law Rule uses the life-in-being-plus-21-years period in a way that does not require the actual tracing of individuals' lives, deaths, marriages, adoptions, and so on. Wait-and-see imposes this burden, however, if measuring lives are used to mark off the permissible vesting period. It is one thing to write a statute specifying who the measuring lives are. It is another to apply the actual-measuring-lives approach in practice. No matter what method is used in the statute for selecting the measuring lives and no matter how unambiguous the statutory language is, actual individuals must be identified as the measuring lives and their lives must be traced to determine who the survivor is and when the survivor dies. The administrative burden is increased if the measuring lives are not a static group, determined once and for all at the beginning, but instead are a rotating group. Adding to the administrative burden is the fact that the perpetuity question will often be raised for the first time long after the interest or power was created. The task of going back in time to reconstruct not only the facts existing when the interest or power was created, but facts occurring thereafter as well may not be worth the effort. In short, not only would births and deaths have to be kept track of, but adoptions, divorces, and possibly assignments and devises, etc., also, over a long period of time. Keeping track of and reconstructing these events to determine the survivor and the time of the survivor's death imposes an administrative burden wise to avoid. The proxy approach makes it feasible to do just that.

The administrative burden of tracing actual measuring lives and the possible uncertainty of their exact make-up, especially at the margin, combine to make the expiration date of the permissible vesting period less than certain in each given case. By making perpetuity challenges more costly to mount and more problematic in result, this might have the effect of allowing dead-hand control to continue, by default, well beyond the permissible vesting period. Marking off the permissible vesting period by using a proxy eliminates this possibility. The date of expiration of the permissible vesting period under the proxy adopted by the Uniform Act—a flat 90 years—is easy to determine and unmistakable.

One final point. If the use of actual measuring lives plus 21 years generated a permissible vesting period that precisely self-adjusted to each situation, there might be objection to replacing the actual-measuring-lives approach with a flat period of 90 years, which obviously cannot replicate such a function. That is not the function performed by the actual-measuring-lives approach, however. That is to say, that approach is not scientifically designed to generate a permissible vesting period that expires at a natural or logical stopping point along the continuum of each disposition, thereby mysteriously marking off the precise time before which actual vesting ought to be allowed and beyond which it ought not to be permitted. Instead, the actual-measuring-lives approach functions in a rather different way: It generates a period of time that almost always *exceeds* the time of actual vesting in cases when actual vesting ought to be allowed to occur. The actual-measuring-lives approach, therefore, performs a margin-of-safety function, and that is a function that *can* be replicated by the use of a proxy such as the flat 90-year period under the Uniform Act.

The following examples briefly demonstrate the margin-of-safety function of the actual-measuring-lives approach:

> *Example (1)—Corpus to Grandchildren Contingent on Reaching an Age in Excess of 21.* G died, bequeathing property in trust, income in equal shares to G's children for the life of the survivor, then in equal shares to G's grandchildren, remainder in corpus to G's grandchildren who reach age 30; if none reaches 30, to a specified charity.

> *Example (2)—Corpus to Descendants Contingent on Surviving Last Living Grandchild.* G died, bequeathing property in trust, income in equal shares to G's children for the life of the survivor, then in equal shares to G's grandchildren for the life of the survivor, and on the death of G's last living grandchild, corpus to G's descendants then living, per stirpes; if none, to a specified charity.

> In both examples, assume that G's family is typical, with two children, four grandchild, eight great-grandchildren, and so on. Assume further that one or more of the grandchildren are living

at G's death, but that one or more are conceived and born thereafter.

As is typical of cases that violate the Common-law Rule and to which wait-and-see applies, these dispositions contain two revealing features: (i) they include beneficiaries born *after* the trust or other arrangement was created, and (ii) in the normal course of events, the final vesting of the interests coincides with the death of the youngest of the after-born beneficiaries (as in Example (2)) or with some event occurring during the lifetime of that youngest after-born beneficiary (such as reaching a certain age in excess of 21, as in Example (1)).

The permissible vesting period, however, is measured by reference to the lives of individuals who must be in being at the creation of the interests. This means that they key players in these dispositions—the after-born beneficiaries—cannot be counted among the measuring lives. Since the after-born beneficiaries in both of these examples are members of the same or an older generation as that of the youngest of the measuring lives, the validity of these examples fits well within the policy of the Rule. See Waggoner, *The Uniform Statutory Rule Against Perpetuities*, 21 Real Prop., Prob., and Tr.J. 569, 579–90 (1986). In consequence, it is clear that a permissible vesting period measured by the lifetime of individuals in being at the creation of the interests plus 21 years is not scientifically designed to and does not in practice expire at the latest point when actual vesting should be allowed—on the death of the last survivor of the after-born beneficiaries. Because of its tack-on 21-year part, the period usually expires at some arbitrary time *after* that beneficiary's death. In Example (2), the period of 21 years following the death of the last survivor of the descendants who were in being at G's death is normally more than sufficient to cover the death of the last survivor of the grandchildren born after G's death.

Thus the actual-measuring-lives approach performs a margin-of-safety function. A proxy for this period performs this function just as well. In fact, in one sense it performs it more reliably because, unlike the actual-measuring-lives approach, the flat 90-year period cannot be cut short by irrelevant events. A key element in the supposition that the tack-on 21-year part of the period is usually ample to cover the births, lives, and deaths of the after-born beneficiaries when it is appropriate to do so is that the measuring lives will live out their statistical life expectancies. This will not necessarily happen, however. They may all die prematurely, thus cutting the permissible vesting period short—possibly too short to cover these post-creation events. Plainly, no rational connection exists between the premature deaths of the measuring lives and the time properly allowable, in Example (1), for the youngest *after-born* grandchild to reach 30 or, in Example (2), for the death of that youngest *after-born* grandchild to occur. A proxy eliminates the possibility of a permissible vesting period cut short by irrelevant events.

Consequently, on this count, too, a flat 90-year period is to be preferred: It performs the same margin-of-safety function as the actual-measuring-lives approach, performs it more reliably, and performs it with a remarkable ease in administration, certainty in result, and absence of complexity as compared with the uncertainty and clumsiness of identifying and tracing actual measuring lives.

Rationale of the 90-year Permissible Vesting Period. The myriad problems associated with the actual-measuring-lives approach are swept aside by shifting away from actual measuring lives and adopting instead a 90-year permissible vesting period as representing a reasonable approximation of—a proxy for—the period of time that would, on average, be produced by identifying and tracing an actual set of measuring lives and then tacking on a 21-year period following the death of the survivor. The selection of 90 years as the period of time reasonably approximating the period that would be produced, on average, by using the set of actual measuring lives identified in the Restatement (Second) or the earlier draft of the Uniform Act is based on a statistical study published in Waggoner, *Perpetuities: A Progress Report on the Draft Uniform Statutory Rule Against Perpetuities,* 20 U.Miami Inst. on Est.Plan. Ch. 7 (1986). This study suggests that the youngest measuring life,[*] on average, is about 6 years old. The remaining life expectancy of a 6-year old is reported as 69.6 years in the U.S. Bureau of the Census, Statistical Abstract of the United States: 1986, Table 108, at p. 69. (In the Statistical Abstract for 1985, 69.3 years was reported.) In the interest of arriving at an end number that is a multiple of five, the Uniform Act utilizes 69 years as an appropriate measure of the remaining life expectancy of a 6-year old, which—with the 21-year

[*] The reference to the youngest measuring life is to the transferor's youngest descendant living when the trust or other property arrangement was created. See Table 1 at p. 7–17, 20 U.Miami Inst. on Est. Plan. (1986). The transferor's youngest then-living descendant is typically the youngest measuring life under a type of perpetuity saving clause routinely used by competent practitioners. As a commonly included beneficiary of a trust or descendant of a beneficiary, the transferor's youngest then-living descendant would typically be the youngest measuring life under the earlier draft of the Uniform Act. As a commonly included beneficiary of a trust, the transferor's youngest then-living descendant would also typically be the youngest measuring life under the Restatement (Second)'s list, as well as under one interpretation of the causal-relationship-to-vesting formula, whether the descendant's beneficial interest is or is not vested when it is created.

tack-on period added—yields a permissible vesting period of 90 years.

The adoption of a flat period of 90 years rather than the use of actual measuring lives is an evolutionary step in the development and refinement of the wait-and-see doctrine. Far from revolutionary, it is well within the tradition of that doctrine. The 90–year period makes wait-and-see simple, fair, and workable. *Aggregate dead-hand control will not be increased beyond that which is already possible by competent drafting under the Common-law Rule.*

Seen as a valid approximation of the period that would be produced under the conventional survivor-of-the-measuring-lives-plus-21-years approach, and in the interest of making the law of perpetuities uniform, *jurisdictions adopting this Act are strongly urged not to adopt a period of time different from the 90-year period.*

Acceptance of the 90–year–period Approach under the Federal Generation-skipping Transfer Tax. Federal regulations, to be promulgated by the U.S. Treasury Department under the generation-skipping transfer tax, will accept the Uniform Act's 90–year period as a valid approximation of the period that, on average, would be produced by lives in being plus 21 years. See Temp. Treas. Reg. § 26.2601–1(b)(1)(v)(B)(2) (as to be revised). When originally promulgated in 1988, this regulation was prepared without knowledge of the Uniform Act, which had been promulgated in 1986; as first promulgated, the regulation only recognized a period measured by actual lives in being plus 21 years. After the 90–year approach of the Uniform Act was brought to the attention of the U.S. Treasury Department, the Department issued a letter of intent to amend the regulation to treat the 90–year period as the equivalent of a lives–in–being–plus–21–years period. Letter from Michael J. Graetz, Deputy Assistant Secretary of the Treasury (Tax Policy), to Lawrence J. Bugge, President, National Conference of Commissioners on Uniform State Laws (Nov. 16, 1990). For further discussion of the coordination of the federal generation-skipping transfer tax with the Uniform Act, see Comment G to Section 1, infra.

The 90–year Period Will Seldom be Used Up. Nearly all trusts (or other property arrangements) will terminate by their own terms long before the 90–year permissible vesting period expires, leaving the permissible vesting period to extend unused (and ignored) into the future long after the contingencies have been resolved and the property distributed. In the unlikely event that the contingencies have not been resolved by the expiration of the permissible vesting period, Section 3 requires the disposition to be reformed by the court so that all contingencies are resolved within the permissible period.

In effect, as noted above, wait-and-see with deferred reformation operates similarly to a traditional perpetuity saving clause, which grants a margin-of-safety period measured by the lives of the transferor's descendants in being at the creation of the trust or other property arrangement (plus 21 years).

No New Learning Required. The Uniform Act does not require the practicing bar to learn a new and unfamiliar set of perpetuity principles. The effect of the Uniform Act on the planning and drafting of documents for clients should be distinguished from the effect on the resolution of actual or potential perpetuity-violation cases. The former affects many more practicing lawyers than the latter.

With respect to the planning and drafting end of the practice, the Uniform Act requires no modification of current practice and no new learning. *Lawyers can and should continue to use the same traditional perpetuity-saving/termination clause, using specified lives in being plus 21 years, they used before enactment.* Lawyers should not shift to a "later-of" type clause that purports to operate upon the *later of* (A) 21 years after the death of the survivor of specified lives in being or (B) 90 years. As explained in more detail in Comment G to Section 1, such a clause is not effective. If such a "later-of" clause is used in a trust that contains a violation of the Common-law Rule, Section 1(a), by itself, would render the clause ineffective, limit the maximum permissible vesting period to 90 years, and render the trust vulnerable to a reformation suit under Section 3. Section 1(e), however, saves documents using this type of clause from this fate. By limiting the effect of such clauses to the 21–year period following the death of the survivor of the specified lives, Section 1(e) in effect transforms this type of clause into a traditional perpetuity-saving/termination clause, bringing the trust into compliance with the Common-law Rule and rendering it invulnerable to a reformation suit under Section 3.

Far fewer in number are those lawyers (and judges) who have an actual or potential perpetuity-violation case. An actual or potential perpetuity-violation case will arise very infrequently under the Uniform Act. When such a case does arise, however, lawyers (or judges) involved in the case will find considerable guidance for its resolution in the detailed analysis contained in the Comments, infra. In short, the detailed analysis in the Comments need not be part of the general learning required of lawyers in the drafting and planning of dispositive documents for their clients.

The detailed analysis is supplied for the assistance in the resolution of an actual violation. Only then need that detailed analysis be consulted and, in such a case, it will prove extremely helpful.

A section-by-section summary of the Uniform Act follows:

SUMMARY OF THE UNIFORM STATUTORY RULE AGAINST PERPETUITIES

Section 1 sets forth the Statutory Rule Against Perpetuities (Statutory Rule). The Statutory Rule and the other provisions of the Act supersede the Common-law Rule Against Perpetuities (Common-law Rule) and replace any statutory version or variation thereof. See Section 9.

Section 1(a) deals with nonvested property interests. Subsections (b) and (c) deal with powers of appointment.

Paragraph (1) of subsections (a), (b), and (c) codifies the validating side of the Common-law Rule. In effect, paragraph (1) of each of these subsections provides that a nonvested property interest or a power of appointment that is valid under the Common-law Rule Against Perpetuities is valid under the Statutory Rule and can be declared so at its inception; in such a case, nothing would be gained and much would be lost by invoking a permissible vesting period during which the validity of the interest or power is in abeyance.

Paragraph (2) of subsections (a), (b), and (c) establishes the wait-and-see rule by providing that an interest or a power of appointment that is not validated by Section 1(a)(1), 1(b)(1), or 1(c)(1), and hence would have been invalid under the Common-law Rule, is nevertheless valid if it does not actually remain nonvested when the 90-year permissible vesting period expires (or, in the case of a power of appointment, if the power ceases to be subject to a condition precedent or is no longer exercisable when the 90-year permissible vesting period expires).

Section 2 defines the time when, for purposes of the Act, a nonvested property interest or a power of appointment is created. The period of time allowed by Section 1 (Statutory Rule Against Perpetuities) is marked off from the time of creation of the nonvested property interest or power of appointment in question. Section 5, with certain exceptions, provides that the Uniform Act applies only to nonvested property interests and powers of appointment created on or after the effective date of the Act.

Section 2(b) provides that, if one person can exercise a power to become the unqualified beneficial owner of a nonvested property interest (or a property interest subject to a power of appointment described in Section 1(b) or 1(c)), the time of creation of the nonvested property interest or the power of appointment is postponed until the power to become unqualified beneficial owner ceases to exist. This is in accord with existing common law.

Section 2(c) provides that nonvested property interests and powers of appointment arising out of transfers to a previously funded trust or other existing property arrangement are created when the nonvested property interest or power of appointment arising out of the original contribution was created. This avoids an administrative difficulty that can arise at common law when subsequent transfers are made to an existing irrevocable trust. Arguably, at common law, each transfer starts the period of the Rule running anew as to that transfer. This difficulty is avoided by subsection (c).

Section 3 directs a court, upon the petition of an interested person, to reform a disposition within the limits of the 90-year permissible vesting period, in the manner deemed by the court most closely to approximate the transferor's manifested plan of distribution, in three circumstances: First, when a nonvested property interest or a power of appointment becomes invalid under the Statutory Rule; second, when a class gift has not but still might become invalid under the Statutory Rule and the time has arrived when the share of a class member is to take effect in possession or enjoyment; and third, when a nonvested property interest can vest, but cannot do so within the 90-year permissible vesting period. It is anticipated that the circumstances requisite to reformation under this section will rarely arise, and consequently that this section will seldom need to be applied.

Section 4 identifies the interests and powers that are excluded from the Statutory Rule Against Perpetuities. This section is in part declaratory of existing common law. All the exclusions from the Common-law Rule recognized at common law and by statute in the state are preserved.

In line with long-standing scholarly commentary, section 4(1) excludes nondonative transfers from the Statutory Rule. The Rule Against Perpetuities is an inappropriate instrument of social policy to use as a control on such arrangements. The period of the Rule—a life in being plus 21 years—is suitable for donative transfers only.

Section 5 provides that the Statutory Rule Against Perpetuities applies only to nonvested property interests or powers of appointment created on or after the Act's effective date. Although the

Statutory Rule does not apply retroactively, Section 5(b) authorizes a court to exercise its equitable power to reform instruments that contain a violation of the state's former Rule Against Perpetuities and to which the Statutory Rule does not apply because the offending property interest or power of appointment was created before the effective date of the Act. Courts are urged in the Comment to consider reforming such dispositions by judicially inserting a saving clause, since a saving clause would probably have been used at the drafting stage of the disposition had it been drafted competently.

Table of Sections

§ 1. Statutory Rule Against Perpetuities

(a) **[Validity of Nonvested Property Interest.]** A nonvested property interest is invalid unless:

(1) when the interest is created, it is certain to vest or terminate no later than 21 years after the death of an individual then alive; or

(2) the interest either vests or terminates within 90 years after its creation.

(b) **[Validity of General Power of Appointment Subject to a Condition Precedent.]** A general power of appointment not presently exercisable because of a condition precedent is invalid unless:

(1) when the power is created, the condition precedent is certain to be satisfied or become impossible to satisfy no later than 21 years after the death of an individual then alive; or

(2) the condition precedent either is satisfied or becomes impossible to satisfy within 90 years after its creation.

(c) [Validity of Nongeneral or Testamentary Power of Appointment.] A nongeneral power of appointment or a general testamentary power of appointment is invalid unless:

(1) when the power is created, it is certain to be irrevocably exercised or otherwise to terminate no later than 21 years after the death of an individual then alive; or

(2) the power is irrevocably exercised or otherwise terminates within 90 years after its creation.

(d) [Possibility of Post-death Child Disregarded.] In determining whether a nonvested property interest or a power of appointment is valid under subsection (a)(1), (b)(1), or (c)(1), the possibility that a child will be born to an individual after the individual's death is disregarded.

(e) [Effect of Certain "Later-of" Type Language.] If, in measuring a period from the creation of a trust or other property arrangement, language in a governing instrument (i) seeks to disallow the vesting or termination of any interest or trust beyond, (ii) seeks to postpone the vesting or termination of any interest or trust until, or (iii) seeks to operate in effect in any similar fashion upon, the later of (A) the expiration of a period of time not exceeding 21 years after the death of the survivor of specified lives in being at the creation of the trust or other property arrangement or (B) the expiration of a period of time that exceeds or might exceed 21 years after the death of the survivor of lives in being at the creation of the trust or other property arrangement, that language is inoperative to the extent it produces a period of time that exceeds 21 years after the death of the survivor of the specified lives.

COMMENT

ping Transfer Tax Regulations With Uniform Act

H.   Subsidiary Common-law Doctrines: Whether Superseded by this Act

———

Common-law Rule Against Perpetuities Superseded. As provided in Section 9, this Act supersedes the common-law Rule Against Perpetuities (Common-law Rule) in jurisdictions previously adhering to it (or repeals any statutory version or variation thereof previously in effect in the jurisdiction). The Common-law Rule (or the statutory version or variation thereof) is replaced by the Statutory Rule Against Perpetuities (Statutory Rule) set forth in this section and by the other provisions in this Act.

Subsidiary Doctrines Continue in Force Except to the Extent the Provisions of Act Conflict With Them. The courts in interpreting the Common-law Rule developed several subsidiary doctrines. In accordance with the general principle of statutory construction that statutes in derogation of the common law are to be construed narrowly, a subsidiary doctrine is superseded by this Act only to the extent the provisions of the Act conflict with it. A listing and discussion of such subsidiary doctrines, such as the constructional preference for validity, the all-or-nothing rule for class gifts, and the doctrine of infectious invalidity, appears later, in Part G of this Comment.

Application. Unless excluded by Section 4, the Statutory Rule Against Perpetuities (Statutory Rule) applies to nonvested property interests and to powers of appoint-

ment over property or property interests that are nongeneral powers, general testamentary powers, or general powers not presently exercisable because of a condition precedent.

The Statutory Rule does not apply to vested property interests (e.g., X's interest in Example (23) of this Comment) or to presently exercisable general powers of appointment (e.g., G's power in Example (19) of this Comment; G's power in Example (1) in the Comment to Section 2; A's power in Example (2) in the Comment to Section 2; X's power in Example (3) in the Comment to Section 2; A's noncumulative power of withdrawal in Example (4) in the Comment to Section 2).

A.   GENERAL PURPOSE

Section 1 sets forth the Statutory Rule Against Perpetuities (Statutory Rule). As explained above, the Statutory Rule supersedes the Common-law Rule Against Perpetuities (Common-law Rule) or any statutory version or variation thereof.

The Common-law Rule's Validating and Invalidating Sides. The Common-law Rule Against Perpetuities is a rule of *initial* validity or invalidity. At common law, a nonvested property interest is either valid or invalid *as of its creation.* Like most rules of property law, the Common-law Rule has both a validating and an invalidating side. Both sides are derived from John Chipman Gray's formulation of the Common-law Rule:

> No [nonvested property] interest is good unless it must vest, if at all, not later than 21

years after some life in being at the creation of the interest.

J. Gray, The Rule Against Perpetuities § 201 (4th ed. 1942). From this formulation, the validating and invalidating sides of the Common-law Rule are derived as follows:

Validating Side of the Common-law Rule: A nonvested property interest is valid when it is created (initially valid) if it is then *certain* to vest or terminate (fail to vest)—one or the other—no later than 21 years after the death of an individual then alive.

Invalidating Side of the Common-law Rule: A nonvested property interest is invalid when it is created (initially invalid) if there is no such certainty.

Notice that the invalidating side focuses on a lack of *certainty,* which means that invalidity under the Common-law Rule is *not* dependent on *actual* post-creation events but only on *possible* post-creation events. *Actual* post-creation events are irrelevant, even those that are known at the time of the lawsuit. It is generally recognized that the *invalidating* side of the Common-law Rule is harsh because it can invalidate interests on the ground of possible post-creation events that are extremely unlikely to happen and that in actuality almost never do happen, if ever.

The Statutory Rule Against Perpetuities. The essential difference between the Common-law Rule and its statutory replacement is that the Statutory Rule preserves the Common-law Rule's overall policy of preventing property from being tied up in unreasonably long or even perpetual family trusts or other property arrangements, while eliminating the harsh potential of the Common-law Rule. The Statutory Rule achieves this result by codifying (in slightly revised form) the validating side of the Common-law Rule and modifying the invalidating side by adopting a wait-and-see element. Under the Statutory Rule, interests that would have been initially valid at common law continue to be initially valid, but interests that would have been initially invalid at common law are invalid only if they do not actually vest or terminate within the permissible vesting period set forth in Section 1(a)(2). Thus the Uniform Act recasts the validating and invalidating sides of the Rule Against Perpetuities as follows:

Validating Side of the Statutory Rule: A nonvested property interest is initially valid if, when it is created, it is then *certain* to vest or terminate (fail to vest)—one or the other—no later than 21 years after the death of an individual then alive. The validity of a nonvested property interest that is not *initially* valid is in abeyance. Such an interest is valid if it vests within the permissible vesting period after its creation.

Invalidating Side of the Statutory Rule: A nonvested property interest that is not *initially* valid becomes invalid (and subject to reformation under Section 3) if it neither vests nor terminates within the permissible vesting period after its creation.

As indicated, this modification of the invalidating side of the Common-law Rule is generally known as the wait-and-see method of perpetuity reform. The wait-and-see method of perpetuity reform was approved by the American Law Institute as part of the Restatement (Second) of Property (Donative Transfers) §§ 1.1–1.6 (1983). For a discussion of the various methods of perpetuity reform, including the wait-and-see method and the Restatement (Second)'s version of wait-and-see, See Waggoner, *Perpetuity Reform,* 81 Mich.L.Rev. 1718 (1983).

B. SECTION 1(a)(1): NONVESTED PROPERTY INTERESTS THAT ARE INITIALLY VALID

Nonvested Property Interest. Section 1(a) sets forth the Statutory Rule Against Perpetuities with respect to nonvested property interests. A nonvested property interest (also called a contingent property interest) is a future interest in property that is subject to an unsatisfied condition precedent. In the case of a class gift, the interests of all the unborn members of the class are nonvested because they are subject to the unsatisfied condition precedent of being born. At common law, the interests of all potential class members must be valid or the class gift is invalid. As pointed out in more detail later in this Comment, this so-called all-or-nothing rule with respect to class gifts is not superseded by this Act, and so remains in effect under the Statutory Rule. Consequently, all class gifts that are subject to open are to be regarded as nonvested property interests for the purposes of this Act.

Section 1(a)(1) Codifies the Validating Side of the Common-law Rule. The validating side of the Common-law Rule is codified in Section 1(a)(1) (and, with respect to powers of appointment, in Sections 1(b)(1) and 1(c)(1)).

A nonvested property interest that satisfies the requirement of Section 1(a)(1) is initially valid. That is, it is valid as of the time of its creation. There is no need to subject such an interest to the waiting period set forth in Section 1(a)(2), nor would it be desirable to do so.

For a nonvested property interest to be valid as of the time of its creation under Section 1(a)(1), there must then be a *certainty* that the interest will either vest or terminate—an interest terminates when vesting becomes impossible—no later than 21 years after the death of an individual then alive. To satisfy this requirement, it must be established that there is no possible chain of events that might arise after the interest was created that would allow the interest to vest or terminate after the expiration of the 21-year period following the death of an individual in being at the creation of the interest. Consequently, initial validity under Section 1(a)(1) can be established only if there is an individual for whom there is a causal connection between the individual's death and the interest's vesting or terminating no later than 21 years thereafter. *The individual described in subsection (a)(1) (and subsections (b)(1) and (c)(1) as well) is often referred to as the "validating life," the term used throughout the Comments to this Act.*

Determining Whether There is a Validating Life. The process for determining whether a validating life exists is to postulate the death of each individual connected in some way to the transaction, and ask the question: Is there with respect to this individual an invalidating chain of possible events? If one individual can be found for whom the answer is No, that individual can serve as the validating life. As to that individual there will be the requisite causal connection between his or her death and the questioned interest's vesting or terminating no later than 21 years thereafter.

In searching for a validating life, only individuals who are connected in some way to the transaction need to be considered, for they are the only ones who have a chance of supplying the requisite causal connection. Such individuals vary from situation to situation, but typically include the beneficiaries of the disposition, including the taker or takers of the nonvested property interest, and individuals related to them by blood or adoption, especially in the ascending and descending lines. There is no point in even considering the life of an individual unconnected to the transaction—an individual from the world at large who happens to be in being at the creation of the interest. No such individual can be a validating life because there will be an invalidating chain of possible events as to every unconnected individual who might be proposed: Any such individual can immediately die after the creation of the nonvested property interest without causing any acceleration of the interest's vesting or termination. (The life expectancy of any unconnected individual, or even the probability that one of a number of new-born babies will live a long life, is irrelevant.)

Example (1)—Parent of Devisees As the Validating Life. G devised property "to A for life, remainder to A's children who

attain 21." G was survived by his son (A), by his daughter (B), by A's wife (W), and by A's two children (X and Y).

The nonvested property interest in favor of A's children who reach 21 satisfies Section 1(a)(1)'s requirement, and the interest is initially valid. When the interest was created (at G's death), the interest was then certain to vest or terminate no later than 21 years after A's death.

The process by which A is determined to be the validating life is one of testing various candidates to see if any of them have the requisite causal connection. As noted above, no one from the world at large can have the requisite causal connection, and so such individuals are disregarded. Once the inquiry is narrowed to the appropriate candidates, the first possible validating life that comes to mind is A, who does in fact fulfill the requirement: Since A's death cuts off the possibility of any more children being born to him, it is impossible, no matter when A dies, for any of A's children to be alive and under the age of 21 beyond 21 years after A's death. (See the discussion of subsection (d), below.)

A is therefore the validating life for the nonvested property interest in favor of A's children who attain 21. None of the other individuals who is connected to this transaction could serve as the validating life because an invalidating chain of possible post-creation events exists as to each one of them. The other individuals who might be considered include W, X, Y, and B. In the case of W, an invalidating chain of events is that she might predecease A, A might remarry and have a child by his new wife, and such child might be alive and under the age of 21 beyond the 21-year period following W's death. With respect to X and Y, an invalidating chain of events is that they might predecease A, A might later have another child, and that child might be alive and under 21 beyond the 21-year period following the death of the survivor of X and Y. As to B, she suffers from the same invalidating chain of events as exists with respect to X and Y. The fact that none of these other individuals can serve as the validating life is of no consequence, however, because only one such individual is required for the validity of a nonvested interest to be established, and that individual is A.

The Rule of Subsection (d). The rule established in subsection (d) plays a significant role in the search for a validating life. Subsection (d) declares that the possibility that a child will be born to an individual after the individual's death is to be disregarded. It is important to note that this rule applies only for the purposes of determining the validity of an interest (or power of appointment) under paragraph (1) of subsection (a), (b), or (c). The rule of subsection (d) does not apply, for example, to questions such as whether or not a child who is born to an individual after the individual's death qualifies as a taker of a beneficial interest—as a member of a class or otherwise. Neither sub-

section (d), nor any other provision of this Act, supersedes the widely accepted common-law principle, sometimes codified, that a child in gestation (a child sometimes described as a child *en ventre sa mere*) who is later born alive is regarded as alive at the commencement of gestation.

The limited purpose of subsection (d) is to solve a perpetuity problem caused by advances in medical science. The problem is illustrated by a case such as Example (1) above— "to A for life, remainder to A's children who reach 21." When the Common-law Rule was developing, the possibility was recognized, strictly speaking, that one or more of A's children might reach 21 more than 21 years after A's death. The possibility existed because A's wife (who might not be a life in being) might be pregnant when A died. If she was, and if the child was born viable a few months after A's death, the child could not reach his or her 21st birthday within 21 years after A's death. The device then invented to validate the interest of A's children was to "extend" the allowable perpetuity period by tacking on a period of gestation, if needed. As a result, the common-law perpetuity period was comprised of three components: (1) a life in being (2) plus 21 years (3) plus a period of gestation, when needed. Today, thanks to sperm banks, frozen embryos, and even the possibility of artificially maintaining the body functions of deceased pregnant women long enough to develop the fetus to viability (see Detroit Free Press, July 31, 1986, at 5A; Ann Arbor News, Act. 30, 1978, at C5 (AP story); N.Y. Times, Dec. 6, 1977, at 30; N.Y. Times, Dec. 2, 1977, at B16)—

advances in medical science unanticipated when the Common-law Rule was in its developmental stages—having a pregnant wife at death is no longer the only way of having children after death. These medical developments, and undoubtedly others to come, make the mere addition of a period of gestation inadequate as a device to confer initial validity under Section 1(a)(1) on the interest of A's children in the above example. The rule of subsection (d), however, *does* insure the initial validity of the children's interest. Disregarding the possibility that children of A will be born after his death allows A to be the validating life. None of his children, under this assumption, can reach 21 more than 21 years after his death.

Note that subsection (d) subsumes not only the case of children conceived after death, but also the more conventional case of children in gestation at death. With subsection (d) in place, the third component of the common-law perpetuity period is unnecessary and has been jettisoned. The perpetuity period recognized in paragraph (1) of subsections (a), (b), and (c) has only two components: (1) a life in being (2) plus 21 years.

As to the legal status of conceived-after-death children, that question has not yet been resolved. For example, if in Example (1) it in fact turns out that A does leave sperm on deposit at a sperm bank and if in fact A's wife does become pregnant as a result of artificial insemination, the child or children produced thereby might not be included at all in the class gift. Cf. Restatement (Second) of Property (Donative Transfers) Introductory

Note to Ch. 26 at pp. 2–3 (Tent. Draft No. 9, 1986). Without trying to predict how *that* matter will be settled in the future, the best way to handle the problem from the perpetuity perspective is subsection (d)'s rule requiring the possibility of post-death children to be disregarded.

Recipients As Their Own Validating Lives. It is well established at common law that, in appropriate cases, the recipient of an interest can be his or her own validating life. See, e.g., Rand v. Bank of California, 236 Or. 619, 388 P.2d 437 (1964). Given the right circumstances, this principle can validate interests that are contingent on the recipient's reaching an age in excess of 21, or are contingent on the recipient's surviving a particular point in time that is or might turn out to be in excess of 21 years after the interest was created or after the death of a person in being at the date of creation.

Example (2)—Devisees As Their Own Validating Lives. G devised real property "to A's children who attain 25." A predeceased G. At G's death, A had three living children, all of whom were under 25.

The nonvested property interest in favor of A's children who attain 25 is validated by Section 1(a)(1). Under subsection (d), the possibility that A will have a child born to him after his death (and since A predeceased G, after G's death) must be disregarded. Consequently, even if A's wife survived G, and even if she was pregnant at G's death or even if A had deposited sperm in a sperm bank prior to his death, it must be assumed that all of A's children are in being at G's death. A's children are, therefore, their own validating lives. (Note that subsection (d) requires that in determining whether an individual is a validating life, the possibility that a child will be born to "an" individual after the individual's death must be disregarded. The validating life and the individual whose having a post-death child is disregarded need not be the same individual.) Each one of A's children, all of whom under subsection (d) are regarded as alive at G's death, will either reach the age of 25 or fail to do so within his or her own lifetime. To say this another way, it is certain to be known no later than at the time of the death of each child whether or not that child survived to the required age.

Validating Life Can Be Survivor of Group. In appropriate cases, the validating life need not be individualized at first. Rather the validating life can initially (i.e., when the interest was created) be the unidentified survivor of a group of individuals. It is common in such cases to say that the members of the group are the validating *lives,* but the true meaning of the statement is that the validating *life* is the member of the group who turns out to live the longest. As the court said in Skatterwood v. Edge, 1 Salk. 229, 91 Eng.Rep. 203 (K.B.1697), "for let the lives be never so many, there must be a survivor, and so it is but the length of that life; for Twisden used to say, the candles were all lighted at once."

Example (3)—Case of Validating Life Being the Survivor of a Group. G devised real property "to such of my grandchildren as attain 21." Some of G's children are living at G's death.

The nonvested property interest in favor of G's grandchildren who attain 21 is valid under Section 1(a)(1). The validating life is that one of G's children who turns out to live the longest. Since under subsection (d) it must be assumed that none of G's children will have post-death children, it is regarded as impossible for any of G's grandchildren to be alive and under 21 beyond the 21-year period following the death of G's last surviving child.

Example (4)—Sperm Bank Case. G devised property in trust, directing the income to be paid to G's children for the life of the survivor, then to G's grandchildren for the life of the survivor, and on the death of G's last surviving grandchild, to pay the corpus to G's great-grandchildren then living. G's children all predeceased him, but several grandchildren were living at G's death. One of G's predeceased children (his son, A) had deposited sperm in a sperm bank. A's widow was living at G's death.

The nonvested property interest in favor of G's great-grandchildren is valid under Section 1(a)(1). The validating life is the last surviving grandchild among the grandchildren living at G's death. Under subsection (d), the possibility that A will have a child conceived after G's death must be disregarded. Note that subsection (d) requires that in determining whether an individual is a validating life, the possibility that a child will be born to "an" individual after the individual's death is disregarded. The validating life and the individual whose having a post-death child is disregarded need not be the same individual. Thus in this example, by disregarding the possibility that A will have a conceived-after-death child, G's *last surviving grandchild* becomes the validating life because G's last surviving grandchild is deemed to have been alive at G's death, when the great-grandchildren's interests were created.

Example (5)—Child in Gestation Case. G devised property in trust, to pay the income equally among G's living children; on the death of G's last surviving child, to accumulate the income for 21 years; on the 21st anniversary of the death of G's last surviving child, to pay the corpus and accumulated income to G's then-living descendants, per stirpes; if none, to X Charity. At G's death his child (A) was 6 years old, and G's wife (W) was pregnant. After G's death, W gave birth to their second child (B).

The nonvested property interests in favor of G's descendants and in favor of X Charity are valid under Section 1(a)(1). The validating life is A. Under subsection (d), the possibility that a child will be born to an individual after the individual's death must be disregarded *for the purposes of determining va-*

lidity under Section 1(a)(1). Consequently, the possibility that a child will be born to G after his death must be disregarded; and the possibility that a child will be born to any of G's descendants after their deaths must also be disregarded.

Note, however, that the rule of subsection (d) does *not* apply to the question of the entitlement of an after-born child to take a beneficial interest in the trust. The common-law rule (sometimes codified) that a child in gestation is treated as alive, if the child is subsequently born viable, applies to *this* question. Thus subsection (d) does *not* prevent B from being an income beneficiary under G's trust, nor does it prevent a descendant in gestation on the 21st anniversary of the death of G's last surviving child from being a member of the class of G's "then-living descendants," as long as such descendant has no then-living ancestor who takes instead.

Different Validating Lives Can and in Some Cases Must Be Used. Dispositions of property sometimes create more than one nonvested property interest. In such cases, the validity of each interest is treated individually. A validating life that validates one interest might or might not validate the other interests. Since it is not necessary that the same validating life be used for all interests created by a disposition, the search for a validating life for each of the other interests must be undertaken separately.

Perpetuity Saving Clauses and Similar Provisions. Knowledgeable lawyers almost routinely insert per-

727

petuity saving clauses into instruments they draft. Saving clauses contain two components, the first of which is the *perpetuity-period component*. This component typically requires the trust or other arrangement to terminate no later than 21 years after the death of the last survivor of a group of individuals designated therein by name or class. (The lives of corporations, animals, or sequoia trees cannot be used.) The second component of saving clauses is the *gift-over component*. This component expressly creates a gift over that is guaranteed to vest at the termination of the period set forth in the perpetuity-period component, but only if the trust or other arrangement has not terminated earlier in accordance with its other terms.

It is important to note that regardless of what group of individuals is designated in the perpetuity-period component of a saving clause, the surviving member of the group is not necessarily the individual who would be the validating life for the nonvested property interest or power of appointment in the absence of the saving clause. Without the saving clause, one or more interests or powers may in fact fail to satisfy the requirement of paragraph (1) of subsections (a), (b), or (c) for initial validity. By being designated in the saving clause, however, the survivor of the group becomes the validating life for all interests and powers in the trust or other arrangement: The saving clause confers on the last surviving member of the designated group the requisite causal connection between his or her death and the impossibility of any interest or power in the trust or other arrangement remaining in existence beyond the 21-year period following such individual's death.

Example (6)—Valid Saving Clause Case. A testamentary trust directs income to be paid to the testator's children for the life of the survivor, then to the testator's grandchildren for the life of the survivor, corpus on the death of the testator's last living grandchild to such of the testator's descendants as the last living grandchild shall by will appoint; in default of appointment, to the testator's then-living descendants, per stirpes. A saving clause in the will terminates the trust, if it has not previously terminated, 21 years after the death of the testator's last surviving descendant who was living at the testator's death. The testator was survived by children.

In the absence of the saving clause, the nongeneral power of appointment in the last living grandchild and the nonvested property interest in the gift-in-default clause in favor of the testator's descendants fail the test of Sections 1(a)(1) and 1(c)(1) for initial validity. That is, were it not for the saving clause, there is no validating life. However, the surviving member of the designated group becomes the validating life, so that the saving clause does confer initial validity on the nongeneral power of appointment and on the nonvested property interest under Sections 1(a)(1) and 1(c)(1).

If the governing instrument designates a group of individuals that would cause it to be impracticable to determine the death of the survivor, the common-law courts have developed the doctrine that the validity of the nonvested property interest or power of appointment is determined as if the provision in the governing instrument did not exist. See cases cited in Restatement (Second) of Property (Donative Transfers) (1983), Reporter's Note No. 3 at p. 45. See also Restatement (Second) of Property (Donative Transfers) § 1.3(1) Comment a (1983); Restatement of Property § 374 & Comment *l* (1944); 6 American Law of Property § 24.13 (A. Casner ed. 1952); 5A R. Powell, The Law of Real Property Para. 766[5] (1985); L. Simes & A. Smith, The Law of Future Interests § 1223 (2d ed. 1956). If, for example, the designated group in Example (6) were the residents of X City (or the members of Y Country Club) living at the time of the testator's death, the saving clause would not validate the power of appointment or the nonvested property interest. Instead, the validity of the power of appointment and the nonvested property interest would be determined as if the provision in the governing instrument did not exist. Since without the saving clause the power of appointment and the nonvested property interest would fail to satisfy the requirements of Sections 1(a)(1) and 1(c)(1) for initial validity, their validity would be governed by Sections 1(a)(2) and 1(c)(2).

The application of the above common-law doctrine, which is not superseded by this Act and so remains in full force, is not limited to saving clauses. It also applies to trusts or other arrangements where the period thereof is directly linked to the life of the survivor of a designated group of individuals. An example is a trust to pay the income to the grantor's descendants from time to time living, per stirpes, for the period of the life of the survivor of a designated group of individuals living when the nonvested property interest or power of appointment in question was created, plus the 21-year period following the survivor's death; at the end of the 21-year period, the corpus is to be divided among the grantor's then-living descendants, per stirpes, and if none, to the XYZ Charity. If the group of individuals so designated is such that it would be impracticable to determine the death of the survivor, the validity of the disposition is determined as if the provision in the governing instrument did not exist. The term of the trust is therefore governed by the 90-year permissible vesting period of paragraph (2) of subsections (a), (b), or (c) of the Statutory Rule.

Additional References. Restatement (Second) of Property (Donative Transfers) § 1.3(1) (1983), and the Comments thereto; Waggoner, *Perpetuity Reform,* 81 Mich.L.Rev. 1718, 1720–1726 (1983).

C. SECTION 1(a)(2): WAIT–AND–SEE — NONVESTED PROPERTY INTERESTS WHOSE VALIDITY IS INITIALLY IN ABEYANCE

Unlike the Common-law Rule, the Statutory Rule Against Perpetuities does not automatically invalidate nonvested property interests for which there is no validating life. A nonvested property interest that does not meet the requirements for validity under Section 1(a)(1) might still be valid under the wait-and-see provisions of Section 1(a)(2). Such an interest is invalid under Section 1(a)(2) only if in actuality it does not vest (or terminate) during the permissible vesting period. Such an interest becomes invalid, in other words, only if it is still in existence and nonvested when the allowable waiting period expires.

1. The 90-Year Permissible Vesting Period

Since a wait-and-see rule against perpetuities, unlike the Common-law Rule, makes validity or invalidity turn on *actual* post-creation events, it requires that an actual period of time be measured off during which the contingencies attached to an interest are allowed to work themselves out to a final resolution. The Statutory Rule Against Perpetuities establishes a permissible vesting period of 90 years. Nonvested property interests that have neither vested nor terminated at the expiration of the 90-year permissible vesting period become invalid.

As explained in the Prefatory Note, the permissible vesting period of 90 years is *not* an arbitrarily selected period of time. On the contrary, the 90-year period represents a reasonable approximation of—a proxy for—the period of time that would, *on average,* be produced through the use of an actual set of measuring lives identified by statute and then adding the traditional 21-year tack-on period after the death of the survivor.

2. Technical Violations of the Common-law Rule

One of the harsh aspects of the invalidating side of the Common-law Rule, against which the adoption of the wait-and-see element in Section 1(a)(2) is designed to relieve, is that nonvested property interests at common law are invalid even though the invalidating chain of possible events *almost* certainly will *not* happen. In such cases, the violation of the Common-law Rule could be said to be merely technical. Nevertheless, at common law, the nonvested property interest is invalid.

Cases of technical violation fall generally into discrete categories, identified and named by Professor Leach in *Perpetuities in a Nutshell,* 51 Harv.L.Rev. 638 (1938), as the fertile octogenarian, the administrative contingency, and the unborn widow. The following three examples illustrate how Section 1(a)(2) affects these categories.

Example (7)—Fertile Octogenarian Case. G devised property in trust, directing the trustee to pay the net income therefrom "to A for life, then to A's children for the life of the survivor, and upon the death of A's last surviving child to pay the corpus of the trust to A's grandchildren." G was survived by A (a female who had passed menopause) and by A's two adult children (X and Y).

The remainder interest in favor of G's grandchildren would be invalid at common law, and consequently is not validated by Section 1(a)(1). There is no validating life because, under the common law's conclusive presumption of lifetime fertility, which is not superseded by this Act (see Part H, below), A *might* have a third child (Z), conceived and born after G's death, who will have a child conceived and born more than 21 years after the death of the survivor of A, X, and Y.

Under Section 1(a)(2), however, the remote possibility of the occurrence of this chain of events does not invalidate the grandchildren's interest. The interest becomes invalid only if it remains in existence and non-vested 90 years after G's death. The chance that the grandchildren's remainder interest will become invalid under Section 1(a)(2) is negligible.

Example (8)—Administrative Contingency Case. G devised property "to such of my grand-children, born before or after my death, as may be living upon final distribution of my estate." G was survived by children and grandchildren.

The remainder interest in favor of A's grandchildren would be invalid at common law, and consequently is not validated by Section 1(a)(1). The final distribution of G's estate *might* not occur within 21 years of G's death, and after G's death grandchildren might be conceived and born who might survive or fail to survive the final distribution of G's estate more than 21 years after the death of the survivor of G's children and grandchildren who were living at G's death.

Under Section 1(a)(2), however, the remote possibility of the occurrence of this chain of events does not invalidate the grandchildren's remainder interest. The interest becomes invalid only if it remains in existence and nonvested 90 years after G's death. Since it is almost certain that the final distribution of G's

estate will occur well within this 90-year period, the chance that the grandchildren's interest will be invalid is negligible.

Example (9)—Unborn Widow Case. G devised property in trust, the income to be paid "to my son A for life, then to A's spouse for her life, and upon the death of the survivor of A and his spouse, the corpus to be delivered to A's then living descendants." G was survived by A, by A's wife (W), and by their adult children (X and Y).

Unless the interest in favor of A's "spouse" is construed to refer only to W, rather than to whoever is A's spouse when he dies, if anyone, the remainder interest in favor of A's descendants would be invalid at common law, and consequently is not validated by Section 1(a)(1). There is no validating life because A's spouse *might* not be W; A's spouse might be someone who was conceived and born after G's death; she might outlive the death of the survivor of A, W, X, and Y by more than 21 years; and descendants of A might be born or die before the death of A's spouse but after the 21-year period following the death of the survivor of A, W, X, and Y.

Under Section 1(a)(2), however, the remote possibility of the occurrence of this chain of events does not invalidate the descendants' remainder interest. The interest becomes invalid only if it remains in existence and nonvested 90 years after G's death. The chance that the descendants' remainder interest will become invalid under the Statutory Rule is small.

Age Contingencies in Excess of 21. Another category of technical violation of the Common-law Rule arises in cases of age contingencies in excess of 21 where the takers cannot be their own validating lives (unlike Example (2), above). The violation of the Common-law Rule falls into the technical category because the insertion of a saving clause would in almost all cases allow the disposition to be carried out as written. In effect, the Statutory Rule operates like the perpetuity-period component of a saving clause.

> *Example (10)—Age Contingency in Excess of 21 Case.* G devised property in trust, directing the trustee to pay the income "to A for life, then to A's children; the corpus of the trust is to be equally divided among A's children who reach the age of 30." G was survived by A, by A's spouse (H), and by A's two children (X and Y), both of whom were under the age of 30 when G died. The remainder interest in favor of A's children who reach 30 is a class gift. At common law, the interests of *all* potential class members must be valid or the class gift is totally invalid. Leake v. Robinson, 2 Mer. 363, 35 Eng.Rep. 979 (Ch. 1817). This Act does not supersede the all-or-nothing rule for class gifts (see Part G, below), and so the all-or-nothing rule continues to apply under this Act. Although X and Y will either reach 30 or die under 30 within their own lifetimes, there is at G's death the possibility that A will have an afterborn child (Z) who will reach 30 or die

under 30 more than 21 years after the death of the survivor of A, H, X, and Y. The class gift would be invalid at common law and consequently is not validated by Section 1(a)(1). Under Section 1(a)(2), however, the possibility of the occurrence of this chain of events does not invalidate the children's remainder interest. The interest becomes invalid only if an interest of a class member remains nonvested 90 years after G's death.

Although unlikely, suppose that at A's death Z's age is such that he could be alive and under the age of 30 at the expiration of the allowable waiting period. Suppose further that at A's death X or Y or both is over the age of 30. The court, upon the petition of an interested person, must under Section 3 reform G's disposition. See Example (3) in the Comment to Section 3.

D. SECTIONS 1(b)(1) and 1(c)(1): POWERS OF APPOINTMENT THAT ARE INITIALLY VALID

Powers of Appointment. Sections 1(b) and 1(c) set forth the Statutory Rule Against Perpetuities with respect to powers of appointment. A power of appointment is the authority, other than as an incident of the beneficial ownership of property, to designate recipients of beneficial interests in or powers of appointment over property. Restatement (Second) of Property (Donative Transfers) § 11.1 (1986). The property or property interest subject to a power of appointment is called the "appointive property."

The various persons connected to a power of appointment are identified by a special terminology. The "donor" is the person who created the power of appointment. The "donee" is the person who holds the power of appointment, i.e., the powerholder. The "objects" are the persons to whom an appointment can be made. The "appointees" are the persons to whom an appointment has been made. The "takers in default" are the persons whose property interests are subject to being defeated by the exercise of the power of appointment and who take the property to the extent the power is not effectively exercised. Restatement (Second) of Property (Donative Transfers) § 11.2 (1986).

A power of appointment is "general" if it is exercisable in favor of the donee of the power, the donee's creditors, the donee's estate, or the creditors of the donee's estate. A power of appointment that is not general is a "nongeneral" power of appointment. Restatement (Second) of Property (Donative Transfers) § 11.4 (1986).

A power of appointment is "presently exercisable" if, at the time in question, the donee can by an exercise of the power create an interest in or a power of appointment over the appointive property. Restatement (Second) of Property (Donative Transfers) § 11.5 (1986). A power of appointment is "testamentary" if the donee can exercise it only in the donee's will. Restatement of Property § 321 (1940). A power of appointment is "not presently exercisable because of a condition precedent" if the only impediment to its present exercisability is a condition precedent, i.e., the occurrence of some uncertain event. Since a power of appointment terminates on the donee's death, a de-

ferral of a power's present exercisability until a future time (even a time certain) imposes a condition precedent that the donee be alive at that future time.

A power of appointment is a "fiduciary" power if it is held by a fiduciary and is exercisable by the fiduciary in a fiduciary capacity. A power of appointment that is exercisable in an individual capacity is a "nonfiduciary" power. As used in this Act, the term "power of appointment" refers to "fiduciary" and to "nonfiduciary" powers, unless the context indicates otherwise.

Although Gray's formulation of the Common-law Rule Against Perpetuities does not speak directly of powers of appointment, the Common-law Rule *is* applicable to powers of appointment (other than presently exercisable general powers of appointment). The principle of subsections (b)(1) and (c)(1) is that a power of appointment that satisfies the Common-law Rule Against Perpetuities is valid under the Statutory Rule Against Perpetuities, and consequently it can be validly exercised, without being subjected to a waiting period during which the power's validity is in abeyance.

Two different tests for validity are employed at common law, depending on what type of power is at issue. In the case of a *nongeneral power* (whether or not presently exercisable) and in the case of a *general testamentary power,* the power is initially valid if, when the power was created, it is certain that the latest possible time that the power can be exercised is no later than 21 years after the death of an individual then in being. In the case of a

733

general power not presently exercisable because of a condition precedent, the power is initially valid if it is then in certain that the condition precedent to its exercise will either be satisfied or become impossible to satisfy no later than 21 years after the death of an individual then in being. Subsections (b)(1) and (c)(1) codify these rules. Under either test, initial validity depends on the existence of a validating life. The procedure for determining whether a validating life exists is essentially the same procedure explained in Part B, above, pertaining to nonvested property interests.

Example (11)—Initially Valid General Testamentary Power Case. G devised property "to A for life, remainder to such persons, including A's estate or the creditors of A's estate, as A shall by will appoint." G was survived by his daughter (A).

A's power, which is a general testamentary power, is valid as of its creation under Section 1(c)(1). The test is whether or not the power can be exercised beyond 21 years after the death of an individual in being when the power was created (G's death). Since A's power cannot be exercised after A's death, the validating life is A, who was in being at G's death.

Example (12)—Initially Valid Nongeneral Power Case. G devised property "to A for life, remainder to such of A's descendants as A shall appoint." G was survived by his daughter (A).

A's power, which is a nongeneral power, is valid as of its creation under Section 1(c)(1). The validating life is A; the analysis leading to validity is the same as applied in Example (11), above.

Example (13)—Case of Initially Valid General Power Not Presently Exercisable Because of a Condition Precedent. G devised property "to A for life, then to A's first born child for life, then to such persons, including A's first born child or such child's estate or creditors, as A's first born child shall appoint." G was survived by his daughter (A), who was then childless.

The power in A's first born child, which is a general power not presently exercisable because of a condition precedent, is valid as of its creation under Section 1(b)(1). The power is subject to a condition precedent—that A have a child—but this is a contingency that under subsection (d) is deemed certain to be resolved one way or the other within A's lifetime. A is therefore the validating life: The power cannot remain subject to the condition precedent after A's death. Note that the latest possible time that the power can be exercised is at the death of A's first born child, which might occur beyond 21 years after the death of A (and anyone else who was alive when G died). Consequently, if the power conferred on A's first born child had been a nongeneral power or a general testamentary power, the power could not be validated by Section 1(c)(1); instead, the power's validity would be governed by Section 1(c)(2).

E. SECTIONS 1(b)(2) and 1(c)(2): WAIT–AND–SEE— POWERS OF APPOINTMENT WHOSE VALIDITY IS INITIALLY IN ABEYANCE

Under the Common-law Rule, a *general power not presently exercisable because of a condition precedent* is invalid as of the time of its creation if the condition *might* neither be satisfied nor become impossible to satisfy within a life in being plus 21 years. A *nongeneral power* (whether or not presently exercisable) or a *general testamentary power* is invalid as of the time of its creation if it *might* not terminate (by irrevocable exercise or otherwise) within a life in being plus 21 years.

Sections 1(b)(2) and 1(c)(2), by adopting the wait-and-see method of perpetuity reform, shift the ground of invalidity from possible to actual post-creation events. Under these subsections, a power of appointment that would have violated the Common-law Rule, and therefore, fails the subsection (b)(1) or (c)(1) tests for *initial* validity, is nevertheless not invalid as of the time of its creation. Instead, its validity is in abeyance. A general power not presently exercisable because of a condition precedent is invalid only if *in actuality* the condition neither is satisfied nor becomes impossible to satisfy within the 90-year permissible vesting period. A nongeneral power or a general testamentary power is invalid only if *in actuality* it does not terminate (by irrevocable exercise or otherwise) within the 90-year permissible period.

Example (14)—General Testamentary Power Case. G devised property "to A for life, then to A's first born child for life, then to such persons, including the estate or the creditors of the estate of A's first born child, as A's first born child shall by will appoint; in default of appointment, to G's grandchildren in equal shares." G was survived by his daughter (A), who was then childless, and by his son (B), who had two children (X and Y).

Since the general testamentary power conferred on A's first born child fails the test of Section 1(c)(1) for *initial* validity, its validity is governed by Section 1(c)(2). If A has a child, such child's death must occur within 90 years of G's death for any provision in the child's will purporting to exercise the power to be valid.

Example (15)—Nongeneral Power Case. G devised property "to A for life, then to A's first born child for life, then to such of G's grandchildren as A's first born child shall appoint; in default of appointment, to the children of G's late nephew, Q." G was survived by his daughter (A), who was then childless, by his son (B), who had two children (X and Y), and by Q's two children (R and S).

Since the nongeneral power conferred on A's first born child fails the test of Section 1(c)(1) for *initial* validity, its validity is governed by Section 1(c)(2). If A has a child, such child must exercise the power within 90 years after G's death or the power becomes invalid.

Example (16)—General Power Not Presently Exercisable Be-

cause of a Condition Precedent.
G devised property "to A for life,
then to A's first born child for
life, then to such persons, including A's first born child or
such child's estate or creditors,
as A's first born child shall appoint after reaching the age of
25; in default of appointment, to
G's grandchildren." G was survived by his daughter (A), who
was then childless, and by his
son (B), who had two children (X
and Y).

The power conferred on A's
first born child is a general power not presently exercisable because of a condition precedent.
Since the power fails the test of
Section 1(b)(1) for *initial* validity, its validity is governed by
Section 1(b)(2). If A has a child,
such child must reach the age of
25 (or die under 25) within 90
years after G's death or the power is invalid.

Fiduciary Powers. Purely administrative fiduciary powers are excluded from the Statutory Rule under Sections 4(2) and (3), but the
only distributive fiduciary power
that is excluded is the power described in Section 4(4). Otherwise,
distributive fiduciary powers are
subject to the Statutory Rule. Such
powers are usually nongeneral powers.

*Example (17)—Trustee's Dis-
cretionary Powers Over Income
and Corpus.* G devised property
in trust, the terms of which were
that the trustee was authorized
to accumulate the income or pay
it or a portion of it out to A
during A's lifetime; after A's
death, the trustee was authorized to accumulate the income
or to distribute it in equal or

unequal shares among A's children until the death of the survivor; and on the death of A's
last surviving child to pay the
corpus and accumulated income
(if any) to B. The trustee was
also granted the discretionary
power to invade the corpus on
behalf of the permissible recipient or recipients of the income.

The trustee's nongeneral
powers to invade corpus and to
accumulate or spray income
among A's children are not excluded by Section 4(4), nor are
they initially valid under Section
1(c)(1). Their validity is, therefore, governed by Section 1(c)(2).
Both powers become invalid
thereunder, and hence no longer
exercisable, 90 years after G's
death. It is doubtful that the
powers will become invalid, because the trust will probably terminate by its own terms earlier
than the expiration of the permissible 90-year period. But if
the powers do become invalid,
and hence no longer exercisable,
they become invalid as of the
time the permissible 90-year period expires. Any exercises of
either power that took place before the expiration of the permissible 90-year period are not
invalidated retroactively. In addition, if the powers do become
invalid, a court in an appropriate
proceeding must reform the instrument in accordance with the
provisions of Section 3.

F. THE VALIDITY OF THE DONEE'S EXERCISE OF A VALID POWER

The fact that a power of appointment is valid, either because it (i)
was not subject to the Statutory

Rule to begin with, (ii) is initially valid under Sections 1(b)(1) or 1(c)(1), or (iii) becomes valid under Sections 1(b)(2) or 1(c)(2), means merely that the power can be validly exercised. It does not mean that any exercise that the donee decides to make is valid. The validity of the interests or powers created by the exercise of a valid power is a separate matter, governed by the provisions of this Act. A key factor in deciding the validity of such appointed interests or appointed powers is determining when they were created for purposes of this Act. Under Section 2, as explained in the Comment thereto, the time of creation is when the power was exercised if it was a presently exercisable general power; and if it was a nongeneral power or a general testamentary power, the time of creation is when the power was created. This is the rule generally accepted at common law (see Restatement (Second) of Property (Donative Transfers) § 1.2, Comment d (1983); Restatement of Property § 392 (1944)), and it is the rule adopted under this Act (except for purposes of Section 5 only, as explained in the Comment to Section 5).

Example (18)—Exercise of a Nongeneral Power of Appointment. G was the life income beneficiary of a trust and the donee of a nongeneral power of appointment over the succeeding remainder interest, exercisable in favor of M's descendants (except G). The trust was created by the will of G's mother, M, who predeceased him. G exercised his power by his will, directing the income to be paid after his death to his brother B's children for the life of the survivor, and upon the death of B's last surviving child, to pay the corpus of the trust to B's grandchildren. B predeceased M; B was survived by his two children, X and Y, who also survived M and G.

G's power and his appointment are valid. The power and the appointed interests were created at M's death when the power was created, not on G's death when it was exercised. See Section 2. G's power passes Section 1(c)(1)'s test for initial validity: G himself is the validating life. G's appointment also passes Section 1(a)(1)'s test for initial validity: Since B was dead at M's death, the validating life is the survivor of B's children, X and Y.

Suppose that G's power was exercisable only in favor of G's own descendants, and that G appointed the identical interests in favor of his own children and grandchildren. Suppose further that at M's death, G had two children, X and Y, and that a third child, Z, was born later. X, Y, and Z survived G. In this case, the remainder interest in favor of G's grandchildren would not pass Section 1(a)(1)'s test for initial validity. Its validity would be governed by Section 1(a)(2), under which it would be valid if G's last surviving child died within 90 years after M's death.

If G's power were a general testamentary power of appointment, rather than a nongeneral power, the solution would be the same. The period of the Statutory Rule with respect to interests created by the exercise of a general testamentary power starts to run when the power was created (at M's death, in this example), not when the power was exercised (at G's death).

Example (19)—Exercise of a Presently Exercisable General Power of Appointment. G was the life income beneficiary of a trust and the donee of a presently exercisable general power of appointment over the succeeding remainder interest. G exercised the power by deed, directing the trustee after his death to pay the income to G's children in equal shares for the life of the survivor, and upon the death of his last surviving child to pay the corpus of the trust to his grandchildren.

The validity of G's power is not in question: A presently exercisable general power of appointment is not subject to the Statutory Rule Against Perpetuities. G's appointment, however, is subject to the Statutory Rule. If G reserved a power to revoke his appointment, the remainder interest in favor of G's grandchildren passes Section 1(a)(1)'s test for initial validity. Under Section 2, the appointed remainder interest was created at G's death. The validating life for his grandchildren's remainder interest is G's last surviving child.

If G's appointment were irrevocable, however, the grandchildren's remainder interest fails the test of Section 1(a)(1) for initial validity. Under Section 2, the appointed remainder interest was created upon delivery of the deed exercising G's power (or when the exercise otherwise became effective). Since the validity of the grandchildren's remainder interest is governed by Section 1(a)(2), the remainder interest becomes invalid, and the disposition becomes subject to reformation under Section 3, if G's last surviving child lives beyond 90 years after the effective date of G's appointment.

Example (20)—Exercises of Successively Created Nongeneral Powers of Appointment. G devised property to A for life, remainder to such of A's descendants as A shall appoint. At his death, A exercised his nongeneral power by appointing to his child B for life, remainder to such of B's descendants as B shall appoint. At his death, B exercised his nongeneral power by appointing to his child C for life, remainder to C's children. A and B were living at G's death. Thereafter, C was born. A later died, survived by B and C. B then died survived by C.

A's nongeneral power passes Section 1(c)(1)'s test for initial validity. A is the validating life. B's nongeneral power, created by A's appointment, also passes Section 1(c)(1)'s test for initial validity. Since under Section 2 the appointed interests and powers are created at G's death, and since B was then alive, B is the validating life for his nongeneral power. (If B had been born after G's death, however, his power would have failed Section 1(c)(1)'s test for initial validity; its validity would be governed by Section 1(c)(2), and would turn on whether or not it was exercised by B within 90 years after G's death).

Although B's power is valid, his exercise may be partly invalid. The remainder interest in favor of C's children fails the test of Section 1(a)(1) for initial validity. The period of the Statutory Rule begins to run at G's death, under Section 2. (Since B's power was a nongeneral power, B's appointment under the common-law relation back doctrine of powers of appointment is treated as having been made by A. If B's appointment related back no further than that, of course, it would have been validated by Section 1(a)(1) because C was alive at A's death. However, A's power was also a nongeneral power, so relation back goes another step. A's appointment—which now includes B's appointment—is treated as having been made by G.) Since C was not alive at G's death, he cannot be the validating life. And, since C might have more children more than 21 years after the deaths of A and B and any other individual who was alive at G's death, the remainder interest in favor of his children is not initially validated by Section 1(a)(1). Instead, its validity is governed by Section 1(a)(2), and turns on whether or not C dies within 90 years after G's death.

Note that if either A's power or B's power (or both) had been a general testamentary power rather than a nongeneral power, the above solution would not change. However, if either A's power or B's power (or both) had

been a presently exercisable general power, B's appointment would have passed Section 1(a)(1)'s test for initial validity. (If A had the presently exercisable general power, the appointed interests and power would be created at A's death, not G's; and if the presently exercisable general power were held by B, the appointed interests and power would be created at B's death.)

Common-Law "Second-look" Doctrine. As indicated above, both at common law and under this Act (except for purposes of Section 5 only, as explained in the Comment to Section 5), appointed interests and powers established by the exercise of a general testamentary power or a nongeneral power are created when the power was created, not when the power was exercised. In applying this principle, the common law recognizes a so-called doctrine of second look, under which the facts existing on the date of the exercise are taken into account in determining the validity of appointed interests and appointed powers. E.g., Warren's Estate, 320 Pa. 112, 182 A. 396 (1930); In re Estate of Bird, 225 Cal.App.2d 196, 37 Cal. Rptr. 288 (1964). The common-law's second-look doctrine in effect constitutes a limited wait-and-see doctrine, and is therefore subsumed under but not totally superseded by this Act. The following example, which is a variation of Example (18) above, illustrates how the second-look doctrine operates at common law and how the situation would be analyzed under this Act.

Example (21)—Second-look Case. G was the life income beneficiary of a trust and the donee of a nongeneral power of appointment over the succeeding remainder interest, exercisable in favor of G's descendants. The trust was created by the will of his mother M, who predeceased him. G exercised his power by his will, directing the income to be paid after his death to his children for the life of the survivor, and upon the death of his last surviving child, to pay the corpus of the trust to his grandchildren. At M's death G had two children, X and Y. No further children were born to G, and at his death X and Y were still living.

The common-law solution of this example is as follows: G's appointment is valid under the Common-law Rule. Although the period of the Rule begins to run at M's death, the facts existing at G's death can be taken into account. This second look at the facts discloses that G had no additional children. Thus the possibility of additional children, which existed at M's death when the period of the Rule began to run, is disregarded. The survivor of X and Y therefore becomes the validating life for the remainder interest in favor of G's grandchildren, and G's appointment is valid. The common-law's second-look doctrine would not, however, save G's appointment if he actually had one or more children after M's death and if at least one of these afterborn children survived G.

Under this Act, if no additional children are born to G after M's death, the common-law second-look doctrine can be invoked as of G's death to declare

G's appointment then to be valid under Section 1(a)(1); no further waiting is necessary. However, if additional children *are* born to G and one or more of them survives G, Section 1(a)(2) applies and the validity of G's appointment depends on G's last surviving child dying within 90 years after M's death.

Additional References. Restatement (Second) of Property (Donative Transfers) § 1.2, Comments d, f, g, and h; § 1.3, Comment g; § 1.4, Comment l (1983).

G. SECTION 1(e): EFFECT OF CERTAIN "LATER–OF" TYPE LANGUAGE; COORDINATION OF GENERATION–SKIPPING TRANSFER TAX REGULATIONS WITH UNIFORM ACT

Effect of Certain "Later-of" Type Language. Section 1(e) was added to the Uniform Act in 1990. It primarily applies to a non-traditional type of "later-of" clause (described below). Use of that type of clause might have produced unintended consequences, which are now rectified by the addition of Section 1(e).

In general, perpetuity saving or termination clauses can be used in either of two ways. The predominant use of such clauses is as an override clause. That is, the clause is not an integral part of the dispositive terms of the trust, but operates independently of the dispositive terms; the clause provides that all interests must vest no later than at a specified time in the future, and sometimes also provides that the trust must then terminate, but only if any interest has not previously vested or if the trust has not previously terminated. The other use of such a clause is as an integral part of the dispositive terms of the trust; that is, the clause is the provision that directly regulates the duration of the trust. Traditional perpetuity saving or termination clauses do not use a "later-of" approach; they mark off the maximum time of vesting or termination only by reference to a 21–year period following the death of the survivor of specified lives in being at the creation of the trust.

Section 1(e) applies to a non-traditional clause called a "later-of" (or "longer-of") clause. Such a clause might provide that the maximum time of vesting or termination of any interest or trust must occur no later than the later of (A) 21 years after the death of the survivor of specified lives in being at the creation of the trust or (B) 90 years after the creation of the trust.

Under the Uniform Act as originally promulgated, this type of "later-of" clause would not achieve a "later-of" result. If used as an override clause in conjunction with a trust whose terms were, by themselves, valid under the Common-law Rule, the "later-of" clause did no harm. The trust would be valid under the Common-law Rule as codified in Section 1(a)(1) because the clause itself would neither postpone the vesting of any interest nor extend the duration of the trust. But, if used either (1) as an override clause in conjunction with a trust

whose terms were not valid under the Common-law Rule or (2) as the provision that directly regulated the duration of the trust, the "later-of" clause would not cure the perpetuity violation in case (1) and would create a perpetuity violation in case (2). In neither case would the clause qualify the trust for validity at common law under Section 1(a)(1) because the clause would not guarantee that all interests will be certain to vest or terminate no later than 21 years after the death of an individual then alive.** In any given case, 90 years can turn out to be longer than the period produced by the specified–lives–in–being–plus–21–years language.

Because the clause would fail to qualify the trust for validity under the Common-law Rule of Section 1(a)(1), the nonvested interests in the trust would be subject to the wait-and-see element of Section 1(a)(2) and vulnerable to a reformation suit under Section 3. Under Section 1(a)(2), an interest that is not valid at common law is invalid unless it actually vests or terminates within 90 years after its creation. Section 1(a)(2) does not grant such nonvested interests a permissible vesting period of either 90 years or a period of 21 years after the death of the survivor of specified lives in being. Section 1(a)(2) only grants such interests a period of 90 years in which to vest.

** By substantial analogous authority, the specified-lives-in-being-plus-21-years prong of the "later of" clause under discussion is not sustained by the separability doctrine (described in Part H of the Comment to § 1). See, e.g., Restatement of Property § 376 Comments e & f & illustration 3 (1944); Easton v. Hall,

323 Ill. 397, 154 N.E. 216 (1926); Thorne v. Continental Nat. Bank & Trust Co., 305 Ill.App. 222, 27 N.E.2d 302 (1940). The inapplicability of the separability doctrine is also supported by perpetuity policy, as described in the text above.

The operation of Section 1(a), as outlined above, is also supported by perpetuity policy. If Section 1(a) allowed a "later-of" clause to achieve a "later-of" result, it would authorize an improper use of the 90–year permissible vesting period of Section 1(a)(2). The 90–year period of Section 1(a)(2) is designed to approximate the period that, *on average,* would be produced by using actual lives in being plus 21 years. Because in any given case the period actually produced by lives in being plus 21 years can be shorter or longer than 90 years, an attempt to utilize a 90–year period in a "later-of" clause improperly seeks to turn the 90–year average into a minimum.

Set against this background, the addition of Section 1(e) is quite beneficial. Section 1(e) limits the effect of this type of "later-of" language to 21 years after the death of the survivor of the specified lives, in effect transforming the clause into a traditional perpetuity saving/termination clause. By doing so, Section 1(e) grants initial validity to the trust under the Common-law Rule as codified in Section 1(a)(1) and precludes a reformation suit under Section 3.

Note that Section 1(e) covers variations of the "later-of" clause described above, such as a clause that postpones vesting until the later of (A) 20 years after the death of the survivor of specified lives in being or (B) 89 years. Section 1(e) does not, however, apply to all dispositions that incorporate a "later-of" approach. To come under Section 1(e), the specified-lives prong must include a tack-on period of up to 21 years. Without a tack-on period, a "later-of" disposition, unless valid at common law, comes under Section 1(a)(2) and is given 90 years in which to vest. An example would be a disposition that creates an interest that is to vest upon "the later of the death of my widow or 30 years after my death."

Coordination of the Federal Generation-skipping Transfer Tax with the Uniform Statutory Rule. In 1990, the Treasury Department announced a decision to coordinate the tax regulations under the "grandfathering" provisions of the federal generation-skipping transfer tax with the Uniform Act. Letter from Michael J. Graetz, Deputy Assistant Secretary of the Treasury (Tax Policy), to Lawrence J. Bugge, President, National Conference of Commissioners on Uniform State Laws (Nov. 16, 1990) (hereinafter *Treasury Letter*).

Section 1433(b)(2) of the Tax Reform Act of 1986 generally exempts ("grandfathers") trusts from the federal generation-skipping transfer tax that were irrevocable on September 25, 1985. This section adds, however, that the exemption shall apply "only to the extent that such transfer is not made out of corpus added to the trust after September 25, 1985." The provisions of Section 1433(b)(2) were first implemented by Temp. Treas. Reg. § 26.2601–1, promulgated by T.D. 8187 on March 14, 1988. Insofar as the Uniform Act is concerned, a key feature of that temporary regulation is the concept that the statutory reference to "corpus added to the trust after September 25, 1985" not only covers actual post–9/25/85 transfers of new property or corpus to a grandfathered trust but "constructive" additions as well. Under the temporary regulation as first promulgated, a "constructive" addition occurs if, after 9/25/85, the donee of a nongeneral power of appointment exercises that power "in a manner that may postpone or suspend the vesting, absolute ownership or power of alienation of an interest in property for a period, measured from the date of creation of the trust, extending beyond any life in being at the date of creation of the trust plus a period of 21 years. If a power is exercised by creating another power it will be deemed to be exercised to whatever extent the second power may be exercised." Temp. Treas. Reg. § 26.2601–1(b)(1)(v)(B)(2) (1988).

Because the Uniform Act was promulgated in 1986 and applies only prospectively, any "grandfathered" trust would have become irrevocable prior to the enactment of the Uniform Act in any state. Nevertheless, the second sentence of Section 5(a) extends the wait-and-see approach to post-effective-date exercises of nongeneral powers even if the power itself was created prior to the effective date of the Uniform Act in any state. Consequently, a post-effective-date exercise of a nongeneral power of appointment created in a "grandfathered" trust could come under the provisions of the Uniform Act.

The literal wording, then, of Temp. Treas. Reg. § 26.2601–1(b)(1)(v)(B)(2) (1988), as first promulgated, could have jeopardized the grandfathered status of an exempt trust if (1) the trust created a nongeneral power of appointment, (2) the donee exercised that nongeneral power, and (3) the Uniform Act is the perpetuity law applicable to the donee's exercise. This possibility arose not only because the do-

nee's exercise itself might come under the 90–year permissible vesting period of Section 1(a)(2) if it otherwise violated the Common-law Rule and hence was not validated under Section 1(a)(1). The possibility also arose in a less obvious way if the donee's exercise created another nongeneral power. The last sentence of the temporary regulation states that "if a power is exercised by creating another power it will be deemed to be exercised to whatever extent the second power may be exercised."

In late March 1990, the National Conference of Commissioners on Uniform State Laws (NCCUSL) filed a formal request with the Treasury Department asking that measures be taken to coordinate the regulation with the Uniform Act. By the Treasury Letter referred to above, the Treasury Department responded by stating that it "will amend the temporary regulations to accommodate the 90–year period under USRAP as originally promulgated [in 1986] or as amended [in 1990 by the addition of subsection (e)]." This should effectively remove the possibility of loss of grandfathered status under the Uniform Act merely because the donee of a nongeneral power created in a grandfathered trust inadvertently exercises that power in violation of the Common-law Rule or merely because the donee exercises that power by creating a second nongeneral power that might, in the future, be inadvertently exercised in violation of the Common-law Rule.

The Treasury Letter states, however, that any effort by the donee of a nongeneral power in a grandfathered trust to obtain a "later-of" specified–lives–in–being–plus–

21–years or 90–years approach will be treated as a constructive addition, unless that effort is nullified by state law. As explained above, the Uniform Act, as originally promulgated in 1986 or as amended in 1990 by the addition of Section 1(e), nullifies any direct effort to obtain a "later-of" approach by the use of a "later-of" clause.

The Treasury Letter states that an indirect effort to obtain a "later-of" approach would also be treated as a constructive addition that would bring grandfathered status to an end, unless the attempt to obtain the later-of approach is nullified by state law. The Treasury Letter indicates that an indirect effort to obtain a "later-of" approach could arise if the donee of a nongeneral power successfully attempts to prolong the duration of a grandfathered trust by switching from a specified–lives–in–being–plus–21–years perpetuity period to a 90–year perpetuity period, or vice versa. Donees of nongeneral powers in grandfathered trusts would therefore be well advised to resist any temptation to wait until it becomes clear or reasonably predictable which perpetuity period will be longer and then make a switch to the longer period if the governing instrument creating the power utilized the shorter period. No such attempted switch and no constructive addition will occur if in each instance a traditional specified–lives–in–being–plus–21–years perpetuity saving clause is used.

Any such attempted switch is likely in any event to be nullified by state law and, if so, the attempted switch will not be treated as a constructive addition. For example, suppose that the original grandfa-

thered trust contained a standard perpetuity saving clause declaring that all interests in the trust must vest no later than 21 years after the death of the survivor of specified lives in being. In exercising a nongeneral power created in that trust, any indirect effort by the donee to obtain a "later-of" approach by adopting a 90–year perpetuity saving clause will likely be nullified by Section 1(e). If that exercise occurs at a time when it has become clear or reasonably predictable that the 90–year period will prove longer, the donee's exercise would constitute language in a governing instrument that seeks to operate in effect to postpone the vesting of any interest until the later of the specified–lives–in–being–plus–21–years period or 90 years. Under Section 1(e), "that language is inoperative to the extent it produces a period of time that exceeds 21 years after the death of the survivor of the specified lives."

Quite apart from Section 1(e), the relation-back doctrine generally recognized in the exercise of nongeneral powers stands as a doctrine that could potentially be invoked to nullify an attempted switch from one perpetuity period to the other perpetuity period. Under that doctrine, interests created by the exercise of a nongeneral power are considered created by the donor of that power. See, e.g., Restatement (Second) of Property, Donative Transfers § 11.1 comment b (1986). As such, the maximum vesting period applicable to interests created by the exercise of a nongeneral power would apparently be covered by the perpetuity saving clause in the document that created the power, not-

744

withstanding any different period the donee purports to adopt.

H. SUBSIDIARY COMMON-LAW DOCTRINES: WHETHER SUPERSEDED BY THIS ACT

As noted at the beginning of this Comment, the courts in interpreting the Common-law Rule developed several subsidiary doctrines. This Act does not supersede those subsidiary doctrines except to the extent the provisions of this Act conflict with them. As explained below, most of these common-law doctrines remain in full force or in force in modified form.

Constructional Preference for Validity. Professor Gray in his treatise on the Common-law Rule Against Perpetuities declared that a will or deed is to be construed without regard to the Rule, and then the Rule is to be "remorselessly" applied to the provisions so construed. J. Gray, The Rule Against Perpetuities § 629 (4th ed. 1942). Some courts may still adhere to this proposition. Colorado Nat'l Bank v. McCabe, 143 Colo. 21, 353 P.2d 385 (1960). Most courts, it is believed, would today be inclined to adopt the proposition put by the Restatement of Property § 375 (1944), which is that where an instrument is ambiguous—that is, where it is fairly susceptible to two or more constructions, one of which causes a Rule violation and the other of which does not—the construction that does not result in a Rule violation should be adopted. Cases supporting this view include Southern Bank & Trust Co. v. Brown, 271 S.C. 260, 246 S.E.2d 598 (1978); Davis v. Rossi, 326 Mo. 911, 34 S.W.2d 8 (1930); Watson v. Goldthwaite, 184 N.E.2d 340, 343 (Mass.

1962); Walker v. Bogle, 244 Ga. 439, 260 S.E.2d 338 (1979); Drach v. Ely, 703 P.2d 746 (Kan.1985).

The constructional preference for validity is not superseded by this Act, but its role is likely to be different. The situation is likely to be that one of the constructions to which the ambiguous instrument is fairly susceptible would result in validity under Section 1(a)(1), 1(b)(1), or 1(c)(1), but the other construction does not necessarily result in invalidity; rather it results in the interest's validity being governed by Section 1(a)(2), 1(b)(2), or 1(c)(2). Nevertheless, even though the result of adopting the other construction is not as harsh as it is at common law, it is expected that the courts will incline toward the construction that validates the disposition under Section 1(a)(1), 1(b)(1), or 1(c)(1).

Conclusive Presumption of Lifetime Fertility. At common law, all individuals—regardless of age, sex, or physical condition—are *conclusively* presumed to be able to have children throughout their entire lifetimes. This principle is not superseded by this Act, and in view of new advances in medical science that allow women to become pregnant after menopause by way of test-tube fertilization (see Sauer, Paulson, & Lobo, *A Preliminary Report on Oocyte Donation Extending Reproductive Potential to Women Over 40,* 323 N.ENG.J.MED. 1157 (1990)) and the widely accepted rule of construction that adopted children are presumptively included in class gifts, the conclusive presumption of lifetime fertility is not unrealistic. Since even elderly individuals probably cannot be excluded from adopting children based on their ages alone, the possibility of having children by adoption is seldom extinct. See generally Waggoner, *In re Lattouf's Will and the Presumption of Lifetime Fertility in Perpetuity Law,* 20 San Diego L.Rev. 763 (1983). Under this Act, the main force of this principle is felt in Example (7), above, where it prevents a nonvested property interest from passing the test for initial validity under Section 1(a)(1).

Act Supersedes Doctrine of Infectious Invalidity. At common law, the invalidity of an interest can, under the doctrine of infectious invalidity, be held to invalidate one or more otherwise valid interests created by the disposition or even invalidate the entire disposition. The question turns on whether the general dispositive scheme of the transferor will be better carried out by eliminating only the invalid interest or by eliminating other interests as well. This is a question that is answered on a case by case basis. Several items are relevant to the question, including who takes the stricken interests in place of those the transferor designated to take.

The doctrine of infectious invalidity is superseded by this Act by Section 3, under which courts, upon the petition of an interested person, are required to *reform* the disposition to approximate as closely as possible the transferor's manifested plan of distribution when an invalidity under the Statutory Rule occurs.

Separability. The common law's separability doctrine is that when an interest is *expressly* subject to alternative contingencies, the situation is treated as if two interests were created in the same person or class. Each interest is judged separately; the invalidity of one of the interests does not necessarily cause the other one to be invalid. This common law principle was established in Longhead v. Phelps, 2 Wm. Bl. 704, 96 Eng.Rep. 414 (K.B. 1770), and is followed in this country. L. Simes & A. Smith, The Law of Future Interests § 1257 (2d ed. 1956); 6 American Law of Property § 24.54 (A. Casner ed. 1952); Restatement of Property § 376 (1944). Under this doctrine, if property is devised "to B if X-event or Y-event happens," B in effect has two interests, one contingent on X-event happening and the other contingent on Y-event happening. If the interest contingent on X-event but not the one contingent on Y-event is invalid, the consequence of separating B's interest into two is that only one of them, the one contingent on X-event, is invalid. B still has a valid interest—the one contingent on the occurrence of Y-event.

The separability principle is not superseded by this Act. As illustrated in the following example, its invocation will usually result in one of the interests being initially validated by Section 1(a)(1) and the validity of the other interests being governed by Section 1(a)(2).

Example (22)—Separability Case. G devised real property "to A for life, then to A's children who survive A and reach 25, but if none of A's children survives A or if none of A's children who survives A reaches 25, then to B." G was survived by his brother (B), by his daughter (A), by A's husband (H), and by A's two minor children (X and Y).

The remainder interest in favor of A's children who reach 25 fails the test of Section 1(a)(1) for initial validity. Its validity is therefore governed by Section 1(a)(2), and depends on each of A's children doing any one of the following things within 90 years after G's death: predeceasing A, surviving A and failing to reach 25, or surviving A and reaching 25.

Under the separability doctrine, B has two interests. One of them is contingent on none of A's children surviving A. That interest passes Section 1(a)(1)'s test for initial validity; the validating life is A. B's other interest, which is contingent on none of A's surviving children reaching 25, fails Section 1(a)(1)'s test for initial validity. Its validity is governed by Section 1(a)(2) and depends on each of A's surviving children either reaching 25 or dying under 25 within 90 years after G's death.

Suppose that after G's death, A has a third child (Z). A subsequently dies, survived by her husband (H) and by X, Y, and Z. This, of course, causes B's interest that was contingent on none of A's children surviving A to terminate. If X, Y, and Z had all reached the age of 25 by the time of A's death, their interest would vest at A's death, and that would end the matter. If one or two, but not all three of them, had reached the age of 25 at A's death, B's other interest—the one that was contingent on none of A's surviving children reaching 25—would also terminate. As for the children's interest, if the after-born child Z's age was

such at A's death that Z could not be alive and under the age of 25 at the expiration of the allowable waiting period, the class gift in favor of the children would be valid under Section 1(a)(2), because none of those then under 25 could fail either to reach 25 or die under 25 after the expiration of the 90-year permissible vesting period. If, however, Z's age at A's death was such that Z could be alive and under the age of 25 at the expiration of the 90-year permissible vesting period, the circumstances requisite to reformation under Section 3(2) would arise, and the court would be justified in reforming G's disposition by reducing the age contingency with respect to Z to the age he would reach on the date when the permissible vesting period is due to expire. See Example (3) in the Comment to Section 3. So reformed, the class gift in favor of A's children could not become invalid under Section 1(a)(2), and the children of A who had already reached 25 by the time of A's death could receive their shares immediately.

The "All-or-Nothing" Rule With Respect to Class Gifts; the Specific Sum and Sub-Class Doctrines. The common law applies an "all-or-nothing" rule with respect to class gifts, under which a class gift stands or falls as a whole. The all-or-nothing rule, usually attributed to Leake v. Robinson, 2 Mer. 363, 35 Eng.Rep. 979 (Ch. 1817), is commonly stated as follows: If the interest of any potential class member *might* vest too remotely, the entire class gift violates the Rule. Although this Act does not supersede the basic idea of the much-maligned "all-or-nothing" rule, the evils sometimes attributed to it are substantially if not entirely eliminated by the wait-and-see feature of the Statutory Rule and by the availability of reformation under Section 3, especially in the circumstances described in Sections 3(2) and (3). For illustrations of the application of the all-or-nothing rule under this Act, see Examples (3), (4), and (6) in the Comment to Section 3.

The common law also recognizes a doctrine called the specific-sum doctrine, which is derived from Storrs v. Benbow, 3 De G.M. & G. 390, 43 Eng.Rep. 153 (Ch. 1853), and states: If a specified sum of money is to be paid to each member of a class, the interest of each class member is entitled to separate treatment and is valid or invalid under the Rule on its own. The common law also recognizes a doctrine called the sub-class doctrine, which is derived from Cattlin v. Brown, 11 Hare 372, 68 Eng.Rep. 1318 (Ch. 1853), and states: If the ultimate takers are not described as a single class but rather as a group of subclasses, and if the share to which each separate subclass is entitled will finally be determined within the period of the Rule, the gifts to the different subclasses are separable for the purpose of the Rule. American Security & Trust Co. v. Cramer, 175 F.Supp. 367 (D.D.C.1959); Restatement of Property § 389 (1944). The specific-sum and subclass doctrines are not superseded by this Act. The operation of the specific-sum doctrine under this Act is illustrated in the following example.

Example (23)—Specific-Sum Case. G bequeathed "$10,000 to each child of A, born before or after my death, who attains 25." G was survived by A and by A's two children (X and Y). X but not Y had already reached 25 at G's death. After G's death a third child (Z) was born to A.

If the phrase "born before or after my death" had been omitted, the class would close as of G's death under the common-law's rule of construction known as the rule of convenience: The after-born child, Z, would not be entitled to a $10,000 bequest, and the interests of both X and Y would be valid upon their creation at G's death. X's interest would be valid because it was initially vested; neither the Common-law Rule nor the Statutory Rule applies to interests that are vested upon their creation. Although the interest of Y was not vested upon its creation, it would be initially valid under Section 1(a)(1) because Y would be his own validating life; Y will either reach 25 or die under 25 within his own lifetime.

The inclusion of the phrase "before or after my death," however, would probably be construed to mean that G intended after-born children to receive a $10,000 bequest. See Earle Estate, 369 Pa. 52, 85 A.2d 90 (1951). Assuming that this construction were adopted, the specific-sum doctrine allows the interest of each child of A to be treated separately from the others for purposes of the Statutory Rule. For the reasons cited above, the interests of X and Y are initially valid under Section 1(a)(1). The nonvested interest of Z, however, fails Section 1(a)(1)'s test for initial validity;

there is no validating life because Z, who was not alive when the interest was created, could reach 25 or die under 25 more than 21 years after the death of the survivor of A, X, and Y. Under Section 1(a)(2), the validity of Z's interest depends on Z's reaching (or failing to reach) 25 within 90 years after G's death.

The operation of the sub-class doctrine under this Act is illustrated in the following example.

Example (24)—Sub-class Case. G devised property in trust, directing the trustee to pay the income "to A for life, then in equal shares to A's children for their respective lives; on the death of each child, the proportionate share of corpus of the one so dying shall go to the children of such child." G was survived by A and by A's two children (X and Y). After G's death, another child (Z) was born to A. A now has died, survived by X, Y, and Z.

Under the sub-class doctrine, each remainder interest in favor of the children of a child of A is treated separately from the others. This allows the remainder interest in favor of X's children and the remainder interest in favor of Y's children to be validated under Section 1(a)(1). X is the validating life for the one, and Y is the validating life for the other.

The remainder interest in favor of the children of Z fails Section 1(a)(1)'s test for initial validity; there is no validating life because Z, who was not alive when the interest was created, could have children more than 21 years after the death of the

survivor of A, X, and Y. Under Section 1(a)(2), the validity of the remainder interest in favor of Z's children depends on Z's dying within 90 years after G's death.

Note why both of the requirements of the sub-class rule are met. The ultimate takers are described as a group of sub-classes rather than as a single class: "children of the child so dying," as opposed to "grandchildren." The share to which each separate sub-class is entitled is certain to be finally determined within a life in being plus 21 years: As of A's death, who is a life in being, it is certain to be known how many children he had surviving him; since in fact there were three, we know that each sub-class will ultimately be entitled to one-third of the corpus, neither more nor less. The possible failure of the one-third share of Z's children does not increase to one-half the share going to X's and Y's children; they still are entitled to only one-third shares. Indeed, should it turn out that X has children but Y does not, this would not increase the one-third share to which X's children are entitled.

Example (25)—General Testamentary Powers—Sub-class Case. G devised property in trust, directing the trustee to pay income "to A for life, then in equal shares to A's children for their respective lives; on the death of each child, the proportionate share of corpus of the one so dying shall go to such persons as the one so dying shall by will appoint; in default of appointment, to G's grandchildren in equal shares." G was survived by A and by A's two children (X and Y). After G's death, another child (Z) was born to A.

The general testamentary powers conferred on each of A's children are entitled to separate treatment under the principles of the sub-class doctrine. See above. Consequently, the powers conferred on X and Y, A's children who were living at G's death, are initially valid under Section 1(c)(1). But the general testamentary power conferred on Z, A's child who was born after G's death, fails the test of Section 1(c)(1) for *initial* validity. The validity of Z's power is governed by Section 1(c)(2). Z's death must occur within 90 years after G's death if any provision in Z's will purporting to exercise his power is to be valid.

Duration of Indestructible Trusts—Termination of Trusts by Beneficiaries. The widely accepted view in American law is that the beneficiaries of a trust other than a charitable trust can compel its premature termination if all beneficiaries consent *and* if such termination is not expressly restrained or impli-

edly restrained by the existence of a "material purpose" of the settlor in establishing the trust. Restatement (Second) of Trusts § 337 (1959); IV A. Scott, The Law of Trusts § 337 (3d ed. 1967). A trust that cannot be terminated by its beneficiaries is called an indestructible trust.

It is generally accepted that the duration of the indestructibility of a trust, other than a charitable trust, is limited to the applicable perpetuity period. See Restatement (Second) of Trusts § 62, Comment o (1959); Restatement (Second) of Property (Donative Transfers) § 2.1 & Legislative Note & Reporter's Note (1983); I A. Scott, The Law of Trusts § 62.10(2) (3d ed. 1967); J. Gray, The Rule Against Perpetuities § 121 (4th ed. 1942); L. Simes & A. Smith, The Law of Future Interests §§ 1391–93 (2d ed. 1956).

Nothing in this Act supersedes this principle. One modification, however, is necessary: As to trusts that contain a nonvested property interest or power of appointment whose validity is governed by the wait-and-see element adopted in Section 1(a)(2), 1(b)(2), or 1(c)(2), the courts can be expected to determine that the applicable perpetuity period is 90 years.

§ 2. When Nonvested Property Interest or Power of Appointment Created

(a) Except as provided in subsections (b) and (c) and in Section 5(a), the time of creation of a nonvested property interest or a power of appointment is determined under general principles of property law.

(b) For purposes of this [Act], if there is a person who alone can exercise a power created by a governing instrument to become the unqualified beneficial owner of (i) a nonvested property interest or

(ii) a property interest subject to a power of appointment described in Section 1(b) or 1(c), the nonvested property interest or power of appointment is created when the power to become the unqualified beneficial owner terminates. [For purposes of this [Act], a joint power with respect to community property or to marital property under the Uniform Marital Property Act held by individuals married to each other is a power exercisable by one person alone.]

(c) For purposes of this [Act], a nonvested property interest or a power of appointment arising from a transfer of property to a previously funded trust or other existing property arrangement is created when the nonvested property interest or power of appointment in the original contribution was created.

COMMENT

Subsection (a): General Principles of Property Law; When Nonvested Property Interests and Powers of Appointment Are Created. Under Section 1, the period of time allowed by the Statutory Rule Against Perpetuities is marked off from the time of creation of the nonvested property interest or power of appointment in question. Section 5, with certain exceptions, provides that the Act applies only to nonvested property interests and powers of appointment created on or after the effective date of the Act.

Except as provided in subsections (b) and (c), and in the second sentence of Section 5(a) for purposes of that section only, the time of creation of nonvested property interests and powers of appointment is determined under general principles of property law.

Since a will becomes effective as a dispositive instrument upon the decedent's death, not upon the execution of the will, general principles of property law determine that the time when a nonvested property interest or a power of appointment created by will is created is at the decedent's death.

With respect to a nonvested property interest or a power of appointment created by inter vivos transfer, the time when the interest or power is created is the date the transfer becomes effective for purposes of property law generally, normally the date of delivery of the deed.

With respect to a nonvested property interest or a power of appointment created by the testamentary or inter vivos exercise of a power of appointment, general principles of property law adopt the "relation back" doctrine. Under that doctrine, the appointed interests or powers are created when the power was *created,* not when it was exercised, if the exercised power was a nongeneral power or a general testamentary power. If the exercised power was a general power presently exercisable, the relation back doctrine is not followed; the time of creation of the appointed property interests or appointed powers is regarded as the time when the power was irrevocably *exercised,* not when the power was created.

Subsection (b): Postponement, for Purposes of this Act, of the Time

751

When a Nonvested Property Interest or a Power of Appointment is Created in Certain Cases. The reason that the significant date for purposes of this Act is the date of creation is that the unilateral control of the interest (or the interest subject to the power) by one person is then relinquished. In certain cases, all beneficial rights in a property interest (including an interest subject to a power of appointment) remain under the unilateral control of one person even after the delivery of the deed or even after the decedent's death. In such cases, under this subsection, the interest or power is created, for purposes of this Act, when no person, acting alone, has a power presently exercisable to become the unqualified beneficial owner of the property interest (or the property interest subject to the power of appointment).

> *Example (1)—Revocable Inter-Vivos Trust Case.* G conveyed property to a trustee, directing the trustee to pay the net income therefrom to himself (G) for life, then to G's son A for his life, then to A's children for the life of the survivor of A's children who are living at G's death, and upon the death of such last surviving child, the corpus of the trust is to be distributed among A's then-living descendants, per stirpes. G retained the power to revoke the trust.

Because of G's reservation of the power to revoke the trust, the creation for purposes of this Act of the nonvested property interests in this case occurs at G's death, not when the trust was established. This is in accordance with common law, for

purposes of the Common-law Rule Against Perpetuities. Cook v. Horn, 214 Ga. 289, 104 S.E.2d 461 (1958).

The rationale that justifies the postponement of the time of creation in such cases is as follows. A person, such as G in the above example, who alone can exercise a power to become the unqualified beneficial owner of a nonvested property interest is in effect the owner of that property interest. Thus, any nonvested property interest subject to such a power is not created for purposes of this Act until the power terminates (by release, expiration at the death of the donee, or otherwise). Similarly, as noted above, any property interest or power of appointment created in an appointee by the irrevocable exercise of such a power is created at the time of the donee's irrevocable exercise.

For the date of creation to be postponed under subsection (b), the power need not be a power to revoke, and it need not be held by the settlor or transferor. A *presently exercisable* power held by *any* person *acting alone* to make himself the unqualified beneficial owner of the nonvested property interest or the property interest subject to a power of appointment is sufficient. If such a power exists, the time when the interest or power is created, for purposes of this Act, is postponed until the termination of the power (by irrevocable exercise, release, contract to exercise or not to exercise, expiration at the death of the donee, or otherwise). An example of such a power that might not be held by the settlor or transferor is a power, held by any person who can act alone, fully to invade the corpus of a trust.

An important consequence of the idea that a power need not be held by the settlor for the time of creation to be postponed under this section is that it makes postponement possible even in cases of testamentary transfers.

Example (2)—Testamentary Trust Case. G devised property in trust, directing the trustee to pay the income "to A for life, remainder to such persons (including A, his creditors, his estate, and the creditors of his estate) as A shall appoint; in default of appointment, the property to remain in trust to pay the income to A's children for the life of the survivor, and upon the death of A's last surviving child, to pay the corpus to A's grandchildren." A survived G.

If A exercises his presently exercisable general power, any nonvested property interest or power of appointment created by A's appointment is created for purposes of this Act when the power is exercised. If A does not exercise the power, the nonvested property interests in G's gift-in-default clause are created when A's power terminates (at A's death). In either case, the postponement is justified because the transaction is the equivalent of G's having devised the full remainder interest (following A's income interest) to A and of A's having in turn transferred that interest in accordance with his exercise of the power or, in the event the power is not exercised, devised that interest at his death in accordance with G's gift-in-default clause.

Note, however, that if G had conferred on A a *nongeneral* power or a general *testamentary* power, A's power of appointment, any nonvested property interest or power of appointment created by A's appointment, if any, and the nonvested property interests in G's gift-in-default clause would be created at G's death.

Unqualified Beneficial Owner of the Nonvested Property Interest or the Property Interest Subject to a Power of Appointment. For the date of creation to be postponed under subsection (b), the presently exercisable power must be one that entitles the donee of the power to become the unqualified beneficial owner of the *nonvested property interest (or the property interest subject to a nongeneral power of appointment, a general testamentary power of appointment, or a general power of appointment not presently exercisable because of a condition precedent).* This requirement was met in Example (2), above, because A could by appointing the remainder interest to himself become the unqualified beneficial owner of all the nonvested property interests in G's gift-in-default clause. In Example (2) it is not revealed whether A, if he exercised the power in his own favor, also had the right as sole beneficiary of the trust to compel the termination of the trust and possess himself as unqualified beneficial owner of the property that was the subject of the trust. Having the power to compel termination of the trust is not necessary. If, for example, the trust in Example (2) was a spendthrift trust or contained any other feature that under the relevant local law (see

753

Claflin v. Claflin, 149 Mass. 19, 20 N.E. 454 (1889); Restatement (Second) of Trusts § 337 (1959)) would prevent A as sole beneficiary from compelling termination of the trust, A's presently exercisable general power over the remainder interest would still postpone the time of creation of the nonvested property interests in G's gift-in-default clause because the power enables A to become the unqualified beneficial owner of such interests.

Furthermore, it is not necessary that the donee of the power have the power to become the unqualified beneficial owner of *all beneficial* rights *in the trust*. In example (2), the property interests in G's gift-in-default clause are not created for purposes of this Act until A's power expires (or on A's appointment, until the power's exercise) even if someone other than A was the income beneficiary of the trust.

Presently Exercisable Power. For the date of creation to be postponed under subsection (b), the power must be presently exercisable. A testamentary power does not qualify. A power not presently exercisable because of a condition precedent does not qualify. If the condition precedent later becomes satisfied, however, so that the power becomes presently exercisable, the interests or powers subject thereto are not created, for purposes of this Act, until the termination of the power. The common-law decision of Fitzpatrick v. Mercantile Safe Deposit Co., 220 Md. 534, 155 A.2d 702 (1959), appears to be in accord with this proposition.

    Example (3)—General Power in Unborn Child Case. G devised property "to A for life, then to A's first-born child for life, then to such persons, including A's first-born child or such child's estate or creditors, as A's first-born child shall appoint." There was a further provision that in default of appointment, the trust would continue for the benefit of G's descendants. G was survived by his daughter (A), who was then childless. After G's death, A had a child, X. A then died, survived by X.

As of G's death, the power of appointment in favor of A's first-born child and the property interests in G's gift-in-default clause would be regarded as having been created at G's death because the power in A's first-born child was then a general power not presently exercisable because of a condition precedent.

At X's birth, X's general power became presently exercisable and excluded from the Statutory Rule. X's power also qualifies as a power exercisable by one person alone to become the unqualified beneficial owner of the property interests in G's gift-in-default clause. Consequently, the nonvested property interests in G's gift-in-default clause are not created, for purposes of this Act, until the termination of X's power. If X exercises his presently exercisable general power, before or after A's death, the appointed interests or powers are created, for purposes of this Act, as of X's exercise of the power.

Partial Powers. For the date of creation to be postponed under subsection (b), the person must have a presently exercisable power to become the unqualified beneficial owner of the full nonvested property interest or the property interest subject to a power of appointment described in Section 1(b) or 1(c). If, for example, the subject of the transfer was an undivided interest such as a one-third tenancy in common, the power qualifies even though it relates only to the undivided one-third interest in the tenancy in common; it need not relate to the whole property. A power to become the unqualified beneficial owner of only part of the nonvested property interest or the property interest subject to a power of appointment, however, does not postpone the time of creation of the interests or powers subject thereto, unless the power is actually exercised.

Example (4)—"5 and 5" Power Case. G devised property in trust, directing the trustee to pay the income "to A for life, remainder to such persons (including A, his creditors, his estate, and the creditors of his estate), as A shall by will appoint;" in default of appointment, the governing instrument provided for the property to continue in trust. A was given a noncumulative power to withdraw the greater of $5,000 or 5% of the corpus of the trust annually. A survived G. A never exercised his noncumulative power of withdrawal.

G's death marks the time of creation of: A's testamentary power of appointment; any nonvested property interest or power of appointment created in G's gift-in-default clause; and any appointed interest or power created by a testamentary exercise of A's power of appointment

over the remainder interest. A's general power of appointment over the remainder interest does not postpone the time of creation because it is not a presently exercisable power. A's noncumulative power to withdraw a portion of the trust each year does not postpone the time of creation as to all or the portion of the trust with respect to which A allowed his power to lapse each year because A's power is a power over only part of any nonvested property interest or property interest subject to a power of appointment in G's gift-in-default clause and over only part of any appointed interest or power created by a testamentary exercise of A's general power of appointment over the remainder interest. The same conclusion has been reached at common law. See Ryan v. Ward, 192 Md. 342, 64 A.2d 258 (1949).

If, however, in any year A exercised his noncumulative power of withdrawal in a way that created a nonvested property interest (or power of appointment) in the withdrawn amount (for example, if A directed the trustee to transfer the amount withdrawn directly into a trust created by A), the appointed interests (or powers) would be created when the power was exercised, not when G died.

Incapacity of the Donee of the Power. The fact that the donee of a power lacks the capacity to exercise it, by reason of minority, mental incompetency, or any other reason, does not prevent the power held by such person from postponing the time of creation under subsection (b), unless the governing instrument extinguishes the power (or prevents it from coming into existence) for that reason.

Joint Powers—Community Property; Marital Property. For the date of creation to be postponed under subsection (b), the power must be exercisable by one person alone. A joint power does not qualify, except that, if the bracketed sentence of subsection (b) is enacted, a joint power over community property or over marital property under the Uniform Marital Property Act held by individuals married to each other is, for purposes of this Act, treated as a power exercisable by one person acting alone. See Restatement (Second) of Property (Donative Transfers) § 1.2, Comment b and illustrations 5, 6, and 7 (1983), for the rationale supporting the enactment of the bracketed sentence and examples illustrating its principle.

Subsection (c): No Staggered Periods. For purposes of this Act, subsection (c) in effect treats a transfer of property to a previously funded trust or other existing property arrangement as having been made when the nonvested property interest or power of appointment in the original contribution was created. The purpose of subsection (c) is to avoid the administrative difficulties that would otherwise result where subsequent transfers are made to an existing irrevocable trust. Without subsection (c), the allowable period under the Statutory Rule would be marked off in such cases from different times with respect to different portions of the same trust.

Example (5)—Series of Transfers Case. In Year One, G created an irrevocable inter vivos trust, funding it with $20,000 cash. In Year Five, when the value of the investments in which the original $20,000 contribution was placed had risen to a value of $30,000, G added $10,000 cash to the trust. G died in Year Ten. G's will poured the residuary of his estate into the trust. G's residuary estate consisted of Blackacre (worth $20,000) and securities (worth $80,000). At G's death, the value of the investments in which the original $20,000 contribution and the subsequent $10,000 contribution were placed had risen to a value of $50,000.

Were it not for subsection (c) the permissible vesting period under the Statutory Rule would be marked off from three different times: Year One, Year Five, and Year Ten. The effect of subsection (c) is that the permissible vesting period under the Statutory Rule starts running only once—in Year One—with respect to the entire trust. This result is defensible not only to prevent the administrative difficulties inherent in recognizing staggered periods. It also is defensible because if G's inter vivos trust had contained a perpetuity saving clause, the perpetuity-period component of the clause would be geared to the time when the original contribution to the trust was made; this clause would cover the subsequent contributions as well. Since the major justification for the adoption by this Act of the wait-and-see method of perpetuity reform is that it amounts to a statutory insertion of a saving clause (see the Prefatory Note), subsection (c) is consistent with the theory of this Act.

Additional References. Restatement (Second) of Property (Donative Transfers) §§ 1.1, 1.2 (1983), and the Comments thereto.

§ 3. Reformation

Upon the petition of an interested person, a court shall reform a disposition in the manner that most closely approximates the transferor's manifested plan of distribution and is within the 90 years allowed by Section 1(a)(2), 1(b)(2), or 1(c)(2) if:

(1) a nonvested property interest or a power of appointment becomes invalid under Section 1 (statutory rule against perpetuities);

(2) a class gift is not but might become invalid under Section 1 (statutory rule against perpetuities) and the time has arrived when the share of any class member is to take effect in possession or enjoyment; or

(3) a nonvested property interest that is not validated by Section 1(a)(1) can vest but not within 90 years after its creation.

COMMENT

Reformation. This section requires a court, upon the petition of an interested person, to reform a disposition *whose validity is governed by the wait-and-see element of Section 1(a)(2), 1(b)(2), or 1(c)(2)* so that the reformed disposition is within the limits of the 90-year period allowed by those subsections, in the manner deemed by the court most closely to approximate the transferor's manifested plan of distribution, in three circumstances: First, when (after the application of the Statutory Rule) a nonvested property interest or a power of appointment becomes invalid under the Statutory Rule; second, when a class gift has not but still might become invalid under the Statutory Rule and the time has arrived when the share of one or more class members is to take effect in possession

or enjoyment; and third, when a nonvested property interest can vest, but cannot do so within the allowable 90-year period under the Statutory Rule.

It is anticipated that the circumstances requisite to reformation will seldom arise, and consequently that this section will be applied infrequently. If, however, one of the three circumstances arises, the court in reforming is authorized to alter existing interests or powers and to create new interests or powers by implication or construction based on the transferor's manifested plan of distribution as a whole. In reforming, the court is urged not to invalidate any vested interest retroactively (the doctrine of infectious invalidity having been superseded by this Act, as indicated in the Comment to Section 1). The court is also urged not to reduce an age contingency in excess of 21 unless it is absolutely necessary, and if it is deemed necessary to reduce such an age contingency, not to reduce it automatically to 21 but rather to reduce it no lower than absolutely necessary. See example (3), below; Waggoner, *Perpetuity Reform*, 81 Mich.L.Rev. 1718, 1755–1759 (1983); Langbein & Waggoner, *Reformation of Wills on the Ground of Mistake: Change of Direction in American Law?*, 130 U.Pa.L.Rev. 521, 546–49 (1982).

Judicial Sale of Land Affected by Future Interests. Although this section—except for cases that fall under subsections (2) or (3)—defers the time when a court is directed to reform a disposition until the expiration of the 90-year permissible vesting period, this section is not to be understood as preventing an earlier application of other remedies. In particular, in the case of interests in land not in trust, the principle, codified in many states, is widely recognized that there is judicial authority, under specified circumstances, to order a sale of land in which there are future interests. See 1 American Law of Property §§ 4.98–.99 (A. Casner ed. 1952); L. Simes & A. Smith, The Law of Future Interests §§ 1941–1946 (2d ed. 1956); see also Restatement of Property § 179 at pp. 485–95 (1936); L. Simes & C. Taylor, Improvement of Conveyancing by Legislation 235–38 (1960). Nothing in Section 3 of this Act should be taken as precluding this type of remedy, if appropriate, before the expiration of the 90-year permissible vesting period.

Duration of the Indestructibility of Trusts—Termination of Trusts by Beneficiaries. As noted in Part G of the Comment to Section 1, it is generally accepted that a trust cannot remain indestructible beyond the period of the rule against perpetuities. Under this Act, the period of the rule against perpetuities applicable to a trust whose validity is governed by the wait-and-see element of Section 1(a)(2), 1(b)(2), or 1(c)(2) is 90 years. The result of any reformation under Section 3 is that all nonvested property interests in the trust will vest *in interest* (or terminate) no later than the 90th anniversary of their creation. In the case of trusts containing a nonvested property interest or a power of appointment whose validity is governed by Section 1(a)(2), 1(b)(2), or 1(c)(2), courts can therefore be expected to adopt the rule that no purpose of the settlor, expressed in or implied from the governing instrument, can prevent the beneficiaries of a trust other than a charitable trust from compelling its termination after 90 years after every nonvested property interest and power of appointment in the trust was created.

Subsection (1): Invalid Property Interest or Power of Appointment. Subsection (1) is illustrated by the following examples.

Example (1)—Multiple Generation Trust. G devised property in trust, directing the trustee to pay the income "to A for life, then to A's children for the life of the survivor, then to A's grandchildren for the life of the survivor, and on the death of A's last surviving grandchild, the corpus of the trust is to be divided among A's then living descendants per stirpes; if none, to" a specified charity. G was survived by his child (A) and by A's two minor children (X and Y). After G's death, another child (Z) was born to A. Subsequently, A died, survived by his children (X, Y and Z) and by three grandchildren (M, N, and O).

There are four interests subject to the Statutory Rule in this example: (1) the income interest in favor of A's children, (2) the income interest in favor of A's grandchildren, (3) the remainder interest in the corpus in favor of A's descendants who survive the death of A's last surviving grandchild, and (4) the alternative remainder interest in the corpus in favor of the specified charity. The first interest is initially valid under Section 1(a)(1); A is the validating life for that interest. There is no validating life for the other three interests, and so their validity is governed by Section 1(a)(2).

If, as is likely, A and A's children all die before the 90th anniversary of G's death, the income interest in favor of A's grandchildren is valid under Section 1(a)(2).

If, as is also likely, some of A's grandchildren are alive on the 90th anniversary of G's death, the alternative remainder interests in the corpus of the trust then become invalid under Section 1(a)(2), giving rise to Section 3(1)'s prerequisite to reformation. A court would be justified in reforming G's disposition by closing the class in favor of A's descendants as of the 90th anniversary of G's death (precluding new entrants thereafter), by moving back the condition of survivorship on the class

so that the remainder interest is in favor of G's descendants who survive the 90th anniversary of G's death (rather than in favor of those who survive the death of A's last surviving grandchild), and by redefining the class so that its makeup is formed as if A's last surviving grandchild died on the 90th anniversary of G's death.

Example (2)—Sub-class Case. G devised property in trust, directing the trustee to pay the income "to A for life, then in equal shares to A's children for their respective lives; on the death of each child the proportionate share of corpus of the one so dying shall go to the descendants of such child surviving at such child's death, per stirpes." G was survived by A and by A's two children (X and Y). After G's death, another child (Z) was born to A. Subsequently, A died, survived by X, Y, and Z.

Under the sub-class doctrine, each remainder interest in favor of the descendants of a child of A is treated separately from the others. Consequently the remainder interest in favor of X's descendants and the remainder interest in favor of Y's descendants are valid under Section 1(a)(1): X is the validating life for the one, and Y is the validating life for the other.

The remainder interest in favor of the descendants of Z is not validated by Section 1(a)(1) because Z, who was not alive when the interest was created, could have descendants more than 21 years after the death of the survivor of A, X, and Y. Instead, the validity of the remainder interest in favor of Z's descendants is governed by Section 1(a)(2), under which its validity depends on Z's dying within 90 years after G's death.

Although unlikely, suppose that Z is still living 90 years after G's death. The remainder interest in favor of Z's descendants will then become invalid under the Statutory Rule, giving rise to subsection (1)'s prerequisite to reformation. In such circumstances, a court would be justified in reforming the remainder interest in favor of Z's descendants by making it indefeasibly vested as of the 90th anniversary of G's death. To do this, the court would reform the disposition by eliminating the condition of survivorship of Z and closing the class to new entrants after the 90th anniversary of G's death.

Subsection (2): Class Gifts Not Yet Invalid. Subsection (2), which, upon the petition of an interested person, requires reformation in certain cases where a class gift has not but still might become invalid under the Statutory Rule, is illustrated by the following examples.

Example (3)—Age Contingency in Excess of 21. G devised property in trust, directing the trustee to pay the income "to A for life, then to A's children; the corpus of the trust is to be equally divided among A's children who reach the age of 30." G was survived by A, by A's spouse (H), and by A's two children (X and Y), both of whom were under the age of 30 when G died.

Since the remainder interest in favor of A's children who reach 30 is a class gift, at common law (Leake v. Robinson, 2 Mer. 363, 35 Eng.Rep. 979 (Ch. 1817)) and under this Act (see Part G of the Comment to Section 1) the interests of *all* potential class members must be valid or the class gift is totally invalid. Although X and Y will either reach 30 or die under 30 within their own lifetimes, there is at G's death the possibility that A will have an afterborn child (Z) who will reach 30 or die under 30 more than 21 years after the death of the survivor of A, H, X, and Y. There is no validating life, and the class gift is therefore not validated by Section 1(a)(1).

Under Section 1(a)(2), the children's remainder interest becomes invalid only if an interest of a class member neither vests nor terminates within 90 years after G's death. If in fact, there is an afterborn child (Z), and if upon A's death, Z has at least reached an age such that he cannot be alive and under the age of 30 on the 90th anniversary of G's death, the class gift is valid. (Note that at Z's *birth* it would have been known whether or not Z could be alive and under the age of 30 on the 90th anniversary of G's death; nevertheless, even if it was *then* certain that Z could *not* be alive and under the age of 30 on the 90th anniversary of G's death, the class gift could not *then* have been declared valid because, A being alive, it was *then* possible for one or more additional children to

760

have later been born to or adopted by A.)

Although unlikely, suppose that at A's death (prior to the expiration of the 90-year period), Z's age was such that he *could* be alive and under the age of 30 on the 90th anniversary of G's death. Suppose further that at A's death X and Y were over the age of 30. Z's interest and hence the class gift as a whole is not yet invalid under the Statutory Rule because Z might die under the age of 30 within the remaining part of the 90-year period following G's death; but the class gift might become invalid because Z might be alive and under the age of 30, 90 years after G's death. Consequently, the prerequisites to reformation set forth in subsection (2) are satisfied, and a court would be justified in reforming G's disposition to provide that Z's interest is contingent on reaching the age he can reach if he lives to the 90th anniversary of G's death. This would render Z's interest valid so far as the Statutory Rule Against Perpetuities is concerned, and allow the class gift as a whole to be declared valid. X and Y would thus be entitled immediately to their one-third shares each. If Z's interest later vested, Z would receive the remaining one-third share. If Z failed to reach the required age under the reformed disposition, the remaining one-third share would be divided equally between X and Y or their successors in interest.

Example (4)—Case Where Subsection (2) Applies, Not Involving an Age Contingency in Excess of 21. G devised property in trust, directing the trustee to pay the income "to A for life, then to A's children; the corpus of the trust is to be equally divided among A's children who graduate from an accredited medical school or law school." G was survived by A, by A's spouse (H), and by A's two minor children (X and Y).

As in Example (3), the remainder interest in favor of A's children is a class gift, and the common-law principle is not superseded by this Act by which the interests of *all* potential class members must be valid or the class gift is totally invalid. Although X and Y will either graduate from an accredited medical or law school, or fail to do so, within their own lifetimes, there is at G's death the possibility that A will have an afterborn child (Z), who will graduate from an accredited medical or law school (or die without having done either) more than 21 years after the death of the survivor of A, H, X, and Y. The class gift would not be valid under the Common-law Rule, and is therefore not validated by Section 1(a)(1).

Under Section 1(a)(2), the children's remainder interest becomes invalid only if an interest of a class member neither vests nor terminates within 90 years after G's death. Suppose in fact that there is an afterborn child (Z), and that at A's death Z was a freshman in college. Suppose further that at A's death X had graduated from an accredited law school and that Y had graduated from an accredited medical school. Z's interest and hence the class gift as a whole is not yet invalid under Section 1(a)(2) because the 90-year period following G's death has not yet expired; but the class gift might become invalid because Z might be alive but not a graduate of an accredited medical or law school 90 years after G's death. Consequently, the prerequisites to reformation set forth in Section 3(2) are satisfied, and a court would be justified in reforming G's disposition to provide that Z's interest is contingent on graduating from an accredited medical or law school within 90 years after G's death. This would render Z's interest valid so far as the Section 1(a)(2) is concerned, and allow the class gift as a whole to be declared valid. X and Y would thus be entitled immediately to their one-third shares each. If Z's interest later vested, Z would receive the remaining one-third share. If Z failed to graduate from an accredited medical or law school within the allowed time under the disposition as so reformed, the remaining one-third share would be divided equally between X and Y or their successors in interest.

Subsection (3): Interests that Can Vest But Not Within the 90-Year Permissible Vesting Period. In exceedingly rare cases, an interest might be created that can vest, but not within the 90-year permissible vesting period of the Statutory Rule. This may be the situation when the interest was created (see Example (5)), or it may become the situation at some time thereafter (see Example (6)). Whenever the situation occurs, the court, upon the petition of an interested person, is required by subsection (3) to reform the disposition within the limits of the 90-year permissible vesting period.

Example (5)—Case of An Interest, As of Its Creation, Being Impossible to Vest Within the 90-Year Period. G devised property in trust, directing the trustee to divide the income, per stirpes, among G's descendants from time to time living, for 100 years. At the end of the 100-year period following G's death, the trustee is to distribute the corpus and accumulated income to G's then-living descendants, per stirpes; if none, to the XYZ Charity.

The nonvested property interest in favor of G's descendants who are living 100 years after G's death can vest, but not within the 90-year period of Section 1(a)(2). The interest would violate the Common-law Rule, and hence is not validated by Section 1(a)(1), because there is no validating life. In these circumstances, a court is required by Section 3(3) to reform G's disposition within the limits of the 90-year period. An appropriate result would be for the court to lower the period following G's death from a 100-year period to a 90-year period.

Note that the circumstance that triggers the direction to reform the disposition under this subsection is that the nonvested property interest still can vest, but cannot vest within the 90-year period of Section 1(a)(2). It is not necessary that the interest be certain to become *invalid* under that subsection. For the interest to be certain to become invalid under Section 1(a)(2), it would have to be certain that it can neither vest *nor terminate* within the 90-year period. In this example, the interest of G's descendants might *terminate* within the period (by all of G's descendants dying within 90 years of G's death). If this were to happen, the interest of XYZ Charity would be valid because it would have vested within the allowable period. However, it was thought desirable to require reformation without waiting to see if this would happen: The only way that G's *descendants,* who are G's *primary* set of beneficiaries, would have a chance to take the property is to reform the disposition within the limits of the 90-year period on the ground that their interest cannot *vest* within the allowable period and subsection (3) so provides.

Example (6)—Case of An Interest After its Creation Becoming Impossible to Vest Within the 90-Year Period. G devised property in trust, with the income to be paid to A. The corpus of the trust was to be divided among A's children who reach 30, each child's share to be paid on the child's 30th birthday; if none

reaches 30, to the XYZ Charity. G was survived by A and by A's two children (X and Y). Neither X nor Y had reached 30 at G's death.

The class gift in favor of A's children who reach 30 would violate the Common-law Rule Against Perpetuities and thus is not validated by Section 1(a)(1). Its validity is therefore governed by Section 1(a)(2).

Suppose that after G's death, and during A's lifetime, X and Y die and a third child (Z) is born to or adopted by A. At A's death, Z is living but her age is such that she cannot reach 30 within the remaining part of the 90-year period following G's death. As of A's death, it has become the situation that Z's interest cannot vest within the allowable period. The circumstances requisite to reformation under subsection (3) have arisen. An appropriate result would be for the court to lower the age contingency to the age Z can reach 90 years after G's death.

Additional References. For additional discussion and illustrations of the application of some of the principles of this section, see the Comments to Restatement (Second) of Property (Donative Transfers) § 1.5 (1983).

§ 4. Exclusions From Statutory Rule Against Perpetuities

Section 1 (statutory rule against perpetuities) does not apply to:

(1) a nonvested property interest or a power of appointment arising out of a nondonative transfer, except a nonvested property interest or a power of appointment arising out of (i) a premarital or postmarital agreement, (ii) a separation or divorce settlement, (iii) a spouse's election, (iv) a similar arrangement arising out of a

prospective, existing, or previous marital relationship between the parties, (v) a contract to make or not to revoke a will or trust, (vi) a contract to exercise or not to exercise a power of appointment, (vii) a transfer in satisfaction of a duty of support, or (viii) a reciprocal transfer;

(2) a fiduciary's power relating to the administration or management of assets, including the power of a fiduciary to sell, lease, or mortgage property, and the power of a fiduciary to determine principal and income;

(3) a power to appoint a fiduciary;

(4) a discretionary power of a trustee to distribute principal before termination of a trust to a beneficiary having an indefeasibly vested interest in the income and principal;

(5) a nonvested property interest held by a charity, government, or governmental agency or subdivision, if the nonvested property interest is preceded by an interest held by another charity, government, or governmental agency or subdivision;

(6) a nonvested property interest in or a power of appointment with respect to a trust or other property arrangement forming part of a pension, profit-sharing, stock bonus, health, disability, death benefit, income deferral, or other current or deferred benefit plan for one or more employees, independent contractors, or their beneficiaries or spouses, to which contributions are made for the purpose of distributing to or for the benefit of the participants or their beneficiaries or spouses the property, income, or principal in the trust or other property arrangement, except a nonvested property interest or a power of appointment that is created by an election of a participant or a beneficiary or spouse; or

(7) a property interest, power of appointment, or arrangement that was not subject to the common-law rule against perpetuities or is excluded by another statute of this State.

COMMENT

Section 4 lists seven exclusions from the Statutory Rule Against Perpetuities (Statutory Rule). Some are declaratory of existing law; others are contrary to existing law. Since the Common-law Rule Against Perpetuities is superseded by this Act (or a statutory version or variation thereof is repealed by this Act), a nonvested property interest, power of appointment, or other arrangement excluded from the Statutory Rule by this section is not subject to any rule against perpetuities, statutory or otherwise.

A. SUBSECTION (1): NON-DONATIVE TRANSFERS EXCLUDED

Rationale. In line with long-standing scholarly commentary, subsection (1) excludes (with certain enumerated exceptions) nonvested property interests and powers of appointment arising out of a nondonative transfer. The rationale for this exclusion is that the Rule Against Perpetuities is a wholly inappropriate instrument of social policy to use as a control over such arrangements. The period of the rule—a life in being plus 21 years—is not suitable for nondonative transfers, and this point applies with equal force to the 90-year allowable waiting period under the wait-and-see element of Section 1 because that period represents an approximation of the period of time that would be produced, on average, by using a statutory list identifying actual measuring lives and adding a 21-year period following the death of the survivor.

No general exclusion from the Common-law Rule Against Perpetuities is recognized for nondonative transfers, and so subsection (1) is contrary to existing common law. (But see Metropolitan Transportation Authority v. Bruken Realty Corp., 67 N.Y.2d 156, 492 N.E.2d 379, 384 (1986), pointing out the inappropriateness of the period of a life in being plus 21 years to cases of commercial and governmental transactions and noting that the Rule Against Perpetuities can invalidate legitimate transactions in such cases.)

Subsection (1) is therefore inconsistent with decisions holding the Common-law Rule to be applicable to the following types of property interests or arrangements when created in a nondonative, commercial-type transaction, as they almost always are: options (e.g., Milner v. Bivens, 335 S.E.2d 288 (Ga.1985)); preemptive rights in the nature of a right of first refusal (e.g., Atchison v. City of Englewood, 170 Colo. 295, 463 P.2d 297 (1969); Robroy Land Co., Inc. v. Prather, 24 Wash.App. 511, 601 P.2d 297 (1969)); leases to commence in the future, at a time certain or on the happening of a future event such as the completion of a building (e.g., Southern Airways Co. v. DeKalb County, 101 Ga. App. 689, 115 S.E.2d 207 (1960)); nonvested easements; top leases and top deeds with respect to interests in minerals (e.g., Peveto v. Starkey, 645 S.W.2d 770 (Tex. 1982)); and so on.

Consideration Does Not Necessarily Make the Transfer Nondonative. A transfer can be supported by consideration and still be donative in character and hence not excluded from the Statutory Rule. A transaction that is essentially gratuitous in nature, accompanied by donative intent on the part of at least one party to the transaction, is not to be regarded as nondonative simply because it is for consideration. Thus, for example, the exclusion would not apply if a parent purchases a parcel of land for full and adequate consideration, and directs the seller to make out the deed in favor of the purchaser's daughter for life, remainder to such of the daughter's children as reach 25. The nonvested property interest of the daughter's children is subject to the Statutory Rule.

Some Transactions Not Excluded Even if Considered Nondonative.

Some types of transactions—although in some sense supported by consideration and hence arguably nondonative—arise out of a domestic situation, and should not be excluded from the Statutory Rule. To avoid uncertainty with respect to such transactions, subsection (1) specifies that nonvested property interests or powers of appointment arising out of any of the following transactions are not excluded by subsection (1)'s nondonative-transfers exclusion: a premarital or postmarital agreement; a separation or divorce settlement; a spouse's election, such as the "widow's election" in community property states; an arrangement similar to any of the foregoing arising out of a prospective, existing, or previous marital relationship between the parties; a contract to make or not to revoke a will or trust; a contract to exercise or not to exercise a power of appointment; a transfer in full or partial satisfaction of a duty of support; or a reciprocal transfer. The term "reciprocal transfer" is to be interpreted in accordance with the reciprocal transfer doctrine in the tax law (see United States v. Estate of Grace, 395 U.S. 316 (1969)).

Other Means of Controlling Some Nondonative Transfers Desirable. Some commercial transactions respecting land or mineral interests, such as options in gross (including rights of first refusal), leases to commence in the future, nonvested easements, and top leases and top deeds in commercial use in the oil and gas industry, directly or indirectly restrain the alienability of property or provide a disincentive to improve the property. Although controlling the duration of such interests is desirable, they are exclud-ed by subsection (1) from the Statutory Rule because, as noted above, the period of a life in being plus 21 years—actual or by the 90-year proxy—is inappropriate for them; that period is appropriate for family-oriented, donative transfers.

The Committee was aware that a few states have adopted statutes on perpetuities that include special limits on certain commercial transactions (e.g., Fla.Stat. § 689.-22(3)(a); Ill.Rev.Stat. ch. 30, § 194(a)), and in fact the Committee itself drafted a comprehensive version of Section 4 that would have imposed a 40-year period-in-gross limitation in specified cases. In the end, however, the Committee did not present that version to the National Conference for approval because it was of the opinion that the control of these interests is better left to other types of statutes, such as marketable title acts (e.g., the Uniform Simplification of Land Transfers Act) and the Uniform Dormant Mineral Interests Act, backed up by the potential application of the common-law rules regarding unreasonable restraints on alienation.

B. SUBSECTIONS (2)–(7): OTHER EXCLUSIONS

Subsection (2)—Administrative Fiduciary Powers. Fiduciary powers are subject to the Statutory Rule Against Perpetuities, unless specifically excluded. Purely administrative fiduciary powers are excluded by subsections (2) and (3), but distributive fiduciary powers are generally speaking not excluded. The only distributive fiduciary power excluded is the one described in subsection (4).

The application of subsection (2) to fiduciary powers can be illustrated by the following example.

Example (1). G devised property in trust, directing the trustee (a bank) to pay the income to A for life, then to A's children for the life of the survivor, and on the death of A's last surviving child to pay the corpus to B. The trustee is granted the discretionary power to sell and to reinvest the trust assets and to invade the corpus on behalf of the income beneficiary or beneficiaries.

The trustee's fiduciary power to sell and reinvest the trust assets is a purely administrative power, and under subsection (2) of this section is not subject to the Statutory Rule.

The trustee's fiduciary power to invade corpus, however, is a nongeneral power of appointment that is not excluded from the Statutory Rule. Its validity, and hence its exercisability, is governed by Section 1. Under that section, since the power is not initially valid under Section 1(c)(1), Section 1(c)(2) applies and the power ceases to be exercisable 90 years after G's death.

Subsection (3)—Powers to Appoint a Fiduciary. Subsection (3) excludes from the Statutory Rule Against Perpetuities powers to appoint a fiduciary (a trustee, successor trustee, or co-trustee, a personal representative, successor personal representative, or co-personal representative, an executor, successor executor, or co-executor, etc.). Sometimes such a power is held by a fiduciary and sometimes not. In either case, the power is excluded from the Statutory Rule.

Subsection (4)—Certain Distributive Fiduciary Power. The only distributive fiduciary power excluded from the Statutory Rule Against Perpetuities is the one described in subsection (4); the excluded power is a discretionary power of a trustee to distribute principal before the termination of a trust to a beneficiary who has an indefeasibly vested interest in the income and principal.

Example (2). G devised property in trust, directing the trustee (a bank) to pay the income to A for life, then to A's children; each child's share of principal is to be paid to the child when he or she reaches 40; if any child dies under 40, the child's share is to be paid to the child's estate as a property interest owned by such child. After A's death, the trustee is given the discretionary power to advance all or a portion of a child's share before the child reaches 40. G was survived by A, who was then childless.

The trustee's discretionary power to distribute principal to a child after A's death but before the child's 40th birthday is excluded from the Statutory Rule Against Perpetuities. (The trustee's *duty* to pay the income to A and after A's death to A's children is not subject to the Statutory Rule because it is a duty, not a power.)

Subsection (5)—Charitable or Governmental Gifts. Subsection (5) codifies the common-law principle that a nonvested property interest held by a charity, a government, or a governmental agency or subdivision is excluded from the Rule

767

Against Perpetuities if the interest was preceded by an interest that is held by another charity, government, or governmental agency or subdivision. See L. Simes & A. Smith, The Law of Future Interests §§ 1278–87 (2d ed. 1956); Restatement (Second) of Property (Donative Transfers) § 1.6 (1983); Restatement of Property § 397 (1944).

Example (3). G devised real property "to the X School District so long as the premises are used for school purposes, and upon the cessation of such use, to Y City."

The nonvested property interest held by Y City (an executory interest) is excluded from the Statutory Rule under subsection (5) because it was preceded by a property interest (a fee simple determinable) held by a governmental subdivision, X School District.

The exclusion of charitable and governmental gifts applies only in the circumstances described. If a nonvested property interest held by a charity is preceded by a property interest that is held by a noncharity, the exclusion does not apply; rather, the validity of the nonvested property interest held by the charity is governed by the other sections of this Act.

Example (4). G devised real property "to A for life, then to such of A's children as reach 25, but if none of A's children reaches 25, to X Charity."

The nonvested property interest held by X Charity is not excluded from the Statutory Rule.

If a nonvested property interest held by a noncharity is preceded by a property interest that is held by a charity, the exclusion does not apply; rather, the validity of the nonvested property interest in favor of the noncharity is governed by the other sections of this Act.

Example (5). G devised real property "to the City of Sidney so long as the premises are used for a public park, and upon the cessation of such use, to my brother, B."

The nonvested property interest held by B is not excluded from the Statutory Rule by subsection (5).

Subsection (6)—Trusts for Employees and Others; Trusts for Self-employed Individuals. Subsection (6) excludes from the Statutory Rule Against Perpetuities nonvested property interests and powers of appointment with respect to a trust or other property arrangement, whether part of a "qualified" or "unqualified" plan under the federal income tax law, forming part of a bona fide benefit plan for employees (including owner-employees), independent contractors, or their beneficiaries or spouses. The exclusion granted by this subsection does not, however, extend to a nonvested property interest or a power of appointment created by an election of a participant or beneficiary or spouse.

Subsection (7)—Pre-existing Exclusions from the Common-Law Rule Against Perpetuities. Subsection (7) assures that all property interests, powers of appointment, or arrangements that were excluded from the Common-law Rule Against Perpetuities or are excluded by another statute of this state are also excluded from the Statutory Rule Against Perpetuities.

Possibilities of reverter and rights of entry (also known as rights of re-entry, rights of entry for condition broken, and powers of termination) are not subject to the Common-law Rule Against Perpetuities, and so are excluded from the Statutory Rule. By statute in some states, possibilities of reverter and rights of entry expire if they do not vest within a specified period of years (such as 40 years). See Fratcher, A Modest Proposal for Trimming the Claws of Legal Future Interests, 1972 Duke L.J. 517, 527–31. See also Uniform Simplification of Land Transfers Act § 3–409. States adopting the Uniform Statutory Rule Against Perpetuities may wish to consider the enactment of some such limit on these interests, if they have not already done so.

§ 5. Prospective Application

(a) Except as extended by subsection (b), this [Act] applies to a nonvested property interest or a power of appointment that is created on or after the effective date of this [Act]. For purposes of this section, a nonvested property interest or a power of appointment created by the exercise of a power of appointment is created when the power is irrevocably exercised or when a revocable exercise becomes irrevocable.

(b) If a nonvested property interest or a power of appointment was created before the effective date of this [Act] and is determined in a judicial proceeding, commenced on or after the effective date of this [Act], to violate this State's rule against perpetuities as that rule existed before the effective date of this [Act], a court upon the petition of an interested person may reform the disposition in the manner that most closely approximates the transferor's manifested plan of distribution and is within the limits of the rule against perpetuities applicable when the nonvested property interest or power of appointment was created.

COMMENT

Subsection (a): Act Not Retroactive. This section provides that, except as provided in subsection (b), the Statutory Rule Against Perpetuities and the other provisions of this Act apply only to nonvested property interests or powers of appointment created on or after the Act's effective date. With one exception, in determining when a nonvested property interest or a power of appointment is created, the principles of Section 2 are applicable. Thus, for example, a property interest (or a power of appointment) created in a revocable inter vivos trust is created when the power to revoke terminates. See Example (1) in the Comment to Section 2.

The second sentence of subsection (a) establishes a special rule for nonvested property interests (and powers of appointment) created by the exercise of a power of appointment. For purposes of this section only, a nonvested property interest (or a power of appointment) created by the exercise of a power of appointment is created when the power is irrevocably exercised or when a revocable exercise of the power becomes irrevocable. Consequently, all the provisions of this Act except Section 5(b) apply to a nonvested property interest (or power of appointment) created by a donee's exercise of a power of appointment where the donee's exercise, whether revocable or irrevocable, occurs on or after the effective date of this Act. All the provisions of this Act except Section 5(b) also apply where the donee's exercise occurred before the effective date of this Act if: (i) that pre-effective-date exercise was revocable *and* (ii) that revocable exercise becomes irrevocable on or after the effective date of this Act. This special rule applies to the exercise of all types of powers of appointment—presently exercisable general powers, general testamentary powers, and nongeneral powers.

If the application of this special rule determines that the provisions of this Act (except Section 5(b)) apply, then for all such purposes, the time of creation of the appointed nonvested property interest (or appointed power of appointment) is determined by reference to Section 2, without regard to the special rule contained in the second sentence of Section 5(a).

If the application of this special rule of Section 5(a) determines that the provisions of this Act (except Section 5(b)) do not apply, then Section 5(b) is the only potentially applicable provision of this Act.

*Example (1)—Testamentary Power Created Before But Exer-*cised *After the Effective Date of this Act.* G was the donee of a general testamentary power of appointment created by the will of his mother, M. M died in 1980. Assume that the effective date of this Act in the jurisdiction is January 1, 1987. G died in 1988, leaving a will that exercised his general testamentary power of appointment.

Under the special rule in the second sentence of Section 5(a), any nonvested property interest (or power of appointment) created by G in his will in exercising his general testamentary power was created (for purposes of Section 5) at G's death in 1988, which was *after* the effective date of this Act.

Consequently, all the provisions of this Act apply (except Section 5(b)). That point having been settled, the next step is to determine whether the nonvested property interests or powers of appointment created by G's testamentary appointment are initially valid under Section 1(a)(1), 1(b)(1), or 1(c)(1), or whether the wait-and-see element established in Section 1(a)(2), 1(b)(2), or 1(c)(2) apply. If the wait-and-see element does apply, it must also be determined when the allowable 90-year waiting period starts to run. In making these determinations, the principles of Section 2 control the time of creation of the nonvested property interests (or powers of appointment); under Section 2, since G's power was a general testamentary power of appointment, the common-law relation-back doctrine applies and the appointed nonvested property interests (and appointed powers of appointment) are created at M's death in 1980.

If G's testamentary power of appointment had been a nongeneral power rather than a general power, the same results as described above would apply.

Example (2)—Presently Exercisable Nongeneral Power Created Before But Exercised After the Effective Date of this Act. Assume the same facts as in Example (1), except that G's power of appointment was a presently exercisable nongeneral power. If G exercised the power in 1988, after the effective date of this Act (or, if a pre-effective-date revocable exercise of his power became irrevocable in 1988, after the effective date of this Act), the same results as described above in Example (1) would apply.

Example (3)—Presently Exercisable General Power Created Before But Exercised After the Effective Date of this Act. Assume the same facts as in Example (1), except that G's power of appointment was a presently exercisable general power. If G exercised the power in 1988, after the effective date of this Act (or, if a pre-effective-date revocable exercise of his power became irrevocable in 1988, after the effective date of this Act), all the provisions of this Act (except Section 5(b)) apply; for such purposes, Section 2 controls the date of creation of the appointed nonvested property interests (or appointed powers of appointment), without regard to the special rule of the second sentence of Section 5(a). With respect to the exercise of a presently exercisable general power, it is possible—indeed, probable—that the special rule of the second sentence of Section 5(a) and the rules of Section 2 agree on the same date of creation for their respective purposes, that date being the date the power was irrevocably exercised (or a revocable exercise thereof became irrevocable).

Subsection (b): Reformation of Pre-existing Instruments. Although the Statutory Rule Against Perpetuities and the other provisions of this Act do not apply retroactively, subsection (b) recognizes a court's authority to exercise its equitable power to reform instruments that contain a violation of the Common-law Rule Against Perpetuities (or of a statutory version or variation thereof) and to which the Statutory Rule does not apply because the offending nonvested property interest or power of appointment in question was created before the effective date of this Act. This equitable power to reform is recognized only where the violation of the former rule against perpetuities is determined in a judicial proceeding that is commenced on or after the effective date of this Act. See below.

Without legislative authorization or direction, the courts in four states—Hawaii, Mississippi, New Hampshire, and West Virginia—have held that they have the power to reform instruments that contain a violation of the Common-law Rule Against Perpetuities. In re Estate of Chun Quan Yee Hop, 52 Hawaii 40, 469 P.2d 183 (1970); Carter v. Berry, 243 Miss. 321, 140 So.2d 843

771

(1962); Edgerly v. Barker, 66 N.H. 434, 31 A. 900 (1891); Berry v. Union Natl. Bank, 262 S.E.2d 766 (W.Va.1980). In four other states— California, Missouri, Oklahoma, and Texas—the legislatures have enacted statutes conferring this power on the courts or directing the courts to reform defective instruments. Cal. Civ.Code § 715.5 (West 1982); Mo. Rev.Stat. § 442.555 (1978); Okla. Stat. tit. 60, §§ 75–78 (1981); Tex.Property Code § 5.043 (Vernon 1984). See also Idaho Code § 55–111 (1948). The California statute is silent as to whether or not it applies to nonvested property interests and powers of appointment created prior to the effective date of the Act; the only significant California appellate decision to apply the statute, Estate of Ghiglia, 42 Cal.App.3d 433, 116 Cal.Rptr. 827 (1974), involved a will where the testator died after the Act's effective date. The Missouri, Oklahoma, and Texas statutes explicitly do not apply retroactively. The Hawaii, Mississippi, New Hampshire, and West Virginia decisions, however, invoked the court's equitable power (sometimes called the cy pres power, and sometimes called the doctrine of equitable approximation or equitable modification) to reform pre-existing instruments that contained a violation of the Common-law Rule. Subsection (b) constitutes statutory authority for a court to exercise its equitable reformation power.

Reformation Experience So Far. The existing judicial opinions and legislative provisions purport to adopt a principle of reformation that is consistent with the theme that the technique of reform should be shaped to grant every appropri-ate opportunity for the property to go to the intended beneficiaries. The New Hampshire court, for example, said that "where there is a general and a particular intent, and the particular one cannot take effect, the words shall be so construed as to give effect to the general intent." Edgerly v. Barker, 66 N.H. 434, 467, 31 A. 900, 912 (1891) (citation omitted). The Hawaii court held that "any interest which would violate the Rule Against Perpetuities shall be reformed within the limits of that rule to approximate most closely the intention of the creator of the interest." In re Estate of Chun Quan Yee Hop, 52 Hawaii 40, 46, 469 P.2d 183, 187 (1970). The Mississippi court described the reformation principle as "a simple rule of judicial construction, designed to aid the court to ascertain and carry out, as nearly as may be, the intention of the donor." Carter v. Berry, 243 Miss. 321, 370, 140 So.2d 843, 852 (1962). The California statute provides that the authority to reform "shall be liberally construed and applied to validate [the] interest to the fullest extent consistent with [the] ascertained intent." Cal.Civ.Code § 715.5.

Unfortunately, all the cases that have arisen so far have been of one general type—contingencies in excess of 21 years—and all of the courts have simply ordered a reduction of the age or period in gross to 21.

Guidance as to How to Reform. The above reformation efforts are unduly narrow. Subsection (b) is to be understood as authorizing a more appropriate technique—judicial insertion of a saving clause into the instrument. See Browder, *Con-*

struction, Reformation, and the Rule Against Perpetuities, 62 Mich. L.Rev. 1 (1963); Waggoner, *Perpetuity Reform,* 81 Mich.L.Rev. 1718, 1755–1759 (1983); Langbein & Waggoner, *Reformation of Wills on the Ground of Mistake: Change of Direction in American Law?,* 130 U.Pa.L.Rev. 521, 546–49 (1982). This method of reformation allows reformation to achieve an after-the-fact duplication of a professionally competent product. Such a technique would have been especially suitable in the cases that have already arisen, for it probably would have allowed the dispositions in all of them to have been rendered valid without disturbing the transferor's intent at all. See Waggoner, *Perpetuity Reform,* 81 Mich.L.Rev. 1718, 1756 n. 103 (1983). The insertion of a saving clause grants a more appropriate opportunity for the property to go to the intended beneficiaries. Furthermore, it would also be a suitable technique in fertile octogenarian, unborn widow, and administrative contingency cases. A saving clause is one of the formalistic devices that a professionally competent lawyer would have used before the fact to assure initial validity in these cases. Insofar as other violations are concerned, the saving clause technique also grants every appropriate opportunity for the property to go to the intended beneficiaries.

In selecting the lives to be used for the perpetuity-period component of the saving clause that in a given case is to be inserted after the fact, the principle to be adopted is the same one that ought to guide lawyers in drafting such a clause before the fact: The group selected should be appropriate to the facts and the disposition. While the exact make-up of the group in each case would be settled by litigation, the individuals designated in Section 1.3(2) of the Restatement (Second) of Property (Donative Transfers) (1983) as the measuring lives would be an appropriate referent for the court to consider. Care should be taken in formulating the gift-over component, so that it is appropriate to the dispositive scheme. Among possible recipients that the court might consider designating are: (i) the persons entitled to the income on the 21st anniversary of the death of the last surviving individual designated by the court for the perpetuity-period component and in the proportions thereof to which they are then so entitled; if no proportions are specified, in equal shares to the permissible recipients of income; or (ii) the grantor's descendants per stirpes who are living 21 years after the death of the last surviving individual designated by the court for the perpetuity-period component; if none, to the grantor's heirs at law determined as if the grantor died 21 years after the death of the last surviving individual designated in the perpetuity-period component.

Violation Must be Determined in a Judicial Proceeding Commenced On or After the Effective Date of this Act. The equitable power to reform is recognized by Section 5(b) only in situations where the violation of the former rule against perpetuities is determined in a judicial proceeding commenced on or after the effective date of this Act. The equitable power to reform would typically be exercised in the same judicial proceeding in which the invalidity is determined.

§ 6. Short Title

This [Act] may be cited as the Uniform Statutory Rule Against Perpetuities.

§ 7. Uniformity of Application and Construction

This [Act] shall be applied and construed to effectuate its general purpose to make uniform the law with respect to the subject of this [Act] among states enacting it.

§ 8. Time of Taking Effect

This [Act] takes effect _____.

§ 9. [Supersession] [Repeal]

This [Act] [supersedes the rule of the common law known as the rule against perpetuities] [repeals. (list statutes to be repealed)].

COMMENT

The first set of bracketed text is provided for states that follow the Common-law Rule Against Perpetuities. The second set of bracketed text is provided for the repeal of statutory adoptions of the Common-law Rule Against Perpetuities, statutory variations of the Common-law Rule Against Perpetuities, or statutory prohibitions on the suspension of the power of alienation for more than a certain period. Some states may find it appropriate to enact both sets of bracketed text by joining them with the word "and." This would be appropriate in states having a statute that declares that the Common-law Rule Against Perpetuities is in force in the state except as modified therein.

A cautionary note for states repealing listed statutes. If the statutes to be repealed contain exclusions from the rule against perpetuities, states should consider whether to repeal or retain those exclusions, in light of Section 4(7) of this Act that excludes from the Uniform Statutory Rule Against Perpetuities property interests, powers of appointment, and other arrangements "excluded by another statute of this State."

UNIFORM CUSTODIAL TRUST ACT

PREFATORY NOTE

This Uniform Act provides for the creation of a statutory custodial trust for adults to be governed by the provisions of the Act whenever property is delivered to another "as custodial trustee under the (Enacting state) Uniform Custodial Trust Act." The provisions of this Act are based on trust analogies to concepts developed and used in establishing custodianships for minors under the Uniform Transfers to Minors Act (UTMA). The Custodial Trust Act is designed to provide a statutory standby inter vivos trust for individuals who typically are not very affluent or sophisticated, and possibly represented by attorneys engaged in general rather than specialized estate practice. The most frequent use of this trust would be in response to the commonly occurring need of elderly individuals to provide for the future management of assets in the event of incapacity. The statute will also be available for accomplishing distribution of funds by judgment debtors and others to incapacitated persons for whom a conservator has not been appointed. Since this Act allows any person, competent to transfer property, to create custodial trusts for the benefit of themselves or others, with the beneficial interest in custodial trust property in the beneficiary and not in the custodial trustee, its potential for use is extensive. Although the most frequent use probably will be by elderly persons, it is also available for a parent to establish a custodial trust for an adult child who may be incapacitated; for adult persons in the military, or those leaving the country temporarily, to place their property with another for management without relinquishing beneficial ownership of their property; or for young people who have received property under the Uniform Transfers to Minors Act to continue a custodial trust as adults in order to obtain the benefit and convenience of management services performed by the custodial trustee.

This Act follows the approach taken by the Uniform Transfers to Minors Act and allows any kind of property, real or personal, tangible or intangible, to be made the subject of a transfer to a custodial trustee for the benefit of a beneficiary. However, the most typical transaction envisioned would involve a person who would transfer intangible property, such as securities or bank accounts, to a custodial trustee but with retention by the transferor of direction over the property. Later, this direction could be relinquished, or it could be lost upon incapacity. The objective of the statute is to provide a simple trust that is uncomplicated in its creation, administration, and termination. The potential for tax problems is minimized by permitting the beneficiary in most instances to retain control while the beneficiary has capacity to manage the assets effectively. The statute contains an asset specific transfer provision that it is believed will be simple to use and will gain the acceptance of the securities and financial industry. A simple transfer document, examples of which are set forth in the Act, and a receipt from the custodian, also in the Act, would provide for identification of beneficiaries or distributees upon death of the beneficiary. Protection is extended to third parties dealing with the custodian. Although the Act is patterned on the Uniform Transfers to Minors Act and meshes into the Uniform Probate Code, it is appropriate for enactment as well in states which have not adopted either UTMA or the UPC.

An adult beneficiary, who is not incapacitated, may: (1) terminate the custodial trust on demand (Section 2(e)); (2) receive so much of the income or custodial property as he or she may request from time to time (Section 9(a)); and (3) give the custodial trustee binding instructions for investment or management (Section 7(b)). In the absence of direction by the beneficiary, who is not incapacitated, the custodial trustee manages the property subject to the standard of care that would be observed by a prudent person dealing with the property of another and is not limited by other statutory restrictions on investments by fiduciaries (Section 7).

A principal feature of the Custodial Trust under this Act is designed to protect the beneficiary and his or her dependents against the perils of the beneficiary's possible future incapacity without the necessity of a conservatorship. Under Section 10, the incapacity of the beneficiary does not terminate (1) the custodial trust, (2) the designation of a successor custodial trustee, (3) any power or authority of the custodial trustee, or (4) the immunities of third persons relying on actions of the custodial trustee. The custodial trustee continues to manage the property as a discretionary trust under the prudent person standard for the benefit of the incapacitated beneficiary.

Means of monitoring and enforcing the custodial trust include provisions requiring the custodial trustee to keep the beneficiary informed, requiring accounting by the custodial trustee (Section 15), providing for removal of the custodial trustee (Section 13), and the distribution of the assets on termination of the custodial trust (Section 17). The custodial trustee is protected in Section 16 by the statutes of limitation on proceedings against the custodial trustee.

CUSTODIAL TRUST

Transactions with the custodial trustee should be executed readily and quickly by third parties because their rights and protections are determined by the Act and a third party acting in good faith has no need to determine the custodial trustee's authority to bind the beneficiary with respect to property and investment matters (Section 11). The Act generally limits the claims of third parties to recourse against the custodial property, with the beneficiary insulated against personal liability unless he or she is personally at fault and the custodial trustee is similarly insulated unless the custodial trustee is personally at fault or failed to disclose the custodial capacity when entering into a contract (Section 12).

As a consequence of the mobility of our population, particularly the mature persons who are most likely to utilize this Act, uniformity of the laws governing custodial trusts is highly desirable, and the Act is designed to avoid conflict of laws problems. A custodial trust created under this Act remains subject to this Act despite a subsequent change in the residence of the transferor, the beneficiary, or the custodial trustee or the removal of the custodial trust property from the state of original location (Section 19).

Table of Sections

Section 1. Definitions

As used in this [Act]:

(1) "Adult" means an individual who is at least 18 years of age.

(2) "Beneficiary" means an individual for whom property has been transferred to or held under a declaration of trust by a custodial trustee for the individual's use and benefit under this [Act].

(3) "Conservator" means a person appointed or qualified by a court to manage the estate of an individual or a person legally authorized to perform substantially the same functions.

(4) "Court" means the [_____] court of this State.

(5) "Custodial trust property" means an interest in property transferred to or held under a declaration of trust by a custodial trustee under this [Act] and the income from and proceeds of that interest.

(6) "Custodial trustee" means a person designated as trustee of a custodial trust under this [Act] or a substitute or successor to the person designated.

(7) "Guardian" means a person appointed or qualified by a court as a guardian of an individual, including a limited guardian, but not a person who is only a guardian ad litem.

(8) "Incapacitated" means lacking the ability to manage property and business affairs effectively by reason of mental illness, mental deficiency, physical illness or disability, chronic use of drugs, chronic intoxication, confinement, detention by a foreign power, disappearance, minority, or other disabling cause.

(9) "Legal representative" means a personal representative or conservator.

(10) "Member of the beneficiary's family" means a beneficiary's spouse, descendant, stepchild, parent, stepparent, grandparent, brother, sister, uncle, or aunt, whether of the whole or half blood or by adoption.

(11) "Person" means an individual, corporation, business trust, estate, trust, partnership, joint venture, association, or any other legal or commercial entity.

(12) "Personal representative" means an executor, administrator, or special administrator of a decedent's estate, a person legally authorized to perform substantially the same functions, or a successor to any of them.

(13) "State" means a state, territory, or possession of the United States, the District of Columbia, or the Commonwealth of Puerto Rico.

(14) "Transferor" means a person who creates a custodial trust by transfer or declaration.

(15) "Trust company" means a financial institution, corporation, or other legal entity, authorized to exercise general trust powers.

COMMENT

(1) "Adult" is a person 18 years of age for the purpose of custodial trusts. The result of this is that a person 18 years of age will be eligible to be a custodial trustee under this Act, although he or she may not be eligible under UTMA since minor custodianships under UTMA may run to age 21 and the minor could in some cases be older than the custodian. As the Comments under Section 1 of UTMA explain, the age of 21 was retained under that Act because the Internal Revenue Code continues to permit a "minority trust" under Section 2053(c), to continue in effect until age 21 and because it was believed that most transferors creating trusts or custodianships for minors would prefer to retain the property under management for the benefit of the young person as long as possible. The difference has little or no practical consequence and serves the purpose of each Act.

(3) "Conservator" is defined broadly to permit identification of a person functioning as a conservator.

(4) "Court" means _____ court. Here the likelihood is that most states would utilize the same court, e.g., the probate court, that deals with conservators and estates.

(5 and 6) The terms, "custodial trust property" and "custodial trustee," are used throughout to identify clearly the statutory trust property and trustee under this Act. The statutory trust concept is used throughout the Act.

(7) A definition of guardian has been included and is based on the Uniform Probate Code Section 5–103(6).

(8) A definition of incapacitated has been included, for the purpose of this Act, because incapacity of the beneficiary converts the trust from a revocable trust to a discretionary trust. The definition is taken from the Uniform Probate Code Section 5–401(c) relating to the person who is unable to manage property. Compare Uniform Probate Code Section 5–103(7). Note that Section 10(a)(ii) permits a transferor to direct that the trust shall be administered as one for an incapacitated person. Section 10 deals specifically with the determination of incapacity.

(10) The beneficiary's family is broadly defined to identify persons who may have standing to seek judicial intervention or accounting (Sections 13 and 15).

(11) The definition of a person is taken from the Uniform Probate Code Section 1–201(29).

(12) Personal representative is broadly defined and the definition reflects that in the Uniform Probate Code Section 1–201(30).

Section 2. Custodial Trust; General

(a) A person may create a custodial trust of property by a written transfer of the property to another person, evidenced by registration or by other instrument of transfer, executed in any lawful manner, naming as beneficiary, an individual who may be the transferor, in which the transferee is designated, in substance, as custodial trustee under the [Enacting state] Uniform Custodial Trust Act.

(b) A person may create a custodial trust of property by a written declaration, evidenced by registration of the property or by other instrument of declaration executed in any lawful manner, describing the property and naming as beneficiary an individual other than the declarant, in which the declarant as titleholder is designated, in substance, as custodial trustee under the [Enacting state] Uniform Custodial Trust Act. A registration or other declaration of trust for the sole benefit of the declarant is not a custodial trust under this [Act].

(c) Title to custodial trust property is in the custodial trustee and the beneficial interest is in the beneficiary.

(d) Except as provided in subsection (e), a transferor may not terminate a custodial trust.

(e) The beneficiary, if not incapacitated, or the conservator of an incapacitated beneficiary, may terminate a custodial trust by delivering to the custodial trustee a writing signed by the beneficiary or conservator declaring the termination. If not previously terminated, the custodial trust terminates on the death of the beneficiary.

(f) Any person may augment existing custodial trust property by the addition of other property pursuant to this [Act].

(g) The transferor may designate, or authorize the designation of, a successor custodial trustee in the trust instrument.

(h) This [Act] does not displace or restrict other means of creating trusts. A trust whose terms do not conform to this [Act] may be enforceable according to its terms under other law.

COMMENT

Section 2 is the principal provision authorizing the creation of a custodial trust and utilizes the concept of incorporation by reference when the transferee or titleholder of property is designated as custodial trustee under the Act. Section 2 sets forth the general effect of such a transfer. Section 18 provides forms which satisfy the requirements of this section and identifies customary methods of transferring assets to create a custodial trust.

Section 2(a) provides that a trust may be created by transfer to another for the benefit of the transferor or another. This is expected to be the most common way in which a custodial trust would be created. However, a custodial trust may also be created by declaration of trust by the owner of property to hold it for the benefit of another as is provided in Section 2(b). A declaration in trust by the owner of property for the sole benefit of the owner is not contemplated by this Act because such an attempt may be considered ineffective as a trust due to the total identity of the trustee and beneficiary. However, the doctrine of merger would not preclude an effective transfer under this Act for the benefit of the transferor and one or more other beneficiaries. See Section 6.

A custodial trust could be created by the exercise of a valid power of attorney or power of appointment given by the owner of property as one of the transfers "consistent with law."

These alternatives permit the major uses of the custodial trust to be accomplished expeditiously. For example, an older person, wishing to be relieved of management of property may transfer property to another for benefit of the transferor or of the transferor's spouse or child. The declaration may be used to establish a trust of which the owner is trustee to continue management of the property for benefit of another, such as a spouse or child. The trust may include a provision for distribution of assets remaining at the beneficiary's death directly to a named distributee.

This Act does not preclude the creation of trusts under other existing law, statutory or nonstatutory, but is designed to facilitate the creation of simple trusts incorporating the provisions of this Act. The written transfer or declaration "consistent with law" requires that the formalities of the transfer of particular property necessary under other law will be observed, e.g., if land is involved, the requirements of a proper deed and recording must be satisfied.

Section 2(c) provides for the retention of the beneficial interest in the custodial trust property in the beneficiary and, of course, not in the custodial trustee. The extensive control and benefit in the beneficiary who is not incapacitated maintains the simplicity of the trust and avoids tax complexity. The custodial trustee is given the title to the property and authority to act with regard to the property only as is authorized by the statute. The custodial trustee's powers are enumerated in Section 8.

Section 2(e) gives the adult beneficiary, who is not incapacitated, the power to terminate the custodial trust at any time during his or her lifetime. This power of termination exists in any beneficiary who is not incapacitated whether the beneficiary was or was not the transferor. A beneficiary may be determined to be incapacitated or the transferor may designate that the trust is to be administered as a trust for an incapacitated beneficiary under Section 10, in which event the beneficiary does not have the power to terminate. However, the designation of incapacity by the transferor can be modified by the trustee or the court by reason of changed circumstances pursuant to Section 10. The Act precludes termination by exercise of a durable power of attorney if the beneficiary is incompetent (Section 7(f)). If the donor prefers not to permit the beneficiary the power to terminate or to designate the beneficiary as incapacitated under Section 10, an individually drafted trust outside the scope of this Act would seem appropriate.

Upon termination of a custodial trust, the custodial trust property must be distributed as provided in Section 17.

A transfer under this Act is irrevocable except to the extent the beneficiary may terminate it. Hence, a transfer to a trustee for benefit of a person other than the transferor is not revocable by the transferor. If a power of revocation were retained by the transferor, that would be a trust outside the scope of this Act and enforceable under general law pursuant to subsection 2(h).

This Act does not provide for protection of the custodial trust assets from the claims of creditors of the beneficiary, whether those are general or governmental creditors. Other laws of the state remain unaffected. In this regard, unusual problems of handicapped persons and the coordination of resources and state or federal services call for special provision and planning outside the scope of this Act.

Section 3. Custodial Trustee for Future Payment or Transfer

(a) A person having the right to designate the recipient of property payable or transferable upon a future event may create a custodial trust upon the occurrence of the future event by designating in writing the recipient, followed in substance by: "as custodial trustee for _____ (name of beneficiary) under the [Enacting state] Uniform Custodial Trust Act."

(b) Persons may be designated as substitute or successor custodial trustees to whom the property must be paid or transferred in the order named if the first designated custodial trustee is unable or unwilling to serve.

(c) A designation under this section may be made in a will, a trust, a deed, a multiple-party account, an insurance policy, an instrument exercising a power of appointment, or a writing designating a beneficiary of contractual rights. Otherwise, to be effective, the designation must be registered with or delivered to the fiduciary, payor, issuer, or obligor of the future right.

COMMENT

This section permits a future custodial trustee to be designated to receive property for the beneficiary of a custodial trust to be effective upon the occurrence of a future event or transfer. To accommodate changes in circumstances during the passage of time, one or more successors or substitute custodial trustees can also be designated. The designation of the future custodial trustee and the beneficiary can be made in an instrument which is revocable or irrevocable depending upon the nature of the transaction or transfer. Any person designated as a future custodial trustee may decline to serve before the transfer occurs or may resign under Section 13 after the transfer.

The source of this section is Section 3 of UTMA.

The enacting state's rule against perpetuities may limit or affect the creation of a custodial trust upon the occurrence of a future event, but because the use of a custodial trust usually contemplates dispositions for the benefit of living persons, perpetuity problems should rarely arise.

Section 4. Form and Effect of Receipt and Acceptance by Custodial Trustee, Jurisdiction

(a) Obligations of a custodial trustee, including the obligation to follow directions of the beneficiary, arise under this [Act] upon the custodial trustee's acceptance, express or implied, of the custodial trust property.

(b) The custodial trustee's acceptance may be evidenced by a writing stating in substance:

CUSTODIAL TRUSTEE'S RECEIPT AND ACCEPTANCE

I, _____ (name of custodial trustee) acknowledge receipt of the custodial trust property described below or in the attached instrument and accept the custodial trust as custodial trustee for _____ (name of beneficiary) under the [Enacting state] Uniform Custodial Trust Act. I undertake to administer and distribute the custodial trust property pursuant to the [Enacting state] Uniform Custodial Trust Act. My obligations as custodial trustee are subject to the directions of the beneficiary unless the beneficiary is designated as, is, or becomes incapacitated. The custodial trust property consists of _____.

Dated: _____

_____
(Signature of Custodial Trustee)

(c) Upon accepting custodial trust property, a person designated as custodial trustee under this [Act] is subject to personal jurisdiction of the court with respect to any matter relating to the custodial trust.

COMMENT

Although a custodial trust is created by a transfer that satisfies Section 2 of the Act, the responsibility and obligations upon the trustee do not arise until the trustee has accepted the transfer. This detailed section is included to call the attention of the parties to the effective receipt and acceptance by the custodial trustee. Once a custodial trustee accepts the transfer of the custodial trust property, the custodial trustee assumes the obligation of a custodial trustee under this Act. The acceptance can be ex-pressed or implied, but it is recommended that the written acceptance provided for in Section 4(b) be utilized. By the acceptance the custodial trustee submits to the personal jurisdiction of the courts of the enacting state for the purpose of the custodial trust, despite subsequent relocation of the parties or of the custodial trust property. The principal sources of these provisions are Sections 8 and 9 of UTMA and the analogous provisions under the Uniform Probate Code, Sections 3–602, 5–208, 5–307, 7–103.

Section 5. Transfer to Custodial Trustee by Fiduciary or Obligor; Facility of Payment

(a) Unless otherwise directed by an instrument designating a custodial trustee pursuant to Section 3, a person, including a fiduciary other than a custodial trustee, who holds property of or owes a debt to an incapacitated individual not having a conservator may make a transfer to an adult member of the beneficiary's family or to a trust company as custodial trustee for the use and benefit of the incapacitated individual. If the value of the property or the debt exceeds [$20,000], the transfer is not effective unless authorized by the court.

(b) A written acknowledgment of delivery, signed by a custodial trustee, is a sufficient receipt and discharge for property transferred to the custodial trustee pursuant to this section.

COMMENT

This section is in the nature of a facility-of-payment provision that permits persons owing money to an incapacitated individual to discharge a fixed obligation by a payment to a custodial trustee under this Act. The section does not au-thorize the custodial trustee to settle claims for disputed amounts but only to acknowledge an effective receipt of property paid or delivered. It is based primarily on Sections 6 and 7 of UTMA and includes the

784

protections of Section 8 of UTMA as well. It permits a custodial trust to be established as a substitute for a conservatorship to receive payments due an incapacitated individual. Also, see Section 11, which protects transferors and other third parties dealing with the custodial trustee.

Section 6. Multiple Beneficiaries; Separate Custodial Trusts; Survivorship

(a) Beneficial interests in a custodial trust created for multiple beneficiaries are deemed to be separate custodial trusts of equal undivided interests for each beneficiary. Except in a transfer or declaration for use and benefit of husband and wife, for whom survivorship is presumed, a right of survivorship does not exist unless the instrument creating the custodial trust specifically provides for survivorship [or survivorship is required as to community or marital property].

(b) Custodial trust property held under this [Act] by the same custodial trustee for the use and benefit of the same beneficiary may be administered as a single custodial trust.

(c) A custodial trustee of custodial trust property held for more than one beneficiary shall separately account to each beneficiary pursuant to Sections 7 and 15 for the administration of the custodial trust.

COMMENT

This Act, unlike UTMA, does not preclude a custodial trust for more than one beneficiary. Adult persons creating custodial trusts are likely to set up custodial trusts in various forms, e.g., parents may wish to set up a custodial trust for their children or for themselves, then for a spouse, etc. However, the interests of each beneficiary are separate and the custodial trustee is obligated under subsection (c) to account separately to each beneficiary for administration of the beneficiary's interest in the custodial trust.

Subsection (b) allows a custodial trustee who is administering multiple custodial trusts for the same beneficiary to administer the custodial trusts as a single custodial trust. For example, if multiple trusts are created for an incapacitated beneficiary, the custodial trustee can administer them as a single custodial trust.

Section 7. General Duties of Custodial Trustee

(a) If appropriate, a custodial trustee shall register or record the instrument vesting title to custodial trust property.

(b) If the beneficiary is not incapacitated, a custodial trustee shall follow the directions of the beneficiary in the management, control, investment, or retention of the custodial trust property. In the absence of effective contrary direction by the beneficiary while not incapacitated, the custodial trustee shall observe the standard of care that would be observed by a prudent person dealing with property of another and is not limited by any other law restricting investments by fiduciaries. However, a custodial trustee, in the custodial trustee's discretion, may retain any custodial trust property received from the transferor. If a custodial trustee has a special skill or expertise or is named custodial trustee on the basis of representation of a special skill or expertise, the custodial trustee shall use that skill or expertise.

(c) Subject to subsection (b), a custodial trustee shall take control of and collect, hold, manage, invest, and reinvest custodial trust property.

(d) A custodial trustee at all times shall keep custodial trust property of which the custodial trustee has control, separate from all other property in a manner sufficient to identify it clearly as custodial trust property of the beneficiary. Custodial trust property, the title to which is subject to recordation, is so identified if an appropriate instrument so identifying the property is recorded, and custodial trust property subject to registration is so identified if it is registered, or held in an account in the name of the custodial trustee, designated in substance: "as custodial trustee for _____ (name of beneficiary) under the [Enacting state] Uniform Custodial Trust Act."

(e) A custodial trustee shall keep records of all transactions with respect to custodial trust property, including information necessary for the preparation of tax returns, and shall make the records and information available at reasonable times to the beneficiary or legal representative of the beneficiary.

(f) The exercise of a durable power of attorney for an incapacitated beneficiary is not effective to terminate or direct the administration or distribution of a custodial trust.

COMMENT

Subsection (b) restates and confirms the control by the beneficiary who is not incapacitated. However, the trustee has a reasonable obligation to act when the beneficiary has not directed him. Under Sections 9 and 10, when a beneficiary becomes incapacitated, the custodial trust becomes a discretionary trust and the trustee is subject to the control of the statute and not the beneficiary's direction. The custodial trustee is subject to the usual trustee's standard as taken from Section 7–302 of the Uniform Probate Code. The statute also imposes a slightly higher standard on professional fiduciaries acting under the statute. Otherwise, much of this section is taken from Section 12 of UTMA. Whenever recordable assets, such as land, are in the custodial trust, the trustee would be expected to record title to the asset. The section is entitled "general duties" because there are additional specific duties identified in other sections such as Section 9.

Section 8. General Powers of Custodial Trustee

(a) A custodial trustee, acting in a fiduciary capacity, has all the rights and powers over custodial trust property which an unmarried adult owner has over individually owned property, but a custodial trustee may exercise those rights and powers in a fiduciary capacity only.

(b) This section does not relieve a custodial trustee from liability for a violation of Section 7.

COMMENT

This section is taken from Section 13 of UTMA. It grants the trustee very broad powers over the property, subject, however, to the Prudent Person Rule and to the obligations set out in the Act. An alternative approach to subsection (a) that might be taken by an enacting state is to refer to the existing statutes granting powers to a trustee, such as the Uniform Trustee's Powers Act. For example: [(a) A custodial trustee has the powers of a trustee under the Uniform Trustee's Powers Act.]

Section 9. Use of Custodial Trust Property

(a) A custodial trustee shall pay to the beneficiary or expend for the beneficiary's use and benefit so much or all of the custodial trust property as the beneficiary while not incapacitated may direct from time to time.

(b) If the beneficiary is incapacitated, the custodial trustee shall expend so much or all of the custodial trust property as the custodial trustee considers advisable for the use and benefit of the beneficiary and individuals who were supported by the beneficiary when the beneficiary became incapacitated, or who are legally entitled to support by the beneficiary. Expenditures may be made in the manner, when, and to the extent that the custodial trustee determines suitable and proper, without court order and without regard to other support, income, or property of the beneficiary.

(c) A custodial trustee may establish checking, savings, or other similar accounts of reasonable amounts under which either the custodial trustee or the beneficiary may withdraw funds from, or draw checks against, the accounts. Funds withdrawn from, or checks written against, the account by the beneficiary are distributions of custodial trust property by the custodial trustee to the beneficiary.

COMMENT

This section provides that the custodial trustee is obligated to follow the directions of the beneficiary who is not incapacitated in paying over or expending custodial trust property. If the beneficiary is incapacitated, this section imposes duties on the custodial trustee to apply funds for the beneficiary similar to those imposed on custodians for minors under Section 14 of UTMA. In addition, however, subsection (b) authorizes a custodial trustee to pay over or expend custodial trust property for the use and benefit of the incapacitated beneficiary's dependents who were supported by the beneficiary at the time the beneficiary became incapacitated or for whom there is a legal obligation to support.

The use-and-benefits standard for the expenditure of custodial property is intended to avoid any implication that the custodial trust property can be used only for the required support of the incapacitated beneficiary.

Subsection (c) allows a custodial trustee to maintain a bank account, of an amount reasonable under the circumstances, with the beneficiary whereby both the beneficiary and the custodial trustee may write checks on the account. This may be used as one method of making money available for the beneficiary's personal needs. Many incapacitated persons, unable to manage business affairs, are still competent to pay personal expenses. This type of arrangement would be important to them. A custodial trustee should maintain, of course, a separate bank account for use in managing the custodial trust property and investments.

An alternative approach might be taken to this section that refers to the distributive powers of a conservator under the laws of the enacting state, in the event that state should prefer that incorporation by reference. For example: [The custodial trustee has the distributive powers of a conservator under the Uniform Probate Code.]

Section 10. Determination of Incapacity; Effect

(a) The custodial trustee shall administer the custodial trust as for an incapacitated beneficiary if (i) the custodial trust was created under Section 5, (ii) the transferor has so directed in the instrument creating the custodial trust, or (iii) the custodial trustee has determined that the beneficiary is incapacitated.

(b) A custodial trustee may determine that the beneficiary is incapacitated in reliance upon (i) previous direction or authority given by the beneficiary while not incapacitated, including direction or authority pursuant to a durable power of attorney, (ii) the certificate of the beneficiary's physician, or (iii) other persuasive evidence.

(c) If a custodial trustee for an incapacitated beneficiary reasonably concludes that the beneficiary's incapacity has ceased, or that circumstances concerning the beneficiary's ability to manage property and business affairs have changed since the creation of a custodial trust directing administration as for an incapacitated beneficiary, the custodial trustee may administer the trust as for a beneficiary who is not incapacitated.

(d) On petition of the beneficiary, the custodial trustee, or other person interested in the custodial trust property or the welfare of the beneficiary, the court shall determine whether the beneficiary is incapacitated.

(e) Absent determination of incapacity of the beneficiary under subsection (b) or (d), a custodial trustee who has reason to believe that the beneficiary is incapacitated shall administer the custodial trust in accordance with the provisions of this [Act] applicable to an incapacitated beneficiary.

(f) Incapacity of a beneficiary does not terminate (i) the custodial trust, (ii) any designation of a successor custodial trustee, (iii) rights or powers of the custodial trustee, or (iv) any immunities of third persons acting on instructions of the custodial trustee.

COMMENT

This is one of the more important sections of the Act under which the custodial trustee may determine that the beneficiary is incapacitated so the trust will change from one subject to the control of the beneficiary to a discretionary trust for the beneficiary. Subsection (b) allows the custodial trustee to determine that the beneficiary is incapacitated provided the determination is based upon the certificate of the beneficiary's physician, the prior direction or authority of the beneficiary, or other reasonable evidence. That authority could be evidenced, for example, by a durable power of attorney executed by the beneficiary prior to becoming incapacitated even though that power of attorney is not otherwise effective to control management or termination of the custodial trust. Such a durable power of attorney could be given to a child, spouse, friend, or other trusted individual. In addition, specific authority is provided in subsection (d) for the beneficiary, the custodial trustee, or other interested person to seek a declaration from the court as to the capacity of the beneficiary for the purposes of this Act. This is important to the custodial trustee, as his duties and responsibilities change on the event of the beneficiary's incapacity.

This section is not a proceeding for the appointment of a conservator, and it is not contemplated that such a declaration would lead to court appointment of a conservator or guardian unless other factors would warrant such appointment. The existence of a comprehensive and well-managed custodial trust would be one factor that would tend to avoid the necessity for the appointment of a conservator or guardian of the estate.

This section also does not provide a proceeding to attack the legal competence of a transferor in setting up a trust under Section 2. Rather, Section 10 relates to a management matter in a validly established custodial trust.

Subsection (f) provides that the incapacity of the beneficiary does not terminate the custodial trust. If the beneficiary becomes incapacitated, the authority of the custodial trustee continues and the custodial trustee must follow the statutory provisions of the Act relating to managing custodial trusts for incapacitated individuals.

Section 11. Exemption of Third Person From Liability

A third person in good faith and without a court order may act on instructions of, or otherwise deal with, a person purporting to make a transfer as, or purporting to act in the capacity of, a custodial trustee. In the absence of knowledge to the contrary, the third person is not responsible for determining:

(1) the validity of the purported custodial trustee's designation;

(2) the propriety of, or the authority under this [Act] for, any action of the purported custodial trustee;

(3) the validity or propriety of an instrument executed or instruction given pursuant to this [Act] either by the person purporting to make a transfer or declaration or by the purported custodial trustee; or

(4) the propriety of the application of property vested in the purported custodial trustee.

COMMENT

This section is based upon Section 16 of the UTMA and protects third persons who deal in good faith with the custodial trustee.

Section 12. Liability to Third Person

(a) A claim based on a contract entered into by a custodial trustee acting in a fiduciary capacity, an obligation arising from the ownership or control of custodial trust property, or a tort committed in the course of administering the custodial trust, may be asserted by a third person against the custodial trust property by proceeding against the custodial trustee in a fiduciary capacity, whether or not the custodial trustee or the beneficiary is personally liable.

(b) A custodial trustee is not personally liable to a third person:

(1) on a contract properly entered into in a fiduciary capacity unless the custodial trustee fails to reveal that capacity or to identify the custodial trust in the contract; or

(2) for an obligation arising from control of custodial trust property or for a tort committed in the course of the administration of the custodial trust unless the custodial trustee is personally at fault.

(c) A beneficiary is not personally liable to a third person for an obligation arising from beneficial ownership of custodial trust property or for a tort committed in the course of administration of the custodial trust unless the beneficiary is personally in possession of the custodial trust property giving rise to the liability or is personally at fault.

(d) Subsections (b) and (c) do not preclude actions or proceedings to establish liability of the custodial trustee or beneficiary to the extent the person sued is protected as the insured by liability insurance.

COMMENT

This section is patterned after Section 17 of the UTMA and that section in turn was based upon Sections 5–428 and 7–306 of the Uniform Probate Code limiting the liability of conservators and trustees. See also Restatement of Trusts, 2d Sections 265 and 277. The effect of this section is to limit the claims of third parties to recourse against custodial trust property as both the custodial trustee and the beneficiary are protected from personal liability absent personal fault on their part. This section does not alter the obligations between the custodial trustee and the beneficiary arising out of the administration of the estate and the accounting for that administration.

There may be cases in which a custodial trustee or beneficiary may have a right to possession of custodial trust property and may insure against liability arising out of possession or control of the property as a named insured, e.g., under homeowner's or automobile liability insurance. In such a case, the beneficiary should be permitted as a party defendant under subsection (d) but only to the extent of the protection of the liability insurance.

Section 13. Declination, Resignation, Incapacity, Death, or Removal of Custodial Trustee, Designation of Successor Custodial Trustee

(a) Before accepting the custodial trust property, a person designated as custodial trustee may decline to serve by notifying the person who made the designation, the transferor, or the transferor's legal representative. If an event giving rise to a transfer has not occurred, the substitute custodial trustee designated under Section 3 becomes the custodial trustee, or, if a substitute custodial trustee has not been designated, the person who made the designation may designate a substitute custodial trustee pursuant to Section 3. In other cases, the transferor or the transferor's legal representative may designate a substitute custodial trustee.

(b) A custodial trustee who has accepted the custodial trust property may resign by (i) delivering written notice to a successor custodial trustee, if any, the beneficiary and, if the beneficiary is incapacitated, to the beneficiary's conservator, if any, and (ii) transferring or registering, or recording an appropriate instrument relating to, the custodial trust property, in the name of, and delivering the records to, the successor custodial trustee identified under subsection (c).

(c) If a custodial trustee or successor custodial trustee is ineligible, resigns, dies, or becomes incapacitated, the successor designated under Section 2(g) or 3 becomes custodial trustee. If there is no effective provision for a successor, the beneficiary, if not incapacitated, may designate a successor custodial trustee. If the beneficiary is incapacitated, or fails to act within 90 days after the ineligibility, resignation, death, or incapacity of the custodial trustee, the beneficiary's conservator becomes successor custodial trustee. If the beneficiary does not have a conservator or the conservator fails to act, the resigning custodial trustee may designate a successor custodial trustee.

(d) If a successor custodial trustee is not designated pursuant to subsection (c), the transferor, the legal representative of the transferor or of the custodial trustee, an adult member of the beneficiary's family, the guardian of the beneficiary, a person interested in the custodial trust property, or a person interested in the welfare of the beneficiary, may petition the court to designate a successor custodial trustee.

(e) A custodial trustee who declines to serve or resigns, or the legal representative of a deceased or incapacitated custodial trustee, as soon as practicable, shall put the custodial trust property and records in the possession and control of the successor custodial trustee. The successor custodial trustee may enforce the obligation to deliver custodial trust property and records and becomes responsible for each item as received.

(f) A beneficiary, the beneficiary's conservator, an adult member of the beneficiary's family, a guardian of the person of the beneficiary, a person interested in the custodial trust property, or a person interested in the welfare of the beneficiary, may petition the court to remove the custodial trustee for cause and designate a successor custodial trustee, to require the custodial trustee to furnish a bond or other security for the faithful performance of fiduciary duties, or for other appropriate relief.

COMMENT

This section follows many of the provisions of Section 18 of UTMA with some substantive changes. It is designed to accommodate in a single section the circumstances in which a custodial trustee would be replaced by another custodial trustee. Under subsection (b), if the beneficiary is incapacitated, a custodial trustee who resigns must give written notice to both the beneficiary and the beneficiary's conservator if one exists. Under subsection (c), a beneficiary who is not incapacitated may designate, without limitation, a successor custodial trustee. If, however, the beneficiary fails to act or is incapacitated, the procedure to be followed is very similar to that found in UTMA except that the nonincapacitated beneficiary has 90 days to act and if the benefi-

ciary has no conservator or if the conservator declines to act, the custodial trustee may eventually designate a successor custodial trustee.

Under subsection (f), the beneficiary, whether or not incapacitated, can petition the court to remove the custodial trustee for cause and to designate a successor trustee, or the court may require the custodial trustee to give bond or other appropriate relief.

This section, unlike Section 18 of UTMA, does not give the custodial trustee the general power to designate a successor custodial trustee but rather limits that power to the situation in which the procedure for designating successor custodial trustees by others has been exhausted.

Section 14. Expenses, Compensation, and Bond of Custodial Trustee

Except as otherwise provided in the instrument creating the custodial trust, in an agreement with the beneficiary, or by court order, a custodial trustee:

(1) is entitled to reimbursement from custodial trust property for reasonable expenses incurred in the performance of fiduciary services;

(2) has a noncumulative election, to be made no later than six months after the end of each calendar year, to charge a reasonable compensation for fiduciary services performed during that year; and

(3) need not furnish a bond or other security for the faithful performance of fiduciary duties.

COMMENT

This section follows the pattern of Section 15 of the UTMA except it does subject the arrangements for payment of expenses, compensation, and bond to provisions in the custodial trust instrument or agreement of the beneficiary or court order.

As in UTMA, the provisions with regard to compensation are designed to avoid imputed compensation to the custodian who waives compensation and also to avoid the accumulation of claims for compensation until the termination of the custodial trust. Although the ability to control these matters by the trust instrument or agreement of the beneficiary seems to be implied, as was assumed in UTMA, it is here expressly stated because of the possibility of informal arrangements with persons as trustees.

Section 15. Reporting and Accounting by Custodial Trustee; Determination of Liability of Custodial Trustee

(a) Upon the acceptance of custodial trust property, the custodial trustee shall provide a written statement describing the custodial trust property and shall thereafter provide a written statement of the administration of the custodial trust property (i) once each year, (ii) upon request at reasonable times by the beneficiary or the beneficiary's legal representative, (iii) upon resignation or removal of the custodial trustee, and (iv) upon termination of the custodial trust. The statements must be provided to the beneficiary or to the beneficiary's legal representative, if any. Upon termination of the beneficiary's interest, the custodial trustee shall furnish a current statement to the person to whom the custodial trust property is to be delivered.

(b) A beneficiary, the beneficiary's legal representative, an adult member of the beneficiary's family, a person interested in the custodial trust property, or a person interested in the welfare of the beneficiary may petition the court for an accounting by the custodial trustee or the custodial trustee's legal representative.

(c) A successor custodial trustee may petition the court for an accounting by a predecessor custodial trustee.

(d) In an action or proceeding under this [Act] or in any other proceeding, the court may require or permit the custodial trustee or the custodial trustee's legal representative to account. The custodial trustee or the custodial trustee's legal representative may petition the court for approval of final accounts.

(e) If a custodial trustee is removed, the court shall require an accounting and order delivery of the custodial trust property and records to the successor custodial trustee and the execution of all instruments required for transfer of the custodial trust property.

(f) On petition of the custodial trustee or any person who could petition for an accounting, the court, after notice to interested persons, may issue instructions to the custodial trustee or review the propriety of the acts of a custodial trustee or the reasonableness of compensation determined by the custodial trustee for the services of the custodial trustee or others.

COMMENT

This section requires that the custodial trustee inform the beneficiary of the initiation of the trust and provide reasonably current reports of the administration of the custodial trust to the beneficiary or the beneficiary's legal representative. Even though some custodial trustees may act informally, it seems appropriate that both the trustee and the beneficiary be expected to exchange complete information concerning the administration of the trust at least once each year. In some cases, more frequent exchanges of information between the custodial trustee and beneficiary would be expected, e.g., when they use a bank account to which both have access. This is particularly true with regard to necessary information for tax reporting by the parties involved. This section assumes the usual minimum components of an account, i.e., assets and values at the beginning of the accounting period, receipts, and disbursements during the accounting period and assets and their values on hand or available for distribution at the close of the accounting period.

Subsection (a) identifies the necessary reports and accountings for the parties, and subsection (b) identifies a broad group of persons who may petition the court for an accounting by the custodial trustee or the custodial trustee's legal representative. Much of the section is drawn from Section 19 of the UTMA modified to fit the custodial trust.

Subsection (f) recognizes the inherent power of the court to instruct trustees and review their actions. This paragraph is patterned after Uniform Probate Code Section 7–205.

Section 16. Limitations of Action Against Custodial Trustee

(a) Except as provided in subsection (c), unless previously barred by adjudication, consent, or limitation, a claim for relief against a custodial trustee for accounting or breach of duty is barred as to a beneficiary, a person to whom custodial trust property is to be paid or delivered, or the legal representative of an incapacitated or deceased beneficiary or payee:

(1) who has received a final account or statement fully disclosing the matter unless an action or proceeding to assert

the claim is commenced within two years after receipt of the final account or statement; or

(2) who has not received a final account or statement fully disclosing the matter unless an action or proceeding to assert the claim is commenced within three years after the termination of the custodial trust.

(b) Except as provided in subsection (c), a claim for relief to recover from a custodial trustee for fraud, misrepresentation, or concealment related to the final settlement of the custodial trust or concealment of the existence of the custodial trust, is barred unless an action or proceeding to assert the claim is commenced within five years after the termination of the custodial trust.

(c) A claim for relief is not barred by this section if the claimant:

(1) is a minor, until the earlier of two years after the claimant becomes an adult or dies;

(2) is an incapacitated adult, until the earliest of two years after (i) the appointment of a conservator, (ii) the removal of the incapacity, or (iii) the death of the claimant; or

(3) was an adult, now deceased, who was not incapacitated, until two years after the claimant's death.

COMMENT

In an effort to provide as comprehensive a statute as possible to inform the parties of substantially all of their obligations and rights, statutes of limitation are provided in this section. The limitations provided in this section are derived from the Uniform Probate Code, Sections 1–106 and 7–307, and from the Missouri Custodial Act.

The nature of the limitations imposed by the section are illustrated by the situation in which a custodial trustee is removed, resigns, or dies. If the former custodial trustee accounts as required under Section 13 on removal or resignation, or the deceased custodial trustee's personal representative accounts, the two-year limitation of subsection (a)(1) applies. Should the former custodial trustee or the personal representative fail to account, then, subsection (a)(2) would apply to limit the time in which a proceeding to assert the claim could be commenced. This time would begin to run on the date the trust terminated. Of course, if the claim is one for fraud or concealment, the longer time limitation of subsection (b) would apply. In any event, should the beneficiary become incapacitated or die before the applicable time limitation had expired, the tolling provision of subsection (c) could postpone the time bar until two years after removal of the disability or death.

Section 17. Distribution on Termination

(a) Upon termination of a custodial trust, the custodial trustee shall transfer the unexpended custodial trust property:

(1) to the beneficiary, if not incapacitated or deceased;

(2) to the conservator or other recipient designated by the court for an incapacitated beneficiary; or

(3) upon the beneficiary's death, in the following order:

(i) as last directed in a writing signed by the deceased beneficiary while not incapacitated and received by the custodial trustee during the life of the deceased beneficiary;

(ii) to the survivor of multiple beneficiaries if survivorship is provided for pursuant to Section 6;

(iii) as designated in the instrument creating the custodial trust; or

(iv) to the estate of the deceased beneficiary.

(b) If, when the custodial trust would otherwise terminate, the distributee is incapacitated, the custodial trust continues for the use and benefit of the distributee as beneficiary until the incapacity is removed or the custodial trust is otherwise terminated.

(c) Death of a beneficiary does not terminate the power of the custodial trustee to discharge obligations of the custodial trustee or beneficiary incurred before the termination of the custodial trust.

COMMENT

This section controls distribution of the custodial trust property when the custodial trust is terminated under Section 2(e). It is designed to provide for efficient and certain distribution without judicial proceedings. Subsection (a)(3) is an important provision for avoiding complications on distribution and provides that distribution may be controlled first, by the direction of the deceased beneficiary or second, by the custodial trust instrument (see Sections 2, 6 and 18) and, only if no effective prior designation for the payment or distribution of the property on the death of the beneficiary has been made, shall it pass through the beneficiary's estate.

The direction to the custodial trustee by the beneficiary, who is not incapacitated, for distribution on termination of the custodial trust may be in any written form clearly identifying the distributee. For example, the following direction would be adequate under the statute:

I, _____ (name of beneficiary) hereby direct _____ (name of trustee) as custodial trustee, to transfer and pay the unexpended balance of the custodial trust property of which I am beneficiary to _____ as distributee on the termination of the trust

at my death. In the event of the
prior death of _____ above
named as distributee, I designate
_____ as distributee of the custodial trust property.

_____ (signature)
Beneficiary
Date_____
Receipt Acknowledged

Signed

_____ (signature)
Custodial Trustee
Date_____

Section 18. Methods and Forms for Creating Custodial Trusts

(a) If a transaction, including a declaration with respect to or a transfer of specific property, otherwise satisfies applicable law, the criteria of Section 2 are satisfied by:

(1) the execution and either delivery to the custodial trustee or recording of an instrument in substantially the following form:

TRANSFER UNDER THE [ENACTING STATE] UNIFORM CUSTODIAL TRUST ACT

I, _____ (name of transferor or name and representative capacity if a fiduciary), transfer to _____ (name of trustee other than transferor), as custodial trustee for _____ (name of beneficiary) as beneficiary and _____ as distributee on termination of the trust in absence of direction by the beneficiary under the [Enacting state] Uniform Custodial Trust Act, the following: (insert a description of the custodial trust property legally sufficient to identify and transfer each item of property).

Dated: _____

_____

(Signature); or

(2) the execution and the recording or giving notice of its execution to the beneficiary of an instrument in substantially the following form:

DECLARATION OF TRUST UNDER THE [ENACTING STATE] UNIFORM CUSTODIAL TRUST ACT

I, _____ (name of owner of property), declare that henceforth I hold as custodial trustee for _____ (name of beneficiary other than transferor) as beneficiary and _____ as distributee on termination of the trust in absence of direction by the beneficiary under the [Enacting state] Uniform Custodial Trust Act, the following:

(Insert a description of the custodial trust property legally sufficient to identify and transfer each item of property).

Dated: _____

_____

(Signature)

(b) Customary methods of transferring or evidencing ownership
of property may be used to create a custodial trust, including any of
the following:

    (1) registration of a security in the name of a trust company,
an adult other than the transferor, or the transferor if the
beneficiary is other than the transferor, designated in substance
"as custodial trustee for _____ (name of beneficiary) under the
[Enacting state] Uniform Custodial Trust Act";

    (2) delivery of a certificated security, or a document neces-
sary for the transfer of an uncertificated security, together with
any necessary endorsement, to an adult other than the transfer-
or or to a trust company as custodial trustee, accompanied by an
instrument in substantially the form prescribed in subsection
(a)(1);

    (3) payment of money or transfer of a security held in the
name of a broker or a financial institution or its nominee to a
broker or financial institution for credit to an account in the
name of a trust company, an adult other than the transferor, or
the transferor if the beneficiary is other than the transferor,
designated in substance: "as custodial trustee for _____
(name of beneficiary) under the [Enacting state] Uniform Custodial Trust Act";

    (4) registration of ownership of a life or endowment insur-
ance policy or annuity contract with the issuer in the name of a
trust company, an adult other than the transferor, or the
transferor if the beneficiary is other than the transferor, designated in substance: "as custodial trustee for _____ (name of
beneficiary) under the [Enacting state] Uniform Custodial Trust
Act";

    (5) delivery of a written assignment to an adult other than
the transferor or to a trust company whose name in the assignment is designated in substance by the words: "as custodial
trustee for _____ (name of beneficiary) under the [Enacting
state] Uniform Custodial Trust Act";

(6) irrevocable exercise of a power of appointment, pursuant to its terms, in favor of a trust company, an adult other than the donee of the power, or the donee who holds the power if the beneficiary is other than the donee, whose name in the appointment is designated in substance: "as custodial trustee for _____ (name of beneficiary) under the [Enacting state] Uniform Custodial Trust Act";

(7) delivery of a written notification or assignment of a right to future payment under a contract to an obligor which transfers the right under the contract to a trust company, an adult other than the transferor, or the transferor if the beneficiary is other than the transferor, whose name in the notification or assignment is designated in substance: "as custodial trustee for _____ (name of beneficiary) under the [Enacting state] Uniform Custodial Trust Act";

(8) execution, delivery, and recordation of a conveyance of an interest in real property in the name of a trust company, an adult other than the transferor, or the transferor if the beneficiary is other than the transferor, designated in substance: "as custodial trustee for _____ (name of beneficiary) under the [Enacting state] Uniform Custodial Trust Act";

(9) issuance of a certificate of title by an agency of a state or of the United States which evidences title to tangible personal property:

(i) issued in the name of a trust company, an adult other than the transferor, or the transferor if the beneficiary is other than the transferor, designated in substance: "as custodial trustee for _____ (name of beneficiary) under the [Enacting state] Uniform Custodial Trust Act"; or

(ii) delivered to a trust company or an adult other than the transferor or endorsed by the transferor to that person, designated in substance: "as custodial trustee for _____ (name of beneficiary) under the [Enacting state] Uniform Custodial Trust Act"; or

(10) execution and delivery of an instrument of gift to a trust company or an adult other than the transferor, designated in substance: "as custodial trustee for _____ (name of beneficiary) under the [Enacting state] Uniform Custodial Trust Act."

COMMENT

This section largely follows Section 9 of UTMA. It provides instructional detail for forms and methods of transferring assets that satisfy the requirements of the statute. Although many of the customary methods of transferring assets are identified, these methods are not intended to be exclusive since any type of property that can be transferred by any legal means is intended to be within the scope of the statute, provided the requirements of Section 2 are met. The method of transfer or conveyance appropriate to the asset should be used, e.g., if land is involved, a deed or conveyance that satisfies the local requirements would be appropriate. In the effort to make the statute as self-contained and as fully explanatory as possible, these provisions for implementation are included in the statute rather than being appended or inserted in the Comments.

Section 19. Applicable Law

(a) This [Act] applies to a transfer or declaration creating a custodial trust that refers to this [Act] if, at the time of the transfer or declaration, the transferor, beneficiary, or custodial trustee is a resident of or has its principal place of business in this State or custodial trust property is located in this State. The custodial trust remains subject to this [Act] despite a later change in residence or principal place of business of the transferor, beneficiary, or custodial trustee, or removal of the custodial trust property from this State.

(b) A transfer made pursuant to an act of another state substantially similar to this [Act] is governed by the law of that state and may be enforced in this State.

COMMENT

This section is designed to avoid confusion in the event a party or assets are removed from the state.

Section 20. Uniformity of Application and Construction

This [Act] shall be applied and construed to effectuate its general purpose to make uniform the law with respect to the subject of this [Act] among states enacting it.

Section 21. Short Title

This [Act] may be cited as the "[Name of Enacting State] Uniform Custodial Trust Act."

Section 22. Severability

If any provision of this [Act] or its application to any person or circumstance is held invalid, the invalidity does not affect other provisions or applications of this [Act] which can be given effect without the invalid provision or application, and to this end the provisions of this [Act] are severable.

Section 23.   Effective Date

This [Act] takes effect _____.

UNIFORM STATUS OF CHILDREN OF ASSISTED CONCEPTION ACT

PREFATORY NOTE

Nuclear energy was at once a breakthrough into untold wonders beyond the wildest hopes and dreams of its mentors, yet its use and development has been resisted by some as an uncontrollable force which threatens incomprehensible destruction. Nuclear energy, a force like many others, can be used for good and for evil, but once created it remains for the prudence or folly of mankind to direct its course. It is not likely ever to be eradicated.

Extraordinary progress in medical technology has produced veritable miracles many of which have been feared and rejected at first, with a master race contemplated by genetic engineering, vascularizing corpses with modern respirators, producing babies in test tubes, yet nuclear energy, genetic engineering, respirators, petrie dishes and other advances developed by human ingenuity are here to stay. Once out, the genie will never return to the bottle.

Ours is the responsibility to acknowledge the reality of these forces and with wisdom and prudence develop order and design in their use and implementation for the good of humanity.

This Conference is faced with the birth of many beautiful, innocent children brought into the world through certain extraordinary procedures which will ultimately require regulation, but meanwhile the status of these children demands our attention. These children are without traditional heritage, or parentage and other fundamentals, they are buffeted by forces beyond their comprehension and control. Although without guile or fault, but because of accident of birth, these children of the new biology have been deprived of certain basic rights.

Children then are the first priority, others can wait, at least until the children are taken care of. One cannot but acknowledge the reality of these extraordinary medical innovations created and developed to overcome the burden of infertility that literally bedevils our society.

An estimated one billion dollars was spent by Americans in the year of 1987 on medical care to combat infertility. Office visits for infertility services rose from $600,000 in 1968 to about $1.6 million in 1984 according to the report of the O.T.A.

803

It is likely that stringent regulatory legislation will become necessary in the near term to provide a social solution to deal with this scourge among those who are now looking with hope and expectation of fulfillment to the recent advances in medical technology. Some 600 surrogate mother arrangements have been concluded to date.

This Act "Status Of Children Under *Assisted Conception* " is not the complete answer to the overwhelming social problem. This Act is not a surrogacy regulatory act nor was it intended to be.

This Act has made only limited tangential use of so-called surrogacy components and then only to augment and clarify the rights of children born under the new technology as well as the rights of the parties to these arrangements.

It is extremely important for all to understand clearly the mandate which has guided the Drafting Committee in the preparation of this Act.

The Committee was given the responsibility to draft an act, a child oriented act, to provide order and design that would inure to the benefit of those children who have been born as a result of this new modern miracle. This was not to be a regulatory act. But the Conference did direct this Drafting Committee, by its almost unanimous vote, to proceed by making use of such limited and monitored surrogacy procedures as might be necessary to accomplish its mandate.

This Act was designed primarily to effect the security and well being of those children born and living in our midst as a result of assisted conception. The Executive Committee and the general Conference, considering the plight of these children, some with five parents, some with no father, some having no one responsible for support, nurturing, health, well being, or rights as a person or a member of society, determined that the greatest priority and first call on the energy and talent of the Drafting Committee was to provide an act which addressed these and other deficiencies.

The Drafting Committee has therefore with conscientious dedication addressed itself to the precise issue of the status of children, their rights, security, and well being. It is drawn with a narrow focus and in many instances, is limited by design to accommodate its mandate. You will find provisions which at first may appear arbitrary and seemingly inequitable, but there is not one word in this Act that was casually drafted.

The narrowness of the Act is designed to limit its applicability to what is best for children. The design of the limitation was also intended to strengthen the focus of this Act in the eyes of legislators and the public as prospective legislation which is needed immediately to provide order, direction, and design with dignity to the unsettled lives of our target children.

Because this Act is sensitive to the treatment of all of the parties, especially the children, it is likely to be more readily accepted by legislators and the public than a full surrogacy regulatory act that is still meeting with intractable opposition in so many places.

Reference is hereby made to the shortness of the Act. It is intended to state clearly essential principles without inordinate elaboration or detailed regulatory procedures.

A woman who gives birth to a child is the child's mother.

A caveat is provided if bracketed Section 5 is to be included.

An alternative is available for those who will not accept even limited, supervised, judicially-guided surrogacy. That alternative provides that any surrogacy agreement, so-called, is void.

There was great urgency on the part of the Drafting Committee to provide a child with two parents, and this established a presumption of paternity in the husband of a married woman who bears a child through assisted conception placing the burden on the husband to show lack of consent.

A donor of sperm, however, is not to be considered the parent of a child conceived through assisted conception unless there has been some agreement beforehand.

We have given our child, conceived under assisted conception, virtually the same rights in property and inheritance as though conceived by natural means.

The bracketed Section 5 relating to limited surrogacy can be accepted or rejected by any jurisdiction. The Committee remains neutral neither opting for nor against surrogacy. The nonsurrogacy sections will stand alone and may be adopted without Section 5.

But for those states which choose to include Section 5, they will be edified by the serious detailed attention to matters which will preserve the best interests of the child, while at the same time developing order and balance in the rights and duties of the parties.

The Drafting Committee considered carefully the respective rights and duties of all parties in interest, the planning and review of all terms and components in the arrangement, the guidance, supervision, and direction of the court, the careful, thoughtful concern for those sensitive issues necessary to provide the greatest protection for the child. All of these and more were considered not only as providing substantial solutions for the problems of the children, but also as being most effective and likely to make a difference even among those who might ordinarily object to general surrogacy legislation.

It is the kind of act that addresses the very issue that troubles everyone—the rights of the child—because of this limited focus, we feel it will tend to eliminate the need for protracted litigation.

The process may in some instances seem to burden the court, and the intended parents must enter these arrangements fully prepared for certain exigencies and risk, but to assure the desired result there must be some burden, some inconvenience and even some risk when the life and well being of a child is in the balance.

The Committee made clear, positive choices in each instance to produce a child-oriented act. There was no boiler plate available to accomplish the task. The litany of restrictions, examinations, investigation, qualifications, and limitations as set out in Section 5 is purposeful in the prosecution of the mandate of the Committee although, in the eyes of some, a burden that may have a chilling effect on the success of the arrangement.

It is, however, through this narrow scope and focus, through these precise specific measures of guidance, limitation, control, and supervision we feel there can be developed a valid viable order that will provide for the best interests of the child and establish with clarity and dignity the rights of all parties in this extended family under Alternative A of this Act. This Act gives equal opportunity for those who are not prepared to accept the new technology. They may opt to elect Alternative B under the Act which will void any arrangement which contemplates surrogacy, so-called, or an agreement whereby a woman relinquishes her rights and duties as a parent of a child. The Act is intended to provide certain basic rights for children under either alternative arrangement.

Table of Sections

---

§ 1. Definitions.

In this [Act]:

(1) "Assisted conception" means a pregnancy resulting from (i) fertilizing an egg of a woman with sperm of a man by means other than sexual intercourse or (ii) implanting an embryo, but the term does not include the pregnancy of a wife resulting from fertilizing her egg with sperm of her husband.

(2) "Donor" means an individual [other than a surrogate] who produces egg or sperm used for assisted conception, whether or not a payment is made for the egg or sperm used, but does not include a woman who gives birth to a resulting child.

[(3) "Intended parents" means a man and woman, married to each other, who enter into an agreement under this [Act] providing that they will be the parents of a child born to a surrogate through assisted conception using egg or sperm of one or both of the intended parents.]

(4) "Surrogate" means an adult woman who enters into an agreement to bear a child conceived through assisted conception for intended parents.

COMMENT

The definition of "assisted conception" establishes the scope of coverage of this Act. It is intended to be a broad definition. Section

1(1)(i) includes both "traditional" artificial insemination with fertilization occurring inside the woman's body and *in vitro* fertilization in which the joinder of sperm and egg takes place outside the body. Section 1(1)(ii) is designed to include within the definition the situation in which fertilization takes place through sexual intercourse and the resulting embryo is transplanted to the womb of another woman.

The final clause of Section 1(1) purposefully excludes husband-wife procreation from the definition of assisted conception. There are two reasons for this exclusion. First, as a policy matter, the rules pertaining to husband-wife procreation ought to be the same regardless of the means utilized for procreation. Thus, if a husband and wife choose to procreate through *in vitro* fertilization or more traditional artificial insemination, the status of the resulting child should be determined by existing laws, such as the Uniform Parentage Act, which govern the status of children produced by sexual intercourse. Second, the rules of this Act designating parentage and status of children are not always appropriate to husband-wife procreation. For example, a husband ought not be permitted, through the use of artificial insemination, to claim the status of a non-parent donor under Section 4(a) of this Act. As a result of the exclusion in Section 1(1), he will not be permitted to claim that status.

It should be noted that while this Act is intended to govern the status of children of assisted conception, it is *not* intended to establish a regulatory scheme establishing the appropriate methods for the performance of such assisted conception. A jur-isdiction may, *e.g.,* choose to enact separate regulations requiring genetic screening when assisted conception is undertaken, requiring that assisted conception be conducted only under certain conditions, etc.

While it may be suggested that the word "donor" ought properly to be limited to those who merely offer genetic material without compensation, Section 1(2) defines the term to include those who receive compensation for their genetic material. The term donor is regularly used to describe those who sell sperm to sperm banks. *See, e.g.,* Curie–Cohen, et al., *Current Practice of Artificial Insemination by Donor,* 300 N.Eng.J.Med. 585 (1979). Also, those who sell their blood to blood banks are usually referred to as blood donors. *See, e.g., Hillsborough County v. Automated Medical Laboratories,* 471 U.S. 707 (1985).

The bracketed language in Section 1(2) should be enacted only if the adopting jurisdiction selects Alternative A, infra, concerning surrogacy. The exception clause at the end of Section 1(2) makes it clear that a woman whose egg is fertilized through assisted conception and who bears the resulting child is not considered a donor. Under Section 2 of the Act she will be the mother of that child, unless a surrogacy arrangement has been approved under Alternative A.

The bracketed language which appears as Section 1(3) should be enacted only if the adopting jurisdiction selects Alternative A concerning surrogacy.

It should be emphasized that regardless of which alternative treatment of surrogacy agreements is chosen by a particular jurisdiction,

Section 1(4) should be enacted. This subsection defines a surrogate. Regardless of what force, if any, an enacting jurisdiction chooses to give to surrogacy agreements, it is necessary to define what is meant by a surrogate.

§ 2. Maternity.

[Except as provided in Sections 5 through 9,] a woman who gives birth to a child is the child's mother.

COMMENT

The unbracketed language in this section codifies existing law concerning maternity and is made necessary only because of the existence and growing use of technology enabling a woman to give birth to a child to which she is not genetically related. This provision makes it clear that unless the enacting jurisdiction has adopted Alternative A, which in some circumstances designates someone other than the woman who gives birth as the mother, the woman who bears a child is the mother of that child. The bracketed language in this section should be enacted only if the adopting jurisdiction selects Alternative A concerning surrogacy.

§ 3. Assisted Conception by Married Woman.

[Except as provided in Sections 5 through 9,] the husband of a woman who bears a child through assisted conception is the father of the child, notwithstanding a declaration of invalidity or annulment of the marriage obtained after the assisted conception, unless within two years after learning of the child's birth he commences an action in which the mother and child are parties and in which it is determined that he did not consent to the assisted conception.

COMMENT

The presumptive paternity of the husband of a married woman who bears a child through assisted conception reflects a concern for the best interests of the children of assisted conception. Any uncertainty concerning the identity of the father of such a child ought to be shouldered by the married woman's husband rather than the child. Thus, the husband (not someone acting on his behalf such as a guardian, administrator or executor) has the obligation to file an action aimed at denying paternity through lack of consent to the assisted conception rather than the child or mother having an obligation to prove the husband's paternity.

It should be noted, however, that if the nonpaternity action is timely filed and the husband's lack of consent is demonstrated, the child will be without a legally-recognized father because the sperm donor is not the father under Section 4(a) of the Act. Also, because the filing of such a nonpaternity action is permitted within two years of the husband's learning of the child's birth, the period of uncertainty concerning the identity of the child's father will be longer than two years in the relatively rare case where the husband is not immediately made aware of the child's birth.

By designating the husband of a woman who bears a child through assisted conception as the father, it is intended that he will be considered the father for purposes of any cause of action which arises before the birth of the child. Thus, for example, he would be the father under any state law authorizing a wrongful death action for the death of an unborn child during pregnancy.

The bracketed language in this section should be enacted only if the adopting jurisdiction selects Alternative A concerning surrogacy. Under that alternative, under certain circumstances the husband of the woman bearing the child will not be the father of the child. Instead, the man whose sperm was used in the creation of the child usually will be the father in such cases.

§ 4. Parental Status of Donors and Deceased Individuals.

[Except as otherwise provided in Sections 5 through 9:]

(a) A donor is not a parent of a child conceived through assisted conception.

(b) An individual who dies before implantation of an embryo, or before a child is conceived other than through sexual intercourse, using the individual's egg or sperm, is not a parent of the resulting child.

COMMENT

Present statutory law is split concerning the parental status of sperm donors. Fifteen states have statutes, patterned after Section 5(b) of the Uniform Parentage Act, specifying that a donor will not be considered the father of a child born of artificial insemination if the semen was provided to a licensed physician for use in artificial insemination of a married woman other than the donor's wife. Fifteen other statutes do not explicitly limit nonparenthood to situations where the semen is provided to a physician. Instead, they shield donors from parenthood in all situations where a married woman is artificially inseminated with her husband's consent.

Subsection 4(a), when read in light of Section 3, opts for the broader protection of donors provided by the latter group of statutes. That is, if a married woman bears a child of assisted conception through the use of a donor's sperm, the donor will not be the father and her husband will be the father unless and until his lack of consent to the assisted conception is proven within two years of his learning of the birth. This provides certainty for prospective donors. It should be noted, however, that under Section 4(a) nonparenthood is also provided for those donors who provide sperm for assisted conception by unmarried women. In that relatively rare situation, the child would have no legally recognized father. It should also be noted that Section 4(a) does not adopt the UPA's requirement that the donor provide the semen to a licensed physician. This is not realistic in light of present practices in the field of artificial insemination.

In providing nonparenthood for "donors," Section 4(a) includes by reference the definition of donor in Section 1(2) which covers those who provide sperm or eggs for assisted conception. Thus, if a woman provided an egg for assisted conception which resulted in another woman bearing the child, the egg donor would not be the child's mother. This would provide no burden on the child in light of Section 2's general rule declaring that the woman who gives birth to a child is that child's mother.

Subsection 4(b) is designed to provide finality for the determination of parenthood of those whose genetic material is utilized in the procreation process after their death. The death of the person whose genetic material is either used in conceiving an embryo or in implanting an already existing embryo into a womb would end the potential parenthood of the deceased. The latter situation, in which cryopreservation is utilized to "freeze" an embryo which has been created *in vitro,* is already in existence and gave rise to much controversy in Australia in the early 1980's.

A married couple died after having created an embryo through *in vitro* fertilization. Among the many questions raised after their simultaneous death in a plane crash was whether posthumous implantation of the embryo would result in children who would be those of the deceased couple. Under Section 4(b), it would be clear that implantation after the death of any genetic parent would not result in that genetic parent being the legally recognized parent. Clearly, under Section 2 of the Act, the woman who bears the child will be the mother. The paternity of such child would presumptively be that of the mother's husband, if she is married, under Section 3 of the Act. For a discussion of recent Australian legislation in the area, see Corns, *Legal Regulation of In Vitro Fertilisation in Victoria,* 58 L.Inst.J. 838 (1984); Note, *Genesis Retold: Legal Issues Raised by the Cryopreservation of Preimplantation Human Embryos,* 36 Syr.L.Rev. 1021, 1029 n. 49 (1985).

Section 4(b) is the only provision of the Act which would deal with procreation by those who are married to each other. It is designed primarily to avoid the problems of intestate succession which could arise if the posthumous use of a person's genetic material could lead to the deceased being termed a parent. Of course, those who want to explicitly provide for such children in their wills may do so.

The bracketed language at the beginning of this section should be adopted only by those jurisdictions enacting Alternative A concerning surrogacy. Under that provision, certain persons who would otherwise be considered donors will be parents.

ALTERNATIVE A

COMMENT

A state that chooses Alternative A should also consider Section 1(3) and the bracketed language in Sections 1(2), 2, 3, and 4.

[§ 5.   Surrogacy Agreement.

(a) A surrogate, her husband, if she is married, and intended parents may enter into a written agreement whereby the surrogate relinquishes all her rights and duties as a parent of a child to be conceived through assisted conception, and the intended parents may become the parents of the child pursuant to Section 8.

(b) If the agreement is not approved by the court under Section 6 before conception, the agreement is void and the surrogate is the mother of a resulting child and the surrogate's husband, if a party to the agreement, is the father of the child. If the surrogate's husband is not a party to the agreement or the surrogate is unmarried, paternity of the child is governed by [the Uniform Parentage Act].

COMMENT

Because of the significant controversy concerning the appropriateness of arrangements under which a woman agrees to bear a child on behalf of another woman, this Act proposes two alternatives. Under Alternative A, in Sections 5 through 9, the adopting state is offered a framework under which such agreements are given effect under limited and prescribed circumstances. This alternative also outlines the parent-child relationships which are established when such agreements are approved by a court.

Alternative B, consisting of alternative Section 5, declares such agreements to be void and describes the parent-child relationships between any child born pursuant to such agreements and the other parties. The strong desire of some childless couples for a biologically-related child together with the technological capacity to utilize the sperm of a husband in impregnating a woman not his wife and the willingness of others to aid such couples in satisfying those desires creates a strong likelihood that such agreements will continue to be written. Therefore, it is crucially important that a state enacting the Act adopt either Alternative A or Alternative B.

Under Section 5(a) of Alternative A, together with the definition of "intended parents" under Section 1(3), a valid surrogacy agreement requires the participation of two intended parents who are married to each other and a surrogate, who is defined by Section 1(4) as an *adult* woman who agrees to bear a child through assisted conception for the intended parents. If the surrogate is married, her husband must also be a party to the surrogacy agreement. Additional requirements for a surrogate and the intended parents are imposed by Section 6 of Alternative A. It should be noted that Section 5(a) simply authorizes such agreements. It does not give them effect in terms of designating parenthood, etc. In order to become effective in such matters, the agreement must be approved by the appropriate court under Section 6.

Section 5(b) makes clear that agreements which are not approved under Section 6 are void. Nonapproved agreements in a jurisdiction which has adopted Alternative A of the Act have the same effect as all surrogacy agreements under Alternative B. That is, the surrogate is the mother of any child of assisted conception born pursuant to such agreements. Her husband, if he is a party to such agreement, shall be the father. If the surrogate's husband is not a party to such agreement or if she is unmarried, paternity of the child will be left to existing law.

§ 6. Petition and Hearing for Approval of Surrogacy Agreement.

(a) The intended parents and the surrogate may file a petition in the [appropriate court] to approve a surrogacy agreement if one of them is a resident of this State. The surrogate's husband, if she is married, must join in the petition. A copy of the agreement must be attached to the petition. The court shall name a [guardian ad litem] to represent the interests of a child to be conceived by the surrogate through assisted conception and [shall] [may] appoint counsel to represent the surrogate.

(b) The court shall hold a hearing on the petition and shall enter an order approving the surrogacy agreement, authorizing assisted conception for a period of 12 months after the date of the order, declaring the intended parents to be the parents of a child to be conceived through assisted conception pursuant to the agreement and discharging the guardian ad litem and attorney for the surrogate, upon finding that:

(1) the court has jurisdiction and all parties have submitted to its jurisdiction under subsection (e) and have agreed that the law of this State governs all matters arising under this [Act] and the agreement;

(2) the intended mother is unable to bear a child or is unable to do so without unreasonable risk to an unborn child or to the physical or mental health of the intended mother or child, and the finding is supported by medical evidence;

(3) the [relevant child-welfare agency] has made a home study of the intended parents and the surrogate and a copy of the report of the home study has been filed with the court;

(4) the intended parents, the surrogate, and the surrogate's husband, if she is married, meet the standards of fitness applicable to adoptive parents in this State;

(5) all parties have voluntarily entered into the agreement and understand its terms, nature, and meaning, and the effect of the proceeding;

(6) the surrogate has had at least one pregnancy and delivery and bearing another child will not pose an unreasonable risk to the unborn child or to the physical or mental health of the surrogate or the child, and this finding is supported by medical evidence;

(7) all parties have received counseling concerning the effect of the surrogacy by [a qualified health-care professional or social worker] and a report containing conclusions about the capacity of the parties to enter into and fulfill the agreement has been filed with the court;

(8) a report of the results of any medical or psychological examination or genetic screening agreed to by the parties or required by law has been filed with the court and made available to the parties;

(9) adequate provision has been made for all reasonable health-care costs associated with the surrogacy until the child's birth including responsibility for those costs if the agreement is terminated pursuant to Section 7; and

(10) the agreement will not be substantially detrimental to the interest of any of the affected individuals.

(c) Unless otherwise provided in the surrogacy agreement, all court costs, attorney's fees, and other costs and expenses associated with the proceeding must be assessed against the intended parents.

(d) Notwithstanding any other law concerning judicial proceedings or vital statistics, the court shall conduct all hearings and proceedings under this section in camera. The court shall keep all records of the proceedings confidential and subject to inspection under the same standards applicable to adoptions. At the request of any party, the court shall take steps necessary to ensure that the identities of the parties are not disclosed.

(e) The court conducting the proceedings has exclusive and continuing jurisdiction of all matters arising out of the surrogacy until a child born after entry of an order under this section is 180 days old.

COMMENT

Section 6, along with Section 8 which deals with parentage under an approved surrogacy, is the core of Alternative A. It provides for state involvement, through supervision by a court, in the surrogacy process before the assisted conception. The purpose of this early involvement is to insure that the parties are appropriate for a surrogacy arrangement, that they understand the consequences of what they are about to do and that the best interests of any child(ren) born of the surrogacy arrangement are considered before the arrangement is authorized.

The forum for state involvement is a petition brought by *all* the parties to the arrangement (including the surrogate's husband if she is married) in which the parties seek a judicial order authorizing the assisted conception contemplated by their agreement. The agreement itself must be submitted to the court. The court must hold a hearing on the petition and, under Section 6(b), must make ten separate findings before the surrogacy arrangement will be allowed to proceed. It should be noted that Section 6(b)(10) requires a finding that the arrangement would not be "substantially detrimental to the interest of any of the affected individuals." This insures the court will retain a measure of discretion to consider and utilize all relevant information.

This pre-conception authorization process is roughly analogous to adoption procedures currently in place in most jurisdictions. Just as adoption contemplates the transfer of parentage of a child from the

natural to the adoptive parents, surrogacy involves the transfer from the surrogate to the intended parents. Section 6 is designed to protect the interests of the child(ren) to be born under the surrogacy arrangement as well as the surrogate and the intended parents. It should be noted that under Section 1(3) at least one of the intended parents will be genetically related to the child(ren) born of the arrangement.

Section 6 seeks to protect the interests of the child(ren) in several ways. The major protection of the interests of the child provided by the Act is the authorization procedure itself. By providing for the court order authorizing the assisted conception and the surrogacy arrangement, the Act establishes closely supervised surrogacy as one of the methods to guarantee the security and well being of the child. Under Section 6(a), a guardian ad litem must be appointed to represent the interests of any child conceived through the surrogacy arrangement. An enacting jurisdiction may choose either mandatory or optional independent representation for the surrogate. Under Section 6(b)(3), the court will be informed of the results of a home study of both the intended parents and the surrogate. A study of the surrogate is required because of the possibility of termination of the agreement under Section 7 in which case the surrogate will be the legally recognized mother.

Further protection of the child is provided by the finding required by Section 6(b)(4) that both intended parents and surrogate (and her husband, if any) satisfy the standards of fitness required of adoptive parents. Under Section 6(b)(6), the court must assure itself, on the basis of medical evidence, that the pregnancy will not be dangerous to the child. While Section 6(b)(8) does not require any medical or genetic screening, it does mandate that if such testing is required by the agreement (or other law) the results will be available to the court and all parties. Section 6(b)(9) requires assurance that health-care costs during pregnancy have been provided. The provisions in Section 6(b)(1) and Section 6(e) dealing with exclusive jurisdiction is designed to minimize the possibility of parallel litigation in different states and the consequent risk of child-napping for strategic purposes.

The interests of the surrogate are also protected by Section 6. The bracketed version of Section 6(a) would require appointed counsel to represent her interests and, at the least, counsel will be permitted for her. The findings required by Section 6(b)(5) and Section 6(b)(7) will protect the surrogate against the possibility of overreaching or fraud. Under Section 6(b)(6), the court must find that the surrogate has had at least one previous pregnancy and delivery. Presumably such a finding helps insure that the surrogate fully understands the nature and experience of pregnancy. The court must also find the contemplated pregnancy and delivery would not pose unreasonable physical or mental health risks to her. The requirement of assurance of provision for health-care costs until birth imposed by Section 6(b)(9) protects the surrogate. Section 6(c) requires that all costs associated

with the hearing be borne by the intended parents, unless otherwise provided in the agreement. If the agreement imposed such costs on the surrogate, the court could find, under Section 6(b)(10), that the agreement was not in the surrogate's interest and refuse to authorize it.

While most surrogacy arrangements apparently involve intended parents and surrogates who have met each other, if the surrogate does not want her identity revealed to the intended parents, she may request (under Section 6(d)) that the court take all steps to insure that anonymity. At any event, Section 6(d) requires all proceedings to be held in camera with sealed records to insure confidentiality. It should be noted that in addition to the protections offered the surrogate by Section 6 at the hearing, she is given the right under Section 7 to terminate the agreement, even after it has been approved.

The intended parents (who are by definition *unable* to procreate through traditional means, Section 6(b)(2)) also have their interests protected through this Section. In addition to the very existence of the court authorization procedure which gives effect to the surrogacy arrangement, Sections 6(b)(5), (6) and (7) help provide assurances to them that the surrogate is capable and is knowingly entering the arrangement. The interest of producing a healthy child is promoted through Section 6(b)(6)'s required finding that a pregnancy by the surrogate will not be unreasonably risky to the child.

Section 6, while constructing a detailed set of requirements for the petition and the findings which must be made before an authorizing order can be issued, nowhere states the consequences of violations of the rules. Because of the variety of types of violations which could possibly occur, it was felt that a bright-line rule concerning the effect of such violations was inappropriate. The question of the consequences of a failure to abide by the rules of Section 6 is left to a case-by-case determination. A court should be guided in making such a determination by the narrow purpose of Alternative A to permit surrogacy arrangements and the equities of a particular situation. Note that Section 7 provides a period for termination of the agreement and vacating of the order. The discovery of a failure to abide by the rules of Section 6 would certainly provide the occasion for terminating the agreement. On the other hand, if a failure to abide by the rules of Section 6 is discovered by a party during a time when Section 7 termination would be permissible, failure to terminate might be an appropriate reason to estop the party from later seeking to overturn or ignore the Section 6 order.

§ 7. Termination of Surrogacy Agreement.

(a) After entry of an order under Section 6, but before the surrogate becomes pregnant through assisted conception, the court for cause, or the surrogate, her husband, or the intended parents may terminate the surrogacy agreement by giving written notice of termination to all other parties and filing notice of the termination with the court. Thereupon, the court shall vacate the order entered under Section 6.

(b) A surrogate who has provided an egg for the assisted conception pursuant to an agreement approved under Section 6 may terminate the agreement by filing written notice with the court within 180 days after the last insemination pursuant to the agreement. Upon finding, after notice to the parties to the agreement and hearing, that the surrogate has voluntarily terminated the agreement and understands the nature, meaning, and effect of the termination, the court shall vacate the order entered under Section 6.

(c) The surrogate is not liable to the intended parents for terminating the agreement pursuant to this section.

COMMENT

Subsections (a) and (b) provide for termination of the surrogacy arrangement after the authorization order in two situations. Under subsection (a), any party or the court for cause may cancel the arrangement before the pregnancy has been established. This provides for a period of cancellation during a time when the interests of the parties would not be unduly prejudiced by such termination. By definition, the procreation process has not begun and, therefore, there is no interest to be asserted on behalf of the child. The intended parents certainly have an expectation interest during this time, but the nature of this interest is little different from that which they would have while they were attempting to create a pregnancy through traditional means.

Subsection (b) gives a surrogate who has provided the egg for the assisted conception 180 days after the last insemination to recant and decide to keep the child as her own. Under most current surrogacy arrangements, the surrogate will have provided the egg. The subsection requires that all parties to the agreement be given notice and that a hearing be held on a filing of an intent to terminate by the surrogate. Such notice, of course, must be provided in a constitutionally acceptable manner. If the court determines that the surrogate's termination is voluntary and she is aware of the consequences of such a termination (see Section 8(b)), it must vacate the authorization order.

This 180-day recantation period can, at one level, be described as a compromise between two polar positions concerning recantation. On one extreme, some argue that once the agreement has been presented to a court which has made the requisite findings under Section 6(b), no recantation should be permitted. After all, the surrogate has entered into an agreement to bear a child for the intended parents and the court has found that she acted knowingly and voluntarily and that she was an appropriate person to fulfill the role of surrogate. It would be argued that the expectation interests of the intended par-

ents ought not be frustrated by the surrogate's unilateral action.

On the other hand, some argue that the surrogate ought to be able to renounce her agreement at any time until after the birth of the child. This position would assimilate the surrogate's rights to those of a birth mother who gives consent to the adoption of her child. Most current adoption statutes provide that valid consent can be given only after birth.

The selection of the 180-day recantation period, however, can be viewed as more than a mere mechanical compromise between the two positions. Instead, this recantation period can be explained by pointing out that the surrogacy arrangement is simply different from both the ordinary contract situation and the ordinary adoption situation and, therefore, ought to be treated differently. Surrogacy is not an ordinary contract because it contemplates the creation of a human being whose interests must be taken into account. It can be argued that the child's interests in a parent-child relationship with his or her biological mother are protected by giving her an extra 180 days to decide if she really wants to give up the child to the intended mother.

On the other hand, surrogacy is different from an adoption and the post-birth consent requirement of adoption is not appropriate for the surrogacy situation. The requirement of post-birth consent in adoption is based on the reality that many birth mothers are young, unmarried women who arrange *during pregnancy* to give their child up for adoption. It is felt that decisions made under such circumstances are often the result of emotional stress created by young women in the midst of an often unwanted pregnancy and, therefore, are pressured in inappropriate ways. Therefore, "pregnant women are irrebuttably presumed incapable of protecting their own interests." Ellman, Kurtz & Stanton, *Family Law: Cases, Text, Problems* 1238 (Michie 1986).

The surrogacy arrangement authorized under this Act is very different. Most importantly, the original decision to give up the child is made *before* the pregnancy by an adult woman who has already experienced a previous pregnancy. It is an arrangement which has been examined and approved by a court under Section 6, with all the protections of the surrogate provided under that section. Any undue pressure which may have been brought to bear on the surrogate to become a surrogate will have been examined at the Section 6 hearing.

Having rejected the contract and adoption analogies, the question of an appropriate time period for recantation remains. Section 7(b)'s 180–day recantation period roughly coincides with the time during which the surrogate has a constitutionally-protected right to terminate the pregnancy. Because the surrogate has this right to choose to *abort,* there is a certain logic in giving the same period in which to decide to *bear* the child and honor her pre-conception agreement. This recantation provision recognizes the right of the surrogate to change her mind well into the pregnancy as well as the interests of the intended parents in the finality of the decision-making process before birth. Note that because the 180–day period begins on the date of the last insemination pursuant to the agreement (a point chosen because of its certainty), it is possible that the recantation period will extend longer than 180 days into pregnancy, if the pregnancy was actually created by an earlier insemination.

A jurisdiction which finds the 180–day period too short can choose not to enact Alternative A at all and opt for Alternative B which provides for no enforcement of surrogacy agreements.

Section 7(c) insures that a recanting surrogate will not be held liable in damages for her recantation, either under subsection (a) or (b). It is intended that no such liability for the surrogate for her recantation can be imposed by the agreement. By creating this immunity for the surrogate, this provision is not intended to *impose* any liability for costs associated with the surrogacy on any other parties to the arrangement. Such obligations, however, may be imposed by the agreement itself, see Section 6(b)(9).

§ 8. Parentage Under Approved Surrogacy Agreement.

(a) The following rules of parentage apply to surrogacy agreements approved under Section 6:

(1) Upon birth of a child to the surrogate, the intended parents are the parents of the child and the surrogate and her husband, if she is married, are not parents of the child unless the court vacates the order pursuant to Section 7(b).

819

(2) If, after notice of termination by the surrogate, the court vacates the order under Section 7(b) the surrogate is the mother of a resulting child, and her husband, if a party to the agreement, is the father. If the surrogate's husband is not a party to the agreement or the surrogate is unmarried, paternity of the child is governed by [the Uniform Parentage Act].

(b) Upon birth of the child, the intended parents shall file a written notice with the court that a child has been born to the surrogate within 300 days after assisted conception. Thereupon, the court shall enter an order directing the [Department of Vital Statistics] to issue a new birth certificate naming the intended parents as parents and to seal the original birth certificate in the records of the [Department of Vital Statistics].

COMMENT

Under Section 8(a), parentage of the child born pursuant to an approved surrogacy is vested in the intended parents where the order under Section 6 is still in effect. Notice of the birth of the child must be filed by the intended parents and the court, upon receipt of the notice, shall direct the issuance of a birth certificate naming the intended parents as parents. It should be noted that a birth certificate issued under this subsection might later be replaced by a birth certificate naming other individuals as parents of the child if an action to dispute the parentage of the intended parents filed under Section 9(d) is successful.

Section 8(b) deals with parentage where the surrogate has exercised her Section 7(b) right of recantation. It makes clear that the surrogate and her husband, if a party to the agreement, are the parents of the child in such a situation. Where the surrogate is unmarried or her husband was not a party to the agreement, paternity is left to the otherwise relevant state law. It should be noted, however, that if the surrogate has married or remarried since the order authorizing the surrogacy, her husband is not the father of the child. See Section 9(c).

Because under the Act (Section 1(3)) at least one intended parent must be genetically related to the child and Section 7(b) recantation is limited to those surrogates who have provided the egg, in all cases arising under Section 8(b) the intended father will be the genetic father. Thus, the interaction of Section 8(b) and the law of paternity may result in the legally recognized father (the intended father) and the legally recognized mother (the surrogate) being in different households. This situation, while regrettable, is not unique in family law and may precipitate litigation over custody. *See In re Baby M,* 537 A.2d 1227 (N.J.1988) and the trial court order on remand, 14 Fam.L.Rep. 1276 (1988).

§ 9. Surrogacy: Miscellaneous Provisions.

(a) A surrogacy agreement that is the basis of an order under Section 6 may provide for the payment of consideration.

(b) A surrogacy agreement may not limit the right of the surrogate to make decisions regarding her health care or that of the embryo or fetus.

(c) After the entry of an order under Section 6, marriage of the surrogate does not affect the validity of the order, and her husband's consent to the surrogacy agreement is not required, nor is he the father of a resulting child.

(d) A child born to a surrogate within 300 days after assisted conception pursuant to an order under Section 6 is presumed to result from the assisted conception. The presumption is conclusive as to all persons who have notice of the birth and who do not commence within 180 days after notice, an action to assert the contrary in which the child and the parties to the agreement are named as parties. The action must be commenced in the court that issued the order under Section 6.

(e) A health-care provider is not liable for recognizing the surrogate as the mother before receipt of a copy of the order entered under Section 6 or for recognizing the intended parents as parents after receipt of an order entered under Section 6.]

COMMENT

Subsection 9(a) is intended to shield surrogacy agreements which include payment of the surrogate from attack under "baby-selling" statutes which prohibit payment of money to the natural mother in adoptions.

Section 9(b) is intended to acknowledge that the surrogate, as a pregnant woman, has a constitutionally-recognized right to provide for her health care and that of the unborn child.

Section 9(c) makes it clear that a man who marries the surrogate after the surrogacy authorization has been issued is neither a party to the original action nor the father of a resulting child, even if the surrogate exercises her recantation right under Section 7(b). It is felt that since he was not a party to the surrogacy agreement, he ought not be burdened with the status of parent. In the case of a recanting surrogate who has married since the original Section 6 order, she will be the mother and the intended father may be the legally recognized father under the jurisdiction's ordinary paternity laws.

Subsection 9(d) should be read in connection with the parentage provision of Section 8(a). The presumption created by Section 9(d) is intended to provide a starting point for the determination of whether a child born to the surrogate was actually the product of the assisted conception performed pursuant to the agreement. For example, a surrogate may assert that the child was created by the union of her egg and her husband's sperm. She and all other persons who have notice of the birth are given 180 days to commence an action to assert that the child was not the product of the assisted conception. It is intended that the substantive and procedural law governing such actions will be governed by the otherwise relevant state statutes concerning disputed parentage of a child.

Subsection 9(e) is designed to provide an incentive to the parties to the surrogacy to make hospital personnel aware of the existence of the arrangement and to protect the health care providers in case such notification has not been made.

[END OF ALTERNATIVE A]

ALTERNATIVE B

COMMENT

A state that chooses Alternative B shall consider Sections 10, 11, 12, 13, 14, 15, and 16, renumbered 6, 7, 8, 9, 10, 11, and 12, respectively.

[§ 5. Surrogate Agreements.

An agreement in which a woman agrees to become a surrogate or to relinquish her rights and duties as parent of a child thereafter conceived through assisted conception is void. However, she is the mother of a resulting child, and her husband, if a party to the agreement, is the father of the child. If her husband is not a party to the agreement or the surrogate is unmarried, paternity of the child is governed by [the Uniform Parentage Act].]

COMMENT

This section should be utilized by a jurisdiction which chooses not to give any efficacy to surrogacy arrangements. It recognizes, however, that some such agreements will continue to be achieved even though they are not enforceable at law. Therefore, it makes provision for the maternity and paternity of children who are born pursuant to such agreements. Note that Alternative B's Section 5 substitutes for Alternative A's Sections 5–9.

[END OF ALTERNATIVE B]

§ 10. Parent and Child Relationship; Status of Child.

(a) A child whose status as a child is declared or negated by this [Act] is the child only of his or her parents as determined under this [Act].

(b) Unless superseded by later events forming or terminating a parent and child relationship, the status of parent and child declared or negated by this [Act] as to a given individual and a child born alive controls for purposes of:

(1) intestate succession;

(2) probate law exemptions, allowances, or other protections for children in a parent's estate; and

(3) determining eligibility of the child or its descendants to share in a donative transfer from any person as a member of a class determined by reference to the relationship.

COMMENT

This provision is parallel to those provisions in adoption statutes which provide that once an adoption creates or negates a parent-child relationship, that relationship or negation of a relationship applies in all circumstances.

While strictly speaking subsection (b) may be redundant in light of subsection (a), it is included because of the importance of the situations listed herein. The introductory clause primarily is designed to deal with situations where a parent-child relationship established under this Act is later severed through the placement of a child for adoption or, conversely, situations where a parent-child relationship is negated by the Act but is later established by an adoption.

§ 11. Uniformity of Application and Construction.

This [Act] shall be applied and construed to effectuate its general purpose to make uniform the law with respect to the subject of this [Act] among states enacting it.

§ 12. Short Title.

This [Act] may be cited as the Uniform Status of Children of Assisted Conception Act.

§ 13. Severability.

If any provision of this [Act] or its application to any person or circumstances is held invalid, the invalidity does not affect other provisions or applications of this [Act] which can be given effect without the invalid provision or application, and to this end the provisions of this [Act] are severable.

§ 14. Effective Date.

This [Act] shall take effect on _____. Its provisions are to be applied prospectively.

§ 15. Repeals.

Acts or parts of acts inconsistent with this [Act] are repealed to the extent of the inconsistency.

§ 16. Application to Existing Relationships.

This [Act] applies to surrogacy agreements entered into after its effective date.

UNIFORM SIMULTANEOUS DEATH ACT

PREFATORY NOTE

The Uniform Simultaneous Death Act (USDA) was first promulgated in 1940. It was amended in 1953 and has been enacted in the District of Columbia and all but three of the States.

The original USDA provided that, when there is no sufficient evidence that two individuals died otherwise than simultaneously, each individual's property is distributed as if he or she survived the other. The advantages of this approach are that each individual's property passes to that individual's relatives rather than to the other individual's relatives and that double administrative costs are avoided because property does not pass from one estate to another estate.

This revision of the USDA does not alter the result of the original Act. Rather, it expands the narrow application of the original Act so that, as revised, it no longer is restricted to situations in which there is no sufficient evidence that two individuals died otherwise than simultaneously. In cases in which both individuals caught in a common tragedy have died by the time third parties arrive at the scene, or shortly thereafter, the narrow application of the original Act has sometimes led to unfortunate litigation in which the representative of one of the individuals attempts, through the use of gruesome medical evidence, to prove that the one he or she represents survived the other by an instant or two. Examples include Janus v. Tarasewicz, 482 N.E.2d 418 (Ill.App.Ct. 1985) (husband's brother died as result of ingesting Tylenol capsules laced with cyanide by unknown perpetrator prior to sale in stores; after learning of his death, but before the cause of his death had been determined, husband and wife returned from their honeymoon and each ingested contaminated Tylenol capsules; upon their arrival at intensive care unit of emergency room, neither showed visible vital signs; hospital personnel never succeeded in establishing in husband any spontaneous blood pressure, pulse, or signs of respiration and pronounced him dead; hospital personnel did succeed in establishing in wife a measurable, though unsatisfactory, blood pressure; although she had very unstable vital signs, remained in a coma, and had fixed and dilated pupils, she was placed on mechanical respirator and remained on the respirator for two days before she was pronounced dead; USDA found inapplicable because there was sufficient evidence that wife survived husband); In re Bucci's Will, 57 Misc.2d 1001, 293 N.Y.S.2d 994

(N.Y.Surr.Ct.1968) (husband and wife found dead when removed from wreckage of their small airplane, which crashed and burned after having collided in air with large airplane; existence of carbon monoxide in wife's blood found sufficient evidence to establish wife's survival of husband, whose skull was fractured and in whose blood no carbon monoxide was found).

Even in cases in which it is indisputable that one of the two survived the other, such as a case in which one is clearly dead at the scene of the accident and the other clearly dies in the ambulance on the way to the hospital, the policy of the original Act plainly should apply.

This version of the USDA, then, extends the application of the original Act to situations in which there *is* sufficient evidence that one of the individuals survived the other one, but the period of survival was insubstantial. This version originated in Sections 2–104 and 2–601 of the Uniform Probate Code of 1969, which imposed a 120–hour requirement of survival for intestate and testate succession, and in the revisions of Article I and II of the Uniform Probate Code that were approved in 1990 and 1991, which extend the 120–hour requirement of survival to provisions of a "governing instrument" and to "co-owners with right of survivorship," as those terms are defined in Section 1. A clear and convincing evidence standard of proof of survival by 120 hours is imposed throughout in order to reduce litigation and to resolve close cases in favor of non-survival.

The sections specifically pertaining to community property and insurance policies contained in the original Act are unnecessary and omitted from the 1991 version. If a decedent spouse dies owning community property, those community property interests are covered by the general provisions of Sections 2 and/or 3. Similarly, insurance is covered by the general provisions of Section 3.

Section 5 of this version, titled "Evidence of Death or Status," covers an area not covered in the original Act. Subsection (1) of Section 5 defines death by reference to the Uniform Determination of Death Act. Subsections (2) through (6) are drawn from Section 1–107 of the Uniform Probate Code as revised in 1991 and provide for evidence of death or status. Note that subsection (6) is made desirable by the introduction of the requirement that survival by 120 hours must be established by clear and convincing evidence. Subsection (6) provides that, in the absence of evidence disputing the time of death stipulated on a document such as a certified copy of a death certificate, such a document that stipulates a time of death 120 hours or more after the time of death of another individual, however the time of death of the other individual is determined, establishes by clear and convincing evidence that the individual survived the other individual by 120 hours.

Section 7 of this version is a new section made desirable by the extension of a 120–hour requirement of survival to all governing instruments, such as life-insurance beneficiary designations, and to co-ownership arrangements with right of survivorship, such as joint tenancies and joint checking accounts. Section 7 grants protection to payors and other third parties who, before receiving written notice of a claimed lack of entitlement under the Act, pay off or in other ways rely on a survivor's apparent entitlement to succeed to property.

This version of the USDA is appropriate for enactment in states that have not enacted Sections 1–107, 2–104, and 2–702 of the Uniform Probate Code (1991) or Sections 002, 104, and 702 of the Uniform Act on Intestacy, Wills, and Donative Transfers (1991).

Reference. This Act is discussed in Halbach & Waggoner, "The UPC's New Survivorship and Antilapse Provisions," 55 Alb.L.Rev. 1091, 1091–99 (1992).

Table of Sections

Section 1. Definitions

In this [Act]:

(1) "Co-owners with right of survivorship" includes joint tenants, tenants by the entireties, and other co-owners of property or accounts held under circumstances that entitles one or

more to the whole of the property or account on the death of the other or others.

(2) "Governing instrument" means a deed, will, trust, insurance or annuity policy, account with POD designation, pension, profit-sharing, retirement, or similar benefit plan, instrument creating or exercising a power of appointment or a power of attorney, or a dispositive, appointive, or nominative instrument of any similar type.

(3) "Payor" means a trustee, insurer, business entity, employer, government, governmental agency or subdivision, or any other person authorized or obligated by law or a governing instrument to make payments.

Section 2. Requirement of Survival by 120 Hours Under Probate Code

Except as provided in Section 6, if the title to property, the devolution of property, the right to elect an interest in property, or the right to exempt property, homestead or family allowance depends upon an individual's survivorship of the death of another individual, an individual who is not established by clear and convincing evidence to have survived the other individual by 120 hours is deemed to have predeceased the other individual. This section does not apply if its application would result in a taking of intestate estate by the state.

COMMENT

By 1993 technical amendment, an anomalous exemption of securities registered under the Uniform TOD Security Registration Act from the 120-hour survival requirement of this section and of Section 3 was eliminated. The exemption reflected a temporary concern attributable to UTODSRA's preparation prior to discussion of inserting a 120-hour survival requirement in this Act.

Section 3. Requirement of Survival by 120 Hours Under Governing Instruments

Except as provided in Section 6, for purposes of a provision of a governing instrument that relates to an individual surviving an event, including the death of another individual, an individual who is not established by clear and convincing evidence to have survived the event by 120 hours is deemed to have predeceased the event.

Section 4. Co-owners With Right of Survivorship; Requirement of Survival by 120 Hours

Except as provided in Section 6, if (i) it is not established by clear and convincing evidence that one of two co-owners with right of survivorship survived the other co-owner by 120 hours, one-half of the property passes as if one had survived by 120 hours and one-half as if the other had survived by 120 hours and (ii) there are more than two co-owners and it is not established by clear and convincing evidence that at least one of them survived the others by 120 hours, the property passes in the proportion that one bears to the whole number of co-owners.

COMMENT

This section applies to property or accounts held by co-owners with right of survivorship. As defined in Section 1, the term "co-owners with right of survivorship" includes multiple-party accounts with right of survivorship. In the case of a joint checking account registered in the name of the decedent and his or her spouse with right of survivorship, the 120–hour requirement of survivorship imposed by this section will not interfere with the surviving spouse's ability to withdraw funds from the account during the 120–hour period following the decedent's death if the state has a facility-of-payment statute such as Section 6–222(1) of the Uniform Probate Code. A state without such a facility-of-payment statute should consider enacting one in conjunction with the enactment of this Act.

Section 5. Evidence of Death or Status

In addition to the rules of evidence in courts of general jurisdiction, the following rules relating to a determination of death and status apply:

(1) Death occurs when an individual [is determined to be dead under the Uniform Determination of Death Act] [has sustained either (1) irreversible cessation of circulatory and respiratory functions or (2) irreversible cessation of all functions of the entire brain, including the brain stem. A determination of death must be made in accordance with accepted medical standards].

(2) A certified or authenticated copy of a death certificate purporting to be issued by an official or agency of the place where the death purportedly occurred is prima facie evidence of the fact, place, date, and time of death and the identity of the decedent.

(3) A certified or authenticated copy of any record or report of a governmental agency, domestic or foreign, that an individu-

al is missing, detained, dead, or alive is prima facie evidence of the status and of the dates, circumstances, and places disclosed by the record or report.

(4) In the absence of prima facie evidence of death under paragraph (2) or (3), the fact of death may be established by clear and convincing evidence, including circumstantial evidence.

(5) An individual whose death is not established under the preceding paragraphs who is absent for a continuous period of five years, during which he [or she] has not been heard from, and whose absence is not satisfactorily explained after diligent search or inquiry, is presumed to be dead. His [or her] death is presumed to have occurred at the end of the period unless there is sufficient evidence for determining that death occurred earlier.

(6) In the absence of evidence disputing the time of death stipulated on a document described in paragraph (2) or (3), a document described in paragraph (2) or (3) that stipulates a time of death 120 hours or more after the time of death of another individual, however the time of death of the other individual is determined, establishes by clear and convincing evidence that the individual survived the other individual by 120 hours.

COMMENT

States that have enacted the Uniform Determination of Death Act should enact the first set of bracketed language in paragraph (1). States that have not enacted the Uniform Determination of Death Act should enact the second set of bracketed language in paragraph (1).

Section 6. Exceptions

Survival by 120 hours is not required if:

(1) the governing instrument contains language dealing explicitly with simultaneous deaths or deaths in a common disaster and that language is operable under the facts of the case;

(2) the governing instrument expressly indicates that an individual is not required to survive an event, including the death of another individual, by any specified period or expressly requires the individual to survive the event for a specified period; but survival of the event or the specified period must be established by clear and convincing evidence;

(3) the imposition of a 120–hour requirement of survival would cause a nonvested property interest or a power of appointment to [be invalid under the Rule Against Perpetuities] [fail to qualify for validity under Section 1(a)(1), (b)(1), or (c)(1) or to become invalid under Section 1(a)(2), (b)(2), or (c)(2), of the Uniform Statutory Rule Against Perpetuities]; but survival must be established by clear and convincing evidence; or

(4) the application of a 120–hour requirement of survival to multiple governing instruments would result in an unintended failure or duplication of a disposition; but survival must be established by clear and convincing evidence.

COMMENT

Subsection (1). Subsection (1) provides that the 120–hour requirement of survival is inapplicable if the governing instrument "contains language dealing explicitly with simultaneous deaths or deaths in a common disaster and that language is operable under the facts of the case." The application of this provision is illustrated by the following example.

Example. G died leaving a will devising her entire estate to her husband, H, adding that "in the event he dies before I do, at the same time that I do, or under circumstances as to make it doubtful who died first," my estate is to go to my brother Melvin. H died about 38 hours after G's death, both having died as a result of injuries sustained in an automobile accident.

Under this section, G's estate passes under the alternative devise to Melvin because H's failure to survive G by 120 hours means that H is deemed to have predeceased G. The language in the governing instrument does not, under subsection (1), nullify the provision that causes H, because of his failure to survive G

by 120 hours, to be deemed to have predeceased G. Although the governing instrument does contain language dealing with simultaneous deaths, that language is not operable under the facts of the case because H did not die before G, at the same time as G, or under circumstances as to make it doubtful who died first.

Subsection (2). Subsection (2) provides that the 120–hour requirement of survival is inapplicable if "the governing instrument expressly indicates that an individual is not required to survive an event, including the death of another individual, by any specified period or expressly requires the individual to survive the event for a stated period."

Mere words of survivorship in a governing instrument do not expressly indicate that an individual is not required to survive an event by any specified period. If, for example, a trust provides that the net income is to be paid to A for life, remainder in corpus to B if B survives A, the 120–hour requirement of survival would still apply. B would have to survive A by 120 hours. If, however, the trust expressly stated that B need not survive A by any specified period, that language would negate the 120–hour requirement of survival.

Language in a governing instrument requiring an individual to survive by a specified period also renders the 120–hour requirement of survival inapplicable. Thus, if a will devises property "to A if A survives me by 30 days," the express 30–day requirement of survival overrides the 120–hour survival period provided by this Act.

Subsection (4). Subsection (4) provides that the 120–hour requirement of survival is inapplicable if "the application of this section to multiple governing instruments would result in an unintended failure or duplication of a disposition." The application of this provision is illustrated by the following example.

> *Example.* Pursuant to a common plan, H and W executed mutual wills with reciprocal provisions. Their intention was that a $50,000 charitable devise would be made on the death of the survivor. To that end, H's will devised $50,000 to the charity if W predeceased him. W's will devised $50,000 to the charity if H predeceased her. Subsequently, H and W were involved

in a common accident. W survived H by 48 hours.

> Were it not for subsection (4), not only would the charitable devise in W's will be effective, because H in fact predeceased W, but the charitable devise in H's will would also be effective, because W's failure to survive H by 120 hours would result in her being deemed to have predeceased H. Because this would result in an unintended duplication of the $50,000 devise, subsection (4) provides that the 120–hour requirement of survival is inapplicable. Thus, only the $50,000 charitable devise in W's will is effective.

Subsection (4) also renders the 120–hour requirement of survival inapplicable had H and W died in circumstances in which it could not be established by clear and convincing evidence that either survived the other. In such a case, an appropriate result might be to give effect to the common plan by paying half of the intended $50,000 devise from H's estate and half from W's estate.

Historical Note. This comment was revised in 1993. For the prior version, see 8B U.L.A. 261 (1993).

Section 7. Protection of Payors, Bona Fide Purchasers, and Other Third Parties; Personal Liability of Recipient

(a) [Protection of Payors and Other Third Parties.]

(1) A payor or other third party is not liable for having made a payment or transferred an item of property or any other benefit to a person designated in a governing instrument who, under this [Act], is not entitled to the payment or item of property, or for having taken any other action in good faith

reliance on the person's apparent entitlement under the terms of the governing instrument, before the payor or other third party received written notice of a claimed lack of entitlement under this [Act]. A payor or other third party is liable for a payment made or other action taken after the payor or other third party received written notice of a claimed lack of entitlement under this [Act].

(2) Written notice of a claimed lack of entitlement under paragraph (1) must be mailed to the payor's or other third party's main office or home by registered or certified mail, return receipt requested, or served upon the payor or other third party in the same manner as a summons in a civil action. Upon receipt of written notice of a claimed lack of entitlement under this [Act], a payor or other third party may pay any amount owed or transfer or deposit any item of property held by it to or with the court having jurisdiction of the probate proceedings relating to the decedent's estate, or if no proceedings have been commenced, to or with the court having jurisdiction of probate proceedings relating to decedents' estates located in the county of the decedent's residence. The court shall hold the funds or item of property and, upon its determination under this [Act], shall order disbursement in accordance with the determination. Payments, transfers, or deposits made to or with the court discharge the payor or other third party from all claims for the value of amounts paid to or items of property transferred to or deposited with the court.

(b) [Protection of Bona Fide Purchasers; Personal Liability of Recipient.]

(1) A person who purchases property for value and without notice, or who receives a payment or other item of property in partial or full satisfaction of a legally enforceable obligation, is neither obligated under this [Act] to return the payment, item of property, or benefit nor liable under this [Act] for the amount of the payment or the value of the item of property or benefit. But a person who, not for value, receives a payment, item of property, or any other benefit to which the person is not entitled under this [Act] is obligated to return the payment, item of property, or benefit, or is personally liable for the amount of the payment or the value of the item of property or benefit, to the person who is entitled to it under this [Act].

(2) If this [Act] or any part of this [Act] is preempted by federal law with respect to a payment, an item of property, or any other benefit covered by this [Act], a person who, not for

value, receives the payment, item of property, or any other benefit to which the person is not entitled under this [Act] is obligated to return the payment, item of property, or benefit, or is personally liable for the amount of the payment or the value of the item of property or benefit, to the person who would have been entitled to it were this [Act] or part of this [Act] not preempted.

Section 8. Uniformity of Application and Construction

This [Act] shall be applied and construed to effectuate its general purpose to make uniform the law with respect to the subject of this [Act] among states enacting it.

Section 9. Short Title

This [Act] may be cited as the Uniform Simultaneous Death Act (1993).

Section 10. Repeal

The following acts and parts of acts are repealed:

(1)

(2)

(3)

Section 11. Severability Clause

If any provision of this [Act] or its application to any persons or circumstance is held invalid, the invalidity does not affect other provisions or applications of the [Act] which can be given effect without the invalid provision or application, and to this end the provisions of this [Act] are severable.

Section 12. Effective Date

(a) This [Act] takes effect _____.

(b) On the effective date of this [Act]:

(1) an act done before the effective date in any proceeding and any accrued right is not impaired by this [Act]. If a right is acquired, extinguished, or barred upon the expiration of a pre-scribed period of time that has commenced to run by the provisions of any statute before the effective date, the provisions remain in force with respect to that right; and

(2) any rule of construction or presumption provided in this [Act] applies to instruments executed and multiple-party ac-

counts opened before the effective date unless there is a clear indication of a contrary intent.

COMMENT

Subsection (b) is adapted from Section 8–101(b)(4) and (5) of the Uniform Probate Code.

Application to Pre-Existing Governing Instruments. For decedents dying after the effective date of enactment, the provisions of this Act apply to governing instruments executed prior to as well as on or after the effective date of enactment. The Joint Editorial Board for the Uniform Probate Code has issued a statement concerning the constitutionality under the Contracts Clause of this feature. The statement, titled "Joint Editorial Board Statement Regarding the Constitutionality of Changes in Default Rules as Applied to Pre-Existing Documents," can be found at 17 Am.C.Tr. & Est.Couns.Notes 184 (1991) or can be obtained from the headquarters office of the National Conference of Commissioners on Uniform State Laws, 676 N. St. Clair St., Suite 1700, Chicago, IL 60611, Phone 312/915–0195, FAX 312/915–0187.

Historical Note. This comment was revised in 1993. For the prior version, see 8B U.L.A. 266 (1993).

UNIFORM HEALTH–CARE DECISIONS ACT

Table of Sections

PREFATORY NOTE

Since the Supreme Court's decision in *Cruzan v. Commissioner, Missouri Department of Health*, 497 U.S. 261 (1990), significant change has occurred in state legislation on health-care decision making. Every state now has legislation authorizing the use of some sort of advance health-care directive. All but a few states authorize what is typically known as a living will. Nearly all states have statutes authorizing the use of powers of attorney for health care. In addition, a majority of states have statutes allowing family members, and in some cases close friends, to make health-care decisions for adult individuals who lack capacity.

This state legislation, however, has developed in fits and starts, resulting in an often fragmented, incomplete, and sometimes inconsistent set of rules. Statutes enacted within a state often conflict and conflicts between statutes of different states are common. In an increasingly mobile society where an advance health-care di-

836

rective given in one state must frequently be implemented in another, there is a need for greater uniformity.

The Health–Care Decisions Act was drafted with this confused situation in mind. The Act is built around the following concepts. *First*, the Act acknowledges the right of a competent individual to decide all aspects of his or her own health care in all circumstances, including the right to decline health care or to direct that health care be discontinued, even if death ensues. An individual's instructions may extend to any and all health-care decisions that might arise and, unless limited by the principal, an agent has authority to make all health-care decisions which the individual could have made. The Act recognizes and validates an individual's authority to define the scope of an instruction or agency as broadly or as narrowly as the individual chooses.

Second, the Act is comprehensive and will enable an enacting jurisdiction to replace its existing legislation on the subject with a single statute. The Act authorizes health-care decisions to be made by an agent who is designated to decide when an individual cannot or does not wish to; by a designated surrogate, family member, or close friend when an individual is unable to act and no guardian or agent has been appointed or is reasonably available; or by a court having jurisdiction as decision maker of last resort.

Third, the Act is designed to simplify and facilitate the making of advance health-care directives. An instruction may be either written or oral. A power of attorney for health care, while it must be in writing, need not be witnessed or acknowledged. In addition, an optional form for the making of a directive is provided.

Fourth, the Act seeks to ensure to the extent possible that decisions about an individual's health care will be governed by the individual's own desires concerning the issues to be resolved. The Act requires an agent or surrogate authorized to make health-care decisions for an individual to make those decisions in accordance with the instructions and other wishes of the individual to the extent known. Otherwise, the agent or surrogate must make those decisions in accordance with the best interest of the individual but in light of the individual's personal values known to the agent or surrogate. Furthermore, the Act requires a guardian to comply with a ward's previously given instructions and prohibits a guardian from revoking the ward's advance health-care directive without express court approval.

Fifth, the Act addresses compliance by health-care providers and institutions. A health-care provider or institution must comply with an instruction of the patient and with a reasonable interpretation of that instruction or other health-care decision made by a person then authorized to make health-care decisions for the patient. The obligation to comply is not absolute, however. A health-care provider or institution may decline to honor an instruction or decision for reasons of conscience or if the instruction or decision requires the provision of medically ineffective care or care contrary to applicable health-care standards.

Sixth, the Act provides a procedure for the resolution of disputes. While the Act is in general to be effectuated without litigation, situations will arise where resort to the courts may be necessary. For that reason, the Act authorizes the court to enjoin or direct a health-care decision or order other equitable relief and specifies who is entitled to bring a petition.

The Health–Care Decisions Act supersedes the Commissioners' Model Health–Care Consent Act (1982), the Uniform Rights of the Terminally Ill Act (1985), and the Uniform Rights of the Terminally Ill Act (1989). A state enacting the Health–Care Decisions Act which has one of these other acts in force should repeal it upon enactment.

Section 1. Definitions.

In this [Act]:

(1) "Advance health-care directive" means an individual instruction or a power of attorney for health care.

(2) "Agent" means an individual designated in a power of attorney for health care to make a health-care decision for the individual granting the power.

(3) "Capacity" means an individual's ability to understand the significant benefits, risks, and alternatives to proposed health care and to make and communicate a health-care decision.

(4) "Guardian" means a judicially appointed guardian or conservator having authority to make a health-care decision for an individual.

(5) "Health care" means any care, treatment, service, or procedure to maintain, diagnose, or otherwise affect an individual's physical or mental condition.

(6) "Health-care decision" means a decision made by an individual or the individual's agent, guardian, or surrogate, regarding the individual's health care, including:

(i) selection and discharge of health-care providers and institutions;

(ii) approval or disapproval of diagnostic tests, surgical procedures, programs of medication, and orders not to resuscitate; and

(iii) directions to provide, withhold, or withdraw artificial nutrition and hydration and all other forms of health care.

(7) "Health-care institution" means an institution, facility, or agency licensed, certified, or otherwise authorized or permitted by law to provide health care in the ordinary course of business.

(8) "Health-care provider" means an individual licensed, certified, or otherwise authorized or permitted by law to provide health care in the ordinary course of business or practice of a profession.

(9) "Individual instruction" means an individual's direction concerning a health-care decision for the individual.

(10) "Person" means an individual, corporation, business trust, estate, trust, partnership, association, joint venture, government, governmental subdivision, agency, or instrumentality, or any other legal or commercial entity.

(11) "Physician" means an individual authorized to practice medicine [or osteopathy] under [appropriate statute].

(12) "Power of attorney for health care" means the designation of an agent to make health-care decisions for the individual granting the power.

(13) "Primary physician" means a physician designated by an individual or the individual's agent, guardian, or surrogate, to have primary responsibility for the individual's health care or, in the absence of a designation or if the designated physician is not reasonably available, a physician who undertakes the responsibility.

(14) "Reasonably available" means readily able to be contacted without undue effort and willing and able to act in a timely manner considering the urgency of the patient's health-care needs.

(15) "State" means a State of the United States, the District of Columbia, the Commonwealth of Puerto Rico, or a territory or insular possession subject to the jurisdiction of the United States.

(16) "Supervising health-care provider" means the primary physician or, if there is no primary physician or the primary physician is not reasonably available, the health-care provider who has undertaken primary responsibility for an individual's health care.

(17) "Surrogate" means an individual, other than a patient's agent or guardian, authorized under this [Act] to make a health-care decision for the patient.

COMMENT

The term "advance health-care directive" (subsection (1)) appears in the federal Patient Self–Determination Act enacted as sections 4206 and 4751 of the Omnibus Budget Reconciliation Act of 1990 and has gained widespread usage among health-care professionals.

The definition of "agent" (subsection (2)) is not limited to a single individual. The Act permits the appointment of co-agents and alternate agents.

The definition of "guardian" (subsection (4)) recognizes that some states grant health-care decision making authority to a conservator of the person.

The definition of "health care" (subsection (5)) is to be given the broadest possible construction. It includes the types of care referred to in the definition of "health-care decision" (subsection (6)), and to care, including custodial care, provided at a "health-care institution" (subsection (7)). It also includes non-medical remedial treatment such as practiced by adherents of Christian Science.

The term "health-care institution" (subsection (7)) includes a hospital, nursing home, residential-care facility, home health agency or hospice.

The term "individual instruction" (subsection (9)) includes any type of written or oral direction concerning health-care treatment. The direction may range from a written document which is intended to be effective at a future time if certain specified conditions arise and for which a form is provided in Section 4, to the written consent required before surgery is per-

formed, to oral directions concerning care recorded in the health-care record. The instruction may relate to a particular health-care decision or to health care in general.

The definition of "person" (subsection (10)) includes a limited liability company, which falls within the category of "other legal or commercial entity."

Because states differ on the classes of professionals who may lawfully practice medicine, the definition of "physician" (subsection (11)) cross-references the appropriate licensing or other statute.

The Act employs the term "primary physician" (subsection (13)) instead of "attending physician." The term "attending physician" could be understood to refer to any physician providing treatment to the individual, and not to the physician whom the individual, or agent, guardian, or surrogate, has designated or, in the absence of a designation, the physician who has undertaken primary responsibility for the individual's health care.

The term "reasonably available" (subsection (14)) is used in the Act to accommodate the reality that individuals will sometimes not be timely available. The term is incorporated into the definition of "supervising health-care provider" (subsection (16)). It appears in the optional statutory form (Section 4) to indicate when an alternate agent may act. In Section 5 it is used to determine when a surrogate will be authorized to make health-care decisions for an individual, and if so, which class of individuals has authority to act.

The definition of "supervising health-care provider" (subsection (16)) accommodates the circumstance that frequently arises where care or supervision by a physician may not be readily available. The individual's primary physician is to assume the role, however, if reasonably available. For the contexts in which the term is used, see Sections 3, 5, and 7.

The definition of "surrogate" (subsection (17)) refers to the individual having present authority under Section 5 to make a health-care decision for a patient. It does not include an individual who might have such authority under a given set of circumstances which have not occurred.

Section 2. Advance Health–Care Directives.

(a) An adult or emancipated minor may give an individual instruction. The instruction may be oral or written. The instruction may be limited to take effect only if a specified condition arises.

(b) An adult or emancipated minor may execute a power of attorney for health care, which may authorize the agent to make any health-care decision the principal could have made while having capacity. The power must be in writing and signed by the principal. The power remains in effect notwithstanding the principal's later incapacity and may include individual instructions. Unless related to the principal by blood, marriage, or adoption, an agent may not be an owner, operator, or employee of [a residential long-term health-care institution] at which the principal is receiving care.

(c) Unless otherwise specified in a power of attorney for health care, the authority of an agent becomes effective only upon a determination that the principal lacks capacity, and ceases to be effective upon a determination that the principal has recovered capacity.

(d) Unless otherwise specified in a written advance health-care directive, a determination that an individual lacks or has recovered capacity, or that another condition exists that affects an individual instruction or the authority of an agent, must be made by the primary physician.

(e) An agent shall make a health-care decision in accordance with the principal's individual instructions, if any, and other wishes to the extent known to the agent. Otherwise, the agent shall make the decision in accordance with the agent's determination of the principal's best interest. In determining the principal's best interest, the agent shall consider the principal's personal values to the extent known to the agent.

(f) A health-care decision made by an agent for a principal is effective without judicial approval.

(g) A written advance health-care directive may include the individual's nomination of a guardian of the person.

(h) An advance health-care directive is valid for purposes of this [Act] if it complies with this [Act], regardless of when or where executed or communicated.

COMMENT

The individual instruction authorized in subsection (a) may but need not be limited to take effect in specified circumstances, such as if the individual is dying. An individual instruction may be either written or oral.

Subsection (b) authorizes a power of attorney for health care to include instructions regarding the principal's health care. This provision has been included in order to validate the practice of designating an agent and giving individual instructions in one document instead of two. The authority of an agent falls within the discretion of the principal as expressed in the instrument creating the power and may extend to any health-care decision the principal could have made while having capacity.

Subsection (b) excludes the oral designation of an agent. Section 5(b) authorizes an individual to orally designate a surrogate by personally informing the supervising health-care provider. A power of attorney for health care, however, must be in writing and signed by the principal, although it need not be witnessed or acknowledged.

Subsection (b) also limits those who may serve as agents to make health-care decisions for another. The subsection addresses the special vulnerability of individuals in residential long-term health-care institutions by protecting a principal against those who may have interests that conflict with the duty to follow the principal's expressed wishes or to determine the principal's best interest. Specifically, the owners, operators or employees of a residential long-term health-care institution at which the principal is receiving care may not act as agents. An exception is made for those related to the principal by blood, marriage or adoption, relationships which are assumed to neutralize any consequence of a conflict of interest adverse to the principal. The phrase "a residential long-term health-care institution" is placed in brackets to indicate to the legislature of an enacting jurisdiction that it should substitute the appropriate terminology used under local law.

Subsection (c) provides that the authority of the agent to make health-care decisions ordinarily does not become effective until the principal is determined to lack capacity and ceases to be effective should the principal recover capacity. A principal may provide, however, that the authority of the agent becomes effective immediately or upon the happening of some event other than the loss of capacity but may do so only by an express provision in the power of attorney. For example, a mother who does not want to make her own health-care decisions but prefers that her daughter make them for her may specify that the daughter as agent is to have authority to make health-care decisions immediately. The mother in that circumstance retains the right to later revoke the power of attorney as provided in Section 3.

Subsection (d) provides that unless otherwise specified in a written advance health-care directive, a determination that a principal has lost or recovered capacity to make health-care decisions must be made by the primary physician. For example, a principal might specify that the determination of capacity is to be made by the agent in consultation with the primary physician. Or a principal, such as a member of the Christian Science faith who relies on a religious method of healing and who has no primary physician, might specify that capacity be determined by other means. In the event that multiple decision makers are specified and they cannot agree, it may be necessary to seek court instruction as authorized by Section 14.

Subsection (d) also provides that unless otherwise specified in a written advance health-care directive, the existence of other conditions which affect an individual instruction or the authority of an agent must be determined by the primary physician. For example, an individual might specify that an agent may withdraw or withhold treatment that keeps the individual alive only if the individual has an incurable and irreversible condition that will result in the individual's death within a relatively short time. In

that event, unless otherwise specified in the advance health-care directive, the determination that the individual has that condition must be made by the primary physician.

Subsection (e) requires the agent to follow the principal's individual instructions and other expressed wishes to the extent known to the agent. To the extent such instructions or other wishes are unknown, the agent must act in the principal's best interest. In determining the principal's best interest, the agent is to consider the principal's personal values to the extent known to the agent. The Act does not prescribe a detailed list of factors for determining the principal's best interest but instead grants the agent discretion to ascertain and weigh the factors likely to be of importance to the principal. The legislature of an enacting jurisdiction that wishes to add such a list may want to consult the Maryland Health–Care Decision Act, Md. Health–Gen. Code Ann. § 5–601.

Subsection (f) provides that a health-care decision made by an agent is effective without judicial approval. A similar provision applies to health-care decisions made by surrogates (Section 5(g)) or guardians (Section 6(c)).

Subsection (g) provides that a written advance health-care directive may include the individual's nomination of a guardian of the person. A nomination cannot guarantee that the nominee will be appointed but in the absence of cause to appoint another the court would likely select the nominee. Moreover, the mere nomination of the agent will reduce the likelihood that a guardianship could be used to thwart the agent's authority.

Subsection (h) validates advance health-care directives which conform to the Act, regardless of when or where executed or communicated. This includes an advance health-care directive which would be valid under the Act but which was made prior to the date of its enactment and failed to comply with the execution requirements then in effect. It also includes an advance health-care directive which was made in another jurisdiction but which does not comply with that jurisdiction's execution or other requirements.

Section 3. Revocation of Advance Health–Care Directive.

(a) An individual may revoke the designation of an agent only by a signed writing or by personally informing the supervising health-care provider.

(b) An individual may revoke all or part of an advance health-care directive, other than the designation of an agent, at any time and in any manner that communicates an intent to revoke.

(c) A health-care provider, agent, guardian, or surrogate who is informed of a revocation shall promptly communicate the fact of the revocation to the supervising health-care provider and to any health-care institution at which the patient is receiving care.

(d) A decree of annulment, divorce, dissolution of marriage, or legal separation revokes a previous designation of a spouse as agent unless otherwise specified in the decree or in a power of attorney for health care.

(e) An advance health-care directive that conflicts with an earlier advance health-care directive revokes the earlier directive to the extent of the conflict.

COMMENT

Subsection (b) provides that an individual may revoke any portion of an advance health-care directive at any time and in any manner that communicates an intent to revoke. However, a more restrictive standard applies to the revocation of the portion of a power of attorney for health care relating to the designation of an agent. Subsection (a) provides that an individual may revoke the designation of an agent only by a signed writing or by personally informing the supervising health-care provider. This higher standard is justified by the risk of a false revocation of an agent's designation or of a misinterpretation or miscommunication of a principal's statement communicated through a third party. For example, without this higher standard, an individual motivated by a desire to gain control over a patient might be able to assume authority to act as agent by falsely informing a health-care provider that the principal no longer wishes the previously designated agent to act but instead wishes to appoint the individual.

Subsection (c) requires any health-care provider, agent, guardian or surrogate who is informed of a revocation to promptly communicate that fact to the supervising health-care provider and to any health-care institution at which the patient is receiving care. The communication triggers the Section 7(b) obligation of the supervising health-care provider to record the revocation in the patient's health-care record and reduces the risk that a health-care provider or agent, guardian or surrogate will rely on a health-care directive that is no longer valid.

Subsection (e) establishes a rule of construction permitting multiple advance health-care directives to be construed together in order to determine the individual's intent, with the later advance health-care directive superseding the former to the extent of any inconsistency.

The section does not specifically address amendment of an advance health-care directive because such reference is not necessary. Subsection (b) specifically authorizes partial revocation, and subsection (e) recognizes that an advance health-care directive may be modified by a later directive.

Section 4. Optional Form.

The following form may, but need not, be used to create an advance health-care directive. The other sections of this [Act] govern the effect of this or any other writing used to create an advance health-care directive. An individual may complete or modify all or any part of the following form:

ADVANCE HEALTH–CARE DIRECTIVE

Explanation

You have the right to give instructions about your own health care. You also have the right to name someone else to make health-care decisions for you. This form lets you do either or both of these things. It also lets you express your wishes regarding donation of organs and the designation of your primary physician. If you use this form, you may complete or modify all or any part of it. You are free to use a different form.

Part 1 of this form is a power of attorney for health care. Part 1 lets you name another individual as agent to make health-care decisions for you if you become incapable of making your own decisions or if you want someone else to make those decisions for you now even though you are still capable. You may also name an alternate agent to act for you if your first choice is not willing, able, or reasonably available to make decisions for you. Unless related to you, your agent may not be an owner, operator, or employee of [a

845

residential long-term health-care institution] at which you are receiving care.

Unless the form you sign limits the authority of your agent, your agent may make all health-care decisions for you. This form has a place for you to limit the authority of your agent. You need not limit the authority of your agent if you wish to rely on your agent for all health-care decisions that may have to be made. If you choose not to limit the authority of your agent, your agent will have the right to:

(a) consent or refuse consent to any care, treatment, service, or procedure to maintain, diagnose, or otherwise affect a physical or mental condition;

(b) select or discharge health-care providers and institutions;

(c) approve or disapprove diagnostic tests, surgical procedures, programs of medication, and orders not to resuscitate; and

(d) direct the provision, withholding, or withdrawal of artificial nutrition and hydration and all other forms of health care.

Part 2 of this form lets you give specific instructions about any aspect of your health care. Choices are provided for you to express your wishes regarding the provision, withholding, or withdrawal of treatment to keep you alive, including the provision of artificial nutrition and hydration, as well as the provision of pain relief. Space is also provided for you to add to the choices you have made or for you to write out any additional wishes.

Part 3 of this form lets you express an intention to donate your bodily organs and tissues following your death.

Part 4 of this form lets you designate a physician to have primary responsibility for your health care.

After completing this form, sign and date the form at the end. It is recommended but not required that you request two other individuals to sign as witnesses. Give a copy of the signed and completed form to your physician, to any other health-care providers you may have, to any health-care institution at which you are receiving care, and to any health-care agents you have named. You should talk to the person you have named as agent to make sure that he or she understands your wishes and is willing to take the responsibility.

You have the right to revoke this advance health-care directive or replace this form at any time.

* * *

PART 1

POWER OF ATTORNEY FOR HEALTH CARE

(1) DESIGNATION OF AGENT: I designate the following individual as my agent to make health-care decisions for me:

_____

(name of individual you choose as agent)

_____

(address)   (city)   (state)   (zip code)

_____

(home phone)   (work phone)

OPTIONAL: If I revoke my agent's authority or if my agent is not willing, able, or reasonably available to make a health-care decision for me, I designate as my first alternate agent:

_____

(name of individual you choose as first alternate agent)

_____

(address)   (city)   (state)   (zip code)

_____

(home phone)   (work phone)

OPTIONAL: If I revoke the authority of my agent and first alternate agent or if neither is willing, able, or reasonably available to make a health-care decision for me, I designate as my second alternate agent:

_____

(name of individual you choose as second alternate agent)

_____

(address)   (city)   (state)   (zip code)

_____

(home phone)   (work phone)

(2) AGENT'S AUTHORITY: My agent is authorized to make all health-care decisions for me, including decisions to provide, withhold, or withdraw artificial nutrition and hydration and all other forms of health care to keep me alive, except as I state here:

_____

_____

_____

(Add additional sheets if needed.)

(3) WHEN AGENT'S AUTHORITY BECOMES EFFECTIVE: My agent's authority becomes effective when my primary physician determines that I am unable to make my own health-care decisions unless I mark the following box. If I mark this box [   ], my agent's authority to make health-care decisions for me takes effect immediately.

(4) AGENT'S OBLIGATION: My agent shall make health-care decisions for me in accordance with this power of attorney for health care, any instructions I give in Part 2 of this form, and my other wishes to the extent known to my agent. To the extent my wishes are unknown, my agent shall make health-care decisions for me in accordance with what my agent determines to be in my best interest. In determining my best interest, my agent shall consider my personal values to the extent known to my agent.

(5) NOMINATION OF GUARDIAN: If a guardian of my person needs to be appointed for me by a court, I nominate the agent designated in this form. If that agent is not willing, able, or reasonably available to act as guardian, I nominate the alternate agents whom I have named, in the order designated.

PART 2

INSTRUCTIONS FOR HEALTH CARE

If you are satisfied to allow your agent to determine what is best for you in making end-of-life decisions, you need not fill out this part of the form. If you do fill out this part of the form, you may strike any wording you do not want.

(6) END–OF–LIFE DECISIONS: I direct that my health-care providers and others involved in my care provide, withhold, or withdraw treatment in accordance with the choice I have marked below:

[   ] (a) Choice Not To Prolong Life

I do not want my life to be prolonged if (i) I have an incurable and irreversible condition that will result in my death within a relatively short time, (ii) I become unconscious and, to a reasonable degree of medical certainty, I will not regain consciousness, or (iii) the likely risks and burdens of treatment would outweigh the expected benefits, OR

[   ] (b) Choice To Prolong Life

I want my life to be prolonged as long as possible within the limits of generally accepted health-care standards.

(7) ARTIFICIAL NUTRITION AND HYDRATION: Artificial nutrition and hydration must be provided, withheld, or withdrawn in accordance with the choice I have made in paragraph (6) unless I mark the following box. If I mark this box [   ], artificial nutrition and hydration must be provided regardless of my condition and regardless of the choice I have made in paragraph (6).

(8) RELIEF FROM PAIN: Except as I state in the following space, I direct that treatment for alleviation of pain or discomfort be provided at all times, even if it hastens my death:

_____

_____

(9) OTHER WISHES: (If you do not agree with any of the optional choices above and wish to write your own, or if you wish to add to the instructions you have given above, you may do so here.) I direct that:

_____

_____

(Add additional sheets if needed.)

PART 3
DONATION OF ORGANS AT DEATH
(OPTIONAL)

(10) Upon my death (mark applicable box)

[   ] (a) I give any needed organs, tissues, or parts, OR

[   ] (b) I give the following organs, tissues, or parts only

_____

    (c) My gift is for the following purposes (strike any of the following you do not want)

    (i) Transplant

    (ii) Therapy

    (iii) Research

    (iv) Education

PART 4
PRIMARY PHYSICIAN
(OPTIONAL)

(11) I designate the following physician as my primary physician:

_____

(name of physician)

_____

(address)   (city)   (state)   (zip code)

_____

(phone)

OPTIONAL: If the physician I have designated above is not willing, able, or reasonably available to act as my primary physician, I designate the following physician as my primary physician:

_____

(name of physician)

_____

(address)   (city)   (state)   (zip code)

_____

(phone)

* * *

(12) EFFECT OF COPY: A copy of this form has the same effect as the original.

(13) SIGNATURES: Sign and date the form here:

_____   _____

(date)   (sign your name)

_____   _____

(address)   (print your name)

_____

(city)   (state)

(Optional) SIGNATURES OF WITNESSES:

First witness   Second witness

_____   _____

(print name)   (print name)

_____   _____

(address)   (address)

850

_____	_____
(city) (state)	(city) (state)
_____	_____
(signature of witness)	(signature of witness)
_____	_____
(date)	(date)

COMMENT

The optional form set forth in this section incorporates the Section 2 requirements applicable to advance health-care directives. There are four parts to the form. An individual may complete all or any parts of the form. Any part of the form left blank is not to be given effect. For example, an individual may complete the instructions for health care part of the form alone. Or an individual may complete the power of attorney for health care part of the form alone. Or an individual may complete both the instructions and power of attorney for health care parts of the form. An individual may also, but need not, complete the parts of the form pertaining to donation of bodily organs and tissue and the designation of a primary physician.

Part 1, the power of attorney for health care, appears first on the form in order to ensure to the extent possible that it will come to the attention of a casual reader. This reflects the reality that the appointment of an agent is a more comprehensive approach to the making of health-care decisions than is the giving of an individual instruction, which cannot possibly anticipate all future circumstances which might arise.

Part 1 (1) of the power of attorney for health care form requires only the designation of a single agent, but with opportunity given to designate a single first alternate and a single second alternate, if the individual chooses. No provision is made in the form for the designation of co-agents in order not to encourage the practice. Designation of co-agents is discouraged because of the difficulties likely to be encountered if the co-agents are not all readily available or do not agree. If co-agents are appointed, the instrument should specify that either is authorized to act if the other is not reasonably available. It should also specify a method for resolving disagreements.

Part 1 (2) of the power of attorney for health care form grants the agent authority to make all health-care decisions for the individual subject to any limitations which the individual may state in the form. Reference is made to artificial nutrition and hydration and other forms of treatment to keep an individual alive in order to ensure that the individual is aware that those are forms of health care that the agent would have the authority to withdraw or withhold absent specific limitation.

Part 1 (3) of the power of attorney for health care form provides that the agent's authority becomes effective upon a determination that the individual lacks capacity, but as authorized by Section 2(c) a box is provided for the individual to indicate that the authority of the agent takes effect immediately.

Part 1 (4) of the power of attorney for health care form directs the agent to make health-care decisions in accordance with the power of attorney, any instructions given by the individual in Part 2 of the form, and the individual's other wishes to the extent known to the agent. To the extent the individual's wishes in the matter are not known, the agent is to make health-care decisions based on what the agent determines to be in the individual's best interest. In determining the individual's best interest, the agent is to consider the individual's personal values to the extent known to the agent. Section 2(e) imposes this standard, whether or not it is included in the form, but its inclusion in the form will bring it to the attention of the individual granting the power, to the agent, to any guardian or surrogate, and to the individual's health-care providers.

Part 1 (5) of the power of attorney for health care form nominates the agent, if available, able, and willing to act, otherwise the alternate agents in order of priority stated, as guardians of the person for the individual. This provision is included in the form for two reasons. First, if an appointment of a guardian becomes necessary the agent is the one whom the individual would most likely want to serve in that role. Second, the nomination of the agent as guardian will reduce the possibility that someone other than the agent will be appointed as guardian who could use the position to thwart the agent's authority.

Because the variety of treatment decisions to which health-care in-

structions may relate is virtually unlimited, Part 2 of the form does not attempt to be comprehensive, but is directed at the types of treatment for which an individual is most likely to have special wishes. Part 2(6) of the form, entitled "End-of-Life Decisions", provides two alternative choices for the expression of wishes concerning the provision, withholding, or withdrawal of treatment. Under the first choice, the individual's life is not to be prolonged if the individual has an incurable and irreversible condition that will result in death within a relatively short time, if the individual becomes unconscious and, to a reasonable degree of medical certainty, will not regain consciousness, or if the likely risks and burdens of treatment would outweigh the expected benefits. Under the second choice, the individual's life is to be prolonged within the limits of generally accepted health-care standards. Part 2(7) of the form provides a box for an individual to mark if the individual wishes to receive artificial nutrition and hydration in all circumstances. Part 2(8) of the form provides space for an individual to specify any circumstance when the individual would prefer not to receive pain relief. Because the choices provided in Parts 2(6) to 2(8) do not cover all possible situations, Part 2(9) of the form provides space for the individual to write out his or her own instructions or to supplement the instructions given in the previous subparts of the form. Should the space be insufficient, the individual is free to add additional pages.

The health-care instructions given in Part 2 of the form are binding on the agent, any guardian, any surrogate, and, subject to exceptions specified in Section 7(e)-(f), on the individual's health-care providers. Pursuant to Section 7(d), a health-care provider must also comply with a reasonable interpretation of those instructions made by an authorized agent, guardian, or surrogate.

Part 3 of the form provides the individual an opportunity to express an intention to donate bodily organs and tissues at death. The options provided are derived from a suggested form in the Comment to Section 2 of the Uniform Anatomical Gift Act (1987).

Part 4 of the form provides space for the individual to designate a primary physician should the individual choose to do so. Space is also provided for the designation of an alternate primary physician should the first designated physician not be available, able, or willing to act.

Paragraph (12) of the form conforms with the provisions of Section 12 by providing that a copy of the form has the same effect as the original.

The Act does not require witnessing, but to encourage the practice the form provides space for the signatures of two witnesses.

The form does not require formal acceptance by an agent. Formal acceptance by an agent has been omitted not because it is an undesirable practice but because it would add another stage to executing an advance health-care directive, thereby further reducing the number of individuals who will follow through and create directives. However, practitioners who wish to adapt this form for use by their clients are strongly encouraged to add a formal acceptance. Designated agents have no duty to act until they accept the office either expressly or through their conduct. Consequently, requiring formal acceptance reduces the risk that a designated agent will decline to act when the need arises. Formal acceptance also makes it more likely that the agent will become familiar with the principal's personal values and views on health care. While the form does not require formal acceptance, the explanation to the form does encourage principals to talk to the person they have named as agent to make certain that the designated agent understands their wishes and is willing to take the responsibility.

Section 5. Decisions by Surrogate.

(a) A surrogate may make a health-care decision for a patient who is an adult or emancipated minor if the patient has been determined by the primary physician to lack capacity and no agent or guardian has been appointed or the agent or guardian is not reasonably available.

(b) An adult or emancipated minor may designate any individual to act as surrogate by personally informing the supervising health-care provider. In the absence of a designation, or if the designee is not reasonably available, any member of the following classes of the patient's family who is reasonably available, in descending order of priority, may act as surrogate:

(1) the spouse, unless legally separated;

(2) an adult child;

(3) a parent; or

(4) an adult brother or sister.

(c) If none of the individuals eligible to act as surrogate under subsection (b) is reasonably available, an adult who has exhibited special care and concern for the patient, who is familiar with the patient's personal values, and who is reasonably available may act as surrogate.

(d) A surrogate shall communicate his or her assumption of authority as promptly as practicable to the members of the patient's family specified in subsection (b) who can be readily contacted.

(e) If more than one member of a class assumes authority to act as surrogate, and they do not agree on a health-care decision and the supervising health-care provider is so informed, the supervising health-care provider shall comply with the decision of a majority of the members of that class who have communicated their views to the provider. If the class is evenly divided concerning the health-care decision and the supervising health-care provider is so informed, that class and all individuals having lower priority are disqualified from making the decision.

(f) A surrogate shall make a health-care decision in accordance with the patient's individual instructions, if any, and other wishes to the extent known to the surrogate. Otherwise, the surrogate shall make the decision in accordance with the surrogate's determination of the patient's best interest. In determining the patient's best interest, the surrogate shall consider the patient's personal values to the extent known to the surrogate.

(g) A health-care decision made by a surrogate for a patient is effective without judicial approval.

(h) An individual at any time may disqualify another, including a member of the individual's family, from acting as the individual's surrogate by a signed writing or by personally informing the supervising health-care provider of the disqualification.

(i) Unless related to the patient by blood, marriage, or adoption, a surrogate may not be an owner, operator, or employee of [a residential long-term health-care institution] at which the patient is receiving care.

(j) A supervising health-care provider may require an individual claiming the right to act as surrogate for a patient to provide a written declaration under penalty of perjury stating facts and circumstances reasonably sufficient to establish the claimed authority.

COMMENT

Subsection (a) authorizes a surrogate to make a health-care decision for a patient who is an adult or emancipated minor if the patient lacks capacity to make health-care decisions and if no agent or guardian has been appointed or the agent or guardian is not reasonably available. Health-care decision making for unemancipated minors is not covered by this section. The subject of consent for treatment of minors is a complex one which in many states is covered by a variety of statutes and is therefore left to other state law.

While a designation of an agent in a written power of attorney for health care is preferred, situations may arise where an individual will not be in a position to execute a power of attorney for health care. In that event, subsection (b) affirms the principle of patient autonomy by allowing an individual to designate a surrogate by personally informing the supervising health-care provider. The supervising health-care provider would then, in accordance with Section 7(b), be obligated to promptly record the designation in the individual's health-care record. An oral designation of a surrogate made by a patient directly to the supervising health-care provider revokes a previous designation of an agent. See Section 3(a).

If an individual does not designate a surrogate or if the designee is not reasonably available, subsection (b) applies a default rule for selecting a family member to act as surrogate. Like all default rules, it is not tailored to every situation, but incorporates the presumed desires of a majority of those who find themselves so situated. The relationships specified in subsection (b) include those of the half-blood and by adoption, in addition to those of the whole blood.

Subsection (c) permits a health-care decision to be made by a more distant relative or unrelated adult with whom the individual enjoys a close relationship but only if all family members specified in subsection (b) decline to act or are otherwise not reasonably available. Consequently, those in non-traditional relationships who want to make certain that health-care decisions are made by their companions should execute powers of attorney for health care designating them as agents or, if that has not been done, should designate them as surrogates.

Subsections (b) and (c) permit any member of a class authorized to serve as surrogate to assume authority to act even though there are other members in the class.

Subsection (d) requires a surrogate who assumes authority to act to immediately so notify the members of the patient's family who in given circumstances would be eligible to act as surrogate. Notice to the specified family members will enable them to follow health-care developments with respect to their now incapacitated relative. It will also alert them to take appropriate action, including the appointment of a guardian or the commencement of judicial proceedings under Section 14, should the need arise.

Subsection (e) addresses the situation where more than one member of the same class has assumed authority to act as surrogate and a disagreement over a health-care decision arises of which the supervising health-care provider is informed. Should that occur, the supervising health-care provider must comply with the decision of a majority of the members of that class who have communicated their views to the provider. If the members of the class who have communicated their views to the provider are evenly divided concerning the health-care decision, however, then the entire class is disqualified from making the decision and no individual having lower priority may act as surrogate. When such a deadlock arises, it may be necessary to seek court determination of the issue as authorized by Section 14.

Subsection (f) imposes on surrogates the same standard for health-care decision making as is prescribed for agents in Section 2(e). The surrogate must follow the patient's individual instructions and other expressed wishes to the extent known to the surrogate. To the extent such instructions or other wishes are unknown, the surrogate must act in the patient's best interest. In determining the patient's best interest, the surrogate is to consider the patient's personal values to the extent known to the surrogate.

Subsection (g) provides that a health-care decision made by a surrogate is effective without judicial approval. A similar provision applies to health-care decisions made by agents (Section 2(f)) or guardians (Section 6(c)).

Subsection (h) permits an individual to disqualify any family member or other individual from acting as the individual's surrogate, including disqualification of a surrogate who was orally designated.

Subsection (i) disqualifies an owner, operator, or employee of a residential long-term health-care institution at which a patient is receiving care from acting as the patient's surrogate unless related to the patient by blood, marriage, or adoption. This disqualification is similar to that for appointed agents. See Section 2(b) and Comment.

Subsection (j) permits a supervising health-care provider to require an individual claiming the right to act as surrogate to provide a written declaration under penalty of perjury stating facts and circumstances reasonably sufficient to establish the claimed relationship. The authority to request a declaration is included to permit the provider to obtain evidence of claimed authority. A supervising health-care provider, however, does not have a duty to investigate the qualifications of an individual claiming authority to act as surrogate, and Section 9(a) protects a health-care provider or institution from liability for complying with the decision of such an individual, absent knowledge that the individual does not in fact have such authority.

Section 6. Decisions by Guardian.

(a) A guardian shall comply with the ward's individual instructions and may not revoke the ward's advance health-care directive unless the appointing court expressly so authorizes.

(b) Absent a court order to the contrary, a health-care decision of an agent takes precedence over that of a guardian.

(c) A health-care decision made by a guardian for the ward is effective without judicial approval.

COMMENT

The Act affirms that health-care decisions should whenever possible be made by a person whom the individual selects to do so. For this reason, subsection (b) provides that a health-care decision of an agent takes precedence over that of a guardian absent a court order to the contrary, and subsection (a) provides that a guardian may not revoke the ward's power of attorney for health care unless the appointing court expressly so authorizes. Without these subsections, a guardian would in many states have authority to revoke the ward's power of attorney for health care even though the court appointing the guardian might not be aware that the principal had made such alternate arrangement.

The Act expresses a strong preference for honoring an individual instruction. Under the Act, an individual instruction must be honored by an agent, by a surrogate, and, subject to exceptions specified in Section 7(e)-(f), by an individual's health-care providers. Subsection (a) extends this principle to guardians by requiring that a guardian effectuate the ward's individual instructions. A guardian may revoke the ward's individual instructions only if the appointing court expressly so authorizes.

Courts have no particular expertise with respect to health-care decision making. Moreover, the delay attendant upon seeking court approval may undermine the effectiveness of the decision ultimately made, particularly but not only when the patient's condition is life-threatening and immediate decisions concerning treatment need to be made. Decisions should whenever possible be made by a patient, or the patient's guardian, agent, or surrogate in consultation with the patient's health-care providers without outside interference. For this reason, subsection (c) provides that a health-care decision made by a guardian for the ward is effective without judicial approval, and the Act includes similar provisions for health-care decisions made by agents (Section 2(f)) or surrogates (Section 5(g)).

Section 7. Obligations of Health–Care Provider.

(a) Before implementing a health-care decision made for a patient, a supervising health-care provider, if possible, shall promptly communicate to the patient the decision made and the identity of the person making the decision.

(b) A supervising health-care provider who knows of the existence of an advance health-care directive, a revocation of an advance health-care directive, or a designation or disqualification of a surrogate, shall promptly record its existence in the patient's health-care record and, if it is in writing, shall request a copy and if one is furnished shall arrange for its maintenance in the health-care record.

(c) A primary physician who makes or is informed of a determination that a patient lacks or has recovered capacity, or that another condition exists which affects an individual instruction or the authority of an agent, guardian, or surrogate, shall promptly record the determination in the patient's health-care record and communicate the determination to the patient, if possible, and to any person then authorized to make health-care decisions for the patient.

(d) Except as provided in subsections (e) and (f), a health-care provider or institution providing care to a patient shall:

(1) comply with an individual instruction of the patient and with a reasonable interpretation of that instruction made by a person then authorized to make health-care decisions for the patient; and

(2) comply with a health-care decision for the patient made by a person then authorized to make health-care decisions for the patient to the same extent as if the decision had been made by the patient while having capacity.

(e) A health-care provider may decline to comply with an individual instruction or health-care decision for reasons of conscience. A health-care institution may decline to comply with an individual instruction or health-care decision if the instruction or decision is contrary to a policy of the institution which is expressly based on reasons of conscience and if the policy was timely communicated to the patient or to a person then authorized to make health-care decisions for the patient.

(f) A health-care provider or institution may decline to comply with an individual instruction or health-care decision that requires medically ineffective health care or health care contrary to generally accepted health-care standards applicable to the health-care provider or institution.

(g) A health-care provider or institution that declines to comply with an individual instruction or health-care decision shall:

(1) promptly so inform the patient, if possible, and any person then authorized to make health-care decisions for the patient;

(2) provide continuing care to the patient until a transfer can be effected; and

(3) unless the patient or person then authorized to make health-care decisions for the patient refuses assistance, immediately make all reasonable efforts to assist in the transfer of the patient to another health-care provider or institution that is willing to comply with the instruction or decision.

(h) A health-care provider or institution may not require or prohibit the execution or revocation of an advance health-care directive as a condition for providing health care.

COMMENT

Subsection (a) further reinforces the Act's respect for patient autonomy by requiring a supervising health-care provider, if possible, to promptly communicate to a patient, prior to implementation, a health-care decision made for the patient and the identity of the person making the decision.

The recording requirement in subsection (b) reduces the risk that a health-care provider or institution, or agent, guardian or surrogate, will rely on an outdated individual instruction or the decision of an individual whose authority has been revoked.

Subsection (c) imposes recording and communication requirements relating to determinations that may trigger the authority of an agent, guardian or surrogate to make health-care decisions on an individual's behalf. The determinations covered by these requirements are those specified in Sections 2(c)-(d) and 5(a).

Subsection (d) requires health-care providers and institutions to comply with a patient's individual instruction and with a reasonable interpretation of that instruction made by a person then authorized to make health-care decisions for the patient. A health-care provider or institution must also comply with a health-care decision made by a person then authorized to make health-care decisions for the patient to the same extent as if the decision had been made by the patient while having capacity. These requirements help to protect the patient's rights to autonomy and self-determination and validate and seek to effectuate the substitute decision making authorized by the Act.

Not all instructions or decisions must be honored, however. Subsection (e) authorizes a health-care provider to decline to comply with an individual instruction or health-care decision for reasons of conscience. Subsection (e) also allows a health-care institution to decline to comply with a health-care instruction or decision if the instruction or decision is contrary to a policy of the institution which is expressly based on reasons of conscience and if the policy was timely communicated to the patient or to an individual then authorized to make health-care decisions for the patient.

Subsection (f) further authorizes a health-care provider or institution to decline to comply with an instruction or decision that requires the provision of care which would be medically ineffective or contrary to generally accepted health-care standards applicable to the provider or institution. "Medically ineffective health care", as used in this section, means treatment which would not offer the patient any significant benefit.

Subsection (g) requires a health-care provider or institution that declines to comply with an individual instruction or health-care decision to promptly communicate the refusal to the patient, if possible, and to any person then authorized to make health-care decisions for the patient. The provider or institution also must provide continuing care to the patient until a transfer can be effected. In addition, unless the patient or person then authorized to make health-care decisions for the patient refuses assistance, the health-care provider or institution must immediately make all reasonable efforts to assist in the transfer of the patient to another health-care provider or institution that is willing to comply with the instruction or decision.

Subsection (h), forbidding a health-care provider or institution to condition provision of health care on execution, non-execution, or revocation of an advance health-care directive, tracks the provisions of the federal Patient Self–Determination Act (42 U.S.C. § 1395cc(f)(1) (C) (Medicare); 42 U.S.C. § 1396a (w)(1)(C) (Medicaid)).

Section 8. Health–Care Information.

Unless otherwise specified in an advance health-care directive, a person then authorized to make health-care decisions for a patient has the same rights as the patient to request, receive, examine, copy, and consent to the disclosure of medical or any other health-care information.

COMMENT

An agent, guardian, or surrogate stands in the shoes of the patient when making health-care decisions. To assure fully informed decision making, this section provides that a person who is then authorized to make health-care decisions for a patient has the same right of access to health-care information as does the patient unless otherwise specified in the patient's advance health-care directive.

Section 9. Immunities.

(a) A health-care provider or institution acting in good faith and in accordance with generally accepted health-care standards applicable to the health-care provider or institution is not subject to civil or criminal liability or to discipline for unprofessional conduct for:

(1) complying with a health-care decision of a person apparently having authority to make a health-care decision for a patient, including a decision to withhold or withdraw health care;

(2) declining to comply with a health-care decision of a person based on a belief that the person then lacked authority; or

(3) complying with an advance health-care directive and assuming that the directive was valid when made and has not been revoked or terminated.

(b) An individual acting as agent or surrogate under this [Act] is not subject to civil or criminal liability or to discipline for unprofessional conduct for health-care decisions made in good faith.

COMMENT

The section grants broad protection from liability for actions taken in good faith. Subsection (a) permits a health-care provider or institution to comply with a health-care decision made by a person appearing to have authority to make health-care decisions for a patient; to decline to comply with a health-care decision made by a person believed to be without authority; and to assume the validity of and to comply with an advance health-care directive. Absent bad faith or actions taken that are not in accord with generally accepted health-care standards, a health-care provider or institution has no duty to investigate a claim of authority or the validity of an advance health-care directive.

Subsection (b) protects agents and surrogates acting in good faith from liability for making a health-care decision for a patient. Also protected from liability are individuals who mistakenly but in good faith believe they have the authority to make a health-care decision for a patient. For example, an individual who has been designated as agent in a power of attorney for health care might assume authority unaware that the power has been revoked. Or a family member might assume authority to act as surrogate unaware that a family member having a higher priority was reasonably available and authorized to act.

Section 10. Statutory Damages.

(a) A health-care provider or institution that intentionally violates this [Act] is subject to liability to the aggrieved individual for damages of $[500] or actual damages resulting from the violation, whichever is greater, plus reasonable attorney's fees.

(b) A person who intentionally falsifies, forges, conceals, defaces, or obliterates an individual's advance health-care directive or a revocation of an advance health-care directive without the individual's consent, or who coerces or fraudulently induces an individual to give, revoke, or not to give an advance health-care directive, is subject to liability to that individual for damages of $[2,500] or actual damages resulting from the action, whichever is greater, plus reasonable attorney's fees.

COMMENT

Conduct which intentionally violates the Act and which interferes with an individual's autonomy to make health-care decisions, either personally or through others as provided under the Act, is subject to civil damages rather than criminal penalties out of a recognition that prosecutions are unlikely to occur. The legislature of an enacting state will have to determine the amount of damages which needs to be authorized in order to encourage the level of potential private enforcement actions necessary to effect compliance with the obligations and responsibilities imposed by the Act. The damages provided by this section do not supersede but are in addition to remedies available under other law.

Section 11. Capacity.

(a) This [Act] does not affect the right of an individual to make health-care decisions while having capacity to do so.

(b) An individual is presumed to have capacity to make a health-care decision, to give or revoke an advance health-care directive, and to designate or disqualify a surrogate.

COMMENT

This section reinforces the principle of patient autonomy by providing a rebuttable presumption that an individual has capacity for all decisions relating to health care referred to in the Act.

Section 12. Effect of Copy.

A copy of a written advance health-care directive, revocation of an advance health-care directive, or designation or disqualification of a surrogate has the same effect as the original.

COMMENT

The need to rely on an advance health-care directive may arise at times when the original is inaccessible. For example, an individual may be receiving care from several health-care providers or may be receiving care at a location distant from that where the original is kept. To facilitate prompt and informed decision making, this section provides that a copy of a valid written advance health-care directive, revocation of an advance health-care directive, or designation

or disqualification of a surrogate
has the same effect as the original.

Section 13. Effect of [Act].

(a) This [Act] does not create a presumption concerning the intention of an individual who has not made or who has revoked an advance health-care directive.

(b) Death resulting from the withholding or withdrawal of health care in accordance with this [Act] does not for any purpose constitute a suicide or homicide or legally impair or invalidate a policy of insurance or an annuity providing a death benefit, notwithstanding any term of the policy or annuity to the contrary.

(c) This [Act] does not authorize mercy killing, assisted suicide, euthanasia, or the provision, withholding, or withdrawal of health care, to the extent prohibited by other statutes of this State.

(d) This [Act] does not authorize or require a health-care provider or institution to provide health care contrary to generally accepted health-care standards applicable to the health-care provider or institution.

[(e) This [Act] does not authorize an agent or surrogate to consent to the admission of an individual to a mental health-care institution unless the individual's written advance health-care directive expressly so provides.]

[(f) This [Act] does not affect other statutes of this State governing treatment for mental illness of an individual involuntarily committed to a [mental health-care institution under appropriate statute].]

COMMENT

Subsection (e) is included to accommodate the legislature of an enacting jurisdiction that wishes to address in this Act rather than by separate statute the authority of an agent or surrogate to consent to the admission of an individual to a mental health-care institution. In recognition of the principle of patient autonomy, however, an individual may authorize an agent or surrogate to consent to an admission to a mental health-care institution but may do so only by express provision in an advance health-care directive. Subsection (e) does not address the authority of a guardian to consent to an admission, leaving that matter to be decided under state guardianship law.

All states surround the involuntary commitment process with procedural safeguards. Moreover, state mental health codes contain detailed provisions relating to the treatment of individuals subject to commitment. Subsection (f) is included in the event that the legislature of an enacting jurisdiction wishes to clarify that a general health-care statute such as this Act is intended to supplement and not supersede these more detailed provisions.

Section 14. Judicial Relief.

On petition of a patient, the patient's agent, guardian, or surrogate, a health-care provider or institution involved with the patient's care, or an individual described in Section 5(b) or (c), the [appropriate] court may enjoin or direct a health-care decision or order other equitable relief. A proceeding under this section is governed by [here insert appropriate reference to the rules of procedure or statutory provisions governing expedited proceedings and proceedings affecting incapacitated persons].

COMMENT

While the provisions of the Act are in general to be effectuated without litigation, situations will arise where judicial proceedings may be appropriate. For example, the members of a class of surrogates authorized to act under Section 5 may be evenly divided with respect to the advisability of a particular health-care decision. In that circumstance, authorization to proceed may have to be obtained from a court. Examples of other legitimate issues that may from time to time arise include whether an agent or surrogate has authority to act and whether an agent or surrogate has complied with the standard of care imposed by Sections 2(e) and 5(f).

This section has a limited scope. The court under this section may grant only equitable relief. Other adequate avenues exist for those who wish to pursue money dam-

ages. The class of potential petitioners is also limited to those with a direct interest in a patient's health care.

The final portion of this section has been placed in brackets in recognition of the fact that states vary widely in the extent to which they codify procedural matters in a substantive act. The legislature of an enacting jurisdiction is encouraged, however, to cross-reference to its rules on expedited proceedings or rules on proceedings affecting incapacitated persons. The legislature of an enacting jurisdiction which wishes to include a detailed procedural provision in its adoption of the Act may want to consult Guidelines for State Court Decision Making in Life–Sustaining Medical Treatment Cases (2d ed. 1992), published by the National Center for State Courts.

Section 15. Uniformity of Application and Construction.

This [Act] shall be applied and construed to effectuate its general purpose to make uniform the law with respect to the subject matter of this [Act] among States enacting it.

Section 16. Short Title.

This [Act] may be cited as the Uniform Health–Care Decisions Act.

Section 17. Severability Clause.

If any provision of this [Act] or its application to any person or circumstance is held invalid, the invalidity does not affect other provisions or applications of this [Act] which can be given effect without the invalid provision or application, and to this end the provisions of this [Act] are severable.

Section 18. Effective Date.

This [Act] takes effect on _____.

Section 19. Repeal.

The following acts and parts of acts are repealed:

(1)

(2)

(3)

UNIFORM PRUDENT INVESTOR ACT

Table of Sections

PREFATORY NOTE

Over the quarter century from the late 1960's the investment practices of fiduciaries experienced significant change. The Uniform Prudent Investor Act (UPIA) undertakes to update trust investment law in recognition of the alterations that have occurred in investment practice. These changes have occurred under the influence of a large and broadly accepted body of empirical and theoretical knowledge about the behavior of capital markets, often described as "modern portfolio theory."

This Act draws upon the revised standards for prudent trust investment promulgated by the American Law Institute in its Restatement (Third) of Trusts: Prudent Investor Rule (1992) [hereinafter Restatement of Trusts 3d: Prudent Investor Rule; also referred to as 1992 Restatement].

Objectives of the Act. UPIA makes five fundamental alterations in the former criteria for prudent investing. All are to be found in the Restatement of Trusts 3d: Prudent Investor Rule.

(1) The standard of prudence is applied to any investment as part of the total portfolio, rather than to individual investments.

866

In the trust setting the term "portfolio" embraces all the trust's assets. UPIA § 2(b).

(2) The tradeoff in all investing between risk and return is identified as the fiduciary's central consideration. UPIA § 2(b).

(3) All categoric restrictions on types of investments have been abrogated; the trustee can invest in anything that plays an appropriate role in achieving the risk/return objectives of the trust and that meets the other requirements of prudent investing. UPIA § 2(e).

(4) The long familiar requirement that fiduciaries diversify their investments has been integrated into the definition of prudent investing. UPIA § 3.

(5) The much criticized former rule of trust law forbidding the trustee to delegate investment and management functions has been reversed. Delegation is now permitted, subject to safeguards. UPIA § 9.

Literature. These changes in trust investment law have been presaged in an extensive body of practical and scholarly writing. See especially the discussion and reporter's notes by Edward C. Halbach, Jr., in Restatement of Trusts 3d: Prudent Investor Rule (1992); see also Edward C. Halbach, Jr., Trust Investment Law in the Third Restatement, 27 Real Property, Probate & Trust J. 407 (1992); Bevis Longstreth, Modern Investment Management and the Prudent Man Rule (1986); Jeffrey N. Gordon, The Puzzling Persistence of the Constrained Prudent Man Rule, 62 N.Y.U.L. Rev. 52 (1987); John H. Langbein & Richard A. Posner, The Revolution in Trust Investment Law, 62 A.B.A.J. 887 (1976); Note, The Regulation of Risky Investments, 83 Harvard L. Rev. 603 (1970). A succinct account of the main findings of modern portfolio theory, written for lawyers, is Jonathan R. Macey, An Introduction to Modern Financial Theory (1991) (American College of Trust & Estate Counsel Foundation). A leading introductory text on modern portfolio theory is R.A. Brealey, An Introduction to Risk and Return from Common Stocks (2d ed. 1983).

Legislation. Most states have legislation governing trust-investment law. This Act promotes uniformity of state law on the basis of the new consensus reflected in the Restatement of Trusts 3d: Prudent Investor Rule. Some states have already acted. California, Delaware, Georgia, Minnesota, Tennessee, and Washington revised their prudent investor legislation to emphasize the total-portfolio standard of care in advance of the 1992 Restatement. These statutes are extracted and discussed in Restatement of

Trusts 3d: Prudent Investor Rule § 227, reporter's note, at 60–66 (1992).

Drafters in Illinois in 1991 worked from the April 1990 "Proposed Final Draft" of the Restatement of Trusts 3d: Prudent Investor Rule and enacted legislation that is closely modeled on the new Restatement. 760 ILCS § 5/5 (prudent investing); and § 5/5.1 (delegation) (1992). As the Comments to this Uniform Prudent Investor Act reflect, the Act draws upon the Illinois statute in several sections. Virginia revised its prudent investor act in a similar vein in 1992. Virginia Code § 26–45.1 (prudent investing) (1992). Florida revised its statute in 1993. Florida Laws, ch. 93–257, amending Florida Statutes § 518.11 (prudent investing) and creating § 518.112 (delegation). New York legislation drawing on the new Restatement and on a preliminary version of this Uniform Prudent Investor Act was enacted in 1994. N.Y. Assembly Bill 11683–B, Ch. 609 (1994), adding Estates, Powers and Trusts Law § 11–2.3 (Prudent Investor Act).

Remedies. This Act does not undertake to address issues of remedy law or the computation of damages in trust matters. Remedies are the subject of a reasonably distinct body of doctrine. See generally Restatement (Second) of Trusts §§ 197–226A (1959) [hereinafter cited as Restatement of Trusts 2d; also referred to as 1959 Restatement].

Implications for charitable and pension trusts. This Act is centrally concerned with the investment responsibilities arising under the private gratuitous trust, which is the common vehicle for conditioned wealth transfer within the family. Nevertheless, the prudent investor rule also bears on charitable and pension trusts, among others. "In making investments of trust funds the trustee of a charitable trust is under a duty similar to that of the trustee of a private trust." Restatement of Trusts 2d § 389 (1959). The Employee Retirement Income Security Act (ERISA), the federal regulatory scheme for pension trusts enacted in 1974, absorbs trust-investment law through the prudence standard of ERISA § 404(a)(1)(B), 29 U.S.C. § 1104(a). The Supreme Court has said: "ERISA's legislative history confirms that the Act's fiduciary responsibility provisions 'codif[y] and mak[e] applicable to [ERISA] fiduciaries certain principles developed in the evolution of the law of trusts.'" *Firestone Tire & Rubber Co. v. Bruch*, 489 U.S. 101, 110–11 (1989) (footnote omitted).

Other fiduciary relationships. The Uniform Prudent Investor Act regulates the investment responsibilities of trustees. Other fiduciaries—such as executors, conservators, and guardians of the property—sometimes have responsibilities over assets that are governed by the standards of prudent investment. It will often be appropriate for states to adapt the law governing investment by trustees under this Act to these other fiduciary regimes, taking account of such changed circumstances as the relatively short duration of most executorships and the intensity of court supervision of conservators and guardians in some jurisdictions. The present Act does not undertake to adjust trust-investment law to the special circumstances of the state schemes for administering decedents' estates or conducting the affairs of protected persons.

Although the Uniform Prudent Investor Act by its terms applies to trusts and not to charitable corporations, the standards of the Act can be expected to inform the investment responsibilities of directors and officers of charitable corporations. As the 1992 Restatement observes, "the duties of the members of the governing board of a charitable corporation are generally similar to the duties of the trustee of a charitable trust." Restatement of Trusts 3d: Prudent Investor Rule § 379, Comment *b*, at 190 (1992). See also id. § 389, Comment *b*, at 190–91 (absent contrary statute or other provision, prudent investor rule applies to investment of funds held for charitable corporations).

Section 1. Prudent Investor Rule.

(a) Except as otherwise provided in subsection (b), a trustee who invests and manages trust assets owes a duty to the beneficiaries of the trust to comply with the prudent investor rule set forth in this [Act].

(b) The prudent investor rule, a default rule, may be expanded, restricted, eliminated, or otherwise altered by the provisions of a trust. A trustee is not liable to a beneficiary to the extent that the trustee acted in reasonable reliance on the provisions of the trust.

COMMENT

This section imposes the obligation of prudence in the conduct of investment functions and identifies further sections of the Act that specify the attributes of prudent conduct.

Origins. The prudence standard for trust investing traces back to *Harvard College v. Amory*, 26 Mass. (9 Pick.) 446 (1830). Trustees should "observe how men of prudence, discretion and intelligence manage their own affairs, not in regard to speculation, but in regard to the permanent disposition of their funds, considering the probable income, as well as the probable safety of the capital to be invested." Id. at 461.

Prior legislation. The Model Prudent Man Rule Statute (1942), sponsored by the American Bankers Association, undertook to codify the language of the *Amory* case. See Mayo A. Shattuck, The Development of the Prudent Man Rule for Fiduciary Investment in the United States in the Twentieth Century, 12 Ohio State L.J. 491, at 501 (1951); for the text of the model act, which inspired many state statutes, see id. at 508–09. Another prominent codification of the *Amory* standard is Uniform Probate Code § 7–302 (1969), which provides that "the trustee shall observe the standards in dealing with the trust assets that would be observed by a prudent man dealing with the property of another...."

Congress has imposed a comparable prudence standard for the administration of pension and employee benefit trusts in the Employee Retirement Income Security Act (ERISA), enacted in 1974. ERISA § 404(a)(1)(B), 29 U.S.C. § 1104(a), provides that "a fiduciary shall discharge his duties with respect to a plan solely in the interest of the participants and beneficiaries and ... with the care, skill, prudence, and diligence under the circumstances then prevailing that a prudent man acting in a like capacity and familiar with such matters would use in the conduct of an enterprise of like character and with like aims...."

Prior Restatement. The Restatement of Trusts 2d (1959) also tracked the language of the *Amory* case: "In making investments of trust funds the trustee is under a duty to the beneficiary ... to make such investments and only such investments as a prudent man would make of his own property having in view the preservation of the estate and the amount and regularity of the income to be derived...." Restatement of Trusts 2d § 227 (1959).

Objective standard. The concept of prudence in the judicial opinions and legislation is essentially relational or comparative. It resembles in this respect the "reasonable person" rule of tort law. A prudent trustee behaves as other trustees similarly situated would behave. The standard is, therefore, objective rather than subjective. Sections 2 through 9 of this Act identify the main factors that bear on prudent investment behavior.

Variation. Almost all of the rules of trust law are default rules, that is, rules that the settlor may alter or abrogate. Subsection (b) carries forward this traditional attribute of trust law. Traditional trust law also allows the beneficiaries of the trust to excuse its performance, when they are all capable and not misinformed. Restatement of Trusts 2d § 216 (1959).

Section 2. Standard of Care; Portfolio Strategy; Risk and Return Objectives.

(a) A trustee shall invest and manage trust assets as a prudent investor would, by considering the purposes, terms, distribution requirements, and other circumstances of the trust. In satisfying this standard, the trustee shall exercise reasonable care, skill, and caution.

(b) A trustee's investment and management decisions respecting individual assets must be evaluated not in isolation but in the context of the trust portfolio as a whole and as a part of an overall investment strategy having risk and return objectives reasonably suited to the trust.

(c) Among circumstances that a trustee shall consider in investing and managing trust assets are such of the following as are relevant to the trust or its beneficiaries:

(1) general economic conditions;

(2) the possible effect of inflation or deflation;

(3) the expected tax consequences of investment decisions or strategies;

(4) the role that each investment or course of action plays within the overall trust portfolio, which may include financial assets, interests in closely held enterprises, tangible and intangible personal property, and real property;

(5) the expected total return from income and the appreciation of capital;

(6) other resources of the beneficiaries;

(7) needs for liquidity, regularity of income, and preservation or appreciation of capital; and

(8) an asset's special relationship or special value, if any, to the purposes of the trust or to one or more of the beneficiaries.

(d) A trustee shall make a reasonable effort to verify facts relevant to the investment and management of trust assets.

(e) A trustee may invest in any kind of property or type of investment consistent with the standards of this [Act].

(f) A trustee who has special skills or expertise, or is named trustee in reliance upon the trustee's representation that the trustee has special skills or expertise, has a duty to use those special skills or expertise.

COMMENT

Section 2 is the heart of the Act. Subsections (a), (b), and (c) are patterned loosely on the language of the Restatement of Trusts 3d: Prudent Investor Rule § 227 (1992), and on the 1991 Illinois statute, 760 § ILCS 5/5a (1992). Subsection (f) is derived from Uniform Probate Code § 7–302 (1969).

Objective standard. Subsection (a) of this Act carries forward the relational and objective standard made familiar in the *Amory* case, in earlier prudent investor legislation, and in the Restatements. Early formulations of the prudent person rule were sometimes troubled by the effort to distinguish between the standard of a prudent person investing for another and investing on his or her own account. The language of subsection (a), by relating the trustee's duty to "the purposes, terms, distribution requirements, and other circumstances of the trust," should put such questions to rest. The standard is the standard of the prudent investor similarly situated.

Portfolio standard. Subsection (b) emphasizes the consolidated portfolio standard for evaluating investment decisions. An investment that might be imprudent standing alone can become prudent if undertaken in sensible relation to other trust assets, or to other nontrust assets. In the trust setting the term "portfolio" embraces the entire trust estate.

Risk and return. Subsection (b) also sounds the main theme of modern investment practice, sensitivity to the risk/return curve. See generally the works cited in the Prefatory Note to this Act, under "Literature." Returns correlate strongly with risk, but tolerance for risk varies greatly with the financial and other circumstances of the investor, or in the case of a trust, with the purposes of the trust and the relevant circumstances of the beneficiaries. A trust whose main purpose is to support an elderly widow of modest means will have a lower risk tolerance than a trust to accumulate for a young scion of great wealth.

Subsection (b) of this Act follows Restatement of Trusts 3d: Prudent Investor Rule § 227(a), which provides that the standard of prudent investing "requires the exercise of reasonable care, skill, and caution, and is to be applied to investments not in isolation but in the context of the trust portfolio and as a part of an overall investment strategy, which should incorporate risk and return objectives reasonably suitable to the trust."

Factors affecting investment. Subsection (c) points to certain of the factors that commonly bear on risk/return preferences in fiduciary investing. This listing is nonexclusive. Tax considerations, such as preserving the stepped up basis on death under Internal Revenue Code § 1014 for low-basis assets, have traditionally been exceptionally important in estate planning for affluent persons. Under the present recognition rules of the federal income tax, taxable investors, including trust beneficiaries, are in general best served by an investment strategy that minimizes the taxation incident to portfolio turnover. See generally Robert H. Jeffrey & Robert D. Arnott, Is Your Alpha Big Enough to Cover Its Taxes?, Journal of Portfolio Management 15 (Spring 1993).

Another familiar example of how tax considerations bear upon trust investing: In a regime of pass-through taxation, it may be prudent for the trust to buy lower yielding tax-exempt securities for high-bracket taxpayers, whereas it would ordinarily be imprudent for the trustees of a charitable trust, whose income is tax exempt, to accept the lowered yields associated with tax-exempt securities.

When tax considerations affect beneficiaries differently, the trustee's duty of impartiality requires attention to the competing interests of each of them.

Subsection (c)(8), allowing the trustee to take into account any preferences of the beneficiaries respecting heirlooms or other prized assets, derives from the Illinois act, 760 ILCS § 5/5(a)(4) (1992).

Duty to monitor. Subsections (a) through (d) apply both to investing and managing trust assets. "Managing" embraces monitoring, that is, the trustee's continuing responsibility for oversight of the suitability of investments already made as well as the trustee's decisions respecting new investments.

Duty to investigate. Subsection (d) carries forward the traditional responsibility of the fiduciary investor to examine information likely to bear importantly on the value or the security of an investment—for example, audit reports or records of title. E.g., *Estate of Collins*, 72 Cal.App.3d 663, 139 Cal. Rptr. 644 (1977) (trustees lent on a junior mortgage on unimproved real estate, failed to have land appraised, and accepted an unaudited financial statement; held liable for losses).

Abrogating categoric restrictions. Subsection 2(e) clarifies that no particular kind of property or type of investment is inherently imprudent. Traditional trust law was encumbered with a variety of categoric exclusions, such as prohibitions on junior mortgages or new ventures. In some states legislation created so-called "legal lists" of approved trust investments. The universe of investment products changes incessantly. Investments that were at one time thought too risky, such as equities, or more recently, futures, are now used in fi-

duciary portfolios. By contrast, the investment that was at one time thought ideal for trusts, the long-term bond, has been discovered to import a level of risk and volatility—in this case, inflation risk—that had not been anticipated. Accordingly, section 2(e) of this Act follows Restatement of Trusts 3d: Prudent Investor Rule in abrogating categoric restrictions. The Restatement says: "Specific investments or techniques are not per se prudent or imprudent. The riskiness of a specific property, and thus the propriety of its inclusion in the trust estate, is not judged in the abstract but in terms of its anticipated effect on the particular trust's portfolio." Restatement of Trusts 3d: Prudent Investor Rule § 227, Comment *f*, at 24 (1992). The premise of subsection 2(e) is that trust beneficiaries are better protected by the Act's emphasis on close attention to risk/return objectives as prescribed in subsection 2(b) than in attempts to identify categories of investment that are per se prudent or imprudent.

The Act impliedly disavows the emphasis in older law on avoiding "speculative" or "risky" investments. Low levels of risk may be appropriate in some trust settings but inappropriate in others. It is the trustee's task to invest at a risk level that is suitable to the purposes of the trust.

The abolition of categoric restrictions against types of investment in no way alters the trustee's conventional duty of loyalty, which is reiterated for the purposes of this Act in Section 5. For example, were the trustee to invest in a second mortgage on a piece of real property owned by the trustee, the investment would be wrongful on account of the trustee's breach of the duty to abstain from self-dealing, even though the investment would no longer automatically offend the former categoric restriction against fiduciary investments in junior mortgages.

Professional fiduciaries. The distinction taken in subsection (f) between amateur and professional trustees is familiar law. The prudent investor standard applies to a range of fiduciaries, from the most sophisticated professional investment management firms and corporate fiduciaries, to family members of minimal experience. Because the standard of prudence is relational, it follows that the standard for professional trustees is the standard of prudent professionals; for amateurs, it is the standard of prudent amateurs. Restatement of Trusts 2d § 174 (1959) provides: "The trustee is under a duty to the beneficiary in administering the trust to exercise such care and skill as a man of ordinary prudence would exercise in dealing with his own property; and if the trustee has or procures his appointment as trustee by representing that he has greater skill than that of a man of ordinary prudence, he is under a duty to exercise such skill." Case law strongly supports the concept of the higher standard of care for the trustee representing itself to be expert or professional. See Annot., Standard of Care Required of Trustee Representing Itself to Have Expert Knowledge or Skill, 91 A.L.R. 3d 904 (1979) & 1992 Supp. at 48–49.

The Drafting Committee declined the suggestion that the Act should create an exception to the prudent investor rule (or to the diversification requirement of Section 3) in the case of smaller trusts. The Committee believes that subsections (b) and (c) of the Act emphasize factors that are sensitive to the traits of small trusts; and that subsection (f) adjusts helpfully for the distinction between professional and amateur trusteeship. Furthermore, it is always open to the settlor of a trust under Section 1(b) of the Act to reduce the trustee's standard of care if the settlor deems such a step appropriate. The official comments to the 1992 Restatement observe that pooled investments, such as mutual funds and bank common trust funds, are especially suitable for small trusts. Restatement of Trusts 3d: Prudent Investor Rule § 227, Comments h, m, at 28, 51; reporter's note to Comment g, id. at 83.

Matters of proof. Although virtually all express trusts are created by written instrument, oral trusts are known, and accordingly, this Act presupposes no formal requirement that trust terms be in writing. When there is a written trust instrument, modern authority strongly favors allowing evidence extrinsic to the instrument to be consulted for the purpose of ascertaining the settlor's intent. See Uniform Probate Code § 2–601 (1990), Comment; Restatement (Third) of Property: Donative Transfers (Preliminary Draft No. 2, ch. 11, Sept. 11, 1992).

Section 3. Diversification.

A trustee shall diversify the investments of the trust unless the trustee reasonably determines that, because of special circumstances, the purposes of the trust are better served without diversifying.

COMMENT

The language of this section derives from Restatement of Trusts 2d § 228 (1959). ERISA insists upon a comparable rule for pension trusts. ERISA § 404(a)(1)(C), 29 U.S.C. § 1104(a)(1)(C). Case law overwhelmingly supports the duty to diversify. See Annot., Duty of Trustee to Diversify Investments, and Liability for Failure to Do So, 24 A.L.R. 3d 730 (1969) & 1992 Supp. at 78–79.

The 1992 Restatement of Trusts takes the significant step of integrating the diversification requirement into the concept of prudent investing. Section 227(b) of the 1992 Restatement treats diversification as one of the fundamental elements of prudent investing, replacing the separate section 228 of the Restatement of Trusts 2d. The message of the 1992 Restatement, carried forward in Section 3 of this Act, is that prudent investing ordinarily requires diversification.

Circumstances can however, overcome the duty to diversify. For example, if a tax-sensitive trust owns an underdiversified block of low-basis securities, the tax costs of recognizing the gain may outweigh the advantages of diversifying the holding. The wish to retain a family business is another situation in which the purposes of the trust sometimes override the conventional duty to diversify.

Rationale for diversification. "Diversification reduces risk ... [because] stock price movements are not uniform. They are imperfectly correlated. This means that if one holds a well diversified portfolio, the gains in one investment will cancel out the losses in another." Jonathan R. Macey, An Introduction to Modern Financial Theory 20 (American College of Trust and Estate Counsel Foundation, 1991). For example, during the Arab oil embargo of 1973, international oil stocks suffered declines, but the shares of domestic oil producers and coal companies benefitted. Holding a broad enough portfolio allowed the investor to set off, to some extent, the losses associated with the embargo.

Modern portfolio theory divides risk into the categories of "compensated" and "uncompensated" risk. The risk of owning shares in a mature and well-managed company in a settled industry is less than the risk of owning shares in a start-up high-technology venture. The investor requires a higher expected return to induce the investor to bear the greater risk of disappointment associated with the start-up firm. This is compensated risk—the firm pays the investor for bearing the risk. By contrast, nobody pays the investor for owning too few stocks. The investor who owned only international oils in 1973 was running a risk that could have been reduced by having configured the portfolio differently—to include investments in different industries. This is uncompensated risk—nobody pays the investor for owning shares in too few industries and too few companies. Risk that can be eliminated by adding different stocks (or bonds) is uncompensated risk. The object of diversification is to minimize this uncompensated risk of having too few investments. "As long as stock prices do not move exactly together, the risk of a diversified portfolio will be less than the average risk of the separate holdings." R.A. Brealey, An Introduction to Risk and Return from Common Stocks 103 (2d ed. 1983).

There is no automatic rule for identifying how much diversification is enough. The 1992 Restatement says: "Significant diversification advantages can be achieved with a small number of well-selected securities representing different industries.... Broader diversification is usually to be preferred in trust investing," and pooled investment vehicles "make thorough diversification practical for most trustees." Restatement of Trusts 3d: Prudent Investor Rule § 227, General Note on Comments *e-h*, at 77 (1992). See also Macey, supra, at 23–24; Brealey, supra, at 111–13.

Diversifying by pooling. It is difficult for a small trust fund to diversify thoroughly by constructing its own portfolio of individually selected investments. Transaction costs such as the round-lot (100 share) trading economies make it relatively expensive for a small investor to assemble a broad enough portfolio to minimize uncompensated risk. For this reason, pooled investment vehicles have become the main mechanism for facilitating di-versification for the investment needs of smaller trusts.

Most states have legislation authorizing common trust funds; see 3 Austin W. Scott & William F. Fratcher, The Law of Trusts § 227.9, at 463–65 n.26 (4th ed. 1988) (collecting citations to state statutes). As of 1992, 35 states and the District of Columbia had enacted the Uniform Common Trust Fund Act (UCTFA) (1938), overcoming the rule against commingling trust assets and expressly enabling banks and trust companies to establish common trust funds. 7 Uniform Laws Ann. 1992 Supp. at 130 (schedule of adopting states). The Prefatory Note to the UCTFA explains: "The purposes of such a common or joint investment fund are to diversify the investment of the several trusts and thus spread the risk of loss, and to make it easy to invest any amount of trust funds quickly and with a small amount of trouble." 7 Uniform Laws Ann. 402 (1985).

Fiduciary investing in mutual funds. Trusts can also achieve diversification by investing in mutual funds. See Restatement of Trusts 3d: Prudent Investor Rule, § 227, Comment *m*, at 99–100 (1992) (endorsing trust investment in mutual funds). ERISA § 401(b)(1), 29 U.S.C. § 1101(b)(1), expressly authorizes pension trusts to invest in mutual funds, identified as securities "issued by an investment company registered under the Investment Company Act of 1940 . . . .".

Section 4.   Duties at Inception of Trusteeship.

Within a reasonable time after accepting a trusteeship or receiving trust assets, a trustee shall review the trust assets and make and implement decisions concerning the retention and disposition of assets, in order to bring the trust portfolio into compliance with the purposes, terms, distribution requirements, and other circumstances of the trust, and with the requirements of this [Act].

COMMENT

Section 4, requiring the trustee to dispose of unsuitable assets within a reasonable time, is old law, codified in Restatement of Trusts 3d: Prudent Investor Rule § 229 (1992), lightly revising Restatement of Trusts 2d § 230 (1959). The duty extends as well to investments that were proper when purchased but subsequently become improper. Restatement of Trusts 2d § 231 (1959). The same standards apply to successor trustees, see Restatement of Trusts 2d § 196 (1959).

The question of what period of time is reasonable turns on the totality of factors affecting the asset and the trust. The 1959 Restatement took the view that "[o]rdinarily any time within a year is reasonable, but under some circumstances a year may be too long a time and under other circumstances a trustee is not liable although he fails to effect the conversion for more than a year." Restatement of Trusts 2d § 230, comment *b* (1959). The 1992 Restatement retreated from this rule of thumb, saying, "No positive rule can be stated with respect to what constitutes a reasonable time for the sale or exchange of securities." Restatement of Trusts 3d: Prudent Investor Rule § 229, comment *b* (1992).

The criteria and circumstances identified in Section 2 of this Act as bearing upon the prudence of decisions to invest and manage trust assets also pertain to the prudence of decisions to retain or dispose of inception assets under this section.

Section 5. Loyalty.

A trustee shall invest and manage the trust assets solely in the interest of the beneficiaries.

COMMENT

The duty of loyalty is perhaps the most characteristic rule of trust law, requiring the trustee to act exclusively for the beneficiaries, as opposed to acting for the trustee's own interest or that of third parties. The language of Section 4 of this Act derives from Restatement of Trusts 3d: Prudent Investor Rule § 170 (1992), which makes minute changes in Restatement of Trusts 2d § 170 (1959).

The concept that the duty of prudence in trust administration, especially in investing and managing trust assets, entails adherence to the duty of loyalty is familiar. ERISA § 404(a)(1)(B), 29 U.S.C. § 1104(a)(1)(B), extracted in the Comment to Section 1 of this Act, effectively merges the requirements of prudence and loyalty. A fiduciary cannot be prudent in the conduct of investment functions if the fiduciary is sacrificing the interests of the beneficiaries.

The duty of loyalty is not limited to settings entailing self-dealing or conflict of interest in which the trustee would benefit personally from the trust. "The trustee is under a duty to the beneficiary in administering the trust not to be guided by the interest of any third person. Thus, it is improper for the trustee to sell trust property to a third person for the purpose of benefitting the third person rather than the trust." Restatement of Trusts 2d § 170, comment q, at 371 (1959).

No form of so-called "social investing" is consistent with the duty of loyalty if the investment activity entails sacrificing the interests of trust beneficiaries—for example, by accepting below-market returns—in favor of the interests of the persons supposedly benefitted by pursuing the particular social cause. See, e.g., John H. Langbein & Richard Posner, Social Investing and the Law of Trusts, 79 Michigan L. Rev. 72, 96–97 (1980) (collecting authority). For pension trust assets, see generally Ian D. Lanoff, The Social Investment of Private Pension Plan Assets: May it Be Done Lawfully

under ERISA?, 31 Labor L.J. 387 (1980). Commentators supporting social investing tend to concede the overriding force of the duty of loyalty. They argue instead that particular schemes of social investing may not result in below-market returns. See, e.g., Marcia O'Brien Hylton, "Socially Responsible" Investing: Doing Good Versus Doing Well in an Inefficient Market, 42 American U.L. Rev. 1 (1992). In 1994 the Department of Labor issued an Interpretive Bulletin reviewing its prior analysis of social investing questions and reiterating that pension trust fiduciaries may invest only in conformity with the prudence and loyalty standards of ERISA §§ 403–404. Interpretive Bulletin 94–1, 59 Fed. Regis. 32606 (Jun. 22, 1994), to be codified as 29 CFR § 2509.94–1. The Bulletin reminds fiduciary investors that they are prohibited from "subordinat[ing] the interests of participants and beneficiaries in their retirement income to unrelated objectives."

Section 6. Impartiality.

If a trust has two or more beneficiaries, the trustee shall act impartially in investing and managing the trust assets, taking into account any differing interests of the beneficiaries.

COMMENT

The duty of impartiality derives from the duty of loyalty. When the trustee owes duties to more than one beneficiary, loyalty requires the trustee to respect the interests of all the beneficiaries. Prudence in investing and administration requires the trustee to take account of the interests of all the beneficiaries for whom the trustee is acting, especially the conflicts between the interests of beneficiaries interested in income and those interested in principal.

The language of Section 6 derives from Restatement of Trusts 2d § 183 (1959); see also id., § 232. Multiple beneficiaries may be beneficiaries in succession (such as life and remainder interests) or beneficiaries with simultaneous interests (as when the income interest in a trust is being divided among several beneficiaries).

The trustee's duty of impartiality commonly affects the conduct of investment and management functions in the sphere of principal and income allocations. This Act prescribes no regime for allocating receipts and expenses. The details of such allocations are commonly handled under specialized legislation, such as the Revised Uniform Principal and Income Act (1962) (which is presently under study by the Uniform Law Commission with a view toward further revision).

Section 7. Investment Costs.

In investing and managing trust assets, a trustee may only incur costs that are appropriate and reasonable in relation to the assets, the purposes of the trust, and the skills of the trustee.

COMMENT

Wasting beneficiaries' money is imprudent. In devising and implementing strategies for the investment and management of trust assets, trustees are obliged to minimize costs.

The language of Section 7 derives from Restatement of Trusts 2d § 188 (1959). The Restatement of Trusts 3d says: "Concerns over compensation and other charges are not an obstacle to a reasonable course of action using mutual funds and other pooling arrangements, but they do require special attention by a trustee.... [I]t is important for trustees to make careful cost comparisons, particularly among similar products of a specific type being considered for a trust portfolio." Restatement of Trusts 3d: Prudent Investor Rule § 227, comment *m*, at 58 (1992).

Section 8. Reviewing Compliance.

Compliance with the prudent investor rule is determined in light of the facts and circumstances existing at the time of a trustee's decision or action and not by hindsight.

COMMENT

This section derives from the 1991 Illinois act, 760 ILCS 5/5(a)(2) (1992), which draws upon Restatement of Trusts 3d: Prudent Investor Rule § 227, comment *b*, at 11 (1992). Trustees are not insurers. Not every investment or management decision will turn out in the light of hindsight to have been successful. Hindsight is not the relevant standard. In the language of law and economics, the standard is ex ante, not ex post.

Section 9. Delegation of Investment and Management Functions.

(a) A trustee may delegate investment and management functions that a prudent trustee of comparable skills could properly delegate under the circumstances. The trustee shall exercise reasonable care, skill, and caution in:

(1) selecting an agent;

(2) establishing the scope and terms of the delegation, consistent with the purposes and terms of the trust; and

(3) periodically reviewing the agent's actions in order to monitor the agent's performance and compliance with the terms of the delegation.

(b) In performing a delegated function, an agent owes a duty to the trust to exercise reasonable care to comply with the terms of the delegation.

(c) A trustee who complies with the requirements of subsection (a) is not liable to the beneficiaries or to the trust for the decisions or actions of the agent to whom the function was delegated.

(d) By accepting the delegation of a trust function from the trustee of a trust that is subject to the law of this State, an agent submits to the jurisdiction of the courts of this State.

COMMENT

This section of the Act reverses the much-criticized rule that forbad trustees to delegate investment and management functions. The language of this section is derived from Restatement of Trusts 3d: Prudent Investor Rule § 171 (1992), discussed infra, and from the 1991 Illinois act, 760 ILCS § 5/5.1(b), (c) (1992).

Former law. The former nondelegation rule survived into the 1959 Restatement: "The trustee is under a duty to the beneficiary not to delegate to others the doing of acts which the trustee can reasonably be required personally to perform." The rule put a premium on the frequently arbitrary task of distinguishing discretionary functions that were thought to be nondelegable from supposedly ministerial functions that the trustee was allowed to delegate. Restatement of Trusts 2d § 171 (1959).

The Restatement of Trusts 2d admitted in a comment that "There is not a clear-cut line dividing the acts which a trustee can properly delegate from those which he cannot properly delegate." Instead, the comment directed attention to a list of factors that "may be of importance: (1) the amount of discretion involved; (2) the value and character of the property involved; (3) whether the property is principal or income; (4) the proximity or remoteness of the subject matter of the trust; (5) the character of the act as one involving professional skill or facilities possessed or not possessed by the trustee himself." Restatement of Trusts 2d § 171, comment *d* (1959). The 1959 Restatement further said: "A trustee cannot properly delegate to another power to select investments." Restatement of Trusts 2d § 171, comment *h* (1959).

For discussion and criticism of the former rule see William L. Cary & Craig B. Bright, The Delegation of Investment Responsibility for Endowment Funds, 74 Columbia L. Rev. 207 (1974); John H. Langbein & Richard A. Posner, Market Funds and Trust–Investment Law, 1976 American Bar Foundation Research J. 1, 18–24.

The modern trend to favor delegation. The trend of subsequent legislation, culminating in the Restatement of Trusts 3d: Prudent Investor Rule, has been strongly hostile to the nondelegation rule. See John H. Langbein, Reversing the Nondelegation Rule of Trust–Investment Law, 59 Missouri L. Rev. 105 (1994).

The delegation rule of the Uniform Trustee Powers Act. The Uniform Trustee Powers Act (1964) effectively abrogates the nondelegation rule. It authorizes trustees "to employ persons, including attorneys, auditors, investment advisors, or agents, even if they are associated with the trustee, to advise or assist the trustee in the performance of his administrative duties; to act without independent investigation upon their recommendations; and instead of acting personally, to employ one or more agents to perform any act of administration, whether or not discretionary...." Uniform Trustee Powers Act § 3(24), 7B Uniform Laws Ann. 743 (1985). The Act has been enacted in 16 states, see "Record of Passage of Uniform and Model Acts as of September 30, 1993," 1993–94 Reference Book of Uniform Law Commissioners (unpaginated, following page 111) (1993).

UMIFA's delegation rule. The Uniform Management of Institutional Funds Act (1972) (UMIFA), authorizes the governing boards of eleemosynary institutions, who are trustee-like fiduciaries, to delegate investment matters either to a committee of the board or to outside investment advisors, investment counsel, managers, banks, or trust companies. UMIFA § 5, 7A Uniform Laws Ann. 705 (1985). UMIFA has been enacted in 38 states, see "Record of Passage of Uniform and Model Acts as of September 30, 1993," 1993–94 Reference Book of Uniform Law Commissioners (unpaginated, following page 111) (1993).

ERISA's delegation rule. The Employee Retirement Income Security Act of 1974, the federal statute that prescribes fiduciary standards for investing the assets of pension and employee benefit plans, allows a pension or employee benefit plan to provide that "authority to manage, acquire or dispose of assets of the plan is delegated to one or more investment managers...." ERISA § 403(a)(2), 29 U.S.C. § 1103(a)(2). Commentators have explained the rationale for ERISA's encouragement of delegation:

> ERISA ... invites the dissolution of unitary trusteeship.... ERISA's fractionation of traditional trusteeship reflects the complexity of the modern pension trust. Because millions, even billions of dollars can be involved, great care is required in investing and safekeeping plan assets. Administering such plans—computing and honoring benefit entitlements across decades of employment and retirement—is also a complex business.... Since, however, neither the sponsor nor any other single entity has a comparative

advantage in performing all these functions, the tendency has been for pension plans to use a variety of specialized providers. A consulting actuary, a plan administration firm, or an insurance company may oversee the design of a plan and arrange for processing benefit claims. Investment industry professionals manage the portfolio (the largest plans spread their pension investments among dozens of money management firms).

John H. Langbein & Bruce A. Wolk, Pension and Employee Benefit Law 496 (1990).

The delegation rule of the 1992 Restatement. The Restatement of Trusts 3d: Prudent Investor Rule (1992) repeals the nondelegation rule of Restatement of Trusts 2d § 171 (1959), extracted supra, and replaces it with substitute text that reads:

> § 171. Duty with Respect to Delegation. A trustee has a duty personally to perform the responsibilities of trusteeship except as a prudent person might delegate those responsibilities to others. In deciding whether, to whom, and in what manner to delegate fiduciary authority in the administration of a trust, and thereafter in supervising agents, the trustee is under a duty to the beneficiaries to exercise fiduciary discretion and to act as a prudent person would act in similar circumstances.

Restatement of Trusts 3d: Prudent Investor Rule § 171 (1992). The 1992 Restatement integrates this delegation standard into the prudent investor rule of section 227, providing that "the trustee must

... act with prudence in deciding whether and how to delegate to others...." Restatement of Trusts 3d: Prudent Investor Rule § 227(c) (1992).

Protecting the beneficiary against unreasonable delegation. There is an intrinsic tension in trust law between granting trustees broad powers that facilitate flexible and efficient trust administration, on the one hand, and protecting trust beneficiaries from the misuse of such powers on the other hand. A broad set of trustees' powers, such as those found in most lawyer-drafted instruments and exemplified in the Uniform Trustees' Powers Act, permits the trustee to act vigorously and expeditiously to maximize the interests of the beneficiaries in a variety of transactions and administrative settings. Trust law relies upon the duties of loyalty and prudent administration, and upon procedural safeguards such as periodic accounting and the availability of judicial oversight, to prevent the misuse of these powers. Delegation, which is a species of trustee power, raises the same tension. If the trustee delegates effectively, the beneficiaries obtain the advantage of the agent's specialized investment skills or whatever other attributes induced the trustee to delegate. But if the trustee delegates to a knave or an incompetent, the delegation can work harm upon the beneficiaries.

Section 9 of the Uniform Prudent Investor Act is designed to strike the appropriate balance between the advantages and the hazards of delegation. Section 9 authorizes delegation under the limitations of subsections (a) and (b). Section 9(a) imposes duties of care, skill, and caution on the trustee in selecting the agent, in establishing the terms of the delegation, and in reviewing the agent's compliance.

The trustee's duties of care, skill, and caution in framing the terms of the delegation should protect the beneficiary against overbroad delegation. For example, a trustee could not prudently agree to an investment management agreement containing an exculpation clause that leaves the trust without recourse against reckless mismanagement. Leaving one's beneficiaries remediless against willful wrongdoing is inconsistent with the duty to use care and caution in formulating the terms of the delegation. This sense that it is imprudent to expose beneficiaries to broad exculpation clauses underlies both federal and state legislation restricting exculpation clauses, e.g., ERISA §§ 404(a)(1)(D), 410(a), 29 U.S.C. §§ 1104(a)(1)(D), 1110(a); New York Est. Powers Trusts Law § 11–1.7 (McKinney 1967).

Although subsection (c) of the Act exonerates the trustee from personal responsibility for the agent's conduct when the delegation satisfies the standards of subsection 9(a), subsection 9(b) makes the agent responsible to the trust. The beneficiaries of the trust can, therefore, rely upon the trustee to enforce the terms of the delegation.

Costs. The duty to minimize costs that is articulated in Section 7 of this Act applies to delegation as well as to other aspects of fiduciary investing. In deciding whether to delegate, the trustee must balance the projected benefits against the likely costs. Similarly, in deciding how to delegate, the trustee must take costs into account. The trustee must be alert to protect the beneficiary from "double dipping." If, for example, the trustee's regular compensation schedule presupposes that the trustee will conduct the investment management function, it should ordinarily follow that the trustee will lower its fee when delegating the investment function to an outside manager.

Section 10. Language Invoking Standard of [Act].

The following terms or comparable language in the provisions of a trust, unless otherwise limited or modified, authorizes any investment or strategy permitted under this [Act]: "investments permissible by law for investment of trust funds," "legal investments," "authorized investments," "using the judgment and care under the circumstances then prevailing that persons of prudence, discretion, and intelligence exercise in the management of their own affairs, not in regard to speculation but in regard to the permanent disposition of their funds, considering the probable income as well as the probable safety of their capital," "prudent man rule," "prudent trustee rule," "prudent person rule," and "prudent investor rule."

COMMENT

This provision is taken from the Illinois act, 760 ILCS § ⅚(d) (1992), and is meant to facilitate incorporation of the Act by means of the formulaic language commonly used in trust instruments.

Section 11. Application to Existing Trusts.

This [Act] applies to trusts existing on and created after its effective date. As applied to trusts existing on its effective date, this [Act] governs only decisions or actions occurring after that date.

Section 12. Uniformity of Application and Construction.

This [Act] shall be applied and construed to effectuate its general purpose to make uniform the law with respect to the subject of this [Act] among the States enacting it.

Section 13. Short Title.

This [Act] may be cited as the "[Name of Enacting State] Uniform Prudent Investor Act."

Section 14. Severability.

If any provision of this [Act] or its application to any person or circumstance is held invalid, the invalidity does not affect other provisions or applications of this [Act] which can be given effect without the invalid provision or application, and to this end the provisions of this [Act] are severable.

Section 15. Effective Date.

This [Act] takes effect _____.

Section 16. Repeals.

The following acts and parts of acts are repealed:

    (1)

    (2)

    (3)

SELECTED
NON–UNIFORM LEGISLATION

UNITED KINGDOM: INHERITANCE (PROVISION FOR FAMILY AND DEPENDANTS) ACT 1975

Table of Sections

§ 1. Application for Financial Provision From Deceased's Estate

(1) Where after the commencement of this Act a person dies domiciled in England and Wales and is survived by any of the following persons:—

886

(*a*) the wife or husband of the deceased;

(*b*) a former wife or former husband of the deceased who has not remarried;

(*c*) a child of the deceased;

(*d*) any person (not being a child of the deceased) who, in the case of any marriage to which the deceased was at any time a party, was treated by the deceased as a child of the family in relation to that marriage;

(*e*) any person (not being a person included in the foregoing paragraphs of this subsection) who immediately before the death of the deceased was being maintained, either wholly or partly, by the deceased;

that person may apply to the court for an order under section 2 of this Act on the ground that the disposition of the deceased's estate effected by his will or the law relating to intestacy, or the combination of his will and that law, is not such as to make reasonable financial provision for the applicant.

(2) In this Act "reasonable financial provision"—

(*a*) in the case of an application made by virtue of subsection (1)(*a*) above by the husband or wife of the deceased (except where the marriage with the deceased was the subject of a decree of judicial separation and at the date of death the decree was in force and the separation was continuing), means such financial provision as it would be reasonable in all the circumstances of the case for a husband or wife to receive, whether or not that provision is required for his or her maintenance;

(*b*) in the case of any other application made by virtue of subsection (1) above, means such financial provision as it would be reasonable in all the circumstances of the case for the applicant to receive for his maintenance.

(3) For the purposes of subsection (1)(*e*) above, a person shall be treated as being maintained by the deceased, either wholly or partly, as the case may be if the deceased, otherwise than for full valuable consideration, was making a substantial contribution in money or money's worth towards the reasonable needs of that person.

§ 2. Powers of Court to Make Orders

(1) Subject to the provisions of this Act, where an application is made for an order under this section, the court may, if it is satisfied that the disposition of the deceased's estate effected by his will or

the law relating to intestacy, or the combination of his will and that
law, is not such as to make reasonable financial provision for the
applicant, make any one or more of the following orders:—

(a) an order for the making to the applicant out of the net
estate of the deceased of such periodical payments and for such
term as may be specified in the order;

(b) an order for the payment to the applicant out of that
estate of a lump sum of such amount as may be so specified;

(c) an order for the transfer to the applicant of such property
comprised in that estate as may be so specified;

(d) an order for the settlement for the benefit of the applicant of such property comprised in that estate as may be so
specified;

(e) an order for the acquisition out of property comprised in
that estate of such property as may be so specified and for the
transfer of the property so acquired to the applicant or for the
settlement thereof for his benefit;

(f) an order varying any ante-nuptial or post-nuptial settlement (including such a settlement made by will) made on the
parties to a marriage to which the deceased was one of the
parties, the variation being for the benefit of the surviving party
to that marriage, or any child of that marriage, or any person
who was treated by the deceased as a child of the family in
relation to that marriage.

(2) An order under subsection (1)(a) above providing for the
making out of the net estate of the deceased of periodical payments
may provide for—

(a) payments of such amount as may be specified in the
order,

(b) payments equal to the whole of the income of the net
estate or of such portion thereof as may be so specified,

(c) payments equal to the whole of the income of such part of
the net estate as the court may direct to be set aside or
appropriated for the making out of the income thereof of payments under this section,

or may provide for the amount of the payments or any of them to
be determined in any other way the court thinks fit.

(3) Where an order under subsection (1)(a) above provides for
the making of payments of an amount specified in the order, the
order may direct that such part of the net estate as may be so
specified shall be set aside or appropriated for the making out of

the income thereof of those payments; but no larger part of the net estate shall be so set aside or appropriated than is sufficient, at the date of the order, to produce by the income thereof the amount required for the making of those payments.

(4) An order under this section may contain such consequential and supplemental provisions as the court thinks necessary or expedient for the purpose of giving effect to the order or for the purpose of securing that the order operates fairly as between one beneficiary of the estate of the deceased and another and may, in particular, but without prejudice to the generality of this subsection—

(a) order any person who holds any property which forms part of the net estate of the deceased to make such payment or transfer such property as may be specified in the order;

(b) vary the disposition of the deceased's estate effected by the will or the law relating to intestacy, or by both the will and the law relating to intestacy, in such manner as the court thinks fair and reasonable having regard to the provisions of the order and all the circumstances of the case;

(c) confer on the trustees of any property which is the subject of an order under this section such powers as appear to the court to be necessary or expedient.

§ 3. Matters to Which Court Is to Have Regard in Exercising Powers Under § 2

(1) Where an application is made for an order under section 2 of this Act, the court shall, in determining whether the disposition of the deceased's estate effected by his will or the law relating to intestacy, or the combination of his will and that law, is such as to make reasonable financial provision for the applicant and, if the court considers that reasonable financial provision has not been made, in determining whether and in what manner it shall exercise its powers under that section, have regard to the following matters, that is to say—

(a) the financial resources and financial needs which the applicant has or is likely to have in the foreseeable future;

(b) the financial resources and financial needs which any other applicant for an order under section 2 of this Act has or is likely to have in the foreseeable future;

(c) the financial resources and financial needs which any beneficiary of the estate of the deceased has or is likely to have in the foreseeable future;

(d) any obligations and responsibilities which the deceased had towards any applicant for an order under the said section 2 or towards any beneficiary of the estate of the deceased;

(e) the size and nature of the net estate of the deceased;

(f) any physical or mental disability of any applicant for an order under the said section 2 or any beneficiary of the estate of the deceased;

(g) any other matter, including the conduct of the applicant or any other person, which in the circumstances of the case the court may consider relevant.

(2) Without prejudice to the generality of paragraph (g) of subsection (1) above, where an application for an order under section 2 of this Act is made by virtue of section 1(1)(a) or 1(1)(b) of this Act, the court shall, in addition to the matters specifically mentioned in paragraphs (a) to (f) of that subsection, have regard to—

(a) the age of the applicant and the duration of the marriage;

(b) the contribution made by the applicant to the welfare of the family of the deceased, including any contribution made by looking after the home or caring for the family;

and, in the case of an application by the wife or husband of the deceased, the court shall also, unless at the date of death a decree of judicial separation was in force and the separation was continuing, have regard to the provision which the applicant might reasonably have expected to receive if on the day on which the deceased died the marriage, instead of being terminated by death, had been terminated by a degree of divorce.

(3) Without prejudice to the generality of paragraph (g) of subsection (1) above, where an application for an order under section 2 of this Act is made by virtue of section 1(1)(c) or 1(1)(d) of this Act, the court shall, in addition to the matters specifically mentioned in paragraphs (a) to (f) of that subsection, have regard to the manner in which the applicant was being or in which he might expect to be educated or trained, and where the application is made by virtue of section 1(1)(d) the court shall also have regard—

(a) to whether the deceased had assumed any responsibility for the applicant's maintenance and, if so, to the extent to which and the basis upon which the deceased assumed that responsibility and to the length of time for which the deceased discharged that responsibility;

(*b*) to whether in assuming and discharging that responsibility the deceased did so knowing that the applicant was not his own child;

(*c*) to the liability of any other person to maintain the applicant.

(4) Without prejudice to the generality of paragraph (*g*) of subsection (1) above, where an application for an order under section 2 of this Act is made by virtue of section 1(1)(*e*) of this Act, the court shall, in addition to the matters specifically mentioned in paragraphs (*a*) to (*f*) of that subsection, have regard to the extent to which and the basis upon which the deceased assumed responsibility for the maintenance of the applicant and to the length of time for which the deceased discharged that responsibility.

(5) In considering the matters to which the court is required to have regard under this section, the court shall take into account the facts as known to the court at the date of the hearing.

(6) In considering the financial resources of any person for the purposes of this section the court shall take into account his earning capacity and in considering the financial needs of any person for the purposes of this section the court shall take into account his financial obligations and responsibilities.

§ 4. Time-Limit for Applications

An application for an order under section 2 of this Act shall not, except with the permission of the court, be made after the end of the period of six months from the date on which representation with respect to the estate of the deceased is first taken out.

§ 5. Interim Orders

(1) Where on an application for an order under section 2 of this Act it appears to the court—

(*a*) that the applicant is in immediate need of financial assistance, but it is not yet possible to determine what order (if any) should be made under that section; and

(*b*) that property forming part of the net estate of the deceased is or can be made available to meet the need of the applicant;

the court may order that, subject to such conditions or restrictions, if any, as the court may impose and to any further order of the court, there shall be paid to the applicant out of the net estate of the deceased such sum or sums and (if more than one) at such intervals as the court thinks reasonable; and the court may order that, subject to the provisions of this Act, such payments are to be made until such date as the court may specify, not being later than the date on which the court either makes an order under the said section 2 or decides not to exercise its powers under that section.

(2) Subsections (2), (3) and (4) of section 2 of this Act shall apply in relation to an order under this section as they apply in relation to an order under that section.

(3) In determining what order, if any, should be made under this section the court shall, so far as the urgency of the case admits, have regard to the same matters as those to which the court is required to have regard under section 3 of this Act.

(4) An order made under section 2 of this Act may provide that any sum paid to the applicant by virtue of this section shall be treated to such an extent and in such manner as may be provided by that order as having been paid on account of any payment provided for by that order.

§ 6. Variation, Discharge, etc. of Orders for Periodical Payments

(1) Subject to the provisions of this Act, where the court has made an order under section 2(1)(a) of this Act (in this section referred to as "the original order") for the making of periodical payments to any person (in this section referred to as "the original recipient"), the court, on an application under this section, shall have power by order to vary or discharge the original order or to suspend any provision of it temporarily and to revive the operation of any provision so suspended.

(2) Without prejudice to the generality of subsection (1) above, an order made on an application for the variation of the original order may—

(a) provide for the making out of any relevant property of such periodical payments and for such term as may be specified in the order to any person who has applied, or would but for section 4 of this Act be entitled to apply, for an order under section 2 of this Act (whether or not, in the case of any application, an order was made in favour of the applicant);

(b) provide for the payment out of any relevant property of a lump sum of such amount as may be so specified to the original recipient or to any such person as is mentioned in paragraph (a) above;

(*c*) provide for the transfer of the relevant property, or such part thereof as may be so specified, to the original recipient or to any such person as is so mentioned.

(3) Where the original order provides that any periodical payments payable thereunder to the original recipient are to cease on the occurrence of an event specified in the order (other than the remarriage of a former wife or former husband) or on the expiration of a period so specified, then, if, before the end of the period of six months from the date of the occurrence of that event or of the expiration of that period, an application is made for an order under this section, the court shall have power to make any order which it would have had power to make if the application had been made before that date (whether in favour of the original recipient or any such person as is mentioned in subsection (2)(*a*) above and whether having effect from that date or from such later date as the court may specify).

(4) Any reference in this section to the original order shall include a reference to an order made under this section and any reference in this section to the original recipient shall include a reference to any person to whom periodical payments are required to be made by virtue of an order under this section.

(5) An application under this section may be made by any of the following persons, that is to say—

(*a*) any person who by virtue of section 1(1) of this Act has applied, or would but for section 4 of this Act be entitled to apply, for an order under section 2 of this Act,

(*b*) the personal representatives of the deceased,

(*c*) the trustees of any relevant property, and

(*d*) any beneficiary of the estate of the deceased.

(6) An order under this section may only affect—

(*a*) property the income of which is at the date of the order applicable wholly or in part for the making of periodical payments to any person who has applied for an order under this Act, or

(*b*) in the case of an application under subsection (3) above in respect of payments which have ceased to be payable on the occurrence of an event or the expiration of a period, property the income of which was so applicable immediately before the occurrence of that event or the expiration of that period, as the case may be, and any such property as is mentioned in paragraph (*a*) or (*b*) above is in subsections (2) and (5) above referred to as "relevant property".

(7) In exercising the powers conferred by this section the court shall have regard to all the circumstances of the case, including any change in any of the matters to which the court was required to have regard when making the order to which the application relates.

(8) Where the court makes an order under this section, it may give such consequential directions as it thinks necessary or expedient having regard to the provisions of the order.

(9) No such order as is mentioned in sections 2(1)(*d*), (*e*) or (*f*), 9, 10 or 11 of this Act shall be made on an application under this section.

(10) For the avoidance of doubt it is hereby declared that, in relation to an order which provides for the making of periodical payments which are to cease on the occurrence of an event specified in the order (other than the remarriage of a former wife or former husband) or on the expiration of a period so specified, the power to vary an order includes power to provide for the making of periodical payments after the expiration of that period or the occurrence of that event.

§ 7. Payment of Lump Sums by Instalments

(1) An order under section 2(1)(*b*) or 6(2)(*b*) of this Act for the payment of a lump sum may provide for the payment of that sum by instalments of such amount as may be specified in the order.

(2) Where an order is made by virtue of subsection (1) above, the court shall have power, on an application made by the person to whom the lump sum is payable, by the personal representatives of the deceased or by the trustees of the property out of which the lump sum is payable, to vary that order by varying the number of instalments payable, the amount of any instalment and the date on which any instalment becomes payable.

PROPERTY AVAILABLE FOR FINANCIAL PROVISION

§ 8. Property Treated as Part of "Net Estate"

(1) Where a deceased person has in accordance with the provisions of any enactment nominated any person to receive any sum of money or other property on his death and that nomination is in force at the time of his death, that sum of money, after deducting

therefrom any capital transfer tax payable in respect thereof, or that other property, to the extent of the value thereof at the date of the death of the deceased after deducting therefrom any capital transfer tax so payable, shall be treated for the purposes of this Act as part of the net estate of the deceased; but this subsection shall not render any person liable for having paid that sum or transferred that other property to the person named in the nomination in accordance with the directions given in the nomination.

(2) Where any sum of money or other property is received by any person as a donatio mortis causa made by a deceased person, that sum of money, after deducting therefrom any capital transfer tax payable thereon, or that other property, to the extent of the value thereof at the date of the death of the deceased after deducting therefrom any capital transfer tax so payable, shall be treated for the purposes of this Act as part of the net estate of the deceased; but this subsection shall not render any person liable for having paid that sum or transferred that other property in order to give effect to that donatio mortis causa.

(3) The amount of capital transfer tax to be deducted for the purposes of this section shall not exceed the amount of that tax which has been borne by the person nominated by the deceased or, as the case may be, the person who has received a sum of money or other property as a donatio mortis causa.

§ 9. Property Held on a Joint Tenancy

(1) Where a deceased person was immediately before his death beneficially entitled to a joint tenancy of any property, then, if, before the end of the period of six months from the date on which representation with respect to the estate of the deceased was first taken out, an application is made for an order under section 2 of this Act, the court for the purpose of facilitating the making of financial provision for the applicant under this Act may order that the deceased's severable share of that property, at the value thereof immediately before his death, shall, to such extent as appears to the court to be just in all the circumstances of the case, be treated for the purposes of this Act as part of the net estate of the deceased.

(2) In determining the extent to which any severable share is to be treated as part of the net estate of the deceased by virtue of an order under subsection (1) above, the court shall have regard to any capital transfer tax payable in respect of that severable share.

(3) Where an order is made under subsection (1) above, the provisions of this section shall not render any person liable for anything done by him before the order was made.

(4) For the avoidance of doubt it is hereby declared that for the purposes of this section there may be a joint tenancy of a chose in action.

POWERS OF COURT IN RELATION TO TRANSACTIONS INTENDED
TO DEFEAT APPLICATIONS FOR FINANCIAL PROVISION

§ 10. Dispositions Intended to Defeat Applications for Financial Provision

(1) Where an application is made to the court for an order under section 2 of this Act, the applicant may, in the proceedings on that application, apply to the court for an order under subsection (2) below.

(2) Where on an application under subsection (1) above the court is satisfied—

(a) that, less than six years before the date of the death of the deceased, the deceased with the intention of defeating an application for financial provision under this Act made a disposition, and

(b) that full valuable consideration for that disposition was not given by the person to whom or for the benefit of whom the disposition was made (in this section referred to as "the donee") or by any other person, and

(c) that the exercise of the powers conferred by this section would facilitate the making of financial provision for the applicant under this Act,

then, subject to the provisions of this section and of sections 12 and 13 of this Act, the court may order the donee (whether or not at the date of the order he holds any interest in the property disposed of to him or for his benefit by the deceased) to provide, for the purpose of the making of that financial provision, such sum of money or other property as may be specified in the order.

(3) Where an order is made under subsection (2) above as respects any disposition made by the deceased which consisted of the payment of money to or for the benefit of the donee, the amount of any sum of money or the value of any property ordered to be provided under that subsection shall not exceed the amount of the payment made by the deceased after deducting therefrom any capital transfer tax borne by the donee in respect of that payment.

(4) Where an order is made under subsection (2) above as respects any disposition made by the deceased which consisted of the transfer of property (other than a sum of money) to or for the

benefit of the donee, the amount of any sum of money or the value of any property ordered to be provided under that subsection shall not exceed the value at the date of the death of the deceased of the property disposed of by him to or for the benefit of the donee (or if that property has been disposed of by the person to whom it was transferred by the deceased, the value at the date of that disposal thereof) after deducting therefrom any capital transfer tax borne by the donee in respect of the transfer of that property by the deceased.

(5) Where an application (in this subsection referred to as "the original application") is made for an order under subsection (2) above in relation to any disposition, then, if on an application under this subsection by the donee or by any applicant for an order under section 2 of this Act the court is satisfied—

(a) that, less than six years before the date of the death of the deceased, the deceased with the intention of defeating an application for financial provision under this Act made a disposition other than the disposition which is the subject of the original application, and

(b) that full valuable consideration for that other disposition was not given by the person to whom or for the benefit of whom that other disposition was made or by any other person,

the court may exercise in relation to the person to whom or for the benefit of whom that other disposition was made the powers which the court would have had under subsection (2) above if the original application had been made in respect of that other disposition and the court had been satisfied as to the matters set out in paragraphs (a), (b) and (c) of that subsection; and where any application is made under this subsection, any reference in this section (except in subsection (2)(b) to the donee shall include a reference to the person to whom or for the benefit of whom that other disposition was made.

(6) In determining whether and in what manner to exercise its powers under this section, the court shall have regard to the circumstances in which any disposition was made and any valuable consideration which was given therefor, the relationship, if any, of the donee to the deceased, the conduct and financial resources of the donee and all the other circumstances of the case.

(7) In this section "disposition" does not include—

(a) any provision in a will, any such nomination as is mentioned in section 8(1) of this Act or any donatio mortis causa, or

(b) any appointment of property made, otherwise than by will, in the exercise of a special power of appointment,

but, subject to these exceptions, includes any payment of money (including the payment of a premium under a policy of assurance) and any conveyance, assurance, appointment or gift of property of any description, whether made by an instrument or otherwise.

(8) The provisions of this section do not apply to any disposition made before the commencement of this Act.

§ 11. Contracts to Leave Property by Will

(1) Where an application is made to a court for an order under section 2 of this Act, the applicant may, in the proceedings on that application, apply to the court for an order under this section.

(2) Where on an application under subsection (1) above the court is satisfied—

(a) that the deceased made a contract by which he agreed to leave by his will a sum of money or other property to any person or by which he agreed that a sum of money or other property would be paid or transferred to any person out of his estate, and

(b) that the deceased made that contract with the intention of defeating an application for financial provision under this Act, and

(c) that when the contract was made full valuable consideration for that contract was not given or promised by the person with whom or for the benefit of whom the contract was made (in this section referred to as "the donee") or by any other person, and

(d) that the exercise of the powers conferred by this section would facilitate the making of financial provision for the applicant under this Act,

then, subject to the provisions of this section and of sections 12 and 13 of this Act, the court may make any one or more of the following orders, that is to say—

(i) if any money has been paid or any other property has been transferred to or for the benefit of the donee in accordance with the contract, an order directing the donee to provide, for the purpose of the making of that financial provision, such sum of money or other property as may be specified in the order;

(ii) if the money or all the money has not been paid or the property or all the property has not been transferred in accordance with the contract, an order directing the personal representatives not to make any payment or transfer any property, or not to make any further payment or transfer any further property, as the case may be, in accordance therewith or directing the personal representatives only to make such payment or transfer such property as may be specified in the order.

(3) Notwithstanding anything in subsection (2) above, the court may exercise its powers thereunder in relation to any contract made by the deceased only to the extent that the court considers that the amount of any sum of money paid or to be paid or the value of any property transferred or to be transferred in accordance with the contract exceeds the value of any valuable consideration given or to be given for that contract, and for this purpose the court shall have regard to the value of property at the date of the hearing.

(4) In determining whether and in what manner to exercise its powers under this section, the court shall have regard to the circumstances in which the contract was made, the relationship, if any, of the donee to the deceased, the conduct and financial resources of the donee and all the other circumstances of the case.

(5) Where an order has been made under subsection (2) above in relation to any contract, the rights of any person to enforce that contract or to recover damages or to obtain other relief for the breach thereof shall be subject to any adjustment made by the court under section 12(3) of this Act and shall survive to such extent only as is consistent with giving effect to the terms of that order.

(6) The provisions of this section do not apply to a contract made before the commencement of this Act.

§ 12. Provisions Supplementary to §§ 10 and 11

(1) Where the exercise of any of the powers conferred by section 10 or 11 of this Act is conditional on the court being satisfied that a disposition or contract was made by a deceased person with the intention of defeating an application for financial provision under this Act, that condition shall be fulfilled if the court is of the opinion that, on a balance of probabilities, the intention of the deceased (though not necessarily his sole intention) in making the disposition or contract was to prevent an order for financial provision being made under this Act or to reduce the amount of the provision which might otherwise be granted by an order thereunder.

(2) Where an application is made under section 11 of this Act with respect to any contract made by the deceased and no valuable consideration was given or promised by any person for that con-

tract then, notwithstanding anything in subsection (1) above, it shall be presumed, unless the contrary is shown, that the deceased made that contract with the intention of defeating an application for financial provision under this Act.

(3) Where the court makes an order under section 10 or 11 of this Act it may give such consequential directions as it thinks fit (including directions requiring the making of any payment or the transfer of any property) for giving effect to the order or for securing a fair adjustment of the rights of the persons affected thereby.

(4) Any power conferred on the court by the said section 10 or 11 to order the donee, in relation to any disposition or contract, to provide any sum of money or other property shall be exercisable in like manner in relation to the personal representative of the donee, and—

(a) any reference in section 10(4) to the disposal of property by the donee shall include a reference to disposal by the personal representative of the donee, and

(b) any reference in section 10(5) to an application by the donee under that subsection shall include a reference to an application by the personal representative of the donee;

but the court shall not have power under the said section 10 or 11 to make an order in respect of any property forming part of the estate of the donee which has been distributed by the personal representative; and the personal representative shall not be liable for having distributed any such property before he has notice of the making of an application under the said section 10 or 11 on the ground that he ought to have taken into account the possibility that such an application would be made.

§ 13. Provisions as to Trustees in Relation to §§ 10 and 11

(1) Where an application is made for—

(a) an order under section 10 of this Act in respect of a disposition made by the deceased to any person as a trustee, or

(b) an order under section 11 of this Act in respect of any payment made or property transferred, in accordance with a contract made by the deceased, to any person as a trustee,

the powers of the court under the said section 10 or 11 to order that trustee to provide a sum of money or other property shall be subject to the following limitation (in addition, in a case of an application under section 10, to any provision regarding the deduction of capital transfer tax) namely, that the amount of any sum of money or the value of any property ordered to be provided—

(i) in the case of an application in respect of a disposition which consisted of the payment of money or an application in respect of the payment of money in accordance with a contract, shall not exceed the aggregate of so much of that money as is at the date of the order in the hands of the trustee and the value at that date of any property which represents that money or is derived therefrom and is at that date in the hands of the trustee;

(ii) in the case of an application in respect of a disposition which consisted of the transfer of property (other than a sum of money) or an application in respect of the transfer of property (other than a sum of money) in accordance with a contract, shall not exceed the aggregate of the value at the date of the order of so much of that property as is at that date in the hands of the trustee and the value at that date of any property which represents the first-mentioned property or is derived therefrom and is at that date in the hands of the trustee.

(2) Where any such application is made in respect of a disposition made to any person as a trustee or in respect of any payment made or property transferred in pursuance of a contract to any person as a trustee, the trustee shall not be liable for having distributed any money or other property on the ground that he ought to have taken into account the possibility that such an application would be made.

(3) Where any such application is made in respect of a disposition made to any person as a trustee or in respect of any payment made or property transferred in accordance with a contract to any person as a trustee, any reference in the said section 10 or 11 to the donee shall be construed as including a reference to the trustee or trustees for the time being of the trust in question and any reference in subsection (1) or (2) above to a trustee shall be construed in the same way.

SPECIAL PROVISIONS RELATING TO CASES OF DIVORCE, SEPARATION ETC.

* * *

MISCELLANEOUS AND SUPPLEMENTARY PROVISIONS

§ 19. Effect, Duration and Form of Orders

(1) Where an order is made under section 2 of this Act then for all purposes, including the purposes of the enactments relating to

capital transfer tax, the will or the law relating to intestacy, or both the will and the law relating to intestacy, as the case may be, shall have effect and be deemed to have had effect as from the deceased's death subject to the provisions of the order.

(2) Any order made under section 2 or 5 of this Act in favour of—

(a) an applicant who was the former husband or former wife of the deceased, or

(b) an applicant who was the husband or wife of the deceased in a case where the marriage with the deceased was the subject of a decree of judicial separation and at the date of death the decree was in force and the separation was continuing,

shall, in so far as it provides for the making of periodical payments, cease to have effect on the remarriage of the applicant, except in relation to any arrears due under the order on the date of the remarriage.

(3) A copy of every order made under this Act shall be sent to the principal registry of the Family Division for entry and filing, and a memorandum of the order shall be endorsed on, or permanently annexed to, the probate or letters of administration under which the estate is being administered.

§ 20. Provisions as to Personal Representatives

(1) The provisions of this Act shall not render the personal representative of a deceased person liable for having distributed any part of the estate of the deceased, after the end of the period of six months from the date on which representation with respect to the estate of the deceased is first taken out, on the ground that he ought to have taken into account the possibility—

(a) that the court might permit the making of an application for an order under section 2 of this Act after the end of that period, or

(b) that, where an order has been made under the said section 2, the court might exercise in relation thereto the powers conferred on it by section 6 of this Act,

but this subsection shall not prejudice any power to recover, by reason of the making of an order under this Act, any part of the estate so distributed.

(2) Where the personal representative of a deceased person pays any sum directed by an order under section 5 of this Act to be paid out of the deceased's net estate, he shall not be under any liability

by reason of that estate not being sufficient to make the payment, unless at the time of making the payment he has reasonable cause to believe that the estate is not sufficient.

(3) Where a deceased person entered into a contract by which he agreed to leave by his will any sum of money or other property to any person or by which he agreed that a sum of money or other property would be paid or transferred to any person out of his estate, then, if the personal representative of the deceased has reason to believe that the deceased entered into the contract with the intention of defeating an application for financial provision under this Act, he may, notwithstanding anything in that contract, postpone the payment of that sum of money or the transfer of that property until the expiration of the period of six months from the date on which representation with respect to the estate of the deceased is first taken out or, if during that period an application is made for an order under section 2 of this Act, until the determination of the proceedings on that application.

§ 21. Admissibility as Evidence of Statements Made by Deceased

In any proceedings under this Act a statement made by the deceased, whether orally or in a document or otherwise, shall be admissible under section 2 of the Civil Evidence Act 1968 as evidence of any fact stated therein in like manner as if the statement were a statement falling within section 2(1) of that Act; and any reference in that Act to a statement admissible, or given or proposed to be given, in evidence under section 2 thereof or to the admissibility or the giving in evidence of a statement by virtue of that section or to any statement falling within section 2(1) of that Act shall be construed accordingly.

* * *

§ 25. Interpretation

(1) In this Act—

"beneficiary", in relation to the estate of a deceased person, means—

(a) a person who under the will of the deceased or under the law relating to intestacy is beneficially interested in the estate or would be so interested if an order had not been made under this Act, and

(b) a person who has received any sum of money or other property which by virtue of section 8(1) or 8(2) of this Act is treated as part of the net estate of the deceased or would have received that sum or other property if an order had not been made under this Act;

"child" includes an illegitimate child and a child en ventre sa mere at the death of the deceased;

"the court" means the High Court, or where a county court has jurisdiction by virtue of section 22 of this Act, a county court;

"former wife" or "former husband" means a person whose marriage with the deceased was during the deceased's lifetime dissolved or annulled by a decree of divorce or of nullity of marriage made under the Matrimonial Causes Act 1973;

"net estate", in relation to a deceased person, means:—

(a) all property of which the deceased had power to dispose by his will (otherwise than by virtue of a special power of appointment) less the amount of his funeral, testamentary and administration expenses, debts and liabilities, including any capital transfer tax payable out of his estate on his death;

(b) any property in respect of which the deceased held a general power of appointment (not being a power exercisable by will) which has not been exercised;

(c) any sum of money or other property which is treated for the purposes of this Act as part of the net estate of the deceased by virtue of section 8(1) or (2) of this Act;

(d) any property which is treated for the purposes of this Act as part of the net estate of the deceased by virtue of an order made under section 9 of the Act;

(e) any sum of money or other property which is, by reason of a disposition or contract made by the deceased, ordered under section 10 or 11 of this Act to be provided for the purpose of the making of financial provision under this Act;

"property" includes any chose in action;

"reasonable financial provision" has the meaning assigned to it by section 1 of this Act;

"valuable consideration" does not include marriage or a promise of marriage;

"will" includes codicil.

* * *

COMMONWEALTH LEGISLATION TREATING EXECUTION ERRORS

South Australia: Wills Act Amendment Act (No. 2) of 1975, amending Wills Act of 1936 to add new Section 12(2).

12(2). Validity of Will

A document purporting to embody the testamentary intentions of a deceased person shall, notwithstanding that it has not been executed with the formalities required by this Act, be deemed to be a will of the deceased person if the Supreme Court, upon application for admission of the document to probate as the last will of the deceased, is satisfied that there can be no reasonable doubt that the deceased intended the document to constitute his will.

Queensland Succession Act of 1981, Section 9.

9. Will to be in Writing and Signed Before Two Witnesses

A will shall not be valid unless it is in writing and executed in manner hereinafter mentioned and required (that is to say) it shall be signed at the foot or end thereof by the testator or by some other person in his presence and by his direction and such signature shall be made or acknowledged by the testator in the presence of two or more witnesses present at the same time and such witnesses shall attest and shall subscribe the will in the presence of the testator but no form of attestation shall be necessary provided that:

(a) the Court may admit to probate a testamentary instrument executed in substantial compliance with the formalities prescribed by this section if the Court is satisfied that the instrument expresses the testamentary intention of the testator; and

(b) the Court may admit extrinsic evidence including evidence of statements made at any time by the testator as to the manner of execution of a testamentary instrument.

Statutes of Manitoba, Wills Act, Section 23 (1983)

23. Substantial Compliance in Execution of Will

Where, upon application, if the court is satisfied that a document or any writing on a document embodies

905

(a) the testamentary intentions of a deceased; or

(b) the intention of a deceased to revoke, alter or revive a will of the deceased or the testamentary intentions of the deceased embodied in a document other than a will;

the court may, notwithstanding that the document or writing was not executed in compliance with all the formal requirements imposed by this Act, order that the document or writing, as the case may be, be fully effective as though it had been executed in compliance with all the formal requirements imposed by this Act as the will of the deceased or as the revocation, alteration or revival of the will of the deceased or of the testamentary intention embodied in that other document, as the case may be.

NORTH DAKOTA ANTE–MORTEM PROBATE ACT

North Dakota Century Code ch. 30.1–08.1

Table of Sections

---

§ 30.1–08.1–01. Declaratory Judgment

Any person who executes a will disposing of his estate in accordance with this title may institute a proceeding under chapter 32–23 for a judgment declaring the validity of the will as to the signature on the will, the required number of witnesses to the signature and their signatures, and the testamentary capacity and freedom from undue influence of the person executing the will.

§ 30.1–08.1–02. Parties—Process

Any beneficiary named in the will and all the testator's present intestate successors shall be named parties to the proceeding. For the purposes of this chapter, any beneficiary named in the will and all the testator's present intestate successors shall be deemed possessed of inchoate property rights.

Service of process upon the parties to the proceeding shall be made in accordance with Rule 4 of the North Dakota Rules of Civil Procedure.

§ 30.1–08.1–03. Finding of Validity—Revocation

If the court finds under chapter 32–23 that the will has been properly executed and that the plaintiff testator has the requisite testamentary capacity and freedom from undue influence, it shall declare the will valid and order it placed on file with the court. For the purposes of section 30.1–12–02, a finding of validity under this chapter shall constitute an adjudication of probate. The will shall be binding in North Dakota unless and until the plaintiff-testator executes a new will and institutes a new proceeding under this chapter naming the appropriate parties to the new proceeding as well as the parties to any former proceeding brought under this chapter.

§ 30.1–08.1–04. Admissibility of Facts—Effect on Other Actions

The facts found in a proceeding brought under this chapter shall not be admissible in evidence in any proceeding other than one brought in North Dakota to determine the validity of a will; nor shall the determination in a proceeding under this chapter be binding, upon the parties to such proceeding, in any action not brought to determine the validity of a will.

†